MONEY, BANKING, AND FINANCIAL MARKETS

MONEY, BANKING, AND FINANCIAL MARKETS

MEIR KOHN
Dartmouth College

The Dryden Press
Chicago Fort Worth San Francisco Philadelphia
Montreal Toronto London Sydney Tokyo

Acquisitions Editor: Jan Richardson
Developmental Editor: Dan Coran
Project Editor: Cate Rzasa
Design Director: Jeanne Calabrese
Production Manager: Barb Bahnsen
Permissions Editor: Cindy Lombardo
Director of Editing, Design, and Production: Jane Perkins

Copy Editor: Mary Englehart
Indexer: Leoni McVey
Text Type: 10/12 Sabon

Library of Congress Cataloging-in-Publication Data
Kohn, Meir G.
    Money, banking, and financial markets / Meir Kohn.
        p. cm.
    Includes bibliographical references and index.
    ISBN 0-03-033334-2
    1. Finance. 2. Banks and banking. 3. Money. 4. Monetary policy.
    5. Banks and banking, International. I. Title
    HG173.K64 1990
    332.1—dc20   90-44518

Printed in the United States of America
 12-032-98765432

Address orders:
The Dryden Press
Orlando, FL 32887

Address editorial correspondence:
The Dryden Press
908 N. Elm St.
Hinsdale, IL 60521

The Dryden Press
Holt, Rinehart and Winston
Saunders College Publishing

Cover source: Island photo © Douglas Peebles.

To my parents

THE DRYDEN PRESS SERIES IN ECONOMICS

Aronson
The Electronic Scorecard

Asch and Seneca
Government and the Marketplace
Second Edition

Breit and Elzinga
**The Antitrust Casebook:
Milestones in Economic Regulation**
Second Edition

Campbell, Campbell, and Dolan
**Money, Banking, and
Monetary Policy**

Dolan and Lindsey
Economics, *Sixth Edition*

Dolan and Lindsey
Macroeconomics, *Sixth Edition*

Dolan and Lindsey
Microeconomics, *Sixth Edition*

Eckert and Leftwich
**The Price System and Resource
Allocation,** *Tenth Edition*

Edgmand, Moomaw, and Olson
**Economics and
Contemporary Issues**

Fort and Lowinger
**Applications and Exercises in
Intermediate Microeconomics**

Gardner
Comparative Economic Systems

Hyman
**Public Finance: A Contemporary
Application of Theory to Policy**
Third Edition

Johnson and Roberts
**Money and Banking: A Market-
Oriented Approach,** *Third Edition*

Kaufman
The Economics of Labor Markets
Third Edition

Kidwell and Peterson
**Financial Institutions, Markets,
and Money,** *Third Edition*

Kohn
**Money, Banking, and Financial
Markets**

Landsburg
Price Theory and Applications

Link, Miller, and Bergman
**EconoGraph II: Interactive Software
for Principles of Economics**

Nicholson
**Intermediate Microeconomics and
Its Application,** *Fifth Edition*

Nicholson
**Microeconomic Theory:
Basic Principles and Extensions**
Fourth Edition

Pappas and Hirschey
**Fundamentals of Managerial
Economics,** *Third Edition*

Pappas and Hirschey
Managerial Economics
Sixth Edition

Puth
American Economic History
Second Edition

Rukstad
**Macroeconomic Decision Making in
the World Economy:
Text and Cases,** *Second Edition*

Thomas
**Economics: Principles and
Applications**

Thomas
**Macroeconomics:
Principles and Applications**

Thomas
**Microeconomics:
Principles and Applications**

Welch and Welch
Economics: Theory and Practice
Third Edition

Yarbrough and Yarbrough
**The World Economy: Trade and
Finance,** *Second Edition*

PREFACE

This text differs from other money and banking textbooks in three important ways. First, it brings financial markets and institutions to life. It does so by describing how financial institutions and financial instruments develop as solutions to problems and as responses to profit opportunities. Instead of being numbed by an avalanche of unconnected facts and figures, the student is stimulated by a coherent and intriguing narrative. The result is a sense of drama and excitement. Understanding *why* institutions and markets are the way they are, students are encouraged to think about the real world in a creative way.

The coverage is very up-to-date. The book takes topics straight out of today's financial pages and makes them comprehensible to the student. Examples include the movement toward interstate banking; the rise of the money market and of the Eurodollar market; the LDC debt crisis; the savings and loan debacle and the crisis in deposit insurance; the rise and fall of the junk bond market; the appearance of new financial instruments—financial futures, options, and swaps and mortgage-backed securities. In each case, the book makes clear what is happening, why it is happening, and why it matters.

The second important way this text differs is in the extra help it provides in the teaching of monetary theory. Because instructors find it difficult to teach ISLM in the limited time available, they often rely exclusively on the AS/AD model. However, AS/AD does not link up well with the part of the course that deals with the financial system. It is also of little help in explaining the mechanics of monetary policy and how monetary changes affect the economy—especially their effect on interest rates and exchange rates. I address this problem by supplementing the AS/AD and ISLM models with a simple and intuitive new framework, the circular flow/loanable funds model. This model is used to explain the immediate impact of monetary and other changes, providing "the missing link" between AS/AD and the financial system. It also provides an intuitive bridge to the ISLM model for those instructors who wish to teach it.

The circular flow/loanable funds model is very easy to use. It relies on the same easy-to-understand behavior used earlier in the book to explain the working of the banking system and of financial markets—bank creation of money through lending, the borrowing and saving behavior of firms and households, and the circular flow of payments. As a result, the monetary-theory part of the course integrates well with the earlier discussion of the financial system. And because of its clear connection with individual behavior, the model lends itself readily to real-world applications.

The circular flow/loanable funds model is particularly good in illuminating a number of key topics: The connection between money demand and velocity; the "liquidity effect" on interest rates of a monetary injection; the effect of inflation on the real rate of interest; the differential liquidity effect on long and short rates; the connection between interest rates and exchange rates; and interest-rate versus money-growth targeting of monetary policy.

The third way in which this text differs from others is in its treatment of international material. Instead of being segregated in a separate section at the end, international material is fully integrated throughout the book. Some examples: The banking structure of the United States is studied in relation to that of other countries; the Eurodollar market is explained as part of the overall development of the money market; foreign exchange and international lending are discussed as part of the normal business of money center banks; connections and parallels are drawn between exchange rates and interest rates throughout; and the macro models are developed for an open economy.

Finally, a number of topics are covered more extensively in this text than is customary. Each of the following receives chapter-length treatment: The causes and consequences of inflation; the Quantity Theory as a theory of the long-run effects of monetary change; the government securities market and its significance for the economy; and the mortgage market and securitization.

ORGANIZATION AND CONTENTS

INTRODUCTION

This short chapter is designed to give the student a feeling for the excitement and drama of financial markets and for their importance to everyday life. What happens when financial markets go wrong? What is it like to be a banker or a bond trader?

PART ONE:
THE FINANCIAL SYSTEM: SOME BASIC IDEAS

Chapter 2 explains the role of financial markets in the economy. Chapter 3 develops carefully the reasons for lending and borrowing, the informational problems involved, and the ways that indirect and direct lending address them. It also considers the economic efficiency of the financial system, including cost efficiency, integration of markets, and competition. Money and the payments system are explained in Chapter 4 in terms of the same sort of informational problems. Chapter 5 establishes the principles of bank profit maximization that will serve as the basis for later discussions of actual bank behavior. Chapter 6 is devoted to interest-rate algebra, interest rates and asset prices, and interest-rate risk.

PART TWO: BANKING AND THE MONEY MARKET

The government securities market is described thoroughly in Chapter 7, as a paradigm for other financial markets, and as the pivot of the money market. The peculiar structure of U.S. banking is explained in Chapter 8 in terms of its historical origins and of the attempts of banks to capture economies of scale. The story of the growth of the money market and of the banks' response is told in Chapters 9 and 10, stressing the role of restrictive regulations and of creative attempts to get around them. Chapter 11, on international banking, explains Eurocurrency banking and the international functions of banks. This section culminates in Chapter 12 with an examination of how banks maximize profits while managing liquidity and risk in the environment of the 1990s (the differences between large and small banks are highlighted).

PART THREE: MORE ABOUT FINANCIAL MARKETS

This part addresses some more advanced topics in financial markets and institutions. Chapter 13 describes how futures, options, and swaps are traded and how they are used, with an emphasis on the underlying economics. Chapter 14 offers a comprehensive treatment of the capital market, stressing parallels with the short-term market, explaining the rise and fall of the junk bond market, and considering the implications of increasing corporate leverage. Chapter 15 is devoted to the development of the mortgage market and to securitization.

PART FOUR: REGULATION AND POLICY

The principles of bank safety are developed in Chapter 16—the nature of bank runs, the role of a lender of last resort, and the moral hazard problems of insurance. The current problems of the saving and loan industry and of deposit insurance are then discussed in Chapter 17 in light of these principles. Suggested solutions to the problems are considered and recent legislation—the new capital standards and the S&L bailout—is described in detail. Chapter 18 brings together the discussion of Parts Three and Four on regulation and deregulation and describes the special responsibility of the Fed for the safety of the financial and payments systems (including a discussion of the problem of daylight overdraft). This leads naturally into the regulation of the quantity of money in Part Five.

PART FIVE: REGULATING THE QUANTITY OF MONEY

The basic principles of multiple deposit expansion are developed carefully in Chapter 19. The Fed's instruments of controls are then discussed in Chapter 20. (Since students already have the basics of multiple expansion, they understand why control matters.) Chapter 21 discusses the reality of multiple expansion from the point of view of a bank's reserve manager and explains the relationships between simple theory and complex practice, and between micro and macro.

PART SIX: MONEY AND THE ECONOMY

Having seen how the quantity of money is controlled, the next step is to see how it affects the economy. First, in Chapter 22 there is a careful treatment of money demand and its connection with velocity. Then Chapter 23 uses the Quantity Theory to explain the long-run effects of monetary change. The circular flow/loanable funds model is developed in Chapter 24 to describe the immediate effects and is expanded to an open economy in Chapter 25. (The open economy model brings out clearly the connections between trade flows and capital flows and between the loanable funds and foreign exchange markets.) Next, Chapter 26 on the ISLM model and Chapter 27 on the AS/AD model are used to connect and integrate the immediate and long-run effects. (Chapter 26 on the ISLM model can be skipped without any loss of continuity; several chapters after 26 have appendixes that use the ISLM model, but these appendixes too can be skipped if desired.) The theory is illustrated extensively with applications.

A thorough discussion of the causes and real effects of inflation in Chapter 28 provides essential motivation for the policy discussion later of attempts to restrain inflation. Chapter 29 covers expectation formation (including rational expectations), the term structure of interest rates, and the international structure of interest rates and exchange rates.

PART SEVEN: MONETARY POLICY

The possible goals of monetary policy are considered in Chapter 30 in the context of different views of the macroeconomic problem (Keynesian, Monetarist, and real business cycles). The mechanics and pros and cons of different targets are discussed (interest rates, exchange rates, and monetary growth rates). This is followed by a discussion of the policy-making process. The evolution of the theory and practice of stabilization policy is described in Chapter 31. Monetarist and Keynesian views on monetary and fiscal policy are explained, including the Phillips curve tradeoff, the Friedman-Phelps critique, the New Classical Economics, and the Lucas critique. The final chapter, Chapter 32, begins with a comprehensive and balanced discussion of the "Monetarist experiment" of 1979–1982, of its effects, and of the problems in its implementation. It goes on to discuss monetary policy since 1982 and some of the remaining issues in monetary policy for the future.

HOW THE BOOK CAN BE USED

The book is designed to allow maximum flexibility without sacrificing depth or rigor. It provides both a thorough treatment of the financial system and a complete development of the macro theory. Clearly, all this material cannot be covered in a single term. By judicious selection of chapters, the book lends itself equally well to money and banking courses that stress the microeconomics of the financial system and to those that stress monetary theory and policy. The book has also been used successfully as the basis for a course in financial institutions and markets and for a course in macroeconomics for business students. Detailed recommendations on which chapters to include for each type of course are provided in the *Instructor's Manual*.

TEACHING PHILOSOPHY AND METHODS

THE ISLAND ECONOMY

The book frequently uses the device of a fictitious South Sea island economy to bring out essential principles without getting bogged down in historical or institutional detail. This is done, for example, in explaining money and the payments system (Chapter 4), bank safety (Chapter 16), and the multiple expansion multiplier (Chapter 19). In each case, the subject is covered twice—once for the simple fictitious economy, then again for the U.S. economy. On the second pass, because the principles are already clear, the historical and institutional details make sense and are not merely arbitrary facts to be remembered. Of course, the repetition also reinforces understanding. The Island economy is also used as the basis for the theoretical models of Part Six. As a result, these models can be simple without being unrealistic. The theoretical argument can be stated clearly first and then applied to the real world.

THE ROLE OF DETAIL

The reason for the wealth of real-world detail in the book is that students find it much easier to grasp abstract concepts when they can understand the actual mechanics: The detail gives students something closer to their own experience that they can hold on to. For example, the multiple expansion multiplier becomes less mysterious when we discuss in Chapter 21 how a bank actually manages its reserve desk, and how reserves are traded in the federal funds market (including the use of Fedwire to transfer funds).

PUTTING THE STUDENT IN THE SHOES OF THE DECISION MAKER

A device that is frequently used is to put students in the shoes of the decision maker and then present them with the issues and problems such a decision maker faces. Such scenarios are quite successful in getting students to think actively about the material rather than just memorize facts. They (and their instructors) are constantly motivated to ask, "How does this work?" "Why is this done?" and even "Why not do this?" Some examples include: An entrepreneur seeking finance in Chapter 2; a trader needing means of payment in Chapter 4; a banker maximizing profits in Chapter 5; a securities dealer making a market in Chapter 7; a corporate treasurer managing liquid assets in Chapter 9; a reserve manager minimizing costs in Chapter 21; and a currency trader speculating on exchange rates in Chapter 29.

EXTENSIVE USE OF EXTRACTS FROM THE FINANCIAL PRESS

A large number of items taken from the financial press are used to reinforce, motivate, and illustrate the material.

EXTENSIVE USE OF NUMERICAL EXAMPLES

Numerical examples are used extensively to illustrate complex ideas throughout the book. Financial transactions are carefully described with T-accounts.

CHECK STATIONS

Students are invited to check their understanding of key quantitative concepts by solving simple in-chapter problems as they proceed. Answers are provided at the back of the book.

TERMS AND DEFINITIONS

Important concepts are elucidated with a marginal glossary. Key terms are listed at the end of each chapter.

GRAPHS

Considerable care has been taken to illustrate concepts visually wherever possible. Graphs are captioned to enhance understanding.

CHAPTER SUMMARIES

Extensive summaries are provided at the end of each chapter.

CLASSROOM TESTING

The text is based on lectures developed over a decade at Dartmouth College and used there and at Boston University, Brandeis University, and UCLA by several instructors with considerable success. In particular, both the narrative approach to financial institutions and the loanable funds treatment of the macroeconomic theory work very well in the classroom.

SUPPLEMENTARY MATERIALS

INSTRUCTOR'S MANUAL/TEST BANK/TRANSPARENCY MASTERS

The *Instructor's Manual* provides alternative outlines for courses stressing the financial system, monetary theory and policy, financial institutions and markets, or macroeconomics. The manual contains chapter overviews and answers to end-of-chapter discussion questions. The *Test Bank*, written by Suzanne Crosby of Iona College, contains approximately 2,100 multiple-choice and essay questions. A set of 130 transparency masters is also provided, featuring key exhibits from the text.

STUDY GUIDE

Written by Tom Odegaard of Baylor University, Mark Vaughan of Washington University, and Jan Hansen of University of Wisconsin, the *Study Guide* provides chapter overviews, outlines, review questions, conceptual problems, and excerpts from the financial press to help students master course material. Special sections called Office Hours provide additional discussions of difficult topics.

SOFTWARE

Developed by William V. Williams of Hamline University, these 12 software simulations give students experience in working with such concepts as the circular flow of payments, bank lending, present value, asset and liability management, open market operations, ISLM, the foreign exchange market, the stock market, monetary and fiscal policy, and the Monetarist/Keynesian debate. Each simulation is tied directly to a chapter in the text. The software is free to instructors upon adoption.

COMPUTERIZED TEST BANK

Through the use of ExaMaster, a powerful, easy-to-use testing program, instructors can generate tests quickly and easily. Instructors can create tests with just a few keystrokes by following ExaMaster's screen prompts. (Available in IBM and Macintosh versions.)

NEWSLETTER

A periodic newsletter will keep adopters up to date on current developments in financial markets and institutions and will provide new examples to illustrate concepts in the text.

ACKNOWLEDGMENTS

First and foremost I owe an immense debt of thanks to Becky Ryan. As economics editor at Dryden, Becky provided energetic support and guidance in every aspect of development and production. Her help resulted in a much better book, produced much more speedily, and with much less pain to the author.

I also wish to thank Cate Rzasa, my production editor at Dryden, for her skill and cheerful patience in handling endless changes and revisions that complicated an already tight production schedule. I thank Jeanne Calabrese for the elegant design of the book and the eye-catching cover. Others at Dryden who earned my thanks include Jan Richardson, who took over from Becky as economics editor; Dan Coran, developmental editor; Mary Englehart, copy editor; Dan Swanson, graphic artist; and Carol Klein and Linda Hopper, who provided production assistance throughout the project. Daniel Kohn provided valuable assistance with the graphics. Joe Rosenfeld provided able research assistance. Steve Marks provided helpful comments and suggestions.

My debt to the many reviewers of the various drafts of the book is enormous. Many of the good ideas are theirs; all of the remaining errors are mine. I thank the following:

Melvin Ayogu
James Madison University
Mitchell Berlin
New York University
Tom Bonsor
Eastern Washington University
Michael Bordo
Rutgers University
Elijah Brewer
Federal Reserve Bank of Chicago
Kathleen Brook
New Mexico State University
Conrad Caligaris
Northeastern University
Suzanne Crosby
Iona College
Berkhart Drees
George Washington University
James Eaton
Bridgewater College
Douglas Evanoff
Federal Reserve Bank of Chicago
John Fender
Penn State University
David Hula
Kansas State University
Ashfaq Ishaq
George Washington University
Arthur James
Texas A & M University
John Kaatz
Georgia Institute of Technology
Magda Kandil
Southern Illinois University at Carbondale
Benjamin Kim
University of Nebraska

Adam Kohn
University of California, Berkeley
Carsten Kowalczyk
Dartmouth College
Ronald McKinnon
Stanford University
George Morgan
Virginia Polytechnic Institute and State University
Rayleen Noreen
Benedictine College
Seonghwan Oh
UCLA
Yakir Plessner
Hebrew University
Dean Popp
San Diego State University
Richard Schatz
St. John's University
Richard Schiming
Mankato State University
Zena Seldon
University of Wisconsin—La Crosse
Frank Steindl
Oklahoma State University
Paul Trescott
Southern Illinois University
John Wassom
Western Kentucky University
Eugene White
Rutgers University
Henry Woudenberg
Kent State University
Alex Zanello
Dartmouth College

I am grateful, too, to my students over the years, who have provided me with invaluable feedback and a wealth of suggestions for improvement.

Meir Kohn
December 1990

ABOUT THE AUTHOR

Meir Kohn (Ph.D., M.I.T.) is a Professor of Economics at Dartmouth. He has also taught at the Hebrew University, University of California at Berkeley, Boston University, the University of Western Ontario, and UCLA. His professional work focuses on monetary theory and macro-economics, and he has published extensively in professional journals.

CONTENTS IN BRIEF

CONTENTS

PART ONE

THE FINANCIAL SYSTEM: SOME BASIC IDEAS
9

CHAPTER 13 | HEDGING RISK WITH FUTURES, OPTIONS, AND SWAPS 317

13.1 Futures 317

Forward Transactions and Their Problems 317 / The Futures Contract as a Solution 318 / Financial Futures 320

Cornering the Silver Market 322

Hedging Interest-Rate Risk with Financial Futures 323 / Some Complications of Futures Trading 326 / How Much Do Banks Actually Use Financial Futures? 331

13.2 Options 332

Hedging Exchange-Rate Risk with Options 332 / The Options Market 335

13.3 Swaps 338

Interest-Rate Swaps 338 / Currency Swaps 344

13.4 Are Futures, Options, and Swaps Good for the Economy? 345

Eliminating Risk of Rising Rates 348

Summary 349

CHAPTER 14 | THE CAPITAL MARKET 353

14.1 The Securities 353
14.2 The Borrowers 355

Firms 355 / Households 357 / Government 357

14.3 The Lenders 357

Life Insurance Companies 358 / Pension Funds 359 / Stock and Bond Mutual Funds 361

14.4 The Market for Debt 362

Secured Debt 362 / Unsecured Debt 363 / The Rise and Fall of the Junk Bond 368 / Eurobonds 371 / Municipal Bonds 373

14.5 The Market for Equities 376

New Issues of Stock 376 / Venture Capital 378 / The Secondary Market: The Stock Exchange 378

Reading the Stock Market Listings 380

Mergers, Acquisitions, and LBOs 380

RJR Finale Will Send Money Coursing 382

Increasing Leverage: Is It a Cause for Concern? 383 / The Global Market for Equities 384 / Who Holds and Trades Stocks? 385 / Derivative Securities and Program Trading 387 / The Crash of 1987 389

Summary 390

PART THREE

MORE ABOUT
FINANCIAL
MARKETS
315

PART FIVE

REGULATING THE
QUANTITY OF
MONEY
511

CHAPTER 19 | THE MULTIPLE EXPANSION OF BANK DEPOSITS:
AN INTRODUCTION 513

19.1   The Basic Relationship between Deposits and Reserves 514

The Effect of a Change in Reserves 519

19.2   A Currency Drain 520

19.3   The Introduction of Time Deposits 521

19.4   What Happens to Bank Lending When a Check Is Deposited? 523

A Check Is Deposited in a Checking Deposit 523 / A Check Is Deposited in a
Time Deposit 524

19.5   The Money Multiplier and the Monetary Base 525

The Money Multiplier 526 / The M2 Multiplier 527 / The Effects of a
Change in the Monetary Base 528

Summary 529

APPENDIX A TO CHAPTER 19: TRACING THE MULTIPLE
EXPANSION OF DEPOSITS THROUGH THE BANKING SYSTEM 532

APPENDIX B TO CHAPTER 19: TRANSFORMING EQUATIONS IN TOTAL
AMOUNTS INTO EQUATIONS IN CHANGES IN THOSE AMOUNTS 535

CHAPTER 20 | THE FED'S INSTRUMENTS OF CONTROL 537

20.1   Definitive Money, Monetary Base, and Reserves in the U.S.
Economy 537

20.2   How the Fed Changes Monetary Base through Open Market
Operations 540

20.3   Other Factors That Affect Monetary Base 543

Discount Loans 544 / Foreign Exchange Transactions 544 / Federal Reserve
Float 545 / Treasury Payments and Receipts 546 / Gold and SDR Certificate
Accounts 547 / Coin 548

20.4   Summary of Factors That Affect Definitive Money, Monetary Base,
and Reserves 549

20.5   Other Instruments of Control 550

Discount Policy 551 / Reserve Requirements 552 / Direct Credit
Controls 554

20.6   What Happens to the Fed's Income? 554

Summary 555

CHAPTER 21 | MULTIPLE EXPANSION AND THE
MONEY MULTIPLIER IN PRACTICE 559

21.1   A Bank's-Eye View of Reserves 559

PART SIX

MONEY AND THE ECONOMY
577

CHAPTER 1

INTRODUCTION

"A monetary system is like a liver: It does not take up very much of our thoughts when it goes right, but it attracts a deal of attention when it goes wrong." So wrote D. H. Robertson in 1922. The subject you are going to study is important. The proper functioning of the monetary and financial system deeply affects the welfare of individuals and of nations. Some historical examples of what life can be like when a monetary system does go wrong should make this clear.

1.1 THE GERMAN HYPERINFLATION

In Germany, prices rose rapidly in the final years of World War I. After the war they stabilized briefly, but in 1921 a combination of economic events threw Germany's economy into disarray. Unable to raise enough revenue through taxation, the government printed money to pay its bills. Prices began to rise again, more and more rapidly. Two years later, in November 1923, prices had risen to over one million million times their prewar level. This is equivalent to the price of a 25¢ stamp rising to $250 trillion, about 50 times the current total income of the United States.

During those two years, prices rose by the hour. It was better to pay for a meal in advance because it would cost more by the time you finished. A young woman from Berlin recollects:

> My allowance and all the money I earned were not worth one cup of coffee. You could go to the baker in the morning and buy two rolls for 20 marks; but go there in the afternoon and the same two rolls were 25 marks...
>
> *(Fergusson, p.121)*

With the mark losing value so fast, workers had to be paid daily—or even twice daily. It became foolish to hold on to money, and people would rush out to spend their earnings immediately:

1

[People] squandered money recklessly; wine would be dearer tomorrow!...Prices would rise from hour to hour; the public was seized with a mania for buying. Stories are told of the old bachelor who bought swaddling clothes because the local shop had nothing else to sell...Shopkeepers countered by closing their shops on various pretexts...

(V.W. Germains in Fergusson, p. 97)

Shopkeepers were never sure of covering the cost of replenishing their stocks, irrespective of the prices at which they sold the goods; many goods had completely disappeared. Factories were no longer interested in selling to the home market against money, the value of which was rapidly vanishing...Shopkeepers treated their customers almost as enemies...buying, like kissing, went by favor.

(Moritz Julius Bond in Ringer, pp. 102–103)

Money was next to worthless. Stories are told of thieves robbing people of the baskets or suitcases in which they carried their money but leaving the money itself behind. Since no one wanted to take money, people found other ways to trade. In the country, they bartered. In the cities, where barter was more difficult, they found other devices:

Communities printed their own money based on goods, on a certain amount of potatoes or rye, for instance. Shoe factories paid their workers in bonds for shoes which they could exchange at the bakery for bread or at the meat market for meat.

(Erna von Pustau in Fergusson, p. 121)

Life became a series of calculations. Every day the newspaper would publish an index of goods and services with a multiplier for that day's price. For example:

- Taxi-autos: Multiply ordinary fare by   600,000
- Bookshops: Multiply ordinary price by   300,000
- Public baths: Multiply ordinary price by   115,000

(Fergusson, p. 163)

Those with foreign money, especially American dollars, were comparatively well off. There is a story of one man who went into a restaurant and handed his waiter an American dollar with the instruction to bring him the best meal it would buy. Before he could finish his lunch, the waiter brought him a second meal, explaining that the mark had once again fallen against the dollar.

With the breakdown of the monetary system, ordinary economic activity became difficult or even impossible. Even if one had the money to pay for a purchase, it required a wheelbarrow or a baby carriage to carry it to the store, and an hour to count it out. Goods ceased to be available and businesses ceased to function effectively. Petty crime was rampant.

In November 1923, a monetary reform brought the hyperinflation to an end, and the economy began to recover. By then, however, the savings of most middle-class Germans had been wiped out. A deep bitterness remained that was to pave the way for the rise of Hitler a few years later.[1]

---

[1]We shall learn about the causes and consequences of inflation in Chapter 28.

1.2 THE GREAT DEPRESSION

Economic disaster is no stranger to our own shores. The Great Depression that afflicted the United States in the 1930s was vastly worse than the German hyperinflation (even though prices actually fell by a third during the Depression). Economists still debate the causes of the Depression, but undoubtedly a general collapse of the monetary and financial system played a major role. Following the stock market crash of October 1929 came a series of bank failures and panics. By 1933, over half the country's banks had closed their doors. Unemployment and poverty reached proportions that this country had never before experienced. Over 40 million people, one-third of the population, sank into poverty and homelessness.

Even those fortunate enough to have jobs could never feel secure. People would show up for work only to find that the factory or business that had employed them the day before had shut down overnight. One Detroit auto worker remembers:

> Before daylight we were on the way to Chevrolet. The police were already on the job, waving us away from the office. "Nothin' doin'. nothin' doin'." Now we were tramping through falling snow. Dodge employment office. A big well-fed man in a heavy overcoat stood at the door saying, "No, no" as we passed before him. On the tramp again...
>
> *(This Fabulous Century, p. 45)*

As the winter of 1930–1931 came closer, efforts were made to help the unemployed. *Time* magazine reported:

> With the cold snap came a new hustle and bustle among public men in many a city to do something about unemployment. During the summer, when men out of work were not perishing of hunger and cold, this major problem was allowed to coast along on the theory that autumn would bring economic improvements. When no business upturn appeared, widespread preparations were started to avoid another winter of long breadlines...With doleful tales of hard times ringing in his ears, the President [Hoover] next appointed a special Cabinet Commission to "formulate...plans continuing and strengthening the organization of federal activities for employment during the winter."...The President did not propose any new or concrete scheme of federal relief to this commission. He reverted to the same abstract principles he set up last year.

People who had lead respectable, middle-class lives found themselves poor overnight with barely the means to survive. Many adults today still remember vividly their Depression-era childhoods:

> I remember all of a sudden we had to move. My father lost his job and we moved into a double garage. The landlord didn't charge us rent for seven years. We had a coal stove, and we had to each take turns, the three of us kids, to warm our legs...In the morning we'd get out and get some snow and put it on the stove and melt it and wash around our faces. Never the neck or anything...my father was pretty sharp in a way...He could always get something to feed us kids. We lived about three months on candy cods, they're little chocolate square things. We had those melted in milk. And he had a part time job in a Chinese restaurant. We lived on fried noodles...He went to delivering Corn Flake samples. We lived on Corn Flake balls, Rice Krispies...
>
> *(Terkel, p. 93)*

|1.3| THE OHIO THRIFT CRISIS OF 1985

In case you think that problems with the monetary and financial system are entirely a thing of the past, consider a more recent episode. In 1985, the collapse of Cincinnati-based Home State Savings Bank lead to a panic that caused the governor of Ohio to close temporarily 71 of the state's thrifts.

Home State had taken a severe loss on some of its investments. Like many savings banks in Ohio, its deposits were insured by the state-sponsored Ohio Deposit Guarantee Fund rather than by the federal government. Unfortunately, this private fund did not have the reserves to cover Home State's loss. The result was a run on the bank by Home State's depositors and similar runs on other banks insured by the fund. *The Wall Street Journal* reported "scenes from the 1930s" as depositors lined up to withdraw their money from banks they felt they could no longer trust:

> Outside Molitor Loan & Building Co. in the Cincinnati suburb of Delhi, more than 100 people waited in line all Thursday night. Bolstered by thermos bottles, sleeping bags, kerosene heaters, and portable television sets, they waited for the thrift to open Friday to get their money out.
>
> "Ohio Deposit Guarantee Fund: All Savings Guaranteed in Full," said the sign over Molitor's glass door. But 35-year-old Christine Wright, unconvinced, had driven 90 miles from her home in Greenville, Ohio to wait in line for her mother.
>
> Her mother, Ms. Wright said, had been hit by a "double whammy." The mother had had $8,000 in cash in Home State Savings but had been lucky enough to get it out in time. Then, she had turned around and put the money in Molitor, which, though financially sound, was being hit by a run of its own. Ms. Wright said her mother has little other income except a minimum social security check. She added: "I wasn't even aware there were two different kinds (of deposit insurance)—state and federal."
>
> Ms. Wright and the others waited in vain. Molitor didn't open Friday morning.
>
> (*The Wall Street Journal*, March 18, 1985)

Within a week of closing, 20 of the 71 thrifts were found eligible for federal deposit insurance and were allowed to reopen. The scale of the Ohio thrift crisis was relatively small. Since then, a much larger thrift crisis has developed, involving thousands of thrifts across the country. This time there are no runs, because these thrifts are federally insured. But their losses are likely to cost taxpayers well in excess of $100 billion.[2]

|1.4| "MASTERS OF THE UNIVERSE"

The subject of money and banking is not all about disasters. Most of the time we shall be talking about the normal, day-to-day operations of banks and financial markets. However, even in normal times the world of money and finance is a place of excitement and even glamour. The mood is well captured by the

---

[2]We will learn about the causes of this crisis in Chapters 16 and 17.

following vivid, if sardonic, description of a fictional bond trading room from Tom Wolfe's *The Bonfire of the Vanities*.

The investment-banking firm of Pierce & Pierce occupied the fiftieth, fifty-first, fifty-second, fifty-third, and fifty-fourth floors of a glass tower that rose up sixty stories from out of the gloomy groin of Wall Street. The bond trading room, where Sherman worked, was on the fiftieth...No sooner did you pass the fake fireplace than you heard an ungodly roar, like the roar of a mob. It came from somewhere around the corner. You couldn't miss it. Sherman McCoy headed straight for it, with relish. On this particular morning, as on every morning, it resonated with his very gizzard.

He turned the corner, and there it was: The bond trading room of Pierce & Pierce. It was a vast space, perhaps sixty by eighty feet, but with the same eight foot ceiling bearing down on your head. It was an oppressive space with a ferocious glare, writhing silhouettes, and the roar. The glare came from a wall of plate glass that faced south, looking out over New York Harbor, the Statue of Liberty, Staten Island, and the Brooklyn and New Jersey shores. The writhing silhouettes were the arms and torsos of young men, few of them older than forty. They had their suit jackets off. They were moving about in an agitated manner and sweating early in the morning and shouting, which created the roar. It was the sound of well-educated young white men baying for money on the bond market.

"Pick up the...phone please!" a chubby, pink-faced member of the Harvard Class of 1976 screamed at someone two rows of desks away. The room was like a newspaper city room in that there were no partitions and no signs of visible rank. Everyone sat at light grey metal desks in front of veal-colored terminals with black screens. Rows of green-diode letters and numbers came skidding across...A member of the Yale Class of 1973 with a neck that seemed to protrude twelve inches out of his shirt stared at a screen and screamed over the telephone at a broker in Paris...

...Sherman sat down before his own telephone and computer terminals. The shouts, the imprecations, the gesticulations, the...fear and greed, enveloped him, and he loved it. He was the number one bond salesman, "the biggest producer," as the phrase went, in the bond trading room of Pierce & Pierce on the fiftieth floor, and he loved the very roar of the storm...The bond market had caught fire, and experienced salesmen such as himself were all at once much in demand. All of a sudden, in investment houses all over Wall Street, the erstwhile Bond Bores were making so much money they took to congregating after work in a bar on Hanover Square called Harry's, to tell war stories...Bonds now represented four-fifths of Pierce & Pierce's business, and the young hotshots...were desperate to get to the bond trading room at Pierce & Pierce...Masters of the Universe! The roar filled Sherman's soul with hope, confidence, esprit de corps...

1.5 THE PLAN OF THE BOOK

Having, I hope, whetted your appetite, here is what lies ahead. In Part One we shall learn the basics. What the financial system does and how it does it. The nature of money and banks and the role they play in the economy. How to understand interest rates. In Parts Two and Three we shall take a more detailed look at the financial system—in Part Two, the focus will be on banking; in Part Three, on financial markets. Enormous changes are taking place in both areas and we shall try to understand why these changes are happening.

In Part Four we shall look at government regulation of the monetary and financial system. Why is regulation necessary? What are the problems? We shall see that the principal regulator is the Fed—a special bank operated by the federal government. The Fed has the responsibility, in addition to its other tasks, of regulating the quantity of money in our economy. In Part Five we shall look at how it does this and in Part Six at what difference it makes to the economy. We shall then be ready, in Part Seven, to talk about monetary policy: How should the Fed regulate the quantity of money?

BIBLIOGRAPHY

Egan, James P., *Money and Banking 90/91*, Guilford, CT: Dushkin, 1990.

Fergusson, Adam, *When Money Dies: The Nightmare of the Weimar Collapse*, London: William Kimber & Co. Limited, 1975.

Galbraith, John Kenneth, *The Great Crash*, Boston: Houghton Mifflin, 1955.

Galbraith, John Kenneth, *Money: Whence it Came, Where it Went*, Boston: Houghton Mifflin, 1975.

Havrilesky, Thomas M., and Robert Schweitzer, *Contemporary Developments in Financial Institutions and Markets*, Arlington Heights, IL: Harlan Davidson, 1987.

Mayer, Martin, *The Money Bazaars*, New York: Mentor, 1984.

McElvaine, Robert S., ed., *Down & Out in the Great Depression: Letters from the Forgotten Man*, Chapel Hill: The University of North Carolina Press, 1983.

Ringer, Fritz K., ed., *The German Inflation of 1923*, New York: Oxford University Press, 1969.

Terkel, Studs, *Hard Times: An Oral History of the Great Depression*, New York: Random House, 1970.

Time-Life Books, *This Fabulous Century: 1930–1940*, New York: Time-Life Books, 1969.

Wilcox, James A., *Current Readings on Money, Banking, and Financial Markets*, Glenview, IL: Scott, Foresman/Little, Brown, 1988.

Wolfe, Tom, *The Bonfire of the Vanities*, New York: Farrar, Strauss, & Giroux Inc., 1987.

PART ONE

THE FINANCIAL SYSTEM
SOME BASIC IDEAS

CHAPTER 2

SAVING AND INVESTMENT

Before we look at the detailed workings of the financial system, we need to have some idea of the big picture: What is the economic function of the financial system? What is its place in the economy as a whole?

Put simply, the function of the financial system is to facilitate borrowing and lending. To understand more, we need to know who borrows, who lends, and why. To begin with, let us take a look at the reasons for borrowing and lending by households and firms.

2.1 WHY DO HOUSEHOLDS SAVE AND LEND?

Why do people sometimes spend more than their incomes and sometimes less? For any individual, income and needs fluctuate from month to month and from year to year. Moreover, needs may be high just when income is low, and vice versa. It would be quite inconvenient to be forced to spend, each month or year, exactly the income of that month or year. Saving and borrowing provide ways to match the pattern of spending more closely to needs.

If you spend *less* than your income, you are saving; if you spend *more* than your income, you are dissaving. How can you spend more than your income? If you saved in the past, you can draw down the savings that you accumulated. Alternatively, if someone will lend to you, you can borrow and repay by saving in the future. Some definitions will clarify matters.

- **Saving:** spending less than income
- **Dissaving:** spending more than income
- **Savings:** wealth gained through saving

Saving can be used either (1) to pay back debts or (2) to increase savings. Dissaving can be accomplished either (1) through borrowing or (2) by drawing

11

EXHIBIT 2.1

LIFE-CYCLE INCOME
AND SPENDING

Income starts low, rises
through middle age, then falls
at retirement. The pattern of
spending over the life cycle is
more even. This is made
possible by borrowing in the
early years, by repayment and
saving in the middle years, and
by dissaving from assets after
retirement.

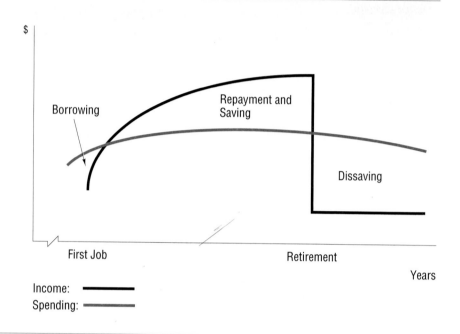

down savings. Saving and dissaving are the result both of fluctuations in income
and of fluctuations in spending. For example, dissaving may be necessary either
because income is low or because spending is high. Let us look at some of the
reasons why income and spending might fluctuate.

FLUCTUATIONS IN INCOME

Unless you are very fortunate, you will, like most people, need to earn your living
by working. Over your lifetime, your income will probably have the sort of
pattern shown in Exhibit 2.1. While you are in school, your income is probably
low. When you graduate and take a high-paying job, your income will take a big
jump. You can expect your income to go on rising steadily into middle age. Then
it will probably reach a plateau. When you retire, your earnings from work will
drop.

Clearly, matching your expenditure precisely to this pattern of income would
be highly inconvenient. In fact, most people borrow in their early years, enabling
them to spend more than their incomes. They then save during the peak earning
years to repay what they have borrowed and to accumulate savings for their later
years. Finally, they use those savings to support spending during retirement. This

pattern of borrowing and repayment, saving and dissaving is called the **life-cycle pattern of saving.**

There are, of course, other reasons why your income might fluctuate—some good and some not so good. The good might include winning the state lottery or inheriting a fortune. In such cases you would probably not want to spend all the money at once. Rather, you would save most of it and spend it gradually over the years. On the less pleasant side, you might lose your job. While your income might dry up temporarily, you would not want to cut back your spending to the same extent. If you have savings to fall back on, you will be able to maintain a reasonable standard of living while you look for a new job.

life-cycle pattern of saving
Pattern of borrowing and repayment, saving and dissaving through a lifetime.

FLUCTUATIONS IN SPENDING

The same sort of unevenness that we have seen on the income side also exists on the spending side. Some needs involve expenditures that are large relative to your annual income—a college education, a home, a car. It would be hard or even impossible to pay for these out of current income. There are two alternatives: Save before you buy (the method favored in Japan) or borrow and repay over time (the method favored in the United States). With the first alternative, a period of saving is followed by a large dissaving; with the second alternative, the dissaving comes first and is followed by a period of saving as you repay the loan.

Some needs are unexpected. Disasters of various kinds—illness, for example—may require large temporary expenditures. There may also be opportunities—a profitable business deal or a special on a trip to Tahiti—that you will miss unless you can call on resources in excess of your current income.

NET SAVING AND LENDING OF HOUSEHOLDS AS A GROUP

We have been looking at the saving behavior of a single household. Can we say anything about the total savings of *all* households taken together—of the **household sector?**

The answer involves some subtlety. For example, just because each individual is going to save for his or her retirement does not mean that the household sector *as a whole* will be saving for this reason. Consider a simple economy in which there are 100 young people each of whom saves $500 a month, and 100 old people each of whom dissaves $500 a month. For this economy, total life-cycle saving of the household sector will be zero.

Or consider an economy in which, each month, 1 person in 100 spends $10,000 on a new car (out of savings or borrowed) and the 99 others each saves $101.01 (either toward their next car or as a payment on the car they already have). Once again saving and dissaving will balance out, and total saving will be zero.

household sector
One of the decision-making divisions of the economy, composed of all individual households.

Similar arguments would apply to saving for unexpected contingencies. Suppose everyone has accumulated a precautionary reserve of the desired size. Suppose too that surprise fluctuations in income and needs average out over the population. Then the dissaving of those drawing down their precautionary reserves should be matched, pretty much, by the saving of those replenishing their reserves.

Nonetheless, as we shall see below when we look at the numbers, the household sector of our own economy *is* a net saver. Why is this?

One reason is that the population is growing. As a result, there are always more young people than old. Since there are more savers (the young) than dissavers (the old), *net* saving will be positive.[1] Another reason there is net saving is that income too is growing. The old draw down the savings they accumulated out of their income when they were young. But income then was less than the income the young are earning today. As a result, the dissaving of the current old is less than the saving of the current young. This effect is reinforced by the tendency of people to save a larger fraction of income as their income rises: The young today save a larger fraction of a larger income.

We can see from these considerations that the net saving of the household sector will depend a great deal on demographics (population growth and age composition) and on the rate of growth of income. Economies whose populations and incomes are growing rapidly will, other things equal, tend to generate a lot of net saving. Economic stagnation or an aging population will lead to reduced net saving. These factors go a long way toward explaining the substantial differences between the saving rates of different countries (see "Differences in National Savings Rates" on page 16).

If the household sector as a whole is a net saver, it is spending less than the income it receives. Although households could just accumulate this unspent income in the form of money, we shall see later that this is not usually an attractive alternative. Generally, the unspent income is lent to other sectors of the economy.

2.2 | WHY DO FIRMS INVEST AND BORROW?

To understand the behavior of firms, it is best to look at some concrete examples.

---

[1]Remember our simple example of 100 young people, each saving $500, and 100 old people, each dissaving $500. Suppose that at the end of each period (say 40 years) all the young become old, the old die, and 100 new young are born. If the population now starts to grow at 1% per period, in the first period there will be 101 young and 100 old, in the second period 102 young and 101 old, and so on. That is, there will always be one "extra" young person and saving will always exceed dissaving by $500.

FINANCING PRODUCTION

Suppose you have a terrific idea for some computer software, a program that you claim will enable the buyer to get rich in the stock market. You have already persuaded Pear Computer, a major manufacturer of personal computers, of the size of the potential market. Pear has agreed to buy the completed program from you for $150,000.

You reckon that to complete the program you will need to hire 4 programmers for 6 months. The monthly costs are as follows:

4 programmers at $3,500/mo.	$14,000
Office space and other expenses	1,000
	$15,000 x 6 mo. = $90,000

Your profit will be $150,000 – $90,000 = $60,000, which is not at all bad. You have only one problem: Where do you get the $90,000 you need to complete the project? The answer, of course, is that you need to borrow.

You take your story, well documented, to your local banker, Harrison Stuyvesant. Impressed with your qualifications and even more so with the commitment from Pear Computer to buy your product, Harrison grants you a **line of credit** for $90,000. That means that you will be able to borrow $15,000 the first month, $15,000 more the second month, and so on, up to a limit of $90,000.

You go ahead with the project. Six months later, you deliver the program to Pear, receive payment, and repay your bank loan. If you close your business, that is the end of it. If in the meantime, however, you have come up with another idea, you will need to continue your line of credit with the bank until you deliver your next program. This sort of loan, one that is alternately growing and being paid off, is called **revolving credit**. You could, of course, sink your profits from the first deal into financing the second, but, as we shall see in a moment, you may have better use for the money.

We have assumed that Pear will pay for the program immediately. In reality, though, businesses usually give each other some time to pay (this is called **trade credit**). If you give Pear 60 days to pay, you will have to ask your bank to increase your credit line to $120,000 (assuming you continue to employ your programmers in the meantime).

In this example, most of the expenses are labor. However, if your business had involved manufacturing, you would have had to finance the materials you used: An automobile manufacturer needs to pay for steel *before* the cars made from that steel are sold. Or if you were a retailer, you would have had to finance your inventory: A shoe store needs to pay for the shoes on its shelves before it sells them. The finance needed to cover the expense incurred in the production and sale of a product or service is called **working capital**. Traditionally, working capital has been provided largely by banks.

line of credit
Arrangement whereby a financial institution guarantees that a business can borrow up to a specified maximum amount of funds during a period of time.

revolving credit
Credit arrangement whereby a business can borrow, repay, and reborrow as it sees fit during a period of time.

trade credit
Time that one business will allow another business to pay for goods or services purchased.

working capital
Finance needed to cover the expense incurred in the production and sale of a product or service.

DIFFERENCES IN NATIONAL SAVINGS RATES

Last year the total savings of OECD households dropped below 10% of their disposable income—the lowest savings ratio for a quarter of a century and down from a peak of more than 14% in the mid-1970s. America's personal-savings ratio has dropped from 8% in 1981 to a 40-year low of below 4% in 1987. Britain's has fallen from 14% in 1980 to just under 6% last year. And in Sweden and Norway personal-savings ratios have become negative recently—i.e., households are borrowing more than they are saving. On the other hand Japanese and West German households remain as thrifty as ever; their savings ratios have actually risen slightly during the 1980s.

To explain these differences, economists have explored people's motives for saving. The most important is probably retirement. This is the basis of the life-cycle hypothesis of household saving, which says that households accumulate wealth during their working years by spending less than they earn. They then eat into those savings once they retire. The precise pattern will depend upon factors such as interest rates, the degree of risk aversion and the functioning of capital markets.

The pure life-cycle model has since been modified to allow for other motives: the desire to leave bequests; precautionary savings against unemployment or sickness; and savings to finance lumpy spending, such as cars and holidays.

This framework for individuals suggests that the savings of an entire country will be influenced by:
• The age structure of the population. The smaller the number of retired people in relation to the working population, the higher the savings ratio. Japan has only 19 retired people for every 100 workers, compared with 26 in America and 35 in Britain. One study found that the differences in the age structure of the populations of Japan and America

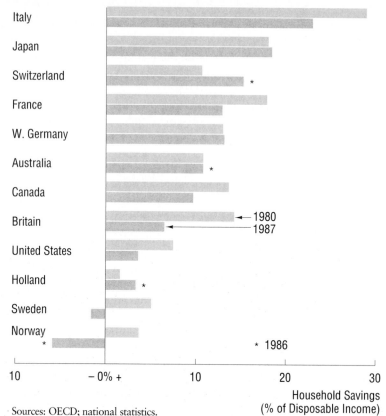

Sources: OECD; national statistics.

can by itself explain most of the disparity in their savings ratios.
• The efficiency of financial markets. Interest-rate ceilings lower the return on savings (as in America in the 1970s), while credit controls restrict access to borrowing. Financial deregulation has resulted in higher consumer borrowing—and hence lower net savings—in many countries, particularly Sweden and Norway.
• Taxation. America and Canada had similar savings rates at the start of the 1970s. One reason why they then diverged sharply was America's tax system, which increasingly favored borrowers. Canada's favored savers.
• The impact of interest rates on savings is ambiguous. Lower interest

rates make saving in, e.g., a bank less attractive; but they may also mean that households need to save more diligently if they are to reach some chosen target.
• Higher inflation encouraged higher savings in the 1970s. Inflation raised the level of savings needed to maintain the real value of financial assets. The sharp fall in inflation during the 1980s is a significant cause of the slump in savings.
• The wealth effect of rising stock prices (until October 1987) and in some countries house prices has reduced the need to save.

Source: "Smaller Savings for Rainy Days," *The Economist*, March 19, 1988, p. 76. Copyright 1988, The Economist. Distributed by Special Features/Syndication Sales.

FINANCING LONG-TERM INVESTMENT

There is another, rather different type of finance that a business might need. Returning to our computer software example, suppose you have been doing so well that in addition to just selling programs you are thinking of branching out into computer services. To do this, you will need to buy your own mainframe computer at a cost of $250,000. You anticipate that the new business should add about $5,000 a month to your net income, making it an attractive investment. This kind of long-term investment in machinery or buildings is called investment in **fixed capital**, in contrast to the working capital we looked at above.

fixed capital
Finance needed for long-term investment in machinery or buildings.

When you approach your local banker, Harrison, for a loan, you are surprised and disappointed to find that he is reluctant. He presents his reasons. First, the loan is rather long-term for his taste: You would need at least 4 to 5 years to pay it off. This means that his money would be tied up for a long time. In contrast, the line of credit could be wound up on fairly short notice. For reasons we shall see later, banks prefer short-term loans that can be turned back into cash quickly. In addition, a lot more can go wrong in 5 years than in 6 months: You might not be able to pay off the loan. Adding to the uncertainty, your estimate of the income from this investment is fairly speculative. When you asked for a working-capital loan, you already had a commitment from Pear to buy your product. Now you have only hopes and expectations: You have not actually sold anything yet. As a result, this loan is much riskier than the working-capital loan—another reason for your banker's reluctance.

However, since Harrison does value you as a customer, he agrees to offer you a 3-year loan for $150,000. To reduce the risk to the bank, the loan is **collateralized** by the computer: If you fail to repay the loan, the computer becomes the property of the bank and can be sold to pay off the loan. With a loan of only $150,000, you still need another $100,000. Also, because the investment itself is unlikely to generate enough revenue within 3 years to pay off the loan, you will need more money later on.

collateralized
Having a borrower's property pledged as a guarantee that a loan will be repaid.

Your situation is typical for a firm wishing to invest in fixed capital. You cannot easily borrow enough to finance the whole investment. To raise the money you need, you will have to find investors with faith in the prospects of your business who are willing to take a long-term risk in exchange for an attractive return. In principle, you could sell stocks or bonds, but in your case the sum you need is much too small to make this worthwhile. Most likely, you will have to rely on your own resources. This is why it would have been unwise to invest your earlier profits in working capital: It is relatively easy to finance working capital, but much harder to finance fixed capital. In fact, most investment in fixed capital is financed out of retained earnings, or **internal funds**, in this way.

internal funds
After-tax profits that are retained by the business and not distributed to stockholders.

NET DISSAVING AND BORROWING OF FIRMS AS A GROUP

We have seen that firms dissave in order to invest both in working capital and in fixed capital. They also save for later investment and to repay past borrowing. In addition, just as households accumulate a precautionary reserve against unexpected contingencies, so too do firms.

Are firms as a whole, then, net savers or dissavers? Normally, our economy is growing: Firms are making new investments and expanding their output. As a result, the dissaving of the firm sector tends to run ahead of its saving, so that generally the firm sector as a whole is a net dissaver.

The amount of net dissaving of the firm sector will depend, of course, on how fast the economy is growing. If the economy slows down, net dissaving of the firm sector will shrink. In a stagnant economy, one with no growth, the dissaving of firms that are currently investing will be balanced by the saving of other firms for future investment or to repay loans for past investment, and the net saving of the firm sector will be zero.

If the firm sector is a net dissaver, it is spending more than its current income. The difference must be borrowed from other sectors of the economy.

2.3 | BRINGING BORROWING AND LENDING TOGETHER

THE CIRCULAR FLOW OF PAYMENTS

To keep things simple, let us begin by pretending that the economy is made up of only the two sectors—households and firms. We shall bring in other sectors, like the government, later on.

We have seen that while some households save and others dissave, as a group households are net savers. Similarly, while some firms save and others dissave, as a group firms are net dissavers. The basic economic role of the financial system is to channel the net saving of the household sector to the firm sector in order to finance its net dissaving. This is illustrated in Exhibit 2.2, a circular flow diagram that shows schematically the flows of payments in our simplified economy.

Households are paid income by firms in the form of wages, dividends, and interest. They spend most of this income directly on goods and services. What they do not spend in one way or another, they lend. This lending is channeled by the financial system to firms. The money firms borrow in this way is added to their own internal funds to be spent on goods and services in the form of investment expenditure. The investment expenditure of one firm—the purchase of plant, equipment, or materials—is the sales revenue of another. So the total revenue of the firm sector is the sum of household expenditure and of firms'

EXHIBIT 2.2

THE CIRCULAR
FLOW OF PAYMENTS

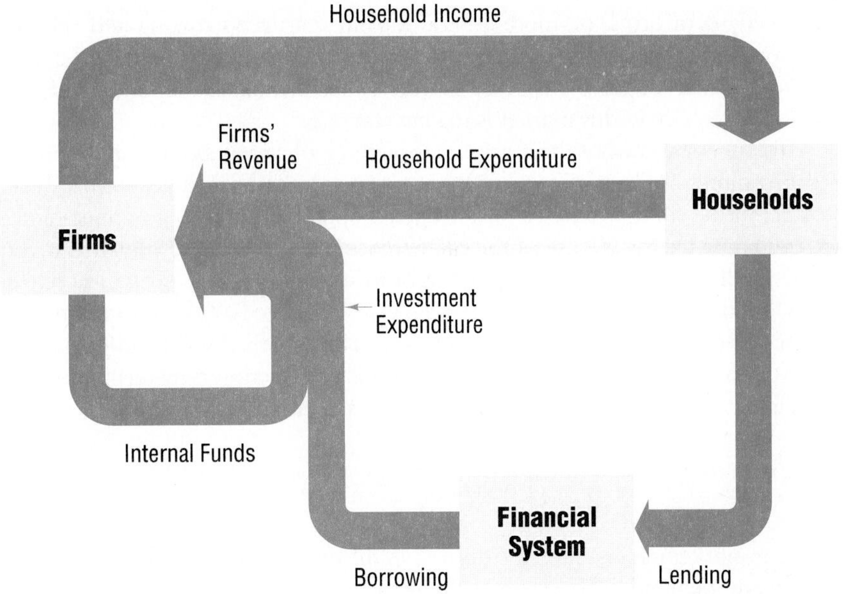

Household Income

Firms' Revenue

Household Expenditure

Households

Firms

Investment Expenditure

Internal Funds

Financial System

Borrowing

Lending

Firms pay income to households. Households either spend this or lend it, through the financial system, to firms. Firms spend what they borrow, plus their own internal funds, on investment. Household expenditure plus firm investment expenditure is the total revenue of all firms. This revenue is split between income that goes to households and internal funds that firms use for investment.

investment expenditure. Firms retain some of this revenue and pay out the rest to households as income, and the cycle begins all over again.[2]

The circular flow diagram simplifies considerably a more complicated reality. In the first place, as we have seen, firms lend as well as borrow, and households borrow as well as lend. Although the diagram shows only the *net* flow from the household sector to firms, these other transactions too will be channeled through the financial system.

Furthermore, households and firms are not the only sectors in the economy: Two others that are important in terms of their effect on the financial system are the government and "foreigners" (firms and households outside our own economy). Later on, as we bring these other sectors into the story, we shall see that the circular flow becomes considerably more complicated.

[2]Some investment, particularly in working capital, represents payments directly to households rather than to other firms. These payments are not shown in Exhibit 2.2.

THE LOANABLE FUNDS MARKET

The role of the financial system, then, is to match the saving of households with the dissaving of firms, or, more generally, to match up borrowing and lending. For some purposes, it is useful to think of the financial system as being a market—a market for loans. This market is usually called the **loanable funds market**. The price in this market is the interest rate.[3]

loanable funds market
Market for funds that lenders are willing to make available to borrowers.

To understand what the interest rate is, think of a loan as a rental of money. Renting money is like renting a car. If you rent a car—say, a Camaro—for a week, you get the use of the Camaro for the agreed-upon period; then you must return it. You pay a fee for the use of the car, perhaps $300 per week. Similarly, if you rent $1 million for a year, you get the use of $1 million for a year. You must return the $1 million at the end of the year and pay a fee, say $50,000. The amount that you have borrowed ($1 million) is called the **principal**; the fee ($50,000) is called the **interest** on the loan. The interest expressed as a fraction or percentage of the principal is called the **interest rate**; in our case the interest rate is[4]

principal
Amount of money borrowed, excluding interest.

interest
Fee paid by a borrower to a lender for the use of the lender's money.

$$\frac{\$50,000}{\$1,000,000} = 0.05, \text{ or } 5\%.$$

interest rate
Cost of borrowing expressed as a percentage of the principal.

The market interest rate, the "price" in the market for loans, will depend on supply and demand. The supply is the net lending of the household sector; the demand is the net borrowing of the firm sector. Let us look at each a little more closely.

SUPPLY AND DEMAND

We have seen why the household sector is a net lender, but what determines the *amount* of its net lending? One determinant is income: The household sector tends to save more, and so lend more, as incomes rise.

The amount of net lending also depends on the interest rate that can be earned from lending or that must be paid for borrowing. Remember that net lending of the household sector is its saving less the amount it borrows:

household net lending = household saving – household borrowing.

The effect of the interest rate on household saving is uncertain in principle, and it does not seem to be large in practice. For reasons that we shall see later, however, household borrowing *is* quite sensitive to the interest rate: As the interest rate rises, household borrowing falls. As a result, *net* lending (saving less borrowing) rises as the interest rate increases.

---

[3]In fact, as we shall see later, there are many different types of loan, each with its own interest rate. We abstract from these complications here.

[4]We shall look at more general interest-rate calculations in Chapter 6.

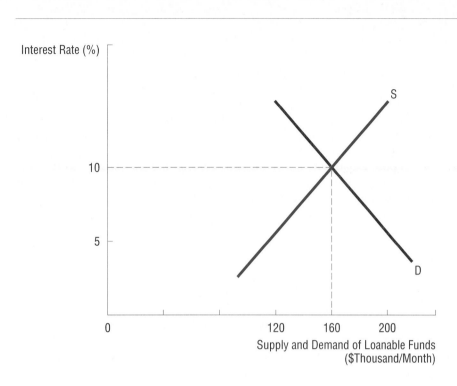

EXHIBIT 2.3

THE LOANABLE FUNDS MARKET

The supply of loanable funds is the net lending of the household sector. The demand is the net borrowing of the firm sector. The market is in equilibrium at an interest rate of 10%, at which both the quantity supplied and the quantity demanded equal $160 million per month.

The resulting positive relationship between the interest rate and household net lending gives us the upward-sloping supply curve for loanable funds shown in Exhibit 2.3. (The numbers are made up for the purpose of illustration: We shall look at some real numbers for the U.S. economy at the end of the chapter.) Note that the supply curve is drawn *given* household income: If income changes, the curve will shift.

The demand curve in Exhibit 2.3 represents the net borrowing of firms. What determines the *amount* they borrow? A firm borrows because it wishes to buy plant and equipment, hire labor, buy inputs, and finally, produce and sell goods. Hence one important determinant of its willingness to borrow is its expectation of profits. How well does the firm think its product will sell? The more optimistic it is, the more willing it will be to borrow money and to commit that money to an investment project.

A second determinant of firm borrowing is the interest rate. To see why, consider an example. Suppose a firm can borrow $5,000 to produce an electronic gizmotron, which will take one year to produce. When it is ready in a year's time, the gizmotron can be sold for $5,500. The investment will be worthwhile if the loan can be repaid out of the $5,500 and something remains for the firm. If the interest rate is 5%, the firm will repay $5,250, and it will be left with $250. If the interest rate is 15%, the firm will have to repay $5,750, and it will make a loss. At 10% it will just break even. We can express this algebraically as follows: The project will be profitable if and only if

$$\$5,000 \times (1 + i) < \$5,500,$$

where i is the interest rate the firm must pay.

break-even interest rate
Interest rate above which a project is unprofitable and below which it is profitable.

For this project 10% is the **break-even interest rate**. At interest rates below 10%, the project is profitable; at interest rates above 10%, the project is unprofitable.[5]

In practice, a firm will face many different investment projects, each with a different break-even interest rate. These projects can be ranked according to their break-even rates (Project A is the gizmotron):

Project	Break-even Rate	Cost
A	10%	$5,000
B	8	4,000
C	7	1,000
D	4	5,000
E	3	2,000

Suppose the firm can borrow at 5%. Then Projects A, B, and C are all profitable, but Projects D and E are not. Hence the firm will borrow $5,000 plus $4,000 plus $1,000—or $10,000 in all—in order to invest in these three projects. If the rate at which it can borrow is 9%, the firm will borrow only $5,000 and invest only in Project A: Projects B and C are no longer profitable if the firm has to pay 9% for finance. The lower the interest rate, the more investment the firm will be willing to undertake.[6]

This negative relationship between the interest rate and firm investment underlies the downward-sloping demand curve in Exhibit 2.3. That curve shows the net borrowing of all firms—total dissaving less total saving (remember that much investment is financed out of savings accumulated from firms' own internal funds). Note that the demand curve is drawn *given* firms' perceptions of profit opportunities: If these perceptions change, the curve will shift.

---

[5]For more complicated projects—those that require more than a single investment or those that pay off at more than one time—there need not be a single break-even interest rate. In Chapter 6 we shall look at a more general way of evaluating an investment project.

[6]You may have encountered this relationship between investment and the interest rate in your principles of economics course under the name *marginal efficiency of investment schedule*.

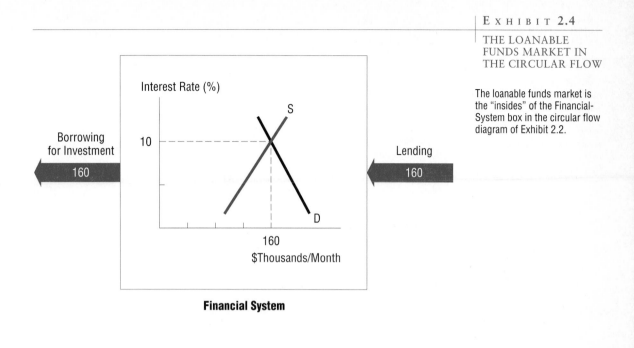

EXHIBIT 2.4

THE LOANABLE
FUNDS MARKET IN
THE CIRCULAR FLOW

The loanable funds market is
the "insides" of the Financial-
System box in the circular flow
diagram of Exhibit 2.2.

EQUILIBRIUM IN THE LOANABLE FUNDS MARKET

The **equilibrium interest rate** is the interest rate at which the quantity of loanable funds demanded equals the quantity supplied. In Exhibit 2.3 it is the rate at which the supply and demand curves intersect—10%. At this interest rate, borrowing and lending both total $160 million per month.

The market interest rate could not long be above the equilibrium value of 10%. If it were, some households offering to lend to firms would not find takers. These households would then offer to lend at a lower rate, and the market rate would be bid down by this competition. Similarly, the market rate could not long be below 10%. If it were, some firms willing to borrow would not find lenders. These firms would offer to pay above the market rate, and the market rate would be bid up. At the equilibrium rate of 10%, things just balance out.

equilibrium interest rate
Interest rate at which the quantity of loanable funds demanded equals the quantity supplied.

THE LOANABLE FUNDS MARKET
IN THE CIRCULAR FLOW

Where does this market for loanable funds fit into the economy as a whole? The loanable funds market is just the "insides" of the financial-system box in the circular flow diagram in Exhibit 2.2. This is illustrated in Exhibit 2.4.

E X H I B I T 2.5

A FALL IN THE
DEMAND FOR
LOANABLE FUNDS

Firms' pessimism about the
economy shifts the demand
curve for loanable funds to the
left. The result is a fall in the
equilibrium interest rate and in
the quantity of loanable funds
borrowed and lent.

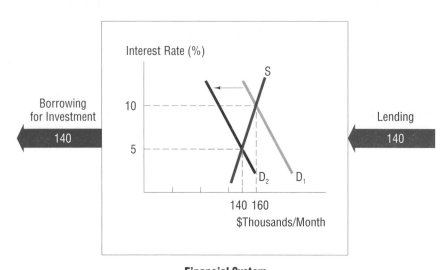

Financial System

In terms of the circular flow, equilibrium in the loanable funds market means that the flow into the financial-system box equals the flow out of it. In our example the equilibrium interest rate is 10%. At this interest rate, the supply of loanable funds and the demand both equal $160 million. The flow into the financial market is $160 million; the flow out of it is $160 million. If the interest rate were higher or lower, the flows would not balance. Since this is impossible, the interest rate must be at its equilibrium level.

This combination of the two diagrams—the supply and demand in the loanable funds market and the circular flow—gives us a simple model that we can use to analyze changes in the economy. As an example, imagine that firms suddenly become more pessimistic about the profitability of investment. As a result, the break-even interest rates on the projects they are considering fall. At any given interest rate, fewer projects now pass the test, and so firms are willing to borrow less than before. This means a shift to the left of the demand curve for loanable funds.

The effect on the loanable funds market is shown in Exhibit 2.5. The demand curve shifts to the left by $40 million (we assume that at any interest rate firms are now willing to borrow $40 million less than they would have been before). The new equilibrium interest rate is 5%. The amount of borrowing at this interest rate is $140 million per month rather than $160 million. Note that the quantity of loanable funds demanded falls by less than the $40 million it would have fallen had the interest rate stayed at 10%. The fall in the interest rate to 5% partly offsets the firm's pessimism about profits, boosting investment somewhat: At 5% firms are willing to invest $20 million more than at the original 10%, so investment and net borrowing fall by only $20 million rather than by the full $40 million.

What are the implications for the circular flow of payments? The amount of loanable funds flowing through the financial system is $20 million less. Where has it gone? If we look at our circular flow diagram, Exhibit 2.2, we see that if the flow to the financial system falls by $20 million, there must be a corresponding increase in household expenditure of the same amount. Therefore, despite the fall in investment expenditure, total expenditure remains the same. Of course, as we shall see later, things may not go so smoothly. Keynesian economists, in particular, believe that such a fall in firms' desire to invest can cause serious problems for the economy. We shall examine their arguments and the remedies they suggest in Chapter 30.

A MORE REALISTIC CIRCULAR FLOW

Of course, the flow of payments in the real world is much more complicated than the simple circular flow of Exhibit 2.2. To make things more realistic, we would need to add additional sectors. One important sector is the government. Exhibit 2.6 shows how the simple circular flow might be modified to include a government sector. Another important sector is "foreigners"—to account for international transactions. Including a foreign sector in the circular flow is a little complicated, so we defer it until Chapter 25.

In Exhibit 2.6 households now pay part of their income to the government as taxes, and the government spends a certain amount on goods and services.[7] Of course, government expenditure and tax revenue need not be equal. If they are not, the difference must be made up in some way: The flows into and out of the government-sector box in the circular flow diagram have to balance. One way they can be made to balance is through borrowing or lending. If the government has a deficit—spends more than it receives in taxes—it can borrow; if it has a surplus, it can lend.[8]

The implications for the loanable funds market are shown in Exhibit 2.7. The demand for loanable funds is now the *sum* of the demand of firms, D^F, and the demand of government, D^G (we depict the government as a borrower, which seems not unrealistic).[9] For simplicity, we assume that D^G is a constant amount, $80 million, determined by policy, and that it is unaffected by the interest rate (we

---

[7]These taxes are *net* taxes—taxes less transfer payments such as social security and welfare. Firms also pay taxes, but these are not shown in the diagram. For simplicity, we also ignore here the effect of taxes on the net lending of households and on the net borrowing of firms. In reality, taxes do have an important effect.

[8]There are other ways to balance things; we shall consider these later on.

[9]Remember that household demand for loanable funds has been subtracted from household saving to give us household net lending—our supply curve.

EXHIBIT 2.6

INCLUDING A GOVERNMENT SECTOR IN THE CIRCULAR FLOW

The government sector collects taxes from households, leaving less for spending and lending. Government expenditure is added to household expenditure and firm investment expenditure to make up the total sales revenue of firms. If government expenditure and taxes are not equal, the difference may be made up by government borrowing or lending.

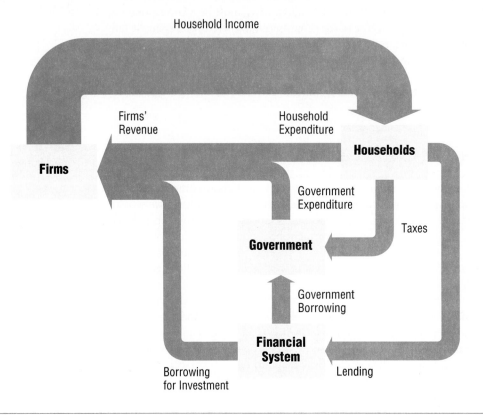

take a more realistic look at this in Chapter 25). We therefore draw total demand as D^F plus this constant amount.

Now, equilibrium in the loanable funds market involves an inflow from households of $200 million, an outflow to firms of $120 million, and an outflow to the government of $80 million. The equilibrium interest rate is now 20%. At this interest rate, households are willing to lend somewhat more and firms are willing to borrow somewhat less. The difference between the amount households are willing to lend at 20% and the amount firms wish to borrow at this rate just equals the amount the government needs to borrow to balance its budget.

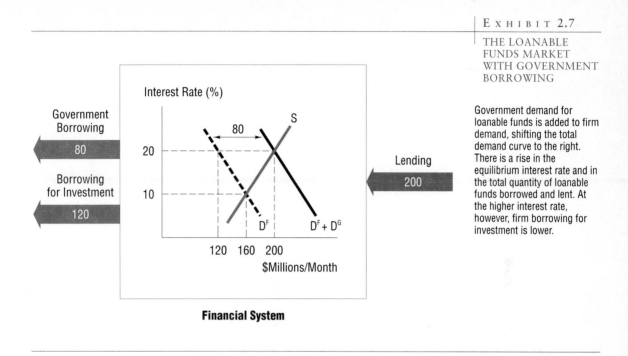

Financial System

EXHIBIT 2.7

THE LOANABLE
FUNDS MARKET
WITH GOVERNMENT
BORROWING

Government demand for
loanable funds is added to firm
demand, shifting the total
demand curve to the right.
There is a rise in the
equilibrium interest rate and in
the total quantity of loanable
funds borrowed and lent. At
the higher interest rate,
however, firm borrowing for
investment is lower.

2.4 | A LOOK AT THE NUMBERS

What do these flows look like in the real world? Exhibit 2.8 presents some estimates. These numbers are taken from the **flow of funds accounts**, the purpose of which is precisely to trace the flows of borrowing and lending in the economy. Exhibit 2.8 shows the borrowing and lending of households, firms, government, and foreigners.[10] For each sector the table shows total lending, total borrowing, and net borrowing or lending.[11] In 1988 households lent a total of $440 billion and borrowed $296 billion, for net lending of $440 – $296 = $144 billion. Firms were net borrowers of $12 billion. However, investment was much larger than the amount that firms borrowed: In addition to their net borrowing in 1988, firms had available to them $470 billion of internal funds. Notice that government was a large net borrower, to the tune of $195 billion. Foreigners were a large net lender, lending the U.S. economy a total of $136 billion. We shall have more to say about these numbers in later chapters.

flow of funds accounts
Record of the amounts
borrowed and lent among
the various sectors of the
economy.

[10]The households category includes personal trusts and nonprofit organizations (such as colleges and some hospitals); "firms" are nonfinancial businesses (the category does not include banks, insurance companies, etc.); "government" includes state, local, and federal governments.

[11]Lending is net acquisition of financial assets (when you lend, you acquire an IOU or a financial asset); borrowing is net increase in liabilities.

EXHIBIT 2.8

BORROWING AND LENDING BY SECTOR, 1988 (BILLIONS OF DOLLARS)

	Total Lending	Total Borrowing	Net Lending	Net Borrowing
Households	440	296	144	
Firms	124	136		12
Government	16	211		195
Foreigners	173	37	136	

Source: Federal Reserve Flow of Funds Accounts.

SUMMARY

- When income exceeds spending, there is saving. Saving is used to repay debt or to increase savings.

- When spending exceeds income, there is dissaving. Dissaving is made possible either by borrowing or by the use of savings.

- Because spending patterns do not match income patterns, households both save and dissave. Income fluctuates both over the life cycle and year to year. Expenditures fluctuate because of the purchase of big-ticket items such as houses and automobiles and because of unexpected events such as illness.

- As a group, households are net savers. This is because population and income are growing. As a result, the saving of younger households more than offsets the dissaving of older households.

- Firms also both save and dissave. They dissave in order to finance investment. This dissaving is made possible by borrowing or by the use of savings out of past profits. Saving is used to repay past borrowing or to accumulate reserves for future investment.

- Firms borrow from banks to finance the working capital they need for production. They finance longer-term investment in fixed capital largely out of retained earnings but also by borrowing directly from investors.

- In the aggregate, firms are net dissavers. This is because the economy is growing. New firms that are being created and old firms that are expanding are dissavers. This new, additional activity means that there is more dissaving than saving, so that the firm sector as a whole is a net borrower.

- The net saving of the household sector is channeled to the firm sector by the financial system. The circular flow diagram in Exhibit 2.2 shows the various flows of payments involved.

- It is useful to think of the financial system as being a market for loanable funds, with household net lending representing the supply and firm net borrowing representing the demand. The interest rate is the price in this market.

- Household net lending is household saving less household borrowing. Household net lending increases as the interest rate rises mainly because household borrowing falls. Changes in the income of the household sector shift the supply curve.

- A firm goes ahead with an investment project if the market rate of interest is below the project's break-even rate. As the market rate falls, more projects meet this criterion, and firm investment and borrowing increase.

- A more realistic circular flow would include sectors other than firms and households. Two important sectors are the government sector and the foreign sector (the latter representing transactions with other countries).

- The flow of funds accounts provide estimates of real-world flows of borrowing and lending. Households are a large net lender and firms a net borrower. In recent years the government has been a large net borrower and the foreign sector a large net lender.

KEY TERMS

saving	trade credit	interest
dissaving	working capital	interest rate
savings	fixed capital	break-even interest rate
life-cycle pattern of saving	collateralized	equilibrium interest rate
household sector	internal funds	flow of funds accounts
line of credit	loanable funds market	
revolving credit	principal	

DISCUSSION QUESTIONS

1. The way the circular flow is set up in Exhibit 2.2, a fall in the demand for loanable funds by firms cannot cause total expenditure to fall. How could the circular flow be modified to allow such a result? (*Hint*: There needs to be some way for money not lent by households *not* to go into extra household expenditure.) Is such a modification realistic?

2. One reason that households are net savers is that population is growing. What would be the effect on the economy (saving, investment, the interest rate) of achieving zero population growth?

3. Suppose the government cut taxes without cutting expenditure. Use the simple model (circular flow diagram plus loanable funds market) to discuss the possible effects on interest rates and investment. How does your answer depend on what households decide to do with the extra income?

BIBLIOGRAPHY

Board of Governors of the Federal Reserve System, *Introduction to the Flow of Funds*, Washington, D.C.: Board of Governors of the Federal Reserve System, 1980.

Fisher, Irving, *The Theory of Interest*, New York: Macmillan, 1930.

Hall, Robert E., and John B. Taylor, *Macroeconomics: Theory, Performance, and Policy*, New York: Norton, 1988.

SOFTWARE EXERCISE FOR THIS CHAPTER

Title: Loanflow

This computer exercise will help you consolidate your understanding of the circular flow of payments and how the financial system channels funds from lenders to borrowers. See your instructor if you wish to use this program.

Did you know that there is a Study Guide available for this text?

Be prepared for your class tests, midterms, and final exams by obtaining a copy of this invaluable resource. It includes:

- chapter overviews
- detailed chapter reviews in outline form
- true/false and multiple choice review questions
- conceptual problems with complete, detailed solutions

If your bookstore does not have the Study Guide in stock, please ask the bookstore manager to order copies for you and your fellow classmates.

To help you prepare for exams, The Dryden Press has made available for sale the following supplement to **Money, Banking, and Financial Markets**

Study Guide
ISBN 0-03-052622-1

If this supplement is not available in your bookstore, please ask the bookstore manager to order copies for you and your fellow students.

The Dryden Press

The Dryden Press

CHAPTER 3

BORROWING AND LENDING

We saw in Chapter 2 that the role of the financial system is to bring borrowers and lenders together. In this chapter we shall see just what that involves. First we shall look at the difficulties of making a loan. Then we shall see how the financial system deals with those difficulties.

We shall generally think of lenders as being households and of borrowers as being firms. Of course, as we saw in Chapter 2, the shoe can sometimes be on the other foot: Households also borrow and firms also lend. In addition, there are other important borrowers and lenders such as the government and foreigners. However, household lending to firms is in many ways the typical case, and our story will be simpler and easier to follow if we focus on it.

3.1 THE BASIC DIFFICULTIES OF MAKING A LOAN

THE RISKS INVOLVED

When you make a loan, you give up money here and now in exchange for a promise. Some examples are:

1. *A savings account.* You hand over $1,000 and are promised your money back whenever you want it, plus annual interest of 5%, compounded daily, to be credited to your account at the end of each month.[1]

2. *A bond.* You hand over $10,000 and are promised your money back at the end of 20 years, plus a check for $500 every 6 months until then.

---

[1]We shall discuss interest rates and compounding fully in Chapter 6.

3.   *A stock*. You give up $5,000 and are promised 0.5 of 1% of the dividends paid out by the company each year.[2]

security
Financial instrument representing ownership or debt that provides a claim to the borrower's future income.

In each case the nature of the promise is spelled out in a document or **security**. The document takes the form of a passbook for the savings account and a certificate for the stock or bond.

The exchange of money here and now for a promise involves risk. That risk is obvious with the stock. You are promised a very definite share of a very *indefinite* amount: What you receive will depend both on the firm's profits and on management's decision on how much of that profit to pay out rather than reinvest in the firm. But there is also a risk with the bond, even though the promise is quite specific. The company issuing the bond may **default**—that is, it may fail to keep its promises to you. Interest payments may be late or, worse, you may not get the principal back. This need not involve any dishonesty: There are all sorts of risks in business, and the company may simply be unable to pay, even though it has done its best to meet its obligations. How about the savings account? Is that at least safe? In the past, it was not: You could have lost your money if the bank failed. Today, however, virtually all deposits are insured by the government.[3]

default
To fail either to make interest payments on schedule or to pay off the amount owed when the financial instrument matures.

THE IMPORTANCE OF INFORMATION

The key to dealing with risk is information: You need to know what you are getting into. If the risk is too great, you may not want to make the loan at all. But some risk may be tolerable if the potential reward is sufficient.

Suppose, for example, that you have the opportunity to invest in a dynamic new company called High Tech Concepts (HTC). You will need information about HTC, and also, perhaps, about what it intends to do with the borrowed money. What is its record? Has it paid off its loans in the past? Is it well managed? What assets does it have to collateralize the loan? What other debts does it owe? What are its prospects? Will it have the cash flow it needs to repay the loan?

Gathering such information is costly—in time and in trouble as well as in dollars. HTC will have to prepare accounting information, or pay an accountant to do so, as well as prepare some sort of presentation about its plans. Credit records will have to be checked. Experts will have to be consulted on the value of collateral. You will have to spend time absorbing all the data and making some sort of judgment.

It may also be hard to get all the information you want. HTC may not want to reveal too much because the information could be valuable to its competitors. Suppose it has a great idea for a new product—a new line of sneakers that squeak out a tune as you walk (Squeakers). To get the financing it needs from you and

---

[2]The owner of a stock, unlike the owner of a bond or a savings account, also acquires the right to make decisions about the management of the company by voting at stockholder meetings.

[3]The reliability of this insurance is a question we shall take up in Chapters 16 and 17.

from others, HTC will have to disclose its idea. But if the idea becomes widely known, others may steal it and get the product to market first.

How much can you rely on the information you do get? HTC clearly has an interest in making itself look good, so it will be selective in what it tells you. It will give you the good news and keep as much of the bad news to itself as it can. Knowing this, even if HTC does tell you the truth, you will tend to discount what it says.

THE LOAN CONTRACT

Even when you have the necessary information, you are unlikely to trust HTC enough to accept a simple promise to repay. You will want something more binding—something that can, if necessary, be enforced by a court of law. You will, therefore, have to negotiate some sort of legal contract. Such negotiation is also costly—in lawyers' fees and in more time and trouble.

You will have to be careful in negotiating the contract: The *nature* of the contract may affect HTC's behavior and thereby affect the risk and return on your investment. For example, suppose you agree to put up $1 million in exchange for 75% of the profits from the production of Squeakers. This is an **equity contract** (stocks are equity contracts). An equity contract may have the effect of reducing the effort that the current owner and manager, Higgins Thornton III, would otherwise put into the venture. From Higgins' point of view, the contract imposes a 75% "tax" on his profits. It seems plausible that he will not work as hard to squeeze out that last dollar of profit if he gets only 25% of it for himself. As a result, the return on your investment may not be as good as you had expected.

To avoid this incentive effect of an equity contract, you could instead negotiate a **debt contract** (bonds are debt contracts). You could lend HTC the $1 million in exchange for a fixed $1.2 million next year. Now Higgins will work harder, because every extra dollar over the $1.2 million he owes you is a whole extra dollar for him.

Unfortunately, there are incentive problems with this sort of contract too. Suppose that if Squeakers sell well (there is a 50% chance), profits will be $2 million. (See Exhibit 3.1.) If they do not sell well (also a 50% chance), profits will be $1.2 million. In either case HTC will be able to pay off its debt to you. The return to Higgins will be the profits less the repayment of the loan—either $800,000 (a 50% chance) or zero (also a 50% chance).

However, Higgins sees a way to improve his potential gains. If he makes the Squeakers luminescent, at little extra cost, the possible profits become $2.2 million for success (the chance is still 50%); however, if the luminescent Squeakers do badly, they will do *so* badly that HTC will be unable to repay its debt to you at all. For Higgins, the riskier project is an improvement: He gets $1 million instead of $800,000 if the venture succeeds, and he still gets zero if it fails. However, *you* now stand a 50% chance of losing your whole investment.

equity contract
Contract representing a claim to a share in the net income and in the assets of a business.

debt contract
Contract stating agreement by the borrower to pay the lender fixed dollar amounts at regular intervals until a specified date when the final payment is made.

Exhibit 3.1

RETURNS FROM TWO
VERSIONS OF THE
SQUEAKERS PROJECT
UNDER A DEBT
CONTRACT

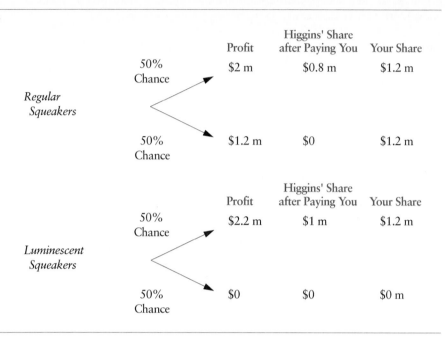

	Profit	Higgins' Share after Paying You	Your Share
Regular Squeakers 50% Chance	$2 m	$0.8 m	$1.2 m
50% Chance	$1.2 m	$0	$1.2 m

	Profit	Higgins' Share after Paying You	Your Share
Luminescent Squeakers 50% Chance	$2.2 m	$1 m	$1.2 m
50% Chance	$0	$0	$0 m

limited liability
Responsibility for
payments of business debts
that does not extend to the
owners' personal assets.

loan covenants
Clauses in a lending
contract that limit the
borrower's behavior in
various ways.

How does Higgins get away with this? Can you not sue him for the money he owes you? Not if HTC is a corporation. As a corporation, HTC is a distinct legal entity. You have lent your money to HTC, not to Higgins personally. The liability of the owners of a corporation for its debts is limited to the money they have put into the corporation—their equity. This institution of **limited liability** is at the root of the incentive problem you face when lending to HTC. Nonetheless, limited liability is a very useful legal institution: Without it, the risks of starting and running a business would be much higher, and there would be many fewer businesses.

Because lending contracts have these sorts of incentive effects, they often contain a variety of clauses, called **loan covenants**, limiting the behavior of the borrower in various ways. For example, you might insist that Higgins put up a certain proportion of the cost of the project himself, so that he too has something to lose if the project fails.

It is not enough simply to write a contract: You will have to *monitor* the behavior of the borrower to make sure the terms of the contract are being honored. You will have to receive regular accounts from HTC, certified by a reliable accountant, in order to check that the loan covenants are being honored. Hence monitoring is also costly.

SOME GENERAL PROBLEMS WITH THE COST OF LENDING

The costs of making a loan are to some extent *indivisible*: Making a $10,000 loan for a month may not cost much less than making a $100 million loan for 30 years. For example, suppose the information and contracting costs are the same in each case, say $20,000, and the monitoring costs are $1,000 a month. The borrower in each case is willing to pay no more than 10% a year in interest for the money. The costs of making the loan are small when compared to the $10 million a year in interest on the big loan, but they would completely swamp the $80 in total interest on the small loan.[4] In these circumstances, the small, short-term loan would simply not be made.

There is also a **free-rider problem.** If you go to the trouble and expense of digging out the information about HTC, negotiating and writing a loan contract, and monitoring its behavior, then someone else can come along and lend to HTC quite safely without incurring all of these costs. They can simply rely on your having done a good job for them. You bear all the costs, but the benefits are shared by all lenders. As a result, each potential lender will wait for someone else to go first, and the loan may never be made.

free-rider problem
Problem of one investor bearing all the cost of research that can also be used by other investors.

LIQUIDITY

Risk is not your only problem when making a loan. What do you do if there is some emergency or opportunity and you want your money back in a hurry? If it is easy for you to do this, we describe the loan as being **liquid.** While you would obviously like to get your money back easily whenever you want it, a borrower needs to have a firm commitment. It is hard for borrowers to do anything useful with the money if they have to be ready at all times to repay it on short notice.

How can these conflicting needs be reconciled? One solution is for you to sell the security to someone else. That way you get your money, but from someone other than the borrower, and the promise of future payment is transferred to the purchaser of the security. If you are allowed to do this, the security is described as being **transferable** or **negotiable.** Stocks and bonds are negotiable. However, savings accounts are not; instead, the bank promises to repay you your money whenever you want it.

Even though stocks and bonds are negotiable, there is no guarantee that, at the time you want to sell, you will be able to get a good price. It all depends on what potential buyers are willing to pay. You may get back less than the amount you invested (you make a **capital loss**), or, if you are lucky, you may get back much more (you make a **capital gain**).

liquid
Capable of ready conversion into cash.

transferable (negotiable)
Transferable from one person to another so that the title passes to the transferee.

capital loss
Loss from the sale of an asset at a price below the original cost.

capital gain
Gain from the sale of an asset at a price higher than the original cost.

---

[4]An annual rate of 10% is equivalent to about 0.8 of 1% a month, so the one-month loan would pay 0.8 of 1% of $10,000, or $80. We shall take a closer look at interest-rate algebra in Chapter 6.

SUMMARY

When making a loan, you must gather and evaluate information. Then you must write a loan contract, taking into account the incentive problems involved, and monitor the fulfillment of the contract. The costs of doing all this can be substantial. Having made the loan, it may be hard to get your money back when you want it.

Indeed, the costs and the problems of making a loan are such that, without the considerable help of the financial system, you would almost never do it. Fortunately, the financial system has devised ways to handle the costs efficiently and to deal with the associated problems. This makes widespread borrowing and lending possible.

There are basically two different ways the problems can be handled—through **direct lending** and through **indirect lending**. We shall look at each in turn.

direct lending
Lending by ultimate lender to ultimate borrower with no intermediary.

indirect lending
Lending by ultimate lender to financial intermediary that then relends to ultimate borrower.

3.2 | ALTERNATIVE SOLUTIONS

SOLUTION 1: DIRECT LENDING

Suppose you have $10,000 that you wish to put away for your retirement. At the same time Megacorp Motors (MM) is planning to build a new assembly plant and needs to borrow. Your respective needs could be matched if you lent MM your $10,000 in exchange for a 30-year bond. MM will repay the money in 30 years and pay the agreed-upon interest every 6 months until then. The deal is strictly between you and MM. It is up to you to do your homework and to decide whether or not MM is a good risk—whether it is likely to pay as promised and whether the return is high enough given the risk.

DEALING WITH THE INFORMATION PROBLEMS Financial markets have developed ways of making your decision easier. The **Securities and Exchange Commission (SEC)**, a government agency, requires companies issuing bonds to file extensive and detailed financial statements, and these financial statements are made available to the public. In addition, the bonds must be sold through a dealer (called an **underwriter**), an investment firm charged with providing full and unbiased information about the securities it sells. The underwriter has reason to take its responsibilities seriously: If the issuer defaults and if the underwriter has not been conscientious, investors can sue it for their losses. The underwriter also negotiates the form of the loan contract, with an eye to making the bond as attractive as possible to the market. **Rating agencies** (Standard & Poor's, Moody's, and others) specialize in investigating the creditworthiness of corporate borrowers and in monitoring their performance. These agencies give each borrower a letter grade for creditworthiness and make further information available to their subscribers.

Securities and Exchange Commission (SEC)
Federal agency that regulates the securities markets and securities brokers and dealers.

underwriter
An investment firm that purchases new securities from an issuer for a price negotiated in advance and then resells them.

rating agencies
Investment advisory firms that rank bonds according to the perceived probability of their default.

All of these arrangements greatly reduce the information, negotiation, and monitoring costs for the individual lender, but only at substantial cost to the borrower. The borrower must prepare the financial statements, pay the rating fees, and pay the underwriting costs. (But note how having the borrower pay the costs eliminates the free-rider problem.) The total costs are substantial, easily running into the hundreds of thousands of dollars for a single bond issue (see "The Cost of a Public Issue" on page 38). The costs are also largely indivisible: They depend little on the total amount to be borrowed. As a result, this sort of direct borrowing by public issue will be unattractive unless the amount to be borrowed is large and the term of the loan long.

LIQUIDITY   The relatively long term of the typical direct loan makes liquidity a particularly serious problem. As we have seen, one way for you to get your money back, without the borrowing company itself having to repay you, is to be allowed to resell the bond to someone else. But just being *allowed* to do this is not enough: It has to be possible in practice to sell the bond relatively easily and at a fair price. This requires that there be an organized resale market permanently available. Such a market is called a **secondary market**, to distinguish it from the **primary market** for new issues.

For a secondary market to be available it has to be *made*. That is, someone has to be ready and willing at all times to do the work of matching up buyers and sellers. This **market maker** will quote prices at which he is willing to buy and sell and will adjust those prices up or down to bring amounts bought and sold roughly into line. For example, suppose he quotes a buying price (a **bid price**) of 90 and a selling price (an **asked, or offered, price**) of 91. He finds that each day he has to buy $1 million worth of bonds, but sells only $800,000. If he lowers the bid and offered prices to 89 and 90, respectively, he will buy less and sell more: Fewer bonds will be sold to him if his bid price is lower, and he will sell more at his lower offered price.

In order to stand behind his quoted prices, the market maker must carry an inventory. The offered price has meaning only if he actually has bonds ready for sale at that price; the bid price has meaning only if he is ready to buy at that price even when he cannot resell immediately.

The market maker will make money from the bid–asked differential. If he buys $1 million worth of bonds at 89 and sells them at 91, he will make a two point profit—2% of $1 million or $20,000. If he is clever, he will also make **trading profits**—adding to his inventory when he thinks the market price will rise, and reducing it when he thinks the market price will fall. If he is successful, he will be "buying low and selling high," the traditional recipe for profitable trading.

The existence of a secondary market for a particular security makes that security more liquid and therefore more attractive to lenders (of course, the risk associated with the uncertain resale price remains). The greater the liquidity, the lower the return the issuer will have to pay on the loan.

However, making a market for a security is costly. We are not talking about the costs of setting up a market for a whole *type* of security—for example, the

secondary market
Financial market in which previously issued securities are traded, such as the New York Stock Exchange.

primary market
Financial market in which securities are sold when they are first issued.

market maker
Someone standing ready to buy and sell securities at declared prices.

bid price
Price at which a market maker will purchase and a customer will sell a debt instrument in the secondary market.

asked (offered) price
Price at which a market maker will sell and a customer will purchase a debt instrument in the secondary market.

trading profits
Profits realized from buying and selling securities.

THE COST OF A PUBLIC ISSUE

Megacorp Motors wants to raise $10,000,000 by issuing debt. If this is its first public offering, the company will incur the following costs:

Underwriter's fee (assuming rate of 2% of face value plus $15,000 expense allowance)	$215,000
Legal fees	75,000
Accounting fees	65,000
Printing costs	50,000
Debt rating by Moody's or Standard & Poor's	25,000
Assorted fees (includes stock exchange, state "blue sky" law, SEC registration, and registrar's fees)	18,000
Total	**$448,000**

This cost is about 4.5% of the amount raised.

If High Tech Concepts wanted to raise $1,000,000 in this way, it would face an underwriter's fee of $35,000 (2% of $1 million, plus $15,000). The other costs would be much the same. The total cost would be $268,000, or nearly 27% of the amount raised.

Sources: Jennings and Marsh, *Securities Regulation: Cases and Materials*, 6th ed., Mineola, NY: Foundation Press, 1987, and Larry D. Soderquist, *Securities Regulation: A Problem Approach*.

New York Stock Exchange for stocks. We are talking about the (marginal) costs of setting up a market for an *individual* security—for example, the stock of Megacorp Motors. These costs include the time a market maker must invest in learning about the company and the time he has to devote to dealing in the stock; they also include the cost of financing the trading inventory.

Many of the costs of making a market are, once again, indivisible. Hence it will not be worthwhile making a market unless there is going to be quite a lot of business. This requires the amount of the security outstanding to be large. As a result, small and short-term borrowers are again at a disadvantage: Because the potential volume of trading in their issues is small, a secondary market will not be made, and their debt will therefore be relatively illiquid. To compensate investors, the return will have to be higher, making direct borrowing an expensive way to raise money.

SOLUTION 2: INDIRECT LENDING

Indirect lending provides an entirely different way of dealing with information and liquidity. Suppose that, instead of lending your $10,000 directly to Megacorp Motors (MM) by buying its bond, you lend the money to a bank, say Metropolis National. That is, you put the $10,000 into a savings account. Metropolis, of course, does not keep the money, but rather *relends* it to some final borrower, say to High Tech Concepts (HTC). In effect, you are lending your $10,000 to HTC indirectly via the bank.

DEALING WITH THE INFORMATION PROBLEMS   Metropolis is not just a simple go-between here: It is a party to the transaction. As far as you are concerned, you are making a loan to Metropolis; as far as HTC is concerned, it is borrowing from Metropolis. For both of you, this indirect loan is very different from a direct one.

In the first place, the risk to you does not depend on the creditworthiness of HTC: You do not even know to whom the money is being lent. Whether or not HTC repays, the savings account is an unconditional obligation of Metropolis to you. If there are any losses, they are Metropolis' problem, not yours. As a result, your only concern is with the creditworthiness of Metropolis itself.

That concern is easily met. The information and monitoring costs of lending to a bank—of making a deposit—are extremely low. In fact, since 1933 most bank deposits have been guaranteed by the federal government, making the information and monitoring costs essentially zero. However, even before federal deposit insurance existed, banks had an obvious interest both in being safe and in being perceived to be safe. That is, they had an interest in reducing the information and monitoring costs of lending to them, so that depositors would be ready to trust them with their money.[5]

While you, as a depositor, no longer need to worry about the creditworthiness of the ultimate borrower, Metropolis obviously does. However, the information and monitoring costs are likely to be much less burdensome for a bank than they are for a small individual investor. There are a number of reasons for this—better information, the large scale of lending, specialization, a continuing relationship with the borrower, and diversification. Let us look at each of these.

If HTC is a customer of Metropolis, Metropolis will have a lot of private information that is not publicly available. It will have direct access to information on HTC's cash flow—payments and receipts—by observing transactions in HTC's checking account. In fact, a common condition for a bank loan will be that the borrower maintain a certain average amount in its checking account (called a **compensating balance**) partly for this reason. In addition, HTC may be more willing to provide information to its bank *in private* than it would be to the public at large: There is less risk of valuable secrets being revealed to its competitors.

We have already noted that many of the costs of a loan are indivisible. As a result, making large loans is relatively less expensive than making small ones. One advantage the bank has over you is that it makes comparatively large loans. For example, the loan Metropolis makes to HTC might be for $1 million. To make such a loan, Metropolis will put together your $10,000 with money it receives from many other depositors. Bank loans are, on average, much larger than individual deposits.

compensating balance
Required minimum balance that a borrower must maintain at a bank, usually in a checking account.

---

[5]Since deposits are insured up to a maximum of $100,000, this does leave large depositors with some risk, at least in principle. Of course, the insurance does not eliminate the information and monitoring problem: It just passes it on to the federal government. We shall take up the whole question of deposit insurance in Chapters 16 and 17.

When you specialize in some activity, you generally get better at it. Banks specialize in assessing the creditworthiness of borrowers and in monitoring their performance. As a result, they tend to be better at it than the average small investor. Because they have seen it all before, they are good at reading between the lines of financial statements, and they are less likely to be taken in. Experience helps them detect the early signs of impending trouble that you might miss. None of this is to say that banks never make mistakes: We shall see some spectacular ones in later chapters. However, because of specialization, banks are able to assess credit risk more successfully on average, and more cheaply, than small, occasional investors.

If you, as an individual investor, lend your money to HTC, the odds are that this will be your first and last loan to that particular company. Once HTC has your money, since it does not expect anything more from you in the future, it does not have a particularly strong incentive to keep you happy. Of course, its treatment of you as a creditor will affect its public reputation and thus its ability to borrow from others. This does place some constraints on its behavior, but it may be able to get away with quite a lot. In contrast, when HTC borrows from Metropolis, it expects to go back to the bank repeatedly for additional loans. If HTC misbehaves on the current loan, Metropolis may not lend to it again. If this happens, HTC cannot simply switch banks: Being cut off by one bank is hardly a recommendation to other banks. Because this continuing relationship is at stake, the borrower has a strong incentive to behave. This makes monitoring less expensive.

pool
To collect a number of different financial assets into a single unit.

THE ADVANTAGES OF POOLING   Metropolis has many deposits and many loans. The resulting ability to **pool** deposits and loans gives the bank a number of advantages over an individual investor.

diversification
Process of acquiring a portfolio of securities that have dissimilar risk-return characteristics such that the overall portfolio risk is reduced.

The first advantage is **diversification**. Let us compare the risks faced by an individual small investor with those faced by a bank. Suppose the minimum feasible size of a loan, because of indivisible costs, is $10,000. With only $10,000 to lend, if you make a loan directly, you will have to lend it all to a single company. The interest on the loan is 15%. Suppose that there is a 1-in-50 chance of default on this loan, and that in case of default you lose all your money.

If Metropolis has 100,000 depositors just like you, each of whom deposits $10,000, it will have a total of $1 billion to invest. Even if it makes larger loans, say of an average size of $1 million, it can lend to 1,000 different companies. Suppose that for each of these loans the risk and potential return are the same as for the loan that you make (the chance of default and total loss is 1 in 50, and the return if things work out is 15%).[6]

What was a gamble for a single loan becomes close to a sure thing for a large pool of loans. Metropolis can rely on about 20 of the 1,000 borrowers defaulting

---

[6]In reality, because of the bank's advantages in information gathering and monitoring, the risk is likely to be less for a given return.

on their loans, resulting in a loss of $20 million. On the other 980 loans Metropolis will earn interest of

$$980 \times 0.15 \times \$1 \text{ million} = \$147 \text{ million.}$$

Subtracting the $20 million loss leaves a return of $127 million, or 12.7% of the $1 billion pool of loans. Of course, there might be slightly more defaults or slightly less, but there is a 95% chance that the return on the pool will be between 11.7% and 13.7%; the chance of the whole amount being lost is less than one in $10^{1,700}$, a truly infinitesimal number.[7]

Note, however, that the magic of diversification will work this well only if the chance of default on one loan is unrelated to the chance of default on the others. For example, if a bank lends only to local farmers and if a drought affects all of them at the same time, they will all tend to default together.

Diversification allows Metropolis to promise a sure return on its deposits, 11% say. This leaves something to cover expenses, unusual losses, and a modest, if well-deserved, profit. This sure 11% may well look more attractive to you as an investor than a gamble on a direct loan that pays 15% if things go well and is a complete loss if they do not.

Pooling deposits has another advantage: It creates liquidity. The loans that Metropolis makes are quite illiquid. The loan to HTC may be for several months or even years, and it is not easily transferable. Even if Metropolis is allowed to sell the loan, it will have trouble finding someone willing to buy it at a reasonable price: It will face the same problems HTC would have faced had it tried to borrow directly. Nonetheless, despite the illiquidity of its loans, Metropolis promises to repay your $10,000 whenever you want it. How is it able to do this?

The key, once again, is pooling. Although the behavior of any single depositor—the timing and size of additional deposits, the timing and size of withdrawals—is fairly unpredictable, the behavior of Metropolis' 100,000 depositors is much easier to predict. With total deposits of about $1 billion, withdrawals will fluctuate, say, between $20 million and $80 million each day, and new deposits will also fluctuate daily between $20 million and $80 million. Moreover, withdrawals and new deposits will tend to offset one another: Only rarely will a day of many withdrawals also be a day of few new deposits. As a result, the chance that the amount withdrawn will exceed new deposits by more than, say, $50 million is quite small. So, by making sure that it can easily lay its hands on $50

[7]For a single loan, the distribution of returns is binomial. The expected return is $1,127,000, and the standard deviation is $160,000. For a pool of 1,000 loans, the expected value is $1,000 \times \$1,127,000 = \$1.127$ billion, and the standard deviation is $\sqrt{1,000} \times \$160,000 = \$0.005$ billion. The distribution of returns for the pool is approximately normal, so that the probability of being within 2 standard deviations of the mean is about 95%. The chance of the whole amount being lost is 0.02 to the power 1,000.

million in cash, Metropolis can promise complete liquidity on the whole $1 billion in deposits.[8]

Occasionally, of course, net withdrawals *will* exceed $50 million, and the bank will have to have a way to deal with this. We will see a variety of ways in Chapter 12. Of course, the magic of pooling works only when withdrawal by one individual is unrelated to withdrawal by another. If all depositors want their money at once (a **bank run**), the bank will be in serious trouble. We shall discuss this possibility, and what can be done about it, in Chapter 16.

bank run
Withdrawal of deposits simultaneously by many of a bank's customers.

THE ADVANTAGES OF INDIRECT LENDING TO THE BORROWER   If indirect lending offers advantages to the lender, it also offers them to the borrower. The natural edge the bank has in gathering information and monitoring allows many of the costs of a public issue to be avoided. Filing with the SEC and rating are unnecessary, and the illiquidity of a loan is much less of a problem for a bank than it would be for individual investors.

Dealing with a single lender also allows greater flexibility if the company gets into trouble and has difficulty paying its debts. There are basically two reasons it might get into such trouble—bad management and bad luck. If the reason is bad management, forcing the borrower into liquidation may be in the best interests of its creditors: Letting it continue in business will only mean more losses, leaving fewer assets left to pay off debts. However, in the case of bad luck, if there is reason to believe that the borrower's luck will change, then liquidation is not such a good idea. The interests of the creditors might best be served by simply rescheduling repayment of the debt.

With direct debt, rescheduling a loan is difficult. The relationship between the borrower and the many, relatively uninformed lenders is necessarily arm's length and legalistic. The only way to deal with default is through formal bankruptcy proceedings (see "Bankruptcy"). This is costly, both in lawyers' fees and in disruption of normal company operations. Also, because monitoring by the many creditors is difficult, it is hard for them to distinguish between bad luck and bad management. As a result, the terms of the loan contract tend to be enforced rigidly in either case.

With indirect lending, the bank is in a much better position to know whether the problem is bad luck or bad management. And, as a single lender, it can alter the terms of the loan without having to obtain the agreement of hundreds or thousands of other creditors. It can reschedule payments, waive some of the restrictions imposed by the loan contract, or even lend additional money to help the borrower over a temporary crisis. In addition, the court costs of a formal bankruptcy proceeding can be avoided.

---

[8]Assume that the expected value of both new deposits and withdrawals is $50 million, that the standard deviations are $15 million, and that both are normally distributed and independent. Then there is a 95% chance that each will be between $20 million and $80 million. The expected value of the difference between new deposits and withdrawals is zero, and the standard deviation is $\sqrt{2} \times \$15$ million = $21 million. There is therefore a 99% probability that total deposits will fall by less than 2.5 standard deviations, or $50 million.

When a company can no longer pay its bills it may file for bankruptcy. If it fails to do so, its unpaid creditors may be able to force it into bankruptcy. Filing initiates a legal process in which *all* claims against the firm are settled to the extent possible. Without such a process, creditors would compete wastefully to be paid first, before the firm ran out of assets; and the last in line would get nothing. In 1984, some 62,000 business firms filed for bankruptcy.

There are two basic types of bankruptcy proceedings—*liquidation* and *reorganization*. In 1984, about two thirds of filings were for liquidation, and the rest were for reorganization.

In a liquidation, the corporation's assets are sold for cash and creditors are paid off (usually not in full) from the proceeds. A liquidation is sometimes called a "Chapter 7" proceeding or "straight bankruptcy." Since the company's assets are sold, it no longer continues in business.

In a reorganization, creditors look not to the present assets of the company but rather to its future earning potential in order to collect. The company reorganizes, presents a plan for future payments to its creditors and to the court, and then continues in existence, implementing the court-approved plan. This type of bankruptcy is known as a "Chapter 11" proceeding.

Sources: David G. Epstein, *Debtor-Creditor Law in a Nutshell*, 2nd ed., (St. Paul: West, 1988); Michelle J. White, "The Corporate Bankruptcy Decision," *Journal of Economic Perspectives* 3(2) 1989: 129–151.

BANKRUPTCY

DIRECT AND INDIRECT LENDING COMPARED

The different ways the different functions and problems of lending are handled by direct and indirect lending are summarized in Exhibit 3.2. What are the advantages and disadvantages of the two types of lending?

For the lender, indirect lending is usually less risky and more liquid. Correspondingly, the average return is usually lower. Less risk, of course, means not only a lower chance of loss, but also a lower chance of gain: You may get rich through clever (or lucky) investments in the stock market, but you cannot do so by investing in a savings account. Another attraction of indirect lending is that it offers some types of security that are simply unavailable in the direct market (we shall see some examples in the next section).

For the borrower, indirect borrowing is usually cheaper for small or short-term loans. This is because of the indivisible nature of many of the costs of direct borrowing and because of the greater flexibility of indirect lending. Most borrowers do not really have a choice, because their lack of credit standing makes direct borrowing virtually impossible. For borrowers who do have the option of going to the direct market, it will often prove cheaper than indirect borrowing if they wish to raise large sums of money. For *very* large sums of money, it may not even be possible to borrow indirectly: The capacity of the direct financial markets is much larger than that of even the largest banks.[9]

---

[9]We shall see in later chapters that banks do get together in consortiums to fund really large loans.

E x h i b i t 3.2

DIRECT AND
INDIRECT LENDING

Function or Problem	Direct Lending (Bond Market)	Indirect Lending (Bank)
Gathering information	SEC filing	Lender needs information only on bank; bank checks up on borrower
Evaluating information	Rating agency	Bank
Writing loan contract	Underwriter	Bank
Monitoring performance	Rating agency	Bank
Indivisibility of costs	Only large loans worthwhile	Pooling of small deposits to make large loans
Free-rider problem	Costs paid by borrower	Bank is the single lender
Liquidity	Secondary market	Pooling of deposits
Default	Formal bankruptcy proceedings	Private renegotiation with the bank

Exhibit 3.3A breaks down the net flow of lending that we saw in Chapter 2 into direct and indirect components. Notice that indirect lending accounts for by far the larger part. Exhibit 3.3A shows *new* lending in various forms in 1988. Exhibit 3.3B, on the other hand, shows the total amount of direct and indirect securities held by households.

|3.3| THE DIFFERENT TYPES OF FINANCIAL INTERMEDIARY

financial intermediary
Institution that borrows by issuing its own securities and relends the funds it raises.

An institution engaged in indirect lending is called a **financial intermediary**. A financial intermediary borrows by issuing its own securities and then relending the funds it raises. All financial intermediaries benefit from the two advantages of pooling—diversification and the creation of liquidity.

There are three main types of financial intermediary—banks, investment companies, and insurance companies.

EXHIBIT 3.3

DIRECT AND INDIRECT LENDING (BILLIONS OF DOLLARS)

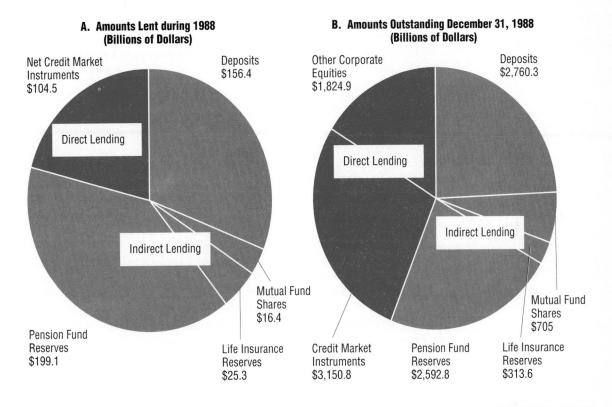

Note that money market fund shares are included with mutual fund shares rather than deposits.

Source: The Federal Reserve's Flow of Fund Accounts, Q3, 1989 and Flow of Funds Accounts Financial Assets and Liabilities, Year-End 1965–1988.

BANKS

Banks are the most important type of financial intermediary. As we have seen, in addition to pooling, banks assess creditworthiness and monitor loan performance. Also, by guaranteeing their depositors a sure return, they bear the credit risk of the loans they make.

Banks offer two types of deposit. **Demand deposits,** or funds in checking accounts, are deposits that may be withdrawn on demand. Because they are transferable, they are used to make payments. **Time deposits,** or funds in savings accounts, may not be withdrawn freely. Some time deposits, called certificates of deposit or CDs, have a fixed maturity, before which they may be withdrawn only with penalty. Others, like a passbook savings account, formally allow the bank to require notice before a withdrawal can be made (in practice, banks usually permit

banks
Financial institutions that accept deposits and make loans.

demand deposits
Funds placed in banks that are payable on demand and transferable by check.

time deposits
Interest-bearing savings accounts that have a specified date of maturity or that require notice before withdrawal.

withdrawal on demand). Time deposits are not generally transferable and are not used to make payments.

Traditionally, one type of bank, called a **commercial bank**, specialized in taking demand deposits and in making loans to firms. Another type, called a **savings bank** or **thrift**, specialized in taking time deposits and in making loans to households. We shall see in later chapters that this distinction has been considerably eroded in recent years.

commercial bank
Financial intermediary that specializes in taking demand deposits and in making loans to business firms.

savings bank (thrift)
Financial institution that specializes in taking time deposits and in making loans to households.

investment company
Financial institution that raises funds to acquire a diversified portfolio of financial instruments by selling stocks or shares of ownership in that portfolio.

bond mutual fund
Fund that pools the investments of a large number of people and purchases bonds.

INVESTMENT COMPANIES

An **investment company** reaps the benefits of pooling without doing many of the other things a bank does. It does not itself assess creditworthiness or monitor performance. Instead, it puts together a pool of publicly traded direct securities and relies on the information and monitoring provided by financial markets in the same way that a small investor might. Some investment pools do nothing more than simple pooling; others attempt to "pick winners" and actively try to choose the best securities to include in their pools.[10]

An investment company also differs from a bank in that it bears no credit risk. Rather than offering its investors a sure return, as a bank does on a deposit, it offers them a share in the return on the pooled securities. If the portfolio does well, so do the investors; if it does not do well, neither do the investors. In neither case are the profits of the investment company affected: The management earns its income entirely from fees.

The main attraction of the investment pool for investors is precisely that it is a pool. Instead of putting all of your $10,000 into one Megacorp Motors (MM) bond, you could invest it, for example, in the shares of a **bond mutual fund** (one type of investment pool). Such a fund might have a total of $10 billion invested in 1,000 companies, possibly including MM. Your $10,000 share in the fund is equivalent to your holding 1,000 $10 bonds, one in each company. Now, if MM defaults, rather than losing your whole $10,000, you stand to lose only $10. By investing in the mutual fund, you gain the advantages of diversification.

An investment pool also offers the second advantage of pooling—liquidity. If you hold a single bond, and you want to sell it, the cost of the transaction can be quite high: You will have to pay a commission to your broker to arrange the sale of the bond in the bond market. On the other hand, if you sell back your share to the bond mutual fund, the cost of an actual sale of bonds can often be avoided. Because sales and purchases of shares will tend to offset one another, the fund will often be able to liquidate your share by selling it to another shareholder, *without* having to sell the underlying bonds in the market. You may still have to pay the mutual fund a fee, but this will be substantially less than the cost of actually selling a bond.

[10]The value of active management of investment pools is unclear. Most economists doubt it has much value.

INSURANCE COMPANIES

Remember from Chapter 2 that one of the reasons for saving is to provide a precautionary reserve against unexpected expenses. However, rather than holding a reserve, you can protect yourself by buying an **insurance policy**.

An insurance policy is a special kind of security, the payout on which is *contingent* on some event. If the specified contingency occurs, you are paid; if it does not, you receive nothing. For example, suppose you insure your $20,000 car by paying a premium of, say, $1,200 a year to the Providential Insurance Company. If all goes well, you get nothing. However, if you total your car, the insurance company pays you $20,000. By paying the $1,200, you protect yourself against the risk of having to pay a much larger sum in the event of a loss.[11]

How can Providential relieve you of this risk without taking on a considerable risk itself? The answer, of course, is pooling. Suppose Providential sells policies to 1 million people, each with 1 chance in 20 of a total loss. Large numbers once again do their magic: The 1 chance in 20 for an individual is transformed by pooling into a fairly reliable loss of one-twentieth of the total. That is, about 50,000 of the 1 million cars insured will be totaled.

Therefore Providential will take in premiums in

$$\$1,200 \times 1 \text{ million} = \$1,200 \text{ million},$$

and it will pay out in claims a fairly reliable

$$50,000 \times \$20,000 = \$1,000 \text{ million}.$$

There is substantially less than a 1% chance that claims will deviate from this amount by more than $15 million. This leaves Providential with a nice, very safe profit.[12]

There is also another source of profit. Suppose that premiums, a total of $1.2 billion, are all received on January 1. Losses occur at a steady rate throughout the year—about 1,000 a week. This means that at the end of the first week Providential will have paid out $2 million in claims and be left with $1,198 million. Its funds will fall week by week in this way by about $2 million each week. By December 31 about $200 million will remain. The average amount held by the

insurance policy
Type of security that provides protection against loss or costs in return for payment of premiums.

---

[11]Typically, you will be compensated for other contingencies as well: damage short of total loss, liability for damages to others, medical expenses in the event of an accident, etc. To keep our example simple, we ignore these other contingencies.

[12]For a single policy the distribution of the claim is binomial, with an expected value of $1,000 and a standard deviation of $4,472. For a pool of 1 million policies, the expected value of claims is 1 million $\times \$1,000 = \$1$ billion, and the standard deviation is $\sqrt{1 \text{ million}} \times \$4,472 = \$4,472,000$. Total claims have a normal distribution, so there is less than a 1% chance of their being more than 3 standard deviations from the mean.

insurance company over the year is

$$\frac{\$1,200 \text{ million} + \$200 \text{ million}}{2} = \$700 \text{ million}.$$

If premiums are paid in uniformly over the year, rather than all at once on January 1, then Providential will be holding a fairly stable fund of $700 million throughout the year.

It would be silly for Providential to keep this fund in cash, and, of course, it does not. It lends it out to earn a return until it needs the money back to pay off claims. The resulting investment income is an additional source of profit.

insurance company
Financial intermediary that sells insurance policies and uses the proceeds to make loans.

An **insurance company**, then, is a financial intermediary in much the same way as a bank. A bank sells claims on itself—deposits—and uses the proceeds to make loans; an insurance company sells claims on itself—policies—and it too uses the proceeds to make loans.

GOVERNMENT FINANCIAL INTERMEDIARIES

In addition to privately owned financial intermediaries, there are a number of intermediaries owned by the government, principally the federal government. The reason for their existence is generally some failure, real or perceived, of private markets and intermediaries in serving some politically influential sector of the economy, such as agriculture, housing, or higher education.

Exhibit 3.4 lists the principal types of financial intermediary and indicates in which of the following chapters they are discussed.

3.4 HOW WELL DOES THE FINANCIAL SYSTEM DO ITS JOB?

Now that we have some idea of what the financial system is supposed to do, we can ask how well it does it.

MAKING SAVING AND INVESTMENT EASIER

It is best to begin with saving. There are various ways to save. One way is by holding on to cash. However, this is not usually very attractive, because cash pays no interest. If you save for your retirement by stuffing $100 bills into a mattress, you will at best have the same amount of dollars you put away. If, instead, you

EXHIBIT 3.4

TYPES OF FINANCIAL INTERMEDIARY

Banklike Intermediaries

Commercial banks	Chapters 4, 5, 8–13, 16–18
Savings and loans	Chapters 15, 17
Savings banks	Chapters 15, 17
Credit unions	Chapter 18
Finance companies[a]	Chapter 9

Investment Companies

Bond mutual funds	Chapter 14
Equity mutual funds	Chapter 14
Money market mutual funds	Chapter 9
Defined contribution pension funds	Chapter 14

Insurance Intermediaries

Casualty insurance companies (auto, home, etc.)	Chapters 14, 18
Life insurance companies	Chapters 14, 18
Defined benefit pension funds	Chapter 14

Government Intermediaries Include:

Federal Reserve Banks	Chapters 4, 5, 10, 16, 17, 18 and Parts Four and Five
Federal Home Loan Banks	Chapter 15
Government National Mortgage Association (investment pool)	Chapter 15
Federal Deposit Insurance Corporation (insurance)	Chapters 16, 17

[a]Finance companies are banklike in the type of loans that they make, but they do not borrow by offering deposits. Instead, they themselves borrow from banks or raise money in the direct financial markets.

invest the money in earning assets that offer some sort of return, you may have much more.[13]

There are many earning assets available. It is useful to divide them into two groups—real and financial. **Real assets** include things like factories, houses, art,

real assets
Property that provides a return or that may increase in value, such as real estate or works of art.

---

[13]Because of inflation, you could wind up with less in terms of actual purchasing power than you put away: The money will buy less when you come to spend it than it would have bought when you stuffed it into your mattress (we shall have more to say about inflation in Chapter 28). To see how much difference the rate of return can make, suppose that you save $5,000 a year for 40 years for your retirement, and that you will be retired for 20 years. If you go the mattress route, you will have $10,000 a year to spend in Florida. However, if you invest in assets with a 5% return, you will have $48,500 a year to spend. We shall see in Chapter 6 how to make this sort of calculation.

and baseball cards. They may provide you with a return in money (factories) or in enjoyment (art), and they may also rise in value over the years to provide you with capital gains.

financial assets
Property that represents loans, such as savings accounts and bonds.

Financial assets, securities like savings accounts and bonds, represent loans. Most of these loans are used, directly or indirectly, to finance the purchase of real assets by someone else. Loans to households go mainly to finance the purchase of homes and consumer durables like cars and appliances; loans to firms are mainly used to finance investment in plant, equipment, and working capital.

So, in a sense, financial assets are a "veil." Your investment in a financial asset represents someone else's investment in a real asset, financed by a loan from you. From the point of view of society as a whole, all investment is investment in real assets.

The quantity and quality of society's real investment is very important for our economic well-being. Economic growth and rising incomes require investment in more and better productive capital. The amount of investment is important, but it is also important that investment be channeled to the best uses.

The efficiency of the financial system is a major determinant of both the quantity and the quality of investment. Such efficiency has three aspects:

1. Efficiency in the transformation of investment characteristics.
2. Cost efficiency.
3. Efficiency in the integration of financial markets.

Let us look at each of these more carefully.

EFFICIENCY IN THE TRANSFORMATION OF INVESTMENT CHARACTERISTICS

Before investing in any asset, there are a number of things you will want to consider: How safe is it? How high a return, on average, can you expect? How liquid is it?

Many of the real assets in our economy, particularly the productive assets, would seem highly unattractive to household investors. For example, consider a steel mill. It is large and indivisible, putting it out of reach of most individual investors. It is risky: The steel business has lots of ups and downs and is subject to savage competition. It is highly illiquid: Try selling a used steel mill on short notice.

However, the financial system can create financial assets that are direct and indirect claims on such real assets and that are far more attractive to household investors. For example, a share of stock in the company that owns the steel mill is a smaller investment and more liquid. A share of a diversified investment pool that includes some of the same stock is even more liquid and considerably less risky. A bank deposit used by a bank to fund a loan to the steel company is far more liquid. An insurance policy, the premiums on which are used by an insurance company to buy the steel company's bonds, is an asset with properties very different from those of the steel mill itself.

The more successful a financial system is in transforming risky and illiquid real assets into the kinds of safe and liquid financial assets that people want, the more funds there will be available for real investment. Different countries have very different financial systems, and these differences are an important determinant of their relative economic success (see "Financial Systems" on page 52).

COST EFFICIENCY

If one measure of a financial system is the quality of the financial products it offers, another is the cost at which it makes them available.

Remember our discussion in Chapter 2 of the financial system as a market for loanable funds. Exhibit 3.5 illustrates equilibrium in that market (the numbers are again made up). There is an important difference, however, between this diagram and Exhibit 2.4. In Chapter 2 we assumed implicitly that borrowing and lending cost nothing; now we know better. That assumption was reflected in the way we drew Exhibit 2.4: The interest rate paid by borrowers was the same as the interest rate received by lenders. In Exhibit 3.5 the two rates are no longer the same: The difference between them is the cost of making loans. You can see that this cost, assumed to be 2%, makes quite a difference. The equilibrium interest rate for borrowers is now such that the quantity of loanable funds demanded at this rate equals the quantity supplied at a rate 2% *lower*.

The "wedge" of 2% between the rate paid by borrowers and the rate received by lenders has three effects:

1. Lenders earn less than they would if lending were costless (9% instead of 10%).

2. Borrowers pay more than they would if lending were costless (11% instead of 10%).

3. The amount of borrowing and lending is less than it would be if lending were costless ($150 million per month instead of $160 million).

Since real investment and borrowing are closely related, we can say that the greater the cost of lending, the less real investment there will be. Therefore, from society's point of view, we would like this cost to be as low as possible.

Let us look at this cost more closely. The 2% "cost" to borrowers and lenders is the price the financial system charges for its services. In the economy described by Exhibit 3.5, banks and insurance companies, underwriters and rating agencies are receiving 2% of $150 million, or $3 million per month, to make borrowing and lending possible. The amount they receive may be broken down into two categories—costs and economic rents.

Costs include all the actual expenses of gathering and evaluating information, writing contracts, and so on. They also include a fair return on real investment in the financial system itself. Any amount charged beyond these true costs is **economic rent**—payment beyond that required to have the service provided.

economic rent
The excess of price over the costs required to provide a service.

All sorts of institutions make up a country's financial system. A well developed system can help a country to grow by ensuring savings are used efficiently. The chart shows the relative importance of different types of assets and institutions. Developing countries generally hold a bigger share of their total financial assets (48%) in banks than do industrial countries (37%). The relative importance of central banks in developing countries is even greater (20% compared to 3%). Industrial countries tend to have more sophisticated and diversified financial systems. France is an exception: bank deposits account for 56% of its financial assets. Britain is notable for contractual savings institutions, like pension funds. They account for 26% of financial assets, a level matched only in Canada.

Source: "Economic and Financial Indicators: Financial Systems," *The Economist*, August 18, 1989. Copyright 1989, The Economist. Distributed by Special Features/Syndication Sales.

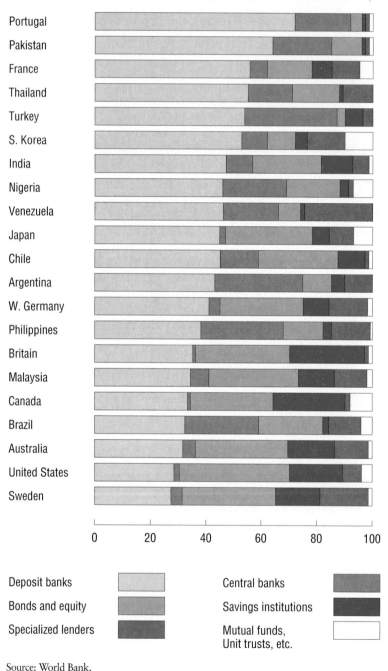

FINANCIAL ASSETS BY TYPE, 1985 (AS A PERCENTAGE OF TOTAL)

Portugal, Pakistan, France, Thailand, Turkey, S. Korea, India, Nigeria, Venezuela, Japan, Chile, Argentina, W. Germany, Philippines, Britain, Malaysia, Canada, Brazil, Australia, United States, Sweden

0 20 40 60 80 100

Deposit banks
Bonds and equity
Specialized lenders
Central banks
Savings institutions
Mutual funds, Unit trusts, etc.

Source: World Bank.

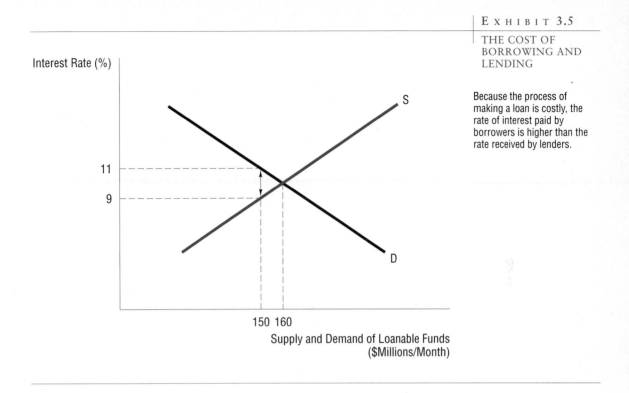

EXHIBIT 3.5

THE COST OF BORROWING AND LENDING

Because the process of making a loan is costly, the rate of interest paid by borrowers is higher than the rate received by lenders.

From society's point of view, we would like the costs to be as low as technology and ingenuity can make them, and we would like the economic rents to be zero. Of course, the banks, underwriters, and other financial institutions have a very different view of things. Reducing costs requires a lot of hard work, and what we call economic rent is in their eyes a much-deserved bonus.

Luckily, society's point of view has a powerful champion—competition. In the presence of competition, economic rents will vanish as each bank or underwriter tries to undercut the other. In a competitive environment, economic rents are hard to come by and temporary at best. They may be earned either by finding a new way to provide existing products more cheaply or by thinking up new products. They will last only until competitors catch on and start to imitate.

In the following chapters we shall have much to say about competition, or its absence, in the financial system. We shall see that even though competition is generally a good thing, there are some special features of the financial system that complicate matters, so that unfettered competition may not always produce exactly the outcome we want.

EFFICIENCY IN THE INTEGRATION OF FINANCIAL MARKETS

The third aspect of efficiency of the financial system is the degree to which the financial markets are integrated. To see why integration is important, consider what would happen if we split the national loanable funds market illustrated in Exhibit 2.4 into two separate parts—one part covering the eastern half of the country and the other the western half. People in each part of the country lend to one another, but they do not lend to people in the other part.[14]

The result of the split is shown in Exhibit 3.6. Comparing this to Exhibit 2.4, you can see that the interest rate in the West is higher than it was and that the interest rate in the East is lower. The higher rate in the West means that loanable funds there are relatively more scarce. There may be several reasons for this: People in the East may save more, for example, or investment opportunities may be better in the West.

With the market split in this way, there is less investment in the West and more in the East than there was when the market was integrated. When the market was integrated, there was a uniform interest rate of 10% all across the country, and investments with a break-even rate above 10% were undertaken everywhere. Now, in the West only projects with a break-even rate above 15% are undertaken, and in the East all projects with a break-even rate above 5%.

This reallocation of investment is inefficient. The investments that are cut back in the West, relative to those that would have been made with an integrated financial market, have break-even rates between 10% and 15%, while those that are added in the East have break-even rates between 5% and 10%. Clearly, society as a whole is made poorer when an investment with a break-even rate of 15% is sacrificed and one with a rate of 5% is substituted. Suppose, for example, that $100 million that would have been invested in biotechnology labs in the West is now invested in button factories in the East. Instead of $15 million being earned on the $100 million, only $5 million is earned. Because the $100 million is invested in less productive real assets in the East, the total income of society as a whole is $10 million lower than it would have been if the money had been invested in the West.

Similar arguments can be made for fragmentation of the market causing inefficiencies in saving. People in the East save "too little" and those in the West "too much." Saving involves a sacrifice, and savers in the West are sacrificing too much given the economy's overall investment opportunities: They are being paid 15% to save, when the "true" value of their saving, in an integrated market, is only 10%. Similarly, savers in the East are saving too little because they are being underpaid for their saving.

Although an integrated market is best for society as a whole, it is obviously not better for *everyone*. If we integrate the market, interest rates will fall in the West and rise in the East. Borrowers in the West and lenders in the East will be

---

[14]We ignore the costs of lending in this discussion.

EXHIBIT 3.6

A FRAGMENTED FINANCIAL SYSTEM

Dividing the loanable funds market shown in Exhibit 2.4 produces two markets each with different interest rates. In the West funds are more scarce and the interest rate is higher; in the East funds are less scarce and the interest rate is lower.

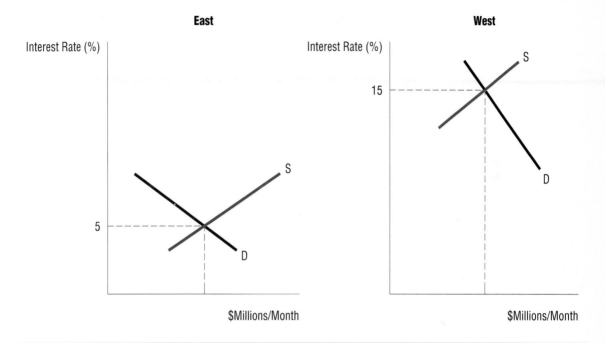

pleased, but borrowers in the East and lenders in the West will not. You will hear lots of self-serving arguments from businessmen in the East about the "importance of investing in the local economy."

However, the gains of the gainers from integration exceed the losses of the losers: gainers could, in principle, compensate losers for their losses and still come out ahead. Given the higher average return on investment with integration, there is more in total to divide up. Thus there is enough to give everyone the income they had before and have something left over.

The problem, of course, is that in practice losers are *not* compensated. As a result, there will be strong political opposition to integration. The potential losers will use their political power to block a change that will make them worse off economically, even though it may be to the general good.

Our example is one of geographic fragmentation, but the same arguments apply to other types of fragmentation. For example, suppose one type of saver provides the funds used to finance long-term investment by firms, and another provides the funds used to finance home mortgages. The two markets are separate. There is no movement of funds between the markets, and the interest rates in the two markets will be different for loans that are essentially similar in terms of risk and liquidity. This sort of fragmentation is inefficient for precisely the same reasons that geographic fragmentation is inefficient: There will be too much of one type of investment and too little of the other; one group will save too much, the other too little.

We shall see that there are a variety of barriers to integration of financial markets in the United States. Some of these barriers are technological: The information and transactions costs of linking up some markets may be too high to make it worthwhile. Clearly, a dynamic and creative financial system will be a help in overcoming such barriers, for if you can come up with a way to do it, you may be able to make a lot of money (those economic rents we talked about before). The nature of the available technology is, of course, important. Computers have done much to reduce the cost of processing information and have made possible transactions that would once have been prohibitively expensive.

There are other barriers to integration of financial markets that are the result of laws and regulations. We shall examine the reasons for these laws and how they affect the functioning of the financial system in the following chapters. We shall also see that there has been rapid progress in recent years in increasing the integration of financial markets, both within the United States and internationally.

SUMMARY

- Making a loan involves giving up money here and now in exchange for a promise of money in the future. This involves risk because the promise may not be kept.
- Information is the key to dealing with risk.
- To make a loan, you need to do the following:
  1. Gather information.
  2. Evaluate that information.
  3. Write a loan contract (taking into account the incentive problems, perhaps imposing covenants and requiring collateral).
  4. Monitor performance.
- The costs involved have some general properties that add to the difficulty: They are largely indivisible (independent of the size of the loan), and there is a free-rider problem.
- Liquidity is also a problem. Lenders would like to be able to get their money back easily; borrowers would like to avoid the need to repay on short notice.
- Loans may be made either directly through financial markets or indirectly through financial intermediaries. Both direct lending and indirect lending deal in their own way with the basic problems involved in lending.

- There are three major types of financial intermediary: (1) banklike intermediaries that take deposits and make loans, (2) investment companies that create pools of publicly issued (direct) securities, and (3) insurance companies that sell policies (contingent securities).

- In addition to these private intermediaries, there are also government-sponsored intermediaries.

- Assets may be divided into real assets and financial assets. Financial assets represent loans that are typically used by the borrower to acquire real assets. The quality and quantity of investment in real assets is important for economic growth and for the well-being of the economy.

- The financial system transforms real assets into financial assets with more desirable characteristics—that is, into assets that are divisible, safe, and liquid and that involve low information costs. How well it does this affects the quantity and quality of real investment.

- The cost of borrowing and lending places a wedge between the rate earned by borrowers and the rate paid by lenders. Because this wedge reduces the amount of investment in real assets, we would like it to be as small as possible. Its size depends on costs and on economic rents.

- Competition helps to reduce costs and to eliminate economic rents.

- The fragmentation of financial markets, both geographically and between different types of loan, is inefficient. However, not everyone gains from integration of financial markets, and potential losers may use political means to block change.

KEY TERMS

security	underwriter	demand deposits
default	rating agencies	time deposits
equity contract	secondary market	commercial bank
debt contract	primary market	savings bank (thrift)
limited liability	market maker	investment company
loan covenants	bid price	bond mutual fund
free-rider problem	asked (offered) price	insurance policy
liquid	trading profits	insurance company
transferable (negotiable)	compensating balance	real assets
capital loss	pool	financial assets
capital gain	diversification	economic rent
direct lending	bank run	
indirect lending	financial intermediary	
Securities and Exchange Commission (SEC)	banks	

DISCUSSION QUESTIONS

1. You could make a one-year loan for $1,000 at 15% interest to your friend Bob. Alternatively, you could put your money in the bank at 6% and let Bob borrow the $1,000 at 15% from the bank. Which would you prefer and why?

2. You are the owner of a small software company, and you need to raise $1 million to expand your business. What are the different ways you might raise the money? What are the relative costs and benefits of the different ways?

3. You are a dealer in corporate securities, and you are considering whether to add Megacorp Motors bonds to the securities that you handle. What are the costs? How will you make a profit? What are the benefits to Megacorp Motors of your making a market in its securities?

4. Summarize the different gains from pooling. How are these gains exploited by different types of financial intermediary?

5. You are the manager of a bank. One of your borrowers is late in making an interest payment. What should you do about it? What can you do?

6. Given all the advantages of indirect lending, why would anyone want to make a direct loan?

7. What are the characteristics of the following investments in terms of divisibility, liquidity, informational costs, monitoring costs, risk, and return?

   a. An automobile plant   e. A pension claim

   b. A refrigerator   f. A life insurance policy

   c. A checking account   g. A share of Megacorp Motors stock

   d. A $20 bill

8. A major problem facing the countries of the Eastern bloc (China, the Soviet Union, Poland, etc.) as they attempt to move toward a free-market economy is that their financial systems are either nonexistent or highly inefficient. In designing a new financial system, what should they have in mind? What are the benefits they should expect from an efficient financial system?

SOFTWARE EXERCISE FOR THIS CHAPTER

Title: Lending

This computer exercise places you in the role of a lender who must decide how to loan out a large sum of money. You will face the tradeoffs discussed in this chapter as you apply your knowledge of risk, liquidity, divisibility, and information and transactions costs. See your instructor if you wish to use this program.

BIBLIOGRAPHY

Berlin, Mitchell, "Bank Loans and Marketable Securities: How Do Financial Contracts Control Borrowing Firms?" *Business Review, Federal Reserve Bank of Philadelphia* July-August 1987, 9–18.

Lewis, M. K., and K. T. Davis, *Domestic and International Banking*. Cambridge, Mass.: M.I.T. Press, 1987.

CHAPTER 4

MONEY AND BANKS

You know what money is: It is the dollar bill you use to pay for your groceries, or the check your parents send to pay for your tuition. But that is just the tip of the iceberg; indeed, most payments in our economy involve neither dollar bills nor checks. The dollar bill and the check are just parts of a complex payments system, the proper functioning of which is vital to our economic welfare.

Rather than tackling the complexities of the U.S. payments system head on, we shall begin by thinking about money in a much simpler setting. Once we understand the problems involved in making payments and how money solves those problems, it will be much easier to make sense of the payments system of the United States.

4.1 THE STORY OF MONEY

Imagine that you live on an idyllic South Sea island. Life is simple. The climate is pleasant. Food is plentiful. Like most islanders, you earn your living as a craftsman. You are a weaver.

Specialization is the key to your prosperity. As a specialized weaver, you have learned to produce cloth better and faster than someone who weaves only occasionally. But specialization makes sense only if you can trade with others. You produce a lot of cloth—much more than you yourself could possibly use. And because you spend all your time weaving, you do not produce any of the other goods you need.

For example, suppose you need a new canoe. In principle, you could build one yourself. However, because you are so good at producing cloth, it makes much more sense to acquire a canoe by trading cloth for it. Moreover, Sulu, the canoe builder, builds a far better canoe than you ever could.

61

You and Sulu agree on a fair price, say, six pigs. However, you do not pay for the canoe there and then: You buy on credit. In exchange for the canoe, you are obliged to provide goods of similar value (six pigs' worth) some time in the future. Most likely, you will pay the debt in cloth. Over the next few years, whenever Sulu needs cloth—for his family or as a gift to others—he will come to you and you will give him what he needs. Each time, the debt will be reduced accordingly. Your deal with Sulu is typical on the island. Goods are generally exchanged for promises of goods of equivalent worth in the future.

Of course, giving up goods in exchange for a promise requires trust. Sulu put a lot of time into that canoe. He will hand it over to you only if he can be sure that he will be paid. The basic problem is this: Once you have the canoe, you have no direct incentive to honor your debt. All the cloth you give him is a net loss from your point of view. Since canoes last a long time, you will not be going back to him for another one any time soon, and you will not lose anything directly by not paying your debt. However, your community is a small one. Everyone knows everyone else. If you fail to honor your debt to Sulu, no one else will trade with you. In this small community, your reputation for honesty is important to you. Reneging on a debt is just not the way to behave.

Notice that no money has been used in this transaction. The price was set in pigs—since pigs are traded quite a lot, it is convenient to set prices in this way—but you did not actually pay for the canoe with pigs. It is easy to translate the price in pigs into a price in cloth: Your cloth trades at six yards per pig, so the price of the canoe is 36 yards of your cloth. Something used in this way, as a sort of measuring rod for prices, is called a **unit of account.**

unit of account
Specific measure in which a price or value is expressed.

The trading system on your island works well. One reason it does so is that the number of goods traded is small. With more goods it would rapidly become impossible to keep track of who owes what to whom. Another reason this trading system works is that the community is small and tight-knit, so that everyone can be sure that debts will be paid.

TRADE WITHOUT TRUST AND COMMODITY MONEY

One day you decide to expand your trading horizons and set off for the Main Island. There is a weekly market there to which people come from far and wide, some traveling for many days. You go to the Main Island because many of the goods on offer there are not available on your own small island.

The trading methods of your own island are simply not appropriate in this big, impersonal market. Trust is out of the question. You trade with people you have never seen before and will probably never see again. Collecting a debt from some far-off island is impractical, and reneging on a debt to a foreigner somehow does not carry the same social stigma as reneging on a debt to a fellow islander. Some method of trade is needed that does not require trust. So credit is out. Each trade must be self-contained—an immediate swap of value for equal value.

barter
Direct exchange of goods for goods without the use of money.

One possibility is **barter**—a direct exchange of goods for goods. You could pay for the jewelry you want with some of your own cloth. The problem is that the jeweler may not happen to want cloth. He may, of course, be willing to accept it with the intention of trading it later for something else he does want. However, he will not be keen to do this, for if he does, he will soon have piles of goods he does not really want. If he agrees at all, it will be at a fairly unfavorable price.

Although barter is a possibility, you will get a much better deal on the jewelry if you offer to pay the jeweler in silver. Why silver? Because the jeweler knows that *other* people prefer to be paid in silver. Since they do, silver is much more useful to him than other goods in making his own purchases. He will therefore be willing to offer you a better deal if you pay in silver. Why do other people prefer to be paid in silver? For the same reason as the jeweler. If this sounds circular, it is. The use of silver in payment is much like the use of a common language. Why did you learn to speak English rather than French or Japanese? Because that is the language that everyone around you spoke. Why did they choose English? For exactly the same reason.

How did silver achieve this privileged position? First, it is widely traded already: There is considerable demand for silver for jewelry and for religious objects. Second, silver is valuable relative to its weight: One can easily carry around a lot of purchasing power. Third, silver is easy to divide into smaller amounts, so that making change is no problem (making change with pigs can be messy). Fourth, silver is uniform: One piece of pure silver is much like any other of the same weight (cloth, for example, may vary in quality). Fifth, silver is durable: It keeps well from the time you receive it in trade until the time you spend it (pigs get sick, fruit rots).

A commodity like silver that has achieved this status of being a common means of payment is called **money**, or, more specifically, **commodity money** (we shall see presently that there are other types of money). Different societies have used different things, but precious metals are often the commodity of choice. Indeed, in many languages the word for money and the word for silver are one and the same.

One practical problem with using silver as money is its purity. Since silver may be alloyed with cheaper metals, you would, in principle, need to assay each piece of silver each time it is traded. This would slow trade considerably. Fortunately, some merchant long ago came up with a solution. After he assayed a piece of silver, he stamped it with his mark, so the next time it came his way he would know it was pure. Others started to do the same, and soon only stamped pieces of silver were readily acceptable in trade. Unstamped metal was acceptable only at a discount.

Then someone had an even better idea. The stamped metal came in all sorts of sizes and had to be weighed for each transaction. So an enterprising merchant made up pieces of stamped silver of standard weight. Because they further reduced the cost of making payment, these **coins** were in great demand and were acceptable at a premium over unstamped silver.

So popular were these coins, let us call them "dollars," that the enterprising merchant abandoned his original trade and specialized in minting them. He made a good living from the difference between what he paid for unstamped silver and

money
Any generally accepted means of payment that will be taken in exchange for goods and services.

commodity money
Something that is used as money and is also bought and sold for its value as a commercial product.

coins
Pieces of metal of certified weight and purity that circulate as money.

seigniorage
Difference between the value of money and its cost of production.

store of value
Something that holds value over time.

the value of the coins he produced. Such a difference between the value of money and its cost of production is called **seigniorage**. (See "A History of Coins.")

These days most trade on the Main Island is conducted in silver dollars. While other types of deal, including direct barter, are possible, you will generally do best by first selling your cloth to a cloth merchant in exchange for silver dollars and then using the dollars to buy whatever you want—including that jewelry you had your eye on. Moreover, because of its ubiquitous use in trade, the dollar has replaced the pig as the unit of account. Prices are generally quoted in dollars.

So, after a busy but enjoyable day's shopping, you head back to your canoe for the trip home. You find that you have some money left over. No problem, you think: You can keep it until the next time you come to the Main Island. You have discovered that money is a **store of value**. In fact, it is a much better store of value than the cloth you had been stockpiling as savings for your old age. You make a mental note to sell the cloth for money and store the money.

One day, on one of your shopping trips to the Main Island, you see offered for sale a new type of loom that you have never seen before. It is much better than the one you have at home, and it would probably double your productivity. The problem is that you do not have the price—$200. You could save up and buy the loom later, but if you could get it now, your income would increase and you could save the needed amount much faster. Unfortunately, buying on credit is out of the question.

Luckily, there is on the Main Island a moneylender. She is a wealthy merchant who has money to lend. She also has extensive trading connections on many other islands, through her large and far-flung family, and these connections provide her with good information on the creditworthiness of potential borrowers. Just to make sure, though, she also employs some very large and muscular debt collectors. You go to her, borrow the $200 you need, and agree to repay $250 in a year's time—the difference compensating her for the possibility of default and for other costs (for example, the muscle needs to be fed).

The use of money makes this sort of generalized credit possible. It differs from the trade credit on your home island in not being tied to any particular trade transaction. You could call on such generalized credit, for instance, to finance the cost of a wedding or of a trading expedition to some other group of islands. All that matters to the moneylender is that you are a good credit risk. To some extent, this generalized credit is a substitute for the more personal type you have at home, but it is not as readily available and it is significantly more expensive. Its existence does facilitate trade in the same sort of way, however, as is shown by your purchase of the new loom.

Let us summarize, then, the functions performed by money in the island economy.

A HISTORY OF COINS

Although Phoenician merchants had traded with bars of precious metals bearing their stamps well before, the first we hear of coins is in Lydia (an Anatolian Greek city) in the seventh century B.C. These coins were simple in design: One side bore parallel lines, and the other, geometric incisions. The metal was *electrum,* a mixture of gold and silver. The art of coinage was later perfected by the Greeks and then the Romans. Early Roman coins bore the image of a steer, and from the Latin word for steer, *pecus*, we get the modern adjective *pecuniary.*

English coins were in short supply in the American colonies, so that other types of money were used widely. Wampum was much in demand among Dutch and English traders, and in seventeenth-century America, wampum making was a thriving industry.

The first mint in the United States was established in Philadelphia by order of the Coinage Act of 1792. It has been in continuous operation ever since. The first coin issued by the federal government was the Franklin cent, designed by Benjamin Franklin in 1787. Perhaps the most famous American coin is the "eagle" series issued intermittently between 1795 and 1933. These gold coins appeared in denominations of $1, $2.50 ("quarter-eagle"), $3, $5 ("half-eagle"), $10 ("eagle"), and $20 ("double-eagle").

- Money is the preferred *means of payment*. In the absence of trust, trade requires the simultaneous exchange of objects of equal value. Money is the object of value most acceptable in trade.[1]

- Money is the *unit of account*. It is convenient to denominate prices in terms of the common means of payment.

- Money is a *store of value*. Its value and durability make it a convenient way to keep one's savings. Also, because it is the common means of payment, it is highly liquid.

- Money is the *standard of deferred payment*. Since money is the common means of payment, it is often more convenient for both borrower and lender to define a loan in terms of a sum of money to be paid rather than in terms of specific goods to be delivered.

WAREHOUSE BANKING

Although there are advantages to keeping your savings in the form of money, there is also one serious disadvantage—the danger of loss or theft. It would be nice if you could keep your money somewhere safe.

While security is a problem for you, it is an even more serious problem for the large merchants, silversmiths, jewelers, and moneylenders on the Main

---

[1]The term *medium of exchange* is sometimes used for this function. We shall use that term slightly differently, as you will see presently.

warehouse banking
The storage and safekeeping of depositors' money.

Island, who have far more to lose. To protect their property, many have invested in secure storage facilities. Since they have these facilities anyhow, some have found it profitable to offer to store money for others, for a fee. We shall call this service **warehouse banking**.[2]

When you leave your hoard of silver at such a warehouse bank, you are given a receipt. You can have your money back whenever you present the receipt. Some other banks, rather than issuing receipts, keep a large ledger in which they write the amounts of money deposited with them by different customers. If someone puts money in or takes it out, they merely change the appropriate entry in their ledger. This arrangement has some advantages—you do not have to worry about losing the receipt, for example—but it does require you to trust the banker.

Meanwhile, with access to bigger markets and new technologies, your weaving business has prospered. You now employ several weavers, and you spend most of your own time selling cloth and buying fiber. To this end, you travel a lot from island to island.

On your travels you often need to make large payments. However, payment in coin is inconvenient. Either you must carry large amounts of money with you, something you are loath to do, or you must arrange with your trading partner to meet you at your bank, so that you can withdraw the money to pay him. This seems particularly silly when he has a deposit at the same bank. You both travel for hours to the bank; you take the money out and give it to him, and he puts it back in the bank.

So, to avoid this waste of time, you make an arrangement with the bank. To make a payment to someone, you simply take your bank receipt and sign it over to him (endorse it to him). He then takes it to the bank, at his convenience, and exchanges it for a new receipt in his own name. Banks with book-entry deposits have an even more convenient arrangement: Depositors can simply write a note to their bank, instructing it to transfer money from their account to that of the payee. Such a note is called a **check**.

check
An order to a bank to pay out of a deposit.

CHECKS AND CLEARING

Being able to endorse receipts and write checks makes it easy to pay those who have deposits at the same bank as you do. Paying others, however, is less convenient. They must take the check or receipt to your bank, get the cash, and then take the cash back to their own bank to deposit it. When they pay you, you have to go through the same rigmarole.

Banks eventually come up with a way to avoid all this hauling of money back and forth. They offer, for a fee, to do the work for you. Now, when you receive a check drawn on another bank, you just give it to your own bank, and it takes care of it.

---

[2]Another name for this service is *cloakroom banking*: The bank is like a cloakroom where you can leave your money, rather than a hat or coat, for safekeeping.

Little is known about banking before the Middle Ages. The Greeks and Mesopotamians had banks, as did the Romans. These civilizations regarded banking as "unnatural," but some banks were allowed to operate. The term *bank* derives from the Latin *bancus*, which refers to the bench on which the banker would keep his money and his records.

Modern banking originated in medieval Italy, despite strong Christian prohibitions against usury (the charging of interest). Florence, Genoa, and Lucca became the centers of finance and trade in the twelfth and thirteenth centuries. Banking slowly spread to the rest of Europe, and by the late thirteenth century, in Barcelona, Spain, even the clergy was engaged in banking. The Germans and Swiss rose to preeminence in the 1480s. England's banking system was well established by the late seventeenth century.

In the American colonies, commercial banking was largely conducted by the major merchant houses. Most actual banks were landowner cooperatives: Landowner members could mortgage their land and receive bank notes in return. The British discouraged this and other forms of banking in the colonies out of fear of overissue and inflation and the consequent loss to British creditors.

THE ORIGINS OF
BANKING

What the banks do initially is this. At the end of each day, each bank sends a messenger to every other bank with the checks it has received drawn on that bank. The messengers hand over the checks, receive dollars in exchange, and bring the dollars back to their own banks.

Messengers from different banks are forever running into one another and having to wait behind one another in line. One day, one of them has a bright idea. Why not all meet at 4 p.m. each day on the beach and simply swap checks? For example, if Palm Tree Bank has $1,000 in checks drawn on Turtle Cove Trust and TCT has $950 in checks drawn on Palm Tree, then the two messengers can simply swap packages of checks and settle the difference with $50 in silver. This practice of **clearing** is a great convenience. The messengers now settle up in about half an hour and have time for a chat and a swim before they head back to their respective banks.

When the banks hear of this, they like the idea. One of them even suggests a way to improve on the arrangement. How about each of the banks keeping some silver on deposit at Palm Tree, the largest of the Main Island's banks? Then the messengers can settle up by writing to one another checks drawn on these clearing deposits. Palm Tree can then debit some accounts and credit others without any actual silver having to be transferred. Since each bank's payments are largely offset by receipts from other banks, the clearing deposits will not need to be large.

With these improvements adopted, very little silver actually needs to be moved around anymore: Most payments are cleared through the banks. Actual transfers of silver dollars are required only if a bank finds that its clearing deposit is running low and needs to be replenished, or if it finds that the clearing deposit has grown too large and decides to bring the excess back to its own vault.

clearing
Exchange of checks between banks in which checks deposited at one bank are set off against those deposited at another.

THE ORIGIN OF BANK NOTES

Paper currency has been in use in China since the ninth or tenth century; Marco Polo wrote of the inflationary problems the Chinese faced with their system. At about the same time, leather currency was being used in Europe: Edgar, King of England, issued leather money from 959 to 975. The use of paper money in Europe can be traced to the Venetians, who, during the battle of Tyre in 1112, paid their troops with banknotes redeemable in metal currency on their return to Venice.

Florence and Venice emerged as world banking centers during the Middle Ages, and banks in these cities regularly exchanged paper notes as a substitute for coin when settling transactions. In England the first paper currency consisted of receipts issued by goldsmiths for coin and plate deposited in their warehouses. These receipts were generally accepted as a means of payment among the nobility and the merchant class.

BANK NOTES

bearer receipts
Receipts conveying ownership to the person in possession of them.

bank notes
Promissory notes issued by a bank that are payable to bearer on demand; acceptable as money.

Once the banks start to think of new ideas, there is no stopping them. Turtle Cove Trust is the next to come up with a good idea. Instead of giving receipts for deposits that specify the owner's name, it issues **bearer receipts** in various denominations—five dollars, tens, and twenties. The amount of silver specified on the receipt is paid by TCT to whoever presents the receipt, not just to the original depositor. TCT calls these bearer receipts, **bank notes**. But because they carry a picture of a green-backed turtle, they come to be known as *greenbacks*.[3]

Greenbacks do have their disadvantages. If they are lost or stolen, that is it. However, as a medium of exchange, they are terrific. Their great advantage is this: When you receive one in payment, you can use it to pay someone else, just as you do with silver. You don't have to take it to your bank to cash it or to have it cleared. Of course, you can if you want to; but you don't have to.

These innovations spread rapidly, and soon check clearing and bank notes are offered by all the banks; the old type of receipt disappears. Few payments are made in silver any more; most involve checks or bank notes.

FRACTIONAL-RESERVE BANKING

The owner of Palm Tree Bank notices that most of the silver dollars on deposit are gathering dust. Even before people used checks and bank notes, the amount of new deposits each day tended to offset withdrawals, so the bank's total stock of silver did not change much. Now, even less silver goes in and out of the vault. The owner of Palm Tree also notices that the moneylender next door is doing

---

[3]This is not, of course, the true origin of the name *greenback*. To help finance the Civil War, the U.S. Treasury issued large amounts of bank notes. The green color of these notes distinguished them from the bank notes of regular banks—hence the name.

very well indeed: As trade has expanded, the demand for credit has grown, and the cost of credit from moneylenders has grown with it.

So how about lending out some of those dusty silver dollars? Palm Tree offers to waive the service fees it charges its depositors for storing silver and clearing checks if they agree to the bank's lending out some of the deposited silver. Palm Tree, of course, guarantees that depositors will still be able to withdraw their silver dollars on demand. The depositors agree, and Palm Tree begins making loans. Of the $100,000 in silver dollars it has in its vault, it lends out $50,000.

Palm Tree's loans prove popular. Because of its relatively cheap source of funds and its informational advantage over the moneylenders (it knows a lot about its customers' business), it can offer loans at lower rates.

Turtle Cove Trust's customers start to ask whether TCT might not also start to make loans. TCT is receptive to the suggestion because it has noticed something interesting about its greenbacks: Very few of them ever come back to be redeemed in silver. So long as people are content to use them as money, they circulate from hand to hand, and almost never come back to the bank for redemption.

So how about printing up some *extra* greenbacks, and, rather than issuing them as receipts, simply lending them out? So long as TCT remains ready to redeem the greenbacks in silver on demand, who will care? TCT prints up $100,000 in greenbacks, in addition to the $100,000 it has already issued, and lends them out to its customers (for a fee, of course).

These two innovations, Palm Tree's and TCT's, are in many ways equivalent: Both result in **fractional-reserve banking**. That is, the silver that each bank now holds is less than the amount of its obligations to redeem in silver. Palm Tree has $100,000 in deposits but only $50,000 in silver in its vault. TCT has $200,000 in greenbacks in circulation but only $100,000 in silver to back them.

fractional-reserve banking Banking in which only a fraction of a bank's deposits is held in the form of liquid reserves, with the balance lent out to earn interest.

There is also a subtle change in the nature of these obligations. Before, the banks were simply custodians of other people's money and providers of transactions services. Deposits and bank notes both represented title to actual silver dollars in the banks' vaults. They were like cloakroom checks: evidence of property left for safekeeping. Now the deposits and bank notes have become *debt* of the bank, IOUs, rather than title to specific silver dollars. The banks have become *financial intermediaries*, issuing their own IOUs and taking the IOUs of others. What is special about these bank IOUs is that they are used as money.

THE BENEFITS AND DANGERS OF FRACTIONAL-RESERVE BANKING

Fractional-reserve banking brings substantial benefits to the Main Island. First, credit is cheaper. Large sums of money, which had been gathering dust, are now available as loans. Second, the real cost of the means of payment has been reduced. Before, when more money was needed, someone had to go down into the silver mines to dig it up. Now, money in the form of bank notes or checking deposits can be created at much lower cost. Labor can be redirected from the production of silver money to the production of other, more useful goods.

PAPER CURRENCY IN THE UNITED STATES

When the First Continental Congress met in 1775 in Philadelphia, the first order of business was to establish a national currency. There were problems with the acceptability of the paper currency issued by the Congress and used by the Revolutionary armies to pay their bills. Although anyone refusing to accept this currency at par was liable to be tried as "an enemy of his country," the paper generally circulated at a value of no more than one-twentieth of face value. The British exacerbated the problem by bringing in shiploads of counterfeit Continental currency so as to further weaken its value.

During the period of relatively unregulated banking before the Civil War, a large number of state-chartered banks operated and issued bank notes. In fact some 7,000 different types of bank notes were in circulation. Telling good notes from bad was not easy. The location of the issuing bank was often unknown, and many notes were not even issued by banks: Corporations, tradesmen, even barbers and bartenders, all issued notes of one kind or another. A promoter even offered help in establishing a "bank." To establish a bank "worth" $100,000, all that was needed was $5,000 for plates to print the notes and another $5,000 for the promoter's fees. Weekly publications known as "bank note detectors" that helped merchants identify the many bills in circulation could not keep up with the spread of new bills. So merchants often relied on tell-tale signs: A bill being worn was a good sign because it indicated that the note had been accepted in the past; tiny pinholes, visible if the note was held up to the light, were a sign that the note had been accepted by a bank (banks stored their notes on pins). One historian writes that it was a wonder, with "nearly every citizen regard[ing] it his constitutional right to issue money, [that] successful trade was possible at all."

The National Banking Act of 1863 effectively taxed out of existence notes issued by state-chartered banks, and subsequently only nationally chartered banks issued notes. During the Civil War, the federal government, hard pressed for funds, issued its own irredeemable notes, which came to be known as "greenbacks." After the Fed was established in 1913, Federal Reserve notes gradually replaced the notes of national banks and the U.S. Treasury.

There are, unfortunately, also dangers. Since it is so easy to produce more money, what stops the banks from producing as much as they wish? With more money chasing the same goods, prices will rise and the value of money will fall. That money you were saving for your retirement will become worthless.

What prevents this from happening is **convertibility**. Remember that bank money is redeemable in silver dollars. For example, some of the greenbacks come back to TCT each day via the clearing. Some people receiving greenbacks deposit them at their own banks; the banks, not wanting to keep them, present them at the clearing for redemption. As TCT expands its lending, more and more greenbacks show up at the clearing. TCT's clearing deposit at Palm Tree runs low,

convertibility
Capability of being exchanged for a specified equivalent, as another currency or security.

and TCT has to take more silver dollars out of its vault to replenish it. Alarmed by this fall in its reserves, TCT scales back its lending and the printing of greenbacks that goes along with it.

But what if *all* the banks expand their issue of bank money at the same time? Then, clearing payments will tend to cancel one another out, and no bank will lose silver reserves. Silver will, however, be lost in other ways. Although bank money is used as a means of payment, so are silver dollars. As the total amount of bank money increases, people will want more silver dollars too. They will withdraw silver dollars from their banks, and the banks' reserves will fall. In addition, as spending increases because of the new loans, people will buy more foreign goods, and there will be a net outflow of silver overseas to pay for them. These drains of silver, internal and external, restrict the ability of the banks to expand the amount of bank money beyond some sort of limit.[4]

There are other dangers. A small bank, Coral Reef Bank, has expanded its lending rather recklessly, and some of its largest borrowers have defaulted. Coral Reef's depositors, hearing of this, rush to the bank to withdraw their deposits. Of course, because Coral Reef is a fractional-reserve bank, it does not have enough silver to pay its depositors all at once. It is forced to close its doors and to turn its depositors away. As Coral Reef's loans are repaid, more money comes in, and the depositors eventually get most of their money back. In the meantime, however, they lose the use of their money and are put to considerable inconvenience and worry.

In the collapse of Coral Reef, the Main Island has experienced its first bank run. Worried islanders press the chief to appoint someone to keep an eye on the banks and to make sure that the depositors' money is safe. The chief appoints one of his many brothers, and the Main Island has its first bank regulator.[5]

THE MAIN ISLAND'S PAYMENTS SYSTEM

By now, after all these innovations, the Main Island has quite a sophisticated and complex payments system. Let us review it. A couple of definitions will help us keep things straight.

- *Medium of exchange*: Something that, by its transfer from buyer to seller, allows a sale to proceed.

- *Means of payment*: An object of value whose transfer constitutes final payment and concludes the transaction.[6]

Silver dollars fit the definition of medium of exchange, but so too do bank notes and checks. How about means of payment? Clearly, silver dollars fit the definition, but the situation is not so clear with respect to checks and bank notes.

---

[4] We shall examine the limit more closely in Chapter 19.

[5] We shall have much more to say about bank safety and regulation in Part Four.

[6] This distinction between medium of exchange and means of payment is, I believe, due to Charles Goodhart.

Let us look at checks first. When you give someone a check, that is not final payment: It is just a promise that final payment will follow when the check is presented to the bank. Of course, the promise may not be good. If you do not have a deposit large enough to cover the check, the check will "bounce."

Is final payment made in silver dollars? Not usually. When a check clears, payment is usually made in bank deposits: The ownership of an amount of bank deposit is transferred from the payor to the payee (there may or may not be a corresponding transfer of silver from bank to bank). The bank deposit is a *title* to silver held in the bank's vault. When payment is made, it is the title that is transferred, not the silver itself. So the means of payment here is the bank deposit.

Unlike checks, bank notes *are* a means of payment. The bank note, like the deposit (but unlike the check), is actual title to silver held by the bank. There is no question of the bank note bouncing.

Because bank notes and deposits are a means of payment, they are a kind of money, just like silver itself. We shall call them **bank money** to distinguish them from silver commodity money. There are some important differences between the two types of money.

bank money
Bank liabilities such as bank notes and deposits that are used as money.

Silver dollars would be valuable even if they could not be used as money: They could be melted down and made into jewelry. In contrast, bank notes and deposits have no intrinsic value. Bank notes cost little to produce, and if you "melt down" bank notes, you will have nothing but worthless ash. Deposits do not even have a physical existence: They are just an abstract idea.

So why are people willing to accept in payment something of no intrinsic value? The simple answer is that people are willing to accept bank money because it is convertible into silver dollars. If you wish, you may take a ten-dollar greenback to Turtle Cove Trust and change it for ten shiny silver dollars. Or you can convert your deposit into silver dollars by making a withdrawal. Of course, since everyone knows that bank money is convertible, there is actually very little reason to convert it. It is far more convenient to use it directly to make payments.

There is also a deeper answer to the question of why people will accept bank money in payment. They will accept it because they expect to be able to use it to pay others. To make this clear, suppose a wizard causes all of the silver reserves in all of the banks' vaults to disappear, so that bank money is no longer, in fact, convertible. No one except the bankers knows this, and they are not about to tell. As long as no one finds out, the economy can go on just as before. People will accept bank notes or deposits in payment because they themselves can use them to make payments to others.

With the use of bank money, then, trade no longer requires the immediate swap of value for equal value. You are now willing, as was Sulu when he sold you a canoe, to part with goods in exchange for a promise. As always when a promise is involved, trust is required. When you accept bank money in payment, you trust that it is indeed convertible (that no wizard, or thief, has caused the banks' reserves of silver dollars to disappear). With the use of bank money, the need for trust in a trading partner—which was easy in the small island community but much harder in a large anonymous market—has been replaced by the need for trust in a bank.

The enormous increase in convenience that results from the use of bank money makes trade much easier, and the Main Island's economy booms.

4.2 THE U.S. PAYMENTS SYSTEM

It is time to leave our imaginary South Sea paradise and to come to grips with the complexities of the real world. How are payments made in the United States?

MEANS OF PAYMENT

FEDERAL RESERVE MONEY Let us begin by looking at our most familiar type of money—a dollar bill. What kind of money is it? Like the greenbacks issued by Turtle Cove Trust, it is a bank note. It has been issued by one of the twelve **Federal Reserve Banks.** You can see which one by looking at the seal to the left of the picture of George Washington.

The **Fed,** as the Federal Reserve Banks are called collectively, is a very special type of bank, called a **central bank,** and is an agency of the U.S. government. In most countries the central bank is called "The Bank of . . ."—for example, The Bank of England, The Bank of Canada, The Bank of Japan. A central bank has many important functions, about which we shall hear later on. Just one of those functions is the provision of hand-to-hand currency like our dollar bill.

The U.S. dollar, unlike the TCT greenback, is *not* convertible into commodity money. It once was, but it no longer is.[7] This raises two interesting questions: Why do people still accept it in payment? What stops the Fed from issuing as many dollars as it pleases?

One reason the Federal Reserve dollar is still acceptable in payment is that it is **legal tender.** If you owe someone $1,000 and pay that debt with Federal Reserve dollars, then the debt is legally discharged. The payee has no legal right to demand payment in any other form, say, in gold. A second reason is that the federal government will always be willing to accept Federal Reserve dollars in payment of tax obligations. However, as with TCT greenbacks, the most important reason people are willing to accept Federal Reserve dollars is that they in turn can use them to pay others. Even in the absence of convertibility, the acceptability of a currency can be self-supporting in this way.

And what restrains the Fed from issuing as many dollars as it pleases? Nothing. There is no legal restraint whatsoever. Yes, this is cause for concern, and we shall later devote a number of chapters to it. But for the moment, we shall assume that the Fed knows what it is doing, and that it issues just the right amount of dollars, whatever that quantity is.

Federal Reserve Banks
The 12 banks that make up the central bank of the United States.

Fed
Federal Reserve Banks.

central bank
Official institution with broad responsibilities for a nation's payment system.

legal tender
Money that the government requires a creditor to accept in discharge of debts.

---

[7]Convertibility into gold coin for private individuals ended in 1933. From then until 1971 foreign governments could convert dollars into gold bullion. Today the dollar is no longer convertible into gold, or into anything else.

definitive money
Money that is not
convertible into anything
else.

fiat money
Money created by
government order.

Federal Reserve dollars are the **definitive money** of our monetary system—the real thing, the ultimate word. They play the same role silver dollars play on the imaginary South Sea island. In our economy, ordinary bank money is convertible into Federal Reserve dollars in the same way that bank money on the Main Island is convertible into silver dollars. Federal Reserve dollars are a kind of "artificial silver" that exists by order of the government. Money of this sort, which exists by government order, or fiat, is called **fiat money**.

Our coins are also created by the government—in this case, by the U.S. Treasury. The coins, like Federal Reserve bank notes, are token money: No precious-metal coins have been minted for general circulation since 1971.[8] There have been suggestions to replace the one-dollar Federal Reserve note with a coin, but the public has resisted the idea (see "A Campaign to Change the Coin of the Realm").

Federal Reserve dollars take the form not only of bank notes of various denominations, but also of book-entry deposits. The Fed really is a bank, and, in addition to issuing bank notes, it accepts deposits. It does not, however, accept them from just anyone. Its principal depositors are the regular banks and the federal government. The regular banks use their deposits at the Fed as clearing deposits, much as banks on the Main Island use their deposits at Palm Tree Bank.

ORDINARY BANK MONEY   In addition to definitive fiat money, we also have ordinary bank money. Banks offer various types of checking accounts that may be used as a means of payment just like the notes and deposits of the Federal Reserve banks. However, ordinary banks in the United States are not allowed to issue their own bank notes: The federal government reserves this valuable right for itself. How valuable is this right? In June 1989 the amount of Federal Reserve notes outstanding was about $230 billion. Not quite all of this is seigniorage. There are the costs of printing new bills and of replacing worn and damaged ones. However, those costs come to only about $120 million a year, so the seigniorage is substantial.

Ordinary bank money in the form of checking accounts is convertible into definitive fiat money. You may go to your bank at any time and make a withdrawal from your account in the form of definitive money, or you may transfer funds to someone else in that form. To be able to meet such withdrawals, banks hold reserves of definitive money, in the form of currency in their vaults and in the form of deposits at the Fed. Ours is a fractional-reserve system, so these reserves are quite small relative to the banks' deposit liabilities. The amount of checkable deposits in June 1989 was $546 billion. For every $100 of this convertible bank money, banks held about $11 in reserves, $5 of it in actual vault cash and the rest in the form of deposits at the Fed.

Our means of payment, then, are Federal Reserve dollars (bank notes and deposits at the Fed), Treasury coins (for small payments), and ordinary bank

---

[8]Precious-metal coins are called *full-bodied* token money because their scrap value approaches their face value. Our coins are non-full-bodied token money.

A CAMPAIGN TO CHANGE THE COIN OF THE REALM

Eleven years ago, faced with growing government deficits, the Carter Administration took an unusual step aimed at reducing the Treasury Department's budget by $50 million a year. It introduced the Susan B. Anthony dollar coin to complement the George Washington dollar bill.

A paper dollar wears out after a year or two in circulation, and millions of replacement bills are printed every year. The Carter Administration was confident it could slash costs by replacing bills with coins, which last an average of two decades. However, the new silver coin, honoring one of the founders of the women's rights movement, made its debut and promptly disappeared. The popular rejection of the Susan B. Anthony dollar was so profound that few since have had the nerve to promote the notion of a dollar coin again.

Among the few is James Benfield, a Washington lobbyist who has begun a campaign to revamp United States money by bringing back the dollar coin and eliminating the dollar bill.

Mr. Benfield said his passion about the subject of bills and coins arises from the enormous potential for savings for consumers and the government. The Treasury now spends $120 million a year replacing worn-out dollar bills and would save virtually all of that by converting completely to a dollar coin. In this decade, at least seven countries have replaced low-denomination bills with coins. Canadians have approved of their recent conversion from bills to coins for their dollars.

The lobbyist points out that from 1957 to 1987 the Consumer Price Index rose 400 percent, meaning the dollar of the Reagan years is equivalent to the quarter of the Eisenhower years.

Where there are vending machines, there are now often dollar-bill changers, which cost about $2,400 each and still manage to spit back many of the notes. Refitting an existing vending machine to accept dollar bills costs about $400. Dollar bills still are not accepted on New York City buses, but Washington, Chicago and Cleveland have all been forced to spend millions to refit their buses with new fare machines that accept dollar bills.

Many of the vending machines, virtually all of those manufactured since the Susan B. Anthony dollar was introduced in 1979, can be easily adjusted to accept dollar coins.

The big negative facing Mr. Benfield's campaign is the public hostility that was shown toward the Susan B. Anthony coin. That experience has made some politicians skeptical of Mr. Benfield's idea, notably Representative Frank Annunzio, the Illinois Democrat who is chairman of the House coinage subcommittee.

But Mr. Benfield is confident the problems can be overcome with a basic design improvement and public relations effort.

The Treasury Department is conducting a formal study of why the Susan B. Anthony coin failed, but Mr. Benfield said the study is wasting time and money.

"You don't have to be a rocket scientist to figure it out," he said.

The obverse, left, and reverse sides of the Susan B. Anthony dollar.

"The Suzie was the same size as a quarter. It had ribbed edges, just like a quarter. It was the same silver color as a quarter. So when people pulled out a pocketful of change, they had trouble telling a dollar from a quarter."

Mr. Benfield's remedy: smooth the edges of the new dollar coin and color it gold; then stamp Christopher Columbus's likeness on it, introduce it before 1992 and aggressively promote it as part of the national celebration of the 500th anniversary of the discovery of America.

Source: "A Campaign to Change the Coin of the Realm," *The New York Times*, April 6, 1988, p. A20. Copyright © 1988 by The New York Times Company. Reprinted by permission.

money (deposits only). A purchase is finally and completely paid for when the seller is paid with one of these. We shall call Federal Reserve dollars *Fed money* and ordinary bank money plain *bank money*.

MEDIA OF EXCHANGE

There are various ways of making a purchase. Sometimes you pay immediately with definitive Fed money. Sometimes, you use some other medium of exchange to initiate the transaction, with final payment to follow—for example, a check, a bank credit card, or customer or trade credit. With these other methods, because there is a promise of payment rather than immediate payment, some degree of trust is required.

The choice of which medium of exchange to use in a given transaction will depend on cost. Generally, the least expensive method will be chosen.

IMMEDIATE PAYMENT AND WIRE TRANSFERS   Immediate payment in Fed money is common, for quite different reasons, both for very small transactions and for very large ones. It is not much used for those in between.

Immediate payment is used for small transactions because there is a large fixed cost associated with promises of payment (remember our discussion in Chapter 3). This makes deferred payment too expensive for small transactions. As a result, when you buy a candy bar at the grocery store, you will generally not be able to pay by check or credit card: You will have to pay with cash.

One reason that payment with Fed money is used for *large* transactions is that it is fast. This matters because delay is costly. For example, suppose you are responsible for handling the cash of a large corporation, and you have a payment due today for $100 million. A check may take several days to clear, and in the meantime you are losing the interest you could be earning. At an annual rate of 10%, daily interest on this amount is about $26,500.[9]

Another reason speed is important is that most large payments (those in the multimillion-dollar range) are related to short-term lending—sometimes for as little as a single day (we shall learn about such loans in later chapters). It makes little sense to make a one-day loan by sending a check that takes several days to clear.

Fedwire
Communications network that links major-bank computers to the Fed's computers.

Large payments are made not by transferring cash but rather by transferring title to deposits at the Fed. These transfers are made over **Fedwire**, a communications network that links the computers of most major banks to the computers of the Fed.

To see how Fedwire works, suppose Chase Manhattan Bank wants to pay $100 million to Citibank. The Fedwire operator at Chase types the appropriate code into the computer—for obvious reasons, security is pretty tight—and then

---

[9]While the delay is a loss to you, the payee, it is a gain to the payor. We shall see in Chapter 28 the sort of games that are played to increase the gains and minimize the losses from delays in payment.

sends a message requesting the Fed to transfer $100 million from Chase's deposit at the Fed to Citi's deposit. A minute or two later a message comes back from the Fed confirming the transfer. At the same time the Fed also sends a message to Citi, notifying it that it has received $100 million from Chase. At that moment the payment has been made: It is exactly as if a suitcase containing $100 million in tens and twenties had been "beamed" from Chase's vault to Citi's vault.

Using the Fedwire is more expensive than using a check. The cost is about $10 per message. So wire transfer is not used for small payments: The average amount is $3.2 million, compared with an average of $1,200 for a check and $10 for a cash payment. In addition to the costs of *using* Fedwire, there are significant costs to being hooked up to the system. As a result, many small banks, whose customers make few payments in the multimillion-dollar range, do not find it worthwhile to be connected.

In addition to Fedwire, there is a clearing system for wire transfers called **CHIPS** (Clearing House Interbank Payment System) that is operated by the New York Clearing House. CHIPS saves both on Fedwire fees and on the size of the clearing deposits that banks need to hold at the Fed. Subscribers to CHIPS include the 12 member banks of the New York Clearing House and over 100 other domestic and foreign banks with offices in New York City. Like Fedwire, CHIPS is computerized.

CHIPS
Clearing House Interbank Payment System, a clearing system for wire transfers.

There are important differences between wire transfers over Fedwire and those over CHIPS. Whereas a Fedwire message is like payment in cash, a CHIPS message is more like a check. It is not an actual payment but rather a promise to make payment by the end of the day. Just as with other promises, this one requires trust. There is a danger the "check" will bounce.

The way that CHIPS clearing works is this. At 4:30 p.m. each day the CHIPS computer sends to each participant a summary of all payments made and received. The summary shows the participant's position relative to each of the other participants. For example, if Citi has sent $5 billion to Chase and received $4 billion, Citi's net position is that it owes Chase $1 billion. The summary also shows the *net net*. For example, if, in addition, Citi is owed $700 million by Chemical Bank of New York and it has no transactions with any other bank, it owes *the system* $1 billion − $700 million = $300 million. Each bank checks the summary against its own records and confirms. If it owes the system money, it must send the amount over Fedwire to a special clearing account at the Fed by 5:30 p.m. By 6:00 p.m., banks that are owed money by the system receive payment, out of the same special account.

CHECKS   Most payments intermediate in size between the small ones made in cash and the very large ones made by wire transfer are made by check. Checks in our economy are exactly like those on the Main Island. When you pay for that $500 stereo by check, you are instructing your bank to pay the store $500. The store will be careful about accepting your check. If, when it is presented to your bank for payment through the clearing system, there is less than $500 in your account, the check will be returned to the store unpaid. The store will then have to go to the trouble of trying to collect the money from you.

check card
Bank-issued card guaranteeing payment, presented by bank customers when writing a check.

traveler's check
Type of insured bank note purchased from a bank or other issuer, refundable from the issuer if lost.

prepaid card
Purchased card that is used to make payments for certain services.

giro payment
Bank service allowing direct transfer of funds among account holders.

on-us clearing
Clearing of a check at the bank on which that check is drawn.

In some countries, like Britain, banks issue their customers a **check card**. If such a card is presented at the time a check is written, the bank will guarantee payment up to some limit (say £100).

An alternative that avoids the bad-check problem is the **traveler's check**. These are issued by a bank or other issuer—the largest issuer, American Express, is not a bank—in fixed denominations, and payment of the face-value amount is guaranteed. Traveler's checks are not checks in the ordinary sense of being drawn on some account that may or may not cover them. Rather, the issuer is paid for the traveler's check ahead of time, so that it already has the money. The main advantage of traveler's checks over cash is that if you lose the checks or they are stolen, you can obtain a refund from the issuer. In this sense, traveler's checks are a kind of insured bank note.

An idea similar to the traveler's check is the **prepaid card**. Such cards are used on many campuses to operate copying machines. You buy the card, often from a vending machine, for, say, $5. To make copies, you insert the card into the copying machine, and the cost of the copies is deducted from the balance on the card until the $5 is used up. Prepaid cards are also used for some other payments—for example, paying for tickets on the Washington, DC, subway system. They are extremely popular in Japan (see "Japanese Take to the Prepaid Plastic Card").

Another alternative to the check that is popular in many foreign countries is the **giro payment**. With a check you give an order to pay, drawn on your bank, to the seller; with a giro payment you give the order to pay *directly* to your own bank. Clearly, you cannot give the order unless there is cover for it, so the seller does not have to worry about the payment bouncing. The problem for the seller is being sure that you will actually issue the order. As a result, giros are used mainly for periodic payments like utility and tax bills. In many countries the post office offers giro accounts (an extension of the money orders offered by our own postal service).

There are several ways to collect payment on a check. The most straightforward is simply to take the check yourself to the bank on which it is drawn and ask to be paid (this is called **on-us clearing**). Although straightforward, this is a lot of trouble. It is worthwhile only when the sum involved is large. For example, a corporation, on receiving a check for $10 million, will find it worthwhile to deliver the check by messenger and request the funds be wired to its own bank.

Most checks go through a complex interbank clearing process. Large cities generally have clearinghouses to clear checks drawn on local banks. Checks from outside the clearinghouse group, or from areas with no clearinghouse, go to the Fed to clear. The Fed itself uses the local clearinghouse to deliver and pick up checks. Where there is no clearinghouse, the Fed must actually deliver checks to individual banks.

Before checks can begin the process of clearing, they must be sorted and processed. The costs, together with the fees charged by the Fed for clearing, are borne by the bank receiving the money. The total costs, especially for checks drawn on banks across the country, can be substantial.

JAPANESE TAKE TO THE PREPAID PLASTIC CARD

The Japanese, who have always shown a propensity to save money, are now taking to the idea of spending it in advance to buy prepaid cards for a wide variety of services and a growing number of goods, including hamburgers.

The prepaid card fever in Japan began back in 1982 when Nippon Telegraph and Telephone introduced prepaid telephone cards ranging in value from Y500 to Y5,000. The cards soon caught on not only for their convenience but also—since smartly designed cards were introduced in 1984—for their uses as promotional giveaways and personal gifts. Last year NTT sold Y138.5bn worth of both standard and designed telephone cards.

Teleca, the company that manages the production and sales of NTT's cards, has made perfumed telephone cards, cards that flash holograms, and cards that carry all sorts of messages ranging from wedding announcements to charity drives. Teleca claims that the variety and ingenuity of card designs has started something of a fad with avid collectors ready to pay several hundred thousand yen for rare and unused cards.

Teleca has started to issue autodial cards which are prepaid telephone cards that will automatically dial a specified number that is pre-recorded onto the card. Taxi companies, for example, can give away cards with their number pre-recorded as promotion material and hope to convince clients of their convenience.

Japan Railways Group introduced a prepaid Orange Card in 1985 and sales have risen steadily, in part helped by a promotional drive in which cards are issued for every imaginable occasion, such as the anniversary of the opening of obscure branch lines. For East Japan Railway Company alone, which operates JR's eastern lines centering in Tokyo, total sales from prepaid cards in 1987 reached Y23.5bn.

Area Links has introduced a prepaid taxi card that will be accepted by a number of taxi companies in the Kansai area (in western Japan). The company hopes eventually to introduce prepaid cards that could be used to pay for dry cleaning, purchases at convenience stores and, as might be expected in Japan, practice swings at the local driving range.

Source: Extracted from "Japanese Take to the Prepaid Plastic Card," *Financial Times*, November 17, 1988. Extract reprinted by permission of the Financial Times.

The use of computers to clear smaller payments to and from households and firms has been relatively slow to catch on: It always seems to be just around the corner. **Automated clearinghouses** allow banks to exchange computer-tape records of payments instead of checks. These are most useful for repeated periodic payments such as payroll payments and Social Security checks (the government is the biggest user of this form of payment). Total volume remains small. There have been experiments with **point-of-sale transfer systems** that link the cash register at a store directly to bank computers. When you buy something, the amount is immediately debited from your bank account and credited to the account of the store.

The electronic device that has proven most successful is the **automated teller machine (ATM)**. These machines are located outside banks and at other locations like shopping malls and airports. They allow customers easy access to their checking accounts, for deposits, withdrawals, and transfers, 24 hours a day, 7 days a week. At the end of 1989 there were some 75,000 ATMs in the United States; transactions on these machines were running at a rate of about 400 million per month, most of them cash withdrawals. A majority of ATMs are connected to at least one of several national networks (the largest are Cirrus and

automated clearinghouse
Clearing of payments through banks' exchange of computer-tape records.

point-of-sale transfer system
System that links stores' cash registers directly to bank computers.

automated teller machine (ATM)
Card-operated facility for making bank deposits and withdrawals.

Plus). These networks allow customers to access their accounts and, in particular, to withdraw cash through the ATMs of banks other than their own. ATM networks are in the process of being extended internationally: Soon you will be able to withdraw cash from ATMs in London, Paris, and Tokyo as well as in New York City and Los Angeles.

The operation of the New York Clearing House is described in "The Physical Side of Banking."

CREDIT The medium of exchange that involves the greatest degree of trust is credit. The costs are such that sales on credit are out of the question unless there are special circumstances that make trust of the purchaser easier or special arrangements that make it unnecessary.

As we saw in Chapter 2, firms that do regular business frequently extend one another trade credit. That is, goods are shipped against a promise of payment in, say, 30, 60, or 90 days. The continuing business relationship between the firms is what makes such trust possible. Failure to pay would sour the relationship.

Stores will often extend credit to their customers. If you live in a small community, the general store will often let you buy "on tab" and let you settle up at the end of the month. This works for the same reason credit worked on the small Island: In a small community everyone knows everyone else, and reputation is important. For different reasons, large department stores, too, will often sell on credit, usually using a **store credit card**. Such stores are large enough to support a credit department of their own to assess creditworthiness and large enough to get some of the benefits of pooling risk.

A different solution to the problem of trust for smaller retailers is the **bank credit card**. Instead of the store extending you credit, it is extended by a bank. The bank relieves the store of the burden of assessing creditworthiness and of collecting payment. If you pay for that $500 stereo with your bank credit card, the credit slip is processed much like a check: The store passes the slip to its own bank, which clears payment with the bank that issued the card.

Although the clearing process is similar, there are important differences between a credit card purchase and a check. In the case of the credit card, the issuing bank pays the store immediately, without debiting your account (in fact, you need not have an account with the bank issuing the credit card). Instead, the bank makes you an automatic loan for the amount of the payment. At the end of the monthly billing period, you will have the choice of paying the $500 immediately, without interest, or of paying it off over time, with interest.

The bank credit card is also a solution to the bad-check problem. In fact, if you do not exploit the option to pay over time, but instead pay immediately the amount due each month, the credit card functions as a sort of guaranteed check. There is still, however, an element of credit in this arrangement—the bank does pay the merchant before it collects payment from you. This element of credit is eliminated with something called a **debit card**. With a debit card, rather than waiting for you to pay at the end of the billing period, the bank automatically debits your checking account immediately with each transaction.

store credit card
Card issued by a store authorizing purchase of goods on credit.

bank credit card
Card allowing holder to purchase goods on credit extended by issuing bank.

debit card
Card authorizing the debiting of the holder's checking account with each transaction.

The Physical Side of Banking

By N. R. Kleinfield

European American Bank arrived first. At a few minutes to 10 a.m., three of its young clerks rattled in with a laundry cart on wheels. Then Bankers Trust trundled in with what looked like a black footlocker. Chemical Bank brought five silver-colored bins.

The carts were laden with billions of dollars worth of canceled checks—checks to Con Ed, checks to the landlord, checks to Uncle Bob.

The messengers seemed unimpressed with their precious cargo, as shown by the following exchange:

"Hey, Joe, what's shaking?"

"Not much. Still moving dough."

This was final settlement time for the big New York banks. Checks, of course, rarely get deposited in the same banks in which the check writers have their accounts, so each day the financial houses must trade their paper with one another and settle up what they owe. Rather than Chase and Irving and Citibank scurrying all over town, the trading occurs each morning at one central location—the New York Clearing House.

Within a small white, two-story building nestled near the foot of Broad Street, hard by Battery Park, the physical side of banking takes place. Each day, roughly $200 billion of paper and paperless electronic checks ebb and flow inside its doors.

On the clearing floor, the clerks hoisted cardboard boxes out of the bins. Inside the boxes were checks sorted for individual banks. The clearing floor is surrounded by a wooden counter. The clerks whipped around the room, dumping the boxes at each bank's location along the counter. They then scooped up checks destined for their own banks.

"Waiting on Manny Hanny," an edgy clearing house official barked at 10:15 a.m. Clerks scanned the morning paper, swapped small talk. At 10:18, Manufacturers Hanover finally trooped in. It was slapped with the $5 fine. Its clerks did not look stricken. All the banks get fined, and the Federal Reserve, which usually carts in the most dollars, typically gets hit the most. Sometimes, there is good reason. Years ago, a truck bearing checks for the Fed from Buffalo swerved off the road and spilled the checks into a river. They had to be reconstructed from microfilm.

A small Datapoint computer in the other room toted up how much each bank had brought and received. The figures were handed to the clerks. Chase learned that it owed $172,951,952.06. Citibank owed $1,602,969,464.34. Morgan was due $1,087,424,207.34. The clerks bade their noisy adieus and left. No money actually changed hands. The Fed was simply notified of the tabulations and it in turn debited and credited the banks' reserves.

The total amount of paper checks cleared for the day was just average: $17,653,476,553.22.

Some of the money, of course, will make an encore. The banks have until 11 p.m. the next day to return so-called rubber checks. That happens to something under 3 percent of the total. The big reason is that old demon: insufficient funds.

In a room adjacent to the clearing floor, employees were now furiously jabbing at the keys of Datapoint 3600 terminals, entering checks into an electronic brain. This was the City Collection Department. Here, checks drawn on 143 foreign banks that had been deposited in New York banks are dropped off, about $1 billion a day. They are toted up on a computer and messengers from the foreign banks stop in at 11:30 a.m., take the checks to their banks, which have an hour and a half to reconcile the numbers and send Federal funds checks back.

At 4:32 p.m., the settlement numbers arrive for the 20 banks that settle on CHIPS. About $180 billion blipped through the system, 10 times the amount of paper checks cleared in the morning. The Bank of New York was owed $533,230,744.02. The Manufacturers and Traders Bank of Buffalo was owed $130,360.33.

"It's rare that you see something under a million," said Bruce Turkstra, who heads the operation.

The average check that goes through CHIPS is a whopping $2.7 million, he added. Every so often, a blip of more than $1 billion arrives.

At 4:33, Manufacturers and Traders wired that it would take its money. A young woman sat before a computer terminal with a sheet in her lap and when the banks wired acknowledgement, she checked them off. By 5:07, all 20 had wired.

Now Bob Tennant, supervisor of telecommunications, phoned the Fed, where a CHIPS account is kept to field money from the paying banks and then send it out to the recipient banks. Every day, there are new passwords to open and close the account. Mr. Tennant spoke the password: "ache."

Within eight minutes, all the money arrived, a little over $2 billion. A minute later, it was gone. Once, one bank mistakenly gave 20 cents too much, and the clearing house had to send back what was the smallest CHIPS check in history.

At 5:32 p.m., Mr. Tennant phoned the Fed again. He said "mean," the password to close the CHIPS account, its balance now $0.00.

"That's it," Mr. Turkstra said. He put on his overcoat and went home.

Source: N. R. Kleinfield, "The Physical Side of Banking," *The New York Times*, December 30, 1987. Copyright © 1987 by The New York Times Company. Reprinted by permission.

There are two major clearing systems for bank credit cards—Visa and MasterCard. Cards similar to bank credit cards are also issued by some financial institutions that are not banks—for example, the American Express card and the Sears Discover card.

Since merchants generally have to pay a fee for credit card transactions—2% to 5% is common—but no fee for clearing a check, they will often charge you more if you pay by credit card. This usually takes the form of a "cash discount" if you do not use a credit card.

Notice that in issuing credit cards, debit cards, and bank cards, banks are combining their two traditional functions. One function, which we have seen in this chapter, is to provide a medium of exchange that facilitates trade. The second function, which we saw in Chapter 3, is to assess creditworthiness and to bear credit risk.

SOME NUMBERS

How much are the different methods of payment and media of exchange used? Exhibit 4.1 shows, for each method, rough estimates of the number of transactions per day, the average size of each transaction, and the total value of daily transactions in 1991.

Although there are many cash transactions, each is small, and so the total value is quite small. Wire transfers, on the other hand, are relatively few but large, and their total volume swamps all other methods of payment. Checks are somewhere in between. Credit-card transactions account for surprisingly little of the total.

SUMMARY

- Money makes trade possible when credit is impossible or too expensive.

- There is an element of circularity in the acceptability of money in exchange: Traders are willing to accept it because they in turn expect others to be willing to accept it.

- The qualities of a commodity that make it suitable for use as money include large trading volume, high value relative to weight, divisibility, homogeneity, and durability.

- The purity and weight of commodity money is standardized and guaranteed by minting into coins. The excess of the exchange value over the cost of producing a money is called seigniorage.

- Money performs several economic functions: It is a means of payment, a medium of exchange, a unit of account, a store of value, and a standard of deferred payment.

EXHIBIT 4.1

USE OF METHODS
OF PAYMENT:
1991 ESTIMATES

	Transactions (per Day)	Average Value of Transaction	Total Value (per Day)
Cash	1–2 billion	$10	$10–$20 billion
Wire transfers			
Fedwire	270 thousand	$3.2 million	$850 billion
CHIPS	170 thousand	$5.4 million	$900 billion
Checks	220 million	$1,200	$260 billion
Credit card	30 million	$75	$2.3 billion

Source: A. N. Berger and D. B. Humphrey, *Market Failure and Resource Use: Economic Incentives to Use Different Payment Instruments*, Finance and Economics Discussion Series, (Washington, DC: Federal Reserve Board, July 1988). Numbers are extrapolated to 1991, using earlier data and estimated growth rates and rate of inflation. Some daily figures are obtained from annual figures assuming 250 business days a year.

- A warehouse bank accepts money for safekeeping. Claims on deposits take the form of receipts or book entries. Payments can be made by endorsement of receipts or by using checks to transfer the ownership of deposits.

- Payments between traders with deposits at different banks are made easier by check clearing. Banks hold deposits at a clearing bank to facilitate the process.

- Bank notes are bearer receipts in standard denominations. They may be used as hand-to-hand currency in the same way as coins.

- A fractional-reserve bank differs from a warehouse bank in that it is a financial intermediary. Its deposits are no longer custodial holdings; they are debt liabilities. A small part of a fractional-reserve bank's assets consists of a reserve of definitive money, held to enable the bank to convert deposits on demand. The remainder consists of earning assets of various types—principally loans.

- Fractional-reserve banks create money. The benefit is that this bank money is much cheaper to produce than commodity money. However, there are also potential problems. One is excessive money creation. This is generally restrained by convertibility. A second problem is bank runs, which may lead to the collapse of fractional-reserve banks.

- The definitive money of the U.S. economy consists primarily of bank notes and deposits of the Federal Reserve Banks (the Fed), the nation's central bank. Fed money is not convertible into anything else. Its acceptability is enhanced by its being legal tender and by the willingness of the government to accept it in payment of taxes. There are no legal constraints on the ability of the Fed to create definitive money.

- In addition to Fed money, our means of payment include coins issued by the U.S. Treasury and ordinary bank money in the form of checkable deposits, which are convertible into definitive Fed money. Fed deposits are used by banks to clear checks.

- Immediate payment with definitive money is the preferred medium of exchange both for small transactions and for very large ones. The very large payments are made by transferring title to Fed deposits using a communications network called Fedwire. There is also a clearing system for such payments called CHIPS.

- Checks are the medium of exchange for most other transactions. Checks are cleared "on us," through local clearinghouses, and through the Fed. Other similar media of exchange include traveler's checks, prepaid cards, and giro payments.

- Electronic payments have yet to catch on in the United States for small payments. However, ATMs have proven very popular, principally as cash dispensers.

- Credit, in the form of trade credit, is a common medium of exchange among firms. Consumer credit is extended by some small stores to local customers and by the credit departments of large retailers. Consumer credit is also provided by financial institutions that specialize in the assessment and bearing of credit risk.

KEY TERMS

unit of account	fractional-reserve banking	traveler's check
barter	convertibility	prepaid card
money	bank money	giro payment
commodity money	Federal Reserve Banks	on-us clearing
coins	Fed	automated clearinghouse
seigniorage	central bank	point-of-sale transfer system
store of value	legal tender	
warehouse banking	definitive money	automated teller machine (ATM)
check	fiat money	
clearing	Fedwire	store credit card
bearer receipts	CHIPS	bank credit card
bank notes	check card	debit card

DISCUSSION QUESTIONS

1. Which of the various economic functions of money are unique to it? For the functions that are not unique to money, give examples of other things that perform these same functions.

2. Why is cash the preferred medium of exchange for drug deals?

3. Do you think that warehouse banks would pay interest on their deposits? Would fractional-reserve banks? Why or why not?

4. Why do you think U.S. banks do not issue check cards? Are there good substitutes?

5. Is an issuer of traveler's checks (like American Express) a financial intermediary? Do traveler's checks fit the definition of a means of payment? Why or why not?

6. Why do merchants ask to see a bank credit card before they will accept a check? Explain how this is an example of the free-rider phenomenon.

7. A bank credit card is an example of financial intermediation; a store credit card is not. Explain.

8. Debit cards have not been very popular in the United States. What is their disadvantage to a consumer relative to credit cards?

9. How can you tell if a payments system is performing its function well? Use our discussion of the efficiency of the *financial* system in Chapter 3 as a guide.

BIBLIOGRAPHY

Einzig, Paul, *Primitive Money*, London: Eyre and Spottiswood, 1948.

Federal Reserve Bank of New York, "Large-Dollar Payment Flows from New York," *Quarterly Review*, Federal Reserve Bank of New York, Winter 1987–8, 6–13.

Groseclose, Elgin, *Money and Man: A Survey of Monetary Experience*, Norman, OK: University of Oklahoma Press, 1977.

Helfferich, Karl, *Money*, translated by Louis Infield, New York: Augustus M. Kelly, 1969.

Humphrey, D. B., *The U.S. Payments System: Costs, Pricing, Competition and Risk*, Monograph Series in Finance and Economics, New York: Salomon Brothers Center for the Study of Financial Institutions, 1984.

Radford, R. A., "The Economic Organization of a P. O. W. Camp," *Economica* 12 (November), 189–201, 1945.

Robertson, D. H., *Money*, Cambridge: James Nisbet, 1922.

Shaw, W. A., *The History of Currency: 1252 to 1894*, 2nd ed. New York: Augustus M. Kelly, 1967.

Stigum, Marcia, *After the Trade: Dealer and Clearing Bank Operations in Money Market and Government Securities*, Homewood, IL: Dow Jones-Irwin, 1988.

Studenik, Paul, et al., *Financial History of the United States*, New York: McGraw-Hill, 1963.

CHAPTER 5

THE BUSINESS OF BANKING AND ITS REGULATION

In Chapters 3 and 4 we looked at the role of banks in the economy. We saw that banks provide two types of service. The first is financial intermediation: Banks borrow in their own name in order to relend to others. The second type of service is the provision of media of exchange: Banks provide an important means of payment—checking deposits—and they play a significant role in the extension of credit to both firms and households.

In this chapter we shall look at banks from a much narrower point of view—that of their owners. From their owners' point of view, the role of banks is simply to make a profit. In this respect banks are no different from car dealerships or drugstores.

We shall see how banks maximize their profits and the risks and opportunities involved. The understanding we gain of bank behavior is important not just for its own sake, but also because it will help us understand how banks respond to changes in their environment. In later chapters this understanding will enable us to make sense of recent events—such as the savings and loan crisis—and to anticipate future developments.

The picture of banking that we paint in this chapter is greatly simplified—really no more than a caricature. We shall fill in most of the details in later chapters, once we absorb the basic ideas.

5.1 LET'S OPEN A BANK

The best way to understand banking is to become a banker yourself. Imagine that you have $2 million to invest. The money has been raised from your own savings and from willing friends, relatives, and classmates. The owners between them receive 2 million shares in the bank.

87

balance sheet
Financial statement that lists a firm's assets, liabilities, and net worth.

assets
Items of value that a business owns.

liabilities
A firm's debts.

net worth (equity)
Net ownership value of a firm.

To get started, you need a charter: You cannot open a bank without one. Charters are granted by state or federal banking regulators. As a citizen of well-known probity—and impeccable political connections—you have no difficulty in obtaining a charter. You rent a building, hang out a shingle with the name "Solid State Bank," and you are open for business.

To keep track of what you are doing and of how well you are doing it, you need a way to describe the condition of the bank. The **balance sheet** does just that. It lists what the bank owns (its **assets**), what it owes to others (its **liabilities**), and the difference between them (its **net worth** or **equity**). That is,

$$\text{net worth} = \text{assets} - \text{liabilities},$$

or, equivalently,

$$\text{assets} = \text{liabilities} + \text{net worth}.$$

In a balance sheet, assets are listed on the left, and liabilities and net worth are listed on the right. For example, the balance sheet of Solid State Bank, as it opens for business, is as follows:

ASSETS		LIABILITIES AND NET WORTH	
Cash	$2m	Liabilities	$ 0
		Equity	2m

Since net worth is always calculated as assets less liabilities, the right-hand column and the left-hand column should always sum to the same amount. That is, they should balance: Hence the name *balance sheet*.

A balance sheet always describes the situation at *a particular moment*. In this case, it is the moment at which the bank opens for business. As we shall see, each new transaction causes the balance sheet to change.

🌴 **CHECK STATION 1**

Jack Flash has the following assets and liabilities: a savings account balance of $15,000, a checking account balance of $5,000, a house worth $200,000, a mortgage for $100,000, credit-card debt of $7,000, a car worth $20,000, a loan on the car of $15,000, and a pension plan worth $100,000.

Construct a balance sheet for Jack. What is his net worth?*

THE BANKS' BANK

Suppose your $2 million in cash is initially in the form of used tens and twenties locked in the vault. There are some fairly obvious reasons why you might not want to keep all this cash on the premises. You decide, therefore, to deposit $1.5

*Answers to check station questions are in Appendix B at the back of the book.

million of it in an account you open at your local Federal Reserve bank. Not only is this safer, but the account at the Fed will prove useful later for clearing checks.[1]

What does your balance sheet look like after you have made this deposit?

ASSETS		LIABILITIES AND NET WORTH	
Cash	$0.5m	Equity	$2m
Deposit at Fed	1.5m		

Items that have changed from the previous balance sheet are shown in **boldface** *type.*

LOANS AND DEPOSITS

Even with your account at the Fed, you are still not much of a banker: You have no deposits and no loans. While you wait for the deposits to start coming in—you have placed ads in all the local newspapers offering a free toaster oven to anyone opening a new account—you decide to get things rolling by lending out some of your own money.

A dynamic local entrepreneur, Hattie Jakes, comes in and makes a persuasive pitch for a $200,000 loan that would enable her to hire more programmers for her software company. You decide to make the loan. How will this affect your balance sheet? The *immediate* effect will be:

ASSETS		LIABILITIES AND NET WORTH	
Cash	$ 0.5m	Checking deposits	
Deposit at Fed	1.5m	Jakes Inc.	$200,000
Loans		Equity	2m
Jakes Inc.	200,000		

Note that a loan is *not* made by handing over cash, but rather by crediting the borrower's checking deposit for the amount of the loan; if necessary, as it is here, you will open an account for this purpose. The loan, then, is a swap of one security or IOU for another. Jakes gives you her security—the signed loan contract. In exchange, you give her your security—the demand deposit, a promise to pay on demand any amount up to $200,000. The reason the swap of IOUs is useful to Jakes is that the bank's IOU is acceptable in payment to others, whereas her own IOU is not. The bank's IOU is money.

The loan appears on your balance sheet as an asset. That is because it is a promise by Jakes to pay you $200,000 in the future. The deposit appears as a liability. It is a promise from you to pay $200,000 on demand.

---

[1]Recall our discussion in Chapter 4 of check clearing and of the role played by deposits at the Fed.

CHECK STATION 2 | **What is the effect of the loan on Jakes's own balance sheet?**

Presumably, Jakes did not take out this loan in order to have the money sit idle. The next day she writes dozens of checks and uses the whole amount to meet her payroll.

Suppose the checks all go to employees with accounts at other banks. Each employee deposits his or her paycheck at his or her own bank. For example, one check for $10,000 is deposited at First National. First National collects payment for its depositor by clearing the check through the Fed. That is, the check is sent to the Fed, which credits First National's account with the Fed for $10,000 and debits your bank's account for the same amount. The ability to clear checks in this way is one of the reasons why an account at the Fed is so useful: Otherwise, First National would have had to send the check to you, and you would have had to send the cash over to them.

Once the check has cleared, your balance sheet reads as follows:

ASSETS		LIABILITIES AND NET WORTH	
Cash	$ 0.5m	Checking deposits	
Deposit at Fed	1,490,000	Jakes Inc.	$190,000
Loans		Equity	2m
Jakes Inc.	200,000		

Notice that your deposit at the Fed has fallen by $10,000 and that you have debited Jakes's account for the same amount.[2]

After all the other checks have cleared, your balance sheet becomes:[3]

ASSETS		LIABILITIES AND NET WORTH	
Cash	$ 0.5m	Checking deposits	
Deposit at Fed	1.3m	Jakes Inc.	$ 0
Loans		Equity	2m
Jakes Inc.	200,000		

Just as you are beginning to worry, new deposits start rolling in, and before you know it, you are out of toaster ovens. All the new deposits are checking deposits.[4] A total of $10 million comes in, in the form of checks drawn on other

---

[2]Actually, there is rather more to the clearing of checks than this. We shall go into the details in Chapters 8 and 20.

[3]We assume here, and throughout this chapter, that all the checks go to people with accounts at *other* banks rather than at your bank. For a small bank, this is a reasonable assumption. We shall have more to say about this assumption in Chapter 19.

[4]Banks also have time deposits, or savings accounts, deposits against which checks cannot be written. We shall have more to say about time deposits later on, but for now our story will be simpler if we leave them out.

banks. You send these checks to the Fed to clear, and once they do, your balance sheet reads:

ASSETS		LIABILITIES AND NET WORTH	
Cash	$ 0.5m	Checking deposits	$10m
Deposit at Fed	11.3m		
Loans	200,000	Equity	2m

New loan applications also start coming in, and you approve $10 million in new loans. As with the loan to Jakes, the new deposits created as you make the loan soon disappear, as checks written on them clear through the Fed. When things settle down, you will have a balance sheet that is fairly typical for a bank:

ASSETS		LIABILITIES AND NET WORTH	
Reserves		Checking deposits	$10m
Cash	$ 0.5m		
Deposit at Fed	1.3m		
Loans	10.2m	Equity	2m

Notice that "Cash" and "Deposit at Fed" are bundled into the category **reserves,** since they both play the role of enabling you to meet any possible excess of withdrawals (in cash or through clearing) over deposits (in cash or through clearing). We shall have more to say about this in a moment.

reserves
Funds that a bank holds in the form of vault cash and deposits at the Fed.

What does your balance sheet look like when you *first* make the $10 million in loans? | 🌴 **CHECK STATION 3**

5.2 HOW TO MAXIMIZE OUR PROFITS

What sort of a profit are you making? The relationship of profits to the items in your balance sheet can be summarized in the following equation:

$$\pi = (L \times i_L) - (D \times i_D) - FC, \qquad [5.1]$$

where

π is profits,
L is the amount of loans,
i_L is the realized interest rate earned on loans,
D is the amount of deposits,
i_D is the cost per dollar of deposits,
FC is fixed costs.

contractual rate
Rate that is charged.

realized rate
Rate that is actually
obtained.

Your revenue is the interest you earn on loans: This is the interest rate on loans times the amount of loans outstanding.[5] The interest rate that matters here is not the **contractual rate**—the rate you charge—but the **realized rate**—the rate you actually get. The two differ because not all loans are repaid as planned. If a loan goes bad, the realized rate on that loan will be below the contractual rate, perhaps well below. Of course, a bad loan need not mean a complete loss; something is usually recovered, often from the sale of collateral.

For example, suppose that you charge a contractual rate of 12% on loans to firms and that you have $5 million of such loans outstanding. Suppose too that one in ten of these loans goes bad and that in such cases you recover, on average, 95% of the loan. On the $4.5 million of good loans, you will earn

$$0.12 \times \$4.5 \text{ million} = \$540,000,$$

and on the $0.5 million of bad ones, you will lose

$$0.05 \times \$0.5 \text{ million} = \$25,000.$$

Your net revenue from the whole portfolio of loans will be

$$\$540,000 - \$25,000 = \$515,000,$$

fixed costs
Costs that do not depend
on the amount of deposits.

explicit interest
Interest paid to depositors.

implicit interest
Interest in the form of
services provided.

for a realized rate of 10.3% on the total $5 million of loans.

Against the revenue from loans, you must set your costs. First, there are the costs that do not depend on the amount of your deposits—**fixed costs.** These include most of the costs of the physical facilities (the building, the computer, etc.) and some of the labor costs. Then there are the costs of the deposits—actual **explicit interest** paid to depositors as well as **implicit interest** in the form of services that you provide. For example, although your customers do not receive interest on their regular checking deposits (explicit interest), they do receive free checking (implicit interest). The checking is free to the customer, but certainly not to you.[6] In Equation 5.1, therefore, i_D includes both explicit and implicit interest.

So what can you do to increase your profits? Given the amount of loans and the amount of deposits, profits will increase if you can raise the realized rate you earn on loans and lower the cost of your deposits. Also, it is clear that the more loans, the better. But from the balance sheet you can see that in order to make more loans, you must either attract more deposits, reduce your reserves, or find more equity. Let us examine each of these possibilities more carefully.

---

[5] In reality, revenue also includes fees for various services that banks provide, and costs include the costs of these services. We shall have more to say about these services in later chapters.

[6] This cost, often more than a dollar a check, is the main reason many banks are not wild about accepting students as customers. Students tend to have low balances on average and to write many checks for small amounts.

You charge an average of 14% on your loans, and one in ten loans defaults, in which case you recover 90%. You pay no explicit interest on your deposits, but the services you provide free to your depositors cost you 8% of the amount of the deposits. Your fixed costs are $100,000 a year.

What are your profits?

🌴 **CHECK STATION 4**

SETTING LOAN RATES AND DEPOSIT RATES

Why not raise the 14% you charge on your $10.2 million in loans to 15% and make an extra $102,000 in profits? If your loan customers have nowhere else to go, you might get away with it. But normally they *do* have somewhere else to go—to other banks, for instance. Such competition limits your ability to raise your loan rates above those that other lenders charge.

Worse yet, if you do raise your rates, not only will you lose customers, but you will tend to lose your *best* ones. This phenomenon is known as **adverse selection.** It is the result of asymmetric information: Your customers know more about their own creditworthiness than you do. For example, in terms of default risk, as far as you can tell, Jakes Inc. looks very much like another of your loan customers, QuicKilling Enterprises. However, unknown to you, QuicKilling is on the verge of going under. When you raise the rate you charge on loans to both companies, Jakes has no trouble switching to another bank, and does so. QuicKilling does not even try: It would rather not attract any attention to its books at the moment. The loan to Jakes is replaced in your portfolio by a loan to a new customer, who is suspiciously undeterred by your higher loan rates.

adverse selection Tendency, in losing customers, to lose the best ones.

So raising the rate you charge on your loans (the contractual rate) will inevitably lower their average quality, and the risk of loss will increase. As a result, the *realized* rate (the contractual rate less loan losses) will rise by less than the contractual rate. For example, if you raise your contractual rate from 14% to 15% while other banks do not raise theirs, your realized rate may rise only from 11% to 11.2%, or it may even *fall* to 10.8%. Since it is the realized rate that matters, you will set the contractual rate at a level that will net you the highest possible realized rate on your loans.

What sort of rate should you pay on your deposits? Here again you are constrained by competition. You would like to pay as little as possible, but if the rate you pay is *too* low, depositors will go elsewhere. The question is: What alternatives do your customers have? Are there many other banks in the area? What rates do these other banks offer, in both explicit and implicit interest? How attractive are investments *other* than bank deposits? In setting your deposit rates, you face a trade-off. The more attractive you make your deposit rates, the more deposits you will have, and the more loans you can make. On the other hand, making your deposit rates more attractive will raise your costs.

🌴CHECK STATION 5 | **Suppose the relationship between the default and recovery rates and the contractual rate on loans is as in the following table. For each contractual rate, calculate the realized rate. (Assume that whatever rate you charge, you will still be able to lend $10.2 million.)**

Contractual Rate	Percentage of Loans That Default	Percentage of Loan Recovery	Realized Rate
12	10	95	?
13	12	95	?
14	12	90	?
15	15	85	?
16	20	75	?

What is the best rate to charge?

RESERVES AND LIQUIDITY

One way you can make more loans, and thus more profit, is by reducing the amount of your reserves. We have seen that when you make a loan, there is initially an increase both in the amount of loans and in the amount of deposits; then as checks are written on the new deposits and as they clear, you lose deposits and reserves. The ultimate net effect of the new loan on your balance sheet is an increase in loans outstanding balanced by a decrease of equal amount in reserves. So, if you are willing to reduce your reserves by $1 million, you can make an extra $1 million in loans. If the realized rate on your loans is 11%, this would raise your profits by $110,000. Should you do it?

Before you do, remember *why* you have the reserves. Your deposits are convertible: Depositors are entitled to withdraw their money (in cash or by writing checks) whenever they please. Generally, the flow of money out will be offset by the flow of money in. Sometimes, though, more will go out. Your portfolio of loans is of no help to you in meeting such an outflow: Essentially, the only way to turn loans into cash is to wait for them to be repaid. Therefore you need some other source of ready money—of **liquidity.**

liquidity
Access to ready cash.

A possible excess of withdrawals is not the only reason you need liquidity. If Hattie Jakes comes in for a new loan, you would like to be able to accommodate her: If you cannot, she might leave in a huff and take her business elsewhere. To be able to make new loans when good customers like Jakes request them, and to be able to exploit other good opportunities when they present themselves, you need liquidity.

One way to provide liquidity is to hold enough reserves. The question is: How much is enough?

required reserve ratio
Minimum ratio between reserves and deposits that financial institutions are required to maintain.

The amount of reserves you hold is not entirely up to you. Banking regulations require you to keep a certain minimum amount that is defined in terms of a ratio between reserves and deposits. That ratio is called the **required reserve ratio.**

For example, if you have $10 million in deposits and the required reserve ratio is 10%, you must hold at least

$$0.10 \times \$10 \text{ million} = \$1 \text{ million.}$$

The amount of reserves that you must hold, $1 million in this case, is called **required reserves.**

Unfortunately, required reserves are of no use at all in providing liquidity. To see why, consider the following allegory. In an earlier time, when travelers crossed the Atlantic by passenger liner rather than by jumbo jet, the S.S. *Majestic* is steaming peacefully toward England with 3,000 passengers aboard. The *Majestic* carries 1,000 life preservers—one for every 3 passengers as required by regulations (lifeboats are also required). One foggy night, following a fantastic party, a passenger falls overboard. The captain faces a dilemma. Regulations require him, on pain of losing his license, to have on board *at all times* one life preserver for every 3 passengers. If he throws a life preserver to the foundering passenger, he is in trouble: He will have 2,999 passengers on board, but only 999 life preservers. On the other hand, if he does not throw him a life preserver. . . .[7]

The moral? Required reserves, like required life preservers, are not available for use. As we shall see in Chapter 19, the real reasons for required reserves is quite unrelated to liquidity: It has to do with controlling the amount of bank money that the banking system can create. So, to provide liquidity, you need something in addition to required reserves.

One thing you could do is hold **excess reserves**—reserves in addition to the required amount. Clearly, the more excess reserves you have, the less likely you are to run out. On the other hand, the more excess reserves you have, the fewer loans you can make and the lower your profits. You will have to decide just how much profit you are willing to give up in order to sleep well at night.[8]

Suppose, weighing the pros and cons, you decide on a reserve ratio of 12%—the 10% required plus excess reserves of 2% that you can actually use. This ratio allows you to reduce your reserves from $1.8 million to $1.2 million and to make an extra $600,000 of loans. Your balance sheet becomes:

required reserves
Minimum amount of reserves a financial institution must hold.

excess reserves
Cash in the vault or deposits at the Fed that exceed the amount of reserves required by law.

ASSETS		LIABILITIES AND NET WORTH	
Reserves		Checking deposits	$10m
Cash	$ 0.5m		
Deposit at Fed	0.7m		
Loans	10.8m	Equity	2m

---

[7]One student suggested the following solution to this ethical dilemma: Throw 2 more passengers overboard, and throw the 3 of them a life preserver.

[8]We shall see in Chapter 12 that there is a lot more to the management of a bank's liquidity than this. In reality, excess reserves do not play a significant role. However, whatever the means, liquidity is costly, and there will be the same trade-off between liquidity and profit.

Of course, whatever your excess reserves, there will still be days when you run short. What to do? One possibility is that some other bank finds itself in the opposite position—temporarily with more reserves than it wants. Because its surplus, like your deficit, is temporary, it will not wish to make more loans. One way to solve both of your problems is for the other bank to lend you its unwanted reserves on a short-term basis (for one day at a time). The market for such loans is called the **fed funds market,** since the loans are made by one bank transferring "federal funds" (deposits at the Fed) to another. These transfers are made using Fedwire. The existence of this market is another reason why it is useful to have a deposit at the Fed. Another way to make up a deficiency in reserves is to borrow from the Fed itself. Such a loan is called a **discount loan.**

fed funds market
Market in which banks borrow reserves from other banks.

discount loan
A bank's borrowing from the Fed.

EQUITY AND SOLVENCY

It is time to check your profits. Suppose your realized rate on loans is 11%, your cost of deposits is 9%, and, to make the arithmetic simple, your fixed costs are zero. Using our formula, your profits are

$$(\$10.8 \text{ million} \times 0.11) - (\$10 \text{ million} \times 0.09) = \$288,000.$$

Is this good? To know whether it is or not, you need to see what sort of return this is on the money you (and your friends, relatives, and classmates) invested in Solid State Bank. To do this, you need to calculate the percentage return on the money invested, or the **return on equity (ROE):**

return on equity (ROE)
Percentage return on money invested.

$$\text{ROE} = \frac{\pi}{E} = \frac{\$288,000}{\$2,000,000} = 0.144, \text{ or } 14.4\%. \qquad [5.2]$$

To see whether this return on equity is good or bad, you have to compare it to something else. What else could have been done with the $2 million the owners invested in Solid State Bank? One possibility would have been to invest it in the stocks of *other* banks of similar risk. If such investments normally pay 16%, then the 14.4% return on your own bank does not look all that impressive. What could you do to improve it?

There are two ways to increase π/E: Increase π or decrease E. Since you have already done all you can to increase π, how about halving E to $1 million? To maintain the balance of the balance sheet, you will have to make a reduction of the same amount on the asset side. Unfortunately, reserves cannot be cut: You need to maintain the 12% reserve ratio that you decided on earlier. So it will have to be loans. Therefore, when $1 million worth of loans is repaid, rather than making new loans, you take out the money yourself and invest it elsewhere. The balance sheet becomes:

ASSETS		LIABILITIES AND NET WORTH	
Reserves		Checking deposits	$10m
Cash	$0.5m		
Deposit at Fed	0.7m		
Loans	9.8m	Equity	1m

Of course, as the amount of loans falls, total profits fall too, to

$$(\$9.8 \text{ million} \times 0.11) - (\$10 \text{ million} \times 0.09) = \$178,000.$$

However, return on equity *rises* to a respectable

$$\frac{\$178,000}{\$1,000,000} = 0.178, \text{ or } 17.8\%.$$

Does this really make you better off? That depends on what you did with the spare $1 million that you took out of Solid State. You could have invested it in bank stocks, or you could have set up another bank just like Solid State. In the latter case, you would be earning profits of

$$2 \times \$178,000 = \$356,000$$

on your $2 million, clearly better than the $288,000 you were earning when you had the whole $2 million invested in Solid State.

Now that we understand the principle, why not take it even further? How about reducing equity to $500,000, or even to $20,000? Let us see what happens in the latter case:

ASSETS		LIABILITIES AND NET WORTH	
Reserves		Checking deposits	$ 10m
Cash	$ 0.5m		
Deposit at Fed	0.7m		
Loans	8,820,000	Equity	20,000

The return on equity is now a very pleasing 350%! Calculate it yourself.

But, of course, there is a catch: *The lower the equity, the greater the chance the bank will fail.*

To understand why, let us see what happens when a loan goes bad. Suppose the inevitable happens and QuicKilling Enterprises goes belly-up. The $200,000 it owes you is a total loss—not a cent will be recovered. You must therefore mark down the asset side of your balance sheet by $200,000. Clearly, to maintain balance, some item on the right-hand side of the balance sheet must be marked down by the same amount. It cannot be deposits. The loss on the loan in no way affects your liability to your depositors. Your debt to them does not depend on how well you do on your loans. All the profits are yours, but so are all the losses. Hence it is equity that must be marked down.

The consequences depend on how much equity you had before the loss.

Case 1. You had $1,000,000 in equity. After the loss your balance sheet will be:

ASSETS		LIABILITIES AND NET WORTH	
Reserves		Checking deposits	$ 10m
Cash	$0.5m		
Deposit at Fed	0.7m		
Loans	9.6m	Equity	0.8m

This is certainly not good news, but it is not the end of the world either. Over the next few years you will need to take out only part of your profits and devote the rest to rebuilding equity, but in the longer run the bank will continue to provide a good return on your initial investment.

Case 2. You had $20,000 in equity before the loss. After the loss your balance sheet will be:

ASSETS			LIABILITIES AND NET WORTH	
Reserves			Checking deposits	$ 10m
Cash	$	0.5m		
Deposit at Fed		0.7m		
Loans		8,620,000	Equity	-180,000

insolvent
Having an excess of liabilities over assets.

What does the negative number for equity mean? It means that the liabilities of the bank exceed its assets. The bank is **insolvent:** Even if all the other loans were to be repaid in full, you would not have enough to pay off the $10 million you owe your depositors. At best, you could pay them $9,820,000. The negative value of equity is the size of the shortfall.

What happens now? When a bank becomes insolvent, it is closed down: Its charter is revoked. Are you personally liable for the $180,000? No. Because the bank is a corporation, its owners are protected by limited liability: They cannot lose more than their investment in the corporation. In the absence of deposit insurance, the depositors would have to bear the loss. The bank would be liquidated, and the depositors would be paid off at a rate of about 98¢ on the dollar.

With complete deposit insurance, the loss would be born by the insurer—the government (which means, ultimately, the taxpayer). The insurer provides the $180,000 so that depositors can be paid in full. In reality, not all deposits are insured. Federal deposit insurance covers a maximum of $100,000 per depositor.

Since many deposits are much larger than this maximum, there exist large amounts of uninsured deposits. So some depositors do stand to take a loss.

This potential loss to depositors from bank failure can be a problem, not only for the depositors, but also for the bank itself. Indeed, even a suspicion of insolvency may mean serious trouble for the bank. To see why, suppose you have uninsured deposits in a bank and you hear the bank has taken large losses on its loans and is in danger of failing. What do you do? So does everyone else. The resulting rush to the bank to withdraw deposits is called a *bank run,* and it is one of the greatest dangers a bank can face. We saw that a bank keeps extra reserves to accommodate unusually large withdrawals, but *no* level of reserves, short of 100%, can provide enough liquidity to accommodate a bank run.[9]

So how can a bank protect itself? We have seen that the more equity a bank has, the smaller the chance of insolvency and, therefore, the smaller the danger of a bank run. Actually, it is not the absolute amount of equity that matters, but the amount relative to the amount of loans. The ratio of the two is called the **equity-to-loan ratio.** We shall use the symbol *e* for this ratio:

equity-to-loan ratio
Ratio of the amount of a bank's equity to the amount of its loans.

$$e = \frac{E}{L}. \qquad\qquad [5.3]$$

The lower is *e*, the greater the danger your bank could become insolvent, and the more jittery your uninsured depositors will be. The more jittery they are, the higher the return you will have to pay them to keep their deposits with you. That is one reason you will not want to lower your equity too far.

There is another reason you will be worried about the danger of insolvency. If your bank is successful, you stand to lose more than just your original stake if it fails. Ownership of the bank is a claim to a stream of future profits: If the bank fails, you lose that claim. If the bank has a good location, good customers, and good prospects for growth, then it may be worth considerably more than the money the owners put into it. For example, although they put only $2 million into the bank, they might now be able to sell it to someone else for as much as, say, $3 million.

The amount of money the owners originally put into the bank, the $2 million that appears on the balance sheet, is called the **book value** of its equity. The amount for which they could sell the bank, $3 million, is called the **market value.** The difference, $1 million in this case, is called **goodwill;** it is the value of the bank's charter. If the shares of the bank are publicly traded (which is unlikely for such a small bank), then the market price of these shares will provide an estimate of its market value.

book value
Accounting value of a bank.

market value
Amount for which a bank can be sold.

If the bank fails and the charter is revoked, the owners will lose, not $2 million, but $3 million. They will lose the value of the charter, or the goodwill, in addition to the money that they put into the bank. So, if the value of the charter is substantial, you will keep a higher equity ratio in order to reduce the risk of losing it.

goodwill
Difference between the market value of a bank and its book value.

---

[9]We shall look at bank runs and deposit insurance in more detail in Chapters 16 and 17.

Before we leave this example, notice how it illustrates two important financial phenomena. The first is *diversification*, or, in this case, the lack thereof. Your loan to QuicKilling was quite large relative to the amount of your equity. The larger the individual loans you make, the greater the chance that a single default will sink you.[10]

leverage
Use of borrowed money to make an investment.

The second phenomenon is the effect of **leverage**—using borrowed money to make an investment. Consider the following example. You can make a $1,000 investment that in a year will pay off either $1,100 or $1,200: Each outcome is equally likely. Your return will be either 10% or 20%. The average return is

$$0.5 \times (10\% + 20\%) = 15\%,$$

so we can describe the return as being 15%, plus or minus 5%.

Now, instead of putting up the whole $1,000 yourself, you could borrow some of it. Suppose you borrow $900 at 12% and put up the remaining $100. Since you are making an investment 10 times the size of the amount that you yourself put up, we say that your **leverage ratio** is 10.

leverage ratio
Ratio of the total amount of an investment to funds actually supplied by an investor.

Let us look at the return on the $100 that you yourself invest. After you repay the loan, the payoff to you will be either

$$\$1,100 - (\$900 \times 1.12) = \$92$$

or

$$\$1,200 - (\$900 \times 1.12) = \$192,$$

each equally likely. Therefore the return will be either –8% or +92%, for an average of 42%. The prospective return is now 42% plus or minus 50%. Notice two things: (1) the average return is higher, and (2) the possible variation about that average—the risk—has increased. In general, the greater the leverage, the higher the average return and the greater the risk.

Your bank is very much like this simple example. The equity is the amount that you yourself (and the other owners) put up. The deposits are the borrowed money. The bank's assets are the investment. If Solid State's equity is $1 million, the leverage ratio is 11—the $11 million in assets divided by the $1 million in equity. The higher the leverage ratio, the higher the average return (return on equity) but the greater the fluctuation in return relative to equity, and so the greater the risk of insolvency.

---

[10]In fact, bank regulations generally forbid a bank to lend to a single borrower an amount greater than 15% of its equity.

In light of these considerations, you weigh the trade-offs and decide that an equity-to-loan ratio of about 6% is reasonable. Your final balance sheet, then, is:

ASSETS		LIABILITIES AND NET WORTH	
Reserves		Checking deposits	$ 10m
Cash	$0.5m		
Deposit at Fed	0.7m		
Loans	9.4m	Equity	0.6m

Suppose you wanted to raise your equity ratio from 6% to 10%. What would your balance sheet look like after you had done it? What are the various ways you could increase your equity?

🌴 **CHECK STATION 6**

SOME NUMBERS

To see how actual banks in the real world decide on the various ratios, look at Exhibit 5.1, which shows a **consolidated balance sheet** for all U.S. commercial banks. Each item on the balance sheet is a total for all banks taken together, with liabilities of one bank to another netted out. For example, a deposit that Citi holds at Chase is not included either in total deposits or in total assets. You can see that the average ratio of reserves to demand deposits is 13% (however, some of these reserves are held against time deposits); the leverage ratio is 25; and the equity-to-loan ratio is 4.8%.

consolidated balance sheet Balance sheet reporting the financial condition of a number of separate entities as if they were a single unified economic entity.

Exhibit 5.2 shows income, expenses, and profits for all U.S. commercial banks. All numbers are expressed as a percentage of assets. Noninterest income is banks' earnings from fees they receive for various services (we shall learn about many of them later); noninterest expense is implicit interest plus fixed costs plus the costs of various services unrelated to deposits; the loss provision is actual plus

EXHIBIT 5.1

CONSOLIDATED BALANCE SHEET OF U.S. COMMERCIAL BANKS YEAR-END, 1987 (BILLIONS OF DOLLARS)

ASSETS		LIABILITIES AND NET WORTH	
Reserves	$ 72	Checking deposits	$ 543
Cash	30	Time deposits	1,373
Deposits at Fed	42	Other liabilities	795
Loans and investments	2,283		
Other assets	394	Equity	110

Source: Federal Reserve, *Flow of Funds Accounts: Financial Assets and Liabilities Year-End, 1964-87.*

E X H I B I T 5.2

INCOME AND
EXPENSES AS A
PERCENTAGE OF
AVERAGE NET
CONSOLIDATED
ASSETS AT U.S.
COMMERCIAL
BANKS

Item	1984	1985	1986	1987	1988
Gross interest income	10.33%	0.96%	8.50%	8.34%	8.95%
Gross interest expense	6.98	6.08	5.11	4.95	5.42
Net interest margin	3.35	3.50	3.39	3.40	3.53
Noninterest income	1.09	1.20	1.28	1.41	1.47
Loss provision	0.57	0.68	0.78	1.27	0.54
Other noninterest expense	3.04	3.17	3.22	3.30	3.33
Securities gains (losses)	−0.01	0.06	0.14	0.05	0.01
Income before taxes	0.83	0.90	0.80	0.28	1.14
Taxes	0.19	0.21	0.19	0.18	0.33
Extraordinary items	0.01	0.01	0.01	0.01	0.03
Net income	**0.64%**	**0.70%**	**0.62%**	**0.11%**	**0.84%**
Cash dividends declared	0.32	0.33	0.33	0.36	0.44
Net retained earnings	0.32	0.37	0.29	−0.24	0.40
Memo:					
Average assets ($ billions)	2,401	2,559	2,753	2,883	2,959
Number of banks	13,952	13,898	13,733	13,273	12,691

Source: *Federal Reserve Bulletin*, July 1989.

expected losses from loan defaults.[11] To find the return on equity, multiply the net income by the leverage ratio of about 25.

5.3 CAN BANKS BE TRUSTED?

We have seen the various ways in which banks can increase their profits: We would expect them to exploit each of them to the fullest. We have also seen that many of these ways of increasing profits carry with them risks. We would expect bankers to be aware of the risks and to be accordingly judicious in their pursuit of gain. Banking is really no different from any other business in this trade-off between risk and return.

Unlike most other businesses, however, banks are subject to an enormous amount of regulation. There are limits on the kinds of assets banks can hold, on their leverage, on the interest rates they may pay on deposits, on their geographic

---

[11]There is a tax advantage to a bank from recording an expected loan loss on its books before the actual loss occurs. The bank can deduct the expected loss from its taxable income immediately, and so pay less tax. When the loan comes due, if it is in fact paid in full, the "loss" that did not happen is a capital gain, and the bank pays tax on it.

expansion, and on the nonlending activities in which they may engage.[12] We seem to trust banks less than we trust other businesses to make the right decisions without outside interference.

What possible justification could there be for such interference? In general, our economic system is one of free enterprise. We believe that the unfettered pursuit of gain by the individual usually achieves what is best for society as a whole: The way to get rich is to provide others with what they want. If this is so, then placing restrictions on the operations of *any* business harms not only the owners of that business, but also its customers and society as a whole.

However, this general argument for unrestricted free enterprise sometimes fails. One occasion on which it may do so is when the pursuit of individual gain has harmful side effects, the costs of which are not borne by those doing the harm. Such costs imposed on others are called **externalities.**

A typical example is pollution. A chemical company dumps waste into the environment, and this waste harms others. The economic problem—and the justification for regulation—is *not* that the waste is harmful, but that the full cost is not borne by the chemical company doing the harm. Because pollution costs the company nothing, it pollutes too much. If it had to pay for the harm, it would pollute less. The existence of this externality may justify regulation of the chemical company to limit its pollution.

Does banking involve such externalities? Suppose a banker makes loans that are risky and, as a result, the bank fails. If the banker bears all the costs, then presumably he will have taken them into account in making his decision, and the loans will not be "too" risky. However, if the failure of the bank harms others in ways that cost the bank nothing, then, because these costs do not matter to it, the bank will tend to make loans that are *too* risky from society's point of view. If such externalities exist, it may make sense to regulate banks to limit the riskiness of the loans they make, and, perhaps, in other ways too.

What might these externalities of bank failure be? History provides some hints, the biggest hint being provided by the catastrophic economic collapse known as the Great Depression. Indeed, most of the banking regulation we have today is a legacy of that single, frightful episode.

externalities
Costs of harmful side effects of a firm's activity that are borne by others and not by the firm.

THE GREAT DEPRESSION AND THE COLLAPSE OF THE FINANCIAL SYSTEM

The "roaring 20s" was a period of sustained economic growth and prosperity. Banks contributed to this prosperity and, in general, shared in it. Reflecting the optimism of the times, the stock market enjoyed an unprecedented boom, with stock prices more than doubling between 1926 and 1929. Although the economy began to slow in 1928, this initially had little impact on the stock market: The Dow Jones Industrial Average (a measure of stock prices) rose from 200 in

---

[12]We shall have more to say about all of these restrictions in later chapters.

January 1928 to 381 in September 1929. Then, in October, the market faltered, and in the week of October 23–29, it crashed. By the end of the year stocks had fallen in value by over a third, and they fell by a third again in 1930. By 1932 the Dow had fallen to 58, about 15% of its peak in 1929.

The collapse of the stock market heralded a more general collapse of the economy. The number of unemployed rose from 1.6 million in 1929 to 12.1 million (one-fourth of the labor force) in 1932. Gross national product, a measure of economic output, fell by a quarter. Prices too fell by a quarter, and farm prices fell by a half. Not only was this the sharpest economic decline in modern history, it was also the longest. The economy did not really recover until World War II. See Exhibit 5.3 for the behavior of prices and unemployment in this period.

As the economy slipped, banks began to fail in large numbers. Of the 24,000 banks in existence in 1929, only about 15,000 remained by the end of 1933. See Exhibit 5.4.

The declining economy led to bank failures, and bank failures contributed to further decline in a vicious circle. The fall in spending led to business losses and to widespread default on loans. The resulting fear of bank insolvency led to bank runs. The bank runs developed into general banking panics as depositors rushed to withdraw deposits from all banks, including those that were still solvent. Many solvent banks were unable to find the needed liquidity and were forced to close. Their closure shut off credit to many small and medium-sized firms, forcing them to cut back their operations and lay off more workers. The resulting fall in spending caused more defaults, and so on.

This vicious circle, demonstrated so graphically in the Great Depression, is the type of externality that may provide a rationale for the regulation of banking. The cost of one bank's failure is not limited to the owners of that bank, or even to its depositors, but may spill over in this way to other banks and ultimately to the economy as a whole.

Of course, the mere existence of an externality does not guarantee that regulation will be helpful in dealing with it: Poorly conceived regulation may well make things worse. Indeed, many economists believe that banking regulation already in place before the Depression contributed substantially to the severity of the problem. (We shall take another look at this, and in particular at the role the Fed played, in Chapter 16.) It is notable that some countries with *less*, rather than more banking regulation, such as Canada and the United Kingdom, weathered the storm without undergoing the same sort of banking collapse that occurred in the United States.

THE REGULATORY LEGACY

The financial regulation we have today is largely the product of a series of acts passed by Congress between 1933 and 1935. The form of this regulation, naturally enough, reflects the beliefs of the time—not necessarily correct—on what exactly had gone wrong.

EXHIBIT 5.3

THE GREAT
DEPRESSION

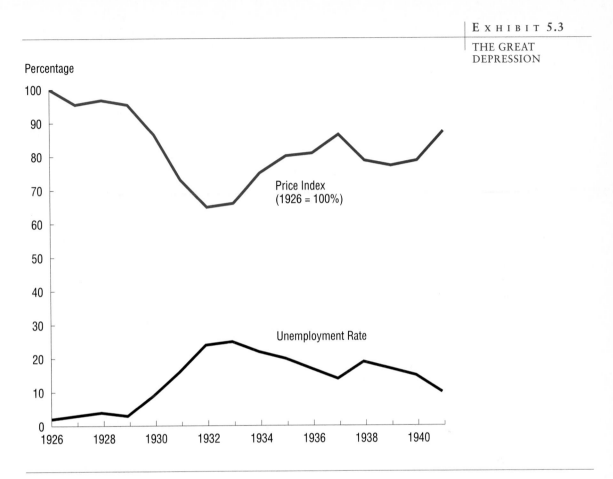

Source: *Economic Report of the President.*

The popular interpretation of events at the time, shared by legislators and by the general public, was that "excessive competition" among banks had led them to make loans that supported "speculation" in the stock market. This speculation, they believed, had led to the stock market boom, which had ended, inevitably, in collapse and disaster. The response of Congress was to limit competition among banks in a number of ways and to keep them out of the securities markets.

Banks had competed with one another for deposits principally by offering better interest rates. No longer. Under the new regulations, they were prohibited from paying interest at all on checking accounts, and a ceiling was placed on the interest they could pay on savings accounts. Since no bank could offer more for deposits than any other, there could be no competition. In addition, limitations on branch banking were strengthened to make it harder for one bank to set up and compete in the market of another.

E X H I B I T 5.4

BANK FAILURES
DURING THE GREAT
DEPRESSION

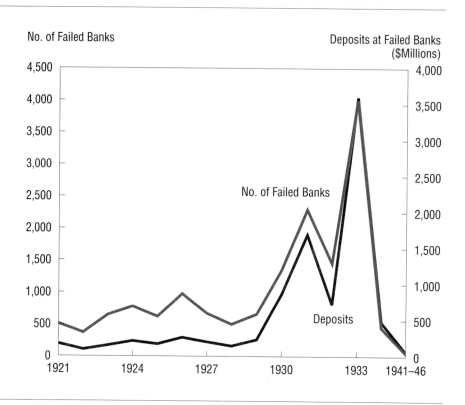

Banks had been very active in the securities markets. They had underwritten new securities and had lent both to securities dealers to finance their inventories and to investors to finance their purchases. When the market plummeted, many of these loans soured, forcing the sale of the securities pledged as collateral. Such sales further fueled the decline in security prices. It was believed that losses on these securities loans were an important factor in bank insolvencies.[13]

Under the new laws, commercial banks were largely barred from participation in the securities markets. Such participation was limited to **investment banks,** which were, in turn, barred from commercial banking. Banks were also restricted

investment banks
Financial institutions engaged in underwriting or brokering publicly traded corporate securities.

---

[13]Buying securities *on margin*, as the purchase of securities with borrowed money is called, is another example of leverage. If you buy stocks worth $100,000 by putting up $10,000 of your own money and borrowing the rest, you are said to buy on 10% margin. The stocks you buy become collateral for the loan. If the stocks go up in value to $110,000, the gain is yours (a 100% gain). If the stocks fall in value to $90,000, the loss too is yours (a 100% loss). If the stocks do fall to $90,000, the lender will want you to repay $9,000 of the loan, so that the $81,000 loan remaining is once again equal to 90% of the value of the stock. This request for partial repayment is known as a *margin call*. If you cannot come up with the money, the lender will sell the stock to pay off the whole loan.

in their ability to hold securities as assets and in their ability to lend with securities as collateral.[14]

Finally, people felt that something had to be done to put an end to banking panics. The Fed had been set up in 1913 with this as one of its major goals. During the collapse, however, for a variety of reasons that we shall explore in Chapter 16, it had been largely ineffectual. A new federal agency was set up, the Federal Deposit Insurance Corporation, or FDIC, to insure deposits against bank failure. Since depositors now knew that they would get their money whether the bank was solvent or not, there was no longer any reason for them to rush to withdraw their deposits. For a long time, consequently, bank runs ceased to be a problem.

IS REGULATION THE SOLUTION OR THE PROBLEM?

Although the idea of externalities did underlie the banking legislation of the 1930s, it would be naive to believe that it provided the sole motivation. For example, restricting competition may be rationalized as an attempt to increase stability. However, as we saw in Chapter 3, restricting competition also reduces pressure to lower costs and increases opportunities for economic rents. Many banks were delighted to see their profits increased and their lives made easier in this way.

Moreover, regulations, even when they are designed purely for the public good, do create problems of their own. First, regulations distort incentives: They alter what it is best for a bank to do to maximize its profits. For example, the existence of deposit insurance allows banks to make riskier loans precisely because depositors are now less worried about their deposits. Second, regulations are slow to change and they reduce flexibility in responding to changing circumstances. When existing regulations stand in the way of profits, considerable ingenuity may be shown in finding ways around the regulations. In Part Two we shall see over and over again, in different contexts, examples of these two phenomena. The interplay between banking regulation and profit-seeking behavior will be a constant theme of our discussion.

SUMMARY

- Banks are in business to make a profit for their owners.
- The state of a bank is summarized at any one moment by its balance sheet. Each new transaction changes the balance sheet. The fundamental identity of the balance sheet is: Assets equal liabilities plus net worth. This is true because net worth is defined as assets less liabilities. The main items on a

---

[14]Investment "banks" are not really banks at all, or even financial intermediaries. We shall have more to say about them in Chapter 14.

bank's balance sheet are:

ASSETS	LIABILITIES AND NET WORTH
Reserves	Deposits
Loans	Equity

- A bank will often keep part of its reserves in a deposit at the Fed. This deposit is useful for clearing checks and as a vehicle for borrowing and lending reserves.

- A bank loan is an exchange of one IOU, the loan contract, for another, a demand deposit.

- The profit of the bank is just its revenue minus its costs. Revenue is the realized interest rate times the amount of loans. The realized interest rate is the contractual rate less an adjustment for bad loans. The bank's costs include fixed costs, the explicit interest paid on deposits, and the cost of various services provided to depositors (implicit interest).

- The interest rate a bank charges on loans and the rate it pays on deposits are constrained by competition.

- Because of adverse selection, raising the contractual rate on loans will reduce the quality of the bank's loan portfolio. The realized rate will therefore rise less and may even fall.

- A bank requires liquidity in order to be able to meet an excess of withdrawals over new deposits and in order to be able to exploit new loan opportunities.

- Regulations require banks to keep reserves equal to a specified percentage of deposits (in the form of cash or deposits at the Fed). These required reserves do not contribute to a bank's liquidity.

- Holding reserves in excess of the amount required is one way to provide the liquidity a bank needs.

- On days on which a bank, nonetheless, is short of reserves, it can borrow reserves from other banks via the fed funds market or directly from the Fed itself.

- Return on equity—profit divided by equity—is a measure of a bank's profitability.

- Return on equity can be increased by decreasing the bank's equity. However, such a reduction also increases the risk of the bank's becoming insolvent.

- The greater the risk of insolvency, the more nervous will be the bank's uninsured depositors, and the greater will be the danger of a bank run.

- In the event of failure, the owners may stand to lose more than their investment in the bank, if its market value exceeds its book value.

- The failure of a bank may have external effects on others. These externalities may justify regulation of banks to reduce the risk of failure.

- Much of our banking regulation is a legacy of the Great Depression. Laws passed in the 1930s sought to curb "excessive competition" by limiting the interest banks could pay on their deposits and by limiting their ability to expand geographically. Banks were also barred (for the most part) from the securities markets. To reduce the risk of banking panics, deposit insurance was instituted.

- Regulations distort incentives and reduce flexibility in responding to changing circumstances. When regulations stand in the way of profits, ways will often be found to get around them.

KEY TERMS

balance sheet	adverse selection	book value
assets	liquidity	market value
liabilities	required reserve ratio	goodwill
net worth (equity)	required reserves	leverage
reserves	excess reserves	leverage ratio
contractual rate	fed funds market	consolidated balance sheet
realized rate	discount loan	externalities
fixed costs	return on equity (ROE)	investment banks
explicit interest	insolvent	
implicit interest	equity-to-loan ratio	

DISCUSSION QUESTIONS

1. What is the fed funds market? Why is it important?

2. Why would a bank both want to encourage regulation and, at the same time, devise methods for innovating around the regulation?

3. Suppose that Solid State Bank is insured by the FDIC. Do you think the FDIC would care about its equity-to-loan ratio? Why or why not?

4. Why do banks require minimum average balances as a condition for free checking?

5. Could the market value of a bank ever be *less* than its book value? In what circumstances?

6. If a new bank opened up next-door to Solid State Bank, what would be the likely effect on the explicit and implicit interest you offer your depositors? What would happen to the value of Solid State's charter if a new bank opened up next-door? How would this affect the equity ratio you choose and the risk of the bank failing?

7. Leverage in banking is much higher than in manufacturing. Why do you think this is?

8. The following table shows the amount of deposits you will have for different levels of cost (explicit plus implicit interest). If your best realized rate on loans is 11%, what is the best cost of deposits? Assume your reserve ratio is 10% and your fixed costs are zero.

Cost of Deposits	Amount of Deposits
4%	$ 8m
5	10m
6	12m
7	13m

BIBLIOGRAPHY

Friedman, Milton and Anna Jacobson Schwartz, *A Monetary History of the United States 1867–1960*, Princeton: Princeton University Press, 1963.

Galbraith, John Kenneth, *The Great Crash*, Boston: Houghton Mifflin, 1955.

Havrilesky, Thomas M., and John Boorman, *Current Perspectives in Banking*, Arlington Heights, IL: Harlan Davidson, 1980.

Koch, Timothy W., *Bank Management*, Hinsdale, IL: Dryden Press, 1988.

Lewis, M. K., and K. T. Davis, *Domestic and International Banking*, Cambridge, Mass.: M.I.T. Press, 1987.

CHAPTER 6

INTEREST RATES AND SECURITY PRICES

We have seen that lending means giving up money here and now in exchange for a promise of money in the future. Two real-world examples of such promises are:

- *A Treasury bill*—a promise of the U.S. government to pay $10,000 in one year's time,
- *An AT&T bond*—a promise of AT&T to pay $1,000 in 20 years' time plus $50 every 6 months until then.

How much money should you give up now in exchange for such promises? That is, how much should you pay for the T-bill or for the AT&T bond? Or, if you are told the price of each, how can you decide which is a better deal? In this chapter we shall address questions such as these.[1]

6.1 SOME BASIC TECHNIQUES

Before we can address these questions, we need to learn some basic techniques.

---

[1]In this chapter we shall limit our discussion to promises that—like the T-bill and the AT&T bond—promise definite amounts of money at specific times. While this type of promise accounts for the overwhelming majority of actual borrowing and lending, there are, as we saw in Chapter 3, other, more complex types of promise. A stock, for example, is a promise to pay a share of a firm's future profits, with the actual amount of those future profits unknown. An insurance policy is a promise to pay some amount contingent on a particular event—for example, the wrecking of your car.

TIME LINES

time line
Graphic representation of amounts promised and their due dates.

The first thing we need is a simple way to represent a promise of payment. The **time line** is a useful way to do this. It shows both the amounts promised and when they are due. For example, the following time line represents the one-year T-bill:

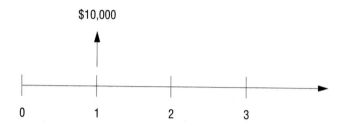

Or consider a $1,000, 5-year zero-coupon bond—a promise to pay $1,000 after 5 years:

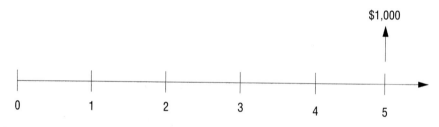

Or a $1,000 5-year bond with $100 annual coupons—a promise to pay $100 each year for 5 years, plus $1,000 at the end of the fifth year:

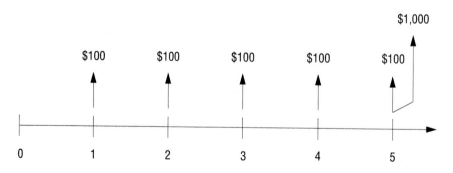

The time line itself represents the continuous passage of time. Time 0 is now, Time 1 is one year from now, a point on the line halfway between Time 1 and Time 2 is one and a half years from now, and so on.

An upward-pointing arrow at a particular point indicates a payment to be received at that time. The amount of the payment is shown above the arrow. The double arrow at Time 5 on the time line for the coupon bond indicates that two payments are due then, one of $100 and the other of $1,000.

Draw a time line for the AT&T bond.   🌴 **CHECK STATION 1**

INTEREST-RATE BASICS

To learn some interest-rate basics, suppose you deposit $1,000 at your local bank and receive in exchange a one-year certificate of deposit (CD) that promises to pay $1,100 one year from now. The CD may be represented by the following time line:

The $1,000 that you lent is called the **principal** and the $100 extra that you get back is called the **interest**. The **interest rate** is the interest expressed as a fraction of the principal,

$$\text{interest rate} = \frac{\$100}{\$1,000} = 0.10, \qquad [6.1]$$

or as a percentage,

$$\text{interest rate} = 0.10 \times 100\% = 10\%. \qquad [6.2]$$

Because the 10% is earned over a period of a year, we call it an *annual* interest rate of 10%.

If you are told that the annual interest rate is 10%, you know that if you deposit $1,000 now, at the end of a year you will receive

$$\$1,000 \times (1 + 0.10) = \$1,100. \qquad [6.3]$$

That is, the $1,000 is multiplied by 1, since you get your principal back, plus 0.10, for the interest.

In general, if you put the amount P into the bank and the interest rate is i, at the end of the year you will have

$$A = P (1 + i). \qquad [6.4]$$

principal
The amount loaned.

interest
The amount repaid in addition to principal.

interest rate
The interest as a percentage of principal.

future value
Value at a time in the future, including accumulated interest, of an amount invested earlier.

(Notice that in this formula the interest rate is always expressed as a fraction, not as a percentage.) The amount you have at the end of the year, A, is called the **future value** of the amount P at an interest rate of i.

🌴 **CHECK STATION 2**

A. How much would you have in the bank one year from now if you deposited $100 today and the annual interest rate were 12%?
B. How much would you have in the bank one year from now if you deposited $100 today and the annual interest rate were 8%?
C. How much would you have in the bank one year from now if you deposited $90.91 today and the annual interest rate were 10%?

COMPOUNDING

compounding
Calculation of interest on interest already earned.

Now consider the possibility of leaving your money in the bank for 2 years rather than one. In the second year you will earn interest, not only on the original $1,000, but also on the $100 interest that you earned in the *first* year. This earning of interest on interest is called **compounding.** Thus at the end of 2 years you will have

$$\$1,100 \times 1.10 = \$1,210, \qquad [6.5]$$

or, in terms of your original deposit,

$$\$1,000 \times 1.10 \times 1.10 = \$1,210. \qquad [6.6]$$

More generally, the future value of an amount invested for 2 years is

$$A = P(1+i)(1+i) = P(1+i)^2. \qquad [6.7]$$

It is easy to extend this formula to calculate the future value of an amount invested for 3 years:

$$A = P(1+i)(1+i)(1+i) = P(1+i)^3, \qquad [6.8]$$

or, indeed, for any number of years:

$$A = P(1+i)(1+i)\cdots(1+i) = P(1+i)^n, \qquad [6.9]$$

where n is the number of years.

EXAMPLE

Calculate the future value of $200 invested in a 5-year CD with an annual interest rate of 7%.
The answer is

$$\$200 \times (1.07)^5.$$

You could calculate the actual amount by multiplying it out, but there are a number of possible shortcuts. If you have a calculator that can raise numbers to a power, then

$$\$200 \times (1.07)^5 = \$200 \times [1.40] = \$280.$$

Financial calculators can calculate future values directly—just follow the instructions for your calculator. If you do not have a suitable calculator, you can find the future-value factor—the number in brackets in the above calculation, [1.40]—in a future-value table, like Table 1 at the back of the book.

CHECK STATION 3

A. How much would you have in the bank 2 years from now if you deposited $100 today and the annual interest rate were 12%?

B. What is the future value 2 years from now of $120 today if the annual interest rate is 15%?

C. How much would you have in the bank 20 years from now if you deposited $10,000 today and the annual interest rate were 12%?

D. What is the future value 10 years from now of $384.54 today if the annual interest rate is 10%?

6.2 PRICING PROMISES OF ANNUAL PAYMENTS

Now that we have laid the groundwork, we are ready to tackle one of the questions we originally set ourselves: How much should you be willing to pay for a particular promise or security?

We shall begin by looking at promises, like the one-year T-bill, that involve payments after whole numbers of years. These are easier to deal with than promises, like the AT&T bond, that involve payments after fractions of years. We shall look at the more complicated type once we understand the basic idea.

BILLS OR ZERO-COUPON BONDS

The simplest type of security is one that promises a *single* payment. The $10,000, one-year T-bill is an example. Securities promising a single payment are usually

bills
Securities of short maturity promising a single payment.

zero-coupon bonds
Single-payment securities having a long maturity.

market price
Price actually paid for a security.

market yield
Annual interest rate calculated from the market price.

called **bills** if their maturity is a year or less and **zero-coupon bonds** if it is longer; we shall use the term *bill* for both.

Suppose the T-bill is selling for $9,500. That is, its **market price** is $9,500. Should you buy it? We cannot answer this question in a vacuum. It all depends on what your alternatives are. Suppose your alternative is a bank CD. To make your decision between the CD and the T-bill, you should compare the relative rewards of investing in each. A natural measure of that reward is the annual interest rate. We know the annual rate on the CD. So, to make the comparison, we need to know the annual rate on the bill.

The principal on the bill—the amount you are lending—is *not* $10,000, the bill's face value: rather, it is $9,500, the amount you pay for the bill. In a year's time you will get back the $9,500 in principal plus $500 in interest—$10,000 in all. The annual interest rate is

$$\frac{\$500}{\$9,500} = .0526, \text{ or } 5.26\%. \qquad [6.10]$$

This annual interest rate, calculated from the market price in this way, is called the **market yield.**

The relationship between the market price of a one-year bill, its face value, and its market yield is

$$\text{market price} \times (1 + \text{market yield}) = \text{face value}. \qquad [6.11]$$

We can also reverse the calculation. If we know the market yield, we can use Equation 6.11 to calculate the market price. For example, if we know that the market yield on one-year T-bills is 10%, then we can solve for the price of the bill, P, where P satisfies

$$P \times 1.10 = \$10,000. \qquad [6.12]$$

Hence

$$P = \frac{\$10,000}{1.10} = \$9,090.91. \qquad [6.13]$$

More generally, if A is the amount due in a year and i is the market yield, then the price is

$$P = \frac{A}{(1 + i)}. \qquad [6.14]$$

present value
Discounted value today of some amount due in the future.

This type of formula is called a *present-value formula*. The **present value** is the value today of some amount due in the future. As can be seen from a comparison of Equations 6.4 and 6.14, there is an inverse relationship between present value and future value. The future value of $9,090.91 at an interest rate of 10% is $10,000; the present value of $10,000 at an interest rate of 10% is $9,090.91. The present value of $10,000 at an interest rate of 10% is just the amount that will grow into $10,000 (have a future value of $10,000) in one year's time at this interest rate.

A. The T-bill sells *at a discount,* at a price below its face value. What would be the yield if it sold *at par,* at a price equal to its face value?

B. If the market yield on one-year T-bills is 6%, what is the market price?

C. What is the present value of $1,000 due one year from now if the annual interest rate is 15%?

⌐☂ **CHECK STATION 4**

What is the present value at 10% of $10,000 due 2 years from now? It is just the amount now that will grow into $10,000 (have a future value of $10,000) in 2 years' time at this interest rate. That is, the present value is P in the following equation:

$$\$10,000 = P \times (1.10)^2. \qquad [6.15]$$

Rewriting this, we have

$$P = \frac{\$10,000}{(1.10)^2}. \qquad [6.16]$$

Or, more generally,

$$P = \frac{A}{(1+i)^2}, \qquad [6.17]$$

where A is the amount due and i is the interest rate.

We can use Equation 6.17 to calculate the market price of a 2-year T-bill. If the face value is $10,000 and the market yield is 11%, then

$$P = \frac{\$10,000}{(1.11)^2} = \$8,116.22. \qquad [6.18]$$

This amount, $8,116.22, is the amount that would grow into $10,000 in 2 years at an annual interest rate of 11%.[2]

It is easy to generalize Equation 6.17 to give the present value of an amount due at *any* time in the future. The present value of A due in n years, if the annual interest rate is i, is

$$P = \frac{A}{(1+i)^n}. \qquad [6.19]$$

That is, P is the amount that would grow into A in n years at this interest rate.

---

[2] Actually, the longest maturity of T-bill sold by the Treasury is one year. However, as we shall see, it is possible to *create* T-bills of longer maturities from longer-maturity coupon bonds.

EXAMPLE

What is the market price of a $1 million, 10-year T-bill if the market yield is 9%?
The answer is

$$P = \frac{\$1,000,000}{(1.09)^{10}} = \$1,000,000 \times [0.42241081] = \$422,410.81.$$

To do this calculation, you can use either a regular calculator or a financial calculator. Or you can use a present-value table, like Table 2 in Appendix A at the back of the book, to find the present-value factor—the term in brackets.

CHECK STATION 5

A. What is the present value of $100 due 2 years from now if the interest rate is 6%?
B. What is the market price of a $1,000, 3-year T-bill if the market yield is 10%?

COUPON BONDS

We are ready to go on to price a more complicated type of security—one that promises multiple payments. Consider for example the 2-year Treasury bond represented by the following time line:

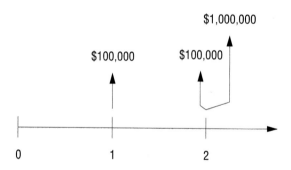

To calculate the market price of this bond, we are going to use what we already know about the pricing of *bills*. First, we break down the payments due on the bond into separate individual payments. The payment due at the end of the first year is:

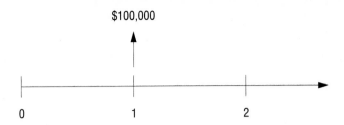

The two payments due at the end of the second year combine to give:

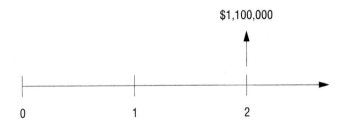

The payment due at the end of the first year and the payment due at the end of the second year are just like two T-bills—a one-year T-bill for $100,000 and a 2-year T-bill for $1,100,000.

Suppose the market yield on one-year T-bills happens to be 7% and on 2-year T-bills, it is 8%. Then the market price of the payment due at the end of the first year is

$$P = \frac{\$100,000}{1.07} = \$93,457.94, \qquad [6.20]$$

and the market price of the payment due at the end of the second year is

$$P = \frac{\$1,100,000}{(1.08)^2} = \$943,072.70. \qquad [6.21]$$

Could the market price of the bond differ from the sum of the market prices of its two component parts? That is, could it be other than

$$P = \$93,457.94 + \$943,072.70 = \$1,036,530.64? \qquad [6.22]$$

If the market price of the bond were more than this, you could "construct" the 2-year bond more cheaply by buying the two constituent parts. That is, you could buy a one-year T-bill and a 2-year T-bill that together would promise you exactly the same payments in the future as the 2-year bond, and pay less for them than you would pay for the bond. Since no one would buy the bond in these circumstances, prices would adjust until the price of the bond was no longer higher than the sum of the prices of the two bills.

TREASURY STRIPS

For reasons we shall explore later in the chapter, investors often prefer long-term bills to ordinary coupon bonds. However, until recently, T-bills were not available at maturities of over a year. The existence of this unsatisfied demand provided a tempting profit opportunity for ingenious financial innovators.

Merrill Lynch was the first to respond. In August 1982 Merrill began to offer TIGRs (Treasury Investment Growth Receipts)—bills collateralized by a portfolio of government securities. For example, Merrill buys $100 million worth of 20-year Treasury bonds with a 10% annual coupon. It stands to receive from the Treasury $10 million every year, plus $100 million after 20 years. Merrill can therefore sell $10 million of one-year TIGRs; $10 million of 2-year, $10 million of 3-year; and so on, out to a maturity of 20 years ($110 million of 20-year TIGRs). All these TIGRs are completely collateralized by the $100 million of 20-year bonds. "Pieces" separated from a security in this way are called **Treasury strips.**

Treasury strips
Government bonds broken up and traded as separate coupon and principal payments.

Merrill's idea proved so successful and so profitable that Salomon soon followed with CATS, and Lehman with LIONS; within a couple of months Wall Street firms had sold over $14 billion of dismembered government bonds.

In August 1984 the Treasury itself got into the act when it announced its own STRIPS program (Separate Trading of Registered Interest and Principal of Securities). This program allowed investors to trade separately the various coupon and principal payments that make up a Treasury security and to register ownership separately for each of the pieces. Why did the Treasury do this? By making its securities more attractive in this way, it could sell them at a lower yield. To put it another way, it was gaining for itself the profit that investment banks had been making by breaking up government bonds into more desirable pieces.

If the market price of the bond were less than $1,036,530.64, you could buy the bond and sell off the two parts separately for more than you paid for the bond. The increased supply of one-year and 2-year bills would drive down their price until the sum of their prices equaled the price of the one-year bond. At that point it would no longer be profitable to break up one-year bonds. Indeed, Treasury bonds are broken down in this way to create long-term bills (see "Treasury Strips").

We can generalize this argument to price any bond by breaking it down into its constituent "bill equivalents." Suppose that the face value is A and the coupon payment C. Using our formula for the market price of a bill, if the market yield on m-year bills is i_m, where m is any number of years, then the market price of a coupon due in m years is

$$\frac{C}{(1 + i_m)^m}.$$

[6.23]

This is just the present value of the coupon payment calculated at the appropriate market interest rate.

The present value, and hence the market price, of an n-year bond is just the sum of the present values of the various payments, with each present value calculated at the appropriate market interest rate. That is,

$$P = \frac{C}{(1 + i_1)} + \frac{C}{(1 + i_2)^2} + \cdots + \frac{(C + A)}{(1 + i_n)^n}. \qquad [6.24]$$

Note that this method of pricing a bond by breaking it down into bills relies on there *being* market yields on bills of the relevant maturities. For T-bills such market yields do exist (see "Treasury Strips"). However, for bonds of issuers other than the U.S. government, they do not. However, our method still tells us *in principle* what a bond should be worth.

EXAMPLE

If the market yield on bills is the same 8% at all maturities, what is the market price of a $1,000, 3-year bond with 11% annual coupons?
The time line is:

The sum of the present values of the three payments (the total of $1,110 at the end of Year 3 counting as one payment) is

$$P = \frac{\$110}{(1.08)} + \frac{\$110}{(1.08)^2} + \frac{\$1,110}{(1.08)^3} = \$1,077.31.$$

A. If the market yield on bills is the same 10% at all maturities, what is the market price of a $1,000, 2-year bond with 12% annual coupons?

B. For the bond in Part A, what is its market price if the market yield on bills is 15% at all maturities? If the market yield on bills is 12%?

🌴 **CHECK STATION 6**

MARKET YIELD ON A COUPON BOND

With bills, the formula relating market price to market yield, Equation 6.19, could be used in either direction. Given the face value, the maturity, and the market yield, it could be used to calculate the market price. Given the face value, the maturity, and the market price, it could be used to calculate the market yield.

We would like to be able to do the same sort of thing with coupon bonds. Given market yields, we have no trouble calculating market price, but when we try to go the other way—to calculate market yield from market price—there is a problem. If we look at our formula for the market price, Equation 6.24, we see not a single rate, but many—one for each payment maturity. It makes no sense to try to solve for these many different rates from our single equation.

So how about replacing these many rates with a single interest rate, and then solving for that single rate? That is, solve for the value of i that, given P, A, and C, satisfies

$$P = \frac{C}{(1 + i)} + \frac{C}{(1 + i)^2} + \cdots + \frac{(C + A)}{(1 + i)^n} \, . \qquad [6.25]$$

average annual yield to maturity
Single interest rate at which the present value of a bond's coupon and principal payments equals its market price.

Notice that in each denominator i_m is replaced with just plain i. The single interest rate that solves this equation is called the **average annual yield to maturity.** The market yield on a bond is defined as the average annual yield to maturity calculated from its market price. Although this does give us a number we can call the market yield of a bond, we shall see later that there are important differences in meaning between this number and the market yield on a bill.

EXAMPLE

What is the average annual yield to maturity of the following 20-year bond if its market price is $803.64?

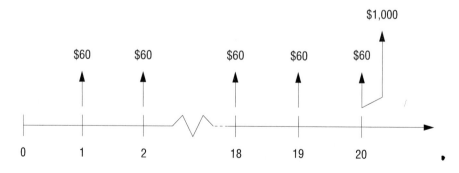

The answer is the value of i that satisfies

$$\$803.64 = \frac{\$60}{(1+i)^1} + \frac{\$60}{(1+i)^2} + \cdots + \frac{(\$60 + \$1,000)}{(1+i)^{20}}. \qquad [6.26]$$

Solving an equation like this is difficult: You generally need a financial calculator or a computer program. In this case the answer turns out to be 8%.

In this example the market price of the bond is below its face value: The bond is **selling at a discount.** However, if the market yield on this bond were 5% instead of 8%, the market price would be $1,124.62, so that the market price would be above face value. This is called **selling at a premium.** If the market yield were 6%—exactly the same as the coupon rate—then the market price would be exactly equal to the face value: The bond would be **selling at par.** If the market yield is above the coupon rate, a bond sells at a discount; if the market yield is below the coupon rate, it sells at a premium.

selling at a discount
Selling at a price below face value.

selling at a premium
Selling at a price above face value.

selling at par
Selling at a price exactly equal to face value.

🌴 **CHECK STATION 7**

(*To be attempted only with a financial calculator*)
A. **What is the market yield on a 10-year bond with a face value of $10,000 and 10% annual coupons, if it is selling for $9,500?**
B. **What is the market price of a $1,000, 3-year bond with 7% annual coupons if the market yield is 11%?**

AMORTIZED LOANS

Consider the following security:

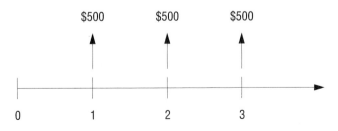

Rather than promising a series of small coupon payments and then a large payment of face value like a coupon bond, it promises a series of equal payments. This type of security is called an **amortized loan** or, if the payments are annual, an **annuity,** and it is quite common. For instance, most automobile loans and home mortgage loans are amortized loans.

amortized loan
Security that promises a series of equal payments.

annuity
Security that promises a series of equal annual payments.

E X A M P L E

You wish to borrow $100,000 to buy a house and to repay the loan in equal annual installments over 30 years.[3] If the annual interest rate on mortgage loans is 10%, how much must you pay each year?

The stream of payments is:

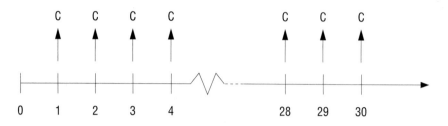

We need to find the value of C such that the present value of the payments at an interest rate of 10% equals the amount borrowed.

$$\$100,000 = \frac{C}{(1.10)^1} + \frac{C}{(1.10)^2} + \cdots + \frac{C}{(1.10)^{30}} \qquad [6.27]$$

$$= C\left[\frac{1}{(1.10)^1} + \frac{1}{(1.10)^2} + \cdots + \frac{1}{(1.10)^{30}}\right].$$

The term in brackets is called an *annuity factor.* Table 3 in Appendix A at the back of the book gives annuity factors for various interest rates and numbers of periods. The factor we need is the entry in the 10% column, 30-period row— 9.427. Hence the annual payment is

$$\frac{\$100,000}{9.427} = \$10,607.93.$$

More generally the relationship between the present value of an annuity, P, the periodic payment, C, and the periodic interest rate, i, is

$$P = \frac{C}{(1+i)} + \frac{C}{(1+i)^2} + \cdots + \frac{C}{(1+i)^n} = C\left[\frac{1}{i}\left\{1 - \frac{1}{(1+i)^n}\right\}\right]. \qquad [6.28]$$

perpetuity
Annuity that is payable forever.

One special type of annuity is called a **perpetuity**. A perpetuity is just an annuity that never ends. Alternatively, you could think of it as a bond that pays coupons forever, with payment of the face value deferred indefinitely.

[3]Actually, mortgage loans usually involve monthly rather than annual payments. We shall see how to calculate monthly payments in the next section.

EXAMPLE

What is the present value of a perpetuity with annual payments of $500 each, beginning a year from now and going on forever, if the annual interest rate is 10%?

With a little ingenuity, we can use the formula for the present value of an annuity to get an answer. Notice that the expression in brackets, the annuity factor, includes the expression

$$\frac{1}{(1 + i)^n} .$$

As n gets very large, the value of this expression approaches zero, so that the value of the expression in square brackets in Equation 6.28 approaches $1/i$. Hence, the present value of our perpetuity is

$$P = C\left[\frac{1}{i}\right] = \frac{\$500}{.10} = \$5,000. \qquad [6.29]$$

The present value, P, of a perpetuity of C, if the interest rate is i, is

$$P = \frac{C}{i} . \qquad [6.30]$$

Perpetuities do exist in the real world. The best known is the Consol—a security issued by the British government in the early 1800s to consolidate the debt of the Napoleonic Wars. The market yield on a perpetuity is particularly easy to calculate: It is simply the annual payment divided by the market price.

A. **What is the market price of a $10,000 annuity that lasts for 10 years if the market yield is 12%?**

B. **What is the market price of a perpetuity with annual payments of $1,000 if the market yield is 5%?**

🌴 **CHECK STATION 8**

6.3 DAYS, MONTHS, AND HALF-YEARS

So far we have looked only at promises that involve annual payments. In reality, most securities involve payments over shorter intervals, such as daily or semiannually. For example, the AT&T bond that we considered at the beginning of the chapter has the time line that appears on the following page.

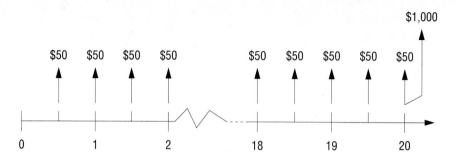

How are we to calculate the price or yield of such a security?

COMPOUNDING AGAIN

Let us start with a savings account. If you walked into a bank, you might see a listing of rates offered on various types of time deposit. For example, the listing for a one-year CD might read:

> One-year CD
> 12% APR (monthly compounding)
> 12.68% effective annual rate

What does all this mean? It will help to define some terms:

compounding period
Period over which interest is calculated.

- **Compounding period.** This is the period over which interest is calculated. For the above CD, the compounding period is one month. At the end of the first month, the bank calculates how much interest it owes you; at the end of the second month it calculates again, including interest on the first month's interest—that is, the interest is compounded.

periodic rate
Rate per compounding period.

- **Periodic rate.** This is the rate per compounding period. For the CD, we shall see in a moment that it is 1%. That is, if you buy a $1,000 CD, then after the first month the bank will owe you

$$\$1,000 \times (1.01) = \$1,010;$$

after the second month it will owe you

$$\$1,010 \times (1.01) = \$1,000 \, (1.01)^2 = \$1,021;$$

and so on.

stated annual rate
Periodic rate multiplied by the number of compounding periods in the year.

- **Stated annual rate.** This is the periodic rate multiplied by the number of compounding periods in the year. In this case it is 1% times 12, which is 12%. The stated annual rate is often called the *annual percentage rate*, or *APR*.

In the listing, the APR is given as 12%, so the periodic rate is 12% divided by 12, the number of compounding periods per year.

- **Effective annual rate.** This is the interest accrued at the end of the year as a percentage of the principal amount. In this case, compounding monthly at a monthly rate of 1% will give us at the end of the year

$$\$1,000 \times (1.01)^{12} = \$1,126.83.$$

effective annual rate
Interest accrued at the end of the year as a percentage of the principal amount.

The effective annual rate is

$$\frac{\$126.83}{\$1,000} = .12683, \text{ or } 12.68\%.$$

The effective annual rate is the rate you should use to make comparisons. For example, is this CD better or worse than one offered by the bank across the street with an APR of 11.9% compounded weekly? The latter CD has a periodic rate of

$$\frac{11.9\%}{52} = 0.229\%.$$

At the end of the year, therefore, the bank will pay you

$$\$1,000 \times (1.00229)^{52} = \$1,126.22.$$

The effective annual rate is 12.62%, slightly lower than that on the first CD: The more frequent compounding does not quite make up for the lower stated annual rate.

We can summarize the relationships between the various concepts as follows:

$$\frac{\text{stated annual rate}}{\text{number of periods}} = \text{periodic rate} \qquad [6.31]$$

and

$$(1 + \text{periodic rate})^{\text{number of periods}} = 1 + \text{effective annual rate}. \qquad [6.32]$$

Equation 6.32 can also be turned around to calculate the periodic rate from the effective annual rate:

$$1 + \text{periodic rate} = (1 + \text{effective annual rate})^{1/\text{number of periods}} \qquad [6.33]$$

EXAMPLE

Suppose we are told that the effective annual rate on a one-year CD is 9.38% and that interest is compounded monthly. What is the periodic interest rate? What is the APR?

Using Equation 6.33, we have

$$1 + \text{periodic rate} = (1.0938)^{1/12} = 1.0075,$$

so that the periodic rate is 0.75% and the APR is

$$0.75\% \times 12 = 9\%.$$

CHECK STATION 9

A. Find the periodic rate and the effective annual rate if the stated annual rate is 7.3% with daily compounding.

B. The effective annual rate is 10.25% with compounding every 6 months. What is the periodic rate? What is the APR?

BILLS OF MATURITY OF LESS THAN A YEAR

Consider the following 3-month T-bill:

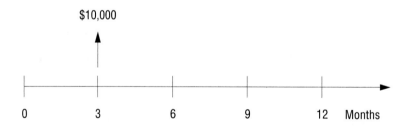

Suppose that it is selling for $9,764.54. How does it compare to the following 6-month T-bill, which sells for $9,491.58?

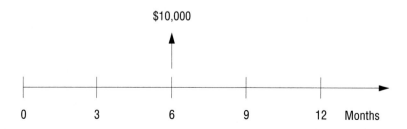

One way to make the comparison is by comparing effective annual rates on the two securities. That is, even though the two securities have different maturities, we can compare them by putting their rates on a common, annual basis.

For the 3-month T-bill, the periodic rate (3 months) is

$$\frac{\$10,000 - \$9,764.54}{\$9,764.54} = \frac{\$235.46}{\$9,764.54} = .0241, \text{ or } 2.41\%.$$

The effective annual rate satisfies

$$(1.0241)^4 = 1.10 = 1 + \text{effective annual rate}$$

and is therefore 10%.

For the 6-month T-bill, the periodic rate (6 months) is

$$\frac{\$10,000 - \$9,491.58}{\$9,491.58} = \frac{\$508.42}{\$9,491.58} = .0536, \text{ or } 5.36\%.$$

The effective annual rate satisfies

$$(1.0536)^2 = 1.11 = 1 + \text{effective annual rate}$$

and is therefore 11%.

Although the 6-month bill seems the better deal, we shall see presently that choosing between securities of different maturities involves more than just a comparison of effective annual yields.

What is the effective annual rate on a T-bill due in 2 months and selling for $9,857.40? | 🌴 **CHECK STATION 10**

BONDS WITH A COUPON PERIOD OF LESS THAN A YEAR

Bonds generally have coupons due at intervals shorter than a year. For example, the AT&T bond that we saw at the beginning of the chapter has coupon periods of 6 months:

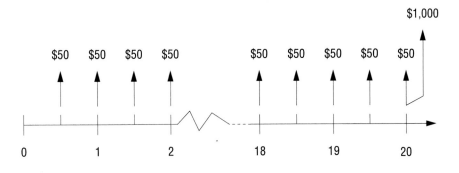

When this bond was issued, it might have been advertised as follows:

> AT&T
> $100 million
> (denominations of $1,000)
> 20-year bonds
> 10% semiannual coupon

The total amount issued is $100 million, in units of face value of $1,000 each. The phrase *10% semiannual coupon* means that coupons are paid semiannually and that the **annual coupon rate** is 10%. The annual coupon rate is a stated annual rate. The periodic (6-month) coupon rate is calculated from the annual coupon rate by dividing by the number of periods per year—2. The periodic coupon rate is therefore 5%. The actual coupon payment is the periodic coupon rate times the face value of the bond—in this case, $50.

annual coupon rate
Stated annual rate used to calculate the periodic coupon rate.

What is this bond worth? In finding an answer, we need to follow the same procedure as we did with a bond having annual coupon payments. We need to calculate, and then sum, the present values of all the payments due, just as we did in Equation 6.25. However, here we need to take into account the fact that payments are due at half-yearly rather than at yearly intervals. Let us begin by changing the unit of time measurement from a year to a half-year, transforming the time line to:

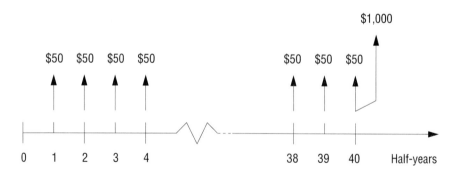

Now we need an interest rate. Suppose the appropriate effective *annual* interest rate is 8% at all maturities. Since we have changed our unit of time measurement to a half-year, we need to convert the effective annual rate into a half-year periodic rate, using Equation 6.33:

$$1 + \text{periodic rate} = (1.08)^{1/2} = 1.039,$$

so the periodic rate is 3.9%.

Applying Equation 6.25 but using the half-year as the period and the half-year periodic rate as the interest rate, we get

$$P = \frac{\$50}{(1.039)} + \frac{\$50}{(1.039)^2} + \cdots + \frac{\$50}{(1.039)^{39}} + \frac{\$1,050}{(1.039)^{40}} = \$1,221.00.$$

What is the market price of a $10,000, one-year bond with 12% quarterly coupons? Use an annual interest rate of 10%. | 🌴 **CHECK STATION 11**

AMORTIZED LOANS WITH MONTHLY PAYMENTS

If you take out a $10,000, 3-year automobile loan to help finance the purchase of a new car, what will your monthly payments be?

Suppose the bank charges an APR of 12% on automobile loans. The periodic rate will be one-twelfth of this, or 1%. Taking a month as the unit of measurement, the time line for the loan is:

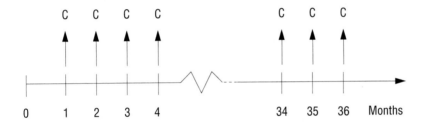

We need to find the value of C such that the present value of the payments at an interest rate of 1% equals the amount borrowed:

$$\$10,000 = \frac{C}{(1.01)^1} + \frac{C}{(1.01)^2} + \cdots + \frac{C}{(1.01)^{36}}.$$

This has exactly the same form as the problem we solved in the case of annual payments (see Equation 6.25). The solution in this case is $332.14.

The bank quotes an APR of 9% on home mortgages. What will be the monthly payment on a 30-year mortgage for $120,000? | 🌴 **CHECK STATION 12**

6.4 | LET'S MAKE AN INVESTMENT

You have now learned quite a lot about yields and prices. You are ready to put your knowledge to use and to make some investments. Suppose you have some money to invest and you decide to buy three bills of differing maturities:

- A one-year bill with a face value of $10,000
- A 5-year bill with a face value of $10,000
- A 30-year bill with a face value of $100,000

The market yields on each of these securities is 6%, so their market prices are, respectively,

$$P = \frac{\$10,000}{1.06} = \$9,433.96,$$

$$P = \frac{\$10,000}{(1.06)^5} = \$7,472.58,$$

and

$$P = \frac{\$100,000}{(1.06)^{30}} = \$17,411.01.$$

THE REALIZED YIELD AND INTEREST-RATE RISK

Suppose that a year after you buy the securities, you need your money and must liquidate your investment portfolio. How much will you have? Since the one-year bill matures at that time, you receive the face value, $10,000. However, in order to turn the other two bills into cash, they must be sold. How much you get for them will depend on market yields *at the time you sell them.*

Suppose the market yield at all maturities has risen from 6% to 8%. Because the 5-year bill has, after a year, become a 4-year bill, its market price is now

$$P = \frac{\$10,000}{(1.08)^4} = \$7,350.30.$$

The 30-year bill is now a 29-year bill. So its market price is

$$P = \frac{\$100,000}{(1.08)^{29}} = \$10,732.75.$$

realized yield
Annual rate of interest that is actually earned on an investment.

Let us see how your three investments have done. The way to do this is to look at the **realized yield** of each. The realized yield is simply the annual rate of interest that you *actually earned* on a given investment. For the three securities in question, the realized yields are as follows:

- For the one-year bill (held to maturity), it is

$$\frac{\$10,000 - \$9,433.96}{\$9,433.96} = .06.$$

- For the 5-year bill (sold after one year), it is

$$\frac{\$7,350.30 - \$7,472.58}{\$7,472.58} = -0.016.$$

- For the 30-year bill (sold after one year), it is

$$\frac{\$10,732.75 - \$17,411.01}{\$17,411.01} = -0.384.$$

What are the lessons to be learned from this little adventure in investing?

- *Lesson 1.* Only if you hold a bill to maturity will its realized yield equal the market yield at the time you bought it.
- *Lesson 2.* For a bill sold before maturity, the realized yield will depend on the market yield *at the time of the sale.*
- *Lesson 3.* The higher the market yield at the time of sale, the lower the market price.
- *Lesson 4.* The greater the bill's remaining time to maturity, the greater the sensitivity of the market price of a bill to its market yield.

There is no mystery here. The results are a direct consequence of applying the present-value formula (Equation 6.19):

$$\text{market price} = \frac{\text{face value}}{(1 + \text{market yield})^{\text{time to maturity}}} \qquad [6.34]$$

The market price of a bill is simply the present value of the bill's face value, calculated using the market yield as the interest rate. The higher the interest rate at which we discount, the smaller the present value. Hence the higher the market yield, the lower the market price. Since the discount factor is raised to a power equal to the remaining time to maturity, the longer that time is, the greater will be the effect on market price of a change in market yield.

Given the outcome, was your initial investment strategy wrong? That all depends. Although it is true that the value of the 30-year bill fell the most as a result of the rise in market yields, if market yields had gone *down* rather than up, the tables would have been turned. The 30-year bill would have gone *up* in value the most, and the gain on the 30-year bill would have been the greatest. For example, suppose the market yields at all maturities had fallen to 4% rather than rising to 8%. The realized yield on the one-year bill would still have been 6%; the realized yield on the 5-year bill would have been 14.4%; and the realized yield on the 30-year bill would have been 84.2%!

So the differential sensitivity to changes in market yield cuts both ways. You can lose more on long-term securities if interest rates rise, but you can also gain more if they fall. The relationship between market yield and price for each of the three bills is illustrated in Exhibit 6.1. This sensitivity of market price to changes

EXHIBIT 6.1

THE RELATIONSHIP
BETWEEN MARKET
YIELD AND PRICE

The market price of a $100,000
Bill with 30 years to maturity
and of $10,000 Bills with 1 and
5 years to maturity is shown as
a function of market yield.

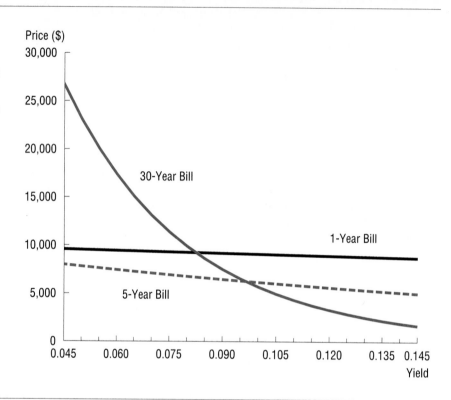

**interest-rate risk
(market risk)**
Risk associated with
changes in market interest
rates.

in market interest rates is called **interest-rate risk** or **market risk**. Longer-maturity
bills have greater interest-rate risk.

THE REALIZED YIELD AND REINVESTMENT RISK

If you want to avoid risk, should you invest only in short-maturity securities? Not
necessarily. To see why not, suppose you do not need your money after a year, but
instead leave it invested for 30 years until you retire. What will your realized yield
be then on the different investments?

In this case, it is the 30-year bill that provides the sure return. It matures after
30 years and you receive the face value of $100,000. The realized yield will satisfy

$$\left(\frac{\$100,000}{\$17,411.01} \right)^{1/30} = 1.06 = 1 + \text{realized yield},$$

so the realized yield will equal the market yield at the time you bought the bill.

How much will you make from your two other investments? That depends on what you did with the money when they matured. Suppose that when the one-year bill matured, you used the money to buy another one-year bill, and so on for 30 years. Then your realized yield will depend on the sequence of one-year market yields over the 30 years: It will be some sort of average. If interest rates fell after the first year, the realized yield will turn out to be less than 6%. If they rose, it will turn out to be more than 6%. Similarly for the 5-year bill: Its realized return will also depend on how you reinvest. The realized yields over 30 years on these shorter-term bills will therefore be subject to **reinvestment risk**—the risk associated with reinvestment at uncertain interest rates.

reinvestment risk
Risk associated with reinvestment at uncertain interest rates.

So what *should* you do. That depends on a number of things. What is your time horizon? Are you putting the money away for a long time or do you expect to need it soon? If you are putting it away for a long time, is there any chance you will need to liquidate before then? Do you want to play it safe or to gamble? If you do want to gamble, which way do you think interest rates will move? No one said investing was going to be easy!

INVESTING IN COUPON BONDS

Coupon bonds are a little more complicated than bills. Let us see to what extent the four lessons we learned about investing in bills have to be modified when it comes to coupon bonds.

Lesson 1. Suppose we buy the following bond at its market price of $803.64 and hold it to maturity:

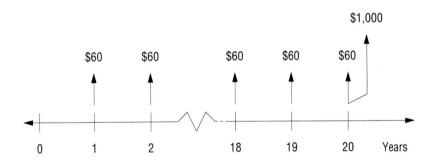

Will the realized yield equal the market yield?

We saw in Section 6.2 that the market yield of a bond is defined as its average annual yield to maturity—the interest rate, i, that satisfies

$$\$803.64 = \frac{\$60}{(1+i)^1} + \frac{\$60}{(1+i)^2} + \cdots + \frac{(\$60 + \$1{,}000)}{(1+i)^{20}} . \qquad [6.35]$$

In this case $i = 8\%$.

If you hold this bond to maturity, then, will you earn a realized yield of 8%? Not necessarily. To see why not, look at the time line. You will receive coupon payments every year. Your realized yield will depend on the interest rate you will be able to earn on them when you reinvest the money. For example, after one year you will receive a check for $60. What you do with this money has nothing to do with the issuer of the bond who paid you the $60. You could put it into a savings account for 19 years; or you could buy a bond or a bill with a maturity of that length, or with a shorter maturity, with the intention of reinvesting again. The total amount that you actually have after 20 years will depend on how successful you are at reinvesting the coupon payments.

If you are actually able to reinvest each of the coupon payments at 8%, then your realized yield will indeed be 8%. If you can only reinvest at a lower rate, your realized yield will be less. When you buy the bond, you do not know at what rate you will be able to reinvest the coupons. As a result the realized yield on a coupon bond is uncertain—subject to reinvestment risk—*even if you hold the bond to maturity.*

Indeed, the attraction of bills relative to coupon bonds is that, if you hold them to maturity, there is *no* reinvestment risk: You know exactly what you will have when the bill matures. That is the reason for the demand for long-term T-Bills, and for the development of Treasury strips to which it gave rise.

Lessons 2 and 3 hold equally for bonds.

Lesson 4. The sensitivity of the market price of a coupon bond does increase with maturity. However, the sensitivity also depends on the size of the coupon payments. Remember that the coupon bond is a composite of payments at different dates and that the market price is the sum of the present values of all the payments. Because the coupons are received before the face value amount, they are relatively less sensitive to changes in the rate used to discount them to the present. If the coupons are large, then a relatively large part of the market price will be attributable to the coupons and the market price will be less sensitive to changes in the market yield.

SUMMARY

- A time line can be used to show, for any security, the amounts promised and when the amounts are due.

- The earning of interest on interest is called compounding.

- The market price of a bill is the present value of its face value, evaluated at the market yield.

- The market price of a coupon bond is the sum of the present values of all the payments.

- Strips actually do break up Treasury Bonds in this way into their constituent payments.

- The market yield on a bond is defined as its average annual yield to maturity.

- Bonds sell at par when the market yield equals the coupon rate, at a discount when market yield is above the coupon rate, and at a premium when market yield is below the coupon rate.

- Promises of equal payments, like home mortgage and automobile loans, are called amortized loans or annuities. An annuity that goes on forever is called a perpetuity.

- Promises that involve payments over intervals that differ from a year can be priced by calculating a periodic rate of interest and using that to find present values.

- Only if a bill is held to maturity will its realized yield be the same as the market yield at the time it was purchased.

- Because of the need to reinvest coupon payments, the realized yield on a coupon bond will not necessarily equal the market yield at the time it was purchased.

- For a security sold before maturity, the realized yield will depend on the market yield *at the time of the sale*.

- The higher the market yield at the time of sale, the lower the market price.

- The greater the time remaining to maturity, the greater the sensitivity of the market price of a security to its market yield—the interest-rate risk.

- Investing in securities that come due before the portfolio is to be liquidated involves reinvestment risk.

KEY TERMS

time line	present value	compounding period
principal	Treasury strips	periodic rate
interest	average annual yield to maturity	stated annual rate
interest rate		effective annual rate
future value	selling at a discount	annual coupon rate
compounding	selling at a premium	realized yield
bills	selling at par	interest-rate risk (market risk)
zero-coupon bonds	amortized loan	
market price	annuity	reinvestment risk
market yield	perpetuity	

SOFTWARE EXERCISE FOR THIS CHAPTER

Title: Presvalu

To understand the relationship between interest rates and securities prices, it is best to look at some specific applications. This exercise will help you determine the present value of assets that provide a stream of future income. It is very useful in understanding the bond market. See your instructor if you wish to use this program.

PART TWO

BANKING AND THE MONEY MARKET

CHAPTER 7

THE GOVERNMENT SECURITIES MARKET

In terms of trading volume, the market for U.S. government securities is by far the largest financial market in the world. Because it is also among the least regulated, it has been at the forefront of innovation: Participants in this market have played a major role in creating some of the other financial markets we shall study in later chapters.[1] Trading in the government securities market by the Fed plays a key role in determining the level of interest rates and the quantity of money in our economy.[2]

We shall study this market in some detail not only because of its importance, but also to get a feeling for how real financial markets work. Just as a bank is in many ways typical of other financial intermediaries, so is this financial market typical of others. If you understand the government securities market, you will have a pretty good idea of how other financial markets work.

7.1 THE BIGGEST BORROWER ON EARTH

The U.S. government is the world's largest debtor: It owes more by far than any other government or institution in the world, and more by several orders of magnitude than any firm or individual. At the end of 1989 its debt was fast approaching $3 *trillion*: that is, $3,000,000,000,000.

How did this come about? Each year, the federal government gathers tax revenue from firms and individuals, and it spends money on defense, welfare, and a host of other things. In principle, tax revenue should cover expenditure. In

---

[1]The money market (Chapter 9), the market for financial futures (Chapter 13), and the market for mortgage-backed securities (Chapter 15).

[2]We shall learn about this in Parts Five, Six, and Seven.

141

E X H I B I T 7.1

FEDERAL DEFICITS
AND DEBT

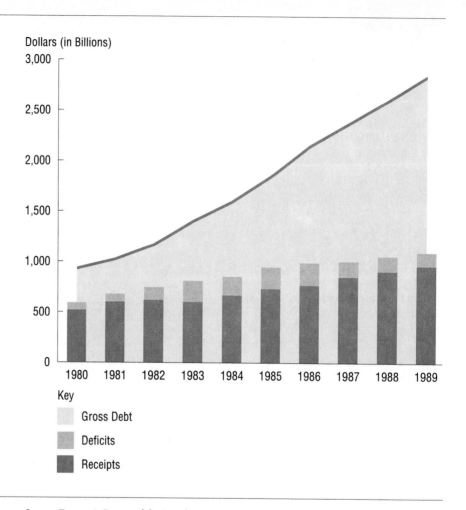

Source: *Economic Report of the President.*

practice, it does not, and the gap must be bridged by borrowing. It is this continued borrowing that has raised the debt to such an astronomical figure.

Exhibit 7.1 shows the numbers. In recent years federal government expenditure has been running ahead of revenue by $100–$200 billion a year. This is 10%–20% of annual federal expenditure of about $1 trillion. As we saw in Chapter 2, government borrowing now dominates total borrowing in the economy. In 1988 the $194 billion of government borrowing far exceeded the $46 billion net borrowing by firms and significantly exceeded the $141 billion net lending by households. The shortfall was made up by substantial borrowing from foreigners.

We can see who lends the U.S. government these enormous sums by looking at the ownership of U.S. government securities. Remember that a security is a record of borrowing: If we think of loans as being money rentals, then securities are the rental contracts. If a security is transferable, or **marketable**, the original lender can transfer the contract to someone else (in exchange for payment, of course). The new owner of the contract, by "carrying" the loan, becomes the lender even though he did not lend the money originally. The borrower repays the new owner of the contract rather than the original lender. Exhibit 7.2 shows who holds U.S. government securities (both marketable and nonmarketable) and, therefore, who lends to the U.S. government.

marketable
Capable of being sold to another person.

Most U.S. securities are marketable, but there are also nonmarketable U.S. securities, which the original purchaser is not allowed to sell to anyone else. The best-known example is U.S. Savings Bonds, which are sold to households, but there are also other nonmarketable securities sold to state and local governments and to foreign governments.

In addition to the debt the U.S. government owes to others, there is a substantial amount that it owes itself. This consists of both marketable and nonmarketable securities held by various agencies of the U.S. government. This debt is an accounting fiction: You are neither richer nor poorer if you write an IOU to yourself for $100 million. Debt owed to yourself is meaningless; only debt owed to others really matters. The reason for this accounting fiction is partly record-keeping, but partly also to hoodwink the public. For example, Social Security is a pay-as-you-go scheme: Payments received in a given year are used to fund benefits in the same year. If there is a surplus, this is "invested" in government securities. Translation: The government gets to spend the surplus. Future Social Security deficits will be funded by redemption of the accumulated securities. Translation: They will be funded out of general tax revenue.[3]

As well as borrowing to finance its own budget deficit, the federal government also borrows to relend the money to others, thus acting as a financial intermediary. Every so often Congress decides that a group close to its heart is not being served sufficiently well by private financial markets. It then sets up a government agency to provide loans to this group. Important examples include mortgage loans to veterans, farmers, and low-income families; commercial loans to farmers and to small businesses; and education loans to students. To be able to make these loans, the federal government borrows the necessary funds. The amounts are quite large: By mid-1988 the amount outstanding of such debt exceeded $350 billion.

---

[3]In early 1990 Senator Moynihan was proposing a cut in Social Security taxes to reduce the Social Security surplus and thereby to do away with this opportunity to conceal the true size of the federal budget deficit.

EXHIBIT 7.2

NET DEBT OF THE
U.S. TREASURY BY
HOLDER

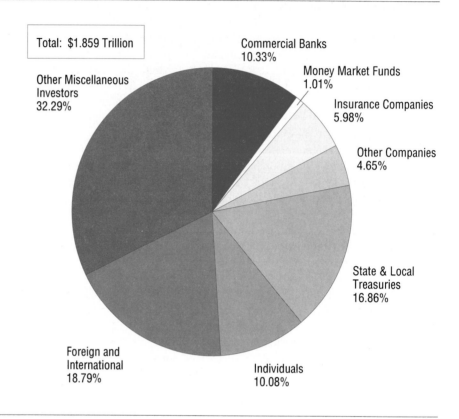

Source: *Federal Reserve Bulletin.*

|7.2| GOVERNMENT BONDS, NOTES, AND BILLS

MARKETABLE TREASURY SECURITIES

Most U.S. government securities are issued by the Department of the Treasury. They are known in the market as *Treasuries* or *governments*. The shortest-maturity Treasuries are 3-, 6-, and 12-month bills in denominations of $10,000 to $1 million. They are known as *T-bills*. Since they pay no coupon interest, T-bills always sell at a discount. In addition to bills, the Treasury also offers coupon securities (called *coupons* by the market) of maturities of from 2 to 30 years. Those of 2- to 10-year maturity are called notes, and those of longer maturity are called *bonds*. Both notes and bonds are available in denominations of $1,000 to $1 million. Coupons are paid semiannually. Depending on market rates of interest, notes and bonds can sell at par, at a discount, or at a premium.

EXHIBIT 7.3

TREASURY BOND

Some notes and bonds are available in the form of handsomely engraved certificates (see Exhibit 7.3). Ownership may be registered with the Treasury, or the certificate may be issued in **bearer** form: That is, possession of the certificate is

bearer security
Security for which possession is primary evidence of ownership.

sole proof of ownership. The advantage of bearer certificates is that they are easier to trade, because the cost of reregistering ownership is avoided. The disadvantage, of course, is that if they are lost or stolen, that is it.[4]

book entry security
Security that exists only as a computer record.

However, notes and bonds issued since 1983 take the form not of certificates, but rather of **book entries**. These are not literally entries in a book, but rather records on a computer. T-bills exist *only* in this form. Book-entry securities are much easier to trade. A computer record can be changed in seconds to reflect a change in ownership, whereas the physical transfer of a piece of paper takes hours or days and is far more costly.

AGENCIES

As we mentioned before, a number of agencies have been set up as financial intermediaries to provide loans to particular favored categories of borrower. Most of the smaller ones borrow from the Treasury through something called the Federal Financing Bank: The Treasury sells securities and the proceeds are used to fund lending by the Federal Financing Bank. In addition, some of the larger agencies issue securities in their own name. These securities are known as **agencies** in the market. Exhibit 7.4 provides a list of the principal agencies and a brief description of what they do.

agencies
Securities issued by certain agencies of the federal government.

UNDERSTANDING TREASURY LISTINGS

The prices and yields on all outstanding Treasury and agency issues are reported daily in the financial press. Exhibit 7.5 shows the listing for January 26, 1990. Issues are arranged in order of maturity date.

callable
Redeemable by issuer at face value before maturity.

Since the bond and note listings are a little simpler, we shall begin with them. The first column gives the maturity date. Notice the issue listed May 93-98. Issues that give a range like this for the maturity date are **callable**: The Treasury may redeem them at face value, whenever it pleases, at any time between the two dates. The letter k, n, or p following the maturity date distinguishes notes from bonds and signifies the taxability for foreign investors.[5] The rate column gives the annual coupon rate: Coupons are semiannual, so the coupon payment is at half the annual rate. The next two columns give the price that dealers will pay for this issue (the **bid price**) and the price at which they will sell it (the **ask price**, or **offer price**).

bid price
Price that dealers will pay for a security.

ask (offer) price
Price at which dealers will sell a security issue.

Bid and ask prices are quoted as a percentage of the face value. For example, the bid price for the 9% notes of November 1993 is 101-24. The 24 means 24/32. That is, for a bond of face value $1 million of this issue, the dealer is

---

[4]A registered certificate, if lost or stolen, will be replaced by the government (the original cannot be cashed by anyone but the registered owner); *partial* compensation may be available for the loss or theft of a bearer certificate, but none is available for lost or stolen coupons.

[5]You will see in Chapter 14 why recent issues of Treasuries have been exempt from tax withholding.

EXHIBIT 7.4

FEDERAL AND FEDERALLY SPONSORED CREDIT AGENCIES

Agency	Debt Outstanding: September 1989 (Millions of Dollars)
Federal Agencies	
Export-Import Bank	$ 10,990
This independent agency of the U.S. government finances exports of U.S. goods and services and offers direct credit to foreign borrowers. It also guarantees loans made by commercial lenders.	
Federal Housing Administration	295
Tennessee Valley Authority	18,847
Coordinates resource conservation, development, and land-use programs in the Tennessee River Valley.	
Federally Sponsored Agencies	
Federal Home Loan Banks	143,578
Provide credit to member savings institutions engaged in mortgage lending.[a]	
Federal Home Loan Mortgage Corporation	26,738
"Freddie Mac" makes mortgage funds available by buying conventional and government-insured mortgages in the secondary market.[a]	
Federal National Mortgage Association	111,507
"Fannie Mae" is a private corporation authorized by Congress to make mortgage funds available by buying mortgages in the secondary market.[a]	
Farm Credit Banks	54,041
Provide credit to farmers.	
Student Loan Marketing Association	27,126
"Sallie Mae" is a government-sponsored corporation that provides funds for student loans.	
Financing Corporation	8,170
Established in August 1987 to recapitalize the Federal Savings and Loan Insurance Corporation (FSLIC).[b]	
Farm Credit Financial Assistance Corporation	847
Provides funds to Farm Credit System.	

[a]We shall discuss the mortgage market in Chapter 15.

[b]We shall discuss deposit insurance in Chapters 16 and 17.

Sources: *Federal Reserve Bulletin*, February 1990, and the *Washington Information Directory*.

EXHIBIT 7.5

TREASURY BILLS, BONDS, AND NOTES

Treasury Bills, Bonds and Notes

Prices in 32d of a point, bill yields in basis points.

TREASURY BILLS

Date	Bid	Ask	Chg.	Yield
-1990-				
Feb 1	7.19	6.97	—0.20	7.07
Feb 8	7.59	7.47	+0.03	7.59
Feb 15	7.66	7.53	+0.07	7.66
Feb 22	6.87	6.75	—0.45	6.87
Mar 1	7.41	7.28	—0.08	7.43
Mar 8	7.63	7.59	—0.01	7.76
Mar 15	7.67	7.63	—0.03	7.81
Mar 22	7.65	7.63	—0.02	7.82
Mar 29	7.60	7.56	—0.04	7.76
Apr 5	7.70	7.66	—0.01	7.87
Apr 12	7.74	7.69	+0.01	7.92
Apr 19	7.79	7.75	+0.01	8.00
Apr 26	7.70	7.66	....	7.91
May 3	7.70	7.66	—0.01	7.92
May 10	7.74	7.69	+0.01	7.97
May 17	7.72	7.69	+0.02	7.98
May 24	7.70	7.66	....	7.96
May 31	7.71	7.66	+0.04	7.97
Jun 7	7.67	7.63	+0.06	7.95
Jun 14	7.74	7.69	+0.07	8.03
Jun 21	7.73	7.69	+0.06	8.04
Jun 28	7.69	7.66	+0.05	8.02
Jul 5	7.75	7.72	+0.05	8.10
Jul 12	7.73	7.69	+0.06	8.08
Jul 19	7.71	7.69	+0.07	8.09
Jul 26	7.68	7.63	+0.06	8.03
Aug 2	7.73	7.69	+0.05	8.11
Aug 30	7.72	7.69	+0.04	8.12
Sep 27	7.65	7.63	+0.05	8.07
Oct 25	7.62	7.59	+0.01	8.06
Nov 23	7.62	7.59	—0.01	8.09
Dec 20	7.55	7.50	—0.01	8.02
-1991-				
Jan 17	7.51	7.47	+0.01	8.02

Source— Bloomberg L.P.

BONDS & NOTES

Source—Bloomberg L.P.

Date	Rate	Bid	Ask	Chg.	Yield
Jan 90 p	7⅜	99-30	100-01	....	4.90
Feb 90	3½	98-21	99-07	....	20.25
Feb 90 p	6½	99-28	99-31	....	6.97
Feb 90 p	7⅛	99-28	99-31	....	7.29
Feb 90 p	11	100-02	100-05	—01	7.24
Mar 90 p	7¼	99-24	99-27	....	8.00
Mar 90 p	7⅜	99-25	99-28	....	7.94
Apr 90 n	10½	100-13	100-16	....	7.83
Apr 90 p	7⅝	99-26	99-29	....	7.86
May 90 p	7⅞	99-27	99-30	....	7.96
May 90	8¼	99-31	100-05	....	7.58
May 90 p	8⅛	99-30	100-01	....	7.92
May 90 p	11⅜	100-27	100-30	—01	7.91
Jun 90 p	7¼	99-18	99-22	....	7.97
Jun 90 p	8	99-27	99-31	....	8.03
Jul 90 n	10¾	101-04	101-08	....	7.91
Jul 90 p	8⅜	100-01	100-05	—01	8.05
Aug 90 p	7⅞	99-25	99-29	—01	8.04
Aug 90 p	9⅞	100-26	100-30	—01	8.07
Aug 90 n	10¾	101-10	101-14	—01	7.99
Aug 90 p	8⅝	100-06	100-10	—01	8.04
Sep 90 p	6¾	99	99-04	....	8.10
Sep 90 p	8½	100-04	100-08	....	8.08
Oct 90 n	11½	102-06	102-10	—01	8.04
Oct 90 p	8¼	99-31	100-03	....	8.09
Nov 90 p	8	99-24	99-28	—02	8.14
Nov 90 n	9⅝	100-31	101-03	—01	8.14
Nov 90 n	13	103-17	103-21	—03	8.10
Nov 90 p	8⅞	100-14	100-18	—01	8.14
Dec 90 p	6⅝	98-18	98-22	....	8.12
Dec 90 p	9⅛	100-23	100-27	—01	8.14
Jan 91 n	11¾	103-03	103-07	—02	8.19
Jan 91 p	9	100-21	100-25	—02	8.17
Feb 91 p	7⅜	99-02	99-06	—01	8.19
Feb 91 p	9⅛	100-27	100-31	....	8.13
Feb 91 p	9⅜	101-02	101-06	....	8.19
Mar 91 p	6¾	98-08	98-12	—01	8.22
Mar 91 p	9¾	101-15	101-19	—02	8.27
Apr 91 n	12⅜	104-15	104-19	—06	8.28
Apr 91 p	9¼	101	101-04	—02	8.27
May 91 p	8⅛	99-23	99-27	—01	8.24
May 91 n	14½	107-28	108	—01	7.84
May 91 p	8¾	100-14	100-18	—03	8.28

BONDS & NOTES

Date	Rate	Bid	Ask	Chg	Yield
Jun 91 n	7⅞	99-11	99-15	—02	8.27
Jun 91 p	8¼	99-27	99-31	—01	8.27
Jul 91 p	7¾	99-05	99-09	—02	8.27
Jul 91 n	13¾	107-07	107-11	—06	8.30
Aug 91 p	7½	98-24	98-29	—03	8.26
Aug 91 p	8¾	100-17	100-21	—01	8.28
Aug 91 n	14⅞	109-29	110-02	—04	7.83
Aug 91 p	8¼	99-25	99-29	—04	8.31
Sep 91 p	8⅜	100	100-03	—01	8.30
Sep 91 p	9⅛	101-04	101-08	—03	8.29
Oct 91 p	7⅝	98-26	98-29	—01	8.30
Oct 91 p	12¼	106-01	106-05	—03	8.29
Nov 91 p	6½	96-30	97-02	—03	8.29
Nov 91 p	8½	100-06	100-10	—04	8.30
Nov 91 n	14¼	110-16	110-20	—04	7.77
Nov 91 p	7¾	98-30	99-01	—01	8.32
Dec 91 p	7⅝	98-24	98-27	—02	8.28
Dec 91 p	8¼	99-26	99-30	—04	8.28
Jan 92 p	11⅝	105-26	105-31	—03	8.26
Feb 92 p	6⅝	96-24	96-28	—04	8.31
Feb 92 p	9⅛	101-13	101-17	—04	8.29
Feb 92 n	14⅝	112-03	112-13	—07	7.93
Mar 92 p	7⅞	99-02	99-06	—06	8.28
Apr 92 k	11¾	106-20	106-25	—02	8.31
May 92 p	6⅝	96-13	96-17	—02	8.31
May 92 p	9	101-07	101-11	—02	8.33
May 92 n	13¾	110-29	111-01	—07	8.35
Jun 92 p	8¼	99-22	99-26	—04	8.33
Jul 92 p	10⅜	104-10	104-14	—02	8.34
Aug 87-92	4¼	90-24	91-26	—03	7.86
Aug 92	7¼	97-13	97-19	—03	8.32
Aug 92 p	8¼	99-21	99-25	—03	8.34
Aug 92 p	7⅞	98-25	98-28	—04	8.37
Sep 92 p	8¾	100-26	100-30	—04	8.34
Oct 92 p	9¾	103-05	103-09	—02	8.36
Nov 92 p	7¾	98-14	98-17	—04	8.34
Nov 92 p	8⅜	99-29	100-02	—03	8.34
Nov 92 n	10½	105-04	105-08	—04	8.34
Dec 92 p	9⅛	101-26	101-30	—04	8.36
Jan 93 p	8¾	100-28	101	—04	8.36
Feb 88-93	4	91-02	92-04	—04	6.91
Feb 93	6¾	95-17	95-29	—04	8.30
Feb 93	7⅞	98-29	99-02	—06	8.23
Feb 93 p	8¼	99-19	99-23	—04	8.35
Feb 93 n	10⅞	106-15	106-19	—05	8.37
Mar 93 p	9⅝	103-07	103-11	—04	8.39
Apr 93 p	7⅜	97-03	97-07	—06	8.37
May 93 p	7⅝	97-23	97-27	—03	8.38
May 93 n	10⅛	104-22	104-26	—07	8.41
Jun 93 p	8⅛	99-03	99-07	—05	8.39
Jul 93 p	7¼	96-16	96-20	—05	8.39
Aug 88-93	7½	97-01	97-11	—05	8.38
Aug 93	8⅝	100-15	100-25	—05	8.36
Aug 93 p	8¾	100-30	101-02	—05	8.39
Aug 93 n	11⅞	110-09	110-15	—06	8.40
Sep 93 p	8¼	99-15	99-19	—04	8.38
Oct 93 p	7⅛	95-28	96	—06	8.40
Nov 93	8⅝	100-18	100-28	—05	8.34
Nov 93 n	11¾	110-14	110-18	—05	8.43
Nov 93 p	9	101-24	101-28	—07	8.41
Dec 93 p	7⅝	97-17	97-20	—06	8.35
Jan 94 p	7	95-08	95-12	—05	8.39
Feb 94	9	101-31	102-05	—06	8.36
Feb 94 p	8⅞	101-15	101-19	—07	8.40
Apr 94 p	7	95	95-04	—03	8.39
May 89-94	4⅛	89-21	90-23	—06	6.64
May 94 p	13⅛	116-15	116-21	—08	8.41
May 94 p	9½	103-21	103-25	—06	8.43
Jul 94 p	8	98-16	98-20	—05	8.37
Aug 94 p	8⅝	100-21	100-25	—05	8.41
Aug 94	8¾	101-04	101-16	—05	8.34
Aug 94 p	12⅝	115-11	115-18	—06	8.43
Oct 94 p	9½	103-29	104-01	—06	8.44
Nov 94	10⅛	106-11	106-17	—06	8.43
Nov 94 p	11⅝	112-06	112-10	—07	8.44
Nov 94 p	8¼	99-09	99-13	—06	8.39
Jan 95 p	8⅝	100-21	100-25	—07	8.43
Feb 95	3	89-26	90-28	—07	5.07
Feb 95	10½	108-01	108-07	—07	8.46
Feb 95 p	11¼	111-04	111-10	—06	8.45
Feb 95 p	7¾	97-14	97-17	—06	8.34
Apr 95 p	8⅜	99-23	99-27	—05	8.41

BONDS & NOTES

Date	Rate	Bid	Ask	Chg	Yield
May 95	10⅜	107-26	108	—06	8.46
May 95 p	11¼	111-16	111-22	—09	8.46
May 95	12⅝	117-10	117-16	—06	8.45
Jul 95 p	8⅞	101-23	101-27	—06	8.45
Aug 95 p	10½	108-20	108-26	—05	8.47
Oct 95 p	8⅝	100-21	100-25	—06	8.44
Nov 95 p	9½	104-15	104-19	—05	8.47
Nov 95	11½	113-15	113-21	—06	8.46
Jan 96 p	9¼	103-13	103-17	—05	8.48
Feb 96 p	8⅞	101-21	101-25	—06	8.49
Apr 96 p	9⅜	104	104-04	—07	8.50
May 96 p	7⅜	94-16	94-20	—07	8.49
Jul 96 p	7⅞	96-27	96-31	—07	8.49
Oct 96 p	8	97-17	97-21	—06	8.46
Nov 96 p	7¼	93-15	93-19	—07	8.51
Ja 97 p	8	97-22	97-25	—07	8.43
May 97 p	8½	99-28	100	—05	8.50
Aug 97 p	8⅝	100-17	100-21	—06	8.50
Nov 97 p	8⅞	101-29	102-01	—05	8.51
Feb 98 p	8⅛	97-19	97-23	—11	8.52
May 98 p	9	102-19	102-23	—10	8.53
Aug 98 p	9¼	104-02	104-06	—13	8.55
May 93-98	7	89-25	90-11	—12	8.65
Nov 98	3½	89-14	90-16	—15	4.84
Nov 98 p	8⅞	101-28	102	—12	8.54
Feb 99 p	8⅞	101-30	102-02	—13	8.54
May 94-99	8½	99-12	99-22	—15	8.55
May 99 p	9⅛	103-18	103-22	—12	8.54
Aug 99 p	8	96-18	96-22	—13	8.51
Nov 99 p	7⅞	95-31	96-02	—13	8.47
Feb 95-00	7⅞	94-29	95-03	—12	8.61
Aug 95-00	8⅜	98-07	98-13	—12	8.61
Feb 01	11¾	121-30	122-04	—15	8.61
May 01	13⅛	132-04	132-10	—16	8.59
Aug 96-01	8	95-19	95-25	—08	8.58
Aug 01	13⅜	134-11	134-17	—16	8.60
Nov 01	15¾	151-29	152-03	—17	8.62
Feb 02	14¼	141-01	141-07	—22	8.67
Nov 02	11⅝	122-09	122-21	—21	8.66
Feb 03	10¾	115-27	116-01	—21	8.67
May 03	10¾	116	116-06	—21	8.67
Aug 03	11⅛	119-03	119-09	—20	8.68
Nov 03	11⅞	125-07	125-13	—23	8.68
May 04	12⅜	129-23	129-29	—24	8.68
Aug 04	13¾	141-15	141-21	—26	8.66
Nov 04 k	11⅝	124-03	124-09	—20	8.68
May 00-05	8¼	96-21	96-27	—19	8.62
May 05 k	12	127-20	127-26	—25	8.68
Aug 05 k	10¾	117-07	117-13	—26	8.69
Feb 06 k	9⅜	106-07	106-13	—26	8.63
Feb 02-07	7⅝	90-31	91-05	—23	8.62
Nov 02-07	7⅞	93-02	93-08	—23	8.62
Aug 03-08	8⅜	97-07	97-13	—23	8.66
Nov 03-08	8¾	100-10	100-16	—21	8.68
May 04-09	9⅛	103-07	103-13	—21	8.70
Nov 04-09	10⅜	113-04	113-10	—24	8.75
Feb 05-10	11¾	124-21	124-27	—27	8.75
May 05-10	10	110-06	110-12	—26	8.75
Nov 05-10	12¾	133-19	133-25	—30	8.76
May 06-11	13⅞	143-24	143-30	—1-01	8.76
Nov 06-11	14	145-15	145-19	—1-02	8.76
Nov 07-12	10⅜	114-18	114-24	—28	8.72
Aug 08-13	12	129-18	129-24	—30	8.73
May 09-14	13¼	141-19	141-25	—1-02	8.73
Aug 09-14k	12½	134-28	135-02	—1-01	8.73
Nov 09-14k	11¾	128-06	128-12	—31	8.71
Feb 15 k	11¼	126-12	126-18	—1-00	8.64
Aug 15 k	10⅝	120-06	120-12	—30	8.64
Nov 15 k	9⅞	112-24	112-30	—29	8.62
Feb 16 k	9¼	106-13	106-19	—28	8.61
May 16 k	7¼	86-01	86-05	—24	8.58
Nov 16 k	7½	88-17	88-21	—25	8.59
May 17 k	8¾	101-17	101-21	—27	8.59
Aug 17 k	8⅞	102-27	102-31	—27	8.59
May 18 k	9⅛	105-24	105-28	—27	8.57
Nov 18 k	9	104-19	104-23	—27	8.55
Feb 19 k	8⅞	103-10	103-14	—29	8.55
Aug 19 k	8⅛	95-15	95-19	—26	8.54

k—Non U. S. citizen exempt from withholding taxes. n—Treasury note. p—Treasury note and non U. S. citizen exempt from withholding taxes.

Source: *New York Times*, Jan. 27, 1990.

willing to pay

$$101\tfrac{24}{32} \times \$1,000,000 = 101.75 \times \$1,000,000 = \$1,017,500.$$

The dealer will pay this bid price plus **accrued interest**. The next coupon payment on this note is due in May 1990. As of January 1990, 2 months of the 6-month coupon period have already passed. The current owner is therefore considered to have earned 2/6 of the next coupon (actually the calculation is done in days rather than in months), and this amount will be added to the bid price when the dealer purchases the security.

The "chg." column gives the change in the bid price over the bid price of the previous day. The 9's of November '93 fell by 7/32 of a point between closing on January 25, 1990, and closing on January 26. The number in the yield column is a measure of yield to maturity. A variety of methods are used to calculate this. As we saw in Chapter 6, this number does not actually tell us the yield that would be realized if a bond were held to maturity.

The bid and ask prices of bills are stated on a "bank discount" basis. The bank discount is defined as

$$\text{bank discount} = \frac{\text{face value} - \text{price}}{\text{face value}} \times \frac{360}{\text{days to maturity}}.$$

Don't ask what this means: It is just a convention. The numbers after the period in this case are not 1/32nds, but decimal fraction—for example, 8.14 means 8 14/100. We can use the above formula to solve for the actual price. For example, for a $10,000 bill due on May 10, the bid price is quoted as 7.74, and there are 104 days to maturity. That means that the bid price satisfies

$$0.0774 = \frac{\$10,000 - \text{price}}{\$10,000} \times \frac{360}{104}.$$

Solving this, we get a bid price of $9,776.40.

THE YIELD CURVE

Notice that the yields in Exhibit 7.5 show a fairly steady rise with increasing maturity. To see this more clearly, we can plot yield against maturity to obtain a **yield curve** as in Exhibit 7.6.[6]

accrued interest
Interest accumulated on a bond since the last coupon payment.

yield curve
Graphic representation of the relationship between yield and maturity of Treasury securities.

---

[6]The yields on some issues deviate markedly from that predicted by a smooth yield curve. These anomalies are mainly the result of peculiar tax treatment. For example, "flower bonds" such as the 3% of February 1995 may be used to pay federal estate taxes *at par*. This makes them particularly attractive to the old, infirm, and very rich, and they therefore offer a significantly lower yield.

E x h i b i t 7.6

YIELD CURVE FOR
GOVERNMENT
SECURITIES
(JANUARY 27, 1990)

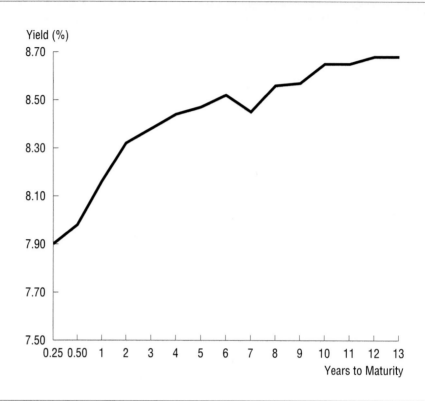

normal yield curve
Yield curve that shows
yields rising with maturity.

inverted yield curve
Yield curve that shows
yields falling with
maturity.

The shape of the yield curve varies over time. The yield curve of Exhibit 7.6 has what is called a **normal** shape: Yields rise steadily with maturity. Sometimes, however, the yield curve becomes **inverted,** with yields falling with maturity, or even humped or U-shaped. We shall see presently that the shape of the yield curve has very important implications for those trading in the government securities market. What determines the shape of the yield curve—the relationship between yields at different maturities? Why does it change? The answers are complicated, and we will need to cover a lot of ground before we finally tackle them in Chapter 29.

7.3 HOW NEW ISSUES ARE SOLD: THE PRIMARY MARKET

Not unnaturally, the Treasury would like to get as good a price as it can for its securities; that is, it would like to pay as low an interest rate as it can on the money it borrows. An excellent way to get a good price is to hold an auction. And that is exactly what the Treasury does.

An average of $8 billion to $9 billion of new issues are auctioned each week. About two-thirds of this represents refinancing of old debt, the money raised being used to pay off old issues that mature. The rest goes to finance the current deficit. There are weekly auctions of bills and regular but less frequent auctions of notes and bonds. The auctions are held by the Federal Reserve Bank of New York. The amount, maturity, and denomination mix of each new issue are announced at least a week in advance, so that the new issue can be absorbed smoothly by the market.

Those wishing to buy part of a new issue must submit a sealed bid to any of the Federal Reserve Banks by the stated deadline. There are two types of bid—a **competitive bid**, which specifies a price, and a **noncompetitive bid**, which does not. To see how an auction works, consider the following example.

competitive bid
Bid for the purchase of a new Treasury issue that specifies a price.

noncompetitive bid
Bid for the purchase of a new Treasury issue that does not specify a price.

EXAMPLE

Suppose that for an issue of $1 billion in one-year T-bills, the New York Fed receives the following bids (bank discounts are translated into actual prices bid):

Competitive (7 bids)
$ 50 million at 91.365
125 million at 91.364
75 million at 91.364
350 million at 91.363
200 million at 91.362
100 million at 91.362
200 million at 91.361

Noncompetitive (many bids)
$ 325 million in total

All the noncompetitive bids are accepted, so subtract the $325 million total of noncompetitive bids from the $1 billion being sold to leave $675 million. This amount is to be divided among the competitive bidders.

Among the competitive bids, the highest are accepted first. The first four bids, at 91.365, 91.364 (two bids), and 91.363, will be accepted in full; the total amount of these four bids is $600 million. Subtracting this from $675 million leaves $75 million.

The $75 million of remaining securities is divided proportionally among those bidding the next highest price, 91.362. Since there is a total $300 million of bids at this price, and only $75 million to go around, each bidder will get one-fourth of the amount bid for.

The weighted average price of the competitive bids that were accepted is 91.363.[7] This is the price the noncompetitive bidders will pay.

---

[7] $(50 \times 91.365 + 200 \times 91.364 + 350 \times 91.363 + 75 \times 91.362)/675 = 91.363$.

Competitive bidders are usually market professionals, such as banks and dealers: If you want to buy an amount of over $1 million, you *must* submit a competitive bid.[8] You can see the considerations involved in submitting such a bid: You want it to be high enough to be accepted, but not so high that you pay too much. The noncompetitive bidders are usually less sophisticated small investors.

If you wish, you too may submit a noncompetitive bid! For your convenience, a copy of a tender form is shown as Exhibit 7.7

7.4 TRADING EXISTING ISSUES: THE SECONDARY MARKET

Suppose your tender is accepted and you buy some T-bills. However, before they mature, you find that you have urgent need of your money. What do you do? You turn to the *secondary market*. The secondary market is the market for existing securities, to be distinguished from the *primary market* for new issues.

While the primary market for governments may seem large, it is tiny compared to the secondary market. In 1987 the volume of transactions reported by the major dealers in the secondary market for U.S. securities averaged over $110 billion *per day*. If we take into account the smaller dealers who do not report their transactions, total trading volume among all market participants is considerably more than this.

Numbers in the billions probably don't impress you any more. So to see how huge the market in governments actually is, compare it with the New York Stock Exchange. On a normal day, trading volume on the NYSE is in the range of $5 billion to $10 billion. Even on "Black Monday," October 19, 1987, when trading volume hit an all-time peak, it reached only $21 billion. This is less than one-fifth of the *normal* trading volume in governments.

HOW THE SECONDARY MARKET IS ORGANIZED

over-the-counter (OTC) market
Secondary market in which dealers at different locations stand ready to buy and sell securities.

Perhaps one reason the market for Treasuries gets less publicity than the stock exchange is that it is an **over-the-counter (OTC) market**. While stocks are traded, photogenically, on the floor of the stock exchange, with lots of excited people shouting and waving their arms at one another, governments are traded quietly over the telephone. This OTC market has no single physical location. However, it too is centered in New York City. The principal participants are *dealers, brokers,* and *clearing banks*.

dealers
Individuals or firms that act as market makers by quoting bids and offers on securities.

Dealers make the market: They quote prices at which they are willing to buy and sell government securities. (It is these bid and ask prices that are quoted in Exhibit 7.5.) To be able to buy and sell at quoted prices, dealers must hold

[8]No single buyer is allowed to buy more than 35% of a given issue.

EXHIBIT 7.7

TENDER FORM

FORM PD 5176-1
(January 1986)

OMB No. 1535-0069
Expires: 01-31-89

TREASURY DIRECT

TENDER FOR 13-WEEK TREASURY BILL

TENDER INFORMATION

AMOUNT OF TENDER: $ _____

BID TYPE (Check One)   ☐ NONCOMPETITIVE   ☐ COMPETITIVE AT ____ . ____ %

ACCOUNT NUMBER ____ - ____ - ____

INVESTOR INFORMATION

ACCOUNT NAME

ADDRESS

CITY   STATE   ZIP CODE

TAXPAYER IDENTIFICATION NUMBER

1ST NAMED OWNER ____ - ____ - ____   OR   ____ - ____
SOCIAL SECURITY NUMBER   EMPLOYER IDENTIFICATION NUMBER

TELEPHONE NUMBERS

WORK (____) ____ - ____   HOME (____) ____ - ____

PAYMENT ATTACHED

TOTAL PAYMENT: $ _____

CASH (01): $ _____   CHECKS (02/03): $ _____

SECURITIES (05): $ _____ $ _____

OTHER (06): $ _____ $ _____

FOR DEPARTMENT USE

TENDER NUMBER
912794

CUSIP

ISSUE DATE

RECEIVED BY

DATE RECEIVED

EXT REG ☐
FOREIGN ☐
BACKUP ☐
REVIEW ☐

CLASS ☐

NUMBERS

DIRECT DEPOSIT INFORMATION

ROUTING NUMBER

FINANCIAL INSTITUTION NAME

ACCOUNT NUMBER   ACCOUNT TYPE (Check One)   ☐ CHECKING

ACCOUNT NAME   ☐ SAVINGS

AUTOMATIC REINVESTMENT

1   2   3   4   5   6   7   8   Circle the number of sequential 13-week reinvestments you want to schedule at this time

AUTHORIZATION

For the notice required under the Privacy and Paperwork Reduction Acts, see the accompanying instructions.

I submit this tender pursuant to the provisions of Department of Treasury Circulars, Public Debt Series Nos. 1-86 and 2-86 and the public announcement issued by the Department of the Treasury.

Under penalties of perjury, I certify that the number shown on this form is my correct taxpayer identification number and that I am not subject to backup withholding because (1) I have not been notified that I am subject to backup withholding as a result of a failure to report all interest or dividends, or (2) the Internal Revenue Service has notified me that I am no longer subject to backup withholding. I further certify that all other information provided on this form is true, correct and complete.

_____ _____
SIGNATURE   DATE

inventories. If someone wants to buy at the ask price, dealers must have the securities available to sell; and if someone wants to sell securities at the bid price, they must be ready to buy them and add them to their inventory. Dealers may buy new issues from the Treasury, trade with investors large and small, and trade with one another. There are two types of dealer—*primary* and *secondary*.

PRIMARY DEALERS

primary dealers
Securities dealers that are large enough and sound enough to be a trading partner with the Fed.

Dealers that are large enough and sound enough to be "recognized" by the Fed as potential trading partners are known as **primary dealers**. As we shall see in Chapter 20, the Fed does an enormous amount of trading in U.S. securities in order to carry out its monetary policy (about $1 trillion per year in transactions). Only primary dealers get a part of this action.

There are other benefits to being a primary dealer. Knowing what the Fed is up to gives you an edge in predicting interest-rate changes. As we shall see presently, being able to do this successfully is the key to making a profit in this business. As a primary dealer, you are connected to a network of brokers, and this gives you further informational advantages. You also gain considerable prestige: Many large institutional investors will trade only with a primary dealer.

inside market
Market in which primary dealers trade among themselves.

Primary dealers do a lot of trading with one another in what is called the **inside market**. It is here that the market price of government securities is really determined. Each dealer looks at the bid and ask prices of each of the others. If he thinks another dealer is bidding too high, he will sell him securities at the bid price ("hit the bid"); or if he thinks the ask price is too low, he will buy the offered securities. In both cases he expects to profit from his competitor's mistake. As a result of such trading, the prices of different traders tend to be brought into line with one another quite rapidly. The resulting common price expresses a market consensus on the "right" price for that security.

In addition to trading with one another, primary dealers trade with the smaller, secondary dealers and with "retail" customers—corporations, financial institutions, and individuals. Competition for retail customers is fierce, and the latter can generally expect to buy and sell at prices close to those on the inside market.

There are costs to being a primary dealer. To be recognized by the Fed, a dealer must show that it has the capital, expertise, and capacity to be a reliable trading partner, and it must submit to quite stringent monitoring. To be considered at all, a dealer must account for at least 1% of the daily trading volume (over $1 billion per day) and must have minimum equity capital of $50 million. Dealers who have applied for recognition and who are in the process of being checked out are called "aspiring" dealers.

As of April 1989 there were 42 primary dealers and several other aspiring dealers (see Exhibit 7.8). Of particular interest are the large number of foreign dealers, particularly the Japanese firms. In recent years Japan has become an increasingly important source of funding for U.S. government debt.

The number of primary dealers has grown recently, along with the growth of the market: In 1970 there were only 24. Some believe that the resulting increase in competition has been the reason for the recent widespread losses among primary dealers. As a result of such losses, two dealers, L. F. Rothschild & Co.

EXHIBIT 7.8

PRIMARY DEALERS IN GOVERNMENT SECURITIES

Bank of America NT & SA

Bankers Trust Company

Bear, Stearns & Co. Inc.

Carroll McEntee & McGinley Incorporated (Hong Kong)

Chase Securities Inc.

Citicorp Securities Markets Inc.

Continental Illinois National Bank and Trust Company of Chicago

CRT Government Securities Ltd.

Daiwa Securities America Inc. (Japan)

Dean Witter Reynolds Inc.

Dillon, Read & Co. Inc.

Discount Corporation of New York

Donaldson, Lufkin and Jenrette Securities Corporation

Drexel Burnham Lambert Government Securities Inc.

The First Boston Corporation

First National Bank of Chicago

Goldman, Sachs & Co.

Greenwich Capital Markets Inc. (Japan)

Harris Government Securities Inc. (Canada)

Irving Securities Inc.

Kidder, Peabody & Co. Inc.

Kleinwort Benson Government Securities Inc. (Britain)

Aubrey G. Lanston & Co. Inc. (Japan)

Manufacturers Hanover Securities Corporation

Merrill Lynch Government Securities Inc.

Midland Mantagu Securities Inc. (Britain)

J. P. Morgan Securities Inc.

Morgan Stanley & Co. Inc.

The Nikko Securities Co. International Inc. (Japan)

Nomura Securities International Inc. (Japan)

Paine Webber Incorporated

Prudential-Bache Securities Inc.

Salomon Brothers Inc.

Sanwa-BGK Securities Co. L.P. (Japan)

Security Pacific National Bank

Shearson Lehman Government Securities Inc.

Smith Barney, Harris Upham & Co. Inc.

Thomson McKinnon Securities Inc.

S. G. Warburg & Co. Inc. (Britain)

Wertheim Schroder & Co. Inc.

Westpac Pollock Government Securities Inc. (Australia)

Yamaichi International (America) Inc. (Japan)

Source: The Federal Reserve Bank of New York's Market Reports Division, as of April 1989.

and National Westminster Bank, have recently given up their primary status and reduced the scope of their business.

SECONDARY DEALERS

In addition to the primary dealers, there are also some 300 smaller, **secondary dealers**. These do not deal directly with the Fed, and they are much less closely monitored than the primary dealers. They buy government securities from the

secondary dealers
Dealers that buy securities from primary dealers and sell them to the public.

primary dealers and sell them to the public. Almost anyone can set up as a secondary dealer.

BROKERS

When dealers in government securities buy and sell, they "take a position" in the securities they trade—that is, they take ownership. Brokers, on the other hand, never take ownership themselves. Their role is just to bring the trading parties together. Think of a used-car *dealer* as opposed to a real estate *broker*. The used-car dealer buys a car from you, temporarily taking ownership, or sells you a car off the lot. The real estate broker brings the parties to a sale together but never personally owns the property.

Brokers are particularly important in the inside market between primary dealers. With so many primary dealers, direct trading among them would be impractical, for each dealer would have to keep in touch simultaneously with 41 other primary dealers. In practice, each dealer quotes prices to a broker, who displays them on computer screens provided to the other dealers. Hence each dealer needs to be in touch with only one or two brokers, rather than with dozens of other dealers. The idea is illustrated in Exhibit 7.9.

In addition to centralizing information in this way, brokers provide dealers with anonymity. A dealer does not want his competitors to know what he is doing. Seeing his trades may convey information that is useful to them, and if his move turns out to be a mistake, he would rather his competitors not get the chance to gloat. Hence the bids and offers on the computer screen do not indicate the source, and in clearing the transaction both securities and payment go through the broker so that anonymity is preserved. The dealer initiating a trade (hitting a bid or taking an offer) pays the broker a commission.

Notice that brokers can function more efficiently the fewer there are of them. With, say, 20 different brokers, there would be little centralization of information: Dealers could do just as well trading with one another directly. Five would be a big improvement. The best, of course, would be a single broker, for then all the information could be displayed on a single computer screen. There are, in fact, only six or seven major brokers of government securities, and in recent years there has been a tendency for them to merge, further reducing their number.

The problem with the small number, of course, is that there is little competitive pressure. Until recently, the commissions that brokers charged—from $12.50 per $1 million face value on 90-day bills to $78.12 per $1 million on coupon securities—had remained unchanged for many years despite the tremendous increase in volume and despite costs that were falling steadily because of technological progress. Brokers were making enormous profits on volumes in the tens of billions of dollars a day each, and dealers were fuming.

In 1986 Salomon Brothers decided to do something about it. Together with some 30 other dealers, it set up a new brokerage house, called Liberty, to compete with existing brokers. Commissions immediately dropped by 50% and then continued to fall. Competition is a wonderful thing!

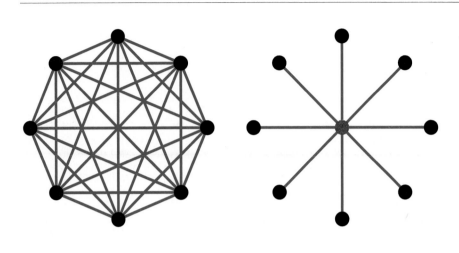

EXHIBIT 7.9

TRADING WITH AND WITHOUT A BROKER

When dealing directly with one another, 8 dealers need 28 links. With a single broker providing the connections, only 8 links are needed.

The fall in commissions has, however, pressured brokers to seek profits elsewhere, and dealers are not entirely pleased with the consequences (see "U.S. Bond Dealers Incensed about Threat to Price-Data Control" on page 158).

CLEARING BANKS

Trades involving dealers and brokers are executed by a number of **clearing banks** that specialize in providing this service. A clearing bank will keep the dealer's inventory of securities in a book-entry account (see "Book-Entry Treasury Securities" on page 159). The bank will also hold a demand deposit to be used in executing trades and, to finance the dealer's trading, it will make loans to the dealer as necessary.

To see how this all works, let us follow an actual trade. Maggie Jones, a trader at XYZ Securities, has just bought $5 million worth of the 12s of 2005 at 130.1. Maggie made the purchase over the phone through Mittelmann, a broker. Maggie fills out a "trade ticket" with the details of the trade and passes this on to Andy in operations. Andy checks the ticket for errors and calculates the amount of money to be paid. He then faxes confirmation of the trade to Mittelmann, and he sends instructions by direct computer link to Calbank, XYZ's clearing bank, to clear the trade. Calbank uses Fedwire to transfer payment of the amount due to Metropolis, Mittelmann's clearing bank (see "Book-Entry Treasury Securities"). The payment comes out of XYZ's demand deposit, or if necessary, Calbank makes XYZ a loan, collateralized by the securities. Calbank receives the securities from Metropolis in exchange. Of course, Mittelmann must arrange to receive the securities from whoever has sold them (Maggie does not know who

clearing bank
A bank that executes trades for a securities dealer or broker.

U.S. BOND DEALERS INCENSED ABOUT THREAT TO PRICE-DATA CONTROL

By Tom Herman

Staff Reporter of The Wall Street Journal

NEW YORK—Big government-bond dealers are up in arms about a threat to their tight control of a preciously guarded asset: information.

At stake is who gets to see the electronic screens of middlemen called bond brokers—screens displaying U.S. government bond prices. Until now, only the largest dealers had access to that information, which is widely considered to give the big dealers an important advantage in trading bonds.

Now one of the largest bond brokers, RMJ Securities Corp., has decided to offer its trading screen to a wider group of customers. It also is changing its role from serving merely as a middleman to guaranteeing trades it handles. And some of its longtime customers, such as bond-trading powerhouse Salomon Brothers Inc., aren't pleased.

Though the big dealers won't talk about it, bond industry sources say that some big firms have stopped doing business through RMJ, a tactic

bond traders call "putting them in the penalty box."

But any blow to the information cartel will delight U.S. government officials, who have long viewed the current structure as an unfair monopoly run by an exclusive club of the nation's biggest bond dealers. And RMJ's move should mean that more investors soon will gain access to the broker screens and more up-to-date information about bond prices.

Until now, RMJ and several other large brokers have restricted access to their screens to the 44 large commercial banks and securities dealers recognized as "primary dealers" by the Federal Reserve Bank of New York, as well as a few other firms that have applied to become primary dealers.

The dispute about who has access to broker screens has raged for years, and the issue is under study by the Justice Department's antitrust division. Lazard Freres & Co., a small but prestigious New York investment

bank, once charged that the current system amounts to a "private club approach" and an unfair "oligopoly," which is control of a commodity or service in a given market by a small number of companies or suppliers.

Some big dealers grumble that if everyone gains access to the brokers' price screens, this would reduce the incentive to being a member of the Fed's primary dealer group. This, they say, might even undermine the tightly knit system through which the Federal Reserve executes monetary policy by buying and selling vast amounts of government securities in the open market.

Source: Tom Herman, "U.S. Bond Dealers Incensed about Threat to Price-Data Control," *The Wall Street Journal*, March 2, 1989. Reprinted by permission of The Wall Street Journal, © Dow Jones & Company, Inc. 1989. All Rights Reserved Worldwide.

this is) and deliver them to XYZ; it must also transfer the funds in return to the anonymous seller.

Most major banks do some clearing, but a few handle most of the business. The largest of these is Manufacturers Hanover, which handles about $100 billion worth of trades each day in governments and other securities; other large clearing banks are Bank of New York, Irving Trust, and Marine Midland.

7.5 HOW TO BE A SECURITIES DEALER

How do dealers make money? What are the opportunities? What are the risks? The best way to find out is to try for yourself. With the banking experience you gained in Chapter 5, you are more than qualified.

BOOK-ENTRY TREASURY SECURITIES

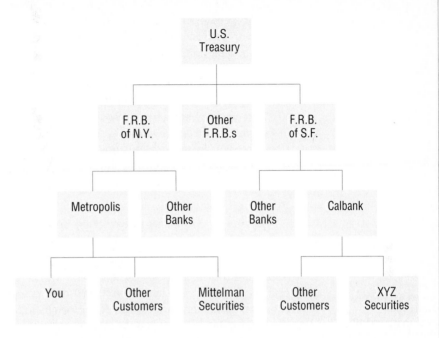

The book-entry system works as follows. Suppose you have a securities account at Metropolis National. That is, Metropolis "keeps" your securities in the form of entries in its computer. Metropolis, in turn, has a securities account at the New York Fed.

When you buy a $10,000 bond (Security No. 234567) from the Treasury, the Treasury records in its computer that Security No. 234567 belongs to the New York Fed; the New York Fed's computer records that Security No. 234567 belongs to Metropolis; and Metropolis's computer records that Security No. 234567 belongs to you. When coupons are due, the Treasury pays the New York Fed, which pays Metropolis, which pays you.

Suppose you sell this bond to XYZ Securities, which has an account at Calbank in San Francisco. This requires the following changes in computer records. Metropolis debits your account and requests over Fedwire that Security No. 234567 be transferred from its own account to that of Calbank, for XYZ Securities. The New York Fed notifies the San Francisco Fed that Security No. 234567 is being transferred to it and debits Metropolis's account. The Treasury transfers Security No. 234567 from the account of the New York Fed to the account of the San Francisco Fed. The San Francisco Fed credits the account of Calbank with Security No. 234567. Finally, Calbank credits the account of XYZ Securities with Security No. 234567.

To start with, you need some equity capital. You raise $2 million from your own resources and from friends, relatives, and classmates. You rent office space and set up in business. In this case no charter or permission is required: The government securities market is very lightly regulated, and anyone can set up as a dealer. There used to be even less regulation until some major scandals in the early 1980s motivated Congress to impose some minimum standards. As a result, you do need to register with some regulatory authority—usually the SEC.

You need a clearing bank, so you put your $2 million into a demand deposit at Metropolis and open a securities account there. You also need market information. Since you are too small to hook up with the major brokers, the best you can do is subscribe to an electronic information service like Reuters or Telerate to receive up-to-date information on bond prices.

BUYING AND SELLING SECURITIES

The bread and butter of your business is buying and selling securities. To have something to sell, you buy $100 million worth of various securities from a primary dealer. How can you buy $100 million worth of securities when you have only $2 million? By getting a **dealer loan** from Metropolis for the difference.

dealer loan
Loan that a securities dealer obtains from a bank for the purpose of buying securities.

Metropolis will lend you the money and hold the securities as collateral. As you sell the securities, your bank will release them against payment, subtracting the money it is owed, and crediting you for the rest. Metropolis is willing to lend you up to $98 million against these securities. This is less than the value of the securities, because their market price might fall, and the bank wants to be sure that the value of the collateral stays above the amount of the loan.

Why would anyone pay you more for these securities than you paid for them yourself? Usually because they want smaller quantities than a primary dealer would be willing to handle. Your trading volume grows steadily, and soon you are taking in a small but steady income from the spread between your bid and ask price. As you buy and sell, your inventory fluctuates, but it stays in the $100 million range.

carry
Difference between the interest rate a dealer pays for financing and the interest rate it receives on the securities it owns.

Besides the bid–ask spread, you have an additional source of profit—**carry**. Unlike the inventory of, say, a shoe store or a supermarket, your inventory earns income. You get the interest the Treasury pays on that $100 million in securities. Regrettably, that interest is not all profit. You have to subtract the interest *you* pay on the dealer loan that finances the inventory. If the interest rate on the securities exceeds the interest rate on the financing, you make a profit—a positive carry. If the interest rate on the securities is less than the cost of financing, you make a loss—a negative carry.

Whether the carry is positive or negative depends on the shape of the yield curve and on the maturity of your securities. The rate you pay to finance your inventory is a short-term rate. You borrow a varying amount day by day, and Metropolis charges you each day a rate one-quarter of a percent above the overnight fed funds rate for that day. Whatever the average maturity of your securities, it is longer than overnight. So if the yield curve has a normal shape—interest rates increasing with maturity—you will earn positive carry—the longer the average maturity of your securities, the greater the carry. Of course, if the yield curve is inverted, carry will be negative, and you will lose money. However, you will have to take your loss: With no inventory you have no business.

REPURCHASE AGREEMENTS

You can increase your profit from carry if you can reduce the cost of financing your inventory. To do this, you will have to find someone else to borrow from. There is, of course, the usual problem of borrowing—trust—but that problem can be minimized if the loan is collateralized by the securities (as with your dealer loan). Such collateralized loans to government securities dealers usually take the form of **repurchase agreements** (alternatively called *repos* or *RPs*). Most repos are overnight, but some are for longer periods (these are called *term repos*).

repurchase agreement (repo)
Simultaneous arrangement to sell securities and to repurchase them later at a specified time and price.

A repo with, say, Megacorp Motors might work like this. You agree to sell Megacorp a specified amount of securities for $10,000,000 and to buy them back (repurchase them) the next day for $10,001,850. While formally this is a sale and repurchase, Megacorp is effectively making you a $10,000,000 loan for one day and the $1,850 excess in the buy-back price represents interest on the loan (roughly 7% at an effective annual rate). The securities sold and bought back are the collateral: Were you to fail to repurchase them (fail to repay the loan), Megacorp could sell the securities to someone else to recover its money. As with a dealer loan, a repo is usually overcollateralized to protect the lender.

The first stage of the agreement, the sale, is executed immediately. Megacorp's bank wires the $10 million to your bank, Metropolis, and most of it goes to repay the dealer loan on those securities. Rather than wire the securities back in exchange, Metropolis transfers them from your account to a special custodial account in the name of Megacorp. This is cheaper than actually transferring ownership through the whole chain of book-entry records.

The next morning you buy back the securities at the agreed price by having your bank wire $10,001,850 to Megacorp's bank, and you regain possession of the securities. Where do you get the money? From your bank. For reasons we shall see later, Metropolis will lend you money *during the day* without charging you interest, so long as you repay the loan by the end of the day. Such a loan is called a daylight loan, or **daylight overdraft** (it is as if you had "overdrawn" your demand deposit). How will you repay this daylight loan? By doing another repo, either with Megacorp again or with someone else. So you finance your inventory by **rolling over** your repo borrowing day after day, bridging the gap between repos with free daylight loans from your clearing bank.

daylight overdraft
Amount of money lent interest-free during the business day.

The reason it is worth going to all this trouble is that the interest rate on repos is generally *below* the fed funds rate and therefore substantially below the rate on dealer loans. For Megacorp, too, the repo is attractive: Although the interest rate is not high, the repo is a very liquid investment and quite safe.

rolling over
Repaying a debt by further borrowing.

E X H I B I T 7.10

YIELDS ON
TREASURY BILLS
AND BONDS

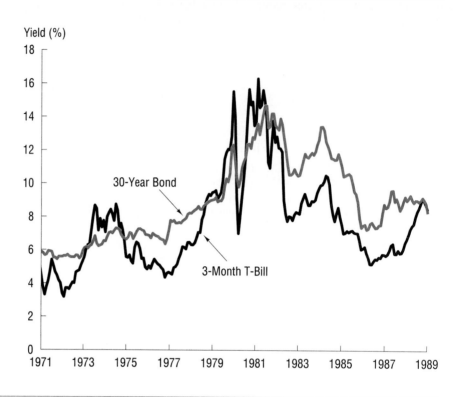

Source: *Economic Report of the President* and *Treasury Bulletin*.

LEVERAGE AND VOLATILITY

Although you may make some profit on the bid–asked spread and on carry, the only (honest) way to make really big money is through capital gains on your position in securities ("position plays").

The potential for gain or loss is substantial. Interest rates have become much more volatile in recent years (see Exhibit 7.10). As we learned in Chapter 6, volatile interest rates mean volatile security prices. It used to be that a daily movement of 1/64 of 1% in bond prices was remarkable—the cause of much discussion among commuters on the Long Island Railroad; today daily movements of 3% are not unheard of.

Your potential for gain or loss as a result of this volatility is magnified enormously by your very considerable leverage. Like most dealers, you are financing 98% to 99% of your inventory of securities with borrowed money. Your balance sheet is:

| Securities | $100m | Borrowing | $98m |
| | | Equity | 2m |

Suppose interest rates fall and the value of your securities rises by 2% to $102 million. The terms under which you have borrowed are not affected by this change in the market value of the securities. If you have repoed the securities, the repurchase price is already set and is unaffected by changes in the market value of the underlying securities. Hence your balance sheet becomes:[9]

| Securities | $102m | Borrowing | $98m |
| | | Equity | 4m |

Remember that equity is calculated as assets minus liabilities. Leverage has magnified the 2% rise in security prices into a doubling of your equity!

This is terrific, but what do you do if you think interest rates are going to *rise*? With this same position, a 2% *fall* in security prices would wipe you out.

SHORT SALES

The thing to do, if you think interest rates are going to rise, is to take a **short position,** or "go short": You do this by borrowing securities and selling them.

Consider an example. First, you sell off your inventory (we shall see in a moment how you can carry on as a dealer without it). Then you borrow $100 million in Treasuries for 10 days from XYZ Securities. You immediately sell these securities and lend the money you obtain for them for 10 days at a fixed rate of interest. For instance, you can lend the money to your bank in the form of a time deposit.[10]

But if you sell the securities, how will you be able to return them to XYZ as you have promised? All you have to do is buy *equivalent* securities in the market: You are not obliged to return the identical securities—just equivalent ones. If you borrow T-bills maturing on a certain date, you have to return the same face value

short position
Position based on borrowing securities and selling them.

---

[9] In this balance sheet, the securities are valued at their market price (*marked to market*). Whereas this is normal for the balance sheets of securities dealers, banks often carry securities and other assets on their balance sheets at purchase price, making a correction only when the securities are actually sold. There are different tax implications to these two different types of accounting procedure.

[10] The interest the Treasury pays on the securities belongs to XYZ, not to you. You also have to pay interest to XYZ, at an agreed rate, on the loan of securities. To calculate your carry on the position, the interest you pay XYZ must be subtracted from the interest you earn on the funds you obtained from selling the securities. The carry may be positive or negative.

of T-bills maturing on the same date; they do not have to have the same serial numbers. It is rather like borrowing money: When you borrow $5 from a friend, you are not expected to return the very same $5 bill.

As a result of the short sale, your balance sheet will be:

| Time deposit | $102m | Securities | $100m |
| | | Equity | 2m |

Rather than having securities and owing money, as you did before, you now have money and owe securities.

Suppose that interest rates rise, just as you expected, and the market price of the securities you borrowed falls by 2%. Your balance sheet becomes:

| Time deposit | $102m | Securities | $98m |
| | | Equity | 4m |

Now, when you buy in the market the securities you must return to XYZ, you will need to pay only $98 million for them. As a result, your equity has doubled.

REVERSE REPOS

reverse repurchase agreement (reverse repo) Simultaneous arrangement to buy securities and to resell them later at a specified time and price.

In reality, the way dealers usually acquire securities for a short sale is not by borrowing them, but through a **reverse repurchase agreement** (also called a "reverse repo," "reverse RP," or simply a "reverse"). A reverse repo is a repo seen from the other side of the transaction: When you repo your securities, the other side of the transaction is doing a reverse repo.

Consider the example illustrated in Exhibit 7.11. XYZ Securities reverses in $10.5 million of T-bills from Friendly Savings and Loan for 3 days. In Stage 1 XYZ sends Friendly $10 million in cash and receives the securities in return. Then, 3 days later in Stage 2, XYZ returns equivalent securities and receives its $10 million plus the agreed-upon interest of $7,837 (an effective annual rate of 10%). From XYZ's point of view, this transaction is a reverse; from Friendly's, it is a regular repo.

RUNNING A BOOK IN REPOS

The market for both repos and reverses has grown enormously. We have seen why repos are attractive to dealers: They provide a cheap way to finance inventory. For other holders of government securities, for example, banks and savings and loans, they provide an easy way to raise money quickly. As a source

EXHIBIT 7.11

A REPO/REVERSE REPO

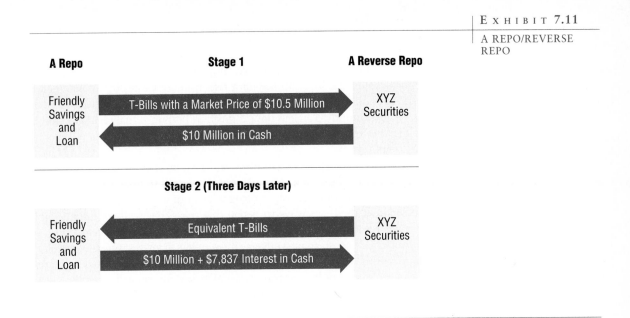

of liquidity, holding government securities and repoing them as needed is an attractive alternative to holding excess reserves.

Who does reverses? As we have seen, dealers (and anyone else) wanting to take a short position. They also provide a way for you, the dealer, to satisfy your customers' orders without having to hold inventory: You can sell securities you do not actually have and reverse them in to make delivery. For example, you might want to do it this way rather than by buying them outright if you know that you will be receiving some of the same securities in a couple of days (say you have bought them at auction).

How are those wanting to do repos and those wanting to do reverses to find one another? How is the "price" (the interest rate on repo loans) to be determined? We need someone to make the market. Naturally enough, the same dealers who make the market in securities also make the market in repos and reverses.[11] That is, they reverse in securities from some clients and then repo them out again to others. This is called **running a book in repos.** The bid and ask "prices" are the rates paid and received on repo loans. The spread earned by the market maker is the rate received on repo loans minus the rate paid on them.

running a book in repos Making a market in repos and reverse repos by reversing in securities from some clients and repoing them out again to others.

[11]Brokers also play the same sort of middleman role in the inside market for repos.

HEDGING

Guessing the way that interest rates will move and taking the appropriate position has become the main source of profits (and losses) for dealers in government securities. You can bet on a rise in interest rates by taking a short position. You can bet on a fall in interest rates by owning securities (this is called taking a *long* position). You can have a position both in actual securities and in repos, and it is your *net* position with respect to both that determines whether you are long or short.

Although you may have to gamble to some extent to make a profit, you may not want to bet the farm. For example, you may wish to hold a fair amount of inventory without taking the risk of being wiped out if interest rates rise.

hedge
Protect against risk.

Fortunately, there are ways to **hedge** this risk. That is, there are available financial instruments, such as futures, options, and swaps, that enable you to insure yourself, at a cost, against adverse movements in interest rates. We shall see exactly how this works in Chapter 13, but the basic idea is that when interest rates change, the gain or loss on your position in, say, futures will offset the loss or gain on your position in the securities themselves.

7.6 HIGH JINKS IN THE GOVERNMENT SECURITIES MARKET

With its rapid growth, in terms both of volume and of new types of financial instrument (repos, reverses, futures, etc.), and with its loose supervision, the government securities market has attracted more than its share of adventurers and crooks. A number of major scandals shook the confidence of the market in the early 1980s and led to tighter regulation.

One fly-by-night operation, Drysdale Government Securities, had built, within a few months of entering the market in 1982, a position of over $6 billion in government bonds. All this was achieved on capital of only $20 million. Drysdale built its position largely by reversing in securities, including over $2 billion worth from Chase.

Drysdale exploited an inconsistency that had resulted from the confusion in this rapidly expanding market. When bonds were reversed in, the owner retained title to any coupon interest due on them, so that the cash loan paid to the owner covered only the securities themselves and not the accrued interest. However, when securities were *sold*, the price did include accrued interest. Hence, by reversing in securities and selling them, Drysdale could generate cash (equal to the accrued interest on the bonds), which it could then use for its own speculations.

When those speculations turned sour, Drysdale was unable to pay the accrued interest on the bonds it had borrowed. In particular, it defaulted on some $160 million it owed to Chase. It turned out, however, that the securities involved had not actually belonged to Chase at all, but rather to its customers. These customers had empowered Chase to repo out their securities in order to make some extra income. So Chase claimed to be an innocent agent in the transaction and therefore not liable for the losses. Confidence in the market was seriously shaken. Ultimately, with help from other major market participants and with some behind-the-scenes arm-twisting, the Fed succeeded in persuading Chase to change its mind and to pick up the loss.

There were two further scandals in 1985, one involving E.S.M. Government Securities and the other Bevill, Bresler, and Schulman. As we have seen, dealers and banks (like Chase) often run a book in repos, repoing out to third parties securities that have been reversed in to them. It seems that these two firms were repoing out the same securities to more than one lender at a time. So, when these two dealers failed after incurring large trading losses, they proved to have fewer securities than they had pledged as collateral.

With a normal repo, of course, this sort of trick is impossible: Because the securities are held in a custodial account at a clearing bank, there is no way to repo them out again. However, there exists an alternative arrangement whereby the dealer retains possession of the securities. The dealer simply sends the lender written notification advising him that the securities have been set aside in his name. This appropriately named "trust me" repo was the kind used by the two dealers in question.

Many of E.S.M.'s customers proved to be thrifts that had been repoing out securities as a cheap source of funds to initiate mortgages destined for mortgage pools.[12] Some of these thrifts, in Ohio and Maryland, were insured by state rather than federal deposit insurance. When the size of the Ohio and Maryland thrifts' losses became known—their losses exceeded the reserves of the state deposit-insurance agencies—they became the victims of the first bank runs since the 1930s, and they were forced to close their doors.[13]

In response to these and other scandals, with total estimated losses to customers of some $750 million, regulation of the market was tightened considerably by the Government Securities Act of 1986. Among its provisions, all dealers (except banks, which are regulated by other agencies) must register with the SEC; and the Secretary of the Treasury is given the authority, in consultation with the Fed and the SEC, to formulate rules on such things as how much capital dealers should have and how repos and reverses should be carried out.

SUMMARY

- The U.S. government is the biggest borrower on earth, owing about $2 trillion. Rapid recent growth in this amount has been due to large federal budget deficits. The federal government also borrows to relend to others.

- Most U.S. debt is marketable. It is held by households, firms, and financial institutions, both at home and overseas.

---

[12]We shall learn about these in Chapter 15.

[13]We read about the bank runs in Ohio in Chapter 1.

- U.S. government securities come in the form of T-bills, of maturity up to a year, and longer-maturity notes and bonds. Mostly, these securities exist only in book-entry form.

- Listings of Treasury securities give the bid and ask price for each issue outstanding and a calculation of the yield to maturity. The actual price paid for coupon securities includes accrued interest.

- A plot of yield against maturity of outstanding issues is called a yield curve. The normal shape of this curve is increasing, but it sometimes becomes inverted.

- New issues of government securities are sold at auction (the primary market). Both competitive and noncompetitive bids may be made.

- Existing issues are traded in the secondary market. This market is enormous, with daily volume of over $110 billion. It is an over-the-counter market made by dealers who quote bid and ask prices and hold inventories.

- Primary dealers, who trade directly with the Fed, play the most important role. Their trading in the inside market largely determines market prices. Primary dealers also trade with smaller, secondary dealers and with retail customers.

- Trading in the inside market is mediated by brokers. The brokers do not themselves take a position in securities. Their role is to provide information and to enable dealers to trade with one another anonymously.

- The smaller the number of brokers, the more efficiently they can perform their function. However, with small numbers there is a potential problem of lack of competition. Recently dealers got together to form a new brokerage house to compete with existing firms, and fees fell dramatically.

- Trades are actually executed through clearing banks and generally involve the transfer of both securities and money via Fedwire. Such transfer is facilitated by the system of book-entry securities.

- Dealers normally operate with very high leverage. The two important sources of finance are dealer loans from clearing banks and repos from other lenders. In both cases the loans are collateralized by securities.

- Dealers may earn profit from carry if the yield curve has a normal shape. However, the biggest potential for profit—and loss—lies in position plays. The potential for profit and loss is magnified by leverage.

- If interest rates are expected to fall, a profit may be made from a leveraged long position in securities. If interest rates are expected to rise, then a short position is indicated. A short position involves the sale of borrowed securities, usually acquired through a reverse repo.

- Repos and reverses have become so important that dealers now make a market in these as well as in the securities themselves.

- Dealers can and do reduce their exposure to interest-rate risk by hedging their positions in futures or options.

- A number of scandals in the early 1980s involving secondary dealers led to passage of the Government Securities Act of 1986, which tightened the rules for the market in government securities.

KEY TERMS

marketable

bearer security

book entry security

agencies

callable

bid price

ask (offer) price

accrued interest

yield curve

normal yield curve

inverted yield curve

competitive bid

noncompetitive bid

over-the-counter (OTC) market

dealers

primary dealers

inside market

secondary dealers

clearing bank

dealer loan

carry

repurchase agreement (repo)

daylight overdraft

rolling over

short position

reverse repurchase agreement (reverse repo)

running a book in repos

hedge

DISCUSSION QUESTIONS

1. Since the government does not raise any money in the secondary market, this market could be eliminated without any harm to the government. Discuss.

2. You have $1,000 and a credit-card limit of $5,000 (no interest is charged if you pay off your credit-card debt within a month). You are absolutely sure that interest rates are going to fall and that bond prices are going to rise 5% sometime in the next month. What is your strategy? What happens if you are wrong and prices fall by 5% instead?

3. In Exhibit 7.5, consider the 8 ¾ of January 1993. What is the semiannual coupon? How much would you have to pay for a $1,000 face value bond (accrued interest is zero)? What is the average effective annual yield to maturity?

4. Dealers make a profit by selling at a higher price than they buy. However, in Exhibit 7.5 the bid price for a T-bill maturing April 19 is 7.79 while the ask price is 7.75. How could a dealer profit in this case?

5. In what circumstances do you think the Treasury will call before maturity a bond that is callable? How does this affect the attractiveness of the bond and its price?

6. The Treasury may pay whatever yield the market requires on bills and notes, but the law places a ceiling of 4.25% on the yield it may pay on bonds. Since the 1960s long-term market rates have been higher than this, so the Treasury has been able to sell bonds only when Congress has granted it a specific

exemption from the law, which it has done from time to time. What is the economic rationale for this restriction on issuing bonds? What, if any, political reason might there be?

7. Why are there no ratings and no underwriters for government securities?

8. Why is the Treasury happy with the lack of regulation in the government securities market?

9. Are government securities dealers financial intermediaries? Are brokers? Are dealers who run a book in repos? Explain.

BIBLIOGRAPHY

Rosengren, Eric S., "Is There a Need for Regulation in the Government Securities Market?" *New England Economic Review*, September-October 1986, 29–40.

Stigum, Marcia, *The Money Market*, 3rd ed., Homewood, IL: Dow-Jones Irwin, 1990.

_____, *After the Trade: Dealer and Clearing Bank Operations in Money Market and Government Securities*, Homewood, IL: Dow-Jones Irwin, 1988.

Tucker, James F., *Buying Treasury Securities at Federal Reserve Banks*, Richmond, VA: Federal Reserve Bank of Richmond, March 1989.

CHAPTER 8

THE INTERSTATE BANKING STORY

You may have noticed that the name of your local bank has changed because it has been taken over by some larger bank. This takeover is just part of a broad movement of mergers and takeovers of banks going on all across the country.

The story of this development, like those of many we shall study in coming chapters, is one of powerful economic forces coming up against, and ultimately defeating, government regulations that stand in their way. In this case the regulations in question are those that restrict where a bank may open new branches; the powerful economic force is what economists call **economies of scale**—cost advantages of size that make large banks more profitable than small ones.

The desire to achieve economies of scale drives banks to grow. If they are allowed to expand freely, larger banks will gobble up smaller ones, until the banking industry consists of a few, very large banks. This has happened in most advanced economies, like Japan and the United Kingdom, but not in the United States.

economies of scale
Declining average cost of operation as the scale of operation is increased.

8.1 | BANKING STRUCTURE IN THE UNITED STATES AND OTHER COUNTRIES

To see how much the United States differs in this respect from other countries, look at Exhibit 8.1. Column 1 shows the total number of banking companies in each country, and Column 2 shows the total number of bank offices (each banking company may have more than one office). Since the countries vary in population, we need to adjust the number of banks for population to see which countries have relatively many banks and which have relatively few. Hence Column 3 shows the population per banking company, and Column 4 shows the population per bank office: The larger the population per banking company or per bank office, the *fewer* the relative number of banks or bank offices.

171

EXHIBIT 8.1

BANK AND BRANCH DENSITY AND DEPOSIT CONCENTRATION OF THE UNITED STATES
AND OTHER INDUSTRIAL COUNTRIES: 1982

Country	Number of Commercial Banks	Number of Bank Offices	Population per Bank	Population per Bank Office	Share of Deposits at 5 Largest Banks
United States	14,451	54,235	15,676	4,177	19.2%
West Germany[a]	243	41,000[d]	254,156	1,506	61.8
Canada	11	7,425	2,221,636	3,296	77.7
United Kingdom[b]	35	14,000	1,601,914	4,004	56.8
Japan[c]	86	13,420	1,378,825	8,835	34.5
France	206	40,200	262,913	1,347	76.1
Italy	1,170	11,970	48,987	4,787	35.1
Switzerland	432	5,501	14,682	1,153	46.7

Note: The fact that institutions and banking laws vary greatly from one country to another makes comparisons difficult.

[a]Although West Germany has 243 commercial banks, 6 largely dominate the market. The remaining banks are 99 regional and 138 private institutions. West Germany also has many cooperative banks which provide credit to small industrial firms and the rural population; mortgage banks which provide credit to home and municipal development builders; and cooperative banks owned by trade unions which provide credit to their own members.

[b]The United Kingdom has 296 "recognized banks" though only 35 are commercial banks owned within the country. In addition to the 35 there are 12 discount houses, 25 consulting banks, and 224 branches of foreign banks.

[c]Japan's commercial banks are made up of 13 city banks, 63 regional, 7 trust, and 3 long-term credit banks.

[d]This number includes all branches of all institutions.

Source: R. F. Styron, "The 'New England Experiment' in Interstate Banking," *New England Economic Review*, March-April 1984, 6. Data from *American Banker*, July 25, 1983; *American Banker*, "Top 500," July 28, 1982; *Bankers Almanac of the United Kingdom*, 1981–1982; *Canadian Statistical Review*, 1983; *Deutsche Bundesbank, Annual Report 1983*; *FDIC Changes Among Banks and Branches*, 1982, Statistics on Banking; *OECD Economic Surveys*, 1983; *Commission de Controle des Banques*, June 1982; *International Monetary Fund*, Research Department; various embassy offices, unpublished banking data.

The United States clearly has many more banking companies relative to its population than do other countries. One possible reason is that this simply reflects a higher level of banking service. However, service is a function not of the number of banking companies, but of the number of bank *offices* available to serve the public: Ten offices run by one company will provide much the same service as ten offices run by ten different companies. So Column 4 gives us the population per bank office: The fewer customers per bank office, the higher the level of service we would expect. We see that by this measure the level of service in the

United States is about average. So the very large number of banks in the United States does not mean more service, just a larger number of bank *companies*.[1]

It is particularly revealing to compare the United States with Canada. In many ways Canada is much like the United States: It has about the same standard of living, and it too covers a large geographic area. Since the United States has about 10 times the population of Canada, for it to have the same number of banking companies relative to population, the United States would need about 10 times the number of banks in Canada—about 110. In fact, it has over 14,000. For the United States to have the same number of bank offices relative to population (and thus the same level of service), the United States would need about 74,000. In fact, the number is only about 54,000.

Despite the large number of banking companies in the United States, it might be that a relatively few large ones account for most of the business and that the rest are unimportant. Column 5 shows that this is not so. The 5 largest banks in the United States account for some 20% of all deposits, compared with nearly 80% for the 5 largest banks in Canada. Most other countries on the list are more like Canada than like the United States in this respect. So the United States really does differ in that its banking system is much less concentrated than those found in other countries.

WHY IS THE UNITED STATES SO DIFFERENT?

The reason for the peculiar structure of banking in the United States is more political and historical than economic. The federal form of government divides responsibilities between the states and Washington. The precise nature of that division has always been controversial, particularly with regard to banking.

In the early years of the United States, banks were chartered by special acts of either the state or the federal legislatures. State-chartered banks were limited to operation within the state in which they were chartered. The first national bank chartered by Congress was the First Bank of the United States, which was chartered in 1791. Its charter expired in 1811 and was not renewed. In 1816 Congress chartered the Second Bank of the United States. The charter of the Second Bank expired in 1836, and a bill renewing its charter was vetoed by President Andrew Jackson.

The reason the charters of the two national banks were not renewed is that the banks had become the object of mounting political opposition. National banking was strongly supported by the Federalists, led by Alexander Hamilton, who wished to see a strong federal government and who saw the economic future of the United States in commerce and industry. A federally chartered bank with nationwide branching increased the power of the federal government and increased the mobility of funds, facilitating the sort of urban economic development the Federalists advocated. On the other hand, the anti-Federalists, notable

---

[1]Some 9,000 of the banking companies in the United States in 1982 had only a single office.

among them Thomas Jefferson, opposed a strong federal government and wanted greater power for the states. They wanted the United States to develop a predominantly rural, agricultural economy. Naturally, they did not see a national bank as being in their interest.

Controversy over the national banks was heightened by their monopoly position and by their involvement in partisan politics. Not only were the First and Second Banks free to open branches in any state, but they were also given the *exclusive* right to do so. This monopoly power, plus financial backing from the federal government, soon gave them a dominant position in banking. Indeed, the Second Bank came to control a full third of all banking assets in the country. The national banks were accused of using their considerable economic power to play politics. Their opponents claimed that they were run by Federalists for the benefit of Federalists. They were accused of discriminating against anti-Federalists in making loans, and the Second Bank was accused of using the granting of loans to buy votes for the Federalists.

The national banks were also strongly opposed by state-chartered banks. The latter also often had government-granted monopolies within their states, and they did not want to see their economic rents eroded by competition from the national banks. Since they could hardly state their opposition in these terms, they used instead the argument that interstate banking would redistribute credit away from rural areas and toward the cities.

Experience with the First and Second Banks gave nationwide banking a bad reputation. The lessons drawn from that experience were that nationwide branching was undesirable and that large banks were to be feared. As we shall see in this chapter, those conclusions were almost certainly mistaken. The problems with the First and Second Banks were more attributable to their monopoly position than to interstate branching or size as such. Nothing would have restrained their misbehavior more than a little competition from *other* national banks.

unit bank
Bank consisting of a single banking office.

This same fear of bank power led to state banking laws that limited the right of banks to open branches. These limits varied from state to state. Some states allowed no branching at all, limiting all banks to a single office under a single roof (called a **unit bank**). Others allowed branching within a city, within a county, or even statewide. There was generally no provision to allow the entry of banks from other states.

No more national banks were chartered until 1864. In that year, for reasons related to the financing of the Civil War, Congress passed a National Banking Act that empowered the Comptroller of the Currency (a Treasury official) to grant national bank charters. The act said nothing specific about branching, but to allay the old fears about interstate banking and the concentration of power, the Comptroller limited national banks to a single office. In 1922 the then Comptroller reversed this position and began to allow limited branching. The McFadden Act of 1927 cleared up the legal status of branching, explicitly permitting branches in the city in which the bank's head office was located as long as state-chartered banks were allowed to do the same. A 1933 amendment to the McFadden Act permitted national banks in a given state the same branching allowed state banks. Since state-chartered banks were not allowed to branch across state lines, the law in effect prohibited interstate branching by national banks.

8.2 PROFITABILITY AND SIZE

This web of legal restrictions on the growth of banks has found itself increasingly in conflict with the basic economics of banking. The technology of banking is such that large banks should be more profitable than small ones. To see why this is so, let us recall our discussion in Chapter 5 of the factors that determine a bank's profitability.

Consider a hypothetical bank described by the following balance sheet:

Reserves (R)	Deposits (D)
Loans (L)	Equity (E)

The best measure of the bank's profitability is its return on equity (ROE),

$$ROE = \frac{\pi}{E},$$
[8.1]

where π is profits. Profits are determined by

$$\pi = (L \times i_L) - (D \times i_D) - FC,$$
[8.2]

where

i_L is the realized interest rate earned on loans,
i_D is the cost per dollar of deposits,
FC is fixed costs.[2]

If large banks and small face the same rates on loans and deposits, then their relative profitability depends on three things:

1. *Fixed costs.* The lower these are, relative to the amount of loans and deposits, the higher the profit.

2. *Reserves.* The lower these are, relative to deposits, the more loans that can be made and the higher the profits will be.[3]

---

[2]Banks also earn noninterest income from fees for services they provide, and their costs include the cost of such services.

[3]Remember that reserves are either cash in the bank's vault or deposits at the Fed. Neither of these earns interest, so neither contributes to a bank's profits. Large and small banks have to keep (roughly) the same ratio of *required* reserves, so we are talking about the amount of excess reserves they choose to keep. (Later, we shall see that banks have other ways to ensure liquidity, but that these other ways are also costly.)

3. *Equity.* The lower the equity-to-loan ratio, the higher the return on equity.[4]

Let us look at each of these in more detail.

FIXED COSTS

variable costs
Bank's costs that vary directly with the amount of deposits or loans.

fixed costs
Bank's costs that do not vary directly with the amount of deposits or loans.

indivisible costs
Items of cost that cannot easily be divided.

If a bank takes in an extra $1 million in deposits, it will have to pay more interest and process more checks (implicit interest): These are its **variable costs**. But it will not have to get a bigger building or bigger computer, nor will it have to hire an extra bank president: The costs of these items are therefore fixed. The **fixed costs** of a bank are those costs that do not vary directly with the amount of deposits or the amount of loans.

Fixed costs are often **indivisible costs**. For example, a bank needs a vault whether it has $1 million in deposits or $100 million: It cannot have half a vault. Of course, it can have a smaller or larger vault, but the vault it needs for $100 million in deposits is not much more expensive than the one it needs for $1 million in deposits. The same is true for the bank's building: Banks that are bigger in terms of the amount of their deposits and loans may have bigger buildings or more buildings, but their costs go up much less than proportionally.

Some labor costs are also indivisible. In the past much of a bank's labor cost was associated with the processing of deposit and loan transactions, work that used to be done by hand. Because the amount of such work depended on the amount of deposits and loans, it was a variable cost. Increasingly, this work has become automated and computerized. Now the required computer hardware, and the staff of programmers and systems analysts needed to service it, are indivisible fixed costs.

In addition, in order to provide services like check processing, investment advice, or international banking, a bank needs a trained staff, with special knowledge and skills. To provide the service at all, it needs a minimum number of people working in each area. In a large bank these employees will have more work to do than in a small bank. As a result, it will be less expensive for the large bank to provide the service.

To sum up, larger banks will generally have higher fixed costs than small banks, but because of indivisibilities, these fixed costs will rise less than proportionally with size.

To see the importance of fixed costs in determining profits, consider an example. Suppose we have two identical banks, Tweedledum National and Tweedledee National. Each has precisely the same balance sheet:

TWEEDLEDUM NATIONAL OR TWEEDLEDEE NATIONAL

Reserves	$12m	Deposits	$100m
Loans	94m	Equity	6m

[4]See Chapter 5 for an explanation.

The realized rate on loans is 12% for each and the variable cost per dollar of deposits is 10%. Fixed costs for each bank are $500,000. Profits for each bank are therefore

$$\pi = \$94 \text{ million} \times 0.12 - \$100 \text{ million} \times 0.10 - \$500,000 = \$780,000,$$

and

$$\text{ROE} = \frac{\$780,000}{\$6,000,000} = 0.13, \text{ or } 13\%.$$

Now suppose the two banks merge into one—call it First Tweedle. The balance sheet of the combined bank will be:

FIRST TWEEDLE

Reserves	$ 24m	Deposits	$200m
Loans	188m	Equity	12m

As a result of the merger, there will be a lot of duplication of facilities—two computers, two sets of systems analysts, and so on. By eliminating the duplication—for instance, by using only one computer for the combined business of both banks, and by letting go one set of systems analysts—the fixed costs of the combined bank can be reduced to, say, $700,000.

The profits of First Tweedle will therefore be

$$\pi = \$188 \text{ million} \times 0.12 - \$200 \text{ million} \times 0.10 - \$700,000 = \$1,860,000.$$

and its return on equity will increase to

$$\text{ROE} = \frac{\$1,860,000}{\$12,000,000} = 0.155, \text{ or } 15.5\%.$$

As an illustration of these sorts of cost savings, in 1988, when Bank of New York ($23.7 billion in assets at year-end 1987) took over Irving Trust ($23.9 billion), it estimated that *total* costs of the combined bank would be 20% below those of the two banks operating separately.[5]

RESERVES

From our discussion of reserves in Chapter 5, recall that because of pooling, new deposits and withdrawals tend to offset one another. On some days, however, there will be an excess of withdrawals, and a bank will need a source of liquidity

[5]Since total costs include both fixed and variable costs, the decrease in fixed costs alone was presumably much more than 20%.

to deal with this. However, *the bigger the pool, the better it works*. This means that a larger bank will need to worry less about liquidity, and it will need to spend less, proportionally, to get the liquidity it requires.

For example, suppose that each of Tweedledum and Tweedledee carries excess reserves sufficient to cover possible excess withdrawals on 19 days out of 20 (on the remaining day the bank turns to the federal funds market). The amount of excess reserves required by each bank is, say, $1 million or 1% of its $100 million in deposits. If the combined bank, First Tweedle, also wants to be able to cover possible excess withdrawals on 19 days out of 20, it will need to hold excess reserves of about $1.4 million, or only 0.7% of its $200 million in deposits. The reason it needs proportionally less is that on many days when the Tweedledum half of the combined bank has a large excess of withdrawals, the Tweedledee half will have an offsetting excess of deposits, and vice versa.[6]

Hence First Tweedle can reduce its reserve ratio from the 12% held by each of Tweedledum and Tweedledee (11% required plus 1% excess) to 11.7% for the combined bank (11% required plus 0.7% excess) and have the same probability of being short of reserves. Its balance sheet becomes:

FIRST TWEEDLE

Reserves	$ 23.4m	Deposits	$200m
Loans	188.6m	Equity	12m

Profits rise to $2,372,000 and the return on equity to 16.1%.[7]

EQUITY

We saw in Chapter 5 that the lower the equity-to-loan ratio, the higher the return on equity. We also saw that a certain minimum of equity is needed to protect the bank against loan losses and possible insolvency. But this cushion of equity is only the final defense: The primary protection against loan losses is diversification, another consequence of pooling.

Here too, the bigger the pool, the better it works. If the loans of Tweedledum and Tweedledee are not related, it is unlikely that a bad year for Tweedledum's loans will also be a bad year for Tweedledee's. As a result, First Tweedle can hold an equity cushion smaller than the combined equity of both banks without

---

[6]Daily net withdrawals from Tweedledum or Tweedledee have a normal distribution with an expected value of zero and a standard deviation of $600,000. There is therefore a 5% chance that net withdrawals will exceed 1.65 standard deviations, or $1 million on any given day. Daily net withdrawals from First Tweedle, the combined bank, have a standard deviation that is $\sqrt{2}$ x $600,000, and there will therefore be a 5% chance that it exceeds $\sqrt{2}$ x $1 million = $1.4 million. In general, the necessary amount of excess reserves rises with the square root of the size of the bank.

[7]Banks do not in reality meet their liquidity needs to any significant extent by holding excess reserves. We shall look at the actual methods they use in Chapter 12. Nonetheless, ensuring liquidity, however it is done, is costly. As a result, because large banks need less liquidity, they have lower costs.

increasing the chance of insolvency. If equity can be reduced by \$3 million, the balance sheet becomes:

FIRST TWEEDLE

Reserves	\$ 23.4m	Deposits	\$200m
Loans	185.6m	Equity	9m

Profits become \$1,572,000 and return on equity rises to 17.5%.

Merging banks improves diversification in other ways too. For diversification to work its magic, the risk of default on different loans must be *unrelated*. For example, a rural bank with a large number of small loans out to local farmers may *look* diversified, but it is not. Many of the events that cause one borrower to default—a drought or a fall in crop prices—will most likely cause many others to default too. The bank's loan portfolio is really more like one big loan than many small ones. Hence combining banks specializing in different *types* of lending will be particularly beneficial. For example, combining two rural banks in different parts of the country, one lending to dairy farmers and the other to orange growers, may reduce considerably the risk of insolvency of the combined bank.

ECONOMIES OF SCALE: WHAT IS THE EVIDENCE?

We have seen, then, that there are two main reasons why we would expect large banks to be more profitable than small ones. First, the indivisible nature of most fixed costs means that large banks can provide the same services more cheaply than small banks. Second, there are financial returns to scale: The pooling that underlies the management of liquidity and risk works better, the bigger the pool.

Of course, there are also diseconomies of scale. Large organizations become increasingly bureaucratic and difficult to control. These difficulties may lead to expensive errors if control is too loose—a single employee losing millions on some unauthorized deal—or to a lack of flexibility in the face of changing circumstances if controls are too tight. At some point the diseconomies of scale will balance the economies, so that banks beyond a certain size may have no significant advantage. We could call this point the **minimum efficient scale.**

minimum efficient scale Point at which the diseconomies of scale balance the economies.

A number of studies have looked for evidence of economies of scale in banking through statistical examination of bank costs and profits.[8] The results have been mixed: Some have found evidence of economies of scale, but many have not. Estimates of the minimum efficient scale have ranged from \$25 million to

[8]This work is reviewed in M. K. Lewis and K. T. Davis, *Domestic and International Banking*, Cambridge, MA: M.I.T. Press, 1987. A number of studies and surveys of studies are cited, and evidence is provided that small banks are failing at higher rates than larger banks, in S. Shaffer, "Challenges to Small Banks' Survival," *Business Review*, Federal Reserve Bank of Philadelphia, September-October 1989.

$25 billion. Even if we accept the $25 million number, some 4,000 banks in the United States in 1988 were below this size.

The interpretation of the statistical evidence, however, is somewhat problematic. What we would like to find out is whether the *technology* of banking exhibits economies of scale: That is, can large banks, *in principle*, operate more cheaply than small ones? What the statistical evidence tells us is whether the profits or costs of *actual* banks of different size in the United States differ. That is not at all the same thing.

If banks are not permitted to expand freely, they will do their best to adapt: They will try to achieve what economies of scale they can by cooperation *between* banks. For example, as we shall see presently, many of the economies of scale are captured by the **correspondent relationship** between large and small banks. As a result of this adaptation, the observed differences in cost are much smaller than the differences inherent in the technology: The correspondent relationship lowers costs for small banks. However, these interbank arrangements may be a relatively inefficient way of achieving economies of scale. Were banks permitted to expand, we might observe costs lower than those we actually do observe.

In fact, the best real-world evidence for economies of scale is the concentrated structure of banking in all countries in which such concentration has not been prevented by law, as well as the unceasing efforts of U.S. banks to get around the laws that limit their expansion.[9]

correspondent relationship
Interbank relationship involving deposits and various services.

|8.3| LIVING WITHIN THE LAW

Because of restrictions on geographic expansion in the United States, banks have tried to capture potential economies of scale *between* banks, rather than *within* a single large bank as banks do in other countries.

THE CORRESPONDENT RELATIONSHIP

correspondent bank
Large bank that provides smaller bank with special services.

respondent bank
Small bank that receives special services from a larger bank.

The primary vehicle for capturing economies of scale between banks is the correspondent relationship between large and small banks. Many important services that large banks offer simply cannot be offered economically by a small bank. As a result, a small bank will usually have a long-run relationship with one or more large banks. The large bank is called the **correspondent** and the small bank the **respondent**.

The services that correspondents provide include:

1. *Transactions services.* Check processing today is highly automated, and the necessary equipment is expensive. Because the volume of checks handled by

---

[9]Besides the returns to *scale* that we have examined in this section, there are also returns to *scope*: It may be cheaper to produce certain products together rather than separately. For example, cars, trucks, and locomotives have many common components. We shall see in Chapter 18 that such economies of scope may exist in the financial sector too.

a small bank does not justify such an investment, it will send its checks to its correspondent for processing. Similarly, the fixed costs of joining the wire-transfer system are substantial. For a small bank with little demand for wire transfers, it makes more sense to rely on its correspondent for access.[10]

2. *Financial-market transactions.* Trading government securities, and other types of securities that we shall encounter later, requires access to the book-entry system and to Fedwire. When customers of a small bank or the small bank itself wish to trade such securities, they rely on the correspondent to carry out the transactions and safeguard the securities.

3. *Market information.* Many small banks have trust departments that manage customers' investment portfolios and provide investment advice. The correspondent will provide a small bank with most of the necessary market information.

4. *International banking.* When one of its customers needs foreign exchange or a letter of credit, a small bank turns to its correspondent to provide this service. (Try selling the French francs left over from your European vacation to a small-town bank, and you will see that it has no experience with foreign exchange and turns rapidly to its correspondent for help.)

5. *Loan-sharing.* Sometimes a customer of a small bank will want a loan that is too large for the bank to handle. The small bank will turn to its correspondent to take on part of the loan. This arrangement is called an **overline**. Sometimes it goes the other way: Even a large bank may face a loan request that is too large for it to take on alone. In such a case, it will farm out parts of the loan to its many respondent banks. This arrangement is called a **loan participation**.

overline Correspondent's assumption of part of a respondent's loan.

loan participation Respondent's assumption of part of a correspondent's loan.

correspondent balances Zero-interest deposits that a respondent holds with its correspondents.

Respondents have various ways to pay for the services provided by the correspondent. Payment used to be made largely through **correspondent balances**: The respondent keeps funds in a zero-interest demand deposit with the correspondent and the interest forgone represents the payment. For example, if Smalltown Bank keeps $1 million with Metropolis, Metropolis can make $1 million in loans, the interest on which pays for the services Metropolis provides to Smalltown. In recent years, for reasons we shall see in Chapter 9, this practice has become less popular. Respondents increasingly pay fees for the services they receive and receive interest on funds kept with the correspondent.

The balances that small banks keep with their correspondents are useful for both parties. For the small banks, they are an important source of liquidity: They

[10]Before 1980 banks that were not members of the Federal Reserve System did not generally have direct access to the Fed's check-clearing services or to Fedwire, but had to go through a correspondent that was a member. The Fed handled directly about 40% of the some 35 billion checks a year that cleared through the system, and correspondents made some $1.7 billion a year processing the rest. With the passage of the DIDMC Act of 1980, as partial compensation for the imposition of reserve requirements, the Fed's services became available to all depository institutions—some 44,000 versus the 5,500 member banks. Although the Fed was now required to charge explicitly for its services, it found itself in direct competition for check-clearing business with the large correspondent banks. The latter were not pleased.

can easily be drawn down if there is a net outflow of customer deposits. (The correspondent will also lend to the respondent if necessary when the latter is short of liquidity.) For the large banks, the balances of their respondents are an important source of funds. Large banks often have hundreds, even thousands, of respondent banks and the total balances can be substantial: The banks with the largest amounts of correspondent balances are listed in Exhibit 8.2. This source of funds is both relatively inexpensive and, since the funds are unlikely to be withdrawn in a hurry, relatively stable.

Thus the correspondent relationship captures both technological and financial economies of scale. Check processing and financial-market transactions are examples of the former. The sharing of loans to increase diversification and the use of correspondent balances to increase liquidity are examples of the latter.

FRANCHISING

franchising
Granting a right to a company to market the franchiser's goods or services in a specific territory, using the franchise name and methods.

Franchising is a refinement of the correspondent relationship. Like that relationship, it achieves many potential economies of scale without actual integration of ownership.

Franchising is common in fast food and in other consumer services—McDonald's, Pizza Hut, Midas Muffler, and 7-Eleven are all well-known examples. The way it works is this. A local businessman, the franchisee, pays the parent corporation, the franchiser, for the right to set up a company using the franchise name and methods. The franchiser provides training, equipment, quality control, and national advertising. It receives in exchange a fee or a share in the profits. The local franchise, however, remains a separate company owned by the franchisee.

This idea of franchising has spread to banking. The most active franchiser is First Interstate Bank of Los Angeles, which by the end of 1988 had franchised 44 banks with 143 banking offices in 11 states and the District of Columbia—for example, First Interstate Bank of Wisconsin and First Interstate Bank of Golden, Colorado. Banks that become franchises adopt the First Interstate name and receive advertising, management training and advice, access to a teller-machine network, and a variety of other services. However, they retain their independent ownership. They therefore do not violate the law against interstate banking.

EDGE ACT CORPORATIONS

Edge Act corporations
Subsidiary corporations set up by U.S. commercial banks to engage in international banking.

One special kind of bank is allowed to operate across state lines. The Edge Act of 1919 allows the federal government to charter special-purpose banks engaged solely in international banking. The purpose of the law was to encourage international trade and to increase the role of American banks in its financing.

These **Edge Act corporations** are allowed to take deposits from foreign sources, deal in foreign exchange, lend to finance foreign trade, and engage in a

EXHIBIT 8.2

BANKS WITH LARGEST CORRESPONDENT BALANCES (JUNE, 1988)

Rank	Bank	Demand Deposits Due to All Banks (Millions of Dollars)
1	Citibank, New York	$3,010
2	Chase Manhattan Bank, New York	2,697
3	Bankers Trust Co., New York	2,606
4	Manufacturers Hanover Trust, New York	2,250
5	Irving Trust Co., New York	1,839
6	Bank of America, San Francisco	1,212
7	Morgan Guaranty Trust, New York	1,118
8	Bank of New York	946
9	Security Pacific National Bank, Los Angeles	851
10	First Interstate Bank, Los Angeles	814
11	First National Bank of Chicago	746
12	Chemical Bank, New York	744
13	Union Bank, Los Angeles	682
14	Philadelphia National Bank	670
15	National Bank of Detroit	510
16	NCNB Texas National Bank, Dallas	509
17	Harris Trust & Savings, Chicago	456
18	Continental Illinois, Chicago	455
19	Mellon Bank, Pittsburgh	426
20	First National Bank, Boston	370

Source: *American Banker*, Nov. 29, 1988.

variety of overseas operations. They may not take deposits from U.S. residents or make general commercial loans, and their deposits are not insured.

What makes them attractive to banks is that they are exempt from the general prohibition on interstate banking: A bank can set up an Edge Act subsidiary that may then open branches wherever it pleases. Although they are not allowed to take deposits from U.S. residents or to make loans unrelated to foreign trade, banks naturally try to interpret the range of permitted activities as broadly as they can.

Many large banks have Edge Act subsidiaries—79 were in existence in 1988 with about 140 offices.[11] Edge Act corporations are particularly popular as a way for banks outside New York to obtain a presence in New York City, the primary center for international banking, and as a way for New York City banks to set up in secondary financial centers such as Chicago, Los Angeles, Houston, and Miami.

[11]The number of Edge Act subsidiaries is down from 143 in 1983. Some have been replaced by other vehicles for international banking that we shall encounter in Chapter 11. Others have been closed because of a general diminution of interest in foreign lending, about which we shall also learn in Chapter 11.

|8.4| GETTING AROUND THE LAW

Given the strong economic incentives for bank expansion and the laws standing in their way, we would expect to find banks using every means available to get around the laws. And they do. Over the years banks have come up with a number of ingenious schemes. We now look at some of them.

BANK HOLDING COMPANIES

holding company
Corporation formed for the purpose of owning or holding stock in other corporations.

Consider the two scenarios illustrated in Exhibit 8.3. Two banks, Bank A and Bank B, are located in two adjacent states. In Scenario 1, Bank A buys Bank B: This is illegal, because it violates the prohibition against interstate banking. In Scenario 2, Bank A sets up a shell corporation called a **holding company** that becomes the legal owner of Bank A. A holding company is a corporation that does no actual business itself: Its sole function is the legal ownership of other corporations. The holding company now buys Bank B. Because the holding company is not itself a bank, the purchase is quite legal.

multibank holding company
Corporation that owns more than a single bank.

This type of holding company, one that owns more than a single bank, is called a **multibank holding company**. Multibank holding companies have existed since the turn of the century, and they have been particularly popular in states, largely in the Midwest and Northwest, that restricted branching even within the state.

Regulators caught up with this maneuver in 1956, when the Douglas Amendment to the Bank Holding Company Act prohibited this method of expansion across state lines unless explicitly permitted by the states involved.[12] However, the law did contain a "grandfather clause" that permitted multibank holding companies already operating across state lines to continue to do so.

After some consolidation, there remained for many years only 7 major multibank holding companies operating across state lines. The largest of these is First Interstate Corporation of Los Angeles, which in 1989 operated 26 banks in 14 different western states, with over 1,000 domestic offices (in addition to the offices of its franchises). First Interstate's $58 billion in assets made it one of the 10 largest banks in the country.[13]

one-bank holding companies
Corporations that own only a single bank.

In addition to multibank holding companies, there are **one-bank holding companies** that own only a single bank. A one-bank holding company may set up subsidiaries (corporations owned by the holding company) that are not themselves legally banks or owned by a bank and that can therefore engage in activities

---

[12]The main purpose of the Bank Holding Company Act was to restrain the growth of bank holding companies and to limit their ability to engage in nonbanking activities. The act was the result of a growing fear of concentrated financial power, a fear largely stimulated by one giant bank holding company in the West—Giannini's Transamerica Corporation. Transamerica owned Bank of America and many other banks in several western states: in 1947 it had 43% of all deposits in California, 45% in Oregon, and 79% in Nevada. Transamerica also owned many nonbanking enterprises.

[13]Transamerica was broken up after 1956. First Interstate consists of most of the banks it owned, except Bank of America.

E X H I B I T 8.3

TWO DIFFERENT
WAYS FOR ONE BANK
TO TAKE OVER
ANOTHER

The acquisition of Bank B by a
bank located in a different
state, Bank A, is not allowed
(Scenario 1). However, by
setting up a holding company
(Scenario 2), Bank A can get
around the law.

Scenario 1

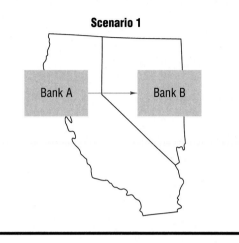

Scenario 2

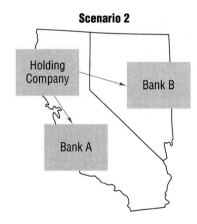

prohibited a bank. Some dealers in government securities (see Chapter 7) are subsidiaries of bank holding companies. We shall see other examples later on.

In 1987 there were 10,279 firms engaged in banking. Of these, 985 were multibank holding companies: They owned 4,465 banks among them, accounted for 70% of total assets of all banks, and their average size was $1,850 million. Another 4,919 firms were one-bank holding companies: They accounted for 21% of total assets, and their average size was $110 million. The 4,375 remaining firms were not holding companies at all: They accounted for only 9% of total assets, and their average size was only $50 million.

Chain banking is a less formal variation on the idea of a multibank holding company. Under this arrangement, an individual or group of individuals owns two or more banks directly, without the benefit of a holding company. This idea,

chain banking
Ownership of two or more banks by an individual or group without the benefit of a holding company.

which also dates from the turn of the century, proved particularly popular in Illinois and Iowa (both of which used to prohibit any branching at all); some 70 such chains still exist in these two states.

NONBANK BANKS

The ban on interstate banking prevents a bank from setting up branches in other states. So how about setting up a branch that is not *legally* a bank branch at all, but is as close to one as we can make it? The legal definition of a bank (in the Bank Holding Company Act of 1956) is an institution that "accepts demand deposits and makes commercial loans." So, if we set up a branch that *either* takes demand deposits (and channels the funds back to us) *or* makes commercial loans (using funds that we provide), but not both, we have something that is not legally speaking a bank. If our branch accepts demand deposits but does not make commercial loans, then we have what is called a **nonbank bank** or *consumer bank*. If we do not accept demand deposits, we have what is called a **nonbank office**. Nonbank banks need a bank charter, nonbank offices do not.

Nonbank banks and offices may be set up either by buying a bank and stripping it of its deposits or its loans, or by opening an office that is from the beginning a nonbank. In addition, many large banks have **nonbank subsidiaries** that engage in activities other than banking. By 1983, 139 bank holding companies were operating 382 nonbanks of various kinds with 5,500 offices outside their home states.

Pressure to restrain the growth of nonbank banks has increased. From 1984 to 1987 they were in a kind of legislative limbo, with a freeze on new charters, and in 1987 Congress passed the Competitive Equality Banking Act prohibiting the opening of any new nonbank banks. Those already in existence were grandfathered—166 existed in 1989—but their assets were allowed to grow by no more than 7% a year. Nonbank offices of various kinds that do not take deposits remain legal.

TELLER MACHINES

Generally, people want their banking services close by. In particular, they want to be able to withdraw cash and to deposit checks conveniently. That used to mean that in order for a bank to have any chance of getting your business, it had to have a branch in your neighborhood. Automated teller machines (ATMs) have changed that. ATMs can dispense cash, accept deposits, and conclude various other transactions at locations far removed from the bank itself. Moreover, the courts have ruled that ATMs are *not* bank branches.

A number of banks have used ATMs to establish a presence in locations that would not otherwise be open to them because of the ban on interstate banking (see " 'Bank' Tops List of Names to Avoid at Citicorp Sales Offices in Omaha").

nonbank bank
Financial institution that accepts deposits but does not make loans.

nonbank office
Financial institution that does not accept deposits.

nonbank subsidiaries
Companies wholly owned by bank holding companies but having no banking functions.

'BANK' TOPS LIST OF NAMES TO AVOID AT CITICORP SALES OFFICES IN OMAHA

By Daniel Hertzberg

Staff Reporter of The Wall Street Journal

Some people in Omaha, Nebraska, may think they're in a bank when they visit the office of the local Citicorp subsidiary. But the New York banking giant insists they're wrong.

The Citicorp Centers that opened earlier this year at two shopping centers are really "sales offices," a spokesman says. "This is not a branch," he stresses.

Good Reason

The Citicorp spokesman has good reason to make the point. After all, banks are generally barred from setting up out-of-state branches that accept deposits from the public.

But customers in the Omaha sales offices can mail deposits to Citicorp's Citibank (South Dakota) subsidiary from mailboxes in the vestibules; Citicorp Center employees will even provide a stamped envelope. And customers can get cash from their ac-

counts in South Dakota by using a Citibank credit card at one of the automated teller machines.

Some Nebraska bankers are up in arms: Citicorp, they contend, is illegally collecting deposits in the state.

"They look like a bank, they offer all the bank services, they advertise like a bank," says William Brandt, general counsel of the Nebraska Bankers Association. "The only conclusion we have is they are a bank."

'Slick Operation'

Roger Beverage, the state's banking director, says Citicorp is "a slick operation." He notes that sales offices don't physically take money and machines, not people, dispense the cash.

Still, he worries that Citicorp "is taking money out of Nebraska and sending it to South Dakota. Nebraska has a tough enough time keeping its capital as it is."

Citicorp is offering depositors in Omaha interest rates on certificates of deposit that are about $1\frac{1}{2}$ percentage points higher than those at local banks. Mr. Beverage says, "They are flooding the Omaha TV market with very impressive spots."

Mr. Brandt says there are rumors Citicorp is seeking $80 million in deposits from Omaha by the end of the year. "By Nebraska standards, that's a lot of money," he says.

The New York bank won't comment.

Source: Daniel Hertzberg, "'Bank' Tops List of Names to Avoid at Citicorp Sales Offices in Omaha," *The Wall Street Journal*, October 23, 1984. Reprinted by permission of The Wall Street Journal, © Dow Jones & Company, Inc. 1983. All Rights Reserved Worldwide.

FOREIGN BANKS: OUTSIDE THE LAW?

Before 1978 banks outside the United States enjoyed an enormous loophole in the regulations governing interstate branching. Many states allowed foreign banks to open a branch, and such a branch would then be regulated by the state more or less in the same way as a bank chartered in that state. Since such a foreign bank was not a national bank, it did not fall under the jurisdiction of the McFadden Act. There was therefore no barrier to its setting up branches in this fashion in as many different states as it pleased.

Foreign banks were not slow to take advantage. Growth was particularly rapid in the 1970s: From 1972 to 1979 the number of foreign banks operating in the United States grew from 209 to 328. The largest contingents were from Japan, the United Kingdom, and Canada, but many other countries were also represented. Most foreign banks were located in the major financial centers—in New York, California, Illinois, and Florida. The 20 foreign banks with the most assets in the United States are listed in Exhibit 8.4.

E x h i b i t 8.4

FOREIGN BANKS WITH THE MOST ASSETS IN THE UNITED STATES:
DECEMBER 31, 1987

U.S. Ranking	Bank	Home Country	Number of U.S. Offices[a]	Assets (Billions of Dollars)[b]
1	Mitsubishi Bank	Japan	7	32.6
2	Bank of Tokyo	Japan	11	28.7
3	Fuji Bank Limited	Japan	7	27.0
4	Hong Kong and Shanghai Bank	Hong Kong	12	25.7
5	Dai-Ichi Kangyo	Japan	5	23.3
6	Industrial Bank of Japan	Japan	7	21.8
7	Sanwa Bank	Japan	7	20.8
8	Sumitomo Bank	Japan	6	19.1
9	Bank of Montreal	Canada	14	17.9
10	Swiss Bank Corporation	Switzerland	6	17.0
11	National Westminster Bank	United Kingdom	6	15.4
12	Tokai Bank	Japan	5	14.8
13	Standard and Chartered	United Kingdom	8	12.6
14	Mitsui Bank	Japan	5	10.8
15	Daiwa Bank	Japan	4	10.2
16	Bank of Nova Scotia	Canada	7	10.1
17	Banca Nazionale Del Lavoro	Italy	5	9.6
18	Barclays Group	United Kingdom	13	9.2
19	Banco di Roma	Italy	4	9.0
20	Sumitomo Trust and Banking Corporation	Japan	3	8.9

[a]Counts each U.S. subsidiary bank as one office, although the bank may have numerous branches of its own.

[b]Includes all assets of U.S. branches and agencies as well as all assets of subsidiary U.S. banks.
Source: J. V. Houpt, "International Trends for U.S. Banks and Banking Markets," Board of Governors of the Federal Reserve System, Staff Study 15b, May 1988.

A foreign bank—for example, Industrial Bank of Japan (IBJ)—can set up in the United States either by opening a branch or by setting up a subsidiary. A branch is the more common alternative. IBJ's branches provide services to Japanese companies trading in the United States, engage in international banking, and make commercial loans to U.S. companies. Typically, however, they do not take consumer deposits or do business with U.S. consumers. To get into consumer banking in the United States, IBJ would need a branch network, a local identity, and federal deposit insurance. The easiest way to get all three is to buy a U.S. bank and to run it as a subsidiary.

By 1986 foreign banks accounted for over a quarter of all bank loans to business (commercial and industrial loans). Growth was most rapid in New York City, the nation's financial center, and on the West Coast. In 1988 a third of bank assets in California were in foreign-owned banks; four of the ten largest banks in California were Japanese or Japanese-owned (see "Besides Doing Business in U.S., the Japanese Increasingly Finance It" on page 190).

The loophole in the interstate banking regulations was closed by the International Banking Act of 1978. Under that act a foreign bank was required to select one state as its "home state" and could not then branch outside that state. (A grandfather clause allowed banks with existing multistate operations to keep them.) The act also closed some other loopholes. Before 1978 foreign banks were generally not subject to reserve requirements, were not required to have deposit insurance, and were allowed (unlike domestic banks) to own affiliates that traded securities. The act extended to foreign banks operating in the United States most regulations that applied to domestic banks.[13]

8.5 GETTING RID OF THE LAW

Under the pressure of the often successful attempts by major banks to get around the laws against interstate banking, those laws themselves have been crumbling. Medium-sized local banks have been pressing the states to permit some form of interstate banking, so that they too could benefit from the economies of scale that have been enjoyed by the major banks. Note that the Bank Holding Company Act of 1956 made it clear that state laws take precedence: Anything the states allow in the way of interstate banking is fine with the federal government.

In 1975 Maine became the first state to open itself to full interstate banking. The law originally required **reciprocity**: Any bank from any state was allowed to open branches in Maine, so long as that bank's home state allowed Maine banks to open branches there. Maine later waived reciprocity in the hope of attracting out-of-state banks that would help its economic development. By 1988 out-of-state banks accounted for almost 90% of Maine's banking business.

reciprocity
Mutual granting of privileges.

REGIONAL INTERSTATE BANKING

In 1982 Massachusetts also passed an interstate banking law. But this law was very different from the Maine law: It allowed reciprocal interstate banking, but *only* with the five other New England states—Connecticut, Rhode Island, Maine, New Hampshire, and Vermont.

To understand the reasons for this restriction, we need to distinguish between three different size classes of commercial bank. The largest banks are

---

[13]Of the 79 Edge Act corporations in 1988, 18 were owned by foreign banks. Since they are now subject to the same geographic restrictions as U.S. banks, foreign banks have started to take an interest in Edge Act subsidiaries.

BESIDES DOING BUSINESS IN U.S., THE JAPANESE INCREASINGLY FINANCE IT

By Michael R. Sesit

Staff Reporter of The Wall Street Journal

The chief financial officer of Gulf States Paper Corp. recalls the day a couple of years ago when someone suggested he try a lender called Industrial Bank of Japan. "I'd never heard of IBJ," says the executive, James O'Brien. "My first question was: Do they lend in dollars?"

The answer was yes. And five months later, the Tuscaloosa, Alabama, paper company borrowed $15 million from IBJ. "They sent down two Japanese guys from the New York office and analyzed the numbers to death," Mr. O'Brien says. In 25 years, the firm's New York bank "never learned our business like the Japanese did. The joke around here was if we didn't understand something in our financial statements, we'd just ask the Japanese to explain it."

The Japanese are on the march again, this time in American banking. They aren't trying anything fancy; their banks here rarely indulge in "creative financing" or other razzmatazz. But by offering standard commercial-banking services—loans, letters of credit, a little leasing—and usually executing them with precision, they are making big inroads.

Nine California banks now are Japanese-owned, and another one soon may be; an unidentified Japanese bank is negotiating a possible purchase of Union Bank in Los Angeles from Britain's Standard Chartered Bank. In Tampa, Florida, Japanese banks have just helped finance the buy-out of Jim Walter Corp.

In the Club

By the middle of last year, in fact, Japanese banks accounted for 9% of U.S. banking assets, the Federal Reserve says. That's more than double their share at the beginning of the decade. Their loans and other assets in this country added up to $270 billion at midyear. While part of this is more or less captive business with Japanese companies here, the sum nonetheless is almost as much as the combined total of J.P. Morgan and Citicorp.

Nobuya Hagura can't help remarking on the change. Twenty years ago, as a Japanese bank representative in the U.S., he tried to join the Wall Street Club atop Chase Manhattan Plaza in New York. U.S. bankers and businessmen who were members wouldn't recommend him, he says. Now he is the president of Dai-Ichi Kangyo, a lender to companies as American as Coca-Cola and General Motors—and the largest bank in the world.

Learning U.S. ways hasn't always been easy. When Japanese banks first tried the U.S. market, says Peter Pawlak, a Sanwa Bank vice president in Atlanta, they would do things like present a borrower with "a five-pound stack of paper" to read and sign, documents laboriously translated from Japanese. Not surprisingly, customers balked. But one strength of the Japanese is flexibility, and they quickly whittled down their paper work.

That didn't get them over the personal-relations hurdles, though. "Very often, a company in the South wants to talk to a Southerner or an American," observes Gregory Brusberg, a senior vice president of Citizens & Southern National Bank in Atlanta. "Very often here, an initial question is: 'Where'd you go to school?'"

Sumitomo Bank tried to prepare Masao Harada to work in the U.S. by sending him to a Dale Carnegie course in Osaka. There, among other exercises, he had to play the role of a carnival barker and practice shouting "Hurry, hurry, hurry—come to the show." He did it, but when he first got to America, he still shrank from answering the phone.

Many Japanese banks have hired local bankers to call on potential customers, but that can be overdone too. The first U.S. calling officer Fuji Bank sent to Georgia-Pacific acted "like he

money center banks
Largest banks located in major financial centers and involved in international banking and the financial markets.

located in the major financial centers—mainly New York City but also Chicago and San Francisco. They differ from other banks not only in their size, but also in the range of their activities: They are far more involved in international banking and in the financial markets. These banks are called **money center banks**. Intermediate in size and in range of activities between these and the thousands of small local banks, there are a few hundred **regional banks**, located in regional financial centers, such as Boston, Los Angeles, and Charlotte.

just fell off a turnip truck," says Danny Huff, the director of corporate finance at Georgia-Pacific Corp. "He tried to outdo the most good ol' boy I've ever seen. He didn't last long."

The newcomers have had better luck when they have tapped into their Japanese business connections. IBJ, for instance, introduced a Japanese steel company, Yamato Kogyo Co., to a U.S. steelmaker, Nucor Corp. of Charlotte, North Carolina. Then it worked patiently for two years to help them agree on a joint venture. Now they are building a $200 million plant in Arkansas, and at some point IBJ figures to get some lending business out of the deal.

"We should be very courteous," says Takeo Otsubo, a senior vice president of an IBJ unit in New York. "In Tokyo, we want foreigners to respect Japanese customs. We should expand our business here and take advantage of opportunities, but we shouldn't strut and spread money."

Source: Michael R. Sesit, "Besides Doing Business in U.S., the Japanese Increasingly Finance It," *The Wall Street Journal*, January 28, 1988. Reprinted by permission of The Wall Street Journal, © Dow Jones & Company, Inc. 1988. All Rights Reserved Worldwide.

JAPAN'S SHARE OF LENDING
Assets of Japanese Banks in the United States as a percentage of total U.S. banking assets.

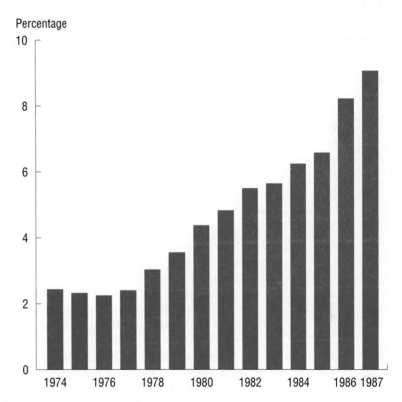

Source: Federal Reserve Board.

Massachusetts is home to a number of these regional banks—for example, Bank of Boston, with $34 billion in assets, and Bank of New England, with $22 billion.[14] Banks such as these wanted to expand and to reap the benefits of economies of scale without being swallowed up themselves by the giant money

regional banks
Medium-sized banks located in regional financial centers.

[14]Year-end 1986.

center banks. The sort of regional interstate arrangement proposed by Massachu-setts would enable them do so while keeping out their most feared competitors.

Connecticut and Rhode Island proved receptive to the idea, since each had regional banks of its own that would benefit—for example, Hartford National, with $14 billion in assets, and Fleet Financial Group of Providence, with $12 billion. They soon came on board with regional reciprocal laws like that of Massachusetts.

The northern New England states, however, were less enthusiastic. To see why, imagine you own a small bank in Vermont. Its current market value of $2 million exceeds its $1 million book value because of its excellent profits.[15] Profits are high because there is relatively little local competition. However, once inter-state banking is allowed, larger banks will move in, either buying a local bank or setting up a subsidiary, and the increased competition will lower the market value of your bank to $1.5 million. So if you do not sell out, you stand to lose.

If you do sell out, your bank may be worth as much as $2.5 million to a potential buyer, even in the more competitive environment. The reason? Econo-mies of scale. Your bank is worth more as part of a larger bank than it is standing alone. However, just because your bank is worth $2.5 million to a potential purchaser does not mean that you will get that amount. It is all a matter of bargaining: For you, anything over $1.5 million is better than not selling; for the purchaser, anything less than $2.5 million is a good deal.

Clearly, the more competition there is to buy your bank, the better for you. If only two or three Boston banks are bidding, you may not get much more than $1.5 million. However, if a dozen or so large banks from all over the country start to take an interest, you are much more likely to get something close to $2.5 million. You would therefore like to see the bidding open to *all* potential buyers—not just the Boston banks, but the New York banks too.

The smaller banks of Vermont and New Hampshire were therefore divided in their attitudes toward regional interstate banking. Many did not wish to be taken over by larger banks at all and opposed interstate banking altogether. Others were ready to be taken over but did not think that *regional* interstate banking was in their own best interests.

In a political compromise, Vermont passed a law in 1987 that allowed regional interstate banking beginning in 1988, and then full national interstate banking beginning in 1990. Many other states have passed similar two-stage laws. New Hampshire has passed a regional interstate banking law.

Naturally enough, when the Massachusetts law was first proposed, the New York banks were furious. With dark mutterings about "the Confederate States of New England," they challenged its constitutionality in court. However, in 1985, the Supreme Court upheld the law, and the idea has since spread to other parts of the country that also have strong regional financial centers, such as the Southeast, the Midwest, and the Northwest.

---

[15]The distinction between market value of equity and book value was discussed in Chapter 5. The difference between the two values is "the value of the bank charter," or goodwill.

By 1989 some 45 states had passed some form of interstate banking legislation. That legislation is summarized in Exhibit 8.5. Many states, but not all, had also abolished within-state restrictions on banking. Current state laws are summarized in Exhibit 8.6.

Notice that a number of states already have national interstate banking laws on their books. Not surprisingly, one of them is New York State. But even New York banks are worried about competition. Following the passage of New York's interstate banking law in 1982, New York began negotiations with California for a reciprocal agreement. These negotiations collapsed when New York suggested the following "irresistible" deal: New York banks would be completely free to set up anywhere in California, and California banks would be completely free to set up anywhere in New York State—except in New York City![16]

THE RISE OF THE "SUPERREGIONALS"

Regional interstate banking has given a major boost to large banks in the regional financial centers. Several have proven so successful that they have come to be known as **superregionals**.[17] These banks now approach the money center banks in size and often exceed them in profitability (see Exhibit 8.7 and "Nothing Could Be Finer, to Bank in Carolina" on page 197). Because these superregionals no longer need to be protected from competition from the money center banks, there is now a trend toward full national interstate banking in some of the regions. In particular, Ohio allowed national reciprocal interstate banking in 1988.

superregionals
Large non-money-center banks that have expanded across state lines.

At the same time the regional agreements were allowing the superregionals to expand rapidly, the money center banks were having a hard time keeping up with the pace of expansion. Nonbank banks had been their principal method of getting around the regional agreements, but this was closed to them after 1984.

A new avenue did open up, however, as a result of the savings and loan crisis. To relieve the burden on the federal government from bailing out failed S&Ls, the Garn-St. Germain Act of 1982 allowed bank holding companies to acquire problem S&Ls across state lines. A number of money center banks took advantage of the opportunity. Citi, for example, acquired large S&Ls in California, Illinois, and Florida: Citicorp Savings of Illinois (the former First Federal of Chicago) has 60 branches, more than any other Chicago-area bank.

The banking crisis in the Southwest has also led states like Texas and Oklahoma to open themselves to full interstate banking, resulting in some big out-of-state acquisitions—for example, the purchase by New York's Chemical Bank of Texas Commerce Bancshares of Houston, a one-time superregional ($19 billion in assets) that had fallen on hard times.

---

[16]California allowed reciprocal national interstate banking January 1, 1991.

[17]A superregional was defined in the *American Banker Yearbook 1988* as a "non-money-center bank, ranked among the top 100 banking firms in total assets, and has merged across state lines to establish a banking presence in another state."

EXHIBIT 8.5

INTERSTATE BANKING LEGISLATION: JANUARY 1, 1991

Currently Nationwide Entry			Regional Entry Only		
State	Reciprocity	Percentage of Total Assets Held by Out-of-State Banks	State	Reciprocity	Percentage of Total Assets Held by Out-of-State Banks
Alaska	no	0.22%	Alabama	yes	0.22%
Arizona	no	58.65	Arkansas	yes	17.71
California	yes	0.10	Connecticut	yes	69.65
Colorado	yes	17.80	District of Columbia	yes	44.93
Delaware	yes	5.58	Florida	yes	34.96
Idaho	no	45.65	Georgia	yes	25.52
Illinois	yes	7.94	Maryland	yes	26.93
Indiana[a]	yes	28.28	Massachusetts	yes	0.00
Kentucky	yes	37.51	Minnesota	yes	2.69
Louisiana	yes	0.73	Mississippi	yes	1.82
Maine	no	86.27	Missouri	yes	.18
Michigan	yes	2.69	New Hampshire	yes	18.51
Nebraska	yes	8.59	North Carolina	yes	0.04
Nevada	no	33.34	South Carolina	yes	47.44
New Jersey	yes	14.76	Tennessee	yes	31.45
New Mexico	no	8.32	Virginia	yes	6.87
New York	yes	2.96	Wisconsin	yes	15.47
Ohio	yes	6.84			
Oklahoma	yes	5.38			
Oregon	no	44.29		No Law	
Pennsylvania	yes	13.71			
Rhode Island	yes	34.44			Percentage of Total Assets Held by
South Dakota	yes	13.31	State		Out-of-State Banks
Texas	no	31.59	Hawaii		0.00%
Utah	no	32.41	Iowa		8.68
Vermont	yes	11.93	Kansas		0.04
Washington	yes	79.34	Montana		36.23
West Virginia	yes	0.93	North Dakota		30.99
Wyoming	no	31.73			

[a]As of 7/1/92.

Note: Average percentage of assets held by all out-of-state banks: 14.19%.

Source: Donald T. Savage, Division of Research and Statistics, Board of Governors of the Federal Reserve System.

EXHIBIT 8.6

STATE BRANCHING LAWS

This listing shows the current distribution of branching laws by state. As indicated, two of the states that now have only limited branching will allow statewide branching in the 1990s.

Statewide Branching		Limited Branching	Unit Banking
Alabama[a]	Nevada	Arkansas[b]	Colorado
Alaska	New Hampshire	Iowa	Illinois
Arizona	New Jersey	Kentucky	Montana
California	New York	Louisiana	Wyoming
Connecticut	North Carolina	Minnesota	
Delaware	North Dakota[a]	Missouri	
Florida a		New Mexico	
Georgia[a]	Ohio	Pennsylvania	
Hawaii	Oklahoma	Tennessee	
Idaho	Oregon	Texas	
Indiana[a]	Rhode Island	Wisconsin	
Kansas[a]	South Carolina		
	South Dakota		
Maine	Utah		
Maryland	Vermont		
Massachusetts	Virginia		
Michigan	Washington		
Mississippi[a]	West Virginia		
Nebraska[a]			

[a]Statewide branching by merger.
[b]Arkansas will permit statewide branching in 1999.
Source: *Federal Reserve Bulletin*, March 1989, p.121.

The difficulties of the money center banks in their competition with the superregionals were compounded by a growing shortage of equity capital. Loan losses on Latin American debt and new, more stringent capital requirements left them without the resources they needed for further acquisitions.[18]

The superregionals, too, have had their problems. As of early 1990, the two largest Boston superregionals, Bank of Boston and Bank of New England, were in trouble as a result of loan losses. Bank of New England's problems were severe enough to raise the prospect of its failure and takeover by federal regulators (parts of the bank's operations were being offered for sale to, among others, Citibank). First Interstate was also in serious trouble, and there was talk of a takeover by BankAmerica, Security Pacific, or Wells Fargo (First Interstate had made an unsuccessful bid for BankAmerica only three years previously). Even NCNB, the prototype of the superregional, was recording significant losses.

Nonetheless, the relative strength of regional and money center banks has changed to something much closer to parity. This was illustrated rather well by

[18]We shall discuss these new capital requirements and the reasons for them in Part Four.

EXHIBIT 8.7

MAJOR SUPERREGIONAL BANKS[a]

Bank	States	Assets (Billions of Dollars)
First Interstate	California, Arizona, Washington, Nevada, Oregon	$51.8
Wells Fargo	California	44.7
PNC Financial	Pennsylvania, Kentucky, Indiana, Ohio	32.7
Bank of Boston	Massachusetts, Connecticut, Maine, Rhode Island	30.5
First Bank System	Minnesota, North Dakota, South Dakota, Montana, Washington, Wisconsin	28.4
First Fidelity Bancorporation	New Jersey, Pennsylvania	27.1
Bank of New England	Massachusetts, Connecticut, Maine, Rhode Island	27.0
SunTrust Banks	Florida, Georgia	25.6
NCNB Corp.	North Carolina, South Carolina, Georgia, Florida, Maryland, Virginia	24.6
First Union	North Carolina, South Carolina, Georgia, Florida	24.5
Shawmut National	Connecticut, Massachusetts, Rhode Island	24.5
Fleet Financial	New York, Rhode Island, Maine	24.4
NBD Corporation	Michigan, Illinois, Indiana	22.6
Banc One	Ohio, Indiana, Kentucky, Michigan, Wisconsin	22.2
Norwest Corp.	Minnesota, Iowa, Nebraska, Wisconsin	20.3
First Wachovia	North Carolina, Georgia	18.8

[a]Ranked by holding company total assets as of June 30, 1987. Includes pending mergers on a pro forma basis.

Source: *The Wall Street Journal*, October 1, 1987.

what happened when Ohio went over to full national interstate banking in October 1988. Nothing happened. On the one hand, Ohio had developed its own strong superregionals such as BancOne of Columbus; on the other, the money center banks had been weakened and were in no position to move in.

INTERSTATE BANKING AND THE CORRESPONDENT RELATIONSHIP

The movement toward interstate banking has placed strains on the correspondent relationship. A small local bank now sees its regional or money center correspondent as a potential competitor, since the correspondent may well end

NOTHING COULD BE FINER, TO BANK IN CAROLINA

In June 1985, when the Supreme Court allowed interstate banking, First Union had just $8.2 billion in assets. Ten minutes after the court decision, First Union's chief executive, Mr. Edward Crutchfield, got on the blower to his friend Mr. Billy Walker of Atlantic Bancorporation of Jacksonville, Florida, which had $3.7 billion in assets. Two days later they had agreed to merge. Just over 18 months later First Union has bought a total of 20 banks, trebling its assets to $28.6 billion, as of March 1988.

Interstate banking laws have swelled First Union's potential market from one state with a 6m population to 13 contiguous states with a combined population of 60m, which is bigger than Britain's. To that can also be added Texas, which any bank can enter. So far, First Union has expanded only in the most populous and economically buoyant of the sunbelt states: Florida, Georgia, the Carolinas and, in a tiny way, Tennessee.

The bank has chosen to centralize most management, including investment decisions, market research, advertising and the bank's name. All the acquired banks' branches now trade under the First Union name, in standard colors (green), supplemented only by "of Florida," or whatever. Big parties and rallies have been used to persuade employees to love their new name, and big advertising campaigns to persuade customers. First Union felt the eventual payback from a common brand for a common set of products would outweigh any immediate dislocation or confusion.

When First Union began its buying spree, it assumed that, if it had to pay prices above a target's book value and thus dilute earnings per share, it would be able to mop up 70% of the dilution by cost savings and 30% by boosting revenues. Actually, the opposite has happened. Around 80% of its gains have come from increasing revenues by selling a wider range of products through a larger number of outlets, only 20% from cost savings.

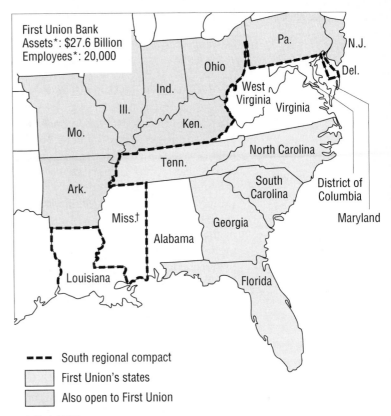

- - - South regional compact

First Union's states

Also open to First Union

* End 1987
† Will allow reciprocal banking with Tennessee, Alabama, Louisana, and Arkansas from July 1, 1988; with rest of south from July 1, 1990

First Union already did an unusually wide range of things for an $8 billion bank, including trust management, mortgages and insurance, through a subsidiary that was allowed to stay in the business ("grandfathered") when insurance was barred to commercial banks. That breadth could then be applied to narrower banks that it bought.

Even so, cost savings have been big. Northwestern's non-interest costs fell about 30% when it merged with First Union. Overlapping branches can be closed, back-office functions like check-processing put through one center in each state. Also, before the merger wave, First Union was already working on a new computer system to handle the assessment, approval and monitoring of commercial loans, at a set-up cost of about $5m. The same system would have cost its Florida and Georgia purchases about $5m each if they had stayed independent. To extend the North Carolina system costs only about $500,000 per state, so the bank is now integrating all its states at a total cost of about $6.5m; separately, as good a system would have cost at least $20m.

Source: "Nothing Could Be Finer, to Bank in Carolina," *The Economist*, March 26, 1988. Copyright 1988, *The Economist*. Distributed by Special Features/Syndication Sales.

banker's banks
Regional service centers
jointly owned by groups of
small banks.

up buying the bank across the street. One response to this problem, particularly in the Midwest, has been for groups of small banks to set up regional service centers under joint ownership—so-called **banker's banks**. These provide many of the same services traditionally provided by a correspondent.

HOW FAR HAVE WE COME?

Despite rapid recent progress, the movement toward full interstate banking is still in its early stages. There are in theory $50 \times 51 = 2,550$ possible entry combinations between different states (DC counts as a "state," and Georgia into Alabama and Alabama into Georgia count as two different possibilities). As of 1989 interstate banking laws permitted 878 of the 2,550, and *actual* entry as a result of the new laws had occurred in only 105 (grandfathered multibank holding companies accounted for another 19). Only 21 bank holding companies owned banks in three or more states other than their own, and First Interstate remained the only holding company to own banks in more than 10 states. Only about 14% of banking assets at insured commercial banks (excluding nonbank banks) were held by bank holding companies headquartered in another state.[19]

Moreover, the new interstate banking laws do not generally allow full interstate branching, just ownership of existing banks by out-of-state holding companies.

8.6 "INTERSTATE" BANKING COMES TO EUROPE

Europe is now undergoing its own movement toward "interstate" banking. While most European countries allow unrestricted branching within the country, there is currently only limited branching across national borders. However, the 12 nations of the European Economic Community plan to remove all barriers to trade among them by 1992. In particular, the Second Banking Directive, adopted by the EEC in December 1989, will grant banks based in any member state a license to operate in any other member state without the need to register or to obtain a charter in that state. The license will also be available on a reciprocal basis to banks from countries outside the EEC as long as their home governments allow free entry by EEC banks.

The Second Directive will create the largest and most integrated banking market in the world: The EEC has a population of some 320 million. The effects should be much like those of the movement toward interstate banking in the United States. It seems reasonable to expect a wave of mergers and acquisitions resulting in fewer, larger banks. Some observers suggest that there may eventually be as few as 800 banks in the EEC (an economy roughly the size of the U.S. economy), as opposed to double that number now.

[19]From D. T. Savage, "Interstate Banking Update," xerox, Board of Governors of the Federal Reserve System, 1989.

8.7 INTERSTATE BANKING: PRO AND CON

As the movement toward full interstate banking progresses in the United States, banks will get larger and the number of banks will shrink. One way to quantify this development is through some measure of concentration; for example, what share of total assets is accounted for by the 25 largest banks, or the 100 largest? At the national level, concentration has already increased noticeably. In 1970 the 25 largest banks accounted for 33% of total assets; the 100 largest, for 50%. By 1988 the share of the 25 largest had grown to 36%; that of the 100 largest, to 63%. Notice that the big change is with respect to the largest 100, not the largest 25: This reflects the growth of the superregionals.[20]

Should we be concerned about this growing concentration of the U.S. banking system? Are all those deep-seated populist fears, stimulated so long ago by the unhappy experience with the First and Second Banks of the United States, justified? There are a number of issues here. Will the improved integration of financial markets harm local communities by draining funds away? Will increasing size lead to monopoly power and the abuses that usually accompany it? Will a concentrated banking system be more or less subject to bank failures and crises?

As we take up these questions, we can learn a great deal by looking at the Canadian example. Remember that Canada has none of our restrictions on the geographic expansion of banks, and therefore has long had a very concentrated banking structure: In 1982 Canada's five largest banks held nearly 80% of all deposits in that country. So, to some extent, Canada is a model for how U.S. banking might look when full interstate banking becomes a reality.

INTEGRATION VERSUS KEEPING MONEY IN THE COMMUNITY

Nationwide banking improves the integration of the financial system and the mobility of funds. Deposits raised in one part of the country can easily be used to fund loans in another. The integration of the financial system brought about by nationwide banking in Canada is reflected in uniform rates on deposits and loans across the country. In the United States, rates vary much more from region to region.

As we saw in Chapter 3, an integrated financial system is economically more efficient because it facilitates the flow of funds to wherever the return is highest. The result is more productive investment and higher income for the nation as a whole. However, as we also saw in Chapter 3, higher income for the nation *as a whole* does not mean that there will be no losers.

Consider an example. Suppose the Rustbelt is in economic decline and the Sunbelt is growing rapidly. Investment opportunities are much better in the Sunbelt. In the absence of interstate banking, because the demand for funds in the

[20]Ibid.

Sunbelt is high relative to the supply, interest rates will be higher there than they are in the Rustbelt. If we allow interstate banking, deposits made in Rustbelt branches will support loans made by branches in the Sunbelt. As a result, interest rates will fall in the Sunbelt and rise in the Rustbelt, and funds will flow out of the latter region and into the former. As a consequence, investment will fall in the Rustbelt, and its decline will be hastened. Jobs will be lost even faster. On the other hand, investment will increase in the Sunbelt and its growth will be even more rapid. New jobs will open up there even faster. And the new jobs in the Sunbelt will pay more than the old jobs lost in the Rustbelt.

So that is the choice. "Keeping money in the community" will slow the decline of declining areas, but it will also slow the growth of growing ones: No money *leaving* the community means that somewhere else no money is *entering* the community. The jobs that are saved will pay less than the jobs that would have been created but are not. So the cost of a rising standard of living is the personal and social cost of picking up and following the money from declining regions to growing ones.

Of course, this discussion rather overstates the effect of nationwide banking on financial integration. In reality, banks have already found ways to bring about considerable mobility of funds. Even in the bad old days of unit banking, money did *not* stay in the community. Interest rate differentials between regions create strong profit incentives: A bank in the Rustbelt will not use local deposits to make local loans if it can lend the money to a bank in the Sunbelt and earn a higher return. Correspondent balances are one way that one bank can lend to another, and we shall see other ways in later chapters.

What this means is that local banks do not necessarily "invest in the community." They pay relatively low interest rates on deposits—protected from the competition of out-of-state banks—and then invest the money themselves outside the community for a higher return. So borrowers in the community gain little from a fragmented banking system, and depositors earn less interest than they should. The "community" bank earns economic rents from the difference between the relatively low rates it pays depositors and the higher rates it earns on loans to banks elsewhere.

Integration of the banking system improves not only the efficiency of the financial system, but also the efficiency of the payments system. Check clearing is more expensive in the United States than it is in Canada. In the United States, when a New York City bank receives a check drawn on a San Francisco bank, the check must pass through many hands and be processed several times before it is finally presented for payment in San Francisco. The process takes days and is quite costly. In Canada, when a Montreal bank receives a check drawn on a Vancouver bank, clearing is much easier. The Vancouver bank is most likely a branch of one of the major national banks, which also has branches in Montreal. Therefore the check can be presented for payment at the local clearinghouse in Montreal and payment received the same day. Also, with a more concentrated banking system, more checks will clear internally within each bank, and fewer will need to clear between banks.

ECONOMIES OF SCALE AND MONOPOLY POWER

In Chapter 3 we saw that an important measure of the efficiency of a financial system is the price it charges for its services, a price that can be measured to a large extent by the difference between the rate lenders receive and the rate borrowers pay. The smaller that difference, the more lending, borrowing, and investing there will be. We saw, too, that prices charged by the financial system depend on two things—costs and competition. The lower the costs and the greater the competition, the lower the price will be.

Because economies of scale reduce costs, large banks should be able to provide their services more cheaply. However, economies of scale lead to greater concentration, and greater concentration makes one worry about market power and reduced competition. Generally speaking, the more concentration in a market, the less competition there will be. With fewer firms, it becomes easier for them to collude, openly or tacitly, to raise prices and to reduce the level of service. If all firms raise prices together, they will lose relatively little business, because there is nowhere else for customers to go.

How concerned should we be about increasing concentration in banking? Should we expect to see interest rates on deposits fall, rates on loans rise, and bank profits increase?

To answer these questions, we need to be clear about what constitutes "the market." Individuals and firms prefer to deal with a bank that is close by (were this not so, restrictions on bank branching would make little difference). The relevant size of the market for individuals is perhaps the town or the county. For firms the relevant market size may be larger. Firms will be willing to deal with banks farther away if those banks offer a better deal. And many firms operate nationally or even internationally, so for them the relevant market will be defined accordingly.

To see how much competition there is, then, we need to see how many banks there are, not in the nation as a whole, but in the specific *local* market. Generally speaking, the United States has relatively little competition at the local level, despite the enormous number of banks nationally. In states that restrict branching within the state, the typical local market may contain as few as two or three banks. In states with more liberal branching laws, despite the smaller total number of banks in the state, the number present in each local market tends to be higher.

So, as branching restrictions disappear, the result may actually be *less* concentration at the level of the local market where it really matters and thus *more* competition. Indeed, studies suggest that there has been a slight decrease in local concentration as a result of interstate expansion.[21]

Of course, the ability to raise prices depends not only on the actual number of firms in a market, but also on potential entry. If raising prices, and thus profits, makes it attractive for new firms to enter the market, firms already there may decide that it is better to keep prices low. Easing the restrictions on interstate banking clearly makes entry into local markets easier.

While geography is one dimension of a market, another is the nature of the product. For example, if you have a monopoly on the production of pink toothpaste, your ability to exploit it is limited: If you raise your price too much, people will switch to white toothpaste. Banks increasingly find themselves in the same position. As we shall see in later chapters, distinctions between different types of financial intermediary have been eroded in recent years. Thrifts, finance companies, and investment banks now offer many of the services once offered only by banks. As a result, the number of effective competitors in the relevant market may be much larger than the number of banks alone.

Some evidence of the potential effect on competition of unrestricted branching is provided by the experience of Canada, which has long enjoyed unrestricted nationwide branching. There, competition is vigorous and customers are well served. Rates on deposits are high relative to rates on loans. Fees for foreign exchange transactions are low. Bank hours seem more attuned to the convenience of customers: Many banks are open until 8 p.m. and on Saturdays. And the offer shown in Exhibit 8.8 is not something you would expect to receive from your typical American bank!

INTEGRATION AND STABILITY

Another advantage of the integrated Canadian system, made up principally of very large banks, over the American system, with its many small banks, is that the Canadian system seems to be much less prone to bank failures and crises.

As we shall see in Chapters 16 and 17, the U.S. banking system is currently in quite a mess. Many of the banks in trouble are small, cost-inefficient ones. Other, larger, problem banks often suffer from poor diversification: For example, some of the Boston superregionals are too heavily dependent on the New England economy and on New England real estate. Another source of trouble is the entry into banking of doubtful operators, in for a quick killing (this phenomenon seems particularly widespread in the Southwest and West). Such entry is

---

[21]The beer industry went through a similar process of national concentration in the 1950s and 1960s. The technology of beer production used to make it difficult to transport beer long distances for sale. As a result, the industry consisted of a large number of brewers nationally, with relatively few in each isolated local market. There was, therefore, little competition in these local markets. Then the technology changed, and it became possible for individual brewers to sell their product nationwide. The total number of brewers in the country shrank rapidly (there are increasing returns in brewing too), and small companies were swallowed up by larger ones. However, the number of firms competing in each *local* market grew significantly. Competition increased and prices fell.

EXHIBIT 8.8
MONEY SPECIALS

MONEY SPECIALS

AT CANADA TRUST

We appreciate your business and hope you'll find these special bonus/discount coupons of value. Bonus/discounts are available at participating branches from January 30 to March 18, 1989.

Coupons can't be transferred or facsimilies used, and there's a limit of one coupon per product. All offers can be discontinued at any time without notice and cannot be used in conjunction with any other offers. Full conditions are available at participating branches.

UP TO $100 FOR ACCOUNT TRANSFERS

This coupon entitles you to a cash bonus of $5 for every $1,000 transferred, if you have us arrange the transfer of a personal savings or chequing account from a competitor to a Canada Trust personal savings or chequing account. Maximum bonus $100.

Full conditions at participating branches.

Coupon valid from January 30 to March 18, 1989.

10% OFF SUPERLOANS

This coupon entitles you to a discount of 10% off the rate for the first six months on a new SuperLoan over $10,000. For example if our regular rate is 12.75% then the offer rate would be 11.25%*. SuperLoan is an open loan for amounts of $10,000 or more, that automatically renews itself every 6 months if payments are up-to-date. The interest rate at each six month renewal will normally be lower than our regular personal loan rate.

Full conditions are at participating branches.

Coupon valid from January 30 to March 18, 1989.

*On a $15,000 loan with 5 year amortization, the monthly payment for the first 6 months would be $328.01 and the cost of the loan $817.07. Funds must be advanced within 30 days of offer ending.

UP TO $20 FOR CREDIT CARD TRANSFERS

This coupon entitles you to $10 when used to transfer a balance of $500 or more from any of your other credit cards to a new or existing Canada Trust MasterCard. Limit two transfers per customer.

Coupon valid January 30 to March 18, 1989.

10% OFF MORTGAGES

This coupon entitles you to a 10% rate reduction for the first six months of a new six month open mortgage over $20,000. For example, if our regular rate is 11.25% then the offer rate would be 10%. Rate reduction applies to the first six months only. If payments are up-to-date, renewal is guaranteed at the then current rate.

Full conditions at participating branches.

Coupon valid from January 30 to March 18, 1989.

much more difficult when new entrants have to compete for customers with efficient and safe nationwide banks.

The Canadian system has experienced nothing like the banking turmoil in the United States. Its large, integrated banks, with good diversification and liquidity, are much better placed to weather economic adversity. It is interesting to note, however, that there have been significantly more bank failures in Canada since deposit insurance was introduced in 1967. With deposit insurance, it is easier for a small bank to compete with large banks for deposits: As far as depositors are concerned, all insured banks are equally safe. Hence, because the deposit insurance nullifies one of the important advantages of scale, more new banks have been able to open. Many of these have subsequently failed.

SUMMARY

- Because of economies of scale, large banks should be more profitable than small ones. Banks will try to become larger in order to be more profitable, and the result should be a banking industry consisting of a few, very large banks.

- In most countries, where this process has not been impeded by regulatory restrictions, the banking industry is indeed highly concentrated. In the United States, however, regulatory restrictions have prevented concentration. There are two types of restriction—those affecting interstate banking and those affecting branching within states.

- The origins of these regulatory restrictions are historical and political rather than economic. Early experiments with nationwide branching, in the form of the First and Second Banks of the United States, aroused strong opposition and were abandoned. Abuses by these banks, however, were probably more a result of monopoly than of size or of nationwide branching.

- The economies of scale in banking are due to (1) indivisibilities in many of the fixed costs (buildings, computers, foreign exchange departments), and (2) the advantages of having a larger pool (a larger pool needs proportionally less reserves to guarantee liquidity and less equity to protect against insolvency).

- Banks have adapted to the regulations preventing their expansion by trying to capture economies of scale between banks rather than within a single bank. The principal vehicle for this is the correspondent relationship between large and small banks. (Franchising takes this idea a little further.)

- Banks have also tried various ways of getting around the law. One, using multibank holding companies, was prohibited in 1956. Another, involving nonbank banks—institutions that take deposits but do not make commercial loans—was blocked in 1984.

- A loophole in the law once allowed foreign banks to operate across state lines. Partly because of this advantage, foreign banks have expanded rapidly in the United States, and they now have a substantial share of the market, particularly in New York and California. The loophole was plugged in 1978 when foreign banks were brought under the same regulations as domestic banks.

- In recent years interstate banking has become legal in many areas. Some states allow unrestricted interstate banking. Some allow interstate banking with reciprocity. Some allow interstate banking with states in specified regions, with or without reciprocity.

- Partly as a result of regional interstate banking agreements, some regional banks have grown into "superregionals" large enough to compete head-on with the money center banks.

- Although the movement toward interstate banking has led to increased concentration at the national level, there are reasons to believe that competition should actually increase in local banking markets.

- Interstate banking should result in a more efficient allocation of funds nationwide by allowing the supply of deposits to be matched to the demand for loans over a much larger market.

- Interstate banking should also result in a safer and more stable banking system because of better diversification and more difficult entry for doubtful operators.

KEY TERMS

economies of scale	loan participation	nonbank bank
unit bank	correspondent balances	nonbank office
fixed costs	franchising	nonbank subsidiaries
variable costs	Edge Act corporations	reciprocity
indivisible costs	holding company	money center banks
minimum efficient scale	multibank holding company	regional banks
correspondent relationship		superregionals
correspondent bank	one-bank holding companies	banker's banks
respondent bank	chain banking	
overline		

DISCUSSION QUESTIONS

1. What do you think is behind populist opposition to "big banking"? Who stands to gain from a fragmented banking system?

2. "Acquisition of local banks by large out-of-state banks will harm small communities." Discuss.

3. Suppose you are a large bank entering a new market. You can do so either by setting up a new subsidiary from scratch or by purchasing a small bank already there. Which would you do and why?

4. What are economies of scale? How are they relevant to banking?

5. Why does pooling involve economies of scale?

6. What is the difference between correspondent banking and franchising?

7. Is there reason to worry about increasing concentration in the banking industry?

8. Most interstate banking laws allow mergers and acquisitions rather than new entry. None allow interstate branching. Why do you think this is?

SOFTWARE EXERCISE FOR THIS CHAPTER

Title: Duobank

This computer exercise simulates competition between two banks. It requires two people, each serving as a bank executive who makes important decisions in a competitive environment. Each bank tries to attract both depositors and loan customers. See your instructor if you wish to use this program.

BIBLIOGRAPHY

Amel, Dean F., and Michael J. Jacowski, "Trends in Banking Structure since the Mid-1970s," *Federal Reserve Bulletin* March 1989, 120–133.

Benson, John N., "The Canadian Experience with Nationwide Banking," *Economic Review of the Federal Reserve Bank of Atlanta* May 1983, 60–65.

Clair, Robert T., and Paula K. Tucker, "Interstate Banking and the Federal Reserve: A Historical Perspective," *Economic Review of the Federal Reserve Bank of Dallas* November 1989, 1–20.

King, B. Frank, Tschinkel, Sheila L., and David D. Whitehead, "Interstate Banking Developments in the 1980s," *Economic Review of the Federal Reserve Bank of Atlanta* May-June 1989, 32–51.

Lewis, M. K., and K. T. Davis, *Domestic and International Banking*, Cambridge, Mass.: M.I.T. Press, 1987.

Savage, Donald T., "Interstate Banking Developments," *Federal Reserve Bulletin* February 1987, 79–92.

_____, Interstate Banking Update, 1989.

Shaffer, S., "Challenges to Small Banks' Survival," *Business Review, Federal Reserve Bank of Philadelphia* Sept.-Oct. 1989.

Syron, Richard F., "The 'New England Experiment' in Interstate Banking," *New England Economic Review* March-April 1984, 5–17.

CHAPTER 9

BANKS AND THE MONEY MARKET

I. THE RISING TIDE

Canute was an English king much revered by his subjects. They believed him to be so powerful that even the tides must obey him. One day, they urged him to demonstrate his mighty power. At low tide, the royal throne was placed on the beach. The king sat on his throne and commanded the waves to stay their onward progress. For a while he seemed successful, and his subjects stood in awe. But within an hour, Canute was sitting in water up to his knees.

The story of this chapter is a modern version of King Canute, with banks playing the king and rising interest rates the tide. Banking regulations enacted in the 1930s limited the interest rates that banks could pay on their deposits. So when, beginning in the late 1960s, economic forces caused other interest rates to rise, banks were unable to raise their rates in response. This gave borrowers and lenders a strong incentive to develop new ways of getting together, ways that did not involve banks. Facing a major loss of business, banks found ways around the regulations and pressed Congress to change them.

This process of challenge and response has altered profoundly the way banks and financial markets operate—not only in the United States, but also around the world. We take up this story in the next three chapters. In the current chapter we shall focus on how banks were squeezed out. In Chapter 10 we shall see how banks found their way back in. In Chapter 11 we shall see the effects on international banking.

9.1 SETTING THE SCENE

SHORT-TERM BORROWING AND LENDING

The principal *demand* for short-term loans comes from firms wishing to finance the outlays on labor and materials, on inventories and trade credit, that they must

207

make before their products are sold (working capital). The *supply* of short-term loans comes from households and firms that need to hold liquid reserves because of fluctuations in current income and expenditure.

In general, there are two ways to bring the supply of lending and the demand for borrowing together. Ultimate lenders can lend directly to ultimate borrowers through a financial market, or they can lend indirectly through a financial intermediary. The short-term financial market is called the **money market** (as distinct from the long-term **capital market**). The principal short-term financial intermediary is the commercial bank.

money market
The short-term financial market.

capital market
The long-term financial market.

Historically, the share of direct lending in the short-term market has been small. Direct lending is not well suited to short-term loans. Many of the costs—the processing of information, the fees paid to rating agencies and underwriters—have a large element of indivisibility: They are much the same whether a loan is large or small, for three months or for thirty years. As we saw in Chapter 3, working-capital loans need to be renewed or rolled over: Although each loan is for only three or six months, once it is paid off, the borrower typically needs to borrow again. This means that many of the fixed costs of making a public issue will have to be paid over and over again, whereas they would have had to be paid only once for a long-term loan. As a result, short-term direct borrowing is relatively expensive unless very large sums are involved.

Moreover, banks have significant natural advantages in the short-term market. A line of credit implies a continuing relationship between borrower and lender, so that the information and contracting costs do not have to be paid over and over again as with a public issue where different lenders are involved each time. Moreover, short-term loans for working capital are mostly unsecured: There is no natural collateral as there is for long-term loans used to finance fixed capital. A bank can more easily take on the risk of such a loan, because the value to the borrower of the continuing relationship with the bank makes default less likely. Banks also have an important advantage in their ability to provide liquidity through pooling: Liquidity is particularly important to short-term lenders.

LOAN RATES, DEPOSIT RATES, AND REGULATION

For any type of lending, direct or indirect, the cost to the borrower exceeds the return to the lender: The difference between them is the payment to the financial system for the service it provides in arranging the loan.

So, naturally, the rates that banks charge on their loans will be higher than the rates that they pay on their deposits. However, the size of this gap will depend on competitive pressure. In a highly competitive environment, economic rents are squeezed to a minimum, and the gap between loan rates and deposit rates will be no greater than the bank's costs. But when competition is absent or restrained, and when banks have market power, they can raise the rates they charge on loans and lower the rates they pay on deposits, leaving them with substantial economic rents.[1]

After the banking catastrophe of the Great Depression, laws were passed to *deliberately* limit competition among banks. It was felt, rightly or wrongly, that the loss in economic efficiency and in consumer welfare was justified by the greater safety this brought to the banking system. The idea was that banks making good profits (economic rents) would be less likely to take chances and do the kinds of things that would get them, and the economy, into trouble.

One way banks had competed with one another had been by bidding for deposits (competition had been particularly fierce for correspondent balances). The Banking Act of 1933—called the Glass-Steagall Act after its congressional sponsors—set out to make this form of competition impossible by imposing limits on the interest rates banks could pay on deposits. Section 11 of the Glass-Steagall Act prohibited the payment of *any* interest on demand deposits. The act also empowered the Federal Reserve Board to regulate the interest rates paid on time deposits. This the Fed did under **Regulation Q**, which set a ceiling on permitted rates.

To see what difference these regulations make, let us consider first what happens when there is no regulation. The rate on loans is determined by supply and demand: Competition among banks and between banks and the direct short-term market ensures that loan rates rise and fall with changes in supply and demand. Because it responds to changes in the market, we say that the loan rate is a *market* rate. But banks cannot make loans without attracting deposits. As loan rates rise with the market, banks will be willing to pay more to attract deposits; competition among them will ensure that they do pay more. As loan rates fall, they will be willing to pay less. So when there is no regulation, the rate on deposits is also a market rate.

The Glass-Steagall regulations place no limit on the interest rate charged on loans.[2] As a result, the rate on loans continues to be a market rate, fluctuating with supply and demand. What happens to the rate on deposits depends on whether the market rate (or what would have been the market rate) is above or below the legal ceiling. As long as the market rate on deposits stays *below* the ceiling, it is as if the ceiling does not exist. Banks compete and depositors receive the market rate.[3] However, when the market rate on deposits rises and comes up against the ceiling, competition for deposits ceases, and depositors receive the

Regulation Q
Federal Reserve regulation that set an interest-rate ceiling on deposits.

---

[1]"Costs" include a fair return on the capital invested in the bank—a "normal" or fair profit. Economic rent is any profit larger than this. See Chapter 3 for more on this.

[2]There do exist limits, called *usury laws*, imposed by many states. However, these limits are quite high and they are not normally effective. They did become effective in some cases in the early 1980s, when market rates reached exceptionally high levels.

[3]It might seem that the ceiling on demand deposits, set at zero, must always bite. But remember *implicit* interest. The interest on a demand deposit is the sum of explicit and implicit interest. When market rates on deposits are low, the implicit interest may be sufficient by itself to equal the market rate, even though the explicit rate is constrained to be zero. In that case the ceiling does not really matter. In Canada explicit interest on demand deposits was zero for many years even though banks were allowed to pay interest on demand deposits.

ceiling rate. Since no bank is allowed to pay more than this, each bank can safely pay the ceiling rate without having to worry that depositors will be lured away by other banks offering more.

The size of the gap between loan rates and deposit rates depends, therefore, on whether market rates are high or low. When they are low, and the ceiling on deposit rates does not bite, competition keeps the gap small. But once market rates rise above the ceiling on deposit rates, competition for deposits ceases and the gap between loan rates and deposit rates grows wider.

THE RISING TREND IN INTEREST RATES

For a long time after the Great Depression—from the 1930s through most of the 1960s—market rates remained low. Then, as a result of a variety of government policies and economic events that we shall study later, they began to rise.

prime rate
Base rate for bank lending.

The results may be seen in Exhibit 9.1. The rate on T-bills is representative of rates in the money market (direct short-term lending). The **prime rate** is the base rate for bank lending: Other loan rates are set at a markup over prime to reflect default risk.[4] You can see that before the late 1960s, market interest rates on loans were rising but remained below 5%. Market rates on deposits—not shown in the exhibit but presumably somewhat below the market rate on loans—barely came up against the maximum (the gradual raising of the maximum helped). However, by the early 1980s the prime had passed the 20% mark and the gap between it and the rate on deposits was enormous.

An enormous gap between loan rates and deposit rates may not sound like much of a problem for banks. What is wrong with collecting high rates on loans and paying low rates on deposits, while placing all the blame on federal regulations? The problem is that the gap provides an incentive to find new ways of bringing borrowers and lenders together—ways that do *not* involve banks. Suppose, for example, that banks are paying 5% on deposits and charging 20% on loans, and that you, as a financial innovator, can find a different way of getting borrowers and lenders together. You can offer lenders 10%, charge borrowers 15%, and still be left with a healthy profit; and you should have little trouble luring business away from the banks.

9.2 | LARGE BORROWERS AND LENDERS SIDESTEP BANKS

As interest rates began to rise, the first to react were corporate treasurers. To see why, put yourself in the shoes of the corporate treasurer at Megacorp. Your responsibilities include managing Megacorp's liquid assets, which are held to

---

[4]The prime rate used to be the rate that banks charged their most creditworthy borrowers. However, after banks began to compete by offering "subprime" rates to some customers, the original meaning of the term was lost.

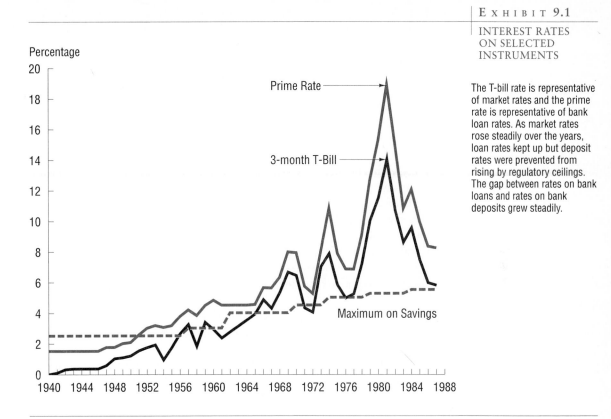

EXHIBIT 9.1

INTEREST RATES ON SELECTED INSTRUMENTS

The T-bill rate is representative of market rates and the prime rate is representative of bank loan rates. As market rates rose steadily over the years, loan rates kept up but deposit rates were prevented from rising by regulatory ceilings. The gap between rates on bank loans and rates on bank deposits grew steadily.

Source: *Economic Report of the President.*

cover differences between fluctuating income and expenditure. Compare your situation in 1951 to your situation in 1980.

It is 1951. You have $1 million in cash to manage. Given that the funds must be kept fairly liquid, what are your choices? One is to keep it all in a zero-interest checking account.[5] Another is to invest part of it in T-bills: You cannot invest all of it, because you need to keep some cash on hand. If you put $900,000 into T-bills, at the 1.2% they pay, you can make an extra $10,800 a year in interest for Megacorp. However, before you do so, you need to look at the costs. If you do invest in T-bills, someone has to make sure that enough cash is always on hand for the company's operations. This will inevitably involve a lot of buying and selling, and the resulting commissions will eat into your gains. Worse, since you do not have the time yourself to worry about this, you will have to hire someone to do it, at a cost of something like $15,000. The game is not worth the candle. You decide to leave your money in the zero-interest checking account.

[5]Corporations are not allowed to hold most forms of time deposit.

Now it is 1981. Market interest rates are over 15%, but because of banking regulation, checking accounts still pay no interest. Your choices have broadened: There are now alternatives other than T-bills that offer higher yields and lower transactions costs (we shall learn about them presently). You can now earn perhaps $450,000 a year from active management of your $3 million in cash. Even though it now costs you $50,000 to hire someone to do the work, it is more than worthwhile. Interest has become a lot more interesting.

Indeed, in the early 1980s many companies earned a better return on their cash management than they did on their core line of business. For example, in 1980 Rockwell International (a major aerospace, automotive, and general manufacturer), with a pre-tax income of $500 million, earned $80 million of that from cash management. The yield on its liquid assets, 14%, was well above its return on the fixed capital it used in actual manufacturing.[6]

On the one hand, then, we have corporate cash managers. As market rates rise in the 1960s, they see the enormous gap between deposit rates and market rates and begin to look for ways of earning more on their liquid assets. On the other hand, we have various bank *borrowers*. They are paying very high rates on their bank loans and are looking for ways to lower their borrowing costs.

DEALER REPURCHASE AGREEMENTS

One important class of borrower is the government securities dealer. You will recall from Chapter 7 that by the very nature of their business, dealers must hold large inventories of securities. The traditional way to finance these inventories is loans from their clearing banks. As interest rates begin to rise, however, these dealer loans become increasingly expensive, and dealers look for an alternative source of finance.

The problem, of course, is how to overcome the relatively high information and transactions costs of short-term direct borrowing. The clearing bank has a natural advantage here: It has a continuing relationship with the dealer that the latter is unlikely to endanger by causing difficulties with its loan. Moreover, since the clearing bank holds the dealer's inventory of securities, it is easy to arrange collateral for the loan.

You, as corporate treasurer of Megacorp, would be happy to lend to a securities dealer, but only if you could be protected from loss, and protected in a way that does not involve enormous costs of information-gathering and monitoring. The **dealer repurchase agreement**, or "repo," provides a solution. As we saw in Chapter 7, it works like this: A dealer agrees to sell you a specified amount of securities for $1,000,000 and to buy them back—say, the next day—for $1,000,185. Although formally this is a sale and a repurchase, in effect it is a collateralized loan. You are lending the dealer $1,000,000 for one day; the $185 excess in the buy-back price is just the interest on the loan (roughly 7% at an

dealer repurchase agreement Arrangement whereby a dealer sells government securities and simultaneously contracts to buy them back at a specific time and price.

[6]*Annual Report for Rockwell International, Fiscal Year Ending 9/30/80.*

annualized rate). The securities are collateral: If the dealer does not repay the loan, you may sell them to recover what is owed to you. Because the loan is collateralized, you do not need to check out the dealer and monitor his performance. This keeps down the cost of making the loan.

For you, the corporate treasurer, such a repo loan to a government securities dealer is a very attractive alternative to actually holding T-bills. First, the constant buying and selling of T-bills is expensive in terms of commissions and other transactions costs. Moving the securities from the dealer's account to a custodial account in your name is cheaper than the full transfer of ownership that is involved in a true purchase or sale. Moreover, the maturity of a repo can easily be tailored to match your needs—from overnight to several weeks—so that there are fewer transactions. Second, if T-bills have to be sold before maturity, as is often the case, there is interest-rate risk: If interest rates rise suddenly, the market value of the T-bills will fall. With a repo, there is no interest-rate risk: The yield is fixed in advance and is unaffected by what happens to the market price of the securities.

The enormous growth in the amount of dealer repos outstanding is shown in Exhibit 9.2. As we saw in Chapter 7, dealers now do a brisk business in both repos and reverses. Their own use of repos as a source of finance is just the amount of repos less the amount of reverses.

COMMERCIAL PAPER

For the corporate treasurer, repos are one alternative to T-bills. Another is **commercial paper**—the short-term, unsecured debt of corporations and financial institutions. While repos are more liquid and have less interest-rate risk than T-bills, they offer a lower yield. Commercial paper, on the other hand, is less liquid and has higher default risk than T-bills, but its yield is higher.

commercial paper
Short-term, unsecured debt of corporations and financial institutions.

Commercial paper has been around a long time. Because of the fragmentation of banking in the United States, large firms located away from the major financial centers have often had trouble financing their working capital with loans from small local banks. In the nineteenth century, they began to turn to the New York market as an alternative, selling commercial paper there to meet their short-term needs.

Since commercial paper is unsecured, only the largest and most creditworthy corporations are considered good enough risks to be able to raise money in this way. The 1,200 or so issuers of commercial paper represent only a small fraction of the approximately 2 million corporations in the United States. However, for these companies, issuing commercial paper provides an attractive alternative to borrowing from a bank.

EXHIBIT 9.2

GROWTH OF
DEALER REPOS

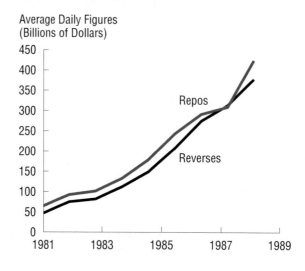

Note: Figures for repos and reverses are each composed of term and overnight funds. 1989 figures are based on the first 11 months.

Source: *Federal Reserve Bulletin*, February 1990.

Commercial paper is sold in denominations as small as $25,000, but multiples of $100,000 are more common. Usually, commercial paper is in the form of a bill, and so, like a T-bill, it sells at a discount below its face value.[7]

Issuing commercial paper carries many of the usual costs of a public issue. The paper must be rated for risk by a rating service such as Moody or Standard & Poor's; this may cost the issuer from $5,000 to $25,000 a year. The paper must then be sold. About half is sold through dealers and brokers, who charge a fee of about 1/8 of 1%. The rest is sold directly to investors by the issuer; this is called **direct placement.** Direct placement saves the issuer the fee that would be paid to dealers, but it is not free: It requires a permanent sales staff to do the work the dealers would have done. Indeed, the costs are so substantial that only the largest issuers, those with $1 billion or more of paper outstanding, find it worthwhile to act as their own dealers in this way. One cost of a public issue is avoided with commercial paper: Securities with an original maturity of under 270 days, sold to finance "current transactions," are exempt from the requirement to file with the SEC.

direct placement
Sale of a security directly to investors without a public issue.

---

[7]Investors have some preference for round lots of securities—$1,000,000 worth rather than $987,566. As a result, an increasing amount of paper is issued in interest-bearing form rather than as discount paper. That is, it is sold at face value, and pays principal plus interest calculated at the market rate at time of issue.

EXHIBIT 9.3

COMMERCIAL PAPER OUTSTANDING

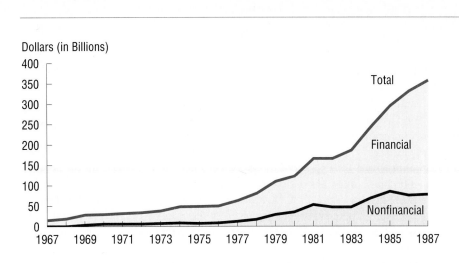

The market for commercial paper has existed for a long time, but it only began to grow rapidly in the 1970s as the widening gap between the rates on bank loans and deposits pushed borrowers and lenders into the direct market.

Given the indivisible nature of many of the costs involved, a borrower needs to issue a large amount of commercial paper to make the whole thing worthwhile. In fact, most issuers issue very large amounts. The average is about $120 million, and the largest issuers have several billions outstanding.

There is not much of a secondary market for commercial paper. Because there are so many different issues outstanding, and the market for any specific issue is small, it is not really worth anyone's while to make a market. Because of the poor secondary market, holders of commercial paper cannot be confident of getting a good price if they need to sell before maturity. To offset this lack of liquidity, the maturity of commercial paper tends to be very short—less than 30 days on average. Since issuers typically need the money for substantially longer than this, the paper is usually "rolled over": That is, new commercial paper is sold to pay off the old.

As you can see from Exhibit 9.3, the market for commercial paper did not amount to much until the 1960s. In the period of low interest rates, rates on commercial paper were not much below those on bank loans; the potential saving in interest did not cover the high fixed costs of issuing commercial paper. When interest rates rose, the demand for commercial paper grew and so, therefore, did the difference between the rate on commercial paper and the rate on bank loans. As a result, an increasing number of companies found commercial paper an attractive way to borrow.

Although the amount outstanding was only $3.7 billion in 1959, it had grown to $52.6 billion by 1976 and to $353 billion by August 1987. Of this $353 billion, $78 billion was issued by nonfinancial corporations such as manufacturers, retailers, and public utilities. The rest, $275 billion, was issued by financial institutions such as bank holding companies, insurance companies, and, especially, finance companies. The latter are of particular importance and interest and deserve a closer look.

FINANCE COMPANIES

Firms that sell durable goods, such as cars, appliances, computers, or machinery, have a particularly large appetite for short-term funds. This is because financing is an important part of marketing their product: It is much easier to sell a car or a refrigerator if you can offer your customer financing at a reasonable rate. So, beginning in the 1920s, corporations such as General Motors set up subsidiaries called **finance companies** to do this (see "GMAC" on page 218).

finance companies
Financial intermediaries that borrow in order to make consumer, mortgage, and business loans.

A finance company like GMAC raises funds either by borrowing from banks or by selling commercial paper. It then uses the funds to lend to buyers of GM products. GMAC also lends to GM dealers to help them finance their inventories and to GM suppliers of automotive parts to finance their working capital. The composition of finance company lending is shown in Exhibit 9.4.

Finance companies are financial intermediaries: They borrow in order to lend to others. They are able to compete with banks in this activity, because the type of loan they make involves relatively low information and monitoring costs. Loans to consumers are collateralized by the product purchased, such as a car or an appliance. Loans to dealers and suppliers are relatively safe, because these are firms with which the parent of the finance company does business and about which it therefore has good information. Moreover, it is clearly not in the interest of dealers and suppliers to sour a continuing relationship with the parent company by poor performance in repaying loans.

Another reason that finance companies can compete with banks is that they escape the costs that bank regulation imposes on banks. Unlike banks, they are not required to hold reserves, they do not have a required equity-to-asset ratio, and they do not have to pay deposit insurance premiums.

THE EFFECT ON BANKS

How does all this redirected borrowing and lending affect banks? Consider the following example. There are two firms—X and Y. Firm X has $1 million in liquid funds for which it has no immediate need. Firm Y, on the other hand, needs to borrow $1 million. Clearly, there is a possible match here. But how is the match to be made?

In the 1950s the match would have been made through a bank. Firm X would have deposited the $1 million in a zero-interest checking account, and the bank would have lent the money to Firm Y at, say, 3%. The difference between the rate on the loan and the rate on the deposit would not have been sufficient to drive either firm to seek a better alternative.

By the late 1970s the rate on such a loan would have been 15%; because of banking regulations, the rate on the checking account was still zero. On the one

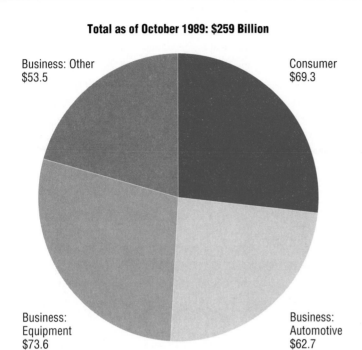

Total as of October 1989: $259 Billion

Business: Other $53.5

Consumer $69.3

Business: Equipment $73.6

Business: Automotive $62.7

Note: Leasing totals were added to business. This underestimates the total for consumers by a relatively small amount.

Source: *Federal Reserve Bulletin.*

hand, Firm X wanted to earn more than zero: The forgone interest was now large enough to make the effort worthwhile. On the other hand, Firm Y wanted to raise money more cheaply: The cost of the loan was sufficiently high to drive it to seek a cheaper alternative. If X could lend Y the money some other way, rather than through a bank, at some rate between 0% and 15%, both would be better off, and only the bank would lose. [8]

Exhibit 9.5 shows some of the ways X can lend to Y without a bank being involved. (There are some additional ways, involving banks overseas, that we shall see in Chapter 11.) If Y is a government securities dealer, then it can borrow from X directly by using a repo. If Y is some large corporation, with good credit, it can borrow directly by selling X commercial paper. The substitution, in these cases, of direct lending for lending via a bank is called **disintermediation**. If Y is a

disintermediation Shifting from bank-intermediated lending to lending in the direct market.

[8]Actually, the room for a deal is not quite this wide. For example, if Y sells commercial paper to X, it bears the cost of issuing commercial paper. This must be covered by interest savings. For X the commercial paper is less liquid and riskier than a bank deposit, so it will require some compensation for this. Nonetheless, there is still plenty of room for a deal at the expense of the bank.

GMAC

General Motors Acceptance Corporation (GMAC) is a wholly owned subsidiary of General Motors, originally set up in 1919 (with a capitalization of only $2.5 million). Its original purpose was to borrow funds and lend them out again to GM dealers and car buyers. In the 1980s, the large automakers realized that their enormous "captive" finance companies had the potential to do considerably more than this. Today, in addition to its traditional role of financing and insuring dealer inventories and customer purchases of GM cars and trucks, GMAC is involved in the leasing of GM products, in mortgage lending, and in various types of insurance. In 1988 GMAC had $99 billion in assets, and rivaled the largest banks in size. GM actually earns more money today from GMAC's loans and mortgages than it does from selling cars and trucks.

Sources: "And You Thought They Just Sold Cars," *Business Month,* November 1987; and *Moody's Bank and Finance Manual.*

smaller company that lacks the credit to issue its own commercial paper, it may still be able to borrow from X *indirectly* via a finance company: The finance company borrows from X by selling it commercial paper, and then lends the money to Y. Such a substitution of a different type of indirect lending, with a finance company rather than a bank acting as the intermediary, could be called **reintermediation.**

reintermediation
Shifting from bank-intermediated lending to other intermediaries.

While both Firm X and Firm Y are delighted with these alternative arrangements—X earns more on its liquid assets and Y borrows more cheaply—both disintermediation and reintermediation are bad news for the banks. Where before they were earning a nice income on the difference between loan rates and deposit rates, now they are earning nothing: Both loans and deposits are gone.

Some extent of the loss due to commercial paper alone can be seen from Exhibit 9.6, which shows the share of commercial paper in short-term finance. Since about half the lending of finance companies is to business, we add half the amount of commercial paper issued by finance companies to the amount of nonfinancial commercial paper, and compare the total with the commercial and industrial loans of banks. For example, at the end of 1987 commercial and industrial loans amounted to $572 billion, and lending to business via commercial paper (directly and indirectly through finance companies) amounted to $145 billion. Thus the share of commercial paper was

$$\frac{\$145 \text{ billion}}{\$145 \text{ billion} + \$572 \text{ billion}} = 0.20, \text{ or } 20\%.$$

Another indication of how much the traditional lending role of banks has been eroded is the fall in the fraction of short-term credit to nonfinancial business supplied by the major banks—from 43% in 1974 to 27% in 1985.

Looking merely at the *amount* of business that has been lost considerably understates the problem for the banks. The *type* of business lost is also important. Remember that only the largest and most creditworthy corporations have access

EXHIBIT 9.5

DIFFERENT WAYS TO ARRANGE SHORT-TERM LENDING

The traditional way for Firm X to lend to Firm Y was through a bank. Alternative ways developed involving direct lending in the money market via repos and commercial paper, and involving other financial intermediaries such as finance companies.

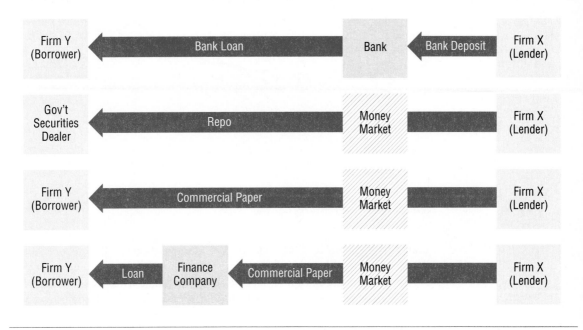

to the money market. The government securities dealers, finance companies, and other large corporations that have found alternatives to borrowing from their banks are among the banks' best customers. Loans to these customers have very little default risk. So the banks have lost many of their best loans. The loans they have left are riskier; as we shall see later, this inevitably has had a bad effect on bank safety.

9.3 SMALL INVESTORS GET IN ON THE ACT

We have seen how the enormous gap between market rates and regulated deposit rates drove corporate treasurers to reduce their deposits and to invest instead in money market paper—T-bills, repos, commercial paper, and in other instruments about which we shall hear later. What about households? They too would have preferred the high market interest rates to the stingy rates on deposits, but for them it was not so easy.

Repurchase agreements, commercial paper, and other money market instruments all have large minimum denominations. The minimum is usually $100,000—

EXHIBIT 9.6

COMMERCIAL-PAPER
SHARE OF SHORT-
TERM FINANCE

From the late 1960s on, the
share of direct short-term
lending grew steadily at the
expense of bank loans.

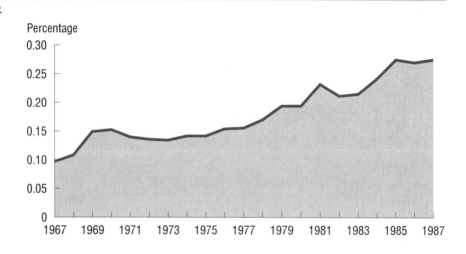

Source: *Economic Report of the President.*

even T-bills start at $10,000—and the typical transaction is in the millions. While this may be no problem for a corporate treasurer with millions to invest, it puts high money market rates well out of reach of the small saver.

But does this not suggest a tremendous profit opportunity? If some ingenious financial innovator can find a way to bring small investors into the money market, the potential business is enormous. Millions stand to be made. But how is it to be done?

Since the problem is the large minimum denomination, some sort of pooling seems to be indicated. What sort of pools, other than banks, are available? In Chapter 3 we saw that investment companies offer a kind of pool called a mutual fund. For example, stock mutual funds pool small amounts from each of many investors and invest in a portfolio of stocks. Why not do the same thing with money market paper?

MONEY MARKET MUTUAL FUNDS

**money market
mutual fund**
Pool of a large number of
small accounts for the
purpose of investing in
diversified portfolios of
money market securities.

The first **money market mutual fund** was offered in 1972. As you can see from Exhibit 9.7 the idea was a tremendous success. By 1975 there were already 35 funds, with 200,000 accounts and $4 billion in assets. By 1982 there were over 450 different funds, with over 3 million accounts, and $240 billion in assets![9]

---

[9]You can see from Exhibit 9.7 that there was a temporary drop in the amount of these funds after 1982. We shall see why in the next chapter.

EXHIBIT 9.7

MONEY MARKET
MUTUAL FUND
ASSETS

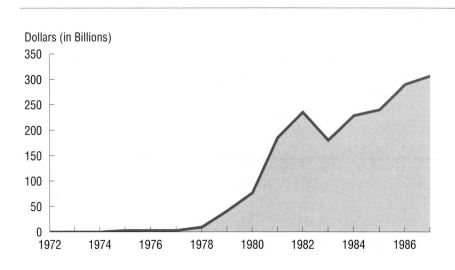

Source: *Economic Report of the President.*

The success of money market mutual funds is due to more than just the high money market rates they offer small investors. Being pools, they have other advantages too. They provide investors with greater liquidity than can be had from owning money market instruments directly: Most withdrawals can be met out of new funds coming in, so cash reserves need not be large, and it is rarely necessary to sell assets before they mature. Because the fund's portfolio is large, diversification works its magic. Indeed, the liquidity and diversification advantages of money market mutual funds makes them attractive even to *large* investors that already have direct access to the money market.

As with other mutual funds, investors in a money market mutual fund buy *shares* in the pool of securities held by the fund. If the securities rise or fall in value, so do the shares. In contrast, with a deposit, the value of the deposit is unaffected by fluctuations in the value of the underlying securities. Since default risk is small, the main reason for potential fluctuation in the value of the securities is fluctuation in market interest rates. However, as we saw in Chapter 6, the price of short-term securities is affected relatively little by fluctuations in market interest rates, and the average maturity of securities held by money market mutual funds is very short indeed—one to two months is typical. Therefore money market mutual fund shares are, in practice, fairly stable in value.

Because of their great liquidity, money market mutual funds are able to offer shareholders limited check-writing privileges.[10] But isn't this illegal? Aren't only banks allowed to offer checking accounts? No problem. Shareholders in a money

[10]There is usually a minimum amount for each check (say $500) and a maximum number of checks per month (say three or four).

CMA ACCOUNTS

Merrill Lynch first offered its Cash Management Account (CMA) in 1977. If you buy and sell stocks, you normally keep a cash account with your broker out of which you pay for your purchases and into which the proceeds of your sales are placed. This cash account does not normally bear interest. The CMA automatically checks the cash account every week and sweeps the balance into a money market mutual fund paying a market rate of interest; if money is needed for a stock purchase, it is automatically taken out of the money market mutual fund. In addition, you receive a checkbook. Checks you write are debited first against any cash in your cash account; if this is insufficient, the money market mutual fund account is tapped; and if this too is insufficient, credit is automatically extended up to an amount equal to 50% of the value of your stock portfolio (your stocks are collateral). You also receive a bank credit card that may be used to access the same line of credit. Since Merrill Lynch is not a bank itself, it may not offer a checking account or a bank credit card. These are actually offered for Merrill Lynch by Bank One of Columbus, Ohio, which receives a fee for the service. The CMA ensures that you earn the highest possible interest on funds with your broker, and it improves enormously the liquidity of your stock portfolio.

The banks challenged the legality of the CMA: Merrill Lynch seemed to be engaged in banking activities prohibited to an investment bank. This challenge was not successful, and banks have been forced to compete with similar products of their own. For example, Citibank offers the Asset Network Account, and Chase Manhattan offers the Universal Account. By the end of 1986 Merrill Lynch had some 1,300,000 CMA accounts, and most other brokerage houses were offering their own versions of the CMA.

market mutual fund have a joint account at a commercial bank on which the checks are drawn, so it is all quite aboveboard. Moreover, because of the benefits of pooling, the balance that needs to be kept in the account is quite small.

Investment companies and investment banks devised a variety of different types of money market mutual fund, often combining them with other accounts and services. One of the most successful, and most widely emulated, was the Cash Management Account offered by Merrill Lynch (see "CMA Accounts").

IMPLICATIONS FOR THE MONEY MARKET AND FOR BANKS

The rapid growth of money market mutual funds has been an important factor in the expansion of the money market itself. The funds have brought into the market billions of dollars that would not otherwise have been available. (Those billions came largely out of time deposits at banks.) Money market mutual funds have become particularly important in the commercial paper market, holding over 28% of the commercial paper outstanding in 1986. (See Exhibit 9.8.) The inflow of funds kept interest rates on commercial paper low relative to bank loans, and this encouraged more companies to issue commercial paper.

EXHIBIT 9.8

COMPOSITION OF MONEY MARKET MUTUAL FUND ASSETS: 1987

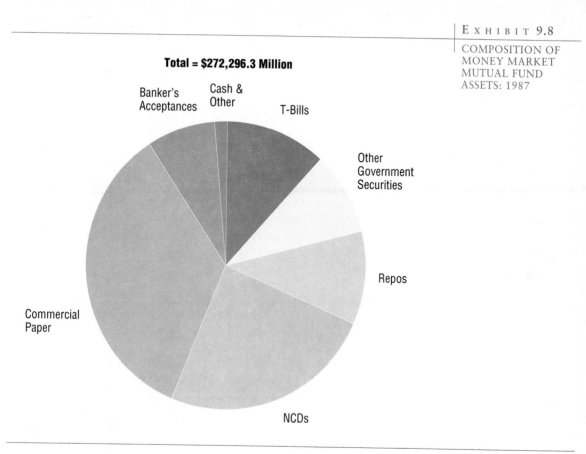

Total = $272,296.3 Million

Source: Investment Company Institute, *Mutual Fund Fact Book.*

The money market mutual funds also added some new ways of arranging short-term lending beyond those shown in Exhibit 9.5. The alternatives shown there were all limited to large lenders. Large lenders can lend directly to large borrowers through repos or commercial paper; they can lend indirectly to small borrowers through finance companies. Exhibit 9.9 shows the new possibilities. Now small lenders can lend to large borrowers through money market mutual funds, and they can lend to small borrowers through a chain involving money market mutual funds and finance companies.

Clearly, these new chains of intermediation come very close to duplicating what a bank can do. As does a bank, a money market mutual fund takes in many small deposits (or something very much like deposits) and pools them to lend to firms and households. Moreover, the money market mutual fund, like the finance company, has some significant cost advantages. It is not required to hold reserves; it has no required equity-to-asset ratio; and it pays no deposit insurance premiums. It also does not have to spend money on gathering credit information, assessing creditworthiness, and so on: Because it buys only publicly traded securities, it can rely on the money market to do the work for it.[11] For all these reasons, the costs of a money market mutual fund are much lower than those of a bank. This means that it can pay a return on its liabilities that is quite close to the return it earns on its assets.

9.4 WAS THE GROWTH OF THE MONEY MARKET GOOD FOR THE ECONOMY?

What are the broader implications of this rapid expansion of the money market? Clearly, ultimate borrowers and lenders are better off: Borrowers can borrow more cheaply, lenders can earn more on their savings. Equally clearly, banks are hurt (although we shall see in the next chapter that they do make a comeback). But how does it affect the economy as a whole?

In one sense it is an improvement. We saw in Chapter 3 that the smaller the difference between borrowing and lending rates, the better. The smaller the difference, the more saving and investment there will be. The developments we have seen certainly had the effect of reducing that difference. But was it a genuine gain? The difference was so large only because of bank regulation—Regulation Q and Section 11 of the Glass-Steagall Act. So the achievement was really just in overcoming this artificial regulatory barrier.

We can gain some perspective on this by once again comparing the United States with Canada. In Canada there were no regulations limiting the interest rates that banks could pay on deposits. As market rates rose, so did the rates on time deposits and on demand deposits. Nothing like the U.S. money market developed there: Most short-term lending in Canada is still intermediated by banks. There has been some shift from low- or zero-interest checking accounts to higher-interest time deposits, but because banks could pay competitive rates, there has been no overall loss of deposits.

Perhaps, after all, the enormous amount of human effort and ingenuity that went into getting around the regulatory restrictions in the United States was something of a waste. Had the regulatory restrictions not been there, all the resources that went into overcoming them could have been put to more productive use.

SUMMARY

- Historically, because direct lending is relatively expensive and because banks have a natural advantage in the short-term market, most short-term lending has been intermediated by banks.

---

[11]In the case of the chain of intermediation involving the finance company, the finance company takes on the credit assessment and loan monitoring that is normally done by a bank.

EXHIBIT 9.9

SHORT-TERM LENDING VIA A MONEY MARKET MUTUAL FUND

Money market mutual funds opened up some new channels of intermediation. Small lenders could now lend indirectly both to large and, through finance companies, to small borrowers.

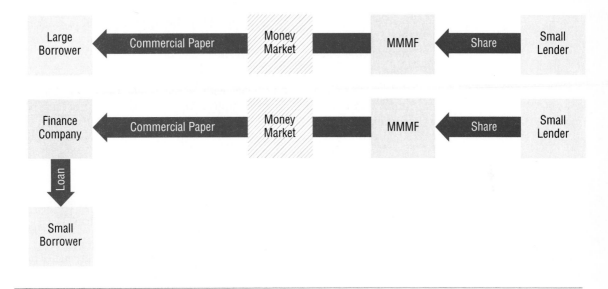

- Following the banking collapse of the Great Depression, the Glass-Steagall Act sought to limit "excessive" competition among banks. Among its provisions, it prohibited the payment of interest on demand deposits and empowered the Fed to limit interest on time deposits under Regulation Q.

- In the 1960s rising interest rates came up against these restrictions on the rates that banks could pay on deposits. The result was a widening gap between the restricted rates on deposits and the market-determined rates on loans. This gap gave borrowers and lenders a strong incentive to develop new ways of getting together, ways that did not involve banks.

- The first to respond to these incentives were corporate treasurers seeking a better return on their cash assets. They began to lend to government securities dealers through dealer repurchase agreements and to other corporations by purchasing commercial paper.

- The biggest borrowers in the commercial-paper market are finance companies. Many of the largest of these were set up to finance the purchase of consumer durables. They are able to compete with banks as financial intermediaries because they specialize in types of lending with relatively low information and monitoring costs and because they escape the regulatory costs and restrictions imposed on banks.

- Both disintermediation—the shift from bank-intermediated lending to the direct market—and reintermediation—the shift to other intermediaries such as finance companies and money market mutual funds—meant a serious loss of business for banks.

- The large denominations traded on the money market, usually $100,000 and up, kept high market rates out of the reach of most households. Money market mutual funds solved this problem, bringing the small investor into the money market, by pooling large numbers of small accounts to invest in diversified portfolios of money market securities.

- While all these innovations did eventually succeed in circumventing the restrictions on bank deposit rates, with a resulting increase in the efficiency of the financial system, the enormous effort involved would not have been necessary had the restrictions not been there in the first place.

KEY TERMS

money market	dealer repurchase agreement	finance companies
capital market		disintermediation
Regulation Q	commercial paper	reintermediation
prime rate	direct placement	money market mutual fund

DISCUSSION QUESTIONS

1. If the effective annual market rate on commercial paper is 10%, what is the discount on a piece of commercial paper due in 30 days?

2. Suppose that Tronics Inc. needs to borrow $3 million. It can either issue commercial paper at 10% or borrow from its bank at 11%. The costs of issuing commercial paper are as follows: There is an annual rating fee of $20,000, and Tronics must pay its dealer a fee of 1/8 of 1% to place each issue (if it issues 90-day paper and rolls it over, it will have to pay the dealer fee 4 times a year). Which is cheaper, the bank loan or the commercial paper? What is the minimum-size issue that would make commercial paper the cheaper alternative?

3. What effect do you think that Section 11 of the Glass-Steagall Act had on the implicit interest paid on demand deposits? What sort of implicit interest is there on correspondent balances?

4. What would you expect banks to do when market rates on loans come up against usury-law ceilings—state laws that set a ceiling on the rate that may be charged on a loan? These ceilings are designed to protect low-income and other high-risk borrowers. Do you think they are likely to succeed in this goal?

5. How meaningful do you think the restriction is that funds raised from the sale of commercial paper must be used for "current transactions" (that is, they must not be used for fixed investment)? Explain.

6. Money market mutual funds and finance companies seem to be producing the same "product" as banks (financial intermediation) but doing so more cheaply. How is this possible?

7. What is the difference between disintermediation and reintermediation?

BIBLIOGRAPHY

Cook, Timothy Q., and Timothy D. Rowe, *Instruments of the Money Market*, Federal Reserve Bank of Richmond, 1986.

Stigum, Marcia L., *The Money Market*, 3rd ed., Homewood, IL: Dow Jones-Irwin, 1990.

CHAPTER 10

BANKS AND THE MONEY MARKET

II. THE BANKS FIGHT BACK

In Chapter 9 we saw how the traditional pattern of indirect short-term lending through banks was changed by the growth of the money market. In response to the widening gap between regulated yields on deposits and rising market interest rates, both depositors and borrowers sought more attractive alternatives.

Corporate treasurers, with large amounts of liquid funds to manage, soon found it worthwhile to invest their cash in short-term securities rather than leave it in zero-interest checking accounts. Their needs were matched by government securities dealers looking for less expensive financing for their inventories and by other corporate treasurers trying to reduce the cost of short-term borrowing. As a result, the markets for repos and commercial paper flourished. Initially kept out of the money market by the large denominations involved, households soon found a way in through the newly created money market mutual funds.

As borrowers and lenders found one another in the money market, either directly or indirectly through nonbank intermediaries such as finance companies and money market mutual funds, the banks found themselves steadily losing business. Bank deposits, which had accounted for two-thirds of all financial assets in 1947, had fallen to one-third by 1980. Not surprisingly, banks sought desperately to fight their way back.

10.1 FINDING WAYS TO PAY INTEREST ON DEMAND DEPOSITS

The first thing banks did was to find ways to pay interest on the demand deposits of their large depositors. Why would a bank *want* to pay interest on its deposits? Because it must. With high market rates of interest, corporations will simply not let their money sit in a zero-interest account. They will either manage the money themselves to earn interest, in the ways we described in Chapter 9, or they will

229

move it to another bank that does find a way to pay them interest. So our bank must either pay up or lose the accounts. An interest-paying deposit will not be as profitable for the bank as a zero-interest deposit, but it will be a lot more profitable than *no* deposit.

BANK REPOS

bank repos
Arrangement to convert a deposit automatically into a repo overnight.

Banks countered dealer repos with their own **bank repos.** Instead of the inconvenience of having to arrange repos with a government securities dealer, a corporate treasurer could have the bank turn the balance of his demand deposit into an overnight repo *automatically* each day.

For example, suppose that at the end of the day, say, at 3:30 p.m., the corporation has a balance of $1 million in its zero-interest checking account. The bank automatically sells the corporation $1 million in T-bills and agrees to buy back the T-bills at 9 a.m. the next day at a price of $1,000,185. At 9 a.m. the next day the account is credited with $1,000,185; during the day money flows in and is paid out. At the end of the second day, the balance is, say, $2 million. Once again, automatically, the bank sells the corporation this amount in T-bills and agrees to buy back the T-bills the following morning for $2,000,370. Usually, the T-bills are transferred to a custodial account *at the bank,* so transactions costs are low.

As far as the depositor is concerned, this arrangement is really nothing more nor less than a checking account that pays interest. Formally, of course, it is a zero-interest checking account by day and a repurchase agreement by night. But since there are no transactions in the account at night, this formal distinction matters very little to the depositor.

Although the formal distinction between a deposit and an overnight repo may not matter to the depositor, it does matter to the bank. To see why, consider the balance sheet of a typical bank, First National (for simplicity, we assume that First National maintains its reserves at precisely the required ratio of 10%):

<table>
<tr><td colspan="4" style="text-align:center">FIRST NATIONAL</td></tr>
<tr><td>Reserves</td><td>$10m</td><td>Deposits</td><td>$100m</td></tr>
<tr><td>T-bills</td><td>15m</td><td>Equity</td><td>5m</td></tr>
<tr><td>Loans</td><td>80m</td><td></td><td></td></tr>
</table>

T-account
Simple accounting statement that lists only the changes that occur in balance sheet items.

Suppose that First National offers repo agreements to several of its largest corporate depositors, with deposits between them of, say, $10 million. The *change* to First National's balance sheet is represented by the following **T-account** (T-accounts are explained more fully in the appendix to this chapter):

EXHIBIT 10.1

OVERNIGHT AND
TERM REPURCHASE
AGREEMENTS

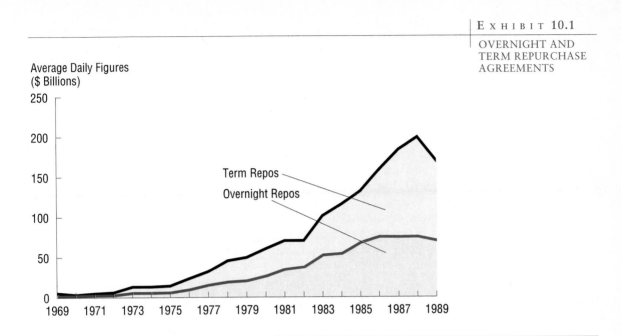

Note: Overnight figures include overnight Eurodollars.
Source: *Economic Report of the President.*

Deposits	−$10m
Securities sold under agreement to repurchase	+10m

Because deposits are down by $10 million, First National may reduce its cash reserves by $1 million, and replace them with earning assets. Say it does so by buying more securities. The change will be:

Reserves	−$1m
T-bills	+1m

But didn't we just say that the bank repo is nothing more than a disguised interest-bearing checking account? Doesn't the bank have to keep reserves against it? Not at all. "Securities sold under agreement to repurchase" are considered by bank regulators to be a "borrowing," not a deposit. Since the repo is not formally a deposit, it is not subject to a reserve requirement.[1] So, at 4 p.m., when the bank counts up its deposits, the $10 million has "vanished."

From Exhibit 10.1 you can see how the use of bank repos skyrocketed in the late 1970s and early 1980s.

THE FEDERAL FUNDS GAMBIT

There is another method for banks to pay interest on checking accounts that has the added advantage to the bank that no collateral in the form of T-bills is required. That method involves federal funds.

We saw in Chapter 5 that banks keep a significant part of their reserves in demand deposits at the regional Fed. These deposits, in addition to being more secure than vault cash, provide a convenient way for banks to transfer funds to one another when clearing checks. They also provide a convenient way for banks to lend one another reserves in the *federal funds market.*

broker market
Market in which large blocks of federal funds are lent.

There are two parts to this market. In the first part, the **broker market,** large sums of federal funds—at least $10 million at a time, $25 million on average—are traded via brokers. There are five large brokers, much like the government securities brokers we met in Chapter 7. A typical broker, with a staff of no more than 25, might arrange $10 *billion* to $20 *billion* in loans each day. The commission is $1 per $1 million per day of the loan. Not bad work if you can get it!

correspondent market
Market in which correspondents convert respondent deposits into federal funds loans.

The second part of the market, the **correspondent market,** is not really a market at all. As we saw in Chapter 8, small banks will generally keep a demand deposit at their correspondent bank (a large bank that provides the small bank with a variety of services). For example, suppose Township State Bank has $5 million in its demand deposit at First National, its correspondent. The services that First National provides to Township are implicit interest on this deposit. However, when market rates are high, the implicit interest is no longer enough: Township would like to earn something closer to the market rate. Although First National would be willing to pay interest to keep the funds, the law prevents it from paying interest on demand deposits. The federal funds market provides a convenient fig leaf that allows the two banks to get around the law.

To see how, consider the following two-stage transaction.

Stage 1. Township withdraws all $5 million from its deposit at First National in the form of federal funds. That is, First National requests over Fedwire that the Fed transfer $5 million from its account to Township's. T-accounts of the changes to the balance sheets of the two banks and of the Fed are:

---

[1]For the repo to be exempt from reserve requirements, the securities repoed must be Treasuries or agencies.

FIRST NATIONAL BANK

Deposit at Fed	−$5m	Deposits Township	−$5m

TOWNSHIP STATE BANK

Deposit at First National	−$5m	
Deposit at Fed	+5m	

FEDERAL RESERVE BANK

	Deposits Township	+$5m
	First National	−5m

Stage 2. Township now turns around and lends First National the $5 million in federal funds. The T-accounts for this second transaction are:

FIRST NATIONAL BANK

Deposit at Fed	+$5m	Federal funds bought Township	+$5m

TOWNSHIP STATE BANK

Deposit at Fed	−$5m	
Federal funds sold First National	+5m	

FEDERAL RESERVE BANK

	Deposits Township	−$5m
	First National	+5m

Note that the loan of federal funds is called a *purchase* from the point of view of the borrower and a *sale* from the point of view of the lender. We can see the total effect of the two stages by consolidating the T-accounts to show the net changes after both stages have been completed. The result is:

FIRST NATIONAL BANK

	Deposits	
	Township	−$5m
	Federal funds bought	
	Township	+5m

TOWNSHIP STATE BANK

Deposit at First National	−$5m	
Federal funds sold		
First National	+5m	

FEDERAL RESERVE BANK

	Deposits	
	Township	Unchanged
	First National	Unchanged

The net effect, then, is to convert Township's deposit at First National into a federal funds loan. In reality, banks carry out the two-stage transaction in one. First National converts the demand deposit into purchased federal funds directly, and the Fed itself is not involved in the transaction (note that the deposits and the withdrawals from the two banks' accounts at the Fed cancel out over the two stages). First National will do this for Township automatically at the end of each day—just as it does with its repo arrangement for corporations—converting the purchased federal funds back into a deposit the next morning.

The conversion of the deposit into a borrowing has two important implications. First, First National is allowed to pay interest on borrowings—in this case, federal funds purchased—even if it is not allowed to pay interest on demand deposits. Second, since federal funds purchased are not *formally* a deposit, First National does not now need to hold reserves against the $5 million. If the required reserve ratio is 10%, it can reduce its reserves by $500,000 and increase its earning assets by the same amount.

An advantage for First National of this federal funds gambit over the similar bank repo ploy is that First National does not have to hold T-bills as collateral: The funds can be used to make loans. With a repo the funds simply finance the securities underlying the repo, and no additional lending is possible. This lack of collateral in the federal funds gambit is, of course, a disadvantage for Township: If First National fails, it is less likely to recover its money. But Township will be compensated for the risk by getting a higher yield than it would earn on repos.

In order for this arrangement to be legal, however, it must be possible in principle to carry out the two-stage transaction as we have described it. That is, both parties must be *allowed* to have accounts at the Fed, although they do not actually have to have an account. The federal funds gambit is, therefore, available only to other banks, thrifts, U.S. agencies, government securities dealers, and domestic offices of foreign banks.

OVERNIGHT EURODOLLARS

A third variation on this "vanishing deposit" ploy involves **Eurodollars**. We shall discuss Eurodollars more thoroughly in Chapter 11. For the moment just think of them as deposits at First National's branch in London, England. As an alternative to a bank repo or a fed funds purchase, First National can offer its customers the following deal.

Eurodollars
Dollar-denominated deposits held in foreign banks.

At the end of each day, the balance in the customer's demand deposit is automatically withdrawn and redeposited at the London branch. Since the branch in London is outside the jurisdiction of U.S. bank regulators, it may pay interest on its deposits. The funds redeposited in London are lent back to the home office. For example, if $1 million is involved, the T-accounts would be:

FIRST NATIONAL

| | | Deposits | −$1m |
| | | Eurodollar borrowings | +1m |

FIRST NATIONAL, LONDON

| Loans | | Deposits | +$1m |
| First National | +$1m | | |

For the customer, the Eurodollar deposit, like the fed funds sale, is an unsecured loan (there is no deposit insurance on Eurodollar deposits). For First National, the Eurodollar borrowing is not as attractive as a fed funds sale because it is subject to a 3% reserve requirement. However, it may be offered to any customer, not just those entitled to have deposits at the Fed. Also, like a fed funds purchase but unlike a repo, there are no restrictions on how the funds may be used.

10.2 MAKING MONEY FROM COMMERCIAL PAPER

The banks' response to the rapid growth of the commercial-paper market has been: "If you can't beat 'em, join 'em." They have done this in a number of ways, the most direct being actually to help companies issue commercial paper.

STANDBY LETTERS OF CREDIT

standby letter of credit
Bank's guarantee that it will lend an issuer of commercial paper the money to pay off maturing paper.

One way a bank can help is by providing a **standby letter of credit.** Remember from Chapter 9 that commercial paper is generally of very short maturity and that issuers typically roll it over—that is, they sell new paper to pay off the old. There is a potential danger here to the buyer of the commercial paper: What if the issuer, for whatever reason, cannot roll over the paper? That is where the standby letter of credit comes in. The standby letter of credit is a guarantee that, if necessary, the bank will lend the issuer the money to pay off the old paper. In effect, the commercial paper will be converted into a bank loan. Banks are able to guarantee commercial paper in this way precisely because they are specialists in evaluating credit risk and in monitoring loan performance. The amount of standby letters of credit outstanding grew rapidly, from $50 billion in 1980 to over $150 billion in 1985.

The standby letter of credit is valuable because it lends the issuer of the commercial paper the "name" (the creditworthiness) of the guaranteeing bank. Since there is less risk to the lender, the paper can be sold at a lower rate of interest than would be necessary without it. The better the creditworthiness of the bank, the lower the rate the issuer pays, so issuers will go to the most creditworthy banks for their standby letters of credit. Because the money center banks have in recent years taken large losses on their loan portfolios, their creditworthiness has deteriorated.[2] As a result, about half the business in standby letters of credit now goes to Japanese banks in the United States, which have excellent credit standings.

Naturally, the bank charges the issuer of the commercial paper for providing the standby letter of credit. The traditional way that the issuer would "pay" the bank would be by holding a *compensating balance*. A fraction of the money raised from selling the commercial paper, say, 10% to 20%, would be kept in a zero-interest demand deposit at the bank that provided the standby letter of credit. The bank would be able to earn interest on the funds so deposited, and there would be the added advantage that the compensating balance would provide useful information about the issuer: Difficulty in maintaining the level of the compensating balance might be an early indication that the borrower was in trouble and that it would have problems paying off its commercial paper. Another way to view this arrangement is that, by providing the corporation with the standby letter of credit, the bank is paying implicit interest on the demand deposit—paying interest in services rather than in cash, thereby getting around the prohibition on explicit interest.

Today, compensating balances are less popular—the implicit interest is too low—and it is more common for the issuer to pay a straight fee for the provision of a standby letter of credit. With corporations now generally earning interest on their liquid assets, rather than leaving them in zero-interest demand deposits, it is easier to reckon the cost of the standby letter of credit by paying for it directly. The fee is typically 0.375% to 0.75%.

---

[2]We shall have more to say about this in Chapter 17.

UNDERWRITING COMMERCIAL PAPER

Apart from providing guarantees, a bank can also help, for a fee, to actually sell the commercial paper. For some time it was unclear whether or not this was legal. As we saw in Chapter 5, the Glass-Steagall Act prohibited commercial banks from underwriting securities: "Helping to sell" looks a lot like underwriting.[3] However, in 1988 the courts ruled that banks' involvement in the sale of commercial paper did not constitute true underwriting and was therefore permissible.[4]

So even though the growth of the commercial-paper market implies disintermediation, banks are far from being excluded entirely. Although they no longer earn a margin on the loan—the difference between the rate on the loan and the rate on the deposit that provides the necessary funds—they do quite well from the fees they earn on the commercial paper.

THE ADVANTAGES TO THE BANK OF COMMERCIAL PAPER

Indeed, in some cases, banks may actually *prefer* helping a customer issue commercial paper to making a loan directly. To see why, consider an example. Megacorp needs to raise $1 million in working capital. It can do so either by taking a one-year loan from its bank, First National, or by issuing commercial paper.[5]

If Megacorp takes a loan, First National must find the funds. The way the loan is funded is shown in Exhibit 10.2. The funds will come partly from deposits and partly from equity; remember that a bank must fund part of its loans from equity to ensure solvency and to protect its depositors from loan losses. If First National has an equity-to-loan ratio of 6%, then $60,000 of the needed $1 million will come from additional equity.

The remaining $940,000 First National needs for the loan will come from additional deposits. But, because of reserve requirements, First National will have to take in *more* than this amount. If the reserve requirement is 3%, First National will have to take in $940,000/0.97 = $969,000 of additional deposits in order to get the $940,000 it needs; the remaining $29,000 will be added to reserves.

How much will all this cost? Because the equity holders are the ones who bear the risk of loan losses, they require a higher return than depositors. Suppose

---

[3]Underwriting is reserved for investment banks, which are prohibited, in turn, from taking deposits and making commercial loans. We shall discuss underwriting and investment banking in more detail in Chapter 14 and the separation of commercial and investment banking in Chapter 18.

[4]Their rationale was that banks do not—as does an underwriter—actually buy the commercial paper for resale: They act as brokers rather than dealers. Also, the commercial paper is typically placed with a few large financial institutions, rather than sold to the public at large, as is the case with true underwriting.

[5]Although commercial paper is not issued with a maturity this long, Megacorp could roll over a shorter-term issue, which would be comparable, for our purposes, to a one-year loan.

EXHIBIT 10.2

FUNDING A
$1 MILLION LOAN

A new loan is funded partly
from new equity and partly
from additional deposits. The
additional deposits are not all
available to be lent: a fraction
must go into reserves.

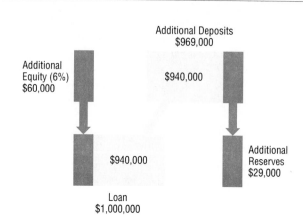

the required rate of return on First National's equity is 15% (if First National earns less than this on the equity in the new loan, it will lower the average return to its equity holders). The interest rate on additional deposits is 8%. In addition to the interest on the deposit, however, First National must also pay a premium for federal deposit insurance of 0.15%. The cost of funding the loan will therefore be

Equity:
$60,000 x 0.15 = $ 9,000

Deposits:
   Interest $969,000 x 0.08 =   77,520
   Deposit insurance $969,000 x 0.0015 =   1,454
Total $87,974

So, just to break even, First National will have to charge 8.8% on the loan.[6]

Instead of making Megacorp a loan itself, First National could help it issue commercial paper. If First National provides a standby letter of credit, the commercial paper will be perceived by the market to be as secure as a loan to First National and will therefore require a rate of interest of, say, 8.1% (a little more than the rate First National must pay on deposits because there is no federal insurance of the commercial paper).

The difference between the 8.1% on the commercial paper and the minimum of 8.8% on the loan can be split between First National and Megacorp, the nature of the split (the amount of fees First National will charge) depending on

---

[6]If there is a risk of default, the contractual rate will have to be above 8.8% to take this into account. The 8.8% is the *realized* rate that Metropolis must be able to expect on the loan. In reality, the whole calculation is more complicated than this because of tax considerations.

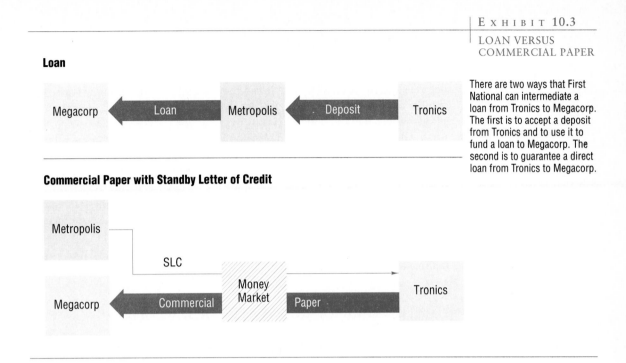

There are two ways that First National can intermediate a loan from Tronics to Megacorp. The first is to accept a deposit from Tronics and to use it to fund a loan to Megacorp. The second is to guarantee a direct loan from Tronics to Megacorp.

the relative bargaining strength of the two. If they split the difference, so that First National charges Megacorp 0.35% in fees, then First National will be making 0.35% more than it would with the straight loan, and Megacorp will be paying 0.35% less.

Exhibit 10.3 illustrates what is happening in the two different lending scenarios. In the first—the straight loan—First National takes in the required new deposit from some other corporation, say Tronics. In the second scenario—the sale of commercial paper—the paper might be sold to the same ultimate lender. So far as Megacorp and Tronics are concerned, the two situations are equivalent, if not quite identical.

For First National too there are strong similarities. In both cases the bank evaluates the credit risk and guarantees payment if the borrower defaults. But there are also significant differences. In the commercial-paper scenario, the loan never appears on First National's balance sheet. This means that it is not subject to the regulations governing equity-to-loan ratios. By effectively making more loans without increasing its capitalization, First National increases its leverage and thus the return on its equity. First National is also relieved of the liquidity concerns that might be associated with having deposits.[7]

---

[7]We discussed leverage and the return on equity in Chapter 5. As we shall see in Chapter 17, regulators have caught up with this ploy, and banks are now required to hold a certain proportion of equity against standby letters of credit.

10.3 BANK BORROWING IN THE MONEY MARKET

Suppose that a bank wants to make a new loan but is "loaned up": Given its deposits and the need to keep required reserves, it has made as many loans as it can. In the example we just looked at, we assumed that First National could somehow get the additional deposits it needed for the loan to Megacorp. But how? There is little a bank can do to increase its ordinary deposits, especially on short notice.

Banks were quick to realize that the growing commercial-paper market offered them not only new ways of lending (as we have seen), but also new ways of *borrowing*. Although banks themselves were not allowed to issue commercial paper, bank holding companies were. A holding company could sell commercial paper and use the proceeds to buy assets from the daughter bank; the money could then be used by the daughter bank to finance additional loans. In this manner additional funds could be raised quite quickly.[8]

NEGOTIABLE CERTIFICATES OF DEPOSIT

negotiable certificate of deposit (NCD)
Time deposit with a fixed maturity that can be bought and sold.

Moreover, banks soon invented a way around the prohibition on the direct issue of commercial paper: the **negotiable certificate of deposit (NCD)**.

A certificate of deposit is a time deposit with a fixed maturity, say, six months or a year. It may be withdrawn before maturity only with a substantial penalty. This, of course, makes it less liquid and therefore less attractive to, for instance, corporate treasurers managing their firms' liquid funds.

The NCD overcomes this problem by being *negotiable*. Although it cannot be redeemed before maturity, it can be sold to someone else. The purchaser may then redeem it from the bank, unless he in turn chooses to sell it. An NCD, because it can be bought and sold in this way, is really more like commercial paper or a T-bill than like an ordinary deposit.

While the rate of interest paid on regular time deposits was restricted by Regulation Q, NCDs of $100,000 or more were exempt and could be sold at market rates of interest.[9] This allowed banks to compete for funds in the money market in a way they could not with regular time deposits.[10]

---

[8]This used to be a way to avoid reserve requirements too. However, in 1970 the Fed imposed a 5% reserve requirement on commercial paper issued by bank holding companies and used to purchase assets from banking subsidiaries.

[9]NCDs of maturity less than 90 days were exempted from Regulation Q in 1970; longer-maturity NCDs were exempted in 1973.

[10]Before 1970, when Regulation Q did apply to NCDs, the Fed generally raised the ceiling rate to keep it above the market rate. In 1968 the Fed tried to restrict NCD rates by failing to raise the ceiling. The attempt was fruitless, because banks simply switched to the Eurodollar market. We shall see how in Chapter 11.

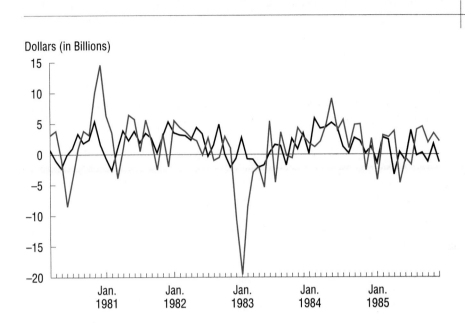

EXHIBIT 10.4

CHANGE IN NCDs OUTSTANDING AND IN BUSINESS LOANS AT LARGE REPORTING COMMERCIAL BANKS (MONTH TO MONTH, THREE-MONTH MOVING AVERAGE)

Source: Federal Reserve Bank of St. Louis.

The first NCD was issued in 1961 by Citibank (then called the First National City Bank of New York). By December 1987 the amount of NCDs outstanding had grown to $325 billion, and trading volume had reached $4 billion a day.

NCDs are issued in large denominations—usually $1 million or more. The market for NCDs, both primary and secondary, is made by the same dealers and brokers that make the market for T-bills and commercial paper (although some large banks place their own NCDs, just like large issuers of commercial paper). NCDs have a minimum maturity of 7 days, but the average is about 5 months.

There are a variety of issuers—mostly large money center banks, but also large regionals, U.S. branches of foreign banks ("Yankee" NCDs), and thrifts. There are also a variety of forms of interest payment: Fixed-coupon NCDs with fixed interest payments; floating-rate NCDs that pay interest varying with some reference market rate (for example, 1% above the current T-bill rate); and zero-coupon NCDs that pay no explicit interest and, like T-Bills, are sold at a discount.

NCDs have become *the* major source of additional funds for banks. With regular deposits, a bank has to sit and wait passively for money to come in: With NCDs, it can actively solicit funds. As the demand for loans goes up and down, so does the amount of NCDs (see Exhibit 10.4).

10.4 GETTING RID OF REGULATION Q

We have seen how banks tried to win back the business they lost from large borrowers and lenders. How did they deal with the defection of households to the money market mutual funds?

First of all, *large* banks did not, on balance, do so badly from this defection. Although they did lose retail deposits, they also gained an important new outlet for their NCDs: Money market mutual funds became major buyers (see Exhibit 9.9).

This new chain of intermediation—through money market mutual funds to large banks—could also be seen as one way around the restrictions on geographic expansion that we discussed in Chapter 8. As far as large banks are concerned, these geographic restrictions are mainly an obstacle to the gathering of deposits from a broader area. They are less of an obstacle to making loans, since potential borrowers are more likely to come to them or to be located in the money centers in the first place. The growth of the money market and the emergence of money market mutual funds in effect allows the large banks, indirectly, to bid deposits away from small local banks (see Exhibit 10.5).

This bidding away of their deposits was, of course, bad news for small local banks. Typically, such banks have had more deposits than good loan opportunities and they have lent the excess to large banks in need of the funds. This was a lucrative business: The small banks took in low-cost time deposits (low-cost because of Regulation Q) and relent the money to large banks at high money market rates (through the federal funds gambit or through NCDs). Money market mutual funds put an end to this by offering depositors a better deal. Depositors could now earn the high money market rates for themselves by lending to large banks (and to others) via the money market mutual funds.

Small banks reacted to this massive loss of deposits by pressing Congress to repeal interest-rate restrictions so that they could compete with the money market mutual funds. Of course, they would have preferred legislation getting rid of the money market mutual funds themselves, but this was politically infeasible. Large banks and consumers would never have allowed it.

Regulation Q was removed in stages by two major banking acts—the *Depository Institution's Deregulation and Monetary Control Act (DIDMCA) of 1980* and the *Garn-St. Germain Act of 1982*.

NOW ACCOUNTS

negotiated order of withdrawal (NOW) account
Time deposit that allows checking.

Even before Congress had had time to react, however, a way had been found to pay interest on household checking accounts—the **negotiated order of withdrawal (NOW) account.** The NOW account was invented by a Massachusetts savings bank looking for a way around a quite different regulation—the one banning savings banks from accepting demand deposits (see "The Creation of NOW Accounts" on page 244).

EXHIBIT 10.5

THE NCD END RUN

The McFadden Act prevents money center banks from nationwide branching to gather deposits. Money market mutual funds, however, can gather funds from all over the country and channel them to the money center banks by buying their NCDs.

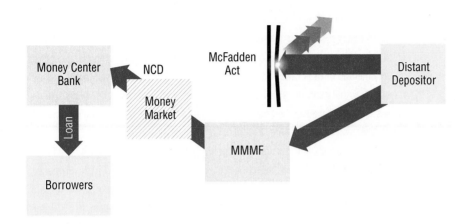

Formally, the negotiated order of withdrawal is a withdrawal slip that you may sign over to someone else. Functionally, of course, it is a check. Suppose you want to buy a can of paint for $20. You could go to your savings bank, write out a withdrawal slip for $20, take the cash, and pay for the paint at the store. With the negotiated order of withdrawal, you write out the withdrawal slip for $20 and sign it over to the store. The store can then present it to the bank to receive the cash, or, more likely, deposit it at its own bank to clear through the clearing system just like a check.

Of course, since the NOW account is formally a time deposit, not a demand deposit, Section 11 of the Glass-Steagall Act does not apply (although Regulation Q does). So not only had a way been found for a savings bank to offer a checking account, but, almost incidentally, a way had also been found to pay interest on a demand deposit.

The NOW account spread first to other savings banks in Massachusetts and then across New England. In 1980 the DIDMCA allowed NOW or similar accounts to virtually all depository institutions across the country. In 1982 SuperNOW (SNOW) accounts were authorized, subject to a $2,500 minimum balance but exempt from interest-rate ceilings (this is what made them "super").

MONEY MARKET DEPOSIT ACCOUNTS

In 1982 the Garn-St. Germain Act created the **money market deposit account,** a variety of time deposit account designed specifically to compete directly with money market mutual funds. It offered basically the same features—a market

money market deposit account
Account with limited check-writing privileges that pays a market rate of interest.

THE CREATION OF NOW ACCOUNTS

In July 1970 the Consumer Savings Bank of Worcester, Massachusetts, offered the first NOW savings account. This account allowed the transfer of funds to a third party through the use of a *negotiated order of withdrawal.* Since the account was technically a savings account, it could pay interest. The Bank Commissioner of Massachusetts initially denied Consumer Savings Bank permission to offer this account, but the Supreme Judicial Court of Massachusetts unanimously overturned the commissioner's decision on May 2, 1972. The court reasoned that a bank was free to offer any method of withdrawal from a savings account that it wished and that therefore the NOW account did not really constitute a new form of account. Following the court's ruling, mutual savings banks and savings and loans throughout Massachusetts and New Hampshire began offering their own versions of the NOW account.

Commercial banks were initially unable to respond by offering their own NOWs: The FDIC and Fed rules that applied to them prohibited them explicitly from offering third-party payments out of savings accounts. However, in 1973 Congress passed a law allowing all thrifts *and* commercial banks in New Hampshire and Massachusetts to offer NOW accounts. In 1976 the permission to offer NOW accounts was expanded to include all of New England. The DIDMCA of 1980 authorized all banks and thrifts nationwide to offer NOW accounts beginning January 1, 1981. Credit unions were authorized in 1974 to issue their own equivalent of the NOW, the *share draft account.*

Sources: Katharine Gibson, "The Early History and Initial Impact of NOW Accounts," *New England Economic Review*, January-February 1975, 17-26; and William Lovett, *Banking and Financial Institutions Law.*

rate of interest, limited check-writing privileges, and a fairly large minimum balance.

The new money market deposit accounts were a tremendous and instantaneous success (see Exhibit 10.6). Within five months of their introduction, in November 1982, they had grown from zero to $350 *billion.* Competition with the money market mutual funds has been fierce. Being bank deposits, money market deposit accounts have an important advantage over money market mutual funds—deposit insurance (although some money market mutual funds have responded with private insurance). As a result, money market deposit accounts have been able to get away with a somewhat lower rate of interest; the gap is smaller in markets, such as New York City, where competition is most intense.

Money market deposit accounts have not, of course, been an unmixed blessing for the banks. Initially, some of their growth came at the expense of the money market mutual funds (see Exhibit 10.6), but mostly it has come at the expense of other, low-interest, time deposits, like passbook savings accounts. Therefore, although banks seem to have been successful in stemming the hemorrhaging of deposits to the money market mutual funds, the cost to them has been enormous. Low-interest time deposits and passbook savings accounts have been replaced on their balance sheets by high-interest money market deposit accounts.

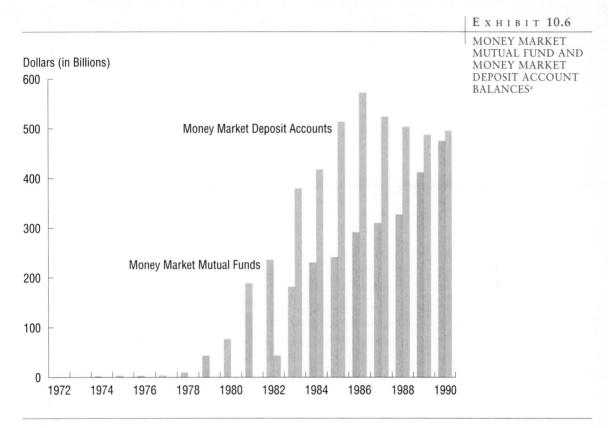

EXHIBIT 10.6

MONEY MARKET MUTUAL FUND AND MONEY MARKET DEPOSIT ACCOUNT BALANCES[a]

[a]Through May 1990.
Source: *Economic Report of the President.*

THE END OF REGULATION Q

The DIDMCA of 1980 provided for the phasing out of Regulation Q by 1986. Today banks are completely free to offer whatever rates they please on all time deposits and NOW accounts. While the payment of interest is still not allowed on regular demand deposits, this is not a problem for individuals and nonprofit institutions: NOW accounts provide a perfect substitute. Corporations, however, are not allowed to hold NOW accounts, although, as we have seen, they do have other alternatives such as the overnight repo.

10.5 | MAKING MONEY BY SELLING SERVICES

We have seen that banks responded to the loss of loan business to the commercial paper market by getting involved in the market in other ways—as dealers and as guarantors of commercial paper. This is not the only way they have tried to profit from developments that have otherwise cost them so much of their traditional business. The growth of cash management and of the money market have provided them with a host of new opportunities. For example, banks play an important, and lucrative, part in helping corporations manage their cash, in clearing transactions in the money market, as custodians of securities, and as sellers of market information.

These various "sidelines" have become increasingly important relative to the traditional business of taking in deposits and making loans. Indeed, some banks have become specialized in the processing of financial information and in the provision of financial services to the exclusion of more traditional banking activities (see "State Street Bucks a Bank-Expansion Trend, and Thrives").

In 1980 the 35 largest banks in the United States derived one-sixth of all their income from the provision of financial services; in 1985 one-third of the income of the 10 largest banks was from noninterest sources.

10.6 | SOME UNINTENDED CONSEQUENCES

While all of these innovations have helped banks hold their own in the face of competition from the money market, they have also increased the banks' cost of funds and squeezed their profits. This pressure on their profits has pushed banks to take more chances. As a result, bank safety has deteriorated significantly in recent years. We shall discuss this fully in Chapters 16 and 17.

Furthermore, many of the financial innovations designed primarily to get around Regulation Q have also undermined other banking regulations. Bank repos and the federal funds gambit create demand deposits that are not counted as such; as a result, it becomes harder to keep track of the total amount of demand deposits in the economy and harder for the Fed to control the quantity of money. The substitution of guaranteeing and placing commercial paper for straightforward bank loans enables banks effectively to increase their leverage, thereby increasing their risk of insolvency. And the growth of money market mutual funds, with a national deposit base, helps large money center banks overcome the geographic restrictions that limit their ability to compete with small local banks for deposits.

STATE STREET BUCKS A BANK-EXPANSION TREND, AND THRIVES: BOSTON COUNTINGHOUSE GROWS FAT ON FINANCIAL DATA-PROCESSING FEES

By Christopher J. Chipello

Staff Reporter of The Wall Street Journal

BOSTON—State Street Boston Corp. sold 23 of its 39 branch banks 4 years ago. Since then it has shuttered 10 more—leaving it with only 6—while its competitors continued to expand rapidly throughout New England.

What's wrong at State Street? Nothing. Indeed, things could hardly be better. With average return on equity of 18.2% over the past 10 years, State Street has become one of the nation's most profitable commercial banks by de-emphasizing banking.

Instead, State Street—New England's seventh-largest bank with assets of about $7 billion—makes most of its money on fees from financial data processing. Essentially a high-tech countinghouse, it keeps track of other people's investments, collects dividends, and the like. But it does so on a scale and with a degree of sophistication that the Ebenezer Scrooges of the world could only have dreamed of.

State Street crunches numbers and spews out statements for more than $500 billion of mutual funds, pension funds and other institutional investors. It may not be the most glamorous work in the investment world, but it pays well. Says Smith Barney, Harris Upham & Co. analyst Thomas Brown, "State Street is one of the banking industry's jewels. It's a growth company masquerading as a bank."

Tighter Lending Policies

The company's shift accelerated in the mid-1970s. Mr. Edgerly, installed after a raft of bad commercial real-estate loans surfaced, imposed more conservative lending policies. At the same time, to capitalize on a 1974 law that tightened reporting requirements for pension funds, State Street set out to apply its mutual-fund expertise to retirement funds. Befitting the bank's heightened emphasis on computer services, strategic officers

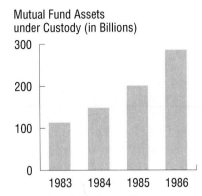

Mutual Fund Assets under Custody (in Billions)

Source: State Street Boston Corp.

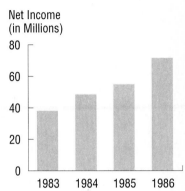

Net Income (in Millions)

now included several executives recruited from IBM.

Then came the 1980s, and mutual funds, helped by falling interest rates and a booming stock market, became the hottest thing since Hula-Hoops. Assets in the mutual-fund industry leapt to more than $700 billion by the end of 1986 from less than $300 billion in 1983. Big funds couldn't handle their burgeoning back-office workloads without outside help, and new funds couldn't afford to set up their own computer operations.

What started out as a niche for State Street began to look like a gold mine. The company today has 40% of the mutual-fund industry's assets under custody, versus 15% for Bank of New York, its nearest rival for the business. And Mr. Edgerly, for one, doesn't believe the industry is about to contract. "I don't think (recent mutual-fund growth) is a flash in the pan," he says. "There's a fundamental trend for people to obtain professional management of their savings."

Assets under Custody

State Street executives refer to their back-office services as the "plumbing" of the financial industry—and expensive plumbing it is. At its massive operations center in Quincy, some

3,000 modern-day Cratchits—many of them clean-cut, young accounting graduates—staff a maze of computer work stations.

Portfolio accountants here phone mutual-fund managers in places like Baltimore and Los Angeles each morning with updates on the funds' assets. The money managers phone back later to tell the accountants how they've shuffled funds. At day's end, net asset values are recalculated and distributed for the next morning's newspapers.

One of State Street's major pushes now is into the global custody business. State Street has set up miniature versions of its Quincy center in London and Sydney. As master custodian for such customers as Rolls-Royce PLC's pension fund, State Street provides services ranging from securities safekeeping to measuring the performance of world-wide investments.

Source: Christopher J. Chipello, "State Street Bucks a Bank-Expansion Trend, and Thrives," *The Wall Street Journal*, June 12, 1987. Reprinted by permission of The Wall Street Journal, © Dow Jones & Company, Inc. 1987. All Rights Reserved Worldwide.

SUMMARY

- Rising interest rates and restrictions on the rates banks could pay on deposits led to a massive loss of business for banks through disintermediation and reintermediation. In order to retain the deposits of their largest customers, banks had to find ways to pay them interest on their balances.

- The methods they invented included the bank repo, the fed funds gambit, and the overnight Eurodollar. With each of these, funds remaining in a demand deposit at the end of the day are swept automatically into an interest-bearing account and then back again into the demand deposit the next morning. As far as the depositor is concerned, the result is an interest-bearing checking account.

- As far as the bank is concerned, there are additional benefits beyond simply not losing the account. Because these devices are not formally deposits, various regulatory impositions, such as required reserves and deposit insurance premiums, can be avoided.

- There are important differences between the brokered federal funds market and the correspondent market. The brokered market is a real market, like the government securities market, in which large banks lend each other reserves. The correspondent market is not really a market at all, but just another name for what we have called here the "federal funds gambit."

- Banks responded to the loss of their best loan customers to the commercial paper market by finding a role for themselves in the issuing of commercial paper. They participated in the market by providing borrowers with standby letters of credit and by underwriting the paper. As a result, fee income replaced the interest income that had been lost.

- There are advantages to the bank in helping a corporation issue commercial paper rather than making it a loan. The need to hold required reserves and pay deposit insurance premiums is avoided, and the bank can avoid equity requirements, increasing its effective leverage.

- Banks have themselves turned increasingly to the money market to raise funds. The primary instrument for this is the negotiable certificate of deposit. NCDs are issued in large denominations and, unlike ordinary CDs, they may be resold, improving their liquidity.

- NCDs have become the large banks' major source of funds for the making of additional loans.

- Large banks were helped more than harmed by money market mutual funds, because the latter channeled funds to the banks by buying their NCDs.

- Small banks, on the other hand, were losing deposits at an alarming rate, and they pressed to be allowed to compete. Regulation Q was removed in stages in the 1980s and there are now no restrictions on the rates banks may pay on time deposits.

- Although the prohibition of interest on checking accounts remains, individuals may open NOW accounts, which are functionally identical to checking accounts and which do pay interest.

- Money market deposit accounts, authorized in 1982, were designed to replicate closely the terms of money market mutual funds. They were a great success, but largely at the expense of other types of time deposit with lower rates of interest.

- Banks have increasingly looked to sources of income other than straight financial intermediation—for example, fees for processing securities transactions, underwriting, and foreign exchange transactions. The share of noninterest income has grown rapidly in recent years.

- These innovations have helped banks to survive, but the result has been a squeeze on their profits that has pushed many of them to take more chances. Moreover, innovations designed to circumvent interest-rate restrictions have also often undermined other regulations, such as reserve requirements, equity requirements, and branching restrictions.

KEY TERMS

bank repos	Eurodollars	negotiated order of withdrawal (NOW) account
T-account	standby letter of credit	
broker market	negotiable certificate of deposit (NCD)	money market deposit account
correspondent market		

DISCUSSION QUESTIONS

1. When all interest-rate restrictions were removed, banks retained minimum balances and limited check writing on money market deposit accounts. Why?

2. Between November 1982 and March 1983, the usual relationship between bank lending and the amount of NCDs issued was disturbed (see Exhibit 10.4). What was happening to disturb it?

3. What are the differences, from the point of view of the ultimate borrower and lender and from the point of view of the bank, between an intermediated loan and bank-guaranteed commercial paper?

4. List all the different possible chains of intermediation between a household lender and a corporation borrower.

5. List all the money market instruments that have been mentioned in this chapter and in Chapter 9. What are the differences between them from the point of view of investors (risk, liquidity, denomination)? Who uses which type to borrow?

6.　What are the different financial intermediaries involved in short-term borrowing and lending? Do they ever lend to one another?

7.　In what ways has the growth of the money market been good for the economy? In what ways has it been bad?

8.　Check with your local bank to see what types of deposits it offers. Does it offer NOWs and SuperNOWs, MMDAs, negotiable and nonnegotiable CDs? What are the interest rates, fees, and restrictions on the different accounts?

BIBLIOGRAPHY

Cook, Timothy Q., and Timothy D. Rowe, *Instruments of the Money Market*, Federal Reserve Bank of Richmond, 1986.

Gilbert, R. Alton, "Requiem for Regulation Q: What It Did and Why It Passed Away," *Economic Review of the Federal Reserve Bank of St. Louis* February 1986, 22–37.

Stigum, Marcia L., *The Money Market*, 3rd ed., Homewood, IL: Dow Jones-Irwin, 1990.

APPENDIX TO CHAPTER 10

USING T-ACCOUNTS

In this and the following chapters, we shall be looking at many balance sheets and at many changes to balance sheets. We can make the task much easier by using a device called a *T-account*.

When we consider a change to a balance sheet, it is a waste to write down the whole thing, since most of the items have not changed. With a T-account we write down just the changes. For example, suppose a check for $1 million is deposited at a bank and the check cleared through the Fed.

Before the check is deposited, the bank's balance sheet is:

Reserves	$ 5m	Deposits	$50m
Loans	47m	Equity	2m

After the check is deposited and cleared, the balance sheet is:

Reserves	**$ 6m**	**Deposits**	**$51m**
Loans	47m	Equity	2m

The change may be represented instead by the following T-account:

Reserves	+$1m	Deposits	+$1m

Notice four things about a T-account: (1) Only the items on the balance sheet that have changed appear on the T-account. (2) All numbers represent changes in balance sheet items, not total amounts of those items. (3) All numbers are preceded by a plus or minus sign—a plus if the change is an increase, a minus if the change is a decrease. (4) Just like a balance sheet, a T-account must balance: The sum of changes on the asset side must equal the sum of changes on the liabilities and net worth side.

To illustrate these principles, let us continue with our example. Suppose the bank now makes a new loan for $1 million. The T-account is:

| Reserves | –$1m | |
| Loans | +1m | |

Notice that only the items that have changed—reserves and loans—appear. Reserves decrease by $1 million, so the amount is preceded by a minus sign; loans increase by $1 million, so that amount is preceded by a plus. The changes on the asset side sum to zero; the changes on the liabilities and net worth side (there are none) also sum to zero.

To find out what the bank's balance sheet looks like after the change, we can add the T-account to the old balance sheet:

old balance sheet + T-account = new balance sheet.

If several changes have taken place, we add them all to the old balance sheet to obtain the new one.

CHECK STATION 1 | **Write T-accounts for the first five balance sheet changes in Chapter 5.**

CHAPTER 11

INTERNATIONAL BANKING

Only 20 years ago, banking and financial markets in the United States were usually studied in isolation. As a student then, you would have paid little attention to developments in the rest of the world. No longer. Today most large banks have "gone international," and for some of the largest, their international business exceeds the business they do in the United States. For example, Citi has 2,135 branches in 89 countries.

Why has this happened? There are three interrelated reasons. The first is the same clash between economic forces and banking regulation that we encountered in Chapters 9 and 10. As we saw, rising market interest rates and the restrictions of Regulation Q led to the growth of the money market at the expense of banks. Banks, fighting back, tried to get around the regulations in various ways. One way was simply to move operations overseas, out of reach of U.S. regulators.

The second reason for the growing importance of international business has been the rapid growth of international trade. Thirty years ago the United States was a fairly isolated market: Imports and exports of goods were each equal to about 5% of the total output of goods and services in the United States. Today that number is closer to 15%. As more and more companies have dealings with customers and suppliers overseas, they expect their banks to provide them with the special services that such dealings require—the particular forms of finance used in international transactions and the conversion of U.S. dollars into the currencies of other countries (**foreign exchange**).

The third reason is that financial markets, too, have become more international. Thirty years ago there was relatively little borrowing and lending across national frontiers: Most countries other than the United States did not even allow it. As a result, U.S. financial markets were relatively isolated from financial markets in other countries. As more and more countries have removed their restrictions on international borrowing and lending, the world has moved closer to having one large, integrated financial market. Today, keeping up with events in

foreign exchange
Conversion of U.S. dollars into the currencies of other countries.

253

London and Tokyo can be as important to a banker as keeping up with events in New York.

In this chapter we shall look both at the activities of U.S. banks overseas and at their activities at home that are international in nature.

11.1 DOLLAR BANKING OVERSEAS

In the late 1960s, when banks in the United States started looking for ways around regulation that was becoming increasingly burdensome, they found already existing in Europe a banking market that took deposits in U.S. dollars and made loans in U.S. dollars. It was therefore relatively easy for them to move a large part of their business into this **Eurodollar market** and out of the reach of U.S. regulators.

Eurodollar market
Market for dollar-denominated deposits and loans in financial institutions outside the United States.

Why were banks in Europe using U.S. dollars? Banks normally accept deposits and make loans in the currency of the country in which they are located. We take it for granted that banks in the United States accept deposits and make loans in U.S. dollars; similarly, banks in France accept deposits and make loans in French francs, and banks in Japan accept deposits and make loans in Japanese yen. So what had driven some European banks to depart from this normal pattern?

THE ORIGINS OF THE EURODOLLAR

Trade between countries is much more complicated and risky than trade within a country. Part of the risk involves the different currencies used by the two parties to a transaction. For example, consider an export of Argentine beef to Italy. If the price is set in Italian lira, the Argentine exporter is taking a risk that the value of the lira will fall before he receives payment, and that he will take a loss; if the price is set in Argentine australs, the Italian importer bears the risk. Either way, the risk is considerable because both these currencies are subject to substantial changes in value. The usual practice, therefore, is to set the price in some relatively stable major currency.

For a long time this role of international currency was played by the British pound sterling. Setting prices for international transactions in pounds made it easier, too, to finance and insure the shipment in London. This was desirable because London boasted the largest and most competitive financial and insurance markets in the world, offering the lowest interest rates and the lowest insurance premiums. The role of the pound as an international currency and the strength of London as a financial center reinforced one another.

After World War II, however, the international role of the pound began to decline. Britain had serious economic problems that were reflected in the increasingly unstable value of the pound. This instability made the pound much less desirable as an international currency. That role was increasingly taken on by a strong U.S. dollar. The United States at that time had by far the strongest economy in the world, and the international monetary system was then based on the U.S. dollar, so that most countries held their foreign exchange reserves in dollars.

The decline of the pound threatened London's preeminence as a world financial center. As usual, bankers found an ingenious solution. If London could not finance world trade in pounds, it would do so in dollars.

But to make dollar loans, the London banks needed dollar deposits. Although they had for years been willing to accept the occasional foreign-currency deposit for the convenience of an international customer, the amounts had been small. Luckily, just as they needed more dollars, the amounts of these dollar deposits began to grow. The reason was the Cold War.[1] Communist countries, too, wanted to hold their foreign exchange reserves in the form of U.S. dollars, but they were reluctant to keep them on deposit in New York. They felt there was too great a danger that the deposits would be seized by the U.S. government. To be safe, they preferred to keep their dollar deposits in London.

This happy coincidence—the need of London banks for dollars to sustain their role in international finance, and the need of countries with strained relations with the United States for a safe place to keep their dollars—was the origin of Eurodollar banking.

THE YANKS ARE COMING

Through the early 1960s, Eurodollar banking grew steadily. But U.S. banks did not participate in this growth. Indeed, few even had branches in London. In 1955 only 7 U.S. banks had any overseas branches at all; these banks had 115 branches between them with $2 billion in assets. By 1968 the numbers had risen, but only to 26 banks, 373 branches, and $23 billion in assets. The big change came after 1968. By 1980 almost every large and medium-sized bank in the United States had become involved in international banking, mainly in the Eurodollar market. In 1980, 159 banks had 787 branches overseas with $344 billion in assets.[2]

What drove U.S. banks into the Eurodollar market? The fear of losing business to London. In the late 1960s the same motives that led firms to abandon their banks for the money market led them to switch their business to the Eurodollar banks in London. Regulation of Eurodollar banking by the Bank of England was minimal: No Regulation Q, no reserve requirements, no required equity ratios, and no deposit insurance premiums. As a result, Eurodollar banks could offer higher rates on deposits and lower rates on loans. Companies that

---

[1]The alliance between the Western nations—the United States, Britain, and France—and Soviet Russia during Word War II broke down almost immediately after the war. The Soviets had occupied Eastern Europe and part of Germany, and they were trying to install Communist governments in these and other countries. Tension grew to the point where relations between East and West were described as being a "cold war," just short of the hostilities of a "hot" war.

[2]The numbers refer only to U.S. banks that are members of the Federal Reserve System. This includes all nationally chartered banks and most large state-chartered banks. The numbers have remained fairly stable since 1980. (In 1986, 164 banks had between them 1,001 branches overseas.)

already did business overseas found it easy to keep some of their liquid assets on deposit in London, where they could earn higher rates of interest than in the United States. They could also get cheaper loans from the same London banks. Worried about this loss of business, U.S. banks with branches in London began to enter the Eurodollar market, and those banks without branches in London started to open them.

The rush became a stampede in 1968 and 1969 when the Fed, in an effort to fight inflation by restricting bank lending, refused to raise the Regulation Q ceiling on rates paid on negotiable certificates of deposit (NCDs). Remember that NCDs had become the banks' main way of competing with the money market for funds. As rising market rates came up against the ceiling, killing off the NCD market, the banks faced a massive loss of business.

Banks responded with the Eurodollar end run.[3] To see how this worked, consider an example. Suppose that Synco is holding a $1 million, 6-month NCD issued by First National that is due to mature today. Since the NCD was issued, market rates have climbed to 11%, above the 10% limit imposed on NCDs by Regulation Q. If First National does nothing, Synco will simply withdraw its money to earn more elsewhere—perhaps in repos or commercial paper. So First National offers to arrange a deposit of the $1 million at its branch in London. Since Regulation Q does not apply outside the United States, First National's London branch can pay a competitive 11% on the deposit. It can then relend the money back to First National in the United States. The home office and the London branch are considered to be two separate institutions, each with its own balance sheet. The effect of the transaction on their balance sheets and on Synco's is:

SYNCO

NCD of First National	−$1m		
Eurodollar deposit at First National, London	+1m		

FIRST NATIONAL

		NCD of First National	−$1m
		Eurodollar borrowing from First National, London	+1m

FIRST NATIONAL, LONDON

Loans First National	+$1m	Deposits Synco	+$1m

---

[3]The Eurodollar end run is very similar to the overnight Eurodollar ploy that we saw in Chapter 10.

Regulation Q was not the only regulation that gave a boost to the Eurodollar market. In the 1960s the U.S. government imposed limits on lending to foreigners. A simple way around these limits was for banks to make such loans out of their overseas offices and to fund them with Eurodollar deposits. For example, a direct loan like the following was prohibited:

FIRST NATIONAL

Loans		NCDs	+$2m
Mexico Petroleum	+$2m		

No problem. First National gets around the regulation by first lending to its overseas subsidiary:

FIRST NATIONAL

Eurodollar deposit at		NCDs	+$2m
First National, London	+$2m		

and then having the overseas subsidiary make the loan:

FIRST NATIONAL, LONDON

Loans		Deposits	
Mexico Petroleum	+$2m	First National	+$2m

The regulation Q limits on NCDs were dropped beginning in 1970, and the restrictions on foreign loans were removed in 1974, but by then U.S. banks were well established in the Eurodollar market.

Banking regulators in the United States have made occasional attempts to impose restrictions on U.S. banks participating in the Eurodollar market. While their authority over the parent bank gives them the power in principle to do this, the highly competitive nature of the Eurodollar market makes it close to impossible in practice. For example, suppose the Fed were to impose reserve requirements on deposits at overseas branches of U.S. banks. This would force those overseas branches to lower the rates they offer on their Eurodollar deposits. Because other Eurodollar banks would not be affected by the regulation—the Fed has no power to require British banks to hold reserves—their rates would remain the same. Naturally enough, depositors would rapidly switch banks to earn the higher rates. The only effect of the reserve requirement would be to drive U.S. banks out of the Eurodollar market.

THE EUROCURRENCY MARKET TODAY

Eurocurrency deposits and loans
Deposits and loans in any currency other than that of the country in which the bank is located.

While the Eurodollar market originally consisted of U.S. dollar deposits and loans in Europe (in London), today its scope is much wider. The market is no longer restricted to London, or even to Europe, and it is no longer limited to U.S. dollars. The term **Eurocurrency** is now used to refer to deposits and loans anywhere in a currency other than that of the country in which the bank is located. For example, deposits of German marks at a bank in Singapore are also "Eurocurrency." The Eurocurrency market has spread to other financial centers in Europe (such as Luxembourg, Paris, and Rome), to the Caribbean (Cayman Islands, Bahamas, and Panama), to the Middle East (Bahrain), and to the Far East (Singapore, Hong Kong, and Tokyo). Today Europe accounts for slightly over half the total, and London itself for only about 30%.

shell branches (booking centers)
Small branch offices, mostly in the Caribbean, that have no contact with the public and whose activities are limited to transactions in the Eurodollar market.

The Eurocurrency banks in the Caribbean are mainly **shell branches** or **booking centers**. Imagine you are in Nassau for spring break. As a customer of First National, you decide to check out the local branch of your bank. What you find is a brass plate bearing the bank's name on the door of a small office—no tellers, no loan officers, no bank business going on. While the "branch" does have hundreds of millions of dollars in loans and deposits, the loans are actually made and the deposits taken in First National's offices in New York City and London. The Nassau "branch" is really no more than a set of books kept by some local people on instructions from elsewhere.

What makes this arrangement so attractive? For smaller U.S. banks, a branch in the Caribbean is an inexpensive way to get into the Eurocurrency market—much cheaper than setting up an office in London. We shall see that these banks do most of their business with other Eurocurrency banks, so the physical location of the branch is not too important. For the large banks, the low tax rates make it advantageous to book business in the Caribbean.[4] An advantage of the Caribbean over other potential locations of a shell branch is that it is in the same time zone as New York, office hours there are the same as at the home office.

international banking facilities (IBFs)
Banking subsidiaries that may operate in the Eurocurrency market from within the United States.

These days you can even find Eurocurrency banking in the United States itself. In 1981, partly to reverse the loss of jobs to overseas shell branches, the Fed authorized banks and Edge Act corporations to establish **international banking facilities (IBFs)** in the United States. An IBF is allowed to operate more or less as a

---

[4]A bank's income from a foreign branch is likely to be taxed both by the United States and by the country in which the branch is located. For example, if Metropolis earned $100 million in London, it might owe $30 million in U.S. federal income tax and $50 million in British taxes. U.S. tax law allows Metropolis to take a credit for its foreign taxes; that is, it may subtract from the amount it owes Uncle Sam the amount it has paid in British taxes. In this case that means that no U.S. tax need be paid, but Metropolis still pays the $50 million British tax. If it shifted half its business to Grand Cayman (where there are no taxes), Metropolis would still owe $30 million in U.S. taxes, but only $25 million in British taxes. It would pay the British tax, and taking that as a credit, would pay another $5 million in U.S. tax, reducing its total tax bill considerably. Furthermore, while income of foreign branches is subject to U.S. federal income tax, it is not subject to state and local taxes. These are substantial in New York City, where many of the major banks are located. So shifting business from New York to a shell branch is also advantageous.

Eurobank: It is not subject to reserve requirements, deposit insurance, or interest-rate ceilings. However, it is not allowed to do business within the United States, except with other IBFs and with the parent bank. Physically, an IBF is usually just a room or even a desk in a regular U.S. bank.

By the end of 1987 over 540 institutions had established IBFs, with over $300 billion in assets between them. IBFs are particularly popular with branches and subsidiaries of foreign banks in the United States, because these anyhow do most of their business with entities outside the United States. Because IBFs are not allowed to offer overnight deposits, their usefulness to U.S. banks is limited, and IBFs have not replaced the Caribbean shell branches as had once been expected.

Before 1985 some 75% to 80% of Eurocurrency deposits were denominated in U.S. dollars. Since then the fall in the value of the dollar relative to other currencies has reduced its attractiveness as an international currency. By 1987 the proportion of Eurocurrency deposits denominated in dollars had fallen to 58%. The German mark, the Swiss franc, and the Japanese yen have correspondingly grown in importance.

The importance of Japanese banks has increased enormously in recent years. When Britain was the big international lender, the pound was the major international currency and London was the world financial center. When Britain declined in economic importance and the United States became the main international lender, the dollar became the international currency and the role of New York and of the American banks increased. Today Japan is the principal international lender, and the importance of Tokyo as a financial center is growing. Japanese banks now play a major role in the Eurocurrency market. For example, in 1986 the 30 Japanese banks in London held 25% of all bank assets in Britain and 36% of international assets.

For an idea of the overall scale of the Eurocurrency market, see Exhibit 11.1. In gauging the real importance of the market, one must realize that the gross sum of liabilities is inflated by a tremendous amount of lending between banks (we shall see the reasons for this in a moment). Hence the best measure of true size is probably *net* liabilities—total liabilities *less* interbank deposits. That number, about a third of the gross figure, was approximately $100 billion in 1973 and had grown to about $500 billion by 1980. (By way of comparison, deposits at U.S. commercial banks were about $1.7 trillion in 1980, over 3 times the amount.) Since 1980 growth of the Eurocurrency market has been slower.

BORROWERS AND LENDERS IN THE EUROCURRENCY MARKET

The customers of the Eurocurrency market have changed over the years. There have been three fairly distinct periods.

In the first period, up to the early 1970s, growth in deposits came mainly from large multinational corporations and from U.S. banks, and lending was largely to governments and government-owned industries in the industrialized nations.

EXHIBIT 11.1

NET LIABILITIES
OF THE
EUROCURRENCY
MARKET
(AT END OF PERIOD)

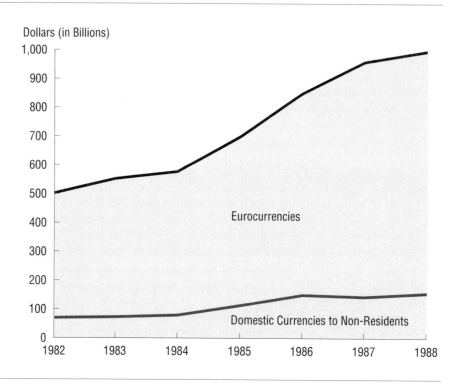

Source: Morgan Guaranty Trust, *World Financial Markets*.

The second period, the one of most rapid growth, came with the rise of the Organization of Petroleum Exporting Countries (OPEC) in the early 1970s. The profits of the oil-exporting nations became a major source of deposits. The main loan customers in this period were countries, mainly less developed countries (LDCs), that needed to borrow to pay their increased oil bills. In the early 1980s oil prices declined, OPEC deposits shrank, and many of the LDC loans turned bad. Since then, new lending to LDCs has more or less dried up and U.S. banks have taken large losses on their LDC debt. We shall have more to say about the causes and consequences of these events in Section 12.5.

In the third period, in the 1980s, the main source of new deposits was the foreign-exchange reserves of small and medium-sized countries, many of them in Asia, with large surpluses in foreign trade. The main borrowers have been corporations in the United States and in other major industrialized countries. Much of the borrowing has been related to the recent wave of mergers and acquisitions in the United States and Europe. For major corporations, the Eurocurrency market has become as routine a source of funds as domestic banks or financial markets—a place to raise large sums of money quickly and relatively cheaply.

WHAT IS A EURODOLLAR?

But what *are* these Eurodollars we have been talking about? *Where* are they? What is the relationship between Eurodollars and plain old U.S. dollars? These questions can best be answered by looking at an example.

Suppose that Megacorp deposits $10 million at Fotherington-Smythe Bank Ltd.(FSB), a London bank. The deposit is made in the form of a check drawn on a New York City bank, say, First National. The effect on the balance sheets of the two banks is:

FSB (LONDON)

Deposit at First National	+$10m	Dollar deposits Megacorp	+$10m

FIRST NATIONAL (NEW YORK)

	Deposits	
	Megacorp	−$10m
	FSB	+10m

Megacorp has traded its $10m in a New York checking account for a Eurodollar time deposit at FSB in London. The actual dollars have not left the United States. All that has happened is that $10 million in deposits at First National in New York has changed ownership and now belongs to FSB instead of to Megacorp.

Suppose that FSB now makes a $10 million Eurodollar loan to Companie Generale S.A. of France. Eurodollar deposits are all time deposits: *Eurodollar banks do not offer dollar demand deposits.* Therefore the loan will not be made by creating a new demand deposit, in the way we saw in Chapter 5. Instead, FSB will make the loan by writing Companie Generale a check on its deposit at First National, New York. If Companie Generale has a checking account at Metropolis National in New York, the effect of the loan on the banks involved will be:

FSB

Deposit at First National	−$10m	
Loans		
Companie Generale	+10m	

FIRST NATIONAL

Deposit at Fed	−$10m	Deposits FSB	−$10m

METROPOLIS

Deposit at Fed	+$10m	Deposits Companie Generale	+$10m

FSB in London now has a dollar liability, Megacorp's time deposit, and a dollar asset, the loan to Companie Generale; thus it has become a financial intermediary in U.S. dollars. The original dollar deposits at First National have been transferred to Metropolis and now belong to Companie Generale.

Notice that all the dollar payments take place in New York: No actual dollar ever leaves the United States. The payments are, in fact, usually made by wire transfer over the CHIPS network that we encountered in Chapter 4. Notice too that none of these Eurodollar transactions changes the amount of dollars in existence. We saw in Chapter 4 that bank lending in the usual manner can create new bank money that did not exist before. We see here, in contrast, that Eurodollar lending creates no new dollars. While Eurodollar banks perform the same intermediary function as U.S. commercial banks, they do not perform the same transactions function. Since they do not offer checking accounts, their deposits are not bank money—not means of payment. So an increase in Eurodollar deposits does not represent an increase in the quantity of money, as does an increase in demand deposits at a U.S. bank.

HOW THE EUROCURRENCY MARKET WORKS

Today, trading in the Eurocurrency market goes on around the clock and around the world. The trading day starts in Singapore. It then moves on to London, which opens early to catch the end of the Singapore market, and then on to New York, which opens early to overlap with London. Borrowing and lending in this market is "wholesale"—$100,000 is the minimum amount and transactions in the tens of millions are commonplace. The maturity of Eurocurrency deposits is mostly under 6 months. However, because such fixed-term deposits are quite illiquid, Eurocurrency NCDs have become increasingly popular in recent years.

floating-rate loans
Loans whose interest rate is adjusted periodically as market rates change.

LIBOR
London Interbank Offered Rate, the rate at which Eurocurrency banks lend to one another.

Eurocurrency loans are often of relatively long maturity (5 to 10 years), and rather than carrying fixed interest rates, they are usually **floating-rate loans**. For example, the loan FSB made to Companie Generale in our example above might have been for 5 years at "LIBOR plus 2%," adjusted every 6 months. What does this mean? **LIBOR** is the London Interbank Offered Rate, the rate at which Eurocurrency banks lend to one another. Loans to nonbank borrowers are set at a premium over LIBOR, the size of which depends on the creditworthiness of the borrower. At the time the loan to Companie Generale is made, LIBOR is, say, 10%. So for the first 6 months, Companie Generale pays at a 12% rate (10% plus the 2% spread). At the end of 6 months, the rate is adjusted. If LIBOR has risen to 11%, Companie Generale will pay interest at a 13% rate (11% plus 2%) for the second 6 months of the loan. If LIBOR has fallen to 8%, it will pay at a

10% rate (8% plus 2%). Six months later, the rate is adjusted again, and so on, for the life of the loan.

Eurocurrency loans are often quite large. Amounts in the billions are not unusual. This is too much for any individual bank to carry: The lack of diversification would be quite worrisome. Indeed, U.S. banking regulation prohibits a bank from lending any single borrower an amount greater than 15% of the bank's equity. (This regulation applies to foreign branches of U.S. banks too.) Since even the largest U.S. banks have equity of less than $10 billion, this would limit them to loans of under $1.5 billion to each borrower.

To make larger loans possible, loans are split up among a number of banks through **loan syndications**. A major bank, called the "lead bank," will put together a syndicate, with each member of the syndicate taking a fraction of the loan; the lead bank earns a fee of 0.375% or more for arranging the syndication. In this way the risk is shared.

loan syndications
Groups of banks that share the risk in making single large loans.

These syndications have provided a way for regional U.S. banks to enter the Eurocurrency market. Such banks would be unlikely to have the international contacts needed to attract much loan business themselves or the expertise needed to evaluate the risk on such loans. The device of the syndication has enabled them to rely on the contacts and expertise of the major international banks. As we shall see, that "expertise" has proven less reliable than the regionals might have hoped.

The Eurocurrency market is characterized by an enormous amount of interbank borrowing and lending. A bank that receives a deposit from a customer will often redeposit some or all of the money with other banks; a bank short of funds for a loan will tap the interbank market for the funds it needs. The market for these interbank deposits is mainly a broker market, very much like the inside market for government securities or the interbank fed funds market in the United States. The brokers centralize information among the hundreds of Eurocurrency banks and provide anonymity in trading.[5] The market is highly competitive and commissions are correspondingly small.

There are several reasons for the very large volume of interbank deposits. A lot of it is the result of transactions between parent banks and their overseas branches, usually made to get around various domestic regulations or to minimize taxes. A good part is related to interest-rate and currency swaps, about which we shall learn in Chapter 13. And much of it is attributable to liquidity considerations and risk sharing.

Because their deposits are typically of much shorter term than their loans, Eurocurrency banks face considerable liquidity risk. If they lent out all their deposits as long-term loans, and if, for any reason, withdrawals were to exceed their ability to find new deposits, they would be in trouble. Holding a significant

---

[5]Of course, banks need to know before the deal is confirmed to whom they are lending. They will typically have credit limits to individual banks, as well as country limits for different Eurocurrency centers. Administering these limits can be complicated because each branch of a bank acts on its own: The London branch of Chase might be lending to Credit Lyonnaise in Paris just as the Singapore branch of Chase is borrowing from Credit Lyonnaise's Hong Kong branch.

amount of deposits at other banks provides them with a cushion of liquidity that they can draw on in such a situation.[6]

We have seen that syndications are a way of sharing default risk among a large groups of banks. But the banks that take a part of a syndicated loan need to find the required funds. Typically, they will not be well enough known to attract a lot of deposits themselves from nonbank customers. However, the major banks do attract a large amount of deposits. So the major banks relend a good part of this to the smaller banks, thereby enabling the smaller banks to fund their part in the syndications that the major banks organize.

The general idea is illustrated in Exhibit 11.2. In Scenario A a single bank is taking all the risk: If the borrower defaults, the bank will have to make up the loss to the depositor; if the depositor withdraws the funds, the bank will have to find new funds to replace them. In Scenario B both the default risk and the liquidity risk are shared. If the borrower defaults, some of the loss will be borne by Banks 1 and 2. If the funds are withdrawn, the lead bank can withdraw its deposits from Banks 1 and 2, and the liquidity problem is passed on to them.

This sort of arrangement has led to some problems. For the arrangement to work, Banks 1 and 2 must be sound: They must have the capital to absorb their share of the loss in case of a default. However, Eurocurrency banks have not been very closely supervised. As a result, some rather doubtful operations were able to set up in business with very little capital in places like Liechtenstein, Luxembourg, or Bahrain. Although such banks were incapable of attracting any customers of their own, they had little trouble plugging into the interbank market both for deposits and for loans. The large banks were so keen to put together deals that they were less careful than they should have been in checking out the banks with which they did business.

Any "risk sharing" in such a case is quite illusory. Suppose we set up a bank, Banco Magnifico of Vaduz, with maybe $500,000 of equity capital, and borrow $100 million in interbank deposits from First National at LIBOR plus 0.25 of 1%. We then take $100.5 million of a First National syndication of a $1 billion loan to Patagonia at LIBOR plus 1%. We will be earning net about $750,000 a year on our initial investment in the bank of $500,000. Not bad.

Someone looking at First National's books would think that it was acting prudently. First National's own exposure on the loan to Patagonia seems to be only $50 million, and in addition First National has this "safe" interbank loan to Banco Magnifico of $100 million. But what happens if the loan goes bad? Who takes the loss? Banco Magnifico will go under and it will quickly become evident that First National's exposure is $150 million, not the $50 million it thought.

After a number of scandals in the early 1980s (see "Banco Ambrosiano" on page 266), the major banks became much more cautious about their interbank lending. As a result, the number of small banks in the market has shrunk considerably. These problems and the problems with many of the large syndicated

---

[6]Correspondent balances and federal funds sold perform a similar function for small banks in the United States.

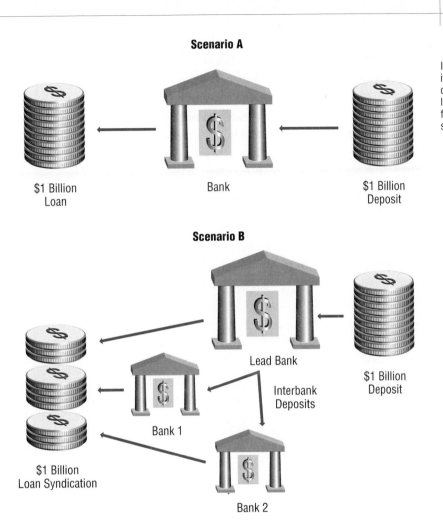

EXHIBIT 11.2

DIFFERENT WAYS TO MAKE A LOAN

If a bank funds a loan directly, it takes on all the liquidity and default risk. If it syndicates the loan, providing the necessary funds to the syndicate banks, it shares the risk with them.

Scenario A

$1 Billion Loan

Bank

$1 Billion Deposit

Scenario B

Lead Bank

$1 Billion Deposit

Bank 1

Interbank Deposits

$1 Billion Loan Syndication

Bank 2

loans to LDCs put a damper on the growth of Eurobank lending in general, and the amount of new syndicated loans fell from $100 billion a year in 1982 to less than $50 billion in 1985. Since then, the market has recovered, rising to nearly $130 billion again in 1988. Almost all the growth has been in lending to private corporations in the developed countries.

There was also a shift in the 1980s in the Eurocurrency market away from bank lending and toward direct lending in the so-called Eurobond market; we shall learn more about this market when we look at the capital market in Chapter

BANCO AMBROSIANO

In June 1982 Roberto Calvi, the head of Banco Ambrosiano, a major Italian bank, was found dead in London. His body was discovered hanging from Blackfriars Bridge—his pockets stuffed with stones, foreign bank notes, and a false passport. Meanwhile, in Italy there was widespread concern over the collapse of the country's largest Catholic bank with massive losses. Implicated in the affair were P-2, a shadowy organization of freemasons, and the Vatican. The scandal would result in the fall of Italy's 44th postwar government.

Calvi had used Ambrosiano's close relationship with the Vatican, and with the Vatican's own bank, the Instituto per le Opere di Religione, as a cover for illicit activities. He had built a complex structure of banks and holding companies in the tax havens of Luxembourg, Liechtenstein, and Switzerland, owning dozens of shell corporations in the Bahamas, Panama, Nicaragua, and Peru. These shells, with names like Manic, Astolfine, Bellatrix, and Erin, were capitalized with as little as $10,000 each and consisted of nothing more than an office with a couple of secretaries and a telex machine. Calvi had Banco Ambrosiano lend these shell companies millions of dollars, which Calvi intended to use to buy a controlling share of the bank itself.

Following its collapse, Banco Ambrosiano was bought by a group of large Italian banks and reorganized under the name of Nuovo Banco Ambrosiano. Some $1,287 million in suspect loans were never recovered.

Source: Rupert Cornwell, *God's Banker* (New York: Dodd, Mead, 1983).

14.[7] Although U.S. banks are prohibited from participation in domestic securities markets by the Glass-Steagall Act, this prohibition does not apply to the activity of their overseas subsidiaries in overseas markets. As a result, U.S. banks have been able to play a significant role in the direct Eurobond market. The market for Eurocommercial paper has also been growing rapidly, reaching $50 billion outstanding in 1988.

11.2 INTERNATIONAL ACTIVITIES OF BANKS IN THE UNITED STATES

Not all international banking involves bank operations overseas. A considerable part of what banks do here in the United States is related to international transactions in one way or another.

For firms, international transactions are much more complicated than domestic ones. In the first place, there are information problems. You have less information about those with whom you are dealing, and they have less information about you. This is a problem because most transactions require an element of trust. The buyer must trust the seller to provide merchandise of the agreed

---

[7]We shall also see in Chapter 13 how swaps enable a borrower to "transform" a fixed-rate bond into something more like a floating-rate bank loan.

quality at the promised time; the seller must trust the buyer to pay as agreed and when agreed. Lack of information makes trust harder; distance, language barriers, and different legal systems make the resolution of disputes more difficult. In addition to these informational problems, there are the difficulties of making international payments. These often involve payment or receipt in currencies other than the U.S. dollar, and the common means of payment, like a simple check, will not work for most international payments.

Banks make international transactions easier in a number of ways. They supply information, provide credit guarantees, and arrange the necessary finance. They buy and sell foreign currencies. And they arrange to make or to receive payments in foreign countries.

FINANCING FOREIGN TRADE

We saw in Chapter 3 that firms do not normally pay immediately for goods or services received. Usually, the supplier provides the purchaser with trade credit. Consider, for example, a purchase by Discount Mart from New England Shoe of $500,000 worth of shoes. New England Shoe will give Discount Mart a period of time, say, 60 days, to pay. During this period Discount Mart expects to sell the shoes and to generate the cash with which to pay its debt. There is usually a charge for such credit, often in the form of a discount for immediate payment rather than an explicit interest charge (the two are, of course, equivalent).

This sort of trade credit is possible only if the seller has good information on the creditworthiness of the buyer and if there is good reason to believe that the account will indeed be paid. A continuing business relationship often provides both the information and the incentive to pay: In our case, Discount Mart is a regular customer of New England Shoe. In the absence of such a relationship, or, more generally, when good information is not readily available, trade credit will not readily be extended.

For example, suppose Discount Mart wishes to buy shoes from Da Silva PLC of Sao Paolo, Brazil. Da Silva knows little about Discount Mart and is therefore unwilling to extend trade credit. Indeed, without payment in advance, or at least some guarantee of payment, Da Silva is reluctant even to ship the shoes. For its part, Discount Mart does not have the cash to pay in advance and needs to find some way to finance the purchase.

Discount Mart could borrow the money directly from its bank, First National, and pay for the shoes in advance. However, it may be reluctant to pay before it has checked that the shipment is satisfactory. An alternative arrangement, one tailored to address the problems of both parties in international transactions, is the **banker's acceptance**. This is how it works:

- *Step 1.* Discount Mart receives a **letter of credit** from First National. This is a promise by the bank to pay Da Silva $500,000 sixty days after confirmed receipt of the shoes. Discount Mart promises to pay First National $500,000 on the same date. This is like a loan, except that instead of receiving bank

banker's acceptance
Short-term credit instrument issued by an importer's bank that guarantees payment of an exporter's invoice.

letter of credit
Financial instrument issued by the importer's bank that obligates the bank to pay the exporter a specified amount once certain conditions are met.

money in exchange for its IOU, Discount Mart receives a letter of credit. Discount Mart sends the letter of credit to Da Silva, which is now willing to ship the merchandise.

time draft
Negotiable financial instrument payable a specified number of days after the date of the draft.

- *Step 2.* When the shoes arrive and Discount Mart acknowledges receipt, Da Silva sends First National an invoice (called a **time draft**) for $500,000, due to be paid in 60 days. First National stamps the time draft "accepted," at which point it becomes a banker's acceptance, an unconditional liability of the bank. The acceptance is returned to Da Silva.

- *Step 3.* Da Silva can hold the acceptance until it matures, but more typically it will prefer to turn it into cash immediately. This it will do by selling the acceptance, which is negotiable, usually to its own bank. (The acceptance is sold at a discount, of course, being a promise to pay in the future.)

- *Step 4.* Da Silva's bank will usually not hold the acceptance to maturity itself, but rather will sell it to a securities dealer in the United States. The securities dealer, in turn, will sell the acceptance to an investor willing to hold it to maturity. That investor may be a financial institution or corporation; it may even be First National itself (an acceptance held by the bank that accepted it is called an "own" acceptance).[8]

Why go to all this trouble? There are two reasons. The first is that it provides a way for the bank to offer its name and creditworthiness to guarantee the deal to Da Silva in place of the unknown (to Da Silva) name and creditworthiness of Discount Mart. The second reason is that banking regulation makes it cheaper to finance the transaction this way.

To see why it is cheaper, consider how our acceptance would appear on the balance sheet of First National:

FIRST NATIONAL

Customer's acceptance Liability Discount Mart	+$500,000	Acceptances outstanding	+$500,000

The customer's acceptance liability is Discount Mart's IOU to First National; the acceptance outstanding is First National's promise to pay whoever eventually presents the acceptance generated by the deal with Da Silva.

Suppose that instead of using an acceptance, Discount Mart had simply borrowed the money from First National and paid Da Silva. Suppose too that

[8]Another way to think of an acceptance is as a guaranteed postdated check (which is a check carrying a future date that cannot be cashed until then). The importer gives the exporter a postdated check drawn on his bank, to be covered by a deposit to be made by him before the date on the check. When the bank stamps it "accepted," it is guaranteeing that the check will be honored.

First National had raised the funds to finance the loan by selling NCDs. Then the change in the bank's balance sheet would have been:

FIRST NATIONAL

Loans		NCDs	+$500,000
Discount Mart	+$500,000		

The two transactions are very similar. In each case: (a) Da Silva gets paid now; (b) the money comes from the sale to the public of a security in First National's name (either an NCD or a banker's acceptance); and (c) the debt of First National to whoever holds the security is balanced by the debt of Discount Mart to the bank.

Although substantively the two transactions are very similar, there are some important differences with respect to cost. Up to a certain total amount of acceptances, no reserves need be held against acceptances outstanding. In addition, since they are not formally deposits, all acceptances are exempt from deposit insurance premiums. This makes acceptances a cheaper source of funding to the bank and to the customer.[9]

The cost advantage is very much like that of a bank helping a firm issue commercial paper rather than making it a direct loan (the bank's "acceptance" of the debt is very similar in substance to its issuing a standby letter of credit in the case of commercial paper). Here, however, the cost advantages have been built into the regulations deliberately.

The reason acceptances were made so attractive was to help New York compete with London as a world financial center. When the regulations were written, before World War I, most international trade was financed with bills of exchange (similar to acceptances) sold on the London market in pounds sterling. Acceptances were given this cost advantage to encourage the development of a similar market in New York in U.S. dollars.

The market has grown rapidly in recent years, along with the general expansion of the money market (see Exhibit 11.3). Traditionally, almost all acceptances were issued by the large money center banks, because the marketability of an acceptance depends on the recognition of the name of the accepting bank.

However, the growth of the market pushed most of these banks up to the maximum amount of acceptances that could be exempted from required reserves: The maximum is calculated as a multiple of the bank's equity capital. As a result, more and more of the business went to medium-sized regional banks that had not traditionally been involved in acceptances. Since 1982, when the limit was raised to 150% of equity (200% with special permission) from 50% (100%

---

[9]Market rates on acceptances are usually a little lower than rates on commercial paper (because of the double guarantee by both the importer and the bank and the implicit collateral of the goods being financed). The cost to the borrower is, of course, higher than this market rate: The borrower usually pays from 25 to 50 basis points to the bank in fees.

E X H I B I T 11.3

U.S. BANKS'
BANKER'S
ACCEPTANCES
OUTSTANDING
(BY BASIS)

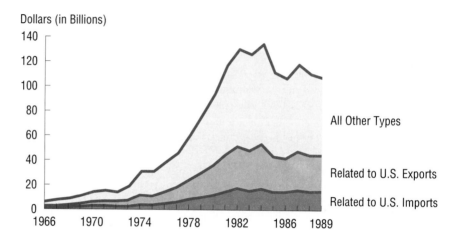

Source: *Federal Reserve Bulletin.*

with permission), the money center banks have made something of a comeback. However, they have also had to contend with increasing competition from foreign banks in the United States, mainly Japanese banks. These have played an increasingly important role in this market, accounting for about a third of the total in 1986.

Banker's acceptances finance about a quarter of all U.S. overseas trade. However, this accounts for only 40% of the banker's acceptances outstanding. Most of the rest are **third-country banker's acceptances.** A large part of world trade *not* involving the United States—third-country trade—is carried out in U.S. dollars. For example, a French electric utility buying oil from Kuwait will be billed for the oil and be expected to pay in U.S. dollars rather than in French francs or in Kuwaiti dinars (because of the large role of American oil companies, oil prices have traditionally been set and the oil trade conducted in U.S. dollars). It is therefore natural that the transaction also be financed in the dollar financial market. As a result, U.S. banker's acceptances play an important role in financing dollar-denominated third-country trade (see Exhibit 11.3).

**third-country
banker's acceptances**
Banker's acceptances used
in international trade that
does not involve the
United States.

FOREIGN EXCHANGE

While many foreign-trade transactions, like Discount Mart's purchase of shoes from Brazil, are paid for in U.S. dollars, some involve payment in foreign currency. This creates additional complications and an additional opportunity for banks to offer their services.

As an example, consider the import of Hermes automobiles from Germany by Teutonic Motors of New Jersey. Teutonic is billed for each car it imports at the rate of DM50,000 per car (the deutsche mark is the German currency). Clearly, Teutonic cannot write a check for this amount: It does not have a checking account in marks. Instead, Teutonic will go to the foreign-exchange department of First National to arrange payment. If the exchange rate is DM1.70 to the dollar, Teutonic will write a check to First National for 50,000/1.70 = $29,400 per car, and First National will pay Hermes the DM50,000 per car in Germany. First National is able to do this because it *does* have a checking account in marks at its branch in Frankfurt.

In fact, Teutonic does not have to pay for the cars it receives immediately (or to arrange for a banker's acceptance). Because Teutonic is an old and valued customer, Hermes will be willing to extend it trade credit: Teutonic will have 90 days to pay (the cost of this credit is included in the price of the car). Although this credit is useful, it exposes Teutonic to **exchange-rate risk**. To see why, consider the following example.

Teutonic receives a shipment of 100 cars. The cost of each car, at the current exchange rate of DM1.70 to the dollar, is $29,400. Teutonic sells the cars to dealers for $32,000 each, so that by the time payment is due 90 days later, Teutonic has accumulated 100 x $32,000 = $3.2 million. It owes Hermes 100 x DM50,000 = DM5 million. When the treasurer of Teutonic goes to First National to arrange payment, he is stunned to hear that the value of the mark has risen to DM1.50 to the dollar (the higher the value of the mark, the *fewer* marks to the dollar). To pay the DM5 million that he owes, he must now write a check to First National for 5 million/1.50 = $3.3 million. Because of the change in the exchange rate, instead of making $260,000 on the deal as expected, Teutonic has lost over $100,000.

Of course, things could have gone the other way. If the value of the mark had fallen instead of risen, say to DM2.00 to the dollar, Teutonic's profit would have been $700,000. What this means is that for importers and exporters like Teutonic, fluctuations in exchange rates could be more important in determining their profits than their skill in running their businesses. Since the management of Teutonic has no special expertise in guessing which way exchange rates will move, it would prefer to get rid of this risk and to concentrate on selling cars—something it understands.

Banks provide importers and exporters with a way of getting rid of this exchange-rate risk by buying and selling foreign exchange in a **forward transaction**. For example, when Teutonic receives the shipment of cars, its treasurer can go to First National and buy forward the DM5 million that it will need to pay in 90 days. That is, First National and Teutonic will enter into an agreement *now*

exchange-rate risk
Risk associated with fluctuations in the exchange rate between different currencies.

forward transaction in foreign exchange
Agreement to buy or sell a foreign currency at a price agreed upon now.

for the sale of DM5 million in 90 days time at an agreed-upon exchange rate. If that rate is DM1.70 to the dollar, First National agrees to provide Teutonic with DM5 million in 90 days time, and Teutonic agrees to pay First National $2,940,000 at that time.[10]

But doesn't this just shift the risk to First National? It does, but First National has a number of ways of dealing with it. In the first place, it will be able to do quite a lot of pooling. Just as it has some customers who want to buy marks forward, it has others—say, exporters to Germany owed payment in marks—who want to *sell* marks forward. So First National can offset a lot of its commitments to sell marks forward with other commitments to buy marks forward. Of course, the amounts may not balance exactly, so First National will turn to the interbank market for foreign exchange either to enter into forward transactions with other banks or to undertake currency swaps.[11]

What is in it for First National? The bank is acting as a dealer in foreign exchange (both spot and forward), and it will earn income in much the same way that dealers in government securities do. One source will be the difference between its bid and ask price. Another will be trading profits earned when the bank takes a position in foreign exchange in a successful gamble on exchange-rate movements.

The interbank market in foreign exchange is a brokered international market that operates 24 hours a day (like the interbank Eurocurrency market). The major centers are London, New York, and Tokyo. In order to participate, U.S. banks must have a presence in New York, and large out-of-state banks generally use Edge Act subsidiaries for this purpose. Increasingly, successful trading also requires a presence in London and Tokyo.

The foreign-exchange market grew rapidly following the abandonment of the gold standard in 1971, but it really exploded with the large increase in exchange-rate volatility that began in the late 1970s. In 1977 foreign-exchange trading volume in New York amounted to about $5 billion a day. By 1989 it had risen to an estimated $130 billion a day—comparable to trading volume in the government securities market. Between 1977 and 1987 the revenues of the top 16 banks from trading in foreign exchange had increased from $279 million a year to $2.3 billion. New York, however, is only part of the worldwide market in foreign exchange. Tokyo accounted for about another $115 billion in daily volume in 1989, and London, still the center of the world market, for a further

---

[10]We shall see how the forward rate is determined in relation to the spot rate (the rate for immediate delivery of foreign exchange) in Chapter 29.

[11]We shall learn about swaps in Chapter 13.

OUR INTREPID REPORTER WHEELS AND DEALS CURRENCIES

By Sarah Bartlett in Dinarland

On an average day, $150 billion pulsates through the currency markets. With no central exchange, a relatively small group of individuals, trading among themselves by phone, collectively determine a currency's value *du jour*. Slavish followers of the latest statistics, traders instantly transmit their reactions to every twitch of the U.S. trade deficit from New York to Tokyo to London. Ultimately they help shape the interest rate on loans from First National on Main Street.

What drives these folks, anyway? It's hard to know without being a trader yourself. Sit in a trading room and you'll do little more than drink in the atmosphere. Listen in on conversations and you'll mostly hear monosyllabic grunts that only jungle-stalking Jane Goodall would appreciate. Persuade a trader to translate, and it sometimes just gets murkier. One day the dollar falls because interest rates fall. The next day the dollar falls because . . . you idiot, interest rates are rising!

That's why when Citicorp said I could try my hand at trading, I leapt at the chance. Chiefly to teach some of its more valued customers, and its own staffers, how to trade foreign currencies, Citi some years ago created the Bourse Game. It shells out $3,500 or so for each corporate customer to play the game for a week. As they note, though, Citi can make

that back in one trade. "It's a form of advertising," explains Heinz Riehl, a Citi senior vice-president who helped originate the game.

Fake Flashes

To run the game, Citi takes over a wing of a hotel and divides the participants into teams of two or three. Each team, or "bank," is set up in a suite and given 100 million fictional dinars. With the help of the hotel's cable hookup, the televisions in each team's room become trading screens. Citi staffers play the roles of both brokers and central bankers. As brokers, they keep the screens filled with prices they elicit from the various banks. Playing central bankers, the Citi folks throw traders off balance by flashing news bulletins at what seem like the worst possible moments. They also intervene, buying or selling currencies to keep them within trading levels known only to them.

It sounded good to me. Sure, everything is vastly simplified. But the game is the next best thing to actually trading—and with no risk of losing millions of dollars for Citi, or of becoming a debtor nation myself.

Citi assigned me to Bank Eleven and gave me two good partners. One, Raul R. Dick, had been working in Dow Corning Corp.'s treasury group for several years. The other, Gary L. Sender, was a 25-year-old live wire

from Merck & Co. Like other corporate participants, they had never made markets in currencies.

No amount of lectures, manual-reading, or hand-holding could prepare us for the first trading session. About 15 minutes before trading begins, the brokers start calling each bank for their bid and offer quotes. We take a stab at it. In this game we are all citizens of Dinarland, and besides the dinar, we will trade in pesos, rials, and francs. The brokers start displaying our prices on the screen. Ready or not, the game is on.

No Thinking

Gary immediately spots an arbitrage opportunity. If he can move fast enough to lock in the spread between a bank offering to sell at an unusually low price and one prepared to buy at an unusually high price, he'll have an automatic profit. To make sure that our bank gets through to the broker first, he repeatedly dials all but the last digit of the broker's number. Then, the second he hears the official go-ahead for trading to begin, he punches in the final number. Presto, a broker is on the line, and Gary gets the deal. The rest of us are still dialing. "Years of trying to win radio contests," Gary chortles.

Raul tries to remain calm, to think things through. But thinking is the worst thing you can do. It gets in the

(continued)

way of knee-jerk reactions. With the phones ringing off the hook—you're obliged to answer—and with prices on the screen changing every split-second, there's no time to worry about a structural deficit in Rialland. All you care about is whether the damn thing's going up or down and which side of the market you want to be on. Soon even Raul is converted. Slamming down the phone after yet another trade, I hear him muttering: "Oh, I love this, I love this, God, how I love this!"

As for me, I decide the best defense is a good offense. My task is to trade the peso. I start phoning the other 10 banks to find out what their buying and selling prices are. As in the real world, they don't know which I want to do. But once they give me quotes, and I say "Done!" they're committed either way. I buy at 1.4650 and sell a minute later to another bank at 1.4820. It's addictive. Buy low, sell high. By the end of the day, I make 300,000 dinars for our bank.

It seemed kind of mean, preying on the weaker banks. But later on, wandering around, I hear Raymond F. Lowry of Dana Corp. do the same. "We'll call Bank Six," he tells his partner. "They're more confused than we are."

Normally, of course, there aren't such wide discrepancies in pricing, so you can't make inordinate profits this

way. Still, the principle holds true: Some banks are market leaders, and others are two or three steps behind. The former can usually make money off the latter. Markets, Citi officials tell us, are all about personalities and psychology. Some people will do anything to gain an edge. Others are content to follow.

Gary clearly liked to be out in front. He decided to "buy the board"—a technique Judith A. Swedek, the Citi vice-president who runs the game in North America, had taught us in class that morning. The idea was to amass a major position in a currency by taking all the offers posted on the brokers' board. You could then nudge a currency up in price and sell at what you have made the peak (in the real world, this maneuver is sometimes called a "power sweep").

High-Wire Act
Gary could hardly wait to try it. As soon as he thought the franc was undervalued, he bought the board. For a brief moment, it was exhilarating. Then a news release flashed on the screen: "Rumors of nuclear meltdown in outer regions of Francland. No news reports available. All communications shut down."

Trading ended soon after, leaving us with a 120 million franc position. Raul was furious. Gary started racing

through the halls. If he couldn't find someone to trade with him in the after-hours "black market," he would be way outside his daily trading limits and in deep trouble with the central bank. Afraid that his high-wire act might destabilize the markets, central banker Swedek bought back some of his francs at a penalty rate—with a warning to be more cautious. Gary kept riding the crests but learned to stay a little more in control. By the end of the week he had made 6.5 million dinars. That was enough to put us ahead of Bank Four, manned by Nayib Neme and Vince Lubrano—and close to a Citi record.

Obviously, the Bourse Game isn't the real world. Still, in microcosm, it helps clarify why market moves can seem so exaggerated. Ultimately, fundamentals drive the market, but along the way, the traders are in charge. To survive as a trader, one has to be able to empty the mind—and be fearless. Gary likened the experience to piloting a jet. I'll take writing any day.

Source: Sarah Bartlett, "Our Intrepid Reporter Wheels and Deals Currencies," reprinted from February 1, 1988 issue of *Business Week*, pp. 70-71, by special permission, copyright © 1988 by McGraw-Hill, Inc.

$190 billion.[12] Some of the excitement of foreign-exchange trading is captured in "Our Intrepid Reporter Wheels and Deals Currencies" on page 273.

Trading volume in foreign exchange is many times larger than the volume of international trade. In fact, most foreign-exchange trading is related to financial rather than trade transactions. For example, if a Japanese pension fund wants to buy U.S. government securities, it must change its yen into dollars to do so. As the volume of these international financial transactions has grown, securities dealers and investment banks have themselves become dealers in foreign exchange, offering this service to their customers themselves, rather than referring them to a commercial bank.

Exchange rates are, of course, determined by supply and demand for foreign exchange. We shall look at the factors underlying supply and demand in Chapters 25 and 29.

SUMMARY

- International banking has become increasingly important to U.S. banks in recent years. One reason is that banks have moved some operations into the Eurocurrency market in order to avoid burdensome regulation. A second reason is that the increase in international trade has increased the demand for the associated bank services. A third reason is that financial markets have become increasingly international.

- The Eurodollar market began as a dollar-denominated banking market located in London. This market sprang up after World War II because it enabled London to remain a major financial center even though the pound sterling was no longer the principal international currency. Today the Eurocurrency market extends around the world and involves currencies other than the dollar.

- Eurocurrency deposits are all time deposits. There are no transactions (checking) accounts. The time deposits are of relatively short maturity, usually under six months.

- Eurocurrency loans are usually of relatively long maturity (five to ten years). Interest on these loans is typically floating-rate, set at a spread over LIBOR.

- Many large loans are syndicated. That is, they are divided up among a syndicate of banks in order to share risk.

---

[12]These numbers were obtained from simultaneous surveys conducted by the Fed, the Bank of England, and the Bank of Japan. A previous survey in 1986 had found daily trading volumes of about $60 billion for New York, $50 billion for Tokyo, and $90 billion for London. Trading volume more than doubled in only three years. The totals for each country are adjusted to eliminate double counting. For example, if Bank A sells Bank B $1 billion in yen, each bank reports a $1 billion trade; one of these reports has to be left out of the total. There was no attempt to eliminate double counting across countries, so adding the numbers for the three markets overestimates the total size of the world market in foreign exchange.

- There is a large amount of interbank deposits (borrowing and lending among banks) to improve liquidity, to reduce risk, and to fund syndications.

- One important way that banks help finance international trade is through the issuance of banker's acceptances. Banker's acceptances can be (and are) traded in the money market. Certain regulatory advantages make acceptances a relatively cheap source of finance.

- Banks also provide foreign-exchange services to their customers. One important service is forward transactions in foreign exchange. This allows customers to lock in an exchange rate for future transactions. Forward contracts shift the exchange-rate risk from the customer to the bank. The bank relies on pooling and other techniques to deal with this risk.

KEY TERMS

foreign exchange	floating-rate loans	third-country banker's acceptances
Eurodollar market	LIBOR	
Eurocurrency deposits and loans	loan syndications	exchange-rate risk
shell branches (booking centers)	banker's acceptance	forward transaction in foreign exchange
	letter of credit	
international banking facilities (IBFs)	time draft	

DISCUSSION QUESTIONS

1. What accounts for the boom in international banking? Why have U.S. and foreign banks expanded their international banking services?

2. What is a Eurodollar? How does it differ from a regular U.S. dollar?

3. Lending in other countries involves risk considerations similar to those found at home, plus some quite different ones. Discuss.

4. What is an Edge Act corporation? What is an IBF? What do they do? How are they different?

5. How do the regulatory authorities encourage international banking? Why do they do it?

6. What are forward contracts? What are they used for?

BIBLIOGRAPHY

Chrystal, K. Alec, "A Guide to Foreign Exchange Markets," *Economic Review of the Federal Reserve Bank of St. Louis* March 1984, 5–18.

Cook, Timothy Q., and Timothy D. Rowe, *Instruments of the Money Market*, Richmond, Virginia: Federal Reserve Bank of Richmond, 1986.

Key, Sydney J., "Activities of International Banking Facilities," *Economic Perspectives of Federal Reserve Bank of Chicago*, 1983, 37–45.

Lewis, M. K., and K. T. Davis, *Domestic and International Banking*. Cambridge, Mass.: M.I.T. Press, 1987.

Stigum, Marcia L., *The Money Market*, 3rd ed., Homewood, Il: Dow Jones-Irwin, 1990.

C H A P T E R 12

BANKING IN THE 1990s
MANAGING LIQUIDITY AND RISK

As we saw in Chapter 5, banking is a business. Just like any other business, its primary purpose is to make as large a profit as possible. The problem is that higher profits can be attained only at the cost of greater risk. The trick in managing a bank successfully is to maximize profit without letting the risks get out of hand.

What are the risks? To understand them, we need to compare the properties of a bank's liabilities with the properties of its assets. Your checking account is a good example of a bank liability. It is highly liquid: You can convert it into cash whenever you want. It is also safe: You are sure of its value. There is no danger of default, and the value of the deposit is not affected by fluctuations in market interest rates or exchange rates.

Unlike its liabilities, most of your bank's assets are illiquid and of uncertain value. Its assets are chiefly loans that cannot readily be turned into cash. Nonetheless, it must be able to honor its commitment to you to convert your deposit into cash on demand. The risk that it may not be able to do so, or that it will prove expensive to do so, is called **liquidity risk**. Not only are the bank's loans illiquid, they are also subject to default. The associated risk of loss to the bank, which cannot pass the losses on to you, is called **credit risk**. Apart from default, the value of your bank's assets may be affected by changes in market interest rates and exchange rates. We saw in Chapter 6 how a rise in market interest rates lowers the value of a security, and we saw in Chapter 11 how a change in exchange rate can cause a loss. Since you are protected from these losses, the resulting **market risk** is borne by the bank.

Taking on these risks is part of a bank's economic function; that is what it does for a living. It will perform its function well, and earn a good profit too in the bargain, if it can handle these risks at the lowest possible cost.

When we first looked at these issues in Chapter 5, we knew little about the real-world environment in which banks operate. That first look was therefore of

liquidity risk
Risk that convertibility into cash may be either impossible or very expensive.

credit risk
Risk that borrowers will not repay their loans.

market risk
Risk that changes in market interest rates or in exchange rates will lead to a capital loss.

279

EXHIBIT 12.1

BALANCE SHEET OF
AMERASIA BANK:
DECEMBER 31, 1989
(MILLIONS OF
DOLLARS)

ASSETS		LIABILITIES AND NET WORTH	
Cash and balances due	$ 3.0	Transactions deposits	$ 2.8
Securities	14.7	Time deposits	39.0
Fed funds sold	5.8	Other liabilities	0.8
Loans	22.4	Equity	5.4
Other	2.1		

Source: *Statement of Condition*, Dec. 31, 1989.

necessity sketchy and naive. Since then we have learned a great deal. We have learned about economies of scale and the geographic restrictions on branching, about the challenges and opportunities of the money market, and about the complexities of international banking. With all this under our belts, we are now ready to take a second, more realistic look at managing a bank in the increasingly competitive and complex world of the 1990s.

12.1 HOW LARGE AND SMALL BANKS DIFFER

There are major differences between the ways that large banks manage risk and the ways that small banks do. Large banks are not just larger, they are different. These differences color both the nature of the risks they face and the methods they use to deal with them.

There are many more small banks in the United States than large ones. In 1989 there were 13,121 commercial banks. Of these, 12,802 (98% of the total number) each had assets of less than $1 billion, and 10,299 banks (78% of the total) each had assets of less than $100 million. Only 40 banks had assets of over $10 billion. However, these few very large banks—regionals and money centers—accounted for over 37% of all bank assets.[1]

The best way to understand the differences between large and small banks is to look at two actual specimens. The small bank we shall examine is Amerasia Bank of Flushing, New York, with $48 million in assets at the end of 1989. The large bank, indeed the largest in the United States, is Citibank of New York, with $143 *billion* in assets at the end of 1988 ($208 billion for Citicorp, its holding company).

[1]*Federal Reserve Bulletin*, March 1989.

A SMALL BANK:
AMERASIA BANK OF FLUSHING, NEW YORK

Exhibit 12.1 shows the balance sheet of Amerasia Bank of Flushing, New York, as of December 31, 1989. The first thing to notice is that Amerasia Bank is **deposit rich**. It has a lot more deposits than loans—$41.8 million in deposits versus $22.4 million in loans.

Amerasia Bank, like most small banks, is principally a **retail bank**: It does most of its business with households and small firms. This means that it has many relatively small deposits and that its opportunities for making loans are rather limited. If it imposes reasonable credit standards, it will be able to lend its customers only fairly small amounts. It has no opportunity to lend directly to creditworthy major corporations that need to borrow large sums.

The big question for Amerasia Bank, then, is what to do with the money "left over." To see how much this is, look at Exhibit 12.2. In addition to its $41.8 million in deposits, Amerasia Bank has $5.4 million in equity and $0.8 million in other liabilities, giving it a total of $48 million of funds in all. If we look at uses, in addition to the loans, about $3 million is taken care of by reserves and other cash and $2.1 million by other assets. That leaves some $21.5 million left over.

These leftover funds are invested in two main categories of asset—government securities and federal funds sold.[2] The federal funds are sold to Amerasia Bank's correspondent bank, Citibank. Successful management of a small bank largely revolves around making good use of these leftover funds, both to increase profits and to deal with the various types of risk. We shall see how this is done after we look at the very different world of a large bank.

A MONEY CENTER BANK: CITIBANK OF NEW YORK

Exhibit 12.3 shows the balance sheet of Citibank as of December 31, 1989. Citibank is owned by the Citicorp holding company. Unlike Amerasia Bank, Citibank is **deposit poor**. Citi has $102 billion of loans, but only $45 billion of domestic deposits.

Citi is a major money center bank. This means that while it does engage in the same sort of small-scale retail banking as Amerasia Bank, much of its business is **wholesale**—large transactions with major corporations, governments, and other financial institutions.[3]

deposit rich
Having a lot of deposits relative to loan opportunities.

retail bank
Bank that does most of its business with households and small firms.

deposit poor
Having a lot of loan opportunities relative to deposits.

wholesale bank
Bank characterized by large transactions with major corporations, governments, and other financial institutions.

---

[2]Securities today generally means U.S. securities. It used to mean state and local government securities too. However, the tax advantages that made it attractive to hold state and local government securities were removed by the Tax Reform Act of 1986.

[3]Actually, Citi is unusual among money center banks in having aggressively expanded its retail business. In 1987 consumer business accounted for 59% of Citicorp's revenue, up from 30% ten years earlier. Citi is the largest issuer of credit cards and student loans in the country and a major mortgage lender. In fact, one in five families in the United States does some banking business with Citi. In contrast, most money center banks have downplayed their retail banking. Indeed, Bankers Trust and Manufacturers Hanover have gone so far as to sell off many of their branches in order to concentrate on their wholesale operations.

E x h i b i t 12.2

AMERASIA BANK:
SOURCES AND USES
OF FUNDS

Sources of Funds

Deposits	$41.8 million	
Equity	5.4 million	
Other	0.8 million	
Total		$48.0 million

Uses of Funds

Loans	$22.4 million	
Cash	3.0 million	
Other	2.1 million	
Leftover Funds	**21.5 million**	
Total		$48.0 million

Source: *Statement of Condition*, Dec. 31,1989.

Citi is heavily involved in the money market. Citicorp has a subsidiary that is a primary dealer in U.S. government securities. In addition, Citibank sells its own NCDs, acceptances, and commercial paper, as well as the commercial paper of its customers. Over 46% of Citicorp's income is from noninterest sources, such as fees and commissions for issuing standby letters of credit, underwriting commercial paper, and trading foreign exchange.

Citi is also very much involved in international banking: It has over 2,000 offices in some 90 countries. These include branches in major Eurocurrency centers such as London and Tokyo as well as subsidiaries engaged in local-currency retail banking in Latin America. Citi is also heavily involved in the trading of foreign exchange: Its revenues from this source rose from $68 million in 1977 to $616 million in 1988. Indeed, Citi does more business overseas than at home. Although this degree of international involvement is unique to Citi, over 30% of the assets of the typical money center bank are international.[4]

Because of its extensive contacts with major corporations, institutions, and governments worldwide, Citi has many opportunities to make loans. In some cases, these opportunities are closer to being obligations. When an important customer, perhaps the source of significant fee income from money market and international transactions, comes in for a loan, Citi will want to oblige. If it does not, the customer will probably take its nonloan business elsewhere, to a more

[4]Most international banking is concentrated in the hands of a few very large banks. In 1987 the big three—Citi, Chase, and BankAmerica—accounted for about one-third of all international assets of U.S. banks; the 25 largest banks accounted for 80%. If foreign exchange and swaps are included, concentration is even greater. Whereas banks used to run their foreign branches and subsidiaries as separate operations, today the trend is increasingly toward managing the whole bank as one single, integrated, global business.

ASSETS		LIABILITIES AND NET WORTH	
Cash and balances due	$ 5.0	Deposits	
Deposits at interest		Noninterest domestic	$10.4
with banks	13.4	Interest-bearing	
Securities	16.6	domestic	34.7
Fed Funds sold and		Overseas	63.9
securities purchased		Purchased funds	19.5
under repo	4.7	Acceptances outstanding	4.2
Loans	101.9	Other liabilities	18.0
Customers' acceptance		Equity	7.6
liability	4.2		
Other	12.4		

Source: *Statement of Condition*, Dec. 31,1989.

accommodating bank. This means that once Citi has set its loan policy—its rates and credit standards—it has little control in the short run over the amount of loans that it must make. It can and does alter its loan policy as circumstances change, but at any time it must be ready to fund the loan opportunities that present themselves.

Given its small domestic deposit base (small only relative to its vast loan opportunities) the problem for Citi, as for other money center banks, is how to fund its loans. To see how much it needs, consider Exhibit 12.4. Domestic deposits, equity, and other sources provide some $71 billion, well short of the $141 billion in loans, cash, and securities. The gap is bridged by $70 billion in net borrowing in the money market—$88 billion in money market liabilities less $18 billion in money market assets.

Amerasia Bank can sit and wait for deposits to come in, but Citi, because it wants to lend more than the amount of its deposits, must go out into the money market and borrow actively. That borrowing takes the form of NCDs, acceptances, commercial paper, federal funds bought, repos, and Eurodollar deposits. Typically, money center banks fund 50% to 60% of their assets with borrowed funds in this way; regionals, 30% to 40%; and small banks, zero. Of course, small banks have no need to borrow funds, and even if they wanted to borrow in the money market, they would lack the credit standing to do so.[5]

Note that although Citi is a net borrower in the money market, it does lend as well as borrow. The reasons for this are partly timing (funds may come in when loan opportunities are not immediately available), partly accommodation of customer needs, and partly a deliberate component in Citi's overall strategy to make profit and to control risk.

---

[5]Small banks usually borrow from their correspondent if the need arises.

EXHIBIT 12.4

CITIBANK: SOURCES
AND USES OF FUNDS

Sources of Funds

Domestic deposits	$45 billion	
Equity	8 billion	
Other	18 billion	
Money market	**88 billion**	
Total		$159 billion

Uses of Funds

Loans	$106 billion	
Cash	5 billion	
Securities	17 billion	
Other	13 billion	
Money market	**18 billion**	
Total		$159 billion

Source: *Citicorp Annual Report*, 1989.[6]

Note too that although Citi is basically short of funds, it is nonetheless holding $17 billion in government securities. Although this amounts to only 11% of its assets, compared to Amerasia Bank's 31%, why does it hold securities at all? The reason is partly cosmetic. Banks have always held government securities, and these are the safest of a bank's assets in terms of default risk. A bank therefore appears insufficiently cautious and conservative if it has no governments on its balance sheet. In addition, Citi is a primary dealer: It is easier to sell a product if you express confidence in it by buying it yourself. Also, government securities are needed as collateral for the overnight repos that serve as disguised interest-bearing demand deposits for Citi's large corporate customers.[7] Perhaps the most important reason, as we shall see later, is that government securities provide Citi with one way of profiting from changes in interest rates.

The basic position of a large bank, then, is that it has more loan opportunities than deposits and must actively borrow to bridge the difference. The successful management of a money center or major regional bank largely revolves around management of its borrowed funds. The choice of *which* source of borrowed funds to tap is crucial both for profitability and for the management of risk. Before we discuss this further, let us look at how large and small banks can be of mutual help to one another.

[6]Money market liabilities include the categories Interest-Bearing and Non-Interest-Bearing Deposits in Overseas Offices (largely Eurodollars), Purchased Funds and Other Borrowings, Acceptances Outstanding. Loans include Customers' Acceptance Liability. Money market assets include Deposits at Interest with Banks, Federal Funds Sold, and Securities Purchased under Resale Agreement.

[7]Government securities are also needed as collateral for discount loans from the Fed.

MATCHING THE NEEDS OF LARGE AND SMALL BANKS

Because of their very different situations, large and small banks have a lot to offer one another. On the one hand, large banks are hungry for funds, while small banks have more than they know what to do with. On the other hand, as we saw in Chapter 8, many important services that large banks offer cannot be offered economically by small banks. There is clearly room for a deal. Small banks usually develop a long-term correspondent relationship with one or more regional or money center banks. For example, Amerasia Bank's principal correspondent is Citibank.

The correspondent offers the small bank (the respondent) a variety of services. Respondents pay for these services by providing the correspondent with funds. They used to do this through zero-interest demand deposits. However, as interest rates rose, this practice died out, and correspondent balances were largely transformed into federal funds sold. As we saw in Chapter 10, these federal funds sold are really just a disguised interest-bearing demand deposit, and are quite distinct from the *brokered* federal funds traded between large banks in the money market. The federal funds sold that we saw on Amerasia Bank's balance sheet are sold to Citibank. Money center and regional banks often have hundreds, or even thousands, of respondent banks, and they obtain a significant amount of funding in this way (see Exhibit 8.2 for some numbers). Another way that large banks borrow funds from smaller ones is through the sale of NCDs. Many small banks and savings and loans hold significant quantities of these.

Correspondents also provide their respondents with additional loan opportunities. One way is through *loan participations* and *loan syndications*. In both cases, large loans are divided up into pieces small enough to be attractive to small and medium-sized banks. In addition to these sorts of arrangement, major banks have increasingly been selling off pools of smaller loans. This practice is known as **securitization**: Loans are turned into tradable securities. The basic reason for securitization is that it frees the selling bank of the need to hold equity capital against the loans that are sold.[8] Small and medium-sized banks have been major purchasers of these securitized loans.

securitization
Practice of converting loans into tradable securities.

Now that we have seen how large and small banks differ and the ways that they interact, we are ready to look at how banks handle the three different types of risk—liquidity risk, market risk, and credit risk. In each case, we shall see that there are important differences between large and small banks in both the nature of the risks and in the ways they deal with them.

---

[8]We shall look at securitization and the reasons for it more closely in Chapter 17.

12.2 | MANAGING LIQUIDITY RISK

Of course, a bank's main source of liquidity is pooling: Withdrawals tend to be offset by new deposits. Sometimes, however, there will be less new deposits than there are withdrawals. The bank must be able to deal with this eventuality. In addition, the bank must be able to make new loans as opportunities present themselves. Since loans are the core of a bank's business, it cannot afford to turn away good loan opportunities. But if it does not have the funds, it cannot make the loan.

To see the various ways a bank can meet its liquidity needs, consider the following schematic balance sheet:

ASSETS	LIABILITIES AND NET WORTH
Reserves	Deposits
Loans and investments	Equity

If there is a demand on liquidity, either because of a fall in the amount of deposits or because of an increase in the amount of loans, then there must be a compensating change somewhere else on the balance sheet to keep things in balance.

How about reserves? We know from Chapter 5 that *required* reserves are of no use: Recall the story of the required life preservers. Our imaginary bank of Chapter 5 relied on *excess* reserves—cash reserves in excess of the required amount—to provide it with the liquidity it needed. However, banks in the real world find this is an unattractive way of doing things. Excess reserves carry too high an opportunity cost. Unlike other assets, they earn no interest. So, in reality, banks keep excess reserves to an absolute minimum.

Barring excess reserves, there are two ways a bank can find liquidity. Either it can sell off existing assets—this approach is called **asset management**—or it can borrow more money as needed—this is called **liability management**.

asset management
Management of a financial institution's asset structure to provide liquidity.

liability management
Management of a financial institution's liability structure to provide liquidity.

ASSET MANAGEMENT

As we have seen, small banks like Amerasia Bank typically have an excess of funds over good loan opportunities. Because they need to invest these funds in some sort of earning asset, for them asset management is a natural. All they need do is choose their asset mix in such a way that it will ensure liquidity.

We saw from the balance sheet of Amerasia Bank that its two principal nonloan assets were federal funds sold (sold to Citibank, its major correspondent) and government securities. The federal funds sold are the more liquid. As we saw in Chapter 10, when we looked at the "federal funds gambit," they are mostly sold overnight, one day at a time, so they can be cashed out at any time. However, they do have disadvantages. First, because they are an *unsecured* and *uninsured* loan to another bank, they are subject to some credit risk. Second, there is an opportunity cost: Other alternatives often offer a higher yield.

EXHIBIT 12.5

YIELD CURVE

The yield curve shows the yields on government securities at different maturities. Normally, the yields at longer maturities are higher.

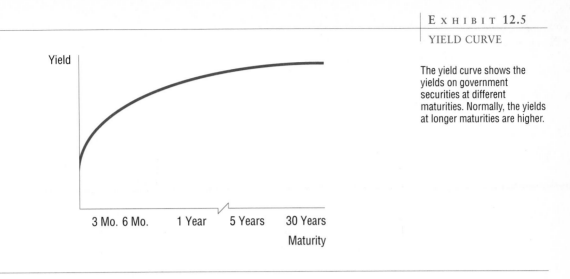

To see why other yields are usually higher, look at the yield curve in Exhibit 12.5. Remember from Chapter 7 that the yield curve is a plot of yields on government securities against maturity. Much of the time, the yield curve has the "normal" shape shown in the exhibit; that is, it is upward-sloping. Since the federal funds rate is usually close to the rate on short-term Treasuries, when the yield curve is normal, the yield on federal funds sold is less than the yield on longer-maturity governments. The opportunity cost of federal funds sold is the yield that could be earned on these government securities.

Government securities have other advantages as an asset: They are free of credit risk and are fairly marketable. They also have disadvantages: Selling them involves transactions costs and possibly a capital loss. Remember that when interest rates rise, security prices fall. So if interest rates have gone up since the bank bought the securities, it will take a loss on the sale. A way to mitigate these disadvantages is to hold the securities to maturity and to repo them rather than sell them when funds are needed. That way, the transactions costs are lower, and no loss need appear on the bank's accounts.[9]

In terms of asset management, then, federal funds sold provide the first line of defense, with government securities providing backup when necessary. The art of asset management consists of trading off the advantages and disadvantages of the two assets and of finding the right proportions between the two. The maturity of the government securities is also an important consideration. If interest rates

[9]Of course, the loss is there whether the securities are sold or not. However, for securities held long-term—in the bank's "investment account"—the loss does not appear on the bank's accounts unless the securities are actually sold. Since bank officers are rewarded according to the bank's accounting profits, it does matter to them whether or not the loss is actually recorded. Securities that are held primarily for resale must be listed on the balance sheet in a separate "trading account" at market price, so that their value on the balance sheet does fluctuate with market interest rates.

are expected to fall, a long maturity maximizes the capital gain; but if they are expected to rise, it maximizes the loss.[10]

LIABILITY MANAGEMENT

Large banks, like Citi, far from having an excess of funds to invest, have a funding gap that has to be bridged by borrowing in the money market. It therefore makes little sense for them to handle liquidity in the same way small banks do, through asset management. If they are faced with a deposit outflow or a new loan request, the natural way for large banks to deal with it is to go to the money market directly to borrow the necessary funds as the need arises. This makes more sense than borrowing first to finance the holding of assets that are then sold to provide liquidity.

The question is, of course: In what form to borrow? The choice, essentially, is between overnight funds and term funds (borrowing longer-term). The options for overnight borrowing include federal funds purchased in the broker market from other large banks; overnight Eurodollars borrowed through brokers in the Eurocurrency market; and repoing government securities through dealers in the government securities market.[11] The options for term borrowing include selling NCDs (large banks generally place them directly themselves); having the holding company sell commercial paper either directly or through dealers; selling acceptances, usually through a dealer, and borrowing term Eurodollars through a Eurocurrency broker.

In choosing among these options, cost is obviously an important consideration. With a normal upward-sloping yield curve, overnight funds are less expensive than term funds, and shorter-maturity term funds are less expensive than longer-maturity funds. However, cost is not everything.

For a bank maintaining its liquidity through liability management, the primary consideration is always being *able* to borrow. To be able to borrow, the bank must, above all else, retain the faith of the market. Most money market borrowings are unsecured: Only repos are fully collateralized. Although NCDs are formally deposits and therefore insured by the FDIC, deposit insurance covers only the first $100,000, and most NCDs are for much larger sums. Because most of the borrowing is unsecured, if the market has the slightest suspicion the bank is in trouble, the rates it pays will rise rapidly. Lenders are conservative. It costs them little to switch their money to another bank that looks safer. Very soon, a

---

[10]Small banks do not have to rely entirely on asset management to provide them with liquidity. Another feature of the correspondent relationship is that a respondent can, in times of need, borrow federal funds from its correspondent.

[11]Another option for overnight borrowing is to borrow from the Fed at the "discount window." We shall have more to say about this in Part Four.

bank perceived to be in trouble may be unable to borrow at any price, leaving it with no alternative but to turn to the Fed for help.[12]

Since even the perception of trouble is dangerous, banks that rely on liability management must be very careful about what they do. For example, relying too heavily on overnight funds looks suspect. The reason it does is that a bank in trouble will have difficulty borrowing term funds. Why would anyone buy an unsecured one-year NCD from a bank that may not be there in a year's time? However, so long as no one expects the bank to collapse *immediately*, there may still be those willing to lend to it overnight. Because you know that other lenders think this way, if you see a bank relying heavily on overnight money, you will begin to wonder whether other lenders know something you do not.

What this means from the point of view of the bank is that, although it may be cheaper to fund a loan with overnight money, doing so will damage the bank's ability to borrow. It is all right to fund a new loan with overnight money initially, but it looks bad if the bank continues to do so. As soon as it can, the bank should replace the overnight funding with NCDs or term Eurodollars.

Choosing between overnight and term funds is not all a bank must worry about. It must also decide on the maturity of its term funds. As we shall see, if interest rates are expected to rise, a long maturity will maximize the gain; if interest rates are expected to fall, a short maturity will minimize the loss.

12.3 MANAGING MARKET RISK

To understand the nature of market risk, it is useful to think of a bank's balance sheet in terms of **market value** rather than **book value**. To understand the distinction, let us consider some examples.

First National Bank has a $1 million T-bill due a year from now. The book value of the T-bill—its value on the bank's balance sheet—is $1 million. If market rates of interest change, this book value is not affected.[13] However, the book value does not represent the true value in terms of what First National could get for the T-bill if it wanted to sell it now. As we saw in Chapter 6, the true market value of a security is the present value of the amount or amounts due, calculated at market rates of interest. In this case, if the market rate on one-year T-bills is 10%, then the market value of the T-bill is $1 million/1.10 = $909,091. Or if the market interest rate is 8%, then the market value is $1 million/1.08 = $925,926.

If an asset is denominated in a foreign currency, its market value depends not only on market interest rates, but also on market exchange rates. For example, suppose First National is holding a one-year, ¥100 million Japanese T-bill. It bought the T-bill at an exchange rate of 150 ¥/$, so its book value is ¥100 million/ ¥150 = $666,667. If the yen exchange rate changes, or if the market rate on

market value
Present value of amount or amounts due, calculated at the market interest rate.

book value
Face or par value with no consideration for market value.

---

[12]In Chapter 17 we shall look at the failure of Continental Illinois, and we shall see how Continental's inability to raise funds in the money market played a major role in its collapse.

[13]We are assuming that this security is in the bank's investment account. Securities held in the trading account appear on the balance sheet at market value.

Japanese T-bills changes, this book value is unaffected. Once again, however, the book value does not tell us what First National could get for the security if it sold it—the security's market value. To calculate this, we need to know the market rate on Japanese T-bills and the *present* exchange rate. If the former is 5% and the latter 140¥/$, then the market value is ¥100 million/1.05 = ¥95.238 million in yen and ¥95.238 million/¥140 = $680,272 in U.S. dollars.

It makes sense to talk of the market value not only of assets, but also of *liabilities*. For example, suppose First National has a $1 million NCD due one year from now. How much is it worth? That is, if First National had to pay someone else now, say another bank, to take on the obligation of paying off the NCD, how much would First National have to pay? The answer, of course, is the market value of the NCD—the present value evaluated at the market interest rate. If that rate is 8.5%, then the market value is $1 million/1.085 = $921,659. This is the amount that First National would have to pay now to rid itself of the obligation to pay off the NCD in a year's time.

Now suppose that you are thinking of buying First National. How much should you be willing to pay for it? The answer is the market value of the bank's equity. This is just the market value of the bank's assets less the market value of its liabilities:

$$\begin{array}{ccccc}
\text{market} & & \text{market} & & \text{market} \\
\text{value of} & = & \text{value of} & - & \text{value of} \\
\text{equity} & & \text{assets} & & \text{liabilities.}
\end{array} \qquad [12.1]$$

The market value of assets is the sum of the market values of the bank's individual assets; the market value of liabilities is the sum of the market values of the bank's individual liabilities.[14]

We have seen that changes in market interest rates or market exchange rates will affect the market values of individual assets and liabilities. They will also, therefore, affect the market value of the bank's equity. For example, suppose that an increase in market interest rates lowers the market value of First National's assets by $50 million and lowers the value of its liabilities by $60 million. The $50 million fall in the value of its assets reduces the market value of the bank's equity by the same amount; however, the $60 million fall in the value of the bank's liabilities *increases* the value of its equity by the same amount (when your debts go down in value, you are wealthier, not poorer). In general,

$$\begin{array}{ccccc}
\text{change in} & & \text{change in} & & \text{change in} \\
\text{market value} & = & \text{market value} & - & \text{market value} \\
\text{of equity} & & \text{of assets} & & \text{of liabilities.}
\end{array} \qquad [12.2]$$

In this particular example, the value of the bank's equity will actually increase by $10 million as a result of the rise in market interest rates. More generally, what

---

[14]For a bank that is publicly traded, we can calculate the market value of its equity by taking the market price of its stock and multiplying by the number of shares outstanding.

happens to the market value of equity will depend on the nature of the different assets and liabilities.

This sensitivity of the value of the bank's equity to changes in market interest rates and market exchange rates is what we mean by market risk. Let us take a closer look, first, at the sensitivity to interest rates—*interest-rate risk*—and then at the sensitivity to exchange rates—*exchange-rate risk*.

INTEREST-RATE RISK

To understand the interest-rate risk intrinsic in a bank's normal operations, consider the following example. Suppose Citi has just made two $1 million loans, one for one year at 8% and one for two years at 9%. It must fund these loans by selling NCDs. Citi has some choice, though, in the maturity of the NCDs, and that choice will determine the degree of interest-rate risk that it bears. Let us look at some alternatives.

Suppose the yield curve is upward-sloping: The rate on one-year NCDs is 7% and the rate on two-year NCDs is 8%. Then the least expensive way to fund the loans is to fund them both with one-year NCDs:

Loans		NCDs	
1-year at 8%	+$1m	1-year at 7%	+$2m
2-year at 9%	+1m		

At the end of the year the one-year loan will be repaid, and Citi can use the funds to pay off $1 million of the NCDs:

Loans	−$1m	NCDs	−$1m

It will have made a margin of 1% on this loan. To obtain the funds it needs to pay off the second $1 million NCD, Citi will have to sell a *new* NCD:

	NCDs	
	Old NCD paid	−$1m
	New NCD sold	+1m

That is, Citi will have to refinance the loan in its second year. Hence this way of funding the two loans is called being in a **refinance position.**

How well Citi does overall on the two-year loan will depend on the interest rate it has to pay on this second NCD. If interest rates stay the same, Citi will pay 7% on the new NCD, and its margin on the two-year loan will now be 2%. If interest rates go up to, say, 10%, the margin in the second year of the two-year

refinance position
Method of funding a loan when the maturity of the loan is longer than the maturity of the liabilities used to fund it.

loan will be negative. On the other hand, if interest rates fall, so that Citi pays less than 7% on the new NCD, its margin on the loan will be more than 2%.

Instead of taking a refinance position, Citi could take a **reinvestment position**. That is, it could finance both of the loans with two-year NCDs:

reinvestment position
Method of funding a loan when the maturity of the liabilities used to fund the loan is longer than the maturity of the loan itself.

Loans		NCDs	
1-year at 8%	+$1m	2-year at 8%	+$2m
2-year at 9%	+1m		

This alternative does not, on the face of it, look very attractive. The margin on the two-year loan is down to 1%, and the margin on the one-year loan is zero.

To see the possible advantages of a reinvestment position, look at what happens at the end of the first year. The one-year loan is repaid, and Citi will have that money available to fund a new one-year loan, since it does not have to pay off any NCDs at that time:

Loans	
Original 1-year	−$1m
New 1-year	+1m

Now suppose interest rates have gone up in the meantime. If the new loan can be made at, say, 15%, the margin will be a whopping 7%. That is, Citi can make a new loan at the current high rate of interest without itself having to borrow at that high rate. By putting itself in a reinvestment position, Citi has locked in funds for the second year at a rate of 8%. Of course, if market rates fall instead of rise, this will not turn out to be a good thing: Citi may have to lend out the funds at a loss.

Thus both the refinance and reinvestment positions involve risk. If interest rates fall, the refinance position makes a gain, but the reinvestment position makes a loss. If interest rates rise, the shoe is on the other foot.

If it chooses to, Citi can eliminate interest-rate risk completely by adopting a third type of position—**matching maturities**. This involves selling NCDs that match precisely the maturities of the loans:

matching maturities
Matching the maturity of the liabilities used to fund a loan with the maturity of the loan to be funded.

Loans		NCDs	
1-year at 8%	+$1m	1-year at 7%	+$1m
2-year at 9%	+1m	2-year at 8%	+1m

Now, whatever happens to interest rates, Citi's margin is unaffected. It will continue to make a safe 1% on each of the loans.

There is a fairly obvious trade-off here between risk and return. A safe, but relatively small, return can be made by matching maturities. To make more than this, a bank will have to bear some risk. Whether it does so by adopting a reinvestment or a refinance position will depend, naturally, on what it believes interest rates are going to do. If the bank believes that interest rates are on the way down or stable, then a refinance position is attractive. If it believes that interest rates are on the way up, then a reinvestment position is the way to go.

The real question, of course, is not whether or not to take a risk, but *how much* risk to take. Banks that play it completely safe will make a very low average margin and therefore earn a low return on equity. Their owners will not be pleased. The owners will generally be willing to take some chance of an occasional loss if that means higher returns on average.

To be able to make sensible decisions, the bank needs to know just what its *overall* exposure to interest-rate risk actually is—not only the exposure on a particular loan-funding combination, but the exposure implicit in the bank's whole balance sheet. That is, it should be able to answer two questions:

1. Is the bank *as a whole* in a refinance or reinvestment position: Will a rise in market interest rates mean an overall loss or gain?

2. For a given change in market interest rates, how large will the loss or gain be?

We can relate these questions to our earlier discussion of the effect of market interest rates on the market value of a bank's equity. We can say that the bank as a whole is in a refinance position if a rise in interest rates *lowers* the market value of the bank's equity; we can say that it is in a reinvestment position if a rise in interest rates *raises* the market value of its equity.

Remember that the change in the market value of a bank's equity equals the change in the market value of its assets less the change in the market value of its liabilities. So to progress further, we need to know exactly how a change in interest rate affects the value of assets and liabilities.

To do this, it is useful to define **duration**. The duration of an asset or a liability is a quantitative measure of the sensitivity of its value to changes in interest rate. A 1% increase in the interest rate will *reduce* the value of an asset or a liability by approximately its duration times 1%. That is:

> **duration**
> Measure of the sensitivity of the value of an asset or a liability to changes in interest rates.

$$\text{percentage change in market value of asset or liability} \approx \\ - \text{ its duration} \times \text{change in interest rate.} \qquad [12.3]$$

For example, if the duration of a bank's assets is 2 years, then an increase in market interest rates of one percentage point will reduce the market value of the bank's assets by approximately 2%. The exact definition of duration and its mathematical derivation are given in the appendix to this chapter.

It is customary to summarize a bank's exposure to interest-rate risk in terms of its **duration gap**. This is defined as:

> **duration gap**
> Difference between asset duration and liability duration times the ratio of liability market value to asset market value.

$$\text{duration gap} = \\ \text{asset duration} - \left(\text{liability duration} \times \frac{\text{market value of liabilities}}{\text{market value of assets}} \right). \qquad [12.4]$$

If the duration gap is positive, the market value of equity will *fall* when interest rates rise: This corresponds to a refinance position for the bank's balance sheet as a whole. If the gap is negative, the market value of equity will *rise* when interest rates rise: This corresponds to a reinvestment position for the balance sheet as a whole. If the gap is zero, the market value of equity will be *unaffected* by changes in interest rate: This corresponds to a maturities-matched position for the balance sheet as a whole. Note that a bank can eliminate interest-rate risk without having to match maturities of *specific* assets and sources of funding: Losses on some combinations can be offset by gains on others.

Important as it is, the duration gap is not easy to estimate in practice, because the maturities of different assets and liabilities are not always clear. What is the maturity of demand deposits, for example? Although, in principle, they may be withdrawn on demand, in practice such deposits may have in indefinite maturity (they are often therefore called *core* deposits). Or what is the maturity of a loan? It may formally be three years, but if interest rates fall, there is a danger that the borrower will pay it off early. Nonetheless, whatever the difficulties, banks do their best to estimate their duration gaps in order to get some idea of their exposure to interest-rate risk.

It is essential that a bank calculate the duration gap for its consolidated balance sheet—the balance sheet that brings together all its operations. For example, to estimate its exposure to interest-rate risk, Citicorp will look at all of its dollar assets and liabilities—those of its securities-dealer subsidiary and Euro-dollar branches and subsidiaries, as well as those of Citibank itself. A positive gap in one part of its operations could be offset by a negative gap elsewhere. It is the overall position that counts.

The type of duration gap the bank will want to have will depend on what it thinks interest rates are going to do. If it believes that interest rates are going to rise, it will want to have a negative duration gap. If it believes rates are going to fall, it will want to have a positive duration gap. The more confident the bank's belief in the direction of change, the larger it will want the duration gap to be. However, as First Bank learned (see "First Bank System Begins to Sell Portfolio of U.S. Bonds"), the dangers can be substantial.

How does a bank deliberately change its duration gap? Once again, small banks and large banks are different. A small bank has little control over the duration of its liabilities, but it can alter the duration of its assets. It can do this by changing the proportion of securities versus federal funds sold and by changing the maturity mix of the securities. For example, if it expects interest rates to fall, it can draw down its federal funds sold and use the funds to buy long-term securities.

A large bank has more options. It can alter its duration gap by changes both on the asset side and on the liability side. For example, if it anticipates a fall in interest rates, the bank can borrow overnight money to purchase long-term securities; if it anticipates a rise in interest rates, it can sell long-maturity NCDs and lend the money overnight.

FIRST BANK SYSTEM BEGINS TO SELL PORTFOLIO OF U.S. BONDS; LOSS IS PUT AT $500 MILLION

By Jeff Bailey

Staff Reporter of The Wall Street Journal

First Bank System Inc. began selling off most of its huge government bond position at an expected loss of $500 million, moving to put behind it one of the worst interest-rate fiascos in modern banking history.

The bank holding company said the bond losses would result in a net loss for 1988 of about $300 million, prompt the sale of its half interest in its Minneapolis headquarters building, and perhaps force it to take other measures to rebuild its capital base.

More than any other major U.S. banking concern in recent years, First Bank aggressively wagered its capital in bond market plays—winning big through 1986, and then losing even bigger beginning in April 1987, when interest rates began rising. Bond prices fall when interest rates rise. The unre-

alized losses in the company's then $8.02 billion bond portfolio hit $640 million on Sept. 30, 1987. Those losses could have widened further had the stock market crash not come, easing interest rates.

But the company's strategy since then—essentially hold and hope for falling interest rates—was costing it tens of millions of dollars in hedging costs, and left it still with enormous interest-rate risk. "We need to get this behind us," D. H. Ankeny Jr., chairman, president and chief executive officer, said in an interview yesterday. Waiting for rates to decline, he said, "is no longer an acceptable strategy."

Between now and the end of the first quarter, First Bank said it would sell $4.6 billion of its current $7.5 billion investment portfolio. Funding

those bonds with deposits was, roughly, costing as much as the bonds were yielding, making them essentially a "nonearning asset," a First Bank official said.

Both Moody's Investors Service and Standard & Poor's Corp. downgraded First Bank's debt ratings yesterday. While selling the bonds reduces the company's interest-rate risk, the lower capital levels will reduce its financial flexibility, the rating concerns noted.

Source: Jeff Bailey, "First Bank System Begins to Sell Portfolio of U.S. Bonds; Loss Is Put at $500 Million," *The Wall Street Journal*, December 20, 1988. Reprined by permission of The Wall Street Journal, © Dow Jones & Company, Inc. 1988. All Rights Reserved Worldwide.

HEDGING INTEREST-RATE RISK IN THE FINANCIAL MARKETS

Rather than reducing its interest-rate risk by taking a maturities-matched position on its assets and liabilities, a bank can allow itself a substantial duration gap on its balance sheet if it hedges by taking an offsetting position in financial futures, options, or swaps. We shall see in Chapter 13 exactly what these instruments are and how they are used, but here is the basic idea.

The bank can promise to buy or sell securities in the future at a price agreed upon now (rather like a forward transaction in foreign exchange). This sort of promise is called a **futures contract**. If interest rates change, the bank will gain or lose money on the promise. For example, suppose the bank enters into a contract with someone to deliver to them a one-year, $1 million T-bill in one year's time at a price of $909,091 (equivalent to a market interest rate of 10%). If, at the time of delivery, the market interest rate actually turns out to be 12%, the bank can go out and buy a one-year T-bill for $892,857. It then has the right to sell it to the other party to the contract for the originally agreed upon price of $909,091. That

futures contract
Contract to buy or sell securities in the future at a price agreed upon in the present.

means a profit of $909,091–$892,857 = $16,234 for the bank and a corresponding loss to the other party. Of course, if the market interest rate had fallen, the bank would have taken a loss and the other party would have made a profit.

Now suppose the bank has a positive duration gap, so that if interest rates rise, the market value of its equity will fall. It can protect itself by taking an offsetting position in futures, selling enough T-bills forward so that if market interest rates rise, the gain on the futures contracts will exactly offset the loss on the bank's balance sheet. If, instead, interest rates fall, the loss on the futures will be exactly offset by the gain on the bank's balance sheet. Taking an offsetting position in this way is called *hedging*. Whatever the bank's duration gap, it can protect itself from interest-rate risk completely (or partially, if it chooses) through an appropriate hedge.

FLOATING-RATE LOANS AND RISK SHIFTING

Yet another way to reduce interest-rate risk is to make *floating-rate loans*. To see how this helps, consider the funding of a particular 2-year loan. The loan has a fixed interest rate of 9%, with interest payments due every 6 months. The loan is funded initially by selling a 6-month NCD at 7%:

Loans		NCDs	
2-year at 9%	+$1m	6-month at 7%	+$1m

The bank is clearly in a refinance position: When the NCD matures, the bank must sell a new NCD to pay off the old one, and it must do this every 6 months over the life of the loan. As we know, if interest rates go up, the bank stands to make a loss.

Suppose, however, that instead of charging a fixed 9%, the bank charges a floating rate that is equal to the rate on 6-month NCDs plus 2%. Since the NCD rate is initially 7%, for the first 6 months, the borrower pays a rate of 9%. If interest rates stay the same, the borrower will continue to pay 9%, just as with the fixed-rate loan. But if the market rate on 6-month NCDs goes up to, say, 10%, the borrower will have to pay a rate of 10% + 2% = 12%. Of course, if the market rate on 6-month NCDs goes down, so will the rate paid by the borrower.

Although the loan has a maturity of 2 years, in terms of the interest-rate risk for the bank, it is as though it were a 6-month loan. For interest-rate risk, it is not maturity that matters, but time until **repricing** (resetting the interest rate). In terms of interest-rate risk, a 2-year loan repriced every 6 months is no different from a sequence of 6-month loans. So, in a sense, making floating-rate loans is a form of maturities matching: The effective maturity of the loan is reduced to match more closely the maturity of the shorter-term liabilities that are used to fund it.

Over the past decade banks have increasingly relied on floating rates for long-term loans. In the Eurodollar market, where loans typically have a long

repricing
Resetting the interest rate.

maturity compared to loans made by banks in the United States, almost all carry a floating rate. This increasing reliance on floating-rate loans is actually a return to what was normal practice before the Great Depression. Then, banks paid market interest rates on deposits and charged floating rates on loans. After the Depression there was a long period of stable interest rates, during which Regulation Q removed most of the uncertainty about the cost of funds. Fixed-rate lending became the norm during this period, but, historically speaking, it was an aberration.

Although floating-rate loans eliminate interest-rate risk for banks, the risk still exists. It is simply shifted to the borrowers. This transfer of risk may not be a particularly good idea for several reasons. First, borrowers may be less able to bear the risk than are banks. Banks specialize in acquiring and using financial information. They are better able to predict interest rates and, if necessary, to hedge their position in the financial markets. Second, the danger of floating-rate loans to borrowers is compounded, because high rates often coincide with times of economic difficulty in which borrowers may already be under severe pressure. A rise in interest payments may be the straw that breaks the camel's back. What this means for banks is that floating-rate loans simply transform one type of risk into another: Interest-rate risk is transformed into credit risk.

One way for borrowers to deal with the interest-rate risk imposed on them by floating-rate loans is to buy insurance. At the height of interest-rate volatility in the early 1980s, an actual insurance policy was offered to small companies to protect them against increases in the floating rates on their loans (see "Small Firms Offered Protection from Rise in Rates on Loans" on page 298).

Insurance is a good idea, but the simplest and most efficient way for borrowers to buy insurance is to buy it from their bank. They do this, in fact, implicitly whenever they borrow at a fixed rate. In order to rid themselves of interest-rate risk, borrowers are willing to pay a fixed rate higher than the average floating rate. The difference can be seen as a kind of "insurance premium" that compensates the bank for carrying the risk. Carrying this risk, and offering the "insurance," is part of the bank's function as a financial intermediary.

The role of the bank here is closely analogous to its role in buying and selling foreign exchange forward. By offering forward transactions in foreign exchange, the bank is relieving its customers of exchange-rate risk: The customers know that they will be able to buy or sell foreign exchange at a predetermined, fixed price. In a similar fashion, by offering longer-term fixed-rate loans, the bank is relieving its customers of interest-rate risk: They know that they will be able to continue to borrow at a predetermined, fixed interest rate. Compared to the risky 2-year floating-rate loan that we looked at above, a 2-year fixed-rate loan sets in advance a forward price on the second, third, and fourth 6-month periods of the loan.

SMALL FIRMS OFFERED PROTECTION FROM RISE IN RATES ON LOANS

By Joanne Lipman

Staff Reporter of The Wall Street Journal

NEW YORK—An insurer's subsidiary is offering nervous borrowers protection against rising interest rates.

AIC Financial Corp., a unit of American Plan Corp. Insurance Group, says that for a fee of 2% of the value of a floating-rate loan, it will pay the difference to the loan holder if rates rise more than 1-1/4 percentage points above what the 13-week Treasury bill is when the policy is written.

The plan is geared toward small businesses that don't qualify for fixed-rate loans and hold variable-rate loans of $100,000 to $5 million. Technically, it isn't insurance, AIC says. Instead, it is a guarantee backed by a surety bond to AIC by American Fidelity Fire Insurance Co. of New York.

"The whole concept of this is, the businessman can't fix his cost of money today," says Abe Jay Lieber, American Plan's president and chief executive officer. "I'm putting him in a position to fix that cost," he says.

AIC began offering the guarantees last week, launching the plan with newspaper advertisements that ask, "Where were you when interest rates went to 20%?" It says it has received about 120 inquiries, many of them from small construction companies or commercial developers. There have not been any requests for the protection on personal loans, but Mr. Lieber says he is willing to consider those too.

Coverage under the plan extends for 15 months, and the loan holder is paid monthly by AIC if interest rates rise beyond the specified level.

Prudential-Bache Securities Inc., which manages the program, is covering AIC's costs partly by selling short 13-week Treasury bill futures for AIC. If interest rates rise, the Treasury bill yield decreases, and AIC's profit can be used to offset the payment to the loan holder. If interest rates fall, the Treasury bill yield increases, but the losses AIC incurs as a result are expected to be absorbed by the fees it has collected.

Some observers note that borrowers just as easily play futures themselves. What AIC is doing "is essentially hedge management . . . and that is why you're paying the premium," says Thomas Russo, a partner in the law firm Cadwalader, Wickersham & Taft. "Someone could do it all himself."

Mr. Lieber concedes "absolutely" that an individual's broker could arrange the same type of protection. But, he says, Prudential-Bache has developed a computer program—based on the past five years of movements in Treasury bills, the prime rate, Eurodollars, certificates of deposit, and Treasury bonds—specifically for AIC's plan.

Source: Joanne Lipman, "Small Firms Offered Protection from Rise in Rates on Loans," *The Wall Street Journal*, September 26, 1983. Reprinted by permission of The Wall Street Journal, © Dow Jones & Company, Inc. 1983. All Rights Reserved Worldwide.

EXCHANGE-RATE RISK

Exchange-rate risk is much like interest-rate risk. A change in a market price—the market exchange rate now, rather than the market interest rate—may have different effects on the value of a bank's assets and on the value of its liabilities. The result is a change in the value of the bank's equity. Most of what we have learned about interest-rate risk carries over to exchange-rate risk.

To understand the nature of exchange-rate risk, consider an example. First National Bank has made a loan in Japanese yen for ¥24 billion and it has only ¥12 billion in yen deposits. The exchange rate is ¥120 to the dollar. The bank's overall balance sheet, *valued in U.S. dollars* is:

Reserves	$ 50m	Deposits	
Loans		In U.S. $	$620m
In U.S. $	500m	In ¥, at 120¥/$	100m
In ¥, at 120¥/$	200m	Equity	30m

Suppose the value of the yen falls, and the exchange rate rises to ¥150 to the dollar. The loan is now worth ¥24 billion/¥150 = $160 million, while the deposit is worth ¥12 billion/¥150 = $80 million. The change in the bank's balance sheet, in market values, is:

Loans		Deposits	
In ¥, at 150¥/$	−40m	In ¥, at 150¥/$	−20m
		Equity	−20m

That is, the bank has lost $20 million.

The risk involved in a currency mismatch is very much like the risk involved in a duration mismatch. A change in exchange rate, just like a change in interest rate, will affect assets and liabilities differently, and the difference will mean a change in the net worth of the bank.

Exchange-rate risk in not just a result of foreign-currency lending. Another major source is a bank's forward commitments to buy and sell foreign exchange. If a bank has sold forward more yen, say, than it has bought, and if the yen rises in value, the bank will take a loss.[15]

Banks avoid exchange-rate risk in much the same way as they avoid interest-rate risk—by "running a matched book." Assets and forward purchases in a given nondollar currency are kept equal to liabilities and forward sales in that currency. For a bank running a matched book, changes in exchange rates have no effect on net worth.

However, banks will not always *want* to run a perfectly matched book. For example, if First National thinks that the value of the yen is going to fall, it might want to have more yen liabilities than yen assets. Or, if it thinks the mark is going to rise, it might want to have more mark assets than mark liabilities. The more confident it is of its prediction, the more it will want to deviate from a perfectly matched book.

---

[15]There are parallels in the realm of interest-rate risk. Just as banks make forward commitments to buy and sell foreign exchange, they also make forward commitments to lend at predetermined interest rates. For example, First National might agree to lend Megacorp $5 million for a year at 10%, the loan to be made 3 months from now. First National will charge a fee for making this commitment, just as it does for a forward transaction in foreign exchange. Such a forward loan commitment exposes First National to interest-rate risk just as a forward foreign-exchange transaction exposes it to exchange-rate risk. If interest rates go up in the next 3 months, the cost of funds will rise, but the loan will still have to be made at the agreed-upon 10% rate.

Naturally, loans denominated in foreign currency are usually made to foreign borrowers (or to U.S. corporations operating overseas). The yen loan of our example, for instance, might have been made to Kamikaze Cycles of Kyoto. The reason Kamikaze wants to borrow in yen rather than in dollars is that borrowing in yen eliminates exchange-rate risk: If it borrows in yen, it does not matter to Kamikaze whether the yen goes up or down relative to the dollar. First National is bearing the exchange-rate risk.

The bank can eliminate this exchange-rate risk for itself by making the loan to Kamikaze in U.S. dollars. The risk, of course, is simply transferred to Kamikaze. Just as floating-rate loans shift interest-rate risk to the borrower, so denominating foreign loans in dollars shifts exchange-rate risk to the borrower. With the loan to Kamikaze denominated in dollars, if the yen falls in value, First National is protected. However, Kamikaze may now be unable to repay: While it has to pay the same number of dollars, the amount of yen it owes has increased. So making foreign loans in dollars transforms exchange-rate risk into credit risk, just as floating-rate loans transform interest-rate risk into credit risk.

Just as a bank can hedge its exposure to interest-rate risk by taking a position in financial futures, options, or swaps, so can it hedge its exposure to exchange-rate risk by taking a position in *currency* futures, options, or swaps. The principle is exactly the same. We shall look at the details in Chapter 13.

12.4 | MANAGING CREDIT RISK

When banks fail, it is almost always because of bad loans. Whereas interest-rate risk has both an up side and a down side, credit risk is all down side. The best that can happen is that the loan is repaid with interest, as agreed. The worst that can happen is a total loss of both interest and principal.

There are two things a bank can do to protect itself against credit risk—it can be careful in making loans and it can diversify. Bank failures are usually the result of reckless lending, a lack of diversification, or both.

KNOW THY BORROWER

Most defaults occur because the borrower is *unable* to repay. Sometimes fraud is involved, but that is the exception rather than the rule. So the essence of careful lending is information—knowing the borrower's capacity to repay. For lending to firms, this involves careful analysis of the firm's financial situation and of its credit record. Much information on these is available from external sources such as Dun & Bradstreet, which publishes reports on the financial history and current credit status of many businesses. Perhaps more important than past history is a firm's future prospects. As we noted in Chapter 3, the bank's long-term customer relationship with a firm may provide it with a valuable informational advantage in assessing the firm's prospects.

For consumer loans, there is less individual information, although credit bureaus do collect and make available credit and employment information on individuals. In making consumer loans, banks tend to rely on "credit scores." The loan applicant gets so many points based on current income, so many for years in current job, so many based on wealth, so many for demographics (for example, married people are better credit risks than singles), and so on. If the total number of points exceeds some threshold value, a loan is granted. The amount the bank is willing to lend will depend, of course, on its assessment of the borrower's ability to repay.

The rate that a bank charges on a loan will depend, to some extent, on the risk of default. There are limits, however, to how much rates can be raised. We saw in Chapter 5 that raising the contractual rate on loans can be counterproductive. Borrowers that look equally risky to the bank may actually differ substantially. Raising the rate on the loan will induce the stronger borrowers to look for a better deal elsewhere, but the weaker borrowers will stay. This process of *adverse selection* will lower the average quality of the loan portfolio, and the realized rate may actually fall. In addition, in some states there is a legal maximum on the rate a bank may charge on its loans. Such limits are called **usury ceilings**. Usury ceilings became a problem in the early 1980s when market interest rates skyrocketed. The effect of the ceilings was to stop banks from lending to their most risky borrowers; for example, credit card lending was severely restricted.

usury ceilings
Legal limits placed on the interest rates that banks may charge.

A bank can reduce the potential loss in case a loan does go bad by demanding collateral—some specific item of value that becomes the property of the bank in case of default. Most consumer lending is collateralized—home mortgages and automobile loans are examples.

DIVERSIFICATION

While it is essential to be as careful as possible in making each loan, mistakes are bound to happen, and even with the best of loans, there is always the chance of a loss. The best defense against these inevitable losses is diversification. The idea is simple enough: Don't put all your eggs in one basket.

Banking regulations attempt to enforce this principle. A bank is not allowed to lend to any one borrower an amount in excess of 15% of its equity (up to 25% if the loan is collateralized). Since equity is generally well below 10% of total assets, this means that no single loan can make up more than 1% to 1.5% of a bank's portfolio. The limit of 15% of equity also means that even the largest U.S. bank, Citibank, with $8 billion in equity, is limited to lending no more than .15 x $8 billion = $1.2 billion to any one borrower.

Although $1.2 billion may sound like a lot of money, there are cases in which borrowers require substantially more—perhaps ten times more (for example, to finance a merger or acquisition). For a long time, Canadian banks had an advantage in making such extremely large loans because their banking regulators imposed no limit on the size of individual loans. In recent years, however, some major Canadian banks have taken massive losses on such large loans, and the

Canadian banks have decided to impose on themselves a voluntary limit of 15%, much like the one regulators impose on U.S. banks.

There is something of a conflict between diversification on the one hand and specialization on the other. In order to make the most of their information, banks often specialize in lending to particular industries and in particular geographic areas. The better use of information means that the individual loans will probably be safer. However, the default risks on loans to firms in the same industry or in the same geographic area are often closely related to one another. This undermines diversification and exposes the bank to increased credit risk. Therefore the costs and benefits of specialization need to be weighed carefully.

LENDING INVOLVING OTHER BANKS

The peculiar structure of U.S. banking that we learned about in Chapter 8 creates some special problems with respect to credit risk. As we saw earlier, small banks lack sufficient loan opportunities and large banks lack sufficient funds. The result is that large banks both share loans with small banks and borrow funds from them.

Loan participations allow the originating bank to make a larger loan than regulations, or prudent diversification, would allow it to make alone. The benefit to participating banks is that it enables them to diversify their loan portfolios. The purchase of securitized loans serves the same function. Both practices offer a partial solution to the specialization–diversification dilemma: Banks can gain the informational benefits by originating loans in an industry or geographic area they know well, while avoiding the lack of diversification by letting other banks actually carry the loans on their balance sheets.

There is a problem, however, with participations and securitizations: They violate the principle of "know thy borrower." In both types of arrangement, one bank is relying on another to do its homework for it. There is a danger that the purchasing bank is taking on more credit risk than it knows or wants.

The other side of the correspondent–respondent relationship—the borrowing of funds by large banks from small—involves credit risk too. Federal funds sold are unsecured loans, and the insurance on correspondent deposits covers only the first $100,000. Another form of interbank lending that is common is the purchase by small banks and savings and loans of NCDs from large banks; here too insurance is limited to the first $100,000.

As we shall see in Chapter 17, some dramatic recent failures have highlighted the dangers of loan sharing and of lending to other banks. As a result, banks today are as careful in assessing the creditworthiness of the banks with which they deal, and in limiting their credit lines to those banks, as they are with any other class of borrower.

As we saw in Chapter 11, the Eurocurrency market is also characterized by substantial interdependence among banks. Syndicated loans play much the same role there as participations do domestically. They enable large loans to be made with the risk being shared by a number of banks. There are also vast amounts of interbank deposits. Some large failures in this market, too, have exposed the risks, and have led banks to become much more cautious in their dealings with one another.

12.5 LDC LOANS: A CASE STUDY IN RISK

The history of one particular type of lending—lending to LDCs (less-developed countries)—illustrates particularly well many of the problems we have been talking about.

Before 1970 there was little lending by banks to LDCs. The latter borrowed mainly from the governments of developed countries rather than from private lenders. By 1982 most such lending had become private, mainly in the form of bank loans. By 1982 U.S. banks held some $107 billion in loans to non-OPEC LDCs. Some $72 billion of these loans were to Latin American countries, with just three—Mexico, Brazil, and Argentina—accounting for the lion's share.

Why did bankers make these loans? The sharp increases in the price of oil engineered by OPEC in 1973 and 1979 left the oil-exporting countries with large amounts of cash. They deposited this with Eurodollar banks, many of them American. The banks, naturally enough, wished to lend the money profitably. International loans, booked overseas, were particularly attractive because they avoided costly reserve requirements and deposit insurance premiums on domestic loans. On the side of demand, the rise in oil prices forced some countries to borrow to pay their oil bills. Others, like Mexico, wanted to borrow against their expected future income as oil producers. Banks fell over each other in the rush to oblige.

Note that there is a special type of credit risk in making a loan to a government (known as **sovereign lending**). Because governments cannot legally be taken to court to recover a debt, lenders have little recourse if a government defaults. If a government does not want to pay, it cannot be made to do so. The only external constraint on its behavior is the constraint of reputation: Defaulting on existing debt will make it harder to borrow in the future. While the banks recognized that some risk was involved in this massive lending to LDCs, there seemed to be a sort of safety in numbers: Since *everyone* was making these loans, they reasoned, the risk couldn't be that great. Perhaps they believed, too, that if things went wrong, the U.S. government would step in to cover the loss rather than allowing a large number of banks to go under.

sovereign lending
Lending to governments.

Many small and medium-sized banks participated in these loans through syndications arranged by the money center banks. They were eager to enter the lucrative Eurodollar market, about which they knew little themselves except that the profits looked attractive. The smaller banks lacked the international contacts and expertise to be able to make loans themselves, so syndications seemed to provide them with an easy way to get a piece of the action. In participating in these syndications, they relied heavily on the savvy of the lead banks that put them together. The international banks, for their part, were happy to include them in: Syndications lowered their own exposure to the LDC loans and provided them with substantial fee income up front. When the crisis struck, some 1,500 U.S. banks were holding LDC debt they had acquired in this way.

The loans were thought to be quite safe in terms of market risk. Because they were floating-rate, interest-rate risk on the loans was minimal. Because the loans were denominated in dollars, matching the banks' deposits, there was no exchange-rate risk either. This absence of risk, however, was illusory. In shifting the interest-rate risk and exchange-rate risk to the borrower, that risk had not really been removed: It had merely been transformed into credit risk.

The true risks became abundantly clear when, in 1980, the Fed sharply tightened monetary policy in the United States, driving interest rates to extraordinarily high levels. The high interest rates precipitated a severe recession in the United States that quickly spread to the other major economies. The worldwide recession greatly reduced the demand for the raw materials that make up a large part of LDC exports. At the same time the rising interest rates in the United States drove up the exchange value of the dollar. All of these factors contributed to the subsequent collapse.

Since the LDC loans were floating-rate, as market interest rates rose, the amount of interest payments the borrowers had to make rose with them. The amount rose in U.S. dollars, but it rose far more in terms of the currencies of the debtor countries because of the rising exchange value of the dollar. While the burden of repayment increased, the capacity of the LDCs to pay decreased as the recession reduced their incomes. As a result, the LDCs found it increasingly difficult to make their payments. In August 1982 Mexico was the first to announce that it was temporarily suspending payments on its debt.

Since then, banks have cut back new lending to LDCs. They have gradually increased their loan loss reserves against the existing loans, recognizing that they are unlikely to be repaid. One-third to one-half of the amount outstanding has been written off in this way. Various deals have been worked out with the debtors, including the rescheduling of interest payments and principal repayment. Losses on these loans have seriously weakened the capital positions of the money center banks that were most involved. Although the smaller banks that participated in the syndications have also taken losses, the amounts involved did not represent as large a fraction of their assets or capital as did the losses of the money center banks.

SUMMARY

- Banks face three types of risk—liquidity risk, market risk, and credit risk. Liquidity risk is the risk that the bank will not have the funds it needs, at reasonable cost, to meet excess withdrawals or to make loans. Market risk is the risk that changes in market interest rates or exchange rates will lead to a capital loss. Credit risk is the risk that borrowers will default on their loans.

- There are important differences in the circumstances of large banks and small banks that affect the risks they face and how they deal with them.

- Small banks are deposit-rich: They have more deposits than good loan opportunities. The basic question for a small bank is what to do with the leftover funds.

- Large banks are deposit-poor: They have more good loan opportunities than deposits. The basic question for a large bank is how to find the extra funds that it needs. Large banks rely mainly on the money market to raise these extra funds.

- Large banks and small can help each other with their respective problems, often through the correspondent relationship. Large banks borrow small banks' excess funds through correspondent balances, through the federal funds gambit, and by selling them NCDs. Large banks provide small banks with additional lending opportunities in the form of participations, syndications, and securitized loans.

- Banks need liquidity both to meet excess withdrawals and to make new loans as opportunities present themselves. The main source of liquidity is pooling.

- Small banks rely on asset management to provide them with the additional liquidity they need. Their excess funds are invested in liquid assets that can be turned into cash as the need arises. The choice is mainly between federal funds sold and government securities. The former are more liquid, but, because the yield curve is normally upward-sloping, the latter usually provide a better return.

- Large banks rely on liability management to provide them with the additional liquidity they need. This means borrowing in the money market. The main choice is between overnight and term funds.

- For a large bank relying on liability management, the primary consideration is always the *ability* to borrow. This means that the bank must be very careful in maintaining the faith of the market.

- The market value of a bank's equity is the market value of its assets less the market value of its liabilities. Changes in market interest rates and in market exchange rates may have different effects on the market value of a bank's assets and of its liabilities, thereby changing the value of its equity.

- The liabilities used to fund a loan will often have a maturity that differs from the maturity of the loan itself. If the maturity of the loan is longer, the bank is in a refinance position; if the maturity of the funding is longer, the bank is in a reinvestment position. If the maturity of loan and funds are the same, the bank is in a maturities-matched position.

- A bank in a refinance position will gain from a fall in market interest rates but lose from a rise. A bank in a reinvestment position will gain from a rise but lose from a fall. A bank in a maturities-matched position will be immune to interest-rate risk.

- To be able to manage its interest-rate risk, a bank needs to know its overall exposure—the exposure for its balance sheet as a whole. One way to measure this is to calculate the bank's duration gap.

- The duration of a bank's assets or liabilities is a weighted average of the maturity of all the payments due. The percentage change in the value of the assets or liabilities is inversely related to the duration.

- The sign and magnitude of the desired duration gap will depend on the bank's expectations about interest-rate movements. By correctly anticipating interest-rate movements, the bank can add substantially to its profits. Mistakes, however, can be costly.

- Banks can change their duration gap by tailoring the maturity of their assets and liabilities. For small banks, this chiefly means altering the maturity composition of their portfolios of government securities. For large banks, it also means changing the maturity mix of their liabilities.

- Interest-rate risk can be hedged by taking a position in financial futures, options, or swaps. If market interest rates change, the capital gain or loss on the hedging instruments will offset the capital loss or gain on the bank's balance sheet.

- Floating-rate loans shift interest-rate risk from lender to borrower. This is not a pure gain for the lender, since interest-rate/risk is largely transformed into credit risk. In general, banks are better qualified to bear the interest-rate risk, and it is part of their function as a financial intermediary to do so (for a fee, of course).

- Exchange-rate risk has many parallels with interest-rate risk. The bank's exposure to exchange-rate risk will depend on the relative amounts of its assets and liabilities denominated in a particular currency. For instance, if it has more assets in that currency than liabilities, a rise in the value of the currency will mean an increase in the value of the bank's equity. The bank can avoid exchange-rate risk entirely by running a matched book, or it can hedge using currency futures, options, or swaps.

- Banks can avoid exchange-rate risk by lending to foreigners in dollars. However, as with floating-rate loans, the risk is merely passed on to the borrower and thereby transformed into credit risk.

- Most bank failures are the result of bad loans. A bank can protect itself from loan losses through the careful use of information and through good diversification.

- Bank regulations impose some degree of diversification by limiting the maximum loan to any one borrower to no more than 15% of a bank's capital.

- Banks do a lot of lending to other banks. Problems in this area have taught banks to be as careful in such dealings as in any other type of lending.

- The sad story of LDC lending provides a good case study in some of the risks involved in bank lending in general.

KEY TERMS

liquidity risk	securitization	matching maturities
credit risk	asset management	duration
market risk	liability management	duration gap
deposit rich	market value	futures contract
retail bank	book value	repricing
deposit poor	refinance position	usury ceilings
wholesale bank	reinvestment position	sovereign lending

DISCUSSION QUESTIONS

1. If Amerasia Bank has more deposits than it needs to fund its loans, why do you think it has such a large amount of repos?

2. Run through a list of the major categories of bank assets and liabilities. For each category, assess its liquidity and risk. How do differences in the risk and liquidity properties of a bank's assets and liabilities impose risks on a bank?

3. What are the main differences between the balance sheets of large and small banks? How do these differences affect the risks these banks face and the way they deal with them?

4. In what ways does the correspondent relationship reduce the risks for the banks involved? In what ways does it increase them?

5. How do the motivations for holding government securities differ between large and small banks?

6. What are the ways a large bank can reduce its exposure to interest-rate risk? What are the costs and benefits of each?

7. What are the dangers of relying on liability management as a way of dealing with liquidity risk?

8. What are the parallels between interest-rate risk and exchange-rate risk?

SOFTWARE EXERCISE FOR THIS CHAPTER

Title: Bank

This computer exercise puts you in the role of a bank executive engaged in the management of an institution's assets and liabilities. You must balance profit maximization against risk in an uncertain world in which random events may confound your plans. See your instructor if you wish to use this program.

BIBLIOGRAPHY

French, George E., "Measuring the Interest-Rate Exposure of Financial Intermediaries," *FDIC Banking Review* Fall 1988, 14–27.

Koch, Timothy W., *Bank Management*, Hinsdale, IL: Dryden, 1988.

Stigum, Marcia, *The Money Market*, 3rd ed., Homewood, IL: Dow Jones-Irwin, 1990.

Stigum, Marcia L. and Rene O. Branch, *Managing Bank Assets and Liabilities: Strategies for Risk Control and Profit*, Homewood, IL: Dow Jones-Irwin, 1983.

APPENDIX TO CHAPTER 12

CALCULATING DURATION

Duration is a useful measure of a bank's exposure to interest-rate risk. In this appendix we shall define duration precisely and see how it is calculated.

Think of the bank's assets as a large number of payments due to be paid to the bank at different times in the future. For example, $5 million might be due in 1 month, $10 million in 3 months, $7 million in 6 months, and so on. Think of the bank's liabilities as a large number of payments due to be paid *by* the bank.

Let us look first at the effect of a change in interest rate on the present value of a single such payment. Remember from Chapter 6 that if the interest rate is i, then the present value, V, of a payment, P, due in t years, is

$$V = \frac{P}{(1+i)^t} .$$

[12A.1]

If the interest rate changes by a small amount, Δi, then the percentage change in the present value, $\Delta V/V$, is given by the simple relation[1]

$$\frac{\Delta V}{V} = -t \frac{\Delta i}{(1+i)} .$$

[12A.2]

Notice the minus sign: An increase in the interest rate *lowers* the present value.

Let us look at an example. Suppose that a payment of $1 million is due in 2 years time and the market interest rate is 11.5%. The present value of this

---

[1] Equation 12A.1 may be written $V = P (1 + i)^{-t}$. Taking a derivative with respect to i, we obtain

$$\frac{dV}{di} = -t P (1+i)^{-t-1} = -t\frac{V}{(1+i)} .$$

Rearranging this and substituting Δ for d, we obtain Equation 12A.2.

payment is

$$\frac{\$1,000,000}{(1.115)^2} = \$804,000. \qquad [12A.3]$$

If the market interest rate increases to 12%, the change in interest rate, Δi, is 12% – 11.5% = 0.5%, and, from Equation 12A.2, the present value of the payment changes by

$$-2 \times \frac{0.005}{1.115} = -0.009. \qquad [12A.4]$$

That is, the present value falls by 0.9% of \$804,000, or \$7,000, to \$797,000.

🌴 **CHECK STATION 1**   A. **Verify this result by calculating the present value of the payment at an interest rate of 12%.**

B. **What is the percentage fall in value if the payment is due in 10 years rather than in 2 years?**

Now, the bank's assets can be seen as a collection of payments due at various times (suppose the most distant is due in seven years). We could show them on the following time line:

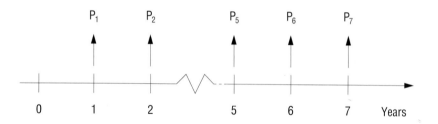

where P_t is the payment due in t years.

The value of the bank's assets, A, is simply the sum of the present values of the various payments:

$$A = V_1 + V_2 + \ldots + V_7, \qquad [12A.5]$$

where V_1 is the present value of P_1, and so on.

Now suppose that market interest rates change by Δi. The change in the value of the bank's assets, ΔA, will be the sum of the changes in the present values of the various payments:

$$\Delta A = \Delta V_1 + \Delta V_2 + \ldots + \Delta V_7. \qquad [12A.6]$$

Dividing ΔV_1 by V_1 and then multiplying by V_1, and doing the same for V_2, and so on, we can rewrite this as

$$\Delta A = \frac{\Delta V_1}{V_1} V_1 + \frac{\Delta V_2}{V_2} V_2 + \ldots + \frac{\Delta V_7}{V_7} V_7. \qquad [12A.7]$$

We can now use Equation 12A.2 to substitute for $\Delta V_1/V_1$, etc., to obtain

$$\Delta A = [-1 \frac{\Delta i}{(1+i)}] V_1 + [-2 \frac{\Delta i}{(1+i)}] V_2 + \ldots + [-7 \frac{\Delta i}{(1+i)}] V_7, \quad [12A.8]$$

or

$$\Delta A = -[1V_1 + 2V_2 + \ldots + 7V_7] \frac{\Delta i}{(1+i)}. \qquad [12A.9]$$

If we divide both sides by A, then we obtain

$$\frac{\Delta A}{A} = -[1 \frac{V_1}{A} + 2 \frac{V_2}{A} + \ldots + 7 \frac{V_7}{A}] \frac{\Delta i}{(1+i)}, \qquad [12A.10]$$

or

$$\frac{\Delta A}{A} = -d_A \frac{\Delta i}{(1+i)}, \qquad [12A.11]$$

where

$$d_A = [1 \frac{V_1}{A} + 2 \frac{V_2}{A} + \ldots + 7 \frac{V_7}{A}] \qquad [12A.12]$$

is called the *duration* of the bank's assets.

Notice that the duration plays exactly the same role in Equation 12A.11 as the maturity of a single payment does in Equation 12A.2. In a sense, the asset duration is the "average maturity" of the bank's assets. Indeed, you can see from Equation 12A.10 that the duration is calculated by taking a weighted average of the maturities of the payments, weighting each payment's maturity by the share of the payment's present value in the total value of the bank's assets.

CHECK STATION 2

A. A bank's assets consists of $5 million due in 1 year, $3 million due in 2 years, and $2 million due in 3 years. If the market interest rate is 9%, calculate the market value of the bank's assets and their duration.

B. If the market interest rate falls to 8.8%, what is the percentage change in the value of the bank's assets? What is the change in their dollar value?

Just like its assets, a bank's liabilities too can be seen as a stream of payments due to be paid in the future. In the same way that we calculated the duration of the bank's assets, we can calculate the duration of its liabilities, call it d_L. That is, if the market interest rate changes by Δi, then the percentage change in the value of the bank's liabilities will be

$$\frac{\Delta L}{L} = -d_L \frac{\Delta i}{(1 + i)} \; .$$ [12A.13]

Remember that the market value of a bank's equity is the value of its assets less the value of its liabilities. Expressed in symbols, this is,

$$E = A - L,$$ [12A.14]

where E is the value of equity. In terms of *changes* in market value,

$$\Delta E = \Delta A - \Delta L.$$ [12A.15]

We are now ready to see how a change in the market interest rate will affect the market value of the bank's equity. First, we divide and then multiply ΔA by A, and do similarly with ΔL,

$$\Delta E = \frac{\Delta A}{A} A - \frac{\Delta L}{L} L.$$ [12A.16]

Next, we substitute for $\Delta A/A$ and $\Delta L/L$ using Equations 12A.11 and 12A.13:

$$\Delta E = \left[-d_A \frac{\Delta i}{(1 + i)} \right] A - \left[-d_L \frac{\Delta i}{(1 + i)} \right] L,$$ [12A.17]

or

$$\Delta E = -\left[d_A A - d_L L \right] \frac{\Delta i}{(1 + i)} \; .$$ [12A.18]

🌴 **CHECK STATION 3** | **The market value of First National's assets is $11.2 billion and the market value of its liabilities is $10.3 billion. The duration of its assets is 2.5 years and the duration of its liabilities is 1.3 years. Suppose the market interest rate goes up from 10.1% to 10.4%. What is the change in the value of the bank's equity?**

It is customary to summarize a bank's exposure to interest-rate risk in terms of its *duration gap*. That is, the expression in brackets in Equation 12A.18 is divided by the value of the bank's assets to give a number that, like maturity and duration, has a dimension of years:

$$dgap = d_A - d_L \frac{L}{A} \; .$$ [12A.19]

DISCUSSION QUESTION

1. Consider the following three ways of repaying a 3-year loan of $10,000 at 10% (each has a present value of $10,000):

   a. A 3-year bill: Principal and accumulated interest are all repaid at the end of 3 years (calculate the amount).

   b. A coupon bond: Annual coupon payments of 10% are paid, and the principal is repaid at the end of 3 years.

   c. An amortized loan: The loan is repaid in three equal annual payments (calculate the size of the annual payment).

   Calculate the duration for each of the above. Which has the longest duration? Which has the shortest? Can you give an intuitive explanation of why?

PART THREE

MORE ABOUT
FINANCIAL MARKETS

CHAPTER 13

HEDGING RISK WITH FUTURES, OPTIONS, AND SWAPS

One of the most exciting developments in the world of finance in the last two decades has been the creation of a variety of financial instruments that offer new ways of dealing with risk. Instruments such as financial futures, options, and swaps, which did not even exist 20 years ago, trade today in volumes of hundreds of billions of dollars. In this chapter we shall learn what each of these new instruments is, how it is traded, and how it can be used.

13.1 FUTURES

The futures contract is a solution to the problems involved in making forward transactions. So before we can understand futures, we need to see what forward transactions are and the problems they involve.

FORWARD TRANSACTIONS AND THEIR PROBLEMS

In **forward transactions**, two parties agree now on the terms of a trade to be carried out at some specified time in the future. In contrast, in **spot transactions**, the trade occurs immediately.

To see why a forward transaction might take place, consider an example. You own a copper mine and are contemplating sinking a new shaft. Over the next year the shaft will produce ore containing one million pounds of metal. You can sell this ore to a smelter, a company that extracts the metal from the ore. The cost, including sinking the shaft and mining the ore, will work out to about $1.00/pound of metal, which is profitable at the current copper price of about $1.40. The problem is that you will not be selling your ore to the smelter immediately, but rather at some time in the future. By then the price of copper

forward transactions
Transactions in which two parties agree in advance on the terms of a trade to be carried out at a specified future time.

spot transaction
Transaction in which the trade occurs immediately.

317

might fall. If it falls below $1.00, you will make a loss instead of a profit. You can eliminate the risk of this happening by contracting *now* to sell your ore to the smelter over the next year at an agreed-upon price, say, $1.35/pound of metal.

This sort of forward transaction creates two types of problem. The first is that you may have trouble finding someone willing to take on the other side of the deal. There may be only one or two smelters to whom you could sell your ore, and they might not be interested in entering into a forward transaction. Moreover, because potential trading partners are scarce, when you do find one, he will have a lot of bargaining power and you may not get a very good deal.

The second problem is that forward transactions involve credit risk. A forward transaction is an exchange of promises. Just as with a loan, there is a danger that the promise will not be kept. For example, suppose the price of copper falls to 50¢. If the smelter honors his obligation to buy one million pounds from you at $1.35, he will be paying $1,350,000 for copper worth only $500,000, for a loss of $850,000. He may even have additional forward commitments that will add to his losses. If he has not hedged his position and if he has insufficient resources, he may not be able to keep his side of the bargain. You will be left with $500,000 worth of copper that cost you $1,000,000 to mine.

To minimize the risk of the smelter reneging on his commitment, you will have to invest time and effort in evaluating his creditworthiness, negotiating the terms of the contract, and monitoring compliance, just as you would if you were making the smelter a loan. And, of course, to protect himself against the possibility that *you* will not fulfill your side of the bargain, the smelter will have to take the same care in his dealings with you. All this will add significantly to the costs of the transaction.[1]

THE FUTURES CONTRACT AS A SOLUTION

Just as financial markets have found ways to reduce the costs of lending, so have they found ways to reduce the costs of forward transactions. The basic method is the *futures contract*. For example, rather than entering into a forward agreement with a particular smelter, you can ask your broker to sell copper futures on COMEX, a commodities exchange in New York that specializes in metals. You can sell 40 contracts, each for 25,000 pounds of copper, for delivery at various future dates to match your anticipated output.

When you sell the futures contracts, you are effectively entering into a deal with COMEX rather than with any particular buyer. Of course, the exchange makes sure that for every seller there is a buyer—prices are raised or lowered until the numbers match—but you do not know and do not care who the correspond-

---

[1]Notice that the forward purchase of foreign exchange from a bank that we saw in Chapter 10 is less liable to these sorts of problems. First, there is plenty of competition among banks. Second, the creditworthiness of the bank is well known and easy to check. Of course, the bank needs to check the creditworthiness of the parties with whom *it* deals, but that is what it does for a living anyway, and those parties are probably loan customers about whom the bank has good information already.

ing buyer is. If the buyer fails to pay up, COMEX guarantees that the contract will be honored. As we shall see, the exchange in turn protects itself against credit risk by demanding collateral from both buyers and sellers. By interposing itself between buyers and sellers in this way, the futures exchange solves the credit-risk problem of forward transactions in much the same way as a bank does in the case of indirect lending.

The futures exchange solves the other problem of forward transactions—the difficulty of finding trading partners—by providing an organized market in which buyers and sellers can easily come together. To increase the potential number of traders, the contracts are standardized: Each specifies a standard amount of a specified grade of commodity to be delivered at a standard time and place. Futures prices are quoted by the exchange for delivery at each of the standard dates (March, June, September, and December for copper futures). The price for immediate delivery is called the **spot price**.

spot price
Price of a commodity that is to be delivered immediately.

Potential buyers and sellers include both *hedgers*, like yourself, and *speculators*. **Hedgers** take a position in futures to offset the risks they face from having a position in the underlying commodity. For example, you are worried about a potential loss on the copper you expect to mine. You can eliminate this risk by selling futures. If the price of copper falls, you will make a capital gain on the futures (we shall see how in a moment), and this gain will offset the loss on the copper. Other hedgers—for instance, a manufacturer of electric motors—rather than having copper, anticipate buying it in the future. Since they are worried about a *rise* in the price of copper, they can hedge their position by *buying* futures. Your position, holding the commodity, is called being **long** the commodity. The position of the motor manufacturer, expecting to buy copper, is called being **short**. A long position in the commodity is hedged by taking a short position in futures—that is, by selling futures. A short position in the commodity is hedged by taking a long position in futures—that is, by buying futures.

hedgers
Traders who take a position in futures to offset the risk they face from having a position in the underlying commodity.

long
Actually holding the commodity.

short
Expecting to purchase a specific commodity.

Unlike hedgers, **speculators** have no position in the underlying commodity. They are willing to bet on price movements in the metal by taking a "naked" position in futures—one not offset by an opposite position in the commodity. For example, suppose you believe that the price of copper will rise to $1.60 next March, well above the current March futures price of $1.30. If you have the courage of your convictions, you can make a profit by buying copper futures. When March comes around, you can sell the copper you are contracted to receive at its market price then. If, as you expected, that price turns out to be $1.60, you will make a profit of $7,500 per contract (25,000 pounds times the difference between the market price and the $1.30 that someone agreed in advance to accept for the copper). Of course, if the price in March is below $1.30, you will make a loss. Since you have no position in the metal itself, the gain or loss on the futures contracts will *not* be offset by an opposite loss or gain on the commodity.

speculators
Futures traders who have no position in the underlying commodity.

The presence of speculators in the market ensures that everyone gets a fair price—a fair price being the market's best estimate of the spot price at the time the contract matures. For example, suppose there are more long hedgers (those having a long position in copper) than short, so that the futures price for March delivery is bid down below what can reasonably be expected to be the spot price then. Speculators will come into the market to buy futures, bidding the price up until it equals the expected March price.

Speculators also help to ensure that new information relevant to the price of the commodity is reflected in futures prices as rapidly as possible. For example, suppose that anticipated cuts in defense spending suggest that there will be a substantial fall in the demand for copper next year. Speculators will rush to sell futures contracts. Their selling will rapidly drive down the futures price until it equals the best estimate of what the spot price will be in light of the new information. Indeed, studies suggest that orange juice futures do a better job of predicting frost in Florida than does the National Weather Service!

The larger the market, in terms of numbers of participants and of trading volume, the less likely that it can be manipulated to any one individual trader's advantage. However, such manipulation is not entirely unknown (see "Cornering the Silver Market" on page 322).

There are a number of futures exchanges, principally in Chicago, London, and New York City. A partial list of contracts currently traded in the United States is presented in Exhibit 13.1.

FINANCIAL FUTURES

As you can see from Exhibit 13.1, there are futures contracts not only for metals and agricultural commodities, but also for securities such as T-bills and Eurodollars, and for foreign currencies such as the Japanese yen and the deutsche mark.

financial futures contract
Contract for the future delivery of securities.

Let us look at one example of such a **financial futures contract**—a contract for future delivery of U.S. Treasury bills.[2] If you sell this contract now for delivery, say, in September, you will have to deliver at that time 90-day T-bills with a face value of $1 million. In exchange, you will receive the futures price at which you sell the contract now. That is, if the futures price *today* for delivery next September is $976,562.50 and you sell one contract, then next September you must hand over 90-day T-bills with a face value of $1 million and you will receive in exchange $976,562.50.

What determines the current futures price? We have seen that it is the market's best estimate of the spot price on the date of delivery. The price of 90-day T-bills in September will depend on the market interest rate at that time. So the futures price today reflects the market's best estimate of the rate on T-bills next September. For example, if the market expects the effective annual interest rate on T-bills to be 10%, then the 90-day periodic rate is expected to be 2.4% and the futures price on your contract will be $1,000,000/1.024 = $976,562.50.

Note that the futures price for T-bills may be quite different from the *spot* price—the price for immediate delivery today. For example, if the effective annual interest rate on T-bills today is 12%, then the periodic rate is 2.9% and the spot

---

[2]To keep things simple, the following discussion is somewhat unrealistic in a number of ways on points of detail. Real-world complications will be introduced in the next section.

EXHIBIT 13.1

MOST WIDELY TRADED FINANCIAL FUTURES IN THE UNITED STATES: JANUARY 5, 1989

Type of Future	Contract Size	Exchange[a]	Total Open Interest
Interest Rates			
U.S. Treasury bonds[b]	$100,000	CBOT[b]	361,658
U.S. Treasury bonds	$50,000	MCE	4,229
Municipal bond index	$100,000	CBOT	12,027
U.S. 10-year Treasury notes	$100,000	CBOT	67,939
U.S. 5-year Treasury notes	$100,000	CBOT	31,532
U.S. five-year Treasury notes	$100,000	FINEX	9,247
U.S. Treasury bills	$1 million	IMM	26,941
U.S. Treasury bills	$500,000	MCE	34
Eurodollar rates[b]	$1 million	IMM[b]	528,913
30-day interest rate	$5 million	CBOT	3,560
Currencies[b]			
U.S. dollar index	500 x index value	FINEX	6,186
Japanese yen	12.5 million yen	IMM	32,647
Japanese yen	6.25 million yen	MCE	289
W. German mark	125,000 D. marks	IMM	35,504
W. German mark	62,500 D. marks	MCE	297
Canadian dollar	$100,000 Canadian	IMM	21,974
British pound	£62,500 British	IMM	16,277
British pound	£12,500 British	MCE	85
Swiss franc	125,000 S. francs	IMM	21,478
Swiss franc	62,500 S. francs	MCE	30
Australian dollar	$100,000 Australian	IMM	1,495
European currency unit	100,000 ECU	FINEX	36
Stock Indexes			
S&P 500	500 x Index	CME	120,511
NYSE Composite Index	500 x Index	NYFE	5,276
Major Market Index	250 x Index	CBOT	6,387
K.C. Value Line Index	500 x Index	KC	1,531
K.C. Mini Value Line	100 x Index	KC	164
Price Indexes			
Commodity Research Bureau (CRB) Index	500 x Index	NYFE	2,431

[a]Exchanges: CBOE (Chicago Board Options Exchange); CBOT (Chicago Board of Trade); CME (Chicago Mercantile Exchange); FINEX (Financial Instrument Exchange Division of New York Cotton Exchange); IMM (International Monetary Market of the Chicago Mercantile Exchange); KC (Kansas City Board of Trade); MCE (MidAmerica Commodity Exchange), and NYFE (New York Futures Exchange).

[b]International (round-the-clock) trading exists in Treasury bonds traded in the United States (on the CBOT and Midwest Commodity Exchange), in London (on the London International Financial Futures Exchange—LIFFE), and in Sydney (on the Sydney Futures Exchange). International trading also exists in Eurodollar interest rate contracts on the LIFFE, Sydney, and Singapore International Monetary (SIMEX) exchanges. Various currency futures contracts trade round the clock on numerous exchanges. The IMM contracts on the yen, German mark, and British pound can be traded on the LIFFE and SIMEX exchanges.

The most actively traded financial futures contracts are the Eurodollar contract, the Treasury bond contracts, the S&P 500 stock index contract, and various currency futures contracts.

Source: Exhibit 22–3, "Most Widely Owned Financial Futures in the United States, January 5, 1989," from *Financial Instititutions, Markets, and Money,* 4th ed. by David S. Kidwell and Richard L. Peterson, p. 563, copyright © 1990 by The Dryden Press, a division of Holt, Rinehart and Winston, Inc., reprinted by permission of the publisher.

CORNERING THE SILVER MARKET

In 1979 members of the oil-billionaire Hunt family, together with associates such as Arab-Brazilian Najib Nahas and the three Saudis, Prince Faysal Ben Abdullah al Saud, Mahmoud Fustok, and Shiek Mohamed al Amoudi, began to buy large amounts of silver. The group soon controlled some 280 million ounces of silver, a substantial share of the world's supply. Much of it was actual bullion, the rest silver futures. Had all the contracts been delivered, the 280,000 one-thousand-ounce bars making up the hoard would have risen to a height of 81,777 feet, well into the stratosphere. The Hunts' buying pushed the price of silver from $6 an ounce to a fleeting high of $50 an ounce in January 1980.

In view of the Hunts' massive purchases of silver and the sharp rise in its price, regulators of the futures markets began to fear that the Hunts were attempting to squeeze or "corner" the market. In a corner, X controls much of the underlying commodity and also buys a large number of futures contracts. (Most futures contracts are normally settled in cash rather than through delivery, so the amount of contracts outstanding can be large relative to available stocks of the commodity.) X then demands actual delivery on the futures contracts. Those who have sold the contracts scramble to buy the commodity. X, of course, does not sell. The price rises steeply, and owners of the commodity, including X, make a large capital gain. To prevent such a corner on the silver market, the futures exchanges imposed a limit of 2,000 on the number of contracts any one trader could buy—equivalent to 10 million ounces, a fraction of the Hunts' holdings.

Following the rule change there were rumors the Hunts would sell off their hoard. The price of silver plummeted. In one day alone—"Black Thursday," March 27, 1980—the price of silver dropped more than 30%. The loss to the Hunts that day was approximately $1 billion. Potential default on loans to the Hunts threatened a number of major banks and brokers with insolvency. Stock prices and the prices of other commodities dropped. A full-scale financial crisis was averted only when the Fed persuaded a group of banks to make new loans to the Hunts, saving them from bankruptcy. The scene had been set for the "greedy '80s."

Source: *Fortune*, August 11, 1980; *The Wall Street Journal*, various, 1980.

price is $1,000,000/1.029 = $972,065$. Thus the futures price reflects not today's rate on T-bills, but what the market expects that rate to be next September.

You can use the T-bill futures contract to speculate on future interest rates. Suppose that your prediction differs from that of the market, and that you think the rate on T-bills next September will be 15%, not 10%. Since you expect the rate to be higher, you expect the price to be lower. You can back your opinion by selling a futures contract now at the market price of $976,562.50. If you are right and the market is wrong, the periodic rate on 90-day T-bills will be 3.6% and their price will be $1,000,000/1.036 = $965,662.89$. You will pay this price for the T-bills you need to make delivery, and you will receive for them the futures price at the time you sold the contract. Hence your profit will be $976,562.50 − $965,662.89 = $10,899.61$. Of course, if your prediction proves wrong, your profit will differ, and it may even be a loss.

Suppose you think the rate on T-bills next September will be 5%. What should you do? If you are right, what will be your profit? If the rate turns out to be 15% instead, what will be your loss?

🌴 CHECK STATION 1

HEDGING INTEREST-RATE RISK WITH FINANCIAL FUTURES

Financial futures can be used not only to speculate, but also to hedge. To see how a bank might use financial futures to hedge interest-rate risk, let us consider an example. Suppose that Metropolis funds a 2-year loan at 12% by selling a 1-year NCD at 10%:

METROPOLIS NATIONAL

Loans		NCDs	
2-year at 12%	+$1m	1-year at 10%	+$1m

Apart from this new loan and the new NCD, Metropolis has a zero duration gap.

Clearly, by funding the loan in this way, Metropolis is exposing itself to refinancing risk. At the end of the first year of the loan, Metropolis will have to pay off the maturing NCD. It will obtain the necessary $1.1 million by selling a second 1-year NCD. This second NCD will mature at the end of the second year, at the same time as the loan. Metropolis's profit from the whole transaction will be the $1 million $\times (1.12)^2 = \$1,254,400$ it receives on the loan *less* what it costs to pay off the second NCD. That cost will depend on the interest rate at the time the second NCD is sold.

Exhibit 13.2 on the following page shows three possible scenarios:

1. *Interest rates are unchanged from the first year.* The second NCD is sold at the same rate as the first (10%) and is paid off at the end of the second year for $1.1 million $\times (1.10) = \$1,210,000$. This leaves Metropolis with a profit of $1,254,400 - \$1,210,000 = \$44,400$. This scenario is what the bank believes to be the most likely, but, of course, it is not certain. Market interest rates could rise or fall by the time the bank has to sell the second NCD.

2. *Interest rates rise.* The second NCD is sold at a rate of 15%, and it is paid off at the end of the second year for $1.1 million $\times (1.15) = \$1,265,000$. This leaves Metropolis with a profit of $1,254,400 - \$1,265,000 = -\$10,600$. That is, the bank suffers a *loss* of $10,600.

3. *Interest rates fall.* The second NCD is sold at a rate of 5%, and is paid off at the end of the second year for $1.1 million $\times (1.05) = \$1,155,000$, leaving Metropolis with a profit of $1,254,400 - \$1,155,000 = \$99,400$.

EXHIBIT 13.2

POSSIBLE PROFITS FROM THE LOAN

	NCD Rate at End of Year 1	Repayment of Second NCD	Profit at End of Year 2 (loan repayment – NCD repayment)
1	10%	$1,000,000 × (1.1) × (1.1)= $1,210,000	$1,254,400 – $1,210,000 = $44,400
2	15	$1,000,000 × (1.1) × (1.15)= $1,265,000	$1,254,400 – $1,265,000 = –$10,600
3	5	$1,000,000 × (1.1) × (1.05)= $1,155,000	$1,254,400 – $1,155,000 = $99,400

The ultimate profitability of the loan, then, will depend on the interest rate at the time the second NCD is sold. Metropolis expects to make $44,400, but it could make as much as $99,400 or lose as much as $10,600.

To lock in a known profit and to avoid this uncertainty, Metropolis hedges its position in the futures market. On the day it makes the loan, the bank sells a futures contract to deliver $1 million face value of 1-year T-bills at the end of the first year; in exchange, it will receive the contract price, specified now, of $917,431. This is the contract price now, because the market expects the rate on 1-year T-bills to be 9% at the beginning of Year 2 and their price, therefore, to be $1 million/1.09 = $917,431.

Metropolis does not now have the T-bills it will need to make delivery: It will buy them at the end of the year. If it can buy them for less than the contract price, it will make a profit; if it has to pay more, it will take a loss. This profit or loss will offset the loss or profit on its loan position.

To see how the hedge works, consider the three interest-rate scenarios we looked at above. The market rate on T-bills is assumed here to be 1% less than that on NCDs: NCDs have some default risk, so they pay a little more than T-bills. The three possible outcomes are illustrated in Exhibit 13.3.

1. *Interest rates are unchanged from the first year.* As expected, Metropolis sells its second NCD at 10%, so that its profit from the loan at the end of Year 2 is $44,400. Also as expected, the T-bill rate is 9%, so the bank pays $917,431 for the T-bills it needs to deliver on its futures contract. It receives for them the same amount, resulting in a wash on its futures position— neither profit nor loss. Therefore the total profit at the end of Year 2 is just the $44,400 profit on the loan.

2. *Interest rates rise.* At the end of Year 1, interest rates have risen 5%, so the NCD rate is 15% and the T-bill rate is 14%. Metropolis therefore stands to lose $10,600 on its 2-year loan (see above). Metropolis pays $1 million/ (1.14) = $877,193 for the T-bills it needs to meet delivery on its futures contract, and it receives for them the contract price of $917,431—a profit of $917,431 – $877,193 = $40,238. Since this money is available at the end of Year 1, and we want to evaluate Metropolis's total profit at the end of Year

EXHIBIT 13.3

POSSIBLE PROFITS FROM THE LOAN WITH HEDGING

	Rate on T-Bills at Year-End	Price of T-Bill	Profit of Futures	Total Profit (profit on loan + profit of futures)
1	9%	$1m/(1.09) = $917,431	$917,431 – $917,431 = 0	$44,000 + 0 = $44,000
2	14%	$1m/(1.14) = $877,193	$917,431 – $877,193 = $40,238	–$10,600 + $40,238 × (1.15) = $35,674
3	4%	$1m/(1.04) = $961,538	$917,431 – $961,538 = –$44,107	$99,400 – $44,107 × (1.05) = $53,088

2, we need to calculate its future value one year later. Metropolis can use the money to fund loans, enabling it to sell fewer NCDs than would otherwise have been necessary. Since those NCDs would have cost Metropolis 15%, that is what the money is worth to it. So the future value of the $40,238 at the end of Year 2 is $40,238 × (1.15) = $46,273. The bank's *total* profit at the end of Year 2, from the hedge in the futures market and from the original loan, will be $46,273 – $10,600 = $35,673.

3. *Interest rates fall.* At the end of Year 1, interest rates have fallen 5%, so that the NCD rate is 5% and the T-bill rate is 4%. Metropolis therefore stands to make a final profit of $99,400 on its loan (see above). It pays $1 million/ (1.04) = $961,538 for the T-bills it needs to meet delivery on its futures contract, and it receives for them the contract price of $917,431—a *loss* of $917,431 – $961,538 = –$44,107. Since this loss occurs at the end of Year 1, and we want to know what Metropolis's total profit will be at the end of Year 2, we need to calculate a future value. Let us assume that Metropolis covers the loss by borrowing $44,107 at 5% (its NCD rate), so that at the end of Year 2 it will owe $44,107 × (1.05) = $46,312. It will pay this out of the profits on its loan. Metropolis's *total* profit at the end of Year 2—the profit from the original loan minus the loss on the futures contract—is $99,400 – $46,312 = $53,088.

The hedge in the futures market makes Metropolis's total profit less variable and therefore less risky. Metropolis cannot hope to gain as much if interest rates fall, but neither does it stand to lose as much if interest rates rise. Gains or losses on the futures position offset losses or gains on the financing of the loan. Total profit varies less—between $35,674 and $53,088, rather than between –$10,600 and +$99,400, as it did without the hedge.

🌴 **CHECK STATION 2** | **Suppose that Metropolis finances a 1-year loan at 12% with a 2-year NCD at 10%.**

A. **What will be its profits at the end of Year 2 if interest rates stay the same, rise 5%, or fall 5%?**

B. **How could Metropolis hedge? What will its profits be if it does?**

SOME COMPLICATIONS OF FUTURES TRADING

The actual payments and receipts resulting from a futures position are rather different from those of our hypothetical example. These differences are important because they affect the cost, and thus the attractiveness, of using futures as a hedge.

margin
Performance bond required of each party in a futures contract.

MARGIN REQUIREMENTS Remember that the futures exchange guarantees fulfillment of the contract to both parties. To protect itself against default, the exchange requires each party to put up collateral. Metropolis, for example, would be required to put up a **margin** of 20% of the face value of the T-bill contract it sells, or $200,000. Meeting this requirement with cash is costly, because the cash does not earn interest, so Metropolis would probably put up $200,000 in Treasury securities and would be entitled to collect the interest they earn. Even so, the margin requirement ties up funds that Metropolis could use more profitably.

daily settlement
Daily payment of gains or losses on a futures contract.

DAILY SETTLEMENT In our hypothetical example, buyers and sellers settle up with one another when the contract matures. In reality, there is **daily settlement**. To see how this works, suppose that on February 1 Zelda enters into a contract with Scott to deliver one ounce of gold in June; the contract price is the current futures price of $400. Suppose that on March 1 Scott and Zelda want to cancel the contract between them. What would be a fair way to do this? In the month since the contract was written, the futures price for June delivery has risen to $450 (the market now expects the price of gold to be $450 in June). Nonetheless, the futures contract still entitles Scott to receive an ounce of gold in exchange for $400. So the value of the contract to Scott is $50, his expected gain if the contract is fulfilled; it is worth –$50 to Zelda, her expected loss. If the contract is to be canceled now, it is only fair that Zelda pay Scott the $50.[3]

marked to market
Daily updating of a futures contract to the current price.

Futures contracts are **marked to market** each day. This means that the old contract is canceled—with the appropriate compensation paid—and a new one is written at the current futures price. For example, suppose that on February 2, the first day after Scott and Zelda write a contract, the futures price of gold rises to $410. The original contract is canceled, Zelda pays Scott $10, and a new contract is written at a price of $410. The next day the futures price falls to $395. The

[3]At the time the contract is written, its value is zero. That is, if Zelda and Scott were to cancel the contract immediately after it was written, neither would need to pay the other any compensation, because neither would be any worse off if the contract were canceled.

contract at $410 is canceled, Scott pays Zelda $15 this time, and a new contract is written at $395. The contract is marked to market in this way each day until it matures in June.

Marking to market makes the exchange's bookkeeping much easier. The exchange does not need to keep track of a host of different contracts, all written at different prices. At any time, all contracts outstanding will have been marked to the *current* futures price and will therefore be identical.

Marking to market, with daily settlement, also reduces the exchange's exposure to default risk. To see why, consider what might happen if contracts were *not* marked to market. When Scott and Zelda wrote the original contract, they each put up an $80 margin (20% of the original price), to be kept in a **margin account** with their broker. Suppose that, by May, the futures price has fallen to $100. Scott faces a potential loss of $300 and Zelda a potential gain of the same amount. If Scott defaults on the contract, he loses his $80 margin but he saves himself $300. Since the exchange guarantees the contract to Zelda, it has to come up with the other $220.[4]

With daily settlement, losses are paid day by day as the futures price falls. The amount is debited automatically from Scott's account and credited to Zelda's. If the sum remaining in Scott's account falls below a certain level (called the **maintenance margin**—usually 75% of the initial margin), Scott will receive a **margin call** from his broker for more collateral. If he does not provide it immediately, the broker will close out Scott's position. That is, after the contract is marked to market that day, it will not be renewed. Proceeding in this way minimizes any default risk to the exchange.[5]

But what happens to Zelda if Scott's position is closed out? She now has a contract to sell gold, but there is no buyer. This is not really a problem: There is, in fact, no specific matching of individual buyers and sellers. The total number of buyers and sellers is brought into balance by raising or lowering the futures price. Both the supply of contracts and the demand depend on the price. So if, after Scott drops out, there are more sellers than buyers at the current price, the price is lowered. At the lower price, fewer potential sellers want to sell and more potential buyers want to buy, so that supply and demand are brought into balance, and there is someone else to take the other side of Zelda's contract. The number of contracts outstanding at any time is called the **open interest**.

SETTLEMENT BY OFFSET With the market organized in this way, it is easy for a trader to close out his position at any time he wishes to do so. In fact, most contracts are closed out before the maturity date, and very few result in actual delivery. Remember that the purpose for most traders is either hedging or

margin account
Cash or collateral deposited by a client with a broker to protect the broker from loss on a contract.

maintenance margin
Predetermined level of a margin account that must be maintained by the client.

margin call
Broker's request for more collateral to bring a client's margin account up to maintenance margin.

open interest
Number of futures contracts outstanding at a specific time.

---

[4]Actually, it is the broker who guarantees the contract to the trader. The exchange guarantees, in turn, that if the broker defaults, it will make up any losses to traders.

[5]Most futures markets have a daily limit on how much the price may be changed in any one day. When that limit is reached, trading stops and is only resumed the next day. This procedure ensures that margin accounts do not get wiped out by large price movements, and that brokers have time to make margin calls to protect themselves from default by their customers.

speculation; hardly anyone actually wants to receive or to provide T-bills. It is usually much more convenient to close out the position than to actually make or take delivery. For example, Metropolis, instead of actually buying a T-bill and making delivery, will cancel out its position just before the contract matures. It will do this by telling its broker to buy the same contract it has sold. Its contract will be marked to market one last time and its position closed out. The contract just bought offsets the contract previously sold, so that Metropolis's net position is zero. This is called **settlement by offset**.

settlement by offset
Closing out a futures contract with an offsetting trade rather than through delivery.

Despite these practices—daily settlement and closing by offset rather than by delivery—the loss or gain from a futures position is much the same as it would be if traders did actually settle by delivery on the date of maturity. This is because sellers always have the *option* of making delivery, and buyers always have the option of taking delivery.[6] As a result, the futures price must approach the spot price as the maturity date gets closer.[7] To see why, suppose that a couple of days before the contract matures, the spot price of T-bills is $950,000 and the futures price is $900,000. Someone can make a substantial profit by buying up contracts and demanding to take delivery. The rush to buy contracts would drive up the futures price until it equaled the spot price.

Since the futures price approaches the spot price at maturity, if the contract is held that long, the cumulative gain or loss is pretty much the same as if delivery had actually taken place. However, the *timing* of the cash flow is very different. In particular, if the futures price fluctuates a great deal over the life of the contract, Metropolis may have to make or receive large payments day by day. This uncertainty about the cash flow—and the resulting need to reinvest or to finance the sums involved—reduces the attractiveness of the hedge.

TRANSACTIONS COSTS Something else that can reduce the attractiveness of a hedge is the cost of the transaction. The operators of the futures market—the brokers and the exchange—need to be paid for their services. Partly, they are paid by commissions: Metropolis will pay its broker a commission when it initiates the contract (the average commission in 1983 was $80 per contract). There is also a small fee to the exchange, and sometimes a small bid–asked spread. Transactions costs in the futures market are generally very low.

HEDGING IMPERFECTIONS You will have noticed from our numerical example that the hedge is imperfect: Although profits fluctuate less with the hedge, they do still fluctuate. The reason is that it is impossible to match the hedge exactly with the underlying loan transaction. A perfect match would require

[6]Doing this is so unusual, however, that exchanges normally require prior notification of the intent to make or to receive actual delivery. Indeed, some financial futures—for example, the stock index futures that we shall encounter in Chapter 14—*must* be closed by offset: There is no such thing as delivery.

[7]For most contracts, the final trading day is either the third Friday of the month, or the next to last business day of the month. For financial futures, delivery must usually be made on the day following the final trading day.

three things: That the contract involve delivery of precisely the object being hedged, that it be for precisely the right amount, and that it be for precisely the right date. In Metropolis's case, that would mean a futures contract for its own NCDs at exactly the maturity and in exactly the amount involved in refinancing the loan. If Metropolis could sell a contract for one $1.1 million NCD at 10% for delivery at the end of Year 1, its profit at the end of Year 2 would be exactly $44,400, regardless of what happened to the NCD rate in the meantime.[8]

A market for such a specific futures contract could not possibly exist. It would be far too small. First of all, a large volume of trading is needed to keep the market competitive: Metropolis would find it too easy to manipulate to its advantage a market devoted entirely to its own NCDs. A large volume of trading is also needed to pay the overhead of running the market. There are substantial fixed costs to setting up a market, and to keep transactions costs low, those fixed costs need to be spread over a large number of transactions.

To ensure a large volume for each contract traded, contracts exist only for standard amounts of relatively few financial instruments for delivery at a few specific dates. For example, actual T-bill contracts are for $1 million face value, for 90-day T-bills only, and for delivery only in March, June, September, and December, going out for 2 years. You cannot write a contract for delivery of $500,000 worth of 6-month T-bills in August.

Given the range of contracts actually available, a hedger will choose the one whose price moves most closely with the price of the commodity or instrument being hedged. If a specific contract for Metropolis NCDs is out of the question, how about one for NCDs in general? Such a contract was traded for a while, with the NCDs of any of the ten largest banks deliverable, but for various reasons this contract proved unsuccessful. There does exist, though, a popular contract in 90-day Eurodollar time deposits, and this may be a good alternative to the T-bill contract.

The financial futures currently available are shown in Exhibit 13.4, in a typical daily listing from *The Wall Street Journal*. The listing shows, for T-bill futures traded on IMM (the International Monetary Market of the Chicago Mercantile Exchange), the opening price, high and low prices, and the final (settlement) price; the change in the settlement price from the previous day; the discount, calculated from the settlement price, and the change from the previous day; and the open interest.

The potential difference between the price of the instrument being hedged and the price of the instrument that is the object of the futures contract is a source of risk called **basis risk**. If the rate on Metropolis's NCDs moves closely with the rate on T-bills, the hedge in our example will work well. The hedge will not, however, protect Metropolis against a rise in the rate on its NCDs *relative* to the T-bill rate. Such a rise could be caused, for instance, by fears about the solvency of

basis risk
Risk that the price of the instrument being hedged will be different from the price of the instrument in the futures contract.

---

[8]The main reason for the imperfection of the hedge in Metropolis's case is the size of the contract. Metropolis would need a contract for $1.21 million in T-bills, but it faces a choice between $1 million or $2 million. With a $1.21 million contract, the range of profits would be reduced to $43,750–$46,240.

E X H I B I T 13.4

T-BILL FUTURES

Source: *The Wall Street Journal*, Apr. 19, 1990, C-16.

Metropolis or about the solvency of banks in general. These things do happen: Exhibit 13.5 shows the effect on NCD rates of the Continental Illinois crisis of 1984.[9]

[9]We shall learn more about this crisis in Chapter 17.

EXHIBIT 13.5

CLOSING PRICES OF NCD AND T-BILL CONTRACTS DURING CONTINENTAL ILLINOIS CRISIS OF MAY 1984

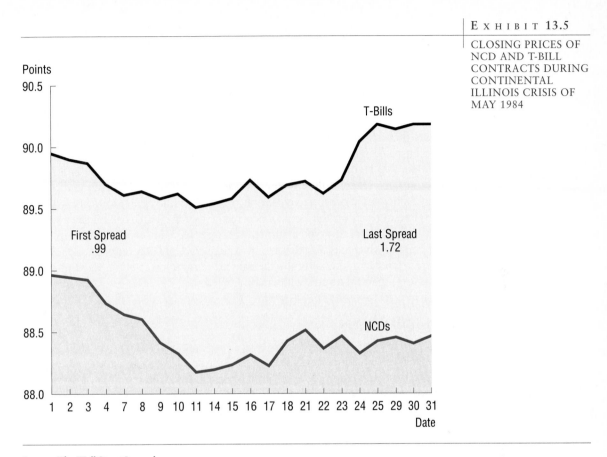

Source: *The Wall Street Journal.*

HOW MUCH DO BANKS ACTUALLY USE FINANCIAL FUTURES?

We have seen how financial futures can be used by a bank to hedge its interest-rate risk externally, rather than dealing with the risk internally by adjusting the duration of its assets and liabilities. To what extent do banks actually do this?

Financial futures are quite widely used by the largest commercial banks: In 1985, 77% of banks with over $5 billion in assets reported taking positions in financial futures. Futures are also popular with the branches and subsidiaries of foreign banks in the United States. Small banks, on the other hand, use financial futures little if at all: Less than 1% of banks with under $100 million in assets reported taking positions in financial futures in 1985. In total, at the end of 1985 commercial banks had positions of about $98 billion in financial futures (about 25% of these were held by foreign banks). Of this total, $90 billion was in Eurodollar futures, $5 billion in T-bill futures, and the rest in long-term Treasury futures.

There are substantial obstacles to the wider use of financial futures. First, their use requires specialized knowledge and considerable sophistication. Smaller banks generally lack trained personnel with the necessary expertise. Second, there are serious regulatory and accounting problems facing all banks wishing to use financial futures.

The main problem is that banks are required to mark to market their futures position but not their cash position. As a result, a bank may record large gains or losses that are entirely illusory. For example, consider the hedge described in Exhibit 13.3. If interest rates fall, there will be a loss on the futures position, but this loss will be offset by a gain when the bank rolls over its NCD at a lower interest rate. Whereas the loss on the futures position must be recorded on the bank's books, the prospective gain on rolling over the NCD is not recorded. It therefore appears on the books, incorrectly, that the bank has taken a loss. A large paper loss of this type might reduce the book value of the bank's capital to the point at which it is closed down by regulators. Until accounting standards are altered to reflect more faithfully the true profits and losses of a hedged position, the use of financial futures will remain limited.

13.2 | OPTIONS

option contract
Agreement that allows the purchase or sale of a specified quantity of an asset at a specified price until the expiration date.

put option
Option to sell.

By hedging with a futures contract, a bank protects itself against a loss if interest rates go up, but it also "protects" itself against a *gain* if interest rates go down. An **option contract** provides the same protection against a loss but leaves the potential for a gain. There is, of course, a snag: Hedging with options is far more expensive.

When Metropolis sells a futures contract, it must deliver a T-bill at the contract price. If, instead, it buys a **put option**, it has the *right* to sell a T-bill for the contract price, but not an obligation. If interest rates go up, Metropolis can exercise that right and make a profit, and that profit will offset the loss on its loan position. If interest rates go down, Metropolis can just tear up the option. It thereby avoids the loss it would have incurred by delivering on a futures contract, and it is left with just the increased profit on its loan position.

Let us study the details using an example involving exchange-rate risk.

HEDGING EXCHANGE-RATE RISK WITH OPTIONS

In Chapter 11 we saw how international trade involves exchange-rate risk. In our example there, Teutonic Motors receives a shipment of 100 cars from Germany for which it has to pay the manufacturer, Hermes, a sum of DM5 million 90 days later. In the meantime, Teutonic expects to sell the cars for a total of $3.2 million. At the exchange rate of DM1.70 to the dollar at the time the cars are received, Teutonic's debt to Hermes in dollars is $5,000,000/1.70 = $2,950,000, leaving it with a profit of $250,000. However, since the debt is to be paid not immediately but 90 days later, there is a risk that the exchange rate will change by then. If the mark falls, the profit will be larger; if the mark rises, the profit will shrink, perhaps even become a loss. We saw that Teutonic can hedge this risk by buying marks forward from its bank.

Let us see how Teutonic can hedge instead by buying **call options**. The option contract specifies an *amount* of marks, DM62,500, an **exercise**, or **strike**, **price**, say, 60¢ (the price is expressed in dollars per mark rather than marks per dollar), and an **expiration date**. The expiration date is, say, 90 days later, in June.[10] There are two types of option contract—American and European. An **American option** gives the purchaser the right to buy the specified amount at the exercise price at any time up to the expiration date of the contract. A **European option** gives the purchaser the right to buy on the expiration date only. Teutonic buys European options. To cover its expected payment to Hermes, it needs to buy 80 contracts (80 x DM62,500 = DM5 million).

At the time it buys the contracts, Teutonic pays a price, or **premium**, to the seller. The premium is, say, 1¢ per mark—a total of 5,000,000 x $.01 = $50,000 for the 80 calls. In exchange for the $50,000, the seller undertakes to provide, in 90 days time, DM5 million in exchange for $3 million (60¢ per mark) *if and only if* Teutonic chooses to exercise the option at that time. The seller keeps the $50,000 premium whether Teutonic chooses to exercise the option or not. Clearly, the seller hopes that when the contract expires, the mark will be below the exercise price (this is called being **out of the money**), so that Teutonic will not choose to exercise. If the mark turns out to be above the exercise price (**in the money**), then Teutonic will exercise and the seller will take a loss. The premium is the seller's reward for accepting the risk of this loss.

The amount of the premium is determined by supply and demand. It is the price at which the number of contracts people want to sell equals the number other people want to buy. The premium will clearly be higher the more likely the option is to be exercised and the higher the mark is likely to go. Therefore the premium will increase the further away is the expiration date, the more variable is the price of the mark, and the lower is the exercise price.

To see how Teutonic's hedge might work out, consider three possible scenarios for the day, 90 days later, that Teutonic must pay its DM5 million to Hermes: (1) the spot price of the mark is still 59¢, (2) it has risen to 65¢, and (3) it has fallen to 54¢. The corresponding outcomes are shown in Exhibit 13.6.

1. *The mark stays at its current price of 59¢.* Since Teutonic can buy the marks it needs in the spot market more cheaply ($2,950,000 versus $3,000,000), it does not exercise its options. Its profit is $198,794: The $3.2 million revenue from selling the cars, less $2,950,000 for the marks it needs to pay Hermes, less the $51,206 cost of the hedge. The $50,000 has to be paid at the *start* of the 90 days, so we need its future value at the end of the 90 days when our calculation is made. Assuming an annual rate of 10%, that future value is $51,206.

call option
Option to buy.

exercise (strike) price
Predetermined price at which an option is surrendered and the underlying transaction takes place.

expiration date
Date at which an option contract terminates.

American option
Option may be exercised any time up to the contract's expiration date.

European option
Option may be exercised only on the contract's expiration date.

premium
Price paid by an option buyer for the rights acquired.

out of the money
Below the exercise price.

in the money
Above the exercise price.

---

[10]The final trading day for the option is the Friday preceding the third Wednesday of the month, and the contract actually expires on the next day—the Saturday.

EXHIBIT 13.6

POSSIBLE PROFITS WITH A HEDGE IN OPTIONS

	Spot Price of Mark	Market Price of DM5m	Exercise Price of Option	Exercise Options?	Overall Profit (revenue from cars – cost of DM5m – premium)
1	59¢	$2.95m	$3m	No	$3.2m – $2.95m – $51,206 = $198,794
2	65¢	$3.25m	$3m	Yes	$3.2m – $3m – $51,206 = $148,794
3	54¢	$2.70m	$3m	No	$3.2m – $2.70m – $51,206 = $448,794

2. *The mark rises to 65¢.* The cost of DM5 million on the spot market is now 5,000,000 x $.65 = $3,250,000. Had Teutonic *not* hedged, it would have had to pay this amount for the marks it needed, giving it a *loss* of $50,000. However, with the hedge in place, Teutonic is able to exercise the calls and pay only $3,000,000. Its profit is therefore $3,200,000 from the sale of the cars, less the $3,000,000 paid for the marks, less the $51,206 cost of the options—$148,794 in all. The hedge guarantees Teutonic a profit of at least $148,794, however high the mark rises.

3. *The mark falls to 54¢.* The cost of DM5 million on the spot market is now 5,000,000 x $.54 = $2,700,000. Naturally, Teutonic does not exercise the options. Its profit is $3,200,000 from the sale of the cars, less the $2,700,000 for the marks, less the $51,206 cost of the options—$448,794 in all. The more the mark falls, the larger the profit.

The advantage, then, of hedging with options rather than with futures or with a forward transaction is that it protects against an adverse price movement but still leaves open the possibility of profit from a favorable one. The disadvantage is the substantial up-front cost in terms of the premium that has to be paid. The premium can be lowered by buying options with a higher exercise price, but this, of course, gives less protection.[11]

---

[11]It is also possible to reduce the cost with something called a *collar.* In addition to buying the call options, Teutonic can sell put options at an exercise price of, say, 57¢. Supposing the premium for the puts is 1¢, the money it receives for the puts will just pay for the calls it needs, with a net cost of zero. The disadvantage, of course, is that with the collar Teutonic's potential profits from a fall in the mark are now limited. Now, if the mark falls below 57¢, the puts will be exercised and Teutonic will have to buy marks at the exercise price of 57¢ instead of at the lower market price.

EXHIBIT 13.7

OPTIONS ON
THE MARK

Philadelphia Exchange

Monday, Feb. 26

Option & Underlying	Strike Price	Calls—Last			Puts—Last		
		Mar	Apr	Jun	Mar	Apr	Jun
62,500 West German Marks-cents per unit.							
DMark	.. 54	r	r	r	r	r	0.17
59.01	...55	4.27	r	r	r	0.08	0.29
59.01	...56	r	r	r	r	r	0.39
59.01	...57	r	r	r	0.09	0.28	r
59.01	.57½	r	s	s	0.11	s	s
59.01	...58	1.28	r	r	0.24	0.46	r
59.01	.58½	1.06	r	s	0.36	r	s
59.01	...59	0.66	0.98	1.58	0.59	0.95	1.40
59.01	.59½	r	r	s	0.70	1.22	s
59.01	...60	0.25	0.58	r	1.03	1.50	1.90
59.01	.60½	r	r	s	1.54	r	s
59.01	...61	r	0.32	r	2.05	r	2.53
59.01	...62	0.05	0.17	0.54	r	r	r
59.01	...63	0.02	r	r	r	r	r
59.01	...64	0.01	r	r	r	r	r

r—Not traded. s—No option offered.
Last is premium (purchase price).

Source: *The Wall Street Journal*, Feb. 27, 1990.

Suppose you are expecting a payment of DM12.5 million in June. The mark is currently at 59¢.

🌴 **CHECK STATION 3**

A. How much do you stand to lose if the mark falls to 50¢?

B. How could you hedge against this risk using options?

C. Using Exhibit 13.7, calculate for each of the options available (1) the potential loss if the mark falls to 50¢ and (2) the cost of the hedge.

THE OPTIONS MARKET

Options are traded on stock and futures exchanges around the world. Exhibit 13.8 gives a partial list of options currently traded on exchanges in the United States.

An example of how options prices are listed in the financial press is shown in Exhibit 13.7 which lists options on the mark traded on the Philadelphia Exchange. Only the three nearest maturities appear in the listing, although options are actually available for the two closest months plus March, June, September, and December, up to nine months into the future. The spot price of the currency appears in the left-hand column—59.01¢ for German marks. The second column gives the exercise prices available. The next three columns list premiums for the various call options; the final three columns list premiums for puts. Notice that the price of the option falls as the exercise price is further removed from the spot price, because the chance that the option will be exercised decreases correspondingly. The price of the option rises with the time left until expiration, since the longer the time, the greater the chance that the price of the currency will move far enough for the option to expire in the money.

EXHIBIT 13.8

U.S. OPTIONS MARKETS

Type of Options	Exchanges at Which Trading Occurs	Indexes or Currencies Traded	Open Interest Dec. 30, 1988
Individual stock options	CBOE	All stock options on CBOE	3,630,235
	AMEX	All stock options on AMEX	2,120,076
	PHLX	All stock options on PHLX	1,218,285
	PSE	All stock options on PSE	991,043
	NYSE	All stock options on NYSE	109,658
Stock index options	CBOE	S&P 500 Stock Index	291,387
	CBOE	S&P 100 Stock Index	554,914
	AMEX	Major Market Index[a]	74,190
	AMEX	Institutional Stock Index	56,883
	AMEX	Computer Technology Index	90
	AMEX	Oil Index	825
	PHLX	Gold/Silver Stock Index	719
	PHLX	Value Line Arithmetic Index	1,433
	PHLX	Over-the-Counter 100 Index	374
	PHLX	Utilities Index	5,999
	PSE	Financial News Composite Index	3,742
	NYSE	NYSE Composite Index	17,601
Options on stock-index futures contracts	CME	S&P 500 Index	21,028
	NYFE	NYSE Composite Index	1,417

Exchanges: AMEX (American Stock Exchange)
CBOE (Chicago Board Options Exchange)
CME (Chicago Mercantile Exchange)
FINEX (Financial Instrument Exchange of the N.Y. Cotton Exchange)
IMM (International Monetary Market of the CME)
NYFE (New York Futures Exchange), PHLX (Philadelphia Exchange)
PSE (Pacific Stock Exchange)

Source: Exhibit 22–8, "U.S. Options Markets," from *Financial Institutions, Markets, and Money*, 4th ed. by David S. Kidwell and Richard L. Peterson, pp. 578–579, copyright © 1990 by The Dryden Press, a division of Holt, Rinehart and Winston, Inc., reprinted by permission of the publisher.

The buyer of an option simply pays the premium: there is no need for collateral. The seller, however, must provide collateral to ensure delivery if the option is exercised. He must either put up the underlying asset as collateral or provide a margin; the calculation of the required margin is complicated. The exercise of an option usually involves actual delivery, but some options (for example, options on stock indexes) are settled in cash.

Options have the same sort of basis risk as futures, and the types of option actually available may not suit precisely the needs of a given hedger with respect to amount, maturity, or underlying asset. For foreign exchange, at least, this

Type of Options	Exchanges at Which Trading Occurs	Indexes or Currencies Traded	Open Interest Dec. 30, 1988
Interest-rate options on futures	CBOT	U.S. Treasury bonds[a]	506,296
	CBOT	U.S. Treasury 10-year notes	55,321
	CBOT	Municipal Bond Index	15,462
	FINEX	5-year Treasury notes	1,940
	IMM	U.S. Treasury bills	266
	CME	Eurodollar interest rates[a]	157,046
Currency options—options on futures	IMM	Japanese yen	92,907
	IMM	West German mark	94,275
	IMM	Canadian dollar	27,071
	IMM	British pound	20,037
	IMM	Swiss franc	34,879
	IMM	Australian dollar	1,279
	FINEX	U.S. Dollar Index	96
Currency options (options for settlement by delivery of currency	PHLX	Japanese yen	132,293
	PHLX	Canadian dollars	12,757
	PHLX	West German mark	119,208
	PHLX	British pound	9,898
	PHLX	Swiss franc	31,802
	PHLX	Australian dollar	7,457
	PHLX	French franc	846
	PHLX	European currency unit (ECU)	121

[a]A number of these options are also traded in foreign countries. Major market index options are traded on the European Options Exchange in Amsterdam before the U.S. market opens. U.S. Treasury bond, Eurodollar rate, and currency options are also traded on the LIFFE exchange in London. Eurodollar rate, Japanese yen, Deutsche mark, and British pound options are traded on the Singapore Exchange (SIMEX). Also, foreign currency options of many denominations, including U.S. dollar options denominated in foreign currencies, are traded on a variety of exchanges around the world. Finally, 24-hour electronic trading should become available for interest-rate, currency, and precious metals options through the CME's "Globex" automated trading system or LIFFE's Telerate Connection.

The most actively traded options series are the stock index options (particularly those based on the Standard & Poor's 100 and Standard & Poor's 500 stock indexes, both of which are traded on the CBOE).

problem is mitigated by the availability of individually tailored options sold by banks in addition to the standard contracts available on the exchanges.

There also exist **options on futures**, which are options to buy and sell futures rather than to buy and sell the underlying commodity or asset. For example, on exercising a call option on T-bill futures, the buyer receives, in exchange for the exercise price, a T-bill futures contract rather than an actual T-bill. Options on futures have some advantages over regular options in terms of liquidity and in terms of the ability to tailor precisely the size of the hedge. The market for options on futures has grown rapidly in recent years.

options on futures
Options to buy and sell futures rather than the underlying commodity or asset.

13.3 | SWAPS

Unlike futures and options, which are very old ideas, the *swap* is a very new one: It first appeared in 1981. By 1983 the amount of swaps outstanding had risen to $3 billion; by 1986, to $300 billion; and by 1988, to over $1 trillion. In 1985 the International Swap Dealers Association was formed to standardize documentation and procedures in this mushrooming market. Swaps are widely used by commercial and investment banks, securities firms, savings and loans, government agencies, and corporations. There are two basic types—*interest-rate swaps* (about 80% of the total) and *currency swaps*. We shall look at each in turn.

INTEREST-RATE SWAPS

interest-rate swap
Exchange of fixed-rate payments for floating-rate payments.

The basic idea of an **interest-rate swap** is illustrated in Exhibit 13.9. Two firms, Megacorp International and Hitec Inc., enter into a five-year swap agreement with one another. Each separately borrows $1 million. Megacorp borrows on the bond market, selling fixed-rate bonds with a 9.5% stated annual rate and semiannual coupons. Hitec takes a floating-rate loan from its bank, paying semiannually a stated annual rate of 1% over LIBOR.[12] Under the swap agreement, the two companies exchange payments every six months for the duration of the two loans. Hitec pays Megacorp a fixed payment at a stated annual rate of 9.75%; Megacorp pays Hitec LIBOR (whatever that is at the time). Hitec is called the **fixed-rate payer** of the swap, and Metropolis is called the **floating-rate payer.**

fixed-rate payer
A party to a swap who agrees to make fixed payments in exchange for LIBOR.

Out of the 9.75% that Megacorp receives from Hitec, it pays the 9.5% on the bonds it has issued, leaving it with a 0.25% gain. Megacorp must pay LIBOR to Hitec, so its net payment is LIBOR *less* the 0.25% gain on the fixed receipts and payments. In total, then, Megacorp pays a floating rate of LIBOR – 0.25%. By entering into the swap agreement, Megacorp has transformed its fixed-rate borrowing into floating-rate borrowing.

floating-rate payer
A party to a swap who agrees to pay LIBOR in exchange for fixed payments.

Hitec receives LIBOR from Megacorp and must add 1% to this in order to pay what it owes on its bank loan. Hitec must also pay Megacorp 9.75%. So Hitec's net payment is this 9.75% plus the 1% over and above what it receives from Megacorp that it pays its bank. In total, Hitec pays a fixed rate of 9.75% + 1% = 10.75%. By entering into the swap agreement, Hitec has transformed its floating-rate borrowing into fixed-rate borrowing.

Each of the two parties remains responsible for repayment of the principal on its own loan, and the $1 million amount of the two underlying loans never actually changes hands between them. However, the amount of the underlying

---

[12]The London Interbank Offered Rate is the rate that Eurodollar banks charge one another for interbank loans. Eurodollar loans are usually made at a markup over this rate.

EXHIBIT 13.9

AN INTEREST-RATE
SWAP IN PRINCIPLE

Floating-Rate Payer   **Fixed-Rate Payer**

9.5% ← Megacorp International ← 9.75% ← Hitec Inc. → LIBOR + 1%

Megacorp International → LIBOR → Hitec Inc.

Net Payment:
LIBOR − 0.25%

Net Payment:
9.75% + 1% = 10.75%

loans—called the **notional principal** of the swap—does determine the size of the payments the two parties must make to one another. Hitec must pay $1 million × 0.0975/2 = $48,750 every 6 months; Megacorp must pay $1 million × LIBOR/2.

notional principal
Amount of the underlying loans in an interest-rate swap.

WHY DO A SWAP? Why do such a strange thing as an interest-rate swap? What is the advantage to the two companies of this complicated arrangement? If Megacorp wants a floating-rate loan, why not simply borrow floating-rate in the first place?

Comparative Advantage Megacorp is a well-known, multinational corporation, and it can borrow at a very good rate both in the direct market and in the indirect market. It pays 0.5% over the Treasury rate on its bonds and 0.25% over LIBOR on its bank loans. Hitec is smaller and less well known, and it pays more to borrow in both markets. It pays 2.5% over the Treasury rate on its bonds and 1% over LIBOR on its bank loans.

Notice, however, that even though Hitec pays more than Megacorp in both markets, it pays a much bigger risk premium in the bond market. An economist would say that Hitec has a *comparative advantage* in the indirect market: It is *relatively* cheaper for it to borrow there. Similarly, Megacorp has a comparative advantage in the direct market. Although it has an *absolute* advantage in both markets (it can borrow more cheaply in both), its advantage is greater in the direct market.

Given these differences in risk premium, a swap enables each of the two companies to borrow more cheaply. Suppose Megacorp wants to borrow short-term for working capital and Hitec wants to borrow long-term at a fixed rate for investment in plant and equipment. There are two ways they could do this. Each could match maturities directly, Megacorp borrowing from its bank and Hitec selling bonds. Or each could go to the market in which it has comparative advantage and then use a swap to transform the effective maturity of the loan. The second route is cheaper.

Suppose the Treasury rate is 9%. Hitec would have to pay 2.5% above this, or 11.5%, on fixed-rate bonds. We have seen that the swap allows it to pay a fixed rate of only 10.75%. Megacorp gains too. If it took a floating-rate loan from its bank, it would have to pay LIBOR + 0.25%. The swap allows it to pay LIBOR – 0.25%.

Why might such a situation of comparative advantage exist? Why do the two markets treat the two firms differently? As we saw in Chapter 3, there are important differences between banks and financial markets in the making of loans. Banks often have better information on small firms and can therefore distinguish between good and bad risks better than can the bond market. Banks are also better at monitoring loan performance and more flexible in dealing with repayment problems. As a result, they may be able to lend to riskier borrowers at a lower risk premium than the bond market would demand.

On the other hand, because of the interest-rate risk involved, banks do not want to make long-term loans at fixed rates of interest. As we saw in Chapter 12, long-term floating-rate loans are not a good solution to this problem, because shifting the interest-rate risk to the borrower does not really get rid of it, it just changes its form. The swap offers a solution: The borrower can use the swap to transform the loan from floating-rate to fixed-rate and thus avoid the interest-rate risk.

The swap allows a separation of interest-rate risk and credit risk. The bond market carries the former, and the bank carries the latter. This is cheaper for Hitec than having either the bond market or the bank carry both types of risk.

Hedging and Speculation   A swap can be seen as a package of forward transactions. In our example the first forward transaction is scheduled to take place 6 months from the start of the agreement. Hitec will pay $48,750 in exchange for 6 months' interest on $1 million, calculated at LIBOR at the start of the swap—say, 7%. So Hitec will receive $1 million x 0.07/2 = $35,000. The second exchange will take place 6 months later, one year from the start of the swap. At that time Hitec will again pay $48,750 and receive 6 months' interest on $1 million, calculated at LIBOR *6 months after the start of the swap*. If by then LIBOR has risen to 10%, Hitec will receive $50,000; if it has fallen to 6%, Hitec will receive $30,000. The third forward transaction is a similar exchange scheduled for 18 months from the start of the swap, at the LIBOR rate after one year, and so on, every 6 months for 5 years.

If interest rates change, the value of the swap to the two parties will change. A rise in interest rates means a capital gain for the fixed-rate payer and a capital loss for the floating-rate payer; a fall in interest rates means a gain for the floating-rate payer and a loss for the fixed-rate payer. In terms of the potential loss or gain, becoming a fixed-rate payer on a swap is similar to *selling* securities forward: The higher the interest rate, the better off you are. So, in terms of potential gains and losses, becoming a fixed-rate payer on a 15-year swap is similar to selling T-bill futures at 6-month intervals going out 15 years. Becoming a floating-rate payer is similar to buying a series of T-bill futures.

Swaps, just like futures and options, provide a way of hedging against interest-rate risk, but they have one important advantage: They allow hedging much farther into the future. Futures and options are available for at most 1 to 2 years, while swaps of 15 years' maturity are not unusual. Let us consider some examples of hedging with swaps.

A U.S. government agency called "Sally Mae" (the Student Loan Marketing Association, or SLMA) provides guaranteed student loans. To finance these loans, it borrows billions in the bond market. Although the loans it makes are floating-rate, it is much easier to sell long-term securities that are fixed-rate. The problem, of course, is that this creates a duration gap with the consequent interest-rate risk. So Sally Mae hedges the risk by becoming a floating-rate payer on swaps.

In Chapter 12 we discussed how floating-rate loans were a bad solution to a bank's interest-rate risk problem. Rather than passing on the interest-rate risk to the borrower, the bank should provide interest-rate "insurance" by lending at a fixed rate and then hedging the risk itself. Eurodollar banks have increasingly been doing this with their long-term loans, making them fixed-rate and using swaps to hedge the interest-rate risk.

More generally, suppose a bank has a positive duration gap on its balance sheet, so that if market interest rates rise, it stands to make a loss. It can hedge this risk by becoming a fixed-rate payer on just the right amount of swaps. The increase in the present value of its position on the swaps will just offset the loss on its balance sheet, or vice versa. Note that to use swaps as a hedge, a bank need not match specific swaps with specific combinations of loans and funding. Rather, it needs to look at its overall position—loans, funding, and hedging instruments, all considered together.

Of course, any instrument used to hedge can also be used to speculate. Suppose that, contrary to the view of the market, you think that interest rates are going to fall. One way to profit is to take a "naked" position as a floating-rate payer. That is, you enter into a swap agreement *without* having any future interest-rate payments to swap. If interest rates fall, you receive the same fixed payments but pay less for them, making a capital gain.

THE MARKET FOR INTEREST-RATE SWAPS Swaps are bundles of forward transactions, and we have seen that there are problems in arranging such transactions directly. First, it may be hard to find suitable partners, and, consequently, it may be hard to get a fair deal.[13] Second, there is the problem of credit risk. If you are a fixed-rate payer and interest rates go up, your partner to the swap may default on the agreement, leaving you with a loss. The swap is really a hedge only as long as you can be sure that the promised payments will actually be made.

---

[13]You may have wondered how Megacorp and Hitec came to an agreement over how to split between them the gains from the swap. We shall see in a moment how a competitive market solves this problem.

We have seen with other types of forward transaction how financial markets and financial intermediaries offer solutions to these problems—for example, the futures and options contracts traded on exchanges and the forward sales of foreign exchange by banks. It should, then, come as no surprise that banks and other intermediaries play a central role in the swap market.

To see how swap agreements work in the real world, let us make the Megacorp–Hitec example a little more realistic. In reality, rather than dealing with one another directly, Megacorp and Hitec would each make a deal with Metropolis National Bank. The bank offers a standard 5-year contract, quoting a price both for fixed-rate and for floating-rate payers. The price is quoted as a spread in **basis points** over the Treasury rate. One hundred basis points equal one percentage point, so that, for example, 0.5% is 50 basis points. The rate on 5-year swaps is quoted, say, as 70 bid and 80 asked. That means that if the yield on 5-year Treasuries is 9%, the fixed-rate payer, Hitec, will pay Metropolis 9% plus the asked price, or 9% + 0.80% = 9.80%, in exchange for LIBOR. The floating-rate payer, Megacorp, will pay Metropolis LIBOR and receive in exchange 9% plus the bid price of 70 basis points: 9% + 0.7% = 9.7%. The flow of payments is shown in Exhibit 13.10.

basis point
One-hundreth of 1% in the yield of an investment.

How is the price of swaps—the size of the spread over the Treasury rate—determined? Like other prices, it is determined by supply and demand. Strong demand by fixed-rate payers like Hitec will drive the spread up. Strong supply by floating-rate payers like Megacorp will drive the spread down. But the market also includes speculators. Speculators will take a fixed-rate position if they think the price is low given the chance of an increase in interest rates; they will take a floating-rate position if they think it is high given the chance of a fall in interest rates. As a result, the price will reflect market expectations about the future behavior of interest rates.[14]

What determines the margin between bid and asked prices? Competition among swap intermediaries. Such intermediaries include not only commercial banks, but also investment banks, like Merrill Lynch and Salomon Brothers, and even some large multinational corporations, like British Petroleum. In our example Metropolis earns 0.1% of $1 million, or $1,000, a year for its services. This amount covers transactions costs and compensates Metropolis for the credit risk it bears.

There is credit risk, because Metropolis is a party to two contracts—one with Hitec and the other with Megacorp. If either Hitec or Megacorp defaults, Metropolis's contract with the other party still stands. If there is a loss as a result of the default, that loss will be borne by Metropolis. Notice that Metropolis here

---

[14]Arbitrage by banks would prevent the spread from ever being negative. If the spread were, say, – 40 basis points, a bank could borrow at LIBOR and buy Treasuries at, say, 7%. It could become a fixed-rate payer, paying 7% – 0.4% = 6.6% and receiving LIBOR: The bank could pocket the 40-basis-point difference between what it was earning on the Treasuries and what it had to pay on the swap. There is no risk, and the bank has to put up no money of its own. Because of the possibility of such arbitrage, a negative spread could never appear.

EXHIBIT 13.10

INTEREST-RATE SWAP IN PRACTICE

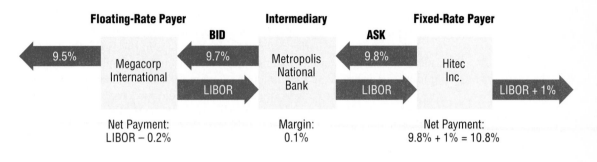

is playing the customary role of a bank—taking a fee to evaluate and to bear credit risk.

How great is the risk? Suppose that, with three years left on the swap, Hitec goes under and is therefore unable to carry out the remaining exchanges of floating-rate for fixed-rate interest payments. Since Metropolis is still bound by its contract with Megacorp, it must now sell a *new* swap to some other party to cover the promised payments. Whether Metropolis gains or loses on this replacement contract depends on the Treasury rate at the time and on the spread. Suppose that the spread is the same—80 basis points—but the Treasury rate has fallen to 8%. Under the terms of the new contract it writes with some new fixed-rate payer, Metropolis will receive every 6 months $1 million × 0.088/2 = $44,000 in exchange for LIBOR. Since Metropolis must still pay Megacorp $48,500 every 6 months in exchange for LIBOR, it will now lose $4,500 on each semiannual payment. The present value of the expected losses on the 6 payments remaining at the time Hitec defaults, calculated at 8%, is about $24,000.

Notice that the loss is fairly small relative to the $1 million of notional principal—on the order of a few percentage points.. The loss from default on a $1 million loan might be much greater. Furthermore, Metropolis could actually *profit* from a default were Hitec considerate enough to default when the Treasury rate is *above* 9%. If the Treasury rate is, say, 10%, the replacement swap pays a semiannual $54,000, leaving Metropolis with a stream of semiannual *profits* of $5,500. In fact, defaults are more common in periods of rising rather than of falling interest rates. Because of the relatively small potential loss, because of the possibility of gain from a default, and because of intense competition among intermediaries, the bid–asked margin tends to be quite small.

Swap intermediaries make a market in swaps, standing ready to provide swaps to fixed-rate and to floating-rate customers at any time at their advertised rates. That is, swap intermediaries do not wait to match up individual fixed- and floating-rate payers. Indeed, parties to swaps, just like parties to futures or options contracts, neither know nor need to know who ultimately takes the other side of the transaction. As far as the customer is concerned, the deal is with the intermediary. Intermediaries also offer a "secondary market" in swaps. In our example, if either Megacorp or Hitec wanted to terminate the swap before it matured, it would be able do so in exchange for an appropriate payment, and Metropolis would find a replacement for the party opting out.

Because intermediaries make a market in swaps in this way, their commitments to fixed-rate and to floating-rate payers are unlikely to match exactly at all times. For example, if the amount of commitments to floating-rate payers exceeds the amount to fixed-rate payers, then the intermediary *itself* is committed to paying a fixed rate in exchange for a floating rate on the difference. If interest rates fall, the intermediary will take a loss; if they rise, it will make a gain.

The intermediary can hedge its open position in swaps with futures or options. Or it can hedge in the securities market by borrowing interbank Eurodollars and using the funds to buy Treasury securities: It will receive fixed payments on the Treasuries and owe variable payments on the Eurodollars, and this will offset its position in swaps as a net fixed-rate payer. Or the intermediary can hedge by having a positive duration gap on its balance sheet. Of course, if it believes interest rates are going to rise, the intermediary may choose not to hedge; instead, it will leave its position open so that it can make a capital gain.

CURRENCY SWAPS

currency swap
Exchange of payments in two different currencies.

In principle, a **currency swap** is very much like an interest-rate swap. The mechanics are similar, with intermediaries again making the market. The motivation too is similar: Comparative advantage and hedging both play a role. The volume of currency swaps written is about one-quarter the volume of interest-rate swaps.

A typical example based on comparative advantage might involve two corporations in two different countries—for example, Megacorp in the United States and Hermes in Germany. Megacorp might be contemplating an investment in Germany, and Hermes might be thinking of producing cars in the United States. Each company will need funds in the currency of the country in which the investment is to be made. However, each company can borrow *relatively* more cheaply in its own country and currency because it is better known to investors there. The swap enables each to reduce its borrowing costs and to obtain the funds in the currency it needs.

This is how it works. Megacorp sells bonds in the United States—for dollars, of course—and Hermes sells bonds in Germany for an equivalent amount of marks. The two corporations then swap the proceeds of the two issues, so that Megacorp gets the marks and Hermes the dollars. Megacorp then pays interest and principal on the mark bonds sold by Hermes, and Hermes pays interest and principal on the dollar bonds sold by Megacorp. In this way each company can borrow where its cost is least and still obtain the funds in the currency it needs.[15]

Currency swaps are useful to banks because they enable them to make loans and to take deposits in whatever currency their customers want, without having to worry about exchange-rate risk. For example, if Megacorp goes to Metropolis National Bank for a Euromark loan, Metropolis will fund it by borrowing interbank Eurodollars and swapping them into marks. Or if a Japanese company wants to make a Euroyen deposit, Metropolis will immediately swap the yen into dollars and lend the dollars on the Eurodollar interbank market. In fact, many banks keep their balance sheets entirely in dollars, automatically swapping into dollars all foreign-currency deposits and loans.

Swaps also allow banks to hedge any mismatch between forward sales and purchases of foreign currency. The currency swap, just like the interest-rate swap, can be seen as a bundle of forward transactions—a series of future exchanges of amounts of one currency for amounts of another. Suppose, for example, that Metropolis has sold more Swiss francs forward than it has bought. It can hedge its short position in "Swissies" by buying a Swiss franc swap that will provide it with a stream of payments in Swiss francs in exchange for dollars. As with interest-rate swaps, the long maturity of currency swaps relative to those of futures and options makes them an attractive hedging instrument.

13.4 | ARE FUTURES, OPTIONS, AND SWAPS GOOD FOR THE ECONOMY?

Financial futures, financial options, and swaps are all part of a wave of recent financial innovations that has been stimulated by a changing economic environment and by changing technology. The increased volatility of interest rates in the early 1980s, the increased volatility of exchange rates since the early 1970s, the increasing integration of world financial markets—all have created a need for new ways of dealing with risk. Advances in computer technology have made possible transactions of a complexity and speed that would have been unthinkable only a few years ago.

But are all these developments really benign? There is much suspicion of these newfangled financial instruments. The media frequently speak of "speculative excesses." There are calls for additional government regulation to protect the public. Are these concerns justified? Let us see what economic function these instruments perform and whether or not there are any serious problems.

All the instruments we have looked at—futures, options, and swaps—can be used both to hedge and to speculate. We have seen specific examples of how futures can be used to hedge interest-rate risk and of how options can be used to

---

[15]In reality, just as with an interest-rate swap, the currency swap will be mediated by an intermediary, which will assess and bear the credit risk. The bank will buy and sell mark swaps at a spread over dollars that reflects differences in interest rates between the two countries.

hedge exchange-rate risk. However, the appropriate futures can also be used to hedge exchange-rate risk, and the appropriate options can be used to hedge interest-rate risk. And we have seen how swaps can be used to hedge both interest-rate and exchange-rate risk. Each of these instruments has its merits. Futures are inexpensive but limit gains as well as losses. Options cost more but allow gains. Swaps permit hedging at much longer terms than either futures or options.

These instruments can be used to hedge other types of risk too. For instance, futures and options provide ways to hedge some types of credit risk. Suppose Metropolis National Bank lends to an oil company. One of the most likely reasons for default is a drop in the price of oil. Metropolis can hedge this risk by buying put options on oil. If the price of oil falls, the loss on the loan will be offset by a rise in the value of the puts.

More general hedges against credit risk are possible. For example, the overall default rate on loans depends a great deal on the state of the economy: If there is a recession, the default rate rises. Banks can hedge some of this general default risk by buying puts on an index of stock prices such as the Standard & Poor's 500 Index. When the economy weakens and stock prices fall, the loan losses will be offset by a rise in the value of the puts.

Commodity swaps are a new instrument that can be used to hedge the risk of changes in commodity prices. In such a swap, one party pays a fixed price for a notional amount of a commodity in exchange for the floating, market price. For example, a copper producer, borrowing to dig a mine, can hedge against future fluctuations in copper prices by becoming a floating-rate payer on a copper swap. An advantage of swaps, relative to futures and options, is that they allow hedging at much longer maturities. The intermediary for a swap is different too—a bank rather than an exchange. Banks have pushed commodity swaps aggressively as a way of entering the commodities trading business in competition with the exchanges.

To understand the economic value of being able to hedge with financial instruments, it is useful to divide the ways of dealing with risk into two general categories—*internal* and *external*. Examples of internal methods include diversification to deal with credit risk and maturities matching and currency matching to deal with interest-rate and exchange-rate risk. These methods are internal in the sense that they impose restrictions on the firm's own balance sheet. Diversification requires that no single asset be large relative to the total portfolio and that risks on different assets be unrelated. Maturities matching and currency matching require, respectively, that the duration and currency denomination of assets and of sources of funding be similar.

The restrictions imposed by these internal methods of dealing with risk may prevent firms from exploiting otherwise attractive profit opportunities. For example, a bank might be unwilling to make a medium-term loan to a good customer, because doing so would increase the bank's duration gap. Or the bank might be unable to exploit relatively low interest rates on deposits in some foreign currency, because taking such deposits would expose it to a currency mismatch. Similarly, if the only funding available to it were short-term, a manufacturing firm might be reluctant to make a promising long-term investment because of the resulting increase in its exposure to interest-rate risk. Also, the need for diversification limits the ability of firms to benefit from specialization.

External methods of dealing with risk involve the use of various financial instruments—including futures, options, and swaps—offered by financial markets and institutions. These external methods free firms from the restrictions that would be imposed by the internal methods. Being able to hedge externally gives a bank or other firm greater freedom in choosing its assets or sources of funding, because any resulting increase in risk can be hedged. For example, our bank can go ahead with its medium-term loan and our manufacturing company with its long-term project. The risks of specializing in a specific market can sometimes be hedged with commodity futures. These external methods of hedging risk are no longer an exotic device reserved for only the most sophisticated: Their use is spreading rapidly to medium-sized and even small businesses (see "Eliminating Risk of Rising Rates" on page 348).

So where does all the risk go? If A hedges interest-rate risk by buying an option from B, is there really any reduction in risk, or is the risk just being passed along? Actually, there are two ways in which the burden of risk can really be reduced by the use of financial instruments. First, if A's duration gap is positive and B's is negative, then they can both reduce their risk by trading the appropriate financial instrument. The financial instrument allows them to cash in on the fact that their combined balance sheet has a better maturity match than each of their balance sheets does separately. Another way to see how financial instruments can help is to observe that a great deal of risk is associated with uncertainty about prices in the future. Much of this risk can be removed by entering into forward transactions. However, as we have seen, forward transactions are hard to arrange. These financial instruments make forward transactions easier.

A second way financial instruments help the economy deal with risk is by allowing risk to be spread. If A has a lot of interest-rate risk and B a little, then B may be quite willing to take on some of A's risk in exchange for an appropriate reward. More generally, large risks are divided up among many "insurers," rather than being borne by a single firm or individual. The idea is illustrated rather well by Lloyd's of London, the insurance exchange. Suppose you want to insure the launch of a $20 million satellite. The actuarial principles of insurance that we looked at in Chapter 3 do not really apply. Pooling is not really possible—there are not enough satellite launches—and the probabilities of loss are not all that clear. So what Lloyd's does is to sign up, say, 1,000 underwriters (usually wealthy individuals) each responsible, in the event of a loss, for one-thousandth of the amount, or $20,000. Each underwriter receives a premium of, say, $1,000. Underwriters usually have a large diversified portfolio of policies. For example, one underwriter might be paid $1 million to insure 1,000 different risks, each of $20,000, for a total of $20 million. Clearly, the position of the underwriter is much less risky than that of the uninsured owner of the satellite, and the latter is happy to pay a premium to the former to bear some of his risk.

Futures, options, and swaps provide a vehicle not only for hedging, but also for speculation. Is this speculation helpful or harmful? As we have seen, specula-

ELIMINATING RISK OF RISING RATES

By Michael Quint

Every spring, L. L. Bean Inc. begins preparing for the Christmas selling season knowing how much it will pay for sweaters, boots and parkas. But until recently, there had always been a question about another important cost—the interest on money it borrows to pay for the yearly buildup of inventory.

Today, that uncertainty has been greatly reduced. The Freeport, Maine, mail-order house has eliminated the risk that a sharp rise in interest rates could cut into its carefully calculated profit margin.

Using a $25 million, two-and-a-half-year agreement with the Continental Bank of Chicago, L. L. Bean paid a one-time fee in return for assurance that during the six months of the year when the company is a borrower, its interest rate will not rise above a specified level.

Lee Surace, comptroller of the family-owned company, declined to disclose the level of the interest-rate cap. "But I can say that it lets me sleep a little better at night," he said. Bean's customers benefit, he said, "because eliminating the interest-rate risk means we can afford to hold the line a bit more on prices."

At the Syracuse Supply Company, a New York distributor and lessor of construction equipment, a five-year interest-rate swap on a $15 million loan with Chemical Bank provided protection against a rise in the bank's prime rate. The company is converting its floating-rate loan, which carried an interest charge slightly higher than the prime rate, into a fixed-rate loan at 10.85 percent.

For the likes of I.B.M. and the Ford Motor Credit Company, arcane products like interest-rate swaps and caps have been a part of their financial strategy for years.

Now bankers are moving aggressively to persuade L. L. Bean and thousands of smaller companies that swaps and caps can help them reduce the risk of higher interest rates.

Swaps and caps, and their offspring, "swaptions" and "captions," which are options to buy swaps or caps, are basically a form of insurance: for a fixed fee, a company can buy protection against higher interest rates, or lock in a fixed borrowing cost to eliminate the uncertainty of floating interest rates. In return for the fee, banks and securities firms assume the risk of interest-rate changes,

protecting themselves by trading futures contracts and Treasury bonds.

"The officers on the line with middle-market companies are clearly becoming more comfortable with the interest-rate-protection products, said Thomas M. Neustaetter, vice president in the corporate finance group at Chemical Bank.

"It's not uncommon to sit down with a treasurer who starts off saying, 'We are a very conservative company, and we don't do anything with futures or options,'" said S. Waite Rawls 3d, vice chairman at Continental. "Our job then is educational, to show that the company is not being conservative if they do nothing to protect themselves against interest-rate risk. Interest-rate swaps and caps are a kind of insurance. Can you imagine a company saying, 'We are conservative and we don't use fire insurance.'"

Source: Michael Quint, "Eliminating Risk of Rising Rates," *The New York Times*, July 31, 1989. Copyright © 1989 by The New York Times Company. Reprinted by permission.

tors perform an important economic function in searching out relevant information and, by trading on it, in causing that information to be integrated into prices. It is this activity of speculators that ensures that forward prices reflect market expectations of prices in the future. So, although speculators do seem to move prices, if that movement reflects new information, it may well be desirable. In addition to this informational role, speculators share the risk of price fluctuations: As a result of their participation in the market, the risk is spread more widely.

In addition to helping the economy handle risk, these financial instruments also contribute by facilitating the integration of financial markets. As we saw in

Chapter 3, such integration enhances economic efficiency. Funds are put to the best uses, investors receive the highest possible returns, and intermediaries are restrained by competition from overcharging for their services.

Swaps play a particularly useful role in "unpackaging" various types of loans. For example, bank loans tend to be floating-rate (or short-maturity), and direct loans via financial markets tend to be fixed-rate; it is hard to get a long-term fixed-rate loan from a bank. Bonds sold in the United States are denominated in dollars, and those sold in Japan are denominated in yen; it is hard to borrow yen in the United States. But with swaps, it is possible to separate the decision on *where* to borrow from the decision on *what form* the borrowing should take. You can borrow from a bank and turn it into a fixed-rate loan with an interest-rate swap. Or you can borrow dollars in the United States and turn them into yen with a currency swap.

Swaps also open up certain financial markets to those who would not normally have access to them. For example, a small firm that would not normally be able to borrow in direct financial markets (for all the reasons we looked at in Chapter 3) can now "swap into" those markets. Firms or banks that would not normally be able to borrow in Japan or in Italy now can do so via currency swaps. Borrowers and lenders can now shop around for the best deal much more freely.

While greater integration of financial markets means greater efficiency, it also puts greater competitive pressure on financial institutions. Profit margins are squeezed, and there is pressure to take more risks. As a result, there may be more failures. We shall look at this problem and at the possible regulatory implications in Part Four.

SUMMARY

- A lot of the risk faced by firms relates to uncertainty about prices for transactions in the future. Much of this uncertainty can be resolved by entering into forward transactions.

- It is hard to find potential partners to forward transactions. As a result of the lack of competition, potential trading partners may have considerable market power, and the terms of the transaction may not be favorable.

- Forward transactions are an exchange of promises. They therefore involve credit risk and all the costs of dealing with such risk.

- The futures contract is a solution to the problems involved in making forward transactions. The existence of an organized market in a standardized commodity increases the number of traders and promotes competition. The credit risk is assumed by the exchange.

- Traders include speculators as well as hedgers. Speculators take a position in futures without having any offsetting position in the underlying commodity or asset.

- Trading by speculators ensures that new information is rapidly integrated into prices and that futures prices reflect market expectations of spot prices in the future.

- Financial futures can be used to hedge interest-rate and exchange-rate risk. For example, a bank in a refinance position can sell T-bill futures. If interest rates rise, the gain on the futures position will offset the loss on the refinancing of the loan.

- Some real-world complications of hedging with futures include: (1) the requirement to put up a margin to guarantee performance; (2) daily settlement (each day, contracts are marked to market, and losers pay gainers); (3) settlement by offset, rather than by actual delivery; (4) transactions costs; (5) hedging imperfections, caused by the impossibility of matching the hedging instrument precisely to the position being hedged.

- Large banks and foreign banks make substantial use of futures, but small banks lack the expertise. Problems in accounting for hedged positions represent an important barrier to wider use.

- Options allow the hedging of downside risk without removing the potential for gain from upside risk. However, they do require an up-front payment of a substantial premium.

- Put options are options to sell; call options are options to buy. An option contract specifies a quantity, an exercise price, and an expiration date.

- Swaps involve the exchange of streams of different types of payment over time. In an interest-rate swap, one party pays a fixed interest rate, the other a floating rate. In a currency swap, payments in two different currencies are exchanged.

- The principal reasons for entering into swaps are hedging, speculation, and comparative advantage. Swaps are attractive to hedgers because they allow hedging further into the future than do other instruments. Swaps allow borrowers to exploit their comparative advantage to borrow more cheaply.

- The market for swaps is made by banks and other intermediaries that quote bid and asked prices and take upon themselves the credit risk of transactions.

- These financial instruments allow firms to hedge risk externally, rather than dealing with it internally by imposing restrictions on their own balance sheets. The increased freedom this allows the firms promotes economic efficiency.

- The use of these instruments allows the economy as a whole to handle risk better in two ways. First, it exploits the fact that the maturity or currency mismatch of the economy as a whole is less than that of individual firms; for example, the positive duration gap of one can be offset by the negative duration gap of another. Second, it allows risks to be spread more widely.

- The existence of these instruments also facilitates the integration of financial markets. Swaps, in particular, allow borrowers and lenders indirect access to markets to which they would not normally have direct access.

KEY TERMS

forward transactions	maintenance margin	premium
spot transaction	margin call	out of the money
spot price	open interest	in the money
hedgers	settlement by offset	options on futures
long	basis risk	interest-rate swap
short	option contract	fixed-rate payer
speculators	put option	floating-rate payer
financial futures contract	call option	notional principal
margin	exercise (strike) price	basis point
daily settlement	expiration date	currency swap
marked to market	American option	
margin account	European option	

DISCUSSION QUESTIONS

1. How are the problems involved in making forward transactions addressed by (a) futures and options contracts and (b) swaps?

2. As a solution to the problems of making forward transactions, are futures contracts more like direct or indirect lending?

3. What are the different ways a bank could hedge its interest-rate risk? What are their relative merits?

4. The rate on 3-month T-bill futures is currently 8%, but you know for sure that in 3 months time the T-bill rate will actually turn out to be 6%. If you buy $1 million in 3-month T-bill futures and hold them until maturity, you will make a sure profit. However, between now and then the rate may fluctuate wildly, perhaps reaching a peak of 20%. How could daily settlement cause you problems? How would the availability to you of liquid resources affect the desirability of taking a position in futures?

5. In the example of Exhibit 13.2, how could Metropolis have used options rather than futures to hedge its position on the loan? What are the relative merits of futures and options?

6. LIBOR and Treasury rates both rise. A floating-rate payer on a swap intermediated by Metropolis defaults with five years remaining. Does Metropolis gain or lose? Explain.

BIBLIOGRAPHY

Arak, Marcelle, Arturo Estrella, Laurie Goodman, and Andrew Silver, "Interest Rate Swaps: An Alternative Explanation," *Journal of the Financial Management Association* 17:2 (Summer 1988), 12–17.

Belongia, Michael T., and G. J. Santoni, "Hedging Interest Rate Risk with Financial Futures: Some Basic Principles," *Economic Review of the Federal Reserve Bank of St. Louis* October 1984, 15–25.

Chance, Don M., *An Introduction to Options and Futures*, Hinsdale, IL: Dryden Press, 1989.

Felgran, Steven D., "Interest Rate Swaps: Use, Risk, and Prices," *New England Economic Review* Nov.-Dec. 1987.

Hull, John, *Options, Futures and Other Derivative Securities*, Englewood Cliffs, NJ: Prentice-Hall, 1989.

Koppenhaver, G. D., "Futures Options and Their Use by Financial Intermediaries," *Economic Perspectives of the Federal Reserve Bank of Chicago* 1986, 18–31.

Kuprianov, Anatoli, "Short-Term Interest Rate Futures," *Economic Review of the Federal Reserve Bank of Richmond* September/October 1986, 12–26.

Parkinson, P., and P. Spindt, *The Use of Interest Rate Futures by Commercial Banks*. In *Financial Futures in the U.S. Economy*, Washington, D.C.: Board of Governors of the Federal Reserve System, 1986.

Smith, Clifford W., Jr., Charles W. Smithson, and Lee Macdonald Wakeman, "The Market for Interest Rate Swaps," *Journal of the Financial Management Association* 17:4 (Winter 1988), 34–44.

Stigum, Marcia L., *The Money Market*, 3rd ed. Homewood, IL: Dow Jones-Irwin, 1990.

Wall, Larry D., and John J. Pringle, "Interest Rate Swaps: A Review of the Issues," *Economic Review of the Federal Reserve Bank of Atlanta* December 1988, 22–40.

CHAPTER 14

THE CAPITAL MARKET

We have learned much about borrowing and lending short-term. It is time to take a look at borrowing and lending long-term. The latter takes place in what is called the **capital market**. We shall see that this long-term market parallels the short-term market in many ways: The underlying problems and the ways of dealing with them are basically the same in both markets. The long-term market, like the short-term market, has informational problems and credit, interest-rate, and liquidity risk. Again like the short-term market, it has direct lending through organized financial markets as well as indirect lending through various types of financial intermediary. These parallels will enable us to understand the capital market relatively quickly and easily.

capital market
Market for financial claims with maturities greater than one year.

We shall look first at the two basic types of security in the capital market—stocks and bonds—and at the principal borrowers and lenders. Then we shall go on to look at the markets for stocks and bonds in greater detail, studying their structure and some recent developments and problems. We shall see that in recent years the capital market, like the money market, has undergone major changes.

14.1 THE SECURITIES

The two main types of long-term security are stocks and bonds. With a bond, as with commercial paper or NCDs, the investor lends money in exchange for a promise to be paid specific amounts at specific times in the future. The promised payments typically take the form of semiannual payments of coupon interest plus repayment of principal on maturity. Variations on this basic structure are possible—for example, zero-coupon bonds that pay nothing until maturity. Stocks, on the other hand, do not pay an amount that is set in advance. With a stock, the investor provides money now in exchange for a share of profits in the future. The investor receives that share in the form of dividend payments and in the form of

353

EXHIBIT 14.1

NEW SECURITY
ISSUES OF U.S.
CORPORATIONS

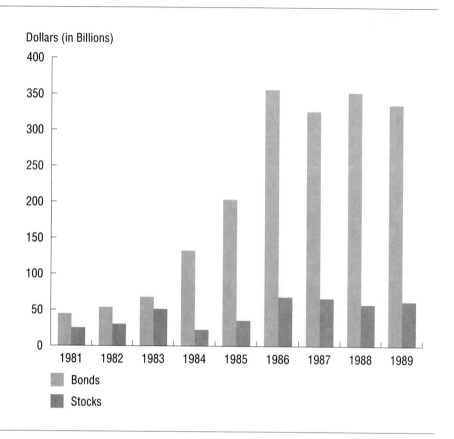

Source: *Federal Reserve Bulletin.*

possible capital gains from increases in the value of the stock. Generally, the investor in stock also receives ownership rights, such as the right to vote each year for the firm's board of directors.

The annual amounts of new issues of stocks and bonds are shown in Exhibit 14.1; the net amounts of funds raised are shown in Exhibit 14.2. Note that the net amount of funds raised is considerably less than the amount of new issues. In 1987, for example, $326 billion of new bonds were sold, but new funds raised through the sale of bonds were only $99 billion. The reason for the difference is that new issues of bonds are offset by bonds that mature and have to be repaid. Similarly, new issues of stocks are offset by stocks that are bought back and "retired." In 1987, $67 billion worth of new stocks were sold, but the net amount of new funds raised in this way was −$77 billion; that is, many more stocks were bought back or retired than were issued.

EXHIBIT 14.2

NET FUNDS
RAISED BY U.S.
CORPORATIONS

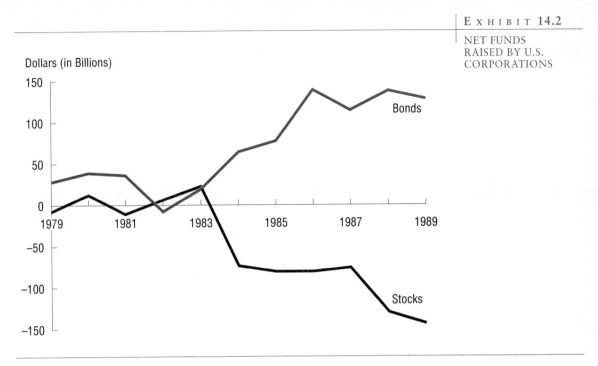

Source: Federal Reserve, *Flow of Funds Account.*

14.2 THE BORROWERS

The principal borrowers in the capital market are firms, households, and the government. Let us look at each in turn.

FIRMS

In Chapter 2 we looked at the financial needs of a typical firm. We saw that it needs finance for two basic reasons. First, it must pay for labor and materials before its output can be produced and sold. This sort of short-term finance for working capital is obtained from banks or in the money market. Second, the firm has to finance investment in fixed capital—in plant and equipment. Because this investment takes a long time to pay off in additional income, it needs to be financed long-term. The firm can finance this long-term investment either by borrowing or by using its own retained earnings—its internal funds.

As you can see from Exhibit 14.3, for firms as a whole, internal funds are by far the larger source. For example in 1987 firms made $380 billion in long-term investments, using $347 billion in internal funds and raising only $33 billion externally by selling securities. This pattern of financing is typical: In most years capital expenditure is greater than the available internal funding, and the differ-

EXHIBIT 14.3

CAPITAL
EXPENDITURES,
INTERNAL FUNDS,
AND EXTERNAL
FINANCING OF
U.S. CORPORATIONS

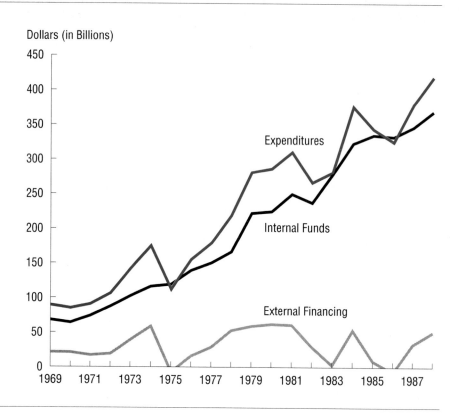

ence must be raised externally. Notice that the need for external finance is greatest in periods, such as the early or late 1970s, in which capital expenditure is increasing rapidly; in periods in which capital expenditure remains constant or falls, as in the mid 1970s, internal funds seem to be sufficient.

Firms generally play it safe by financing long-term investment with long-term funds raised in the capital market. Matching maturities in this way minimizes the interest-rate risk. However, firms will sometimes take a refinance position, financing some long-term investment by rolling over short-term debt. For example, firms required $33 billion in external funding in 1987 to bridge the gap between internal funds and capital expenditure. They raised $99 billion in the bond market, but most of this was used to cover the $77 billion net reduction in equity. Only $22 billion was left to cover part of the gap between capital expenditure and internal funds; the rest was filled by short-term borrowing.

Why do firms rely so heavily on internal funding? They do so because of the serious informational problems involved in external funding. The main reason for these informational problems is that the owners of a firm know much more about its prospects than do outsiders. Because of this asymmetry of information between firms and investors, and because all firms naturally claim to be promising prospects, potential investors find it hard to differentiate between firms that really are ("good firms") and firms that merely say they are ("bad firms"). As a result, investors tend to discount all they are told and to demand a rate of return from all firms that is more appropriate for the bad ones. Therefore good firms find external finance expensive and avoid it. Even bad firms cannot show themselves too willing to rely on external finance without revealing by their very willingness that they *are* bad firms, thereby driving up the rates they must pay.

HOUSEHOLDS

Households are, of course, the principal lender in the long-term market, but they are also the largest borrower. This borrowing is almost all mortgage borrowing to finance the purchase of housing. The mortgage market is such an important topic that we shall devote a complete chapter to it—Chapter 15.

GOVERNMENT

Most U.S. Treasury debt is short- or medium-term, but the amount of long-term borrowing is still substantial. In recent years the Treasury has raised some $20–$30 billion a year in new funds in the long-term market. Having covered the government securities market in Chapter 7, there is little we need add here. We saw in Chapter 7 how new issues are sold and how the secondary market is organized.

Various agencies of the U.S. government play an important role as intermediaries in the long-term market, particularly in the mortgage market, and we shall have more to say about these agencies in Chapter 15.

State and local governments are major borrowers in the long-term market, mainly to finance investment in infrastructure such as roads, bridges, and schools. The market for their securities, called *municipals,* will be discussed later in this chapter.

14.3 THE LENDERS

Households are the ultimate source of all long-term funds, either through the direct purchase of stocks and bonds or indirectly through the purchase of liabilities of financial intermediaries that in turn invest in long-term securities. The principal intermediaries in the capital market are life insurance companies, pension funds, mutual funds, and thrifts. Banks, however, are generally prohibited from owning stocks and bonds: As we saw in Chapter 5, banking regulation enacted in the 1930s was designed explicitly to keep banks out of the capital market. However, as usual, banks have found ways to get a piece of the action.

We shall see that in recent years there have been significant changes in the balance between direct and indirect lending in the capital market and in the relative importance of the various intermediaries involved.

LIFE INSURANCE COMPANIES

As we saw in Chapter 3, an insurance company is a special kind of financial intermediary. Just like a bank, it sells its liabilities and uses the proceeds to buy earning assets. However, insurance companies differ from banks in the nature of their liabilities: Banks offer deposits, and insurance companies offer insurance policies. The two main types of insurance are **life insurance** and **property/casualty insurance**. Life insurance pays off on the death of the policyholder: The idea is to protect dependents from the loss of income. Property/casualty insurance includes most other types of insurance—automobile, homeowners' and commercial, transportation, liability, and health insurance. The companies that sell life insurance—known in the market as **lifes**—are the more important in terms of providing long-term funds.[1]

To see why life insurance policies take the form they do, you have to understand a basic marketing problem. Life insurance is really death insurance. The basic policy, called the **term life policy,** pays off only if the policyholder dies. Because people do not like to think about dying, they may not want to talk to a life insurance salesman. To get their salesmen through the door, lifes came up with something psychologically more appealing than term life—the **whole life policy**. This is a policy that wraps the insurance inside a saving scheme and that therefore can be sold as a way of saving for retirement. You make annual or monthly payments that accumulate at a guaranteed rate of interest until the policy matures at, say, age 65. The accumulated fund can then either be withdrawn in cash or be turned into an annuity (an amount paid to you regularly until you die). This saving scheme has the added feature that if you should die before the policy matures, your heirs will be paid a substantial benefit, even though you failed to make all the payments on the policy. Doesn't that sound a lot more friendly than death insurance?[2]

However, whole life insurance has one serious shortcoming as a vehicle for saving: It lacks liquidity. What happens if you need the money before you retire

---

life insurance
Insurance that pays off on the death of the policyholder.

property/casualty insurance
All insurance other than life insurance: automobile, homeowners, transportation, liability, and health.

lifes
Companies that sell life insurance.

term life policy
Policy that pays off only if the policyholder dies.

whole life policy
Policy that includes a saving plan.

---

[1] There is a third component in the insurance industry—reinsurance. Property/casualty companies pay reinsurers part of the premium to take on some of the risk of a claim. Doing this is particularly important when the potential claims may be large—for example, in the case of air crashes or product liability suits. The largest market for reinsurance is Lloyd's of London.

[2] Whole life also solves another problem inherent in term insurance. The premiums on term life rise with age (an uncomfortable reminder of mortality). With whole life, the premiums are kept constant. You pay more than the fair premium when young and less when old, with the accumulated saving part of the policy being used to smooth things out. For example, if the fair premium for term life is $100 when you are 25 and $300 when you are 50, with whole life you pay $200 at both ages. The excess at age 25 accumulates with interest, and some of it is used to make up the premium when you are 50.

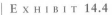

EXHIBIT 14.4

TOTAL ASSETS OF
U.S. LIFE INSURANCE
COMPANIES:
JANUARY 1989

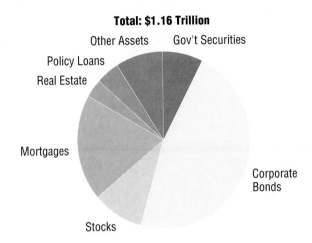

Total: $1.16 Trillion

Other Assets — Gov't Securities — Policy Loans — Real Estate — Mortgages — Stocks — Corporate Bonds

Source: *Federal Reserve Bulletin.*

(or die)? The insurance companies came up with a solution—the **policy loan**. This allows you to borrow any amount, up to the current cash value of the policy, at a rate of interest specified in advance (the rate is somewhat higher than the rate at which the policy accumulates to make borrowing unattractive unless there is a real need). We shall see that policy loans became a major headache for the lifes in the early 1980s.

Since life insurance policies are long-term liabilities, lifes, to minimize their interest-rate risk, tend to match maturities and to invest mostly in long-term assets (see Exhibit 14.4).

PENSION FUNDS

For a long time whole-life insurance was the favorite vehicle for retirement savings. However, since World War II it has been steadily overtaken in popularity by various types of pension fund (see Exhibit 14.5). Pension funds take in monthly payments from worker or employer, and they promise in return an income when the worker retires. The main reason for the switch from insurance policies to pension funds is the **Employee Retirement Income Security Act of 1974 (ERISA)**, which required employers to offer pension plans to their workers.

There are two basic types of pension plan—the **defined benefit plan** and the **defined contribution plan**. With a defined benefit plan, a firm promises its workers a certain level of benefits on retirement, usually linked to earnings in the last years of work. The firm sets up a fund and commits itself to contribute enough year by year to cover the benefits it has promised under the plan. If the fund's

policy loan
Loan to the policyholder of an amount up to the cash value of the life insurance policy.

ERISA
Legislation requiring employers to offer pension plans to their workers.

defined benefit plan
Pension plan wherein a company promises a certain level of retirement benefits and funds the plan to cover those benefits.

defined contribution plan
Pension plan wherein a company contributes a fixed amount annually for each employee.

E X H I B I T 14.5

PENSION FUND
ASSETS AND LIFE
INSURANCE ASSETS
AS PERCENTAGE OF
HOUSEHOLD NET
WORTH

Year	Pension Fund Assets	Life Insurance Assets	Household Net Worth	Pensions as a % of Net Worth	Life Assets as a % of Net Worth
1950	24.3	49.1	939.0	2.6	5.2%
1955	50.5	63.5	1,348.4	3.7	4.7
1960	90.8	78.8	1,743.0	5.2	4.5
1965	154.8	98.9	2,326.6	6.7	4.2
1970	240.8	123.3	3,162.4	7.6	3.9
1975	444.0	158.5	4,743.8	9.4	3.3
1980	916.1	207.4	8,927.0	10.3	2.3
1985	1,801.6	246.5	12,691.0	14.2	1.9
1988	2,592.8	302.5	15,640.0	16.6	1.9

Note: Assets and household net worth in billions of dollars. Figures for private pension funds include life insurance companies' pension fund reserves.

Source: Federal Reserve Board's Flow of Funds Accounts Outstanding, 1946 - 1975 and 1965 - 1988.

investments do poorly, the firm has to make up the difference; if they do well, the firm can reduce its contributions. With a defined contribution plan, on the other hand, the firm contributes a fixed amount each year for each worker. On retirement, the accumulated fund is paid to the worker either in cash or as an annuity. The size of the accumulated fund will depend on how well the contributions have been invested: The risk is borne by the worker, not by the firm. Currently, defined benefit plans account for some two-thirds of the total, but in recent years defined contribution plans have been growing more rapidly, so the balance is shifting.

Just as with lifes, maturities matching has pushed pension funds into the long-term market. Most pension fund assets are invested in diversified portfolios of stocks and bonds (see Exhibit 14.6). Defined benefit plans tend to invest more in bonds, and defined contribution funds, more in stocks. The reason defined benefit plans have a preference for bonds is that their liabilities involve the future payment of fixed dollar amounts. Their demand for matching assets has been an important factor in shaping the types of new financial product that have emerged in recent years.[3]

The competition between lifes and pension funds in the long-term market has in some ways paralleled that between banks and money market mutual funds in the short-term market. As interest rates rose in the late 1970s, lifes were slow to raise the yields they offered savers. For this reason and because of ERISA,

[3]See Zvi Bodie, "Pension Funds and Financial Innovation," xeroxed, Boston University School of Management, January 1990. The particular products that have emerged include Treasury strips (Chapter 6), index futures (discussed later in this chapter), and derivative mortgage securities (Chapter 15).

EXHIBIT 14.6

ASSETS OF
PENSION FUNDS

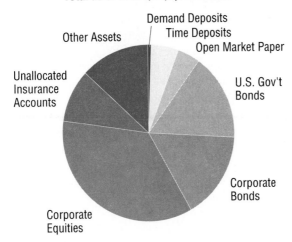

Total as of 1988 Q1: $2,140 Billion

pension funds took away a good part of their business. Like banks, lifes do a lot of private lending to firms, with all the credit assessment and monitoring that this involves. On the other hand, pension funds, like money market mutual funds, tend to invest in publicly traded securities, relying on the financial markets to do the work for them. Just like the banks, lifes have made up for some of their loss of business by providing services to their competitors: Pension funds often pay lifes to administer their investments.[4]

The assets of U.S. pension funds represent the biggest single pool of investable funds in the world—some $2.6 trillion in 1989 (the size of this pool has tripled in a decade); the investment return on this amount in 1989 was $340 billion. Competition to manage this vast pool of funds has been intense, and we shall see later how this competition has affected the financial markets.

STOCK AND BOND MUTUAL FUNDS

As we saw in Chapter 3, mutual funds are a sort of minimal financial intermediary. They put together pools of securities and sell shares in the pool to investors. These shares gain the two principal advantages of pooling—less risk, because of

---

[4]Lifes have also provided investment vehicles specially tailored to meet the needs of pension funds. One example is the guaranteed investment contract, or GIC, which is much like a bank CD except that it is sold by an insurance company. GICs have grown from $40 billion to $150 billion in the last 10 years and are particularly popular with defined contribution plans.

diversification, and greater liquidity, because of offsetting purchases and sales by shareholders. Mutual funds are minimal in that they do none of the credit assessment and monitoring that, say, banks do in lending directly to borrowers. Instead, mutual funds invest entirely in publicly traded securities, relying on financial markets to provide the needed credit assessment and monitoring.

In the short-term market, we encountered the money market mutual funds that invest in all sorts of money market paper—T-bills, commercial paper, banker's acceptances, NCDs. In the long-term market, there are a variety of mutual funds that invest in different types of stocks and bonds. The growth of these funds is shown in Exhibit 14.7.

Having seen the principal securities and the principal borrowers and lenders in the capital market, we are now ready to look at how the market actually operates. It is useful to divide the capital market, according to the type of security sold, into the market for debt and the market for equity.

$\left|14.4\right|$ THE MARKET FOR DEBT

Most of the external long-term funds that firms raise to cover the gap between their capital expenditures and their internally available funds are raised from the sale of debt rather than from the sale of equity (we shall see why later in the chapter). Debt securities promise fixed payments of specific amounts at specific dates in the future.

unsecured debt
Debt backed only by the general credit of the borrower.

secured debt
Debt backed by a specific asset.

Long-term corporate debt may be either **unsecured** or **secured**. Unsecured debt is backed only by the general credit of the borrower. If the borrower defaults, the lender can force bankruptcy and liquidation of all the borrower's assets, but he must line up with other lenders to be repaid out of the proceeds. Secured debt, on the other hand, is backed by some specific asset. In this case, if the borrower defaults, that specific asset may be taken and sold by the lender to recover the debt. Bankruptcy proceedings are not required: The lender just calls in the "repo man."

commercial mortgage
Private loan secured by commercial property.

mortgage bond
Mortgage that is issued publicly and that can be traded.

lease
Contract whereby equipment is lent to a firm for a specific fee and time period.

SECURED DEBT

The most common form of secured debt is the **commercial mortgage**—a private loan secured by fixed property, such as land or buildings. Because of their relative lack of risk, commercial mortgages are particularly attractive to banks and thrifts, and they account for most of the involvement of these institutions in long-term lending to firms. A **mortgage bond** is similar to a mortgage except that it is issued publicly and can be traded. Other types of bond may be secured by movable property, such as airplanes or railroad equipment.

A particularly attractive and rapidly growing form of secured intermediate-term debt (five to fifteen years) is the **lease**. For example, rather than lending a firm money to buy a computer, the bank itself buys the computer and lends it to the firm. There are two advantages to the computer belonging to the bank rather

EXHIBIT 14.7

TOTAL MARKET VALUE OF STOCK AND BOND MUTUAL FUNDS

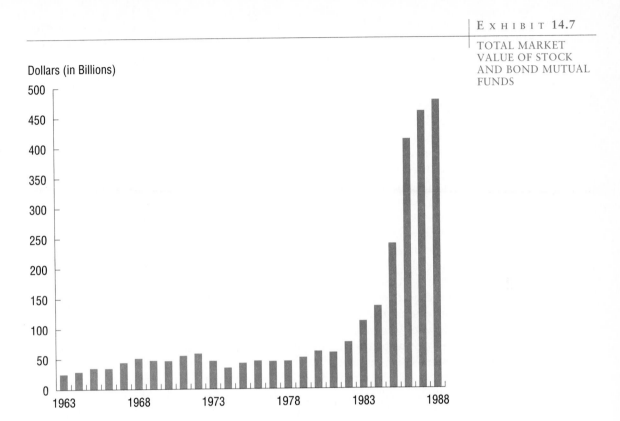

Source: Federal Reserve Board.

than to the firm. First, in case of default, repossession is easy. Second, the bank enjoys the tax advantages of ownership, such as depreciation allowances and investment tax credits. If the bank is in a higher tax bracket than the firm, these tax advantages are worth more to it than to the firm. The bank makes the arrangement worthwhile to the firm by making the lease less expensive than a straight loan. Leases are a popular form of long-term lending for banks and finance companies, being generally used to finance the purchase of transportation equipment (trucks, cars, planes, ships) and office equipment (mainly computers).[5]

UNSECURED DEBT

Unsecured debt may be divided into two categories—that placed privately and that sold to the general public. This distinction between private placements and public issues in the long-term market closely parallels that between bank loans

[5]Much of the leasing is done by specialized subsidiaries of bank holding companies rather than by banks themselves.

and commercial paper in the short-term market. Private placements are sold directly to financial institutions, which assess credit and monitor performance. Public issues require the disclosure of information and the payment of substantial fixed costs and so are worthwhile only when large sums need to be raised.

private placement
Long-term loan made to a firm by a financial intermediary.

PRIVATE PLACEMENTS   A **private placement** is essentially a long-term loan made to a firm by a financial intermediary—the long-term equivalent of a bank loan. The role of "bank" in this market has traditionally been played by life insurance companies: Lifes used to account for some 90% of private placements, with the 10 largest alone accounting for 55% to 65%. Today other financial institutions, particularly pension funds, are playing an increasing role.

The market for private placements grew after World War II. Lifes had large amounts of money to invest but were dissatisfied with the low interest rates available on publicly traded corporate bonds. They were therefore willing to lend to smaller, riskier firms that were willing to pay more for credit. These firms either did not have the credit standing needed for a public issue or did not borrow in large enough amounts to justify the substantial fixed costs. To control their exposure to credit risk, lifes began to specialize in credit assessment and monitoring, and to develop long-term relationships with particular borrowers, in much the same way as banks.

Private placements are highly illiquid. Not only are the borrowers relatively unknown, but until recently there were also legal restrictions on the transferability of privately placed debt. This means that the lending institution should expect to hold the debt until maturity. As a result of the illiquidity, the maturity of private placements tends to be shorter than that of public issues—15 years on average rather than 25.

The mutually beneficial relationship between lifes and small and medium-sized firms came under strain beginning in the late 1970s. Whole-life policies generally paid savers a very low yield: One study in 1979 found it to be as little as 1.3%. This was not too terrible when market rates were low and Regulation Q kept a lid on deposit rates. But when rates on alternative forms of saving—like money market mutual funds and the new high-interest deposits—began to skyrocket, lifes experienced a massive outflow of funds. This outflow took the form of policy loans. The rate on these loans had been set when contracts had been written at what then looked like a prohibitive level—say 5%. But when you can invest your money in a money market mutual fund at 18%, borrowing at 5% looks pretty good.

The result of this outflow of funds from the lifes was a sharp drop in the availability of funds for private placements (see Exhibit 14.8) and corresponding hardship for firms that had relied on this form of finance.

Later, as interest rates came down and as lifes developed new, more attractive, types of policy, they once again started to take in large sums of money, and the private placement market revived. Indeed, recently the private placement market has been used extensively by large companies that had previously shunned it in favor of public issues. For them the main advantages of private placement are speed and secrecy: It allows them to avoid the disclosure requirements and the

Exhibit 14.8

PRIVATE
PLACEMENTS

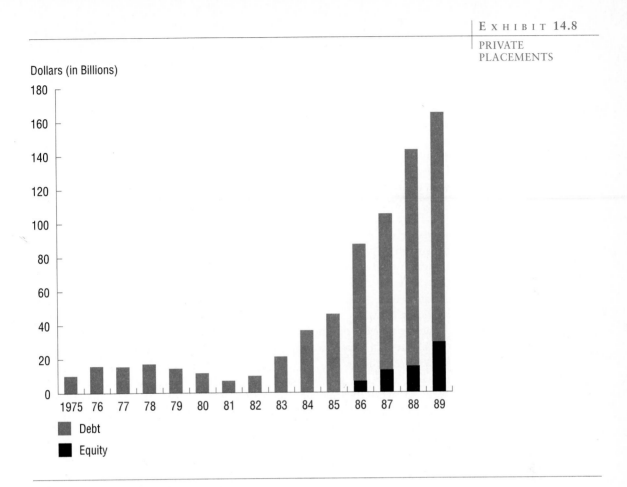

Dollars (in Billions)

Debt

Equity

considerable delays of a public issue. These advantages are particularly important if the borrowing is needed as part of a corporate takeover: Then there is need to move quickly and discreetly.

The market for private placements received a major boost in April 1990, when the SEC passed **Rule 144a,** which permits trading in privately placed securities among institutions with at least $100 million in assets. This will allow a secondary market for private placements to develop, enhancing their liquidity and increasing their appeal. The rule is expected to make private placements particularly attractive to foreign companies wishing to raise funds in the United States. In the past such companies have balked at the disclosure of information required for a public issue—usually much more than that required in their domestic markets.

PUBLIC ISSUES AND UNDERWRITING If a private placement is the long-term equivalent of a bank loan, a **public issue** is the long-term equivalent of commercial paper. Most public issues are unsecured. These **debentures,** as they are called,

Rule 144a
SEC rule that permits trading in private placements among large financial institutions.

public issue
Securities sold to the public at large.

debenture
Corporate security backed by the general credit of the issuing firm.

carry fairly standardized rates and terms and have traditionally been issued only by the largest and most creditworthy corporations. As with commercial paper, the public issue of debentures is expensive and therefore worthwhile only for large amounts.

Each new issue requires the borrowing firm to register with the SEC and to disclose a great deal of financial information. The issue must be rated for credit risk by a rating agency such as Standard & Poor or Moody.[6]

underwriter
Investment bank that buys an entire securities issue and resells it piecemeal to the public.

The actual sale of a new issue is handled by an **underwriter**. This is an investment bank, or a syndicate of investment banks, that buys the entire issue from the firm and then resells it piecemeal to the public. The price the underwriter pays is based on an estimate of the bonds' market value. The top underwriters in 1989 are shown in Exhibit 14.9.

There are two sources of risk to the underwriter. The first is that the market will perceive the issue to be more risky relative to Treasuries than anticipated, so that it can be sold only at a greater spread. For example, in April 1988 First Boston, a major investment bank, agreed to buy a $125 million issue of Connecticut Light and Power at a yield spread of 0.70% (that is, First Boston guaranteed a price that implied a yield of 0.70% over the Treasury rate). However, investors were willing to buy the bonds only at a spread of 0.85%. Assuming that the duration of the bonds was about 10 years and the Treasury rate about 10%, First Boston would have lost about $125 million x 10 x .0015/ (1.1) = $1.7 million.[7]

The really big risk, though, is interest-rate risk. If market interest rates *change* between the time the underwriter buys the issue and the time the bonds are resold, there will be a capital gain or loss. For example, in October 1979, IBM decided to float a $1 billion bond issue. Competition to underwrite it was fierce, and a syndicate led by Salomon and Merrill Lynch won out over IBM's usual underwriter, Morgan Stanley. On October 3 the syndicate agreed on a yield of 9.5%, at a spread of only 0.1% above the Treasury rate of 9.4%. Later that same day the yield on Treasuries jumped to 9.8% in anticipation of a major tightening of monetary policy. That tightening was indeed announced several days later, sending the yield on Treasuries even higher, to over 10%. At that time the underwriters still held some $350 million worth of the bonds. Naturally, as the price of Treasuries fell, so did the price of the IBM bonds. While Salomon and Merrill Lynch were understandably reticent about the extent of their losses, estimates on Wall Street ran as high as $20 million, presumably providing Morgan Stanley with considerable satisfaction.

To compensate them for the risks and for the services they provide, underwriters receive a fee: For the IBM issue the fee was about $5 million. In recent years the risks have become greater, but the fees have become smaller. The greater

---

[6]The value of bond ratings is controversial. The rating agencies generally use the same information that is made available publicly in the filing with the SEC, so the rating is really little more than a summary of that information.

[7]This calculation uses Equation 12A.11 in the appendix to Chapter 12, which you should see for further explanation.

EXHIBIT 14.9

TOP U.S. DEBT
UNDERWRITERS: 1989

Manager	Amount (In Billions)	Market Share
Merrill Lynch	$ 40.28	14.5%
Goldman Sachs	37.81	13.6
First Boston	35.86	12.9
Salomon Brothers	31.01	11.2
Morgan Stanley	27.14	9.8
Shearson Lehman	21.97	7.9
Bear Stearns	16.78	6.1
Drexel Burnham	16.42	5.9
Prudential-Bache	15.71	5.7
Kidder Peabody	8.32	3.0
Subtotals	$251.30	90.6%
Industry Totals	$277.15	100.0%

Source: *The Wall Street Journal*, Jan. 2, 1990.

risk is the result of the increased volatility in interest rates. The lower fees are the result of **Rule 415**.

Under this new SEC regulation, a corporation may register a new issue with the SEC and then wait up to two years to sell it (this is called **shelf registration**). This gives issuers greater flexibility in timing, allowing them to sell when they think rates are relatively low. Furthermore, under Rule 415 issuers are no longer required to name an underwriter at the time they register a new issue. This gives them much greater bargaining power in negotiating a deal with an underwriter. The issue is all set and waiting to go; they can simply ask for offers and take the best one.

As fee income has shrunk under the pressure of competition—it totaled only $3 billion in 1989, down from a record $5.7 billion in 1986—investment banks have been tempted to take larger and larger positions in the bonds they trade, in the hope of profiting from interest-rate movements. Rather than selling as quickly as possible, they have held on to large amounts of bonds, financing their positions with overnight money. As interest rates fell from 1984–1986, they did rather well. When rates rose sharply in 1987, they did somewhat less well. Since then they have trimmed their inventories and hedged what remains.

The secondary market for bonds is generally an "over-the-counter" market (an over-the-telephone market), although the bonds of a few of the largest companies do trade face-to-face on the stock exchanges. The over-the-counter market for bonds operates much like the government securities market that we saw in Chapter 7, with dealers "making the market" by quoting bid and ask prices for the various issues. The bond market, however, particularly for the smaller issues, is much "thinner" than the market for governments. Since there is not much trading in these issues, relatively few dealers will bother to carry them,

Rule 415
SEC rule that permits shelf registration.

shelf registration
Corporation's registration of a new issue with the SEC as long as two years before selling it.

and because of the lack of competition and the high fixed costs to the dealers, bid–ask spreads may be large.

THE RISE AND FALL OF THE JUNK BOND

investment-grade bonds
Bonds with a rating of Baa or BBB or above.

Bonds with a rating of Baa (Moody) or BBB (Standard & Poor) or above are called **investment-grade bonds**. Those with lower ratings are called **"high-yield bonds"** by bond salesmen—the lower the rating, the higher the risk and therefore the higher the yield—and **junk bonds** by everyone else. The issuing of junk bonds grew rapidly during the 1980s (see Exhibit 14.10).

junk (high-yield) bonds
Bonds with a rating below Baa or BBB.

Historically, the market for bonds with ratings below investment grade had been small. The demand was limited: Many institutional investors were limited by regulation to buying investment-grade paper. Companies unable to obtain a good rating would avoid public issues because of the high underwriting costs and the limited demand; they would rely instead on private placements or long-term bank loans. Indeed, most junk bonds on the market had not been originally issued as junk, but were rather "fallen angels"—bonds whose ratings had been downgraded.

The market for junk began to grow in the 1980s for a number of reasons. One was the crunch in the private-placement market caused by the problems of the life insurance companies that we have already discussed. Companies unable to borrow through private placements were forced to turn to public offerings despite the cost.

A second reason was the steady increase in corporate leverage—an increasing reliance on debt rather than equity finance. As the leverage of a firm increases, its debt becomes riskier and its rating falls. To see why, consider a simple example. Suppose there is an investment that costs $225 now and will pay off either $550 or $50 in a year's time. If you finance the investment by borrowing $25 at 10% and putting up $200 of your own money, the debt is perfectly safe: Even if the investment does badly (the $50 outcome), there will be enough to pay off the $27.50 you owe. If you raise the debt–equity ratio from $25/$200=0.123 to $75/$150=0.5 by borrowing $75 and putting up only $150 of your own money, the default risk goes up. If the investment does badly, the $50 is not enough to pay off the $82.50 that you owe.

leveraged buyout (LBO)
Purchase of a corporation's outstanding stock that is financed by issuing debt.

A third reason for the growth of the junk bond market was the increasing popularity of the **leveraged buyout (LBO)**. In an LBO the outstanding stock of a corporation is purchased, often by its managers, with the purchase financed by issuing debt. Since the LBO replaces outstanding equity with debt, thereby increasing leverage, the rating of the acquired company's debt declines. We shall look at the reasons for LBOs and for the increasing reliance on debt in general later on in the chapter.

The explosive growth of the junk bond market was largely the accomplishment of a single individual, Michael Milken, an investment banker with Drexel Burnham Lambert. Arguing that the higher yield on junk bonds more than compensated investors for the increased default risk, Milken marketed junk

EXHIBIT 14.10

OUTSTANDING
JUNK BONDS

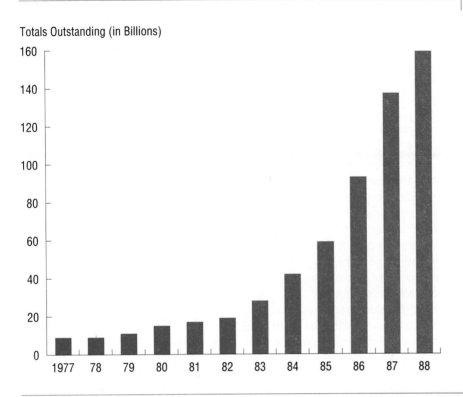

Totals Outstanding (in Billions)

Source: "High-Yield Bonds," report issued by GAO, March 1989.

bonds aggressively to financial institutions such as lifes, pension funds, and savings and loans. The fat underwriting fees on junk bonds—2% versus 0.4%–0.7% on investment-quality issues—transformed Drexel from a minor investment bank in the 1970s into the most profitable firm on Wall Street by 1987. Milken himself earned over $1 billion in compensation from Drexel between 1983 and 1987.

To promote the growth of the market, Milken had to address two problems that are particularly critical for high-risk bonds. The first is that investors in bonds are always worried about liquidity: Will they be able to get a decent price if they have to sell the bond? The better the liquidity, the lower the yield investors will demand when they purchase the bond. With high-risk bonds, liquidity is particularly important, because fears that the bonds will be hard to resell can drive their price down rapidly, and this increases the risk of holding them. Generally, the liquidity of an issue is assured by the underwriter, who promises implicitly to make a market in the bond: That is, the underwriter is willing to buy back the bonds and hold them until they can be resold to other investors. Drexel was particularly important in playing this role of market maker in the market for junk bonds.

The second problem facing junk bonds is potentially high bankruptcy costs. One reason that high-risk borrowers prefer to borrow from a financial institution rather than through a public issue is that it allows more flexibility if they face temporary problems: With a private placement, the terms of the debt can be renegotiated; with a public issue, default and bankruptcy are the more likely outcomes. For low-risk borrowers, since the probability of trouble is small, this disadvantage of a public issue is relatively unimportant. For high-risk borrowers the potential loss is substantial. Drexel, and Milken in particular, acted to minimize this loss by standing ready to help issuers of junk when they were in trouble. To avoid default, Milken arranged in some cases for the debt to be refinanced; in other cases, he arranged additional finance. The availability of this help, rather like that provided by a bank to its borrowers, made junk bonds more attractive both to borrowers and to investors.

The heavy dependence of the junk bond market on Drexel and on Milken became a problem when both were implicated in a growing scandal involving insider trading on Wall Street.[8] The scandal broke in 1986, when Dennis Levine of Drexel pleaded guilty to securities fraud and began to provide evidence on the involvement of others. By 1988 SEC investigators accused Drexel and Milken of involvement. To avoid racketeering charges, Drexel agreed to plead guilty to securities fraud, to pay $650 million in fines, and to fire Milken. Milken challenged this agreement and was indicted in March 1989; he finally left Drexel in July. Drexel's guilty plea on the criminal charge left it open to potentially large civil suits, with damaging effects on its credit standing.

The Drexel safety net under the junk bond market began to fray. In June 1989 Drexel was unable to help a major customer, Integrated Resources, which defaulted on a $1 billion issue, badly shaking the market. Prices of junk bonds fell further in August, when President Bush signed a law requiring savings and loans to divest themselves of their junk bond holdings by 1994. In September Campeau, another big user of junk bonds began to have liquidity problems. In October UAL, the parent of United Airlines, failed to secure financing for a planned LBO, and other issues of junk were deferred. Prices continued to fall.

In December, because of Drexel's problems, the rating on its commercial paper was downgraded, making it impossible to roll over. Because of the problems in the market, the banks found Drexel's inventory of junk bonds unsuitable collateral for a loan to cover payment on commercial paper coming due (Drexel did not have ironclad standby letters of credit). Drexel managed to pay off $550 million of the $700 million in commercial paper that it owed, but it was unable to find another $50 million it needed to pay off more paper coming due. In February 1990, after declaring a loss of $40 million on 1989 revenues of $4.1 billion, Drexel was forced to file for bankruptcy under Chapter 11.

The demise of Drexel left the junk bond market "orphaned," with many more defaults likely. By early 1990 prices had stabilized, but losses had been

---

[8]Insiders, such as company officers and investment bank advisers, are not allowed to trade in securities on the basis of privileged information until that information becomes available to the general public.

substantial. Compared to a return of 17% that would have been earned on an investment in Treasury securities from December 1988 to December 1989, the highest-grade junk would have yielded 12% over this period and the lowest-grade would have yielded, –13.6%. In the first quarter of 1990 there were only $246 million worth of new issues, compared with the usual rate of about $5 billion a quarter previously. A shakeout is expected in the junk bond market, but it will probably continue to function, albeit on a reduced scale. Despite its problems, the market has been a valuable source of funds for many medium-sized firms.[9]

The collapse of the market has threatened some insurance companies, mutual funds, and savings and loans that were heavy investors in junk. For example, First Executive, a big Los Angeles insurer, had $8 billion of its $19 billion in assets in junk, and it had probably taken a loss of $2 billion by the end of 1989. The price of First Executive's stock plummeted, and customers started to worry about the safety of their life insurance policies and pension annuities. There was talk of a possible "run" creating liquidity problems, which could result in a merger with another company or a takeover by California regulators.

EUROBONDS

We have seen how regulation of banking in the United States stimulated the growth of Eurodollar banking. In a similar way, regulation of the capital market has stimulated growth of an overseas market in bonds—the market for **Eurobonds.** Like Eurocurrency banking, the Eurobond market began in London in U.S. dollars and has since spread to other countries and to other currencies.

In the 1960s there was a large potential market overseas for high-quality dollar-denominated bonds. Potential buyers were mainly wealthy individuals, in Europe and elsewhere, who kept funds outside their home countries, often in Swiss bank accounts. As an example, consider the Italian industrialist Leonardo Michelangelo. Leonardo had two main concerns in investing his considerable wealth: To avoid paying taxes and to protect himself against the falling value of the Italian lira. High-quality U.S.-dollar corporate bonds had stable value, but they were taxed. Issuers were obliged to register ownership of the bonds and to withhold a 30% tax on interest payments. Not only did Leonardo object emphatically to paying the 30% tax, but he was also very unhappy with there being any record of his owning the bonds, since he had smuggled his money out of Italy illegally (at this time most countries other than the United States did not allow their residents to take their money out of the country freely).

Eurobonds addressed both the problems Leonardo had with regular U.S. corporate bonds. Since Eurobonds were issued as bearer bonds, there was no record of ownership: The bond simply belonged to whoever had physical possession (the bearer). And no tax was withheld.

Eurobonds
Bonds denominated in a currency other than that of the country in which they are issued.

---

[9]Some issuers of junk bonds have been taking advantage of the slump in the market by offering to buy back their debt at a fraction of its face value.

Since there were thousands like Leonardo in Italy, France, Latin America, and elsewhere, Eurobonds proved an enormous success. Such a success, indeed, that corporations could sell Eurobonds at yields *below* those on comparable Treasuries. This gave them the opportunity, which many could not resist, of selling Eurobonds and investing the proceeds in Treasury securities to make a riskless profit.[10]

Somewhat miffed, the U.S. Treasury acted to make securities issued in the United States more attractive to international investors. In 1984 tax withholding on foreign-owned securities was ended, and corporations were allowed to sell bearer bonds to foreign investors. Although the Treasury itself does not now issue bearer bonds, it does allow banks to sell bearer certificates backed by Treasury bonds. As a result, since 1984 yields on Eurobonds and bonds issued in the United States have more or less equalized.

Nonetheless, the Eurobond market has continued to prosper: Lack of regulation still makes it attractive. Borrowers can raise money more quickly and at lower transactions costs, because they avoid the expense and delay of filing with the SEC, and because fierce competition among underwriters has kept fees and commissions low.[11] Indeed, competition has been so fierce that most underwriters and dealers have lost money, with the result that market making and thus liquidity have suffered.[12]

The Eurobond market has given U.S. commercial banks an opportunity to get into the business of underwriting long-term bonds. The Glass-Steagall Act, which excludes commercial banks from this activity, does not apply outside the United States. Thus many major U.S. banks have set up subsidiaries overseas to underwrite Eurobonds. A secondary reason for their heavy involvement is the close relationship between the Eurobond market and the swap market: Perhaps 70% of all Eurobond issues are related to swaps. As we saw in Chapter 13, swaps have opened up the bond market indirectly to firms and institutions that otherwise would not have had access to it.

Exhibit 14.11 shows the volume of new issues in the Eurobond market. Notice the rapid growth in the early 1980s, to a level comparable with that of the U.S. bond market. Note, too, the growing proportion of nondollar bonds, from 16% in 1982 to 58% in 1988.

In recent years the Japanese in particular have entered the market in a big way, first as buyers, then as issuers and underwriters. Japanese companies prefer the Eurobond market to their own heavily regulated domestic bond market,

---

[10]To eliminate any interest-rate risk, they sold zero-coupon bonds and bought zero-coupon strips.

[11]Issuers of new securities in the United States must file a registration statement with the SEC, then wait 20 days before selling the securities. There are exemptions for firms that sell less than $1.5 million per year, for private placements, and for debt with maturity of less than 270 days (money market paper). The need for filing, and the delay, are eliminated with a Eurobond issue. A lot of takeovers have also been financed in the Euro syndicated loan market, where large amounts can be raised quickly and quietly: No public disclosure is required of the purpose for which the money is being raised, as it is with a bond issue.

[12]Competition from the Eurobond market is another reason why underwriting fees in the U.S. bond market have fallen.

EXHIBIT 14.11

NEW ISSUES OF
EUROBONDS

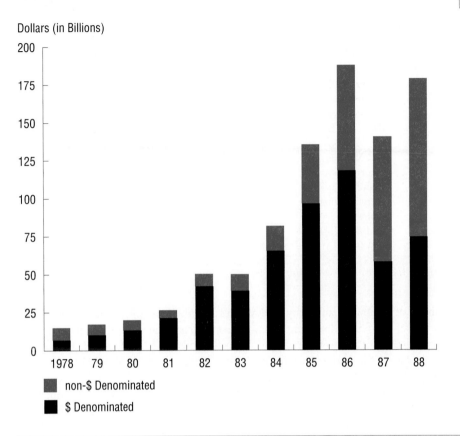

Dollars (in Billions)

Source: *Financial Market Trends*, OECD.

although pending deregulation in Japan may change that in the future. The Eurobond market was originally dominated by British and European banks from its beginnings in the 1960s until 1975. Then U.S. banks and investment banks started to take over. However, the 52% share of underwriting by U.S. institutions in 1984 had fallen to 25% by 1987, while the share of the Japanese investment banks had risen from 9% to 31%. The top Euromarket underwriters in 1989 are listed in Exhibit 14.12.

MUNICIPAL BONDS

State and local governments sell bonds to finance investment in public infrastructure—things like roads, sewers, bridges, airports, and power plants, as well as schools, hospitals, and colleges. Such bonds are called generically **municipal bonds,** or **munis.** There are two main types. **General obligation bonds** are backed by the

municipal bonds (munis)
Bonds sold by state and local governments.

general obligation bonds
Bonds backed by the ability of the issuing authority to levy taxes; repayable from general tax revenue.

EXHIBIT 14.12

TOP EUROMARKET
UNDERWRITERS: 1989
(NON-U.S. DEBT AND
EQUITY)

| Manager | 1989 | | 1988 |
	Amount (In Billions)	Percentage of Market	Percentage of Market
Nomura Securities	$ 33.36	15.4	10.1
Yamaichi Securities	16.96	7.8	4.1
Daiwa Securities	16.82	7.7	5.3
Nikko Securities	15.31	7.1	3.9
Deutsche Bank	10.23	4.7	6.8
CS First Boston	9.65	4.4	7.8
J.P. Morgan	7.64	3.5	3.1
Morgan Stanley	7.06	3.3	2.3
Banque Paribas	6.68	3.1	3.4
Merrill Lynch	6.55	3.0	3.5
Subtotals	$130.26	60.0%	50.4%
Industry Totals	$217.18	100.0%	100.0%

Source: *The Wall Street Journal*, Jan. 2, 1990.

revenue bonds
Bonds repayable only from
the specific revenue of the
project they finance.

ability of the issuing authority to levy taxes and are repayable from its general tax revenue. **Revenue bonds** are repayable only from the specific revenue of the project they finance—for example, from the tolls on a road. If that revenue is insufficient, the issuing authority is not obliged to pay the difference out of general revenue.

The interest on munis is exempt from federal taxation. It is often exempt also from state and local taxes. For example, residents of New York State who hold New York State bonds are exempt from New York State taxes and local taxes on income from them.

This tax exemption allows state and local governments to borrow more cheaply. To see why, suppose your marginal tax rate is 40% and you are considering investing in corporate bonds with a yield of 10%.[13] Because the income from these bonds is taxable, the *after-tax* yield is only 60% of 10%—that is, 6%. If you had the alternative of investing in tax-free munis with the same default risk, how much would they have to yield for you to be willing to buy them? Since the income from munis is *not* taxable, 6% would give you the same yield after tax as 10% on the corporate bonds. Therefore, when corporations have to pay 10% on their bonds, state and local governments can get away with paying only 6%.

Clearly, munis will be most attractive to investors in the highest tax brackets. For an investor paying a marginal tax rate of 50%, a rate on munis of 6% is equivalent to a rate on corporate bonds of 12%; for an investor paying a

[13]The marginal tax rate is the rate you pay on the last dollar earned. This is the relevant rate when you are considering increases in your taxable income.

EXHIBIT 14.13

NEW ISSUES
OF MUNIS

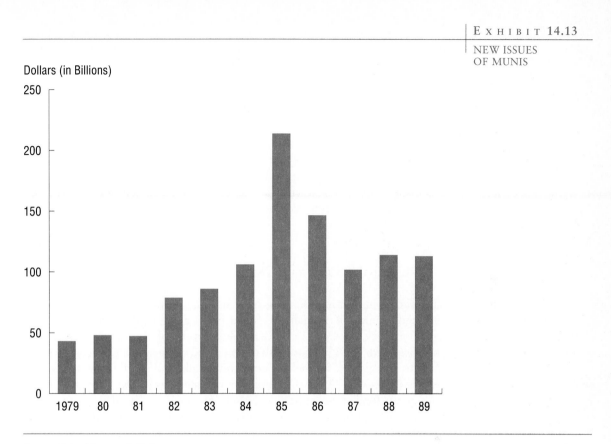

Dollars (in Billions)

Source: *Federal Reserve Bulletin.*

marginal tax rate of 33%, a rate on munis of 6% is equivalent to a rate on corporate bonds of only 9%. Hence the difference between municipal and corporate yields will depend on the level of the marginal tax rate. The reduction of the highest marginal rates in 1986 therefore had the effect of reducing the difference between municipal and corporate yields.

The muni market flourished in the early 1980s as local governments found they could get away with floating tax-free issues for various favored clienteles. Examples included cheap development loans for businesses that would locate in the area, low-interest mortgages for first-time home buyers, and low-interest student loans. The Tax Reform Act of 1986 put an end to most of this when it prohibited the sale of municipal bonds for the benefit of companies, private institutions, or individuals. The act also eliminated a tax break for banks that had made munis a favorite investment—the ability to deduct the interest they paid on money borrowed to buy munis. The end of this deductibility greatly reduced the attractiveness of munis and effectively took banks out of the muni market.

These tax changes have caused a slump in the muni market (see Exhibit 14.13). Note the rush of issues in 1985 trying to get in ahead of the tax reform.

Savage competition among underwriters for what little business remained has driven fees down to half their previous level. As a result, many underwriters have cut back their operations or quit the market altogether.

14.5 THE MARKET FOR EQUITIES

The market for equities receives a great deal of attention: Daily movements in stock prices are routinely reported on the evening news, and large movements get headline treatment. Despite its prominence in the media, the stock market is *not* a major source of funding for firms. After exploring the reasons for this, we shall look at how the market for equities operates and at some of the recent developments in this market.

NEW ISSUES OF STOCK

initial public offering (IPO) First issue of a corporation's stock.

The primary market for equities is quite small compared to the primary market for bonds: Only a very small amount of fixed capital is financed through new issues of stock. In 1989 only $31 billion worth of new stock was issued, compared with $277 billion worth of new bonds. The amount of money raised by firms selling stock for the first time (this is called *going public*) was only $14 billion. There were 245 of these **initial public offerings (IPOs)**. Moreover, if we look at *net* funds raised through the sale of equity, we see that it is actually *negative*. In recent years firms have been buying back more stock than they sell: In 1989 stock bought back was expected to exceed new issues by over $150 billion.[14]

Despite these numbers, equity remains a more important source of long-term finance than debt. Although the share of debt has been growing, for reasons we shall examine in a moment, the value of stock *outstanding* still exceeds the value of debt outstanding by a large margin. At the end of 1988 the value of bonds outstanding was $862 billion and the value of commercial mortgages was $706 billion, whereas the market value of corporate equities was $3,594 billion.

How to resolve this apparent contradiction? First, equity is "forever." Unlike debt, it does not mature. It therefore does not need to be repaid or rolled over. If you raise $1 million by selling stock, you only have to sell one issue; if you raise $1 million by selling bonds and you want to keep the money, you must make repeated issues—each new issue funding the repayment of the last.

Second, selling stock is not the only way to increase equity. Equity also increases when corporations retain earnings rather than paying them out as dividends to stockholders. For example, suppose Megacorp has profits of $1

---

[14]See Exhibits 14.1 and 14.2 for previous years. Note the decline in new issues following the stock market crash of 1987, which is discussed later in the chapter. IPOs in 1989 were well down from the $24 billion of 1988: The delayed reaction to the crash is the result of the long lead time in preparing an IPO.

billion and is planning a $1.5 billion investment in new technology. It raises $500 million through the sale of new bonds and needs a further $1 billion in new equity. Megacorp has two ways to find the $1 billion. It can pay out this year's $1 billion in profits as dividends and simultaneously float a new stock issue of $1 billion. Or it can cancel the dividend payment and use the $1 billion in profits directly to fund the new investment. The first alternative is wasteful. Registration and underwriting costs of a new issue could easily total 5% of the amount raised, $50 million in this case. Megacorp could save the $50 million by using retained earnings.

But don't retained earnings cheat stockholders out of their dividends? Not at all. Even if Megacorp just kept the $1 billion as cash, the value of the stock should rise by this amount. Remember that the value of the stock equals the value of Megacorp's assets less the value of its debt. Because the retained earnings have increased the value of Megacorp's assets by $1 billion, stockholders enjoy a $1 billion increase in the value of their stock. Moreover, if the tax rate on capital gains is less than the tax rate on dividend income (as it was before 1986), they will *prefer* an increase in the value of the stock to an equivalent cash dividend.

A further reason why companies are reluctant to issue new stock is that the market perceives it as a bad signal about their future profits. The problem is one of asymmetric information. The managers of Megacorp know more than outsiders about the company's future prospects. If they think the company is going to do well, they have an incentive to finance new investment by issuing debt. That way the money "left over" for existing stockholders will be greater. Why let new stockholders in on a good deal? On the other hand, if the managers think Megacorp is going to do poorly, they have an incentive to finance new investment by issuing equity. Issuing more debt in these circumstances is dangerous because it increases the risk of bankruptcy: Interest payments have to be made, whereas dividends can be skipped. Since the market understands these incentives, the market value of a firm's stock generally drops when a new issue is announced.[15]

One solution to this informational problem is **convertible bonds**. These are bonds that may be converted into stock at the option of the investor at some predetermined price. If the company does poorly and the market price of the stock falls, the investor need not convert and will continue to receive interest payments. If the company does well and the market price of the stock rises, the investor converts at the predetermined price, which is now below the market price. For a company that expects to do well, this is a way of selling stock (indirectly—the bonds will become stock after conversion) without sending the market a bad signal and depressing the current value of its stock. Convertible bonds have become an increasingly popular way for corporations to raise new equity.

convertible bonds
Bonds that may be converted into stock at the option of the investor at a predetermined price.

---

[15]This is the reason that shelf registration is much less popular for stocks than it is for bonds. The value of outstanding stock falls immediately when a new issue is announced, whether the issue is actually sold immediately or "put on the shelf." For a shelf registration, this cost of a new issue is paid immediately, but the benefit—the funds raised—is received only later, when the stock is actually sold. So, if a firm is going to float a new issue, it makes more sense to go ahead and sell the stock immediately.

VENTURE CAPITAL

The difficulties of raising equity funds through the sale of stock are particularly severe for small start-up companies. In addition to all the informational problems, the fixed costs of an IPO loom large relative to the amounts needed. One increasingly popular solution to this problem, particularly for high-tech firms, is provided by **venture capital**. Venture capital is equity funding provided by specialized institutions that usually also demand some degree of control over the management of the firm.

venture capital
Equity funding by a specialized institution that usually demands some control over the firm in which it invests.

The amount of venture capital grew rapidly from about $5 billion in 1980 to over $30 billion in 1988. Venture capital is provided principally by over 800, mainly small, independent venture capital funds (typically managing $30 million to $40 million). These institutions raise funds mainly from pension funds, insurance companies, and nonprofit institutions. A smaller amount of venture capital is provided by subsidiaries of some large corporations, including banks and lifes. Venture capitalists expect to have their funds tied up for between three and ten years in a given investment. Investments are high-risk, although close monitoring helps. When they succeed, however, the returns can be spectacular.

THE SECONDARY MARKET: THE STOCK EXCHANGE

If you buy a bond, the principal is repaid when the bond matures. If you buy a stock, the issuing company need never repay you. You are entitled to a share in the company's dividends, but, unless the company is liquidated or the stock is bought back, there is no way to get your money back from the company. The only way to turn the stock back into cash is for you to sell it to somebody else. It is not surprising, then, that the secondary market for stocks is particularly well developed.

Stocks are traded on organized exchanges and over the counter (OTC) like government securities. Trading on the exchanges is conducted face-to-face, with a fair amount of shouting and waving of arms; trading on the OTC market is conducted through computers and over the telephone, with considerably less drama. The largest exchange by far is the New York Stock Exchange. Others include the American Stock Exchange (also in New York City) and five major regional exchanges—the Midwest, Pacific, Philadelphia-Baltimore-Washington, Boston, and Cincinnati exchanges.   Although the OTC market is growing, the exchanges still get most of the total trading volume and carry the stocks of the largest and best-known corporations.

The proportion of companies with publicly traded stocks is quite small. Of the over 1 million active corporations in the United States, the stocks of only 2,332 were listed on the New York Stock Exchange in 1985. A couple of thousand more were listed on the other exchanges, and some 30,000 companies were traded on the OTC market, about 4,000 of them regularly. However, these relatively few corporations make up a large part of the economy: Companies traded on the exchanges accounted for some 65% of all corporate assets in 1985.

The New York Stock Exchange is organized around a group of 54 broker-dealer firms called **specialists**. Each stock is carried by only a single specialist—hence the name—but each specialist typically carries more than one stock. The specialist organizes the market in each stock by matching buy and sell orders. In return for a monopoly in trading the stock, the specialist is expected to use his inventory to even out short-run discrepancies between buy and sell orders that might otherwise cause the price of the stock to fluctuate wildly. Nonetheless, being a monopoly does not seem to hurt profits: Specialists are reputed to earn an annual return on equity in excess of 50%.[16]

specialists
Broker-dealer firms that organize the market in specific stocks by matching buy and sell orders.

Suppose you want to buy 100 shares of IBM. You cannot approach a specialist directly. Instead, you must go to a stockbroker, who in turn will place your order with a specialist. It should be easy to find a broker: There are 5,300 brokerage firms registered with the SEC, having some 200,000 employees licensed to deal with the public. If you deal with a large firm, it will have its own representative on the floor of the exchange who can place your order with a specialist. A small firm will not have a representative of its own, relying instead on a "floor broker"—an independent trader on the floor of the exchange—to place your order.

The specialist system is increasingly coming under attack: Two government reports due in 1990 (one from the General Accounting Office, the other from the Office of Technology Assessment) are expected to be highly critical. They are expected to argue, in particular, that the specialist monopoly is standing in the way of technological progress in stock trading. The role of the specialists in the stock market crash of 1987 (on which more below) did not win them many friends.

The New York Stock Exchange faces increasing competition from other exchanges. A "second market" for many listed stocks exists on the London Stock Exchange, the Midwest Stock Exchange in Chicago, and other regional exchanges and is taking an increasing share of the business. The regional exchanges have been aggressive in introducing new trading technologies and in linking up with stock exchanges overseas. There is also a "third market" involving direct, off-exchange trading between institutions, mostly in the hours that the New York Stock Exchange is closed. This market is technologically advanced, matching trades on several computer systems, and is growing rapidly: It accounted for 3.2% of all trades in 1989.

The most dangerous competitor for the New York Stock Exchange, however, is the OTC (over the counter) market. Volume on the OTC market has grown rapidly, and is approaching that of the New York Stock Exchange itself. Much of the trading in the OTC market is conducted through a computer system called NASDAQ. Dealers in a particular stock (there may be several for each stock on the OTC market) list bid and ask prices on a computer screen, and a broker wishing to buy or sell can do so by hitting a button.

---

[16]*Fortune*, Feb. 1, 1988. Because specialists are mostly privately owned companies and are under no obligation to make financial statements available to the public, information on their profits is hard to come by.

READING
THE STOCK
MARKET LISTINGS

Shown below is a typical stock market listing from *The Wall Street Journal* (listings also appear in the business sections of other daily newspapers):

| 52 Weeks | | | | | Yld | | Vol | | | | Net |
Hi	Lo	Stock	Sym	Div	%	PE	100s	Hi	Lo	Close	Chg
$3\frac{1}{8}$	$\frac{1}{8}$	Equitec	EFG	..	...		13	$\frac{13}{32}$	$\frac{13}{32}$	$\frac{13}{32}$	...
$47\frac{1}{8}$	$32\frac{3}{8}$	EsselteBusn	ESB	.96	2.0	18	74	47	47	47	...
$14\frac{1}{4}$	$9\frac{7}{8}$	Esterline	ESL	...	...	11	21	$11\frac{1}{2}$	$11\frac{3}{8}$	$11\frac{1}{2}$	...
29	$22\frac{7}{8}$	EthylCp	EY	.60a	2.4	13	1913	$25\frac{5}{8}$	$25\frac{1}{4}$	$25\frac{5}{8}$	...
$16\frac{1}{2}$	$14\frac{5}{8}$	Excelsior	EIS	1.39e	8.8	...	4	16	$15\frac{7}{8}$	$15\frac{7}{8}$	$- \frac{1}{8}$
$51\frac{5}{8}$	$41\frac{1}{2}$	Exxon	XON	2.40	5.2	20	6285	$46\frac{5}{8}$	$46\frac{1}{4}$	$46\frac{1}{4}$	$- \frac{3}{8}$

Quotations as of 4:30 p.m. Eastern Time
Wednesday, March 28, 1990

Source: *The Wall Street Journal*, Mar. 29, 1990.

The price of a single share of stock is quoted in dollars and fractions of a dollar, down to one-eighth. The two columns before the company's name give high and low prices for the preceding year: For Exxon, these are $51⅝ and $41½. The column after the company's name gives the symbol for the company used in ticker-tape quotations: For Exxon it is XON. The next three columns give dividend information: For Exxon its most recent dividend was $2.40 per share, which was 5.2% of its current price, and which gave a price–earnings, or PE, ratio (current price divided by dividend) of 20. The next column gives trading volume—the number of shares traded that day: For Exxon it was 628,500 shares. The final four columns give trading information for the day: The daily high for Exxon was $46 ⅝, and the daily low was, $46 ¼; the closing trade was at $46 ¼; and the closing price was down ⅜ from the previous close.

MERGERS, ACQUISITIONS, AND LBOs

In recent years much of the action in equity markets has revolved around *mergers and acquisitions,* which include the leveraged buyouts we discussed above, as well as takeovers of one company by another. Two of the biggest takeovers were the purchase of Standard Oil by British Petroleum for $8 billion and the purchase of Unilever by Cheesebrough-Pond for $3 billion, both in 1987. The wave of banking mergers we discussed in Chapter 8 also falls into this category. Mergers and acquisitions generate substantial fee income for the investment banks that put the deals together. For example, Goldman Sachs made $8 million and First Boston made $10 million from the British Petroleum deal.[17]

Why this recent wave of mergers and acquisitions? One factor has been deregulation, not just in banking, but in other areas too—air travel, for example.

---

[17]Fees are often paid even if the deal does not go through. After the UAL leveraged buyout collapsed because of trouble in the junk bond market, some $50 million in fees still had to be paid to banks, investment banks, and lawyers (Lazard Frères alone received $8.25 million).

This deregulation and a more relaxed attitude by the Justice Department toward antitrust enforcement have allowed mergers and takeovers that are aimed at exploiting economies of scale and of scope in many industries.

Another reason often given for takeovers is "managerial slack." Although managers are supposed to run a company to maximize returns to its owners, it is not surprising that they often put their own interests first. For example, they may spend excessive amounts to improve their own comfort and prestige (corporate jets, country club memberships, and the like). They may purchase other companies to expand their empires, even when the return to stockholders is small or negative. They may sit on large amounts of cash, rather than investing it or paying it out as dividends, in order to increase their liquidity and security. In principle, stockholders have control over their managers through their ability to appoint or fire directors. In practice, when ownership of the stock is spread over thousands or even millions of individuals and institutions, it is hard to exert any discipline.

For example, suppose that you, a legendary corporate raider, want to buy Megacorp, which you believe is being mismanaged. The market value of its stock is currently $10 billion. You believe that if you could take it over and reorganize its management, the company's real value would be more like $15 billion. To make sure you get enough stock to be able to exert control, you need to offer $12 billion for it. A minor difficulty: You have nothing like that amount of money. The solution? Borrow the money. An investment bank will help you raise the $12 billion (for a fee, of course), largely in the form of bank loans. Once you buy Megacorp, you simply have it issue bonds to pay off the money you borrowed. Because this new debt raises Megacorp's debt–equity ratio to astronomic levels, the new bonds are issued as junk bonds, and whatever existing bonds Megacorp has outstanding *become* junk. You have just carried out a leveraged buyout.

The financing, on February 9, 1989, of the biggest LBO of all is described in "RJR Finale Will Send Money Coursing" on page 382. Kohlberg Kravis Roberts found $18.9 billion to buy up 74% of RJR Nabisco's stock. Most of the $5 billion in short-term notes used in the deal were paid off in May 1989 with a $4 billion issue of junk bonds—the largest bond issue of *any* kind ever.[18] Investment banks have earned a fortune in fees from putting together such deals: The fees for RJR Nabisco came to over $600 million.

Increasingly, investment banks are putting up their own money to retain part ownership of the bought-out company—an activity known as **merchant banking**. Examples include Prudential-Bache's purchase of 49% of Dr Pepper/Seven-Up, Morgan Stanley's purchase of 40% of Burlington Industries (America's largest textile company), and Merrill Lynch's purchase of Borg Warner and Supermarkets General. Rewards can be substantial if the company does well. As part of one buyout, Morgan Stanley acquired a 25% equity interest for $7 million, then resold it later for $315 million. Of course, the risks are substantial too.

merchant banking
Use of an investment bank's own money to retain part ownership of a bought-out company.

---

[18]As a result of the collapse of the junk bond market, in February 1990, Moody's downgraded its ratings of these RJR Nabisco bonds, causing them to fall in value by 20% in two days.

RJR FINALE WILL SEND MONEY COURSING

By George Anders

Staff Reporter of The Wall Street Journal

NEW YORK—Starting at 8 a.m. today, bankers will gather at Manufacturers Hanover Corp. and three other New York banks to complete the biggest commercial financing in history.

It's the record $25 billion acquisition of RJR Nabisco Inc. by Kohlberg Kravis Roberts & Co. The bulk of that money is being collected today in a series of handoffs and passes that seems more appropriate to a razzle-dazzle football play than the world of high finance.

But if everything goes smoothly, Kohlberg Kravis by the end of the day will have collected $18.9 billion from its bankers, equity investors and Drexel Burnham Lambert Inc. That will let Kohlberg Kravis buy 74% of RJR's stock for $109 a share; the remainder of RJR's share will later be exchanged for new securities.

Sense of Scale

To give some sense of scale, the RJR transfer is six times as big as last year's eye-popping movement of $3 billion to settle Pennzoil Co.'s legal claims against Texaco Inc. Today's transfer is vast enough to cause a bulge in the U.S. money supply statistics, economists say. What's more, it will involve amounts so large that the Federal Reserve System's wire transfer mechanisms can't handle all the money at once; it will have to be broken into "smaller" pieces.

The Fed's interbank wire transfer system can't cope with amounts larger than $999 million. Most days that isn't a problem. But bankers today will be forced to break up some of the big RJR transfers into batches of, say, a mere $900 million or so, repeated as often as necessary.

About the only calamity that could disrupt today's plans would be a power failure in New York City, says Robert Woods, a senior Citibank executive. But Mr. Woods says there's even a contingency plan for a blackout. People would simply use printed Federal Reserve checks instead of wire transfers, and have the checks hand-delivered at each stage of the transactions.

So here's how all the money for RJR is coming together:

The smallest part of the financing, $2 billion, is also the simplest. That money is coming from Kohlberg Kravis's equity investors and will represent ownership in RJR after the deal is completed. The $2 billion was deposited in a Kohlberg Kravis bank account last Friday and will simply be moved to the central RJR account today.

But there's more excitement involved with the $11.9 billion of bank loans. That's the core of the financing, and it's coming from 45 U.S., Japanese, European and Canadian banks. Yesterday, all that money was being transferred to the four U.S. banks that are leading the loan syndicate: Manufacturers Hanover Trust Co., Bankers Trust, Citibank and Chase Manhattan Bank.

This morning, Bankers Trust, Citibank and Chase will start lobbing those funds into a Kohlberg Kravis escrow account at Manufacturers Hanover. To make it easier to keep track of which bank is sending how much, Citibank's transfers will be in $800 million chunks. Bankers Trust will use $950 million pieces, and Chase will use $900 million amounts.

Any leftovers will be dealt with in separate checks for what bankers are quaintly calling the "clean-up amount."

Meanwhile, Drexel Burnham, which has raised $5 billion for Kohlberg Kravis by selling notes to other investors, will start sending its money along, too. These funds are likely to come in the form of checks drawn on the New York Fed.

Kohlberg Kravis officials hope to have all the $18.9 billion gathered by 9:30 a.m. But they won't be able to play hooky for the rest of the day. Because of delays in paying off RJR shareholders, Kohlberg Kravis wants to reinvest all that money before nightfall, so it can earn interest before the money actually needs to be paid out to RJR shareholders. At current short-term interest rates of 9%, the return on $18.9 billion amounts to $4.7 million a day. Even to buy-out giant Kohlberg Kravis, that's nothing to sneeze at.

So Kohlberg Kravis is expected to spread its $18.9 billion among 70 or so different short-term investments, such as commercial paper and certificates of deposit, starting this afternoon.

It will take a little more than a week for Manufacturers Hanover to sort out all the shares. Kohlberg Kravis expects to pay shareholders February 21.

Source: George Anders, "RJR Finale Will Send Money Coursing," *The Wall Street Journal*, February 9, 1989, pp. C1, C18. Reprinted by permission of The Wall Street Journal, © Dow Jones & Company, Inc. 1989. All Rights Reserved Worldwide.

The collapse of the junk bond market has slowed considerably the number of new takeovers announced in 1989 and 1990 relative to 1988. There has also been a tendency to rely exclusively on bank finance rather than on bond issues. For example, Bankers Trust played the central role in the 1989 LBO of NWA, the parent of Northwest Airlines, valued at $3.65 billion. Bankers Trust provided advice, equity, and loans—the latter syndicated, many to Japanese banks.

INCREASING LEVERAGE:
IS IT A CAUSE FOR CONCERN?

Since most of the acquisitions, like the LBOs, have been financed largely with debt, the result has been the removal of a large amount of existing stock from the market and its replacement with debt. In addition, many companies have issued debt to buy back part of their own stock. In all, something like one-sixth of the stock outstanding in 1980 has been removed from the market. The result has been a sharp increase in corporate leverage—in the ratio of debt to equity. See Exhibit 14.14.

Considerable concern has been expressed about this trend. As we saw in Chapter 5, higher leverage means higher risk. The greater the reliance on debt, the higher the proportion of the company's prospective cash flow that must be committed to interest payments. If the company gets into trouble, say, as the result of a recession, and its cash flow shrinks, it may be unable to meet its payments and it may be forced into bankruptcy.

This concern may be exaggerated. Today's leverage, although it is higher than it has been in recent years, is not particularly high by historical standards. Leverage today is comparable to what it was earlier in the century (see Exhibit 14.14): Rather than current leverage being unusually high, it would be more accurate to say that leverage in the years following World War II was unusually low. Moreover, as Exhibit 14.15 shows, leverage in the United States is low compared to that in Japan and Germany. There is an important difference, however, in the nature of the debt. German and Japanese firms rely much more than U.S. (or British) firms on indirect borrowing from financial institutions rather than on direct borrowing through financial markets. As a result, these firms are much more closely monitored by lenders. If things go wrong, say, in a recession, it is much easier for them to renegotiate and to receive support instead of being forced into bankruptcy as would be the case with U.S. firms relying on more arm's-length direct financing.

Why the trend toward increasing leverage in the United States? One reason is a strong tax incentive for corporations to finance their investments with debt rather than with equity: Interest payments to bondholders are tax-deductible, whereas dividend payments to stockholders are not. That means that by increasing its leverage, a corporation reduces its tax bill so that it has more income in total to pay out. For example, consider a firm with an annual income of $5 million that is all equity-financed and that pays $1 million in tax (at a 20% rate). The after-tax income left for the owners is $4 million. Suppose that the firm

EXHIBIT 14.14

RATIO OF LIABILITIES
TO REPLACEMENT
VALUE ASSETS,
NONFINANCIAL
CORPORATE
BUSINESS

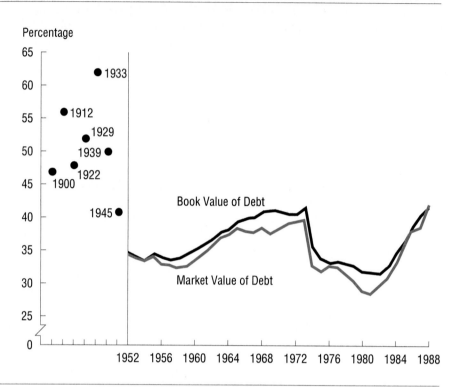

Source: Materials from Goldsmith, Lipsey, and Mendelson 1963; Board of Governors of the
Federal Reserve System, *Balance Sheets for the U.S. Economy, 1949-88*, as presented in Richard W.
Kopcke, "The Roles of Debt and Equity in Financing Corporate Investments," *New England
Economic Review*, July–August 1989, 27. Reprinted with permission.

replaces a part of its equity with debt (it sells bonds and uses the proceeds to buy
back some of its stock) and therefore now has to pay $2 million a year in interest.
Because the interest is deductible, the firm now pays only $600,000 in taxes—0.2
x ($5 million – $2 million)—leaving it with an after-tax income of $5 million –
$600,000 = $4,400,000. Thus the reduction in its tax bill leaves the firm with
$400,000 more income than it had before. This tax incentive for debt has always
been there, but it was strengthened somewhat by the 1986 tax reform.

THE GLOBAL MARKET FOR EQUITIES

The market for equities, like the markets for long-term and short-term debt, has
become increasingly international in recent years. A number of countries, most
notably Great Britain and Japan, have removed restrictions that used to prevent
their residents from buying foreign securities. Financial institutions in those

Country	1966–1973	1974–1979	1980–1985	1986
United States	.35	.49	.46	.46
Japan	.75	.77	.72	.63
West Germany	.70	.77	.78	.79
France	.54	.58	.59	.56
United Kingdom	.40	.58	.48	.42
Canada	.50	.55	.54	.57

EXHIBIT 14.15

INTERNATIONAL DEBT-TO-ASSETS RATIOS FOR NONFINANCIAL CORPORATE BUSINESS: SELECTED COUNTRIES, 1966–1986

Note: Data at market valuation except for France and Canada, where data are shown at book value.
Source: Material from Bank for International Settlements, *Fifty-Sixth Annual Report,* 1986; OECD, *Financial Statistics,* as presented in Richard W. Kopcke, "The Roles of Debt and Equity in Financing Corporate Investments," *New England Economic Review,* July–August 1989, 29. Reprinted with permission.

countries, particularly pension funds and lifes, have grabbed the opportunity and bought large amounts of foreign stocks to diversify their portfolios. Foreign stocks have also become increasingly popular with U.S. investors. The volume of cross-border stock purchases has grown rapidly (see Exhibit 14.16). By 1988 these cross-border transactions accounted for over 11% of all trading on domestic stock exchanges. There is also a small but growing market in **Euroequities** and in equity-related Eurobonds (convertibles and others).

Euroequities
Equities issued by firms in a country other than their own.

To cash in on this increasing globalization of capital markets, an increasing number of U.S. and foreign commercial and investment banks now have a presence in all the major financial centers. Citicorp and Merrill Lynch, Nomura and Daiwa of Japan, Midland Bank and National Westminster of England, Deutsche Bank of Germany—all of these are active in the stock and bond markets in London, New York, and Tokyo. There has also been a trend toward cooperative agreements between institutions in different countries to allow the expertise of one to be applied in the market of the other: For example, Salomon Brothers announced an agreement with Italy's second largest bank, San Paolo di Torino, to cooperate in the U.S. and Italian securities market, and Chase Manhattan announced plans to form a venture capital fund with Gemina S.p.A., a Milan firm.

WHO HOLDS AND TRADES STOCKS?

There have been some interesting changes in stock ownership. Although households remain the largest owners of stocks, they have, since World War II, steadily been reducing their holdings: Today they own some 55% of stocks outstanding, as opposed to 80% in 1971. Their place in the market has increasingly been taken by financial institutions—particularly pension funds and equity mutual

E X H I B I T **14.16**

GROSS PURCHASES
AND SALES OF
DOMESTIC STOCKS
BY NONRESIDENTS

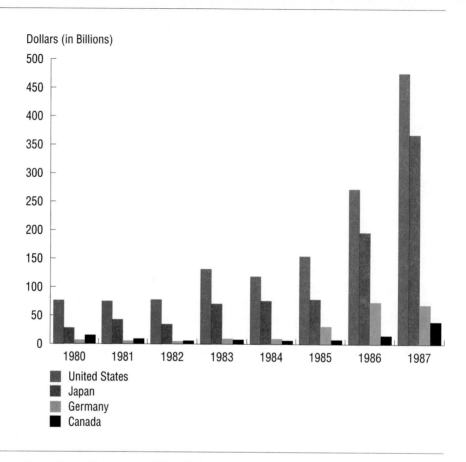

Source: Federal Reserve Bank of New York, *Quarterly Review.*

funds.[19] Lifes, which traditionally preferred bonds, have also been increasing their holdings of equities.

Institutional portfolios are enormous—amounting to about $1.5 trillion in 1984, of which about two-thirds was in pension funds. There has been tremendous competition among lifes, commercial banks, and investment banks for the fees to be earned from managing these portfolios. In 1984 those fees amounted to some $11 billion.

The way to get more money to manage is to show high returns on the money you manage already. The pressure to show success has driven money managers to engage in a tremendous amount of trading. In 1983 pension funds sold over 60% of the stocks they owned to replace them with other stocks, whereas 10 years

[19]Household ownership is very concentrated: In 1971, 80% of all stock held by households was held by just 1% of the population.

before it had been normal to "churn" no more than 20% of a portfolio in this way.[20]

Transactions costs are not much of an obstacle to this churning, because trading is much cheaper for pension funds than it is for individuals. Because they are tax-exempt, pension funds pay no taxes on realized capital gains. Also, most of their trading involves "block trades"—direct sales of large blocks of stock between institutions—that avoid the payment of commissions to brokers.

Trading by institutions now dominates the market. Recent estimates suggest that institutional investors now account for more than 80% of total volume. It has been suggested that this domination of the market by institutional investors, desperately trying to show good short-term results, has added to the volatility of stock prices in recent years.

DERIVATIVE SECURITIES AND PROGRAM TRADING

Another factor that has contributed to the volume of institutional trading and perhaps to an increase in stock price volatility is the creation and trading of new **derivative securities**—futures and options in stocks and in stock indexes (they are called *derivative* securities because they are "derived" from other securities). These futures and options are much like the T-bill futures and options we studied in Chapter 13, except that the underlying "commodity" is a stock or a stock index rather than a Treasury security.

derivative securities
Futures and options in stocks and stock indexes.

For example, a put option on IBM at 150 gives the buyer the right to sell a certain number of IBM shares at $150 per share until a specified date. An index futures contract is a little more complicated. Rather than being based on a single stock, it is based on a stock index—for example, the Standard & Poor's (S&P) 500. The S&P 500 is a broad index of stock prices calculated by taking a weighted average of the prices of the 500 most important stocks (most of them are traded on the New York Stock Exchange), the weights being the total values outstanding of each stock. One S&P 500 futures contract obliges the buyer to pay the agreed futures price in exchange for $500 times the Standard & Poor's 500 Index on the date of maturity. For example, if you have bought one S&P 500 contract at a price of 320, and the S&P 500 Index turns out to be 330 when the contract matures, your gain will be $500 \times (330 - 320) = $5,000.[21]

Just like the derivative securities we studied in Chapter 13, these futures and options can be used both for hedging and for speculation. One particular kind of hedging is called **dynamic hedging** or **portfolio insurance**. We saw in Chapter 13 that options can be used to reduce downside risk while leaving an opportunity for upside appreciation. Hedging a portfolio with options can be replicated by selling futures to cover *part* of the portfolio. If you sell futures to cover all of the portfolio, it is as if you have sold the stocks for the futures price: You cannot lose

dynamic hedging (portfolio insurance)
Hedging a stock portfolio by trading in index futures.

---

[20]There is evidence that turnover rates have fallen in recent years.

[21]Index futures are always closed by offset (see Chapter 13): There is never actual delivery.

if stocks go down—your gain on the futures contract will exactly offset your loss on the stock—but you cannot gain if the stock goes up. A partial hedge, on the other hand, gives you partial protection: You will gain a little or lose a little as the stock goes up or down. If you can *increase* the fraction of the portfolio hedged as stock prices fall and *decrease* it as they rise, you can guarantee yourself a floor and still leave open the possibility of a gain on the upside. This sort of hedging provides the same type of protection as do put options, but at much lower transactions costs.

The key to successful dynamic hedging is always being able to adjust your position rapidly as stock prices change. Today such rapid adjustment is possible through the use of computers. Computers track stock prices and automatically generate the required orders to buy and sell. This use of computers to control trading is called **program trading**. Program trading is essential to dynamic hedging.

program trading
Use of computers to track and control equities trading.

Program trading is also essential for another activity known as **index arbitrage**. A situation will sometimes occur in which you can buy a portfolio of the actual stocks used to make up the S&P 500 Index at a price slightly above or below the price of the index futures. This creates an arbitrage possibility. Suppose, for example, that the stocks are selling for $1 million, the futures index for delivery a year from now is trading at $1.1 million, and the interest rate on one-year Treasuries is 9%. You can buy the stocks now and sell index futures. When the contract expires, you sell the stocks to cover the contract. Whatever the price of the stocks at the time, you receive $1.1 million. The return on your $1 million investment is a risk-free 10%—better than the risk-free 9% you could have earned on Treasuries. Vigilant computers identify such arbitrage possibilities as soon as they occur. They then automatically generate the appropriate buy and sell orders for both stock and futures exchanges.

index arbitrage
Simultaneous trading in index futures and in the underlying stocks to exploit price differences.

Program trading can generate massive trading volume and move prices sharply. This is particularly likely to happen on days that futures contracts expire, when the positions generated by arbitrage plays are "unwound." Every three months, stock index options, stock index futures, and options on individual stocks all expire at the same time. These so-called "triple witching hours" often herald large swings in stock prices.

Program trading, in its various forms, has been highly controversial. Opponents have blamed it for increasing the volatility of stock prices and for being a major factor in the stock market crash of 1987 (on which more below). They argue that this increased volatility has scared away small investors, and this has reduced market liquidity, adding further to the volatility. However, most studies have found little evidence that volatility has in fact increased in recent years or that program trading has increased it. However, although overall volatility does not seem to have increased, there does seem to have been an increase in the frequency of large one-day price movements.

Much of the opposition to program trading has come from the New York Stock Exchange. There is resentment there of the increasing role of the Chicago futures exchanges in the equity market and of the resultant loss of business. Instead of buying and selling actual stocks on the stock exchange, customers can adjust their positions more cheaply by buying and selling futures and options. Moreover, specialist market-makers are vulnerable to losses from the large one-day movements in prices that seem to be associated with program trading. The pressure the stock exchange has exerted on brokers to refrain from program trading has driven many of them to move their trading to London and to the "third market." Trying to lure back this business, and in the spirit of "if you can't beat them, join them," the New York Stock Exchange recently initiated trading in Exchange Stock Portfolios (ESPs): These allow the simultaneous buying or selling of all the S&P 500 stocks, actually making program trading easier to execute.

THE CRASH OF 1987

In the 1980s the stock market enjoyed a long period of steadily rising prices (a "bull market"). The Dow-Jones Industrials Index, the most widely quoted index of stock prices, rose from 1,000 points in 1982 to 1,500 in 1985 and then accelerated to over 2,500 in October 1987.

In the week of October 12–16 the market faltered. The Dow-Jones fell steadily from 2,500 on Monday to 2,250 on Friday, as daily volume rose from a normal 150 million shares a day to over 300 million. There was widespread concern that weekend over what Monday might bring.

The market fell sharply on Monday morning. Alan Greenspan, the chairman of the Federal Reserve Board, was on a flight to Texas during most of the afternoon. When he landed, he immediately asked about the market. "It's down five-o-eight," he was told. He breathed a sigh of relief, believing that the market was down only 5.08 points for the day. His relief was short-lived: The market had actually fallen 508 points. This 22.5% decline in a single day (on a volume of over 600 million shares) far exceeded the previous record—the 12.8% decline on October 28, 1929, that had ushered in the Great Depression.

There was considerable concern that there would be a repeat of the general collapse that had followed the crash of 1929, and some economic forecasters predicted a severe recession for 1988. However, no recession materialized, and there was remarkably little impact on the economy. One implication is that the Great Depression itself may have been less a result of the stock market crash than of faulty economic policy in the years that followed. We shall have more to say about this in later chapters.

The crash of 1987 did, however, have a major impact on the capital market itself. Investors lost much of their enthusiasm for stocks, as can be seen by the drop in mutual fund sales (exclusive of money market mutual funds) from $172 billion in 1987 to $78 billion in 1988. The consequent reduction in trading volume has had a severe impact on the earnings of Wall Street firms and has resulted in the layoff of some 45,000 employees. The industry remains in something of a slump.

A presidential task force was appointed to look into the causes of the crash. Contrary to much popular sentiment, it did not place the blame on portfolio insurance, program trading, or index arbitrage. Rather it found that the market, particularly the specialist system of trading, had simply fallen apart under the massive volume of trading. Specialist market-makers lacked the capital to absorb the large excess of sell orders. Some of them had panicked, and instead of buying to stabilize the market in the face of falling prices, they had dumped their own inventories, adding to the downward pressure.

The task force's main recommendations were a number of technical changes in trading mechanisms, designed to ensure orderly trading if similar circumstances were ever to recur. One of these changes was the introduction of "circuit breakers." This meant that if prices fell by some prespecified amount, trading would be halted temporarily to give traders time to assess new information; they would place more buy orders to snap up bargains and this would slow the fall. The New York Stock Exchange also raised the minimum equity requirement for specialists from $100,000 (a ridiculously small sum) to $1 million (still small). It also raised the minimum share inventory that specialists must be able to maintain from 5,000 to 15,000.

A minicrash occurred on Friday, October 13, 1989, with the market dropping 190 points. Circuit breakers halted trading on the futures and options exchanges in Chicago but not on the New York Stock Exchange. There was considerable confusion as large gaps developed between prices on the two sets of markets. This confusion probably contributed to the fall in stock prices. One lesson of the 1989 episode is that if circuit breakers are to help stability, they must be coordinated across the different markets: If trading is halted on one market, it should also be halted on the others.

SUMMARY

- The capital market is the market for long-term borrowing and lending. The primary instruments of the capital market are stocks and bonds (equity and debt).

- The amount of new issues of bonds greatly exceeds the amount of new issues of stock. The amount of net funds raised in each market is significantly less than the amount of new issues, because of redemption of bonds and buying back of stocks. In recent years the net amount of funds raised through stock issues has actually been negative.

- Although firms fund most of their capital expenditure with internal funds, they need to supplement these with funds raised externally in the capital market. A principal reason for the reliance on internal funds is the information problem involved in external borrowing.

- Households are major borrowers, mainly for mortgage finance. Federal, state, and local governments also borrow in the long-term market.

- Households are the ultimate source of most lending in the capital market. This lending takes place either directly through the purchase of stocks and bonds or indirectly through financial intermediaries, such as life insurance companies, pension funds, and mutual funds.

- Life insurance used to be the main vehicle for retirement saving, but it has been overtaken in recent years by pension funds. Both defined-benefit and defined-contribution pension funds have grown enormously in recent years. Competition to manage this vast pool of funds has been intense. Stock and bond mutual funds have also grown rapidly in recent years.

- Because their liabilities are long-term, lifes and pension funds match maturities by investing in long-term securities.

- Corporate debt may be secured (if backed by a particular piece of property) or unsecured (if backed by the general earning power of the firm), and it may be sold privately (private placement) or to the general public (a public issue).

- In a private placement, stocks or bonds are sold directly to specific financial institutions. In a public offering, stocks or bonds are sold to the general public at large.

- New issues are handled by underwriters, who buy the whole issue at an agreed-upon price and hold it until it can be sold to the public. Despite increasing risk, fees for underwriting have decreased because of increased competition.

- The secondary market for corporate bonds is mostly over the counter, although a few issues are traded on exchanges.

- Junk bonds are bonds that have a relatively high risk of default and consequently a high yield. The junk bond market grew significantly in the 1980s, but it ran into serious trouble at the end of the decade.

- Eurobonds are bonds denominated in currencies other than that of the country in which they are issued (for example, U.S. dollar bonds sold in London). The Eurobond market has grown to rival the U.S. domestic bond market in size. Its main attraction, like that of the Eurocurrency banking market, is its lack of regulation.

- Municipal bonds, known as munis, are issued by government units below the federal level (that is, by states, counties, cities, etc.). They are generally exempt from federal taxes. Changes in the tax law have caused a slump in this market.

- Venture capital has become an important source of equity funding for small and medium-sized firms.

- Stocks are sold both on organized exchanges—the largest is the New York Stock Exchange—and over the counter. Trading on the New York Stock Exchange is organized around specialists who make the market in different stocks.

- Much of the recent activity in the stock market has been related to a wave of mergers and acquisitions. These have been prompted by deregulation and by the lax management of some large corporations.

- Concern has been expressed about the increased leverage that has resulted from mergers and acquisitions, from stock buybacks, and from an increased reliance on debt in general. However, leverage does not seem high by historical standards or when compared to leverage in other countries.

- The market for equities has become increasingly globalized as investors have diversified across national boundaries.

- Direct stock ownership by households has fallen steadily, and indirect ownership through institutions has increased. Institutional trading has come to dominate the markets.

- Derivative securities (futures and options) have become popular in recent years, particularly with institutions, as instruments for hedging, speculation, and arbitrage. Program trading plays an important role in their use for portfolio insurance and for index arbitrage.

- The stock market crash of October 1987, although dramatic, did not signal a repeat of the Great Depression, as had been feared. Investigators have found that program trading and derivative securities did not play a major role, and that the main problem was a breakdown in the trading mechanism.

KEY TERMS

capital market	lease	revenue bonds
life insurance	private placement	initial public offering
property/casualty insurance	Rule 144a	convertible bonds
lifes	public issue	venture capital
term life policy	debenture	specialists
whole life policy	underwriter	merchant banking
policy loan	Rule 415	Euroequities
ERISA	shelf registration	derivative securities
defined benefit plan	investment-grade bonds	dynamic hedging (portfolio insurance)
defined contribution plan	junk (high-yield) bonds	
unsecured debt	leveraged buyout (LBO)	program trading
secured debt	Eurobonds	index arbitrage
commercial mortgage	municipal bonds (munis)	
mortgage bond	general obligation bonds	

DISCUSSION QUESTIONS

1. Summarize the parallels between short-term and long-term markets.
2. What role do banks play in the capital market?
3. What type of investor would be most interested in munis and why?
4. Why do issuers of stocks and bonds use underwriters?

5. What are the relative advantages of internal versus external finance? Of debt versus equity?

6. How has the relative importance of direct and indirect lending changed in the long-term market and why?

7. What were the reasons for (a) the rise of the junk bond market, and (b) its current crisis? Is some regulation needed?

8. What were the original reasons for the growth of the Eurobond market? Why does it continue to thrive?

9. What are the different ways that a firm can increase its equity capital? What are their relative merits?

10. How does the secondary market for stocks differ from the secondary market for bonds? What are the problems in the secondary market for stocks? What do you think needs to be done about them?

BIBLIOGRAPHY

American Council of Life Insurance, *Life Insurance Fact Book*, Washington, D.C. (annual).

American Council of Life Insurance, *Pension Facts*, Washington, D.C. (annual).

Bernanke, Ben, "Is There Too Much Corporate Debt?" *Business Review of the Federal Reserve Bank of Philadelphia* September/October 1989, 3–.

Henderson, Yolanda K., "The Emergence of the Venture Capital Industry," *New England Economic Review* July-August 1989, 64–79.

Investment Company Institute, *Mutual Fund Fact Book*, Washington, D.C. (annual).

Kopcke, Richard W., "The Roles of Debt and Equity in Financing Corporate Investments," *New England Economic Review* July-August 1989, 25–48.

Wall, Larry D., "Leverage Ratios of U.S. Nonfinancial Corporations," *Economic Review of the Federal Reserve Bank of Atlanta* May-June 1988, 12–29.

Warshawsky, Mark J., "Pension Plans: Funding, Assets, and Regulatory Environment," *Federal Reserve Bulletin* November 1988, 717–730.

CHAPTER 15

THE MORTGAGE MARKET

When you buy a home, it will probably be the largest purchase of your life. To pay for it, you will have to take out a loan. Because of the large amount involved, you will need a long time to pay it back—25 or 30 years is typical. The loan will be secured by the property you buy: If you fail to make your payments, the lender may sell the property to recover the debt. This type of loan is called a **mortgage**.

The market for mortgage lending is of particular interest. First, it is enormous. As you can see from Exhibit 15.1, it accounts for a large fraction of all long-term lending. Second, it has been plagued by a number of serious problems, and attempts to deal with these problems have led to several ingenious financial innovations. In this chapter we shall explore the mortgage market and the innovations to which it has given rise.

mortgage
Long-term loan secured by real estate.

15.1 WHAT IS A MORTGAGE?

To understand the mortgage market, we need first to understand the nature of the mortgage instrument.

CALCULATING THE PAYMENTS

In many parts of the country, the average home costs five or more times the annual income of the average homebuyer. Since the amount of the mortgage is so large relative to the borrower's income, it makes sense for the principal to be paid off slowly in small installments over the life of the loan, rather than all at once at the end. The standard **fixed-rate mortgage** is therefore an amortized loan, structured to keep monthly payments the same throughout the life of the mortgage. Initially, most of the payment consists of interest on the amount outstanding,

fixed-rate mortgage
Mortgage that is amortized by fixed monthly payments over the life of the loan.

395

EXHIBIT 15.1

LONG-TERM DEBT
OUTSTANDING:
DECEMBER 1988

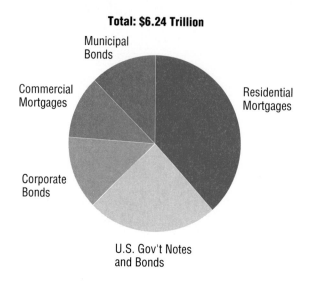

Total: $6.24 Trillion

Source: *Federal Reserve Bulletin.*

with relatively little repayment of principal. Then, as the loan is paid off, the interest part of the payment slowly declines and the repayment of principal speeds up.

To see how it works, suppose you take out a 30-year mortgage for $100,000 with a 12% APR from Gotham Savings and Loan. Since the compounding period is one month, the interest rate for the compounding period is $12\% \div 12 = 1\%$. The effective annual rate is 12.68%:

$$(1.01)^{12} = 1.1268.$$

To calculate your monthly payment, we need to find a monthly annuity that has a present value of $100,000. That is, we need to find the value of C that satisfies

$$\$100,000 = \frac{C}{(1.01)} + \frac{C}{(1.01)^2} + \cdots + \frac{C}{(1.01)^{360}}.$$

The solution is $C = \$1,028.61.$[1]

Your monthly payments may be broken down into interest and principal repayment as shown in Exhibit 15.2.

---

[1]This can be found with a financial calculator or by dividing $100,000 by the appropriate annuity factor. See Chapter 6 for further explanation.

EXHIBIT 15.2

CALCULATION OF MORTGAGE PAYMENTS

Month t	Principal Owed at Beginning of Month	Interest Paid (1% of Principal) I_t	Principal Payment P_t	Total Payment $C = I_t + P_t$
1	$100,000.00	$1,000.00	$28.61	$1,028.61
2	99,971.39	999.71	28.90	1,028.61
3	99,942.49	999.42	29.19	1,028.61
⋮	⋮	⋮	⋮	⋮
360	1,018.43	10.18	1,018.43	1,028.61

At the beginning of the first month, the principal owed is the full $100,000. Interest on this at the monthly rate of 1% is $1,000. The remainder of the $1,028.61 payment, $28.61, is applied to repaying principal. This brings the remaining principal at the start of the second month to

$$\$100,000 - \$28.61 = \$99,971.39.$$

The interest on this at 1% is $999.71. The remainder of the payment,

$$\$1,028.61 - \$999.71 = \$28.90,$$

is again applied to repaying the principal. And so on. The changing share of interest and principal repayment over the life of the mortgage is illustrated in Exhibit 15.3.

Banks often charge a fee for arranging a mortgage. The fee commonly takes the form of **points**. For example, suppose Gotham charges you "2 points." This means that Gotham will deduct a 2% fee from the amount it lends you: Instead of receiving the full $100,000, you will receive only $98,000. The monthly payments, however, will still be calculated on the basis of the full $100,000.

points
Percentage of the face value of a mortgage charged by the lending bank as a fee.

Clearly, the points make the mortgage more expensive. A $100,000 mortgage with 2 points is really the same as a $98,000 mortgage *without points* at some higher interest rate. To find out what that rate is, solve for the monthly rate, i, that satisfies

$$\$98,000 = \frac{\$1,028.61}{(1+i)} + \frac{\$1,028.61}{(1+i)^2} + \cdots + \frac{\$1,028.61}{(1+i)^{360}}.$$

The solution is $i = 1.023\%$ (this may be calculated using a financial calculator). The effective annual interest rate is given by

$$(1.01023)^{12} = 1.1299,$$

and is therefore 12.99%. So, in this case, charging 2 points is equivalent to increasing the effective annual interest rate from 12.68% to 12.99%.

EXHIBIT 15.3

CASH FLOW OF A
$100,000, 30-YEAR
MORTGAGE
(ASSUMING A
YEARLY INTEREST
RATE OF 12.68%)

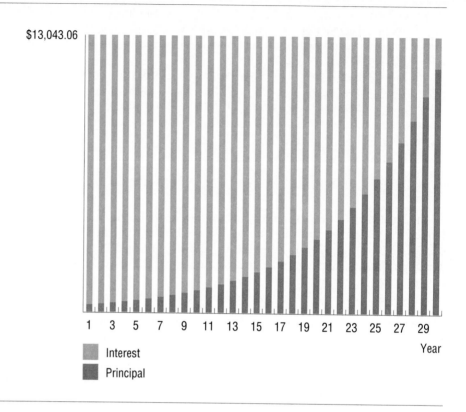

This calculation assumes that you pay the mortgage over the full 30 years. If you pay it off early, the deduction of points will raise the effective annual interest rate even more. For example, if you pay it off after 5 years, the effective annual interest rate becomes 13.93%. This makes the mortgage significantly more expensive if it is paid off early.

COLLATERALIZATION

When you take out your mortgage from Gotham to buy a house, the house becomes collateral for the loan. If you default, Gotham can foreclose and sell the house to recover the amount you still owe; anything left over from the sale goes to you. There is a lien on the property—a clause in the title document that prevents you from selling unless the mortgage loan is repaid.

To be on the safe side, and to make sure it gets all its money in case of default, Gotham would like the value of the house to be *greater* than the amount of the mortgage. As a result, the bank will lend you less than the full current value of the house. For example, if the house is worth $125,000, Gotham will expect you to pay, say, $25,000 yourself, and it will lend you the remaining $100,000. Then, if you default, it can be fairly sure that it will recover its money, even if the value of the house has fallen somewhat in the meantime or if it made an error in assessing its value.

Although Gotham can foreclose if you default, this is a last resort. Foreclosure is costly and the amount recovered from the sale of the house uncertain. Gotham would much rather you paid the mortgage as scheduled. To minimize the chance of default, Gotham will lend you no more than it thinks you can repay. Specifically, it will not lend you an amount for which the payments exceed some fraction, say, 25%, of your income.

For example, as we calculated above, the monthly payment on your mortgage is $1,028.61. Gotham will make the loan only if this is no more than 25% of your income or, equivalently, if your income is at least four times this amount—that is, about $4,100 a month, or $49,200 a year. If your income is less than this, you will not qualify for a mortgage of this size. Either you will have to come up with a larger down payment or you will have to find a less expensive house.

PREPAYMENT

You are unlikely to go on paying your mortgage for the full 30 years. For various reasons, most borrowers pay off their mortgages early. Paying off a mortgage early is called **prepayment.** You may have to sell the house if you are moving out of town, or you may want to buy a larger house. Most mortgages must be repaid if the house is sold: This is called a **due-on-sale provision.** Or you may want to repay the mortgage if you can replace it with another mortgage at a lower rate of interest. This is called *refinancing.*

Let us look at refinancing more closely. Suppose it is 5 years since you took out your mortgage and mortgage interest rates have fallen to an APR of 9.6%. Should you refinance by taking out a new mortgage to pay off the remaining principal on the old one? How much is the remaining principal? We can figure that out by taking the present value of the remaining payments, discounted at the monthly rate of the original mortgage (300 payments remain):

prepayment
Repayment of a loan before it matures.

due-on-sale provision
Mortgage contract stipulation that the mortgage must be repaid if the property is sold.

$$\frac{\$1,028.61}{(1.01)} + \frac{\$1,028.61}{(1.01)^2} + \cdots + \frac{\$1,028.61}{(1.01)^{300}} = \$97,662.97.$$

To pay off the old mortgage, you will have to take out a new one for this amount *plus* any fees. Suppose Gotham charges 3 points to refinance a mortgage. Then the total amount you will need to borrow is

$$\frac{\$97,662.97}{.97} = \$100,683.47.$$

The monthly interest rate is now 9.6% ÷ 12 = 0.8%. So the monthly payment on the new mortgage is the value of C that satisfies

$$\$100,683.47 = \frac{C}{(1.008)} + \frac{C}{(1.008)^2} + \cdots + \frac{C}{(1.008)^{300}}.$$

That C is \$886.68. Since refinancing saves you \$141.93 a month, it is well worth doing.[2]

We shall see that this option to refinance, which is obviously good for borrowers, represents a serious problem for lenders.

15.2 INFORMATIONAL PROBLEMS AND THE TRADITIONAL MORTGAGE MARKET

There are a number of things about the residential mortgage that make it a difficult type of loan from the point of view of the lender:

- The amount of the loan is small compared to the typical loan made to a firm.

- The information requirements—especially in relation to the sum involved—are large: the lender needs information about the borrower *and* about the property. How likely is the borrower to default? How much is the property actually worth? To assess the value of the property, the lender must know the local real estate market. A lender in New York, for example, cannot know directly the value of property in Nashville.

- The servicing of a mortgage loan can be costly in time and effort. The monthly payments must be collected and processed. Sometimes, when payments are late, the borrower needs to be reminded and perhaps cajoled. In case of default, the property must be repossessed and sold.

- Mortgages are very heterogeneous. Not only is the borrower and the collateral different in each case, but also the terms may vary. For example, one mortgage may have a prepayment penalty, and another may not. Or one may require the borrower to take out life insurance to pay off the mortgage if he dies, and another may not. The heterogeneity adds to the burden of investing in mortgages because it adds to the information costs.

All these qualities make a mortgage an unlikely prospect for direct lending. To see why, compare a mortgage to a typical direct security—a corporate debenture. The debenture is issued in large amounts; information costs are small relative to the amount borrowed and are largely paid by the borrower; terms are homogeneous (the terms of one debenture are much like the terms of another);

---

[2]Another way to see that refinancing is worthwhile is to look at the market value of the mortgage. At a monthly rate of 0.8%, the present value of the payments on the old mortgage is \$116,800.16. This is what the mortgage would be worth if it could be sold like a bond. So it costs you \$100,683.47 to pay off a debt with a market value of \$116,800.16: This is certainly worthwhile. The gain of \$116,800.16 - \$100,683.47 = \$16,116.69 is the present value of the payments you save.

the large amount of essentially interchangeable debentures supports a good secondary market, which makes debentures fairly liquid.

It is not surprising, then, that mortgage lending has traditionally been concentrated in the hands of financial intermediaries, particularly those specialized in mortgage lending—**savings banks** and **savings and loans (S&Ls)**. These two types of financial institution, generically called **thrifts,** were indeed first established in the early nineteenth century with the specific aim of taking in savings deposits from households and using the money to make residential mortgage loans. At that time commercial banks were not much interested in writing mortgages. Today commercial banks do make mortgage loans, but much residential mortgage lending is still in the hands of thrifts.

| 15.3 | THE PROBLEMS OF MORTGAGE FINANCE

The way that mortgage finance is organized—principally through thrift intermediaries—has been the cause of a number of serious problems. These include a susceptibility of the housing market to severe recession when interest rates rise, a fragmented mortgage market, and a dangerous susceptibility of thrifts to interest-rate risk.

MORTGAGE LENDING AND RECESSIONS

Mortgage lending has played a prominent role in postwar recessions. Under Regulation Q, the scenario used to run as follows. Market interest rates go up. Because thrifts cannot raise deposit rates to match market rates, households withdraw their money and buy T-bills (this outflow of funds is called *disintermediation*). Because of this outflow and of the lack of new funds coming in, thrifts stop writing new mortgages. Because mortgages are unavailable, people stop buying houses, and the housing industry goes into a slump. Construction firms and laid-off construction workers cut back their spending, and the slump spreads to the rest of the economy.

FRAGMENTATION OF THE MORTGAGE MARKET

The mortgage market has in the past been badly fragmented. Mortgage lending was concentrated in the hands of thrifts that raised funds locally to make mortgages locally. Deposit-taking was limited by branching restrictions that limited thrifts' geographic expansion. Furthermore, lending was restricted to a "normal lending territory" within a distance of 50 miles from the bank (the limit was later increased to 100 miles and finally abolished in 1980 by the DIDMCA). In areas where the housing market was booming, such as California, mortgage money was scarce and rates were high; in areas where the housing market was in a slump, such as Michigan, mortgages were plentiful and rates were low.

savings banks and savings and loans (S&Ls)
Financial institutions originally established to accept savings deposits and to make loans to households.

thrifts
Generic term for savings banks and savings and loans.

As we saw in Chapter 3, such fragmentation is economically inefficient. This inefficiency is exactly like the inefficiency that would arise if each area of the country, instead of buying its food from areas where food production is least expensive, decided to grow its own food locally. Bread would be cheap in South Dakota but dear in Maine. Less wheat would be grown in South Dakota, where costs are low, and more would be grown in Maine, where costs are high. For economic efficiency, we would like to see integrated markets and the same price everywhere. This is just as true for mortgages as it is for bread.

The fragmentation of the thrift industry also led to a lack of diversification. Although a thrift might have had thousands of mortgages outstanding, these were not independent risks. If the local economy soured, many borrowers would default simultaneously. On the other hand, the resulting specialization did have some advantages: Because loan officers got to know the local real estate market pretty well, they could make mortgage loans quickly and with few errors of judgment.

In other countries mortgage markets are much less fragmented. In Canada and Great Britain, for example, although most mortgage lending is handled by specialized thrifts much like our own, those thrifts, unlike ours, have branches all across the country. Thrifts in Canada and Great Britain are therefore able to move funds from low-demand areas to high-demand areas and to keep mortgage rates fairly uniform nationwide. In the United States this sort of integration is ruled out by the prohibition against interstate banking.

INTEREST-RATE RISK

Traditionally, thrifts borrowed by taking in time deposits and then lent the money out as mortgage loans: Almost all their assets were mortgages. Since the duration of the mortgages was significantly longer than that of their deposits, thrifts faced a substantial duration gap and were highly exposed to interest-rate risk.[3]

This interest-rate risk is made much worse by the way prepayment is affected by changes in interest rates. When interest rates go down, borrowers rush to refinance their mortgages at the lower rates; when interest rates go up, they avoid prepayment if they can (moving to a new house becomes less attractive when you have to give up a 7.5% mortgage on the old house and take out a 15% mortgage on the new one). From the point of view of the thrift, instead of making a capital gain on outstanding mortgages when interest rates fall, it finds many of them prepaid and is forced to reinvest the money at a lower interest rate. If interest rates

---

[3]Because the principal of a mortgage is repaid gradually over time, rather than all at once at the end, the duration of a mortgage is not as long as you might think from its maturity. For example, that 30-year mortgage at 12.68% that you took out has a duration of only 7.5 years—if it is not prepaid. Since the average mortgage is prepaid well before maturity, effective duration is reduced even further. For example, if only one in 20 outstanding mortgages is prepaid each year, the 7.5-year duration of a 30-year mortgage falls to under 6 years.

EXHIBIT 15.4

RETURN ON
MORTGAGES VERSUS
COST OF DEPOSIT

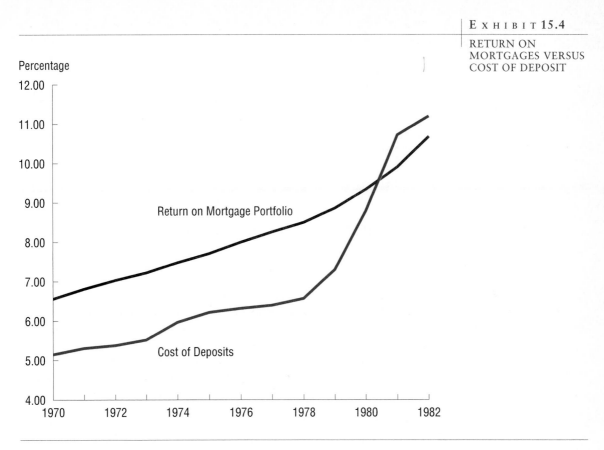

Source: Office of Thrift Supervision, *Savings and Home Financing Sourcebook*, 1988.

rise, fewer mortgages are prepaid, and the thrift is stuck with assets paying the old, lower rates.[4]

During the long postwar period of relatively stable market rates and even more stable deposit rates (because of Regulation Q), the thrifts' exposure to interest-rate risk was not an obvious problem. However, when interest rates rose sharply and began to fluctuate in the late 1970s, and Regulation Q was phased out in the early 1980s, the full danger of their position became horribly apparent.

Exhibit 15.4 shows how the cost of deposits rose steadily relative to the return on mortgages. The result was some staggering losses. The industry lost $6 billion in 1981 and $5 billion in 1982. The small profits for the industry as a whole in 1983–1986 masked continuing losses for about one-third of the thrifts. The number of savings and loans fell from 5,050 in 1980 to 4,100 in 1983, and then to 3,200 by 1986. The continuing crisis in the savings and loan industry,

---

[4]Due-on-sale provisions help the mortgage lender here, forcing prepayment when it is not in the borrower's interest to do so.

which we shall look at in Chapter 17, has its origins in these losses of the early 1980s.

15.4 SOME SOLUTIONS

The chronic problems of the mortgage market—cyclical sensitivity, fragmentation, and exposure to interest-rate risk—brought about a serious crisis in the early 1980s. The response to these problems, both by regulators and by private markets and institutions, has helped to some extent and has completely transformed the way the mortgage market operates.

THE DEMISE OF REGULATION Q

As we saw in Chapter 10, Regulation Q limits on interest rates were largely ineffective by the early 1980s and were abolished completely by 1986. Today thrifts can pay their depositors fully competitive rates on CDs and money market deposit accounts. They can even offer checking, something they could not do in the past, in the form of NOW accounts. There is now no longer any reason for depositors to pull their money out when market rates go up. This should prevent disintermediation and the associated cyclical problems of the housing industry.

However, as the recession of 1980–1982 showed, the problem has not gone away; it has merely changed its form. By 1980 thrifts had ways around Regulation Q that enabled them to pay competitive rates, so that when market rates went up, there was no disintermediation. But because the cost of funds was rising, thrifts raised the rates they charged on mortgages. At these higher rates, monthly payments were higher, pushing up the income required to qualify for a mortgage of a given size. Because fewer households qualified, there was a slowdown in borrowing to buy housing, and the rest of the story proceeded as before.

Under Regulation Q, mortgage rates did not go up much when market rates rose, because thrifts' cost of funds did not rise with market rates. Had you gone to Gotham Savings and Loan for a mortgage in those days, the good news would have been that mortgage rates were only 8%; the bad news would have been that no mortgages were actually available. Had you gone to Gotham after Regulation Q had been abolished, the good news would have been that mortgage money was available; the bad news would have been that the rate was 18%.

Exhibit 15.5 illustrates the different pattern in interest rates, but the same pattern in housing starts, in the recessions of 1973–1974 and 1980–1982. Before the late 1970s, in particular in the recession of 1973–1974, mortgage rates changed little with fluctuations in market rates (represented here by the 6-month T-bill rate). Housing starts fell dramatically in the recession of 1973–1974 because of a lack of availability of mortgage funds. In 1980–1982 there was no lack of availability, but, as you can see, mortgage rates rose sharply with market rates.

EXHIBIT 15.5

INTEREST RATES AND MORTGAGE LENDING

In 1966, 1969, and 1973, when market rates rose, mortgage rates rose little, but the poor availability of mortgages led to a slowdown in home building. In 1980 mortgage rates rose with market rates, and mortgages, although available, were expensive. The result again was a slowdown in home building.

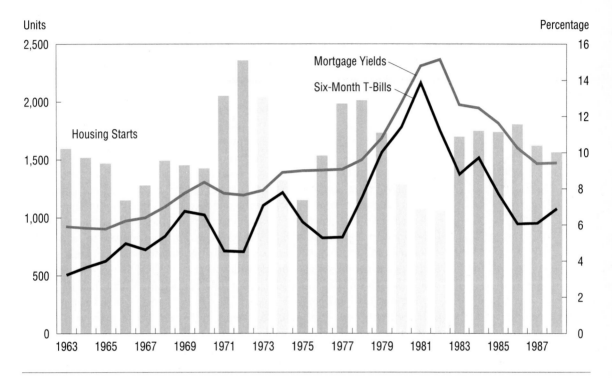

Source: *Economic Report of the President.*

It seems, then, not to matter much for borrowers whether mortgage money is unavailable or simply too expensive. So far as thrifts are concerned, however, it turns out to matter quite a lot. From their point of view, the abolition of Regulation Q has proven to be a disaster. Having to pay market rates on their deposits while being stuck with long-term fixed-rate mortgages has caused them enormous losses.

There does not seem to be much that can be done about the cyclical sensitivity. Whenever credit is tightened and interest rates rise, borrowing must be cut back by someone. Neither government nor business borrowing seems to be very sensitive to changes in interest rates. That leaves households. Most household borrowing is mortgage borrowing. So when credit is tightened, households are the ones that must borrow less, and, in particular, mortgage borrowing must fall. The mechanism that brings this about may change, as it did when Regulation Q was abolished, but the outcome must be the same.

DEREGULATION

One way to reduce the interest-rate risk faced by thrifts is to allow them to expand their range of assets and liabilities to include more than just the traditional mortgages and time deposits. This was the idea behind the thrift deregulation embodied in the DIDMCA of 1980 and the Garn-St. Germain Act of 1982.

For the first time thrifts were permitted to lend to firms as well as to households. They were allowed to buy commercial paper and corporate bonds, to write commercial mortgages, and to have up to 10% of their assets in the form of commercial loans to firms. In addition, their lending to households was broadened to include consumer loans other than mortgages.[5] Savings and loans were also allowed to invest up to 3% of their assets in subsidiaries called **service companies**. These service companies could sell their own debt and invest in a wide variety of activities, such as commercial lending and real estate development. In May 1983 regulators permitted federal S&Ls to invest up to 11% of their assets in junk bonds. In the same period many state regulators broadened the range of permitted assets even more: Some allowed considerable direct investment in real estate, corporate equities, and subsidiary service companies (California, for example, allowed unlimited investment in service companies).

service companies
Subsidiaries of thrifts that may engage in activities not allowed to thrifts.

There was also deregulation of the type of liabilities that thrifts could issue. In addition to their traditional time deposits, thrifts were allowed to offer NOW accounts and even regular demand deposits in the form of compensating balances for their commercial-loan customers.

Deregulation also extended to geographic restrictions. These started to break down in 1981, when Congress allowed failed savings and loans to be acquired by out-of-state thrifts. Then in 1982 Congress allowed the acquisition of failing thrifts by out-of-state commercial banks too.

The effect of these changes was to make thrifts less distinctive and more like commercial banks. Instead of being limited to illiquid long-term mortgages, they were allowed to invest in a range of assets that were shorter-term, like commercial loans, or more liquid, like corporate bonds. Instead of being limited to interest-rate-sensitive time deposits, they were allowed to take in less interest-rate-sensitive NOW accounts and regular checking accounts.[6]

Some thrifts took full advantage of these new opportunities (see "More Thrifts Grow Big by Investing in Areas Other Than Mortgages"). But with the new opportunities came new risks. Running a thrift used to be pretty straightforward: There was little credit risk in mortgage lending, and the interest-rate risk and liquidity risk were largely ignored. Deregulation helped to reduce the inter-

[5]Actually, mutual savings banks had had considerable freedom before 1980. The new regulations allowed this same freedom to savings and loans.

[6]When market interest rates rise, depositors are quick to shift money out of their time deposits and into, say, money market mutual funds. However, they are slower to shift money out of their checkable deposits, like NOW accounts. As a result, although banks must adjust the rates they offer on time deposits to match market rates, they can get away with little change in the rates they offer on checkable deposits.

MORE THRIFTS GROW BIG BY INVESTING IN AREAS OTHER THAN MORTGAGES

By David B. Hilder

Staff Reporter of The Wall Street Journal

OTTAWA, Kan.—This is a farming town of 11,000, where the tallest structure is the local co-op's grain elevator and Main Street has fewer than a dozen traffic lights.

It is also the home of Franklin Savings Association, one of the nation's fastest growing, most profitable and most sophisticated thrifts.

Some residents refer to Franklin's two-story white stucco and concrete headquarters as "that vulgar display of wealth." But then Franklin didn't grow to nearly $9 billion in assets from $300 million in 1982 by making mortgage loans to the people in its hometown. The thrift, which originated less than $10 million of local mortgages last year, put nearly $2 billion of new assets on its books in the first two months of 1987 by buying mortgage-backed securities from Wall Street dealers.

Franklin is one of a growing number of thrifts that are growing large quickly by making nontraditional investments like junk bonds, stocks, real estate, mortgage-backed securities and financial futures and options. New tax-law provisions are likely to accelerate the trend. The thrifts contend that such strategies offer bigger profits than traditional mortgage-making and that careful hedging techniques will help them survive periods of volatile interest rates like the one last month.

Return on Equity

At Columbia Savings, the annual return on average equity—an important measure of profitability—has ranged from 44% to 114% since 1982. At Franklin Savings, it has ranged from 62% to 98% since 1983. And at American Continental Corp., the parent of Lincoln Savings, it has ranged from 28% to 54% since the thrift was acquired in 1984. In contrast, the overall thrift industry's return on equity last year was less than 3%. And the average return of companies in the Standard & Poor's 500 index was stuck between 11% and 13% from 1982 to 1986.

One reason for the high return is that nontraditional savings and loans are taking advantage of the tremendous capital leverage that thrifts are allowed, which magnifies the effect of profits or losses. Until this year, thrifts generally had to maintain a capital-to-assets ratio of only 3%, compared with about 6% for commercial banks. (That means that if the owners of a new thrift put up $3 million of their own capital, the thrift could invest in $100 million of assets such as loans, securities or real estate. An annual profit of just 1% on that $100 million would mean a 33% return on the capital. On the other hand, a 1% loss would wipe out a third of the initial investment.)

One advantage of investing in mortgage-backed securities and junk bonds is relatively low overhead costs. At Franklin, for example, about half a dozen people handle the paperwork associated with more than 90% of the thrift's assets. Dozens of employees are needed to process the paperwork for the thrift's tiny mortgage loan portfolio and its retail deposit accounts.

est-rate risk and liquidity risk, but it increased the credit risk enormously. Thrifts were ill equipped to handle it. Commercial banks are specialists in assessing and bearing credit risk, but thrifts are not. So, given the new freedom, many thrifts managed to get themselves into serious trouble, as we shall see in Chapter 17. All of the thrifts mentioned in the accompanying article were in serious trouble by early 1990.

ADJUSTABLE-RATE MORTGAGES

adjustable-rate mortgage (ARM)
Mortgage on which the interest rate adjusts with market interest rates.

In Chapter 12 we saw that one way to reduce the interest-rate risk involved in using short-term funds to lend long-term is to lend at a floating rate. This essentially converts a long-term loan into a series of short-term loans, rolled over automatically but rolled over at the current rate of interest. The application of this idea to mortgage lending takes the form of the **adjustable-rate mortgage (ARM)**. With an ARM the interest rate payable on a mortgage is linked to some short-term market rate rather than being fixed for the life of the mortgage. ARMs come in a variety of forms, varying as to how often the rate is adjusted and as to which market rate the mortgage rate is pegged.

For example, let us convert your $100,000 fixed-rate mortgage from Gotham Savings and Loan into an adjustable-rate mortgage. You will be pleased to hear that your monthly payment will be less, at least initially. Because it is you who now bear the interest-rate risk rather than the bank, the bank will charge you a lower rate—say, an effective annual rate of 9.5% instead of 12.68%. Your monthly payment falls from $1,028.61 to $812.54.

Under the terms of your ARM, you will continue to pay this rate for one year. At the end of the year, the rate will be adjusted to 1% above the 6-month T-bill rate at that time. Suppose that rate is 10%. The rate on your mortgage will go up to 10% +1%=11%. The amount of principal remaining at the end of the first year will be $99,332.13, so at the new rate your monthly payment will go up to $903.13. This will continue for another year, and the rate will then be adjusted again.

This looks pretty good. Gotham has rid itself of the interest-rate risk: Mortgage payments coming in will go up whenever the rate it pays on deposits goes up. And you are still paying less, even though rates have gone up a little.

But what if interest rates go way up? Suppose the T-bill rate goes up to 18%, raising your mortgage rate to 18%+1%=19%. Your monthly payment will now be $1,459.82. And therein lies a problem—not only for you, but for Gotham too. If you could barely afford the original $812.54 a month, there is no way you can pay the $1,459.82. You are forced to default. Gotham sells the house to cover the loan, but it finds that housing prices are depressed because of high interest rates, and it must take a loss on the loan.

So shifting the interest-rate risk to the borrower may not be such a good idea. Just as we saw with floating-rate business loans, the reduction in interest-rate risk comes at the expense of an increase in credit risk. As we asked then, who is better able to deal with interest-rate risk, borrower or lender? Surely the lender has better information, more expertise, and more means at its disposal to hedge the risk. The borrower should be happy to pay a premium, in the form of a fixed rate higher than the average floating rate, to have the lender bear the risk.

To reduce the credit risk, many ARMs have a cap on how much the rate may be raised each time and a cap on how much it may be raised over the life of the mortgage. While such caps reduce credit risk, they also reduce the lender's protection against interest-rate risk. Other ARMs have a cap on the monthly payment. If this maximum monthly payment proves insufficient even to cover the interest due, then the remaining principal is *increased* by the difference. When interest rates come down again, principal repayment resumes, but the term of the mortgage may need to be extended.

The popularity of ARMs with borrowers varies with the difference between the rates on fixed-rate and adjustable-rate mortgages. When the gap is large, ARMs look attractive. Also, when *both* rates are high, more borrowers may resort to ARMs: Many such borrowers will not qualify for a mortgage at the higher fixed rate but will qualify at the lower ARM rate.

HEDGING INTEREST-RATE RISK

If borrowers prefer to borrow at a fixed rate, and if they are willing to pay a premium to avoid taking on interest-rate risk, how can lenders accommodate them without having to bear the interest-rate risk themselves? The answer, of course, is hedging. As we saw in Chapter 13, financial markets provide a number of ways to hedge interest-rate risk—futures, options, and swaps.

Swaps would seem to be ideal. By selling swaps a thrift can turn a constant stream of payments from a fixed-rate mortgage into a variable stream that matches the market interest rates it must pay on its deposits. But what if the mortgage is prepaid? That is most likely to happen if interest rates fall. If so, the thrift will take a loss on the swap it has sold, because the fall in interest rate will raise the market value of the liability under the swap agreement. As a result, swaps are not a good hedge.

Options provide a way of hedging prepayment risk. By allowing prepayment, the thrift has implicitly given the mortgage borrower an option that becomes valuable if interest rates fall. The thrift can hedge this implicit option by buying actual call options on financial futures. If interest rates fall, the value of these call options will rise and will offset the loss caused by prepayment.

Thrifts have been slow to hedge externally because they generally lack the necessary expertise and because of problems of accounting.[7]

15.5 SECURITIZATION AND THE SECONDARY MARKET FOR MORTGAGES

The methods of dealing with interest-rate risk presented above take it for granted that mortgages must be funded with short-term deposits. But what if they could be funded with *long-term* liabilities? Then there would be no interest-rate risk.

There are two ways this might be done. One is to have thrifts sell long-term bonds instead of deposits. Some larger thrifts have indeed done this, selling

---

[7]See Chapter 13. The troubles of Franklin Savings in 1990, mentioned above, were related to its dealings in financial futures.

mortgage-backed bonds
Long-term bonds
collateralized by portfolios
of mortgages.

mortgage-backed bonds collateralized by portfolios of mortgages. However, heterogeneity and relatively high credit risk have limited the popularity of these bonds; the total outstanding at the end of 1987 was only about $12 billion. Moreover, most thrifts are too small to contemplate a public issue.

The other way to fund mortgages with long-term liabilities is to have a different financial intermediary do the lending, one that already has long-term liabilities. Lifes would seem an obvious candidate. The problem, of course, is the inherent difficulty of mortgage lending—high information costs, small denominations, heterogeneity of terms, and high processing costs. That is why we have specialized mortgage lenders in the first place.

What is needed is some way to separate the origination and servicing of mortgages, which thrifts do well, from the funding of mortgages, which they do badly. Such a separation requires that illiquid mortgage loans be turned into securities that can be sold on a secondary market for mortgages. This process of turning illiquid loans into marketable securities is called *securitization.*

THE ORIGINS OF THE SECONDARY MARKET

The secondary market in mortgages is largely a creation of the federal government. The reason for government involvement, however, was not really concern about interest-rate risk. It was, rather, concern about the availability of mortgages, both to certain classes of borrowers (the poor, farmers, returning veterans) and in certain geographic areas.

The government first got into the mortgage business during the Great Depression. Housing finance had been part of the general collapse: There had been numerous defaults and foreclosures and a large number of thrifts had failed. As part of its reconstruction program, the government set up a number of agencies to help revive the mortgage market.

The Federal National Mortgage Association (FNMA, or "Fannie Mae") was authorized to buy existing mortgages from thrifts and to sell bonds to raise the necessary funds. This enabled the thrifts to generate liquidity whenever they needed it by selling off existing mortgages for cash.

The Federal Housing Administration (FHA) was authorized to insure mortgages made to certain categories of borrower. Such insurance made it easier to sell those mortgages on the secondary market because it reduced the information cost to the buyer. Because the mortgages were insured, the buyer had no need to check out the value of the collateral: If the borrower defaulted and the property was worth less than the unpaid principal, the insurer would pick up the difference. After World War II government insurance was extended, through the Veteran's Administration (VA), to mortgages made to veterans.

In order to qualify for government insurance, mortgages had to be written using a standard, approved loan contract. The use of this standard contract overcame two more obstacles to the secondary sale of mortgages—their heterogeneity and their small size. Mortgages that were insured were all alike—the same terms and no credit risk. It was therefore easy to bundle them into million-dollar packages and sell the packages to large institutional investors.

In the 1940s, 1950s, and 1960s many veterans and others took advantage of these programs, and a large number of insured mortgages were written. In this period insured mortgages made up about 45% of the total. The major investors in insured mortgages were mutual savings banks and life insurance companies.

Because mortgage insurance makes it possible to resell mortgages, origination and servicing can be separated from funding. **Mortgage banking companies** were set up specifically just to originate and service insured mortgages. Once such a company puts together a package of mortgages, it sells the package to an investor, rather than keeping the mortgages itself as an asset. It therefore needs to fund the mortgages only for the short time it takes to put the package together—a few months at most.

mortgage banking companies
Companies that originate and service insured mortgages.

Mortgage banking companies earn income from origination fees—points from the borrower—and from servicing fees paid by the investor for collecting payments and dealing with the borrower. They may also earn income from positive carry, just like the government securities dealers we discussed in Chapter 7. If the yield curve is "normal" (upward-sloping), the long-term rate on the mortgages they hold will be higher than the short-term rate they pay on the money they borrow to fund them. Mortgage bankers may also make a trading profit on any unhedged inventory of mortgages if long-term rates fall between the time of origination of a mortgage and the time of its resale.

Because mortgage bankers are not restricted in their geographic expansion, they may and do operate nationwide. See Exhibit 15.6 for a list of the largest mortgage banking companies. Note that the list includes subsidiaries of banks, finance companies, insurance companies, and retailers, as well as specialized mortgage lenders.[8]

This parallel structure of mortgage lending—separate origination by mortgage bankers and funding by insurance companies and mutual savings banks—competed extremely successfully with S&Ls that performed both functions within the same institution. Indeed, the parallel structure had some major advantages—returns to scale and access to the national capital market—and, by undercutting the S&Ls, managed to capture most of the business of writing insured mortgages. The S&Ls were left with the noninsured, and therefore nonmarketable, mortgages (investors are reluctant to buy uninsured mortgages because of possible costs and losses in case of default).

The insured market generally functioned better than the conventional (uninsured) market. Although the conventional market was fragmented, with rates varying across the country, the insured market was well integrated: Rates would be the same for insured mortgages everywhere. There was also less interest-rate risk, because insured mortgages were held by institutions with longer-term liabilities.

[8]The top-ranked mortgage company, GMAC Mortgage, had grown to nearly $30 billion by early 1990. At that time it bought out Residential Funding Corporation, adding nearly $8 billion more to its portfolio of mortgages.

EXHIBIT 15.6

TOP 12 MORTGAGE COMPANIES[a]

Rank	Mortgage Company	Dollar Volume of Mortgages Serviced (Billions)	Number of Mortgages Serviced
1	GMAC Mortgage Co., Elkins Park, Pa.	$23,886	372,592
2	Lomas & Nettleton Financial Corp., Dallas	21,503	653,152
3	Fireman's Fund Mortgage Corp., Farmington Hills, Mich.	15,461	369,703
4	Metmor Financial, Inc., Los Angeles	13,835	253,639
5	Commonwealth Mortgage Corp. of America, Houston	12,769	238,961
6	BancBoston Mortgage Corp., Jacksonville, Fla.	12,336	281,000
7	Fleet Mortgage Corp., Milwaukee, Wis.	11,830	300,370
8	Weyerhaeuser Mortgage Co., Los Angeles	11,535	192,040
9	Goldome Realty Credit Corp., Buffalo, N.Y.	10,870	181,418
10	First Union Mortgage Corp., Charlotte, N.C.	10,474	193,777
11	First Interstate Mortgage Co., Pasadena, Calif.	10,130	95,862
12	Sears Mortgage Corp., Lincolnshire, Ill.	10,004	159,500

[a]Based on volume of permanent mortgages serviced on June 30, 1987.

Source: Compiled by *American Banker*, copyright 1987.

However, as the number of veterans taking out mortgages declined in the 1960s, so did the importance of the secondary market. The share of insured mortgages fell to about 30% in 1970. In the same period the problems of the conventional market grew more obvious. So between 1968 and 1970 the government took steps to extend the secondary market to conventional mortgages and to expand its scope by developing a market for mortgage-backed securities.

MORTGAGE-BACKED SECURITIES

mortgage-backed securities (MBSs)
Securities backed either by insured or by conventional mortgages.

Before 1970 the secondary market had largely been a market for "private placements": Most of the mortgages originated by mortgage banking companies had been placed with lifes and mutual savings banks. The government now acted to open up a market for **mortgage-backed securities (MBSs)** that could be traded publicly.

FNMA, which had not been particularly active until then, was reorganized and two new agencies were created—the Government National Mortgage Association (GNMA, or "Ginnie Mae") and the Federal Home Loan Mortgage Corporation (FHLMC, or "Freddie Mac"). The three agencies were authorized to issue and to guarantee a variety of mortgage-related securities, backed both by insured and, for the first time, by conventional mortgages.

pass-through security
Direct share in a pool of mortgages; principal and interest payments on the pool are passed through to the purchaser of the security.

The basic mortgage-related security is the **pass-through security**. This is a share in a pool of mortgages—rather like a share in a mutual fund. A large number of mortgages are put together into a pool, and shares in the pool are sold. The

EXHIBIT 15.7

OUTSTANDING
AMOUNT
OF PASS THROUGH
SECURITIES
(BILLIONS OF
DOLLARS)

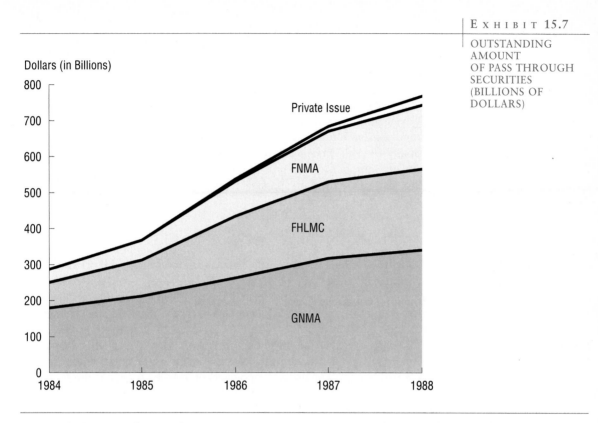

Source: *Federal Reserve Bulletin*, October 1989.

purchaser of, say, a 1% share in the pool receives 1% of all the payments on all the mortgages in the pool, less service fees to the originators and insurance premiums to the insurer. The payments are "passed through" to the purchaser.

The first pass-through was developed by GNMA in 1970, using mortgages insured by the FHA and VA. In 1971 FHLMC began to issue pass-throughs based on conventional loans, and in 1977 BankAmerica sold the first private pass-through without a government guarantee. Pass-throughs have proven extremely popular: From 1971 to 1988 the amount outstanding has grown at an average rate of 40% per year to more than $800 billion by the end of 1988 (see Exhibit 15.7). An increasing proportion of all new mortgages have found their way into pass-throughs.

The large volume of pass-throughs has facilitated the development of an active secondary market. In 1985 trading volume in this market exceeded $2 trillion, putting it ahead of the NYSE in size. The organization of the market is very similar to that of the secondary market in government securities and is, in fact, closely related to it. Many of the same dealers and brokers participate in both markets. There are repos and reverses in pass-throughs much like those in Treasuries.

Pass-throughs have become an increasingly popular investment with thrifts, lifes, commercial banks, and other financial institutions. The government guarantee removes any credit risk, and the good secondary market makes these securities almost as liquid as Treasuries. And they generally carry a higher yield than Treasuries: The higher yield is to compensate for the prepayment risk.

Because purchasers of pass-throughs receive a share of *all* receipts from the underlying mortgages, they also receive a share of prepayments. For investors like lifes and pension funds that want assets to match their long-term liabilities, the possibility of prepayment is a serious drawback. Not only does prepayment shorten the duration of the pass-through, but, as we saw earlier, prepayment tends to increase at the worst possible time—when interest rates fall.

CMOs, REMICs, AND STRIPs

collateralized mortgage obligation (CMO)
Security backed by pass-throughs that pays principal and interest like bonds.

One solution to this problem is the **collateralized mortgage obligation (CMO)**, which was first developed by FHLMC in 1983. An agency or a private financial institution buys pass-throughs and uses them as backing for several classes, or **tranches,** of bond, each with different claims on the payment stream from the portfolio of pass-throughs.

tranches
Classes of bonds that have specific claims on the payment stream of a collateralized mortgage obligation.

In the simplest version, there might be two tranches—A and B. Tranche A has a right to one-third of the principal and Tranche B a right to two-thirds; if the pass-throughs pay 12% interest, the owners of Tranche A get one-third, or 4%, and the owners of Tranche B get 8%. The principal repayment and prepayment from the pass-throughs are not paid out immediately, but go into a redemption fund. At the end of each 6-month period, depending on the amount in the redemption fund, a corresponding amount of bonds is called—bought back at par by the issuer. The bonds to be called are picked by lottery from Tranche A *alone.* Only when all the Tranche A bonds have been called does the issuer of the CMO start to call Tranche B bonds. The first tranche has a short duration and carries much of the prepayment risk; the second tranche has a longer duration and less prepayment risk. In reality, there may be several tranches, each with progressively longer duration and less prepayment risk.

real estate mortgage investment conduit (REMIC)
Type of collateralized mortgage obligation that splits up the cash flow on a mortgage in various ways.

A more recent variation on the CMO is the **real estate mortgage investment conduit (REMIC)**, which splits up the cash flow on a mortgage in a variety of creative ways (see "A Loan's Odyssey" on page 416). One type of REMIC is the **mortgage strip.** The payments received on a portfolio of pass-throughs are divided into interest payments and principal payments (including prepayments). Interest-only strips (**IO strips**) are sold with a right to receive all the interest payments; principal-only strips (**PO strips**) are sold with the right to receive all the principal payments, including prepayments.

mortgage strip
Type of real estate mortgage investment conduit that divides pass-through payments into interest payments and principal payments.

IO strip
Type of mortgage strip that is sold with a right to receive all of the interest payments on a portfolio of pass-through securities.

The value of these strips is particularly sensitive to changes in interest rates: PO strips fall sharply in value and IO strips rise sharply in value when interest rates rise (see the appendix at the end of this chapter for an explanation). This extreme interest-rate sensitivity makes strips an attractive hedging instrument. Long-term investors, like lifes, can hedge the holding of otherwise attractive

PO strip
Type of mortgage strip that is sold with a right to receive all of the principal payments on a portfolio of pass-through securities.

short-term assets with an appropriate amount of PO strips; short-term investors, like banks, can take on more long-term assets and hedge them by holding some IO strips.

The extreme interest-rate sensitivity of strips also makes them dangerous to hold unhedged, as Merrill Lynch, an active dealer in strips, found to its cost and embarrassment. In April 1987 Merrill was caught holding a large amount of unhedged PO strips when long-term rates rose suddenly. Merrill's loss was estimated at $250 million—large even by Wall Street standards. Merrill was not alone in its losses: Other investment banks, mortgage banks, and thrifts with unhedged positions in various mortgage-backed securities also took a beating.

These losses sent a shudder of fear through the market, somewhat reducing demand for mortgage-backed securities. At the same time, a rise in interest rates reduced the number of households wanting new mortgages, shrinking the supply. As a result, the previously rapid growth of the mortgage-backed securities market has slowed, at least temporarily (see Exhibit 15.7).

PRIVATIZATION OF THE SECONDARY MARKET

The secondary market for mortgages is dominated by government agencies. As much as 80% of new mortgages written in 1986 conformed to agency guidelines and so were eligible for securitization. Half of all conforming fixed-rate mortgages were, in fact, securitized.[9] Is this degree of government involvement in the mortgage market desirable?

One reason it may not be desirable is that the federal guarantee in effect extends a subsidy to borrowers with securitized mortgages. Estimates suggest that the rate on conforming mortgages is about 25 basis points below that on nonconforming mortgages. Since these mortgages go even to quite well-to-do borrowers, this subsidy may be inappropriate.

Another reason government involvement may be undesirable is that it constitutes unfair competition with private financial institutions. No private institution can compete with the credit standing of the federal government. There have been suggestions in recent years to turn the government agencies involved in mortgage lending into private companies without government backing.

Private institutions have already carved out a role in some areas. Although pass-throughs are mostly issued by the agencies, private institutions have played an active role in creating CMOs and strips, "hitching a ride" on the government guarantee of the underlying pass-throughs.

The unwillingness of the agencies to accept mortgages above a certain maximum value—$168,00 in 1988—presents another opportunity. Investment banks, thrifts, home builders, mortgage bankers, insurance companies, and commercial banks have all been active in packaging such "jumbo mortgages"

---

[9]Only 10% of ARMs were securitized in the same year. ARMs are less standardized than fixed-rate mortgages, making securitization more difficult. In any case, because they carry less interest-rate risk, ARMs are the mortgages that S&Ls prefer to hold on to.

A LOAN'S ODYSSEY

By George Anders

Staff Reporter of The Wall Street Journal

WEST COVINA, Calif.—Each month, Jim and Erica Vogel send their $1,108.92 mortgage check to a local savings and loan association. For them, that is the end of the transaction.

In fact, their payment is only the first step in a chain of transactions in a vast new financial network: the mortgage-trading business.

Mortgage interest is one of the biggest monthly cash flows in the U.S. economy, and many new investors want some of it. Barely three months after the Vogels bought their home, their local S&L had already sold off their mortgage. Since then, it has been resold and split up so much that part of the young couple's payments now end up everywhere from an Oklahoma thrift institution to a London bank.

How It Started

The story starts in Southern California last August, when Mr. Vogel, a 31-year-old who sells scaffolding equipment, and his wife, who is 26 and sells class rings, decided they wanted a bigger home.

The Vogels spent a month searching before settling on a four-bedroom, $160,000 ranch-style home in San Dimas. They rustled up a 25% down payment, mainly by selling their previous home. Seeking a mortgage for the rest, they took their real estate agent's advice and tried a local lender, First Federal of San Gabriel. Their application sailed through the income and credit checks; three weeks after applying, they got a 30-year loan for $120,000 at 10 ⅝% interest.

First Federal is the sort of neighborhood S&L that might belong in a sentimental Jimmy Stewart movie. It has just 150 employees, in seven branches northeast of Los Angeles. Its four-story headquarters building in West Covina, California, sits next to a suburban shopping mall; its emblem includes a stylized American flag.

In the past five years, however, First Federal has become a savvy seller of mortgages. "Selling off mortgages has let us make another $200 million in mortgage loans that we couldn't have done otherwise," explains Barrett Anderson, the S&L's president.

So, as soon as the Vogels' mortgage entered its books, First Federal planned to sell it. With little chance of finding investors on its own, First Federal waited until it had several other fixed-rate mortgages on hand. Then, it turned to the quasi-governmental agencies that function as mortgage clearinghouses, bundling up mortgages into standardized pools, providing guarantees against default and reselling them to investors.

Along with thousands of other mortgages, the Vogels' arrived at Freddie Mac's Reston, Va., offices one day in mid-December with all the fanfare of an oxygen atom entering a room. It was put into Freddie Mac Pool No. 360018, $443 million of fixed-rate loans from all over the United States.

Wall Street's Problem

As much as the Freddie Mac pool was designed to appeal to investors, that was, for Wall Street, just a first step. Wall Street's problem: Although

most mortgages are drawn up for 30 years, they can be paid off much sooner if people sell their homes or refinance their loan at lower rates. That uncertainty makes it hard for institutional investors to predict how much interest their mortgage investments will provide. "We want to keep that variability to a minimum," says Janice Maseji, a portfolio manager at Teachers Insurance Annuity Association.

So, Wall Street number-crunchers have figured out ways to repackage mortgage pools into securities—the Remics—that behave like corporate bonds, money-market funds or other more-desirable investments. Although agencies such as Freddie Mac or the Federal National Mortgage Administration (Fannie Mae) formally issue Remics, the operation is largely masterminded by big Wall Street firms.

Sure enough, demand for a new Remic began to build in May. First, a Florida S&L, seeking to hedge against rising interest rates, contacted First Boston. Then, insurance companies said they wanted mortgage securities that traded like 10-year corporate bonds; new corporates happened to be scarce then.

Enter Adrian Katz, a curly-haired computer expert at First Boston, just three years out of Princeton. Mr. Katz says he spends 16-hour days looking for ways to make Remics. In mid-May, he found one. He would buy $550 million of mortgage pools—hundreds of pools totaling more than 10,000 mortgages—and divide them into eight new securities, or "tranches." Four tranches would trade like bonds, three had variable interest rates a bit like money-market funds, and one provided a hedge against rising rates.

'Financial Sculpture'

The whole process is "a bit like a financial sculpture," says Dexter Senft, a managing director at First Boston. "You chip away the pieces people don't want, and create something they do want."

Freddie Mac liked the plan. On May 25, it decided to go ahead with the Remic. The next two steps were up to First Boston. It still didn't own all the mortgages needed for the Remic, and so its traders began buying mortgage pools—including part of Pool No. 360018, the one with the Vogels' mortgage. Meanwhile, First Boston's 100 bond salesmen called institutional investors, lining up orders for parts of the Remic once they were assembled.

The Remic tranches resembling long-term corporate bonds were bought up by insurance companies. Among the buyers was Pamela Cornell, an assistant vice president of Cigna Investments Inc., a unit of Cigna Corp. The Hartford, Connecticut, insurer is nearly always in the market for 10-year bonds, which fit in well with the pension investments it manages. "Our traders talk to First Boston every day," Ms. Cornell says. This time First Boston had something Ms. Cornell liked: One of the long-term tranches had a 10.3% interest rate and an expected average life of 10.9 years. She bought $10 million of it.

Other Possibilities

Other tranches don't have such rigid formulas about how much money goes in. Their funding goes up and down depending on short-term interest rates. One tranche, for example, pays 0.65 percentage point above the one-month London interbank offered rate. Such tranches behave a bit like money-market funds and are most popular with thrift institutions because the interest income closely matches their cost of funds.

That part of the Remic appealed to Glenn Wells, a financial officer at Globe Savings Bank of El Reno, Oklahoma. He bought $66 million of a Remic section with a floating interest rate, initially yielding 9.21%. That rate was high enough to be profitable for Globe—about 0.6 percentage point more than its cost of raising money through certificates of deposit or other means.

For Mr. Wells, Remics were sound assets that he couldn't find in the depressed local economy. "We couldn't begin to originate loans of that size and quality in Oklahoma," Mr. Wells says. This way, Globe adds $66 million of triple-A-rated loans to its books with just a single phone call.

Other Remic buyers ranged from a British bank to a Pittsburgh S&L. Comments Mr. Anderson at the S&L that originated the Vogels' mortgage: "We're almost like cattle producers now. We ship the whole animal to market and let other people divide up the prime cuts."

After the seven main tranches are filled, a little money usually remains—the "residual tranche." It's a financial wild card, whose value can change greatly if homeowners either pay off their mortgages quickly or let them run the full 30 years.

In First Boston's Remic, the residual tranche increases in value if long-term interest rates rise. That's because high rates prevent homeowners from refinancing mortgages at attractive new terms. So people are more likely to let their mortgages run longer, and over time more money spills into the residual tranche. And that's why the Florida S&L paid $40 million for the residual tranche—as a nifty hedge against rising interest rates.

The Vogels aren't quite so impressed. They are due to spend the next 29 years and three months sending mortgage checks into this vast financial pipeline.

"It would be nice if it lowered our payments," Mr. Vogel says. "They're plenty high enough."

Source: George Anders, "A Loan's Odyssey: How a Home Mortgage Got into a Huge Pool That Lured Investors," *The Wall Street Journal*, August 17, 1988. Reprinted by permission of The Wall Street Journal, © Dow Jones & Company, Inc. 1988. All Rights Reserved Worldwide.

into private pass-throughs or using them as collateral for private mortgage-backed bonds. Since the agencies will not insure or guarantee jumbos, insurance is provided by private insurance companies.

Another area of private initiative is the origination of mortgages. Today this is no longer limited to thrifts and mortgage banks. Realtors and builders can now act as mortgage brokers, connecting their clients with a lender through one of several computerized networks. The largest are Shelternet, owned by First Boston, and Mortgage One, owned by Coldwell Banker, a Sears subsidiary. These link the broker to many mortgage originators and find the borrower the best rate automatically. Mortgages originated on Shelternet are packaged and sold by First Boston as pass-throughs.

|15.6| THE BENEFITS AND POTENTIAL DANGERS OF SECURITIZATION

There is no question that mortgage securitization has been beneficial. It has greatly reduced the inefficiencies of geographic fragmentation: Thrifts with surplus funds can now buy pass-throughs, and those with more mortgage applications than deposits can sell off the excess in the secondary market. Thrifts can improve the geographic diversification of their mortgage portfolios by selling some of their own mortgages and buying pass-throughs of mortgages from other parts of the country. Holding pass-throughs also improves the thrifts' liquidity: Unlike mortgages, they may be sold or repoed at a moment's notice if cash is needed.

By separating the funding from the origination and servicing of mortgages and by transferring the funding to institutions with long-term liabilities, securitization has greatly reduced the problem of interest-rate risk. Thrifts bear interest-rate risk on the mortgages they originate only for the short time it takes them to put together a marketable bundle of mortgages. They can hedge even this, for a fee, by obtaining a forward commitment from an agency to buy the mortgages at an agreed-upon price.

Securitization has also given mortgage borrowers access to the national capital market, breaking down the barrier between the mortgage market and the rest of the capital market. Evidence of this is that mortgage rates today move much more closely with long-term market rates than they once did.

Securitization is such a good idea that it has spread to other types of loan in addition to mortgages. For example, banks have sold securities backed by automobile loans—known as CARs—and securities backed by credit card receivables—known as "plastic bonds." Plastic bonds, in particular, have been popular, with some $10 billion issued in 1988 and even more in 1990. The way a plastic bond might work is as follows. The underlying credit card debt earns 19% on the amount of the debt. The bond promises investors 9%, costs are 2%, and the default rate is 5%. This leaves a $19\% - 9\% - 2\% - 5\% = 3\%$ cushion to cover unusual defaults; if there are none, the issuing bank keeps the 3%. Banks have also securitized regular commercial loans and portfolios of junk bonds (see Chapter 17).

There are, however, some potential problems with securitization. There is a moral-hazard problem when the originator of a loan sells it off to someone else: The seller may be tempted to get rid of the bad loans and keep the good ones. There is also a question whether the originator will be as determined in pursuing delinquent loans when his own money is not at stake. So far, there is little evidence of these being actual rather than potential problems, but only time will tell.

SUMMARY

- A mortgage is a loan collateralized by property, usually real property (land and structures).

- The mortgage market accounts for a large part of the market for long-term debt.

- Most mortgages involve equal monthly payments. Each payment includes both interest and repayment of some principal. Early payments are mostly interest, with the proportion of principal repayment increasing over the life of the mortgage.

- Mortgages are often prepaid before maturity when people sell their homes or when they refinance by taking out another mortgage at a lower interest rate.

- Because mortgage lending requires the lender to check both the borrower and the property, information requirements and servicing costs are high relative to the amounts involved. Mortgages also vary a lot with respect to their conditions.

- Because of the nature of mortgage lending, it traditionally relied on indirect lending by local, specialized thrifts (savings and loans and savings banks), which raised the necessary funds by taking in local time deposits.

- The mortgage market, organized in this way, suffered from three chronic problems: cyclical disintermediation, with a severe impact on the housing industry and on the economy; fragmentation, with rates and availability varying from region to region; and extreme vulnerability to interest-rate risk.

- Disintermediation ceased to be a problem with the demise of Regulation Q, but having to pay market rates on their deposits increased the exposure of thrifts to interest-rate risk. The end of disintermediation had little effect on the cyclical sensitivity of housing: Borrowers were now priced out of the market rather than rationed out.

- Deregulation allowed thrifts to diversify by investing in many assets other than mortgages. It also allowed them to offer a broader range of liabilities, including various checkable deposits.

- Thrifts were also allowed to offer adjustable-rate mortgages, on which the interest rate adjusts with market rates rather than being fixed for the life of the mortgage. Such mortgages shift most of the interest-rate risk to the borrower, thereby increasing credit risk.

- Thrifts can also hedge interest-rate risk by using futures, options, and swaps.

- Securitization addresses interest-rate risk in a different way—by separating the origination of mortgages from the funding, and by allowing the funding to be done by institutions (such as lifes and pensions) with long-term liabilities.

- The secondary market for securitized mortgages has been developed largely by the federal government. Mortgages are bought by federal and quasi-federal agencies that package them into pools and then either sell bonds backed by these pools or sell direct shares in these pools (pass-throughs).

- Much mortgage origination is now done by specialized mortgage banks or mortgage companies that take in no deposits at all. Instead, they sell on the secondary market all the mortgages that they originate and service.

- A problem with pass-throughs is their susceptibility to reinvestment risk because of prepayment of the underlying mortgages. The market has come up with some ingenious solutions in the form of CMOs and in the form of REMICs such as the IO and PO strips.

- As the secondary market for mortgages matures, there is pressure to reduce government involvement and to rely more on private institutions and markets.

- Securitization has helped to reduce the fragmentation of the mortgage market, to improve thrift diversification, and to reduce interest-rate risk. The idea is spreading to other types of bank loan. However, there is a potential for some moral-hazard problems with this type of arrangement.

KEY TERMS

mortgage	adjustable-rate mortgage (ARM)	tranches
fixed-rate mortgage		real estate mortgage investment conduit (REMIC)
points	mortgage-backed bonds	
prepayment	mortgage banking companies	
due-on-sale provision		mortgage strip
savings banks	mortgage-backed securities (MBSs)	IO strip
savings and loans (S&Ls)		PO strip
thrifts	pass-through security	
service companies	collateralized mortgage obligation (CMO)	

DISCUSSION QUESTIONS

1. What is special about a mortgage loan that makes mortgage lending a problem? What are the different ways that the mortgage market has organized itself in order to deal with the problem?

2. How did the combination of regulatory restrictions and changes in the economic environment adversely affect thrifts?

3. What has been the role of the federal government in the development of the secondary mortgage market? Why was government intervention necessary?

4. How do rising interest rates affect the housing market? How has this changed in recent years? Should the government make sure that home buyers have affordable mortgages even when interest rates are high?

5. From the point of view of both borrowers and lenders, what are the relative advantages and risks of fixed-rate versus adjustable-rate mortgages?

6. Why does prepayment happen? Why is it a problem for mortgage lenders? What are the ways that this problem has been addressed?

7. Why was the U.S. mortgage market fragmented? Why was this a problem? What has happened to alleviate the problem? Are there other possible solutions?

8. How did the demise of Regulation Q affect thrifts? What were the good results? What were the bad results?

9. How did deregulation affect thrifts? What were the good results? What were the bad results?

BIBLIOGRAPHY

Becketti, Sean, "The Prepayment Risk of Mortgage-Backed Securities," *Economic Review of the Federal Reserve Bank of Kansas City* February 1989, 43–57.

Marcus, Alan J., and Arnold Kling, "Interest-Only/Principal-Only Mortgage-Backed Strips: A Valuation and Risk Analysis," NBER Working Paper #2340, August 1987.

Morris, Charles S., and Thomas J. Merfield, "New Methods for Savings and Loans to Hedge Interest Rate Risk," *Economic Review of the Federal Reserve Bank of Kansas City* March 1988, 3–16.

Sellon, Gordon H., Jr., and Deana VanNahmen, "The Securitization of Housing Finance," *Economic Review of the Federal Reserve Bank of Kansas City* July-August 1988, 3–20.

APPENDIX TO CHAPTER 15

THE INTEREST-RATE SENSITIVITY OF MORTGAGE STRIPS

To calculate the value of an IO strip and of a PO strip, look at Exhibit 15.1 at the beginning of the chapter, which shows for a single mortgage the division of payments, C, into principal, P_t, and interest, I_t. Consider first an IO strip that is a claim to the interest payments on this single mortgage and a PO strip that is a claim to the principal repayment.

Suppose first that there is no prepayment. Then the value of the PO strip is

$$V_{PO} = \frac{P_1}{(1.01)} + \frac{P_2}{(1.01)^2} + \cdots + \frac{P_{360}}{(1.01)^{360}} = \frac{\$28.61}{(1.01)} + \frac{\$28.90}{(1.01)^2} + \cdots + \frac{\$1,018.43}{(1.01)^{360}},$$

and the value of the IO strip is

$$V_{IO} = \frac{I_1}{(1.01)} + \frac{I_2}{(1.01)^2} + \cdots + \frac{I_{360}}{(1.01)^{360}} = \frac{\$1,000.00}{(1.01)} + \frac{\$999.71}{(1.01)^2} + \cdots + \frac{\$10.18}{(1.01)^{360}}.$$

The value of both strips declines over time as payments are made: At any date the residual value of the strip is just the present value of the remaining payments.

Since the interest payments start large and then decline, as opposed to the principal payments, which start small and then grow, V_{IO} is substantially larger than V_{PO}—in fact, about twice as large. (The sum of the two values, of course, must equal the value of the underlying mortgage.) Also, as a result of the different patterns of the two streams of payments, the duration of the IO strip is much shorter than that of the PO strip.

What happens to the values of the two strips if the mortgage is prepaid, say, after 60 months? The stream of interest on the mortgage stops, so the value of the IO strip, which is the present value of the remaining 300 interest payments, drops to zero. The PO strip is a claim on the 300 remaining principal payments, which now become zero, *and* on the prepayment. Thus when the mortgage is prepaid, the total amount received by the owner of the PO strip does not change: The sum of the remaining principal payments equals the amount paid on prepayment. However, that amount is now received *earlier*, and earlier, of course, is more valuable. So the value of the PO strip rises as a result of prepayment.

Consider now the value of IO and PO strips based on a pass-through that includes *thousands* of mortgages rather than strips based on just a single mortgage. Routinely, a certain proportion of the mortgages will be prepaid each year as people sell their houses. These expected prepayments over the life of the mortgages will make the PO strips more valuable than the simple present value of the principal repayments as calculated above, and it will make the IO strips less valuable.

What happens to the value of the two types of strip when market interest rates fall? Assume, first, that there is no change in the pattern of prepayment and so the stream of future payments stays the same. When market interest rates fall, the future payments on each strip are discounted to the present at a lower rate, and the present value of both types of strip rises. Call this effect the *discounting effect*.

The assumption of no change in prepayment is, of course, unrealistic. As we saw earlier, when interest rates fall, prepayments increase as borrowers refinance their mortgages. As we have seen, prepayment affects the stream of payments to PO strips and to IO strips quite differently. For PO strips, principal payments are received earlier than expected. This increases their value. For IO strips, when mortgages are prepaid, interest payments on these mortgages cease. Therefore prepayment reduces the stream of future payments, and the value of the IO strip falls. Call the effect of increased prepayment the *prepayment effect*. The prepayment effect raises the value of PO strips and lowers the value of IO strips.

Now consider the discounting effect and prepayment effect together. For the PO strips, the prepayment effect reinforces the discounting effect, and their value rises sharply. A 1% fall in market interest rates might increase the value of a PO strip by as much as 60%. This makes the sensitivity of the value of a PO strip to interest rates about the same as that of a T-bill with a duration of 60 years.

For the IO strip, the prepayment effect *offsets* the discounting effect. In fact, it offsets it so much that the value of IO strips actually *falls* when interest rates fall. A 1% fall in market interest rates might *decrease* the value of an IO strip by as much as 30%. This makes the sensitivity of the value of an IO strip to interest rates the same as that of a T-bill with a *negative* duration of −30 years, were such a thing to exist.

PART FOUR

REGULATION AND POLICY

C H A P T E R 16

BANK SAFETY

THE ISSUES

Banking is in more trouble today than at any time since the Great Depression. Banks and savings and loans have been failing at an alarming rate, and the costs to the taxpayer are expected to be astronomical. In Chapter 17 we shall look at why this is happening, what can be done about it, and what is being done. Before we go into the specifics of the current crisis, however, we need to gain some perspective. There are two things we need to understand. The first is why bank safety is more of a problem than the safety of any other type of business. What is special about banking in this respect? The second is why bank safety seems to be a much more serious problem in the United States than it is in other countries. What is special about banking in the United States?

16.1 BANK RUNS AND BANKING PANICS

In order to separate the general issue of bank safety from the specific problems of the United States, let us begin by looking at banking on the South Sea island that we first visited in Chapter 4.

The island has developed a system of fractional-reserve banking much like our own. Fractional-reserve banking has advantages in efficiency over the more primitive system of warehouse banking that it replaced, but it also has dangers. The most serious danger is the possibility of a *bank run*—a simultaneous withdrawal of deposits by a large number of depositors. To understand what happens in a bank run, put yourselves in the shoes of a depositor.

427

THE PSYCHOLOGY OF A BANK RUN

You are a depositor at one of the smaller banks on the Island, Coral Reef Bank. When Coral Reef was a warehouse bank, your deposit really was just that: The $200 you had placed with the bank sat safely in its vault. Now that Coral Reef has gone over to fractional-reserve banking, your "deposit" has become no more than a claim on the bank. The bank owes you $200, but it no longer actually has the money in the vault to pay you. Instead of holding cash equal to the amount of its deposits, Coral Reef now holds only a small amount of cash reserves; the rest of its assets consists of loans.

You are not unhappy about this change to fractional-reserve banking. Because Coral Reef now holds earning assets rather than just cash, it can offer you free checking and even pay you some interest on your deposit. And Coral Reef still promises to give you back your money whenever you want it. It is able to make this promise because of pooling. Most of the time, withdrawals and new deposits offset one another. Thus Coral Reef can keep its promise to you by holding only a small reserve of cash, just in case there is a temporary excess of withdrawals over new deposits.

Still, you now have two worries you did not have when Coral Reef was a warehouse bank. You now need to worry about its solvency and about its liquidity. The reason you need to worry about solvency is that Coral Reef's ability to pay you depends on its being paid in turn by its borrowers. If Coral Reef's borrowers default, you may never get your money back. You are protected to some extent by the bank's equity. As long as loan losses do not exceed this amount, enough will remain to pay off the depositors. But if loan losses exceed equity, the bank will be insolvent. Then, even if all other loans are repaid in full, the amount will be insufficient to pay off the deposits, and you will stand to lose some of your money.

Your second concern is liquidity. If, for whatever reason, Coral Reef's cash reserves run out, you may be unable to withdraw your money even if the bank is solvent. Most of the bank's assets are in the form of relatively illiquid loans. These loans are not easy to turn into cash. If, because it has run out of reserves, Coral Reef tries to sell its loans to obtain the cash it needs to pay you, it may not get a very good price for them. By being forced to sell off its assets in a hurry at "fire sale" prices, Coral Reef may actually *become* insolvent, even though it was perfectly sound to begin with.

There is, then, an inherent instability in the situation of a fractional-reserve bank. You know quite well that there is insufficient cash to pay off all the deposits. You also know that if, for whatever reason, people start to withdraw their money, the reserves will soon run out. If that happens, however solvent the bank may have been to begin with, it may become insolvent. What this means for you is that if you think other depositors are going to withdraw their money from Coral Reef, you will rush to withdraw yours first. Naturally, others will behave in the same way. Such a concerted rush, with everyone trying to be first, is what constitutes a bank run.

What could cause such a run? Suppose you hear that Coral Reef is in trouble. Some of its loans have soured and it has taken a loss, but you know that the losses are smaller than its capital and that Coral Reef remains solvent. Will you therefore be content to leave your money there? That depends on what you think *other* depositors will do. What if they lack your confidence in the bank and start to withdraw their deposits? You may lament their lack of judgment, but you will still try to get there first to take your money out. There is, therefore, an element of self-fulfilling prophecy about bank runs. If people believe the bank is in trouble, it *is* in trouble. As a depositor, you care less about the true situation—whether the bank is really solvent or not—than you do about what other people *believe* to be true, or what they believe other people believe.

So there you are, waiting in line at Coral Reef Bank to withdraw your money. Luckily, you are near the head of the line. Facing long lines of anxious depositors, what is the bank to do? Although its cash reserves can handle normal day-to-day demands on its liquidity, they are quite inadequate in the face of a bank run.[1] However, even though it fears that its reserves will soon run out, Coral Reef must meet demands for cash quickly and without hesitation. Hesitation will only make matters worse, because it will confirm the depositors' belief that the bank is in trouble.

HOW BANKS CAN HELP ONE ANOTHER

With its reserves disappearing rapidly, Coral Reef Bank is in serious need of help. A natural source of such help is other banks. So Coral Reef arranges to borrow cash from some of the other banks on the Island. The loan is organized by the clearinghouse association. Remember that the banks have set up a clearinghouse to clear payments among them. The clearinghouse association has become a sort of bankers' club. One of the things it has done is to set up emergency procedures for just such an event as this—a run on one of its members. When it hears of the run, the clearinghouse rapidly arranges for other banks to lend Coral Reef the cash it needs.

Such help from one bank to another is not pure altruism, or even merely mutual aid. Bank runs are like fires: They tend to spread. If Coral Reef is forced to close its doors, public confidence in banks in general may be shaken. As a result, there may be runs on other banks. So it is in the interest of all banks to stop a run before it spreads. They can do this by providing the victim of the run with the cash it needs to meet depositors' withdrawals.

Soon, a messenger arrives at Coral Reef, bearing bags of silver dollars. You and the other depositors see that there is, after all, no problem in withdrawing your money. The money seems safe enough where it is. Why not leave it there? You quit the line and go home. Many others do the same, and the run is over.

---

[1] A bank run is a collapse of the pooling principle on which fractional-reserve banking depends—the chance of one withdrawal being unrelated to the chance of another.

Mutual aid, then, can be a significant stabilizer, particularly if depositors know of its existence in advance. Had you known that Coral Reef could borrow cash from other banks, you would not have bothered to go and withdraw your money. You knew the bank was sound; you were just worried that the run itself would drive it under.

PANICS AND THE LIMITATIONS OF MUTUAL AID

Mutual aid is a help, but it does have its limitations. First, there is a public-good problem. Although it is obviously in the interest of all the banks that Coral Reef be helped, each bank will prefer that someone else do the helping. To help Coral Reef, Turtle Cove Trust (TCT) will have to run down its own reserves, making itself more vulnerable if there is a run on its own deposits. The worse things get in terms of the number of banks in trouble, the more reluctant each bank will be to compromise its own liquidity to help another bank.

Second, there is a conflict of interests: Coral Reef is a competitor of the other banks. TCT understands that it has an interest in helping another bank in a liquidity crisis. However, it is very tempting for it to be a little slow in sending over the cash and thereby rid itself of a rival.

banking panic
A run on many banks simultaneously.

Third, and by far the most important, there is little the banks can do if the run develops into a full-fledged **banking panic**. So long as the run is limited to a single bank or to a few, money withdrawn from one bank will most likely be redeposited at another. The reason there are banks to begin with is that people would rather not keep their money at home. What is happening is just a "flight to quality": People are moving their money from banks they consider unsafe to those in which they have more faith. So, as the reserves of Coral Reef decline, those of Palm Tree Bank and TCT will grow. If the clearinghouse can recycle those reserves back to Coral Reef, then all should be well.

However, if depositors lose faith, not just in a single bank, but in *all* banks, we are in deep trouble. If the banking system looks so shaky that people prefer to hold their money in the form of cash, despite the risk and inconvenience, then money withdrawn from one bank will not be redeposited at another, and the system will soon run out of reserves. Remember that the monetary system consists of two parts—a large amount of bank money (deposits) and a small amount of definitive money (cash). If the public loses its faith in bank money and all at once tries to convert a large part of it into definitive money—a "flight to cash"—there simply will not be enough to go round, and the monetary system will collapse.

What could cause such a general banking panic? As one example, suppose a typhoon hits the Island and wipes out a good part of the fishing fleet. Many fishermen, deprived of an income, default on their bank loans. Losses are substantial and widespread. Fearing for the solvency of their banks, many Islanders decide to take their money out and hold cash instead. There are simultaneous runs on many banks. Despite the best efforts of the clearinghouse, a number of banks close their doors, and many depositors take a loss.

Trade on the Island slumps. No one wants to be paid in bank money: Everyone wants cash (another reason for you to take your money out of the bank). Since liquidity is tight, no one is willing to grant credit, and the banks cannot or will not make new loans. With a large part of the Island's bank money now out of use, the total amount of money available shrinks. Because money is scarce, spending is down and prices fall. Falling prices cause more borrowers to default. The economy is in the grip of a vicious downward spiral.

The recession eventually bottoms out, and the economy begins to recover.[2] Islanders ask themselves whether something could not be done to prevent the recurrence of such a disaster. The chief, under pressure to do something, appoints a commission of inquiry.

THE LENDER OF LAST RESORT

In its investigation into the crisis, the commission finds that, despite the loss of faith in bank money in general, the bank notes of some of the larger banks continued to circulate much as before. While checks drawn on the smaller banks were accepted only at a substantial discount—a check for $25 being needed to pay a debt of $20—the bank notes of Palm Tree Bank had been treated with the same respect as that accorded actual silver dollars.

There are good reasons for this. Palm Tree is the largest bank on the Island. Other banks keep their clearing deposits there to clear payments among themselves. Because it holds such a large amount of silver, Palm Tree has invested in a particularly secure vault. Consequently, many banks prefer to keep most of their own reserves of silver with Palm Tree. In fact, most of the silver reserves of the Island have found their way into Palm Tree's vault. Because everyone knows of its substantial reserves, faith in Palm Tree and in its bank notes is almost beyond question.

The commission recommends that Palm Tree's already special status be strengthened by turning it into an official **central bank**. To free it from the public-good and competitive problems that might prevent a private bank from giving wholehearted assistance to other banks in a time of crisis, Palm Tree is purchased from its owners and set up as a public, nonprofit institution. Now, instead of cutting back its lending to other banks in order to improve its own liquidity, as a private bank might, it will be ready to expand its lending to protect the banking system. To reflect its new official status, it is renamed Bank of the Island. It soon comes to be known simply as "the Bank."

central bank
Financial institution established to help maintain the liquidity of private banks.

The ability of the Bank to create as much currency as is needed will protect the banking system from panics. In a panic many people simultaneously try to convert large amounts of bank money into definitive money. The problem is that there is simply not enough definitive money available. Now, the Bank can satisfy

---

[2]The resemblance of this scenario to the description of the Great Depression in Chapter 5 is not coincidental. There we argued that the disastrous effects of a monetary collapse on the economy as a whole constitute the kind of externality that may justify some sort of government intervention.

this demand for conversion with its own notes. Although there is no rapid way to increase the amount of silver coins available (except to borrow silver from banks on other islands), the Bank can print up as many of its own notes as people want. As long as these notes are acceptable in place of definitive money, the panic can be contained.

lender of last resort
Financial institution that stands ready to lend to banks in times of crisis.

The Bank of the Island, then, is to act as a **lender of last resort**. It will stand ready, in times of crisis, to lend to other banks in the form of its own bank notes. The other banks will be able to use these bank notes to meet withdrawals.

Since the notes of the Bank are themselves convertible into silver, everything depends on people being willing to hold them rather than to demand conversion. People will be willing to hold them if they can be sure they are acceptable to others in payment. So, to reinforce their acceptability, the chief announces that they will always be accepted at par in payment of taxes. He also declares them to be **legal tender**. That is, if you owe someone $100, that person *must* accept these bank notes in payment: He cannot go to court and demand to be paid in silver instead.

legal tender
Money that must be accepted in payment of debts.

THE FOUR PRINCIPLES   Although the establishment of a lender of last resort greatly reduces the chance of a banking panic, it does have some potential problems of its own. Mindful of these problems, the chief's commission lays down four principles to guide the Bank in its operations:[3]

1.   The Bank will lend only against good collateral.
2.   The Bank will accept all good collateral.
3.   The Bank will charge a high rate of interest on its loans.
4.   These policies of the Bank will be made known to the public.

The first principle makes it clear that the Bank is to help *illiquid* banks, not *insolvent* ones. The Bank's goal is to protect the banking system and the economy from banking panics, not to bail out banks that have made bad loans. Insolvent banks, lacking good collateral, will be allowed to fail.

If the central bank were to lend without good collateral, banks could always be sure of being able to pay off their depositors. They could always borrow enough from the Bank to do so: Their debt to their depositors would simply be replaced by debt to the Bank. As a result, depositors would never take a loss when a bank failed: The loss would be borne by the central bank instead. However, if the central bank does demand good collateral, a bank's losses will be borne by its owners and by its depositors. Depositors will therefore have every incentive to keep an eye on their banks, and the banks, knowing this, will have every incentive to exercise caution.

The second principle ensures that no solvent bank, whatever its assets, will be allowed to fail for lack of liquidity. As a result, while runs on insolvent banks

---

[3]These principles are based on those developed in the nineteenth century by two British economists, Henry Thornton and Walter Bagehot. The principles they suggested guided the policy of the Bank of England, the first central bank to act as a lender of last resort.

will remain a possibility, there is no reason to expect a run on a sound bank. If your bank is sound, you need no longer fear that a run will drive it under. Rather than having to liquidate its assets at fire sale prices, it will now be able to borrow against them at their fair market value from the lender of last resort. Knowing this, you have no reason to withdraw your deposit. Even if, in cases of doubt, there is a run on a sound bank, the run will do no harm. When it becomes clear that the bank is sound, its deposits will return.

The third principle addresses a different kind of problem. Maintaining liquidity is costly. Banks must either keep reserves that earn no interest, or they must take costly loans from other banks as cash is needed. If the Bank lends them cash whenever they are short, at little cost, why should they keep reserves or take expensive loans elsewhere? There is a double danger here. First, if all the banks behave in this way, the overall liquidity of the system will be reduced. Second, all this borrowing will raise the amount of the notes of the Bank in circulation, putting pressure on their convertibility and on the silver reserves of the Bank.[4] By making borrowing from the Bank expensive, the third principle ensures that such borrowing really will be a last resort. Such borrowing should be too expensive for banks to utilize it routinely as part of their normal liquidity management. Only those that really have no other choice will go to the Bank for a loan.

The fourth principle recognizes that in order to get the maximum benefit from having a lender of last resort, people need to know about it. Knowing that the central bank is there to give support will increase the public's confidence in the banking system and reduce the chance of a banking panic. In this game, beliefs and expectations are everything.

DEPOSIT INSURANCE AND THE MORAL-HAZARD PROBLEM

In its deliberations the chief's commission also considered, but did not recommend, an alternative way to protect the banking system from bank runs—deposit insurance. This would require the setting up of a government agency—call it the Deposit Insurance Fund—that would simply guarantee the safety of deposits.

To understand the implications of such a guarantee, consider your own reaction to deposit insurance, were it instituted. Whatever happens to Coral Reef Bank now, your money is safe. There is no longer any need for you to rush to withdraw your deposit at the first hint of trouble. *Even if the bank is insolvent,* you know that the Deposit Insurance Fund will make up any loss and that you will get back all of your money. Not only does deposit insurance allow you to sleep better at night, it also relieves you of the effort of having to constantly keep an eye on your bank, checking its soundness.

---

[4]The principal mechanism for this would be an "external drain." The increased availability of money will lead to increased spending. Some of the increased spending will be on goods imported from other islands. Banks on other islands, receiving more payments from our island than they are making to it, will ask for the difference in silver, since the notes of the Bank of the Island are not generally acceptable in payment outside the Island.

The owners of Coral Reef are well aware of this change in your attitude. They know that you and its other depositors will no longer look over their shoulder the way you used to. They will therefore take a few more chances and cut a few more corners. Their loans will become a bit more speculative, and they will reduce their equity to raise their return on equity. Before, such behavior would have lost them deposits or required them to pay higher interest on their deposits to keep depositors from moving their money elsewhere. Now, since your deposit is guaranteed, you neither know nor care what the bank is doing. As far as you are concerned, all deposits are the same: They are all perfectly safe because they are all guaranteed by the Deposit Insurance Fund.

Whereas the change in Coral Reef's behavior is of no concern to you, it is of concern to the Deposit Insurance Fund. Whenever a bank fails, the fund will have to pay depositors the difference between the value of the bank's deposits and the value of its assets. The more risks that Coral Reef and the other banks take, the more likely it is that they will fail and the larger their losses are likely to be.

moral hazard
The tendency of the insured to take more risk because he has insurance.

This sort of problem is common to all forms of insurance: It is known as the **moral-hazard** problem. For example, if you have fire insurance on your store, there is less incentive for you to spend a lot of money on fire prevention. Hence, because the insurance is there, the risk of fire goes up. The presence of the insurance reduces your incentive to take care, and with less care, losses to the insurance company increase.

deductible
Initial amount of a loss paid by the insured.

coinsurance
Percentage of a loss paid by the insured.

There are several ways insurance companies deal with the moral-hazard problem. One is to offer less than complete protection. For example, in case of a fire, you have to bear the first $10,000 of loss yourself (a **deductible**) or you are paid only 80% of the amount of the loss (**coinsurance**). In both cases, you stand to lose something yourself from a fire, and that restores your incentive to take care. Or the insurance company could *require* you to take care as a condition for the insurance. For example, it might require you to install a sprinkler system. It could also monitor your behavior by periodically sending an inspector to determine whether you are taking more risks. If the inspector does find that you are taking more risks—say, by storing hazardous material—the insurance company can raise your premium accordingly. All of these ideas can, in principle, be applied to deposit insurance.

In deciding what sort of protection to provide depositors—a lender of last resort or deposit insurance or both—the commission faces a trade-off. The more comprehensive the protection of deposits, the safer the system is from runs and panics. However, the more comprehensive the protection, the riskier will be the behavior of banks and the greater the cost of the protection. Deposit insurance offers depositors much more protection than does a lender of last resort. Not only are the depositors of illiquid banks protected, but so too are the depositors of *insolvent* banks. On the one hand, this blanket protection makes bank runs unlikely: Since deposits are guaranteed, there is no reason to withdraw them. On the other hand, it creates a significant moral-hazard problem. On balance, then, the commission decides that a lender of last resort alone, without deposit insurance, provides sufficient protection but avoids a significant and expensive increase in risk taking by banks.

16.2 BANK SAFETY IN THE UNITED STATES: A BRIEF HISTORY

Now that we have some understanding of the nature of the problem of bank safety and of the possible ways of dealing with it, let us look at the history of bank safety in the United States.

Bank safety has always been more of a problem in the United States than it has been in other countries. The reason is the peculiar structure of U.S. banking. As we saw in Chapter 8, laws and regulations have restricted bank branching and have created a banking system made up of a large number of relatively small local banks. This structure has created a number of problems in terms of bank safety.

The fragmented structure of U.S. banking forfeits many of the natural economies of scale, mostly the result of better pooling, that contribute to bank safety. Our many small local banks are less well diversified than large banks with national branching in other countries. They also have poorer liquidity. Lack of diversification increases the chance of insolvency. This makes depositors more nervous and more likely to run on the bank. Poorer liquidity makes the bank more vulnerable to a run when one does occur.

Unable to capture economies of scale within a single large bank, U.S. banks have tried to capture them through arrangements between banks. (We discussed these in Chapter 8.) These arrangements have contributed to the vulnerability of the system to runs and to panics. In particular, we shall see how the correspondent relationship between small banks and large has repeatedly played a role in U.S. banking crises.

THE PANICS OF THE NATIONAL BANKING ERA

The "national banking era," between 1863 and 1914, saw a series of banking panics—in 1873, 1884, 1890, 1893, and 1907. Correspondent banking was a significant contributor to the development and severity of these panics. Small country banks placed substantial balances with larger city banks, which in turn placed funds with banks in the financial centers, particularly in New York City. This practice led to a dangerous pyramiding of reserves. The country banks relied for liquidity on their ability to withdraw funds on short notice from the city banks, and these in turn relied on their ability to withdraw funds from their deposits with the money center banks.

The reserves of the money center banks supported not just the liquidity of the money center banks themselves, but the liquidity of the whole system. A run on a country bank would lead that bank, and others fearful of potential runs, to make large withdrawals from the city banks, compromising their liquidity. As a result, other country banks, worried about the safety of the city banks, would then

EXAMPLE OF A BANK RUN: THE UNION TRUST COMPANY

Among the first manifestations of the universal panic prevailing yesterday was a run on the Union Trust Company. Several hours before the doors of the institution were thrown open, eager crowds of excited depositors had collected around the building, and when at length ingress was afforded a frantic rush of those in waiting to secure advantageous places ensued. The work of paying out money commenced at once, and was continued without intermission until 4 p.m. The halls and corridors of the building continued jammed with depositors all day, and at the hour of closing there were still several hundred persons in the line who were finally obliged to depart without having obtained their money. A reporter of *The Times* had an interview with Mr. Augustus Schell, Vice President of the Company. Mr. Schell assured the reporter that there was not the slightest doubt of the entire solvency of the institution. Their investments, he said, were of a character that enabled them to realize readily, and every depositor on applying for it could have his money. Beyond the general panic that prevailed he was utterly at a loss to account for the rumors afloat affecting the stability of the Company, which, he added, had always transacted a large and conservative business. The officers of the Company declined to state the amount which had been paid out during the day. It was no doubt, however, a very considerable sum. It was stated that several persons who in the morning had withdrawn their money, subsequently becoming convinced of the solvency of the Company, returned and deposited it again.

Source: *The New York Times*, September 20, 1873, Vol. XXIII, No. 6867.

withdraw their correspondent balances—a bank run by banks. The city banks would, in a similar fashion, pass on the problem to the money center banks.[5]

A series of worsening crises of this sort culminated in the panic of 1907. There was a widespread flight to cash: Depositors converted their deposits into cash and stored much of it in safety deposit boxes. Banks withdrew their correspondent balances and added to their vault cash. The resulting monetary contraction led to a sharp recession. The faith of the public in the banking system was severely shaken and demands for reform received increasing attention.

THE CLEARINGHOUSE ASSOCIATIONS

During the national-banking era there was no central bank and no deposit insurance. However, banks did do their best to provide each other with mutual aid. These efforts were usually organized by the local clearinghouse.

The first U.S. clearinghouse was established in New York City in 1854. To be a member, a New York bank needed a minimum capital of $500,000 (a large sum in those days); it had to open its books to the clearinghouse for scrutiny; and it had to pay fees proportional to its use of clearinghouse services. The success of

---

[5]During such panics, bank notes, as opposed to deposits, were considered completely safe. The notes of national banks were completely backed by government bonds that had to be deposited with the Comptroller of the Currency. If a bank failed, the Comptroller could sell the bonds to redeem the notes.

the New York Clearing House led to its imitation in most major cities: 162 clearinghouses were operating by 1913.

During a crisis the clearinghouse would arrange for members to lend reserves to banks under pressure. It would also issue its own **loan certificates** to be used for interbank payments in place of cash: If Bank A had a negative balance with Bank B at the clearing, it would pay the difference with loan certificates, rather than with cash. The use of loan certificates for interbank transactions freed the banks' cash reserves for payment to the public. So if there was no way to create extra cash to meet demands for conversion, then its use by the banks could at least be economized. In the panic of 1893 at least a dozen clearinghouses issued over $68 million in loan certificates; some were even issued in small denominations and circulated with the public as currency. In 1907 some $500 million worth of various types of cash substitute was created by the clearinghouses, a significant addition to the $3,000 million of currency then in existence.

loan certificates
Certificates used for interbank payments in place of cash.

When these measures proved inadequate, the clearinghouses would declare a partial **suspension of convertibility** for all banks in the association. Cash withdrawals by depositors would usually be limited to a certain amount per day, with exceptions made only for employers needing cash to pay wages. Despite this restriction, other bank business went on as usual. In particular, payments using checks could be made in the normal fashion, and the clearing process proceeded quite normally. As a result, the damage to the economy was far less than it would have been from the widespread failure of banks that the suspension of convertibility prevented.

suspension of convertibility
Limitation of the amounts depositors can withdraw daily from a bank.

THE CREATION OF THE FED

Private arrangements such as these, however, proved unable to contain major panics. In particular, the severity of the panic of 1907 and of the accompanying recession persuaded both the financial community and Congress that some sort of reform was needed. After much debate and political bargaining, Congress passed the **Federal Reserve Act of 1913,** and President Wilson signed it into law on December 23.

Federal Reserve Act of 1913
Legislation that established the Federal Reserve System.

In Europe lenders of last resort had been highly successful in containing panics. There had been no panic in England since 1866, when the crisis of that year persuaded the Bank of England to take on the full responsibility of lender of last resort. However, this European model was not entirely acceptable in the United States. It came up against the old populist fear of concentrated power in Washington and against the vested interests and political influence of thousands of small banks.

As a result of this opposition, the Federal Reserve System was set up on the model of a government-run correspondent-clearinghouse rather than of a true central bank in the mold of the Bank of England. The Federal Reserve Banks were presented to a skeptical banking community more as a safe place for country banks to keep their reserves than as a lender of last resort. They were to be a substitute for the wicked New York City banks that used their correspondent balances to support stock market speculation. (The stock market was about as respectable then as the junk bond market is today.) The ability of the Federal Reserve Banks to create additional cash in a crisis, to act as lender of last resort, was seen as an additional, but not central, benefit.

Twelve Federal Reserve Banks were set up across the country, with a coordinating board in Washington, DC. As a concession to the opponents of central control, most of the power was invested in the regional Banks rather than in the Federal Reserve Board in Washington. Nationally chartered banks were required to become members of the system, and it was hoped that state banks would join voluntarily. However, the state banks were unenthusiastic: Membership was expensive as well as restrictive in terms of reserve requirements and allowable assets; the correspondent system continued to provide a viable alternative both for clearing and for the holding of liquid reserves.

The Federal Reserve Banks were to provide an "elastic currency" that could satisfy the public's demand for conversion of bank money in times of panic. To this end, a new kind of currency was created—Federal Reserve notes. Although these notes were convertible into gold, the hope was that backing by the "full faith and credit of the United States" would give them an acceptability close to that of definitive money.[6]

Member banks were required to keep reserve deposits at the Fed. These reserves could be converted at any time into Federal Reserve notes. Member banks could borrow from the Fed to cover their reserve requirements, or they could borrow directly in the form of notes. A bank wishing to borrow was required to post collateral. Acceptable collateral—called **eligible paper**—was limited to commercial loans to business.[7]

eligible paper
Paper acceptable as collateral for a bank's borrowing from the Fed.

The Fed was required to hold reserves against its deposits and against the Federal Reserve notes it issued. The reserves were to be at least 35% in gold for deposits and 40% for notes, with the rest either gold or eligible paper.[8] Since the Fed was not a profit-seeking institution, and it was not motivated to lend to the maximum extent possible, it was expected to have excess reserves of gold that would enable it to expand its lending in a time of crisis.

Dealing with panics was not the only reason for an "elastic currency." The relative shortage of gold and currency in the 1880s and 1890s had limited the growth of the quantity of bank money. The result of this scarcity of money had

---

[6]The convertibility of Federal Reserve notes into gold was limited in 1933 and eliminated entirely in 1971. See note 10.

[7]The reason for this restriction on the type of collateral that would be accepted had its origin in the "real bills doctrine." This theory maintained that as long as banks lent only to finance legitimate requests for working capital, it would be impossible for them to create excessive amounts of bank money and to cause a rise in prices. This theory, highly controversial at the time, has since been discredited. The alternative view was that only convertibility into gold would limit excessive creation of bank money (see the argument in Chapter 4). The Federal Reserve Act was an uncomfortable compromise between adherents of these two conflicting views.

[8]Against its deposits the Fed was required to hold reserves of 35% in "lawful money," which included gold, Federal Reserve notes, and the various other types of currency then in existence—national bank notes, silver certificates, greenbacks, and Treasury notes.

been a steady rise in its value and a corresponding fall in the prices of goods. The falling prices had been a drag on the economy. Since the Fed now had the ability to supplement the reserves of the banking system, it was expected to do so in such a way as to allow the quantity of money to expand along with economic growth.[9]

In addition to providing an elastic currency, the Fed was also charged with correcting some problems of the payments system. The most serious of these was the difficulty of clearing checks on banks outside a given clearinghouse area. As a result of this difficulty, checks drawn on distant banks were sometimes not honored at par. The Fed was expected to end "nonpar checking" by setting up an efficient national clearing system. Another perceived problem was the still large number of types of paper currency in circulation. In addition to several types that had been issued by the federal government—greenbacks, silver certificates, and Treasury notes—national banks issued bank notes of their own. Federal Reserve notes were supposed eventually to replace all of these as the only form of paper currency.

THE FED FLUNKS ITS FIRST MAJOR TEST

The boom of the 1920s ended with the crash of 1929. A series of banking panics and bank failures in unprecedented numbers contributed significantly to the Great Depression that followed. The number of banks shrank by a third. The quantity of money fell by about the same proportion and so did the level of prices. Faith in the banking system fell to an all-time low: Between 1929 and 1933 the public increased its holdings of currency by 50%, while demand deposits shrank by about a third. Banks responded to this pressure on their liquidity by increasing their own reserves from 15% of deposits in 1930 to 22% in 1932.

The Fed failed this first serious test dismally. Although it did expand its lending in the face of the overwhelming demand for conversion of bank money, the expansion was far less than the occasion required. Partly this was the result of confusion and ineptitude: The division of authority between the regional Federal Reserve Banks and the Federal Reserve Board in Washington was unclear, and Fed officials lacked experience in managing a central bank in a crisis. However, the main reason for the Fed's failure was its limited ability to provide the needed liquidity.

One problem was the linkage to gold. This became an issue at the height of the crisis when gold started to flow out of the United States. Britain had suspended the convertibility of its currency into gold, and there were fears that the United States would soon follow. Foreigners converted their dollars into gold and transferred the gold elsewhere. Rather than expanding its lending as the

[9]Another problem the elastic currency was expected to solve was the annual struggle of farm banks to satisfy the seasonal demand for currency associated with the harvest cycle: Farmers liked to be paid in cash for their crops. The Fed was expected to accommodate this demand for currency by lending to farm banks.

domestic situation required, the Federal Reserve Bank of New York felt it necessary to restrict its lending to protect its gold reserves against this external drain. By raising the rate of interest at which it was willing to lend, the New York Fed pushed up interest rates in the United States and made it more attractive for foreigners to leave their money here. The higher interest rates, however, reduced borrowing and further hurt the economy.

A second serious problem was the restriction that limited acceptable collateral to commercial loans. Since such loans made up only a small part of many banks' assets, they were unable to borrow as much from the Fed as they needed. Remember the second principle: Lend against *all* good collateral. This principle the Fed was legally unable to follow. The Fed's ability to lend was further restricted in that it was allowed to lend only to member banks. Of course, most of the banks in trouble were small country banks that were not members of the Federal Reserve System. However, had the Fed been able to provide sufficient liquidity to member banks, the pressure on these nonmember banks would have been significantly reduced.

A SECOND TRY AT PROTECTING THE BANKING SYSTEM

The failure of the Fed to handle the crisis led to a new wave of banking legislation in the 1930s. One part of this legislation improved the Fed's ability to act as a lender of last resort. The definition of acceptable collateral was expanded to include government securities and a broad range of bank assets. Convertibility into gold was temporarily suspended and then reestablished in a more limited form.[10] Power over the Federal Reserve System was placed firmly in Washington, in the hands of a newly created Board of Governors.

Lest even these steps prove insufficient, Congress added an additional layer of protection in the form of federal deposit insurance. State-sponsored deposit insurance had already been set up by eight Western and Southern states after 1907. There had been serious moral-hazard problems with these state insurance schemes: Under their protection banks in those states had expanded their lending rapidly, and many new banks had sprung up. With the agricultural depression of the 1920s, loans had soured, banks had failed, and the insurance schemes, lacking sufficient funds, had all collapsed.

Federal Deposit Insurance Corporation (FDIC) Government agency established to insure deposits in commercial banks up to a specified amount.

Learning from some of the mistakes of the state schemes, the federal government set up the **Federal Deposit Insurance Corporation (FDIC)** to insure deposits up to a limit of $2,500 per depositor. All banks, not only members of the

---

[10]The official price of gold was raised from $20.67 to $35.00 per ounce. This meant that the dollar was convertible, but into less gold than before. Moreover, only foreign central banks had the right to convert their dollars into gold (in the form of bullion rather than gold coins); currency held by residents of the United States was no longer convertible into gold. Gold held by U.S. residents was nationalized: Private individuals and institutions were required to sell their gold coin and bullion to the government. The external convertibility of the dollar was ended in 1971. Since 1975 U.S. residents have again been allowed to own gold.

Federal Reserve System, were eligible for this insurance. A parallel system was set up for savings and loans under the Federal Savings and Loan Insurance Corporation (FSLIC—pronounced "fizlik").

Federal deposit insurance faced considerable opposition. Many legislators were concerned about moral hazard. There was no precedent for government deposit insurance: No country in the world had ever had government deposit insurance, and none had thought it necessary. There was also strong resistance from the large banks, which opposed deposit insurance for two reasons. First, they felt it would require the sound banks (them) to pay for the losses of the unsound, small banks. Second, it would nullify one of their main competitive advantages over small banks. Economies of scale make large banks safer than small ones, but deposit insurance makes safety irrelevant for depositors. As a result, depositors are just as happy placing their money with a small bank as with a large one.

These effects of the introduction of deposit insurance are well illustrated by the Canadian experience. The introduction of deposit insurance in Canada in 1968 made it much easier for small banks to compete for funds, and many new small banks were opened (new regulations also made it easier for them to receive a bank charter). Although there had been virtually no bank failures in Canada before it had deposit insurance—even during the Great Depression—quite a few of the small banks set up after 1968 did fail.

16.3 BANK SAFETY IN THE UNITED STATES TODAY

The guarantees of bank safety set up in the 1930s, slightly modified by subsequent legislation, are the ones we have today. Our banking system is supported by both belt and suspenders: The belt is deposit insurance, and the suspenders are the lender of last resort.

FEDERAL DEPOSIT INSURANCE

The deposit insurance system is currently in serious trouble. We shall look at its problems and at what is being done about them in the next chapter. Before we do, let us see how deposit insurance actually works.

The FDIC now insures about $2.2 trillion in deposits at some 14,800 banks and about another $900 billion in deposits at some 3,000 S&Ls. Until 1989 the FDIC insured only banks; S&Ls were insured by a separate agency, FSLIC. However the S&L crisis bankrupted FSLIC, and it was taken over by the FDIC. The two insurance funds are still kept separate by the FDIC. Banks are covered by the Bank Insurance Fund (BIF); S&Ls are covered by a separate Savings Association Insurance Fund (SAIF). Only banks are allowed to display the FDIC logo; S&Ls must display a different logo that grudgingly admits insurance by the federal government but does not specifically mention the FDIC. Some 15,700 credit unions with assets of over $200 billion are insured by a separate government agency, the National Credit Union Share Insurance Fund of the National Credit Union Administration.

Each depositor is insured up to a maximum of $100,000 in principal and accrued interest.[11] Although 99% of all depositors are fully covered by this insurance, the remaining 1% of depositors hold some 28% of all deposits. Uninsured deposits are concentrated at the largest banks, which is, of course, where large depositors tend to have their accounts. Whereas less than 10% of total deposits are uninsured for banks with less than $100 million, the number for banks with more than $5 billion in assets is over 50%.

Banks pay an insurance premium of 15¢ per $100 of deposits on *all* deposits, even those that are not fully covered by the insurance. This is, of course, a particular burden for the large banks, which have a lot of uninsured deposits. The premium was raised in 1989 from 8¢. Before 1985, because claims were few, the FDIC rebated part of the premium, bringing the cost down to about 3¢. The rates for S&Ls have risen even more: S&Ls are currently required to pay 23¢ per $100 of deposits. The law allows the Fed to increase premiums as necessary up to a maximum of 32.5¢.

In the long, happy period from the 1930s through the 1970s during which bank failures were few and far between, the FDIC and FSLIC accumulated substantial reserve funds. The reserves of the FDIC remain substantial, as shown in Exhibit 16.1. The FDIC has a considerable annual income from premiums and from interest on the reserve fund. For example, in the first half of 1987 its income was $1.7 billion; it spent $1,436 million on 96 bank failures and $96 million on operating expenses; this left $164 million to be added to its reserves. The FDIC reserve fund experienced its first decline ever in 1988, when it lost some $4 billion on bank failures, mainly in Texas. It lost $851 million in 1989 and expected to lose some $2 billion more in 1990. The FDIC's reserve fund is not very liquid, since some two-thirds of it is "invested" in problem loans of banks that have failed. FSLIC became insolvent in 1986, and its successor, SAIF, is in the process of being rebuilt.

The fund insuring credit unions is in much better shape than the FDIC. Its reserves are over 50% larger relative to the deposits it insures, and its losses have been much smaller. Instead of paying an annual insurance premium, each credit union is required to place capital of 1% of its insured deposits with the insurance fund. If this reserve is ever used up because of losses, the credit unions are required to replenish it out of their own resources. So, unlike the situation with banks and S&Ls, there can be no cost to the taxpayer until the credit unions have used up all of their own capital.

---

[11]It is possible to extend the coverage in various ways by the use of joint accounts, trust accounts, IRAs, etc.

EXHIBIT 16.1

INSURANCE FUND RESERVES

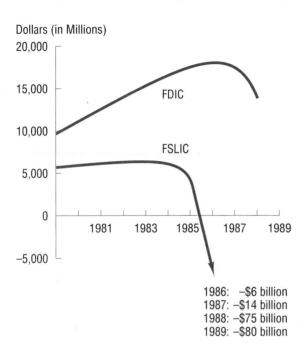

WHAT HAPPENS WHEN A BANK FAILS? The FDIC inspects the books of insured banks periodically to check on their solvency. If a bank is insolvent, it is closed down. The FDIC does not itself have the authority to close a bank: That rests with whoever granted the bank a charter—the Comptroller of the Currency (a Treasury official) for nationally chartered banks or the state banking authority for state-chartered banks. These authorities will close a bank on the advice of the FDIC.

There is a difference between ordinary corporations and banks with respect to insolvency and bankruptcy. An ordinary corporation can be insolvent and continue to operate: Only when its obligations come due and it defaults can its creditors have it declared bankrupt. Banks, on the other hand, are not subject to bankruptcy law. But they are subject to closure by banking regulators as soon as they become insolvent: Actual default is not necessary.

There are essentially two ways to handle a bank failure—*payout* or *purchase and assumption*. In a **payout,** the bank is liquidated and ceases to exist. The FDIC pays all insured depositors the value of their deposits up to the insurance maximum. It then sells off the bank's assets and uses the proceeds to pay off the bank's *un*insured creditors, including the FDIC itself.

payout
Complete liquidation of a failed bank.

purchase and assumption
A failed bank is purchased and its liabilities are assumed by another bank.

In a **purchase and assumption,** on the other hand, the bank is preserved as a going concern, but under new management. The FDIC arranges for some other bank to purchase the failed bank and to take over (to assume) its liabilities. The idea behind a purchase and assumption is that the purchasing bank should be willing to pay something for the value of the failed bank's customer relations and contacts—its goodwill. The value of this goodwill is lost if a bank is liquidated; in a purchase and assumption it is captured and reduces the cost of the failure to the FDIC. Banks interested in acquiring the failed bank submit bids to the FDIC, which takes the highest acceptable bid. A typical purchase and assumption is described in "FDIC Sets Up Takeover of Failed Bank in Oregon."

There are two variations on the purchase and assumption. In the "clean bank" version, the purchasing bank takes over the failed bank's liabilities but not its assets. The FDIC pays it the cash value of the liabilities, less the amount of the purchaser's bid. The FDIC then liquidates the failed bank's assets and keeps the proceeds. In the "whole bank" version, the purchasing bank takes over some or all of the failed bank's assets as well as its liabilities. The FDIC pays it the value of the liabilities, less the market value of those assets, less the purchaser's bid. As the amount of assets under liquidation by the FDIC has soared from $2 billion in 1982 to $11 billion in 1987, the FDIC has increasingly leaned toward whole-bank purchases and assumptions.

A major consideration in the choice between payout and purchase and assumption is cost. A payout is usually cheaper. In a payout, the FDIC pays only the *insured* depositors. The value of the failed bank's goodwill, which is lost in the case of a payout, is generally less than the value of the bank's uninsured liabilities. In a purchase and assumption, *all* liabilities of the failed bank are covered by the FDIC: Uninsured deposits are covered as well as insured, and nondeposit liabilities, such as borrowings of federal funds, as well as deposits.

Nonetheless, there are several reasons why the FDIC may prefer a purchase and assumption over a less expensive payout. Remember that the primary purpose of deposit insurance is to protect the banking system. If the FDIC feels that liquidation of the bank, and the consequent losses to uninsured depositors and creditors, would shake confidence in the banking system, it may prefer to bear the cost of a purchase and assumption.

Moreover, although a payout may ultimately be cheaper, a purchase and assumption may be less of a drain on FDIC funds in the short run. The short-run cost matters to the FDIC, because for political reasons it does not want to show an operating loss and to see its reserve fund shrink. So long as its reserve fund looks relatively healthy, Congress will presume that it is doing its job well and not ask too many questions. There is a strong political incentive to brush problems under the rug. Moreover, some of the long-run costs of a purchase and assumption—such as tax deductions for losses on assumed assets—may not be charged to the FDIC directly, although they are paid by the taxpayer.[12]

---

[12]A payout also ties up cash for a long time: After depositors are paid off, it takes an average of 12 years to liquidate all of a failed bank's assets.

FDIC SETS UP TAKEOVER OF FAILED BANK IN OREGON

By a *Wall Street Journal* Staff Reporter

WASHINGTON—The Federal Deposit Insurance Corp. arranged the takeover of failed Bear Creek Valley Bank in Phoenix, Oregon, by Valley of the Rogue Bank of Rogue River, Oregon.

Bear Creek Valley Bank was closed Friday by the state banking superintendent, John Olin, who said that "serious loan losses" and other liquidity problems experienced over the past year "finally exhausted the bank's capital funds," according to an FDIC spokesman. The FDIC was named receiver.

The single office of Bear Creek Valley Bank will reopen today as a branch of Valley of the Rogue Bank. The depositors of Bear Creek Valley Bank will automatically become depositors of Valley of the Rogue Bank.

To pave the way for the takeover, the FDIC agreed to advance $8.7 million to Valley of the Rogue Bank and to retain assets of the failed bank with a book value totaling $10.4 million.

Valley of the Rogue Bank agreed to assume about $11.3 million in deposits and other liabilities of the failed bank and to pay the FDIC a purchase premium of $150,000, the agency said.

The FDIC said that, including Bear Creek Valley Bank, 12 banks have failed so far this year. Last year 42 banks failed, said the agency, which insures deposits of as much as $100,000.

Source: "FDIC Sets Up Takeover of Failed Bank in Oregon," *The Wall Street Journal*, March 28, 1983. Reprinted by permission of The Wall Street Journal, © Dow Jones & Company, Inc. 1983. All Rights Reserved Worldwide.

Finally, a purchase and assumption is much more popular politically. Those bailed out are happy, and the general taxpayer does not feel the cost so long as the reserve fund holds up. Even when the taxpayer does start to bear the burden, it is not felt directly or immediately.

Despite the several attractions of a purchase and assumption, however, it is not always possible. State laws on branching and interstate banking may limit the pool of possible bidders, although this problem has been eased by the Banking Act of 1982, which permits interstate acquisitions of failed institutions. The size of the failed bank may also be a problem: There were no bidders for Continental Illinois, a $40-billion bank that failed in 1984 (we shall learn more about this case in Chapter 17).

In the case of Continental Illinois, and in some others, when purchase and assumption is impossible and a payout undesirable, the FDIC has resorted to direct assistance. In this case, it makes the failed bank a loan to keep it going until it can be returned to profitability. In exchange, the FDIC receives equity shares in the bank and appoints a board of directors of its choosing. This is essentially nationalization—a government takeover of the bank; the temporary, government-owned bank is known as a **bridge bank**. In the case of direct assistance, not only are all liabilities covered, but even the owners of the bank may come away with something.

bridge bank
Temporary, government-owned bank resulting from direct FDIC assistance to a failed bank.

As we have seen, deposit insurance involves a moral-hazard problem. How bank failures are resolved has a significant effect on the severity of this problem. With a payout, uninsured depositors and other creditors stand to take a loss; with a purchase and assumption, they do not. If uninsured depositors and creditors expect there to be a payout in the event of a failure, they will have every incentive to monitor the bank's performance. If they expect a purchase and assumption, they need not bother.

During most of its history, the FDIC has preferred to rely on purchase and assumption: Between 1934 and 1980, of 712 banks that failed, only 13 were payouts. However, as the number of bank failures rose in the early 1980s, the FDIC became more concerned about the moral-hazard problem, and, in an effort to crack down, it began to rely more heavily on payouts: Of some 800 failures, 99 were payouts. Perceptions of this change in policy had serious effects on the behavior of uninsured depositors, as we shall see in Chapter 17.

Because of the moral-hazard problem, the FDIC has an interest in monitoring and regulating the behavior of insured banks. Regulation can reduce both the probability of failure and the cost of failure if it occurs. For example, banks can be required to hold more equity, and restrictions can control the nature and diversification of their assets. Losses to the FDIC can also be reduced if a bank in trouble can be shut down promptly. A bank already in trouble will be more inclined to play long shots: If the long shot pays off, the situation is saved; if it does not, there is little to lose since losses will be borne by the FDIC. The loss to the FDIC can be reduced if the bank can be shut down before it engages in this sort of behavior. (We shall look at these issues again, in greater detail, in Chapter 17.)

THE DISCOUNT WINDOW

Deposit insurance tends to steal the limelight when it comes to bank safety. With the belt of deposit insurance in place, most depositors are unaware that they are protected too by the suspenders of a lender of last resort.

The Fed, as lender of last resort, stands ready to lend to banks in trouble against suitable collateral. In addition to such emergency loans, the Fed also lends routinely to help banks meet their reserve requirements and to help banks meet seasonal demands for credit—from farmers and from the tourist industry, for example.

discount window
When borrowing from the Fed, one is said to be going to the discount window.

discount rate
Rate charged for borrowing from the Fed.

Borrowing from the Fed is known as borrowing at the **discount window,** and the rate that is charged is known as the **discount rate.** The reason for these names is that bank loans used to be made by discounting commercial bills. A firm with a bill due from a customer, say for $1,000 payable in 90 days, would turn it into cash by discounting the bill at its bank. That is, the firm would sell the bill to the bank for its present, or discounted, value. For example, if the annual rate were 10%, the bank would buy the bill for $976. The bank, in its turn, could then *re*discount the bill at the Fed. If the discount rate were 12%, the bank could sell the bill to the Fed for $972. Today, most lending by the Fed no longer takes this form. Rather, the Fed makes the bank an *advance,* a straight loan secured by collateral. Despite the change in form, the name persists.[13]

The rules governing discount lending have been altered to reflect the lessons of the Depression. One problem then was that the Fed could accept only commercial bills as collateral. Today just about any asset is acceptable. Banks usually offer U.S. government securities, but the Fed will take almost anything in a pinch—including foreign assets and even the bank's buildings. Generally, to protect the Fed against loss due to credit or market risk, the collateral is worth more than the amount of the loan.

A second problem during the Depression was the linkage to gold. This is no longer an issue: Since the complete abandonment of convertibility into gold in 1971, Fed liabilities have been definitive money. There are now no restrictions on the amount of this definitive money that the Fed can provide in a time of crisis.

A third problem—the limitation of lending to member banks—has also disappeared. In 1978 the right to borrow routinely was extended to foreign banks operating in the United States, and in 1980 it was extended to all depository institutions. Moreover, the Fed is authorized, in a crisis, to lend to anyone it sees fit—to any financial institution, to corporations, or even to individuals. In practice, the Fed has been very reluctant to extend its lending, generally preferring to lend to others indirectly through banks.

Thrift institutions have their own "lender of next-to-last resort" in the form of the Federal Home Loan Banks. These institutions, 12 in number to parallel the Federal Reserve Banks, were set up by the banking legislation of the 1930s to provide loans to creditworthy thrifts with liquidity problems. The Federal Home Loan Banks raise the funds they need by selling bonds. Unlike the Fed, they cannot create definitive money. In a crisis, if help from the Federal Home Loan Banks is insufficient, the Fed will provide the necessary funds.

The discount rate is generally set by the Fed at a level that follows market rates, but with a lag. Contrary to the third of our four principles for a lender of last resort, the Fed does not set the discount rate at a level above market rates to discourage non-emergency borrowing. Therefore, to prevent banks from constantly borrowing large amounts at this bargain rate, the Fed lays down guidelines on the maximum that a bank *not* in trouble should borrow. A bank that exceeds these guidelines will immediately attract unwanted attention from bank regulators.

WHERE DOES THE BUCK STOP?

In 1985 E.S.M. Government Securities, a secondary dealer in U.S. government securities, collapsed, causing losses of some $300 million to its customers. Among those customers were a number of state-chartered thrifts in Ohio and

---

[13]The relationship between the two types of lending is rather like that between a direct sale of a security and a repo: The advance is like a repo, because the interest-rate risk on the underlying security is borne by the borrowing bank.

Maryland that were repoing out their government securities through E.S.M. These thrifts were not insured by the FDIC or FSLIC, but by private insurance agencies. Because the losses of the thrifts exceeded the reserve funds of these agencies, depositors became worried about the safety of their deposits. There were runs on a number of banks, including some that had not suffered losses but that were insured by the same potentially insolvent insurers (see "Closing of Ohio S&Ls after Run on Deposits Is One for the Books").[14]

On the other hand, when FSLIC, the federal agency that insured S&L deposits, became insolvent in 1986, there were no runs on the institutions that it insured. Why not? Because behind FSLIC there stood the Fed with its ability to create all the dollars depositors might want.

The *ultimate* guarantor of bank safety, then, remains the lender of last resort. Deposit insurance removes any incentive for a run or for a general banking panic only insofar as the insurance is credible. The federal deposit insurance is credible ultimately because it is backed by the ability of the Fed to satisfy the public's demand to convert bank money into definitive money by creating as much definitive money as is needed. Although the losses of FSLIC will eventually be paid through higher federal taxes, depositors know that they will not have to wait years to get their money, as they might have had to do with a state-funded bailout in Ohio or Maryland. It is this ability of the Fed to act fast in an emergency that ensures depositors that their deposits are safe *and* liquid.

16.4 | WHO IS RESPONSIBLE FOR THE EUROCURRENCY BANKS?

The FDIC and the Fed are responsible for the safety of U.S. domestic banks, but it is not really clear who is responsible for the safety of Eurocurrency banks.

In 1974 the failure of Bankhaus Herstatt, a medium-sized German bank heavily involved in Eurocurrency banking, caused a crisis of confidence in the Eurocurrency market. Depositors, particularly those from the Middle East, withdrew large amounts from non-U.S. banks and redeposited their money with the largest U.S. Eurocurrency institutions. The latter immediately lent the money out in the interbank market, forestalling a liquidity crisis for those banks facing the large withdrawals. (This is a good example of how banks can help one another during a "flight to quality.")

Although the Eurocurrency market weathered this crisis reasonably well, Herstatt demonstrated the potential for more serious problems. Extensive interbank lending seems to make the Eurocurrency market particularly vulnerable to a panic. Fears about one bank can easily grow into fears about the whole system. And there is, of course, no deposit insurance and no explicit lender of last resort.

---

[14]The Ohio deposit insurance agency covered $4.1 billion in deposits with a reserve fund of $123 million. The losses of a single Ohio thrift, Home State Savings of Cincinnati, exceeded the total resources of that state's insurance fund. There were similar problems in Maryland, where a state-sponsored agency covered $6.5 billion in deposits with a reserve fund of $170 million.

CLOSING OF OHIO S&Ls AFTER RUN ON DEPOSITS IS ONE FOR THE BOOKS

"I've gone from kindergarten to first grade in learning about banking," says Ohio Gov. Richard Celeste, who on Friday ordered 71 state-chartered savings and loan institutions closed for at least three days. "Ten days ago," he adds, "I couldn't have told you the difference" between federal and state-sponsored insurance funds.

The governor isn't the only one befuddled about how to handle the depositor runs at some of the state's thrift institutions.

"I've got manuals here on how to manage a savings and loan, but there's nothing written about this," complains William Garman, vice president of Jefferson Building & Savings Bank of Steubenville, Ohio. The thrift institution hesitated, opened briefly on Friday in defiance of the governor's order but then closed early after learning that banks weren't honoring its checks.

The Democratic governor ordered the closings after a surge of withdrawals at a number of Ohio thrift institutions in the wake of the failure of Home State Savings Bank of Cincinnati, which had depositor insurance through the state-sponsored but private Ohio Deposit Guarantee Fund and didn't have federal insurance. Home State was closed earlier and put up for sale after runs stemming from heavy losses in its dealings with the failed E.S.M. Government Securities Inc., of Fort Lauderdale, Florida.

Mr. Celeste today will ask the state legislature to pass a bill requiring the 71 thrifts to apply for federal insurance before they can reopen.

Source: "Closing of Ohio S&Ls After Run on Deposits Is One for the Books," *The Wall Street Journal*, March 18, 1985. Reprinted by permission of The Wall Street Journal, © Dow Jones & Company, Inc. 1985. All Rights Reserved Worldwide.

The Herstatt crisis also raised the question of who was responsible for the safety and stability of Eurocurrency banking. Who is responsible, for example, for the London subsidiary of a French bank taking deposits and making loans in U.S. dollars? The Bank of England, because the lending is done in London? The Bank of France, because the bank involved is a subsidiary of a French bank? Or the Fed, because the lending is done in U.S. dollars?

There are some peculiar difficulties for a bank operating in a non-native currency. If a U.S. bank faces a loss of Euro deposits, it can easily replace them with funds borrowed in the United States. For a foreign bank, it is much more difficult. Its ability to borrow in the United States is limited. If it turns to its own central bank, that institution will be hard pressed to help: The Bank of France can create as many francs as it needs, but its supply of U.S. dollars is limited. A foreign central bank can, of course, borrow dollars from the Fed, but this will expose it to exchange-rate risk.

So a foreign bank operating in U.S. dollars needs some reliable source of liquidity in case of an emergency. What it frequently does is establish a standby line of credit with a U.S. bank. Under this arrangement the U.S. bank will act as the foreign bank's lender of last resort with respect to its U.S.-dollar liabilities. Similarly, of course, a U.S. bank operating in, say, German marks, will establish a standby line of credit with a German bank. Sometimes these arrangements are reciprocal, with no explicit payment on either side. Not surprisingly, the interest of banks in standby lines grew considerably after the Herstatt crisis.

Basel concordat
1974 agreement that each central bank should be responsible for the foreign subsidiaries of its own bank.

In 1974, following the Herstatt crisis, central bankers met at a conference in Basel to draw lines of responsibility. According to the resulting agreement, known as the **Basel concordat,** each central bank is responsible for the foreign subsidiaries of its own banks. Hence, although there is no formal lender of last resort for Eurocurrency banks, each central bank is expected to take care of its own.[15]

The Basel concordat was brought into question by the Bank of Italy's handling of the Banco Ambrosiano scandal in 1982 (see Chapter 11). The scandal involved a subsidiary of Banco Ambrosiano—Banco Ambrosiano Holdings, S.A., a financial holding company located in Luxembourg. The Bank of Italy supported Banco Ambrosiano itself, but refused to assume the debts of Banco Ambrosiano Holdings on the grounds that it was not a bank and not in Italy. Luxembourg also denied responsibility on the grounds that Banco Ambrosiano Holdings was not a bank. Eurodollar banks had lent Banco Ambrosiano Holdings over $500 million.

SUMMARY

- Fractional-reserve banking has considerable advantages over warehouse banking in terms of efficiency. Its main problem is its susceptibility to bank runs and to banking panics.

- Depositors will run on a bank not only when they believe the bank is in trouble, but also when they think other depositors think the bank is in trouble. Fears of a run can cause a run.

- Banks can help one another deal with bank runs by sharing reserves. They have an interest in doing so, because bank runs can be contagious. There are, however, limitations on the efficacy of mutual aid, particularly in the face of a loss of confidence in the whole banking system.

- A lender of last resort can provide the liquidity needed to deal with a general banking panic. Its ability to do so is much enhanced by its being able to create definitive or near-definitive money.

- The four principles laid down to guide the lender of last resort are: (1) Lend only against *good* collateral; (2) accept *all* good collateral; (3) charge a high rate of interest; and (4) make your policies known to the public.

- An alternative way to protect banks against runs and panics is deposit insurance. Deposit insurance involves a serious moral-hazard problem.

- Banks in the United States have had more safety problems than those in other countries because of the peculiar structure of U.S. banking—a large number of geographically restricted small banks.

[15]Unfortunately, Hong Kong, a major Eurocurrency center, has no central bank of its own. Presumably, in a crisis the Bank of England would step in.

- During the national banking era, the only protection banks had was mutual aid. This was organized by the clearinghouse associations.

- A series of banking panics led to the establishment of the Federal Reserve System in 1913. Because of political opposition, the Fed was originally set up in a way that limited its ability to act as a lender of last resort. As a result, it failed badly in handling the banking panics of the Great Depression.

- New banking legislation in the 1930s rectified some of the problems with the Fed and added federal deposit insurance. That legislation created the banking structure we have today.

- The FDIC insures deposits at banks and S&Ls; credit unions have their own agency. Depositors are insured up to a maximum of $100,000 in exchange for an insurance premium paid by the banks.

- When a bank fails, the FDIC may either liquidate it and pay off insured depositors (a payout) or it may arrange for a takeover by a healthy bank (a purchase and assumption). Recently, the FDIC has also sometimes arranged for a bank to continue in operation under government control (a bridge bank). The severity of the moral-hazard problem will depend on which method depositors expect to be used.

- The Fed, as lender of last resort, makes loans to banks via the discount window. It also lends to banks routinely for other reasons.

- The effectiveness of deposit insurance in preventing runs depends on its credibility. The credibility of federal insurance rests on the ability of the Fed to create unlimited liquidity in a crisis.

- Although there is no official safety net for Eurocurrency banks, under the Basel concordat of 1974 central banks agreed to be responsible for their own banks. There remain doubts about how this commitment is to be interpreted.

KEY TERMS

banking panic	loan certificates	payout
central bank	suspension of convertibility	purchase and assumption
lender of last resort	Federal Reserve Act of 1913	bridge bank
legal tender	eligible paper	discount window
moral hazard	Federal Deposit Insurance Corporation (FDIC)	discount rate
deductible		Basel concordat
coinsurance		

DISCUSSION QUESTIONS

1. Suppose you are managing a bank. The rate on bank loans is 12% and the discount rate is 9%. How much would you pay for a $1 million, 90-day commercial bill? How much could you sell it for to the Fed? How much of this would you like to do?

2. Which of the four principles of a lender of last resort did the Fed satisfy when it was first set up? Which does it satisfy now?

3. What are the comparative advantages and disadvantages of a lender of last resort and of deposit insurance as ways of ensuring bank safety?

4. Why was the United States the first country to institute government deposit insurance?

5. How did the banking legislation of the 1930s address the problems of bank safety in the United States? How successful was it? What more, if anything, could have been done?

6. What are the relative advantages of the various methods of dealing with a failed bank?

7. What are the particular problems of Eurocurrency banking in the area of safety? How are they dealt with?

8. Deposit insurance suffers from a moral-hazard problem. What are the ways of dealing with this problem?

BIBLIOGRAPHY

Bovenzi, John F., and Arthur J. Murton, "Resolution Costs of Bank Failures," *FDIC Banking Review* Fall 1988, 1–13.

Dwyer, Gerald P., Jr., and R. Alton Gilbert, "Bank Runs and Private Remedies," *Economic Review of the Federal Reserve Bank of St. Louis* May-June 1989, 43–61.

Friedman, Milton, and Anna Jacobson Schwartz, *A Monetary History of the United States 1867–1960*, Princeton: Princeton University Press, 1963.

Humphrey, Thomas M., "Lender of Last Resort: The Concept in History," *Economic Review of the Federal Reserve Bank of Richmond* March-April 1989, 8–16.

Lewis, M. K., and K. T. Davis, *Domestic and International Banking*, Cambridge, Mass.: M.I.T. Press, 1987.

Parthemos, James, "The Federal Reserve Act of 1913 in the Stream of U.S. Monetary History," *Economic Review of the Federal Reserve Bank of Richmond* July-August 1988, 19–28.

White, E. N., *The Regulation and Reform of the American Banking System, 1900–1929*, Princeton: Princeton University Press, 1983.

CHAPTER 17

THE DEPOSIT INSURANCE CRISIS

Banking legislation in the 1930s improved the Fed's ability to function as a lender of last resort and set up the FDIC to insure deposits. The new system seemed to work well for nearly half a century: There were few bank failures and no bank runs or banking panics. Then, in the early 1980s, things started to come apart. Today, commercial banking is in serious trouble. As Exhibits 17.1 A and B show, the number of failures has risen steadily over the last decade, as has the amount of bank assets involved. Actual failures are only the tip of the iceberg: The number of banks in trouble is far greater. Well over 1,000 banks were on the FDIC's problem list in 1989. But the problems of the commercial banks are dwarfed by those of the savings and loan industry. Widespread losses there threaten to reduce the number of S&Ls to perhaps 1,500 from over 4,000 a decade ago. The eventual cost to the taxpayer may be as high as $200 billion—about $800 for every man, woman, and child in the United States.

What went wrong and why? What should be done? What is being done? These are the questions we shall address in this chapter.

17.1 THE BACKGROUND

That 40-year period of stability was an easy time for bankers. It was the era of "3-6-3" banking: Pay 3% for deposits, charge 6% on loans, be on the golf course by 3 p.m. Interest rates and exchange rates were stable, so there was little market risk. Regulation Q and branching restrictions protected banks from competition. Cushioned by market power, and in a stable environment, little could or did go wrong.

453

E x h i b i t 17.1A

BANK FAILURES

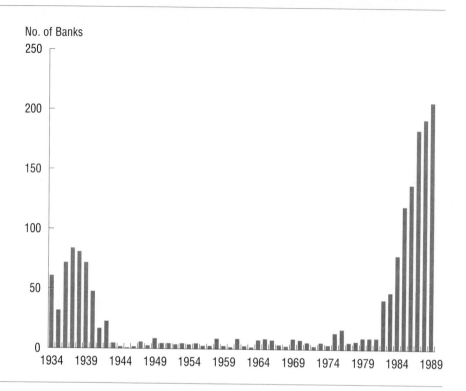

Source: Federal Deposit Insurance Corporation.

COMPETITIVE PRESSURES

Then, beginning in the late 1960s, interest rates began to climb. With the growth of the money market and the crumbling of Regulation Q, banks started to face increasing competition, both from other banks and from other intermediaries and financial markets. The cost of funds increased: The rates paid on deposits went up, and banks started to rely increasingly on relatively expensive funds bought in the money market. Some of the best borrowers were lost to commercial paper.

At the same time, restrictions on geographic expansion were circumvented or removed. Cosy local markets were invaded by outsiders competing for deposits and for loan business. In the rush to reap economies of scale, expansion became a condition for survival.

The growth of the money market made it easier for banks to get the funds they needed for rapid expansion. Banks no longer had to rely on growing deposits to support growth in their loan portfolios: Now they could go out into the money market and bid for funds with commercial paper, NCDs, overnight repos, and purchases of federal funds.

EXHIBIT 17.1B

ASSETS OF
FAILED BANKS

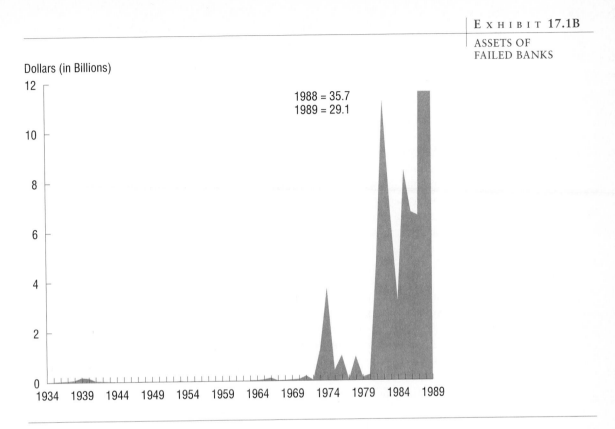

Dollars (in Billions)

1988 = 35.7
1989 = 29.1

Source: Federal Deposit Insurance Corporation.

The increase in the cost of funds, plus the pressure to expand loan portfolios, led to a lowering of lending standards. If you want to earn more on your loans, you have to accept more risk. If you want to expand your lending in a hurry, you have to be less picky. Bank of America, for example, had a policy of expanding its loan portfolio by 10% a year, and its loan officers were rewarded according to the quantity of new loans written—not an incentive designed to promote careful lending. First Chicago tripled its lending between 1969 and 1974 to become the ninth largest bank in the United States; in 1976 bank examiners found problem loans equal in value to double the bank's equity. For small banks without much access themselves to large borrowers, the growth in participations and syndications made it easier to expand their lending. But in making such loans, they trusted others to do the credit assessment for them. For many banks, both large and small, rapid expansion was the prelude to rapid decline.

Increased competition also provided another, more subtle incentive to risk taking. When a bank is protected from competition and has market power, its profits are large. In those circumstances, a bank charter is valuable: It is a license to earn economic rents. If the bank fails, the owners stand to lose the value of the charter in addition to the equity they put into the bank. With more to lose if the bank fails, the owners are more cautious in operating the bank. However, competition whittles away at the value of the charter: When entry into the market is easy, a bank charter is no longer worth very much. With less to lose if the bank fails, taking risks becomes more attractive.

THE ROLE OF DEPOSIT INSURANCE

The increase in risk taking is, of course, aggravated by the existence of deposit insurance. With no deposit insurance, when a bank takes more risks in its lending, the safety of its deposits is reduced, and depositors demand to be compensated, withdrawing their deposits if they are not. Since risk taking raises the cost of funds in this way, banks may not find it profitable to increase their risk taking very much. However, with deposit insurance in place, depositors could care less about the riskiness of a bank's loans, and the brake on risk taking is removed. This is the moral-hazard problem we discussed in Chapter 16.

The connection between risk taking and deposit insurance, and the resulting moral-hazard problem, are illustrated particularly well by the phenomenon of **brokered deposits.** The idea is simple enough. Assume you are a corporate treasurer with $10 million in cash that you want to keep liquid. Because insurance is limited to $100,000 per deposit, you are worried about putting all your money into a single bank. No problem. A **money broker**—usually an investment bank—will offer you the following service. Give them the $10 million, and they will break it up into $100,000 packages. These they will then deposit, each at a different bank. Since each package is fully insured, there is no need to worry about the soundness of the bank, and the broker can simply offer the money to the highest bidder.

brokered deposits
Large amounts of money divided into small portions for deposit with a number of banks.

money broker
Financial institution that manages brokered-deposit accounts for large investors.

Brokered deposits proved a boon to small banks that were rapidly expanding their lending. There was no way such banks could borrow funds by selling NCDs in the money market: Only banks with well-known names and excellent credit standing could do so. However, it was easy for them to get hold of any amount of brokered money.

A particularly dramatic example of the potential dangers of brokered deposits was provided by Empire Savings and Loan of Mesquite, Texas. Empire's deposits grew from $17 million to $309 million in the two years before it failed in March 1984. Eighty-five percent of its deposits were brokered; nearly all its loans involved real estate speculation in the Dallas market, and many of them were fraudulent. Empire's failure was expected to cost FSLIC over $160 million.

The largest money broker in the early 1980s was Merrill Lynch. Of the $22.5 billion of brokered deposits outstanding in 1984, it was responsible for $12.5 billion. The FDIC described Merrill's claim that it was careful in checking out banks with which it placed money as "nonsense." The FDIC tried to put an end to brokered deposits in 1984 by announcing that in future payouts it would regard all deposits placed by the same broker as belonging to a single depositor. For example, if Merrill had placed $5 million at a failed bank (50 packages of $100,000, each belonging to a different client), the $100,000 limit would apply to the whole $5 million, rather than to each individual package. But the courts found this practice illegal, and the FDIC was forced to abandon it. Brokered deposits continue to thrive: As of May 1989, 804 banks were holding brokered deposits amounting to almost $52 billion.[1]

A MOUNTAIN OF PROBLEM LOANS

In the 1970s and 1980s the hunger for high-yield loans has driven banks into a number of areas of lending that have turned out, in retrospect, to be disasters.

LDC DEBT   The biggest problem for money center banks has been their lending to LDCs (less-developed countries), mostly in Latin America. We looked at this lending in Chapter 12 as a case study in risk. Between 1970 and 1982 U.S. banks increased such lending from almost zero to $72 billion. The tightening of monetary policy by the Fed in the 1980–1982 period raised interest rates, raised the value of the dollar, and caused a major worldwide recession. The debtor nations, facing higher rates on their floating-rate loans, a more expensive dollar, and reduced exports, were unable to meet their payments. In August 1982 Mexico was the first to announce that it was temporarily suspending payments on its debt, threatening many banks with insolvency.

Many small and medium-sized banks participated in the LDC loans through syndications. When the crisis struck, some 1,500 U.S. banks were holding LDC debt they had acquired in this way. Syndications offered an easy and lucrative way for these banks to enter the international market, about which they knew next to nothing. They relied on the savvy of the lead banks that put together the syndications.

Since 1982 banks have cut back new lending to LDCs, and they have gradually increased their loan-loss reserves against existing loans, recognizing that the loans are unlikely to be repaid. Various deals have been worked out, including the rescheduling of interest and principal repayment. Losses on these loans have seriously weakened the capital positions of the money center banks that were most involved. The smaller banks involved in the syndications have also taken losses, but the amounts involved did not represent as large a fraction of their assets as they did for the money center banks.

Losses on these loans continue: Large losses were declared in 1987 and again in 1989, when $6.3 billion of write-offs in the third quarter by 5 of the 10 largest banks gave the industry as a whole a net loss for the quarter. In 1988 the money

---

[1] A similar issue in insurance has cropped up in recent years with respect to bank investment contracts (BICs). These are like CDs, with a maturity of 2 to 6 years and a rate guaranteed for any amount deposited during a "window" of, usually, one year. Funds can be withdrawn at any time without penalty. BICs are mainly sold to pension plans in competition with the GICs offered by insurance companies (see Chapter 14). Formally, the BIC, often in very large amounts, belongs to a single depositor—the pension plan—so that most of it would not be covered by insurance. However, banks have offered to pass through the $100,000 FDIC guarantee to each plan *participant*, and the FDIC has allowed this. In early 1990 there was about $50 billion worth of BICs outstanding.

center banks still held $58.5 billion in LDC debt, equal to 91% of their equity capital. Substantial write-offs against these loans were expected to continue well into the 1990s.

ENERGY LOANS The OPEC price rises of 1973 and 1979 set off a wave of energy exploration in the United States, particularly in the Southwest. Banks in the region found themselves swamped with loan requests. They met this demand by selling participations to banks elsewhere, including some money center banks. In this way they returned the favor of the LDC syndications. The regional banks knew nothing about foreign lending, and they took part in syndications in the belief that the money center lead banks knew what they were doing. Similarly, the money center banks knew nothing about oil exploration, and they took part in participations put together by banks in Texas and Oklahoma in the belief that the local banks could tell a good oil loan from a bad one. In 1981 oil prices started to slide, and many more of these loans turned out to be bad than good.

REAL ESTATE Driven partly by growth of the energy industry, the Sunbelt enjoyed a boom in residential and commercial real estate in the late 1970s and early 1980s. Deregulation allowed banks and, particularly, savings and loans to play a large role in financing speculative construction. Then, partly as a result of the collapse of the energy industry and partly as a result of overbuilding, the boom became a bust and defaults were widespread.

During the 1980s rapid growth in New England, New Jersey, the Southeast, and California led to real estate booms in those areas. Regional and superregional banks rapidly expanded their lending to real estate developers. Commercial real estate rose to 18% of bank assets in 1989 from 10% in 1980. In 1989 the real estate market began to soften and the banks began to take losses. The Bank of New England, a hot superregional bank, was in particularly serious trouble, having lost some $1.1 billion in 1989. Real estate loans are proving to be a particular problem for regional banks because most of their lending tends to be concentrated in one geographic area.

AGRICULTURE The rise in oil prices in the early 1970s was part of a more general rise in commodity prices. The newspapers were full of stories about how the world was going to run out of everything. Food prices, in particular, shot up. Many farmers, tempted by the high prices, borrowed to buy more land and equipment. This boom also came to an end. Foreclosures abounded, but with land prices falling, loan losses were substantial.

THE RECESSION OF 1980–1982 Recessions always bring waves of business failures and loan defaults. The recession of 1980–1982 was the worst since the Great Depression. The rise in the value of the dollar compounded the problem, because it made U.S. goods more expensive relative to foreign goods. Automobiles, agricultural and construction equipment, and steel were particularly hard hit by increasing competition from imports and by falling exports.

LBOs Different estimates suggest that banks hold $70 billion to $250 billion in debt related to LBOs and to highly leveraged restructurings (see Chapter 14). This amount has been growing rapidly, since the collapse of the junk bond market has led borrowers to rely more on bank finance. Some individual money center banks are very heavily involved. As with LDC debt, syndications have played a major role here. Many foreign banks, especially Japanese banks, have been involved in this lending. There have been no major problems so far, but there could be in the event of an economic downturn. Because of high leverage and a high ratio of interest payments to current income, the borrowers are particularly likely to default if their incomes fall in a recession.

THE ROLE OF FRAUD A certain number of defaults are only to be expected. Business is risky, and some investments that initially looked promising will eventually turn out to be duds. However, many bad loans turn out to be the result not of adverse business circumstances, but of outright fraud. For the managers of a bank, the easiest way to steal is to arrange bogus loans to friends, relatives, and associates with no intention that the loans be repaid. Studies suggest that this type of fraud plays a major role in many bank failures.

One indicator of the extent to which fraud has played a role is the cost of a bank's failure to the FDIC as a percentage of the bank's assets. Historically, that figure has been around 10%. Recently, it has been rising, exceeding 50% in some cases. Losses of this magnitude are generally not the result of honest mistakes. In 1989 Attorney General Richard Thornburgh estimated that fraud and insider abuse were involved in 25% to 30% of S&L failures and had resulted in over $2 billion worth of losses in 1988 alone (others think this estimate may be conservative).

THE EXTENT OF THE PROBLEM By the mid-1980s many banks were in serious trouble. As Exhibit 17.2 shows, several classes of banks were involved. A number of large money center banks had taken significant losses on LDC, energy-related, and industrial loans. Farm banks throughout the Midwest were in trouble because of the slump in agriculture. Banks and savings and loans in the Southwest and West became insolvent in droves as the energy economy collapsed and real estate values plummeted.

INCREASING MARKET RISK Market risk increased dramatically in the 1970s. As interest rates rose from the late 1960s, they also became more volatile. In 1979 a major change in monetary policy (which we shall discuss in detail in later chapters) had the effect of further increasing the volatility of interest rates. The new policy and the increased volatility continued through 1982. The Bretton Woods agreement, under which exchange rates were fixed within narrow bounds, was abandoned in 1971. In the years that followed, exchange rates were allowed to fluctuate much more widely.

The increased volatility of interest rates and of exchange rates caught many institutions unprepared. Their balance sheets had long been vulnerable to market risk, but because actual fluctuations had been small, they had done little to address the problem. The prime example of this is the savings and loan industry, with its frightening duration gap—the result of funding long-term mortgages with short-term deposits.

Of course, the increased volatility was not just a danger: It was also an opportunity. Successful speculation on interest-rate and exchange-rate movements became a tempting way for banks to supplement their earnings. The temptation was particularly great, because the banks' traditional business of intermediation had become much less profitable under the pressure of competition. The same forces that led banks to make doubtful loans led them to gamble on interest-rate and exchange-rate movements. Several of the more spectacular bank failures of the 1970s were the result of interest-rate and exchange-rate gambles that turned sour.

In 1973 Franklin National, a bank that had expanded rapidly by making poor loans, tried to recoup its losses by betting that interest rates would continue to fall and that the dollar would continue to rise. It shortened the duration of its liabilities, lengthened the duration of its assets, and took a short position in foreign currencies. In 1974 interest rates rose sharply to unprecedented highs and the dollar dropped 10%. Following a liquidity crisis that required the Fed to lend it $1.8 billion, Franklin failed—the largest failure to that date. Foreign-exchange speculation also played a major role in the Herstatt failure that shook the Eurodollar market in the same year. The rise in interest rates in 1979 sank First Pennsylvania, which had been funding a large bond portfolio with short-term money; that bailout cost the FDIC $1.5 billion.

THE FDIC GETS TOUGH: PENN SQUARE

As the number and cost of bank failures increased in the late 1970s and early 1980s, the moral-hazard problem that had always been implicit in deposit insurance became more obvious. In an attempt to impose greater "market discipline," the FDIC started to rely more on payouts and less on purchase and assumptions in its resolution of bank failures. Although there did seem to be a shift in its policy for resolving the failures of small banks, the big question in everyone's mind was whether the FDIC would allow uninsured depositors in a *large* bank to take a loss.

That question was answered with the collapse of Penn Square Bank of Oklahoma City in July 1982. Penn Square's assets had grown from $30 million to over $500 million in five years; some 80% of its loans were energy-related. When it failed, 25% of Penn Square's deposits were brokered. As early as 1980, regulators had detected problems with its loans (possibly involving fraud), but it took two more years until extensive defaults drove it under. In addition to its own lending, Penn Square had also sold $2.1 billion of loan participations to other banks: Continental Illinois had bought $1 billion, Seafirst $400 million, and Chase $200 million to $300 million. These participations also proved to be bad.

Rather than arrange a purchase and assumption of Penn Square, the FDIC decided on a payout. It is not clear whether this really was the result of a get-

EXHIBIT 17.2

BANK FAILURES BY STATE: 1982–MAY 1990

Source: Federal Deposit Insurance Corporation.

tough policy. There were special circumstances that made a purchase and assumption difficult: Oklahoma's branching restrictions made it hard to find a purchaser, and possible liability in lawsuits arising from the alleged criminal violations made the future costs of a purchase and assumption very uncertain. Whatever the FDIC's motives, uninsured depositors—among them several small banks, savings and loans, and credit unions—stood to take a substantial loss. Losses to uninsured depositors, which accounted for more than half the bank's deposits, were expected at the time to be at least $38 million.

The Penn Square payout seemed to provide proof that money really could be lost on uninsured deposits. The good old days of de facto 100% insurance were over. Naturally, this made large depositors much more nervous. (Brokered deposits received a major boost.) Although this increased nervousness on the part of depositors was perhaps intended—it was supposed to make banks more cautious and thereby reduce the moral-hazard problem—the results proved more dramatic than anyone had anticipated.

17.2 THE CRISIS ERUPTS: THE COLLAPSE OF CONTINENTAL ILLINOIS

The problems of commercial banking came to a head with the collapse of Continental Illinois of Chicago in 1984. One could hardly ask for a better case study in the problems of U.S. banking.

In 1973, under its new chairman, Roger Anderson, the Continental Illinois National Bank and Trust Co. of Chicago began a period of aggressive growth. Its goal was to outdo its archrival, First Chicago, and to enter the top tier of money center banks. Continental's loan officers were encouraged to lend, lend, lend. They offered bargain rates to lure business away from competitors. They fought for the lion's share in syndications and participations. By 1983 Continental had accumulated over $42 billion in assets, making it the seventh largest bank in the United States.

Continental's problems began with the rise in interest rates in 1979. Earnings deteriorated and loan losses mounted. Things reached the crisis point when Penn Square collapsed in July 1982: Continental had $1 billion in energy-loan participations from Penn Square itself and had passed on more to its own respondents. It was forced to add $220 million to its growing list of problem loans. That list was already long. It included other energy loans, among them a $300 million loan to NuCorp Energy and one to Dome Petroleum, the focus of a financial scandal in Canada. It also included loans to LDCs; real estate loans—including some to American Invesco, a controversial Chicago developer; and industrial loans to Braniff, International Harvester, Massey-Ferguson, and Chrysler—all either bankrupt or on the verge of bankruptcy.

Because of its rapidly worsening financial situation, Continental found it increasingly difficult to sell its NCDs in the money market. It was forced to remove itself from the "no name" list—the list of top banks whose paper was accepted interchangeably in NCD trading and in delivery on futures contracts.

Continental's worsening position in the money market was particularly dangerous because of its unusually heavy reliance on bought funds. Because its home state of Illinois then allowed no branching, Continental had limited access to domestic demand and time deposits: In fact, such deposits made up no more than 25% of its funds. The remainder came from NCDs, Eurodollars, fed funds, and repos. Continental relied on domestic interbank liabilities for 16% of its funds and on international interbank liabilities for 40% more. None of these interbank liabilities were insured.

The NCDs that Continental was losing could be replaced, for the time being, by even heavier reliance on fed funds and short-term Eurodollars. No one

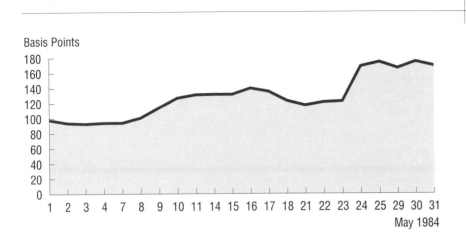

Information is based on the closing prices of futures contracts for June 1984 delivery.
Source: *The Wall Street Journal.*

expected Continental to close overnight. However, it was forced to pay a premium for these funds, and the additional cost added to its problems.

Over the following year, loan losses mounted and the deposit outflow continued. In April 1984 Continental announced the addition of another $400 million to its list of problem loans, bringing the total to $2.3 billion, an amount in excess of its equity. For the first time, there was talk of imminent failure.

On Thursday, May 10, a rumor began to circulate that Continental was about to be closed. (The source of the rumor is unknown, but it seems to have originated in Hong Kong.) The next day, Friday, Continental was unable to roll over its overnight borrowing—Penn Square was still fresh in lenders' minds—and it was forced to go to the Chicago Fed (conveniently located across the street) for a loan of $3.5 billion.

Over the weekend a group of 16 major banks led by J. P. Morgan put together a $4.5 billion line of credit to restore confidence in Continental Illinois. The banks had reason to be concerned. Continental's problems were affecting the ability of all of them to sell NCDs. Exhibit 17.3 shows how the risk premium on NCDs relative to Treasuries increased, and Exhibit 17.4 shows how bank stock prices fell.

By Tuesday of the following week, it was clear that mutual aid was not enough. Continental's need for overnight money had mushroomed to $8 billion—$4 billion from the Fed, $2.25 billion from the rescue group, and the rest from other sources. On Wednesday the Fed injected $1.5 billion of new capital with a purchase of subordinated debt, and it arranged for the rescue group, now numbering 28 banks, to increase Continental's credit line to $5.5 billion and to provide $500 million in equity. Even this was not enough.

EXHIBIT 17.4

STOCK PRICES OF THE TEN LARGEST BANKS DURING THE CONTINENTAL ILLINOIS CRISIS

Bank	May 10, 1984	May 18, 1984	Percentage Change
Citicorp	$32 $\frac{7}{8}$[a]	$31 $\frac{3}{4}$[a]	–3.54%
Bank of America	19	18 $\frac{3}{8}$	–3.40
Chase Manhattan	48 $\frac{1}{4}$	44 $\frac{3}{4}$	–7.82
Manufacturers Hanover	35 $\frac{1}{4}$	32 $\frac{5}{8}$	–8.05
J. P. Morgan	71 $\frac{3}{4}$	67 $\frac{3}{4}$	–5.90
Chemical	31 $\frac{1}{4}$	29 $\frac{7}{8}$	–4.76
First Interstate Bancorp	34 $\frac{7}{8}$	34 $\frac{1}{4}$	–1.82
Bankers Trust	43 $\frac{1}{8}$	41 $\frac{1}{4}$	–4.55
Continental Illinois	12	10 $\frac{3}{8}$	–15.66
Security Pacific	44 $\frac{3}{4}$	43 $\frac{7}{8}$	–1.99

[a]Prices refer to closing of common stock on trading day listed.

Source: *The Wall Street Journal.*

On Thursday, May 17, the FDIC took the extraordinary step of announcing that it would guarantee *all* of Continental's deposits—not just the first $100,000— and all of its *nondeposit* liabilities. The crisis moderated but did not end: The announcement was vague on specifics. Would interest as well as principal be covered? Would the guarantee continue if Continental were merged with another bank? Without answers to these questions, depositors could not feel that their deposits were completely safe.

Continental continued to lose deposits. Why take a chance on Continental, when you could deposit your money safely at Citi or Morgan? By July, although Continental's balance sheet had shrunk by $5 billion, its need for overnight funds had further increased to $10 billion. The growth in lending by the Fed is shown in Exhibit 17.5. A record second-quarter loss of $1.1 billion was announced.

On July 26, 1984, after all attempts to arrange a purchase and assumption had failed (Illinois had even agreed to an out-of-state merger), Continental was taken over by the federal government. The FDIC injected $1 billion of new capital in exchange for an 80% ownership stake in the failed bank. It also assumed the $3.5 billion loan from the Fed in exchange for $4.5 billion worth of the bank's problem loans.

By March 1985 Continental's assets had shrunk from $42 billion to $30 billion. Nonetheless, Continental still required $8 billion of special funding. The final cost of the bailout is still unknown—it depends on how much the FDIC can recover on the bad loans—but recent estimates place it at about $1.7 billion.[2]

---

[2]At 4% of the failed bank's assets, this is quite good compared to the average of a 10% loss for banks closed by the FDIC. The cost of the Continental bailout did not hold the record for long: The 1988 failure of First RepublicBank of Dallas is expected to cost over $3 billion.

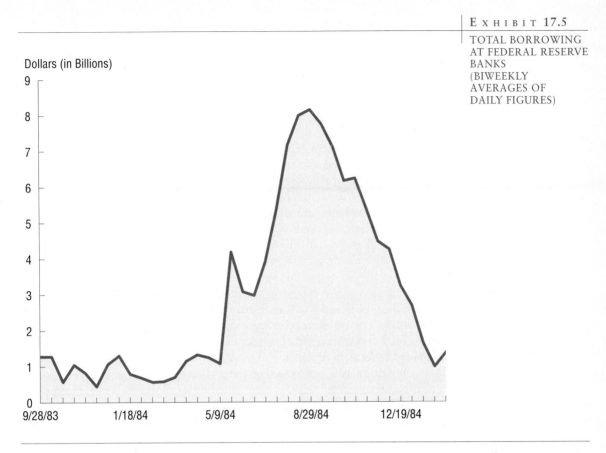

EXHIBIT 17.5

TOTAL BORROWING AT FEDERAL RESERVE BANKS (BIWEEKLY AVERAGES OF DAILY FIGURES)

Source: *Federal Reserve Bulletin.*

SOME LESSONS FROM THE FAILURE OF CONTINENTAL ILLINOIS

THE "QUIET BANK RUN" Today's bank runs are different. Gone is the Depression-style run on a small country bank, with lines of anxious depositors demanding their money back. Instead, it is now the large money-center banks that face a run. Such a run is quiet and almost instantaneous: Lenders of bought funds simply decline to roll over their lending. The result can be the withdrawal of billions of dollars in a single day. The potential for this new type of **quiet bank run** has been created by the growth of the money market and the large banks' increasing reliance on liability management.[3]

quiet bank run
A massive loss of funds due to lenders of bought funds declining to roll over their lending.

[3]Continental was not the first to experience a quiet bank run. Earlier, Franklin National had faced the same sort of run, but on a smaller scale.

Continental Illinois was particularly vulnerable given its exceptionally heavy reliance on bought funds. By comparison, another major bank, Bank of America, encountered similar problems with its loan portfolio at about the same time. Although Bank of America shrank from a peak of over $120 billion in assets in the late 1970s to $94 billion in 1988, it suffered no liquidity crisis. Due to California's much more liberal branching laws, it had a significantly broader base of stable deposits and was correspondingly less dependent on volatile bought funds.

INCREASING INTERDEPENDENCE AMONG BANKS   The failure of Continental Illinois focused attention on the increasing interdependence among banks. This interdependence involves both loans and deposits.

Hunger for loans has stimulated a rapid growth in participations and syndications. As a result, carelessness or dishonesty on the part of an originator of participations, such as Penn Square, can threaten the solvency of all the banks that have taken part of the originator's loans. In the case of Penn Square, Continental itself certainly shared the blame: It had been less than meticulous in examining the loans and in demanding proper documentation (its officer in charge of oil and gas lending in Oklahoma was later indicted for taking more than $500,000 in kickbacks on loans bought from Penn Square). Continental was not the only bank to be brought down by Penn Square: Seafirst of Seattle, with $400 million in participations from Penn Square, also failed and was acquired by Bank of America.

Continental had itself passed on parts of its participations from Penn Square to its own respondent banks. There is generally an implicit understanding in such cases that the correspondent will guarantee the loans to its respondents. This "gentlemen's agreement" proved, in the event, to be worthless: The FDIC refused to honor it. Many of the respondents took substantial losses.

A second channel of interdependence involves correspondent balances and federal funds sold. When Continental collapsed, it had some $6 billion in uninsured deposits and liabilities from over 2,300 small banks. For 66 of these banks, their lending to Continental exceeded their total capital, and for 113 more it exceeded 50% of their capital. Depending on the extent of the losses on these interbank loans, many of the small respondents could have failed. (In the unlikely event of a total loss, over 100 would have folded.)

FAILURE OF THE FDIC'S GET-TOUGH POLICY   The FDIC's attempt to deal with the moral-hazard problem by letting uninsured depositors and creditors take a loss in the event of a bank failure was not a great success. The Penn Square episode set the scene for the run on Continental Illinois. In September 1984 the Comptroller of the Currency (the regulator of national banks) declared in testimony to Congress that the 11 largest banks would not be allowed to fail. That is, in the event of insolvency, the FDIC would bail them out and no depositor or creditor would take a loss. These banks rapidly came to be known as the "too-big-to-fail" banks.

In contrast, the FDIC continued to be tough in its resolution of failures of small banks, essentially setting up a double standard. When the FDIC paid off all the depositors and creditors of the failed First RepublicBank of Dallas (a $27-billion bank) at a cost of over $3 billion, there were howls of protest. Just before, in liquidations of a number of small Texas banks, some 3,000 depositors had lost over $58 million. Not too surprisingly, there has been a flow of deposits out of small banks and into the large banks that have implicit 100% insurance.

17.3 THE S&L MESS: MORAL HAZARD AT ITS WORST

The cost of bailing out failed commercial banks—Continental Illinois, First RepublicBank, and others—was substantial, but it was soon dwarfed by the potentially staggering cost of bailing out a collapsing savings and loan industry. We studied the origins of the savings and loan problem when we looked at the mortgage market in Chapter 15. Mortgage lending had been heavily concentrated in the hands of thrifts that had raised funds primarily from short-term time deposits. This exposed them to significant interest-rate risk. When interest rates rose steeply in 1979, the industry took a beating.

The regulatory response to the difficulties of the early 1980s created a full-blown crisis by the end of the decade. There were two parts to this regulatory response. The first was a reluctance to face up to the problem: Rather than insolvent institutions being closed immediately, they were allowed to continue in operation. This policy was given the virtuous-sounding name of *forbearance*. The second part of the regulatory response was a considerable easing of the restrictions on the type of assets in which S&Ls were allowed to invest: Instead of being limited to residential mortgages, they were allowed to invest in a broad range of nonmortgage assets. As we shall see, the combination of these two policies proved disastrous.

Why the regulatory forbearance? Closing down all the thrifts that were insolvent in 1982 would have cost FSLIC some $20 billion. Since this was well in excess of its reserves, the agency would have had to declare itself bankrupt. Such an action would, of course, have raised a lot of questions about the competence of regulators and of their congressional supervisors and about the wisdom of past policies. If the collapse could be deferred, many of those involved would have left office and the problem would have been passed on to others.

So, in order to put off the day of reckoning, the insolvent thrifts were allowed to continue to operate and to lose money. The result was that by 1988, when the problem was finally addressed, closing all the insolvent thrifts was expected to cost not $20 billion, but $70 billion, and this cost was rising at a rate of $15 billion for each year of further delay.

The case of Lincoln Savings and Loan of Irvine, California, provides an excellent example of what was going on. In 1984 American Continental, a Phoenix real estate development company controlled by Charles H. Keating, Jr., purchased Lincoln Savings and Loan for $51 million. Lincoln used insured deposits to finance real estate developments, including those of American Continental. By 1987 regulators realized that Lincoln was in serious trouble. However, they were dissuaded from doing anything by five U.S. Senators—"the Keating five"—who intervened on Keating's behalf. When Lincoln was eventually closed down in 1989, its assets had grown from their 1987 level of $3.9 billion to $5.5 billion, and the expected cost of the bailout to the taxpayer had ballooned from $1 billion to $2.5 billion. Civil racketeering charges were filed against Keating, and the five Senators suffered considerable embarrassment.

Since regulators must, by law, close an insolvent bank, the policy of forbearance required some creative accounting. Insolvency is, of course, a matter of definition: It depends on how you add up assets, liabilities, and capital. While the most sensible way is to use market values, accountants tend to rely on book or historical values. The system generally used is called GAAP (generally accepted accounting procedures). Thrift regulators, however, used a more lenient system called RAP (regulatory accounting procedures) to decide if an institution was insolvent. To illustrate the difference, one study estimated that in 1982 *total* industry net worth was 3.7% of assets according to RAP; 3% according to GAAP; and –12% using market values. However, even under RAP, many thrifts had dangerously low levels of capital. To allow them to keep operating, equity standards were lowered. The required equity ratio was lowered from 5% to 4% in 1980, and then lowered again to 3% in 1982.

With a shrinking reserve fund and a shrinking staff (due to the Reagan budget cuts), FSLIC was unable to keep up with the growing scale of the problem. The number of insolvent thrifts increased: By 1988, of the remaining 3,024 thrifts 350 were GAAP-insolvent (200 others had already been closed or reorganized) and 1,000 more were barely solvent. Despite this, the number of banks actually closed each year declined. In June 1988 over 60% of problem thrifts had been insolvent for over two years, and 35% had been insolvent for over four years.

The closer a bank is to insolvency, the more serious the moral-hazard problem becomes. Speculative investments cease to have much downside risk: The equity is already gone, so equity holders have nothing to lose, and the insurer will cover any loss to depositors. On the upside, if things turn out well, the bank can be saved, and the equity holders will get the gains. The delay in closing insolvent thrifts left hundreds of institutions in this position—with little or nothing to lose from a gamble and everything to gain.

If the delay provided the motive to gamble, the new freedom to invest in nonmortgage assets provided the opportunity. The intention of granting this new freedom had been to reduce interest-rate risk and to improve diversification by allowing thrifts a broader range of assets. Thrifts were allowed to take on commercial as well as residential mortgages, to make direct investments in real estate, and to invest in junk bonds.

The combination of insured deposits, lax supervision, and the freedom to invest in highly speculative ventures proved to be a recipe for disaster. The problem was worst in states like Florida, California, and Texas, where state-chartered thrifts operated with almost unlimited freedom (see "Texas S&L Disasters Are Blamed, in Part, on Freewheeling Style").

Texas S&L Disasters are Blamed, in Part, on Freewheeling Style

by Leonard M. Apcar

Staff Reporter of The Wall Street Journal

DALLAS—After buying a Texas savings and loan association in 1983, Thomas M. Gaubert wasn't particularly impressed with his more-experienced competitors, comparing them to "a Rotary Club luncheon in Hamtramck, Michigan."

Mr. Gaubert has never had much patience with small-town guys with small-time ideas. Citizens Savings & Loan Association of Grand Prairie, Texas, had a modest $40.5 million in assets when he bought control of it for about $1 million. He renamed it Independent American Savings Association and launched a program of explosive growth. At its zenith, the S&L had $1.86 billion in assets, and Mr. Gaubert envisioned a financial-services and real-estate empire that would provide funds for home builders like himself in good times and bad.

Instead, he was ousted from his S&L by federal regulators in 1984. Independent American is insolvent and in the hands of the Federal Savings and Loan Insurance Corp., it is operating as Independent American Savings Association, F.S.L.A.

Deregulation and a Boom

Deregulation of S&Ls in the early 1980s opened up commercial lending to the industry at a time when the Texas economy was booming. Overnight, Texas became a financial playground for Mr. Gaubert and several other Dallas real-estate high rollers. They saw the thrift business as a vehicle for their big ambitions and expensive tastes, as offering a chance to become lenders instead of borrowers.

"I am tired of playing Monopoly with my money," one developer-turned-banker confided in the early days. "This way, we can use the depositors' money."

For some developers, "owning a Texas thrift was a dream come true—

a virtual printing press to provide money to develop real estate," says William K. Black, who, until July 1, was the FSLIC's deputy director. He is now a high official at the Federal Home Loan Bank, of San Francisco.

Today, of 280 Texas S&Ls, about 60 are insolvent. Regulators say about two-thirds of those are "brain dead," open but sustaining losses and likely to collapse. Besides Mr. Gaubert, three other leading players who piloted Texas thrifts have been removed from their S&Ls by regulators:

—Don R. Dixon, another Dallas home builder, who bought sleepy Vernon Savings & Loan Association in North Texas and converted it into a personal piggy bank with $1.3 billion in assets to finance a yacht, lavish California homes, a fleet of planes and loans to cronies. About 96% of Vernon's loans were in default when regulators took control of it last March and accused Vernon officers of looting. He has filed for personal bankruptcy and has taken the Fifth Amendment when questioned by government investigators.

—Jarrett E. Woods Jr., a Dallas real-estate investor, who bought another small-town Texas S&L, had a fancy for million-dollar loans without borrower equity. Among them were loans to a network of other Texas S&L insiders. The seizure by federal regulators last fall of his Western Savings Association, with $2 billion in assets, was the third-largest on record.

—Edwin T. McBirney III, a 35-year-old Dallas real-estate millionaire who merged six small, mostly unprofitable S&Ls into Sunbelt Savings Association, which at its peak was one of Texas's largest, with $3.2 billion in assets. He lent money with such eye-popping speed that would-be borrowers crowded into Sunbelt's waiting room or staked out one of his favorite restaurants.

Of the four S&L executives, federal regulators have accused only Dixon and Woods of wrongdoing in federal court.

At the local level, the Texas thrift debacle has left thousands of depositors worried about the safety of their funds, and the recession-struck real-estate market reeling from a glut of projects thrown together with easy money. Dallas has about 38 million square feet of unused office space, equivalent to 17 Empire State Buildings.

Tracking the Billions

Regulators concede that high-flying lending operations in Texas S&Ls simply spun out of their control and still aren't in hand.

Even though the newly minted lenders were doubling and redoubling the size of their new S&Ls, thrift examiners were taking up to two years to schedule a visit. And when the regional Federal Home Loan Bank was moved to Dallas from Little Rock in late 1983, the number of agents and supervisors shrank to 12 from 34.

The S&Ls often didn't plan to make money by earning interest on the loans. Instead, they generated profits by charging hefty loan origination fees—sometimes as much as 5% of the loan. And they put part of the loan on the books as interest, and often invested directly in projects, hoping to cash in on the real-estate boom itself.

Source: Leonard M. Apcar, "Loose Lending: Texas S&L Disasters Are Blamed, in Part, on Freewheeling Style," *The Wall Street Journal*, July 13, 1987. Reprinted by permission of The Wall Street Journal, © Dow Jones & Company, Inc. 1987. All Rights Reserved Worldwide.

The rapid expansion of thrifts into nonmortgage lending was fueled by the availability of brokered deposits. An outstanding example is provided by Columbia Savings and Loan of Beverly Hills, California. In the six years up to 1989, Columbia grew from $1 billion in assets to $12 billion. About one-sixth of its business was traditional mortgage lending funded by time deposits, and the rest involved bought funds and marketable securities. A third of its assets consisted of junk bonds, and a third of its liabilities were brokered deposits. Its return on equity in 1986 was 46.3%. In March 1990, after the collapse of the junk bond market wiped out most of its capital, Columbia was struggling to avoid a takeover by federal regulators.

17.4 | SUGGESTIONS FOR REFORMING DEPOSIT INSURANCE

The problems of Continental Illinois on the one hand and of the thrifts on the other clearly demonstrate the basic dilemma of deposit insurance: Too little insurance and there is a danger of bank runs and financial collapse; too much and the moral-hazard problem leads to abuse and fraud. Some sort of reform of the existing system clearly seems in order. Let us look at a number of suggestions that have been made about how to go about it.

REDUCE COVERAGE

Initially, deposit insurance covered only the first $2,500 for each depositor. Even adjusting for inflation, that is equivalent to less than $20,000 today. It has been argued that the current limit of $100,000 is high enough to protect not only widows and orphans, but also many who should be able to look after themselves. The high limit also makes deposit brokering relatively easy. If, the argument continues, the maximum were cut to, say, $20,000, most small depositors would still be protected, while the nervousness of the large depositors would provide just the market discipline that is needed.

The problem with this argument is that it misses the real purpose of deposit insurance. Deposit insurance is not there to protect widows and orphans—however noble that goal: It is there to protect banks. Reduced coverage will make another Continental Illinois that much more likely.

LIMIT INSURANCE TO NARROW BANKS

narrow banks
Banks allowed to invest only in safe liquid assets.

Another suggestion is to limit the insurance of deposits to special **narrow banks.** These would be separate institutions, or separate subsidiaries of bank holding companies, that would be allowed to invest only in safe liquid assets such as

Treasury bills, and perhaps commercial paper and Eurodollars. Only these narrow banks would be eligible for federal insurance.[4]

The transactions function of commercial banks could be taken over by such "checking banks," but the lending function would have to be taken over by finance-company-like intermediaries that would raise funds by selling (uninsured) commercial paper and NCDs. These "loan banks" would need to be unrestricted geographically to ensure that credit would be available to small local businesses. Checking banks and loan banks could share the same premises, and even be subsidiaries of the same bank holding company, but their books would have to be kept separate.

Narrow banks, and thus the nation's transactions balances, would be quite safe from runs and panics. Deposit insurance would ensure this but would largely be unnecessary, since transactions accounts would be completely collateralized by cash and high-quality marketable securities. As the record of money market mutual funds testifies, insurance is not really necessary in these circumstances. The restriction on the permissible assets of the narrowly defined checking banks would largely eliminate the moral-hazard problem.[5]

LET PREMIUMS REFLECT RISK

One way insurance companies deal with moral hazard is by charging premiums that reflect risk. For example, if you install smoke detectors, your fire insurance premiums will fall; if you quit smoking, the cost of your life insurance will go down. Risk-related premiums can, in principle, counteract the incentives for excessive risk taking. Charge a bank with risky assets a higher premium than one that plays it safe, and the gain from riskier investment will be offset by the added cost of the insurance, making excessive risk taking unattractive.

There are two problems with this idea. First, *how much* more should we charge riskier banks? For the incentives to be correct, it is important to get the numbers right, but it is hard to know what the right risk premium might be. Most suggestions involve steps like halving or doubling existing premiums, but such changes of a few basis points one way or another are unlikely to have much of an incentive effect.

The second problem is that we need to estimate the risk *ahead of time*. The bank needs to know that if it engages in risky behavior its premiums will rise.

---

[4]There are parallels to the restrictions that were imposed on the bank notes of national banks before the creation of the Fed. Bank notes had to be backed by U.S. securities. Although there were runs on bank *deposits* (demands to convert them into currency), there was never any loss of public faith in these bank notes, even during banking panics.

[5]One variation on this idea would have the transactions accounts be shares rather than debt liabilities—along the lines of a money market mutual fund—to further reduce susceptibility to a run. Another variation would allow banks to offer different classes of deposit: Insured, which would be fully backed but have a low interest rate, and uninsured, which would be less fully backed and have a higher yield. Depositors could make their own choice. However, there would be a possibility of a run on the unbacked deposits.

However, we typically find out that a bank has engaged in risky behavior only when some of its gambles fail. By then it is too late: The decision we wished to affect with our incentive has already been made.[6]

RELY ON PRIVATE INSURANCE

A related suggestion is to replace or supplement federal deposit insurance with private insurance. For example, let banks rely on private insurance for deposits over $100,000. The idea is that private insurers will somehow be able to make their premiums reflect the riskiness of the bank's assets.

Here too there are problems. Remember the basic purpose of the insurance—to protect the system against a panic. Private insurers do not have the resources to provide a credible guarantee: Remember the runs on the Ohio and Maryland thrifts. Who is going to insure Citibank with its more than $80 billion of uninsured deposits and liabilities? In fact, the only reason that *federal* insurance is credible is that behind it stands a lender of last resort with an unlimited ability to create definitive money.

The other problem is that private insurers lack the coercive power of the government to impose regulations and to close troubled institutions. The inability of the Ohio Deposit Guarantee Fund to close Home State Savings immediately was a major factor in the Ohio crisis.

INCREASE CAPITAL REQUIREMENTS

Another method used by insurance companies to control the moral-hazard problem is to have a deductible. For example, if you yourself have to pay the first $200 toward repairing a fender bender, you will drive more carefully. Applying this idea to deposit insurance, the more of their own money the owners of a bank have at stake, the less attractive risk taking becomes. One way to reduce the moral-hazard problem, then, is to require banks to have a higher equity ratio.[7]

Bank equity has fallen steadily since the 1930s (see Exhibit 17.6). There are good reasons for this. As we know, increasing leverage increases the return on equity, but it also increases the risk of insolvency. In the absence of deposit insurance, the increased risk of insolvency raises the cost of funds and increases the likelihood of a run. At some point, the cost of increased leverage more than

---

[6]For banks with publicly traded debt, the risk premium on their bonds might be an indicator. However, most banks are not publicly traded. Moreover, it is not clear that the market has good enough information on the risk of the bank's portfolio: Regulators generally have better information that they do not make public.

[7]Another way to look at this is to consider the cost to the FDIC of resolving a bank failure. That cost, in the case of a purchase and assumption, is the difference between the total liabilities of the bank and the true market value of its assets (the cost is less in the case of a payout). Since 1980 the average resolution cost has risen from about 4% of a failed bank's assets to about 10%. But, even now, requiring an equity ratio of, say, 20% would protect the FDIC from most losses.

EXHIBIT 17.6

EQUITY TO TOTAL
FINANCIAL ASSETS
AND TO TOTAL RISK
ASSETS AT U.S.
COMMERCIAL BANKS

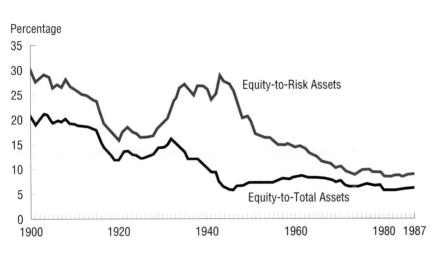

Source: U.S. Department of Commerce.

offsets its advantages. With the introduction of deposit insurance, however, the cost of increased leverage falls: Deposits of all banks became risk-free, because they are all insured, so the cost of funds no longer rises with the leverage of the bank, and bank runs cease to be a problem.[8]

However, the mere desire of banks to increase their leverage is not enough if they do not have the means. Banks may increase their leverage either by expanding or by contracting. In the case of expansion, the bank increases both its assets and its liabilities, leaving its equity the same. In the case of contraction, the bank decreases both its assets and its equity, leaving its liabilities the same. Because of economies of scale, expansion is the more attractive alternative: Banks want to grow, not shrink. Expansion has been made much easier by the growth of the money market and by banks' increasing reliance on bought funds.

If we want to force banks to increase their equity ratio in order to reduce the cost of deposit insurance, there are several potential problems. The first is defining equity. We saw how permissive accounting contributed to the S&L problem. Clearly, the most sensible definition of equity relies on market values. However, it is hard to estimate market values for banks that are not publicly

---

[8]A lower capital ratio is not always desirable: In some circumstances equity can be a useful source of funds. Facing extremely high reserve requirements on their deposits, banks in Israel turned to the stock market as a way to fund their lending. To make their stock attractive and more "depositlike," they guaranteed a rate of return by supporting its price. This they did by buying back stock if the market price started to fall. The amount of bank stock outstanding grew at a tremendous rate until the whole system collapsed in 1983. Fearing a devaluation, the public sold large amounts of bank stock in order to buy dollars; the banks were unable to support the price and prices plummeted. In the face of this strange version of a bank run, the government stepped in to rescue investors and essentially nationalized the banks.

traded: Since most of their assets are not marketable, there is little evidence on how the market might value them.

The second problem is deciding how much capital is enough. Is 5% enough, or 10%? The level is clearly going to be fairly arbitrary. In calculating the amount of capital required for a particular bank, it should be recognized that some assets are more risky than others. For example, there is zero risk with cash reserves and very little with short-term Treasuries. On the other hand, junk bonds and investments in commercial real estate are very risky.

The third problem is determining at what level of equity to shut down a bank. The sooner it is done, the smaller the cost to the FDIC. Using actual book-value insolvency as the criterion may be too slow: By that time, the market value of equity will be well into the red, and the FDIC is sure to take a substantial loss. Perhaps the bank should be closed when its equity falls to some percentage greater than zero—say 1.5%.

A very general problem with trying to increase safety by forcing banks to hold more capital than they desire is that they will try to find ways around the rules. In particular, they will try to compensate for having "too much" capital by increasing their exposure to risk in other ways. Lowering leverage lowers the return on equity; increasing exposure to risk raises it back up again.

One way banks can increase their exposure to risk and add to their income without needing more capital is to make commitments that do not appear on their balance sheets. For example, if a bank makes a customer a direct loan, that loan appears on the bank's balance sheet. But if, instead, it helps the customer issue commercial paper and provides a standby letter of credit (SLC), nothing appears on its balance sheet. However, the risk to the bank is the same in both cases. If equity requirements apply only to balance sheet items, the bank can avoid them by going the SLC route rather than making a direct loan. Such **off-balance-sheet banking** has increased dramatically in the 1980s as regulators have raised capital standards (see Exhibit 17.7).

off-balance-sheet banking
The making of commitments by a bank that do not appear on its balance sheet.

Another way to take business off the balance sheet is securitization. Make a loan in the normal way, and then put it into a package of loans that you sell off to investors. This is very much like the securitization of mortgages that we saw in Chapter 15. There is one important difference, however: Securitized mortgages are collateralized by property, and they are often insured as well. So, to make securitized loans more marketable, banks often sell them **with recourse**; that is, the selling bank guarantees the loans against default. Here too the bank assumes the credit risk but nothing appears on its balance sheet. An added attraction of both securitization with recourse and SLCs is that they enable banks to engage in

with recourse
With a bank guarantee against default.

EXHIBIT 17.7

OFF-BALANCE-SHEET ACTIVITIES OF REPORTING U.S. BANKS

	1984	1985	1986	June 1987
Loan commitments	$ 494	$ 531	$ 572	$ 586
Standby letters of credit	146	175	170	167
Foreign exchange commitment	584	735	893	1,419
Interest rate swaps	0	187	367	521
Other commitments[a]	140	212	340	447
Annual totals	$1,364	$1,840	$2,342	$3,140

[a]Other commitments consist of commitments to buy and sell futures and forward contracts, securities to be issued at a later date, obligations to buy and sell under option contracts, commercial letters of credit, participations in acceptances bought, and other miscellaneous significant commitments.

Source: The General Accounting Office, "Banking: Off-Balance-Sheet Activities," March 1988.

credit assessment and risk bearing—activities in which they have special advantages—without bearing the interest-rate risk.[9]

Other commitments that do not appear on the balance sheet, but expose the bank to risk nonetheless, include forward purchases and sales of foreign exchange, forward commitments to make loans, interest-rate and foreign-exchange options, and interest-rate and currency swaps.

PUNISH BANK OFFICERS DIRECTLY

One final suggestion for dealing with the moral-hazard problem is to impose discipline by punishing bank officers directly. In the case of Continental Illinois, the CEO was fired and ten directors were forced off the board. However, in keeping with his contract, the CEO received a $500,000 "golden parachute." Moreover, since directors are often officers of the bank's largest customers, getting rid of them may not be very good for business.

---

[9]The selling of loans *without* recourse has grown rapidly. A recent survey found a 40% growth in the 15 months ending June 1988, to $53 billion. The sellers are mainly money center banks, and 80% of the buyers are other banks. A large percentage of the buying banks are domestic branches and subsidiaries of foreign banks. Presumably, the buying banks have a lower cost of capital, cheaper sources of funds, or a demand for diversification. Nonbank purchasers include other financial institutions such as lifes and thrifts. Loans sold this way used to be mostly high quality, but recently they have increasingly been below investment grade: Over 40% have been related to LBOs and other high-leverage restructurings.

|17.5| RECENT ATTEMPTS AT REFORM

The growing problems of commercial banks and the S&L crisis have led to two recent changes in bank regulation—the imposition of new capital standards and a program to bail out the thrift industry.

THE BIS CAPITAL STANDARDS

Before 1981 banks were free to set their equity ratios pretty much as they saw fit. Since then, however, regulators have imposed increasingly strict standards. The current regulations were adopted in November 1988 by the United States and 12 other member nations of the Bank for International Settlements (BIS), an international clearing bank for central banks. The reason for adopting international standards is that raising capital requirements in one country alone puts banks in that country at a competitive disadvantage in the international market relative to banks in countries with less strict standards. The *BIS capital standards* address many of the problems involved in setting capital standards that we discussed above, but they still rely on a book-value definition of capital rather than on a market-value definition.

core capital
Book value of stock plus retained earnings.

total capital
Core capital plus supplemental capital.

risk-adjusted assets
Total assets calculated by assigning risk weights to each type of asset.

Under the new standards, there are requirements for **core capital** and for **total capital.** Core capital is defined as book value of stock plus retained earnings. Total capital is defined as core capital plus supplemental capital (loan-loss reserves plus subordinated debt).[10] The amount of capital of the two types that must be held is determined as the greater of two measures—one based on **risk-adjusted assets** and one based on total assets.

The amount of risk-adjusted assets is calculated by assigning different weights to different types of asset according to their risk. The less risky the asset, the lower the weighting. For example, regular loans are counted at 100% of their value, mortgages at 50%, interbank deposits at 20%, and T-bills and cash at 0%. Off-balance-sheet activities are also to be included in the total of risk-adjusted assets. This is done by converting each off-balance-sheet item into a "credit equivalent" of an on-balance-sheet item. For example, a standby letter of credit is counted in full on the grounds that it exposes the bank to the same default risk as a direct loan of the same amount. Once converted to an on-balance-sheet equivalent, each item is assigned to one of the four weighting categories of credit risk.

---

[10]Subordinated debt is long-term debt that is paid off, if the bank becomes insolvent, only after depositors and other creditors have been paid. It therefore provides depositors and other creditors with protection against insolvency in the same way that equity does. Some small banks, including Lincoln Savings and Loan (discussed above) have been accused of selling $1,000 subordinated capital notes over the counter to their retail customers as a kind of high-yield "savings account," without exactly stressing that they are not deposits and not insured.

To see how this all works, consider a bank with the following assets:

Cash	$10m
Federal funds sold	10m
Loans	60m

The bank also has $10 million worth of SLCs outstanding to corporate issuers of commercial paper.

The on-balance-sheet items would contribute

$$0 \times \$10m + 0.2 \times \$10m + 1 \times \$60m = \$62m$$

to risk-adjusted assets. The SLCs are the full credit equivalent of commercial loans and add $10 million to risk-adjusted assets. The total of risk-adjusted assets is therefore $72 million.

The new standards require banks to have total capital of at least 7.25% of risk-adjusted assets by 1990 and 8% by 1992. Core capital should be no less than 3.25% of risk-adjusted assets by 1990 and 4% by 1992. For the bank in our example above, that means that by 1990 it should have at least

$$0.0325 \times \$72m = \$2,340,000$$

of core capital and at least

$$0.0725 \times \$72m = \$5,220,000$$

of total capital.

In addition to the requirement with respect to risk-adjusted assets, there is also a **leverage requirement** stated in terms of total assets. The total assets of our bank are simply the unweighted sum of all its assets:

leverage requirement Requirement based on the unweighted sum of a bank's assets.

$$\$10m + \$10m + \$60m = \$80m.$$

Off-balance-sheet items contribute nothing to total assets. A bank must have core capital at least equal to 3% of total assets. For our bank that means

$$0.03 \times \$80m = \$2,400,000.$$

There is no leverage requirement in terms of total capital.

A bank must meet whichever of the requirements—risk-adjusted or leverage—is the more stringent. In our example, the leverage requirement is the more stringent ($2,400,000 versus $2,340,000), so the bank must have $2,400,000 of core capital. It must also have $5,220,000 of total capital (only the risk-adjusted requirement matters).[11]

Meeting these standards will put a lot of pressure both on money center banks and on small banks. Many money center banks have taken substantial losses on their LDC loans, shrinking their equity. The need to replenish and even raise their equity will make it hard for them to expand their lending or to take over other banks in the rush toward interstate expansion; in early 1990 the money center banks were actually decreasing their commercial and industrial loans in an attempt to raise their capital ratios, sending borrowers into the commercial-paper market in large numbers (see "Manufacturers Hanover Learns"). The regionals are in much better shape in terms of equity, and the new capital standards give them an edge over the money centers. Small banks have a different problem: Because they have little or no access to the equity market, there is no way they can raise capital externally. They will have to raise their equity ratios by shrinking their balance sheets or be taken over by larger banks.

The new rules will, of course, give banks incentives to try to get around them. We have seen that requiring banks to hold more capital than they desire pushes them to increase the riskiness of their assets in order to restore their return on equity. But won't the risk-adjusted standard then require them to hold more capital? Not if they increase the riskiness of assets *within* each risk category. For example, all loans to corporations are counted at 100%. But while safe commercial loans earn about 1% over the cost of funds, loans to finance LBOs earn 2.5% to 4% over cost. What would you expect to happen to the proportion of such high-risk loans? Although the new standards address the problem of off-balance-sheet banking by requiring capital to be held against such activities, no one will be very surprised if banks come up with some new items that are *not* covered by the standards.

THE S&L BAILOUT OF 1989

In February 1989 President Bush announced a plan to deal with the thrift crisis. A modified version of the plan was passed by Congress and signed into law in August of that year as the *Financial Institutions Reform, Recovery and Enforcement Act of 1989 (FIRREA)*.

Office of Thrift Supervision (OTS)
Federal agency established in 1989 to assume the regulatory functions of the Federal Home Loan Bank Board.

The new law put an end to a distinct thrift industry, subject to its own regulations and regulators. The Federal Home Loan Bank Board (FHLBB), which had been responsible for thrift regulation, was abolished. Its regulatory functions were taken over by a new **Office of Thrift Supervision (OTS)** within the Treasury. The FHLBB's function in supervising the Home Loan Bank System,

---

[11]Responding to pressure from the FDIC, which is concerned that the standards are not tough enough, the Fed has proposed that only the healthiest banks (about one in five of all banks) be allowed a leverage requirement of 3%. Others, depending on their situation, would be required to have from 4% to 6%.

MANUFACTURERS HANOVER LEARNS THE ART OF SHRINKING

By Robert Guenther

Staff Reporter of The Wall Street Journal

NEW YORK—After trying to grow out of its developing-country debt problems, Manufacturers Hanover Corp. has decided to shrink out of them.

Manufacturers Hanover will drop in size to about $57 billion in assets, down from $74.36 billion at its peak in 1986, if a possible sale of a controlling interest in its CIT Group Inc. goes through. Manufacturers may sell control of the asset-based lending subsidiary to Dai-Ichi Kangyo Bank Ltd. for about $1.2 billion.

The expected transaction means that Manufacturers, seeking at all cost to avoid a merger, will likely fall to the nation's ninth largest banking company from the seventh spot.

In banking, where asset size is synonymous with importance and power, that prospect is enough to ruin any self-respecting banker's golf game.

But it is one that Manufacturers Chairman John F. McGillicuddy must take if the bank is to bolster its capital base in the face of $8.25 billion in developing-country debt and avoid a merger with another bank in the years ahead.

Source: Robert Guenther, "Manufacturers Hanover Learns the Art of Shrinking," *The Wall Street Journal*, September 13, 1989, p. A10. Reprinted by permission of The Wall Street Journal, © Dow Jones & Company, Inc. 1989. All Rights Reserved Worldwide.

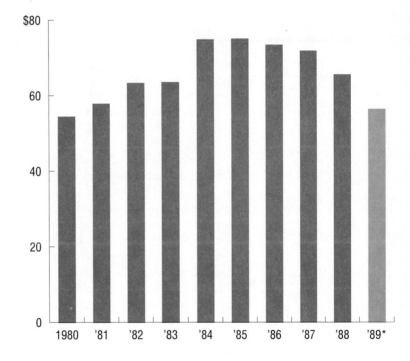

MANUFACTURERS HANOVER SCALES DOWN
(TOTAL YEAR-END ASSETS IN BILLIONS OF DOLLARS)

*Reflects sale of CIT Group subsidiary.

which provided funds to S&Ls in much the same way as the Fed does to banks, was taken over by a new Federal Housing Finance Board.

FSLIC was abolished. The insurance of deposits at S&Ls was taken over by a new Savings Association Insurance Fund (SAIF) at the FDIC. Insurance of banks was placed under the Bank Insurance Fund. Each fund is required to maintain reserves equal to at least 1.25% of estimated insured deposits, which may be raised to 1.5% if circumstances warrant. Insurance premiums were raised both for S&Ls and for banks. The premiums for S&Ls are to remain above those for banks until at least 1998, to help fund the bailout and to rebuild an insurance fund for S&Ls. Institutions that give up their S&L charters in exchange for bank charters must remain in SAIF, with its higher premiums, for five years. The FDIC can terminate insurance more rapidly to banks that are misbehaving; within six months instead of over two years. The power of the FDIC to close institutions is also broadened.

The stricter accounting practices used by commercial banks are to be applied to thrifts. Capital requirements are tightened. Core capital is required to be at least 1.5% of assets by the end of 1989, and 3% by 1995. Total capital is required to be at least 6.4% of risk-weighted assets, rising to 8% in 1992. The new capital requirements are roughly double the old.

Although the new law does not adopt market-value accounting or risk-based premiums, it does commission studies of their feasibility. These studies are to be completed by 1991.

The new law reverses much of the deregulation of the early 1980s that gave thrifts the freedom to invest in a broad range of assets. Thrifts are now required to keep at least 70% of their assets in mortgage-related investments (including mortgage-backed securities). Commercial real estate loans are restricted to no more than four times capital. High-risk investments, such as junk bonds and direct investments in real estate and in equity, are to be marked to market and moved to separately capitalized subsidiaries.[12] For thrifts that fail to meet the capital standards, OTS has broad powers to further restrict their assets and liabilities (brokered deposits, for example). In March 1990 OTS ruled that thrifts may lend to a single borrower no more than 15% of their capital (instead of 100%) or $500,000, whichever is greater.

Resolution Trust Corporation (RTC)
Federal agency established in 1989 to oversee the liquidation of insolvent thrifts.

FIRREA set up a new agency, the **Resolution Trust Corporation (RTC)**, to supervise the liquidation of currently insolvent thrifts. These include some 200 already taken over by FSLIC, plus all those to be closed through 1992. The total cost through 1999 was estimated at the time to be $166 billion, but the estimate has steadily been rising: An April 1990 study by the General Accounting Office estimated the cost at between $157 billion and $192 billion over three decades, depending on how much can be recovered from the sale of assets.

To fund the bailout, the Resolution Funding Corporation (Refcorp) was authorized to make an initial issue of $50 billion in bonds (these bonds have come to be known in the market as "bailout bonds"). This money was to be used to bring up to zero the capital of failed institutions to enable purchase and assumption. An additional $40 billion—from insurance premiums, from the sale of repossessed assets, and from other sources—was to be used for institutions

---

[12]The thrift industry as a whole sold or wrote down 22% of its junk bond holdings in the fourth quarter of 1989—to $10.6 billion from $13.5 billion. Of the 198 thrifts holding junk bonds at year-end, 36 had failed, including 7 of the largest 15.

expected to be closed within the next few years. It was expected that the RTC might eventually have to dispose of as much as $400 billion in repossessed real estate.

FIRREA allows banks, for the first time, to take over sound thrift institutions and even to integrate them into their existing branch networks. Thrifts are also allowed to convert themselves into commercial banks.

Finally, FIRREA imposes new civil penalties for "knowing and reckless violations of lending practices" and criminal penalties for fraud and embezzlement. It also provides the Justice Department with $65 million a year for stricter enforcement.

When FIRREA capital standards were imposed in December 1989, some 800 of the 2,600 remaining thrifts failed to meet them. These institutions were given one month to submit plans to meet the standards; most such plans have been rejected. Since increasing capital is difficult or impossible for many thrifts, they have instead been trying to reduce their assets. In particular, they have been selling off marketable assets such as mortgage-backed securities. New mortgage lending has also been curtailed: The thrifts' share of mortgage originations shrank to 28% at the end of 1989, the lowest level since the 1950s.

Meanwhile S&L losses continue to grow. In 1989 the industry lost $19 billion, compared to $13 billion in 1988. (The 1989 loss was bloated by write-downs of junk bonds.) Delays in shutting down insolvent institutions are still adding to the costs: The operating losses of thrifts already under government control or targeted to be closed amounted to $2.6 billion in the fourth quarter of 1989. By April 1990 only 52 failed thrifts had been sold, but plans were announced to sell 140 more in the following three months. At that time S&L failures were spreading beyond the Southwest to the East and West Coasts as real estate markets there weakened. In the fourth quarter of 1989 losses in both the San Francisco and the New York City districts exceeded those in the Dallas district for the first time.

MODIFYING THE "TOO BIG TO FAIL" DOCTRINE

The FDIC was expected to announce in June 1990 modifications to its "too big to fail" doctrine. Although this doctrine does protect large banks from bank runs, it is potentially very expensive. Suggestions for change include compensating uninsured depositors for only 90% of their deposits, having the large banks themselves set up a fund to cover losses of uninsured depositors, and extending formal insurance to nondeposit liabilities so that insurance premiums can be collected on them too.

17.6 SOME MORE RADICAL SOLUTIONS TO THE SAFETY PROBLEM

The legislative response to the current crisis has been to patch up the system without addressing the structural problems that are its root cause. As we have seen, the U.S. banking system is particularly vulnerable to problems because of its fragmented structure—the result of geographic restrictions on branching. The record of the Great Depression illustrates quite well the importance of structure. In California, with unrestricted statewide branching, only one bank failed. In Canada, with unrestricted nationwide branching, no banks failed.

The restrictions on interstate branching have left us, compared to other countries, with a relatively large number of small and medium-sized banks. These banks are less stable than large banks because they lack the financial advantages of scale. In particular, they tend to be poorly diversified: Their borrowers are all in the same geographic region and often in the same industry. A bank limited to Detroit will not do well when the auto industry is in trouble; a nationwide bank with branches in Detroit will be much less affected.

Some of the practices that have grown up to compensate for limited geographic mobility have themselves reduced stability. When banks can branch freely, as in Canada, funds are moved to where they are most needed *within* the bank: Deposits gathered in Nova Scotia can be used by the same bank to fund loans in Toronto or Vancouver. In the United States the same sort of mobility is achieved through the money market and through loan sharing. Deposits gathered by small banks in Iowa find their way to Chicago money center banks through correspondent balances and correspondent federal funds, or to New York through brokered fed funds or the purchase of NCDs.[13] Loan participations and syndications can be seen as an attempt to achieve the improved diversification that is blocked by the ban on branching. However, as we saw in the case of Continental Illinois, these arrangements add to the system's instability. Interbank borrowings represent "hot money" that can vanish at a moment's notice. Loan sharing creates serious incentive problems: Bank A earns fees for setting up a loan, but Bank B takes the loss if the loan goes bad.

So rather than tinkering with deposit insurance, we could get at the root causes of the problem by speeding up the movement toward full interstate banking. A banking industry consisting of a few hundred large banks would be much less prone to problems and much easier to supervise. In other countries in the past, such banking systems supported by lenders of last resort have functioned well even without deposit insurance. Even today, most other countries have much less extensive deposit insurance than the United States (see Exhibit 17.8). The most radical suggestion for reforming deposit insurance, therefore, is to change the structure to make safety less of a problem and to do away with deposit insurance altogether.

---

[13]The purchase of NCDs by money market funds achieves the same sort of result.

EXHIBIT 17.8

BANK DEPOSIT GUARANTEE SCHEMES IN VARIOUS COUNTRIES

Country	Level of Protection (Maximum per Depositor)	Voluntary or Compulsory Membership	Officially or Privately Administered Scheme
United States	$100,000	Compulsory[a]	Officially
Britain	75 % of deposit up to £20,000 ($32,000)	Compulsory	Officially
France	FFr400,000 ($70,000)	Compulsory	Privately
Japan	¥10m ($66,000)	Compulsory	Privately
Switzerland	SFr30,000 ($20,000)	Voluntary	Privately
W. Germany	30% of bank's equity capital	Voluntary	Privately

[a]Only optional for nonmember state banks.

Source: "International Banking Survey," *The Economist*, April 7, 1990, p. 65. Copyright 1990, The Economist. Distributed by Special Features/Syndication Sales.

Tackling the safety problem by reforming the structure of U.S. banking is not a new idea: It came up before 1913 in the discussions that preceded the founding of the Fed, and it came up again in the debate over deposit insurance in the 1930s. However, then as now, Congress decided to bolster the safety net rather than to reform the structure.

Both structural reform and the reduction or removal of deposit insurance would certainly face serious political problems. Politicians do very well from the current structure—the story of the Keating five is a good example. A banking system of relatively few large banks might not be such a generous source of campaign contributions. Moreover, deposit insurance has enormous popular appeal: It would be very hard to convince the electorate to support its removal or substantial reduction. To quote William Seidman, the chairman of the FDIC, "Next to Social Security, deposit insurance is the government program least likely to be changed or tampered with."

17.7 GOVERNMENT GUARANTEES IN OTHER AREAS

Deposit insurance for banks and S&Ls is not the only program of government guarantees. Some 15,700 credit unions, with assets of $203 billion in 1988, are insured by the National Credit Union Share Insurance Fund. The NCUSIF is stronger than the FDIC: Its reserves are over 50% larger relative to its deposits, and its losses have been much smaller. Although there have been some abuses similar to those at S&Ls, credit unions are generally quite conservative. They are nonprofit (tax-exempt) organizations owned by their members, and there is little incentive for their managements to pursue profit too aggressively.

Pension Benefit Guaranty Corporation (PBGC)
Federal agency that insures the assets of defined benefit pension plans.

The **Pension Benefit Guaranty Corporation (PBGC)** insures over $800 billion in defined benefit pension assets, covering pension plans for some 40 million U.S. workers. The PBGC is funded by insurance premiums paid by participating plans. There are some similarities to deposit insurance—a moral-hazard problem, a very large number of plans that make supervision difficult. And there have been hints of possible trouble. In 1988, by its own accounting, PBGC's liabilities exceeded its assets by $4 billion (according to a study by the New York Fed the number was more like $17 billion).

The federal government also guarantees a large number of loans made through government-sponsored financial intermediaries. These include mortgages, student loans, farm loans, and loans made through the Export–Import Bank to promote trade. In 1988 the total amount of loans guaranteed came to over $550 billion.

The same questions that arose with respect to federal deposit insurance arise with respect to all these other guarantee programs. Are government guarantees necessary or appropriate? Are there moral-hazard or other problems that are likely to end up costing the taxpayer large sums of money?

SUMMARY

- The bank safety net established after the Depression—deposit insurance and lender of last resort—worked well up until the 1980s. However, the past decade has seen rapid growth in the number of bank failures, with substantial losses to the taxpayer.

- The abolition of Regulation Q, the growth of the money market, and increasing freedom to expand geographically have created considerable competitive pressure on banks. As a result, many have lowered their lending standards and taken more risks.

- Deposit insurance has allowed banks to increase risk taking without alarming depositors. This moral-hazard problem is illustrated particularly well by the phenomenon of brokered deposits.

- Credit risk has been a serious problem: The 1980s saw one type of bank lending after another turn into major disasters—LDC lending, energy, real estate, agriculture. Market risk has also increased as both interest rates and exchange rates have became more volatile.

- The FDIC, concerned about the moral-hazard problem, has attempted to impose greater market discipline by relying more on payouts and less on purchases and assumptions. Penn Square was a landmark case.

- The consequent nervousness of depositors contributed to the collapse of Continental Illinois. This collapse illustrates the vulnerability of large money center banks to a "quiet run" and shows how interdependence can spread problems from one bank to another. After Continental Illinois, the FDIC abandoned its get-tough policy and adopted the "too big to fail" doctrine.

- The S&L crisis has its origins in the early 1980s, when rising interest rates caused massive losses to S&Ls. The S&Ls had been funding long-term mortgages with short-term deposits.

- The regulatory response made things much worse: Deregulation allowed S&Ls to take on more credit risk, and insolvent institutions were allowed to continue to operate, exacerbating the moral-hazard problem. Losses grew rapidly.

- Suggestions to reform deposit insurance include reduced coverage, limiting insurance to narrow banks, using risk-related premiums, substituting private insurance, increasing the "deductible" by increasing capital requirements, and punishing bank officers directly.

- New international capital standards recognize the different credit risk in different types of assets. They also recognize the credit risk in various off-balance-sheet activities.

- Meeting the new standards has been a problem for many banks. Many have been forced to limit or even to reduce their lending, and the sale or securitization of assets has been growing.

- FIRREA ended separate regulation of the S&L industry, raised deposit insurance premiums, imposed tighter capital standards on thrifts, largely revoked the freedom given to S&Ls to invest in nonmortgage assets, and set up the Resolution Trust Corporation to supervise the liquidation of insolvent thrifts.

- A more radical solution to the bank safety problem would be to address the root cause—restrictions on interstate banking—and possibly to abolish deposit insurance altogether. Such a radical solution faces probably insuperable political opposition.

- The government also guarantees credit unions, defined benefit pension plans, and a variety of government-intermediated loans. All these guarantees have the potential for problems similar to those of bank deposit insurance.

KEY TERMS

brokered deposits	with recourse	Office of Thrift Supervision (OTS)
money broker	core capital	Resolution Trust Corporation (RTC)
quiet bank run	total capital	
narrow banks	risk-adjusted assets	Pension Benefit Guaranty Corporation (PBGC)
off-balance-sheet banking	leverage requirement	

DISCUSSION QUESTIONS

1. What drove banks to start taking more risks in their lending? Was this increased risk taking evidence of bad management in the sense of managers not doing what was best for bank owners?

2. How did the rise of the money market contribute to the bank safety problem?

3. Do the BIS capital standards remove the incentive for banks to help their customers issue commercial paper rather than making them loans directly?

4. Why did the FDIC try to impose increased market discipline on banks? What were the consequences of this policy?

5. Why did Continental Illinois collapse? How did restrictions on branching contribute to its problems?

6. How and why did the S&L problems of the early 1980s grow into the costly crisis of today?

7. What are the pros and cons of various methods of reforming deposit insurance? Which were adopted by FIRREA? Are these measures sufficient to deal with the problem?

8. How do uniform capital standards on all banks affect the relative profitability of large and small banks?

BIBLIOGRAPHY

Alfriend, Malcolm C., "International Risk-Based Capital Standard: History and Explanation," *Economic Review of the Federal Reserve Bank of Richmond* November-December 1988, 28–34.

Benston, George J., and George G. Kaufman, *Risk and Solvency Regulation of Depository Institutions: Past Policies and Current Options*, Monograph Series in Finance and Economics, Salomon Brothers Center for the Study of Financial Institutions, 1988.

Brewer, Elijah, III., "Full-Blown Crisis, Half-Measure Cure," *Economic Perspectives of the Federal Reserve Bank of Chicago* November-December 1989, 2–17.

Brumbaugh, R. Dan., Jr., Andrew S. Carron, and Robert E. Litan, "Cleaning Up the Depository Institutions Mess," *Brooking Papers on Economic Activity* (1) 1989, 243–295.

Calomiris, Charles W., "Deposit Insurance: Lessons from the Record," *Economic Perspectives of the Federal Reserve Bank of Chicago* May–June 10–30, 1990.

Jaffee, Dwight M., Lawrence J. White, and Edward J. Kane, "Symposium on Federal Deposit Insurance," *Journal of Economic Perspectives* 3:4 (Fall): 3–47, 1989.

Kane, Edward J., *The S & L Insurance Mess: How Did It Happen?* Washington, D.C.: Urban Institute Press, 1989.

Wall, Larry D., "Capital Requirements for Banks: A Look at the 1981 and 1988 Standards," *Economic Review of the Federal Reserve Bank of Atlanta* March-April 1989, 14–29.

White, E. N. *The Regulation and Reform of the American Banking System, 1900–1929*, Princeton: Princeton University Press, 1983.

CHAPTER 18

THE REGULATION OF BANKING AND FINANCIAL MARKETS IN THE 1990s

In the preceding chapters we have seen how financial institutions and financial markets function and how they are regulated. In this chapter we shall take stock, reviewing the reasons for the existing regulatory structure and seeing how that structure has changed and how it continues to change.

We shall see that the Fed plays a particularly important role in the regulatory structure. Not only does it have primary responsibility for the safety and stability of the financial and payments systems, but it also regulates the quantity of money in our economy.

18.1 WHY REGULATE?

As we saw in Chapter 5, one idea underlying the regulation of financial institutions and markets is the idea of externalities. When a banker decides how much risk to take, he considers the possible losses he himself will bear if things go wrong, but he is unlikely to consider, or perhaps even to be aware of, the possible losses to others. Yet the failure of his bank might trigger a banking panic, and the panic might disrupt lending and payments to such an extent that a recession ensues. So if left to himself, the banker might follow a policy that is "too risky" in the sense that it ignores these external costs to others. Hence regulation that limits the riskiness of his assets or forces him to increase his equity may be in the public interest, and it may be a justifiable interference with the free market.

The banking collapse of the Great Depression was viewed, rightly or wrongly, as being the result of excessive risk taking by banks. The legislation of the 1930s attempted to reduce such risk taking in a number of ways. As we saw in Chapters 8 and 9, it limited competition among banks by strengthening the existing restrictions on geographic competition and by capping the rates banks could pay on deposits. It also segmented the financial structure to limit competition and to keep banks out of areas thought to be "too risky." Under the new rules, commercial banks were to accept demand deposits and make commercial loans; investment banks were to underwrite and broker securities; thrifts were to accept time deposits and write mortgages; insurance companies were to engage in insurance. No type of financial institution was to invade the turf of any other.

The principal vehicle of this segmentation was the Glass-Steagall Act of 1933 which separated commercial and investment banking. With this law there was no grandfather clause, and commercial banks were required to divest themselves of their existing securities operations. Banking was set further apart by the Bank Holding Company Act of 1956, which restricted the affiliation of banking and nonfinancial corporations ("the separation of banking and commerce"). The S&L Holding Company Act of 1969 did the same for S&Ls. In addition, various state laws restricted the permissible activities of insurance companies.

In addition to these measures to limit competition and risk taking, the government sought to promote stability directly by providing a guarantee in the form of deposit insurance. If depositors know they are protected, they have no reason to run on the bank. We saw in Chapters 16 and 17 that deposit insurance involves a moral-hazard problem and that this creates a need to supervise and to constrain the behavior of those banks protected by the insurance.

Guarantees of financial institutions are not limited to federal insurance of bank deposits. Insurance policies are generally guaranteed by funds set up by the states, and the customers of securities and futures brokers are protected by private insurance schemes. Retail customers of securities brokers are protected by the **Securities Investor Protection Corporation (SIPC)** for up to $500,000 of their cash and securities.[1] Customers of futures brokers are protected by the futures exchanges.

One function of such guarantees is to protect financial institutions from runs and panics, and another is to protect small depositors and investors from exploitation and manipulation by financially more sophisticated institutions. The underlying problem can be described in terms of asymmetric information. Small depositors and investors have less information than large financial institutions, and they are therefore at a disadvantage.

The desire to protect the unsophisticated from asymmetries of information also underlies the *Securities Acts of 1933 and 1934*. These acts require issuers of new securities to register with the SEC and to disclose all relevant information. Corporations whose securities are traded publicly are required to continue to disclose information periodically. The Securities Acts also prohibit insiders— employees of the corporation or of its agents—from profiting from privileged information. For example, if you know before the public at large that your company is the target of a takeover, you can buy its stock and sell it later after the news has become public and the price has gone up. Regulation, however,

Securities Investor Protection Corporation (SIPC)
Private insurance agency that protects the retail customers of securities brokers.

---

[1]Creation of the SIPC was mandated by Congress in 1970. It is funded by assessments on its members, which include most of the brokerage firms registered with the SEC. In its 20 years of operation, the SIPC has paid out over $180 million to help some 200,000 investors recover more than $1 billion from brokerage firms that went under.

prohibits such **insider trading**. If you come by the information as an insider, you are not supposed to profit from it. The idea is to protect investors that would have sold you the stock at less than its "fair" value. Violations of these laws are what led to the downfall of Michael Milken and of Drexel (see Chapter 14).

There are regulations to protect not only the small investor, but also the small borrower. The *Consumer Credit Protection Act of 1968*, also known as the *Truth in Lending Act*, requires lenders to provide borrowers with accurate information about the cost of credit so that they can more readily shop around. The *Equal Credit Opportunity Act of 1974* prohibits discrimination in credit evaluation. The Fed is charged with administering these laws.

insider trading
Use of privileged information by a corporation's employees or agents to profit from trading the corporation's securities.

18.2 SOME PROBLEMS WITH REGULATION

As we have seen, regulation designed to solve one problem often creates others. Regulation that promotes stability may also hurt efficiency. Regulation may distort incentives in undesirable ways. Overlap and conflict between different regulations and regulators may create confusion and inefficiency. Let us look at each of these problems in turn.

STABILITY VERSUS EFFICIENCY

We saw in Chapter 3 how the efficiency of the financial system is promoted by competition. The costs of borrowing and lending place a wedge between the rates paid by borrowers and the rates received by lenders. The larger this wedge, the less attractive borrowing and lending are, and the less saving and investment there will be. Less saving and investment means slower economic growth. The size of the wedge between the rates for borrowing and for lending depends on the actual costs of making the loans and on the economic rents of intermediaries and middlemen. Competition both reduces economic rents and provides the stimulus for innovation to reduce costs.

The government, under antitrust laws administered by the Department of Justice, generally tries to promote competition in the economy and to prevent collusion to exploit market power. However, because of its interest in stability, the government has often acted to prevent competition in the financial system. An interesting conflict arose between the two principles when, in 1968, the Department of Justice accused stockbrokers of illegal collusion to fix commissions on stock trades. The collusion had, in fact, occurred with the full knowledge and consent of the SEC. The conflict was resolved on the side of competition when the *Securities Acts Amendments of 1975* prohibited further collusion and paved the way for discount brokerage and a general lowering of commissions.

We saw in Chapter 3 that efficiency of the financial system is best served by integration. Interest rates should be uniform across regions and across borrowers of similar creditworthiness. If borrowers and depositors in Maine and California face different interest rates, or if mortgage borrowers pay more for credit than corporations of similar risk, then the financial system is inefficient. The deliberate segmentation of the financial system clearly stands in conflict with this principle, as do the restrictions on bank branching.

THE DISTORTION OF INCENTIVES

Regulations distort the incentives faced by economic agents. The most striking example in the financial system is the moral-hazard problem created by deposit insurance. As we saw in Chapters 16 and 17, the purpose of deposit insurance is to relieve depositors of the need to worry about the safety of their deposits. However, if depositors are not worried about their deposits, then banks can make riskier investments. The cost is ultimately borne by the insurer—in this case, the taxpayer.

REGULATORY CONFUSION

The segmentation of the financial system is matched by segmentation of regulatory responsibility. Exhibit 18.1 shows who regulates what.

dual banking
Banking regulated by both the state and federal governments.

Notice that banks are subject to either (or both) state and federal regulation. This situation—known as **dual banking**—is the result of the historical fight over banking jurisdiction between state and federal government.

Today there are, in fact, four classes of banks and thrifts from the point of view of regulation:[2]

1. *Banks with a national charter (in 1983, 33% of banks, with 60% of total assets).* The Office of the Comptroller of the Currency grants charters, approves mergers and new branches, examines these banks, and, if necessary, closes them. These banks must be members of the Federal Reserve System and must be insured by the FDIC. They are subject to all federal laws and regulations.

2. *State-chartered banks that are members of the Fed (7% of banks, 18% of assets).* State regulators grant charters, approve mergers and new branches, and, if necessary, close these banks. They are examined by the Fed and sometimes also by the state. They must be insured by the FDIC.

3. *State-chartered banks that are not members of the Fed but are insured by the FDIC (60% of banks, 22% of assets).* Regulated as in Category 2, except that examination is by the FDIC.

4. *State-chartered banks not insured by the FDIC (a few small banks).* Regulated as in Category 2, except that examination is by state regulators.

---

[2]Thrifts lost their independent regulation in 1989 and became subject to essentially the same regulators as banks.

EXHIBIT 18.1

REGULATORS OF FINANCIAL INTERMEDIARIES AND FINANCIAL MARKETS

Financial Intermediaries	
Banks and thrifts	*Federal*: Office of the Comptroller of the Currency and Office of Thrift Supervision (Treasury), FDIC, the Fed *State*: State banking commissioner
Credit unions	*Federal*: National Credit Union Administration *State*: State banking commissioner
Finance companies	State permission to open new offices, FTC for consumer protection
Investment companies (mutual funds)	SEC
Insurance companies	State insurance commissioner
Pension funds	Department of Labor, PBGC

Financial Markets (Primary and Secondary)	
Securities firms	SEC, SIPC, NYSE and other exchanges, NASD (self-regulation)
U.S. securities and agencies	The Fed (primary dealers), SEC
Money market (commercial paper, NCDs, BAs)	None
Mortgage-backed securities	None
Stocks and bonds	SEC, the Fed (margin requirements)
Financial futures	Commodity Futures Trading Commission, National Futures Association (self-regulation)
Financial options	SEC (futures options regulated by CFTC), Options Clearing Corporation (self-regulation)

The Bank Holding Company Act of 1956 gave the Fed jurisdiction over all bank holding companies, and in 1980 all institutions offering transactions accounts became subject to reserve requirements set by the Fed. The runs on state-insured thrifts in Ohio and Maryland and the lax regulation of state-chartered thrifts have further served to reduce the authority of the states in this area.

This overlapping patchwork of regulation has been criticized for its duplication and lack of clear lines of authority. For example, although the FDIC may examine a state-chartered nonmember bank, the FDIC must turn to state regulators to close the bank if the bank is found to be insolvent.

The system is also criticized for encouraging regulators to compete in signing up banks by offering less strict rules. (Banks may change their charters from state to federal or vice versa.) For example, before Fed reserve requirements were imposed on all banks, nonmember banks enjoyed substantially easier state-imposed reserve requirements; not surprisingly, many banks switched to state charters and Fed membership declined.

On the other hand, if you believe that banking is overregulated anyhow, all this confusion may not be entirely bad. Regulatory competition provides plenty of loopholes, and it has helped the process of deregulation in a number of areas. A good example is provided by the Massachusetts state thrift regulators who were the first to allow NOW accounts. It is also the state regulators who have been responsible for the movement toward interstate banking. Without competition from state regulators, federal bureaucrats might be less flexible and responsive.

Untidiness in regulation is not limited to banking: There are similar problems in the securities markets. Trading in stocks is regulated by the SEC. However, trading in stock index futures is regulated by the Commodity Futures Trading Commission. The crash of 1987 vividly illustrated the close connection between the two markets. Since then there have been calls to unify regulation of the two markets. In early 1990 there was discussion in Congress of new legislation that would bring the financial futures markets under the control of the SEC. (The political power of the futures industry, and hence its ability to resist this takeover, had been weakened substantially by an FBI sting operation that had revealed major abuses by traders on the two largest futures exchanges.)

18.3 THE PROCESS OF DEREGULATION

Recent years have seen a steady breaking down of the regulatory structure. This has happened partly because strong profit incentives have driven institutions to find ways around the rules and partly because changes in legislation have canceled some regulations and modified others.

BANKING

We saw in Chapter 8 how economies of scale have driven banks to grow and expand and to find ways around the restrictions on interstate banking and how the restrictions themselves have been crumbling. We saw in Chapters 9, 10, and 11 how competition from an emerging money market, both at home and abroad, led to the removal of interest-rate restrictions on bank deposits. We saw in Chapter 15 how the development of a secondary market for mortgages helped to reshape the mortgage market.

FINANCIAL MARKETS

The regulation of financial markets has also been under pressure. As we saw in Chapter 14, competition has been stimulated both by shelf registration and by rivalry from a growing Eurobond market. The abolition of fixed commissions has also helped.

Investment banks have tried to free themselves from SEC regulation by setting themselves up in holding company form. A parent holding company is set up that owns underwriting and securities subsidiaries that are regulated by the SEC as well as other subsidiaries that are not. These other subsidiaries can engage in merchant banking (bridge loans for LBOs and takeovers, equity positions in nonfinancial corporations), commodities trading, insurance, and other activities not permitted a regulated securities firm. By 1990 investment banks had built up assets of some $80 billion in such unregulated activities.

BREAKING DOWN THE BARRIERS

In addition to the erosion of regulation within banking and within the securities industry, there has also been an erosion of the regulations that separate them. The same market forces we saw at work undermining other regulation have been active here too. The segmentation instituted in the 1930s is beginning to break down.

We saw in Chapter 9 how rising interest rates created a tremendous opportunity for nonbanks to compete with banks hobbled by Regulation Q. Investment banks offered money market mutual funds, thrifts offered NOW accounts, credit unions offered share draft accounts. As we saw in Chapter 17, the deregulation of the early 1980s allowed thrifts into commercial lending. And credit unions too became increasingly banklike. Their status as nonprofit institutions exempts them from paying taxes and allows them to undercut banks on loan rates, and they have increasingly been making loans not just to households but also to businesses.[3]

Investment banks have found other ways to expand into commercial banking. One is to buy a bank and turn it into a "nonbank" bank. For example, Merrill Lynch set up Merrill Lynch Bank and Trust Company in New Jersey without demand deposits but with insured time deposits and commercial loans. (Owning a bank also gives Merrill Lynch direct access to the payments system.)

---

[3]The law prohibiting interest on business checking accounts does not specifically mention credit unions, and the credit unions have begun to exploit this loophole.

Although the expansion of nonbank banks was halted in 1987, another method is still open—the acquisition of failing thrifts.[4] Moreover, since the Glass-Steagall Act does not apply overseas, several investment banks have overseas subsidiaries engaged in Eurodollar banking.

Commercial banks, finding their turf invaded in this way, have retaliated by trying to get into investment banking. This seemed particularly attractive because investment banks appeared to be doing so much better than commercial banks. The Glass-Steagall Act had set up a highly protected environment, and investment banks earned a return on equity consistently higher than that earned by commercial banks and corporations in general; their employees were also paid more.

Of course, the exclusion of commercial banks from the securities markets had never been absolute. Exhibit 18.2 shows the securities activities already permitted to banks. Subsidiaries of bank holding companies have always been permitted to deal in Treasury securities and to underwrite general-obligation municipal bonds. Indeed, through such subsidiaries, several major banks are primary dealers in government securities, and banks underwrite about half of all general-obligation bonds. In addition, the Glass-Steagall Act does not extend to banks' activities overseas: U.S. banks underwrite about 10% of new issues of Eurobonds (vigorous competition in this market has kept their share small). Banks have also been important underwriters of commercial paper since the courts decided that this did not violate the Glass-Steagall Act. And banks have been increasingly active in brokering private placements: The market share of commercial banks rose from 12% in 1984 to 26% in 1987. Bankers Trust is now one of the biggest players in private placements.

Recently, even the Glass-Steagall exclusion of commercial banks from the market for long-term corporate securities has been crumbling. In 1982 and 1983 the Fed and then the Office of the Comptroller of the Currency permitted banks to engage in discount brokerage (executing trades without offering investment advice), and over 2,000 banks now offer this service. In 1989 the Fed allowed bank securities affiliates to engage in limited underwriting of corporate bonds (such underwriting was to constitute no more than 10% of their business). Bankers Trust, Chase, Citi, and J.P. Morgan were quick to sign up. The limits were expected to be raised and the permission extended to include corporate equities.[5]

Despite the banks' enthusiasm, investment banking may prove less lucrative than banks had hoped. Just as banks have been entering, competition has increased and profitability has fallen. Shelf registration, the Eurobond market, and the growth of discount brokerage have all contributed to the trend (see Chapter 14). Since the crash of 1987 the securities industry has been in a slump,

---

[4]The 1989 bailout bill has made this route even more attractive: The owner of a thrift is no longer prohibited from using it to market other products, such as credit cards, mutual funds, or insurance.

[5]These enhanced securities powers will undoubtedly increase the role of commercial banks in leveraged buyouts. Banks have also received permission to start selling their own securitized loans (previously they had to pay commissions to an investment bank to do this). To keep the banks honest, the paper must receive an investment-grade rating from an independent rating agency.

Exhibit 18.2

PERMISSIBLE
SECURITIES
ACTIVITIES OF
COMMERCIAL
BANKS[a]

Activity	Year Started[b]
Underwriting, distributing, and dealing	
U.S. Treasury securities	Always
U.S. federal agency securities	Various years
Commercial paper (third party)	1988
Mortgage and consumer paper-backed securities	1988
Municipal securities	
General obligation	Nearly always
Some revenue bonds	1968
All revenue bonds	1988
Corporate bonds (limited)	1989
Private placement (agency capacity)	Always
Mergers and acquisitions	Always
Offshore dealing in Eurodollar securities	Always
Brokerage	
Limited customer	Always
Public retail (discount)	1982
Securities swapping	Always
Financial and precious metal futures brokerage and dealing	1983[c]
Financial advising and managing	
Closed-end funds	1974
Mutual funds	1974
Restricted	Always
Research advice to investors	
Separate from brokerage	1983
Combined with brokerage	
Institutional	1986
Retail	1987

[a]Federal Reserve member banks or bank holding company affiliates.

[b]After the Civil War. Different dates may apply to national and state banks and among state banks. With some exceptions, the earliest date is shown. Regulatory rulings frequently concluded that a specific activity was permissible before the date of ruling. If the activity was halted by enactment of the Glass-Steagall Act, the date of renewed activity is given.

[c]Restricted to futures contracts for which banks may hold the underlying security or that are settled only in cash.

Source: Updated from B. Dole, "The Grass May Be Greener," *Economic Perspectives*, Federal Reserve Bank of Chicago, November-December 1988.

with widespread layoffs. The example of British banks in this respect is not encouraging. They were allowed to enter investment banking in 1986. Since then their profits have been slim, and several that rushed in have since withdrawn.

Today, actual repeal of Glass-Steagall seems increasingly likely. In December 1989 the Securities Industry Association, one of the main opponents of repeal, reversed its position and began to lobby for it. Apparently scared by the crash of

'87, investment banks would like to have the same sort of safety net enjoyed by banks. They also want to be able to borrow on the overnight market and to have access to the payments system. Moreover, they are worried about competition from a Europe that is moving toward full financial integration by 1992.

The partition between commercial and investment banking is not the only one that is breaking down. Insurance companies have been expanding their activities into both investment and commercial banking. For example, Prudential, one of the largest insurance companies, has purchased an investment bank, Bache, which has grown into the third largest retail stockbroker, Pru-Bache. Prudential has also set up nonbank bank subsidiaries and was the first to apply to buy a thrift after passage of the 1989 bailout bill. Prudential subsidiaries now offer residential mortgages, credit card services, retail brokerage of securities and commodities, and investment and merchant banking. Banks would like to be able to reciprocate by selling insurance, but they have not yet been allowed to do so, although some state regulators have allowed bank holding companies to sell insurance through their nonbank subsidiaries.

The separation of banking and commerce is being eroded too. Banks have been restrained from moving into commerce by a law that limits them to owning no more than a 5% voting share in a nonfinancial company. However, a number of nonfinancial corporations have expanded into the financial sector and into commercial banking. Here too nonbank banks and the acquisition of thrifts have played a major role.

Sears, Roebuck and Company has been aggressive in expanding into finance (see Exhibit 18.3). Its involvement in finance is not new: Sears has long been the largest issuer of retail credit cards, and it began offering installment credit in 1911, before any bank did so. Sears has offered automobile insurance since the 1920s, and its subsidiary, Allstate, is one of the largest insurance companies. In 1985 Sears acquired Coldwell Banker, a major real estate broker, and Dean Witter, a large investment bank. It has launched a credit card, Discover, to compete with the Visa and MasterCard bank cards. (Discover is doing well: Unlike bank cards, it has no annual fee, and it offers a 1% cash rebate on purchases.) Sears has acquired a California thrift with some $6 billion in assets, and it is active in mortgage banking and in the secondary mortgage market; Coldwell Banker is able to offer in-house finance for its real estate sales. However, Sears expansion into the financial arena has not been without problems. The in-store offices of Coldwell Banker and Dean Witter have not proven a success (those of the former are being eliminated and those of the latter halved in number). In 1989 Sears sold off Coldwell Banker's Commercial Group.

The major automobile companies have continued to expand their financial activities through their finance company subsidiaries. In 1987 GMAC extended more consumer credit than Citibank—$55 billion (excluding mortgages) versus $44 billion. The Ford Motor Company is expanding its financial operations, planning ultimately to earn about 30% of its income from financial services. Through its subsidiary, First Nationwide Financial Corporation, Ford intends to become the nation's largest thrift holding company.

EXHIBIT 18.3

Source: San Francisco Chronicle, Special Features, 1983.

The credit subsidiaries of General Electric, Westinghouse, Weyerhaeuser, and IBM are all major lenders to firms. GECC is by far the largest: Most of its lending is not GE-related, and it includes LBOs, commercial real estate, and leasing. GECC owns 90% of Kidder Peabody, a major investment bank.

Even the phone company is getting into the act. In 1990 AT&T introduced a bank credit card called Universal, to be marketed to holders of phone calling cards, and designed to compete with Visa and MasterCard. (Universal is issued through a Columbus, Georgia, bank holding company.) AT&T hired away some managers from Citi to run the operation, and Citi, the biggest issuer of bank credit cards, retaliated by switching $30 million of its telecommunications business to MCI, AT&T's main competitor (MCI does not yet offer a credit card).

18.4 | ENDING FINANCIAL SEGMENTATION: PRO AND CON

economies of scope
Reduction in costs
resulting from engaging in
complementary activities.

Is this breaking down of barriers a good thing? On the positive side, it may make it easier to capture **economies of scope**. These are reductions in cost that result from engaging in activities that are complementary. For example, if a bank has invested in acquiring information about a corporation in order to make it a loan, it can use that same information, at no extra cost, to underwrite a bond issue or to write an insurance policy. Or the bank can use the relationships it has developed with its depositors to help it market other products, such as insurance and investments, at relatively low cost. Consumers may enjoy economies of "one-stop shopping" if they can obtain all the financial services they need in one location. All these reductions in cost represent increases in economic efficiency.[6] Letting a bank own equity in a borrower gives it more direct control, enabling it to restrain the excessive risk taking that may be a consequence of debt finance (we discussed this problem in Chapter 3).

One possible reason for concern about ending the separation of commercial and investment banking is the potential for conflicts of interest. To see how these could arise, consider two examples:

- A corporation is about to default on a bank loan. Its bank arranges a public issue to be used to pay off the loan, shifting the risk to unsuspecting small investors. In order to sell the securities, the bank is less than forthcoming with information about the corporation's troubles.

- A bank, underwriting securities, has trouble selling a new issue at a profitable price. So it sells the securities to customers of its trust department and to its innocent respondent banks. Alternatively, it offers cheap bank loans to encourage the purchase of the unsold securities. The bank avoids a loss by selling the securities for more than they are worth.

Concern about such abuses played a role in the debate that preceded passage of the Glass-Steagall Act. Although there was some anecdotal evidence that these sorts of things did actually happen, such abuses do not seem to have been widespread.

A more serious problem with lowering the barriers that separate banking from other activities is that it may worsen the deposit insurance problem. Deposit insurance gives banks a competitive advantage over other types of financial institutions in that it allows them to borrow at the risk-free rate: Their deposits are essentially government debt. Deposit insurance therefore constitutes a taxpayer subsidy to banks. Because of this subsidy, banks are able to undercut other types of financial institution. For example, if investment banks and commercial banks compete in underwriting, and the investment banks have to pay a risk

---

[6]Some banks have tried to capture these economies, despite the regulatory ban on various activities by banks, by renting out floor space in their branches to investment consultants, insurance companies, and realtors.

premium on the funds they use while commercial banks do not, then investment banks will be at a disadvantage. On the other hand, if investment banks gain access to insured deposits by expanding into banking, then the deposit-insurance subsidy will be extended to a whole new range of activities.

While there may be some justification for subsidies when deposit insurance helps to stabilize the banking system (because of the externalities of bank failure), it is hard to justify the extension of subsidies to other activities such as investment banking or insurance, let alone to the development of commercial real estate or the holding of junk bonds (see Chapter 17). Indeed, the use of brokered deposits to finance portfolios of junk bonds is the best current example of abusive exploitation of the deposit-insurance subsidy. The extension of the deposit-insurance subsidy to activities other than banking proper is not only unjustifiable in terms of economic efficiency, it will also inevitably raise the cost of deposit insurance to the taxpayer.

One possible solution to the problem is to insulate the bank part of a financial institution from the rest of its activities along the lines of the "narrow bank" we discussed in Chapter 17. If banking can be separated from other activities *within* a financial firm, then the coverage of deposit insurance can be limited to banking alone. There remains the question, however, of what would happen if, say, the insurance subsidiary of a bank in the "too-big-to-fail" category became insolvent. Would the parent holding company not step in to cover its debts? If it did, and if this resulted in the insolvency of the holding company, would regulators not step in to save it? Limiting *explicit* insurance is not much help if there exist broader implicit guarantees.

Regulators have differed in their attitudes toward the expansion of permissible activities (an example of regulatory competition at work). The Fed, which has the ultimate responsibility when things go wrong, has traditionally been the least enthusiastic, although its current chairman, Alan Greenspan, has long been an advocate of deregulation. The FDIC, on the other hand, has generally favored the removal of barriers (see "The FDIC's Arguments for Bank Deregulation" on page 500). Most enthusiastic have been the state regulators: Various states have allowed banks to become involved in investment banking, insurance, and real estate. The final word rests with Congress, which so far has put off making any decisions.

18.5 DEREGULATION AROUND THE WORLD

The trend toward deregulation in the United States has been matched by similar trends in other countries. There has been a general liberalization of capital and exchange controls, making it easier for investors in one country to purchase securities in another. There has been a worldwide deregulation and modernization of stock exchanges, easing the trading of foreign stocks and the entry of foreign securities firms. The regulation of bank deposits and assets has also been eased. Money markets and markets for derivative securities have been introduced

THE FDIC'S ARGUMENTS FOR BANK DEREGULATION
By George Melloan

L. William Seidman has had a lot of interesting jobs, ranging from advising President Ford on economic policy in the mid-1970s to running Arizona State's business school. His reputation as a trouble-shooter landed him two years ago in one of Washington's hottest spots, running the Federal Deposit Insurance Corp. at a time when failures of small banks had been rising steadily and even some larger institutions were not entirely healthy.

Since Mr. Seidman's job is to protect depositors when banks crash, it is not surprising that he has some thoughts about how to put banking on a sounder footing. One thought is to further deregulate banking by repealing many of the constraints embodied in the Banking Act of 1933, better known as the Glass-Steagall Act.

The FDIC in August released a study forecasting the effects of further deregulation. It launched the study to find out whether bank safety could be maintained, and even improved, after deregulation. Drawing heavily on the views of its own bank supervisors, it concluded it would indeed be possible to protect strictly banking operations at the same time it allowed banks to engage in other activities.

"Fundamentally," says Mr. Seidman, "the study says we don't need Glass-Steagall and we don't need the bank holding company act." Mr. Seidman concluded that diversified financial-services companies are inevitably stronger than highly specialized banks. He says the dangers of tight restrictions on banks show up particularly in states that prohibit branch banking through what are euphemistically known as "unit" banking laws.

"Whoever invented unit banking really cost the insurance fund a bundle," says Mr. Seidman. "I keep saying we ought to raise the premium to every state that maintains unit banking. You look at the FDIC history and it's right there. We have practically no banks failing east of the Mississippi. There's practically no unit banking there. Places like Georgia have recessions but few banks fail. The bank failures we are having are primarily in Texas and Oklahoma, both unit banking states. Both changed their laws when they got into trouble."

Mr. Seidman doesn't want "big-bang" style deregulation. He prefers a "time-release" bang. "We believe banking always will have to be government regulated or supervised for safety and soundness because you have deposit insurance, and deposit insurance means you are borrowing on somebody else's credit. As long as you are borrowing on somebody else's credit, somebody has to be around to see what you do with the money."

Deposit insurance obviously is here to stay, so the goal should be to "limit regulation to the narrowest we can and still insure safety of the system."

As banks are allowed to do more things, the basic problem, in Mr. Seidman's view, is how to prevent conflicts of interest. But supervisors pointed out to him that there is a potential for conflict of interest even in today's banking industry. "Its directors are by and large its borrowers throughout the system, therefore regulating conflict of interest is fundamental. While there have been instances of abuse, the record shows that this can be handled in an appropriate manner. The reason is that 90% of the people are honest. The job of safety supervision is to make sure that the 5% or 10% don't ruin the system." He believes the FDIC needs stronger powers to supervise transactions between banks and related parties.

"But whatever is not allowed inside the wall would be allowed outside through a subsidiary. With respect to antitrust, that kind of problem ought to be governed by normal antitrust rules. If this could be accomplished we would eliminate huge layers of regulatory problems, delay and cost-inefficiency."

Source: George Melloan, "The FDIC's Arguments for Bank Deregulation," *The Wall Street Journal*, November 24, 1987, p. 29. Reprinted by permission of The Wall Street Journal, © Dow Jones & Company, Inc. 1987. All Rights Reserved Worldwide.

in many countries. And the separation between different types of financial institutions has been breaking down.

As the world financial system becomes more integrated, deregulation in one country stimulates deregulation in others. For example, U.S. banks and securities firms have found themselves increasingly competing for business, both at home and abroad, with Japanese and European rivals. If there are indeed important economies of scope, then U.S. financial institutions that are restricted in the range of their activities will be at a competitive disadvantage with respect to foreign institutions that are not so restricted. Of course, deregulation in the United States places the same sort of pressure on foreign countries.

Let us look at the developments in some of the major countries.

CANADA

Although Canadian banking has historically been much less regulated than banking in the United States, the securities markets have been quite tightly regulated and banks have been excluded from the securities markets. The Canadian stock market is quite substantial, being the fourth largest after the United States, Japan, and Great Britain.

In June 1987 Canada deregulated its securities markets and allowed any firm, including banks and insurance companies, to open securities subsidiaries. The distinctions between securities firms, commercial banks, and saving banks (called *trusts* in Canada) were effectively removed. Canadian and U.S. banks have moved into the securities market, mostly by buying up existing Canadian investment banks.

The recent Free Trade Agreement between Canada and the United States will stimulate further deregulation and integration of the two financial systems. Under the new agreement, most of the restrictions limiting access of U.S. financial institutions to the Canadian market will be removed.

JAPAN

Postwar regulation in Japan segmented the financial system on the U.S. model. It created a number of distinct types of bank—long-term credit banks, commercial banks, and trust banks—and separate securities firms. Japan's Article 65 is its equivalent of the Glass-Steagall Act. However, although banks may not underwrite securities, they are allowed to own equity in other corporations. Indeed, banks and their affiliates own some 30% of all equity in Japan. Cross shareholding across banks, insurance companies, securities firms, and nonfinancial corporations in so-called *keiretsu* groups is widespread. This arrangement allows significant integration in practice, despite the regulations that prohibit it.

There has been some deregulation of banking in Japan. The removal of ceilings on deposit interest rates has reduced margins on loans and, as in the United States, has led banks to seek income from fees and commissions. (Japanese banks have been very active in financing merger and acquisitions activity in the United States.) The BIS capital standards were expected to be particularly hard on Japanese banks, because of their very low equity ratios. However, they have had little trouble raising enormous amounts of capital on the stock exchange (the five biggest banks raised some $21 billion by 1989), already putting them over the 8% equity ratio required for 1992.

There has been a gradual liberalization of financial markets in Japan. Options and futures markets have opened. The government bond market has been expanded and liberalized. A short-term money market has emerged. Companies have increasingly turned to the financial markets, relying less than in the past on bank finance. The Tokyo stock exchange has been opened to some foreign firms, but the market remains protected, with high fixed commissions; it is still dominated by four giant securities firms. Although Japanese banks underwrite securities abroad and Japanese securities firms engage in banking abroad, Article 65 remains in effect domestically.

Since 1984 there has been a series of talks with U.S. trade negotiators, called the "Yen–Dollar talks," aimed at opening up the Japanese financial system to foreigners.

EUROPE

The European Community plans to remove all barriers to trade in goods and services within the Community by 1992. Plans include the creation of a fully integrated European Financial Area. The Second Banking Directive, to be operative by January 1, 1993, will allow credit institutions to operate in any member country without requiring permission of the host country. Credit institutions will be allowed to engage in both commercial and investment banking: The model is the **universal banks** of Germany that are free to do more or less whatever they please. A proposed Investment Services Directive will allow the same freedom to securities firms, which may or may not be credit institutions. There are more restricted plans for integrating insurance markets (credit institutions will not yet be allowed to engage in insurance).[7]

universal banks
Banks that are permitted to engage in any activity they wish.

There has been a process of "competitive deregulation" of the European stock markets. Great Britain started it off with its "Big Bang" of 1986, when London's domestic financial market was opened to foreign banks and securities firms (the London Euromarket, which was open already, had been kept quite separate from the domestic market). Fixed brokerage commissions and a stamp tax on securities trades were abolished, leading to much lower transactions costs, and a computerized trading system was introduced. The result was a significant increase in the trading of European and U.S. shares in London, forcing other exchanges to respond. For example, after losing something like 15% of its trading volume to London, Paris moved to open its Bourse to foreign firms and to introduce improved trading technology.

---

[7]Some countries already allow links between banks and insurance companies. In France banks hold one-third of the life insurance market. The French call this integration *bancassurance*; the Germans call it *Allfinanz*.

|18.6| THE CENTRAL ROLE OF THE FED

Deregulation, both at home and abroad, has complicated the task of the Fed, the pivotal regulator in the United States and in the world. The Fed's responsibilities extend to three closely related areas: The stability of the financial system, the stability of the payments system, and the regulation of the quantity of money.

STABILITY OF THE FINANCIAL SYSTEM

Although banking is its primary responsibility, the Fed must pay attention to other parts of the financial system too. No crisis anywhere in the financial system, at home or abroad, will leave banks unaffected, especially as their involvement in other activities and countries increases.

Consequently, the Fed has intervened repeatedly to prop up a variety of failing markets and institutions. Some examples:

- When the Penn Central railroad failed in June 1970 with over $200 million in commercial paper outstanding, the commercial-paper market dried up, resulting in a shortage of working capital for many firms. The Fed encouraged banks to take up the slack by expanding their lending, and it increased its own lending to banks to make this possible.

- When Franklin National failed in 1974 with a large amount of NCDs outstanding, the NCD market experienced difficulties: The premium over T-bills increased from 45 to 470 basis points. The Fed helped by itself lending money to the banks to replace the funds they were temporarily unable to raise in the money market.

- In 1980 a multibillion-dollar speculation in the silver market by the Hunt family of Texas collapsed (see Chapter 13). The Hunts' potential default threatened with insolvency the six broker-dealers carrying their accounts (the largest were Merrill Lynch and Bache). The COMEX was threatened with collapse. The Fed helped a consortium of major banks put together a $1.1 billion rescue package for the Hunts that prevented their default.

- During the stock market crash of 1987, specialists and securities firms needed to expand their borrowing considerably. Because of potential capital losses and customer defaults, they looked like poor credit risks, and the banks stopped lending to them. Had the specialists and brokers not been able to borrow, the Stock Exchange would have had to close. The Fed stepped in to pressure banks to resume their lending. Again in the minicrash of 1989 the Fed announced that it would provide ample credit to banks to lend to brokerage houses and other large investors that wished to buy stocks.

- In contrast, when Drexel collapsed in 1990, the Fed and the SEC saw no reason to intervene, and, in fact, no problems arose. The Fed could have pressured banks to lend to Drexel in order to save it, but it chose not to do so. Contrary to some expectations, the "too-big-to-fail" doctrine was not applied to this securities firm.

THE SAFETY OF THE PAYMENTS SYSTEM

The Fed's concerns about the stability of the financial system are compounded by its parallel responsibility for the safety of the payments system—in particular, the wire transfer system. We saw in Chapter 4 that wire transfers are made through two networks—Fedwire and CHIPS. Each has its problems.

daylight overdraft
Overdraft during the business day.

Fedwire's problem is **daylight overdraft**. To understand the nature of the problem, consider an example. Chase transfers $500 million to Citi over Fedwire. The Fed immediately credits Citi for the $500 million. If Chase *has* $500 million in its account, it is debited. If not, the Fed automatically makes Chase a loan to cover the transfer. Such an automatic loan, used to cover a payment, is called an

overdraft
Automatic loan to cover payment in excess of depositor's balance.

overdraft.[8] Chase is expected to repay the loan by the close of business the same day—hence, *daylight* overdraft. Because the Fed charges no interest on daylight overdrafts, banks have made liberal use of this free credit, and the total amount has mushroomed. In June 1989 the total amount of daylight overdraft on Fedwire averaged over $118 billion a day, roughly twice end-of-day reserve balances. The overdraft on CHIPS averaged $53 billion.[9]

Daylight overdraft exposes the Fed to considerable credit risk. If a bank fails with an overdraft outstanding, the Fed may be left with a very large bad debt. The collapse of Continental Illinois provides a good example. Continental paid off its overnight borrowing as usual by drawing on daylight overdraft, but then was unable to borrow in the market the funds it needed to pay off its debt to the Fed. The Fed was forced to convert the $3.5 billion overdraft into a discount loan: It could hardly have refused, since the loan had in effect already been made.

Large as it is, the loan to Continental Illinois does not hold the record. That distinction goes to Bank of New York, the largest clearing bank for the government securities market. Because of a computer failure, on November 21, 1985, Bank of New York was left with an uncleared daylight overdraft of $30 billion. The Fed had no choice but to make it a discount loan of $28.6 billion to carry it over to the next day. Despite the $5 million in interest the Fed earned on the loan (at 7.5%), it was not amused.

systemic risk
Risk relating to the possibility that the failure of one bank will cause the failure of other banks.

CHIPS has a different problem—**systemic risk**. Payments on CHIPS, unlike those on Fedwire, are provisional; they become final only at the end of the day when clearing takes place. The danger is that a CHIPS participant will fail during the day. If this were to happen, its payments would have to be canceled and the net positions of the other banks recalculated. Many banks would find themselves

---

[8]In many countries banks allow overdrafts on regular checking accounts. In those countries overdrafts are often the main form of consumer credit.

[9]The Fedwire overdraft includes daylight overdraft on the securities wire as well as on the funds wire. The average is the average of the daily peak overdraft.

with large deficits that they could not cover. A domino effect might bring down a large number of banks. It has generally been assumed that the Fed would step in to prevent a collapse. But many participants in CHIPS are foreign banks. Would the Fed help them? Would their own central banks?[10]

Deregulation has compounded the problems. Currently, only banks have access to these networks. However, there is concern that as the barriers between banking and the rest of the financial system fall, nonbank institutions will gain access too. The Fed could wind up making interest-free, unsecured loans to Prudential and to Ford, as well as to Chemical and Bankers Trust. Or the failure of an investment bank that owned a CHIPS participant could threaten collapse of the system.

In recent years the Fed has tried to do something about these problems. In 1982 it suggested that banks "voluntarily" reduce their daylight overdraft to no more than a given multiple of their equity. Since then the caps have been reduced twice. In 1989 the Fed published for comment a proposal to impose a charge for daylight overdraft. The charge would be a fixed 25 basis points on the average daily overdraft in both funds and book-entry securities. (The charge would apply to overdraft in excess of a deductible of 10% of the institution's capital.) The charge would be phased in over three years.

Clearly, the problems of Fedwire and CHIPS must be addressed together; otherwise the only effect of tightening up on Fedwire will be to shift transactions onto CHIPS. Under pressure from the Fed, CHIPS too is making some changes. Soon it will introduce payments finality. This means that payments will be guaranteed by a risk-sharing agreement among participants: All participants will share the loss of any participant unable to cover its deficit position.

There are a number a ways banks can cut down on daylight overdraft, now that they have an incentive to do so. Instead of repaying fed funds each morning and then borrowing again from the same lender in the afternoon, a bank can negotiate a continuing loan at a floating daily rate, or a term loan can be substituted. Banks can delay sending payments on behalf of customers until they actually have a positive balance in their Fed account. Exposure to credit risk on CHIPS can be reduced by adopting the "netting by novation" method of trading used on the London foreign-exchange market. There, two parties keep track of their net bilateral position, trade by trade, and are liable only for the net, to be paid at the end of the trading day. The advantages are that most individual trades do not result in actual payments and that credit-risk exposure to specific participants is closely monitored.

The Swiss banking system has managed to abolish daylight overdraft completely. Since 1987 each payment goes into a central computer, which executes it only if the bank's balance will cover it. If not, the payment goes into a queue. As funds come in, payments are executed on a first-in-first-out basis. Any payments left at the end of the day are canceled. The danger, of course, is gridlock: Everyone

---

[10]It is finality of payment on Fedwire that eliminates any systemic risk there. A failure of one participant there would have no domino effect on others. Instead, the Fed would take the loss.

waiting for everyone else to pay. So far, however, the system has worked well. Its success is helped by the relatively small number of banks in Switzerland—156, versus the more than 7,000 on Fedwire.

REGULATION OF THE QUANTITY OF MONEY

When the Fed was set up as lender of last resort, as guarantor of the stability and safety of the financial and payments systems, it was also given the charge of regulating the quantity of money in the economy. The two functions are closely related.

To be able to rescue institutions or markets in distress—whether because of a run on Continental Illinois or because of a lack of credit to specialists and brokers during the crash of 1987—it is very handy to be able to create as much money as is needed. The Fed can do this. Since its own notes and deposits are definitive money and not convertible into anything else, the Fed can create as much money as it needs.

The Fed's ability to control the quantity of definitive money is important for other reasons too. As we shall see in Chapter 19, it enables the Fed to regulate the total quantity of money in the economy. The quantity of money is, in turn, an important determinant of the price level, of interest rates and exchange rates, and of the general level of economic activity. Hence, through its ability to control the quantity of definitive money, the Fed possesses enormous power over the economy. The question of how it should exercise that power—the question of *monetary policy*—will be our principal concern in the remaining chapters of this book.

SUMMARY

- The externalities involved in a financial collapse are a major reason for regulation of the financial system. Regulation has sought to promote stability by limiting competition—curbs on geographic expansion, caps on deposit rates, and the segmentation of financial institutions.

- Government and private guarantees, such as deposit insurance and the insurance of accounts with brokers, both promote stability and protect individuals from exploitation by better-informed traders. The latter function is also served by disclosure requirements, limits on insider trading, and truth-in-lending laws.

- Regulation creates its own problems. Limited competition and geographic and functional segmentation harm economic efficiency. Regulation distorts incentives.

- Division of regulatory responsibility leads to confusion and duplication. However, because of competition among regulators, it may also make regulation less burdensome.

- Regulation of banking and of financial markets has been eroded in recent years, both by innovation to get around it and by legislation to modify or remove it.

- The separation of banking from the securities markets and from commerce has been breaking down. Banks have recently been granted limited powers to underwrite corporate securities. Securities firms and nonfinancial corporations have found ways into banking.

- Ending this separation allows firms to reap economies of scope. There may, however, be problems of conflict of interest, and the deposit insurance problem may worsen as government guarantees are extended to a broader range of activities.

- The trend toward deregulation is worldwide. Deregulation in one country puts pressure on other countries to deregulate in order to preserve the competitiveness of their financial institutions and markets.

- The Fed plays a special role as the pivotal regulator of the financial system. It intervenes when necessary to ensure the stability and safety of financial markets and institutions. It is currently trying to improve the safety of the payments system, where daylight overdraft and systemic risk are serious concerns. It is responsible for regulating the quantity of money in the economy.

KEY TERMS

Securities Investor Protection Corporation (SIPC)	dual banking	daylight overdraft
	economies of scope	overdraft
insider trading	universal banks	systemic risk

DISCUSSION QUESTIONS

1. Some people argue that regulatory agencies are "captured" by the very institutions that they are supposed to regulate: They begin to serve the interests of those institutions rather than the interests of the public. What are examples of this in the financial system? What are the consequences of such "regulatory capture"?

2. What are the arguments for regulating the financial system? What are the arguments against it? Do we have too much regulation today or too little? Explain.

3. What have been the important changes in financial regulation in the last 20 years? Why did they occur? Have these changes been beneficial? Explain.

4. What are the arguments for separating banking from the securities markets? From commerce? What are the arguments for removing this separation? Explain why you think the separation should or should not continue.

5. If you could redesign the U.S. regulatory structure, what changes would you make and why?

6. Why is the Fed worried about the safety of the payments system? What is being done? What could be done?

BIBLIOGRAPHY

Aguilar, Linda, "Still Toe-to-Toe: Banks and Nonbanks at the End of the '80s," *Economic Perspectives of the Federal Reserve Bank of Chicago*: 12–23, 1990.

Berlin Mitchell, "Banking Reform: An Overview of the Restructuring Debate," *Economic Review of the Federal Reserve Bank of Philadelphia* July-August 1988, 3–14.

Cargill, Thomas F., and Gillian G. Garcia, *Financial Reform in the 1980s*, Stanford, CA: Hoover Institution, 1985.

Cumming, Christine M., and Lawrence M. Sweet, "Financial Structure of the G-10 Countries: How Does the United States Compare? *FRBNY Quarterly Review* Winter 1987–88, 14–25.

Gilbert, R. Alton, "Payments System Risk: What Is It and What Will Happen If We Try To Reduce It?" *Economic Review of the Federal Reserve Bank of St. Louis* January-February 1989, 3–17.

Humphrey, D. B., "Market Responses to Pricing Fedwire Daylight Overdrafts," *Economic Review of the Federal Reserve Bank of Richmond* May-June 1989.

Key, Sydney J., "Mutual Recognition: Integration of the Financial Sector in the European Community," *Federal Reserve Bulletin* September 1989, 591–609.

VanHoose, David D., and Gordon H. Sellon Jr., "Daylight Overdrafts, Payment System Risk, and Public Policy," *Economic Review of the Federal Reserve Bank of Kansas City* September-October 1989, 9–29.

Vital, Christian, and David L. Mengle, "SIC: Switzerland's New Electronic Interbank Payment System," *Economic Review of the Federal Reserve Bank of Richmond* November-December 1988, 12–26.

PART FIVE

REGULATING THE QUANTITY OF MONEY

CHAPTER 19

THE MULTIPLE EXPANSION OF BANK DEPOSITS

AN INTRODUCTION

When the Fed was created, in addition to its role as lender of last resort, it was also given the task of regulating the quantity of money. That charge is an important one: The quantity of money plays a major role in determining prices, interest rates, exchange rates, and the level of economic activity.

In talking about the quantity of money, we need to distinguish between the two different types of money that we learned about in Chapter 4—*definitive money* and *ordinary bank money*. Definitive money is the "final word": In our economy it consists of coins, Federal Reserve notes, and deposits at the Fed. In our economy bank money consists of transactions accounts at banks and at other depository institutions. It is convertible into definitive money on demand.

The Fed can control the amount of definitive money directly because definitive money is a liability of the Fed. It can control the amount of bank money indirectly through the availability of definitive-money reserves and through the setting of reserve requirements. As we saw in Chapter 5, reserve requirements and the need to meet demands for conversion constrain the ability of depository institutions to create bank money.

In this chapter we shall learn the basic principles of the link between definitive money and bank money. We shall then rely on those principles in Chapters 20 and 21 as we examine the role of the Fed and of the banking system in determining the quantity of money in our economy. Following that, in Part Six we shall see how the quantity of money affects the economy, and in Part Seven we shall discuss how the Fed should use its ability to control the quantity of money.

|19.1| THE BASIC RELATIONSHIP BETWEEN DEPOSITS AND RESERVES

In studying the basic relationships that determine the quantity of money in an economy, it is best to keep things as simple as possible. Therefore let us begin with an economy much simpler than our own—the economy of the fictional South Seas island that we first encountered in Chapter 4.

Definitive money on the Island consists of silver coins. Bank money consists of deposits. To begin with, let us suppose that all banking on the Island is *warehouse banking*: Banks hold one dollar in silver for every dollar of deposits. The balance sheet of a typical bank—the Bank of Coconut Grove—is as follows: [1]

BANK OF COCONUT GROVE

Reserves		Checking deposits	$100,000
Silver in vault	$90,000		
Deposit at Palm Tree Bank	10,000		

As a warehouse bank, Coconut Grove holds silver reserves equal to the amount of its deposits. Some of this silver is held in its own vault; the rest is deposited with Palm Tree Bank to enable Coconut Grove to clear checks with other banks.[2]

There are about 100 banks of varying size on the Island. The consolidated balance sheet of the banking system is:[3]

BANKING SYSTEM

Reserves	$10,000,000	Checking deposits	$10,000,000

Banks on the Island find that most of the silver in their vaults is gathering dust. Most payments are made by check. New deposits and withdrawals of coin at each bank roughly balance each day, and the amount of checks the other banks collect on each bank roughly balances the amount that that bank collects from them. Although each bank's holdings of silver fluctuate, they do so by only small amounts.

---

[1]For simplicity, we ignore equity in our discussion. As long as the bank remains a warehouse bank, there is in fact no need for equity to protect the depositors.

[2]See Chapter 4 for a discussion of check clearing.

[3]The consolidated balance sheet shows only the claims of the banking system on others and of others on it, not the claims of one bank on another. We obtain the consolidated balance sheet by summing the assets and summing the liabilities of all the banks and then subtracting from these totals the claims of one bank against another. For example, among the assets of Coconut Grove, there is a $10,000 deposit at Palm Tree Bank; this deposit also appears as a liability on Palm Tree's balance sheet. In preparing the consolidated balance sheet, we need to subtract this $10,000 deposit from total assets and from total liabilities.

Observing this pattern, the Bank of Coconut Grove is the first to decide to switch to fractional reserve banking. It decides to back some of its deposits with loans rather than with silver. That way it can offer depositors a better return, both in interest and in services. It can also, of course, increase its own profits.

How much can Coconut Grove safely lend? To answer this, let us see what happens when the bank makes a loan of $1,000 to Surf Enterprises. As we saw in Chapter 5, the loan is made, not by paying out silver, but rather by crediting the deposit of Surf Enterprises for the amount of the loan. The bank's balance sheet becomes:

BANK OF COCONUT GROVE

Reserves	$100,000	Checking deposits	
Loans	1,000	Old	$100,000
		New: Surf	1,000

Surf Enterprises can then spend the money it has borrowed by writing a check on its deposit.

Surf Enterprises writes the check to Seashell Inc. Since Coconut Grove is a small bank, it is unlikely that the recipient of the check will have a deposit with the same bank. Indeed, Seashell Inc. has a deposit at another bank, Turtle Cove Trust. So the check is presented for payment through the clearing system, and Coconut Grove loses silver from its clearing deposit. The effect on its balance sheet is:

BANK OF COCONUT GROVE

Reserves	$99,000	Checking deposits	$100,000
Loans	1,000		

Since every dollar of lending will lose Coconut Grove a dollar of silver, the bank must decide how much silver it can afford to lose. Another way of saying this is that the bank must decide how much silver it needs to retain as reserves against its deposits. Suppose that Coconut Grove decides that it needs a reserve ratio of 20%: that is, it needs to hold 20¢ of silver reserves for every $1 of deposits. It believes that if it does so, there will be little chance of any liquidity problems. Since Coconut Grove has $100,000 in deposits, if it wishes to maintain a 20% reserve ratio, it will have to retain $20,000 of silver. That means that it can afford to lose $80,000 of its original holding of $100,000 in silver. That is the amount of loans that it can make.

So Coconut Grove makes a total of $80,000 of loans (including its $1,000 loan to Surf Enterprises). This creates $80,000 of new deposits:

BANK OF COCONUT GROVE

Reserves	$100,000	Checking deposits	
Loans	80,000	Old	$100,000
		New	80,000

As checks are written on these new deposits to people at other banks, Coconut Grove loses the new deposits and an equal amount of reserves until its balance sheet becomes:

BANK OF COCONUT GROVE

Reserves	$20,000	Checking deposits	$100,000
Loans	80,000		

This leaves Coconut Grove with its desired reserve ratio of 20%.

🌴 **CHECK STATION 1** | **If Bank of Coconut Grove wants a reserve ratio of 10%, how much can it lend? What will be the immediate increase in its deposits? What will be the amount of its deposits once the loans are spent? What will be the amount of its reserves?**

Let us now look at Coconut Grove's lending from the point of view of the banking system as a whole. When the loans are first made, the effect on the consolidated balance sheet of the banking system is:

BANKING SYSTEM

Reserves	$10,000,000	Checking deposits	
		Old	$10,000,000
Loans	80,000	New (at Coconut	80,000
		Grove)	

That is, Coconut Grove's lending increases the *total* amount of deposits in the economy: The total amount of bank money on the Island increases by $80,000.

As checks are written on the newly created deposits, Coconut Grove loses deposits and reserves, *but these deposits and these reserves are not lost to the banking system as a whole.* To see why, let us look at what happens to the loan that Coconut Grove made to Surf Enterprises. Remember that Surf wrote a check on its new deposit to Seashell Inc., which had a deposit at another bank, Turtle Cove Trust. When the check clears, the effect on the two banks is:

BANK OF COCONUT GROVE

Reserves	−$1,000	Checking deposits Surf	−$1,000

TURTLE COVE TRUST

Reserves	+$1,000	Checking deposits Seashell	+$1,000

In terms of the banking system as a whole, there is no loss of deposits here and no loss of reserves. All that happens is that the deposits and the reserves move from one bank to another.

If Coconut Grove lends a total of $80,000, the total amount of deposits in the economy will be increased by $80,000 and will *remain* increased by this amount, even after the deposits are lost to Coconut Grove itself. The deposits, and the reserves, will just move to other banks. So the ultimate effect of Coconut Grove's lending on the banking system is:

BANKING SYSTEM

Reserves	$10,000,000	Checking deposits Old	$10,000,000
Loans	80,000	New (at other banks)	80,000

Now suppose that Coconut Grove is not alone in converting to fractional-reserve banking: *All* the banks do it. Let us suppose that they all desire a reserve ratio of 20%. How much can they all lend? By how much will the total amount of deposits increase? We can answer these questions by relying on two important lessons from our experiment with Coconut Grove:

1. After a bank switches to fractional-reserve banking with a 20% reserve ratio, its reserves of silver will equal 20% of its deposits.

2. Although the individual bank loses reserves as it expands its lending, those reserves simply move to other banks. The banking system does not lose any reserves.

From the first lesson we can deduce that when all the banks have switched to fractional-reserve banking with a 20% reserve ratio, the total reserves of silver of the banking system will equal 20% of its total deposits. From the second lesson we can deduce that the total reserves of the banking system will be the same after the switch to fractional-reserve banking as they were before. That is, they will remain at $10,000,000. Combining these two deductions, $10,000,000 must be 20% of the total amount of deposits:

$$\$10,000,000 = 0.20 \times \text{total deposits}. \tag{19.1}$$

So the amount of total deposits must be $50,000,000. The balance sheet of the banking system will therefore be:

BANKING SYSTEM

Reserves	$10,000,000	Checking deposits	
		Old	$10,000,000
Loans	40,000,000	New (at all banks)	40,000,000

Each bank will have a reserve ratio of 20%.[4]

🌴 **CHECK STATION 2** | **What would be the balance sheet of the banking system if banks wanted a reserve ratio of 10%?**

It should be clear, then, that the total amount of deposits in a fractional-reserve banking system will depend on two things—the total amount of reserves and the reserve ratio. We can summarize the relationship in the following equation:

$$R = r \times D, \tag{19.2}$$

where

R = total reserves of the banking system,
r = the reserve ratio,
D = total deposits of the banking system.

We can restate this relationship in a more useful way by rearranging Equation 19.2 as follows:

$$D = \frac{1}{r} \times R. \tag{19.3}$$

simple deposit multiplier
Factor by which total reserves are multiplied to arrive at total deposits.

The factor $1/r$ is called the **simple deposit multiplier.** We can restate this in words:

$$\text{total deposits} = \text{simple deposit multiplier} \times \text{total reserves}. \tag{19.4}$$

In our case, when r = 20%, the simple deposit multiplier is 5. That is, total deposits are 5 times total reserves.

---

[4]Clearly, this substantial increase in lending and in the quantity of money will have a major impact on the economy. We shall look at the nature of this impact in Part Six.

A. What would be the simple deposit multiplier if banks desired a reserve ratio of 10%?

B. A neighboring island has reserves of $15 million and a desired reserve ratio of 30%. What is the amount of deposits in its banking system?

🌴 **CHECK STATION 3**

THE EFFECT OF A CHANGE IN RESERVES

What happens when *additional* reserves of silver are added to the banking system? Suppose, for example, that Surf Enterprises receives payment of $2,000 for goods sold to another island. Payment is made in silver coin, which Surf now deposits with its bank, Bank of Coconut Grove. The effect on the bank's balance sheet is:

BANK OF COCONUT GROVE

Reserves	+$2,000	Checking deposits	+$2,000

The increase in reserves and the increase in deposits represent increases not just for Coconut Grove, but also for the banking system as a whole. The total amount of reserves in the banking system has increased from $10,000,000 to $10,002,000.

With additional reserves, Coconut Grove can make more loans. As it does so, and as checks are written on the deposits it has created, it will lose some of the additional reserves to other banks. These other banks will in turn increase their own lending.[5] How much will the amount of deposits have increased by the time the process is complete? We can use Equation 19.4 to answer this question. With the new reserves,

$$\text{total deposits} = 5 \times \$10,002,000 = \$50,010,000. \qquad [19.5]$$

That is, comparing this to Equation 19.4, we see that deposits increase by 5 times the increase in reserves.

Generalizing this result, we have this equation:

$$\text{change in total deposits} = \text{simple deposit multiplier} \qquad [19.6]$$
$$\times \text{ change in total reserves,}$$

or, in symbols,

$$\Delta D = \frac{1}{r} \times \Delta R, \qquad [19.7]$$

---

[5]The process is traced through in Appendix A to this chapter.

where the Greek letter Δ (delta) before a variable denotes a change in that variable.[6]

🌴 **CHECK STATION 4** | **Surf Enterprises pays $5,000 to foreign suppliers of raw materials, so that the banking system loses $5,000 in reserves. What is the effect on the amount of deposits? On the amount of loans outstanding?**

19.2 A CURRENCY DRAIN

We have assumed that the substantial increase in the amount of bank deposits has no effect on the amount of hand-to-hand currency (silver coins) that people use. In fact, people are likely to want to carry more cash as the amount of their deposits increases. They will therefore withdraw cash from their bank deposits, causing bank reserves to fall. This loss of reserves, or **currency drain,** reduces the ability of the banking system to expand its deposits.

currency drain
Loss of reserves caused by depositors withdrawing cash.

Let us look in more detail at how a currency drain works. To keep things simple, we shall assume that people maintain a roughly fixed proportion between the amount of checking deposits they hold and their holdings of cash. That is, we shall assume that the currency held by the public, C, is a fixed proportion, c, of deposits:

$$C = c \times D. \qquad [19.8]$$

currency/checking-deposit ratio
Ratio of publicly held currency to checking deposits.

If, for example, $c = 0.1$, then for every $1 of checking deposit they hold, people will hold on average 10¢ of cash. The coefficient c is called the **currency/checking-deposit ratio.**[7]

Initially, before banks went over to fractional-reserve banking, when there was only $10,000,000 in deposits, people on the Island therefore held

$$C = 0.1 \times \$10,000,000 = \$1,000,000 \qquad [19.9]$$

in silver coin. So the total amount of silver on the Island was $11,000,000—the $1,000,000 that circulated as currency plus the $10,000,000 in bank vaults. Or, if B is the total amount of silver, then

$$B = C + R = \$1,000,000 + \$10,000,000 = \$11,000,000. \qquad [19.10]$$

When the banking system makes the transition to fractional-reserve banking, the amount of deposits, the amount of currency, and the amount of reserves

---

[6]Appendix B to this chapter shows how an equation like Equation 19.3, which relates total amounts, may be transformed directly into an equation like Equation 19.7, which relates *changes* in those amounts.

[7]In reality, this ratio will not be a fixed number, but will depend on the relative returns on cash and deposits and on the relative convenience of using each as a means of payment. We will look at these factors more closely in Chapter 21.

all change. However, Equations 19.2, 19.8, and 19.10 that relate these three quantities to one another still hold. We can therefore use these equations to solve for the final amounts of deposits, currency, and reserves in the economy after the transition.

First, use Equations 19.8 and 19.2 to substitute for C and R, respectively, in Equation 19.10:

$$B = (c \times D) + (r \times D) = (c + r) \times D. \qquad [19.11]$$

Now rearrange this to yield

$$D = \frac{1}{c + r} \times B. \qquad [19.12]$$

Using our actual numbers for c, r, and B, the total amount of deposits after the transition to fractional-reserve banking will be

$$D = \frac{1}{0.1 + 0.2} \times \$11,000,000 = \$36,666,667. \qquad [19.13]$$

This number is less than the $50,000,000 we obtained before, because now as deposits expand people withdraw more currency from their banks. This currency drain reduces the amount of reserves in the banking system, putting a brake on deposit expansion.

CHECK STATION 5

A. What is the amount of currency held by the public? What is the amount of reserves? Do these add up to the total amount of silver?

B. If the desired reserve ratio were 10% and the currency/checking-deposit ratio were 5%, what would be the total amount of checking deposits?

19.3 THE INTRODUCTION OF TIME DEPOSITS

Another factor that can complicate the relationship between the quantity of silver and the amount of checking deposits is the existence of time deposits. The existence of time deposits will affect the amount of checking deposits the banking system can support, because some reserves that would otherwise have been available to support checking deposits will now be "set aside" to support time deposits.

To see why, suppose that banks on the island decide to introduce time deposits and that they decide to hold 5% reserves against them. Call this desired reserve ratio r_T, so that

$$R_T = r_T \times T, \qquad [19.14]$$

where R_T is the total amount of reserves held against time deposits and T is the total amount of time deposits.

Now suppose that when people get used to the new time deposits, they find that they generally have \$2 in time deposits for every \$1 in their checking deposits.[8] That is,

$$T = t \times D, \qquad\qquad [19.15]$$

time-deposit/checking-deposit ratio
Ratio of time deposits to checking deposits.

where t is called the **time-deposit/checking-deposit ratio.** In our case, t is 2.

So now we have reserves against time deposits, R_T, as well as reserves against checking deposits, which we shall now denote R_D. We must therefore replace Equation 19.10 with

$$B = C + R_D + R_T. \qquad\qquad [19.16]$$

Using Equation 19.14 to substitute for R_T in Equation 19.16, we replace Equation 19.11 with

$$B = (c \times D) + (r \times D) + (r_T \times T). \qquad\qquad [19.17]$$

Using Equation 19.15 to substitute for T in Equation 19.17, we obtain

$$B = (c \times D) + (r \times D) + (r_T \times t \times D) = [c + r + (r_T \times t)] \times D. \qquad [19.18]$$

Rearranging this, we now replace Equation 19.12 with

$$D = \frac{1}{c + r + (r_T \times t)} \times B. \qquad\qquad [19.19]$$

The greater the amount of silver coin, the greater the amount of checking deposits. The greater the ratios c, r, r_T, and t, the smaller the amount of checking deposits.

Using the actual numbers, the total amount of checking deposits after time deposits have been introduced falls from \$36,666,667 to

$$D = \frac{1}{0.1 + 0.2 + 0.05 \times 2} \times \$11,000,000 = \$27,500,000. \qquad [19.20]$$

The amount of checking deposits is lower because now that some of the reserves of the banking system have to be held against the new time deposits, there are less reserves available to support checking deposits.

🌴 **CHECK STATION 6** | **A. What is the amount of time deposits?**

---

[8]This fixed ratio is not realistic. We assume it here just to keep the algebra simple. In reality, the ratio will depend on the relative attractiveness of the two types of deposit. We shall have more to say about this in Chapter 21.

B. What is the amount of currency in the hands of the public, the amount of reserves held against checking deposits, and the amount of reserves held against time deposits? Do these three add up to the total amount of silver?

19.4 WHAT HAPPENS TO BANK LENDING WHEN A CHECK IS DEPOSITED?

We saw earlier how an increase in reserves sets in motion new bank lending that increases the total amount of deposits in the banking system. What happens when you deposit a check at your bank? Does that lead to an increase in bank lending and to a multiple expansion of deposits? The answer depends on whether you deposit the check in your checking deposit or in your time deposit. Let us illustrate this with two examples.

A CHECK IS DEPOSITED IN A CHECKING DEPOSIT

Suppose that Bill deposits a check from Pamela in his checking deposit at his bank, Bank of Coconut Grove. Pamela's check is drawn on her account at a different bank, Turtle Cove Trust. The effect on Coconut Grove's balance sheet is:

BANK OF COCONUT GROVE

Reserves	+$1,000	Checking deposits Bill	+$1,000

Coconut Grove now has $800 of reserves more than it needs, and it can expand its lending by that amount.

However, the gain of Coconut Grove is the loss of Turtle Cove Trust. When the check clears, the effect on the balance sheet of Turtle Cove Trust is:

TURTLE COVE TRUST

Reserves	−$1,000	Checking deposits Pamela	−$1,000

Because Turtle Cove Trust has lost $1,000 in deposits, it needs $200 less in reserves. However, it has lost a full $1,000. That means that it has $800 *less* in reserves than it needs. To bring its reserves back up to the desired level, Turtle Cove Trust will have to *reduce* its lending by $800. For example, when an $800 loan is repaid, the bank will not renew it.

We can look at what has happened from the perspective of the banking system as a whole. When Bill deposits his check from Pamela, the effect on the banking system is:

BANKING SYSTEM

Reserves	Unchanged	Checking deposits	
Loans	Unchanged	Pamela	−$1,000
		Bill	+$1,000

That is, there is no change in the amount of reserves of the banking system as a whole. Reserves merely move from one bank to another. As a result, there is no change in the total amount of bank loans outstanding. When one bank expands its lending, another must contract it.

A CHECK IS DEPOSITED IN A TIME DEPOSIT

The story is somewhat different if Bill deposits his check to his time deposit rather than to his checking deposit. Turtle Cove Trust will still find itself short $800 in reserves after the check clears. However, Coconut Grove will have more than an extra $800. The reason is that banks hold smaller reserves against time deposits than they do against checking deposits. For simplicity, suppose Coconut Grove holds zero reserves against time deposits: It will then have $1,000 more in reserves than it needs, and it will be able to expand its lending by that amount. For the banking system as a whole, it is as though it had an extra $200 in reserves—the $1,000 extra of Coconut Grove less the $800 deficit of Turtle Cove Trust. There will therefore be a net expansion of deposits.

From the point of view of the banking system, the effect of Bill's depositing Pamela's check is:

BANKING SYSTEM

Total reserves	Unchanged	Checking deposits	
Needed	−$200	Pamela	−$1,000
Left over	+$200	Time deposits	
Loans	Unchanged	Bill	+$1,000

The left-over reserves enable the banking system to expand its lending, and as it does so, the amount of checking deposits will increase. Eventually, enough new deposits will be created to need all of the spare $200. Since the reserve ratio is 20%, that means that $1,000 in new deposits will be created.

When the process is complete, the total effect on the banking system will be:

BANKING SYSTEM

Total reserves	Unchanged	Checking deposits	
		Pamela	−$1,000
		New deposits	+$1,000
		Time deposits	
Loans	+$1,000	Bill	+$1,000

That is, the $1,000 of new checking deposits created will just offset the $1,000 removed when Pamela's check cleared: The total amount of checking deposits will be unchanged from its original amount.[9] Total lending by the banking system will increase by $1,000.

To summarize: Depositing a check in your checking deposit does not allow the banking system to expand its lending. Depositing a check in your time deposit does allow the banking system to expand its lending, because it frees up reserves.

19.5 THE MONEY MULTIPLIER AND THE MONETARY BASE

Having derived, in the form of Equation 19.19, the relationship between the quantity of silver coin and the amount of checking deposits, we are now ready to develop the relationship between the quantity of silver coin and the *total* quantity of money. We shall define the total quantity of money, M, as the amount of checking deposits, D, plus the amount of silver currency in circulation, C. That is,

$$M = D + C. \qquad [19.21]$$

We define money here to be means of payment in the hands of the public. Notice that not all silver coin is included in M. The amount held in bank vaults as reserves is excluded, because the public cannot use it to make payments: Only the silver the public itself holds, C, is available for that purpose. Notice too that M does not include time deposits. Time deposits are not a means of payment: Since checks may not be written on them, time deposits cannot be used directly to make payments.

From Equation 19.21 and the numbers above, the total quantity of money on the Island is

$$M = \$27,500,000 + \$2,750,000 = \$30,250,000. \qquad [19.22]$$

---

[9]The total amount must equal the reserve multiplier, 5, times total reserves.

THE MONEY MULTIPLIER

money multiplier, m
Ratio of the total quantity
of money to the quantity
of monetary base.

The ratio of the total quantity of money to the quantity of silver is called the **money multiplier, m.** That is,

$$m = \frac{M}{B}.$$

[19.23]

For the Island, the money multiplier is

$$m = \frac{\$30,250,000}{\$11,000,000} = 2.75$$

[19.24]

Equation 19.23 can be rewritten as

$$M = m \times B.$$

[19.25]

monetary base
Quantity of definitive
money used to determine
the money multiplier.

In the context of this equation, it is customary to call the quantity of silver the **monetary base.** Thus

$$\text{total quantity of money} = \text{money multiplier} \times \text{monetary base.}$$

[19.26]

Therefore we can think of the total quantity of money as depending on two things—on the size of the monetary base (the amount of silver) and on the size of the money multiplier.

On what does the size of the money multiplier depend? To find out, let us begin by using Equation 19.18 to substitute for C in Equation 19.21 to obtain

$$M = D + (c \times D) = (1 + c) \times D.$$

[19.27]

Then we can use Equation 19.19 to substitute for D in Equation 19.27 to obtain

$$M = \frac{1 + c}{c + r + (r_T \times t)} B.$$

[19.28]

By comparing Equation 19.28 to Equation 19.25, we see that

$$m = \frac{c + 1}{c + r + (r_T \times t)}.$$

[19.29]

That is, the size of the money multiplier depends on the currency/checking-deposit ratio, c, on the checking-deposit reserve ratio, r; on the time-deposit reserve ratio, r_T; and on the time-deposit/checking-deposit ratio, t. *An increase in any of these ratios will reduce the money multiplier.*

Using the actual numbers for the various ratios, the money multiplier for the Island is

$$m = \frac{1 + 0.1}{0.1 + 0.2 + (0.05 \times 2)} = 2.75. \qquad [19.30]$$

That is, on the Island the total quantity of money will be 2.75 times the quantity of silver coin.

CHECK STATION 7

A. If the quantity of silver coin on the Island were $12 million, what would be the total quantity of money?

B. If the desired reserve ratio for checking deposits were 12%, the desired reserve ratio for time deposits were 3%, the currency/checking-deposit ratio were 20%, and the time-deposit/checking-deposit ratio were 3, what would be the value of the money multiplier?

THE M2 MULTIPLIER

The definition of money that we have used includes only means of payment. We shall see later that for some purposes it may be useful to consider broader definitions of money that include other stores of value that are not means of payment. Let us call our current narrow definition **M1,** so that

M1
Narrow definition of money, consisting only of means of payment.

$$M = M1 = C + D. \qquad [19.31]$$

A broader definition—let us call it **M2**—might also include time deposits. That is,

$$M2 = M1 + T. \qquad [19.32]$$

M2
Definition of money that includes both means of payment (M1) and time deposits.

We can define two different money multipliers corresponding to these two different definitions of money:

$$m1 = \frac{M1}{B} \qquad [19.33]$$

and

$$m2 = \frac{M2}{B}. \qquad [19.34]$$

Since M1 is the same as M, $m1$ is the same as m in Equation 19.29. To find $m2$, we can use Equations 19.8 and 19.15 to substitute for C and T in Equation 19.32, to obtain

$$M2 = (c \times D) + D + (t \times D) = (c + 1 + t) \times D. \qquad [19.35]$$

Then we can use Equation 19.19 to substitute for D in Equation 19.35 to obtain

$$M2 = \frac{c + 1 + t}{c + r + (r_T \times t)} \; B. \qquad\qquad [19.36]$$

Therefore

$$m2 = \frac{c + 1 + t}{c + r + (r_T \times t)} \; . \qquad\qquad [19.37]$$

The M2 multiplier depends on the same ratios as the M1 multiplier, and, as can be seen by comparing Equation 19.29 with Equation 19.37, the M2 multiplier must be the larger of the two.

CHECK STATION 8   A.   What is the value of *m2* for the Island?

B.   What would it be if the time-deposit/checking-deposit ratio increased to 3?

THE EFFECTS OF A CHANGE IN THE MONETARY BASE

Suppose that $1,000,000 in new silver comes into the Island's economy (as payment for goods sold to other islands) and is deposited at one of the banks. What will be the effect on the total quantity of money? On checking deposits, time deposits, and bank lending? On bank reserves and currency in circulation?

Equation 19.25, which shows the relationship between total amounts of monetary base and money, can be transformed into an equation that shows the relationship between *changes* in the monetary base and *changes* in the total quantity of money:[10]

$$\Delta M = m \times \Delta B. \qquad\qquad [19.38]$$

The change in the total quantity of money is the money multiplier times the change in the monetary base.

In our case,

$$\Delta M = 2.75 \times \$1,000,000 = \$2,750,000. \qquad\qquad [19.39]$$

In order to find the change in the quantity of checking deposits, rewrite Equation 19.27 in terms of differences. We then obtain

$$\$2,750,000 = (1 + 0.1) \, \Delta D, \qquad\qquad [19.40]$$

[10]This transformation is explained in Appendix B to this chapter.

Variable	Change	Equation Used	
			EXHIBIT 19.1
			CHANGES THAT RESULT FROM A $1,000,000 INCREASE IN THE MONETARY BASE
Demand deposits (ΔD)	+$2,500,000	19.27	
Time deposits (ΔT)	5,000,000	19.15	
Reserves against checking deposits (ΔR_D)	500,000	19.2	
Reserves against time deposits (ΔR_T)	250,000	19.14	
Currency held by public (ΔC)	250,000	19.8	
Quantity of money, M1 ($\Delta D + \Delta C$)	2,750,000	19.21	
Broadly defined money, M2 ($\Delta D + \Delta C + \Delta T$)	7,750,000	19.32	
Monetary base ($\Delta R_D + \Delta R_T + \Delta C$)	1,000,000	19.16	

so that

$$\Delta D = \frac{\$2,7500,000}{1.1} = \$2,500,000. \qquad [19.41]$$

That is, checking deposits increase by $2,500,000.

Changes in all the monetary variables can be calculated in a similar fashion. The results are summarized in Exhibit 19.1.

Calculate the changes corresponding to those shown in Exhibit 19.1 for a $500,000 *decrease* **in the monetary base.**   🌴 **CHECK STATION 9**

We have seen how the quantity of money and its various components are related to the monetary base in the island economy. Very similar relationships hold for the United States: We shall look at them in detail in Chapter 21. Before we do so, in Chapter 20 we shall examine the instruments the Fed has at its disposal to control the amount of monetary base and to affect the size of the money multiplier. These instruments enable the Fed to regulate the quantity of money.

SUMMARY

- Definitive money in our economy consists of coins, Federal Reserve notes, and deposits at the Fed. Ordinary bank money consists of checking deposits at banks. This chapter examines the link between the quantity of definitive money in an economy and the total quantity of money.

- A small bank can expect to lose reserves when it makes a loan. Hence it cannot lend more than the reserves it is ready to lose. However, these reserves simply move to another bank; they are not lost to the banking system as a whole.

- If all banks desire a reserve ratio of r, then the banking system can expand its deposits to $1/r$ times the amount of its reserves. The factor $1/r$ is called the simple deposit multiplier. If reserves change, the change in the amount of deposits will be $1/r$ times the change in reserves.

- If the amount of currency used by the public increases with the amount of checking deposits, then the expansion of deposits will cause a currency drain as deposits are converted into currency.

- If reserves are held against time deposits, then some definitive money will be tied up in this form and will therefore not be available to be used as reserves against checking deposits.

- When a check is deposited to a checking account, the total amount of reserves in the banking system does not change, so no new lending is possible. The increased lending of the bank in which the check is deposited is exactly offset by the decreased lending of the bank on which the check is drawn.

- When a check is deposited to a time deposit, reserves are freed up and additional loans can be made.

- The money multiplier, m, is the ratio of the total amount of money to the monetary base. An increase in the currency/checking-deposit ratio, c, the checking-deposit reserve ratio, r, the time-deposit reserve ratio, r_T, or the time-deposit/checking-deposit ratio, t, will reduce the money multiplier.

- Money multipliers can be defined for narrow money, M1, which includes only means of payment, and for broad money, M2, which also includes time deposits.

- A change in the monetary base will lead to a change in the total quantity of money that is m times as large.

KEY TERMS

simple deposit multiplier	time-deposit/checking-deposit ratio	M1
currency drain		M2
currency/checking-deposit ratio	money multiplier, m	
	monetary base	

DISCUSSION QUESTIONS

1. Surf Enterprises repays its $1,000 loan to the Bank of Coconut Grove.

   a. What is the effect on Coconut Grove's balance sheet if Surf repays the loan with a check drawn on a deposit at another bank?

   b. What is the effect on Coconut Grove's balance sheet if Surf repays the loan with a check drawn on its deposit at Coconut Grove itself?

2. On a neighboring island, the amount of silver coin is $5 million. Banks have a desired reserve ratio against checking deposits of 10% and hold no reserves against time deposits. The currency/checking-deposit ratio is 30%. What is the quantity of money?

3. On the Island, there is a loss of confidence in the banking system and people start to convert their bank deposits into cash. If the currency/checking-deposit ratio increases to 50%, what is the effect on the total quantity of money on the Island? (Monetary base and the other ratios are as in the chapter.)

SOFTWARE EXERCISE FOR THIS CHAPTER

Title: Deposit

This computer exercise illustrates the process by which the banking system creates money. It allows you to explore how changes in the reserve and currency ratios affect the quantity of money via the money multiplier. See your instructor if you wish to use this program.

BIBLIOGRAPHY

Nichols, Dorothy M., *Modern Money Mechanics: A Workbook on Deposits, Currency, and Bank Reserves*, Chicago: Federal Reserve Bank of Chicago, 1975.

APPENDIX A
TO CHAPTER 19

TRACING THE MULTIPLE EXPANSION OF DEPOSITS THROUGH THE BANKING SYSTEM

In examining the multiple expansion of deposits that follows an injection of reserves from outside the banking system, we went directly from a single bank to the banking system as a whole. It may help to trace through the process of multiple expansion as reserves and deposits move from bank to bank. We assume that all of the banks are small, so that they each lose all the new deposits they create once the checks written on those deposits clear.

Let us call the bank where the new reserves first arrive Bank One. The new deposit of $1,000 changes Bank One's balance sheet as follows:

BANK ONE			
Reserves	+$1,000	Deposits	+$1,000

If Bank One wishes to maintain a 20% reserve ratio, it can afford to lose

$$0.8 \times \$1,000 = \$800$$

of reserves. That means that it can make $800 in new loans. The final effect of the $1,000 deposit on its balance sheet will therefore be:

BANK ONE			
Reserves	+$200	Deposits	+$1,000
Loans	+800		

Suppose that the checks that were written on the new deposits created by Bank One's new loans are all paid to depositors at Bank Two. When the checks clear, the effect on Bank Two's balance sheet is:

BANK TWO			
Reserves	+$800	Deposits	+$800

If Bank Two, like Bank One, wishes to maintain a 20% reserve ratio, it can afford to lose

$$0.8 \times \$800 = \$640$$

of reserves. That means that it can make $640 in new loans. The final effect of the $800 deposit on its balance sheet will therefore be:

BANK TWO			
Reserves	+$160	Deposits	+$800
Loans	+640		

The checks written on the $640 of new deposits created by Bank Two are paid to depositors at Bank Three, and so on.

The pattern should be clear. As a result of the injection of $1,000 of new reserves into the banking system, Bank One has $1,000 of new deposits. Bank Two has

$$0.8 \times \$1,000 = \$800$$

of new deposits, Bank Three has

$$0.8 \times \$800 = 0.8 \times 0.8 \times \$1,000 = \$640,$$

Bank Four has

$$0.8 \times \$640 = 0.8 \times 0.8 \times 0.8 \times \$1,000 = \$512,$$

and so on. If r is the reserve ratio, then Bank One has 1 times the amount of new reserves; Bank Two has $(1 - r)$ times the amount of new reserves; Bank Three has $(1 - r)^2$ times the amount of new reserves; Bank Four has $(1 - r)^3$ times the amount of new reserves; and so on.

The total amount of new deposits created is

$$\Delta D = \Delta R + (1 - r)\Delta R + (1 - r)^2 \Delta R + (1 - r)^3 \Delta R + \cdots \qquad [19A.1]$$
$$= [1 + (1 - r) + (1 - r)^2 + (1 - r)^3 + \cdots] \Delta R.$$

The sum of the series in brackets is

$$1 + (1-r) + (1-r)^2 + (1-r)^3 + \cdots = \frac{1}{1-(1-r)} = \frac{1}{r} . \qquad \text{[19A.2]}$$

Hence, substituting $1/r$ for the term in brackets in Equation 19A.1, we have

$$\Delta D = \frac{1}{r} \times \Delta R. \qquad \text{[19A.3]}$$

By comparing this with Equation 19.7, you can see that the result of tracing through the process in this way is precisely the same as the result we obtained by looking directly at the banking system as a whole.

APPENDIX B
TO CHAPTER 19

TRANSFORMING EQUATIONS IN TOTAL AMOUNTS INTO EQUATIONS IN CHANGES IN THOSE AMOUNTS

Many of the equations we developed in this chapter tell us the relationships between the *total amounts* of different things. They have the form

$$X = a \times Y, \qquad\qquad [19B.1]$$

where X and Y are total amounts and a is a constant number. For example, in Equation 19.3, X is the total amount of checking deposits, Y is the total amount of monetary base, and a is the simple deposit multiplier. Suppose that $a = 2$, $Y = 100$, and $X = 200$.

Equations like Equation 19.B.1 can be transformed quite easily to tell us the relationship between *changes* in X and *changes* in Y. Let Y change from 100 to 110. Call the change ΔY, where the Greek letter Δ (delta) signifies "change." In this case $\Delta Y = 10$. The new value of Y is simply the old value plus ΔY, or $(Y + \Delta Y)$.

Call the new value of X, $(X + \Delta X)$. Then Equation 19B.1 holds for the new values of X and Y:

$$(X + \Delta X) = a \times (Y + \Delta Y). \qquad\qquad [19B.2]$$

If we multiply this out, we obtain

$$X + \Delta X = a \times Y + a \times \Delta Y. \qquad\qquad [19B.3]$$

Now subtract X from the left-hand side of Equation 19B.3 and $a \times Y$ from the right-hand side (the two are equal from Equation 19B.1) to obtain

$$\Delta X = a \times \Delta Y. \qquad\qquad [19B.4]$$

535

That is, the change in X is a times the change in Y. If $\Delta Y = 10$, then

$$\Delta X = 2 \times 10 = 20.$$

We can use this transformation to transform any equation like Equation 19B.1 relating total amounts into an equation like Equation 19B.4 relating changes in those amounts.

CHECK STATION 1 | **Use Equation 19.15 to calculate the change in time deposits that would result from a $1 million increase in checking deposits.**

CHAPTER 20

THE FED'S INSTRUMENTS OF CONTROL

The Fed is charged with regulating the quantity of money in our economy. In this chapter we shall study how the Fed is able to do this. The Fed has several instruments of control. Its most important is its ability to change the monetary base by buying and selling securities. Such purchases and sales are called **open market operations.** We shall see that monetary base can also change for other reasons that are not the direct result of the Fed's actions. We shall examine how such changes occur and how the Fed can offset them. We shall also look at some other instruments of control that enable the Fed to influence the money multiplier.

It is useful to think about the Fed's instruments of control in terms of the relationship we developed in Chapter 19 involving the quantity of money, the money multiplier, and the monetary base:

$$\text{quantity of money} = \text{money multiplier} \times \text{monetary base}. \qquad [20.1]$$

The Fed can increase or decrease the quantity of money either by increasing or decreasing the money multiplier or by increasing or decreasing the monetary base.

open market operations
The purchase or sale of government securities by the Federal Reserve.

20.1 DEFINITIVE MONEY, MONETARY BASE, AND RESERVES IN THE U.S. ECONOMY

Before we look at the Fed's instruments of control, we need to be clear about what constitutes definitive money and monetary base in the U.S. economy. On the South Seas island of Chapter 19, definitive money is silver coin. In our own economy, definitive money is Fed liabilities in the form of Federal Reserve notes, bank deposits at the Fed, and coins issued by the Treasury. These play the same

537

EXHIBIT 20.1

FEDERAL RESERVE BANKS: CONSOLIDATED BALANCE SHEET, MAY 1989 (BILLIONS OF DOLLARS)

Gold certificate account	$ 11.1	Federal Reserve notes			$229.4
SDR certificate account	8.5	Deposits			39.8
Coin	0.4	Banks		33.6	
Discount loans	2.0	U.S. Treasury–			
		General Account		5.3	
Securities		Foreign central banks		0.4	
Acceptances	0	Other		0.5	
U.S. government	230.2				
Items in process of collection	10.4	Deferred credit items			8.4
Foreign-currency assets	13.7	Other liabilities			3.2
Other assets	8.8	Equity			4.3

Source: *Federal Reserve Bulletin.*

role in our economy as silver does on the Island. On the Island, the monetary base includes *all* definitive money. In our own economy, some definitive money is *not* included in the monetary base. To understand why, we need to look at some balance sheets.

Exhibit 20.1 shows the balance sheet of the Fed: This is the consolidated balance sheet of the 12 Federal Reserve Banks. Exhibit 20.2 shows a partial balance sheet of the U.S. Treasury.[1] Definitive money in our economy consists of the $229.4 billion of Federal Reserve notes and the $39.8 billion of deposits at the Fed (shown in Exhibit 20.1) plus the $19 billion of currency issued by the Treasury (shown in Exhibit 20.2).[2] That is,

$$\text{definitive money} = \text{Fed notes} + \text{Fed deposits} + \text{Treasury currency.} \quad [20.2]$$
$$(\$288.2b) \qquad (\$229.4b) \qquad (\$39.8b) \qquad\qquad (\$19b)$$

Monetary base includes only the definitive money that is held by firms, households, and institutions within the United States. It does not include the definitive money that is held by the federal government and by foreigners. To calculate the amount of monetary base, therefore, we need to make the following adjustments:

• From Federal Reserve notes we need to subtract the $0.5 billion cash holdings of the Treasury, leaving $228.9 billion. We would also like to subtract the amount of Federal Reserve notes held outside the United States.

---

[1]This "balance" sheet is incomplete, and it therefore does not balance. It includes only the items that are of interest to us in this chapter.

[2]Almost all of this is coins. Although the Treasury no longer issues notes, some notes issued by the Treasury in the past are still outstanding.

EXHIBIT 20.2

U.S. TREASURY:
PARTIAL BALANCE
SHEET, MAY 1989
(BILLIONS OF
DOLLARS)

Gold	$11.1	Gold certificates	$ 11.1
SDRs	8.5	SDR certificates	8.5
Cash holdings	0.5	Treasury currency	19.0
Deposit at Fed	5.3	Marketable debt[a]	1,871.7
Deposits and tax and loan accounts at commercial banks	34.3		

[a]First quarter 1989.

Source: *Federal Reserve Bulletin.*

The Fed estimates that this may be two-thirds or more of the total. Unfortunately, we have no idea what the exact amount is.[3]

- From Fed deposits we need to subtract the $5.3 billion of deposits held by the U.S. Treasury, the $0.4 billion held by foreign central banks, and the $0.5 billion in other deposits (mainly deposits of U.S. agencies and international organizations such as the International Monetary Fund). This leaves only the $33.6 billion held by banks.[4]

- From currency issued by the Treasury we need to subtract the $0.4 billion in coin held by the Fed, leaving $18.6 billion.

Thus total subtractions of definitive money held by the federal government, by foreign central banks, and by international organizations add up to

$$\$0.5b + \$5.3b + \$0.4b + \$0.5b + \$0.4b = \$7.1b,$$

and

$$\text{monetary base} = \text{total definitive money} - \text{total subtractions.} \quad [20.3]$$
$$(\$281.1b) \qquad\qquad (\$288.2b) \qquad\qquad (\$7.1b)$$

Monetary base may be divided into two components—Fed deposits and currency outstanding. The former is the Fed deposits of banks—$33.6 billion; the latter is the sum of Federal Reserve notes and Treasury currency that is not held by the government—$228.9 billion plus $18.6 billion, for a total of $247.5 billion. That is,

$$\text{monetary base} = \text{bank deposits at Fed} + \text{currency outstanding.} \quad [20.4]$$
$$(\$281.1b) \qquad\qquad (\$33.6b) \qquad\qquad (\$247.5b)$$

[3]We shall have more to say about this problem in Chapter 32.

[4]*Banks* here includes other depository institutions—thrifts and credit unions—that offer transactions accounts. For simplicity of language, we shall generally use *bank* for *depository institution.*

Monetary base may be divided up in another way—into reserves of banks and currency in the hands of the public. The reserves of banks consist of their deposits at the Fed, $33.6 billion, plus the currency they hold in their vaults, $27.2 billion.[5] That is,

$$\text{reserves} = \text{bank deposits at Fed} + \text{vault cash.} \qquad [20.5]$$
$$(\$60.8b) \qquad\qquad (\$33.6b) \qquad\qquad (\$27.2b)$$

Currency in the hands of the public is just currency outstanding less vault cash:

$$\text{currency in the hands of the public} = \text{currency outstanding} - \text{vault cash.} \quad [20.6]$$
$$(\$220.3b) \qquad\qquad\qquad (\$247.5b) \qquad\qquad (\$27.2b)$$

Hence

$$\text{monetary base} = \text{reserves} + \text{currency in the hands of the public.} \quad [20.7]$$
$$(\$281.1b) \qquad (\$60.8b) \qquad\qquad (\$220.3b)$$

20.2 | HOW THE FED CHANGES MONETARY BASE THROUGH OPEN MARKET OPERATIONS

How does the Fed increase or decrease the amount of definitive money? Any loan or purchase by the Fed increases its liabilities; any repayment of a loan or sale by the Fed decreases its liabilities. Since its liabilities are definitive money, any such transaction changes the amount of definitive money.

For example, suppose the Fed buys $1 million in Treasury securities from Citibank. The Fed pays for the securities by crediting Citibank's deposit at the Fed for $1 million. The effect on the Fed's balance sheet is:

THE FED

U.S. securities	+$1m	Deposits Citibank	+$1m

The crediting of $1 million to Citibank's deposit represents a net increase in the total amount of Fed deposits. That is, the Fed pays for the securities with $1 million in new definitive money that it creates for the purpose.

In the above example, the increase in definitive money is also an increase in monetary base: The newly created definitive money goes to a private economic agent within the U.S. economy. The increase in monetary base is also an increase in reserves: The recipient of the new definitive money is a bank.

However, an increase in definitive money need not increase monetary base or reserves. Consider another example—the purchase by the Fed of $2 million in

---

[5]This number does not appear in Exhibits 20.1 or 20.2.

foreign exchange from a foreign central bank. In this case the change in the Fed's balance sheet is:

THE FED

| Foreign currency assets | +$2m | Deposits | |
| | | Foreign central bank | +$2m |

Since deposits at the Fed held by foreign central banks do not count as monetary base, this transaction adds to definitive money but does not add to monetary base. Since deposits at the Fed held by foreign central banks are not bank reserves, there is no increase in reserves.

These two examples illustrate some important principles:

- Whenever the Fed buys or sells anything, it changes the amount of definitive money.

- If the purchase or sale involves a U.S. resident other than the federal government, it changes the amount of monetary base.

- If the purchase or sale involves a U.S. bank, it changes the amount of reserves.

In practice, whenever the Fed deliberately wishes to change monetary base or reserves, it buys or sells one particular asset—U.S. government securities. Such a purchase or sale is called an *open market operation*. In May 1989 the Fed held some $230 billion in U.S. securities that it had acquired in this way (see Exhibit 20.1).

Why does the Fed choose to trade in U.S. government securities? First, it prefers to buy an earning asset: We shall see later that the Fed earns a considerable income from its holdings of government securities. Second, it is desirable to trade in a large market. In a large market, competition among market makers will keep transactions costs low. Also, purchases and sales by the Fed in a large market will have a smaller impact on price than they will in a small market. As we saw in Chapter 7, the market for government securities is large indeed.

Open market operations are executed by the System Account Manager at the Federal Reserve Bank of New York under direction of the chief policy-making body of the Fed, the Federal Open Market Committee, or FOMC. We shall have more to say about the FOMC when we discuss monetary policy in later chapters. Here we assume that a monetary policy is already in place, and we examine how it is actually executed.

If the System Account Manager wishes to purchase, say, $1 billion in 90-day T-bills, he asks each primary dealer to tender an offer of price and quantity. He then accepts offers, beginning with the lowest price, until he has the $1 billion he needs.[6]

---

[6]See Chapter 7 for a general description of the government securities market and for an explanation of such terms as *primary dealer.*

To see the effect of the open market purchase, suppose that XYZ Securities makes one of the successful tenders, and that the Fed buys $200 million worth of T-bills from XYZ. XYZ's clearing bank is Metropolis National. The Fed pays for the securities by crediting Metropolis's account at the Fed for $200 million, and in return Metropolis transfers ownership of the T-bills from XYZ's securities account to the Fed (all this is done by Fedwire). The effects on the balance sheets of the Fed and of Metropolis are:

THE FED

U.S. securities	+$200m	Deposits Metropolis	+$200m

METROPOLIS

Deposit at Fed	+$200m	Deposits XYZ Securities	+$200m

The effect of the open market purchase, therefore, is to increase the reserves of some clearing bank (or banks) by the amount of the purchase. These additional reserves represent an increase, not only for the clearing bank involved, but also for the banking system as a whole. The extra reserves do not come from any other bank: They are freshly created by the Fed. The increase in reserves is also, of course, an increase in the amount of monetary base and of definitive money.

The Fed has another way to change the amount of its liabilities through securities transactions. The Fed acts as an agent for many foreign central banks and several international agencies, holding their U.S. securities for them and executing purchases and sales as requested (in May 1989 the Fed held a total of $235 billion of such securities).

Suppose, for example, that the Bank of Japan (the Japanese central bank) notifies the Fed that it wishes to sell $1 billion in T-bills. Normally the Fed will ask primary dealers for bids. However, if it just happens that the Fed itself wishes to buy T-bills in this amount, it will carry out the transaction "in-house" by buying the T-bills that the Bank of Japan wishes to sell. The immediate effect on the Fed's balance sheet is:

THE FED

U.S. securities	+$1b	Deposits Bank of Japan	+$1b

Since the Bank of Japan is *not* a U.S. resident or bank, there is no immediate effect on monetary base or on reserves. However, the Bank of Japan does not normally leave money in its account at the Fed, because that account bears no interest. Indeed, that is why it holds U.S. securities in the first place. If it sold the securities, it was because it wanted to buy something else. Suppose the Bank of Japan uses the money to buy yen on the spot foreign-exchange market from Metropolis National in New York. When it pays for the yen, it does so by transferring the $1 billion in its account at the Fed to Metropolis:

THE FED

	Deposits	
	Bank of Japan	–$1b
	Metropolis	+$1b

At this point the reserves of U.S. banks, and monetary base, do increase by $1 billion. Therefore, as long as the Bank of Japan spends the money, the *ultimate* effect of the Fed's buying securities from the Bank of Japan is the same as if it had bought them from a primary dealer.

Sometimes the Fed will want to increase bank reserves only temporarily (we shall see why in a moment). In such cases, it often makes sense for the Fed to do a reverse repurchase agreement with primary dealers rather than an outright purchase.[7] The temporary effect on reserves, for the duration of the repo, will be identical to that of an outright purchase.

What is the effect on bank reserves of an open market sale of securities to XYZ Securities?   🌴 **CHECK STATION 1**

20.3 | OTHER FACTORS THAT AFFECT MONETARY BASE

Although open market operations provide the Fed with a way of *deliberately* changing the monetary base, the base will also change for reasons that are not the direct result of any decision by the Fed. Let us look at the various ways that this can happen.

DISCOUNT LOANS

We saw in Chapter 16 that, as lender of last resort, the Fed stands ready to lend definitive money through the discount window to banks in trouble or to banks short of reserves. As Exhibit 20.1 shows, the Fed had about $2.0 billion of such loans outstanding in May 1989.

Since discount lending is done at the initiative of the borrowing bank, the Fed has little direct control over its amount. Of course, changes in the rate the Fed charges for such loans and in the terms on which they are made will affect the

---

[7]See Chapter 7 for an explanation of repurchase agreements.

quantity demanded. However, for reasons we shall discuss below, the discount rate is changed infrequently, and it therefore has little effect on day-to-day variations in bank borrowing.

To see the effect of a discount loan on the Fed's balance sheet, suppose that Metropolis borrows $100 million:

	THE FED		
Discount loans	+$100m	Deposits	
		Metropolis	+$100m

As you can see, a discount loan will immediately increase the amount of bank reserves by the amount of the loan.

FOREIGN EXCHANGE TRANSACTIONS

For reasons we shall look into in Chapter 25, the Fed periodically buys and sells foreign exchange. Once it acquires foreign exchange, the Fed usually uses it to buy securities denominated in that currency rather than holding it as cash. As Exhibit 20.1 shows, the Fed was holding some $13.7 billion in foreign currency assets in May 1989.

To see the effects of such a purchase of foreign currency, suppose the Fed buys $100 million worth of deutsche marks from Metropolis. The effect on the Fed's balance sheet is:

	THE FED		
Foreign currency assets	+$100m	Deposits	
		Metropolis	+$100m

The effect on Metropolis's balance sheet is:

	METROPOLIS	
Deposit at Fed	+$100m	
Foreign currency assets	−$100m	

The effect on monetary base and on reserves, then, is much like that of an open market operation. Indeed, the central banks of some countries use trading in the foreign exchange market as a way of deliberately changing monetary base. The Fed, however, does not do so.

FEDERAL RESERVE FLOAT

The process of clearing checks through the Fed affects the total amount of bank reserves. To see why, consider an example: Megacorp receives a check for $1 million from Syntec in Silicon Valley, drawn on Syntec's bank, First Pacific of San Francisco. Megacorp deposits the check with its own bank, Metropolis National, in New York. Metropolis passes the check on to the New York Fed, which sends it by air to the San Francisco Fed, which passes it on to First Pacific. If First Pacific does not inform the San Francisco Fed that the check is bad, First Pacific's account at the Fed will be debited for $1 million. If the Fed were simply to credit Metropolis at the same time it debited First Pacific, things would be simple. However, that is not the way it works.

When the Federal Reserve System was created, one of the inducements to join was rapid credit for checks cleared. The Fed promised to credit the payee bank within two business days, no matter how long it actually took to present the check to the payor bank. In our example, although it might take four or five days to get the check to First Pacific, Metropolis would be credited after two days. How does this affect the Fed's balance sheet?

When the New York Fed receives the check, the effect on its balance sheet is:

THE FED

Items in process of collection		Deferred credit items	
First Pacific	+$1m	Metropolis	+$1m

The entry on the liability side is a conditional liability to Metropolis: If the check does not bounce, the Fed will credit Metropolis with $1 million. Metropolis may not draw on this amount yet, and it is not counted as part of its reserves. This liability is matched by an asset—the amount that the Fed expects to collect from First Pacific when the check clears.

Two days later, the Fed credits Metropolis's account, even though the check has not yet cleared:

THE FED

	Deposits	
	Metropolis	+$1m
	Deferred credit items	
	Metropolis	−$1m

At this point, because Metropolis has gained $1 million in reserves and First Pacific has as yet lost none, the total reserves of the banking system have increased by $1 million.

Several days later, when the check has been presented to First Pacific and First Pacific has been given time to examine the check, its account is debited:

THE FED

Items in process of collection		Deposits	
First Pacific	–$1m	First Pacific	–$1m

The total amount of reserves of the banking system now returns to what it was before.

Because checks are constantly flowing through the clearing system, the amount of items in process of collection is always greater than the amount of deferred credit items. The difference is called **Fed float**; that is,

Fed float
The difference in amount between items in process of collection and deferred credit items.

$$\text{Fed float} = \text{items in process of collection} - \text{deferred credit items.} \quad [20.8]$$

As Exhibit 20.1 shows, items in process of collection amounted to $10.4 billion in May 1989 and deferred credit items amounted to $8.4 billion. Fed float was therefore $2.0 billion.

Fed float is a source of additional reserves to the banking system. It fluctuates day by day, and the Fed has no direct control over its amount. We shall see in Chapter 32 that the size of Fed float became a problem in the early 1980s when banks tried to use it as a source of cheap credit.

TREASURY PAYMENTS AND RECEIPTS

When the U.S. government makes a payment—a Social Security check, the paycheck of an FBI agent, or payment for an F16 jet fighter—it does so by writing a check on its account at the Fed. The U.S. Treasury uses the Fed as its regular bank. Its deposit at the Fed is called the **General Account**. In May 1989 the General Account amounted to $5.3 billion (see Exhibit 20.1).

General Account
U.S. government's checking deposit at the Federal Reserve Banks.

To see the effect of a payment out of the General Account, suppose that Lou Davis receives a Social Security check for $800 and deposits it at his bank, Metropolis National. Metropolis passes the check on to the Fed. The Fed credits Metropolis and debits the Treasury:

THE FED

		Deposits	
		Metropolis	+$800
		U.S. Treasury	–$800

As a result of Lou's cashing his Social Security check, the reserves of Metropolis, *and of the banking system as a whole*, increase by $800.

In fact, whenever the federal government makes a payment, reserves and monetary base increase, and whenever the federal government receives a payment, reserves and monetary base decrease. The reason is that the General Account is a part of definitive money but is not a part of monetary base.

The volume of payments in and out of the General Account is large. The federal government spends over $1 trillion a year, or an average of $4 billion to $5 billion per business day. Daily receipts and expenditures vary quite a lot, so the balance in the General Account normally fluctuates between $2 billion and $20 billion. Since total deposits of the banking system at the Fed are only about $35 billion, the effects on bank reserves of these fluctuations in the General Account could be significant.

The Treasury tries to balance daily receipts and payments to minimize their impact on bank reserves. Most payments to the Treasury—for example, tax deducted from your paycheck—are paid initially into special accounts that the Treasury keeps at most local banks. These accounts are called **Treasury tax and loan accounts (TT&Ls)**. In May 1989 these accounts totaled $34.3 billion (see Exhibit 20.2). When the Treasury transfers money from the tax and loan accounts to its deposit at the Fed, bank reserves fall by that amount. The Treasury times such transfers to balance, more or less, its payments out of the General Account, so that the net impact on bank reserves is minimized.

Treasury tax and loan accounts (TT&Ls) U.S. government deposits at local banks.

Tax and loan accounts used to be a nice source of zero-interest deposits for the banks. However, since 1978 the Treasury has been less generous. Banks may now keep the funds in a zero-interest account for only a single business day (reserves are required against this account). They must then transfer the funds either to the Fed or to a "note account" at the bank itself, on which the bank must pay the Treasury 0.25% below the weekly average fed funds rate. (No reserves are required on the note account.)[8]

The Fed also acts as the regular banker for foreign central banks and for various international agencies such as the World Bank (see the example above involving the Bank of Japan). Fluctuations in these accounts affect the reserves of the banking system in much the same way as do fluctuations in the General Account, although their magnitude is much smaller.

GOLD AND SDR CERTIFICATE ACCOUNTS

The U.S. government owns a large amount of gold that is held in a very secure vault at Fort Knox. It also owns an amount of **Special Drawing Rights (SDRs)**, which are liabilities of the International Monetary Fund—a sort of international

Special Drawing Rights (SDRs) Liabilities of the International Monetary Fund that serve as international fiat money.

---

[8]This is like the fed funds deal that correspondent banks offer their respondents (see Chapter 10). Banks also receive fees from the Treasury for handling TT&L transactions. Since 1986 the Fed has been developing an on-line computer system on which banks can report their TT&L deposits. The system automatically generates all the reports required by the Treasury and calculates the charges due; it also allows the Fed to know exactly how much is in TT&L accounts at any time.

fiat money. In May 1989 the Treasury held $11.1 billion of gold and $8.5 billion of SDRs (see Exhibit 20.2).

The Treasury can turn gold and SDRs into usable cash by depositing certificates backed by these assets with the Fed. The Fed credits the Treasury's account for the same amount and adds the certificates to its own assets. For example, in the case of gold, the effect on the Fed's balance sheet would be:

THE FED

Gold certificate account	+$10m	Deposits U.S. Treasury	+$10m

The amount of definitive money is immediately increased by $10 million. If and when the Treasury spends the $10 million, there will be an increase in monetary base. The effect of the Treasury depositing SDR certificates would be similar. In May 1989 all of the Treasury's gold and SDRs had been used to generate cash in this way (see Exhibits 20.1 and 20.2). If the Treasury sells gold on the open market, it must redeem from the Fed the certificates backed by that gold.[9]

COIN

The coins we use are minted by the U.S. Treasury. The Treasury sells these coins to the Fed at face value, making a tidy profit.[10] The Fed then issues the coins to banks as needed. The amount sold to the Fed, but not yet issued, appears as an asset on the Fed's balance sheet. In May 1989 it amounted to $0.4 billion (see Exhibit 20.1).

Neither the purchase of the coins from the Treasury nor their purchase from the Fed by banks directly affects the amount of bank reserves. For example, when the Fed purchases $20 million in new coins from the Treasury, the effect on its balance sheet is:

THE FED

Coin	+$20m	Deposits U.S. Treasury	+$20m

---

[9]Gold is valued on the books of the Fed and of the Treasury at an official price that is well below its market value. When the Treasury sells gold, it realizes a substantial capital gain.

[10]This profit is called *seigniorage* (see Chapter 4).

If Metropolis orders $1 million in quarters, the effect on the Fed's balance sheet is:

THE FED			
Coin	–$1m	Deposits	
		Metropolis	–$1m

and the effect on Metropolis's balance sheet is:

METROPOLIS		
Deposit at Fed	–$1m	
Vault cash	+$1m	

Metropolis loses $1 million in reserves in the form of deposits at the Fed, but this is offset by a gain of the same amount in vault cash. Only when the quarters are actually withdrawn by Metropolis's customers will its reserves fall.

20.4 SUMMARY OF FACTORS THAT AFFECT DEFINITIVE MONEY, MONETARY BASE, AND RESERVES

We can summarize all the factors that affect the amount of definitive money in the following equation, which is derived from the Fed's balance sheet in Exhibit 20.1. The amount of definitive money is simply the sum of the Fed's assets—the items on the left-hand side of the balance sheet—less those items on the right-hand side that are not definitive money. Denoting a change in X as $\Delta[X]$, the equation is

$$\Delta[\text{definitive money}] = \Delta[\text{assets}] - \Delta[\text{nonmoney liabilities and equity}] \qquad [20.9]$$

or

$$\Delta[\text{definitive money}] = \Delta[\text{securities held by Fed}] + \Delta[\text{discount loans}] \qquad [20.10]$$
$$+ \Delta[\text{coin, gold certificates, and SDR certificates}$$
$$\text{purchased from Treasury}]$$
$$+ \Delta[\text{float}] + \Delta[\text{foreign-currency assets}]$$
$$+ \Delta[\text{other assets}] - \Delta[\text{nonmoney liabilities and equity}].$$

The change in monetary base is then[11]

$$\Delta[\text{monetary base}] = \Delta[\text{definitive money}] \quad\quad\quad [20.11]$$
$$- \Delta[\text{U.S. Treasury, foreign, and other deposits}]$$
$$- \Delta[\text{U.S. Treasury cash holdings}]$$

The change in bank reserves is[12]

$$\Delta[\text{bank reserves}] = \Delta[\text{monetary base}] \quad\quad\quad [20.12]$$
$$- \Delta[\text{Federal Reserve notes}] + \Delta[\text{vault cash}].$$

In conducting monetary policy, the Fed changes the amount of monetary base and of bank reserves through open market operations. Open market operations intended to offset changes in monetary base or in reserves caused by other factors are called *defensive*. Open market operations intended deliberately to change the level of monetary base or of reserves are called *dynamic*.

As an example of a defensive open market operation, suppose there is an inflow of $20 billion in tax payments to the General Account:

THE FED

		Deposits	
		Banks	−$20b
		U.S. Treasury	+$20b

The Fed can offset this with an open market operation of the same size:

THE FED

U.S securities	+$20b	Deposits	
		Banks	+$20b

Since the inflow to the Treasury is likely to be reversed as soon as the Treasury spends the money, the Fed might well use a reverse repurchase agreement rather than an outright purchase to offset it.

20.5 | OTHER INSTRUMENTS OF CONTROL

The Fed's main instrument of monetary control is its ability to change the amount of monetary base and bank reserves through open market operations. In addition, the level at which the Fed sets the discount rate will have some effect on the

---

[11] From Exhibit 20.2.

[12] From bank balance sheets; not in Exhibit 20.1 or Exhibit 20.2.

amount of reserves that banks borrow at the discount window. In addition to these two instruments of control over monetary base, the Fed has two instruments that can affect the money multiplier: It can set reserve requirements, and it can exert some direct control over bank lending.

DISCOUNT POLICY

At the time the Fed was established, discount lending was expected to be the main instrument of monetary control. Since the 1930s, however, discount lending has increasingly been supplanted in this role by open market operations. The reason is that if the Fed wants to change bank reserves, it is much easier to do so directly through an open market operation rather than indirectly by changing the attractiveness of discount borrowing. Today, the role of the discount window in monetary policy is a subsidiary one.

Discount loans are routinely available to all depository institutions offering transactions accounts—domestic commercial banks, branches and agencies of foreign banks, thrifts, and credit unions. Today such a loan is usually an advance rather than a discount, but the old terminology persists. The borrower is required to put up collateral, usually in the form of Treasury securities, securities of government agencies, or mortgage-backed securities. In an emergency, the Fed, as lender of last resort, may lend to anyone it deems fit, but no such loans to nonbanks have been made since the Great Depression.

Discount lending falls into two categories. **Adjustment credit** may be sought by banks having temporary difficulty in meeting their statutory reserve requirements; such loans are usually made for only a few days. **Extended credit** is available for longer periods. Some extended credit is made available to meet the seasonal demands for funds of small institutions that do not have good access to the money market—for example, small agricultural banks and small banks in tourist areas. A second use of extended credit is to help banks in trouble. The lending to Continental Illinois that we saw in Chapter 17 and the lending to ailing thrifts in the early 1980s both fall in this category.

Discount loans are made by the individual Federal Reserve Banks. Formally, each Bank sets its own rate. The rate is determined by the bank's board of directors, subject to approval by the Fed's Board of Governors. In reality, the Board sets the rate, which is the same for all banks. The basic discount rate applies to all adjustment credit and to seasonal extended credit. The Fed generally charges more for emergency extended credit—a 1% premium after the first 60 days and a 2% premium after 150 days. For extremely long-term loans, the Fed may charge a rate linked to market rates rather than to the discount rate.

The basic discount rate is generally set below the market rate of interest.[13] Banks, naturally, wish to exploit this cheap source of funds to the maximum.

adjustment credit
Discount lending for short periods of time.

extended credit
Discount lending for lengthy time periods.

---

[13]This policy violates the third of the four principles of central banking that we saw in Chapter 16.

They are restrained, however, by a set of guidelines that limits their borrowing.[14] As we shall see in Chapter 21, this presents banks with an interesting problem in how best to exploit their borrowing privileges.

Since the discount rate is set below market rates, its actual level will have little direct effect on bank borrowing. If market rates are, say, 10%, and the discount rate is 8%, banks will wish to borrow as much as they can. If the discount rate is raised to 8.5% or lowered to 7.5%, banks will still wish to borrow as much as they can. Changes in the discount rate do, however, have an "announcement effect." Changes in the discount rate are often used by the Fed to send a message—to underline a change in its policy. We shall look at announcement effects more closely in Chapter 29.

RESERVE REQUIREMENTS

The current reserve requirements, imposed by the Monetary Control Act of 1980, are shown in Exhibit 20.3. Transactions accounts include regular checking accounts, NOW accounts, and credit-union share drafts, but not money market deposit accounts (which are classified as time deposits). Nonpersonal time deposits (mostly NCDs) are those owned by corporations and institutions rather than by households. The lower reserve requirement for the initial amounts of transactions accounts is simply a break for small banks.

These reserve requirements apply to *all* depository institutions—commercial banks, mutual savings banks, savings and loans, credit unions, branches and agencies of foreign banks in the United States, and Edge Act corporations. Reserves may be held as deposits with the Federal Reserve or as vault cash. Depository institutions that are not members of the Federal Reserve System may hold reserves in special "pass-through" correspondent balances against which the correspondent must hold 100% reserves.[15]

The Fed has the authority to change reserve requirements within bounds set by law. The permissible range for the basic ratio on transactions deposits is 8% to 14%. The range for nonpersonal time deposits is 0% to 9%, and the Fed may set the ratio for Eurodollar liabilities as it pleases.

---

[14]Banks should not borrow more than one to two weeks consecutively, three to four weeks in a quarter, or four to five weeks in six months. They should not borrow, at any one time, more than 1% of their domestic deposits. Nor should they be selling fed funds or repoing in securities at the same time they are borrowing.

[15]Before 1980 the Fed's reserve requirements applied only to member banks: Nonmembers were subject to reserve requirements imposed by state banking regulations. State reserve requirements were generally less stringent than those of the Fed. For example, some states counted T-bills as reserves. As a result, there was a steady stream of banks leaving the Federal Reserve System. (It was estimated at the time that Citibank could have added $200 million to its annual income by switching to a New York State charter.) Extending the Fed's reserve requirements to all depository institutions was a direct response to this exodus, which the Fed believed was weakening its ability to control the quantity of money.

EXHIBIT 20.3

RESERVE REQUIREMENTS, SEPTEMBER 1989

Type of Deposit	Percent of Deposit
Transactions accounts:	
$0–$41.5 million[a]	3%
Any amount over $41.5 million[a]	12
Nonpersonal time deposits with maturity under 1.5 years	3
Other time deposits	0
Eurodollar liabilities	3
First $3.4 million[a] of accounts subject to reserve requirements	0

[a]Amounts adjusted annually.

Source: *Federal Reserve Bulletin.*

Reserve requirements are an important determinant of the money multiplier. Remember from Chapter 19 that the money multiplier is

$$m = \frac{1 + c}{c + r + r_T \times t},$$ [20.13]

where c is the currency/checking-deposit ratio, r is the reserve ratio on transactions deposits, r_T is the reserve ratio on time deposits, and t is the time-deposit/checking-deposit ratio. From Equation 20.13 it should be clear that an increase in reserve ratios means a decrease in the money multiplier. Therefore, if the monetary base is unchanged, an increase in reserve ratios also means a decrease in the total quantity of money (see Equation 20.1).

The reserve ratios in the money multiplier equation, r and r_T, are the ratios that banks *actually* hold against their deposits, not the required reserve ratios. Actual ratios cannot be less than required ratios, but they may be greater. Banks may wish to hold more reserves than are required. The difference between actual reserves and required reserves is called **excess reserves**. In practice, as we shall see in Chapter 21, banks keep excess reserves quite small. Hence actual reserve ratios are close to required reserve ratios. A change in the required reserve ratio will therefore change the actual reserve ratio by approximately the same amount.

excess reserves
Difference between actual reserves and required reserves.

The effect on the quantity of money of a change in the required reserve ratio is substantial. For example, in May 1989 banks had about $544 billion of transactions deposits. Increasing the reserve ratio from 12% to 13% would have increased the amount of required reserves on these deposits by 1% of $544 billion, or $5.44 billion. Therefore such an increase in the reserve ratio would have been equivalent in its effect on the banking system to an open market sale of $5.44 billion—a *very* large open market sale.

Changes in the required reserve ratio are thus a rather blunt instrument: Their effect is too large to make them very useful. It makes much more sense to bring about a desired change in the quantity of money through open market operations. Indeed, changes in required reserve ratios are never used in practice as an instrument of monetary control.

DIRECT CREDIT CONTROLS

Anything that restricts the ability of banks to increase their lending will restrict the expansion of deposits that follows an expansion of bank reserves. Such restrictions therefore reduce the money multiplier.

The Credit Control Act of 1969 provided that "[w]henever the President determines that such action is necessary or appropriate for the purpose of preventing or controlling inflation generated by the extension of credit in an excessive volume, the President may authorize the Board [of Governors] to regulate and control any and all extensions of credit." President Carter gave such authorization in early 1980, and the Fed imposed across-the-board restrictions on the growth of most types of bank credit. The effects on the economy were dramatic, so dramatic that the controls were quickly dropped (we shall have more to say about this episode in Chapter 32). The Credit Control Act expired in June 1982 and was not renewed, so the Fed no longer has the power to control credit directly in this way. Nonetheless, even if the Fed cannot order banks to restrict their lending, it can ask them politely to do so (this is called **moral suasion**). The Fed has not done this in recent years.

moral suasion
The Fed's use of informal means to restrict bank lending.

In some other countries, such as Japan, moral suasion plays an important role. Also, in some other countries, central banks may control bank lending through the regulation of various categories of loan. For example, consumer borrowing may be controlled by requiring minimum down payments on installment credit. By raising the required down payment on a car from 10% to 20%, some potential buyers will be squeezed out and the growth of automobile loans will be slowed.

20.6 WHAT HAPPENS TO THE FED'S INCOME?

Looking at the Fed's balance sheet, you can see that its income must be substantial. Most of its assets pay interest, while most of its liabilities do not. If the average interest rate on its assets is, say, 8%, net interest income will be about $20 billion. Add to this fees for various services, mostly related to clearing, and subtract the costs of operating the Federal Reserve banks, and there still remains a healthy piece of change. What happens to this income?

Formally, the Fed belongs to its member banks: When a bank joins the Federal Reserve System, it must purchase shares equal in value to a certain fraction of its own equity. However, the Fed's profits are not paid out to its shareholders. That payout is limited to 6% of the amount of the shares. The rest, about 95% of the Fed's net earnings, is paid to the U.S. Treasury.

SUMMARY

- The Fed's most important instrument of control is its ability to change monetary base through open market operations. Its other instruments are discount policy, the setting of reserve requirements, and direct influence over bank lending.

- Definitive money in the United States consists of coins issued by the Treasury and Fed liabilities in the form of deposits and of Federal Reserve notes.

- Monetary base is definitive money less the amount held by the federal government and by foreign official institutions.

- Monetary base may be broken down into Fed deposits of banks plus currency outstanding, or it may be broken down into bank reserves plus currency in the hands of the public.

- *Any* purchase or sale by the Fed changes the amount of definitive money. If the transaction is not with the federal government or with a foreign official institution, it will also change the amount of monetary base. If the transaction involves a bank, it will change reserves.

- When the Fed wishes deliberately to change monetary base, the Fed usually buys or sells U.S. government securities in the open market. These are called dynamic open market operations.

- The Fed also engages in defensive open market operations to offset other factors that may change monetary base. Such other factors include discount loans, foreign-exchange transactions of the Fed, Federal Reserve float, and transactions involving the U.S. government.

- Discount loans are made at the initiative of the borrowing bank. The discount rate has little effect on the demand for such loans, because it is normally below market rates.

- Discount lending includes short-term adjustment credit to banks that are short of reserves and long-term extended credit to banks with large seasonal demands for funds or to banks in trouble.

- Fed float is created when the Fed credits the bank receiving a check before it debits the bank on which the check is drawn.

- The U.S. government uses the Fed as its bank. As a result, payments to or from the U.S. government decrease or increase bank reserves. The Treasury tries to offset large fluctuations by drawing on the Treasury tax and loan accounts that it keeps at most banks.

- The Treasury deposits certificates backed by gold and SDRs with the Fed in order to turn these assets into usable cash. The Treasury also sells the Fed, at face value, coins that it mints.

- The Fed has the power to set reserve requirements within bounds determined by law. The basic rates are 12% on transactions deposits, 3% on nonpersonal time deposits (NCDs) and Eurodollar borrowings, and 0% on other time deposits. Changes in reserve requirements have such large effects that they are never used in practice as an instrument of monetary control.

- The Fed's authority to impose direct credit controls expired in 1982, but it can still pressure banks to limit their lending.

- The Fed earns a substantial income on its assets. Most of this income goes to the U.S. Treasury.

KEY TERMS

open market operations	Special Drawing Rights (SDRs)	excess reserves
Fed float		moral suasion
General Account	adjustment credit	
Treasury tax and loan accounts (TT&Ls)	extended credit	

DISCUSSION QUESTIONS

1. The following changes have occurred in the Fed's balance sheet:

SDR certificates	+$1 billion
Discount loans	+$0.5 billion
Government securities	−$0.7 billion
Items in process of collection	+$1 billion
Federal Reserve notes	+$1 billion
General Account	−$1.2 billion
Deferred credit items	+$1.5 billion
Deposits of banks	+$0.5 billion

   What are the changes in definitive money, monetary base, and float? If vault cash is unchanged, what is the change in reserves?

2. When banks such as Chase order $5 million in new $20 bills from the Fed, what will be the effect on its balance sheet? What will be the effect on the Fed's balance sheet?

3. Suppose the Fed has printed, at the Treasury's Bureau of Printing and Engraving, $1 billion in new $5 Federal Reserve notes. Where will these appear on the Fed's balance sheet?

4. Suppose the required reserve ratio on transactions deposits were halved and the amount of reserves adjusted to leave the total quantity of bank money the same. What would be the banks' reaction to this? The Treasury's reaction?

5. Suppose the Treasury decided to move its checking deposit from the Fed to Citibank. What would be the effect on the amount of bank reserves and on the stability of bank reserves over time? Why doesn't it do so?

6. What is the effect of each of the following on monetary base, on definitive money, and on banks' reserves?

   a. A snowstorm in Chicago delays presentment of checks for $2 billion that are in the process of being cleared.

   b. The Fed lends Continental Illinois $3.5 billion through the discount window.

   c. The Fed buys $1 billion worth of Japanese yen.

   d. The Treasury withdraws $5 billion from its TT&L accounts.

   e. The Treasury sells gold having an official value of $3 billion.

7. Why does the Fed prefer open market operations to the other instruments of monetary control at its disposal?

SOFTWARE EXERCISE FOR THIS CHAPTER

Title: FOMC

This computer exercise places you in the role of manager of the Federal Open Market account at the New York Federal Reserve Bank. It demonstrates how conducting open market operations from this position is not as easy as it appears to be. See your instructor if you wish to use this program.

BIBLIOGRAPHY

Duro, Lorraine, E., "The Federal Reserve Discount Mechanism," *Economic Review of the Federal Reserve Bank of Cleveland*, April 1983, 1–9.

Goodfriend, Marvin, "A Historical Assessment of the Rationales and Functions of Reserve Requirements," *Economic Review of the Federal Reserve Bank of Richmond*, March-April 1983, 3–21.

Meek, Paul, *U.S. Monetary Policy and Financial Markets*, New York: Federal Reserve Bank of New York, 1982.

CHAPTER 21

MULTIPLE EXPANSION AND THE MONEY MULTIPLIER IN PRACTICE

In this chapter we shall see how the principles of multiple expansion and the money multiplier that we studied in Chapter 19 apply in practice. We shall begin by looking at the multiple expansion process from the point of view of a bank, seeing how it calculates its reserve requirements and how it manages its reserve position. We shall go on to see how bank lending responds to increases in reserves. Finally, we shall see how the behavior of banks and of others determines the size of the money multiplier.

Throughout this chapter *checking deposit* will mean any transactions deposit that may be drawn upon by check or checklike instrument: The term includes NOW accounts and other such devices as well as regular checking accounts. *Bank* will mean any depository institution that offers such checking deposits.

21.1 A BANK'S-EYE VIEW OF RESERVES

In Chapter 20 we saw how the Fed imposes reserve requirements. Here we shall see what that means to a bank. How does a bank calculate the amount of reserves it must hold? How does it manage its reserve position to minimize the cost of meeting the requirement?

CALCULATING REQUIRED RESERVES

Imagine what would happen if banks had to maintain required reserves on a minute-by-minute basis. For example, as you withdraw $100 from the teller machine, the bank's required reserves fall by $12 but its actual reserves fall by the full $100. The bank would have to rush to the fed funds market to borrow the missing $88. Such tight control, however, is not necessary. The goal of reserve requirements is to control the ability of banks to expand their deposits. What matters is the amount of deposits over weeks and months, not the amount minute by minute. So reserve requirements are imposed accordingly.

To see how it works, imagine you are managing reserves for a large bank—Metropolis National. Each day you must fill out a report listing the amount of each of the following that the bank has at the close of business:

- Vault cash
- Time deposits subject to reserve requirements
- Checking deposits subject to reserve requirements
- Deposits at the Fed

This reserve report is sent to the Fed each week and is used to calculate the bank's reserve requirements.

The basic idea is simple. Required reserves are calculated day by day based on the reserve reports. The average required reserve is calculated for a given period. The average *actual* reserves are supposed to be at least the average required reserves. The practical execution of this idea, illustrated in Exhibit 21.1, is a little more complex.

computation period
Two-week time period for calculating a bank's required reserves.

The period for calculating required reserves is called the **computation period**. Each computation period is two weeks long, beginning on a Tuesday and ending on the Monday two weeks later. When one computation period ends, the next one begins immediately. The two computation periods shown in Exhibit 21.1 that are relevant to our discussion are

A. Tuesday, February 1, through Monday, February 14

B. Tuesday, March 1, through Monday, March 14

However, there are other computation periods before A, between A and B, and after B.

maintenance period
Two-week time period over which a bank's actual reserves are calculated.

The period over which average actual reserves must be held is called the **maintenance period**. Like the computation period, each maintenance period is two weeks long. However, the maintenance period begins and ends two days later than the computation period. It begins on a Thursday and ends on the Wednesday two weeks later. When one maintenance period ends, the next begins. The maintenance period shown in Exhibit 21.1 that we shall focus on is

B′. Thursday, March 3, through Wednesday, March 16

There are, of course, other computation periods before and after this one.

Let us see how reserves are calculated for Maintenance Period B′. The amount of reserves you need to hold depends on your checking deposits over Computation Period B and on your vault cash and reservable time deposits over Computation Period A.

Suppose your reservable time deposits in Computation Period A averaged $6 billion. The reserve requirement on such deposits is 3%, so you will need to hold $180 million (3% of $6 billion) against them. You will need to hold that $180

EXHIBIT 21.1

RESERVE COMPUTATION AND MAINTENANCE PERIODS

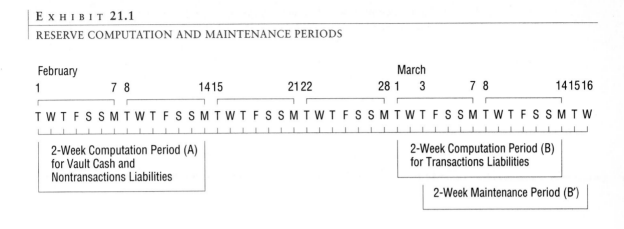

million *now*, during Maintenance Period B′. Suppose, too, that in Computation Period A your vault cash averaged $300 million. That $300 million will count as reserves *now*, in Maintenance Period B′.

The amount of reserves you need to hold against checking deposits is calculated from their daily average over Computation Period B, which overlaps with Maintenance Period B′. At the start of the maintenance period, you know the amounts for the first two days, but not for the rest. Additional information comes in day by day, and you will have the final report on the Monday afternoon two days before the current maintenance period ends. Until then, you will have to estimate the amount of checking deposits for the rest of the computation period and tailor your reserves accordingly.

Suppose you expect the daily average of your checking deposits to be about $8 billion. The reserve requirement is 12%, so you will need to hold $960 million (12% of $8 billion) against those deposits. Add to this the $180 million we calculated above that you need to cover your time deposits, for a total of $1,140 million. Now subtract from this the $300 million in vault cash you held in that earlier reserve computation period. Your deposit at the Fed over the coming two weeks will therefore have to average about $840 million. You will have a closer estimate as the two-week period progresses, and you will know the exact amount when the current reserve computation period ends.[1]

---

[1] For very small banks, with total reservable liabilities of less than $15 million, the reserve computation period for transactions liabilities is the same as that for nontransactions liabilities, beginning a month before the reserve maintenance period. This simplifies matters considerably for these banks. They are also required to report to the Fed less frequently than the larger banks.

🌴 **CHECK STATION 1** | **In the computation period January 18 through January 31, vault cash averaged $290 million and reservable time deposits averaged $6.5 billion. In the computation period February 15 through February 28, checking deposits averaged $7.9 billion. What was the average required amount in your Fed deposit during the maintenance period February 17 through March 2?**

Suppose that on Monday, March 14, it turns out that your average checking deposits for the computation period have been $8.4 billion. Because this is $400 million more than you anticipated, you need an extra 0.12 x $400 million = $48 million of reserves. Your deposits at the Fed during the current maintenance period have averaged $840 million through the Monday. By Wednesday you need to raise this average by $48 million to $888 million. To do this, you will have to increase your Fed deposit considerably on the last two days of the maintenance period. You might, for instance, increase it from $840 million to $1,176 million for Tuesday and Wednesday, giving you a 14-day average of

$$\frac{12 \times \$840m + 2 \times \$1,176m}{14} = \$888 \text{ million},$$

as required.

As we shall see, such a large adjustment can be quite expensive, so you will avoid leaving things to the last minute in this way. Instead, you will keep careful track of what is happening to your bank's checking deposits and reserves, and you will manage your Fed deposits to meet your reserve requirements as inexpensively as possible.

MANAGING A BANK'S RESERVE POSITION

Keeping track of your Fed deposits is quite a task. Their amount fluctuates wildly through the day as large volumes of wire payments go in and out. For much of the day you will be in overdraft.[2] Toward the end of the day you will make a payment or receive one to close out your position on CHIPS.[3] You need to anticipate incoming and outgoing payments, and you must make sure that you end the day with enough to cover your daylight overdraft plus your reserve requirement.

There are a number of ways you can acquire extra Fed deposits. You can borrow federal funds or overnight Eurodollars, sell or repo securities, or borrow directly from the Fed through the discount window. If you have more Fed deposits than you need, you can use the same methods in reverse to dispose of the excess. You will try to acquire the extra Fed deposits you need as inexpensively as possible, and you will try to earn as much as possible on excess funds.

---

[2]See Chapter 18 for a discussion of daylight overdraft.
[3]See Chapter 4 for a discussion of clearing over CHIPS.

The cheapest source of funds is almost always the discount window. However, discount borrowing is rationed.[4] This leaves you with an interesting timing problem: Once you borrow from the window, you must wait some time until you can borrow again. The trick is to borrow when the gain is greatest—that is, when the differential between the discount rate and other rates is at a maximum. This usually happens when other rates go up. The Fed may fail to raise the discount rate at all if the rise in market rates is temporary, and even if it decides to raise the discount rate, it usually takes it some time to decide. So you will try to anticipate when rates are likely to rise and save your discount borrowing for then.

The timing of your other borrowing is important too. Let us say that you will need an average of $850 million. You could try to achieve this average by having somewhat more than this early in the maintenance period and somewhat less toward the end; or you could do just the opposite. Which strategy you choose will depend on whether you think interest rates will rise or fall toward the end of the current maintenance period. Of course, if you guess wrong, it can be expensive.

Remember that all the other banks are in the same situation—trying to balance their reserve positions. On the last Tuesday and Wednesday of the reserve maintenance period, it may turn out that everyone is short of reserves. If so, the Fed funds rate and related rates will go up. Or it could be just the opposite: Everyone may have more than they need, and the Fed funds rate will drop. If you have guessed right, you will be able to exploit the situation. If you have not, you will pay for your mistake.

Plan and scheme as you might, things could go wrong at the last moment. Late on Wednesday afternoon Metropolis could receive a large, unexpected payment, or it could face a large unexpected withdrawal. (See "Irving's Snafu" on page 564 for an idea of just how seriously things can go wrong.)   If you are short, you can go to the discount window at the last minute—one reason you want to be careful about using up your borrowing privileges. If you have more reserves than needed, it is more of a problem, since you may have trouble unloading the excess late in the day.

There is some margin for error. Since 1980 the Fed has charged for its check-clearing services. Payment can be either direct or in the form of excess reserve balances, much like paying a correspondent with a compensating balance. So if you have an excess, some of it can be used in this way. If you have more than that, you are allowed to carry over up to 2% of your reserve requirement to the next reserve maintenance period. For example, if you have $870 million instead of the $850 million you need, $10 million of the excess might cover the cost of the services you receive from the Fed, and you could subtract the remaining $10 million from your reserve requirement in the next reserve maintenance period.[5]

---

[4]See Chapter 20 for details.

[5]You can also carry over a deficit. That is, if you are short up to 2% ($17 million), you can simply add that to your reserve requirement for the next period.

IRVING'S SNAFU

One fine day a clerk set a switch on an Irving Bank computer so that instructions that were supposed to go out over the Fedwire were all written to disk instead. As a result, Irving could accept deliveries of securities, but it could not make them. "We were," said an ex-Irving officer, "acting as a kind of black hole for securities."

"This occurred," he continued, "on a Wednesday. Fortunately, we'd been thinking that funds were going to tighten, so we were long 1 ½ billion of funds on which we planned to make, when we sold them, some nickels. Around 3:15 p.m., just after the Fedwire closed, we discovered that we had, thanks to our mis-set computer switch, a problem: We had not received $4 billion of funds that we thought we had. When we told our funds trader that, he just walked around holding his head. He could not believe that you could go from 1.5 long to 2.5 short in less than five minutes. We did just that and had to start buying funds.

"We became a black hole for funds. No offer rate [in the funds market] was too high for us. Finally, when we had scrimped something like 800 million out of the funds market, we found that we had bought everything there was; there were no nickels, dimes, or anything left. At that point, we still had about 1.7 billion to go. To get that, we had to go to the Fed. Unfortunately, we had only 350 million of collateral at the Fed—at first, the Fed viewed that as a problem. Finally, however, they graciously decided that, since we were long about 4 billion in securities anyway, we could use those securities as collateral. So we were able to get our 1.7 billion from the Fed."

Computer errors can be costly. Interest on $1.7 billion, even on an overnight borrowing, is bound to amount to a tidy sum.

Source: Marcia Stigum, *The Money Market* (Homewood, IL: Dow Jones-Irwin, 1983).

21.2 | THE REALITY OF MULTIPLE EXPANSION

In our discussion of multiple expansion in Chapter 19, we had banks look at their reserve position and expand their lending if they found they had more reserves than they wished to keep. Although that presentation led to an understanding of the multiple expansion multiplier, we have just seen that increased or decreased lending plays no explicit role in the management of a bank's reserve position.

Moreover, when we looked at bank lending in Chapter 12, we saw that banks do not determine their lending according to the level of their reserves. Small banks are deposit-rich and lack good loan opportunities. Because they are not constrained by a lack of funds, an increase in reserves will not make them lend more. Large banks are reserve-poor, because they have more good loan opportunities than deposits. Their lending is not limited by reserves either: They simply borrow the reserves they need in the money market. Once banks, large and small, have set a rate for their loans and a policy for evaluating loan applications, they accept all loans that qualify. The manager of the bank's reserve position is then expected to make sure that the bank has the right amount of reserves.

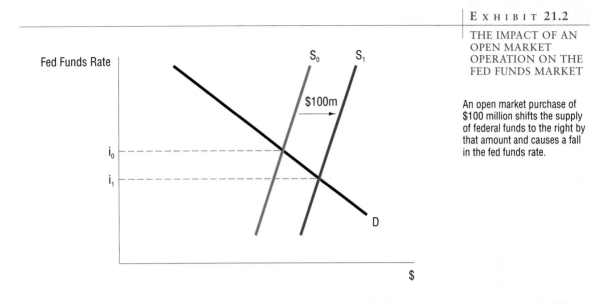

An open market purchase of $100 million shifts the supply of federal funds to the right by that amount and causes a fall in the fed funds rate.

Although no individual bank pays attention to its reserve position when making loans, the connection between reserves and lending remains in effect for the banking system as a whole. When the Fed changes the amount of reserves available to the banking system as a whole, the amount of bank money and the amount of loans do change. Let us see how this happens by tracing through the effects of a particular open market operation.

Suppose the Fed increases the amount of reserves through a $100 million open market purchase of government securities. The reserve managers of the clearing banks involved (the clearing banks of the primary dealers who sold the securities) will find themselves with extra reserves. They will immediately unload these extra reserves on the fed funds market. However, although these particular banks can "unload" their extra reserves in this way, the banking system as a whole cannot do so. The extra reserves represent a net increase in the total supply of fed funds for the banking system as a whole. There are simply $100 million more in reserves available to the system, and someone will have to hold them.

Exhibit 21.2 shows the effect on the fed funds market of this sale of unwanted reserves. The fed funds supply curve shifts to the right by $100 million from S_0 to S_1, and the fed funds rate falls from i_0 to i_1. As the fed funds rate falls relative to the rate on T-bills, banks find it worthwhile to borrow funds in order to buy securities. This is what accounts for the increase in the quantity of fed funds demanded as we move along the demand curve in Exhibit 21.2. To see why the quantity of fed funds demanded increases, let us see what happens when banks increase their holdings of securities.

Since we are talking here of an increase in the holding of securities by the banking system as a whole, the additional securities must be bought from nonbanks—most likely, from securities dealers. When a bank purchases securities from XYZ Securities, it pays for the securities by crediting XYZ's deposit:

BANK

Securities	+$1m	Deposits	
		XYZ Securities	+$1m

The increase in deposits that results is exactly like the increase in deposits that would result from a new bank loan.[6] So a purchase of securities by the banking system increases the total amount of deposits in the same way as does an increase in lending. As the amount of deposits increases, so does the amount of reserves that banks must hold against them. Thus the increased holding of securities expands deposits and soaks up extra reserves.

If the fed funds rate stays down, banks will eventually lower the rates they charge on loans. At the lower rates, more potential borrowers will apply for loans. To satisfy the increased demand, banks will borrow, pushing up the cost of funds. With funds more expensive, banks will sell off some securities. Eventually, on the balance sheet of the banking system, new loans will replace a good part of the extra securities the banks initially bought.

The ultimate effect of the open market operation, then, is an increase in lending and an increase in deposits. Even though the mechanism is quite different, the end result is precisely what we found in Chapter 19.

21.3 THE MONEY MULTIPLIER IN PRACTICE

We have just seen how an open market operation leads to an expansion of bank deposits. The extent of the expansion and the total effect on the quantity of money will depend on the size of the money multiplier.

In Chapter 19 we saw that the magnitude of the money multiplier is given by the following equation:

$$m = \frac{1 + c}{c + r + r_T \times t} .$$ [21.1]

That is, the size of the money multiplier depends on the ratio between currency and checking deposits, c; on the checking-deposit reserve ratio, r; on the time-deposit reserve ratio, r_T, and on the ratio between time deposits and checking deposits, t. Let us look at the factors that determine each of these ratios.

---

[6]In a sense, by purchasing a government security, the bank is funding a loan to the federal government.

THE DETERMINANTS OF THE RESERVE RATIOS

REQUIRED RESERVES AND EXCESS RESERVES The reserve ratios r and r_T represent the proportion of reserves that banks *actually* hold against checking deposits and time deposits, respectively. Banks cannot, of course, hold less reserves than required, but they can hold more. The reserves they hold beyond those required are called *excess reserves*.

If banks hold no excess reserves, then the reserve ratios in the money multiplier equation simply equal the required reserve ratios. However, if banks *do* hold excess reserves, then the actual reserve ratios in the money multiplier equation will exceed the required reserve ratios. The greater the excess reserves and thus the greater the actual reserve ratios, the smaller will be the money multiplier.

So the question is: Do banks hold excess reserves and, if so, how much? To answer this question, we need to ask what reserves banks would hold voluntarily if there were no formal requirements. They would certainly hold some reserves in the form of vault cash, although they might hold less than they do today. Small banks might also hold some reserve deposits: We have seen that small banks ensure liquidity through asset management, and a certain amount of reserve deposits would likely play some role in such a policy. On the other hand, large banks rely on liability management. Given the choice, they would probably hold very little in the way of reserve deposits. While reserve deposits are of some use in clearing wire payments, the availability of daylight overdraft makes a positive balance largely unnecessary.[7] In countries with no reserve requirements, large banks hold very little reserves—on the order of 1% or less of their deposits.[8]

If the amount of reserves that banks wish to hold voluntarily is higher than required reserves, then the requirements do not matter: Banks will decide on their reserves as if the requirements did not exist. However, in the United States requirements seem to be substantially above the amount that banks would wish to hold voluntarily. As a result, we would expect them to hold no more than the amount required. This is more or less the situation. Exhibit 21.3 shows the behavior over time of excess reserves as a percentage of required reserves.

Excess reserves are not exactly zero because, as we have seen, managing reserves is tricky and costly. Mistakes occur and banks are left with more reserves than they intended. For small banks in particular, it may be cheaper to allow some excess reserves than to invest a lot of time and trouble in managing reserves more precisely. The amount of excess reserves permitted in this way should be sensitive to market interest rates. The higher market interest rates are, the greater is the opportunity cost of holding excess reserves, and the more effort banks will make to eliminate them.

---

[7]See Chapter 18 for a discussion of daylight overdraft.

[8]Switzerland recently abolished reserve requirements at the same time that it abolished daylight overdraft (see Chapter 18). Great Britain has a reserve requirement of 0.5%. Canada is in the process of phasing out its reserve requirement.

EXHIBIT 21.3

EXCESS RESERVES AS
A PERCENTAGE OF
REQUIRED RESERVES

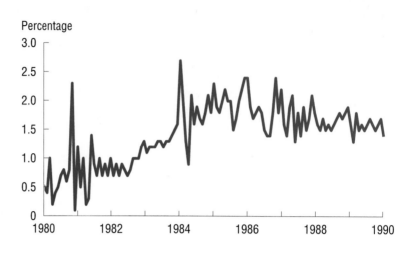

Source: *Federal Reserve Bulletin*, various issues.

CHECK STATION 2 | **What effect would an increase in excess reserves have on the money multiplier? What effect would it have on M1 if the amount of reserves in the banking system were unchanged?**

FORMAL REQUIREMENTS AND EFFECTIVE REQUIREMENTS   The reserve requirement for checking deposits is 12%. However, as we saw in Chapter 10, banks have incentives to "disguise" their checking deposits. By disguising some checking deposits as overnight repos, overnight Eurodollars, or fed funds bought, banks are able to pay their customers interest on those deposits, thereby avoiding the loss of their accounts.

But these disguised checking deposits also avoid reserve requirements. Suppose there are $550 billion of regular checking deposits in the United States and about $150 billion of the disguised variety, for a total of $700 billion. Reserves need be held only against the regular deposits: The amount is 12% of $550 billion, or $66 billion. As a percentage of *total* checking deposits, regular and disguised, these reserves are only

$$\frac{\$66 \text{ billion}}{\$700 \text{ billion}} \times 100 = 9.4\%.$$

effective reserve ratio
The ratio of reserves to
deposits, both regular and
disguised.

This 9.4% is the **effective reserve ratio.** The effective reserve ratio is generally less than the formal reserve requirement, and the more successful banks are at disguising checking deposits, the lower it will be. If we count disguised checking deposits as part of the quantity of money, then we should use the effective reserve ratio in calculating the corresponding effective money multiplier. The more

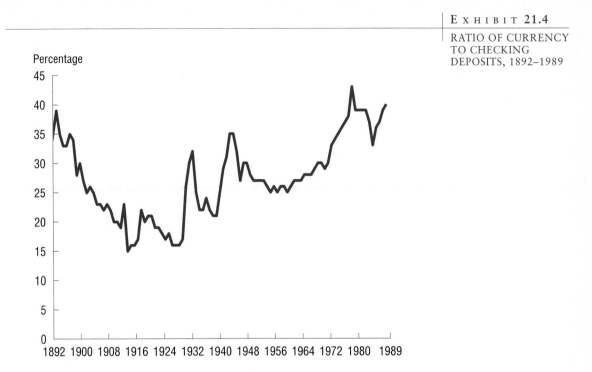

Source: Board of Governors of the Federal Reserve System.

successful banks are at disguising checking deposits, the greater the effective money multiplier will be.

THE DETERMINANTS OF THE OTHER RATIOS

THE CURRENCY/CHECKING-DEPOSIT RATIO In Chapter 19, to keep the algebra simple, we assumed that the ratio between the amount of currency that people use and the amount of their checking deposits is a constant. Exhibit 21.4 shows that in reality it is not.

The size of this ratio clearly depends on the relative attractiveness of currency and checking deposits as means of payment. The following factors play a role:

- *Relative rates of return.* Deposits may pay interest (for example, NOW accounts), whereas currency does not. The higher the interest on deposits, the more attractive they are relative to cash.

- *Desirability of records.* Payment by check generates a record of the transaction; payment in cash does not. People use cash if they want there to be no record. For example, criminals and tax evaders prefer to be paid in cash.

- *Relative ease of use.* How easy is it to pay by check? How easy is it to withdraw cash? Changes in the relative ease of use will affect how much currency people hold relative to deposits.

- *Relative security.* We saw in Chapter 16 that a loss of faith in the banking system may cause a "flight to cash." This happened in the 1930s. On the other hand, an increase in street crime may make it hazardous to carry large amounts of currency.

THE TIME-DEPOSIT/CHECKING-DEPOSIT RATIO   The ratio between time deposits and checking deposits, which we also assumed to be constant in Chapter 19, is not a constant either. Exhibit 21.5 shows the behavior of this ratio over time.

The size of this ratio depends on the relative attractiveness of time deposits and checking deposits. The following factors play a role:

- *Relative rates of return.* Time deposits generally pay a higher interest rate than checking deposits. The difference between the rates on the two types of deposits affects their relative attractiveness. If the difference is small, little is lost by keeping money in a more convenient checking account. If the difference is large, depositors will tolerate a little inconvenience to earn a substantially higher return.

- *Rates on time deposits relative to other assets.* Time deposits are an alternative not only to checking deposits but also to other types of assets—for example, T-bills and money market mutual funds. If such alternative assets offer much better yields, people will invest in them and reduce their time deposits. Since the amount held in checking accounts is not much affected by such a decision, the ratio of time deposits to checking deposits will fall.

- *Liquidity of time deposits.* Time deposits are generally not means of payment. To use the funds in a time deposit to make payments, these funds generally must first be transferred to a checking deposit. The easier it is to do this, the less will be kept in checking deposits and the more will be kept in time deposits.[9]

SOME NUMBERS ON THE MONEY MULTIPLIER

Definitions of the total quantity of money and of the money multiplier in our economy are more complicated than those for the simple Island economy of Chapter 19. There are two reasons: (1) In the United States there is a substantial government sector, and (2) the U.S. economy is involved in international as well

---

[9]Some time deposits, for example, money market deposit accounts, do allow limited direct payment. See Chapter 10 (Section 10.4) for details.

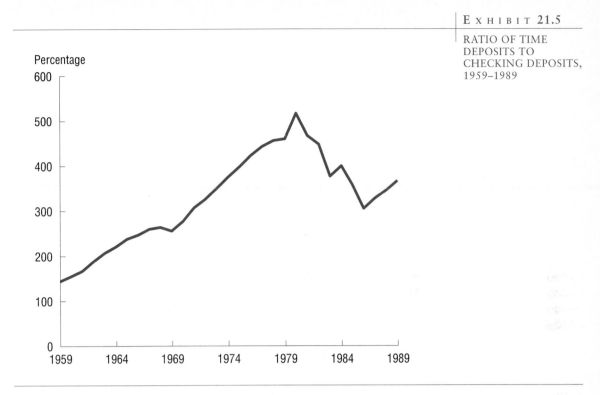

EXHIBIT 21.5

RATIO OF TIME DEPOSITS TO CHECKING DEPOSITS, 1959–1989

Source: Federal Reserve Board.

as domestic transactions. Our monetary statistics try to exclude money held by the government and by foreigners from the totals.

The total quantity of money in our economy that corresponds to M on the Island is called M1. It consists of all means of payment in the hands of domestic nonbank economic agents. It includes (1) cash in the form of Federal Reserve notes and coins (definitive money) and (2) checking deposits and traveler's checks (bank money).

The amount of cash in the hands of the public is just monetary base less bank reserves. In May 1989 it amounted to $216 billion. The amount of checking deposits held by the public is just total checking deposits less those that banks have with each other, those due to the federal government (tax and loan accounts), and those due to foreign governments and financial institutions. In May 1989 the amount of checking deposits held by the public was $550 billion ($278 billion of demand deposits plus $272 billion of other checkable deposits); the amount of traveler's checks was $7 billion. Total bank money was

$$\$550 \text{ billion} + \$7 \text{ billion} = \$557 \text{ billion},$$

and total M1 was

$$\$216 \text{ billion} + \$557 \text{ billion} = \$773 \text{ billion}.$$

In May 1989 monetary base, B, was \$278 billion, so the M1 money multiplier was

$$m1 = \frac{M1}{B} = \frac{\$773 \text{ billion}}{\$278 \text{ billion}} = 2.8.$$

The behavior over time of the M1 money multiplier is shown in Exhibit 21.6.

M2 is M1 plus overnight repos, overnight Eurodollars, money market mutual fund balances, money market deposit accounts, and savings and small time deposits (large CDs are excluded).[10] In May 1989 M2 amounted to \$3,073 billion.[11] The M2 money multiplier was

$$m2 = \frac{M2}{B} = \frac{\$3,073 \text{ billion}}{\$278 \text{ billion}} = 11.0.$$

The behavior of the M2 money multiplier over time is also shown in Exhibit 21.6.

We shall see in later chapters that fluctuations in the money multiplier that result from changes in the various ratios make it quite difficult for the Fed to control the quantity of money.

SUMMARY

- Banks are not required to maintain required reserve ratios on a minute-by-minute basis. Rather, average reserves over a maintenance period should be the required percentage of average deposits over a given computation period.

- Banks submit to the Fed weekly reports on the daily amounts of their checking deposits, time deposits, vault cash, and deposits at the Fed. These reports are used to calculate the amount of required reserves.

- Computation periods last from Tuesday through Monday; maintenance periods from Thursday through Wednesday. When a computation period ends, therefore, there remain two days in the concurrent maintenance period, which banks can use to adjust their reserve positions.

- Banks try to anticipate the amount of deposits they will have and thus the amount of reserves they will need. Large last-minute adjustments can be expensive.

---

[10]Note that disguised transactions deposits—overnight repos and overnight Eurodollars—are included in M2 but not in M1.

[11]There is a broader monetary aggregate, called M3, that also includes large time deposits, term Eurodollars, and term repos. In May 1989 M3 was \$3,954.4 billion.

EXHIBIT 21.6

M1 AND M2 MONEY MULTIPLIERS, 1959–1989

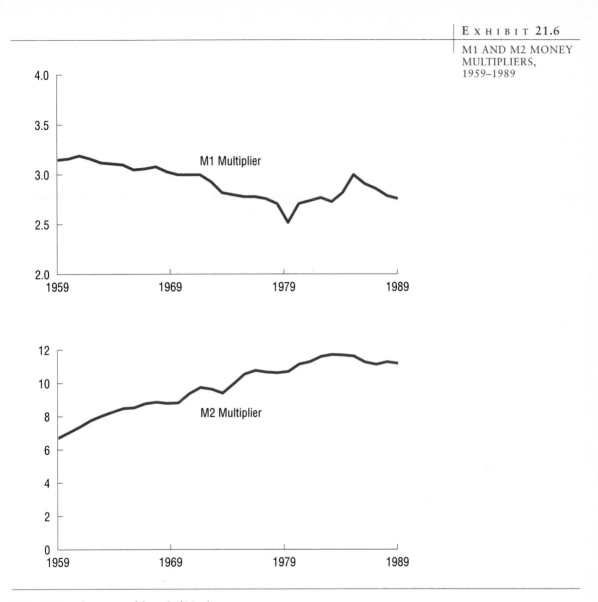

Note: 1990 numbers are as of the end of March.

Source: Board of Governors of the Federal Reserve System and *Economic Report of the President.*

- Banks also try to time their borrowing and lending of reserves, including borrowing at the discount window, so as to minimize the cost of meeting their reserve requirements. Correctly anticipating movements in interest rates is the key to success.

- Contrary to the simple multiple expansion story of Chapter 19, banks do not set their lending according to the availability of reserves. Rather, they set a lending policy in terms of loan rates and credit standards and fund all loans that meet those standards. Reserves are then adjusted as necessary.

- Nonetheless, lending of the banking system is constrained by the availability of reserves.

- Changes in the availability of reserves are conveyed to the individual bank via changes in the fed funds rate. Changes in the fed funds rate induce banks to change their holdings of securities and ultimately their lending.

- The "constants" that go to make up the money multiplier are not, in fact, constant. Their values change in response to economic incentives.

- The reserve ratios in the money multiplier are quite close to the required ratios because excess reserves are generally small. Excess reserves are small because banks are required to hold much more than they would hold voluntarily. Higher interest rates will prod banks to manage their reserves more carefully and will therefore lead to smaller excess reserves.

- Bank ingenuity in disguising checking deposits as nondeposits reduces the effective reserve ratio below the formal reserve ratio.

- The currency/checking-deposit ratio depends on the rate of return on deposits, on the volume of transactions for which records are *not* desired, on the relative ease of use of cash and checks, and on their relative security.

- The time-deposit/checking-deposit ratio depends on the relative rates of return on time deposits and checking deposits, on the rates on time deposits relative to those on other assets, and on the liquidity of time deposits.

KEY TERMS

computation period

maintenance period

effective reserve ratio

DISCUSSION QUESTIONS

1. Suppose you were managing reserves for a *small* bank. What would be your choices? If there were an increase in reserves in the banking system, how would this affect you? How would you respond?

2. How would you expect the following events to affect the various "constants" that make up the money multiplier? How would you expect them to affect the money multiplier itself?

   a. The widespread use of automated teller machines.

   b. The introduction of money market deposit accounts.

    c.   The introduction of NOW accounts.

    d.   The eradication of illicit drug sales as a result of the war on drugs.

3.   What would be the effect on the money multiplier of abolishing reserve requirements?

4.   If the Fed started paying interest on reserves, what would be the effect on the money multiplier?

5.   If you were managing a large bank's reserve position and you thought that interest rates were going to fall over the current maintenance period, what would you do?

BIBLIOGRAPHY

Cagan, Phillip, *Determinants and Effects of Changes in the Stock of Money 1875–1960*, New York: Columbia University Press for the NBER, 1965.

Goodfriend, Marvin, "A Model of Money Stock Determination with Loan Demand and a Banking System Balance Sheet Constraint," *Economic Review of the Federal Reserve Bank of Richmond*, January-February 1982, 3–16.

Tobin, James, *Commercial Banks as Creators of Money, in Banking and Monetary Studies*, edited by D. Carson, Homewood, IL: Irwin, 1963.

PART SIX

MONEY AND THE ECONOMY

CHAPTER 22

VELOCITY AND THE DEMAND FOR MONEY

In Part Five we saw how the Fed regulates the quantity of money. Now in Part Six we shall see how the quantity of money and changes in the quantity of money affect the economy. Once we understand that, we shall be ready in Part Seven to think about monetary policy—how the Fed's power to regulate the quantity of money should best be used.

In this chapter we shall examine the connection between the quantity of money and the amount of spending that takes place. We shall first develop a simple model based on the circular flow diagrams we saw in Chapter 2. We shall see that the relationship between the quantity of money and expenditure depends on the speed at which money circulates through the economy—that is, on the velocity of money. Velocity, in turn, depends on the way that firms and households manage their money balances. After examining this, we shall integrate what we learn into our circular flow model to see how the management of money balances can affect velocity and expenditure.

22.1 A CIRCULAR FLOW MODEL OF THE ISLAND ECONOMY

In studying how money affects the economy, it is best initially to keep things as simple as possible. So instead of tackling immediately the complexities of the U.S. economy, we shall develop the basic principles using a model of a much simpler economy—the economy of the same South Seas island that we have visited from time to time in previous chapters.

You can think of the model we are going to develop in one of two ways—as an *exact* description of the economy of the South Seas island or as an *approximate* description of the economy of the United States. It is easy to set up an exact model of the Island economy, because we can, if necessary, change the economy to fit the model. Unfortunately (or perhaps fortunately), we cannot do the same with the U.S. economy. We shall use the model to trace out the effects of various changes. For example, we shall trace out how an open-market operation affects interest rates. Because the circular flow model is an exact description of the Island economy, our conclusion will be *precisely* correct for that economy. Because the model is only an approximate description of the U.S. economy, our conclusions will be only *roughly* correct for the U.S. economy—how roughly depending on how much the U.S. economy differs from the fictional economy.

THE CIRCULAR FLOW REVISITED

Exhibit 22.1 shows the money flows in the Island economy for a typical month.[1] At the beginning of each month, firms pay out all the previous month's receipts as income to households—a total of $1,000 million. Firms retain no earnings and pay no taxes in this economy. Households pay $100 million in taxes to the government, save $200 million by purchasing securities, and spend the remaining $700 million on consumption. Firms borrow $120 million a month to finance their investment.[2] Also, since the government spends more than it collects in taxes, it must borrow $80 million to cover its deficit. Total expenditure, the sum of spending by households, firms, and government, is $1,000 million. This amount is received by firms in exchange for the goods and services they provide, and it is then paid out again to households as income. The cycle then begins all over again. We shall assume that the Island economy stays the same from month to month, repeating the same pattern of payments.[3]

THE FLOW OF PAYMENTS THROUGH THE MONETARY SYSTEM

The Island has a fractional-reserve banking system. The payments system is so efficient that all payments are made by check: No hand-to-hand currency is used at all. Definitive money consists of $150 million of deposits at the Island's central bank, the Bank of the Island. Since no hand-to-hand currency is used, all this definitive money is bank reserves. Checks are cleared by transferring central-bank deposits from bank to bank. The reserve ratio is 10%, so bank deposits are

---

[1]Exhibit 22.1 reproduces Exhibit 2.6 from Chapter 2.

[2]For simplicity, households do not invest. The climate is so benign that permanent shelter is unnecessary, and there is therefore no investment in residential construction.

[3]The assumption that the economy stays the same from month to month makes it much simpler for us to analyze it. It is not very realistic though, even for the fictional economy. Households are accumulating securities at the rate of $200 million per month, firms are investing, and government debt is growing. All of these changes are likely to affect the behavior of the different economic agents. However, it may not be too unrealistic to say that in the short run at least these changes are not too important, so that the assumption of an unchanging economy is not too bad an approximation.

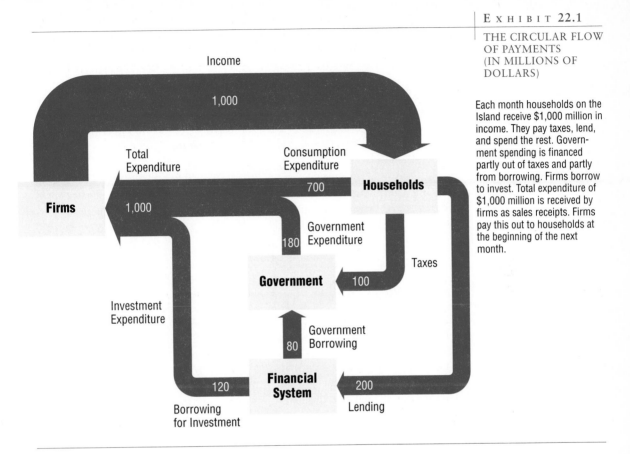

EXHIBIT 22.1

THE CIRCULAR FLOW OF PAYMENTS (IN MILLIONS OF DOLLARS)

Each month households on the Island receive $1,000 million in income. They pay taxes, lend, and spend the rest. Government spending is financed partly out of taxes and partly from borrowing. Firms borrow to invest. Total expenditure of $1,000 million is received by firms as sales receipts. Firms pay this out to households at the beginning of the next month.

10 times reserves, or $1,500 million. Since no hand-to-hand currency is used, the amount of money in the economy *is* the amount of bank deposits. The consolidated balance sheet of the banking system is:[4]

BANKING SYSTEM

Reserves	$ 150m	Deposits	$1,500m
Loans	1,350m		

To understand the relationship between expenditure on the Island and the quantity of money, it will prove useful to trace the economy's monthly flow of payments as they pass through the deposits of the various agents.

---

[4]Because everyone on the Island is honest and there is no uncertainty, loans are always repaid. There is therefore no need for bank equity.

STAGE 1 At the beginning of the month households have just received their monthly income payments. At that time all the Island's money is in the hands of households:[5]

BANKING SYSTEM

	Deposits	
	Households	$1,500m
	Firms	0
	Government	0

STAGE 2 Households immediately pay their taxes—$100 million. Their deposits are debited by this amount, and the government's deposit is credited.[6] The effect is:

BANKING SYSTEM

	Deposits	
	Households	$1,400m
	Firms	0
	Government	100m

STAGE 3 Next, households lend $200 million by buying $80 million in securities from the government and $120 million in securities from firms. When the checks clear, the balance sheet is:

BANKING SYSTEM

	Deposits	
	Households	$1,200m
	Firms	
	Borrowing account	120m
	Sales receipt account	0
	Government	
	Borrowing account	80m
	Tax account	100m

To help us keep track of what is going on, the government keeps its tax receipts and its borrowings in two separate accounts, and firms keep borrowings and sales receipts in two separate accounts.

---

[5]Since the banks' assets do not change during the month, we shall leave them off the next few balance sheets.

[6]Unlike the U.S. government, the government of the Island banks with a private bank rather than with the central bank. This is convenient because it eliminates some of the complications that concerned us in Chapter 20.

STAGE 4 During the month households, firms, and the government make various purchases. Households spend the remaining $700 million of their incomes on consumption, firms spend the $120 million they have borrowed on investment, and the government spends its $100 million in taxes plus the $80 million it has borrowed on a variety of worthy projects. All of this spending represents sales for one firm or another. In particular, when one firm buys, say, machinery, that purchase represents sales for some other firm. So by the end of the month total sales receipts for all the firms are $1,000 million:

BANKING SYSTEM

Deposits	
Households	$ 500m
Firms	
Borrowing account	0
Sales receipt account	1,000m
Government	
Borrowing account	0
Tax account	0

Notice that the households have not spent all the money in their deposits: Some of it will be carried over to the following month. We shall call this amount *asset balances.*[7] These asset balances will play an important role in our discussion of the relationship between the quantity of money and expenditure.

At the beginning of the following month, firms pay out again as income to households their $1,000 million in sales receipts. When the checks clear, the balance sheet of the banking system is once again as it was in Stage 1, and we are ready to begin the story all over again.

22.2 VELOCITY AND THE EQUATION OF EXCHANGE

For a given quantity of money, the faster money circulates through the economy, the greater will be total expenditure. One measure of the speed at which money circulates is called **velocity**. Velocity, V, is defined as the ratio of spending on final goods and services to the quantity of money. That is,

velocity
Speed at which money circulates in the economy.

$$V = \frac{E}{M},$$ [22.1]

[7]For simplicity, we assume that firms and government hold no asset balances.

where E is total expenditure and M is the quantity of money. On the Island M is $1,500 million and E is $1,000 million per month, so

$$V_{monthly} = \frac{\$1,000 \text{ million per month}}{\$1,500 \text{ million}} = \frac{2}{3} \text{ per month.} \qquad [22.2]$$

Velocity is the rate at which money is being spent on final goods and services. In this case, two-thirds of the total quantity of money is spent each month.[8]

Notice that velocity, like expenditure, relates to a particular unit of time. We used a month as our unit, but we could just as easily have used a year. To find *annual*, rather than monthly, velocity, all we need do is use annual, rather than monthly, expenditure. Annual expenditure is just 12 times monthly expenditure—$12 billion. So annual velocity is

$$V_{annual} = \frac{\$12,000 \text{ million per year}}{\$1,500 \text{ million}} = 8 \text{ per year.} \qquad [22.3]$$

🌴 **CHECK STATION 1** | **Calculate annual velocity for the U.S. economy. In 1989, total expenditure was $5,233 billion and the quantity of money was $798 billion. Calculate monthly velocity.**

It is customary to rearrange Equation 22.1 as

$$M \times V = E. \qquad [22.4]$$

equation of exchange
Expression of the relationship between the quantity of money and expenditure.

This equation is called the **equation of exchange**.[9] The use of this equation to express the relationship between the quantity of money and expenditure goes back at least to the seventeenth and eighteenth centuries, to writers such as John Locke, David Hume, and Richard Cantillon.

Looking at the equation, we can see that for a given quantity of money, expenditure can be greater or smaller only if velocity is greater or smaller. For example, in order for expenditure to be $1,125 million per month, velocity on the Island would have to be ¾ per month instead of ⅔:

$$\$1,500 \text{ million} \times \tfrac{3}{4} \text{ per month} = \$1,125 \text{ million per month.} \qquad [22.5]$$

We shall see that velocity depends on how people manage their holdings of money. Intuitively, if people spend or lend most of their money as soon as they receive it, and hold on to relatively little for any length of time, then money will circulate rapidly and velocity will be high. If, on the other hand, people hold large

---

[8]Money is spent in other ways too. If we count the payment of money as income at the beginning of the month, the payment of taxes, the payment of money for securities, and perhaps the payments of firms to each other for inputs used in production, then money is spent many more times than this measure of velocity suggests. However, this particular measure of velocity is the most useful because the connection between money and final expenditure is precisely what concerns us.

[9]Note that, because V is defined as the ratio of E and M, the equation of exchange is always satisfied regardless of what the values of M and E are. An equation that is always satisfied in this way is called an *identity*.

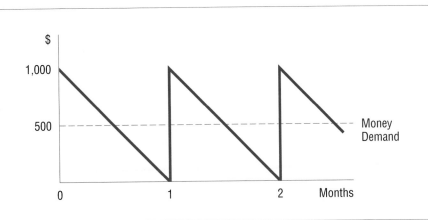

EXHIBIT 22.2

MONEY HOLDINGS OVER TIME AND MONEY DEMAND WITH MONTHLY PAYMENT

At the beginning of each month you receive a $1,000 paycheck. You spend this steadily through the month, running out of money just before your next paycheck. The average balance in your deposit—your money demand—is $500.

amounts of money for long periods of time, then money will circulate slowly and velocity will be low. To understand velocity, then, we need to take a closer look at how people manage their holdings of money.

22.3 THE DEMAND FOR MONEY

Why do you hold money? There are basically two reasons. The first is to pay for the things you buy: Money is means of payment. This reason is called the **transactions motive.** The second reason is that money is a convenient asset: Money is a store of value. This is called the **asset motive.** Let us look into each of these motives more carefully.

transactions motive
Holding money for use as means of payment.

asset motive
Holding money as a store of value.

THE TRANSACTIONS MOTIVE

You hold money to pay for your purchases. How much you hold for this reason will depend on how often you are paid, on how carefully you manage your money, and on the availability of other media of exchange that do not require immediate payment (credit cards, for example).

THE EFFECT OF FREQUENCY OF PAYMENT Let us consider the simplest possible case first. Suppose you are paid $1,000 on the first of every month and during the month you spend it all, so that by the end of the month you have nothing left. At the beginning of each month, on payday, your money balance is $1,000; at the end of each month, the day before you receive your next paycheck, it is zero. Exhibit 22.2 shows how your holdings of money change over time.

The *average* amount of money you hold is called your **demand for money,** (M^D). Since you spend at a fairly steady rate over the month, your average

demand for money (M^D)
Average amount of money held.

EXHIBIT 22.3

MONEY HOLDINGS
OVER TIME AND
MONEY DEMAND
WITH PAYMENT
TWICE A MONTH

Now you are paid twice a month: Each paycheck is for $500. If your spending habits remain the same, the average balance in your deposit will fall to half what it was—$250.

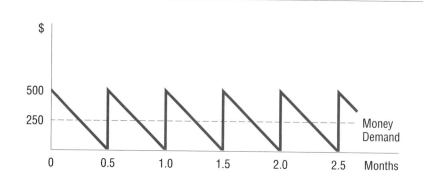

holding of money is simply the average of the beginning-of-month and end-of-month amounts:

$$M^D = \frac{\$1,000 + \$0}{2} = \$500. \qquad [22.6]$$

The pattern of your money holdings, and thus your money demand, will depend on how often you are paid. For example, if you are paid twice a month instead of once, the pattern of your money holdings will change from the one shown in Exhibit 22.2 to the one shown in Exhibit 22.3. Since you are now paid twice a month, your paycheck will be for $500 rather than for $1,000, and your average money holding—your money demand—will be

$$M^D = \frac{\$500 + \$0}{2} = \$250. \qquad [22.7]$$

The frequency with which you are paid depends on a number of things. Because there is a substantial fixed cost to preparing a payroll, your employer will prefer less frequent payments. On the other hand, you will prefer not to wait too long for your paycheck. How long you are willing to wait will depend on the cost of waiting. For example, waiting a month for your pay during the German hyperinflation (see Chapter 1) meant losing most of the value of your pay. Prices rose so rapidly that any delay in payment meant a serious reduction in the value of the money received. As a result, the payment period shortened steadily as the inflation worsened. By the end, with prices doubling daily, workers were paid twice a day—at lunchtime and again at the end of the day.

CHECK STATION 2 | **What would be your money demand if you were paid every three months?**

CASH MANAGEMENT AND OPPORTUNITY COST   During the German hyperinflation there was a considerable cost not only to waiting for money, but

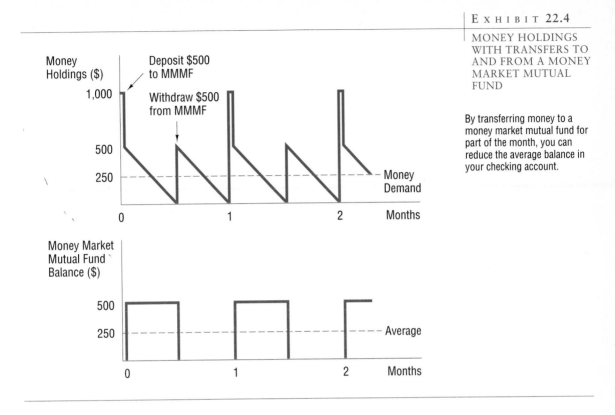

EXHIBIT 22.4

MONEY HOLDINGS WITH TRANSFERS TO AND FROM A MONEY MARKET MUTUAL FUND

By transferring money to a money market mutual fund for part of the month, you can reduce the average balance in your checking account.

also to holding it. Money that was held fell in value just as surely as did money that was owed. As a result, everyone tried to reduce their holdings of money as much as they could.

Although it is not so obvious under more normal circumstances, the cost of holding money is always there. Instead of holding money, you could be holding something that yields a higher return—for example, shares in a money market mutual fund. The return you sacrifice by holding money is its *opportunity cost*. The higher the opportunity cost, the more you will try to reduce your holdings of money.

The amount of money you hold for transactions purposes can be reduced by careful management. For example, suppose you are paid monthly, as shown in Exhibit 22.2. You can reduce the average amount of money you hold over the month by depositing $500 to a money market mutual fund at the beginning of each month and then withdrawing it in the middle of the month. Your money holdings over the month and the balance in your money market mutual fund are shown in Exhibit 22.4.

As you can see from Exhibit 22.4, managing your money holdings in this way reduces your money demand from $500 to $250. What is the reward for all this effort? You can see that the average balance in your money market mutual fund will be $250; if the fund pays a return of 10%, then you will earn $25 a year for your trouble.

In this case the effort hardly seems worthwhile: There must be easier ways to earn $25. However, two things can greatly increase the benefits of active cash management. The first is having more money to manage. Suppose, for example, that you are a corporate treasurer with average money holdings of $1 million. By reducing that amount to $500,000 in much the same way, you can earn $25,000 a year. The second thing that would make active cash management more attractive is a higher opportunity cost: The higher the return on assets other than money, the more attractive it becomes. In Chapter 9 we saw both these factors at work as rising interest rates drove corporate treasurers to seek ways to reduce their cash.

Two economists, William Baumol and James Tobin, looked at the problem of cash management mathematically.[10] How much cash should you hold for transactions purposes so as to minimize your costs? The answer turned out to be

$$M_{tr}^D = \sqrt{\frac{C \times E}{2 \times i_{oc}}}, \qquad\qquad [22.8]$$

where

C = cost of each transfer into or out of money,
E = annual expenditure (equal to annual income),
i_{oc} = opportunity cost of holding money.

For example, if the cost of each transfer into or out of money is $3, your annual expenditure is $15,000, and the opportunity cost of holding money is 10%, then the amount of money you should hold is

$$M_{tr}^D = \sqrt{\frac{\$3 \times \$15,000}{2 \times 0.10}} = \$474.$$

From Equation 22.8 you can see that there is a positive relationship between money demand and expenditure, and that there is a negative relationship between money demand and the opportunity cost of holding money (the difference between the return on money and the return on the alternative asset). There is also a positive relationship between money demand and C, the fixed cost of making a transfer into or out of money. The greater this cost, the less frequently will it be worthwhile to make transfers and the greater will be money demand.

What might affect the cost of a transfer, C? We saw some examples in Chapter 10. Banks offered corporations overnight repos, and they offered households money market deposit accounts. Both of these devices reduced the cost of

[10]William J. Baumol, "The Transactions Demand for Cash: An Inventory Theoretic Approach," *Quarterly Journal of Economics* 66 (1952), 545–556; James Tobin, "The Interest-Elasticity of the Transactions Demand for Cash," *Review of Economics and Statistics* 38 (1956), 241–247.

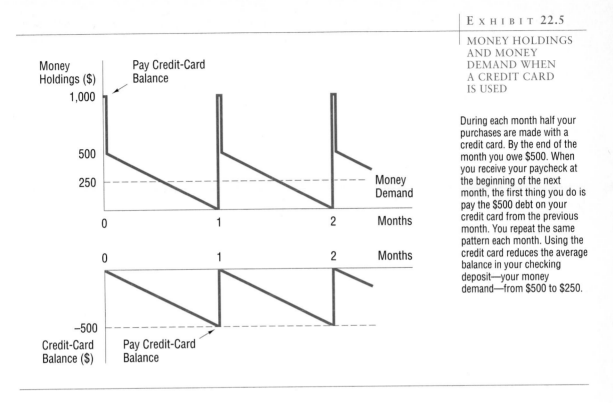

EXHIBIT 22.5

MONEY HOLDINGS AND MONEY DEMAND WHEN A CREDIT CARD IS USED

During each month half your purchases are made with a credit card. By the end of the month you owe $500. When you receive your paycheck at the beginning of the next month, the first thing you do is pay the $500 debt on your credit card from the previous month. You repeat the same pattern each month. Using the credit card reduces the average balance in your checking deposit—your money demand—from $500 to $250.

transferring into and out of money. According to the Baumol-Tobin formula, we would expect such innovations to reduce the demand for money.

Your annual income is $20,000, the cost of each transfer into or out of money is $5, and the opportunity cost of holding money is 5%. Use the Baumol-Tobin formula to calculate how much money you should hold for transactions purposes. 🌴 **CHECK STATION 3**

THE USE OF OTHER MEDIA OF EXCHANGE Money is the only means of payment, but it is not the only medium of exchange. We saw in Chapter 4 that not every purchase requires immediate payment in money: Many purchases are made on credit.

The availability of credit affects the amount of money you need to hold to carry out your normal transactions. For example, suppose you pay for half your purchases during the month with a credit card and that you must pay off your outstanding credit-card balance at the end of each month. The patterns of your money holding and of your credit-card balance are shown in Exhibit 22.5. (The credit-card balance is shown as a negative number, since it is an amount that you owe.) The credit card allows you to hold less money because it improves the synchronization of your payments and receipts. Before, you received all your income at once at the beginning of the month, but you had to pay for purchases day by day throughout the month. Now, by using your credit card, you can defer payment for half your purchases and pay for them all at once when your next income payment comes in.

🌴 **CHECK STATION 4**   **How much money would you need to hold if you could pay for *everything* with a credit card?**

MONEY AS AN ASSET

You hold money, not only to cover your planned transactions, but also as an asset—as a reserve of purchasing power. How much will you hold for this reason? We can divide this question into two parts: (1) What is the total amount of assets you will want to hold? (2) What part of that total will you want to hold as money?

In Chapter 2 we saw that there are two main reasons to save. The first is life-cycle saving to smooth consumption over your lifetime. In particular, you will save to provide for your retirement. The second reason is provision of a precautionary reserve against unplanned expenses or fluctuations in income. You will want a reserve to protect you in case of unemployment or illness or to allow you to take advantage of business or leisure opportunities that may crop up.

The amount of assets you accumulate will depend on your lifetime income. The greater this is, the more you will save. The amount you save will also depend on the rate of return the assets earn. A higher rate of return will make saving more attractive, but it will also reduce the *need* to save: You need to put away less now to provide the same amount in the future. So the net effect is unclear. Increased uncertainty or insecurity should increase the amount of precautionary assets you want to hold.

How much of your wealth will you want to hold as money? In deciding between alternative assets, the main considerations are safety, expected return, and liquidity. Money is safe (because of deposit insurance) and liquid, but its expected return is relatively low.

precautionary motive
Holding money for use for unanticipated expenditures.

THE PRECAUTIONARY MOTIVE   For the assets you hold as a precautionary reserve, liquidity is particularly important. You need to be able to turn them into cash rapidly without loss. Money narrowly defined, M1, is the most liquid of assets: It may be spent directly. Anything else has to be turned into cash first. However, if other assets offer a higher return, you may be willing to sacrifice a little liquidity. Time deposits and money market mutual funds, included in M2, are almost as liquid as money and offer a substantially higher return. The holding of money as part of precautionary reserves is called the **precautionary motive** for holding money.

How much of your precautionary reserves you hold in the form of money and how much you hold in other forms will depend on *relative yields*—on the *difference* between respective rates of return. To see how this works, let us look at an example.

Your checking account will probably be a NOW account that pays something like 5%. A fairly close alternative is an MMDA (money market deposit account), which pays a rate of interest that fluctuates with market rates. The MMDA allows limited checking—a minimum amount for each check, say, $500, and a limited number of checks each month, say three—so it is not quite as liquid as the NOW account.

Suppose you have accumulated $5,000 in your NOW account above what you need for your regular expenses (that is, you have about $5,000 left in your account at the end of each month). Should you transfer the $5,000 to the MMDA? Suppose the yield on the MMDA is 7%. If you transfer the $5,000, you will earn an extra

$$\$5,000 \times (0.07 - 0.05) = \$100$$

per year. This may not seem worth the trouble. Suppose, however, that market rates go up and the yield on the MMDA increases to 12%. Now the potential gain is

$$\$5,000 \times (0.12 - 0.05) = \$350,$$

which may make the effort worthwhile.

LONG-TERM ASSETS AND THE SPECULATIVE MOTIVE For the assets you hold long term—principally your life-cycle savings—liquidity is much less important than yield. Since you do not expect to draw on these assets for a long time, you are not concerned about your ability to turn them into cash rapidly. Money would therefore seem to be an unattractive long-term asset.

There are circumstances, however, in which you might want to hold some of your long-term assets as money. To see why, suppose that your life-cycle savings are in the form of a defined contribution pension fund. The fund offers three investment options—a stock fund, a bond fund, and a money market fund. You are allowed to split your contributions as you please among the three funds, and you are allowed to shift accumulated amounts between funds. You have decided to split your $3,000 annual contribution fifty-fifty between stocks and bonds, and you have so far accumulated about $20,000 in each. Because of its lower average yield, you have not invested anything in the money market fund.

Suppose now that interest rates start to rise and that you believe the trend may continue. If so, the market value of your stocks and bonds will fall. To protect yourself against this possible capital loss, you move $10,000 out of each of your stock and bond funds and into the money market fund: The market value of money market securities is much less sensitive to changes in interest rates.

Although the money market fund is not part of M1, it is part of M2. So your action has increased your holding of broadly defined money. This motive for holding money—protection from capital loss on long-term assets as a result of a rise in interest rates—is called the **speculative motive.**

speculative motive
Holding money for use as protection from capital loss on long-term assets.

EXHIBIT 22.6

FACTORS THAT
AFFECT MONEY
DEMAND

Factor	Effect on Holding of Money for:		
	Transactions Motive	Precautionary Motive	Speculative Motive (mainly M2)
Increase in wealth		Increase	
Increase in spending	Increase		
Improvement in payments technology	Decrease		
Increase in opportunity cost of holding money	Decrease	Decrease	
Expectation of rise in interest rates or increase in uncertainty about them			Increase

This theory of the speculative motive was first developed by Keynes in the 1930s.[11] It was later refined by James Tobin.[12] In Keynes's version, the speculative demand is an all-or-nothing proposition: If you do not expect interest rates to rise, you hold no money at all for this reason. Tobin argued that *uncertainty* about the direction of interest rates would be enough to make people want to hold some of their assets in the form of money, as a kind of insurance. A well-diversified portfolio should include some cash assets as protection against interest-rate risk. If you followed Tobin's advice, you might hold some of your pension assets in the money market fund on a regular basis, perhaps increasing the proportion when you thought interest rates might rise or when uncertainty about interest rates increased.

THE DEMAND FOR MONEY

Let us summarize the reasons that people hold money. There is a *transactions motive* and an *asset motive*. We have further divided the asset motive into *precautionary* and *speculative* elements. The amount held for transactions purposes will depend on the amount of spending planned and on the opportunity cost of holding money. The amount held for asset purposes will depend on wealth and on opportunity cost. (In both cases, the opportunity cost is the difference between the yield on money and the yield on other fairly liquid assets.) The effects of various changes on money demand are shown in Exhibit 22.6.

It is customary and useful to divide up the amount of money held according to the various motives for holding it. The division is artificial, of course, because

---

[11]John Maynard Keynes, *A Treatise on Money* (1930) and *The General Theory of Employment, Interest, and Money* (1936).

[12]James Tobin, "Liquidity Preference as Behavior Towards Risk," *Review of Economic Studies* 25 (1958), 65–86.

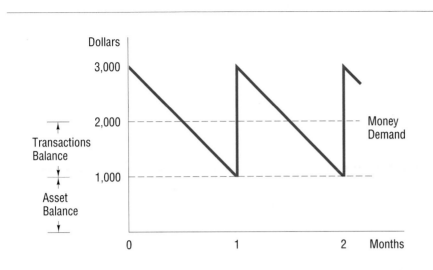

EXHIBIT 22.7

ASSET BALANCES, TRANSACTIONS BALANCES, AND MONEY DEMAND

The balance in your checking account varies from $3,000 on payday to $1,000 at the end of the month. Your average balance of $2,000—your money demand—may be divided conceptually into a $1,000 asset balance and a $1,000 transactions balance.

the same dollar can perform more than one function at once: It may be held as part of a precautionary reserve, but its presence will make cash management that much easier. Nonetheless, our discussion will be simpler if we divide money holdings this way into transactions balances, held for transactions motives, and asset balances, held for asset motives. That is,

$$\text{money demand} = \text{transactions balance} + \text{asset balance}. \qquad [22.9]$$

To see how we can make this division, suppose the balance in your checking account behaves as in Exhibit 22.7. The balance varies over the month between $3,000 and $1,000. At the beginning of each month you receive an income payment of $2,000 that you spend during the month, and you carry over an additional $1,000 from month to month. Your money demand—your average money holding—is $2,000.[13] We can divide this conceptually into a $1,000 asset balance (the $1,000 that remains from month to month) and a $1,000 transactions balance (the average amount of a balance that fluctuates between $2,000 and zero). *Note that the division is purely conceptual.* Your transactions balance and your asset balance are not held separately: Both are included in the same checking account.

---

[13]Remember that we are assuming that no one uses currency directly. If you held currency as well as a checking account, we would have to include it as part of your money demand.

E X H I B I T 22.8

MONEY BALANCES
OVER TIME

At the beginning of each month
firms pay households $1,000
million in income—the amount
of the previous month's sales
receipts. During the month
households, the government,
and the firms that have
borrowed spend this $1,000
million so that it finds its way
back into firms' sales receipt
accounts. It is then paid out
again as income.

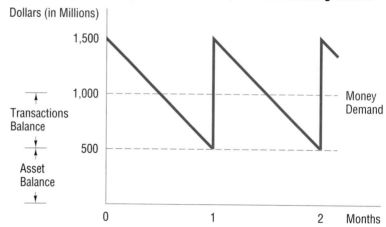

Spenders' Deposits: Households, Government, and Firm Borrowing Account

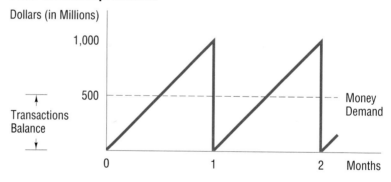

Firms' Sales Receipt Accounts

|22.4| VELOCITY AND THE DEMAND FOR MONEY

Having examined the various factors that affect money demand, we are now
ready to go back to the connection between money demand and velocity.

THE AGGREGATE DEMAND FOR MONEY

Exhibit 22.8 shows the behavior over time of money balances on the Island. The
upper panel shows the behavior of deposits held by spenders—household deposits, government deposits, and firms' borrowing-account deposits all added together. The lower panel shows the behavior of the sales receipt accounts of firms

into which all spending flows. At the beginning of each month, households hold all $1,500 million of the Island's money. Then $100 million in taxes and $200 million in lending are paid into the deposits of other spenders (this has no effect on the diagram). During the month the spenders—households, government, and firms that have borrowed—spend $1,000 million. This amount finds its way into the sales receipt accounts of firms. At the beginning of the next month, the whole amount is paid out again to households.

We can therefore divide all of the money on the Island into transactions balances and asset balances. The upper panel shows that spenders hold an average of $500 million in transactions balances. These transactions balances fall from $1,000 million at the beginning of the month to zero at the end of the month. Firms, in their sales receipt accounts, hold an average of $500 million in transactions balances. These rise from zero at the beginning of the month to $1,000 million at the end of the month. As the transactions balances in the upper panel fall, those in the lower panel rise. There is therefore always a total of $1,000 million in transactions balances. In addition, households hold an extra $500 million in asset balances (on the Island, firms and government hold no asset balances).

The average money holdings of all economic agents on the Island—the sum of all transactions and all asset balances—is called the **aggregate demand for money.** Since all the money in existence must be held by *someone* at all times, *the aggregate demand for money must equal the total amount of money in existence.* We can verify that this is true for the Island:

aggregate demand for money
Average money holdings for all economic agents.

$$\text{total quantity of money} = \text{aggregate demand for money} \qquad [22.10]$$
$$\text{\$1,500m} \qquad\qquad\qquad \text{\$1,500m}$$

$$= \text{transactions balances} + \text{asset balances.}$$
$$\text{\$1,000m} \qquad\qquad \text{\$500m}$$

We can think of the aggregate demand for money as being determined by the same sort of factors that determine the money demand of individual agents. A particularly simple formulation of the aggregate demand for money is the one suggested by Keynes:[14]

$$M^D = kE + f\,(i - i_M)\,W. \qquad [22.11]$$

This formulation makes two assumptions: (1) Transactions balances are proportional to expenditure with k the constant of proportionality.[15] (2) Asset balances

---

[14]Other economists have suggested other formulations, as we shall see in Chapter 27.

[15]More generally, k could depend on the opportunity cost of holding money and on the transactions technology. Expenditure here is expenditure on final goods and services produced in the current period. It might reasonably be argued that the demand for transactions balances will depend on *all* transactions—including those involving financial assets, goods used in the process of production, and goods not currently produced (real estate, used cars, yard sales, etc.). However, if the ratio of total transactions to those involving final goods and services remains fairly constant, then no harm is done by using the latter instead of the former. A change in the ratio would simply change k.

are proportional to wealth, W, with the proportion a decreasing function of the opportunity cost of holding money: f decreases with an increase in the difference between the market rate of interest, i, and the yield on money, i_M.[16]

Using the Keynesian money demand formulation, Equation 22.10 becomes

$$M = kE + f (i - i_M) W. \qquad [22.12]$$

The total quantity of money may be divided into transactions balances, which are proportional to expenditure, and asset balances, which are proportional to wealth, the proportion depending on the relative yield on money.

MONEY DEMAND IN THE CIRCULAR FLOW MODEL

Exhibit 22.9 shows how money demand can be integrated into the simple circular flow model of Exhibit 22.1. On the right of the exhibit we see that the quantity of money on the Island, $1,500 million, may be divided between $1,000 million in transactions balances and $500 million in asset balances.

For the Island economy there is a particularly simple relationship between total expenditure for the month and transactions balances (both highlighted in Exhibit 22.9): The two are equal. (In terms of the Keynesian money demand formulation, the constant k is 1.) Unfortunately, this direct relationship between transactions balances and total expenditure does not hold true for the U.S. economy: It is the result of the peculiarly simple structure of the Island economy. However, a somewhat more indirect relationship does hold true. Money demand determines velocity, and velocity is related, through the equation of exchange, to total expenditure.

THE CONNECTION BETWEEN VELOCITY AND MONEY DEMAND

We can see the connection between velocity and money demand by comparing Equation 22.12 with Equation 22.4:

$$M \times V = E. \qquad [22.4]$$

[16]More generally, uncertainty about i could be an argument in f.

EXHIBIT 22.9

THE CIRCULAR FLOW OF PAYMENTS AND MONEY BALANCES FOR THE ISLAND ECONOMY (IN MILLIONS OF DOLLARS)

The $1,500 million of money that is used on the Island may be divided into $1,000 million in transactions balances and $500 million in asset balances. The amount of transactions balances exactly equals the total amount of expenditure.

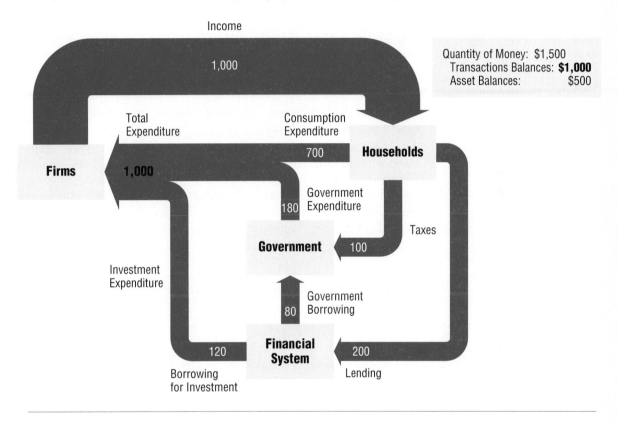

The relationship between the two equations becomes clearer if we rearrange Equation 22.12 to obtain[17]

$$M \times \frac{1}{k} \left[1 - f(i - i_M) \frac{W}{M} \right] = E. \qquad [22.13]$$

[17]Take $f(i - i_M) W$ over to the left-hand side to give

$$M - f(i - i_M) W = kE.$$

Now multiply and divide $f(i - i_M) W$ by M to give

$$M - f(i - i_M)W \times \frac{M}{M} = M \times \left[1 - f(i - i_M) \frac{W}{M} \right] = kE.$$

Finally, divide both sides by k to obtain Equation 22.13.

The expression multiplying M on the left-hand side of Equation 22.13 must equal whatever multiplies M on the left-hand side of Equation 22.4—that is, it must equal velocity. Therefore

$$V = \frac{1}{k}\left[1 - f(i - i_M)\frac{W}{M}\right]. \qquad [22.14]$$

From Equation 22.14 we can see that the same factors that affect money demand also affect velocity too, and we can see how they do so.

1. Anything that increases k reduces velocity. Remember that k is the ratio between transactions balances and expenditure. An improvement in transactions technology, for example, will reduce k and increase velocity.

2. An increase in the opportunity cost of holding money, $i - i_M$, decreases $f(i - i_M)$ (decreasing asset balances) and causes velocity to increase. The Keynesian money demand formulation assumes that k does not depend on the opportunity cost of holding money. However, if it did, an increase in the opportunity cost of holding money would cause k to fall, and this too would increase velocity, reinforcing the effect through asset balances.

3. An increase in wealth would increase the demand for asset balances, and this would reduce velocity.

22.5 | APPLICATION: THE BEHAVIOR OF VELOCITY IN THE U.S. ECONOMY

We can use the ideas we have developed in this chapter to understand the behavior of velocity in the U.S. economy over the years. Exhibit 22.10 shows velocity in the U.S. economy from 1915 to 1989. Velocity is defined as the ratio of M1 to annual expenditure on final goods and services.

We can explain some of the movements in velocity in terms of the factors we have been discussing. For example, velocity fell during the Depression as the opportunity cost of holding money fell and as rising uncertainty increased the precautionary demand for money. We saw in Chapter 9 that the opportunity cost of holding money rose steadily after World War II and that firms, and eventually households, increasingly found ways to reduce their money demand (through improvements in the transactions technology such as credit cards and overnight repos). As Exhibit 22.10 shows, velocity rose steadily throughout the period. In the 1980s the opportunity cost of holding money fell sharply as banks were allowed to pay interest on certain types of checking deposits; the result was a fall in velocity.

EXHIBIT 22.10

VELOCITY 1915–1989

SUMMARY

- The relationship between the quantity of money and expenditure depends on the speed at which money circulates through the economy, that is, on the velocity of money. Velocity, in turn, depends on the way that firms and households manage their money balances.

- Velocity is defined as the ratio of expenditure per unit of time to the quantity of money. Velocity is defined for the same unit of time as expenditure.

- The equation of exchange states that expenditure equals the quantity of money times velocity.

- Money is held for two reasons: as a means of payment (the transactions motive) and as a store of value (the asset motive).

- The amount of money held for transactions purposes depends on the frequency of payment and on the effort devoted to cash management. Both these depend in turn on the opportunity cost of holding money. The amount held also depends on the availability of other media of exchange.

- The amount of money held as an asset depends on the total amount of assets held and on the relative attractiveness of money relative to other assets.

- The asset motive may be subdivided into a precautionary and a speculative motive. Money is an attractive precautionary asset because of its liquidity. It is not generally attractive as a long-term asset because of its low relative return. Broadly defined money may sometimes be held in long-term portfolios, however, because it is less liable to interest-rate risk than assets of longer maturity.

- A person's demand for money is that person's average holding of money. Money demand may be divided conceptually into balances held for transactions purposes and balances held for asset purposes.

- The aggregate demand for money equals the total quantity of money in existence. It may be divided conceptually into transactions balances and asset balances.

- Anything that changes the demand for money also changes velocity. For example, an increase in wealth increases the demand for asset balances, and this reduces velocity.

KEY TERMS

velocity	asset motive	speculative motive
equation of exchange	demand for money (M^D)	aggregate demand for money
transactions motive	precautionary motive	

DISCUSSION QUESTION

What effect would each of the following events have on transactions balances, asset balances, and the velocity of money? Explain.

a. Credit cards become increasingly popular.

b. Deregulation allows the payment of interest on checking accounts.

c. Banks offer cash management services to corporations.

d. Teller machines make it easier to move money between checking deposits and time deposits.

e. A stock market crash makes investors wary of investing in stocks.

BIBLIOGRAPHY

Bordo, Michael D., "Equation of Exchange," in *The New Palgrave: Money,* edited by John Eatwell, Murray Milgate, and Peter Newman, New York: Norton, 1989.

Fisher, Irving, *The Purchasing Power of Money*, New York: MacMillan, 1911.

Laidler, David, *The Demand for Money: Theories, Evidence, and Problems,* 3rd ed., New York: Harper & Row, 1985.

CHAPTER 23

MONEY, PRICES, AND INTEREST RATES IN THE LONG RUN

We have seen that the Fed has the power to regulate the quantity of money. To know how the Fed should use this power, we need to know how changes in the quantity of money affect the economy. We shall divide our discussion into two parts: (1) the short-run effects of a change in the quantity of money and (2) the long-run effects. For example, suppose we want to know the effect of an open market operation on interest rates. The short-run question is: What happens to interest rates immediately and over the next few weeks or months? The long-run question is: What is the *ultimate* effect on interest rates once the economy has had time to adjust completely, say, after several years?

Answering the long-run question is easier, so that is where we shall begin. In this chapter we shall use the Quantity Theory of Money to understand the long-run effects of a monetary change on prices, interest rates, quantities of goods traded, and velocity. In the following chapters we shall take up the more difficult issue of the short-run effects. Much of our discussion will be in terms of the fictional economy of the South Seas island. This will enable us to abstract from some of the complexities of the real world and to get a clearer view of the underlying principles.

23.1 THE QUANTITY THEORY OF MONEY

The distinction between the short-run and long-run effects of changes in the quantity of money goes back at least to 1752, to an essay by David Hume. The basic idea is simple. An increase in the quantity of money disturbs the economy. All sorts of changes may occur: Interest rates may fall, for example, or the pace of economic activity may quicken.[1] Eventually, however, the disturbance will pass, and the economy will adjust to possessing a larger quantity of money. Once that has happened, interest rates and the pace of economic activity will return to normal. The only lasting effect will be on prices: Prices will increase in proportion to the increase in the quantity of money. This view of the long-run effects of an increase in the quantity of money is known as the **Quantity Theory of Money.**[2]

Quantity Theory of Money
Theory of the long-run effects of an increase in the quantity of money.

The easiest way to state the Quantity Theory is in terms of the *equation of exchange* that we developed in Chapter 22. The equation of exchange shows that total expenditure over a period of time equals the quantity of money times the velocity per period of time:

$$M \times V = E, \tag{23.1}$$

where

M = the quantity of money ($1,500 million on the Island),
V = velocity per period (2/3 per month),
E = total expenditure per period ($1,000 million per month).

To apply the Quantity Theory, we need to break down total expenditure into its constituent parts. For example, $2 million of the $1,000 million total monthly expenditure is spent on bread. The price is $1 per loaf, and two million loaves are sold each month. Another $100,000 is spent on bicycles. The price of a bicycle is $100, and 1,000 new bicycles are sold each month. We can therefore break down expenditure as follows:

$$E = p_1 y_1 + p_2 y_2 + \cdots + p_{2,007} y_{2,007}, \tag{23.2}$$

where

p_1 = the price of bread ($1),
y_1 = the quantity of bread sold each month (2 million loaves),
p_2 = the price of a bicycle ($100),
y_2 = the number of bicycles sold each month (1,000),

and so on, for each of the 2,007 different goods sold on the Island.

Using Equation 23.2 to substitute for E in Equation 23.1, the latter may be rewritten

$$MV = p_1 y_1 + p_2 y_2 + \cdots + p_{2,007} y_{2,007}. \tag{23.3}$$

In terms of Equation 23.3, the question we are asking is: When the economy has fully adjusted to a change in M, how will the other variables in the equation have

---

[1]We shall look at these short-run effects in Chapters 24 through 27.

[2]This version of the Quantity Theory is often called the *Classical* Quantity Theory to distinguish it from the Modern Quantity Theory of Milton Friedman, which is a theory of the short-run effects of changes in the quantity of money. We shall look at the Modern Quantity Theory in Chapter 27.

changed? It is obvious that some or all of them must indeed change: If V, the p's, and the y's all stayed the same while M changed, the equation would no longer balance.

The Quantity Theory asserts that a change in the quantity of money will ultimately have no effect on velocity or on the quantities of goods traded; the only effect will be a proportional change in all the prices. That is, V and the y's will be the same, and all the p's will change in proportion to M.

For example, if M increases tenfold—from \$1.5 billion to \$15 billion—in the long run all the prices will increase tenfold, and no other variable will change. That is, the variables in the equation of exchange will change from

Before: \$1.5b × 2/3 = \$1.0b = \$1 × 2m + \$100 × 1,000 + · · ·

to

After: \$15b × 2/3 = \$10b = \$10 × 2m + \$1,000 × 1,000 + · · · ,

so that for each of the 2,007 goods sold on the Island, the price is ten times what it was and the quantity sold is unchanged.

If the quantity of money on the Island were halved, what would be the long-run effect on the variables that appear in the equation of exchange? | 🌴 **CHECK STATION 1**

23.2 THE LOGIC BEHIND THE QUANTITY THEORY

The Quantity Theory is so basic a proposition, and so central to our discussion, that we need to understand the logic behind it. That logic rests on the distinction between nominal and real variables—nominal and real prices, nominal and real interest rates, and nominal and real money balances.

NOMINAL AND REAL PRICES

Exhibit 23.1A shows the prices of a number of goods before the above tenfold increase in the quantity of money. Exhibit 23.1B shows the prices of the same goods, as predicted by the Quantity Theory, long after the process of adjustment to the increase in the quantity of money is over and everything is stable again. The second column of each table lists the **nominal price**, or money price, of each good. The nominal price is what we normally think of as *the* price: It is what we see marked on price tags. In accordance with the Quantity Theory, the nominal prices in Exhibit 23.1B are ten times those in Exhibit 23.1A.

Although the nominal price is the one we see on price tags, it is not the relevant price for making economic decisions. For example, when you are deciding whether or not to buy a bicycle, what matters is not the amount of

nominal price
Price measured in terms of dollars, as distinct from real price, which is measured in opportunity cost.

dollars you pay, but the sacrifice involved. One way to measure that sacrifice is in terms of the hours of work required to earn the money you need to pay for the bicycle. From Exhibit 23.1A we see that before the change 20 hours of work are required. Another way to measure the sacrifice is in terms of the *opportunity cost*— the other goods you could have bought instead. From Exhibit 23.1A the opportunity cost of a bicycle is 100 loaves of bread (what you pay for a bicycle would buy 100 loaves of bread) or one-fiftieth of a canoe. These various measures of sacrifice are alternative but equivalent estimates of the **real price**.

real price
Price in terms of opportunity cost.

If, as the Quantity Theory suggests, nominal prices are all ten times higher after the increase in M, then *real* prices are exactly the same. If the price of a bicycle is $1,000 instead of $100, but your wage is $50 an hour instead of $5, you will still have to work 20 hours to pay for a bicycle.

🌴 CHECK STATION 2   **What are the real prices, in terms of bicycles, of bread, and of canoes before and after the monetary change?**

Since real prices are the same, and since economic decisions are made on the basis of real prices, all economic decisions are the same. For example, in deciding whether or not to buy a bicycle, consumers base their decision on its real price. If before the change, at a real price of 20 hours of work, consumers wished to buy 1,000 bicycles a month, then after the change, at the same real price, they will still wish to buy 1,000 bicycles a month. Similarly, in deciding how many bicycles to make, producers also base their decisions on the real price. If before the change, at a real price of 20 hours of work, producers manufactured 1,000 bicycles a month, then after the change, at the same real price, they will still manufacture 1,000 bicycles a month.

Consequently, if before the change the supply and demand for bicycles are in equilibrium at a real price of 20 hours of work and a quantity of 1,000 bicycles a month, then after the change supply and demand should still be in equilibrium at the same real price and at the same quantity. The tenfold increase in all nominal prices should make no difference. Similarly, in all other markets equilibrium real prices and quantities should be the same.

From this we can see that the predictions of the Quantity Theory for prices and quantities are mutually consistent. The prediction that all prices increase proportionally is consistent with the prediction that the quantities of goods traded—the y's in the equation of exchange—remain unchanged.

NOMINAL AND REAL INTEREST RATES

One price that warrants special attention is the interest rate. We saw in Chapter 2 that the interest rate is the (rental) price of loanable funds. What does the Quantity Theory have to say about this particular price?

EXHIBIT 23.1A

NOMINAL AND REAL PRICES BEFORE THE CHANGE IN M

Good	Nominal Price	Real Price (Wage assumed to be $5/hour)
Bread	$1	1/5 hour of labor
Bicycle	$100	20 hours of labor
Canoe	$5,000	6 months of labor (1,000 hours)

EXHIBIT 23.1B

NOMINAL AND REAL PRICES AFTER THE CHANGE IN M

Good	Money Price	Real Price (Wage assumed to be $50/hour)
Bread	$10	1/5 hour of labor
Bicycle	$1,000	20 hours of labor
Canoe	$50,000	6 months of labor (1,000 hours)

We should begin by distinguishing between the *nominal interest rate* and the *real interest rate*. The **nominal interest rate** is the ratio of money interest paid on a loan to the amount of money lent. For example, if you lend $100 for a year and are repaid $110, then the nominal interest rate is 10%. All the interest rates we have talked about until now have been nominal interest rates. Nominal interest rates are the ones we actually observe in markets.

nominal interest rate
Interest rate measured in money terms.

The **real interest** rate measures the rental price of the loan, not in terms of money, but in terms of *purchasing power*. Suppose, for example, that prices double between the time the loan is made and the time it is repaid a year later, so that the wage is $5 at the beginning of the year and $10 at the end of it. In terms of purchasing power, the $100 you lent was, when you lent it, the equivalent of 20 hours of work. The $110 dollars you are repaid, however, is worth only the equivalent of $110/$10 = 11 hours of work. The real interest rate, r, is the return on your loan calculated in real terms—in terms of hours of work lent and hours of work repaid. That is,

real interest rate
Interest rate measured in terms of purchasing power.

$$1 + r = \frac{11}{20} = 0.55. \qquad [23.4]$$

That is, the real interest rate is -45%. Although you are repaid 10% more money than you lent (the nominal interest rate), it is worth 45% *less* in terms of what it will buy (the real interest rate).

We can express the relationship between nominal and real interest rates in terms of the rate at which prices change between the beginning of the year and the end of the year. Let us define the **inflation rate**, n, as the percentage change in prices over the year. For example, if prices double the inflation rate is 100% and $n = 1.0$. The relationship between the nominal interest rate, i, and the real interest rate is then

inflation rate
Percentage change in prices over a period of time.

$$1 + r = \frac{1 + i}{1 + n} \,. \qquad\qquad [23.5]$$

For our example,

$$1 + r = \frac{1 + 0.1}{1 + 1.0} = 0.55. \qquad\qquad [23.6]$$

In general, we can see from Equation 23.5 that if prices are rising (n is positive), the real interest rate will be less than the nominal interest rate. If prices are falling (n is negative), the real interest rate will be greater than the nominal interest rate. And if prices stay the same (n is zero), the real interest rate will be the same as the nominal interest rate.[3]

🌴 **CHECK STATION 3** | **If the nominal interest rate is 7%, what is the real interest rate if inflation is 5%? If it is –5%? If it is 0%?**

Just as, in general, economic decisions depend on real rather than nominal prices, so do they depend, in particular, on real rather than nominal interest rates. For example, the decisions of those supplying and demanding loanable funds are made in terms of the real rather than the nominal interest rate.

Let us therefore look at the loanable funds market on our fictional South Seas island before and after the tenfold increase in money. Consider one particular lender—call her Janet. Before the change, given her income of $1,000 a month and the market interest rate of 20%, Janet is willing to lend (to save) $100 a month. She makes her decision in real terms. Her income in real terms is the equivalent of 200 hours of work (at the prevailing wage of $5 an hour). Since prices stay the same from month to month (n is zero), the real interest rate is the same as the nominal interest rate—20%. At this real interest rate, Janet is willing to lend the equivalent of 20 hours of work, which is $100. Other lenders and borrowers make their decisions in a similar way. At a real interest rate of 20%, total lending in the economy equals total borrowing and the loanable funds market is in equilibrium.

Long after the monetary change, when everything has settled down again, Janet's income is $10,000 a month in dollars, but it is still the equivalent of the same 200 hours of work in real terms (at a wage now of $50 an hour). At a real interest rate of 20%, Janet is still willing to lend the equivalent of 20 hours of

---

[3]We shall have more to say about Equation 23.6 in Chapter 28, when we discuss the causes and consequences of inflation.

work: In dollars this now amounts to $1,000. Other lenders and borrowers find themselves in similar situations: At a real interest rate of 20%, they will be willing to lend or borrow the same amounts as before in real terms and ten times as much in dollars. So if the loanable funds market was in equilibrium before at a real interest rate of 20%, it will be in equilibrium now at a real interest rate of 20%. The total amounts borrowed and lent will be the same in real terms (equivalents of hours of work) but ten times as much in dollars.

How about the nominal interest rate—the rate we actually observe in the market? Clearly, if prices eventually increase tenfold, there must be a period of time during which they are rising from month to month. During that period real and nominal interest rates will differ. However, in the long run, *after* this period of adjustment, *prices are once again stable from month to month*. Then n is once again zero, and the nominal interest rate again equals the real interest rate. Therefore, if the real interest rate is 20%, so too is the nominal interest rate.

The Quantity Theory predicts that a monetary change will leave real quantities of goods bought and sold unchanged in the long run and will cause prices to rise proportionally. If so, there should be no change in the real amount of loanable funds lent, in the real rate of interest, or in the nominal rate of interest. The dollar amount of loanable funds lent will change proportionally with nominal prices.

NOMINAL AND REAL MONEY BALANCES

The Quantity Theory predicts that a once-and-for-all change in the quantity of money will have no ultimate effect on velocity. To understand why, we need to look at the demand for money: As we saw in Chapter 22, that is what determines velocity. Let us see what happens, respectively, to the demand for transactions balances and to the demand for asset balances.

The demand for transactions balances depends on expenditure (on the volume of transactions to be undertaken) and on the way cash balances are managed. According to the Quantity Theory, expenditure will, in the long run, increase in proportion to the change in the quantity of money: Real transactions will be as before, and all nominal prices will change in proportion to the change in the quantity of money. Hence if before the tenfold increase in M you received $1,000 in income and spent it all during the month, then after things have fully adjusted you will receive $10,000 in income and spend it all during the month.

The amount of transactions balances depends not only on expenditure but also on how payments are made and on how cash is managed. For example, as we saw in Chapter 22, if you receive your income twice a month rather than once a month, your transactions balance will be halved. Or if you switch funds back and forth between your checking deposit and a money market mutual fund, you can reduce your transactions balance. However, payments practices and cash management are determined by real costs. If, as the Quantity Theory suggests, real costs are not affected, then payments practices and cash management will remain the same. Hence transactions balances will rise in proportion to expenditure and prices.[4]

Asset balances depend on wealth and on opportunity cost. Real wealth is unchanged (wealth in dollars is ten times greater); real opportunity cost is unchanged (interest rates are the same). Thus if asset balances are proportional to wealth, in a proportion that depends on opportunity cost, then asset balances too will increase in proportion to prices. If prices increase tenfold, asset balances will also increase tenfold.

Since both transactions balances and asset balances increase in proportion to the increase in money and in prices, total money demand increases in proportion too. We can distinguish between *nominal balances* and *real balances*. The **nominal balance** is the amount of money held, in dollars. The **real balance** is the amount held, measured not in dollars, but in terms of purchasing power—in terms of what the money will buy. In the long run, as a result of a change in the quantity of money, nominal balances increase in proportion to the increase in prices, but real balances remain unchanged.

For example, suppose that Frank holds an average of $1,000 in his checking deposit before the monetary change. When we observe him again much later, after prices have increased tenfold, we find that he now holds an average of $10,000. Frank's *nominal* balance has increased tenfold, but his *real* balance is just the same as it was before. According to Exhibit 23.1A, the $1,000 he holds before the change will buy 1,000 loaves of bread or 10 bicycles; according to Exhibit 23.1B, the $10,000 that he holds after the change will buy exactly the same thing—1,000 loaves of bread or 10 bicycles. Thus Frank's real balance is unaltered.[5]

Since the *real* demand for money, both for transactions and for asset purposes, is unchanged, so too is velocity.

CONCLUSIONS

The conclusions of the Quantity Theory about the long-run effects of a change in the quantity of money, M, on real and on nominal variables are summarized in Exhibit 23.2.

The general rule is that real variables are unchanged and that nominal variables are scaled up in proportion to the change in M. Money is that unit of

nominal balance
Amount of money held measured in dollars.

real balance
Amount of money held measured in purchasing power.

---

[4]This can be illustrated with the Baumol-Tobin formula, Equation 22.8. Both C and E increase tenfold (real cost and real expenditure are the same, but prices are up tenfold), and i_{OC} is the same. Hence the demand for money for transactions purposes increases tenfold.

[5]We can illustrate this with the Keynesian money demand formulation (Equation 22.11):

$$M^D = kE + f(i - i_M) W,$$

where k is a constant that depends on the real costs of cash management, W is wealth, and f is a decreasing function of the opportunity cost of holding money. The constant k is unchanged. Since i and i_M are unchanged, so is $f(i - i_M)$. W and E increase in proportion to the increase in prices. As a result, M^D increases in proportion to the increase in prices. Since nominal money demand increases in proportion to prices, real money demand is unaltered.

	Real	Nominal
Prices of goods and services	No change	Change in proportion to change in M
Quantities of goods and services	No change	—
Money demand	No change	Change in proportion to change in M
Interest rates	No change	No change

EXHIBIT 23.2

THE LONG-RUN EFFECT OF A CHANGE IN M

account—the measuring stick of value. The increase in M changes the length of the measuring stick. Therefore measurements of value, such as dollar prices, have to change in proportion. If $10 now represents the same amount of value as $1 did before, then prices in dollars will have to be 10 times what they were then.

Nominal interest rates, however, do not change. The reason is that the interest rate is a *ratio* of money values—money interest received over sum of money lent. If both money interest and sum of money lent increase tenfold, then the nominal interest rate stays the same. However, as we have seen, if prices *continue* to rise, the nominal interest rate will differ from the real interest rate. We shall discuss prices that continue to rise—*inflation*—in Chapter 28.

The Quantity Theory tells us that prices will eventually change in proportion to the change in the quantity of money. It does not tell us how or why this will happen. What makes prices change? To get an answer, we shall have to look at the short-run effects of a monetary change. That will be our goal in Chapters 24 through 27.

23.3 APPLICATION: GERMAN MONETARY UNION

The Quantity Theory is a simple, rather abstract idea. Nonetheless, it can be useful in discussing policy problems in the real world. An interesting example is provided by the monetary union of East Germany and West Germany that took place in July 1990.

Before monetary union, East Germany and West Germany had separate economies and used different currencies. East Germans used ostmarks; West Germans used deutsche marks. The economies were to be unified, and the unified economy was to use deutsche marks only. As a preliminary to unification, ostmarks were to be converted into deutsche marks. The question was: At what rate? That is, when East Germans exchange their ostmarks, how many deutsche marks should they receive?

The two Germanys agreed that East Germans would each be able to convert up to 4,000 ostmarks one for one, and any further amount two for one. Many considerations, both political and economic, played a role in this decision. One of the major economic considerations was the effect the conversion would have on the level of prices in the unified economy. The Quantity Theory provided a useful guide as to what that effect was likely to be.

Suppose the volume of real transactions in East Germany was about one-tenth of that in West Germany, so that the unified economy would have about 10% more real transactions than West Germany alone before unification. Suppose, too, that velocity in the unified economy would be about the same as it had been in West Germany. Then the Quantity Theory tells us that in order for prices in the unified economy to be the same as in West Germany before unification, the quantity of deutsche marks needed to increase by about 10%. That means that to avoid a rise in prices, the conversion should add no more than 10% to the existing quantity of deutsche marks. If it added more, then prices would rise.

In fact, the monetary union proceeded smoothly and there was no increase in prices.

SUMMARY

- The Quantity Theory of Money answers the question: What are the long-run effects of a monetary change on the economy?

- The predictions of the Quantity Theory may be stated in terms of the variables that appear in the equation of exchange. The Quantity Theory predicts that, in the long run, velocity and the quantities of goods traded will be unaffected and prices will change in proportion to the monetary change.

- The logic behind the Quantity Theory rests on the distinction between real and nominal variables and on the observation that economic decisions are based on real values.

- Nominal prices are prices in terms of dollars; real prices are prices in terms of opportunity cost.

- If all nominal prices change in proportion to a monetary change, as the Quantity Theory predicts, then real prices, economic decisions, and quantities of goods traded are unchanged.

- The nominal interest rate is the rate in terms of dollars. The real interest rate is the rate in terms of purchasing power. Borrowing and lending decisions are based on the real rate.

- A once-and-for-all monetary change leaves the real interest rate unaffected. Once prices stabilize again, the nominal rate will equal the real rate, and so the nominal interest rate, too, is unaffected in the long run by a once-and-for-all monetary change.

- Nominal balances are the amount of money held measured in dollars; real balances are the amount of money held measured in purchasing power. In the long run, real balances are unaffected by a monetary change, and nominal balances increase in proportion to prices.

KEY TERMS

Quantity Theory of Money   nominal interest rate   nominal balance

nominal price   real interest rate   real balance

real price   inflation rate

DISCUSSION QUESTIONS

1. Suppose the quantities of all goods traded grow by a uniform 10%, but the quantity of money does not change. What will be the long-run effect on prices?

2. Suppose there is no change in the quantity of money or in the quantities of goods traded, but that velocity doubles. What will be the long-run effect on prices?

BIBLIOGRAPHY

Fisher, Irving, *The Purchasing Power of Money*, New York: Macmillan, 1911.

Patinkin, Don, *Money, Interest and Prices*, 2nd (abridged) ed., Cambridge, Mass.: M.I.T. Press, 1989.

CHAPTER 24

THE FIRST EFFECTS OF A MONETARY CHANGE

When the Fed increases the quantity of money, what is the effect on the economy? The Quantity Theory tells us the ultimate effects, after any initial disturbance has passed and the economy has adjusted fully to having more money. But what *is* the initial disturbance? What is the short-run effect of a monetary change on prices, interest rates, exchange rates, and economic activity? How long does it last? We shall address these questions in the next few chapters.

In the current chapter and in the next we shall focus on the *very* short run, on an economy's first reaction to a change in the quantity of money. (Think of the relevant period as being perhaps a few weeks.) In this chapter we shall focus on a closed economy—an economy with no foreign trade; in Chapter 25 we shall extend our discussion to an open economy—one that does engage in trade. *We shall assume in both chapters that in this very short run prices do not change.* Since prices do not change, we need not distinguish between real and nominal variables—for example, between real and nominal interest rates.[1]

Our first task is to expand the simple circular flow model that we developed in Chapter 22 to include a market for loanable funds. We shall use the expanded model to examine the effects on the economy of an increase in government deficit spending, of a change in money demand, and of a change in the quantity of money. We shall conclude by using the model to shed light on a particular episode of monetary change in the U.S. economy.

---

[1]We shall look at changing prices and at their effect in Chapters 27 and 28.

24.1 THE CIRCULAR FLOW MODEL WITH A LOANABLE FUNDS MARKET

Exhibit 24.1 (which reproduces Exhibit 22.9 from Chapter 22) shows money flows and money balances for the Island economy during a typical month. At the beginning of each month, firms pay out all their previous month's receipts as income to households—a total of $1,000 million. (Firms retain no earnings and pay no taxes.) Households pay $100 million in taxes, save $200 million by lending it in exchange for securities, and spend the remaining $700 million of their incomes on consumption. Of the $200 million a month that households lend, firms borrow $120 million to finance their investment and the government borrows the remaining $80 million to cover its deficit. Total expenditure of households, firms, and government is $1,000 million. The same pattern of payments is repeated month after month.

The Island has a fractional-reserve banking system. Definitive money consists of $150 million of deposits at the Island's central bank. Since no hand-to-hand currency is used (all payments are made by check), all the definitive money is held by banks as reserves.[2] The reserve ratio is 10%, so the amount of bank deposits is 10 times bank reserves, or $1,500 million. Since no hand-to-hand currency is used, the $1,500 million of bank deposits *is* the total amount of money in the economy, as shown in Exhibit 24.1. Of this total, $1,000 million is transactions balances and $500 million is asset balances. Transactions balances in this economy exactly equal total expenditure.

The balance sheet of the banking system is:

BANKING SYSTEM

Reserves	$ 150m	Deposits	$1,500m
Loans	1,100m		
Securities	250m		

In addition to their portfolio of loans to firms, banks hold some government securities. Banks have no equity: Because no one ever defaults on this idyllic island, none is necessary.

---

[2]On the Island, since the government keeps its deposit with private banks rather than with the central bank, definitive money equals monetary base. Since no hand-to-hand currency is used, monetary base equals reserves. As a result, the money multiplier equals the simple deposit multiplier. (In Equation 19.29 c and t are zero, and B equals R.)

EXHIBIT 24.1

THE CIRCULAR FLOW OF PAYMENTS AND MONEY BALANCES FOR THE ISLAND ECONOMY
(IN MILLIONS OF DOLLARS)

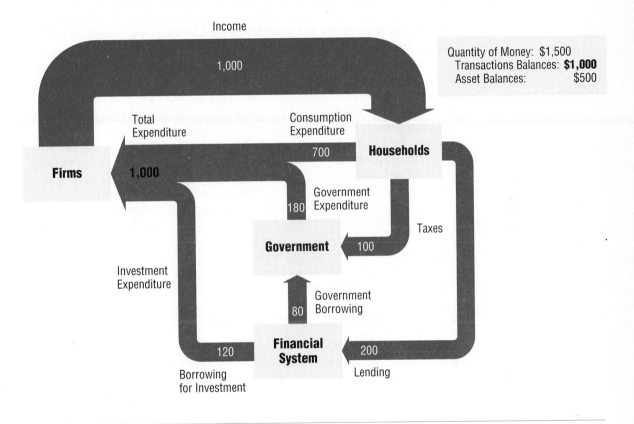

The financial system through which all borrowing and lending takes place can be viewed as a market for loanable funds. Exhibit 24.2 shows equilibrium in this market. The demand of firms for loanable funds is the downward-sloping curve D^F: The lower the interest rate, the more firms will want to invest and the more they will therefore borrow. Government borrowing, D^G, is a fixed $80 million: The government borrows this amount whatever the interest rate. The total demand for loanable funds, labeled $D^F + D^G$, is the sum of firm borrowing and of government borrowing (it is the curve D^F shifted to the right by $80 million). Household lending, labeled S^H, is upward-sloping: Households will lend more if the interest rate is higher.[3] Equilibrium in the loanable funds market occurs at an interest rate of 20%. At that rate the $200 million a month that households are willing to lend just equals the $120 a month that firms want to borrow plus the $80 million a month of government borrowing.

To avoid having to complicate our story with multiple interest rates, we shall assume that bank loans are equivalent to loans made via the direct market and that therefore they bear the same interest rate. For the moment, banks add nothing to the supply of new loanable funds. As long as bank reserves remain the same, the total amount of bank lending cannot increase. Of course, banks do make new loans. However, these new loans are balanced by the repayment of old ones, so the *total* amount of bank lending remains the same. We shall see presently how an increase in reserves does allow banks to increase the total amount of their lending and to contribute to the supply of loanable funds.[4]

24.2 GETTING TO KNOW THE MODEL

Before we look at a monetary change, we need to learn how the circular flow model works. We shall do this by using it to examine the effects on the economy of two changes that are somewhat easier to analyze than a change in the quantity of money. The first is an increase in government spending funded by additional borrowing; the second is an increase in the demand for money. In each case we shall study the effects on borrowing and lending, on total expenditure, and on the way that the total quantity of money is divided between transactions balances and asset balances.

The numbers you will see are as fictitious as the Island economy itself. You should pay attention not to the numbers themselves, but to the *nature* of the changes that occur. Although the numbers for the U.S. economy are very different, the nature of the changes is quite similar.

---

[3]We shall assume that households do not themselves borrow, so that S^H is total household lending. It would complicate things only a little if we assumed instead, more realistically, that S^H was *net* household lending, with lending of one household to another subtracted from the total.

[4]Banks on the Island do not offer time deposits. If they did, then some of the $200 million of new lending by households could be channeled through the banks. For example, suppose that households were adding $40 million a month to their time deposits; banks could then increase their lending by this amount each month. (This assumes that banks do not hold reserves against time deposits.)

E X H I B I T 24.2

EQUILIBRIUM IN THE LOANABLE FUNDS MARKET
(IN MILLIONS OF DOLLARS)

The "insides" of the financial system is a market for loanable funds. The supply of loanable funds is household lending. The demand is borrowing for investment plus government borrowing.

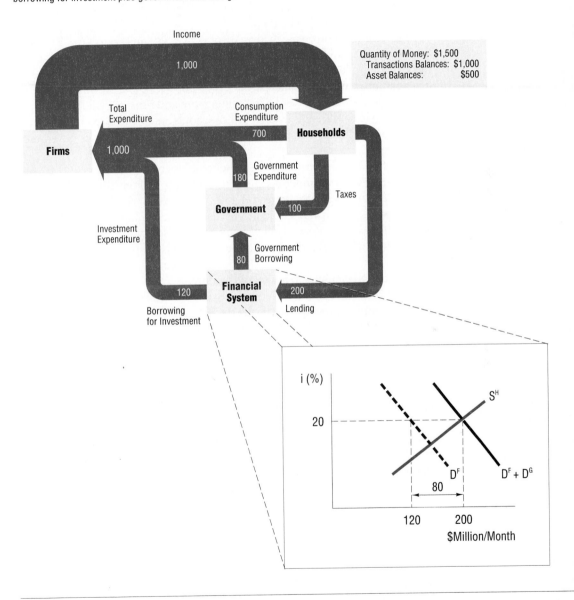

THE FIRST EFFECTS OF AN INCREASE IN GOVERNMENT DEFICIT SPENDING

The government of the Island decides to build a new harbor, the construction of which will cost $30 million a month for several years. Not wishing to anger voters by raising taxes, the government borrows to pay for the project. The immediate effect on the Island economy of the increase in government deficit spending is shown in Exhibit 24.3.

Government borrowing increases from D_0^G = $80 million to D_1^G = $110 million. This increased borrowing shifts the demand curve for loanable funds to the right by $30 million from $D^F + D_0^G$ to $D^F + D_1^G$. The increase in the demand for loanable funds raises the interest rate from 20% to 24%. At this higher rate, households are willing to lend $20 million more and firms are willing to borrow $10 million less. The extra lending by households and the reduced borrowing by firms provide the $30 million needed to satisfy the increase in government borrowing.

The $20 million extra lending by households comes from two sources. One is a decrease in consumption expenditure of $10 million. Because the higher interest rate makes saving more attractive, households spend less and save more. The second source is household asset balances. At the higher interest rate, the opportunity cost of money is higher, and households wish to hold less of their wealth as money and more as securities. So they use $10 million of their asset balances to buy extra securities: This additional purchase of securities accounts for the extra $10 million in household lending.

Government expenditure increases by the $30 million the government borrows. Investment expenditure falls by the $10 million reduction in firm borrowing. Consumption expenditure falls by $10 million. Total expenditure therefore increases by $30 million – $10 million – $10 million = $10 million.

The $10 million increase in total expenditure means an increase in transactions balances of the same amount. The increase in transactions balances equals the $10 million fall in asset balances. The two changes must be equal and opposite since the total quantity of money has not changed.

Clearly, the changes of the current month will have repercussions in the following month and in the months after that. In particular, total expenditure this month is up $10 million, so household income next month will be up by the same amount. We make no attempt to trace through the consequences here: The circular flow model has taken us as far as it can. In Chapter 26 we shall look at a more sophisticated model that does allow us to take the analysis further.

THE FIRST EFFECTS OF AN INCREASE IN MONEY DEMAND

The economy is again as shown in Exhibit 24.2, as it was before the change in government expenditure. Competition for customers' accounts leads banks on the Island to raise the interest they offer on checking deposits from zero to 10%.

EXHIBIT 24.3

THE EFFECT OF AN INCREASE IN GOVERNMENT SPENDING
(IN MILLIONS OF DOLLARS)

The increase in government borrowing shifts the demand for loanable funds to the right. At the higher interest rate that results, household lending rises and borrowing for investment falls. Increased household lending reflects both increased saving and a decrease in asset balances. Total expenditure rises by less than the increase in government expenditure because both consumption expenditure and investment expenditure fall.

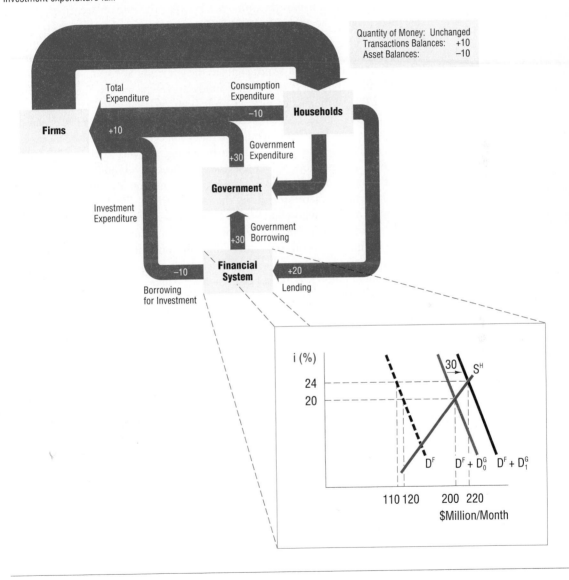

This change makes asset balances more attractive relative to securities as a way of holding wealth, and households increase their asset balances. The immediate effects on the Island economy are shown in Exhibit 24.4.

Because of the higher interest rate on checking deposits, households wish to increase the proportion of their wealth they hold as asset balances of money and decrease the proportion they hold as securities. The actual amount by which they wish to increase their asset balances depends on the interest rate on securities. What matters, of course, is the *difference* between the rate on securities and the rate on deposits. The effect of raising the rate on deposits, therefore, is to reduce household demand for new securities, the extent of the reduction depending on the interest rate on securities. In terms of the loanable funds market, that means that the supply of loanable funds shifts to the left from S_0^H to S_1^H.

The fall in the supply of loanable funds causes the interest rate to rise from 20% to 28%. With higher interest rates both on securities and on deposits, households save more, reducing their expenditure by $15 million. Despite this increase in saving, household lending actually *falls*. The reason is the increase in asset balances: The extra $15 million in saving, together with a $20 million reduction in lending, goes to increase asset balances by $35 million.

At the higher interest rate, firms borrow $20 million less, and firm expenditure on investment therefore falls by the same amount. The fall in consumption expenditure of $15 million and the unchanged government expenditure together means that total expenditure is down by $35 million. The fall in total expenditure means a fall in transactions balances of the same amount. The fall in transactions balances equals the $35 million increase in asset balances, as it must, since the total quantity of money is unchanged. For asset balances to increase, transactions balances must fall.

With total expenditure down $35 million, income next period will be down by the same amount, and further adjustments will take place.

🌴CHECK STATION 1 | **By how much does household saving increase as a result of the increased attractiveness of asset balances?**

| 24.3 | THE FIRST EFFECTS OF AN INCREASE IN THE QUANTITY OF MONEY

Now that we have seen how it works, we are ready to use the circular flow model to look at the effects of an increase in the quantity of money.

Suppose the economy is initially as shown in Exhibit 24.2. At the beginning of one particular month, the central bank purchases $1 million in securities from

EXHIBIT 24.4

THE EFFECT OF AN INCREASE IN DEMAND FOR ASSET BALANCES
(IN MILLIONS OF DOLLARS)

The increased attractiveness of asset balances shifts the supply of loanable funds to the left, raising the interest rate. Household lending and borrowing for investment both fall. The fall in household lending and the fall in consumption expenditure both contribute to the increase in asset balances. The parallel decreases in total expenditure and in transactions balances equal the increase in asset balances.

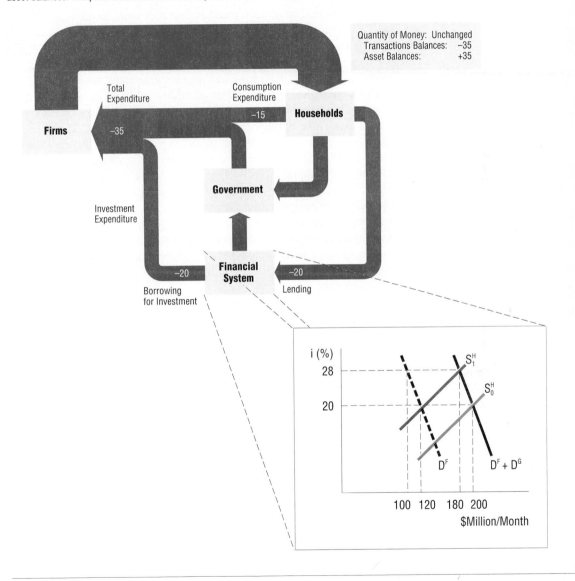

one of the commercial banks. The effect on the banking system's balance sheet is:

BANKING SYSTEM

Reserves	+$1m	
Securities	−$1m	

Banks now have $1 million more in reserves than they need, so they can expand their lending. The reserve ratio is 10% and the simple deposit multiplier (see Chapter 19) is 10, so the banking system can expand deposits and lending by 10 times $1 million, or $10 million.

The effect of the additional bank lending on the loanable funds market can be seen in Exhibit 24.5. The $10 million of additional bank loans is added to whatever amount households lend, shifting the supply curve to the right by $10 million. As a result, the equilibrium interest rate falls to 18%. At the lower interest rate, firms borrow $5 million more ($125 million), and households lend $5 million less ($195 million). Government borrowing is unchanged. So the extra $10 million in bank lending is partly offset by the $5 million drop in lending by households: The net increase in lending is $5 million. This net increase in lending equals the increase in borrowing for investment.

The $5 million reduction in household lending goes to increase consumption expenditure and to increase asset balances. The lower interest rate makes saving less attractive, so households spend $3 million more. The lower interest rate also makes asset balances more attractive relative to securities, so households increase their asset balances by $2 million.

Expenditure on investment increases by $5 million, the amount of additional borrowing; consumption expenditure increases by $3 million; and government expenditure is unchanged. So total expenditure increases by $8 million.

The $8 million increase in total expenditure means an increase in transactions balances of the same amount. As we have seen, asset balances also increase by $2 million. So money balances increase by a total of $10 million. This exactly equals the increase in the quantity of money.

The increased total expenditure this month means that households will receive a higher income next month. This will affect their expenditure and their lending and lead to further repercussions in the loanable funds market. We shall not attempt to trace through these repercussions here.

TRACING A MONETARY CHANGE THROUGH THE BALANCE SHEET OF THE BANKING SYSTEM

To make the immediate effect of the monetary change completely clear, let us trace the month's transactions through the balance sheet of the banking system.[5] At each stage, changes from the preceding stage are highlighted.

---

[5]See Section 22.1 for a parallel description of the transactions during a typical month *before* the monetary change. You may find it useful to compare the two descriptions.

EXHIBIT 24.5

THE IMMEDIATE EFFECT ON THE ECONOMY OF AN INCREASE IN THE QUANTITY OF MONEY
(IN MILLIONS OF DOLLARS)

The increase in the quantity of money shifts the supply of loanable funds to the right, lowering the interest rate. Firms borrow more; households lend less, partly offsetting the increase in the supply of loanable funds. The fall in household lending reflects an increase in consumption expenditure and an increase in asset balances. Total expenditure increases and with it transactions balances.

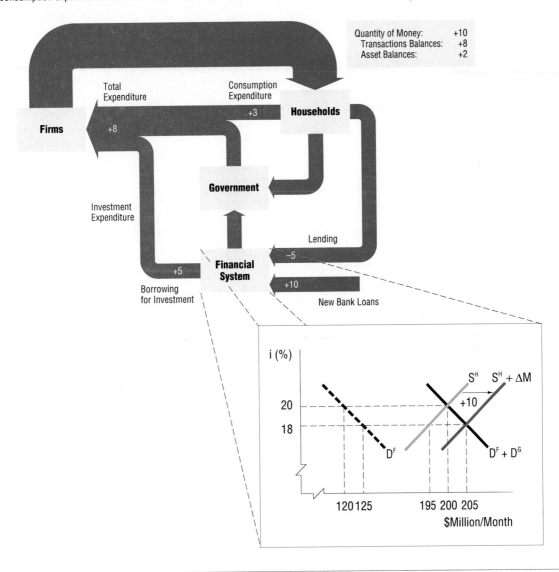

STAGE 1 At the beginning of the month, households receive $1,000 million in income payments. Together with the $500 million in asset balances they already hold, this amounts to all of the money on the Island:

BANKING SYSTEM

Reserves	$ 150m	Deposits	
Loans	1,100m	Households	$1,500m
Securities	250m	Firms	
		Borrowing account	0
		Sales receipts	0
		Government	0

STAGE 2 Households pay $100 million in taxes. Their deposits are debited by this amount, and the government's deposit is credited:

BANKING SYSTEM

Reserves	$ 150m	Deposits	
Loans	1,100m	Households	$1,400m
Securities	250m	Firms	
		Borrowing account	0
		Sales receipts	0
		Government	100m

STAGE 3 The central bank purchases $1 million in securities from the banking system:

BANKING SYSTEM

Reserves	$ 151m	Deposits	
Loans	1,100m	Households	$1,400m
Securities	249m	Firms	
		Borrowing account	0
		Sales receipts	0
		Government	100m

STAGE 4 Banks expand their lending by $10 million:

BANKING SYSTEM

Reserves	$ 151m	Deposits	
Loans	1,110m	Households	$1,400m
Securities	249m	Firms	
		Borrowing account	10m
		Sales receipts	0
		Government	100m

STAGE 5 Households lend $80 million to the government and $115 million to firms (adding to the $10 million that firms have already borrowed from banks):

BANKING SYSTEM

Reserves	$ 151m	Deposits	
Loans	1,110m	Households	$1,205m
Securities	249m	Firms	
		Borrowing account	125m
		Sales receipts	0
		Government	180m

STAGE 6 During the month households, firms, and the government do their spending. Households spend $703 million; firms spend the $125 million they have borrowed; and the government spends the $180 million it has raised in taxes and borrowing. All of this spending ends up in the sales receipts account of firms. Total sales receipts are $1,008 million. At the end of the month, $502 million remain in household deposits. These are asset balances.

BANKING SYSTEM

Reserves	$ 151m	Deposits	
Loans	1,110m	Households	$ 502m
Securities	249m	Firms	
		Borrowing account	0
		Sales receipts	1,008m
		Government	0

To summarize: The increase in the quantity of money means an increase in bank lending. The increase in lending causes the interest rate to fall. We will call this effect of an increase in the quantity of money the **loan-supply effect**.[6] As a result of the fall in the interest rate, borrowing for investment increases and household lending decreases. The fall in household lending reflects both an increase in consumption expenditure and an increase in asset balances. Total spending increases and with it transactions balances. The increase in transactions balances and the increase in asset balances together exactly absorb the increase in the quantity of money.

loan-supply effect
Decrease in interest rate due to increased bank lending.

24.4 APPLICATION: FED POLICY IN 1979-1980

Although the U.S. economy cannot be described exactly by anything so simple as our circular flow model of the Island economy, its structure is basically similar. The U.S. economy reacts to monetary changes in much the same way as the

---

[6]Later on we shall see that there may be other effects involving changes in expectations resulting from the central bank's action, but we shall ignore these for the moment. The loan-supply effect is often also called the *liquidity effect*.

circular flow model, although, of course, the actual numbers are very different. This similarity is brought out quite clearly by a particular episode of sharp monetary change in 1979–1980.

As we shall see in Chapter 32, by late 1979 the Fed was under increasing pressure to do something to reduce the rate of growth of the quantity of money. On October 6 it announced a tough new policy, and over the next several months the quantity of money stopped growing and even declined (see Exhibit 24.6A). The effect of such a monetary *contraction* is just the opposite of the effect of the monetary *expansion* we studied above. Interest rates rose sharply (see Exhibit 24.6B), and total expenditure stopped growing and even declined (see Exhibit 24.6C). Indeed, so dramatic was the effect of the new policy on the economy that by the summer of 1980 the Fed was seriously worried that it might cause a major recession. It therefore reversed its policy and allowed the quantity of money to grow rapidly again (see Exhibit 24.6A). Interest rates immediately dropped as rapidly as they had risen (see Exhibit 24.6B), and total expenditure recovered (see Exhibit 24.6C).

SUMMARY

- The circular flow model describes the first effects of an economic change on the economy. The model assumes that prices stay the same within this time horizon.

- The first effect of an increase in deficit spending is an increase in the demand for loanable funds and a rise in the interest rate. Total expenditure rises by less than the increase in government expenditure because both consumption expenditure and investment expenditure fall.

- An increase in the attractiveness of asset balances causes a decrease in lending that raises the interest rate. With consumption expenditure and investment expenditure both down, total expenditure and transactions balances fall. The fall in transactions balances is necessary to accommodate the increase in asset balances.

- An open market purchase increases bank reserves and allows the banking system to increase its lending. The addition to the supply of loanable funds lowers the interest rate—the loan-supply effect. With consumption expenditure and investment expenditure both up, total expenditure increases.

KEY TERM

loan-supply effect

EXHIBIT 24.6A–C

M1, FED FUNDS, AND THE GNP

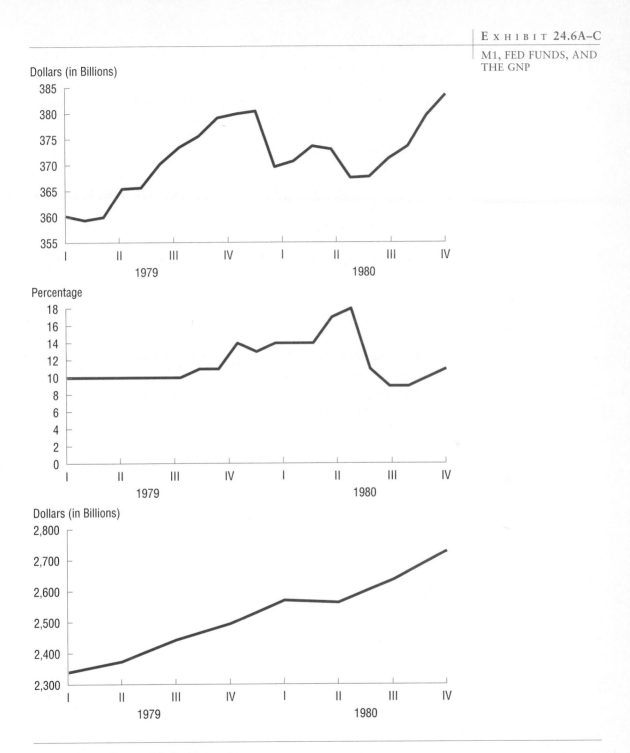

Source: *Economic Report of the President*, various years.

DISCUSSION QUESTIONS

1. Compare the first effects of a change in the quantity of money to the long-run effects that we saw in Chapter 23. Prepare a table showing first effects and long-run effects on (a) the interest rate, (b) total expenditure, (c) prices, (d) quantities of goods traded, and (e) velocity.

2. The Fed conducts a large open market sale. What are the first effects on the economy? What variables change and in which direction?

3. With the discovery of cold fusion, there is an investment boom in the United States. What is the effect on the loanable funds market? What are the other effects on the economy?

4. Suppose the central bank of the Island buys $3 million in government securities *at the same time* that the government increases its deficit spending by $30 million. What is the effect on the economy of these two changes taken together?

BIBLIOGRAPHY

Friedman, Milton, "Factors Affecting the Level of Interest Rates," in *Proceedings of the 1968 Conference on Savings and Residential Finance*, edited by U.S. Savings & Loan League, Chicago: The League, 1969.

Kohn, Meir, "In Defense of the Finance Constraint," *Economic Inquiry* 19:2 (April 1981), 177–196.

Kohn, Meir, "A Loanable Funds Theory of Unemployment and Monetary Disequilibrium," *American Economic Review* 71:5 (December 1981), 859–879.

CHAPTER 25

THE OPEN ECONOMY AND EXCHANGE RATES

In the early 1980s the exchange value of the dollar rose dramatically. As a result, U.S. consumers enjoyed bargain vacations abroad and low-priced VCRs and cameras at home. At the same time, thousands of U.S. workers in the steel and automobile industries lost their jobs as imports took away their markets. Although the U.S. economy could once have been understood with little attention paid to foreign trade and international lending, that is no longer true. Imports accounted for only 3% of total U.S. expenditure in 1960, but by 1989 they accounted for 9%. In 1960 the United States was a net lender of $1.8 billion; by 1988 the United States had become a net borrower of $123 billion (16% of funds raised in U.S. credit markets). To understand the behavior of the U.S. economy today, we must recognize that it is an **open economy**—an economy in which foreign trade and international lending are of major importance.

open economy
Economy in which foreign trade and international lending play major roles.

In Chapter 24 we developed a circular flow model to help us understand the short-run effects on the economy of monetary and other changes. To keep the model simple as we learned the basic relationships, we assumed that the economy was closed to foreign trade and to international lending. In this chapter we shall expand the model to bring in the economy's connections with the rest of the world, and we shall see how these connections complicate the ways in which monetary and other changes affect the economy.

Our first task will be to understand how imports and exports generate supply and demand for foreign exchange and how the market for foreign exchange determines the exchange rate. We shall then see how international lending affects the foreign-exchange market and the loanable funds market. The next step will be to integrate all of this into the circular flow model, seeing how the foreign-exchange market fits into the circular flow of payments. We shall use the model to trace the effects in an open economy of an increase in government deficit spending and of a change in the quantity of money, and to see how these effects differ from those we saw in Chapter 24 for a closed economy.

25.1 INTERNATIONAL TRADE AND THE EXCHANGE RATE

As is our custom, we shall illustrate the basic ideas first in the fictional Island economy before moving on to the complexities of the real world. The numbers are, of course, fictitious: Their purpose is merely to make the discussion more concrete. Our Island trades with the Atoll. The Atoll's monetary system, like the Island's, is based on definitive fiat money that is a liability of its central bank. The unit of money on the Atoll is the yen. We shall assume initially that there is no borrowing or lending between the two countries.

IMPORTS, EXPORTS, AND THE FOREIGN EXCHANGE MARKET

Because the Island's economy is by far the larger of the two economies, all trade between the two countries is conducted in dollars. When traders from the Island buy goods from the Atoll, they pay in dollars; when traders from the Atoll buy goods from the Island, they too pay in dollars. While this arrangement is convenient for natives of the Island, it is a complication for natives of the Atoll. For example, when Toma, a coconut grower on the Atoll, sells a shipment of coconuts to the Island, he is paid with a dollar check written on an Island bank. The dollars are of little direct use to him: He cannot spend them at home, because people on the Atoll expect to be paid in yen. So he needs to sell the dollars in exchange for yen. On the other hand, Melua buys sarongs on the Island to sell on the Atoll, and she must pay for her purchases in dollars. Being a resident of the Atoll, she has no dollars, only yen. So she must buy the dollars she needs. To answer the needs of Toma and Melua and of others like them, a *foreign exchange market* has sprung up where dollars are bought and sold in exchange for yen.[1]

Exhibit 25.1 illustrates equilibrium in this foreign exchange market. On the horizontal axis are millions of dollars traded per month; on the vertical axis is the price in yen per dollar (¥/$) at which they trade. The demand for dollars in the foreign exchange market is equal to the the total value of Island exports. Atoll traders like Melua need dollars to pay for Island exports: Every dollar's worth of Island exports generates demand for one dollar on the foreign exchange market. Similarly, the supply of dollars is equal to the total value of Island imports. Atoll traders like Toma who sell on the Island need to exchange dollars for yen: Every dollar's worth of Island imports generates a supply of one dollar to the foreign exchange market. Equilibrium in the foreign exchange market therefore implies that trade between the two countries must balance. If supply equals demand, then the total value of Island exports ($50 million) must equal the total value of Island imports (also $50 million).

---

[1] The foreign exchange market happens to be located on the Island because the Island has a more sophisticated financial system.

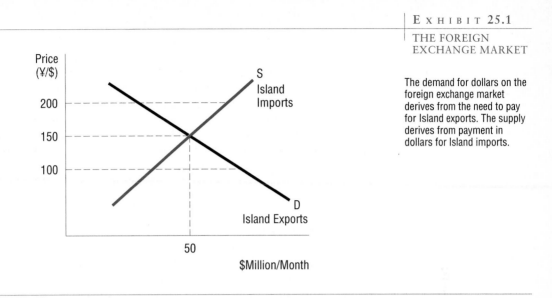

EXHIBIT 25.1

THE FOREIGN EXCHANGE MARKET

The demand for dollars on the foreign exchange market derives from the need to pay for Island exports. The supply derives from payment in dollars for Island imports.

The equilibrium price that balances supply and demand is 150¥/$. If the price were higher, say 200¥/$, then traders like Toma would be delighted. Toma would still get the same dollar price for his coconuts, but he would now get more yen when he sold the dollars. As a result, he would try to sell more coconuts on the Island, increasing his supply of dollars to the foreign exchange market. On the other hand, traders like Melua would not be pleased with the higher exchange rate. Melua would have to pay the same price in dollars for the sarongs she buys, but she would have to charge her customers a higher price in yen. She would therefore be able to sell fewer sarongs, reducing her demand for dollars on the foreign exchange market. So at an exchange rate of 200¥/$, supply would exceed demand. Conversely, at an exchange rate of 100¥/$, demand would exceed supply: Sarong exports from the Island would boom, and coconut imports to the Island would plummet. At the equilibrium price of 150¥/$, supply and demand just balance.

THE EXCHANGE RATE IN THE LONG RUN

Why is it, though, that supply and demand balance at 150¥/$ rather than at some other level? That is, what determines the level of the equilibrium exchange rate? For an answer we need to look more closely at the economic behavior that underlies the supply and demand for foreign exchange.

Let us begin by looking at foreign trade from the point of view of Ran, a coconut processor on the Island. Ran buys coconuts and turns them into oil and fiber, which he then sells. Before there is trade with the Atoll, Ran buys all his coconuts on the Island at a price of $120 per ton. When trade opens up, he has the alternative of buying his coconuts from Toma on the Atoll. The price on the Atoll is ¥12,000 per ton. Since, at that time, the exchange rate happens to be 200¥/$, Toma is willing to quote a price to Ran of ¥12,000/¥200 = $60. Since Atoll coconuts are just as good as Island coconuts, Ran starts to order his supplies from Toma.

Ran's decision to switch, and the decisions of others like him, affect three distinct markets. The demand for coconuts on the Island falls, putting downward pressure on its $120 price. The supply of dollars on the foreign exchange market increases as Toma and other growers on the Atoll convert more dollars into yen, putting downward pressure on the 200¥/$ exchange rate. And the demand for coconuts on the Atoll rises, putting upward pressure on the ¥12,000 price of coconuts there. All three effects push the prices of coconuts in the two countries closer together until, eventually, the prices equalize.[2]

In the long run the price of coconuts on the Island settles at $100, the price on the Atoll settles at ¥15,000, and the exchange rate settles at 150¥/$. At these prices and at this exchange rate, Ran and others like him are indifferent between the two sources of supply, no one switches from one market to the other, and there is no further pressure for prices to change. The tendency of prices in the two countries to equalize in this way is an example of what economists call the **law of one price**: Market forces ensure that the price of a good will tend to be the same in different locations.

The same forces that are at work in the market for coconuts are at work in the markets for *all* goods that could be traded between the two countries. In each case, the changing pattern of trade exerts its own pressure on the foreign exchange market. Whether the exchange rate actually rises or falls depends on the relative strength of all these pressures. Eventually, in the long run, prices and exchange rate settle down and the law of one price holds for all traded goods.

When the prices of all traded goods are equal in two countries at the prevailing exchange rate, **purchasing-power parity** is said to be satisfied. The purchasing power of a dollar is the quantity of goods and services it will buy. When purchasing-power parity is satisfied, the purchasing power of a dollar on the Island, in terms of traded goods, is the same as its purchasing power on the Atoll after being converted into yen at the prevailing exchange rate.

Notice the qualification—purchasing power *in terms of traded goods*. There is no reason why the purchasing power of the dollar should be the same in terms of goods that *cannot* be traded (goods for which transportation costs are very high). The price of a haircut or of beachfront property may well be very different in the two countries.

So, in the long run, once trade patterns have settled down, prices in the two countries and the exchange rate between the two currencies will satisfy purchasing-power parity. In our example, that requires an exchange rate of 150¥/$. The actual level of the exchange rate depends on the underlying supplies and demands for all goods that are traded between the two countries.

law of one price
Principle that market forces ensure that the price of a good will tend to be the same in different locations.

purchasing-power parity
Equivalence of a price for traded goods expressed in one currency to its price expressed in another currency.

---

[2] Taking into account the cost of transporting coconuts between the two markets.

How well does purchasing-power parity hold in practice? The "McDonald's standard" provides a rough guide (see "The Hamburger Standard" on page 649). As you can see, there are some substantial deviations from purchasing-power parity according to this measure. One reason is that the measure is not all that good: The Big Mac is not a good example of a traded good, because locally provided service is a large element of its cost. Another reason, as we shall see, is that a number of factors can cause the *actual* exchange rate to deviate from its long-run equilibrium value for substantial periods of time.

A. If bicycles cost $100 on the Island and ¥15,000 on the Atoll, and canoes are $1,000 on the Island and ¥150,000 on the Atoll, is this consistent with purchasing-power parity?

B. If, at the same time, a dancing lesson costs $50 on the Island and ¥10,000 on the Atoll, is this consistent with purchasing-power parity?

🌴 CHECK STATION 1

25.2 INTERNATIONAL LENDING

Meanwhile, back in the South Seas, borrowing and lending between the Island and the Atoll have been permitted. Because the initial 25% interest rate on the Island is higher than that on the Atoll, Atoll investors start to buy Island securities. This increase in the supply of loanable funds on the Island lowers the interest rate there. Because Atoll investors are supplying loanable funds to the Island instead of to their own loanable funds market, the interest rate on the Atoll rises. As a result, the gap between the two rates shrinks.[3] After a period of adjustment, the two economies stabilize again in a new equilibrium. Let us examine the effects of international lending on the loanable funds market and on the foreign exchange market in this new equilibrium.

THE LOANABLE FUNDS MARKET

As a result of opening itself to foreign borrowing and lending, the Island finds that its interest rate has fallen to 20% and that Atoll lenders are now supplying $20 million a month to the Island's loanable funds market. The relationship between the Island interest rate and the amount of foreign net lending to the Island is shown in Exhibit 25.2. The net supply of foreign lending to the Island is labeled S^{FO}. The higher the interest rate on the Island, the greater the net supply of foreign loanable funds. For example, at an interest rate of 20%, foreigners lend

[3]The gap need not close completely, because securities in the two countries are not exactly the same "good." We shall see in Chapter 29 that investors do more than just compare the two interest rates: The return to Atoll investors from investing in dollar securities depends as well on what happens to the exchange rate in the future. As a result, the two types of security are not exactly equivalent: Island securities involve exchange-rate risk for Atoll investors, and vice versa. The remaining gap between the two interest rates will reflect this differential exchange-rate risk.

E X H I B I T 25.2

FOREIGN NET
LENDING TO THE
ISLAND

The net supply of lending by
foreigners increases with the
interest rate on the Island. At
low values of the Island
interest rate, foreigners will
borrow rather than lend, so net
lending will be negative.

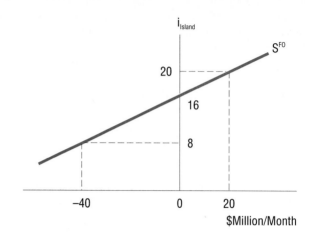

the Island $20 million a month; at a rate of 16%, they lend the Island zero; and at a rate of 8%, foreigners borrow $40 million on the Island (net *lending* to the Island is –$40 million).

To find the effect of international lending on the Island's loanable funds market, we need to add this foreign net supply of loanable funds to the net supply of loanable funds from households to obtain the total supply, as shown in Exhibit 25.3. The total supply of loanable funds, that of households plus that of foreigners, is labeled $S^H + S^{FO}$. At an interest rate of 20%, foreigners contribute an additional supply of $20 million; at an interest rate of 16%, they contribute nothing, so the total supply of loanable funds is just the supply of households; and at an interest rate of 8%, foreigners *borrow* $40 million, so that they *subtract* that amount from the supply of households.

The new equilibrium in the loanable funds market is shown in Exhibit 25.4. At the equilibrium interest rate of 20%, firms are borrowing $120 million a month, the government is borrowing $100 million, households are lending $200 million, and foreigners are lending $20 million.

CHECK STATION 2

A. In Exhibit 25.4, did opening the Island's loanable funds market to borrowing and lending raise or lower the interest rate? What effect did it have on the amount of household lending? On borrowing for investment?

B. What were the corresponding effects on the Atoll's loanable funds market?

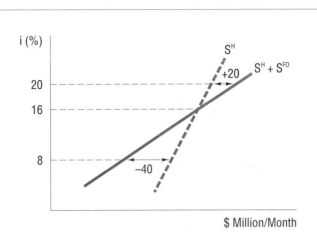

EXHIBIT 25.3

THE TOTAL SUPPLY
OF LOANABLE FUNDS

The total supply of loanable
funds on the Island is the sum
of the supply of lending by
households and the supply of
lending by foreigners.

THE FOREIGN EXCHANGE MARKET

To buy Island securities, Atoll investors need dollars: Dollar-denominated securities cannot be bought with yen. To obtain the $20 million they need, they must go to the foreign exchange market. Their demand for dollars is added to the demand for dollars of buyers of Island exports. The total demand for dollars is therefore shifted to the right by $20 million, as shown in Exhibit 25.5. The resulting equilibrium is at an exchange rate of 180¥/$. At this exchange rate, Island

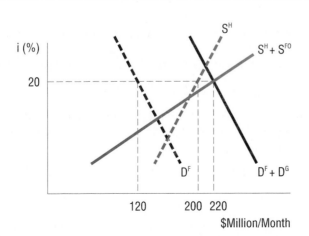

EXHIBIT 25.4

THE EFFECT OF
INTERNATIONAL
LENDING ON THE
LOANABLE FUNDS
MARKET

In the open economy the total
supply of loanable funds is the
supply of households plus the
net supply of foreigners; the
total demand is the demand for
borrowing to finance
investment plus the demand
for government borrowing to
cover its budget deficit.

EXHIBIT 25.5

THE EFFECT OF INTERNATIONAL LENDING ON THE FOREIGN EXCHANGE MARKET

With international lending, foreign investors need dollars in order to buy Island securities. This demand for dollars is added to the demand that originates with buyers of Island exports.

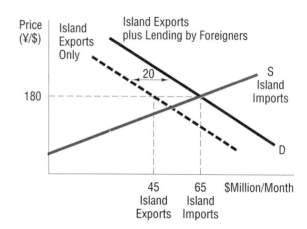

imports are $65 million, and Island exports are $45 million. The $20 million difference between imports and exports is the amount of dollars bought by foreign investors to lend on the Island.

Notice that once international lending is allowed, it is no longer true that equilibrium in the foreign exchange market implies that exports equal imports. Equilibrium now implies that imports equal exports *plus net lending by foreigners*. Stated differently, if trade is balanced, net international lending must be zero.

25.3 A CIRCULAR FLOW MODEL OF THE OPEN ECONOMY

We now need to integrate foreign trade, foreign lending, and the foreign exchange market into our circular flow model of the economy. Exhibit 25.6 shows how this can be done. Compared to our earlier circular flow diagrams (for example, Exhibit 24.1), there is now an additional sector—"Foreigners." Into the box that represents the foreign sector flow the payments made by Island residents for imports to the Island. Out of the Foreigners box flow the payments foreigners make for Island exports and the payments they make for Island securities (net lending by foreigners).[4]

---

[4]Government spending in Exhibit 25.6 has been made $20 million higher than shown in Exhibit 24.1, so that the interest rate remains at 20%. This increase in government spending is not a result of opening the economy: It is made purely for convenience of presentation.

EXHIBIT 25.6

THE CIRCULAR FLOW WITH FOREIGN TRADE AND INTERNATIONAL LENDING
(IN MILLIONS OF DOLLARS)

When a foreign sector is added to the circular flow diagram, absorption need no longer equal total sales receipts and income. Some domestic spending goes on imports, and foreign spending on exports adds to sales receipts. As with other boxes, the flows into and out of the Foreigners box must balance.

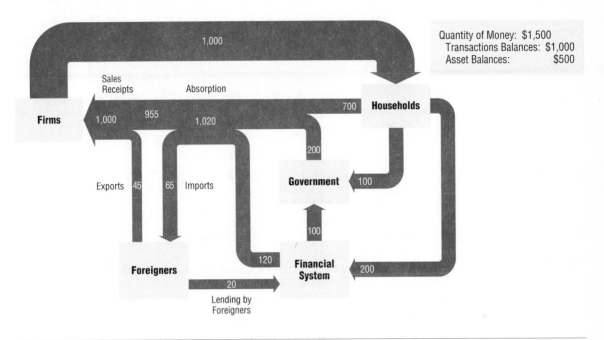

Two important truths about an open economy are evident from Exhibit 25.6:

1. *Even with foreign trade and international lending, no dollars actually leave the economy.* Although Island imports exceed Island exports by $20 million, these $20 million do not leave the Island. In principle, foreigners could accumulate asset balances of money, but, even then, these balances would be in the form of dollar deposits at Island banks. In practice, foreigners prefer to accumulate securities that pay interest rather than asset balances that do not. So the dollars they acquire through their export surplus find their way back into circulation through the financial system.

2. *For an open economy, income no longer equals the total expenditure of domestic agents.* Households, firms, and government on the Island spend a total of $1,020 million. In the open economy, not all of this represents sales revenue to *domestic* firms: Some of it is spent on imports—so representing sales revenue to foreign firms. Imports here are $65 million, so that domestic

expenditure on *domestic* goods and services is $1,020 million – $65 million = $955 million. But in an open economy domestic firms also sell to *foreign* customers. So we have to add the $45 million of exports for a total sales revenue of $1,000 million. This total sales revenue is equal to household income.

To make these distinctions clear, we will call the total expenditure of domestic agents **absorption**. Absorption is the total spending (use of resources) by domestic households, firms, and government. The relation between absorption and income is

absorption
Total expenditure by
households, firms, and
the government.

$$\begin{array}{c} \text{income} = \text{absorption} - \text{imports} + \text{exports.} \\ (\$1,000\text{m}) \quad (\$1,020\text{m}) \quad (\$65\text{m}) \quad (\$45\text{m}) \end{array} \qquad [25.1]$$

You might ask how domestic agents are able to spend more than their incomes. The answer is that they borrow the difference, $20 million, from foreigners. That is:

$$\begin{array}{c} \text{absorption} = \text{income} + \text{net lending by foreigners.} \\ (\$1,020\text{m}) \quad (\$1,000\text{m}) \qquad\qquad (\$20\text{m}) \end{array} \qquad [25.2]$$

The foreign exchange market is the "insides" of the Foreigners box, just as the loanable funds market is the "insides" of the Financial System box. Exhibit 25.7 shows the circular flow model with both markets displayed. We have seen that equilibrium in the loanable funds market ensures that the total of flows into the financial systems box equals the total of flows out of it. Similarly, equilibrium in the foreign exchange market ensures that the total of flows into the foreigners box equals the total of flows out of it.

25.4 UNDERSTANDING THE U.S. BALANCE OF PAYMENTS

Now that we understand the basics of an economy open to trade and capital flows, we are ready to look at some numbers for the United States. Exhibit 25.8 shows the balance of payments for the United States in 1988. The entries correspond roughly to the various flows we discussed above. Flows of payments into the United States are shown as positive numbers; flows of payments out of the United States are shown as negative numbers.

U.S. merchandise imports were $446 billion. They included such things as Japanese cars and VCRs, German machinery, and petroleum from the Middle East and Mexico. They also included television sets, toys, and personal computers manufactured by U.S. corporations abroad, in countries like Brazil and Taiwan. U.S. exports were $320 billion. They included aircraft, computers, construction equipment, lumber, and grain. Imports exceeded exports by $126 billion. The difference between merchandise exports and imports is called the **balance of trade**.

balance of trade
Difference between
merchandise exports and
imports.

EXHIBIT 25.7

THE CIRCULAR FLOW MODEL WITH LOANABLE FUNDS AND FOREIGN EXCHANGE MARKETS
(IN MILLIONS OF DOLLARS)

Equilibrium in the foreign exchange market ensures that flows into and out of the Foreigners box balance, in the same way that equilibrium
in the loanable funds market ensures balance between the flows into and out of the Financial System box.

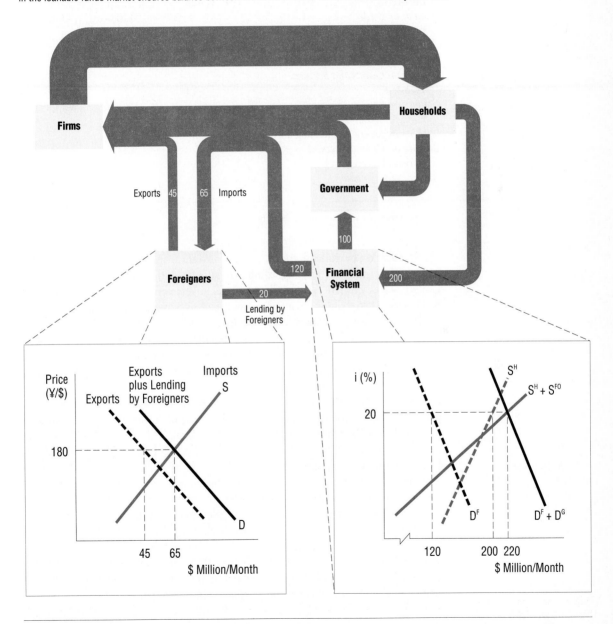

EXHIBIT 25.8

U.S BALANCE OF PAYMENTS IN 1988 (IN BILLIONS OF DOLLARS)

		Balance	Cumulative Balance
Exports	320		
Imports	−446		
Balance of Trade		−126	−126
Income on U.S. assets abroad	108		
Income on foreign assets in U.S.	−106		
Other services, net	1		
Balance on Goods and Services			−123
Transfers	−14		
Balance on Current Account			−137
Foreign investment and lending in U.S.	212		
U.S. investment and lending abroad	−89		
Balance on Capital Account		123	
Statistical discrepancy	14		
Balance of Payments			0

Source: *Survey of Current Business*, March 1989.

In addition to trade in goods, there is also trade in services. One "service" is lending. International lending results in interest and dividend payments. The United States earned $108 billion on its investments overseas, and it paid foreigners $106 billion in income on their investments here. Other services, including tourism, transportation, and military sales and expenditure, netted out at $1 billion. Combining these with the balance of trade, the balance on goods and services was in deficit to the amount of $123 billion.

Both the federal government and private residents make unilateral transfers (gifts) overseas: The U.S. government provides aid to a number of foreign governments, including Israel, Egypt, and the Philippines; private charities also provide aid of various types, such as food shipments during the African famine. The total of such transfers in 1988 was $14 billion. The cumulative balance on goods, services, and transfers was a deficit of $137 billion. This is called the **balance on current account.**

balance on current account
Cumulative balance on goods, services, and transfers.

Foreign investment and lending in the United States amounted to $212 billion. Foreign investment included assembly plants for Japanese automobiles, real estate in New York City and Los Angeles, and the purchase of a number of U.S. banks and securities firms. Lending included the purchase of Treasury and corporate securities and deposits made in U.S. banks. U.S. investment and lending abroad amounted to $89 billion. U.S. investments abroad included McDonald's and Kentucky Fried Chicken restaurants in Europe, television assembly plants in Mexico, and Disney World theme parks in Japan and France. Lending included the purchase of government and private securities abroad and deposits in banks abroad. *Net* foreign investment and lending in the United States, the **balance on capital account,** was $123 billion.

balance on capital account
Net foreign investment and lending in the United States.

EXHIBIT 25.9

U.S. CURRENT ACCOUNT AND NET CAPITAL FLOW, 1960–1989

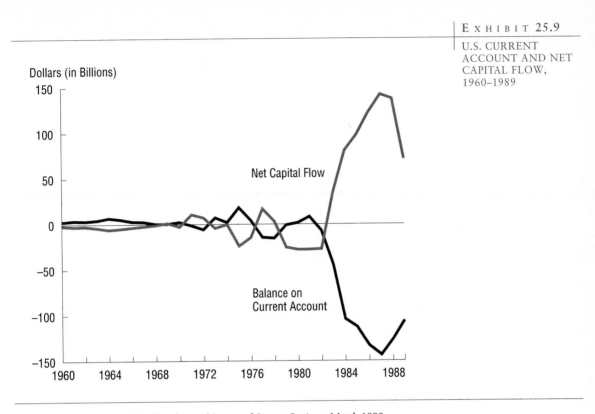

Source: *Economic Report of the President* and *Survey of Current Business*, March 1990.

Equilibrium in the foreign exchange markets implies that the cumulative balance of current-account transactions and foreign net lending, the **balance of payments,** should be zero. However, since many of the numbers are inaccurate, we are left with a $14 billion statistical discrepancy.

balance of payments Cumulative balance on current and capital account.

Exhibit 25.9 shows how the U.S. balance of payments has behaved in recent years. The current account was roughly balanced until the early 1970s. The United States then ran a surplus until the early 1980s, with considerable foreign lending. In the early 1980s the situation reversed, and the United States began to run large current-account deficits and to borrow heavily abroad. We shall see why in the following sections.

There is a great deal of confusion in the media and on the part of politicians about the connection between trade flows and capital flows. For example, the large U.S. current-account deficit is a cause of much concern, being seen as a sign of economic weakness and of a loss of "international competitiveness." At the same time, the willingness of foreigners to invest in the United States is a source of considerable pride: It is interpreted as evidence of the strength of the U.S. economy and of foreigners' confidence in it. But the two phenomena are just mirror images of one another. The large current-account deficit could not happen without an equal and opposite capital flow; foreign investment in the United

States could not happen without an equal and opposite current-account deficit. Concern is often expressed over what would happen if foreigners stopped lending to us. One consequence we can be sure of: It would put a rapid end to our current-account deficit.

25.5 | THE FIRST EFFECTS OF AN INCREASE IN GOVERNMENT SPENDING

Before we look at the effects of a monetary change, we need to see how the open economy model works. We shall do this by examining the effects on the economy of an increase in government deficit spending. This is the same exercise we went through with the closed economy model in Section 24.2.[5] As in Section 24.2, the government of the Island decides to build a new harbor, the construction of which costs $30 million a month for several years. The government finances construction by borrowing in the loanable funds market. The immediate effects on the Island economy are shown in Exhibit 25.10.

We shall assume throughout our analysis that prices of domestic goods stay the same. That is, the prices that producers on the Island charge in dollars and the prices producers on the Atoll charge in yen do not change. Prices of imports and exports will change as the exchange rate changes.

Let us start with the loanable funds market. Government borrowing increases from D_0^G = $100 million to D_1^G = $130 million. This increased borrowing shifts the demand for loanable funds to the right by $30 million, from $D^F + D_0^G$ to $D^F + D_1^G$. The shift in the demand for loanable funds raises the interest rate from 20% to 22%. At this higher rate households lend $10 million more, foreigners lend $15 million more, and firms borrow $5 million less. Looking at the changes in the flows into and out of the Financial System box, we see that the extra lending by households and foreigners and the reduced borrowing by firms provide exactly the extra $30 million borrowed by the government.

The $10 million extra lending of households comes from two sources. One is a decrease in consumption expenditure of $5 million. The higher interest rate makes saving more attractive, so households consume less and save more. The second source is a decrease in asset balances. At the higher interest rate, the opportunity cost of money is higher, and households wish to hold less of their wealth as money and more as securities. So they use $5 million of their asset balances to buy extra securities.

Now look at the foreign-exchange market. The $15 million extra lending by foreigners obliges them to go to the foreign-exchange market for more dollars. As a result, the demand for foreign exchange shifts to the right by $15 million, from D_0 to D_1, and the exchange rate increases to 200¥/$. Such a rise in the exchange

[5]As in Chapter 24, while actual numbers are used for concreteness, all the numbers are fictitious. The purpose of the exercise is to understand the nature of the changes involved, not to learn the particular numbers. Although the numbers for the U.S. economy are very different, the nature of the effects is similar.

EXHIBIT 25.10

THE EFFECT OF AN INCREASE IN GOVERNMENT DEFICIT SPENDING IN AN OPEN ECONOMY
(IN MILLIONS OF DOLLARS)

The increase in government borrowing shifts the demand for loanable funds to the right. At the higher interest rate that results, household and foreign lending rises and borrowing for investment falls. Increased foreign lending shifts the demand for foreign exchange to the right, causing the exchange rate to appreciate.

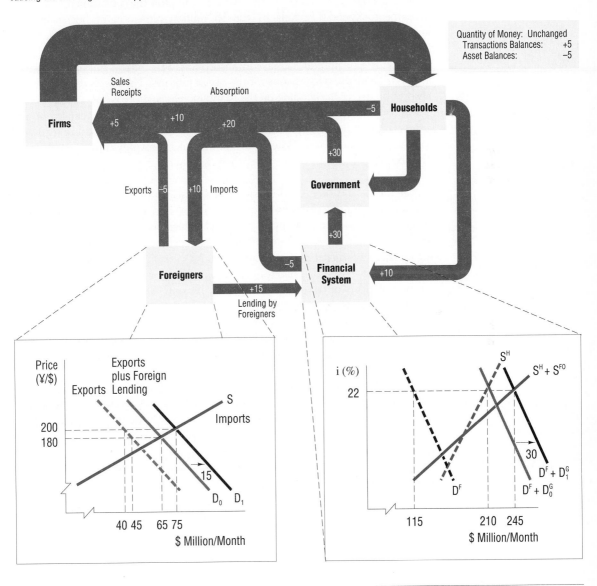

appreciation
Increase in the exchange rate of one currency against another.

rate is called an **appreciation** of the dollar. At the higher exchange rate, exports from the Island are $5 million lower and imports are $10 million higher (we shall see below why imports and exports change). The increase in the gap between imports and exports provides the $15 million extra dollars Atoll investors need in order to purchase additional securities on the Island.

Turning to the flows of expenditure in Exhibit 25.10, we see that government expenditure increases by the extra $30 million the government borrows. Investment expenditure falls by the $5 million reduction in borrowing for investment, and consumption expenditure falls by $5 million. Absorption therefore increases by only $20 million.

Of this $20 million increase in absorption, $10 million goes on increased imports. There are two reasons for the rise in imports. The first is the increase in absorption itself: As spending on the Island increases, more is spent on imported goods too. The second reason is the fall in the price of imports caused by the appreciation of the dollar. Goods on the Atoll cost the same in yen, but their cost to residents of the Island is lower because the dollar now buys more yen. Because imported goods are less expensive, there is a switching of expenditure toward imports.

Domestic spending on domestic goods increases by the increase in absorption less the increase in imports, or $10 million. Foreign spending on domestic goods—exports—decreases by $5 million. The reason for the fall in exports is the appreciation of the dollar. Domestic goods still cost the same in dollars, but at the higher exchange rate they cost more in yen. As a result, Atoll residents buy fewer goods from the Island. Therefore total expenditure on domestic goods—sales receipts of firms on the Island—increases by only $5 million, the increase in absorption minus the fall in exports.

The $5 million increase in total expenditure on domestic goods means an increase in transactions balances by the same amount. The increase in transactions balances equals the $5 million fall in asset balances. The two changes must be equal and opposite since the total quantity of money has not changed.

Clearly, the changes of the current month will have repercussions in the following month and in the months after that: Total sales receipts this month are up $5 million, so household income next month will be up by the same amount. We postpone discussion of the consequences to Chapter 26.

CHECK STATION 3 | **Suppose that, before the change, at 180¥/$, purchasing-power parity held. Does it still hold after the change?**

DIFFERENCES BETWEEN THE EFFECTS IN OPEN AND CLOSED ECONOMIES

Let us compare our results here with those we obtained in Chapter 24 for the effects of a similar change in a closed economy.[6] In comparing Exhibit 25.10 with Exhibit 24.3, we see the following differences:

1. The effect of the increased government borrowing on the interest rate is smaller in the open economy: The interest rate rises to 22% rather than to 24%. The reason the interest rate rises less in the open economy is the increase in lending by foreigners, who now find it more attractive to lend in the dollar-denominated loanable funds market.

2. Because the interest rate rises less, there is less of a fall in firm borrowing—by $5 million instead of by $10 million—and less of an increase in household lending—by $10 million rather than by $20 million. Investment expenditure and consumption expenditure correspondingly fall less, and absorption increases more—by $20 million instead of by $10 million.

3. Although the effect on absorption is greater in the open economy, the effect on sales receipts (and thus on subsequent income) need not be greater, once the effects of dollar appreciation on imports and exports is added in. On the Island these effects are large enough to leave the increase in sales receipts smaller than in the closed economy.

25.6 THE FIRST EFFECTS OF A MONETARY CHANGE

Having seen how the open economy model works, we are ready to use it to examine the first effects of a change in the quantity of money. In an open economy we need to distinguish between two different sources of monetary change. Until now, we have always assumed that a change in the quantity of money was initiated by a purchase or sale of government securities (an open market operation). In the open economy the object of the purchase or sale may also be foreign exchange. We shall look first at the more familiar case of an open market operation and then at the case of a purchase or sale of foreign exchange. Before we do so, however, let us take a moment to note the *long-run* effects of a monetary change.

---

[6]Government borrowing before the increase, by assumption, is $20 million higher in the open economy than it is in the closed economy.

THE LONG-RUN EFFECTS OF A MONETARY CHANGE

To understand the long-run effects of a change in the quantity of money, all we need do is bring together the Quantity Theory of Money and purchasing-power parity. Suppose that things have been stable for some time and that purchasing-power parity holds at an exchange rate of 150¥/$. Then, the quantity of dollars on the Island increases tenfold. What will be the ultimate effect on the exchange rate, once all necessary adjustments have been made?

We saw in Chapter 22 that according to the Quantity Theory real prices on the Island will be unaffected in the long run and nominal prices will be 10 times higher than they were originally. For example, the dollar price of coconuts on the Island will eventually rise from $100 a ton to $1,000. What will happen to the price on the Atoll? The Quantity Theory tells us that, since the quantity of money on the Atoll is unchanged, the price of coconuts in yen will not change either: It will remain at ¥15,000 a ton.

Nonetheless, we know from purchasing-power parity that in the long run the price of coconuts in the two countries must be equivalent. For this to be true, the new exchange rate must be

$$\frac{¥15,000}{\$1,000} = 15¥/\$.$$

Since purchasing-power parity holds, we could have made this calculation in terms of *any* traded good and obtained the same answer.

In terms of the Quantity Theory, trade flows and the relative prices of goods traded join the list of real variables that are not affected in the long run by changes in the quantity of money. The exchange rate joins the list of nominal variables that in the long run change in proportion to the change in the quantity of money.[7]

🌴 CHECK STATION 4

A. The exchange rate is initially 180¥/$. What is the exchange rate in the long run if the quantity of yen falls by 50%?

B. The exchange rate is initially 180¥/$. What is the exchange rate in the long run if the quantity of dollars increases by 10% and the quantity of yen increases by 10%?

---

[7]Corresponding to the usual distinction between real and nominal prices, we can define a *real* exchange rate as the real price of imported goods in terms of exported goods—say, the cost of coconuts in terms of sarongs. The real exchange rate is unaffected in the long run by a monetary change. The *nominal* exchange rate is the one with which we are familiar, the price of one money in terms of the other. The nominal exchange rate changes in proportion to changes in the relative quantities of the two moneys.

THE HAMBURGER STANDARD

The McDonald's standard is based on the theory of purchasing-power parity (PPP), which argues that in the long run the exchange rate between two currencies should equate the price of an identical basket of goods and services in the respective countries. Our "basket" is simply a Big Mac, which has the virtue of being made locally in more than 50 countries and of tasting virtually the same from Manchester to Moscow.

In America the average price of a Big Mac (including tax) is about $2.20. In Tokyo our correspondent had to fork out ¥370 for this gastronomic delight. Dividing the yen price by the dollar price gives an implied PPP for the dollar of ¥168, compared with the current exchange rate of ¥159. So even after the recent slide in the yen, the dollar still looks to be 5% undervalued against the yen on PPP grounds. It also looks 14% undervalued against the D-mark, with a Mac-PPP of DM1.95.

Economists who have calculated PPPs by more sophisticated means come up with remarkably similar results. Professor Ronald McKinnon of Stanford University, one of the leading proponents of the theory of purchasing-power parity, comes up with mid-point estimates for the dollar's PPP of ¥165 and DM2.00.

Mac-currencies are now becoming truly global: the opening of the first McDonald's in Moscow has allowed us to add the rouble to our sample. Muscovites have to pay the equivalent of $6.25 (converting at the official exchange rate) for a Big Mac, which makes it the most expensive hamburger in our sample. In other

BIG MACCURRENCIES: HAMBURGER PRICES

Country	Price* in Local Currency	Implied PPP† of the Dollar	Actual Exchange Rate 4/30/90	% Over (+) or Under (−) Valuation of the Dollar
Australia	A$ 2.30	1.05	1.32	+26
Belgium	BFr 97	44.00	34.65	−21
Britain	£ 1.40	0.64	0.61	−5
Canada	C$ 2.19	1.00	1.16	+16
Denmark	DKr 25.50	11.60	6.39	−45
France	FFr 17.70	8.05	5.63	−30
Holland	FL 5.25	2.39	1.88	−21
Hong Kong	HK$ 8.60	3.90	7.79	+100
Ireland	IR£ 1.30	0.59	0.63	+7
Italy	Lire 3900	1773	1230	−31
Japan	¥ 370	168	159	−5
Singapore	S$ 2.60	1.18	1.88	+59
S. Korea	Won 2100	955	707	−26
Soviet Union	Rouble 3.75	1.70	0.60	−65
Spain	Ptas 295	134	106	−21
Sweden	SKr 24	10.90	6.10	−44
United States††	$ 2.20	—	—	—
W. Germany	DM 4.30	1.95	1.68	−14
Yugoslavia	Dinar 16	7.27	11.72	+61

*Prices may vary between branches.
†Purchasing-power parity: foreign price divided by dollar price.
††Average of New York, Chicago, San Francisco, and Atlanta.
Source: McDonald's; *Economist* correspondents.

words, the rouble is overvalued against the dollar to a greater degree than any other currency, with an implied PPP of 1.70 roubles, compared with an official rate against the dollar of 0.60 roubles.

Yet this overlooks one crucial fact: in Moscow fast food comes slow, with two-to-three hour queues. If this time is valued at average Soviet hourly wages, then the true cost of gorging

on a Big Mac is roughly double the cash price. This implies a "queue-adjusted" Mac-PPP of 3.40 roubles. Indigestion, Mikhail?

Source: "The Hamburger Standard," *The Economist*, May 5, 1990, p. 92. Copyright 1990, The Economist. Distributed by Special Features/Syndication Sales.

THE FIRST EFFECTS OF AN OPEN MARKET OPERATION

The economy is initially as shown in Exhibit 25.6. The central bank purchases $1 million in securities from one of the commercial banks. As a result, banks have $1 million more in reserves than they need, and they expand their lending. The reserve ratio is 10% and the simple deposit multiplier (see Chapter 19) is 10, so the banking system expands its deposits and lending by 10 times $1 million, or $10 million. The effect of the additional bank lending can be seen in Exhibit 25.11.

Let us start with the loanable funds market. The $10 million of additional bank loans is added to whatever amount households and foreigners lend, shifting the supply curve to the right by $10 million, from $S^H + S^{FO}$ to $S^H + S^{FO} + \Delta M$. As a result, the equilibrium interest rate falls to 19%. At the lower interest rate, firms borrow $3 million more, households lend $2 million less, and foreigners lend $5 million less; government borrowing is unchanged. You can see the changes in the flows into and out of the Financial System box.

The extra $10 million in bank lending is therefore partly offset by the drop in lending by households and the drop in lending by foreigners. Total borrowing and lending are as follows:

$$\begin{array}{ccccccccc} \text{household} & + & \text{lending by} & + & \text{new bank} & = & \text{firm} & + & \text{government} \\ \text{lending} & & \text{foreigners} & & \text{loans} & & \text{borrowing} & & \text{borrowing} \\ \$198m & & \$15m & & \$10m & & \$123m & & \$100m \end{array} \qquad [25.3]$$

The $2 million drop in household lending goes both to increase consumption expenditure and to increase asset balances. The lower interest rate makes saving less attractive, so households spend $1 million more. The lower interest rate also makes asset balances more attractive relative to securities, so households increase their asset balances by $1 million.

Now look at the foreign exchange market. The $5 million less lending by foreign investors means that they need to buy $5 million less on the foreign exchange market. The result is a shift to the left of the demand for foreign exchange by $5 million, from D_0 to D_1, and a fall in the exchange rate to 174¥/$. A fall in the exchange rate, because it means the dollar buys fewer yen, is called a **depreciation** of the dollar.

depreciation
Decrease in the exchange rate of one currency against another.

At the lower exchange rate, exports from the Island are up $3 million and imports are down $2 million. Looking at the flows into and out of the Foreigners box, the $5 million decrease in the gap between imports and exports equals the $5 million reduction in the amount of dollars that Atoll investors need in order to purchase securities on the Island.

Turning to the expenditure flows, we see that investment expenditure increases by $3 million, the amount of additional borrowing for investment; consumption expenditure increases by $1 million; and government expenditure is unchanged. Absorption therefore increases by $4 million.

EXHIBIT 25.11

THE EFFECT OF AN INCREASE IN THE QUANTITY OF MONEY IN AN OPEN ECONOMY (IN MILLIONS OF DOLLARS)

The increase in the quantity of money shifts the supply of loanable funds to the right, lowering the interest rate. Firms borrow more, but households and foreigners lend less. The fall in foreign lending shifts the demand for foreign exchange to the left, causing a depreciation of the exchange rate.

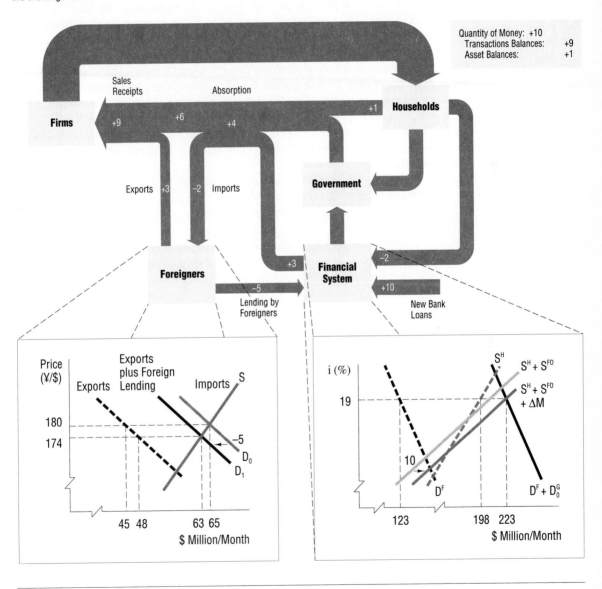

Domestic spending on domestic goods increases by the increase in absorption *plus* the decrease in imports, a total of $6 million. The decrease in imports is the outcome of two effects. The first effect tends to increase imports: As Island residents spend more, they tend to spend more on imported goods too. The second effect tends to work in the opposite direction. The depreciation of the dollar raises the price of imports, making them relatively less attractive. Goods on the Atoll cost the same in yen, but their cost to residents of the Island is higher, because the dollar now buys fewer yen. As a result, expenditure shifts away from imports. In this particular case, the price effect dominates, and imports actually fall. In general, it could go either way.

Foreign spending on domestic goods—Island exports—increases by $3 million. The reason is the depreciation of the dollar. Island goods still cost the same in dollars, but at the lower exchange rate they cost less in yen. As a result, Atoll residents buy more goods from the Island. Therefore total expenditure on domestic goods (sales receipts of firms on the Island) increases by a total of $9 million—the increase in absorption plus the drop in imports plus the increase in exports.

The $9 million increase in total expenditure means an increase in transactions balances by the same amount. As we have seen, asset balances also increase by $1 million. So money balances increase by a total of $10 million, exactly equaling the increase in the quantity of money.

The increased expenditure this month means that households will receive a higher income next month. This will affect their expenditure and their lending and lead to further repercussions in the loanable funds and foreign exchange markets.

DIFFERENCES BETWEEN THE EFFECTS IN OPEN AND CLOSED ECONOMIES

Let us compare our results here with those we obtained in Chapter 24 for a similar monetary change in a closed economy. In comparing Exhibit 25.11 with Exhibit 24.5, we see the following differences:

1. The loan-supply effect of the monetary expansion on the interest rate is smaller in the open economy: The interest rate falls to 19% rather than to 18%. The reason the loan-supply effect is smaller is the reduction in lending by foreigners. As the interest rate falls, foreigners find it less attractive to lend in the dollar-denominated loanable funds market, and their reduction in lending partly offsets the increase in lending by banks.

2. Because the interest rate falls less, there is less of an increase in borrowing for investment—by $3 million instead of by $5 million—and less of a decrease in household lending—by $2 million rather than by $5 million. Investment expenditure and consumption expenditure correspondingly rise less, and absorption increases less—by $4 million instead of by $8 million.

3. Although the effect on absorption is smaller in the open economy, the effect on sales receipts (and thus on subsequent income) is greater once the effect of dollar depreciation on imports and exports is added in. Sales receipts rise by $9 million in the open economy as opposed to a rise of $8 million in the closed economy.

THE MONETARY EFFECTS OF CENTRAL-BANK INTERVENTION IN THE FOREIGN EXCHANGE MARKET

In addition to buying and selling government securities, central banks frequently buy and sell foreign exchange. They do so in order to influence the exchange rate. The exchange rate affects imports and exports, and these affect total sales by firms, which in turn affect income. So the level of the exchange rate matters, and a central bank may therefore intervene in the foreign exchange market to try to affect it.

For example, if there are large temporary gyrations in the exchange rate, it may make sense for the central bank to step in and "maintain an orderly market." By stabilizing the exchange rate, it may be possible to prevent the dislocation that would be caused in the economy by large temporary fluctuations in imports and exports. The central bank might also intervene if it believed the market-determined exchange rate to be "too high" or "too low." We shall discuss the wisdom of such intervention in Part Seven, when we look at monetary policy in general.

Until now, we have assumed that the exchange rate is freely determined by supply and demand in the foreign exchange market without any such official intervention. Such a situation is described as one of a **freely floating exchange rate.** When market forces normally determine the rate, but with occasional central-bank intervention, the situation is called a **dirty float.** When central banks intervene regularly to prevent all fluctuations in the exchange rate, the exchange rate is described as a **fixed exchange rate.**

What are the monetary effects of intervention in the foreign exchange market? Suppose the Island's central bank wishes to lower the exchange rate in the hope of reducing imports and increasing exports. It does this by selling $1 million on the foreign exchange market. Given its ability to *create* definitive dollars, the central bank has no difficulty in finding the $1 million. In exchange for the dollars it sells, the central bank receives yen, which it uses to buy yen-denominated securities.

As we saw in Chapter 20, when the central bank sells dollars (buys yen), it increases bank reserves by the amount of the sale. So the $1 million sale of dollars on the foreign exchange market will have a monetary effect similar to the $1 million open market purchase that we have just studied. In particular, the interest rate will fall, reducing lending by foreigners. The resulting reduction of foreign investors' demand for dollars on the foreign exchange market will add substantially to the downward pressure on the dollar. In fact, the monetary effects of the intervention may have substantially more impact on the exchange rate than the intervention itself.

freely floating exchange rate
Exchange rate determined solely by supply and demand.

dirty float
Exchange rate determined by supply and demand but with occasional central-bank intervention.

fixed exchange rate
Nonfluctuating exchange rate that is determined by central banks.

The other effects of the foreign exchange intervention on the economy—on firm and consumption expenditure, on absorption, and on total sales by firms—will be much the same as for an open market operation. Indeed, as we shall see in Part Seven, monetary policy can in principle be conducted via the foreign exchange market rather than via the market for government securities.

Very often, however, central banks will use defensive open market operations to offset the monetary effects of exchange-rate intervention. This is called a **sterilized intervention**. For example, in the case at hand, the Island central bank could sell $1 million of government securities to "soak up" the $1 million of additional reserves that the foreign exchange intervention created. With a sterilized intervention, the reinforcing monetary effect through a fall in the interest rate is prevented, and the total impact of the intervention on the exchange rate will be much smaller.

sterilized intervention
Central-bank use of open market operations to offset the monetary effects of exchange-rate intervention.

25.7 | APPLICATION: THE APPRECIATION OF THE U.S. DOLLAR IN THE EARLY 1980s

Although the simple open-economy model that we have developed cannot be seen as a literal description of the U.S. economy, it does react to changes in much the same way. Although the actual numbers are very different, the nature of the reaction is similar. We can demonstrate this by using the model to explain the substantial appreciation of the U.S. dollar against most major currencies that occurred in the early 1980s. The appreciation of the dollar against the yen and the mark, the two most important foreign currencies, is shown in Exhibit 25.12A.

In the early 1980s the Reagan administration cut taxes and at the same time increased government spending. The result, as can be seen in Exhibit 25.12B, was a rapid increase in the federal deficit and in government borrowing. At the same time, the Fed was attempting to restrain monetary growth. The effect of the two policies was a combination of the policy we saw in Section 25.5 with the *opposite* of the policy we saw in Section 25.6.

The consequences were much as our model would have predicted. An increase in deficit spending and monetary restraint both tend to raise interest rates and appreciate the currency: Exhibit 25.12C shows the rise in the U.S. interest rate relative to the interest rates of Japan and Germany, and Exhibit 25.12A shows the appreciation of the dollar. The effect on the balance of payments was a predictable increase in the current-account deficit and a corresponding increase in lending by foreigners: Exhibit 25.9 shows the growing current-account deficit and the corresponding capital inflow.

EXHIBIT 25.12A

YEN AND MARK
EXCHANGE RATES,
1979–1985

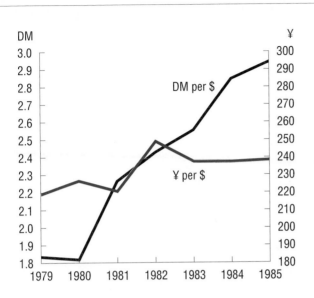

Source: *Economic Report of the President.*

EXHIBIT 25.12B

FEDERAL BUDGET
DEFICIT, 1979–1985

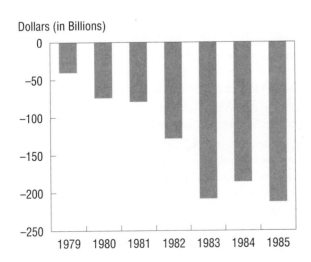

Source: *Economic Report of the President.*

EXHIBIT 25.12C

LONG-TERM REAL
INTEREST RATES,
1979–1985

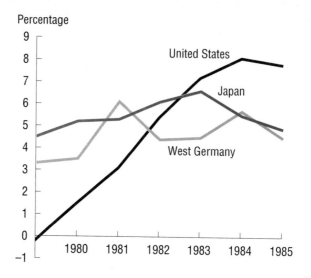

Source: OECD's *Economic Outlook: Historical Statistics.*

SUMMARY

- To understand the behavior of the U.S. economy today, we must recognize that it is an *open* economy—an economy in which foreign trade and international lending are of major importance.

- The foreign exchange market serves the needs of traders who are paid or who must pay in currencies other than their own. It also serves the needs of those who wish to borrow or lend in currencies other than their own.

- Equilibrium in the foreign exchange market implies that imports equal exports plus net lending by foreigners.

- The value of the exchange rate between two currencies depends in the long run on the supplies and demands for all traded goods in both countries. At the long-run equilibrium value of the exchange rate, there is purchasing-power parity between the two currencies.

- Even with foreign trade and international lending, no dollars actually leave the economy.

- For an open economy, income no longer equals total domestic expenditure (absorption). Income equals absorption minus imports plus exports.

- The U.S. trade deficit and the capital inflow into the United States are mirror images of one another: Neither could happen without the other.

- For an open economy, an increase in government deficit spending raises the interest rate and appreciates the currency. The effect on the interest rate is smaller than in a closed economy, and sales receipts and income may rise less.

- In the long run, the exchange rate changes in proportion to a change in the quantity of money.

- In the short run, an increase in the quantity of money in an open economy lowers the interest rate and depreciates the currency. The loan-supply effect is smaller than in a closed economy. The effect on total sales receipts is greater.

- Central banks often intervene in the foreign exchange market to affect the exchange rate. The monetary effects of such an intervention are similar to those of an open market operation.

KEY TERMS

open economy

law of one price

purchasing-power parity

absorption

balance of trade

balance on current account

balance on capital account

balance of payments

appreciation

depreciation

freely floating exchange rate

dirty float

fixed exchange rate

sterilized intervention

DISCUSSION QUESTIONS

1. For a very small open economy, the supply curve of lending by foreigners is perfectly elastic (horizontal). Therefore, the interest rate in its loanable funds market stays the same regardless of the changes that occur in the economy. How does this affect the results of an increase in government deficit spending? Of an increase in the quantity of money?

2. Because of German reunification there is an increase in investment opportunities in Germany, and the interest rate there rises. What is the effect on foreign lending to the United States? (That is, what happens to the supply of foreign loanable funds to the U.S. loanable funds market?) What is the effect on the foreign exchange market? What are the effects on the U.S. economy?

3. The Fed sells U.S. government securities. What are the effects on the loanable funds market? On the foreign exchange market? What are the effects on the economy?

4. Japan is currently lending large sums to the United States. Is this good for the United States? Is it good for Japan? Before you answer, review the discussions in Chapters 3 and 8 of fragmentation and integration of financial markets.

5. Czechoslovakia has a well-trained and potentially productive labor force. However, there has been little investment over the past 40 years, and its

capital stock is antiquated. As a result, productivity is low and unemployment high. In 1991 Czechoslovakia liberalizes its domestic capital market and allows full international capital mobility (foreign borrowing and lending). Assume that the Czech interest rate is high relative to the rest of the world, given the enormous investment potential. What would be the effect on the Czech loanable funds market? On the exchange rate of the Czech crown? On the Czech current account?

SOFTWARE EXERCISE FOR THIS CHAPTER

Title: FXMKT

This computer exercise challenges you to analyze the effects of various events on the foreign exchange market. Specifically, you are asked to predict whether the events will increase, decrease, or have no effect on the demand, supply, price, and quantity sold of foreign exchange. See your instructor if you wish to use this program.

BIBLIOGRAPHY

Bordo, Michael D., "The Classical Gold Standard: Some Lessons for Today," *Review of the Federal Reserve Bank of St. Louis*, May, 1981.

Caves, Richard E., Jeffrey A. Frankel, and Ronald W. Jones, *World Trade and Payments: An Introduction*, Glenview, IL: Scott, Foresman, 1990.

Strongin, Steven, "International Credit Market Connections," *Economic Perspectives of the Federal Reserve Bank of Chicago* July-August 1990, 2–10.

APPENDIX TO CHAPTER 25

A BRIEF HISTORY OF EXCHANGE-RATE REGIMES

Currently, the exchange rates of the major currencies are determined, more or less, by market forces—a regime of floating exchange rates. This situation is fairly recent, going back only to the early 1970s. Before that, exchange rates had generally been fixed. For most of the nineteenth and early twentieth centuries they were fixed in terms of gold. Such a regime is called a **commodity standard.** We shall see how international payments operate under a commodity standard, and then we shall take a brief look at the history of the gold standard. The gold standard broke down in the early twentieth century and was replaced after World War II by the Bretton Woods System of fixed exchange rates; we shall also take a brief look at this.

commodity standard
Exchange rates fixed in terms of a commodity.

HOW A COMMODITY STANDARD WORKS

Let us first see how a commodity standard works in the fictional world of the Island and the Atoll. Instead of fiat definitive moneys, each of the countries uses silver coin as its definitive money. That is, bank money is convertible into silver rather than into liabilities of the central bank.

A ¥100 coin contains half as much silver as a $1 coin, so the exchange rate must be exactly 200¥/$. To see why, consider how you could make money if the exchange rate were higher. You could buy yen for dollars, melt the yen down into silver, and have the silver minted into more dollars than you started with. Similarly, if the exchange rate were below 200¥/$, a profit could be made by turning dollars into yen. Since the exchange rate must be fixed at 200¥/$, there is really no need for a foreign-exchange market.[1]

---

[1]In fact, transporting coin, melting it down, and reminting it is costly, so that there will be a foreign exchange market and the exchange rate will fluctuate in a narrow interval around 200¥/$. We abstract from this minor complication here.

How are international payments made under this regime? Assume first that there are no capital flows. Suppose that the Island buys $55 million worth of goods from the Atoll, and that it sells $50 million worth. Importers pay for the goods they receive by writing checks on their banks. The checks clear and at the end of the clearing process, banks on the Island owe banks on the Atoll $5 million. They pay the $5 million by shipping silver coin in this amount to the Atoll. Notice that under a commodity standard *trade need not be balanced.* The deficit or surplus will be matched by a flow of the commodity money in the appropriate direction.

The shipment of the $5 million in coin from the Island has monetary implications. The banking system on the Island has lost $5 million in reserves. As a result, it reduces its lending. The monetary contraction tends to raise interest rates, lower expenditure and income, and lower prices. Lower income tends to reduce imports, and lower prices on the Island tend to make imports more expensive and exports cheaper. So the imbalance in trade sets in motion forces that tend to restore balance (although the process may be long and painful).

If we allow capital flows, the adjustment mechanism works better. The rise in interest rates that results from the monetary contraction immediately stimulates a capital flow to the Island. Because, under a commodity standard, there is now no worry about possible changes in exchange rate, even small differences in interest rates between the two countries will cause large capital flows.

What happens under this regime if something occurs to stimulate a capital flow in one direction? Clearly, exchange rates cannot change as they would under a floating exchange-rate regime. Suppose that new investment opportunities emerge on the Atoll, causing the interest rate there to rise, and capital flows in from the Island. When the checks Island investors use to pay for the securities clear, banks on the Island find they have to ship silver to the Atoll. Income and prices rise on the Atoll and fall on the Island, so imports to the Atoll increase and its exports decrease. The resulting trade deficit balances the capital inflow. Thus in this respect too the commodity-based system automatically tends to restore balance.

THE GOLD STANDARD

For most of the nineteenth century, exchange rates were set according to commodity standards. Most countries had adopted a gold standard, although some chose silver. The United States officially had a bimetallic standard based on gold and silver until 1861, although it was effectively a silver standard until 1834 and a gold standard after that. From 1862 until 1878 the convertibility of the U.S. dollar was suspended, but a gold standard was reestablished in 1879 and lasted until 1933.

The international gold standard essentially broke down during World War I, and attempts to reestablish it in the interwar years were only partially successful. The reason the regime broke down was that countries were not willing to tolerate the automatic economic adjustments of a commodity standard that we described above. For example, a country out of which gold was flowing would experience monetary contraction, with high interest rates and falling income. Although this would reverse the flow and maintain the exchange rate, the effects on the economy might be painful. It was much easier simply to go off the gold standard, and one country after another did so.

THE BRETTON WOODS AGREEMENT

After World War II an attempt was made to reinstitute a modified gold standard. The rules were spelled out in an agreement signed by the Allies at **Bretton Woods,** New Hampshire, in 1944. Some of the key features of the new regime were:

Bretton Woods
New Hampshire town where the post–WWII system of fixed exchange rates and the International Monetary Fund were established by international agreement in 1944.

1. The U.S. dollar was to be convertible into gold at the rate of $35 per ounce.[2]

2. Other currencies were to be convertible into U.S. dollars at specified fixed exchange rates (and so indirectly convertible into gold).

3. Foreign governments were expected to intervene in the foreign-exchange markets to maintain these fixed exchange rates.

4. The **International Monetary Fund (IMF)** was set up as a sort of international central bank to monitor compliance and to help countries that had difficulty maintaining their exchange rates. It could do this by lending them gold or foreign exchange or by lending them its own liabilities (known as *special drawing rights, or SDRs*).

International Monetary Fund (IMF)
International organization established in 1944 to monitor exchange rates and to promote orderly international financial conditions.

5. If a country could not succeed in maintaining its fixed exchange rate, even with the help of the IMF, it could be allowed, with the agreement of the IMF, to change its exchange rate with the dollar.

The Bretton Woods regime functioned relatively well for over 20 years, but it finally broke down in the early 1970s, for reasons we shall discuss in Part Seven. We shall see there that some economists are unhappy with the current regime of (more or less) floating exchange rates, and that they therefore advocate a return to either a fixed exchange-rate regime or a gold standard.

KEY TERMS

commodity standard
Bretton Woods
International Monetary
   Fund (IMF)

---

[2]The dollar was convertible only for foreign central banks, not for U.S. residents. The Bank of France could, and did, convert dollars that it acquired into gold bullion. But U.S. residents were not allowed even to own gold coin or bullion, let alone convert their dollars into gold.

CHAPTER 26

THE ISLM MODEL

The circular flow model of Chapters 24 and 25 helped us understand the first effects of monetary and other changes on the economy. It was clear, however, that the process of adjustment would continue as income and expenditure continued to change. The Quantity Theory of Chapter 22 gave us some idea of the ultimate effects, once all adjustments had been made. But what happens in between? What does the adjustment process look like?

We shall look at the adjustment process in two stages. In this chapter we shall look at the mutual adjustment of income and expenditure, *assuming prices do not change*. In Chapter 27 we shall look at the adjustment of prices. Taken together, the two chapters will give us a picture of how the economy behaves in the intermediate run, over a period of, say, one or two years.

The theory of the mutual adjustment of income and expenditure was developed in the 1930s by John Maynard Keynes, a British economist, and was published as his *General Theory of Employment, Interest and Money*. The model we shall study in this chapter is called the ISLM model. It was developed by John Hicks, another British economist, to express Keynes's ideas in mathematical form. However, as we shall see, the ISLM model is flexible enough to express views that differ substantially from those of Keynes himself.

26.1 | THE MACROECONOMIC AGGREGATES

A key element in the Keynesian approach to understanding the economy is a system of **national income accounting** that defines and measures **macroeconomic aggregates**. A macroeconomic aggregate is a measure of some variable for the economy as a whole rather than for any individual. For example, aggregate consumption is consumption of all households taken together, as opposed to the consumption of some individual household. The system of national income

national income accounting
Definition and measurement of macroeconomic aggregates.

macroeconomic aggregate
Measure of some variable for the economy as a whole.

663

E X H I B I T **26.1**

THE CIRCULAR FLOW
OF PAYMENTS

The macroeconomic
aggregates of the national
income accounts may be
understood in terms of the
circular flow of payments.

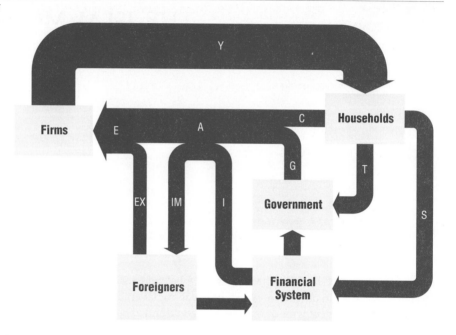

accounting can be understood in terms of the circular flow diagram of Exhibit 26.1.

Total spending by domestic residents, or absorption, denoted A, is made up of three components—consumption, investment, and government expenditure. Consumption, C, is household expenditure less residential investment (investment in new homes). Investment, I, is investment by firms plus residential investment by households. Government expenditure, G, is the purchase of goods and services by the government.[1] Hence

$$A = C + I + G. \qquad [26.1]$$

Total expenditure, E, is what we have called until now the sales receipts of domestic firms. To get from absorption (total spending by domestic residents) to total expenditure (sales receipts of domestic firms), we must subtract imports and

---

[1]Investment in residential housing, which we had before assumed to be zero, is now included in investment. Government expenditure includes spending on goods and services by federal, state, and local governments combined. In 1989, the federal government spent \$404 billion on goods and services, and state and local governments spent \$633 billion. Government expenditure does not include transfer payments such as Social Security and the payment of interest on government debt.

add exports. Domestic expenditure on imports does not represent sales for domestic firms; expenditure by foreigners on domestic goods does represent sales for domestic firms. That is,

$$E = A + EX - IM. \qquad [26.2]$$

If we define *net* exports, X, as exports, EX, less imports IM—

$$X = EX - IM \qquad [26.3]$$

—and if we use Equation 26.1 to substitute for A, then Equation 26.2 becomes

$$E = C + I + G + X. \qquad [26.4]$$

As you can see from Exhibit 26.1, firms pay out all their sales receipts as income, Y.[2] Therefore income, Y, equals expenditure:

$$Y = E. \qquad [26.5]$$

The U.S. national income accounts for 1989 are shown in Exhibit 26.2. Consumption expenditure was $3,470 billion. This included $473 billion spent on durables (cars, household appliances, etc.); $1,123 billion spent on nondurables (food, clothing, etc.); and $1,874 billion spent on services (medical care, education, tourism, etc.). Fixed investment was $747 billion. It included $235 billion of residential investment (new houses and apartments) and $512 billion of fixed investment by firms (new factories, power stations, ships, etc.). Government expenditure was $1,037 billion. Absorption, the sum of these three categories of expenditure, was $5,254 billion. Net exports were –$47 billion, the $626 billion of exports less the $673 billion of imports. Total final sales, the sum of absorption and net exports, were $5,207 billion.

We can rewrite Equation 26.4 using these numbers:

E	=	C	+	I	+	G	+	X
(5,207)		(3,470)		(747)		(1,037)		(–47)

Gross national product (GNP) is a measure of goods and services *produced* during a year rather than of those actually *sold*. The two need not be the same. Firms may sell goods out of inventory that were produced in previous years, and they may add to inventory, rather than sell, goods produced during the current

gross national product (GNP)
All of the goods and services produced by the economy during a year.

[2]If the period in Exhibit 26.1 is taken to be a month, as it is in the circular flow model, then next month's income equals this month's expenditure. If the flow of payments stays the same from month to month, as we assume in this chapter, then *this* month's income also equals this month's expenditure.

year. To obtain GNP, therefore, the $27 billion increase in inventories must be added to total sales, giving a total of $5,234 billion.[3]

26.2 BALANCE BETWEEN INCOME AND EXPENDITURE

We saw in Chapters 24 and 25 that when something happens to disturb the economy—a change in government expenditure, say, or a change in the quantity of money—expenditure changes. Since this month's expenditure is also next month's income, next month's income changes too. With income different next month, expenditure will be different too. This will affect income in the following month, and so on. A key element of Keynes's theory was the realization that this process of expenditure affecting income and income affecting expenditure would eventually come to an end, with income and expenditure once again in balance.

We shall look at the process of adjustment in two stages. First, in order to understand the basic mechanism as clearly as possible, we shall examine it in this section under the assumption that the interest rate does not change. In the next section we shall see how the mechanism works when we allow the interest rate to change as income and expenditure change.

In the process of mutual adjustment, expenditure becomes income and income determines expenditure. So we need to see *how* income determines expenditure. To that end, we shall look in turn at the behavior that determines each of the different components of expenditure.

THE KEYNESIAN CONSUMPTION FUNCTION

disposable income
Total household income less taxes.

Consumption depends on the income that households have available to spend, on *disposable income*. **Disposable income**, Y_d, is total income less taxes, T:[4]

$$Y_d = Y - T. \qquad [26.6]$$

To simplify things, we shall assume that taxes are a fixed proportion, t, of total income, so that

$$T = t\,Y. \qquad [26.7]$$

---

[3]Income, as defined above to be equal to final sales, is income received during the year. GNP is a measure of income earned or accrued. In what follows, we shall ignore this accounting distinction and use GNP as if it measures income in both senses.

[4]Taxes are *net* taxes—taxes actually paid *less* government transfer payments to individuals, such as Social Security and welfare payments. The definition of G, correspondingly, does not include these transfers, only actual purchases of goods and services by the government (defense procurement, federal, state, and local employees' salaries, etc.).

EXHIBIT 26.2

U.S. NATIONAL
INCOME ACCOUNTS
FOR 1989
(BILLIONS OF
DOLLARS)

Consumption expenditure		$3,470	
Durables	$ 473		
Nondurables	1,123		
Services	1,874		
Investment expenditure		747	
Residential	235		
Firms, fixed	512		
Government expenditure		1,037	
Absorption			$5,254
Net exports		−47	
Exports	$ 626		
Imports	−673		
Final Sales			$5,207
Increase in inventory		$27	
Gross National Product			$5,234

Source: *Federal Reserve Bulletin*, June 1990.

For example, if the tax rate, t, is 10% and Y is $1,000 million, then

$$T = 0.1 \times 1,000 = 100. \qquad [26.8]$$

That is, total taxes are $100 million.

Equation 26.7 can be used to substitute for T in Equation 26.6 to obtain

$$Y_d = Y - t\,Y = (1 - t)\,Y. \qquad [26.9]$$

For example, if t is 10%, then disposable income is 90% of total income.

Keynes postulated that the relationship between consumption and disposable income took the form of the following **consumption function**:

$$C = a + b\,Y_d, \qquad [26.10]$$

where a and b are positive constants. The constant a is called **autonomous consumption**—consumption expenditure that is independent of the level of income—and the constant b is called the **marginal propensity to consume.**[5]

The meaning of the consumption function may be illustrated with some numbers for our fictitious South Seas island. Suppose that for the Island, $a = \$70$

consumption function
Relationship of consumption spending to the level of income.

autonomous consumption
Consumption expenditure that is independent of the level of income.

marginal propensity to consume
Amount consumed out of each additional dollar of income.

[5]Equation 26.10 has consumption expenditure depending on nominal income. The consumption function should determine *real* consumption in terms of *real* disposable income: As we saw in Chapter 23, economic behavior is determined by real variables, not nominal ones. However, with prices constant as we assume here, we can use real and nominal magnitudes interchangeably. The same liberty is taken with the other behavioral equations later in this chapter.

million and $b = 0.7$, so that the consumption function is

$$C = 70 + 0.7\ Y_d. \qquad [26.11]$$

Therefore, if disposable income is $900 million, then

$$C = 70 + 0.7 \times 900 = 700. \qquad [26.12]$$

To see why the constant b is called the marginal propensity to consume, consider what happens to consumption if disposable income increases from $900 million to $1,000 million:

$$C = 70 + 0.7 \times 1,000 = 770. \qquad [26.13]$$

When disposable income increases by $100 million, consumption increases by only $b \times \$100$ million, or $70 million. The coefficient b shows what fraction of additional (or marginal) income households will consume.

Equation 26.9 can be used to substitute for Y_d in Equation 26.10 to obtain consumption as a function of *total* income:

$$C = a + b\ (1 - t)\ Y. \qquad [26.14]$$

This is the equation we shall use in developing the Keynesian model. For the Island,

$$C = 70 + 0.7\ (1 - 0.1)\ Y = 70 + 0.63\ Y. \qquad [26.15]$$

🌴 **CHECK STATION 1** | **How much does consumption change if income on the Island falls $200 million?**

THE OTHER ELEMENTS OF EXPENDITURE

How does income affect the other elements of expenditure—investment, government, and net exports? Investment, as we saw in Chapter 2, depends on the interest rate and on investment opportunities, but not on income. For the moment, since we take the interest rate as fixed, investment can be taken to be a fixed amount, I^*. Similarly, government expenditure is largely determined by the political process, independent both of the interest rate and of income, so it too can be taken to be a fixed amount, $\overline{G}$.[6] For the Island economy, $I^* = \$120$ million and $\overline{G} = \$200$ million.

Net exports are exports minus imports. As we saw in Chapter 25, exports decrease with the exchange rate and imports increase with the exchange rate and increase with income. Assume for the moment that the exchange rate, like the

---

[6]In reality, aggregate income and the level of interest rates do affect the government budget, but principally through T rather than through G.

interest rate, does not change. Then we may regard exports as being fixed and imports as depending only on income. Net exports may therefore be written

$$X = X^* - g\, Y, \qquad\qquad [26.16]$$

where X^* and g are constants. The constant X^* is **autonomous net exports** (the part of net exports that does not depend on income), and g is the positive **marginal propensity to import.**

For the Island economy, $X^* = \$30$ million and $g = 0.05$, so that

$$X = 30 - 0.05\, Y. \qquad\qquad [26.17]$$

The meaning of the marginal propensity to import is much like the meaning of the marginal propensity to consume: A \$1 million increase in income will increase imports—and *decrease* net exports—by 0.05 x \$1 million = \$50,000.

How much do net exports change if income on the Island falls \$200 million?

autonomous net exports
Part of net exports that is independent of income.

marginal propensity to import
Amount imported out of each additional dollar of income.

🌴 **CHECK STATION 2**

TOTAL EXPENDITURE AND INCOME

Having seen how each category of expenditure depends on income, we are now ready to see how *total* expenditure depends on income. All that is necessary is to substitute for the various categories of expenditure in Equation 26.4, using Equations 26.14 and 26.16 for C and X and using the fixed values of I and G:

$$E = [a + b\,(1 - t)\, Y] + I^* + \overline{G} + [X^* - g\, Y]. \qquad\qquad [26.18]$$

For the Island, using Equations 26.15 and 26.17 for C and X and substituting \$120 million for I and \$180 million for G, this becomes:

$$E = (70 + 0.63\, Y) + 120 + 200 + (30 - 0.05\, Y). \qquad\qquad [26.19]$$

Equation 26.19 can be used to trace the process of mutual adjustment of income and expenditure. Suppose that at the beginning of some month, call it Month 1, households receive \$1,100 million in income. Using Equation 26.19, expenditure for the month will be

$$E_1 = (70 + 0.63 \times 1,100) + 120 + 200 + (30 - 0.05 \times 1,100) = 1,058. \quad [26.20]$$

The expenditure of Month 1 is paid out at the beginning of Month 2 as income. So income in Month 2 is \$1,058 million. Using Equation 26.19 again, expenditure in Month 2 is

$$E_2 = (70 + 0.63 \times 1,063) + 120 + 200 + (30 - 0.05 \times 1,063) = 1,037. \quad [26.21]$$

So income for Month 3 will be \$1,037 million. And so on.

From these examples it is clear that each month expenditure is less than income and that income is therefore falling from month to month. It also looks as though the gap between income and expenditure is closing. If it closes completely, so that expenditure equals the income that generated it, then income next month will equal income this month. That is, income will stop falling and it will remain the same from month to month. At that point income and expenditure will be in balance. We would like to be able to find the level of income at which this happens, that is, the level of income for which

$$E = Y.$$ [26.22]

CHECK STATION 3 | **What is expenditure in Month 3? What is income in Month 4?**

THE KEYNESIAN CROSS

One way to find the level of income at which income and expenditure balance is to use a diagram called the *Keynesian cross*. An example is shown in Exhibit 26.3, using the numbers for the Island economy. The vertical axis represents expenditure and the horizontal axis represents income. A $45°$ line is drawn from the origin. For any point on the $45°$ line, the value along the vertical axis (expenditure) equals the value along the horizontal axis (income). So the $45°$ line represents the balance condition, Equation 26.22. The solid line shows total expenditure as a function of income, Equation 26.19. Call this the *expenditure line*. For any level of income, the corresponding level of total expenditure may be read from the expenditure line. The point of balance is the point at which the expenditure line intersects the $45°$ line. At that level of income, expenditure equals the income that generates it. For this example, balance occurs at $1,000 million.

CHECK STATION 4 | **What would be the effect on the expenditure line of an increase in investment? What would be the effect on the level of income at which income and expenditure are in balance?**

AN ALGEBRAIC SOLUTION

Instead of using the Keynesian cross diagram to find the point of balance, we can solve for it directly by finding the value of Y that satisfies Equations 26.18 and 26.22 simultaneously. To find that value of Y, just use Equation 26.18 to substitute for E in Equation 26.22, to obtain

$$[a + b (1 - t) Y] + I^* + \overline{G} + [X^* - g Y] = Y.$$ [26.23]

Then gather terms in Y:

$$[a + I^* + \overline{G} + X^*] = \{1 - b (1 - t) + g\} Y.$$ [26.24]

EXHIBIT 26.3

THE KEYNESIAN CROSS

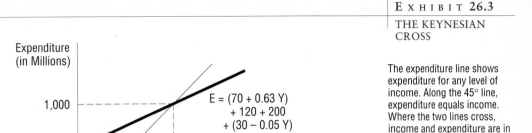

The expenditure line shows expenditure for any level of income. Along the 45° line, expenditure equals income. Where the two lines cross, income and expenditure are in balance.

Finally, divide both sides by the term in braces:

$$Y = \frac{1}{\{1 - b(1-t) + g\}} [a + I^* + \overline{G} + X^*]. \qquad [26.25]$$

This value of Y is precisely the one at which the expenditure line and the 45° line intersect. To see this, substitute the numbers for the Island economy into Equation 26.25:

$$Y = \frac{1}{\{1 - 0.7(1-0.1) + 0.05\}} [70 + 120 + 200 + 30] = 1,000. \quad [26.26]$$

THE INCOME MULTIPLIER

We can see from Equation 26.25 what factors determine the level of income at which balance occurs between income and expenditure. The term in brackets is called **autonomous expenditure**. The term that multiplies autonomous expenditure is called the **income multiplier**.[7] Equation 26.25 may therefore be written in words:

$$\begin{matrix} \text{income at which} \\ \text{balance occurs} \end{matrix} = \begin{matrix} \text{income} \\ \text{multiplier} \end{matrix} \times \begin{matrix} \text{autonomous} \\ \text{expenditure} \end{matrix} \qquad [26.27]$$

autonomous expenditure
Expenditure that is independent of the level of income.

income multiplier
The ratio of income to autonomous expenditure.

[7]Not to be confused with the *money* multiplier that we encountered in Chapter 19.

The greater the autonomous expenditure and the greater the value of the income multiplier, the greater the level of income at which balance occurs.

Autonomous expenditure is the sum of autonomous consumption, a, investment, I^*, government expenditure, $\overline{G}$, and autonomous net exports, X^*. An increase in any one of these will increase the level of income at which balance occurs.

The income multiplier is

$$\frac{1}{\{1 - b\,(1 - t) + g\}}.$$

An increase in the marginal propensity to consume, b, increases the multiplier. An increase in the tax rate, t, or in the marginal propensity to import, g, decreases the multiplier. For the Island economy, with $b = 0.7$, $t = 0.1$, and $g = 0.05$, the multiplier is

$$\frac{1}{1 - 0.7\,(1 - 0.1) + 0.05} = 2.381.$$

We can use the multiplier to see by how much income will change when autonomous expenditure changes—that is, by how much income will have risen once the process of mutual adjustment of income and expenditure is over. To do this, translate Equation 26.27 from levels to changes as follows:[8]

$$\begin{matrix} \text{change in income at} \\ \text{which balance occurs} \end{matrix} = \begin{matrix} \text{income} \\ \text{multiplier} \end{matrix} \times \begin{matrix} \text{change in autonomous} \\ \text{expenditure} \end{matrix} \qquad [26.28]$$

For example, if the government of the Island increases its expenditure by $30 million, autonomous expenditure increases by the same amount, and income will eventually rise by 2.38 times the increase in autonomous expenditure, or $71.4 million.

🌴 **CHECK STATION 5**

A. **Does the $30 million increase in government expenditure pay for itself? To see, use Equation 26.7 to calculate the increase in taxes, and compare it to the increase in expenditure.**

B. **By how much would a drop in investment of $10 million change the income of the Island?**

APPLICATION: AUTONOMOUS EXPENDITURE IN THE GREAT DEPRESSION

The multiplier model can be useful in interpreting real-world events. As an example, let us consider the behavior of expenditure during the Great Depres-

---

[8]See Appendix B to Chapter 19 if the transition from levels to changes is not clear to you.

Year	Investment Expenditure	Government Expenditure	Net Exports	Total Expenditure
1929	$16.2	$8.5	$1.1	$103.1
1930	10.1	9.2	1.0	90.4
1931	5.6	9.2	0.5	75.8
1932	1.0	8.1	0.4	58.0
1933	1.4	8.0	0.4	55.6
1934	3.3	9.8	0.6	65.1
1935	6.4	10.0	0.1	72.2
1936	8.5	12.0	0.1	82.5
1937	11.8	11.9	0.3	90.4
1938	6.5	13.0	1.3	84.7
1939	9.3	13.3	1.1	90.5
1940	13.1	14.0	1.7	99.7
1941	17.9	24.8	1.3	124.5

Source: *Economic Report of the President*, various years; *Historical Statistics of the United States*, U.S. Department of Commerce.

sion. Exhibit 26.4 shows what happened to the various elements of autonomous expenditure and to total expenditure for the years 1929–1941.

Between 1929, the year of the Crash, and 1932, investment declined from $16.2 billion to $1.0 billion. The Smoot-Hawley Tariff Act of 1930 erected substantial barriers to trade in a misguided attempt to protect jobs, contributing to a fall in net exports from $1.1 billion to $0.4 billion. Government expenditure rose initially but then fell as the government, perversely, tried to balance its budget. In all, autonomous expenditure fell from $25.8 billion in 1929 to $9.5 billion in 1932. As the multiplier model suggests, total expenditure fell by a far greater amount—from $103.1 billion to $58.0 billion. In 1934 government expenditure began to increase again as a result of President Roosevelt's New Deal programs, and investment recovered somewhat. As a result, total expenditure began to recover too. Recovery was not complete, however, until government expenditure, and with it autonomous expenditure, rose dramatically with the outbreak of World War II.

26.3 EQUILIBRIUM OF INCOME AND INTEREST RATE

The multiplier model suggests that a $30 million increase in government expenditure on the Island will increase income by several times as much, by $71.4 million. This result is in stark contrast with what we found when we looked at the effects of the same increase in government expenditure using the circular flow model in Section 25.5. There we found that a $30 million increase in government expenditure would lead to an increase in income of only $5 million—much *less* than the increase in government expenditure.

There are two reasons for this difference. The first, of course, is the multiplier process. The circular flow model describes only the *first* effect of an increase in government expenditure, whereas the multiplier model describes the final effect, when the process of expenditure raising income and of income raising expenditure has worked itself out. It is perfectly reasonable that the multiplier process should amplify the impact of the initial change.

The second reason for the difference is our assumption here that there is no change in the interest rate. This assumption, although convenient, is unrealistic. The circular flow model shows that increased government borrowing raises the interest rate. The higher interest rate causes other types of expenditure to fall, and their fall partially offsets the increase in government expenditure. So the simple multiplier model is not really satisfactory. We need to expand it to take account of changes in the interest rate and of their effect on expenditure and income.

AUTONOMOUS EXPENDITURE AND THE INTEREST RATE

The first step is to see how the interest rate affects expenditure. The Keynesian assumption is that consumption and government expenditure do not depend on the interest rate, but that investment and net exports do.

THE INVESTMENT FUNCTION   Investment is a decreasing function of the interest rate. With respect to business investment, we saw in Chapter 2 that the higher the rate of interest, the fewer profitable investment projects there are and the less firms will invest. With respect to residential investment, we saw in Chapter 15 that the higher the rate of interest, the less mortgage borrowing there is and the less new construction.

investment function
Relationship of investment to the interest rate.

The dependence of investment on the interest rate can be expressed in the form of the following **investment function**:

$$I = c - d\,i, \tag{26.29}$$

where c and d are positive constants. The meaning of these constants may be illustrated with some numbers for the Island economy. Suppose that $c = \$200$ million and $d = 400$. If the interest rate is 20%, investment will be

$$I = 200 - 400 \times 0.2 = 120. \tag{26.30}$$

If the interest rate rises to 30%, investment will fall to $80 million; if the interest rate falls to 10%, investment will rise to $160 million. So d is a measure of the sensitivity of investment to changes in interest rate: The larger is d, the more sensitive is investment.

THE NET EXPORT FUNCTION We saw in Chapter 25 that exports and imports depend on the exchange rate: The higher the value of the dollar, the lower are exports and the higher are imports. We saw too that imports also depend on the level of spending: The more is spent in total, the more is spent on imports. These relationships may be summarized as

$$X = EX(e) - IM(e,Y). \qquad [26.31]$$

Thus an increase in the value of the dollar, e, will decrease net exports because it will reduce exports and increase imports; an increase in income, and therefore an increase in expenditure, will decrease net exports because it will increase imports.

We can infer from Equation 26.31 what effect the *interest rate* will have on net exports. We found in Chapter 25 that an increase in interest rate means an increase in the value of the dollar. Since an increase in the value of the dollar means a fall in net exports, we can infer that an increase in interest rate will *reduce* net exports.

The dependence of net exports on the interest rate and on income is expressed in the following **net export function:**

$$X = f - h\,i - g\,Y, \qquad [26.32]$$

net export function
Relationship of net exports to the interest rate and to income.

where f, g, and h are positive constants. The meaning of these constants may be illustrated using some numbers for the Island economy. Suppose that $f = \$110$ million, $h = 400$, and $g = 0.05$. Then, if the interest rate is 20% and income is $1,000 million, net exports for the Island will be

$$X = 110 - 400 \times 0.20 - 0.05 \times 1000 = -20. \qquad [26.33]$$

That is, the Island will be a net *importer* of $20 million.

As we saw in Section 26.2, the constant g is the *marginal propensity to import*. It shows the sensitivity of imports, and so of net exports, to changes in income. The constant h shows the sensitivity of net exports to changes in interest rate.

By comparing Equation 26.32 to Equation 26.16, we see that

$$X = f - h\,i - g\,Y = X^* - g\,Y, \qquad [26.34]$$

so that autonomous net exports must be

$$X^* = f - h\,i. \qquad [26.35]$$

THE IS CURVE

The income multiplier equation, Equation 26.27, shows how the level of income at which balance occurs is related to autonomous expenditure. We have just seen that autonomous expenditure in turn depends on the rate of interest (through the

EXHIBIT 26.5

POINT-OF-BALANCE
INCOME AT VARIOUS
INTEREST RATES

Interest Rate, i	Autonomous Expenditure	Times Income Multiplier	Equals Income, Y
10%	500	× 2.381	1,191
20	420	× 2.381	1,000
30	340	× 2.381	810

dependence of investment and net exports). These two relationships may be combined to show how the level of income at which balance occurs is related to the interest rate. To do this, just use Equations 26.29 and 26.35 to substitute for I^* and X^* in Equation 26.25:

$$Y = \frac{1}{\{1 - b(1-t) + g\}} [a + (c - d\,i) + \overline{G} + (f - h\,i)]. \qquad [26.36]$$

This equation gives point-of-balance income as a function of the interest rate. The higher the interest rate, the lower are investment and net exports, and—through the multiplier—the lower is income. For example, using the numbers for the Island economy,

$$Y = \frac{1}{\{1 - 0.7(1 - 0.1) + 0.05\}} [70 + (200 - 400 \times i) + 200 + (110 - 400 \times i)]. \qquad [26.37]$$

Solving Equation 26.37 for Y at different values of i gives the numbers shown in Exhibit 26.5. These numbers can be used to plot the graph in Exhibit 26.6. This graph shows at what level income and expenditure would balance for each value of the interest rate. The graph is called the **IS curve** (for Investment-Saving). It is usual to draw the graph with the interest rate on the vertical axis and income on the horizontal axis.

IS curve
Graph showing the levels at which income and expenditure are in balance for different values of the interest rate.

Equation 26.36 is the general formula of the IS curve. *Any change to the equation that increases* Y *for a given value of* i *shifts the IS curve to the right.* Two sorts of change will do this. The first is any change that increases the value of the income multiplier:

- An increase in the marginal propensity to consume, *b*.
- A decrease in the tax rate, *t*.
- A decrease in the marginal propensity to import, *g*.

The second sort of change that will increase Y and shift the IS curve to the right is anything that increases autonomous expenditure for a given interest rate:

EXHIBIT 26.6

THE IS CURVE

The IS curve shows at what level income and expenditure balance for each value of the interest rate.

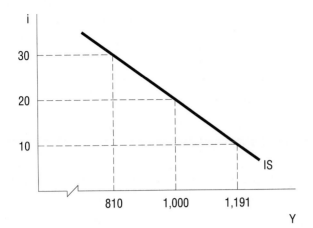

- An increase in autonomous consumption, a.
- An increase in government expenditure, $\overline{G}$.
- An increase in the constant c—representing an increased desire to invest at a given interest rate.
- An increase in the constant f—representing an increase in net exports at a given interest rate.

The slope of the IS curve depends on whatever multiplies the interest rate, i, in Equation 26.36. The larger this number, the greater the change in Y for a given change in i, and therefore the *flatter* the IS curve. The following will make the IS curve flatter:

- An increase in the multiplier.
- An increase in d, the sensitivity of investment to the interest rate.
- An increase in h, the sensitivity of net exports to the interest rate.

Use the IS equation of the Island (Equation 26.37) to calculate how much income would increase if the interest rate fell by 2%. | 🌴 **CHECK STATION 6**

E X H I B I T 26.7

COMBINATIONS OF Y
AND i FOR WHICH
MONEY DEMAND
EQUALS $1,500
MILLION

Interest Rate, i	Asset Balances	Income, Y	Transactions Balances	Total Money Demand = Asset + Transactions Balances
10%	600	900	900	1,500
20	500	1,000	1,000	1,500
30	400	1,100	1,100	1,500

THE LM CURVE

The IS curve tells us, for any interest rate, the level at which income and expenditure balance. But what *is* the interest rate? To answer this question, Keynes postulated an additional relationship between income and the interest rate, this time derived from the demand for money. Using the two relationships together, much as one uses supply and demand curves, we shall be able to find the equilibrium values of the interest rate and income.

In Chapter 22 we saw that the Keynesian formulation of the aggregate demand for money divided it into a transactions demand and an asset demand:

$$M^D = k\,Y + (x - z\,i), \qquad [26.38]$$

where k, x, and z are constants. Transactions balances are proportional to income, with k the constant of proportionality. Asset balances are a declining function of the interest rate, with z determining the degree of sensitivity.[9]

We also saw in Chapter 22 that, since all of the money in existence must be held by someone, the aggregate demand for money must equal the total amount in existence. That is,

$$M = M^D. \qquad [26.39]$$

Using Equation 26.38 to substitute for M^D in Equation 26.39, we obtain

$$M = k\,Y + (x - z\,i). \qquad [26.40]$$

Equation 26.40 shows, for a given level of income, what the interest rate must be so that the demand for money will equal the quantity in existence. The higher the level of income, the greater transactions balances will be. If the quantity of money is unchanged, the only way that transactions balances can be greater is for asset balances to be smaller. Asset balances will be smaller if the

---

[9]Equation 26.38 is a modified version of Equation 22.13: $M^D = kE + f(i - i_M)\,W$. We assume here that income and expenditure are in balance, so Y may stand in for E as a determinant of transactions balances. We assume too that wealth, W, and the interest rate on money, i_M, are fixed so that asset balances may be seen simply as a decreasing function of the interest rate on securities.

EXHIBIT 26.8

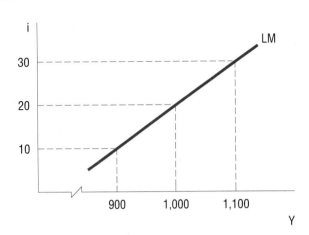

The LM curve shows all combinations of income and interest rate that generate a money demand equal to the quantity of money.

interest rate is higher. So the higher is income, the higher the interest rate must be to satisfy Equation 26.40.

This may be illustrated with some numbers for the Island economy. For the Island, $k = 1$, $x = \$700$ million, and $z = 1,000$; the quantity of money, M, is $1,500 million. So Equation 26.40 becomes

$$1,500 = Y + (700 - 1,000 \times i). \qquad [26.41]$$

For any Y, there is a single i that satisfies Equation 26.41, and for any i, a single Y. Some combinations that satisfy the equation are shown in Exhibit 26.7.

The numbers in Exhibit 26.7 can be used to plot the graph shown in Exhibit 26.8. This graph shows all combinations of income and interest rate that generate a money demand equal to the quantity of money. The graph is called the **LM curve** (demand for Liquidity equals quantity of Money). It is customary to draw the graph with the interest rate on the vertical axis and income on the horizontal axis.

Equation 26.40 is the general formula of the LM curve. It is useful to rearrange it as follows:

$$Y = \frac{M - (x - z\,i)}{k}. \qquad [26.42]$$

LM curve
Graph showing the combinations of income and interest rate for which money demand equals the quantity of money.

For any value of i, Equation 26.42 gives the value of Y for which the demand for money equals M. *Any change to the equation that increases Y for a given value of* i *shifts the LM curve to the right.* The following changes will do this:

EXHIBIT 26.9

IS AND LM CURVES

Where the IS and LM curves intersect (a) income and expenditure are in balance for that interest rate (the IS curve), *and* (b) income and interest rate are such that money demand equals the quantity of money (the LM curve). In this example, equilibrium income is $1,000 million and the equilibrium interest rate is 20%.

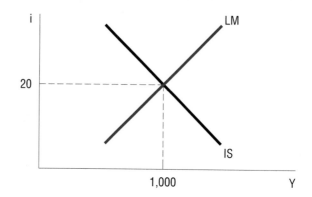

- An increase in M.
- A decrease in x—representing a decrease in the demand for asset balances at a given interest rate.
- A decrease in k.

The slope of the LM curve depends on whatever multiplies the interest rate in Equation 26.42. The larger this number, the greater the change in Y for a given change in i, and therefore the *flatter* the LM curve. The following will make the LM curve flatter:

- An increase in z, the sensitivity of asset balances to the interest rate.
- A decrease in k.

CHECK STATION 7 | **Use the LM equation for the Island (Equation 26.41) to calculate how much income would need to change if the interest rate increased by 1%.**

IS AND LM CURVES TOGETHER

We now have two relationships linking income and the interest rate. The IS curve gives the point-of-balance income corresponding to a given interest rate. The LM curve gives combinations of income and interest rate for which the demand for money equals the quantity of money. The *actual* combination of income and interest rate that we observe in the economy must satisfy both relationships. Therefore the point representing the actual combination of income and interest rate must be on *both* curves. There is only one such point—the point at which the two curves intersect.

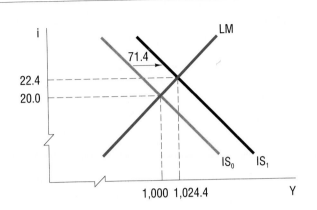

EXHIBIT 26.10

AN INCREASE IN
GOVERNMENT
EXPENDITURE SHIFTS
THE IS CURVE

An increase in government
expenditure moves the IS
curve to the right along an
unchanged LM curve, raising
equilibrium income and the
equilibrium interest rate.

Exhibit 26.9 brings together the IS and the LM curves. The level of income at which the curves intersect is $1,000 million; the interest rate is 20%. We will call these *equilibrium income* and the *equilibrium interest rate*. Setting $Y = 1000$ and $i = 0.20$ satisfies both Equation 26.37 and Equation 26.41.

26.4 USING THE ISLM MODEL

Given some change in the economy, the simple multiplier model gives the new level at which income and expenditure balance, under the assumption that the interest rate is unaffected by the change. The ISLM model gives the new level at which income and expenditure balance, *allowing the interest rate to adjust too*. We shall use the ISLM model to examine the effects on the economy of an increase in government expenditure, of an increase in money demand, and of an increase in the quantity of money.

THE EFFECT OF AN INCREASE IN GOVERNMENT EXPENDITURE

The effect of an increase in government expenditure of $30 million on the Island is shown in Exhibit 26.10. Looking at the formula for the IS curve, Equation 26.36, we see that the increase in government expenditure, G, represents an increase in autonomous expenditure. The IS curve therefore shifts to the *right* by the multiplier times the change in autonomous expenditure—that is, by 2.38 x $30 million = $71.4 million. Looking at the formula for the LM curve, Equation 26.42, we see that the LM curve is *not* affected by this change. Therefore the IS curve moves along the same LM curve to a new point of equilibrium at an income of $1,024.4 million and an interest rate of 22.4%.

EXHIBIT 26.11

DEFICITS, GNP, AND
INTEREST RATES
1965–1969

	Federal Deficit	Short-Term Interest Rate	Nominal GNP
1965	–1.596	4.4	684.9
1966	–3.796	5.6	749.9
1967	–8.702	5.1	793.9
1968	–25.161	5.9	864.2
1969	3.236	7.8	930.3

Source: *Economic Report of the President.*

Comparing this result with the one we obtained from the multiplier model in Section 26.2, the increase in income is much smaller—$24.4 million versus $71.4 million. The reason is as follows: The increased expenditure requires larger transactions balances; transactions balances can be larger only if asset balances are smaller; smaller asset balances require a higher interest rate; the higher interest rate means that investment expenditure and net exports are lower, partly offsetting the effect on total expenditure of the original increase in government expenditure.

Comparing this result with the one we obtained from the circular flow model in Section 25.5, the increase in income is much larger—$24.4 million versus $5 million. The reason is that the circular flow model gives only the first effect, whereas the ISLM model gives the final effect once the process of mutual adjustment of income and expenditure is over and income and expenditure are once again in balance.

🌴 **CHECK STATION 8** | **By how much do net exports change as a result of this change in government expenditure?**

APPLICATION: THE VIETNAM WAR AND ITS ECONOMIC IMPLICATIONS

From the mid-1960s the United States escalated its involvement in the Vietnam War, and military spending rose rapidly. At the same time the Great Society social programs began to raise civilian spending. As you can see from Exhibit 26.11, the two combined to produce a steadily rising government deficit. As the ISLM model predicts, there was an increase in income and an increase in interest rates. In Chapters 9 and 10 we saw the impact on the financial system of this increase in interest rates.

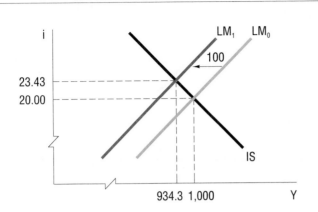

EXHIBIT 26.12

THE PAYMENT OF INTEREST ON CHECKING DEPOSITS SHIFTS THE LM CURVE

An increase in money demand moves the LM curve to the left along an unchanged IS curve, lowering equilibrium income and raising the equilibrium interest rate.

THE EFFECT OF A SHIFT IN MONEY DEMAND

To understand the effect on the economy of a shift in money demand, suppose that banks on the Island begin paying interest on checking deposits. This reduces the opportunity cost of asset balances and makes them more attractive. The effects are shown in Exhibit 26.12. We can represent the increased attractiveness of asset balances by an increase in the value of the constant x in Equation 26.42. As x increases, say, from 700 to 800, the LM curve shifts to the *left* by 100. Looking at the formula for the IS curve, Equation 26.36, we see that it is not affected. Therefore the LM curve moves along an unchanged IS curve to a new point of equilibrium at an income of $934.3 million and an interest rate of 23.43%.

The increase in asset balances requires a decrease in transactions balances, since the total quantity of money is unchanged. Transactions balances can be lower only if expenditure and income are lower. The increase in the interest rate lowers autonomous expenditure, through its effect on investment and on net exports, and so lowers income and expenditure by the required amount.

THE EFFECT OF A MONETARY EXPANSION

To understand the effect of a monetary expansion on the economy, suppose the central bank of the Island purchases $1 million in government securities. This leads to an expansion of bank lending and an expansion in the quantity of money of $10 million. The ISLM model shows the effects of this monetary expansion once income and expenditure have settled down and are once again in balance. The result is shown in Exhibit 26.13. Looking at the formula for the LM curve, Equation 26.42, we see that the increase in the quantity of money, M, shifts the curve to the right by the same amount (k for the Island is 1)—$10 million. From

E X H I B I T 26.13

AN INCREASE IN
THE QUANTITY OF
MONEY SHIFTS
THE LM CURVE

An increase in the quantity of
money moves the LM curve to
the right along an unchanged
IS curve, lowering the
equilibrium interest rate and
raising equilibrium income.

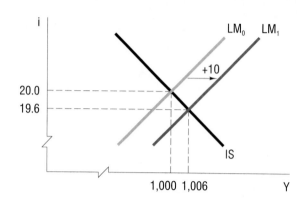

Equation 26.36, we see that the change in the quantity of money has no effect on the IS curve. Therefore the LM curve moves along an unchanged IS curve to a new equilibrium at an income of $1,006 million and an interest rate of 19.6%.

Comparing these results with those we obtained from the circular flow model in Section 25.6, the increase in income is smaller—$6 million versus $9 million—and the fall in the interest rate is smaller—to 19.6% rather than to 19%. The reason is that the increase in the quantity of money is a *one-time* change: The *single* open market operation adds to the supply of loanable funds only in the period in which it occurs. The ISLM model shows what the economy will look like some time later, by which time much of the initial impact has faded. In contrast, the increase in government expenditure we considered before is a *continuing* change: Government expenditure is *permanently* higher, adding to the demand for loanable funds in *every* period after the change. Therefore, its impact continues to grow for a while until income and expenditure have adjusted completely to the change.

APPLICATION:
MARGARET THATCHER'S MONETARY POLICY

In May 1979, Margaret Thatcher was elected Prime Minister of the United Kingdom. She embarked on a policy of severe monetary restraint to bring the rapidly rising price level under control. While the quantity of money continued to grow, the *rate of growth* was reduced. A reduction in the rate of growth of the quantity of money is equivalent in its effect, in terms of the ISLM model, to that of a reduction in the actual quantity of money. As you can see from Exhibit 26.14, the effects of Thatcher's policy were consistent with the results of a shift to the left of the LM curve. Exhibit 26.14 shows the growth rate of the quantity of

EXHIBIT 26.14

MONETARY RESTRAINT IN THE UNITED KINGDOM 1979–1982

Year	Monetary Growth[a]	Income[b]	Interest Rate[c]	Exchange Rate[d]
1978	22.1%	£198	11.91%	81.5
1979	12.3	201	16.49	87.3
1980	6.6	196	13.45	96.1
1981	10.0	194	15.35	95.3
1982	8.0	198	10.20	90.7

[a]Monetary growth = percentage change in M1.
[b]Income = real gross domestic product in billions, 1980 prices.
[c]Interest rate = T-bill rate.
[d]Exchange rate = trade-weighted average of exchange rate against other currencies.
Source: Central Statistical Office, *Economic Trends* (London, Her Majesty's Stationery Office), 1983 and 1984.

money, income, the T-bill rate, and the exchange rate of the British pound. As monetary growth slowed, income fell and the interest rate and exchange rate rose.

26.5 | MAKING PREDICTIONS WITH THE ISLM MODEL

We have seen how useful the ISLM model can be for working out the implications for the economy of particular economic changes. We shall learn some general rules for using ISLM in this way and then look at how the model can be used to make quantitative predictions—predictions of the actual size of the effects.

UNDERSTANDING THE IMPLICATIONS OF ECONOMIC CHANGES

Let us see how the ISLM model can be used to predict the effect of an economic change. As an example, suppose that cold fusion turns out, after all, to be a reality and that limitless cheap energy is therefore a real possibility. As a result, investment becomes a lot more attractive. What are the implications for the economy?

When looking at any change in terms of the ISLM model, the first question is: Where will it have an impact? *Does it affect the IS curve or the LM curve?* To find out, look at Equations 26.36 and 26.42. What effect does the change in question have on each of the equations?

For our example, there is no effect on the LM curve: The quantity of money is unchanged and nothing has happened that would change money demand. However, there is an effect on the IS curve. If investment is more attractive, then investment will be higher at any interest rate. That means an increase in the constant c.

The next question is: *Does the change move the curve left or right or affect its slope?* Anything that increases Y for a given interest rate moves the curve to the *right*; anything that reduces Y for a given interest rate moves the curve to the *left*. Anything that increases whatever multiplies i in the equation makes the curve *flatter*; anything that decreases it makes the curve *steeper*.

For our example, an increase in c increases Y for a given interest rate, so the IS curve moves to the right. Because nothing that multiplies i in the equation is affected, the slope of the IS curve is unchanged. Thus there is a parallel movement of the IS curve to the right, much like the effect of increased government expenditure shown in Exhibit 26.10. Both income and the interest rate will rise.

We can use ISLM to analyze the effects on the economy of any economic change in a similar fashion.

MAKING QUANTITATIVE PREDICTIONS

While it is good to be able to understand the nature of the effects of some economic change, it would be even better if we could make quantitative predictions. It would be nice, for example, to know by *how much* U.S. income and interest rates would change as a result of a $1 billion open market purchase by the Fed.

The numbers we have used for the constants in the various equations of the model are clearly of no use in this respect. They describe our fictional Island economy; they were never meant to describe the U.S. economy. However, economists have tried to estimate statistically what values of these constants would best describe the U.S. economy. A model using such estimates is called an *econometric model*. We shall see in Part Seven that such models play an important role in formulating economic policy.

SUMMARY

- The circular flow model shows the first effects of monetary and other changes; the ISLM model shows the effect after income and expenditure are once again in balance with one another.

- The Keynesian theory describes the economy in terms of macroeconomic aggregates—aggregate income, aggregate consumption, and so on. The system of national income accounting measures these aggregates.

- The multiplier model shows at what level income and expenditure will balance, assuming a fixed interest rate. Consumption and net exports are seen as depending on income; investment and government expenditure are seen as autonomous.

- The level of income at which income and expenditure are in balance can be determined by using the Keynesian cross diagram or algebraically by using the multiplier equation.

- The IS curve gives the level of income at which income and expenditure are in balance at different values of the interest rate. The level changes because the higher the interest rate, the lower are investment and net exports.

- The LM curve shows the combinations of income and interest rate for which money demand equals the quantity of money.

- At the point of intersection of the IS and LM curves, income and the interest rate are in equilibrium: Income and expenditure are in balance for that interest rate (the IS curve); income and interest rate are such that money demand equals the quantity of money (the LM curve).

- An increase in government expenditure moves the IS curve to the right along an unchanged LM curve, raising equilibrium income and the equilibrium interest rate.

- An increase in money demand moves the LM curve to the left along an unchanged IS curve, lowering equilibrium income and raising the equilibrium interest rate.

- An increase in the quantity of money moves the LM curve to the right along an unchanged IS curve, lowering the equilibrium interest rate and raising equilibrium income.

- The ISLM model can be used in this way to predict the effects on the economy of many different changes.

KEY TERMS

national income accounting

macroeconomic aggregate

gross national product (GNP)

disposable income

consumption function

autonomous consumption

marginal propensity to consume

autonomous net exports

marginal propensity to import

autonomous expenditure

income multiplier

investment function

net export function

IS curve

LM curve

DISCUSSION QUESTIONS

1. In the early 1980s "Reaganomics" combined a tight monetary policy with an expansionary fiscal policy. Use the ISLM diagram to show the effect of such a policy: Think of it as combining an increase in government expenditure with a decrease in the quantity of money.

2. Use the ISLM model to analyze the effect on the economy of each of the following changes:

   a. A decrease in the tax rate.

   b. An increase in autonomous consumption.

   c. An increased foreign demand for U.S. goods.

   d. A reduction in transactions balances due to better cash management.

3. The marginal propensity to save is $1 -$ marginal propensity to consume. The marginal propensity to save on the Island is therefore $1 - 0.7 = 0.3$. If the marginal propensity to save increases from 0.3 to 0.4, then:

   a. What is the effect on the multiplier?

   b. What is the effect on the IS curve?

   c. What is the effect on equilibrium income?

   d. What is the effect on the total amount of saving $(Y - C)$?

4. In the ISLM model, the effect on income of an increase in government expenditure is less than it is in the multiplier model, because in the former a rise in the interest rate causes other categories of expenditure to fall. What could the central bank do to prevent the interest rate from rising in this way?

5. What would be the effect on equilibrium income of an increase in government expenditure if the demand for asset balances were completely insensitive to the interest rate $(z = 0)$?

6. What would be the effect on equilibrium income of an increase in the quantity of money if investment were totally insensitive to the interest rate $(d = 0)$?

SOFTWARE EXERCISE FOR THIS CHAPTER

Title: ISLM

As you have seen from this chapter, the ISLM model ties together the behavior of several variables. This computer exercise will help you understand how the responsiveness of these variables to one another influences the effectiveness of monetary policy. See your instructor if you wish to use this program.

BIBLIOGRAPHY

Fischer, Stanley, and Rudiger Dornbusch, *Macroeconomics*, New York: McGraw-Hill, 1987.

Hall, Robert E., and John B. Taylor, *Macroeconomics: Theory, Performance, and Policy*, New York: Norton, 1988.

Hicks, John R., "Mr. Keynes and the 'Classics': A Suggested Interpretation," *Econometrica* 5 April 1937, 147–159.

Keynes, John Maynard, *The General Theory of Employment Interest and Money*, London: Macmillan, 1936.

APPENDIX TO CHAPTER 26

THE LIQUIDITY PREFERENCE THEORY OF THE INTEREST RATE

In Chapter 2 we showed how the interest rate is determined in the market for loanable funds. The ISLM model provides an alternative way of looking at the determination of the interest rate.

Remember the condition that money demand equal the quantity of money (Equation 26.40):

$$M = k\,Y + (x - z\,i). \qquad\qquad [26.40]$$

If we take income as given, we can think of this equation as determining the interest rate. The interest rate must be such that, at that interest rate, people will want to hold the quantity of money in existence. This is called the *liquidity preference theory* of the interest rate.

We can use the liquidity preference theory to predict the effect of various changes on the interest rate. For example, consider the effect of an increase in government expenditure. According to the *loanable funds theory*, this directly increases the demand for loanable funds and causes the interest rate to rise. According to the liquidity preference theory, the increase in government expenditure leads to an increase in equilibrium income. At the higher level of income, a larger part of the quantity of money is required to facilitate transactions. To "squeeze out" this extra money from asset balances, the interest rate must rise.

We have already seen the predictions of the two theories for the effect of an open market operation. The loanable funds theory predicts a fall in the interest rate through a *loan-supply effect* as the monetary expansion adds directly to the supply of loanable funds. The liquidity preference theory also predicts a fall in the interest rate, but for a different reason. The open market operation increases the quantity of money; equilibrium income rises and the interest rate falls, so that the demand for money will increase in parallel. This effect on the interest rate is called a *liquidity effect*.

These two theories arrive at similar conclusions, but they do so by rather different routes. The route of the loanable funds theory is more direct; the route of the liquidity preference theory is more roundabout, but it takes into account more of the repercussions that result from the initial change.

CHAPTER 27

AGGREGATE SUPPLY AND AGGREGATE DEMAND

In studying the effects of monetary and other changes on the economy, we have looked at short-run effects under the assumption that prices do not change (in Chapters 24 through 26) and at long-run effects under the assumption that prices change freely (in Chapter 23). We need to bridge the gap between the short run and the long run. That is, we need to understand how and why prices change.

To be able to talk about the level of prices in general, we shall first develop the idea of a price index and the related idea of an aggregate measure of output. Then we shall look at the relationship between the output that firms produce and the prices that they charge—that is, at the *aggregate supply* relationship. Of course, supply alone is not enough to determine price: We need demand as well. We shall see how an *aggregate demand* relationship can be derived from our models of the short run. Bringing aggregate demand and aggregate supply together, we shall see how various changes affect output and prices in the economy. In addition to those changes that affect aggregate demand—such as changes in government expenditure and in the quantity of money—we shall look at other changes that affect aggregate supply—such as the OPEC oil-price shocks. Finally, we shall use the aggregate-demand/aggregate-supply framework to integrate our understanding of the short run with our understanding of the long run.

27.1 AGGREGATE PRICE AND OUTPUT

If we are going to talk about prices and quantities of goods and services in general, it will be much easier if we can refer to price and quantity *aggregates* rather than to thousands of individual prices and quantities.

691

PRICE INDEXES

consumer price index (CPI)
Index that measures the cost of living for a typical urban family.

The most widely known price aggregate is the **consumer price index (CPI)**. This index measures the cost of living for a typical urban family: It is representative of the prices the typical family pays for the goods and services it consumes. If the CPI goes up 10%, that means that the typical family will have to pay 10% more dollars to buy the same basket of goods and services.

The index is calculated as follows. Every 10 years or so, the Bureau of Labor Statistics (BLS) conducts a survey of the buying habits of American families. From this survey the BLS constructs a typical basket of goods and services consumed by the average urban household, including everything from groceries to medical care. Each month the BLS sends out surveyors to price this basket of goods. The CPI is calculated by comparing the cost of this basket in any particular month with the cost in some base period, usually the period of the most recent survey of spending habits:

$$\text{CPI for December 1990} = \frac{\text{cost of same basket in December 1990}}{\text{cost of typical basket in 1982--1984}} \times 100.$$

[27.1]

The CPI for the base period is therefore 100. A CPI of 150 in December 1990 means that the reference basket costs 50% more then than it did in 1982–1984.

cost-of-living adjustment (COLA)
Clause in a wage contract requiring that wages be raised over the life of the contract to reflect change in the consumer price index.

The CPI is widely used as a measure of purchasing power. For example, Social Security payments are raised annually to reflect changes in the CPI. Many wage contracts include a **cost-of-living adjustment (COLA)** clause requiring that wages be raised over the life of the contract to reflect changes in the CPI. The intention in both cases is to ensure that the payment remains the same in *real* terms—in terms of purchasing power. Linking payments to the CPI or to some other index in this way is called **indexation**.

indexation
Linkage of payments to a published price index.

A different index, less widely quoted but more useful for our purposes, is the **GNP implicit price deflator**. Instead of being based on the basket of goods bought by the typical urban consumer, as is the CPI, this index is based on the basket of final goods and services produced by the economy—the goods and services that make up the *gross national product (GNP)*. This latter basket includes, for example, F16 jet fighters, which are not bought by your average consumer, and it excludes used cars, which are purchased but are not part of the current output of final goods and services. The GNP deflator is calculated just like the CPI, except that a different basket of goods is used. We shall find it convenient to call the level in the base year 1.0 rather than 100. Hence if the GNP deflator was 1.28 in 1989, compared with its level of 1.0 in the base year of 1982, this means that the average price of the final goods and services produced had increased by 28% between the two years.[1]

GNP implicit price deflator
Price index based on the basket of final goods and services produced by the economy.

---

[1]There are actually two GNP implicit price deflators published: One uses a base-period basket of goods as described above, and the other uses a basket of goods that changes from year to year (this is called a *chain* index).

A MEASURE OF OUTPUT

We would like to be able to talk about the total output of final goods and services produced in the economy as a single number. A convenient way to do this is to take the dollar value of final goods and services, **nominal GNP,** and divide by the GNP deflator. The resulting measure is called **real GNP.** For example, nominal GNP in the United States in 1989 was $5.34 trillion. The GNP deflator in 1989 was 1.28. Real GNP in 1989 was therefore

nominal GNP
Dollar value of final goods and services produced by the economy.

$$\text{real GNP} = \frac{\text{nominal GNP}}{\text{GNP deflator}} = \frac{\$5.34 \text{ trillion}}{1.28} = \$4.17 \text{ trillion}. \quad [27.2]$$

real GNP
Nominal GNP divided by the GNP deflator; a measure of real output.

Real GNP is a measure of what the goods and services produced in 1989 would have cost had they been valued in 1982 (base-year) prices instead of 1989 prices.

To see why real GNP is a measure of quantity, let us use it to compare the final goods and services produced by the economy in 1988 and 1989. In 1989 real GNP of $4.17 trillion was 2.5% higher than the 1988 figure of $4.07 trillion. Since real GNP values the goods and services in the two years in constant 1982 prices, the difference in real GNP between the two years is an indicator of the change in the quantities of goods and services produced.

|27.2| AGGREGATE SUPPLY

In Chapters 24 through 26, when we looked at the effects of various changes on the economy, we assumed that prices remained constant. For example, when an increase in the quantity of money caused total expenditure to rise, we assumed implicitly that the rise in expenditure meant an equal rise in the quantities of goods and services sold, with no increase in prices. But will firms really respond to an increase in the demand for their goods by increasing output rather than by raising prices? Or if they do raise prices, by how much will they raise them? We can describe their response with an *aggregate supply curve.*

THE AGGREGATE SUPPLY CURVE

An **aggregate supply curve** shows what prices firms will charge at any level of output. Exhibit 27.1 shows the aggregate supply curve for the Island. On the vertical axis is the price level, P. Think of it as corresponding to the GNP implicit price deflator. On the horizontal axis is aggregate output, y. Think of it as corresponding to real GNP.[2] At an aggregate output of 1,000, firms will charge an aggregate price of 1.0; at an aggregate output of 1,100, firms will charge 1.05. That is, they will produce more only at a higher price.

aggregate supply curve
Curve showing the prices firms will charge at different levels of output.

---

[2]In units, P is a pure number and y is measured in base-period dollars.

The *slope* of the aggregate supply curve shows how firms respond to an increase in demand for their products. If they are slow to raise prices, then an increase in demand will largely result in increased output; in this case, the aggregate supply curve will be relatively flat. If they are quick to raise prices, then an increase in demand will largely result in higher prices and less in an increase in output; in this case, the aggregate supply curve will be relatively steep.

WHAT LIES BEHIND THE AGGREGATE SUPPLY CURVE?

To understand the aggregate supply curve, we need to look at the behavior that lies behind it. Different types of firm respond differently to changes in demand. In some industries—agriculture is a good example—firms take prices as given. Prices are determined by market makers on exchange-like markets rather than being set by individual producers. An increase in demand immediately raises the market price, and firms respond by increasing their output to the point at which rising costs make further expansion unprofitable. In other industries, firms have some degree of market power: They set prices themselves rather than taking them as given by the market. Computer manufacturers and hospitals are examples. Of course, the prices such firms can set are constrained by demand, but they do have some discretion over pricing, and they set their prices to maximize profits. Where they set their prices will depend on costs. As demand increases price-setting firms will respond first by raising output, but as their costs rise, they will eventually raise their prices too.

So, for both for price-taking and price-setting industries, an increase in demand will bring forth greater output and lead to higher prices. In both cases, the extent of the price rise will depend on the behavior of costs. To understand the aggregate supply relationship, therefore, we need to understand what determines costs. The determinants of costs are labor, capital, natural resources, and technology.

LABOR   The number of people working in an economy depends on both demographic and economic factors. The age composition and size of the population are important, as is the extent to which men, women, and children participate in the labor force. For example, a larger proportion of women work for pay in the United States than in Japan, and a larger proportion of men are in the military. Decisions about whether or not to work depend on economic as well as on cultural factors: The higher the pay, the more attractive work becomes.

potential employment
Amount of labor employed if everyone willing to work at current pay can find a suitable job.

We can describe the labor available to an economy in terms of **potential employment**. This is the amount of labor employed if everyone willing to work at current pay can find a suitable job with no more than normal difficulty. Note that potential employment is not the maximum possible amount of labor—it is the amount that is available at current pay. Note too that it does not mean that everyone who wants to is working. Some unemployment is only to be expected: As new workers come into the labor force and as others lose their jobs, it takes time for them to find new jobs. The level of unemployment that corresponds to

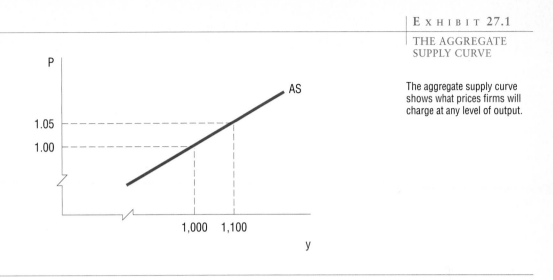

EXHIBIT 27.1

THE AGGREGATE
SUPPLY CURVE

The aggregate supply curve
shows what prices firms will
charge at any level of output.

this normal search process is called the **natural rate of unemployment.** When unemployment is at its natural rate, employment is at its potential. Sometimes, however, dislocations to the economy throw large numbers of people out of work: Unemployment then is above the natural rate and employment is below its potential. At other times, during a boom, jobs are unusually easy to find; unemployment is below the natural rate and employment is above the level of potential employment.

natural rate of unemployment
Level of unemployment resulting from new workers coming into the labor force and from normal turnover.

Labor costs are *the* major element of costs. As firms expand their output, they hire more workers. If labor is plentiful, they may be able to find more workers at the same wage they already pay. If labor is scarce, they may have to offer more. Because higher wages raise costs, prices rise too. Therefore, how fast wages rise in response to an increase in the demand for labor is a major determinant of the slope of the aggregate supply curve.

CAPITAL The total amount of physical capital in the economy—factories and equipment—is the result of investment over a long period of time. It is hard to change it quickly. The availability of capital is an important determinant of costs. If capital is already working at capacity, increasing output may require special and expensive measures—for example, adding a night shift. However, if capital is lying idle, then output can be expanded relatively cheaply. The measure of employment of capital is called the **capacity utilization rate.** As with labor, full utilization of capital does not mean that none of it is idle: Some capital will normally be "down" for maintenance and model changes.

capacity utilization rate
Measure of the employment of physical capital in the economy.

NATURAL RESOURCES The production of goods and services relies on natural as well as human resources. Land and water are needed for agriculture and recreation, raw materials are needed for manufacturing, and energy is needed for everything. Increasing output requires more of these natural resources, and more can be had only at greater cost. Changes in the availability of resources—for example, a restriction of oil output by OPEC—can have immediate and substantial effects on costs.

TECHNOLOGY   The technology available to an economy determines how much output can be produced for given amounts of labor, capital, and natural resources. Changes in technology can have a major impact on costs. For example, computer technology has increased productivity enormously.

MOVEMENTS OF THE AGGREGATE SUPPLY CURVE

Changes in any of the factors that affect costs will shift the aggregate supply curve. We can list the effects as follows.

Changes that shift the aggregate supply curve to the *right*:

- An increase in potential employment.
- An increase in available capital.
- An increase in the availability of natural resources.
- An improvement in the technology of production.

Changes that shift the aggregate supply curve to the *left*:

- A decrease in potential employment.
- A decrease in available capital.
- A decrease in the availability of natural resources.
- A deterioration in the technology of production.

🌴 **CHECK STATION 1**   **What is the effect on the aggregate supply curve of the following changes?**

A.   **The size of the military is reduced by 50%.**

B.   **Cold fusion provides cheap energy.**

C.   **Computers improve productivity in the service sector.**

THE SLOPE OF THE AGGREGATE SUPPLY CURVE

The slope of the aggregate supply curve shows by how much prices will rise as output is increased. The slope clearly depends on all of the factors we have enumerated, but it also depends on the time horizon in question. That is, it depends on whether we are talking about the short-run response of prices as output increases or about the long-run response.

potential output
Level of output that can be produced with available technology and natural resources, with capital utilized at full capacity, and with labor at potential employment.

It is useful to begin by defining **potential output**. Potential output is the level of output that an economy can produce with the technology and natural resources available, with capital utilized at full capacity, and with labor at potential

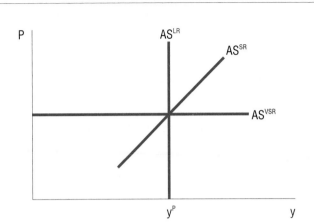

EXHIBIT 27.2

AGGREGATE SUPPLY
AT VARIOUS TIME
HORIZONS

The very-short-run aggregate
supply curve is horizontal. The
long-run aggregate supply
curve is vertical. The short-run
aggregate supply curve has a
positive slope.

employment. If left undisturbed, an economy will eventually settle at potential output.

Potential output is the norm. However, changes in demand may cause output to deviate from this norm. For example, if demand increases, firms will expand their output and hire more workers. Costs may not rise much initially, and prices therefore will not rise much either. But if output is maintained above its normal level for long, costs will rise more rapidly. A tight labor market will mean rising wages as firms compete for workers, and rising wages will mean rising prices. So the shorter the period for which we draw the aggregate supply curve, the flatter it will be: Over a shorter period, an increase or decrease in output will involve a smaller change in prices.

Exhibit 27.2 shows three different aggregate supply curves. Each describes how prices and output respond to an increase in demand, but each describes the response over a different time horizon. The curve labeled AS^{VSR} is horizontal. It describes the response in the very short run—perhaps a month or two—the period that corresponds to the first effects of a change that we examined with the circular flow model. In this very short time horizon, prices do not change at all. The curve labeled AS^{SR} describes the response in a longer time horizon—perhaps a year or two—the period that corresponds to the horizon of the ISLM model. The curve labeled AS^{LR} describes the response of the economy to an increase in demand in the long run. It is drawn vertical at y^P, potential output.

Many economists believe that output cannot be sustained at an abnormal level indefinitely. Eventually, whatever the level of aggregate demand, output will return to normal—that is, to potential output. This view is consistent with the Quantity Theory of Money that we learned about in Chapter 23.

The aggregate demand curve
shows the demand for output
at any price level.

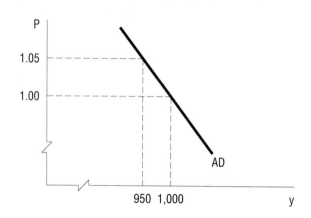

27.3 | AGGREGATE DEMAND

Equilibrium of output and prices in the economy occurs at the point at which the aggregate supply curve intersects an aggregate demand curve. Our next task is to derive such an aggregate demand curve.

THE AGGREGATE DEMAND CURVE

In Chapters 24 through 26, when we looked at how various changes affected expenditure and income, we assumed that prices remained the same. When we talked about decisions on expenditure—how much households consume, how much firms invest—we were implicitly talking about decisions on *quantities* of goods and services. The dollar expenditures were just the quantities demanded multiplied by the constant prices. Now that we are allowing prices to change, however, we need to ask how the quantities demanded will be affected by changing prices. The aggregate demand curve provides the answer.

aggregate demand curve
Curve showing the demand for output at different price levels.

The **aggregate demand curve** shows the demand for output at any price level. Exhibit 27.3 shows the aggregate demand curve for the Island. On the vertical axis is the price level, P. On the horizontal axis is aggregate output, y. At an aggregate price level of 1.0, the output demanded is 1,000. At a price level of 1.05, the output demanded is 950. That is, the higher the price, the lower the output demanded.

THE SLOPE OF THE AGGREGATE DEMAND CURVE

Why does the aggregate demand curve slope downward? There are three reasons. The first is a **wealth effect**. When the price level rises, nominal assets lose some of their value. If you hold $100 or are owed $1,000 and prices double, then those assets are worth half what they were in terms of real purchasing power. As a result of the loss, you will be poorer and you will consume less. Of course, if you *owe* $1,000, the rise in prices will make you richer—the real value of your debt will fall. So the overall effect on demand will depend on the net gains and losses on nominal assets and liabilities.

wealth effect
Effects on aggregate demand caused by net gains and losses on nominal assets and liabilities.

The second reason for the downward slope of the aggregate demand curve is an **interest-rate effect**. One of the nominal assets that loses value when prices rise is balances of money. As we saw in Chapter 22, the demand for money is a demand for *real* balances. So people will try to restore the real value of their money balances by increasing the dollar amount to compensate for the rise in prices. As we have seen, any attempt to increase money balances reduces lending and raises interest rates. The rise in interest rates causes expenditure to fall.

interest-rate effect
Effect on aggregate demand caused by changes in interest rate.

The third reason for the downward slope of the aggregate demand curve is a **foreign-trade effect**. If the rise in prices is not matched by a fall in exchange rate, as it may not be in the short run, then domestic goods will become more expensive relative to foreign goods. Imports will rise and exports will fall. As a result, total expenditure on domestic goods will decline.[3]

foreign-trade effect
Effect on aggregate demand caused by changes in relative price of foreign and domestic goods.

MOVEMENTS OF THE AGGREGATE DEMAND CURVE

What causes the aggregate demand curve to shift? To answer this, we can use what we have already learned about factors that cause expenditure to change, assuming prices are fixed. Anything that *increases* expenditure at fixed prices shifts the aggregate demand curve to the *right*; anything that *decreases* expenditure at fixed prices shifts the aggregate demand curve to the *left*.

The principle is illustrated in Exhibit 27.4. Suppose, for example, that we know that a change in the quantity of money increases expenditure from $1,000 million to $1,100 million if prices are fixed. Before the change, the price level was 1.0 and output was 1,000 million. This combination of price and output is marked X_0 in Exhibit 27.4. The aggregate demand curve before the change, AD_0, must pass through X_0. The aggregate demand curve shows for *all* price levels the quantity of output demanded. Since we know that for the *particular* price level of 1.0, the output demanded is 1,000 million, the aggregate demand curve must go through this point.

By similar reasoning, the aggregate demand curve after the change, AD_1, must go through the point marked X_1 in Exhibit 27.4. This point corresponds to a

[3]In an appendix to this chapter, an aggregate demand curve is derived mathematically from the ISLM model, and it is shown to be downward-sloping.

price level of 1.0 and an output of 1,100 million. We know that if the price level is 1.0, then after the increase in the quantity of money, output demanded is 1,100 million. So the point X_1 must be on the new aggregate demand curve. By similar reasoning, any change that causes expenditure to rise, prices fixed, causes the aggregate demand curve to shift to the right, and any change that causes expenditure to fall, prices fixed, causes the aggregate demand curve to shift to the left.

In Chapters 24 through 26 we saw a number of changes that affect expenditure. It is quite straightforward to translate those effects on expenditure into effects on aggregate demand. Some important examples are as follows.

Changes that shift the aggregate demand curve to the *right*:

- An increase in government expenditure.
- A decrease in taxes.
- A decrease in the attractiveness of holding money as an asset.
- An increase in the quantity of money.

Changes that shift the aggregate demand curve to the *left*:

- A decrease in government expenditure.
- An increase in taxes.
- An increase in the attractiveness of holding money as an asset.
- A decrease in the quantity of money.

THE MODERN QUANTITY THEORY AND AGGREGATE DEMAND

Modern Quantity Theory
Theory of the short-run effects of an increase in the quantity of money; favored by Monetarists.

Monetarists
Economists who stress the importance of controlling the quantity of money.

An alternative approach to aggregate demand is provided by Milton Friedman's **Modern Quantity Theory**. This approach is favored by a school of economists called **Monetarists** who, as we shall see in later chapters, disagree quite sharply with the Keynesians about many issues. The Modern Quantity Theory differs from the Classical Quantity Theory that we encountered in Chapter 23 in that it is a theory of the short run. The Classical Quantity Theory is a theory of the long run.

The basic building block of the Modern Quantity Theory is a theory of money demand that differs somewhat from the Keynesian theory we saw in Chapter 22. Money demand is seen as a stable function of wealth and the yields on alternative assets. Wealth includes "permanent income"—a measure of lifetime earnings—and all other assets. As we saw in Chapter 22, there is a close relationship between money demand and velocity. Thus Friedman's views on money demand may be translated into the following formulation of velocity:

$$V = F(\text{real wealth, yields on alternative assets}). \qquad [27.3]$$

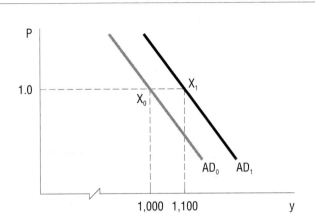

A SHIFT IN THE
AGGREGATE
DEMAND CURVE

A change in the economy that
has the effect of raising
expenditure at constant prices
also has the effect of shifting
the aggregate demand curve to
the right.

Substituting this formulation of velocity into the equation of exchange we derived in Chapter 22, we obtain

$$M \times F(\text{real wealth, yields on alternative assets}) = E. \qquad [27.4]$$

Equation 27.4 is a theory of aggregate demand. Anything that increases the left-hand side increases expenditure. Since real wealth changes little and slowly, and the yields on alternative assets are assumed to have relatively little effect on velocity, the main thing that causes changes in expenditure is changes in the quantity of money. An increase in the quantity of money raises expenditure and so shifts the aggregate demand curve to the right. A decrease in the quantity of money lowers expenditure and moves the aggregate demand curve to the left.

Although the Modern Quantity Theory agrees with the circular flow model and with the ISLM model on the effects of a monetary change, it differs on the effects of other changes. Consider, for example, an increase in government expenditure. Looking at Equation 27.4, we see that there is no effect on wealth, and although the yields on alternative assets may rise, this has little effect on velocity. As a result, there will be little change in expenditure and the aggregate demand curve will move little if at all.

27.4 USING AGGREGATE SUPPLY AND AGGREGATE DEMAND

Now that we have both aggregate supply and aggregate demand, we can bring them together to determine the equilibrium price level and equilibrium output.

EXHIBIT 27.5

AGGREGATE
DEMAND AND
AGGREGATE SUPPLY
FOR THE ISLAND
ECONOMY

The intersection of aggregate
demand and aggregate supply
curves determines equilibrium
output and the equilibrium
price level.

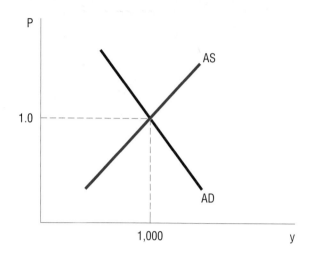

Exhibit 27.5 shows aggregate supply and aggregate demand for the Island economy. The two curves intersect at a price level of 1.0 and an output of 1,000 million. At this price level, the quantity of goods and services produced by the economy equals the quantity that people wish to buy. These are therefore the *equilibrium price level* and *equilibrium output* for the economy.

To see how useful aggregate supply and aggregate demand can be in analyzing the consequences of various economic changes, let us consider some applications.

APPLICATION: THE VIETNAM WAR

We saw in Section 26.4 that in the late 1960s, mainly because of the escalation of the Vietnam War, there was a substantial increase in total expenditure. This represented a shift to the *right* of the aggregate demand curve from AD_0 to AD_1, as shown in Exhibit 27.6. The actual effect on prices and output is shown in Exhibit 27.7. As the aggregate demand curve moved along an unchanged aggregate supply curve, equilibrium output and the equilibrium price level both rose.

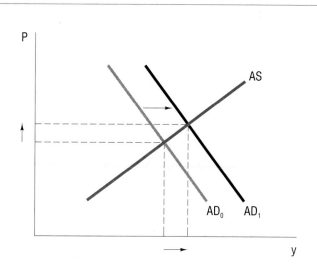

Exhibit 27.6

AN INCREASE IN
TOTAL EXPENDITURE
SHIFTS THE
AGGREGATE
DEMAND CURVE
TO THE RIGHT

Increased government
spending in the late 1960s,
caused largely by the Vietnam
War, increased aggregate
demand. Output and the price
level both rose.

Exhibit 27.7

THE U.S. ECONOMY
1960–1972

	Nominal GNP (Billions)	GNP in 1982 Dollars (Billions)	GNP Implicit Price Deflator (1982=100)
1960	515.3	1,665.3	30.9
1961	533.8	1,708.7	31.2
1962	574.6	1,799.4	31.9
1963	606.9	1,873.3	32.4
1964	649.8	1,973.3	32.9
1965	705.1	2,087.6	33.8
1966	772.0	2,208.3	35.0
1967	816.4	2,271.4	35.9
1968	892.7	2,365.6	37.7
1969	963.9	2,423.3	39.8
1970	1,015.5	2,416.2	42.0
1971	1,102.7	2,484.8	44.4
1972	1,212.8	2,608.5	46.5

Source: *Economic Report of the President*, 1990.

EXHIBIT 27.8

A DECREASE IN TOTAL EXPENDITURE SHIFTS THE AGGREGATE DEMAND CURVE TO THE LEFT

During the Great Depression aggregate demand fell precipitously. Both output and the price level fell.

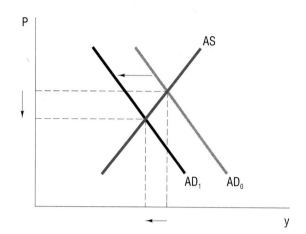

EXHIBIT 27.9

THE U.S. ECONOMY 1929 AND 1933

	Nominal GNP (Billions)	GNP in 1982 Dollars (Billions)	GNP Implicit Price Deflator (1982=100)
1929	103.9	709.6	14.6
1933	56.0	498.5	11.2

Source: *Economic Report of the President*, 1990.

APPLICATION: THE GREAT DEPRESSION

During the Great Depression there was a massive fall in total expenditure. This represented a shift to the *left* of the aggregate demand curve from AD_0 to AD_1, as shown in Exhibit 27.8. The effect on prices and output is shown in Exhibit 27.9. As the aggregate demand curve moved along an unchanged aggregate supply curve, equilibrium output and the equilibrium price level both fell.

APPLICATION: THE OPEC OIL-PRICE SHOCK

The Arab-Israeli war of 1973 provided the Organization of Petroleum Exporting Countries (OPEC) with an opportunity to organize as a cartel, restrict the supply of oil, and raise prices. At the same time, crop failures around the world led to a steep rise in food prices, and the prices of other raw materials rose too. As we saw

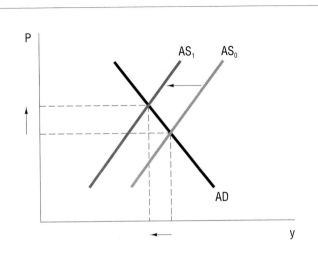

E X H I B I T 27.10

A FALL IN THE
SUPPLY OF NATURAL
RESOURCES SHIFTS
THE AGGREGATE
SUPPLY CURVE TO
THE LEFT

The OPEC oil price increase in
1973 shifted the aggregate
supply curve to the left. Output
fell and the price level rose.

E X H I B I T 27.11

U.S. ECONOMY
1973–1975

	Nominal GNP (Billions)	GNP in 1982 Dollars (Billions)	GNP Implicit Price Deflator (1982=100)
1973	1,359.3	2,744.1	49.5
1974	1,472.8	2,729.3	54.0
1975	1,598.4	2,695.0	59.3

Source: *Economic Report of the President*, 1990.

above, a reduction in the availability of natural resources, which these changes represent, has the effect of shifting the aggregate supply curve to the *left*, from AS_0 to AS_1, as shown in Exhibit 27.10. The effect on prices and output in the United States is shown in Exhibit 27.11. As the aggregate supply curve moved along an unchanged aggregate demand curve, equilibrium output fell and the equilibrium price level rose.

27.5 FROM THE SHORT RUN TO THE LONG RUN

We can use the framework of aggregate demand and aggregate supply to reconcile what we learned in Chapters 24 through 26 about the short-run effects of a monetary change with what we learned in Chapter 23 about the long-run effects.

E X H I B I T **27.12**

THE EFFECTS OF A
MONETARY CHANGE
IN THE SHORT RUN
AND IN THE LONG
RUN

The very-short-run effect of a
change in aggregate demand is
entirely on output. The long-
run effect is entirely on prices.
In the short run there is an
effect on both output and
prices.

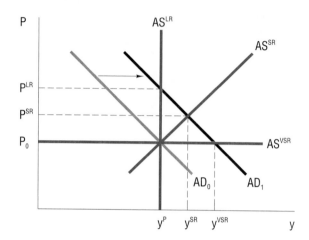

Exhibit 27.12 shows the shift in the aggregate demand curve from AD_0 to AD_1 that results from an increase in the quantity of money. It also shows the aggregate supply curves for the very short run, the short run, and the long run that appear in Exhibit 27.2. The first effect of the monetary change, which we analyzed with the circular flow model, is a movement along the very-short-run aggregate supply curve, AS^{VSR}. Initially, prices remain constant at P_0 and output increases to y^{VSR}. Over a longer period of time, the time horizon of the ISLM model or of the Modern Quantity Theory, prices are more flexible and the relevant aggregate supply curve becomes AS^{SR}. The equilibrium in this short run is at a price level of P^{SR} and an output of y^{SR}. In the long run—the time horizon of the Classical Quantity Theory of Chapter 23—prices are completely flexible and output must return to potential output, y^P. Prices rise in proportion to the increase in the quantity of money, to P^{LR}.[4]

The conceptual distinction between the short run and the long run is clear. However, it is a matter of great practical importance just how long the long run actually is. How long does it take for the effects of a monetary change on output to fade and for all of the effect to be on prices? We shall see in coming chapters that the answer to this question is of vital importance to monetary policy. We shall see too that it is the subject of considerable controversy among economists.

[4]For simplicity, in Exhibit 27.12 a single aggregate demand curve represents the effect of the monetary change for all time horizons. In fact, as we have seen, the effect of the change on aggregate demand differs at different time horizons. The general conclusion, however, is the same. The initial effect is all on output; the ultimate effect is all on prices; and for an intermediate time horizon, there is some effect on each.

SUMMARY

- A price index is a single number that measures the level of prices. The consumer price index measures the level of prices paid by the typical urban family. The GNP deflator measures the level of prices of goods and services produced in the economy. Real GNP is a measure of the economy's output of goods and services.

- The aggregate supply curve describes the level of prices that firms will charge at different levels of output. The steeper it is, the more prices will rise for a given increase in output.

- The principal determinant of aggregate supply is costs. The costs of production depend on labor, capital, natural resources, and technology.

- The number of people employed depends on demographic factors and on wages. The amount of capital is more or less fixed at any time, changing only slowly with investment. When employment is at its full potential and capital is fully utilized, output is at potential output.

- Increases in the supply of labor, capital, and natural resources, and improvements in technology increase aggregate supply (shift the aggregate supply curve to the right).

- The slope of the aggregate supply curve depends on the time period considered. In the very short run it is horizontal; in the long run it is vertical; and in the short run it has a positive slope.

- The aggregate demand curve describes the demand for output at different price levels. It slopes downward because of income and wealth effects, the interest-rate effect, and the foreign-trade effect.

- Any change that increases expenditure at a fixed price level moves the aggregate demand curve to the right. Some examples are an increase in government expenditure, a decrease in money demand, and an increase in the quantity of money.

- Friedman's Modern Quantity Theory suggests that velocity changes little and that therefore the quantity of money is the principal determinant of aggregate demand. An increase in the quantity of money moves the aggregate demand curve to the right.

- The intersection of aggregate demand and aggregate supply curves determines equilibrium output and the equilibrium price level.

- In the very short run, a monetary change will mainly affect output and have little effect on prices. In the long run, there is no effect on output and prices change in proportion to the monetary change. In the short run, both prices and output are affected.

KEY TERMS

consumer price index (CPI)

cost-of-living adjustment (COLA)

indexation

GNP implicit price deflator

nominal GNP

real GNP

aggregate supply curve

potential employment

natural rate of unemployment

capacity utilization rate

potential output

aggregate demand curve

wealth effect

interest-rate effect

foreign-trade effect

Modern Quantity Theory

Monetarists

DISCUSSION QUESTIONS

1. The Soviet Union is the world's largest producer of oil and a major exporter. In 1992 civil unrest in the Soviet Union, particularly in the oil-producing Caucasus region, leads to a severe drop in oil output. As a result, world oil prices rise sharply.

   a. Describe the effect on the U.S. economy in terms of aggregate supply and aggregate demand.

   b. Suppose the Fed wanted to reduce the impact of the oil price rise on equilibrium income in the United States. What could it do?

   c. What are the long-run implications of the oil-price shock for the price level (1) if the Fed does nothing, and (2) if it does what you suggest in Part b?

2. In the United States in the early 1980s there was a tax cut and a tightening of monetary policy (equivalent, in terms of this chapter, to a reduction in the quantity of money). Describe the effects on the economy in terms of aggregate supply and aggregate demand.

3. Worries about instability in Eastern Europe make dollar securities relatively more attractive, causing the dollar to appreciate. Describe the effects on the economy in terms of aggregate supply and aggregate demand.

4. Aggregate demand collapsed in the Great Depression. What would be the Keynesian explanation for the collapse, based on the ISLM model? What would be the Monetarist explanation, based on the Modern Quantity Theory?

5. Congress passes and the states ratify a constitutional amendment requiring a balanced government budget. As a result, the government cuts expenditure and raises taxes. Describe the effects on the economy in terms of aggregate supply and aggregate demand.

BIBLIOGRAPHY

Friedman, Milton, *The Quantity Theory of Money: A Restatement.* In *Studies in the Quantity Theory of Money.* Edited by M. Friedman. Chicago: University of Chicago Press.

Hall, Robert E., and John B. Taylor, *Macroeconomics: Theory, Performance, and Policy,* New York: Norton, 1988.

Webb, Roy H., and Rob Willemse, "Macroeconomic Price Indexes," *Economic Review of the Federal Reserve Bank of Richmond,* July–August 1989, 22–32.

APPENDIX TO CHAPTER 27

AGGREGATE DEMAND AND THE ISLM MODEL

ISLM AND AGGREGATE DEMAND

In terms of the ISLM model of Chapter 26, we can be more specific about the kinds of changes that will cause the aggregate demand curve to shift. In the ISLM model, when the IS curve or the LM curve moves to the right, equilibrium income increases and therefore expenditure increases. An increase in expenditure means that the aggregate demand curve moves to the right. Thus *anything that moves the IS curve moves the aggregate demand curve in the same direction, and anything that moves the LM curve moves the aggregate demand curve in the same direction.* We saw that increases in autonomous expenditure and increases in the multiplier shift the IS curve, and changes in the quantity of money or in the demand for money shift the LM curve.

As an example, recall the $30 million increase in government expenditure we looked at in Chapter 26. The effect on equilibrium income and on the interest rate are shown in Exhibit 27A.1A. The IS curve shifts to the right by $71.4 million from IS_0 to IS_1. Equilibrium income increases from $1,000 million to $1,024.4 million. Since total expenditure equals equilibrium income, it too increases from $1,000 million to $1,024.4 million. By assumption, the price level remains fixed at 1.0, so total expenditure of $1,000 million before the change corresponds to an output of 1,000 million—the point X_0 in Exhibit 27A.1B. This point must be on the initial aggregate demand curve, AD_0. Total expenditure of $1,024.4 million after the change corresponds to an output of 1,024.4—the point X_1 in Exhibit 27A.1B, which must be on the new aggregate demand curve, AD_1.

E X H I B I T 27A.1

A MOVEMENT OF THE IS CURVE MOVES THE AGGREGATE DEMAND CURVE
IN THE SAME DIRECTION

A. An increase in government expenditure shifts the IS curve to the right.

B. The aggregate demand curve also shifts to the right.

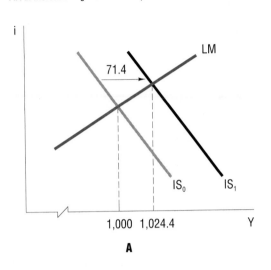

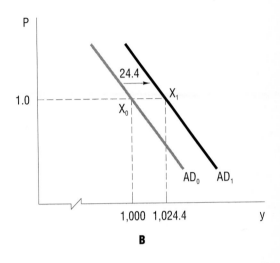

What are the effects on aggregate demand of the following changes?

A. There is an increase in autonomous consumption.

B. There is a decrease in the tax rate.

C. Cash management reduces the demand for transactions balances.

CHECK STATION 1

DERIVING THE SLOPE OF THE AGGREGATE DEMAND CURVE

In Chapter 26 we derived the ISLM model under the assumption that prices were constant. Consequently, we did not distinguish between nominal and real values: When prices are constant, the two are the same. Now, however, because we wish to see the effect of price changes on the equilibrium of the ISLM model, the distinction between real and nominal will have to be made.

The IS curve is the condition for balance between spending and income. Although we talked about spending and income in nominal terms in Chapter 26, if we have balance in nominal terms, we also have balance in real terms. So we

EXHIBIT 27A.2

IS AND LM CURVES
IN REAL TERMS

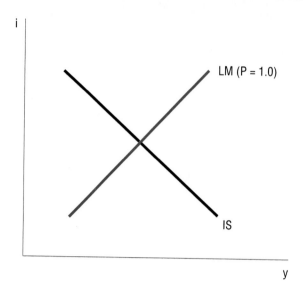

can rewrite the IS condition, Equation 26.36, as

$$y = \frac{1}{\{1 - b(1 - t) + g\}} [a + (c - d\,i) + \overline{G} + (f - h\,i)], \qquad [27A.1]$$

where y, real income or output, replaces Y, nominal income.[1]

The LM curve is the condition that transactions balances and asset balances add up to the total quantity of money. In Chapter 23 we saw that the demand for money balances is a demand for *real* balances: The demand for real transactions balances depends on real income; the demand for real asset balances depends on the interest rate. The amount of *actual* dollars that people want to hold is their demand for real balances times the price level. So we can write the demand for money as[2]

$$M^D = [k\,y + (x - z\,i)] \times P. \qquad [27A.2]$$

[1]The units of all the constants are now real amounts rather than dollars. Actually, we can think of them as always having been in real amounts. For example, the investment function describes *real* investment expenditure as a function of the interest rate, and government expenditure is set in goods and services purchased rather than in dollars. In Chapter 26 we converted these real quantities into dollar amounts by multiplying by the price level. Since the price level was 1.0, no change in the constants was necessary (except in their units).

[2]Equation 26.38 can be seen as Equation 27A.2 with $P = 1.0$.

E x h i b i t 27A.3

ISLM EQUILIBRIUM AT DIFFERENT PRICE LEVELS AND THE AGGREGATE DEMAND CURVE

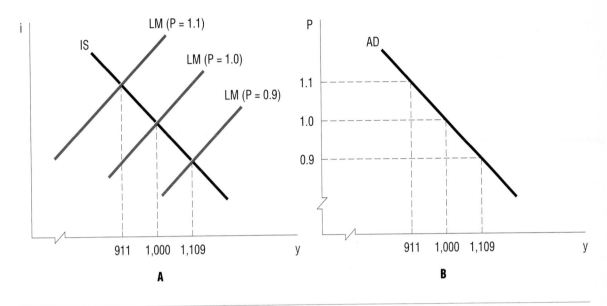

Using Equation 27A.2 for the demand for money, we see that the LM condition becomes

$$M = [k \, y + (x - z \, i)] \times P, \qquad [27A.3]$$

or

$$y = \frac{1}{k} \left[\frac{M}{P} - (x - z \, i) \right]. \qquad [27A.4]$$

The new IS and LM curves are shown in Exhibit 27A.2. There are two differences between this diagram and the parallel one in Chapter 26—Exhibit 26.9. The first difference is that the horizontal axis is labeled y instead of Y—that is, real income or output instead of nominal income. The second is that the position of the LM curve here depends on the price level. The curve is drawn for $P = 1.0$, so that its actual position is the same as in Exhibit 26.9.

What happens if the price level changes? We can see the answer from Equation 27A.4. An increase in P reduces real balances, M/P, so that for a given interest rate, y must be smaller. If the interest rate is the same, the demand for real asset balances is the same too. With a smaller amount of real balances available to the economy, the demand for real transactions balances must be smaller for the LM condition to be satisfied. Real transactions balances can be smaller only if real income is smaller. So a higher value of P means a lower value of y for any value of i; that is, the LM curve shifts to the *left*.

Exhibit 27A.3A shows how the ISLM equilibrium changes with different values of P. A higher price level shifts the LM curve to the *left* and gives a lower equilibrium real income and a higher equilibrium interest rate; a lower price level shifts the LM curve to the *right* and gives a higher equilibrium real income and a lower equilibrium interest rate. If we plot the price level against the equilibrium real income that is consistent with it, we obtain the curve in Exhibit 27A.3B. That is, we obtain an aggregate demand curve.

CHAPTER 28

INFLATION

ITS CAUSES AND CONSEQUENCES

Many countries around the world suffer from serious inflation. In the worst cases, prices may double every few weeks.[1] We saw in Chapter 1 how severe inflation can bring an economy to a complete standstill. But even low rates of inflation can be harmful. Indeed, the Fed believed a 12% inflation in the United States in the late 1970s to be so harmful that it was willing to bring about a serious recession in order to stop it. Was stopping inflation worth this price? Why is inflation harmful? Why does it happen?

In Chapter 27 we looked at some possible reasons why prices might rise. But in each case the price rise was limited. Such a limited increase in prices does not constitute inflation. **Inflation** is a continuing and sustained rise in prices over a substantial period of time. We shall see that inflation is possible only if there is continuing growth in the quantity of money. We shall then look at the effects of inflation on the economy—in particular, its effects on the interest rate, on the exchange rate, on the financial markets, and on the government budget.

inflation
Continuing and sustained rise in prices over a substantial period of time.

28.1 THE CONNECTION BETWEEN MONEY AND INFLATION

The connection between money and inflation can best be understood in terms of the equation of exchange.

[1]The world record is the Hungarian hyperinflation after World War II. For a year, prices doubled on average every four days. In the peak month they doubled twice daily.

THE EQUATION OF EXCHANGE IN A CHANGING ECONOMY

The equation of exchange, which we derived in Chapter 22, is

$$M \times V = P \times y, \qquad [28.1]$$

where M is the quantity of money, V is velocity, P is the price level, and y is the economy's output of goods and services.[2] From this equation relating the *levels* of the four variables, we can derive an equation relating their *rates of growth*. The **rate of inflation** is the rate of growth of the price level.

rate of inflation
Rate of growth of the price level in an economy.

The equation relating the rates of growth may best be illustrated with an example. Suppose the values of the four variables in two consecutive years are as follows:

Year	M	V	P	y
1	1,500	0.667	1.00	1,000
2	1,650	0.660	1.06	1,030

Between the two years M increases by 10%, V falls by 1%, P increases by 6%, and y increases by 3%.

Denote M in Year 1, M_1; V in Year 1, V_1; and so on. Denote the rate of growth of M, or the percentage increase, between the two years, g_M. Denote the rates of growth of the other variables g_V, g_P, and g_Y. Then the quantity of money in Year 2 can be represented in terms of the quantity of money in Year 1 and the rate of growth between the two years as follows:

$$1,650 = 1,500 \times (1 + 0.10) = M_1 \times (1 + g_M), \qquad [28.2]$$

where M_1 is 1,000 and g_M is 0.10. The values of the other variables in Year 2 may be represented in a similar fashion in terms of their values in Year 1 and their rates of growth.

The equation of exchange in terms of the values for Year 2 is

$$1,650 \times 0.660 = 1.06 \times 1,030. \qquad [28.3]$$

Now we replace the value of each variable for Year 2 in Equation 28.3 with its representation in terms of its value in Year 1 and its growth rate (e.g., replace the quantity of money in Year 2, 1,650, with $1,500 \times (1 + 0.10)$). That gives us

$$[1,500 \times (1+0.10)] \times [0.667 \times (1-0.01)] = [1.0 \times (1+0.06)] \times [1,000 \times (1+0.03)].$$

$$[28.4]$$

---

[2]In Chapter 22 we had total expenditure, E, on the right-hand side of the equation. But we saw in Chapter 27 that total expenditure can be seen as the product of a price aggregate, such as the GNP deflator, and a quantity aggregate, such as real GNP.

Using symbols, this becomes

$$M_1 (1 + g_M) V_1 (1 + g_V) = P_1 (1 + g_P) y_1 (1 + g_Y). \qquad [28.5]$$

Since the equation of exchange for Year 1 is, in symbols,

$$M_1 \times V_1 = P_1 \times y_1, \qquad [28.6]$$

we can divide the left-hand side of Equation 28.5 by $M_1 \times V_1$ and the right-hand side by $P_1 \times y_1$ to obtain

$$(1 + g_M) (1 + g_V) = (1 + g_P) (1 + g_Y). \qquad [28.7]$$

We multiply this out to get

$$1 + g_M + g_V + g_M g_V = 1 + g_P + g_Y + g_P g_Y. \qquad [28.8]$$

Finally, we subtract 1 from each side and drop the product terms. The product terms may be dropped because they are relatively small: In our case $g_M g_V = 0.001$ and $g_P g_Y = 0.002$. The result is

$$g_M + g_V \cong g_P + g_Y, \qquad [28.9]$$

where $\cong$ means "approximately equal to." In our example, the approximation is quite good:

$$0.10 + (-0.01) \cong 0.06 + 0.03. \qquad [28.10]$$

Let us restate Equation 28.9 in words:

$$\text{rate of growth of quantity of money} + \text{rate of growth of velocity} \cong \text{rate of inflation} + \text{rate of growth of output.} \qquad [28.11]$$

CHECK STATION 1

A. If velocity increases by 3%, income increases by 2%, and the quantity of money grows by 10%, what is the rate of inflation?

B. For the same growth rates of velocity and income, at what rate must the quantity of money grow to keep prices constant?

Exhibit 28.1 shows the historic behavior of the U.S. economy in terms of the growth rates of Equation 28.11. Notice in particular how both the quantity of money and velocity fell during the Great Depression.

INFLATION AND MONETARY GROWTH

Equation 28.11 is the key to understanding the relationship between the rate of inflation and the rate of growth of the quantity of money. For the moment, suppose the growth rates of velocity and output are constant. Then, from Equation 28.11, it is clear that a change in the rate of inflation can occur *if and only if* there is a corresponding change in the rate of growth of the quantity of money. For example, suppose that initially the growth rates are as in Equation 28.10, with the inflation rate at 6%. With the growth rates of velocity and income fixed, the inflation rate can increase from 6% to 10% if and only if the growth rate of the quantity of money increases from 10% to 14%. This basic truth has been summed up by Milton Friedman in a famous dictum: "Inflation is always and everywhere a monetary phenomenon."

It is important to understand exactly what this means. It means that inflation cannot occur without monetary growth. It does *not* mean that monetary growth is the only immediate cause of inflation. To make this clear, let us look at some cases.

demand–pull inflation
Inflation caused by more money chasing the same quantity of goods.

Case 1   Governments sometimes spend more than they can raise in taxes or borrow. To bridge the gap, they print new money to pay for their purchases. This is done today by Brazil and Argentina, and it was done during the Revolutionary and Civil Wars by the United States. With more money chasing the same quantity of goods, prices rise steadily. This is the classic case of inflation and is called **demand–pull inflation.**

cost–push inflation
Inflation resulting from spiraling increases in wages and prices.

Case 2   When OPEC raised the price of oil in 1973 and again in 1979, the prices of many other goods increased too: Energy, particularly in the form of transportation, is an important element of cost for most goods. The rise in prices stimulated demands for wage increases; the wage increases led to further price rises; the price rises led to further wage increases; and so on in a *wage–price spiral*. This type of inflation is called a **cost–push inflation.**

Case 3   In its early stages, the German hyperinflation was a standard demand–pull inflation. But in its final stages the mechanism changed somewhat. The price level was rising so fast that sellers did not know hour by hour what prices to charge. So people took the exchange rate as a guide. If the mark fell 5% against the dollar, they raised their prices by 5%. However, as we shall see later in the chapter, the price level is an important determinant of the exchange rate. So as prices rose in response to the exchange rate, the exchange rate fell even further, and this stimulated further increases in prices.

In Cases 2 and 3 monetary growth is not the *immediate* cause of rising prices, so in what sense is inflation "a monetary phenomenon"? In both cases, inflation *could not have continued* had the quantity of money not grown fast

EXHIBIT 28.1

AVERAGE RATES
OF CHANGE FOR
MONEY STOCK,
VELOCITY, PRICES,
AND OUTPUT

	g_M (M1)	g_V (Velocity)	g_P (GNP deflator)	g_y (Real GNP)
1929–33	−6.7	−8.1	−6.4	−8.4
1934–39	10.4	−2.1	2.1	6.2
1940–49	11.7	−0.9	6.3	4.5
1950–59	2.5	4.0	2.6	3.9
1960–69	3.7	3.0	2.7	4.0
1970–79	6.6	3.2	7.0	2.8
1980–89	7.5	0.0	4.9	2.6

Sources: *Economic Report of the President*, 1990, and *Monetary Statistics of the United States* by Milton Friedman and Anna J. Schwartz, New York: National Bureau of Economic Research, 1970.

enough to accommodate it. If the quantity of money had not grown fast enough, prices could not have continued to rise. If, in a cost–push inflation, money does not grow along with prices, then sales fall and workers are laid off; increasing unemployment then restrains wage increases, and the process comes to a halt. So even when monetary growth does not *directly* cause an inflation, it is necessary to sustain it.[3]

The relationship between monetary growth and inflation is illustrated in Exhibit 28.2, which plots the average rate of inflation against the average rate of monetary growth for a number of high-inflation countries. The relationship becomes particularly clear when monetary growth is rapid, because then the rates of change in velocity and output are small by comparison.

28.2 DO MONETARY GROWTH AND INFLATION HAVE REAL EFFECTS?

To understand the effects of monetary growth and inflation on an economy, let us return to our South Seas island. In Chapters 23 through 26 we saw the consequences of a one-time increase in the quantity of money. Now we want to see what happens when there is a *continuing* increase. To produce such a continuing increase, the central bank must continue its open market purchases month after month. For simplicity, we shall suppose it purchases enough securities each month to keep the quantity of money growing at a *constant* rate. There will be an initial period of adjustment to this constantly growing quantity of money, just as there was to the one-time increase, but eventually the economy will settle down into some sort of steady pattern. What will this pattern look like?

---

[3]In fact, prices in Germany were rising *faster* than the increase in the quantity of money, and money was becoming very scarce (only in real terms, of course!). The scarcity of money made it difficult to buy and sell, and it was an important element in the collapse of economic activity toward the end of the hyperinflation. In terms of Equation 28.11, the negative growth rate of income allowed inflation to exceed monetary growth.

It is tempting to look to the Quantity Theory for an answer. In Chapter 23 we argued that in the long run a single change in the quantity of money does not affect real variables: The supply and demand for goods and services, the real rate of interest, and velocity all remain the same. The only long-run effect is a scaling up of all nominal prices in proportion to the increase in the quantity of money. However, here we are talking not about a single change, but about a continuing change.

As we saw in Chapters 24 through 26, a single change in the quantity of money does have real effects in the short run. However, the Quantity Theory relies on these real effects being far enough in the past for them to have faded completely. It assumes that enough time has passed so that they no longer affect the current state of the economy. When the quantity of money *continues* to change, however, the real effects continue as well. Each month additional new money enters the economy, disturbing the economy afresh. So the Quantity Theory does not apply to a continuing change in the quantity of money.

inflation "tax"
Money's loss of value due to rising prices.

One of the persistent real effects of a continuing monetary expansion is the **inflation "tax."** As prices rise, money loses value. For example, if prices rise by 1% a month, then the money you hold at the beginning of each month will buy 1% fewer goods and services by the end of that month. In the Island economy, at the beginning of each month, all the money is in the hands of households. Some is the income they have just received, and the rest is asset balances carried over from the previous month. If households hold $1,500 million at the start of the month and prices rise by 1%, that money falls in value by $15 million by the end of the month. By the end of the month it will buy only $1,485 million worth of goods in terms of beginning-of-month prices. So the loss due to the 1% inflation is exactly like the loss that would be due to a 1% tax on money balances paid at the beginning of the month.

This tax, like any other, affects people's behavior. First, like any other tax, it reduces their income. As a result, households will most likely both consume less and save less. Second, like any other tax, it changes the relative price of the good that is taxed. In this case, the "tax" is on money, making money more expensive to hold. As we shall see later in the chapter, this affects the way money balances are managed and therefore affects the demand for money.

Monetary growth and inflation, then, can be expected to have real effects on the economy. Quantities of goods traded, real prices, real interest rates, real exchange rates, real balances, and velocity: All of these may change. In the following sections we shall look at how they change.

28.3 | INFLATION AND INTEREST RATES

Monetary growth and inflation have a number of effects on interest rates. To understand them, we need to take another look at the distinction between real and nominal interest rates.

EXHIBIT 28.2

INFLATION AND MONETARY GROWTH IN HIGH INFLATION COUNTRIES

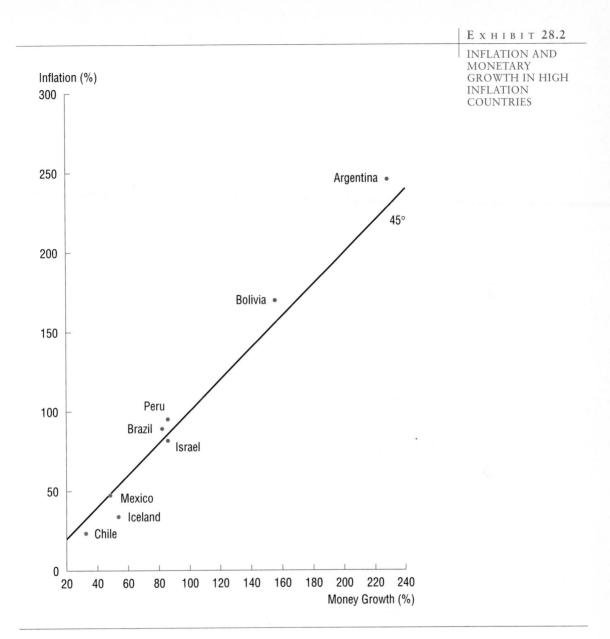

Averages for Bolivia are for 1977–1988.
Averages for Brazil and Chile are for 1977–1985.

Source: International Monetary Fund, *International Financial Statistics.*

REAL AND NOMINAL INTEREST RATES

In Chapter 23 we learned the distinction between nominal and real rates of interest. The *nominal* rate is a rate in terms of money: If you lend for a year at a 5% nominal rate, it means that you get back 5% more money than you gave up when you made the loan. The *real* rate is the rate in terms of purchasing power: A 5% real rate on a one-year loan means that you get back enough money to enable you to buy 5% more goods and services than you could have bought with the money you gave up when you made the loan. In Chapter 23 this distinction between nominal and real rates was an empty one. Since prices were constant over time, the real rate and the nominal rate were always the same. But now, with prices changing, the two rates differ and the distinction matters.

As we saw in Chapter 23, the relationship between real and nominal interest rates can be expressed by the following equation:[4]

$$(1 + i) = (1 + n)(1 + r) \qquad [28.12]$$

where

i = nominal interest rate,
n = rate of inflation,
r = real interest rate.

Equation 28.12 expresses, for a given nominal rate, the relationship between the *actual* real rate on a loan and the *actual* rate of inflation. Of course, if we look at a loan *before* it is made, the actual rate of inflation over the life of the loan is unknown. However, the borrower and lender will have some expectation of what that rate of inflation will be—let us call it n^e. Given that expectation, their expectation of the real rate on the loan, r^e, must satisfy this equation:

$$(1 + i) = (1 + n^e)(1 + r^e). \qquad [28.13]$$

For example, if the nominal rate is 12% and the expected rate of inflation is 5%, then the expected real rate is 6.7%:

$$1 + r^e = \frac{1 + i}{1 + n^e} = \frac{1.12}{1.05} = 1.067. \qquad [28.14]$$

Or, if the nominal rate is still 12% but the expected rate of inflation is 10%, then the expected real rate is only 1.8%:

$$1 + r^e = \frac{1.12}{1.10} = 1.018. \qquad [28.15]$$

[4]Equation 28.12 is simply a rearrangement of Equation 23.6.

There is a useful approximation to Equation 28.13:[5]

$$i \cong r^e + n^e. \qquad [28.16]$$

Equation 28.16 is known as the **Fisher equation**.[6] Restated in words, it is

$$\text{nominal rate} \cong \text{expected real rate} + \text{expected rate of inflation.} \qquad [28.17]$$

Can we infer from the Fisher equation that the only effect of inflation is to raise nominal interest rates by the amount of the inflation? That is, suppose that when inflation is zero, both real and nominal interest rates are 10%. Will the effect of a 5% inflation be merely to raise the nominal rate to 15%? That depends on what happens to the *real* rate. If the inflation has no effect on the real rate, then that is indeed all there is to it. As we shall see, however, there are reasons to believe that the real interest rate *will* be affected.

Fisher equation
Equation stating that the nominal rate of interest approximates the expected real rate plus the expected rate of inflation.

If the real interest rate is 4% and expected inflation is 5%, what is the nominal interest rate?

🌴**CHECK STATION 2**

THE REAL SUPPLY AND DEMAND FOR LOANABLE FUNDS

To understand the effect of inflation on the real interest rate, we need to reformulate the supply and demand for loanable funds in real terms. As we saw in Chapter 23, when making decisions on how much to lend or borrow, it is *real* considerations that matter. So we need to reformulate the supply and demand in terms of the real interest rate and the real amount of loanable funds.

Exhibit 24.2 in Chapter 24 showed supply and demand in the loanable funds market in nominal terms. Exhibit 28.3 translates this into real terms. Notice that the units on the horizontal axis are in *base-period* dollars. Plain dollars will no longer do because prices are no longer constant. For example, if prices are rising at 1% a month, the same amount of real purchasing power will be represented by $200 million in the first month, $202 million in the second month, $204.2 million in the third month, and so on. So the amounts of loanable funds supplied and demanded are measured in terms of real purchasing power, in base-period dollars. For convenience, we shall take as the base period the month before the monetary expansion begins—Month 0—and measure the amount of real loanable funds in dollars of that month; that is, $100 of real loanable funds is the amount needed to buy what $100 would have bought before the inflation begins.

---

[5]Multiplying out the right-hand side and subtracting one from each side, we get $i = r^e + n^e + r^e n^e$. Dropping $r^e n^e$ as relatively small, we obtain Equation 28.16.

[6]Irving Fisher was the first economist to discuss systematically the distinction between real and nominal rates.

EXHIBIT 28.3

THE REAL SUPPLY
AND DEMAND FOR
LOANABLE FUNDS

The supply and demand for
real loanable funds (in base-
period dollars) depend on the
real interest rate.

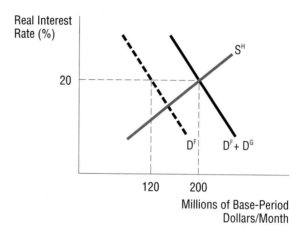

THE EFFECTS OF INFLATION AND MONETARY GROWTH

The supply and demand curves in Exhibit 28.3 appear in the same place as in Exhibit 24.2. The only change is the way the axes are labeled. This assumes that the real supply and demand for loanable funds are unaffected by monetary expansion and inflation. Is this assumption reasonable? There is little reason to think that the real demand is much affected, but there are two effects on the real supply.[7]

The first effect on supply is the effect of the inflation "tax" we discussed above. The inflation tax lowers household disposable income, and we can expect this to reduce the supply of loanable funds. This effect shifts the supply of loanable funds to the left and tends to raise the real rate of interest.

The second effect is a continuing *loan-supply effect*. Let us see how this works in the Island economy. Suppose the economy has adjusted to steady monetary growth of 1% per month. Real variables have stabilized at some constant level. They are not necessarily the same as they were before monetary growth began, but they are constant over time. It follows from Equation 28.10 that with V and y stabilized, the rate of inflation equals the rate of monetary growth. Since the

[7]In this case, Exhibit 28.3 is correctly drawn only if the inflation rate is zero.

(1) Month	(2) Quantity of Money at Start of Month	(3) Price Level P	(4) Increase in Quantity of Money ΔM	(5) New Bank Loans in Real Terms $\Delta M/P$
0	$1,500.0	1.0000	0	0
1	1,500.0	1.0000	15 (1% of 1,500)	$\dfrac{15}{1.0000} = 15$
⋮	⋮	⋮	⋮	⋮
t	3,000.0	2.0000	30 (1% of 3,000)	$\dfrac{30}{2.0000} = 15$
$t+1$	3,030.0	2.0200	30.3 (1% of 3,030)	$\dfrac{30.3}{2.0200} = 15$
$t+2$	3,060.3	2.0402	30.603 (1% of 3,060.3)	$\dfrac{30.603}{2.0402} = 15$

EXHIBIT 28.4

THE LOAN-SUPPLY EFFECT OF A CONTINUING MONETARY EXPANSION (QUANTITIES IN MILLIONS OF DOLLARS)

rate of monetary growth is a constant 1% per month, so also is the rate of inflation. Exhibit 28.4 shows what will happen to money and prices over time.

Column 2 in the exhibit shows the quantity of money at the beginning of each month. Month 1 is the first month of the monetary expansion. The table skips over the many months of adjustment and resumes at Month t, by which time the quantity of money has doubled from $1,500 million to $3,000 million. The quantity of money continues to grow after that at the same rate of 1% a month. The increase in the quantity of money, ΔM, is shown in Column 4.

By Month t the economy has adjusted to the continuing monetary growth and all real variables have stopped changing. The price level in Month t is just double its original value, and it continues to rise at a rate of 1% a month. The price level in each month, P, is shown in Column 3. Column 5 shows the *real* amount of new bank loans that is added to the supply of loanable funds each month. When the quantity of money increases by ΔM, that means that banks lend an additional ΔM dollars in the loanable funds market. To find how much that is in real terms, we must divide by the price level, P. You can see that because P increases month by month at the same rate as ΔM, the real addition of loanable funds is a constant 15 million base-period dollars.[8]

---

[8]The price level will be exactly double only if velocity and output are unchanged from their original values or if the changes just offset one another. However, even if the price level is not exactly double, it will still continue to rise at 1%. The real amount of bank loans will be a constant amount from month to month, even if that amount differs from $15 million. We shall discuss below how velocity and output are actually affected by inflation.

EXHIBIT 28.5

THE MARKET FOR
REAL LOANABLE
FUNDS WITH
MONETARY
GROWTH

In a continuing monetary
expansion, there is a
continuing addition to the real
supply of loanable funds.

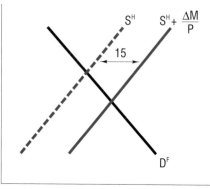

The effect of the continuing monetary injection on the loanable funds market is shown in Exhibit 28.5. There is a *continuing* addition to the total supply of real loanable funds equal to the real value of the continuing monetary injection. There is an important difference, then, between a continuing monetary expansion and the single, once-and-for-all increase in the quantity of money we looked at in Chapter 24 (see Exhibit 24.5). In that case, the new money made available as loans by the banking system added to the supply of loanable funds *only in the initial month*. In the long run, households once again became the sole source of loanable funds, and the loanable funds market eventually returned to its original equilibrium. With a continuing monetary expansion, that is not the case. Now, the banking system is providing additional loans not just once, but *every month*. This amount is a continuing addition to the supply of loanable funds by households. Thus this loan-supply effect shifts the real supply curve to the right and tends to *lower* the real interest rate.

inflation-tax effect
Decrease in real supply of
loanable funds due to the
inflation "tax."

Inflation and monetary growth, then, have no effect on the real demand for loanable funds and two offsetting effects on the real supply. The **inflation-tax effect** tends to lower the supply and raise the real interest rate, and the **continuing loan-supply effect** tends to increase the supply and lower the real interest rate. What is the net effect?

continuing loan-supply effect
Increase in real supply of
loanable funds due to
increased bank lending.

CHECK STATION 3   **During the Great Depression prices fell as the quantity of bank money shrank. What was the nature of the loan-supply effect on the supply of real loanable funds?**

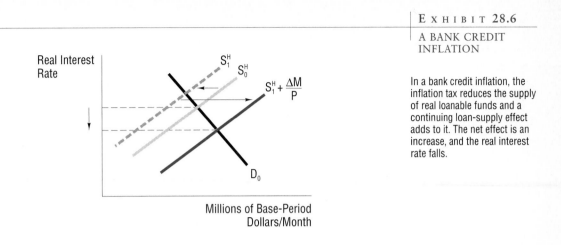

EXHIBIT 28.6

A BANK CREDIT INFLATION

In a bank credit inflation, the inflation tax reduces the supply of real loanable funds and a continuing loan-supply effect adds to it. The net effect is an increase, and the real interest rate falls.

INFLATION AND INTEREST RATES: TWO SCENARIOS

In different cases of inflation in different countries, the circumstances may differ substantially. There are, however, two particular scenarios that are of special interest. Actual inflations may be like one or the other, or possibly somewhere in between.

SCENARIO 1: A BANK CREDIT INFLATION Some moderate inflations are the result of monetary expansion by the banking system that has little or nothing to do with government deficit spending. The result is shown in Exhibit 28.6. The inflation-tax effect reduces the real supply of loanable funds of households from S_0^H to S_1^H, the continuing loan-supply effect adds to this a supply of real loanable funds of $\Delta M/P$, giving a *total* supply of loanable funds of $S_1^H + \Delta M/P$. The continuing loan-supply effect tends to be greater than the inflation-tax effect, so there is a net increase in the real supply of loanable funds and the real interest rate *falls*. To find the nominal rate, we apply the Fisher equation, Equation 28.17. That is, the nominal rate is the new, lower real rate plus the rate of inflation. Generally, the fall in the real rate is less than the rate of inflation, so the nominal rate *rises*.

SCENARIO 2: A GOVERNMENT-SPENDING INFLATION The most common cause of *high* rates of inflation, such as those in Latin America, is the financing of government spending with money creation. The way this works is that the central bank expands the money supply so that the increase in bank lending is enough to

E X H I B I T 28.7

A GOVERNMENT-
SPENDING
INFLATION

In government-spending
inflation, increased government borrowing cancels out
the loan-supply effect, leaving
the inflation tax to raise the
real interest rate.

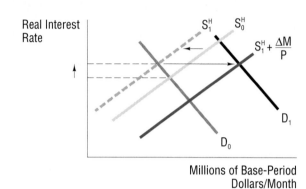

finance the increased borrowing of the government. This is illustrated in Exhibit 28.7. As in Scenario 1, the inflation-tax effect reduces the real supply of loanable funds of households from S_0^H to S_1^H and the continuing loan-supply effect adds to this a supply of real loanable funds of $\Delta M/P$, giving a total supply of loanable funds of $S_1^H + \Delta M/P$. But in Scenario 2, the continuing loan-supply effect is exactly offset by a continuing increase in the *demand* for loanable funds on the part of the government by the same amount (the demand for real loanable funds increases from D_0 to D_1). Since the loan-supply effect is canceled out in this way, we are left with just the inflation-tax effect, so the net result is a *rise* in the real interest rate. To find the new *nominal* rate, we apply the Fisher equation, Equation 28.17. That is, the nominal rate is the new, higher real rate *plus* the rate of inflation.

APPLICATION: U.S. INFLATION AND REAL INTEREST RATES IN THE 1960s AND 1970s

Exhibit 28.8 shows inflation rates and real interest rates on three-month T-bills between 1960 and 1989. The real rate is calculated as the nominal rate less the *actual* rate of inflation (the assumption being that, at any time, expectations of inflation over the next three months are roughly correct).

EXHIBIT 28.8

INFLATION RATES
AND REAL INTEREST
RATES, 1960–1989

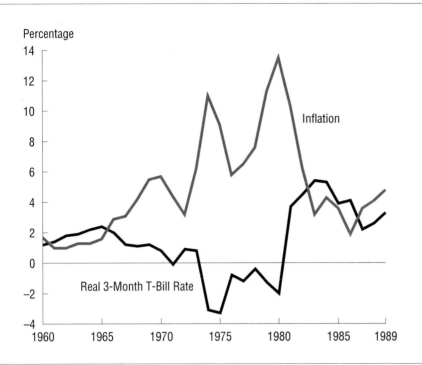

Source: *Economic Report of the President.*

On the whole, as you can see, increasing inflation in the 1960s and 1970s corresponded more to Scenario 1 than to Scenario 2: Real interest rates tended to fall as inflation increased. This suggests that the continuing loan-supply effect during this period substantially exceeded increased government borrowing to finance the deficit. Remember that this was the period, particularly in the later years, when ingenious banks were inventing new forms of transactions deposit that did not officially count as money, but nonetheless did expand its effective quantity.

28.4 INFLATION AND EXCHANGE RATES

How does inflation affect exchange rates? In Chapter 25 we used the Quantity Theory and the principle of purchasing-power parity to argue that, in the long run, the exchange rate between two currencies will change in proportion to changes in quantities of money or, equivalently, to changes in price levels. For example, if prices in Japan double while those in the United States remain the same, we would expect—in the long run—that the dollar will buy twice as many yen as before.

EXHIBIT 28.9

INFLATION AND CHANGES IN EXCHANGE RATES 1973–1989

	Japan	West Germany	United Kingdom	Italy	Argentina (1977–1989)	Israel (1974–1989)
Average inflation-average U.S. inflation	−4.4%	−3.1%	2.5%	5.0%	356.5%	71.8%
Average rate of change in $ exchange rate	−1.5	−3.3	4.0	6.9	333.4	83.0

Sources: The UN's *Monthly Bulletin of Statistics*, June 1978, 1984, and 1990 issues (exchange rates) and the IMF's *International Financial Statistics* (consumer prices).

We can express this relationship in terms of the rates of inflation in the two countries:

$$\text{rate of change of ¥/\$ exchange rate = ¥ inflation rate − \$ inflation rate.} \quad [28.18]$$

It should be stressed that this is a *long-run* relationship. As we saw in Chapter 25, exchange rates can and do deviate from purchasing-power parity for substantial periods of time.

APPLICATION: INFLATION AND EXCHANGE RATES IN THE 1970s AND 1980s

Exhibit 28.9 tests Equation 28.18 for a number of exchange rates over the period 1973–1989. As you can see, the relationship holds up reasonably well, but far from perfectly. For West Germany and Argentina the relationship seems to hold quite well, but for Japan, the United Kingdom, Italy, and Israel it is less exact.

🌴 **CHECK STATION 4**   **Assume that the yen/dollar exchange rate in 1991 is 155¥/$. If inflation in the United States over the 1990s is 4% and in Japan it is 2%, what will the yen/dollar exchange rate be in the year 2000?**

28.5 | INFLATION AND FINANCIAL MARKETS

Inflation has substantial effects on saving and investment and on the financial system that intermediates between them. We shall see that inflation alters the relative desirability of different types of assets and liabilities. There are three comparisons that are affected by inflation:

1. Real assets versus financial assets.

2. Long-term financial assets versus short-term financial assets.

3. Money versus interest-paying assets.

We shall look at each in turn. Before we do, however, we need to understand the distinction between *anticipated inflation* and *unanticipated inflation* and the nature of *inflation risk*.

ANTICIPATED AND UNANTICIPATED INFLATION

In the previous sections, we assumed that monetary growth was steady and therefore that inflation proceeded at a constant rate. In such circumstances, it is reasonable to assume that everyone correctly anticipates the inflation. Such an **anticipated inflation** will be taken into account in writing loan and other contracts. In reality, inflation is rarely like this. Episodes of relatively high inflation often come as a surprise and drastically alter the real terms of contracts that were written on the assumption that inflation would be lower.[9]

To see how such **unanticipated inflation** may change the terms of a loan, let us look at an example. Janet lends Harry $1,000 for a year. They agree on a real rate of interest of 5%, and they anticipate an inflation rate of 3%, so the loan contract requires Harry to repay $1,080 at the end of the year. If inflation is indeed 3%, then Janet will earn a 5% real return on the loan, as intended. However, suppose the economy unexpectedly undergoes a period of severe inflation of 100%. Then the real value of the $1,080 will be only $540, and Janet's *real* return will be –46%.

Of course, things could go the other way—to Janet's advantage rather than Harry's. If Janet and Harry anticipate 100% inflation, then to give an intended real return of 5%, they will agree on repayment of $2,100 at the end of the year. But suppose that the price level rises by only 20%. The real value of the repayment is $1,750, for a *real* return of 75%.

As you can see, inflation higher than anticipated is a windfall to borrowers; inflation lower than anticipated is a boon to lenders.[10] So if it is uncertain what the rate of inflation will be, that uncertainty will make it hard for borrowers and lenders to agree on the terms of a loan. Whatever nominal rate they agreed upon, both parties face considerable risk that the realized real return may differ substantially from the expected real return. We shall call the risk that the actual inflation rate will deviate from the anticipated rate **inflation risk.**

anticipated inflation
Inflation that is expected by most people.

unanticipated inflation
Inflation that is not expected by most people.

inflation risk
Risk that the realized real interest rate on a loan will be changed by unanticipated inflation.

---

[9]In Chapter 29, we shall discuss how expectations of inflation are formed.

[10]Unless, as is often the case, the increased real value of the debt causes borrowers to default.

EXHIBIT 28.10

BUSINESS FAILURES,
1960–1989

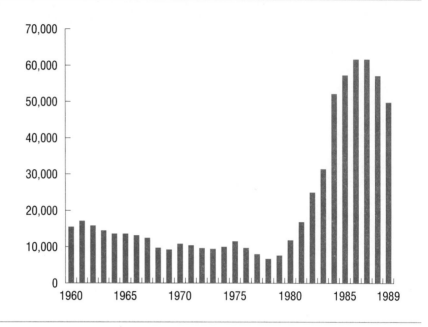

Source: *Economic Report of the President* and *Survey of Current Business*, May 1990.

APPLICATION: INFLATION AND BUSINESS FAILURES   Exhibit 28.10 shows the rate at which business firms have failed over the years. Of course, there are many reasons why businesses fail. However, since businesses are net borrowers, a rise in inflation reduces the value of their debt, making them better off and less likely to fail, whereas a fall in inflation has just the opposite effect. As inflation rose through the 1960s and 1970s, the failure rate declined steadily. As inflation dropped sharply in the early 1980s, the failure rate rose steeply.

REAL VERSUS FINANCIAL ASSETS

Inflation affects the relative attractiveness of real assets as opposed to financial assets. To see why this is so, compare two 20-year investments, one financial and one real. The financial investment is a $100,000 bond with 10% annual coupons. The real investment is a $100,000 house. The house provides you with services worth $10,000 a year—what it would cost you to rent the house. Assume initially that there is no inflation. The flow of returns from the two investments is essentially the same: Each pays $10,000 a year—one in cash, the other in services. At the end of 20 years the bond repays the principal of $100,000, and you can sell the house for $100,000 (assume, with no inflation, that real estate prices remain constant). If the market rate of interest is 10%, both investments have a market value of $100,000.

Now suppose that immediately after you make the two investments, the inflation rate jumps unexpectedly from zero to 10% and is expected to stay there. The market value of the bond falls dramatically. If the real rate of interest stays at 10%, the nominal market rate rises, according to Equation 28.13, to 21%. The market value of the bond is therefore

$$\frac{\$10,000}{(1.21)} + \frac{\$10,000}{(1.21)^2} + \cdots + \frac{\$10,000}{(1.21)^{20}} + \frac{\$100,000}{(1.21)^{20}} = \$48,776. \qquad [28.19]$$

What about the house? The real services it provides are not affected by the inflation, so their dollar value rises with the price level. That is, house rents in dollar terms rise at the rate of 10% a year. Moreover, the price of the house also rises with inflation at the rate of 10% a year. Therefore the market value of the house is now

$$\frac{(1.1) \times \$10,000}{(1.21)} + \frac{(1.1)^2 \times \$10,000}{(1.21)^2} + \cdots \qquad [28.20]$$

$$+ \frac{(1.1)^{20} \times \$10,000}{(1.21)^{20}} + \frac{(1.1)^{20} \times \$100,000}{(1.21)^{20}} = \$100,000.$$

So while the unanticipated increase in inflation cuts the market value of the bond roughly in half, it leaves the market value of the house unaffected. That makes the house a much safer investment in terms of inflation risk. Other real assets, such as precious metals, works of art, and baseball cards, are also relatively safe in terms of inflation risk.[11]

Because real assets are a hedge against inflation risk, when inflation and fears about inflation increase, people tend to shift their wealth out of financial assets and into real ones. Consider, for example, the effect on the market for real estate,

---

[11]This does not mean, of course, that they are not risky in other ways. The prices of such assets are notoriously volatile.

EXHIBIT 28.11

INFLATION AND THE
REAL ESTATE
MARKET

Inflation increases the demand
for real assets, such as real
estate, because they are seen
as a hedge against inflation
risk. As a result, their real price
rises.

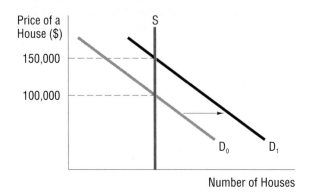

as shown in Exhibit 28.11. Increasing fear of inflation increases demand, moving the demand curve to the right from D_0 to D_1. The supply of real estate is fixed in the short run, so the principal effect is a rise in the average price of existing homes from \$100,000 to \$150,000.[12] In terms of our comparison of financial and real investments, as people rush to sell bonds, the market value of bonds falls even further; as they rush to buy houses, the market value of real estate rises.

The shift in demand from financial to real assets has consequences for the economy. Remember from Chapter 3 that when households acquire financial assets, they are lending to firms to enable the firms to make productive investments. Thus less demand for financial assets on the part of households means less productive investment by firms. In addition, the rise in value of real estate leads to increased investment in housing. So a rise in inflation (or in the fear of inflation) affects the *type* of real investment that takes place in the economy: There is less investment in new factories and more in housing.

One asset is, in a sense, both financial and real—stocks. Stocks are a financial asset in that they promise a flow of dollar payments in the form of dividends. However, these payments are "real" in the sense that the dollar value of dividends should rise with inflation. When there is no inflation, the market value of a stock is

$$S = \frac{D_1}{(1+r)} + \frac{D_2}{(1+r)^2} + \cdots, \qquad [28.21]$$

where D_1 is the dividend in Year 1, and so on, and r is the real—and the nominal—interest rate. Suppose now that inflation is $n\%$. If the real rate is unaffected,

---

[12]This is an increase in the *real* price. The increase occurs now, the inflation is anticipated for the future.

EXHIBIT 28.12

STOCK PRICES AND
INFLATION:
1960–1989

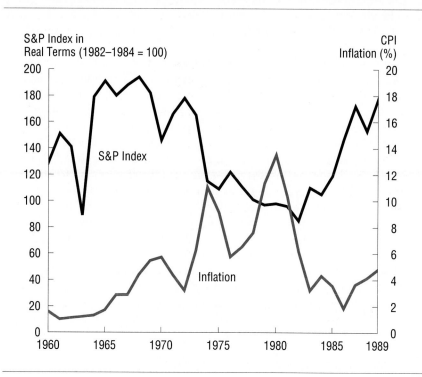

Source: *Economic Report of the President.*

and if real profits are unaffected, then the market value of the stock should stay
the same:

$$S = \frac{D_1(1+n)}{(1+r)(1+n)} + \frac{D_2(1+n)^2}{(1+r)^2(1+n)^2} + \cdots . \qquad [28.22]$$

Dividends in dollar terms should increase with the price level, offsetting the
higher nominal rate of interest at which the cash flow is discounted.

APPLICATION: THE STOCK MARKET IN THE 1970s AND 1980s   In practice, as
Exhibit 28.12 shows, during the 1970s when inflation was rising, stocks did very
poorly. For reasons that may or may not have something to do with inflation,
profits in this period were poor. However, when inflation dropped in the early
1980s, profits improved and stocks made a dramatic recovery.

LONG-TERM VERSUS SHORT-TERM ASSETS

A second comparison that is affected by inflation is the one between long-term
and short-term borrowing and lending. Clearly, the longer the term of a loan, the

greater the inflation risk. The risk that the rate of inflation will change drastically over the life of a 30-year bond is much greater than the risk that it will change over the life of a T-bill or of commercial paper. The greater inflation risk involved in long-term securities affects both lenders and borrowers.

Lenders will want to hold more short-term securities and less long-term: Indeed, the fraction of household portfolios invested in short-term securities rose from 30% in 1965 to 45% in 1977. Moreover, because of their greater inflation risk, long-term securities will need to offer a higher yield relative to short-term securities in order for investors to be willing to hold them.

Inflation risk is also of concern to borrowers. They are not, of course, worried that inflation will rise, but they are worried that it will fall. Firms contemplating long-term investments are in a difficult position. To eliminate interest-rate risk, they need to borrow at a fixed real rate for a term that is the same as the term of the investment (for them to make a profit, this real rate should be below the real return on the investment). A fixed *nominal* rate achieves this only if inflation is constant. If firms finance their investment with long-term debt and the rate of inflation falls, they will be saddled with a high real rate and possibly a loss on the project. If they finance the investment by rolling over short-term debt, they face the usual interest-rate risk that results from a maturity mismatch: The *real* market rate may rise. Firms responded to the inflation of the 1970s both by reducing investment and by relying more on short-term finance.

THE COST OF HOLDING MONEY

Money is an asset that is particularly hard hit by inflation. Since currency and regular demand deposits pay no interest, the opportunity cost of holding money is the interest that could be earned on alternative assets, like T-bills or shares in money market mutual funds. So, as inflation raises the nominal rate of interest, it also raises the opportunity cost of holding money. When the real interest rate is 3% and inflation is zero, the opportunity cost of holding money is 3%. When the real interest rate is still 3%, but inflation is 12%, the opportunity cost of holding money is 15%. This is the *real* opportunity cost: You could have had 15% more real purchasing power had you held another asset.[13]

---

[13]The real return on the alternative asset is the nominal return minus the rate of inflation. The real return on money is just zero minus the rate of inflation. So the *difference* in the real rates equals the nominal return on the alternative asset.

CASH JUGGLING A WAY OF LIFE

It was a dull Memorial Day three years ago for the skeletal staff on duty at the Chemical Bank until the arrival, by courier from overseas, of $100 million in checks drawn on a small bank in Illinois.

The staff was supposed to rush the processing of such large checks, to get an extra day's use of the funds. But the only way to do that in the case of this Illinois bank would be for someone to grab a flight to Chicago that evening and personally hand over the checks.

"We asked one of our supervisors if she had ever been to Chicago," recalled Allen M. Silverstein, a senior vice president at Chemical. "She hadn't. I bought her a ticket on my American Express card. A day's worth of interest on $100 million was $23,000. The plane ticket, hotel room and meals were about $500."

Flying checks around to get an extra day's interest income is just one of the ways that banks and corporations try to maximize their interest income. In the quest for "float"—in its broadest sense, the money in checks that have not yet cleared—companies have developed all kinds of ways to manage their cash.

Amid the competition for float, cash management has become big business. Banks advise clients how to minimize the balances in checking accounts that do not bear interest. Consultants advise corporations how to speed up receipts and delay paying expenses. Books, articles and conferences report the latest techniques.

A. J. (Jack) King, a small-city banker in Montana, said he was stunned a few years ago when a major oil company called him up and asked if it could write all its checks on an account on his bank.

"They were going to clear all checks around the world through Kalispell, Montana—and you can't get more remote than we are," recalled Mr. King, who is chairman of the Valley Bank of Kalispell. Situated in the northwestern corner of the state, near Glacier National Park, Kalispell has a population of almost 11,000.

If the company wrote checks on Mr. King's remote bank, the checks would take an extra day or two after being deposited in banks elsewhere to wend their way through the banking system and be debited from the corporation's Kalispell account. On as much as $30 million of checks a day, the extra days' interest adds up to millions of dollars during a year.

That idea—which did not work out, largely because the parties could not agree on an appropriate fee—illustrates one of the most common ways that corporations try to get the most interest income possible.

Ways to Postpone Payment

Companies can get more interest by delaying expenditures if they do not mind antagonizing customers.

"Another method sometimes used by corporations is delayed postmarks," writes Paul J. Beehler in "Contemporary Cash Management," a book that appeared in 1983. "This is important because discounts are based generally on postmarked dates, not the actual date received. Consequently, a company could postmark a payable on Friday, have it mailed on Monday and gain three days' float on the funds as well as gaining the cash discount.

"This technique is not generally recommended since credibility with suppliers is jeopardized. Mailing funds from remotely located post offices can also help to maximize the length of time it takes payments to reach vendors."

Besides delaying payments, cash management involves accelerating receipts. For example, instead of regularly billing a major customer, a company may arrange automatic withdrawals from the customer's account at the start of every month.

For larger amounts, funds may be transferred electronically. Such transfers in the United States now involve nine times the amount of money paid for in checks and cash. But 99 percent of all transactions are still paid for by check or cash.

Another way in which companies speed up receipts is to use lockboxes. These are post office boxes to which customers send payments. They are opened not by the company but by the company's bank. The bank immediately deposits all checks into a customer's account and only later forwards the invoices to the company.

The final element in cash management is putting as much money as possible to work. That means keeping as little money as possible in checking accounts that draw no interest. One way is zero balance accounts. In effect, the company keeps no money in its checking account but arranges for the bank to transfer funds from interest-bearing accounts to cover checks as they come in. The bank charges a fee for the service.

Companies "sweep out" their checking accounts each evening and invest their funds overnight. Computer technology has made this much easier, allowing companies with a flick of a button to buy securities in the afternoon and arrange to resell them for a slightly higher price in the morning.

Source: Nicholas D. Kristof, "Squeezing Profits from Float," *The New York Times*, May 27, 1985. Copyright © 1985 by The New York Times Company. Reprinted by permission.

Not surprisingly, as inflation increases, firms and households try to reduce their money balances. We saw in Chapters 9 and 10 how, from the late 1960s on, the pressure to get out of cash led to improvements in cash management, to the rapid development of the money market, and to a transformation of commercial banking. High nominal interest rates made it worthwhile to invest considerable resources and ingenuity in slowing down payments and in speeding up receipts. Some of the methods that were used are described in "Cash Juggling a Way of Life" on 737. As firms and households hold less money, velocity increases, and this adds fuel to the inflation.

28.6 | ADJUSTING TO INFLATION

Many financial contracts and other arrangements are ill-suited to an inflationary environment. They are designed for a world in which "a dollar is a dollar." When a dollar is no longer a (base-period) dollar, serious distortions occur.

TAXES

Some of the most serious distortions involve taxes. One example is the taxation of interest income. Remember our example of the $1,000 loan that Janet made to Harry? The intended real rate was 5% and, anticipating 3% inflation, the agreed nominal rate was 8%. Harry had to pay $80 in interest at the end of the year. For tax purposes, all the $80 interest is considered as income for Janet: If the tax rate is 25%, she will have to pay 0.25 x $80 = $20 in tax. But if inflation is 3% as Janet and Harry anticipated, only $50 is really income; the other $30 just compensates Janet for the loss in value of the principal amount. After paying tax, Janet has only $60, so the after-tax nominal rate is 6% and the after-tax real rate is only 3%.

The higher the inflation the worse this distortion becomes, as Exhibit 28.13 shows. Since it is the real after-tax yield that lenders care about—that is their real reward—this tax distortion will reduce the supply of lending as inflation increases, tending to drive up before-tax rates and reduce the amount of lending.

The same sort of problem occurs with other taxes. One example is the tax on capital gains. If you buy a house for $100,000 and sell it for $200,000 twenty years later, you will have to pay taxes on the $100,000 capital gain. However, if the price level has doubled over those twenty years, the real capital gain is zero.

MORTGAGES

Mortgage contracts are distorted particularly badly by inflation. Even if inflation is correctly anticipated, so that the nominal rate correctly compensates for the falling value of money, the terms of the mortgage contract are changed drastically.

To see why, consider this example. The real rate on a $50,000 thirty-year mortgage is 4%. Let us compare the real payments on the mortgage in two

EXHIBIT 28.13

THE EFFECT OF INFLATION ON THE AFTER-TAX REAL RATE

Real Rate before Tax	Rate of Inflation	Nominal Rate		Real Rate After Tax
		Before Tax	After Tax (25%)	
5%	0%	5%	3.75%	3.75%
5	3	8	6	3
5	12	17.6	13.2	1
5	20	26	19.5	−0.5
5	40	47	35.25	−3.4

situations. In the first, there is no inflation; in the second, there is a fully anticipated inflation of 12%.

- *No inflation:* The nominal interest rate is the same as the real rate—4%. The monthly payment is $239, and this payment remains the same for the life of the mortgage, both in dollars and in real terms.

- *Inflation is 12%:* The inflation is fully anticipated, so the nominal interest rate is 16%. The monthly payment increases to $672. This payment remains the same *in dollars* for the life of the mortgage. But in real terms it declines. In fact, the real value of the final payment is only $22 in Year 1 dollars.

In both cases the contract is "fair": The terms for both borrower and lender are just as planned and agreed upon. However, the patterns of repayment in the two cases are very different. With the 12% inflation, the first month's payment is nearly three times higher in real terms and the last month's payment is ten times lower. This pattern of repayment is hard for the typical borrower to handle: Payments are high when income is low—when he or she is young—and then drop in real terms as income increases. Remember that the whole purpose of this type of mortgage is to make repayment easier by having equal monthly payments. Inflation defeats this purpose.

There have been various suggestions for redesigning the mortgage contract to deal with the distortion caused by inflation. The simplest suggestion is the **price-level-adjusted mortgage.** Under this arrangement, the *real* monthly payment remains constant. In our example, with a real rate of 4%, the monthly payment is a *real* $239. For the real payment to remain the same, the payment in dollars must increase if the price level rises. For example, if inflation is 12% over the life of the mortgage, the final payment will be $7,160. This may seem terrifying, but remember that by the time that final payment is made, the price level will be some 30 times higher than it was originally. As a result, salaries also

price-level-adjusted mortgage
Mortgage in which monthly payments increase as the price level rises.

will be 30 times higher, so that the $7,160 final payment will be no more onerous than was the $239 first payment.[14]

INDEXATION

The price-level adjusted mortgage is just one example of a more general idea—*indexation*. As we saw in Chapter 27, a financial or other type of contract is indexed if it stipulates dollar payments that are linked to some published price index. For example, a $10,000 bond might pay 4% real interest with interest and principal repayment linked to the Consumer Price Index (CPI). If the index is 100 when the bond is issued, and 103 when the first annual coupon payment is due, the dollar amount paid is

$$\$10,000 \times 0.04 \times \frac{103}{100} = \$412 .$$

Indexation is quite common in high-inflation countries such as Brazil, Argentina, and Israel. Indeed, indexation is the reason that inflation rates of several hundred percent are "tolerable." Because wages are indexed, savings accounts are indexed, and so on, life can proceed relatively normally: The situation is not nearly so bad as it was during the German hyperinflation (see Chapter 1). Some critics argue, however, that by making inflation tolerable, indexation helps to perpetuate it, because it removes any political pressure on the government to do something about it.

Because inflation has been less severe in the United States, indexation is less common here. However, some wage contracts are indexed, containing COLAs, or cost-of-living adjustment clauses; parts of the tax code are now index-linked; and Social Security payments are linked to the CPI. There have even been a few attempts to introduce index-linked financial instruments. One is described in "A CD That's Guaranteed to Beat the Inflation Rate."

| 28.7 | INFLATION AND THE GOVERNMENT BUDGET

When inflation is caused by a government printing money to pay its bills, the government is obviously a beneficiary of the inflation. It enjoys the revenue from the inflation "tax" paid by households and firms. But even when inflation is caused by a bank-credit expansion not used to finance a budget deficit, inflation has major effects on the government budget.

---

[14]Another advantage of the price-level adjusted mortgage is that it does away with inflation risk. The dollar amounts of future payments need not be fixed in advance, according to some anticipated rate of inflation, but can be determined at the time according to the inflation that has actually taken place.

A CD THAT'S GUARANTEED TO BEAT THE INFLATION RATE

Although long-term Treasury bond yields exceed 12%, more than eight percentage points over the inflation rate, First City National Bank of Houston has unveiled a new investment for pension funds with a "real" yield of only half that—4%. But buyers are already lining up for what many predict will touch off a boom in inflation-indexed pension investments.

In what appears to be a first, the trust department at First City—through several as-yet-unidentified savings and loan associations—plans to offer 30-year, federally insured certificates of deposit guaranteed to yield the inflation rate plus 4%, or 8% at today's level. (The CDs are insured by the Federal Savings & Loan Insurance Corp. (FSLIC) up to $100,000 per pension-fund participant.) Although 4% is far below today's real yields, it is still twice the inflation-adjusted return on bond portfolios from 1929 to 1982.

Low-Cost Hedge

Such an indexed investment would also bolster the performance of pension funds, which are criticized for lagging behind inflation. Among the loudest critics is Robert A. G. Monks, head of the federal Office of Pension & Welfare Benefit Programs, who has proposed that the U.S. Treasury issue inflation-indexed bonds for pension investors.

The face amount of these new certificates increases in step with the consumer price index, thus compensating for inflation. And the CD pays 4% on the adjusted principal. The program is also designed to allow pension plans to keep the CDs on the books at face value. First City says its CDs are superior to "guaranteed investment contracts," which are also carried at face value because they can be traded on the secondary market. "It's a low-cost hedge against inflation for institutions managing pensions," says Lewis J. Spellman, a Uni-

versity of Texas professor and CEO of Trans Texas Holdings Corp., which will assemble the variable-rate loans to back the deposits.

First City, whose own trust department has fared no better than average in managing its $7 billion in assets, will merely broker the CDs. The deal permits cash-strapped S&Ls to bolster their balance sheets with long-term deposits to match their long-term loans. First City still needs final approval from the FSLIC, among others, but it hopes to place $250 million in indexed CDs in the first year.

Source: "A CD That's Guaranteed to Beat the Inflation Rate," reprinted from October 15, 1984 issue of *Business Week*, by special permission, copyright © 1984 by McGraw-Hill, Inc.

INFLATION AND TAXES

Inflation generally increases the government's tax revenue. We have already seen how failure of the tax code to take inflation into account increases the revenue from taxes on interest income and on capital gains. Similar increases occur with other taxes.

One way that inflation increases tax revenue is through **bracket creep.** Income tax is progressive: The tax rate increases as income rises. For example, someone earning $30,000 a year pays only 15¢ in income tax out of each additional dollar, while someone earning $50,000 pays 28¢ out of each additional dollar. The switch from the 15% tax bracket to the 28% tax bracket comes at a specified level of income. It used to be that this level was fixed in terms of dollars. This meant that as inflation raised dollar incomes, but did not necessarily raise *real* incomes, taxpayers found themselves in increasingly higher tax brackets, paying ever higher tax rates.

bracket creep
Movement to a higher tax bracket caused by rising income.

Bracket creep is particularly attractive to legislators as a way of increasing taxes, because it happens automatically: No one has to go on record as voting for a tax increase. The tax reforms of the 1980s eliminated bracket creep by linking tax brackets to the CPI. Whenever Congress is particularly hard-pressed for revenue, though, there are always suggestions to remove the linkage and bring back the government's "inflation bonus."

However, at very high rates of inflation, as in the German hyperinflation, tax revenues fall in real terms. The reason is the delay in collecting the tax. The tax is set in nominal terms—income tax as a percentage of nominal income, for example. By the time the tax is paid, say at the end of the year, the value of the tax payment in real terms has dropped significantly.

INFLATION AND GOVERNMENT DEBT

We have seen that inflation is a boon to borrowers because it reduces the real burden of debt repayment. In most countries the biggest borrower is the government. Indeed, some governments have borrowed so much that it is hard to see how they will ever be able to raise enough taxes to repay their debt or even to pay interest on it. (Italy is often cited as an example.) A private borrower in such a bind might declare bankruptcy and repay only a part of what he owes. Governments do not like to default, however, and because of inflation they do not need to. Remember that the rate of inflation is largely under the control of the central bank. The central bank is, after all, a government agency. If the burden of the debt becomes intolerable, the central bank can often be persuaded to engineer an inflation to reduce its real value.

This conflict of interests is well understood by investors, who therefore become understandably nervous about purchasing government debt when the amount outstanding becomes very large. Although the risk of literal default is low, the risk of "repudiation through inflation" is substantial. In these circumstances, the government may have to issue indexed debt or debt denominated in foreign currency in order to be able to continue to borrow.

SUMMARY

- Inflation is a continuing and sustained rise in prices over a substantial period of time.

- In terms of the equation of exchange: Rate of growth of the quantity of money + rate of growth of velocity $\cong$ rate of inflation + rate of growth of output.

- "Inflation is always and everywhere a monetary phenomenon." Whatever the immediate cause of rising prices, inflation cannot continue unless the quantity of money grows fast enough to accommodate it.

- Unlike a one-time-only change in the quantity of money, a continuing monetary expansion does have real effects, even in the long run.

- Inflation is like a tax on money balances.

- The Fisher equation expresses the relationship between real and nominal rates of interest: Nominal rate $\cong$ expected real rate + expected rate of inflation.

- In a government-spending inflation, the inflation "tax" reduces the supply of real loanable funds and raises the real rate of interest. In a bank-credit inflation, there is an additional effect: The continuing loan-supply effect adds to the supply. The net effect is an increase in the supply of real loanable funds and a fall in the real interest rate.

- In the long run the relationship between the exchange rate and inflation is: Rate of change of ¥/$ exchange rate = ¥ inflation rate – $ inflation rate.

- When inflation is uncertain, borrowers and lenders face considerable risk that the realized real return may differ substantially from the expected real return. This is known as inflation risk.

- Real assets are unaffected by inflation risk, making them relatively more attractive than financial assets in times of inflation. The increased attractiveness of real estate as a hedge against inflation distorts real investment in the economy: There is less productive investment by firms and more residential construction.

- Long-term loans are more subject to inflation risk than short-term loans. As a result, in times of inflation there is a shift toward short-term debt. There is also a reduction in the amount of borrowing and lending.

- The opportunity cost of holding money is the nominal interest rate. Therefore rising inflation encourages the reduction of money holdings. Considerable resources may be invested in cash management.

- Many financial contracts and other arrangements are ill-suited to an inflationary environment. When a dollar is no longer a (base-period) dollar, serious distortions occur.

- Some of the most serious distortions involve taxes. Interest income, capital gains taxes, and bracket creep are some of the examples.

- Mortgages are also seriously distorted. Even if the inflation is anticipated, the pattern of real payments is altered. One solution is to link mortgage payments to a price index.

- Indexation of contracts and tax laws reduces these distortions, but by making an inflation more tolerable, it also reduces pressure on politicians to halt the inflation.

- Moderate inflation usually increases tax revenue, but an extreme inflation reduces it. The real value of government debt is reduced by inflation, tempting governments to "repudiate through inflation."

KEY TERMS

inflation	Fisher equation	unanticipated inflation
rate of inflation	inflation-tax effect	inflation risk
demand–pull inflation	continuing loan-supply effect	price-level-adjusted mortgage
cost–push inflation		
inflation "tax"	anticipated inflation	bracket creep

DISCUSSION QUESTIONS

1. If a bank is lending at 10% when the rate of inflation is 12%, is it losing money? Explain.

2. All the tricks in "Cash Juggling a Way of Life" (page 737) are rewarding to the firms that undertake them. Are they a socially useful utilization of resources? Discuss.

3. Does a fall in the value of the dollar cause inflation? Why or why not?

4. Many believe that inflation in the 1970s was caused by the OPEC oil-price increases. Discuss whether this contradicts Friedman's dictum that "inflation is always and everywhere a monetary phenomenon."

5. List all the ways that inflation damages an economy.

6. In what way is inflation like a tax?

7. The Quantity Theory states that changes in the quantity of money have no real effect in the long run. Therefore, inflation has no long-run real effects. Discuss.

8. How does inflation affect the sorts of assets that households hold? How does it affect the way that firms finance their investment?

9. The quantity of money, velocity, price level, and output for the United States in 1988 and 1989 are shown in the following table. Calculate the rates of growth of each. Show that they satisfy Equation 28.9.

Year	M	V	P	y
1988	790.3	6.18	121.3	4,023.6
1989	797.6	6.56	126.3	4,143.5

BIBLIOGRAPHY

Hall, Robert E., *Inflation: Its Causes and Effects*, Chicago: University of Chicago Press.

Leijonhufvud, Axel, "Costs and Consequences of Inflation." In *Information and Coordination* by A. Leijonhufvud. New York: Oxford University Press, 1981.

CHAPTER 29

EXPECTATIONS, INTEREST RATES, AND EXCHANGE RATES

As we have seen, monetary expansion can affect interest rates and exchange rates both directly and indirectly through its effect on expected inflation. Although we have looked at each of these effects separately, in reality they all happen at the same time. In this chapter we shall bring together the different parts of the story.

First we shall look at how expectations are formed. Then we shall begin to sort out the different effects of a monetary expansion by differentiating between the effects on short-term and on long-term interest rates. This will lead us into a consideration of the different theories of the relationship between short-term and long-term rates and of the role of expectations in that relationship. We shall then look at how interest rates, exchange rates, and expectations are related. Finally, we shall see how changing expectations can simultaneously affect both exchange rates and interest rates.

29.1 THE FORMATION OF EXPECTATIONS

Since expectations are so central to our discussion in this chapter, we begin by examining how people form their expectations. That is, how do people predict the future values of important economic variables?

ADAPTIVE EXPECTATIONS

The simplest type of expectations is **naive expectations:** The future is expected to be the same as the present. For instance, if the inflation rate is now 5%, the naive expectation is that it will continue to be 5% indefinitely into the future. In talking about our fictional Island economy, we have generally assumed that the economy

naive expectations
Expectations that the future will be the same as the present.

745

regressive expectations
Expectations that in the future the value of a variable will return to the norm.

is stationary—nothing changes from month to month. When nothing changes, naive expectations are always correct.

However, the real world is not stationary: It changes constantly. Before the economy has had time to adjust to one shock, something else stirs it up again. How do people form expectations in such an environment? Suppose, for example, that inflation has recently jumped from 2% to 5% after having been at 2% for a long time. Rather than expecting the 5% inflation to continue indefinitely, people might reasonably expect it to return to "normal"—to fall back toward 2%. This sort of expectation is called **regressive**—things are expected to regress to the norm.

extrapolative expectations
Expectations that in the future the value of a variable will continue its present trend.

Regressive expectations make sense only in an economy that does tend to return to some sort of norm. Suppose, however, that the current 5% inflation is observed in the context of a steady increase in the rate of inflation over a period of years. It might then be more reasonable for expectations to be **extrapolative**—to expect the trend to continue—and to expect that the inflation rate will go on rising.

adaptive expectations
Expectations that are based only on past and current values of a variable.

All these methods of predicting future inflation are adaptive: They are based only on past and current inflation. **Adaptive expectations** have the advantage of being simple, but they do not give the best possible forecast because they ignore other information that is relevant. For example, we know that monetary growth affects inflation. We also know that it takes time to do so. So information about today's monetary growth can help to predict tomorrow's inflation.

RATIONAL EXPECTATIONS

Other information, even more indirect, may also be useful. Monetary expansion is largely controlled by the Fed. So any information about the Fed's intentions will be helpful, because it will give some idea of what future monetary expansion, and therefore future inflation, is likely to be. But the Fed is extremely secretive. So just as there are professional "sovietologists" who try to fathom what is going on in the Kremlin, there are also professional "Fed watchers" who devote their lives to trying to figure out just what the Fed is up to. "Should Fed Hide Its Moves, Leaving Markets Confused?" describes the hardships of being a Fed watcher.

announcement effect
Effect on expectations of an announcement of a change in the discount rate.

Given the mystery surrounding the Fed's intentions, actions that would otherwise seem of little importance take on much greater significance. For example, we saw in Chapter 20 that the level of the discount rate has little direct effect on anything. However, when the Fed raises or lowers the discount rate, the action is generally seen as signaling a policy change. So the **announcement effect** on expectations of a change in the discount rate can be considerable.

rational expectations
Expectations that take into account all available information.

Expectations that take *all* available information into account, to make the best possible forecast, are called **rational expectations**. The name is a little misleading because it suggests that anything else is "irrational." This is not the case. Rational expectations are expensive expectations: It takes time, trouble, and expense to gather and process information. People will weigh the costs against the benefits. In a fairly stationary world, simpler methods of expectation forma-

SHOULD FED HIDE ITS MOVES, LEAVING MARKETS CONFUSED?

by David Wessel and Tom Herman

Staff Reporters of The Wall Street Journal

The Federal Reserve has settled one mystery, but in the process it has re-opened an old debate: Should the Fed be less secretive?

Last Wednesday morning, the Fed unintentionally misled many traders and Fed watchers into concluding that it was easing its grip on credit. The misimpression lingered until Monday morning, when the Fed sent an un-ambiguous signal to financial mar-kets that it had not eased.

That made it clear that the Fed wasn't trying to push down interest rates last week. And it left some economists and traders arguing that the Fed could have avoided all the confusion.

"Given the events of the past couple of weeks, I think the Fed should simply have a spokesman announce immediately after the fact: Yes, folks, we have eased . . . and take all the guesswork out of it," says Edward Yardeni, chief economist at Pruden-tial-Bache Securities Inc.

The Fed doesn't do that. Instead, policy moves are cloaked in secrecy, forcing Fed watchers to divine the Fed's intentions by studying minute movements in interest rates and pro-jections of banking reserves. Only weeks later, when it releases summa-ries of the deliberations of its policy-making committee, does the Fed con-firm that it has made a change in policy.

The Fed executes policy changes by buying or selling billions of dollars of government securities. These transactions determine the supply of credit in the economy and directly influence the key federal funds rate—and indirectly other short-term inter-est rates.

For years, the Fed wouldn't so much as admit when it had conducted a transaction in the money markets. Even now, it makes no announce-ments of such transactions.

But in February 1983, the Federal Reserve Bank of New York began confirming information that report-ers and others picked up from the securities dealers doing business with the Fed. The Fed refuses, however, to say whether those transactions involve mere technical adjustments to the fi-nancial system—or whether they rep-resent changes in monetary policy. And that's the rub.

Officially, the Fed sees no reason to change that. "The issue hasn't been addressed because we believe the re-grettable confusion [last week] re-sulted from a misunderstanding of our action on the part of the mar-ket," a Fed spokesman said yester-day.

Back in October, Fed Chairman Alan Greenspan told Congress that mandating announcement of changes in policy "would yield only marginal rewards, but could significantly re-duce the effectiveness of policy."

"It would reduce our flexibility to implement decisions quietly at times to achieve a desired effect, while minimizing possible financial market disruptions," he added.

Many players in financial markets disagree. "Markets are perfectly ca-pable of digesting that information without undue volatility," says David M. Jones, senior vice president of Aubrey G. Lanston & Co. and au-thor of a book on Fed watching.

Some prominent academic stu-dents of the Fed concur. "I can't see any value to fooling people in the marketplace," says Alan Meltzer, a monetarist economist at Carnegie Mellon University in Pittsburgh. "I can't imagine what would be a secret action that the Fed could take that shouldn't be disclosed."

Even some current Fed governors publicly have favored quicker disclo-sure of the minutes taken at meetings of the Fed's policy-making open mar-

ket committee; the minutes now are released when they're six weeks old.

A bill proposed by Rep. Lee Hamilton (D., Indiana) would force the Fed to disclose immediately any decisions of the open market com-mittee. "Secrecy makes markets oper-ate inefficiently," Rep. Hamilton says. "Secrecy is unfair to small investors . . . who don't have resources to em-ploy Fed watchers to interpret Fed policy changes."

Rep. Hamilton's bill, though given little chance of passage, is the kind of reform that would have eliminated last week's confusion. Had they known the Fed wasn't changing policy, the financial markets would have brushed off last Wednesday's injec-tion of reserves as the technical ad-justment that it was.

Even on Wall Street, some see dangers in forcing the Fed to say more sooner. They fear that the Fed might be less willing to fight inflation by raising interest rates, particularly just before an election, if it had to state publicly that it was doing so.

"If the Fed officially announced every single policy shift, it would at-tract excessive political attention—and that might intimidate the Fed and cause it to not fight inflation as much as it should," says Mr. Jones, the Aubrey Lanston economist who gen-erally favors quicker disclosure.

But Prudential-Bache's Mr. Yardeni figures, "If they are chicken and they're not going to do something about inflation, then we should all know about it."

Source: David Wessel and Tom Herman, "Should Fed Hide Its Moves, Leaving Markets Confused?" *The Wall Street Journal*, November 29, 1989. Reprinted by permission of The Wall Street Journal, © Dow Jones & Company, Inc. 1989. All Rights Reserved Worldwide.

tion may be almost as good and a lot less expensive. However, the more volatile the environment and the more that is at risk, the greater the payoff to improved prediction, and the more likely that actual expectation formation will come close to the "rational" ideal. For example, firms, having much more at stake, hire professional forecasters to make economic predictions; households do not. Americans, facing a moderate rate of inflation, make little effort to predict inflation and are slow to adapt to changes in it; Brazilians, facing much higher rates of inflation, give it much more attention and respond immediately to the slightest change.[1]

THE INFORMATIONAL VALUE OF AN INCREASE IN THE QUANTITY OF MONEY

Let us apply these ideas to understanding the informational significance of an increase in the quantity of money. When we looked at the effect of a change in the quantity of money in earlier chapters, we ignored expectations. In the context of rational expectations, however, such an increase may have considerable informational value. News about an increase in the quantity of money may tell us something about the Fed's current policy and about possible changes in that policy.

The interpretation of that information will depend on context. For example, if the Fed is trying to keep money growth at 7% and a large increase in the quantity of money is announced, say, one implying a 10% growth rate, there are at least two possibilities. The first is that the Fed has slipped up and that the quantity of money has grown faster than intended . In this case, the Fed may take steps to correct its mistake by reducing monetary expansion in the future. The second possibility is that the Fed has, in fact, changed its policy, even though it has not yet announced the change. If so, the current expansion would signal greater expansion in the future. Which is the case? Ask your Fed watcher.

29.2 | MONETARY EXPANSION AND INTEREST RATES: LOAN-SUPPLY AND INFLATION-EXPECTATIONS EFFECTS

An increase in the quantity of money, therefore, has two distinct effects on the interest rate. We can best understand them in terms of the Fisher equation:

$$i \cong r^e + n^e, \qquad\qquad [29.1]$$

---

[1]Another difference between adaptive and rational expectations is that the former may consistently under- or overestimate the variable being predicted while the latter does not. For example, as inflation rose steadily in the United States in the 1970s, with expectations that seemed adaptive, people tended to underestimate the rate of inflation year after year. In Brazil, where inflationary expectations seem more like the rational ideal, people often guess incorrectly, but there is no systematic tendency to underestimate or to overestimate the rate of inflation.

where i is the (nominal) market interest rate, r^e is the equilibrium expected real interest rate, and n^e is the expected rate of inflation. The first effect is an increase in the supply of loanable funds—the *loan-supply effect*. This tends to lower the equilibrium real interest rate. The second effect involves information. A change in the quantity of money may provide information on Fed policy and therefore on the rate of monetary expansion in the future. If we assume that current expansion means that future expansion is more likely, then expectations of greater future inflation will tend to raise the nominal interest rate: We shall call this the **inflation-expectations effect**.[2] Because the two effects work in opposite directions, the net effect on the nominal interest rate is ambiguous.

We can untangle the two offsetting effects somewhat if we drop our simplifying assumption of a *single* interest rate. Instead, let us divide the financial market into two parts—a short-term market and a long-term market. Think of the short-term market as corresponding to bank intermediation and the money market, and think of the long-term market as corresponding to the capital market.

Assume for the moment that the short-term market and the long-term market are completely separate. Everybody matches maturities. Households invest their life-cycle saving in long-term securities, which firms issue to finance their capital investment. Households keep their precautionary assets in the short-term market, which firms use to finance their working capital. What happens in one segment of the market has no direct effect on what happens in the other. What will the two effects of a monetary change do to each of these two markets?

inflation-expectations effect
Increase in nominal interest rate because of increase in expected inflation.

THE SHORT-TERM MARKET

The loan-supply effect on the short-term market is large. The increase in the quantity of money means an increase in bank lending. Bank loans are short-term loans. Thus the increase in the quantity of money increases the supply of loanable funds in the short-term market and drives down the short-term real rate.

The inflation-expectations effect, on the other hand, is small. The effect of monetary expansion on inflation takes time. For the short-term market, the relevant rate of inflation is the rate over, say, the next three months. Over so short a period, the inflation rate is unlikely to change much, whatever happens to the rate of growth of the quantity of money.

Therefore, looking at the Fisher equation for the short-term interest rate, we find that the equilibrium expected real rate, r^e, falls and the expected inflation rate, n^e, remains the same; so the nominal market interest rate, i, falls.

---

[2]For the sake of concreteness, we make the assumption that current monetary expansion signals future inflation. More generally, the information effect could be considerably more complex.

THE LONG-TERM MARKET

Assuming that banks make only short-term loans, the loan-supply effect on the long-term market is zero. There is no increase in the supply of loanable funds to the long-term market and therefore no effect on the long-term real rate.

In contrast, the inflation-expectations effect is large. The relevant time horizon here is, say, 30 years. Over this period, changes in monetary growth will have plenty of time to affect prices. So the expectations effect will be strong.

Therefore, looking at the Fisher equation for the long-term interest rate, we find that the equilibrium expected real rate, r^e, stays the same and the expected inflation rate, π^e, rises; so the nominal market interest rate, i, rises.

It would not be surprising, then, to see monetary expansion leading simultaneously to a drop in the short-term rate (the loan-supply effect dominating) and to a rise in the long-term rate (the inflation-expectations effect dominating). Conversely, a restriction in monetary growth might well drive up the short-term rate and simultaneously bring down the long-term rate.

Unfortunately, this neat compartmentalization of the two effects is unrealistic. It relies on the implausible assumption that long-term and short-term markets are completely unrelated. As we shall see, both borrowers and lenders will be ready to switch markets if conditions warrant. We need to investigate what this implies for the relationship between long-term and short-term rates.

29.3 THE TERM STRUCTURE OF INTEREST RATES

term structure of interest rates
Relationship between interest rates at different maturities.

The relationship between interest rates at different maturities is called the **term structure of interest rates**. Until now we have thought in terms of only two rates, a short-term rate and a long-term rate, but there are, in fact, many rates at different maturities, ranging from overnight to 30 years and more.

As we saw in Chapter 7 when we looked at the government securities market, the rates at different maturities may be plotted on a *yield curve*. Some examples of yield curves at different dates are shown in Exhibit 29.1. As you can see, the yield curve sometimes has a positive slope, with long-term rates higher than short-term rates; and it sometimes has a negative slope, with long-term rates lower than short-term rates. A theory of the term structure should explain the shape of the yield curve and why it changes.

THE SEGMENTED-MARKET THEORY AND ITS PROBLEMS

segmented-market theory
Theory that markets at different maturities are completely separate.

The simplest theory of the term structure is the one we relied upon in the previous section—the **segmented-market theory**. This theory assumes that markets at different maturities are completely separate. Neither borrowers nor lenders are willing to switch from one market to another. The relationship between rates at

EXHIBIT 29.1

YIELD CURVE SHAPES

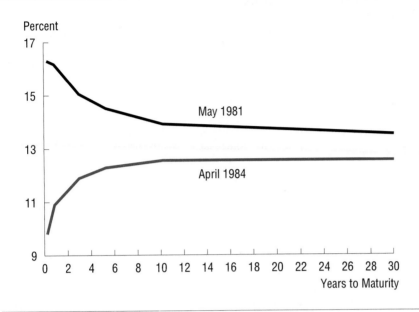

Source: C. Alan Garner, "The Yield Curve and Inflation Expectations," *Economic Review,* Federal Reserve Bank of Kansas City, September-October 1987, 4.

different maturities simply reflects different supply and demand conditions in the separate markets. Changes in the supply or demand at one maturity bear no relation to changes at any other maturity.

Although the segmented-market theory has the advantage of simplicity, the evidence seems to contradict it. For example, long-term rates and short-term rates often move together. This is illustrated in Exhibit 29.2: The entire yield curve often moves up or down in parallel, suggesting that something is affecting *all* rates in much the same way. This parallel movement should not happen if there is no connection between markets at different maturities.

Moreover, the assumed unwillingness of borrowers and lenders to switch markets does not make sense. For example, suppose that you are building a factory. The bond rate is 20%, and the commercial paper rate is 5%. You would, in principle, prefer to match maturities and finance the factory with a bond issue. However, if you expect current rates to persist, it is certainly tempting to finance by rolling over commercial paper. It is surely worth taking *some* interest-rate risk to save 15%.

Indeed, there are circumstances in which it is tempting to finance short term, even though short-term rates are *higher* than long-term rates. Suppose that the short-term rate is 25% and the long-term rate is 20%. But suppose too that you expect the long-term rates to fall in the near future. Then it is better to pay 25% on a bank loan now and refinance with a bond issue later, at a lower long-term

BAFFLED BORROWERS: CORPORATE TREASURERS FIND THE RATE OUTLOOK UNUSUALLY CONFUSING

By Ralph E. Winter

Staff Reporter of The Wall Street Journal

Is it a window or a door?

That question, seemingly appropriate for two-year-olds, has many corporate finance officers stumped. They are trying to decide whether the recent drop in interest rates is a brief dip (a "window") or a "door" leading to a lengthy period of generally lower long-term interest rates.

Right now, a prudent finance executive whose company is borrowing $100 million at short term can save about $10,000 a day just by doing nothing. Because short-term rates have fallen much further than long-term rates, there's a big saving in staying with commercial paper—essentially, short-term IOUs—instead of selling bonds. Over a 10-year period, however, inaction could cost the company $20 million or more if it misses a window and later has to sell $100 million of bonds at a higher interest cost.

Corporate executive are paid well to make such decisions, of course, but seldom do they have to do so when the outlook is so murky.

For corporate officials looking for advice, economists aren't much help. Many predict the interest rates will be lower a year from now. But Allen

Sinai senior vice president of Data Resources Inc., a Lexington, Mass., economic-consulting firm, warns: "Corporate treasurers had better take advantage of this window. If they don't, they may regret it."

Difficult Task

O. Gordon Brewer Jr., the vice president and treasurer of Alco Standard Corp., calls financing "a very difficult subject" now, adding, "It's hard to go to the board of directors and tell them that we want to do long-term financing about 400 basis points (four percentage points) above what we're paying in the short-term market." The official of the diversified machinery manufacturer and distribution company has decided to wait.

Forecasting interest rates has always been tricky because nobody knows what will happen next week, much less six months or a year hence. Even Henry Kaufman, the Salomon Brothers economist, was reversing his previous prediction when he sparked the August rally in the bond and stock markets. He switched from predicting that late this year interest rates would rival the highs of last fall to predicting that rates will drift lower

over the next year, although he expects temporary bounces.

Errors Costly

Moreover, the penalty for being wrong is much higher than it used to be, finance men lament, because interest rates have become so volatile. Twenty years ago, bond rates moved only fractions of a percentage point for months at a time, and corporate treasurers and underwriters would sometimes haggle for hours over $1/32$ of a point, veteran finance men recall. But in just 15 months, from mid-1980 to last fall, bond interest rates soared almost six percentage points. A company that missed the 1980 window and borrowed $100 million last September could pay an extra $60 million of interest over 10 years.

Source: Ralph E. Winter, "Baffled Borrowers: Corporate Treasurers Find the Rate Outlook Unusually Confusing," *The Wall Street Journal*, September 22, 1982. Reprinted by permission of The Wall Street Journal, © Dow Jones & Company, Inc. 1982. All Rights Reserved Worldwide.

rate, than it is to issue bonds now at the current high rate. Of course, there is a risk that things will move the other way, but here too, if the potential gain is great enough, it will be worth taking some interest-rate risk. The headache that this sort of problem gives corporate treasurers is described in "Baffled Borrowers."

Lenders too may be tempted to switch between markets. If the short-term rate is 20% and the long-term rate is 5%, and both rates are expected to remain

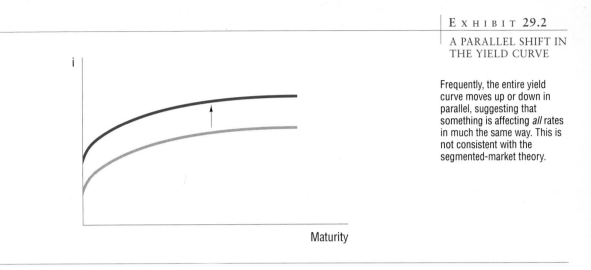

EXHIBIT 29.2

A PARALLEL SHIFT IN THE YIELD CURVE

Frequently, the entire yield curve moves up or down in parallel, suggesting that something is affecting *all* rates in much the same way. This is not consistent with the segmented-market theory.

at these levels, it will be attractive to place life-cycle savings in short-term securities. With such a difference in rates, it will be worth taking some interest-rate risk. Or if the short-term rate is 5% and the long-term rate is 10%, but the long-term rate is expected to rise, it is tempting to place your savings in short-term securities temporarily and switch back into long-term securities later when their price falls.

So, contrary to the assumption of market segmentation, there is clearly some substitutability, both for borrowers and for lenders, between short-term and long-term securities. As you can see from the examples, the willingness to substitute will depend a great deal on expectations.

There is, in fact, a theory that explains the term structure *entirely* in terms of expectations: It is called, not surprisingly, the **expectations theory**. The expectations theory makes just the opposite assumption about borrowers and lenders from that made by the segmented-market theory. It assumes that borrowers and lenders are completely indifferent to interest-rate risk and therefore do not care at all about maturity. Borrowers wish only to finance at the lowest expected rate; lenders wish only to earn the highest expected rate.

expectations theory
Theory that assumes that borrowers and lenders care only about expected yields.

THE IMPLICIT FORWARD INTEREST RATE

To see what this different assumption implies for the term structure, it is useful to begin by defining the *implicit forward interest rate*. Suppose we have a yield curve for T-bills.[3] The 1-year rate is 5%; the 2-year rate is 6%. Now compare two

---

[3] As we saw in Chapter 6, there exists a market for long-term bills in the form of Treasury strips.

different 2-year investment strategies:

- *Strategy 1*: Invest in a 2-year bill.
- *Strategy 2*: Invest in a 1-year bill; when it matures, reinvest in a second 1-year bill.

implicit forward interest rate
Rate required in the future to equalize expected yield on bills of different maturities.

Strategy 1 will earn a rate of 6%. How much Strategy 2 will earn clearly depends on the rate earned on the second 1-year bill. The **implicit forward interest rate** is the rate the second 1-year bill would need to pay in order for the two strategies to give the same return over the 2 years. That is, it is the value of i_1^f that satisfies the following equation:

$$(1 + 0.06)^2 = (1 + 0.05)(1 + i_1^f). \qquad [29.2]$$

The solution is $i_1^f = 0.07$.

The implicit forward rate in Equation 29.2 has the subscript "1" because it is the implicit forward rate for *one year from now*. We can define in a similar fashion an implicit forward rate for *two* years from now, i_2^f. This is the rate a 1-year bill would need to pay 2 years from now so that the following three strategies would give the same return: (1) investing in a 3-year bill; (2) investing in a 2-year bill and then reinvesting in a 1-year bill; and (3) reinvesting in 3 one-year bills. That is, if the rate on a 3-year bill is 6.5%, then i_2^f satisfies

$$(1 + 0.065)^3 = (1 + 0.06)^2 (1 + i_2^f) = (1 + 0.05)(1 + i_1^f)(1 + i_2^f), \qquad [29.3]$$

so that $i_2^f = 7.5\%$. In a similar fashion, we can define the implicit forward rates for 3 years, 10 years, or any number of years from now.

If we make the current actual one-year rate an "honorary" implicit forward rate (zero years from now) with subscript zero, then the relationship between the actual rate on a t-year bill, i_t, and all the implicit forward rates up to year t is

$$(1 + i_t)^t = (1 + i_0^f)(1 + i_1^f) \cdots (1 + i_{t-1}^f). \qquad [29.4]$$

In our example i_3, the rate on a 3-year bill, is 6.5%. The implicit forward rates are $i_0^f = 5\%$, $i_1^f = 7\%$, and $i_2^f = 7.5\%$, so

$$(1.065)^3 = (1.05)(1.07)(1.075). \qquad [29.5]$$

If we take the tth root of both sides of Equation 29.4, we get

$$(1 + i_t) = \sqrt[t]{(1 + i_0^f)(1 + i_1^f)\cdots(1 + i_{t-1}^f)}. \qquad [29.6]$$

That is, the rate on t-year bills is just the geometric mean of the implicit forward rates over the next t years.

As an approximation to Equation 29.6, we can take the arithmetic rather than the geometric mean:

$$i_t \cong \frac{i_0^f + i_1^f + \cdots + i_{t-1}^f}{t} \,. \qquad [29.7]$$

For our example, the approximation works well:

$$6.5\% \cong \frac{5\% + 7\% + 7.5\%}{3} \,. \qquad [29.8]$$

There is a fairly obvious relationship between implicit forward rates and the shape of the yield curve: A *rising* yield curve implies that implicit forward rates *rise* over time (as in the numerical example above); a *falling* yield curve implies that implicit forward rates *fall* over time.

A. The 2-year rate is 6% and the 3-year rate is 7%. What is the implicit 1-year rate 2 years from now?

🌴 **CHECK STATION 1**

B. Implicit forward rates for the next 3 years are 5%, 6%, and 6.25%. What is the 3-year rate?

THE EXPECTATIONS THEORY

Under the assumptions of the expectations theory about the behavior of borrowers and lenders, *the implicit forward interest rate must equal the expected rate.* To see why, suppose the two rates differ. As in our numerical example, the 1-year rate is 5% and the 2-year rate is 6%, so the implicit forward rate is 7%. But investors *expect* the 1-year rate a year from now to be 6%. What does this imply for the demand *now* for 1-year bills and for 2-year bills? Since investors care only about the expected return, they will all choose Strategy 1 and purchase 2-year bills. As a result, the price of 2-year bills will rise and the price of 1-year bills will fall. The two prices will continue to change until the implicit 1-year forward rate equals the expected rate. Then investors will be indifferent between the two maturities and they will no longer have any reason to shift from one market to the other. The same sort of behavior with respect to bills of other maturities will ensure that implicit forward rates equal expected rates at all maturities.

If the expectations theory is correct, then the rate on *t*-year bills is just the average of the expected one-year rates over the next *t* years.

$$i_t \cong \frac{i_{1,0}^e + i_{1,1}^e + \cdots + i_{1,t-1}^e}{t} \,, \qquad [29.9]$$

where $i_{1,t}^e$ is the expected 1-year rate t years from now.[4]

For example, suppose that the 1-year rate is currently 10% and that the 1-year rate is expected to fall to 8% next year and to stay there. Then according to the expectations theory, the 3-year rate now should be

$$i_3 \cong \frac{10\% + 8\% + 8\%}{3} = 8.7\%. \qquad [29.10]$$

So, explaining the shape of the yield curve according to the expectations theory is pretty straightforward. A *rising* yield curve implies that short-term rates are expected to *rise*, and a *falling* yield curve implies that they are expected to *fall*. This is illustrated in Exhibit 29.3.

🌴 **CHECK STATION 2**

A. If the yield curve falls initially and then rises, what does this say about expected future interest rates?

B. The 1-year rate is 5%. It is expected to rise to 6% next year and to remain at that level. According to the expectations theory, what are the 2-year and 3-year interest rates?

THE PREFERRED-HABITAT THEORY

We have now seen the implications of two extreme and opposite assumptions about the willingness of borrowers and lenders to switch maturities. The *segmented-market theory* assumes that they are totally unwilling to switch. The *expectations theory* assumes that they are perfectly willing to switch, having no inherent preference for one maturity over another. A third theory, the **preferred-habitat theory**, takes an intermediate position. It assumes that borrowers and lenders do have a preferred maturity, but not to the extent that they are completely unwilling to consider any other. If they expect a maturity other than their preferred one to be more advantageous, they will be willing to switch to some degree.

What does the preferred-habitat theory imply for the relationship between implicit forward interest rates and expected interest rates? Unlike the segmented-market theory, the preferred-habitat theory implies that there will be some connection. Unlike the expectations theory, it does not imply that forward rates and expected future rates will necessarily be exactly equal.

We can express the preferred-habitat theory in terms of an equation. The theory implies that the interest rate at any maturity is

$$i_t \cong \frac{i_{1,0}^e + i_{1,1}^e + \cdots + i_{1,t-1}^e}{t} + pr_t, \qquad [29.11]$$

preferred-habitat theory Theory of the term structure that assumes borrowers and lenders care about both maturity and expected yield.

---

[4]If we look at a yield curve for coupon securities rather than for bills, the relationship is more complicated, but similar: Long-term rates will be some kind of average of expected short-term rates.

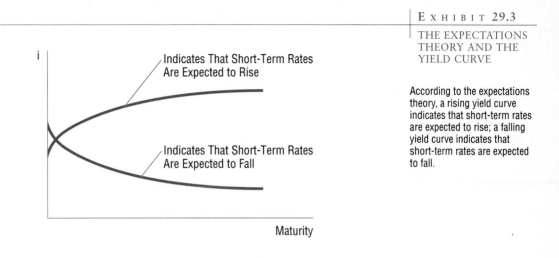

EXHIBIT 29.3

THE EXPECTATIONS
THEORY AND THE
YIELD CURVE

According to the expectations
theory, a rising yield curve
indicates that short-term rates
are expected to rise; a falling
yield curve indicates that
short-term rates are expected
to fall.

where pr_t is the **term premium** at maturity t. The term premium, which might be positive or negative, reflects the relative preference of borrowers and lenders for one maturity over another and the specific supply and demand conditions at that maturity.

The preferred-habitat theory, as expressed in Equation 29.11, implies that interest rates are determined *both* by expectations *and* by a term premium. In comparison, the expectations theory, as seen in Equation 29.9, implies that the interest rate is determined *solely* by expectations.   The segmented-market theory implies that the interest rate at any maturity is determined *solely* by the term premium:

$$i_t \cong pr_t, \qquad\qquad [29.12]$$

In practice, there seems to be a positive term premium for longer-term securities. This is sometimes called a "liquidity premium," because it suggests that, other things equal, investors prefer more liquid (shorter-term) securities. As a result of this positive term premium, the "normal" yield curve—the yield curve when there are no clear expectations of a rise or fall in short-term rates—has a positive slope, rather than being flat as the expectations theory would predict. Since the yield curve does generally have a positive slope, this lends support to the preferred-habitat theory.

Under the preferred-habitat theory, *changes* in expectations will affect the yield curve in much the same way as they do under the expectations theory. For example, if the 1-year rate is 10% and is expected to remain there, and the 3-year

term premium
Quantity reflecting relative preference of borrowers and lenders for one maturity over another.

EXHIBIT 29.4

THE LOAN-SUPPLY
EFFECT OF A MON-
ETARY EXPANSION
ON THE YIELD
CURVE

The loan-supply effect directly
lowers short-term rates. Since
long-term rates are an average
of current and future expected
short-term rates, long-term
rates fall too, but by less the
longer the maturity.

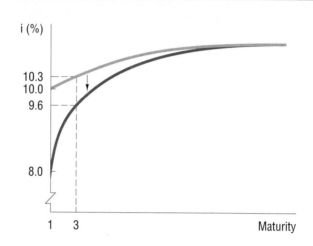

term premium is 0.3%, the 3-year rate will be

$$i_3 \cong \frac{10\% + 10\% + 10\%}{3} + 0.3\% = 10.3\%. \qquad [29.13]$$

Now suppose that expectations change so that the 1-year rate is expected to rise in a year's time to 10.5% and to remain there. The term premium is not affected. The new 3-year rate will be

$$i_3 \cong \frac{10\% + 10.5\% + 10.5\%}{3} + 0.3\% = 10.6\%. \qquad [29.14]$$

That is, the 3-year rate increases just as it would under the expectations theory. So an expected rise in short-term rates will make the yield curve steeper, and an expected fall will make it flatter or even give it a negative slope.

🌴 CHECK STATION 3

A. Is it possible for the term premium to be negative? What would that signify?

B. The 1-year rate is 5%. It is expected to rise to 6% next year and to remain at that level. Term premiums are 0.2% and 0.3% at 2 and 3 years, respectively. What are the 2-year and 3-year interest rates?

LOAN-SUPPLY AND INFLATION-EXPECTATIONS EFFECTS AGAIN

Let us take another look at the loan-supply and inflation-expectations effects of a monetary expansion in light of what we have just learned about the term

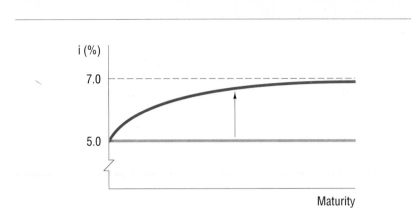

EXHIBIT 29.5

THE INFLATION-
EXPECTATIONS
EFFECT ON THE
YIELD CURVE

Monetary growth raises
expected inflation in the future
with the effect greater the
further into the future.
Expected future short-term
rates rise, and since long-term
rates are an average of these
expected future rates, they rise
too, with the effect greatest at
the longest maturity.

structure. When we assumed market segmentation, the loan-supply effect affected only the short-term market. Now it seems reasonable that it will "spill over" into other maturities. Borrowers will move into the cheaper short-term market, and lenders into the higher-rate long-term market.

In terms of the expectations and preferred-habitat theories, the loan-supply effect will lower current short-term rates. Even if short-term rates are expected to return to what they were, the lower current rate will be averaged into long-term rates, bringing *them* down too. For example, suppose the situation is initially as described in Equation 29.13, and the loan-supply effect lowers the current 1-year rate to 8%. The 3-year rate will fall from 10.3% to

$$i_3 = \frac{8\% + 10\% + 10\%}{3} + 0.3\% = 9.6\% \qquad [29.15]$$

So the loan-supply effect will also lower long-term rates, with the effect diminishing as maturity increases. The yield curve will change as shown in Exhibit 29.4.

The inflation-expectations effect on long-term rates can also be understood in terms of the expectations and preferred-habitat theories. Higher expected inflation in the future means that short-term rates will be higher then: Long-term rates are just an average of these expected future short-term rates. For example, suppose that initially short-term rates are 5% and are expected to remain at that level; for simplicity, term premiums are all zero. Then initially the yield curve is flat at 5%. Now, the rate of monetary expansion increases by 2%. This means that eventually inflation too will increase by 2%, and short-term rates will rise from 5% to 7%. The effect is illustrated in Exhibit 29.5. Since interest rates at longer maturities give more weight to later short-term rates that are more affected by inflation, they will rise more.

If both the loan-supply effect and the inflation-expectations effect are operative, then the total effect on the yield curve will be a combination of those shown in Exhibits 29.4 and 29.5. There will be a tendency for the yield curve to fall and at the same time for the slope to become more positive.

29.4 INTEREST RATES AND EXCHANGE RATES

Just as loanable-funds markets at different maturities are related, so are loanable-funds markets in different *currencies*. In this case too, borrowers and lenders are willing to some extent to substitute between markets.[5] This willingness to substitute will imply certain relationships between interest rates in different currencies, relationships that depend on expectations.

IMPLICIT FORWARD EXCHANGE RATES

When we looked at the term structure, we began by defining an implicit forward interest rate. Here we shall begin by defining an implicit forward *exchange* rate. It is easiest to illustrate the idea with an example. Suppose the rate on 1-year T-bills is 10% in the United States and 5% in Japan. The spot exchange rate—the price you pay in yen for dollars now—is 150¥/$. Consider two investment strategies:

- *Strategy 1*: Invest in a 1-year U.S. T-bill.
- *Strategy 2*: Sell your dollars for yen; buy a Japanese 1-year T-bill; then, when it matures, change the yen back into dollars.

Strategy 1 will earn a rate of 10%. How much Strategy 2 will earn clearly depends on the rate at which you change the yen back into dollars: that is, it depends on the exchange rate one year from now. The **implicit forward exchange rate**, e_1^f, is the exchange rate that would make the return from the two strategies the same. That is, it is the value of e_1^f that satisfies

implicit forward exchange rate
Rate that would equalize the expected return from securities in different currencies.

$$\$1 \times (1.10) = \$1 \times 150 \text{ ¥/\$} \times (1.05) \times \frac{1}{e_1^f \text{ ¥/\$}} \, . \qquad [29.16]$$

The left-hand side of Equation 29.16 is what you would earn from investing $1 in U.S. T-bills. At the end of the year you would have $1 x 1.10 = $1.10. The right-hand side is what you would earn from investing your dollar in Japanese T-bills. First you would have to sell your dollar for yen at the rate of 150¥/$, giving you

[5]We saw in Chapter 13 how currency swaps make it easy to do so.

¥150. You would earn 5% on these yen over the year, giving you ¥150 x 1.05 = ¥157.5. Finally, you would sell the yen at an exchange rate of e_1^f ¥/$, giving you ¥157.5/$e_1^f$ dollars. We want the value of e_1^f that makes the dollar return from investing in Japanese T-bills, ¥157.5/e_1^f, equal the return from investing in U.S. T-bills, $1.10.

The value of e_1^f that satisfies Equation 29.16 is 143.2¥/$. That is, ¥157.5/(143.2¥/$) = $1.10. In other words, if the exchange rate turns out to be 143.2¥/$, the return from Strategies 1 and 2 will be identical. Because the interest rate is lower on *yen* T-bills, the yen must appreciate over the year (the dollar depreciate) for the two strategies to have the same return.

We can write Equation 29.16 in general terms as follows:

$$(1 + i_1^\$) = e \times (1 + i_1^\yen) \times \frac{1}{e_1^f}, \qquad\qquad [29.17]$$

where

$i_1^\$$ = the 1-year dollar interest rate,
$i_1^\yen$ = the 1-year yen interest rate,
e = the spot exchange rate,
e_1^f = the 1-year implicit forward exchange rate.

We can rewrite Equation 29.17 to give the implicit forward rate:

$$e_1^f = e \times \frac{(1 + i_1^\yen)}{(1 + i_1^\$)}. \qquad\qquad [29.18]$$

The implicit forward exchange rate in Equation 29.18 has the subscript "1" because it is the rate for one year from now. We can define in a similar way implicit forward exchange rates at any maturity.[6] We can also, of course, define implicit forward exchange rates for other currencies, such as the pound sterling and the mark.

The exchange rate is 200¥/$. The 1-year interest rate is 5% in the United States and 10% in Japan. What is the implicit 1-year forward exchange rate?   🌴 **CHECK STATION 4**

IMPLICIT AND ACTUAL FORWARD EXCHANGE RATES: COVERED INTEREST ARBITRAGE

As we saw in Chapter 11, there exist markets in which foreign exchange can *actually* be bought and sold forward. What is the relationship between the prices

---

[6]The appropriate equation would be

$$e_t^f = e \times \frac{(1 + i_t^\yen)^t}{(1 + i_t^\$)^t}.$$

in these markets—the *actual* forward exchange rates—and the *implicit* forward exchange rates that we have derived from interest rates in the two currencies?

For an answer, let us return to our numerical example. We found the implicit 1-year forward yen rate to be 143.2¥/$. Suppose the *actual* 1-year forward rate is 140.0¥/$. The spot rate remains 150¥/$. How can you make some money?

- *Step 1*: Borrow $1 million at 10%.[7] (You will have to repay $1 million x 1.10 = $1,100,000 at the end of the year.)

- *Step 2*: Sell the $1 million now at the spot rate of 150¥/$ for $1,000,000 x 150¥/$ = ¥150 million.

- *Step 3*: Invest the ¥150 million now in Japanese T-bills. These will pay ¥150 million x 1.05 = ¥157.5 million at the end of the year.

- *Step 4*: Sell the ¥157.5 million you will receive at the end of the year *now* on the forward market. At the forward rate of 140¥/$, the ¥157.5 million will bring ¥157.5 million/(140¥/$) = $1,125,000. You will receive the $1,125,000 at the end of the year when you hand over the ¥157.5 million.

Your position is now complete. You need do nothing but wait. At the end of the year, when your Japanese T-bills mature, you will receive ¥157.5 million. You will hand over the ¥157.5 million in exchange for $1,125,000 as agreed in your forward contract. Out of the $1,125,000, you will pay the $1,100,000 you owe on the dollar loan of Step 1, leaving you with a profit of $25,000. This trading strategy is called **covered interest arbitrage**.

covered interest arbitrage Trading strategy that exploits differences between implicit forward exchange rates and actual forward exchange rates.

Notice two things about covered interest arbitrage. First, you have put up no money of your own. Second, you have taken absolutely no risk. All four steps are taken simultaneously at the beginning of the year, so the profit is certain. You have to wait a year to collect it, but the amount of the profit is not in doubt. As a result, there is no reason not to take as large a position as you can. A $1 billion position will earn you a thousand times as much—$137.5 million—still with no risk.

Covered interest arbitrage pushes implicit and forward rates toward one another. In our example your borrowing of dollars puts upward pressure on the dollar interest rate; your spot sale of dollars puts downward pressure on the spot exchange rate; your purchase of Japanese T-bills puts downward pressure on the yen interest rate. Looking at Equation 29.18, we see that all of these pressures together tend to *lower* the implicit forward rate. In addition, your forward purchase of dollars puts *upward* pressure on the actual forward rate.

interest-rate parity Equality of actual and implicit forward exchange rates.

Whenever actual and implicit forward rates differ by even a small amount, currency traders will engage in covered interest arbitrage to make a safe profit. Their trading will put pressure on all of the rates involved, tending to eliminate the difference and bring the actual and implicit rates closer together. Hence gaps of the size in our example will simply never occur. The equality of actual and implicit forward rates is called **interest-rate parity**.

[7]Assume you work for a large bank, so that you can borrow at close to the T-bill rate.

Does interest-rate parity hold in practice? One cannot tell from the numbers published in the financial press: The data are simply not detailed enough. To test interest-rate parity, we need the bid and offered exchange rates and interest rates for precisely the same moment. Studies have been done using such detailed data. In one, the author personally gathered dollar-sterling and dollar-mark rates at ten-minute intervals in the London foreign-exchange market for three days in 1985.[8] Of the 3,500 potential arbitrage opportunities in this period, only one would have yielded a small profit. After paying brokerage costs, even this one opportunity would not have been profitable. Studies such as this have confirmed that profitable arbitrage opportunities are extremely rare and therefore that interest-rate parity does hold.

A PURE EXPECTATIONS THEORY

Just as when we looked at interest rates at different *maturities*, it is simplest to begin with a theory of interest rates in different *currencies* that depends *only* on expectations. We shall assume that borrowers and lenders do not care about currency risk and therefore have no preference for borrowing or lending in any particular currency. Borrowers care only about paying the lowest expected rate; lenders care only about earning the highest expected return. A pure expectations theory of exchange rates can be stated quite simply: *The forward exchange rate (implicit and actual) must equal the expected exchange rate.*

Let us look at an example. Suppose that the rates are as follows (interest-rate parity holds, so that actual and implicit forward rates are the same):

$i_1^\$$ (the 1-year dollar interest rate) = 10%,

$i_1^\yen$ (the 1-year yen interest rate) = 5%,

e (the spot exchange rate) = 150¥/$,

e_1^f (the 1-year forward exchange rate) = 143.2¥/$.

Suppose, too, that the forward rate is *not* equal to the expected rate: People expect the exchange rate to be 145¥/$ one year from now.

As an investor, you have the choice of buying U.S. T-bills or Japanese T-bills. If you invest a dollar in U.S. T-bills, you will have $1.10 in a year's time. If you buy Japanese T-bills, for every dollar you invest you will get ¥150 and these will yield ¥150 x 1.05 = ¥157.5 in a year's time. If you do *not* sell these yen forward, the amount you will have in dollars will depend on the exchange rate in one year's time. If you expect that exchange rate to be 145¥/$, as we assume, you will expect to receive ¥157.5/(145¥/$) = $1.086.

What this means is that you will expect a higher return on U.S. T-bills, and you will therefore invest in those and not in Japanese T-bills. If all investors, including investors in Japan, share your expectations about the exchange rate,

[8]Mark P. Taylor, "Covered Interest Parity: A High-Frequency, High-Quality Data Study," *Economica* 54 (November 1987), 429–438.

they will all prefer U.S. T-bills. This will put downward pressure on the U.S. T-bill rate, upward pressure on the Japanese T-bill rate, and upward pressure on the exchange rate (as Japanese investors buy the dollars they need to purchase U.S. T-bills). From Equation 29.18, all of these pressures will tend to *raise* the forward rate (implicit and actual forward rates moving together because of covered interest arbitrage). The pressure will continue until the forward rate is pushed up to 145¥/$, the expected exchange rate. At that point investors will be indifferent between investing in the two types of T-bill and there will be no further change.

The pressure on the markets from "true" investors will be reinforced by pressure from currency traders taking speculative positions. If, as assumed, the forward rate is 143.2¥/$ and you expect the exchange rate to be 145¥/$, you will expect to make a profit by borrowing yen, turning them into dollars, and buying U.S. T-bills. If you do this with ¥1 billion, you will owe ¥1 billion x 1.05 = ¥1.05 billion at the end of the year. The yen you borrow will enable you to buy ¥1 billion/(150¥/$) = $6.67 million in U.S. T-bills, which will yield $6.67 million x 1.10 = $7.33 million at the end of the year. If you are correct in your expectations about the exchange rate, the $7.33 million will be worth ¥1.063 billion, leaving you with a profit of ¥1.063 billion – ¥1.05 billion = ¥13 million.

Most of the trading that takes place in the foreign-exchange market (over $400 billion a day[9]) is related to the two types of transactions we have just seen—investors switching their portfolios from one currency to another and currency traders taking speculative positions, both based on expectations of what exchange rates will be in the future.

Notice that there *is* currency risk in both types of transaction: Investors and currency speculators are *not* hedging their positions in the forward market.[10] Therefore for the pressure on markets to be sufficient to drive the forward and expected exchange rates together, investors and speculators must be willing to accept that currency risk.

If the expectations theory is correct, and forward and expected exchange rates are indeed equal, then the following relationship will hold between interest rates in the two currencies:

$$\text{yen interest rate} = \text{dollar interest rate} + \text{expected percentage change in yen/dollar exchange rate} \qquad [29.19]$$

or

$$i_1^{¥} = i_1^{\$} + \frac{e_1^e - e}{e} , \qquad [29.20]$$

---

[9]See Chapter 11.

[10]Were they to do so, there would be no profit, because of interest-rate parity. There is an *expected* profit only because the expected exchange rate differs from the forward rate and because they do *not* hedge in the forward market.

		EXHIBIT 29.6
United States	8.5%	RATES ON 5-YEAR GOVERNMENT BONDS (BONDS MATURING IN 1995, PRICES AS OF JUNE 1990)
Japan	6.6	
United Kingdom	11.8	
Germany	8.8	
Canada	11.4	

Source: *The Wall Street Journal*, June 25, 1990.

where e_1^e is the expected yen/dollar exchange rate in one year's time.[11] A relationship similar to Equation 29.20 will hold at every maturity and for every currency.

For example, according to the expectations theory, if the 1-year T-bill rate is 10% in the United States and 5% in Japan, that must mean that the market expects the dollar to *depreciate* against the yen by 5% over the coming year:

$$\frac{e_1^e - e}{e} = i_1^¥ - i_1^\$ = 5\% - 10\% = -5\%. \qquad [29.21]$$

Intuitively, the expected 5% depreciation of the dollar makes the expected yield on U.S. T-bills equal to that on Japanese T-bills.

If the expectations theory is correct, we have a simple explanation of why interest rates are higher in one country than in another. If interest rates are higher in the United States than in Japan, it must be that the dollar is expected to depreciate against the yen at a rate equal to the difference in interest rates. If interest rates are lower in the United States than in Japan, it must be that the dollar is expected to appreciate against the yen at a rate equal to the difference in interest rates.

As an example, consider the rates on 5-year government bonds in various countries as shown in Exhibit 29.6. According to the expectations theory, the reason the rate on 5-year government bonds in Canada is 2.9% higher than in the United States is that the Canadian dollar is expected to depreciate against the U.S. dollar by 2.9% per year over the next 5 years. Is the expectations theory true? Since expectations are hard to measure, it is difficult to know. However, sophisticated statistical tests of the expectations theory generally do not find that it holds exactly.

[11]Equation 29.20 can be derived from Equation 29.18 by substituting the expected exchange rate for the forward rate.

🌴 CHECK STATION 5 | **Use Exhibit 29.6 to calculate the expected appreciation or depreciation of the U.S. dollar against the British pound and against the German mark.**

A PREFERRED-HABITAT THEORY OF INTEREST RATES AND EXCHANGE RATES

The validity of the expectations theory depends on investors and currency speculators being *completely* indifferent to currency risk. If they are not, then there may be insufficient pressure on the markets to push forward exchange rates into exact equality with expected exchange rates. Although changes in expectations about exchange rates will still affect relative interest rates, Equation 29.20 will no longer hold exactly. Instead of a pure expectations theory, we will have a *preferred-habitat* theory of exchange rates. The preferred-habitat theory modifies Equation 29.20 by adding to it a **currency premium**:

currency premium
Quantity reflecting the market's relative preference for securities denominated in one currency over those denominated in another.

$$\begin{array}{ccccc} \text{yen} & & \text{dollar} & \text{expected percentage} & \text{yen/} \\ \text{interest} & = & \text{interest} + & \text{change in yen/dollar} + & \text{dollar} \\ \text{rate} & & \text{rate} & \text{exchange rate} & \text{premium} \end{array} \qquad [29.22]$$

or

$$i^{\yen}_1 = i^{\$}_1 + \frac{e^e_1 - e}{e} + pr^1_{\yen/\$}, \qquad [29.23]$$

where $pr^1_{\yen/\$}$ is the 1-year yen/dollar premium. A relationship similar to Equation 29.24 will hold at every maturity and for every currency.

For example, if the one-year T-bill rate is 8% in the United States and 5% in Japan, and if the market expects the dollar to depreciate against the yen by 6% over the coming year, then the 1-year yen/dollar premium is

$$pr^1_{\yen/\$} = i^{\yen}_1 - i^{\$}_1 - \frac{e^e_1 - e}{e} = 5\% - 8\% + 6\% = 3\%. \qquad [29.24]$$

The currency premium indicates the degree of the market's preference for securities denominated in one currency over those denominated in another. In our example, dollar securities are preferred over yen securities with the same expected yield, so the market requires a 3% higher expected yield on yen securities to make them as attractive as dollar securities. The currency premium depends on currency risk and on other types of risk. For example, if most investors in the market face less currency risk from dollar-denominated securities, the yen-dollar premium will be positive. Or if the United States is regarded as safer and more stable than Japan, then this too will tend to make the yen/dollar premium positive.

So the preferred-habitat theory gives us a different explanation for the interest-rate differentials that we observe in Exhibit 29.6. For example, the 2.9% higher rate in Canada than in the United States reflects *both* the expected change in the Canadian/U.S. dollar exchange rate and the Canadian/U.S. dollar premium.

29.5 CHANGING EXPECTATIONS AND THEIR EFFECTS ON EXCHANGE RATES AND INTEREST RATES

We can see from Equation 29.22 that market expectations of a change in the exchange rate will affect relative interest rates. To illustrate this, let us look at an example. Suppose that initially the 1-year yen/dollar premium is 2% and that the exchange rate is 150 ¥/$ now and is not expected to change. The 1-year interest rate in the United States is 5%. The 1-year interest rate in Japan is 7%. These rates satisfy Equation 29.23:

$$0.07 = 0.05 + \frac{150 - 150}{150} + 0.02. \qquad [29.25]$$

Now suppose, for reasons that we shall look at in a moment, market expectations change and the dollar is expected to appreciate against the yen and reach 160¥/$ within a year. At current interest rates and the current exchange rate, investors in both the United States and Japan will now find U.S. securities more attractive than Japanese securities. They will therefore sell Japanese securities and buy U.S. securities. This will put downward pressure on the interest rate in the United States and upward pressure on the interest rate in Japan. At the same time, investors switching between the two markets will be buying dollars in exchange for yen, driving up the spot exchange rate. It is hard to know in principle how each of these rates will change, but suppose for purposes of illustration that the spot exchange rate rises to 156 ¥/$, the U.S. interest rate falls to 4%, the Japanese interest rate rises to 8.56%, and the yen/dollar premium is unchanged. These new rates will once again satisfy Equation 29.23:

$$0.0856 = 0.04 + \frac{160 - 156}{156} + 0.02. \qquad [29.26]$$

What could cause the market to expect the exchange rate to change? We shall look at two important factors—one a long-run factor, the other a short-run factor.

LONG-TERM EXPECTATIONS AND INFLATION

We saw in Chapter 28 that in the long run the rate of change in the exchange rate is equal to the difference in the inflation rates. That is,

$$\frac{e_1^e - e}{e} = n_\yen^e - n_\$^e, \qquad\qquad [29.27]$$

where $n_\yen^e$ is the expected rate of inflation in Japan over the next year and $n_\$^e$ is the expected rate of inflation in the United States.

Thus anything that affects expectations about future inflation rates affects expectations about future exchange rates. As we saw in Section 29.3, the most likely reason for a change in the expected rate of inflation is a change, or the expectation of a change, in the rate of monetary expansion. A change in expectations about future exchange rates will affect interest rates in the two countries and the *current* exchange rate. This effect of expected inflation on long-term interest rates, via international capital markets, reinforces the more direct effect that we saw in Section 29.3.

Equation 29.27 may be combined with Equation 29.23 to give a relationship between *real* interest rates in the two countries. Just use Equation 29.27 to substitute for the expected percentage change in the yen/dollar exchange rate; this gives

$$i_1^\yen = i_1^\$ + (n_\yen^e - n_\$^e) + pr_{\yen/\$} \qquad\qquad [29.28]$$

Rearranging this, we obtain

$$(i_1^\yen - n_\yen^e) = (i_1^\$ - n_\$^e) + pr_{\yen/\$}, \qquad\qquad [29.29]$$

or

$$r_1^\yen = r_1^\$ + pr_{\yen/\$}. \qquad\qquad [29.30]$$

That is, the real rate in Japan is just the real rate in the United States plus the yen/dollar premium.

🌴 **CHECK STATION 6** | **The U.S. expected inflation rate is about 5%. Assuming that currency premiums are zero, use Exhibit 29.6 to calculate the expected rates of inflation in the countries listed.**

APPLICATION: GERMAN REUNIFICATION AND INTEREST RATES IN GERMANY AND THE UNITED STATES

In early 1990, as German reunification became more likely, interest rates in West Germany rose. Reunification had several different economic implications. First, monetary union between East and West Germany aroused fears of a higher rate of inflation. Second, the prospect of large-scale investment in East Germany led the market to anticipate higher real interest rates in the future. Third, fears of possibly adverse Soviet reactions to reunification raised the possibility of political instability.

Commentators at the time stressed the first of these factors, the fear of increased inflation. Were they right? We can use our theory to find out. If an increase in expected inflation in Germany was what caused interest rates to rise there, then the mark should have depreciated against the dollar, and dollar interest rates should have fallen. In fact, the exchange rate stayed put, and interest rates rose in the United States. This suggests that it was the *real* rate that rose in Germany rather than inflationary expectations. According to Equation 29.30, if the mark/dollar premium remained the same, then a rise in the real rate in Germany would raise the real rate in the United States. That is what seems to have happened.

SHORT-TERM EXPECTATIONS AND INTERVENTION

Central banks intervene in foreign-exchange markets to affect the value of their currencies, and they conduct open market operations that affect short-term interest rates. So one of the most important factors in short-term expectations about exchange rates and interest rates is guessing the possible actions of central banks. For example, suppose the Bank of Japan is expected to intervene to bring down the value of the yen (to raise the yen/dollar exchange rate). From our analysis at the beginning of this section, this expectation should raise the yen/dollar exchange rate *now*, and it should raise short-term interest rates in Japan and lower short-term interest rates in the United States.

SELF-FULFILLING EXPECTATIONS AND VOLATILITY

Notice that a change in expectations is enough *by itself* to cause exchange rates and interest rates to move. The expectations need not prove correct. For example, fears of future inflation may prove unfounded and the expected central-bank intervention in the foreign-exchange market may not materialize. But if these events are *expected*, the expectations alone are enough to cause interest rates and exchange rates to change. In a sense, expectations are self-fulfilling. An expectation that the exchange rate will rise will drive up the exchange rate. An expectation that interest rates are about to fall will drive down interest rates.

Expectations are very volatile, affected each day by a flood of new information, rumor, and conjecture. Since these expectations can have a strong effect on interest rates and exchange rates, it is not surprising that interest rates and exchange rates too are very volatile. However, interest rates and exchange rates are of interest not just to speculators. They are important prices that affect real decisions in the economy. Interest rates affect saving and investment, and exchange rates affect imports and exports. So this volatility may not be a particularly good thing. It is often suggested, therefore, that it might be desirable to stabilize exchange rates or interest rates to dampen this volatility. We shall consider the merits of such stabilization in the next chapter.

SUMMARY

- Adaptive expectations use past values of a variable, such as inflation, to predict future values. Rational expectations rely on all available information including current policies and events that are likely to affect the value of the variable in the future.

- Changes in the quantity of money have informational value because they may provide a clue to future monetary growth and so to future interest rates and inflation.

- The loan-supply effect of a monetary change is likely to be greatest on short-term interest rates. The inflation-expectations effect is likely to be greatest on long-term interest rates.

- The segmented-market theory of the term structure assumes that borrowers and lenders are completely unwilling to switch maturities. Rates are determined independently by supply and demand at the different maturities.

- The expectations theory assumes that borrowers and lenders are perfectly willing to switch maturities, caring only about expected yields, and that they are indifferent to interest risk. According to this theory, the implicit forward rates are equal to expected rates. Hence an upward-sloping yield curve means that rates are expected to rise, and a downward-sloping yield curve means that they are expected to fall.

- The preferred-habitat theory takes an intermediate position. Borrowers and lenders care about maturity, but they are willing to switch to some degree.

- Just as loanable-funds markets at different maturities are related, so are loanable-funds markets in different *currencies*. The theories of the currency structure parallel those of the term structure.

- Covered interest arbitrage ensures interest-rate parity—the equality of implicit forward exchange rates and actual forward exchange rates.

- The expectations theory of exchange rates assumes that international borrowers, lenders, and speculators are indifferent to currency risk, caring only about expected yields in different currencies. Under these assumptions, implicit forward rates must equal expected rates. Interest rates in different currencies will differ only if exchange rates are expected to change.

- The preferred-habitat theory modifies the expectations theory by adding a currency premium. The currency premium indicates the degree of the market's preference for securities denominated in one currency over those denominated in another.

- Changing expectations of future exchange rates or interest rates will affect exchange rates and interest rates now. Since expectations are volatile, there is also considerable volatility in exchange rates and interest rates.

KEY TERMS

naive expectations

regressive expectations

extrapolative expectations

adaptive expectations

announcement effect

rational expectations

inflation-expectations effect

term structure of interest rates

segmented-market theory

expectations theory

implicit forward interest rate

preferred-habitat theory

term premium

implicit forward exchange rate

covered interest arbitrage

interest-rate parity

currency premium

DISCUSSION QUESTIONS

1. The president announces at a press conference that he believes the yen/dollar exchange rate to be too high. What is the likely effect on exchange rates, on short-term and long-term interest rates in the United States, and on interest rates in Japan?

2. The Fed, concerned about inflation, slows the rate of monetary growth. What is the likely effect on short-term and long-term interest rates in the United States, on exchange rates, and on interest rates abroad?

3. What are the three theories of the term structure of interest rates? How do they differ in their assumptions and in their implications?

4. We have seen an expectations theory of exchange rates and a preferred-habitat theory, but not a segmented-market theory. What would be the assumptions and implications of such a theory?

5. What are the different methods of expectations formation? How do they differ? Are Americans "irrational" if they form adaptive expectations about inflation?

6. Would you expect expectations about stock prices and about horse races to be adaptive or rational? Explain.

7. If the implicit forward mark exchange rate were 1.90 DM/$ and the actual forward rate were 2.00 DM/$, how could you make some money? Explain in detail what you would do. What are the potential risks?

8. The forward rate on the mark is 1.90 DM/$. You believe that because of reunification, the German trade balance will go from surplus to deficit and the mark will depreciate against the dollar. How could you make some money? Explain in detail what you would do. What are the potential risks?

SOFTWARE EXERCISE FOR THIS CHAPTER

Title: Stockmkt

This computer exercise extends the discussion of expectations in Chapter 29 to the stock market. You can try your luck at trading stocks and see what difference expectations can make to your success in that financial market. See your instructor if you wish to use this program.

BIBLIOGRAPHY

Caves, Richard E., Jeffrey A. Frankel, and Ronald W. Jones, *World Trade and Payments: An Introduction*, Glenview, IL: Scott Foresman, 1990.

Garner, C. Alan, "The Yield Curve and Inflation Expectations," *Economic Review of the Federal Reserve Bank of Kansas City* September-October 1987, 3–15.

Malkiel, Burton G., *The Term Structure of Interest Rates: Theory, Empirical Evidence, and Applications*, Silver Burdett, 1970.

Taylor, Mark P., "Covered Interest Parity: A High-Frequency, High-Quality Data Study," *Economica* 54: 429–38, 1987.

PART SEVEN

MONETARY POLICY

CHAPTER 30

THE FORMATION OF MONETARY POLICY

The Fed can, by creating fiat definitive money, change the quantity of money in our economy. We have seen that such a change affects interest rates, exchange rates, the price level, and output. The Fed, therefore, has enormous power to influence the course of the economy. How should it use this power?

This question—the question of **monetary policy**—can be divided into several parts. First, what needs to be done? What problems might economic policy address? Then, what can be done? Just because a problem exists does not mean that monetary policy can solve it. Finally, monetary policy is not the only kind of economic policy. What should be its role relative to fiscal policy?

There is considerable controversy among economists over these questions. They disagree both about what needs to be done and about what can be done. In this chapter we shall set the stage for a discussion of the different views on monetary policy in the following two chapters. We shall look at the possible goals of economic policy in general and of monetary policy in particular, and then at the different ways monetary policy can be conducted to achieve those goals. We shall also look at the political process that determines monetary policy.

monetary policy
Deliberate control of the money supply to achieve economic goals.

30.1 THE POSSIBLE GOALS OF MONETARY POLICY

Monetary change can affect interest rates, exchange rates, the price level, and output. How should it be used to affect these variables? Let us look at some possible goals.

777

EXHIBIT 30.1

OUTPUT AND
UNEMPLOYMENT
FROM 1900

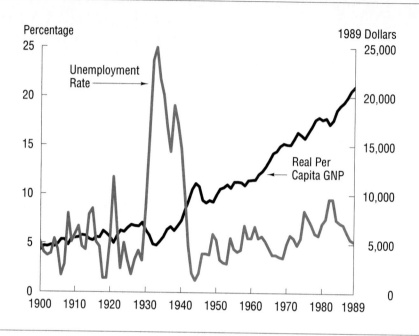

Source: *Economic Report of the President* and *Historical Statistics of the United States: Colonial Times to 1970.*

STABILIZE THE LEVEL OF ECONOMIC ACTIVITY

As you can see from Exhibit 30.1, the level of economic activity fluctuates over time. Output has grown enormously over the years, but its growth has been erratic. Fluctuations in output have been accompanied by fluctuations in employment: When output falls, workers are laid off. Exhibit 30.1 shows the unemployment rate—the percentage of people willing to work who cannot find jobs. Growth in output has raised our standard of living enormously in this century, but periodic bouts of unemployment have caused considerable misery to those affected by them.

What causes these fluctuations in output and employment? Whether anything needs to be done, and if so what, depends on why the fluctuations occur. There are several schools of thought, each with its own view on the appropriate policy:

- *The economy is inherently stable.* If left alone, it would continue to grow steadily with few fluctuations. Most of the fluctuations that do occur are the *result* of erratic, and therefore bad, monetary policy. There is no need for policy to stabilize the economy; all it need do is not *destabilize* it. This is the *Monetarist* view.

- *The economy is stable, but growth is an uneven process.* Fluctuations in economic activity are perfectly natural and even desirable. They are mainly the result of changes in technology and changes in economic opportunities. The discovery of some important new technology stimulates intense activity as it is applied to production; once this is done, the economy "rests" for a while. Nothing need be done about these fluctuations. Indeed, any attempt to even them out will be harmful and will interfere with the process of growth. This sort of view has a long history, but the most recent version is associated with the *real business cycle* school.

- *The economy is inherently unstable.* Small external shocks are magnified by this instability into large fluctuations in economic activity. These fluctuations represent breakdowns, failures of coordination. Policy can be used to offset the external shocks and to keep the economy on a stable growth path. This is the *Keynesian* view. Keynesians believe that the primary policy tool for stabilization is fiscal policy, but that monetary policy can play an important supporting role.

We shall have more to say about Keynesians and Monetarists and their conflicting views on stabilization policy in Chapter 31.

STABILIZE THE PRICE LEVEL

While economists differ in their views about fluctuations in output, there is wide agreement that fluctuations in the price level are harmful. We saw the reasons in Chapter 28. Because contracts are written in nominal terms, unanticipated changes in the price level redistribute wealth arbitrarily between borrower and lender and between employer and employee. Uncertainty about the price level inhibits borrowing and lending and other transactions and leads to a deterioration in the quantity and quality of investment. The high nominal interest rates that result from inflation encourage unproductive game playing to avoid the holding of money.

STABILIZE INTEREST RATES

Are fluctuations in the interest rate harmful? We have seen that interest-rate volatility makes life difficult for financial institutions and markets. However, we must not forget that the interest rate is a price and that prices convey information. A high price indicates that the good in question is scarce and provides an incentive to economize on its use. So a fluctuating interest rate might be necessary to signal the changing scarcity of loanable funds and to stimulate the appropriate changes in supply and demand. Artificially stabilizing a fluctuating price might make things more comfortable, but it might also lead to serious economic inefficiency and waste.

The question, then, is do fluctuations in the interest rate really reflect changes in the scarcity of loanable funds, or do they merely reflect monetary changes or changes in expectations of little fundamental consequence? A couple of cases will illustrate the distinction:

- *Case 1: Cold fusion really works.* As a result, enormous investment possibilities open up—a nuclear furnace in every home, a fusion-driven car in every garage. Interest rates rise, indicating that loanable funds are scarce relative to the opportunities to employ them. In response, saving increases: Given the high return to these new types of investment, it makes sense to put off some less essential items of consumption. Because of the rise in interest rates, other, less profitable investments are cut back to make way for the fusion revolution.

- *Case 2: The demand for money increases.* As a result of banking deregulation in the early 1980s, banks in the United States began to pay interest on checking deposits, reducing the opportunity cost of holding money. As we saw in Chapter 24, an increase in the demand for money reduces household lending and drives up interest rates. Higher interest rates in the early 1980s encouraged saving and discouraged investment, prolonging an already severe recession.

Stabilizing interest rates in the first case would be wrong: Preventing the interest rate from rising would also prevent the appropriate response in terms of saving and investment behavior. On the other hand, stabilizing interest rates in the second case would be quite appropriate: It would prevent an *in*appropriate response in terms of saving and investment. There is really no reason why saving should increase and investment fall as a result of the increase in the demand for money. A successful monetary policy should distinguish between these two types of cases.

PROMOTE GROWTH

Can economic policy affect the growth rate of per capita GNP? Over a period of years, small differences in growth rate cumulate to have enormous effects on the standard of living. For example, suppose the U.S. standard of living is double that of Singapore and the U.S. economy is growing at 3% a year. If the Singapore economy can grow at a 10% rate, its standard of living will catch up with ours in only 10 years.[1] Thus if policy can do anything to increase the growth rate, the potential benefits are enormous.

We have seen that monetary expansion can lower the real interest rate. That should stimulate investment and so promote growth: At a lower real interest rate more potential investment projects are attractive. But inflation, another result of monetary expansion, makes investment more difficult. Which of these two effects is stronger?

---

[1]$(1 + 0.03)^{10} = 1.3; (1 + 0.10)^{10} = 2.6.$

STABILIZE EXCHANGE RATES OR PROMOTE BALANCED TRADE

Like interest-rate instability, exchange-rate instability per se is bad. Both international trade and international investment are economically beneficial, but exchange-rate risk makes both less attractive and so inhibits them. However, exchange rates, like interest rates, are prices that convey important information. Changes in exchange rate may indicate a change in the most efficient mix of goods and services that the economy should produce. For example, a rise in the value of the yen might indicate that Japan should stop producing steel and start producing computers instead. On the other hand, changes in exchange rates might indicate nothing more than currency traders trying to anticipate intervention by central banks. In the latter case, major industries could close and thousands of workers lose their jobs for no good reason. So whether the exchange rate should be stabilized depends a lot on *why* it fluctuates.

As with the interest rate, not just the variability of the exchange rate but also its level matters. If current trade flows are "unsatisfactory," monetary policy may be able to influence them by altering the real exchange rate. For example, the United States is running a substantial trade deficit. Some economists believe this is bad and that the deficit could be reduced if the exchange value of the dollar were lowered. Others believe there is nothing wrong with a trade deficit and that alterations in exchange rates would not affect it much anyway.

ENSURE STABILITY OF THE FINANCIAL SYSTEM

Monetary policy affects the stability of the financial system. Instability in interest rates and in exchange rates creates interest-rate and exchange-rate risk and results in capital gains and losses. Capital losses can result in the collapse of some institutions and in a domino effect on others. Moreover, rising interest rates directly harm intermediaries such as thrifts that have a positive duration gap. They may also harm others indirectly through an increase in the number of defaults, as borrowers find it harder to meet their interest payments. (The LDC debt crisis that we discussed in Chapter 12 is an example of this.) Therefore stable interest rates and *low* interest rates promote the stability of the financial system.

THE TRADEOFFS BETWEEN ALTERNATIVE GOALS

Depending on one's views, then, the goals of monetary policy might include stabilizing the level of economic activity, stabilizing prices, stabilizing interest rates, promoting growth, stabilizing exchange rates, promoting trade balance, and promoting stability of the financial system.

Despite the multiplicity of possible goals, there are really only two things we can do with monetary policy: We can increase the rate of monetary expansion (*ease* policy) or we can slow monetary expansion (*tighten* policy). We can also vary how much we ease or tighten, but that is about it. How can we further so many goals with such a limited instrument?

Whether we ease or tighten, there will be some results we like and others we do not. Some examples:

1. We wish to stimulate employment. This requires easing, but the easing will certainly lead eventually to a higher price level.

2. We wish to reduce inflation. This requires tightening, but the tightening will raise interest rates and may put intolerable strain on the financial system.

3. We wish to improve the trade balance by lowering the exchange value of the dollar. This requires easing, but the easing may well mean higher inflation.

Inevitably, then, policy choices involve *tradeoffs* among the various goals. The same monetary policy that furthers one goal will be deleterious to another. Policymakers must decide on the relative importance of different goals. For example, how much inflation is it worth enduring in order to reduce the unemployment rate?[2]

30.2 DEFINING MONETARY POLICY IN TERMS OF A TARGET

Monetary policy can be eased or it can be tightened. The effects of easing are shown in Exhibit 30.2A.[3] The central bank increases bank reserves by ΔR through an open market purchase (or through foreign-exchange transactions or discount lending).[4] The increase in the amount of reserves allows the banking system to increase its lending by ΔM.[5] This increased bank lending shifts the supply of loanable funds to the right from S to $S + \Delta M$, lowering the interest rate from i_0 to i_1.

Exhibit 30.2B shows the effects of a tightening of monetary policy. The central bank decreases the amount of reserves of the banking system by an amount ΔR through an open market sale (or through foreign-exchange transactions or reduced discount lending). The decrease in the amount of reserves forces the banking system to decrease its outstanding loans by ΔM. This fall in bank lending shifts the supply of loanable funds to the right from S to $S - \Delta M$, because some of the new lending of households is now used to refinance loans that had previously been funded by banks. The reduction in the supply of loanable funds raises the interest rate from i_0 to i_1.

---

[2]The tradeoff dilemma would be eased considerably if we had several *independent* types of policy that could be used to pursue the different goals. For example, monetary policy could concentrate on keeping prices stable, while fiscal policy could concentrate on keeping employment high. As we shall see in Chapter 31, however, fiscal policy in practice is not that independent of monetary policy.

[3]Exhibit 30.2 shows the loanable funds market for a closed economy. For the sake of simplicity, international considerations are left out of the following discussion.

[4]See Chapter 20 for a discussion of how the Fed controls reserves.

[5]See Chapters 19 and 21 for discussions of the deposit expansion process.

EXHIBIT 30.2

THE NATURE OF
MONETARY POLICY

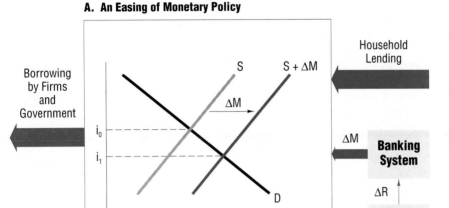

A. An Easing of Monetary Policy

A. The central bank eases
monetary policy by providing
more reserves to the banking
system: Banks increase their
lending, and this brings down
the interest rate.

B. The central bank tightens
monetary policy by reducing
bank reserves: Banks reduce
their lending, and this raises
the interest rate.

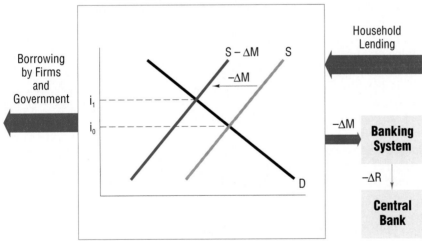

B. A Tightening of Monetary Policy

MONETARY-GROWTH TARGETS
AND INTEREST-RATE TARGETS

As you can see from Exhibit 30.2, monetary policy and changes in it directly affect the rate of growth of the quantity of money, ΔM, and indirectly affect the interest rate, i. Therefore monetary policy can be defined either in terms of ΔM or

monetary-growth target
Monetary policy specified in terms of a desired rate of monetary growth.

interest-rate target
Monetary policy specified in terms of a desired level of some interest rate.

in terms of i. That is, monetary policy can be defined either in terms of a **monetary-growth target** or in terms of an **interest-rate target.**

If policy is defined in terms of a monetary-growth target, the central bank simply decides on the appropriate rate of growth. It sets ΔM to, say, $\Delta M^* = 5\%$. The central bank then increases reserves through open market operations at a rate that will achieve this target.[6] It may sometimes be necessary to change the target growth rate, ΔM^*. The reason might be a change in goals: Worries about inflation might give way to worries about unemployment. Or the current policy might be failing to achieve its desired goal: Inflation might be higher or lower than intended. If an easing of monetary policy is needed, the target growth rate can be raised—for example, from 5% to 7%; if a tightening is called for, the target rate can be lowered—for example, from 5% to 3%.

If policy is defined instead in terms of an interest-rate target, the central bank decides on the level of i that it wishes to achieve, say $i^* = 10\%$. It then lets ΔM be whatever is needed to achieve that target. If the interest rate is above target, increasing the rate of growth of reserves will increase monetary growth and bring the interest rate down. If the interest rate is below target, reducing the rate of growth of reserves will decrease monetary growth and bring the interest rate up. How much of a reduction or increase in reserves is needed can be found by trial and error: If a $100 million open market purchase does not bring the interest rate down enough, then another $100 million can be purchased.

If goals change or if the current interest-rate target is not achieving its desired goal, then the target rate, i^*, can be raised or lowered. For example, if a target rate of 10% is producing too much inflation, monetary policy can be tightened by raising the target to, say 11%. Or, if a target rate of 10% is slowing the economy too much, then policy can be eased by lowering the target interest rate to, say 9%.

In practice, the specific interest rate the Fed chooses as its target is the fed funds rate. Because this is the market rate for borrowing and lending reserves, the Fed can control it quite tightly through open market operations, which have an immediate impact on the availability of reserves. Through the connections we studied in Chapter 29, the fed funds rate will influence other interest rates. Instead of controlling the fed funds rate, the Fed could control the yield on T-bills. It could do this by simply standing ready to buy and sell T-bills at a declared price.

THE CONSEQUENCES OF THE CHOICE OF TARGET

The choice of target—monetary-growth target or interest-rate target—has implications for how the economy will respond to different types of change. This will be brought out most clearly by looking at two examples.

---

[6] We shall see in Chapter 32 that although a monetary-growth target is simple in principle, it is not so simple in practice.

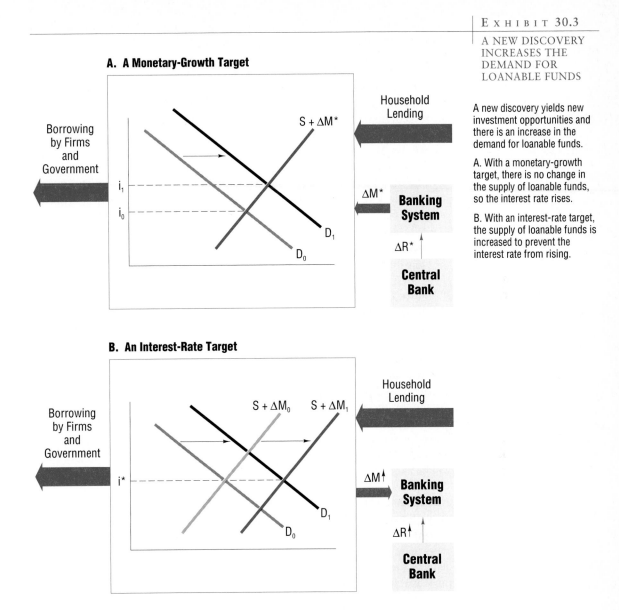

A. A Monetary-Growth Target

B. An Interest-Rate Target

EXHIBIT 30.3

A NEW DISCOVERY INCREASES THE DEMAND FOR LOANABLE FUNDS

A new discovery yields new investment opportunities and there is an increase in the demand for loanable funds.

A. With a monetary-growth target, there is no change in the supply of loanable funds, so the interest rate rises.

B. With an interest-rate target, the supply of loanable funds is increased to prevent the interest rate from rising.

EXAMPLE 1. THE DISCOVERY OF COLD FUSION INCREASES THE DEMAND FOR LOANABLE FUNDS Suppose the discovery of cold fusion opens up thousands of new and exciting investment opportunities. Exhibit 30.3 shows the impact on the loanable funds market under the two alternative targets.

Under a monetary-growth target, as shown in Panel A, the rate of monetary growth remains at its target level of ΔM^*, so the supply of loanable funds does not change. The new investment possibilities shift the demand curve to the right from D_0 to D_1 along the unchanged supply curve, raising the interest rate from i_0 to i_1. As a result of the higher interest rate, households save more and some investment projects that would have been undertaken at i_0 are deferred. There is an increase in total expenditure and an increase in output.

Under an interest-rate target, as shown in Panel B, the interest rate remains at the target rate of i^*. As the demand curve shifts to the right from D_0 to D_1, any tendency for the interest rate to rise is offset by the central bank. By increasing the reserves of the banking system, the central bank allows banks to increase their lending to accommodate completely the increased demand for loanable funds. Because the interest rate does not rise, there is no reason for households to save more or for less profitable investment projects to be deferred. Expenditure and output increase by more than they would under a monetary-growth target.

Which kind of target does best? What do we *want* to happen here? With the new discovery making investment more attractive, we would like to see a shift of resources away from consumption and into investment. We would also like to see them shifted to the new, more profitable types of investment from other, less profitable ones. Output should increase: Given the new opportunities, it seems reasonable that the economy should work "overtime"—above potential output—for a while. With a monetary-growth target, that is exactly what happens.

With an interest-rate target, the response of the economy is different in a number of ways. Because the interest rate does not rise, there is no reallocation of resources from consumption to investment or from one type of investment to another. Also because the interest rate does not rise, total expenditure and output expand by more than they would under a monetary-growth target. On the positive side, this means that investment in the new technology will proceed faster. On the negative side, because this new investment is financed by increased monetary expansion, there will be a price to pay in the future. Eventually, there will be increased inflation.

EXAMPLE 2. THE DEMAND FOR MONEY INCREASES   Suppose that, as in the early 1980s in the United States, banks are allowed to pay interest on checking deposits, reducing the opportunity cost of holding money. Consequently, there is an increase in the demand for money. As we saw in Chapter 24, an increase in the demand for money reduces household lending. Exhibit 30.4 shows the impact on the loanable funds market under alternative monetary-policy targets.

Under a monetary-growth target, as shown in Panel A, the rate of monetary growth remains at the target rate of ΔM^*. So as the supply of loanable funds from households drops from S_0 to S_1, and the total supply of loanable funds falls from $S_0 + \Delta M^*$ to $S_1 + \Delta M^*$, the interest rate rises from i_0 to i_1. As a result of the higher interest rate, households save more and some investment projects that would have been undertaken at i_0 are deferred. There is a fall in total expenditure and a fall in output.

Under an interest-rate target, as shown in Panel B, the interest rate remains at the target rate of i^*. As the supply of loanable funds from households falls from S_0 to S_1, any tendency for the interest rate to rise is offset by the central bank. By

EXHIBIT 30.4

AN INCREASE IN
THE DEMAND FOR
MONEY REDUCES
THE SUPPLY OF
LOANABLE FUNDS

A. A Monetary-Growth Target

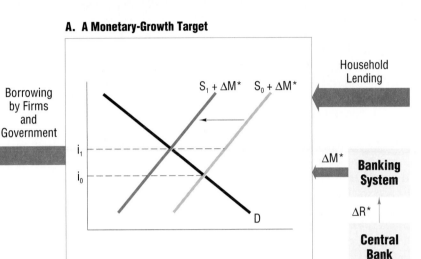

An increase in the demand for money reduces the supply of loanable funds.

A. Under a monetary-growth target, there is no compensating increase in bank lending and the total supply of loanable funds falls, raising the interest rate.

B. Under an interest-rate target, the fall in household lending is completely offset by an increase in bank lending, and there is no effect on the interest rate.

B. An Interest-Rate Target

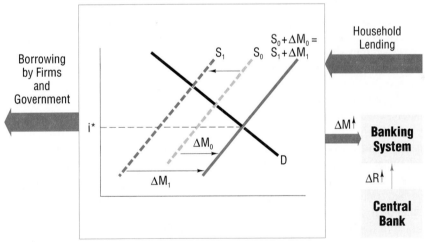

increasing the reserves of the banking system, the central bank allows banks to increase their lending to offset completely the decreased supply of loanable funds from households. Monetary growth increases from ΔM_0 to ΔM_1. The *total* supply of loanable funds remains the same: $S_0 + \Delta M_0 = S_1 + \Delta M_1$. Because the interest rate does not rise, there is no reason for households to save more or for less profitable investment projects to be deferred. Expenditure and output remain the same.

Which type of target does best in this case? What do we want to happen here? The change in the demand for money should not affect the real activity of the economy. There is no reason to reallocate resources away from consumption and toward investment, and there is certainly no reason to reduce output below its potential. But these are the results under a monetary-growth target. On the other hand, the interest-rate target allows the increased demand for money to be satisfied without any disturbance to the allocation of resources. In essence, the central bank gives households the extra money they want with minimum disturbance to the rest of the economy.

WHICH TARGET IS BEST OVERALL? Neither type of target is a clear winner. Since the monetary-growth target stabilizes the rate of monetary growth, real changes like the new discovery that should have no effect on monetary growth do not do so. This protects the economy from unnecessary inflations or deflations. On the other hand, monetary changes like the change in money demand that *should* affect monetary growth, do not do so either, and they therefore cause unnecessary real disruption. While the rate of monetary growth is stabilized, the interest rate is free to vary and does so freely, both when it should—the new discovery—and when it should not—the change in money demand. With this sort of target, interest rates will be quite volatile. As we know, this has consequences for financial stability.

With the interest-rate target, everything is reversed. Interest rates are now stabilized and monetary growth is volatile. Real changes, like the new discovery, instead of changing the interest rate as they should, change the rate of monetary growth as they should not and affect the price level. On the other hand, monetary changes, like the change in money demand, which should have no effect on the interest rate or on the allocation of resources, indeed have none.

Each type of rule, then, has its advantages and its disadvantages. Unfortunately, we cannot have it both ways: Monetary policy cannot simultaneously pursue both a monetary-growth target and an interest-rate target. We have to decide which type of error is likely to have the worse consequences. In the following chapters we shall see that different views about the goals of monetary policy imply different views about the relative severity of the two types of error and so a different choice of targets. We shall also see that there are important differences in how easy it is to pursue the two types of target.

Our discussion of the relative merits of the two types of target has assumed that the level of the target is not altered in the face of the various changes. If the target rate of monetary growth or the target interest rate can be altered appropriately and immediately in response to every change in circumstances, then the choice of target does not matter. For example, if the target interest rate can be raised immediately in response to the new discovery, the outcome is identical to that under the monetary-growth target. Or if the rate of monetary growth can be raised immediately in response to the change in money demand, the outcome is identical to that under the interest-rate target. As we shall see, however, such responsiveness is unrealistic. At the time it is generally hard to know what is going on in the economy. Even hindsight does not always help: Economists are still fighting over what happened during the Great Depression. So the choice of target matters, and no choice will be perfect.

AN EXCHANGE-RATE TARGET

We have described the two alternatives as a monetary-growth target and an interest-rate target. This is reasonable given our assumption that monetary policy is conducted through the loanable funds market. However, it could be conducted instead through the foreign-exchange market. We saw in Chapter 20 (Section 20.3) that purchases and sales of foreign exchange by the central bank have monetary consequences similar to those of purchases and sales of securities. We saw in Chapter 25 (Section 25.6) that central banks can intervene in foreign-exchange markets to influence the exchange rate.

So a central bank could define its monetary policy in terms of an exchange-rate target. That is, it could buy or sell foreign exchange in order to keep the exchange rate at the target level. Easing monetary policy would mean lowering the target exchange rate (a depreciation); tightening would mean raising the exchange rate (an appreciation). The exchange rate is a common target of monetary policy in some smaller countries. For example, Holland, Belgium, and Denmark define their monetary policies in terms of a target exchange rate of their currencies against the German mark.

In terms of how the economy responds to various types of change, an exchange-rate target is much like an interest-rate target. For example, an increase in money demand in Holland would tend to raise interest rates and so appreciate the guilder. The central bank would intervene to prevent the appreciation by buying dollars for guilders. The increased rate of monetary growth would prevent the rise in the interest rate and satisfy the increased demand for money.

30.3 THE POLICY-MAKING PROCESS

We have seen the different possible goals of monetary policy and the different possible targets in terms of which it can be formulated. How are the actual goals and targets chosen? Who decides? The formal answer is: The Fed. So we need to see how the Fed is organized and how it makes decisions. In reality, the Fed is not entirely free to do as it pleases. We shall see what the constraints are. We shall also consider some of the arguments for and against giving the Fed complete independence in conducting monetary policy.

THE FORMAL STRUCTURE OF THE FED

As we saw in Chapter 16, the Fed was originally set up in 1913 as a lender of last resort in response to the recurrent banking crises that had wracked the U.S. economy. Because of strong political opposition to centralized control of bank-

EXHIBIT 30.5

ORGANIZATION OF THE FEDERAL RESERVE SYSTEM

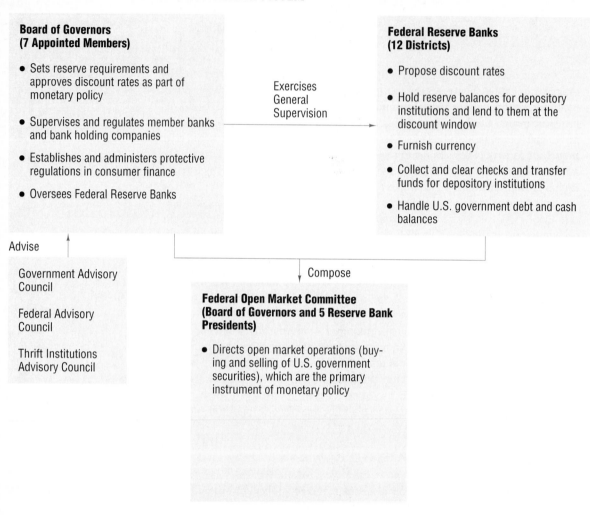

**Board of Governors
(7 Appointed Members)**

- Sets reserve requirements and approves discount rates as part of monetary policy

- Supervises and regulates member banks and bank holding companies

- Establishes and administers protective regulations in consumer finance

- Oversees Federal Reserve Banks

Exercises General Supervision

**Federal Reserve Banks
(12 Districts)**

- Propose discount rates

- Hold reserve balances for depository institutions and lend to them at the discount window

- Furnish currency

- Collect and clear checks and transfer funds for depository institutions

- Handle U.S. government debt and cash balances

Advise

Government Advisory Council

Federal Advisory Council

Thrift Institutions Advisory Council

Compose

**Federal Open Market Committee
(Board of Governors and 5 Reserve Bank Presidents)**

- Directs open market operations (buying and selling of U.S. government securities), which are the primary instrument of monetary policy

Source: *The Federal Reserve System: Purposes and Functions*, 1984.

ing, the United States did not adopt the usual model of a single central bank. Instead, a system was set up with twelve regional Federal Reserve Banks and a coordinating Board in Washington. The division of powers between the regional Banks and the Board was unclear, and the resulting confusion contributed to the Fed's poor performance during the Great Depression. In light of this experience, the Fed was restructured in its present form in the 1930s, with the power firmly placed in Washington. Its formal structure is outlined in Exhibit 30.5.

THE BOARD OF GOVERNORS The Federal Reserve System is controlled by the Board of Governors in Washington, DC. The seven members of the Board are appointed by the president with the advice and consent of the Senate. To promote independence, governors are appointed for a fourteen-year, nonrenewable term. Terms are staggered so that at least one new governor must be appointed every two years.[7] Governors are chosen from different parts of the country to provide equitable regional representation.

The chairman and vice chairman of the Board are named by the president from among the seven governors, subject to confirmation by the Senate, for a four-year term. They may be reappointed so long as their terms as governors have not expired; it is usual for a chairman who is not reappointed to resign from the Board. The term of the chairman does not coincide with the presidential term, so a new president often inherits a chairman from his predecessor in office.

The Board of Governors plays a major role in determining monetary policy. All seven governors are voting members of the Federal Open Market Committee that directs open market operations. The Board sets reserve requirements, within the bounds specified by law, and effectively sets the rate and terms at which the regional Banks may make discount loans.

The Board also plays a major role in regulating the banking system and in preserving the stability of the financial system (as we saw in Chapter 18). It is the primary regulator for member banks, bank holding companies, international banking facilities, Edge Act corporations, and the U.S. branches and agencies of foreign banks. In addition, it has responsibility for the smooth functioning of the payments system and implementation of various federal laws relating to consumer credit—for example, the Truth in Lending Act.

The Board has broad authority over the operations of the twelve regional Federal Reserve Banks. The regional Banks must submit their budgets to the Board for its approval. The Board appoints three of the nine members of each Bank's board of directors and must approve the appointment of the president and first vice president of each Bank.

The Board is required to submit reports to Congress—an annual report on its operations, as well as special reports twice yearly on the state of the economy and on its monetary-policy objectives. The Board is *not* dependent on Congress for budgetary approval. It is financed through an assessment on the incomes of the Federal Reserve Banks.[8]

THE FEDERAL RESERVE BANKS The country is divided into twelve Federal Reserve districts (see Exhibit 30.6). Each district has one Federal Reserve Bank and may have additional branches in major cities. The division into districts reflects the reality of 1913 rather than that of the 1990s: For example, Richmond, Virginia, has its own Federal Reserve Bank, whereas Los Angeles has only a branch of the San Francisco Bank. The three largest regional Banks in terms of

---

[7]Appointments are actually more frequent because some governors do not complete their terms.

[8]As we saw in Chapter 20, the Federal Reserve Banks earn a considerable income from their holdings of government securities and other assets.

assets are located in the money center cities of Chicago, San Francisco, and New York. The New York Fed, because of its proximity to the nation's financial center, is the most important and influential of the regional banks.

The regional Banks carry most of the operational burden of the System. They are responsible for check clearing, the distribution of coin and currency, the making of discount loans to individual banks, the examination of state-chartered member banks, and fiscal-agency functions for the Treasury. The New York Fed, in addition, executes trades in government securities and in foreign exchange for the System and for the U.S. and foreign governments.

Of the nine members of the board of directors of each regional Bank, six are elected by the member banks of the district (three are bankers and three are not) and three are appointed by the Board of Governors. One of the Board-appointed directors is designated chairman. The board of directors oversees, subject to Board approval, the operation of the Bank. The board appoints the Bank's president and first vice president and sets their salaries.

Federal Open Market Committee (FOMC)
Chief policy-making body of the Federal Reserve System.

THE FEDERAL OPEN MARKET COMMITTEE The **Federal Open Market Committee (FOMC)** is the chief policy-making body of the Federal Reserve System. All seven governors are full voting members, as is the president of the New York Fed. The presidents of the eleven other regional Banks all attend meetings, but only four may vote. The right to vote rotates among them, each voting for a period of one year.

The FOMC meets about eight times a year to decide on open market operations and on intervention in the foreign-exchange market. The meetings also provide a forum for the discussion of monetary policy in general. Policy decisions are passed on for execution in the form of **FOMC policy directives** to the Manager for Domestic Operations, System Open Market Account, and to the Manager for Foreign Operations, System Open Market Account, at the New York Fed (see Chapter 20). Day-to-day operations are conducted by the System Account Managers, who keep in constant touch with designated members of the FOMC by telephone.

FOMC policy directives
Federal Reserve policy decisions sent to the New York Fed for execution.

WHERE THE POWER REALLY LIES The formal structure of the Fed is largely a legacy of the anti-centralist sentiments that molded the original Federal Reserve Act. In reality, the Fed today is a central bank much like any other. It is effectively a single bank, headquartered in Washington, with twelve regional branches. The regional Banks have little power, and the function of their boards of directors is mainly public relations.

In Washington, power is largely concentrated in the hands of the chairman. Although decisions of the FOMC are made by majority vote, it is extremely unusual for the views of the chairman not to prevail. The chairman sets the agenda for FOMC meetings and supervises the staff of economists and statisticians who provide the committee with information and advice. (The regional Banks each have their own research departments that inform and advise their respective presidents.)

EXHIBIT 30.6

THE FEDERAL RESERVE SYSTEM

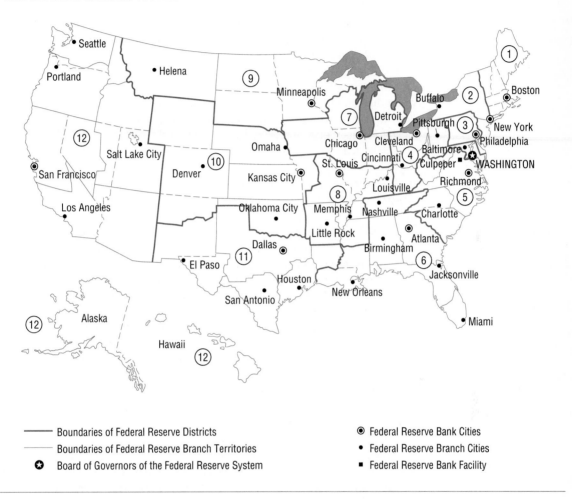

Boundaries of Federal Reserve Districts
Boundaries of Federal Reserve Branch Territories
Board of Governors of the Federal Reserve System

Federal Reserve Bank Cities
Federal Reserve Branch Cities
Federal Reserve Bank Facility

Source: *The Federal Reserve System: Purposes and Functions*, 1984.

In principle, the Fed is an independent agency within the government, and it has considerable freedom in formulating monetary policy. It is a part of neither the executive nor the legislative branches, and its decisions are therefore subject to ratification by neither. Because the Fed has its own source of income, it is immune to budgetary blackmail. The terms of appointment of governors are such that their susceptibility to pressure is minimized. Nonetheless, the Fed is subject to pressures.

PRESSURES FROM THE PRESIDENT AND CONGRESS

The president and the Congress take a close interest in monetary policy. Naturally, they care about the effect of monetary policy on the overall health of the economy. But they also care about monetary policy for a more narrow reason: Monetary policy affects the federal budget.

Monetary policy affects the budget directly through its effect on the amount of interest the government must pay on its debt. A tightening of monetary policy means higher interest rates. The interest the government pays on its outstanding debt is sensitive to current market rates because much of it is short term. Therefore much of it must be rolled over at current market rates. For example, in 1989, the federal government paid $169 billion in interest on a net debt of $2,100 billion. The average interest rate it paid was 7.7%. Had the average rate been 1% higher, the amount of interest the government would have had to pay would have increased by 0.01 x $2,100 billion = $21 billion. This would have increased the budget deficit by the same amount.

Monetary policy also affects the government budget indirectly through its affect on income and growth. The government budget is quite sensitive to the level of income. As income rises, tax receipts increase and some transfers (such as unemployment insurance and food stamps) decrease. These developments tend to reduce the deficit. If monetary policy lowers the interest rate, the level of income rises and the budget deficit is reduced. On the other hand, if monetary policy causes the interest rate to rise, the level of income falls and the budget deficit is increased.

Clearly, then, the conduct of monetary policy will be of intense interest to those involved in the budgetary process—the president and the Congress. Not surprisingly, there will be no shortage of calls for the Fed to do whatever will ease the problems of the budget, or of expressions of impatience when it is slow to do so (see "Bush Takes Steps to Quiet Speculation He Won't Reappoint Greenspan at Fed").

The Fed's independence was granted to it by the Congress, and Congress can just as easily take it away. Whenever Fed policy is too much at variance with what Congress or the president would wish, there is dark talk of new legislation to bring the Fed to heel. It is therefore only natural that the Fed is sensitive to the views of the president and Congress.

OTHER PRESSURES ON THE FED

Because of its responsibility for the stability of the financial system, the Fed is also sensitive to political pressure from the financial community. The New York Fed, in particular, has traditionally represented the interests of Wall Street. Those interests may not always coincide with those of the rest of the economy. For example, as we saw in Chapter 12, interest rates rose in the early 1980s as a result of a tightened monetary policy, causing many LDC borrowers to default. There was considerable pressure on the Fed from the money center banks to bring interest rates down and to help the banks with their LDC debt.

BUSH TAKES STEPS TO QUIET SPECULATION HE WON'T REAPPOINT GREENSPAN AT FED

By Gerald F. Seib

Staff Reporter of The Wall Street Journal

Washington—President Bush tried to quash speculation that he won't reappoint Federal Reserve Board Chairman Alan Greenspan next year, but in the process hinted again that he wants more aggresive Fed action to lower interest rates.

"There is no bubbling war with Alan Greenspan," Mr. Bush said at a White House news conference. Regarding whether he might decide against reappointing Mr. Greenspan, whose four-year term expires in August 1991, Mr. Bush asserted: "There is no discussion of that nature at all."

But when asked whether the Fed is dragging its feet about lowering interest rates, Mr. Bush replied, "I think some feel that way." He quickly added, though, that "some" probably also agree with the "inflationary concerns" that the Fed has expressed when pressed to lower interest rates.

Mr. Bush was responding to a report last week in the Los Angeles Times quoting an unidentified Bush adviser as saying the president was so angry about the Fed's failure to push interest rates down that he probably wouldn't reappoint Mr. Greenspan.

Mr. Greenspan is a longtime friend and adviser of the president, and administration officials indicated last week that his personal standing with Mr. Bush make it unlikely he would be asked to leave. But officials also acknowledge in private that they think the Fed could be more "cooperative" in ensuring that economic growth continues. Aside from the political problems the president would encounter from an economic slump, any slowdown in economic activity also would cut government revenues and exacerbate the budget deficit.

"If the question is, am I happy with interest rates . . . every president would like to see interest rates lower," Mr. Bush said. "There's no question."

But the president insisted that he isn't in a "Fed-bashing mode." He said that differences of opinion over the level of interest rates are "always built into a conflict between the president and the chairman of the Fed, and I don't want to get into that game because I don't feel that way."

Source: Gerald F. Seib, "Bush Takes Steps to Quiet Speculation He Won't Reappoint Greenspan at Fed," *The Wall Street Journal*, March 14, 1990. Reprinted by permission of The Wall Street Journal, © Dow Jones & Company, Inc. 1990. All Rights Reserved Worldwide.

The Fed is also sensitive to the views of the general public. Public dissatisfaction with Fed policies lends support to those in Congress who would limit its independence. As we shall see in Chapter 31, there is significant interaction between monetary policy and fiscal policy—policy relating to government spending and taxation that is determined by Congress. If the economy sinks into a recession, neither the Congress nor the Fed wants to take the blame, and each will do its best to redirect public dissatisfaction toward the other. The Fed will blame fiscal policy; the Congress will blame monetary policy.

The chairman is subject to substantial peer pressure from the central bankers of other major economies, with whom he meets frequently. Monetary policy in one country cannot be conducted without regard for monetary policy in others. For example, if one country tightens its monetary policy relative to that of other countries, thereby raising its interest rates relative to theirs, this will have an impact on its exchange rate and on its foreign trade. The consequent changes in international trade and lending will affect the other economies. (We shall have more to say about this in Chapter 32.) Since some degree of international cooperation is essential, the influence of foreign central bankers can be considerable. Indeed, the most drastic change in U.S. monetary policy to occur in recent years took place in October 1979, immediately after then-Chairman Paul Volcker was hauled over the coals by fellow central bankers at a meeting in Yugoslavia.

In addition to various types of political influence, the Fed is also subject to intellectual influence. To quote Keynes:

> The ideas of economists and political philosophers, both when they are right and when they are wrong, are more powerful than is commonly understood. Indeed the world is ruled by little else. Practical men, who believe themselves to be quite exempt from any intellectual influences, are usually the slaves of some defunct economist. Madmen in authority, who hear voices in the air, are distilling their frenzy from some academic scribbler of a few years back. I am sure that the power of vested interests is vastly exaggerated compared with the gradual encroachment of ideas.

The Fed must justify what it does, both to itself and to others. Such justification will inevitably rely heavily on the ideas of economists. Those ideas find their way into the policy discussion through the staff economists of the FOMC and of the research departments of the Board and of the regional Banks. Perhaps even more important, many governors and chairmen, past and present, have themselves been economists. Naturally, new ideas have the greatest chance of being heard when things are going badly. Two examples that we shall study in the following chapters are the Keynesian ideas that were adopted after the Great Depression, and the Monetarist ideas that were adopted after the poor performance of the economy in the 1970s.

HOW INDEPENDENT SHOULD THE FED BE?

Is the Fed's independence, such as it is, a good thing? Some economists have argued that it is not. It may be naive to think of the Fed as selflessly pursuing the public good. The Fed is a bureaucracy with its own interests—greater power and prestige—that it is likely to put first. For example, the Fed has long resisted suggestions that it announce its policy decisions immediately. It is hard to think of any good economic reason for keeping these decisions secret, but, with a horde of Fed watchers hanging on every word, this secrecy certainly adds to the aura of drama and importance surrounding the institution.

Milton Friedman, in particular, has long argued that the Fed should be made more accountable for its actions. The Fed should have clearly stated goals—as we shall see, Friedman has some very definite ideas about what those goals should be—and its performance should be judged by how well it attains them. If the goals are not attained, the governors should be fired. Friedman has even argued for making the Fed a bureau of the Treasury. There would then be a single address for complaints about economic policy. Under the current arrangement, when things go wrong, the Fed and the Treasury can blame each other.

Advocates of Fed independence, on the other hand, see it as necessary to insulate monetary policy from the immediate political pressures of the moment. As we have seen, easing or tightening of monetary policy has both good effects and bad. The good effects of easing tend to come in the short run and the bad

America's Federal Reserve Bank is under scrutiny by Congress. Politicians have long been uneasy about its independence—the very quality which the markets admire. The House Banking Committee started public hearings on October 25th over a bill, backed by two House Democrats, which seeks to make the Fed more accountable to politicians.

The Hamilton-Dorgan bill has three main proposals: the treasury secretary should meet the Fed's policy-making Open Market Committee at least twice a year; each new president should be free to pick a new chairman for the Fed; and the Fed should publish its policy decisions immediately instead of six weeks later. A second bill, which the Fed's chairman, Mr. Alan Greenspan, favors, seeks to clarify the Fed's job, by requiring it to eliminate inflation over the next five years.

Congress would be wise to leave the Fed alone. A study* by Mr. Alberto Alesina of Harvard University finds a strong inverse relationship between the degree of independence of a central bank and a country's inflation rate. Central banks are ranked by their independence (see chart): the least independent has a value of 1, the most independent, 4. This is judged on the basis of the formal relationship between the central bank and the government, informal contacts and the existence of rules forcing the central bank, say, to accommodate the fiscal deficit by printing more money.

Only two central banks are worthy of four stars: West Germany's Bundesbank and the Swiss National Bank. The Germans, with nightmares

* "Politics and business cycles in industrial democracies" by A. Alesina. *Economic Policy*, April 1989.

of wheelbarrow inflation, have charged the Bundesbank with the statutory duty of guarding the purchasing power of the currency. The Fed and the Bank of Japan both get three stars. These four banks' countries had among the lowest inflation rates in 1973-86. The countries with the least independent central banks, Italy, Spain and New Zealand, had the highest rates.

The chart also confirms that lower inflation was not achieved simply by running a higher jobless rate: the countries with three- and four-star banks have a lower than average rate of unemployment.

Source: "Free, but Not Easy, with Money," *The Economist*, October 28, 1989, p. 84. Copyright 1989. The Economist. Distributed by Special Features/Syndication Sales.

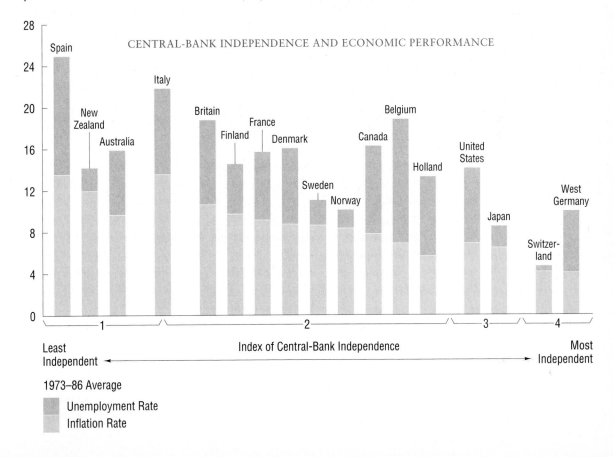

CENTRAL-BANK INDEPENDENCE AND ECONOMIC PERFORMANCE

Least Independent ← Index of Central-Bank Independence → Most Independent

1973–86 Average
Unemployment Rate
Inflation Rate

effects in the long run (the reverse for tightening). Politicians tend to have a very short time horizon—the next election. The proper conduct of monetary policy, on the other hand, requires a concern for the long run as well as the short. So making monetary policy more subject to political control by reducing the Fed's independence seems to many economists a poor recipe for improved performance (see "Free, but Not Easy, with Money" on page 797).

The present arrangement also has its advantages for the politicians. The Fed is a very convenient whipping boy. When monetary policy needs to be tightened, the politicians can avoid taking the blame by pointing a finger at the "independent" Fed. If the Fed were formally accountable to the president or to Congress, this ploy would not work.

In practice, then, although it is subject to influence and pressure, the Fed has and is likely to retain a great deal of discretion in choosing the goals and targets of monetary policy. In the following chapters we shall see which goals and targets it has chosen and the effects those choices have had on the economy.

SUMMARY

- Economists disagree about whether monetary policy has a role in stabilizing the economy. Monetarists and members of the real business cycle school see no need for such a role, the former because they believe the economy is stable, the latter because they believe that fluctuations are necessary. Keynesians believe that the economy is unstable and should be stabilized.

- Economists generally agree that fluctuations in the price level are harmful.

- Fluctuations in interest rates are potentially harmful to the financial system. However, fluctuations in interest rates may provide important information about the changing scarcity of loanable funds. Ideally, policy should allow such appropriate fluctuations while preventing inappropriate ones.

- Monetary policy can lower interest rates, and this may promote growth. But the same policy that lowers interest rates now will likely lead to more inflation in the future, and inflation is harmful to growth.

- The arguments for and against stabilizing or changing interest rates apply in equal measure to stabilizing or changing exchange rates.

- The stability of the financial system is always a major concern of monetary policy. High interest rates and volatile interest rates are harmful to that stability.

- There are inevitably tradeoffs among the various goals of monetary policy: A policy designed to further one goal will often be harmful to another.

- Monetary policy may be defined in terms of a monetary-growth target, in terms of an interest-rate target, or in terms of an exchange-rate target.

- Under a monetary-growth target, a real change in the economy (like the discovery of a new technology) that should affect interest rates actually does so; under an interest-rate target, it does not. Under an interest-rate target, a monetary change that should not affect interest rates does not do so; under a monetary-growth target, it does. The properties of an exchange-rate target are much like those of an interest-rate target.

- The Fed is controlled by the Board of Governors, with the chairman having a dominant voice. Monetary policy is decided by the FOMC, whose membership consists of the Board of Governors and the presidents of the regional Banks.

- Formally, the Fed has complete independence in the formulation of monetary policy. However, it is subject to pressure from the president and Congress, as well as from other quarters.

KEY TERMS

monetary policy

monetary-growth target

interest-rate target

Federal Open Market
Committee (FOMC)

FOMC policy directives

DISCUSSION QUESTIONS

1. What are the different possible goals of monetary policy? Can the Fed achieve all of them simultaneously?

2. What are the pros and cons of stabilizing interest rates and exchange rates?

3. What are the relative merits of interest-rate and monetary-growth targets for monetary policy?

4. What are the various pressures on the Fed? How responsive should the Fed be to these pressures?

5. What are the arguments for and against Fed independence?

BIBLIOGRAPHY

Board of Governors of the Federal Reserve System, *The Federal Reserve System: Purposes and Functions*, 7th ed., Washington, D.C.: Board of Governors of the Federal Reserve System, 1984.

Friedman, Milton, "The Case for Overhauling the Federal Reserve," *Challenge* July–August 1985, 4–12.

Friedman, Milton, and Anna Jacobson Schwartz, *A Monetary History of the United States 1867–1960*, Princeton: Princeton University Press, 1963.

Kane, Edward J., *External Pressures and the Operations of the Fed*. In *Political Economy of International and Domestic Monetary Relations*, edited by R.E. Lombra and W.E. Witte, Ames, Iowa: Iowa State University Press, 1982.

Poole, William, "Optimal Choice of Monetary Policy Instruments in a Simple Stochastic Macro Model," *Quarterly Journal of Economics* 84 May 1970, 197–216.

Strongin, Steven, "Real Boats Rock: Monetary Policy and Real Business Cycles," *Economic Perspectives, Federal Reserve Bank of Chicago* November-December 1988, 21–28.

APPENDIX TO CHAPTER 30
ALTERNATIVE TARGETS IN TERMS OF THE LIQUIDITY PREFERENCE THEORY

The working of a monetary-growth target or an interest-rate target can be explained in terms of the *liquidity preference theory* described in the Appendix to Chapter 26. There we saw that the LM condition—the condition that the demand for money equal the quantity of money in existence—could be thought of as determining the interest rate. That condition is

$$M = kY + (x - z\,i) \qquad\qquad [30A.1]$$

where M is the quantity of money, Y is income, i is the interest rate, and k, x, and z are constants.

A policy that targets monetary growth also determines at any given time the quantity of money, M. A change in autonomous expenditure, like the discovery of cold fusion, causes Y to change. Since M is fixed, i must change in order to satisfy the LM condition, Equation 30A.1. A change in money demand changes x, and since M is fixed, the result will be changes in Y and i.

A policy that targets i keeps i fixed by adjusting M to satisfy the LM condition, Equation 30A.1. An increase in autonomous expenditure that increases Y will now have no effect on i: M will expand to keep i from rising. An increase in money demand (an increase in x) will not affect i either: Once again, M will expand to keep i constant.

CHAPTER 31

THE EVOLUTION OF STABILIZATION POLICY

The most controversial of the possible goals of economic policy is the stabilization of the level of economic activity. In Chapter 30 we saw that economists do not agree on why economic activity fluctuates or on what to do about it. In this chapter we shall look at the evolution of the theory and of the practice of stabilization policy.

We shall divide the differing views on stabilization policy into two broad and opposing schools of thought—*Keynesian* and *Monetarist*. This division is not entirely fair: There is considerable diversity of opinion within each school, and many economists really belong to neither. However, framing the debate in these terms helps to bring out the basic issues.

After examining the two schools' basic positions on stabilization policy, we shall look at the implementation of stabilization policy in the United States and at its results. The lessons that have been learned from this experience have given rise to additional schools of thought—the *New Classical* school, and the *New Keynesian* school.

| 31.1 | THE KEYNESIAN VIEW OF STABILIZATION POLICY

Before the Great Depression most respectable economists thought the economy was inherently stable and believed government intervention to be unnecessary.[1] In his *General Theory of Employment, Interest and Prices*, published in 1936, Keynes presented a very different view. He argued that the economy was inherently *un*stable and that therefore there was a need for a government policy to

---

[1] Some "cranks" outside the mainstream argued otherwise, but little attention was paid to them.

stabilize it. By 1946 this Keynesian view had become the official policy of the U.S. government. The Employment Act of that year instructed the government to pursue a goal of "high employment consistent with a stable price level."

The Keynesian view of stabilization was molded by the catastrophic economic breakdown of the Great Depression. Keynesians attribute that collapse to a major fall in investment, the result in turn of a failure of business confidence. The fall in investment reduced incomes, which further reduced spending. A downward spiral of falling income and falling expenditure left the economy in a state of massive unemployment with no clear end in sight.

The lesson Keynesians distilled from this traumatic episode was that demand shocks, like a reduced desire to invest, can be magnified by an essentially unstable economy into much larger movements of aggregate demand. These movements result in large changes in output and employment. Keynesians believe such fluctuations in output and employment to be undesirable. They also believe them to be preventable, because the initial demand shock can be offset by economic policy. For example, if business investment falters, the slack can be taken up by an increase in government spending. In this way the downward spiral can be stopped before it gets started. Let us use the circular flow model to look more closely at the problem and at the proposed solution.

THE NATURE OF THE PROBLEM

Exhibit 31.1 illustrates the Keynesian story in terms of the circular flow model of our fictitious Island economy.[2] A failure of business confidence makes investment less attractive. As a result, the demand for loanable funds shifts to the left from D_0^F to D_1^F. Firm borrowing and investment expenditure fall by $40 million and the interest rate falls from 20% to 10%. Household lending falls by the same $40 million. Because of the fall in the interest rate, households save less and consume more: Consumption expenditure increases by $10 million. Also because of the fall in the interest rate, the opportunity cost of holding money falls, and households increase their asset balances of money by $30 million. So total expenditure falls by $30 million—the $40 million fall in investment less the $10 million increase in consumption. Lower total expenditure this period means lower income next period. Because of their lower incomes, households will consume less, causing total expenditure to fall even further in a downward spiral.[3]

[2]For the sake of simplicity, we shall use the closed economy model of Chapter 24 rather than the open economy model of Chapter 25. The government budget is initially assumed to be balanced, so that the government is not borrowing.

[3]We saw the outcome of this downward spiral in the multiplier process of Chapter 26.

EXHIBIT 31.1

A FALL IN INVESTMENT UNDER KEYNESIAN ASSUMPTIONS

A fall in the desire to invest reduces the demand for loanable funds. The interest rate falls, as do borrowing and lending. As a result of the fall in interest rate, consumption and asset balances rise. Total expenditure falls, reducing the next month's income and leading to further falls in expenditure.

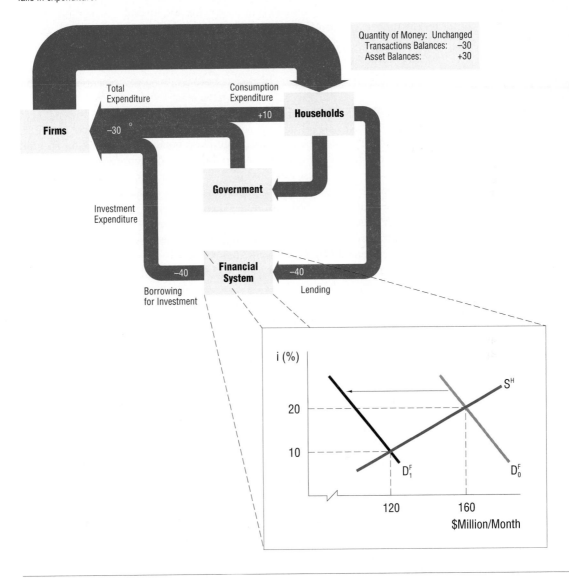

THE ROLE OF FISCAL POLICY

A simple way to prevent the downward spiral is to have the government offset the fall in investment with an increase in its own expenditure financed by borrowing. The effect is shown in Exhibit 31.2. As firms' demand for loanable funds falls from D_0^F to D_1^F, government expenditure increases by the same amount, so that $D_1^F + D^G = D_0^F$. Although firm borrowing and investment expenditure fall by $60 million, government borrowing and expenditure rise by the same amount. Therefore total borrowing and lending and the interest rate remain the same, and so does total expenditure. With no change in total expenditure, there is no downward spiral.

THE ROLE OF MONETARY POLICY

Could monetary policy be used instead of fiscal policy to prevent a fall in total expenditure? The answer depends on two things: (1) the sensitivity of investment expenditure to the interest rate, and (2) the sensitivity of the demand for asset balances to the interest rate. Keynesians assume that investment is *not* very sensitive to the interest rate and that money demand *is* quite sensitive.

Under these Keynesian assumptions, monetary policy is relatively ineffective. First, because investment is not very sensitive to the interest rate, the interest rate needs to be brought down a lot to revive investment. At best, this requires a very large monetary expansion; at worst, it might be impossible to bring the interest rate down far enough to do any good. Second, as the interest rate falls, because of the significant sensitivity of the demand for asset balances, there is a substantial increase in the demand for money. This makes it harder for monetary policy to bring the interest rate down: The new bank lending is largely offset by a fall in household lending as households add to their asset balances.

Under the same assumptions that render monetary policy ineffective, fiscal policy works well. In principle, government borrowing raises the interest rate. As the interest rate rises, investment falls, so total expenditure rises by less than the increase in government spending. This is called **crowding out**. For example, comparing Exhibit 31.2 to Exhibit 31.1, we see that government borrowing raises the interest rate from 10% to 20%, and investment consequently falls by $60 million rather than by the original $40 million. So government expenditure crowds out an extra $20 million of investment. Consequently, it takes a $60 million increase in government expenditure to offset the original $40 million fall in investment.

Under the Keynesian assumptions, crowding out will not be too severe a problem. If the demand for money is highly sensitive to the interest rate, then as interest rates rise, households will reduce their asset balances and add to their lending. Therefore government borrowing will not raise the interest rate as much. Moreover, because investment is not very sensitive to the interest rate, whatever rise there is will not reduce investment a great deal.

Monetary policy can minimize the extent of crowding out by preventing interest rates from rising. This is called the **monetary accommodation of fiscal**

crowding out
Reduction in the amount of investment owing to government borrowing.

monetary accommodation of fiscal policy
A monetary policy that minimizes the effect of fiscal policy on interest rates.

EXHIBIT 31.2

OFFSETTING A FALL IN INVESTMENT EXPENDITURE WITH AN
INCREASE IN GOVERNMENT EXPENDITURE

The fall in the demand for loanable funds is offset by an increase in government borrowing. Since the rise in government expenditure offsets the fall in investment, there is no change in total expenditure.

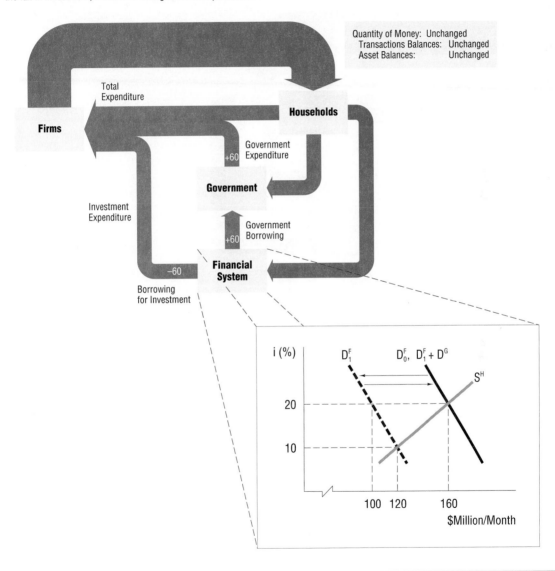

EXHIBIT 31.3

FISCAL POLICY WITH MONETARY ACCOMMODATION

Monetary accommodation of the fiscal expansion reduces the rise in the interest rate and the consequent crowding out. Total expenditure is stabilized with a smaller increase in government expenditure.

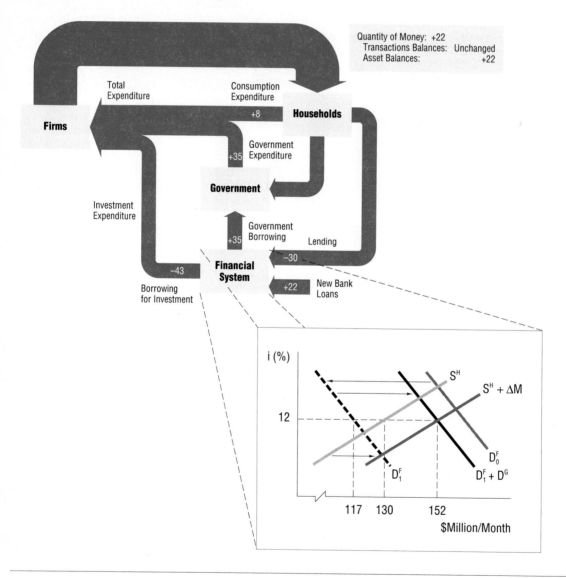

policy. The results of such monetary accommodation are shown in Exhibit 31.3. In addition to the increase in government deficit spending of $35 million, a monetary expansion adds $22 million of new bank loans to the loanable funds market. Compared to the case of Exhibit 31.2, there is a smaller increase in the

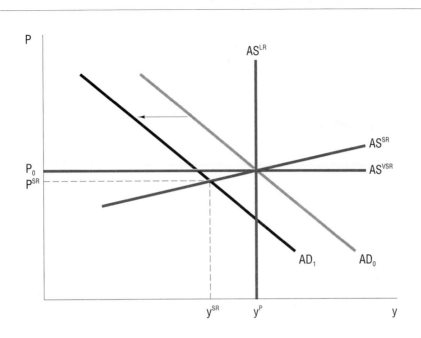

EXHIBIT 31.4

THE KEYNESIAN
ASSUMPTION ABOUT
AGGREGATE SUPPLY

Under the Keynesian
assumption that the short-run
aggregate supply curve is
relatively flat, changes in
aggregate demand have a large
effect on output and a small
effect on the price level.

demand for loanable funds and an increase in supply. As a result, the interest rate rises much less—to 12% rather than to 20%, and there is therefore much less crowding out. Investment is $117 million rather than $100 million. As you can see, when there is monetary accommodation, *less* fiscal expansion is needed to achieve the same degree of stabilization: Here, total expenditure is stabilized by a $35 million fiscal expansion rather than by the $60 million required in Exhibit 31.2 when there was no monetary accommodation. So even if monetary policy is not a substitute for fiscal policy, it can be a useful complement.

If the role of monetary policy is to accommodate fiscal policy, then the appropriate *target* is the interest rate. If the central bank targets the interest rate, monetary policy will ease automatically to prevent a rise in the interest rate caused by an increase in government borrowing.

AGGREGATE SUPPLY

We have seen how changes in the desire to invest can have large effects on total expenditure and how fiscal policy and monetary policy can be used to offset those effects. But fluctuations in total expenditure really matter only if they result in fluctuations in output and employment. Whether they do or not depends on aggregate supply.

We saw in Chapter 27 that a change in total expenditure moves the aggregate demand curve along the aggregate supply curve as shown in Exhibit 31.4. The result is a change in output and a change in the price level. How much there is of each depends on the slope of the aggregate supply curve. If it is flat, most of the effect will be on output. If it is steep, most of the effect will be on the price level.

Most economists agree that in the very short run the aggregate supply curve is flat (AS^{VSR}) and that in the very long run it is vertical (AS^{LR}). The more controversial question is: How steep is the short-run aggregate supply curve (AS^{SR})? That is, how steep is the aggregate supply curve over a period of a year or two? The Keynesian assumption is that the short-run aggregate supply curve is flat enough so that fluctuations in spending can have significant effects on output and employment. Therefore some sort of stabilization policy is necessary to prevent such fluctuations.

To summarize, the *Keynesian assumptions* are as follows:

1. Investment is *not* very sensitive to the interest rate.
2. Money demand *is* quite sensitive to the interest rate.
3. The short-run aggregate supply curve is fairly flat.

Under these Keynesian assumptions, changes in the desire to invest can cause large fluctuations in total expenditure, and these result in large fluctuations in output and employment. Fiscal policy is effective in offsetting such fluctuations. Monetary policy alone is not effective, but it can be useful as a complement to fiscal policy.

31.2 | THE MONETARIST VIEW

The *Monetarist assumptions* are just the reverse of the Keynesian assumptions:

1. Investment *is* sensitive to the interest rate.
2. Money demand is *not* very sensitive to the interest rate.
3. The short-run aggregate supply curve is fairly steep.

IS STABILIZATION NECESSARY?

Under Monetarist assumptions, changes in the desire to invest will have much less of an impact on total expenditure. This is illustrated in Exhibit 31.5. Because investment is more sensitive to the interest rate, the demand for loanable funds, D^F, is drawn flatter than it is in Exhibit 31.1. A given change in interest rate will have a greater effect on the amount of loanable funds demanded for investment. Because the demand for money is not very sensitive to the interest rate, the supply of loanable funds is drawn steeper. A fall in the interest rate will not increase the demand for asset balances much and so will not much reduce the amount of loanable funds supplied. As a result of these differences, the interest rate falls to 15% instead of to 10%, and the amount of borrowing and lending falls by $10 million instead of by $40 million. Asset balances increase by only $5 million

EXHIBIT 31.5

A FALL IN INVESTMENT UNDER MONETARIST ASSUMPTIONS

Under Monetarist assumptions about the sensitivity of investment and of money demand to the interest rate, a fall in the desire to invest has a smaller effect on the interest rate, on borrowing and lending, and on total expenditure.

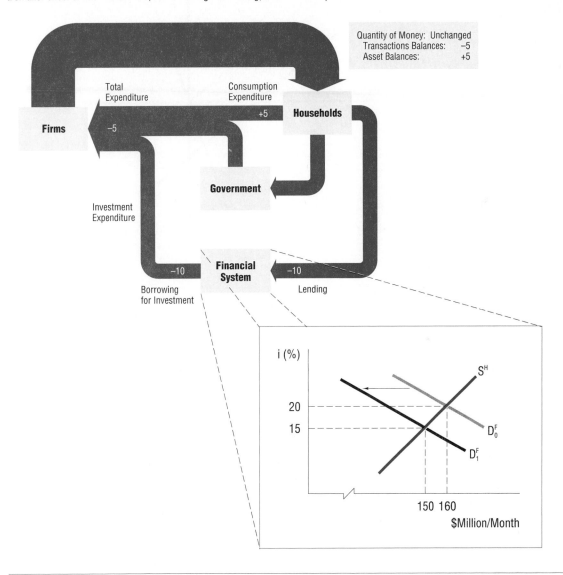

instead of the $30 million of Exhibit 31.1. Therefore total expenditure falls by $5 million rather than by the $30 million it fell under the Keynesian assumptions.

E X H I B I T 31.6

THE MONETARIST
ASSUMPTION ABOUT
AGGREGATE SUPPLY

Under the Monetarist
assumption that the short-run
aggregate supply curve is
relatively steep, changes in
aggregate demand mainly
affect the price level, with
relatively little effect on output.

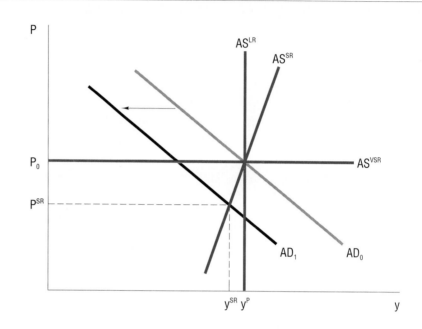

Not only will total expenditure fall less under the Monetarist assumptions, but a given fall in total expenditure will have less of an effect on output and employment. This is illustrated in Exhibit 31.6. Because the short-run aggregate supply curve, AS^{SR}, is fairly steep, the shift in aggregate demand—anyhow smaller than under Keynesian assumptions—mainly affects the price level and has little effect on output and employment.

FISCAL AND MONETARY POLICY UNDER MONETARIST ASSUMPTIONS

Under the Monetarist assumptions, the relative effectiveness of fiscal and monetary policy is reversed: Fiscal policy is weak and monetary policy is powerful.

Fiscal policy is weak because of crowding out. Government borrowing raises the interest rate significantly: Because money demand is insensitive to the interest rate, there is little offsetting increase in household lending as interest rates rise. Because investment is sensitive to the interest rate, the increase in the interest rate reduces investment substantially. Because the fall in investment largely offsets the increase in government expenditure, there is little effect on total expenditure.

Monetary policy, in contrast, is powerful. Because investment is sensitive to the interest rate, the interest rate needs to be lowered relatively little to stimulate investment. So only a small monetary expansion is required. Since money demand is not very sensitive to the interest rate, monetary expansion will not be "wasted" on increasing asset balances and will therefore be relatively effective in lowering the interest rate.

Note that a fiscal policy accommodated by monetary policy will be effective under *both* sets of assumptions. Under Keynesian assumptions, it is fiscal policy that does most of the work; monetary policy plays only a secondary role in preventing a rise in interest rates and the consequent crowding out. Under Monetarist assumptions, it is monetary policy that is doing most of the work: Since *most* of the fiscal expansion is offset by crowding out, preventing crowding out is no secondary matter—it is everything.

31.3 STABILIZATION POLICY IN THE UNITED STATES

Stabilization policy in the United States goes back to the Great Depression. As we shall see, the record of stabilization policy sheds some light on the debate between Keynesians and Monetarists and reveals some additional problems with such a policy.

FISCAL POLICY

The Roosevelt administration came to office in 1933 at the height of the Great Depression. It adopted an extensive program of public works, funded by government borrowing, in an attempt to revive the economy. That policy proved partially successful, but it was not until the massive government spending of World War II that the health of the economy was fully restored.[4]

The Employment Act of 1946 officially adopted a Keynesian view of the government's responsibility to stabilize the economy and to fight unemployment. However, it had little impact initially on economic policy. The Eisenhower administration (1953–1961) was not sympathetic to the Keynesian point of view and favored a conservative fiscal policy, trying to keep budgets balanced. It made no deliberate fiscal response to the two recessions of 1953–1954 and 1958, leaving office with the economy sluggish and unemployment high.

The Kennedy administration, which came to office in 1961, was much more sympathetic to Keynesian ideas. Indeed, several of Kennedy's economic advisers were prominent Keynesians. By June 1962 the administration had decided to stimulate the economy through a deliberate increase in deficit spending. This was to be done by cutting taxes with no cut in expenditure. Although many in the administration would have preferred an increase in spending to a tax cut, the latter seemed politically more expedient, and the needed 40% increase in govern-

---

[4]Roosevelt's New Deal was "Keynesian" before Keynes. Roosevelt was not, in fact, much influenced by the ideas of Keynes himself.

ment spending would have taken a long time to implement. The president announced his new policy in a commencement speech at Yale, in which he attacked traditional notions of fiscal responsibility and "persistent, persuasive, and unrealistic myths" relating to deficit spending. The tax cut became law in 1964. Government spending and deficits continued to rise through the 1960s under subsequent administrations as a result of the Vietnam War and the Great Society social programs.

MONETARY POLICY

During World War II the Fed pegged interest rates on Treasury securities to keep down the interest burden of war finance.[5] Wage and price controls kept the price level from rising as a consequence of the resulting monetary expansion. At the end of the war the Treasury resisted any suggestion that the Fed stop pegging interest rates. Higher interest rates would have raised the cost of government borrowing.

As a result of renewed government deficits during the Korean War, now without wage and price controls, prices began to rise rapidly. So in March 1951, at the urging of a Fed increasingly worried about inflation, an agreement was reached that freed the Fed from any further obligation to peg interest rates. That agreement is known as the **Treasury–Federal Reserve Accord.**

Treasury–Federal Reserve Accord
1951 agreement that freed the Fed from its obligation to peg interest rates on Treasury securities.

After 1953 the Fed pursued a somewhat ill-defined policy of stabilization. It used an array of measures to evaluate economic activity and inflationary pressures. In the 1950s and early 1960s its target was bank lending. (In terms of our discussion in Chapter 30, this is equivalent to a monetary-growth target.) When the economy was weak, the Fed would ease by adding reserves to stimulate bank lending; when the economy was strong, the Fed would tighten by slowing reserve growth to reduce bank lending.[6] The System Account Manager conducted open market operations to achieve a target level of reserves. However, he also kept an eye on the T-bill rate and on "money market conditions"—the rates on dealer loans and their availability—because high T-bill rates or poor availability of dealer loans might suggest that reserves were actually tighter than they seemed.

The fed funds rate started to play a role in monetary policy in the 1960s as the fed funds market grew in importance and as large banks came to rely increasingly on liability management to manage their reserve positions. By the late 1960s the Fed had lost faith in targeting bank credit and reserve position because their connection with overall economic activity had become increasingly unpredictable. The fed funds rate slowly replaced them as the target of monetary policy.

From the late 1960s until 1979, the Fed pegged the fed funds rate within a narrow range (as little as 1/4 of 1%), moving the target range up or down to

---

[5]Three-eighths of 1% on T-bills, 2.5% on long-term bonds.

[6]The measure of reserves the Fed used was *free reserves*—excess reserves less borrowing from the discount window.

tighten or ease monetary policy. Because these movements tended to be small, the fed funds rate generally trailed changes in the economy. When the economy slowed, it took a long time for the Fed to bring the rate down; when the economy quickened, it took a long time for the Fed to raise the rate.

This type of monetary policy—an **interest-rate peg**—fits in quite well with Keynesian ideas since it has the effect of *automatically* accommodating changes in fiscal policy. As deficits increased with the Kennedy tax cuts or with the financing of the Vietnam War, interest rates were not allowed to rise (or rose less): Monetary expansion provided the extra lending needed to keep interest rates from rising.

Note that pegging the interest rate in this way is more than just having an interest-rate target. Of course, an interest-rate peg does involve having an interest-rate target, but it also involves a reluctance to *change* the level of the target in response to changing circumstances.

This combination of fiscal and monetary policy provided little evidence as to whether Monetarists or Keynesians were right about the relative effectiveness of the two types of policy. To determine that, we would need a pure fiscal policy or a pure monetary policy: Both schools agree that fiscal policy with monetary accommodation should be effective, even though they differ as to why. But monetary accommodation was precisely what happened in this period, providing little evidence as to which view was correct. However, the 1960s and 1970s did teach some other lessons about stabilization policy that were quite valuable.[7]

interest-rate peg
A monetary policy that pegs interest rates at a fixed level.

31.4 SOME PRACTICAL PROBLEMS

The experience of the 1960s and 1970s revealed some serious difficulties with the practical implementation of stabilization policy.

TIMING

Timing is the key to successful stabilization. The aim is to offset fluctuations in other sectors with immediate changes in the government budget so that aggregate demand is stabilized. That turns out to be a lot harder than it sounds, because a number of lags in the process make it hard to react in time:

- *Data lag*: It takes time to gather the numbers that describe the state of the economy. Figures on GNP, the most common measure of output, are published at the end of each quarter but are then revised several times as additional information comes in. The final numbers are often very different from the initial estimates.

---

[7]In Chapter 32 we shall see that the evidence of the 1980s has been more informative about the relative effectiveness of the two types of policy.

- *Recognition lag*: Suppose that GNP numbers are down. Is this a real weakening of the economy or just a random blip that will be reversed next quarter? We will have to wait to find out. In reality, recessions often go unnoticed until they are over. For example, a serious downturn began in November 1973 and ended in March 1975. However, as late as January 1974 the president's Council of Economic Advisers did not know the economy was in trouble and indeed did not even believe there was any *prospect* of a recession. By August of that year the chairman of the Fed recognized that a recession was taking place but informed Congress it was probably already at an end. In actuality, the economy was only half way into its most severe contraction since the Great Depression.

- *Implementation lag*: Fiscal policy involves changes in federal taxes or spending. These take time to get through Congress. For example, it took three years to get the Kennedy tax cuts into law. Monetary policy, however, can react more quickly.

- *Effectiveness lag*: Once a policy is implemented, it may take considerable time to achieve the desired effects. The economy may not respond immediately to an easing in monetary policy or to fiscal stimulus.

HOW MUCH STIMULUS OR RESTRAINT?

Supposing we could get the timing right, how *much* stimulus or restraint is needed to offset a recessionary or inflationary tendency in the economy? Should taxes be cut by $1 billion, $10 billion, or $100 billion? Should the Fed sell $10 million in Treasury securities or $10 billion? Since we do not want to under- or over-compensate, getting the amount of stimulus right is very important.

To help them decide on the size of the appropriate policy response, policymakers rely on *econometric models*. These models take a theoretical framework of the type we have been using and try to make it operational.[8] Statistical methods are used to calibrate the model to the observed behavior of the economy. The calibrated model is then used to predict the effects of particular policy actions.

There are a number of difficulties in going from a simple theoretical model to a useful econometric model. The U.S. economy is much more complex than that of our fictitious South Seas island. These complexities must be taken into account. Defining and measuring variables is a problem. We have seen, for example, that the quantity of money is a slippery concept. The theory is usually not sufficiently detailed. For example, adjustment processes are important, but the theory usually tells us only the final position and has little to say on how we get there.

---

[8]Most rely on the ISLM model of Chapter 26, although some rely on the Modern Quantity Theory of Chapter 27.

The economists who build econometric models have to do the best they can to make up for these deficiencies. This requires them, for example, to make decisions about definitions of variables and assumptions about adjustment processes. Different economists, even when they agree about the basic theory, will make different decisions and assumptions. Consequently, the econometric models they construct will differ enormously in their predictions about the effects of economic policy. Of course, disagreement about the basic theory will lead to even wider differences. Obviously, they cannot all be right. This lack of consensus makes it hard to have much confidence in any particular model's predictions, and no one model has a consistently good track record. Not knowing the exact effect of policy actions makes effective stabilization difficult.[9]

These technical difficulties—the lags and the difficulty of knowing how much stimulus or restraint to apply—were not a serious problem in the depths of the Great Depression. The need for stimulus was clear, and overstimulus seemed a remote danger. With milder fluctuations, however, these technical difficulties become more of an obstacle. A policy intended to offset mildly the downward pressure of a recession may instead reinforce strongly the upward pressure of the subsequent boom.

Monetarists argue that, because of these difficulties, attempts to **fine-tune** the economy in this way are more likely to do harm than good. In their view the record shows that attempts to stabilize the economy have, on the whole, destabilized it. Keynesians are more optimistic. Citing the Kennedy tax cuts as an example, they believe that stabilization can work despite the difficulties: The economy certainly picked up steam in the late 1960s after the tax cuts.

fine-tune
To stabilize an economy by continuous, small-scale fiscal and monetary manipulations.

31.5 | AN INFLATIONARY BIAS?

In the 1960s and 1970s Keynesian ideas about fiscal policy gained ground and a quasi-Keynesian monetary policy of pegging the interest rate came into being. In this policy environment, growing government expenditure and a series of supply shocks led to increasing inflation. Monetarists believe this to be no accident: They believe that Keynesian policy has an inherent inflationary bias.

THE POLITICS OF STABILIZATION

One reason for the inflationary bias is political. In principle, stabilization requires stimulus at some times and restraint at others. On average and over time, the two should roughly balance out. Unfortunately, stimulus is politically much more popular than restraint. It is much easier for Congress to approve a tax cut or an

---

[9]Predicting the effect of a change in policy is called *conditional prediction.* Econometric models are much more successful at *unconditional prediction*—the prediction of economic variables assuming a continuation of current policies and trends.

increase in spending than to approve a tax increase or a cut in spending. Similarly, the Fed is everyone's friend when it lowers interest rates, but it faces a lot of criticism when it raises them. As a result, there tends to be a good deal more stimulus than restraint.

Moreover, Keynesian ideas about fiscal policy give politicians an excuse for fiscal deficits. Once the "persistent, persuasive, and unrealistic myths" about deficit spending have been laid to rest, politicians are free to spend without raising taxes. In the late 1960s and early 1970s, spending increased rapidly with the escalation of the Vietnam War and the beginning of a host of new social programs. The government was slow to increase taxes, and instead increased its borrowing.[10] The Fed, following its policy of accommodation through pegging the interest rate, slowed any resulting rise in interest rates by monetary expansion. The monetary expansion led to steadily increasing inflation.

SUPPLY SHOCKS

The Keynesian view of the world stresses the destabilizing effects of demand shocks—for instance, a change in the desire to invest. But, as we saw in Chapter 27, there are also supply shocks.

The effect of a supply shock depends on the nature of monetary policy. This is illustrated in Exhibit 31.7. A negative supply shock—for example, the OPEC oil-price shock of 1973—shifts the aggregate supply curve to the left from AS_0 to AD_1. (Since costs are higher, less output is produced by firms at any level of prices.)

If monetary policy is targeting monetary growth, there is no monetary response and therefore no change in aggregate demand. The aggregate demand curve remains at AD_0, and the result is a rise in prices from P_0 to P_1 and a fall in output from y_0 to y_1. This is the case we looked at in Section 27.4.

Suppose, instead, that monetary policy is pegging the interest rate. Because rising prices tend to raise the interest rate, increased monetary expansion is needed to keep it down.[11] The monetary expansion increases total expenditure, shifting the aggregate demand curve to the right from AD_0 to AD_1. As a result, there is less of an effect on output (in Exhibit 31.7 output remains at y_0) and more of an effect on the price level: Prices rise to P_2 rather than P_1. Such a policy is described as *accommodating* the supply shock.[12]

Is accommodation the right policy response to a supply shock? It is clear that a supply shock requires the economy to make difficult adjustments. A good policy will make those adjustments as easy as possible. Accommodation certainly reduces the *immediate* effect on output and employment. But it does so at the cost

---

[10]Despite warnings from many economists, including Keynesians.

[11]In terms of the circular flow model, the higher prices increase the demand for nominal loanable funds. In terms of the ISLM model, the higher price level shifts the LM curve to the left (see the Appendix to Chapter 27).

[12]There are obvious parallels to accommodating a change in fiscal policy.

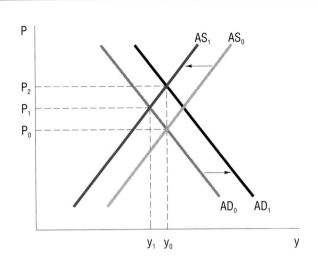

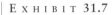

EXHIBIT 31.7

EFFECTS OF A SUPPLY SHOCK

A supply shock moves the aggregate supply curve to the left. Monetary accommodation increases aggregate demand, reducing the effect of the supply shock on output but increasing the effect on the price level.

of increased inflation. If the increased inflation requires a tightening of monetary policy later to control it, then the pain is merely being deferred. Keynesians generally favor at least some accommodation, arguing that it is better to give the economy more time to adjust. Monetarists see no advantage in gradual adjustment and are more concerned than Keynesians about the cost in terms of inflation.

With both the first OPEC oil-price shock in 1973 and the second in 1979 (the latter the result of the Iran-Iraq war and the Iranian revolution), monetary accommodation in the United States reduced the immediate effect on output and employment. However, in both cases the consequent inflation had to be restrained with a severe tightening of monetary policy, resulting in two very serious recessions.[13]

EXPORTING INFLATION AND THE COLLAPSE OF BRETTON WOODS

The rising inflation in the United States led to the collapse of the Bretton Woods system of fixed exchange rates that had been in place since World War II.[14] Under that system the values of the currencies of the major industrial countries were

---

[13]The monetary accommodation of both government deficits and supply shocks provides good examples of how monetary expansion is necessary for inflation, even when it is not the immediate cause. See Chapter 28 for further discussion.

[14]See the Appendix to Chapter 25.

fixed in terms of the dollar, and the dollar was convertible into gold at a fixed price of $35 an ounce. The Bretton Woods system was designed to replace the currency chaos of the interwar years with an environment in which exchange-rate risk was minimized and trade could therefore flourish. The system worked well from 1946, when it was instituted, until rising U.S. inflation in the late 1960s placed it under intolerable strain.

In Chapter 28 we saw how inflation affects the exchange rate when the exchange rate is freely floating. The relationship is

$$\text{rate of change of ¥/\$ exchange rate} = \text{¥ inflation rate} - \text{\$ inflation rate.} \quad [31.1]$$

Thus under a freely floating exchange rate the higher rate of inflation in the United States in the 1960s would have led to a depreciation of the dollar against other countries.

Under the fixed exchange rates of the Bretton Woods system, however, other countries were committed to maintain their exchange rate with the U.S. dollar. For example, to prevent the yen from appreciating against the dollar, the Bank of Japan was obliged to intervene in the foreign-exchange market and buy dollars for yen. As we saw in Chapter 20, such purchases of foreign exchange have the same effect on bank reserves as open market purchases of government securities. Hence the efforts of foreign governments to prevent their currencies from appreciating against the dollar led to more rapid monetary expansion in those countries and to increased inflation there. From Equation 31.1, once the inflation rate in Japan equals that in the United States, there is no longer any tendency for the yen to appreciate. Causing inflation in this way, by defending a fixed exchange rate in the face of inflation abroad, is called *importing inflation.*

As a result of their intervention to prevent their currencies from appreciating, foreign central banks found themselves accumulating more dollars than they really wanted. Under the Bretton Woods rules, they were allowed to convert these unwanted dollars into gold. Indeed, gold was a bargain: Its nominal price had remained at $35 an ounce despite the rise in the dollar price level, so its real price had declined substantially. As foreign central banks converted more and more dollars into gold, it became clear that the situation could not continue: Fort Knox would soon be empty. In 1971 President Nixon suspended convertibility of the dollar into gold. By 1973 attempts to maintain fixed exchange rates had largely been abandoned, and exchange rates were allowed to fluctuate freely with relatively little intervention by central banks.

The abandonment of fixed exchange rates was viewed with favor by most economists. Floating exchange rates would enable each country to control its own inflation rate, independently of the monetary policies of others.

EXHIBIT 31.8

PHILLIPS CURVE, 1956–1969

The data for this period seem to show a fairly stable relationship between inflation and unemployment.

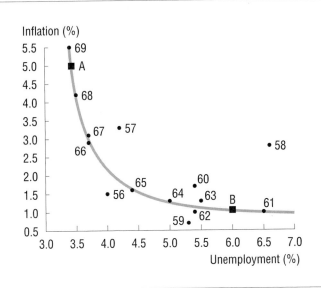

Source: *Economic Report of the President.*

31.6 A TRADEOFF BETWEEN INFLATION AND UNEMPLOYMENT?

As the inflationary consequences of Keynesian policies became increasingly clear, the Keynesian response was to justify the inflation as a necessary price for lower unemployment. Inflation is bad, they argued, but unemployment is worse.

Keynesian economists postulated the existence of a "tradeoff" between inflation and unemployment: Higher inflation bought lower unemployment. They argued that it was worth a little inflation to keep unemployment down. The postulated tradeoff was based on a historical relationship between wage inflation and unemployment published by A. W. Phillips in 1958. A **Phillips curve** for the United States for the 1948–1969 period is shown in Exhibit 31.8. The curve shows that when unemployment is high, prices tend to rise more slowly, and that when unemployment is low, they tend to rise faster.[15]

The Phillips curve was believed by Keynesians to present policymakers with a menu of choices. By choosing a particular rate of growth of aggregate demand, policy could pick a particular combination of inflation and unemployment on the Phillips curve. A policymaker who favored low unemployment could choose a point on the Phillips curve like *A* in Exhibit 31.8. At that point unemployment is low (about 3.5%), but there is some inflation (about 5%). A policymaker who

Phillips curve
Graphical representation of the relationship between inflation and unemployment.

[15]The original Phillips curve had wage inflation on the vertical axis rather than price inflation, but the two are roughly equivalent.

found this level of inflation too high could choose a point like B, at which inflation is lower (about 1%). However, the cost of this lower inflation would be higher unemployment (about 6%).

An appropriate combination of fiscal policy and monetary accommodation would bring the economy to the desired point. Moving up the Phillips curve, say, from B to A, required boosting aggregate demand through increased government spending or a tax cut accommodated by an easy monetary policy. Moving down the Phillips curve, say, from A to B, required restraining aggregate demand through cuts in government spending, higher taxes, and monetary tightening.

The Keynesian preference was for a point like A: Unemployment was seen as the greater evil. Monetarists, seeing inflation as the greater evil, were invited to pick a point like B. The Monetarists, however, refused to play. Instead of picking a point, they cast doubt on the whole idea of a tradeoff between inflation and unemployment.

Friedman–Phelps critique
Argument that the Phillips-curve relationship relies on inflation being unanticipated.

THE FRIEDMAN–PHELPS CRITIQUE

The strongest objection to the idea of a tradeoff was raised independently by Milton Friedman and Edmund Phelps. Friedman and Phelps argued that the whole idea of the Phillips-curve tradeoff was flawed because it ignored expectations.

Friedman and Phelps interpreted the Phillips-curve relationship to be the result of the slowness of wages to adjust to changes in the price level. Firms set wages in nominal terms in wage contracts that run from one to several years. The nominal wage is generally set with some *real* wage in mind. For example, the intention might be to provide a real weekly wage of $w^* = 200$ base-period dollars—a wage that would buy the same goods and services that $200 bought in some base period. If the price level is expected to be $P^e = 1.2$ over the life of the contract, then the nominal wage, W, will be set at

$$W = P^e \times w^* = 1.2 \times 200 = \$240. \qquad [31.2]$$

The *actual* real wage that is paid and received, w, depends on what the price level, P, actually turns out to be. For example, suppose that inflation is higher than expected and that $P = 1.25$. Then the actual real wage is

$$w = \frac{W}{P} = \frac{\$240}{1.25} = 192 \text{ base-period dollars.} \qquad [31.3]$$

So unexpected inflation has the effect of reducing real wages. Because real wages are lower, firms are willing to hire more workers, reducing unemployment.

🌴 **CHECK STATION 1**   The intended real wage is 150 base-period dollars. If the price level is expected to be 2.0, what is the nominal wage? If the actual price level turns out to be 1.8, what is the actual real wage?

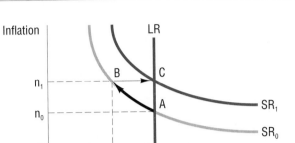

EXHIBIT 31.9

SHORT-RUN AND LONG-RUN PHILLIPS CURVES

An increase in inflation initially reduces unemployment, the economy moving from *A* to *B*. However, as the inflation comes to be anticipated, unemployment rises back to its original level and the economy moves from *B* to *C*.

Notice, though, that for unemployment to fall, the increase in the price level must be *unexpected*. If the price level had been expected to rise to 1.25, the wage contract would have taken this into account and set the nominal wage accordingly at W = 1.25 x 200 = $250.

If this view of the Phillips curve is correct, then the Phillips curve does not represent an exploitable tradeoff, at least in the long run. Stimulating aggregate demand will cause prices to rise. So long as the rise in prices comes as a surprise, real wages will fall and employment will increase. As people come to expect the inflation, however, it will be taken into account by wage agreements, and real wages and the unemployment rate will return to where they were before. Inflation buys increased employment only temporarily—so long as people are caught by surprise. Keeping unemployment below its normal level requires keeping people perpetually surprised.[16] That requires inflation always to be higher than expected and that means that the level of inflation must constantly be rising.

These ideas may be expressed in terms of short-run and long-run Phillips curves, as shown in Exhibit 31.9. Suppose the economy is initially at point A. A rate of inflation n_0 has obtained for some time and is fully anticipated in all contracts. Unemployment is at its normal level, u^n. Now suppose that expansionary fiscal and monetary policies raise the rate of inflation to n_1. For the reasons we discussed above, the unemployment rate falls to u_1. That is, the economy moves to point B along a *short-run* Phillips curve, labeled SR_0 in Exhibit 31.9. Over time, however, firms and workers come to expect the new, higher rate of inflation and to take it into account in setting wages. As a result, the economy moves back to point C with inflation at n_1 but unemployment back at its normal level u^n. Points A and C lie on the *long-run* Phillips curve, labeled *LR*, which is vertical. Now that an inflation rate of n_1 is anticipated, there is a new short-run Phillips curve, SR_1, that passes through point C.

[16]See Chapter 27 for an explanation of normal unemployment.

E X H I B I T 31.10

PHILLIPS CURVE,
1956–1989

After 1969, the seemingly
stable relationship between
inflation and unemployment
breaks down. Points for later
years do not lie on the curve
that fits the earlier data.

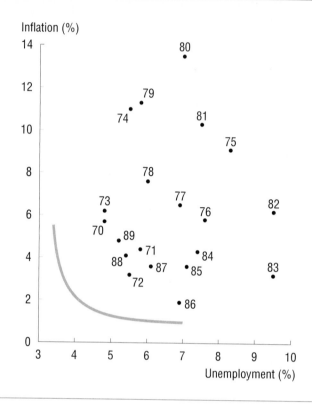

Source: *Economic Report of the President.*

As you can see from Exhibit 31.9, a prediction of the Friedman–Phelps theory is that the observed Phillips curve will move upward if there is a persistent rise in inflation. As Exhibit 31.10 shows, the experience of the 1970s bears out this prediction. The Phillips curve in Exhibit 31.10 is the same as in Exhibit 31.8. It corresponds to SR_0 in Exhibit 31.9. If there really does exist a stable tradeoff, then points for subsequent years should lie on this same curve. If, on the other hand, the Friedman–Phelps theory is correct, then as higher inflation comes to be anticipated, the curve itself will move upward, and the new points will lie above the original curve. That is what actually happened.

31.7 THE RATIONAL-EXPECTATIONS CRITIQUE OF STABILIZATION POLICY

rational-expectations critique
Argument that the effect of economic-policy actions depends on whether or not they are expected.

The Friedman–Phelps critique of the Phillips-curve tradeoff was extended by Robert Lucas, Thomas Sargent, and others into a much more general critique of Keynesian stabilization policy and of the sort of reasoning on which it was based. This has come to be known as the **rational-expectations critique.**

POLICY ACTIONS VERSUS POLICY RULES

The first element of the critique is an insistence that economic policy be evaluated in terms of **policy rules** rather than in terms of individual policy actions. In looking at the effects on the economy of an increase in deficit spending or an increase in the quantity of money, economists often used to analyze these actions as if they were taken in isolation. This is not realistic. Individual policy actions are usually taken in the context of some policy rule. The Fed does not ease or tighten monetary policy in an arbitrary or random way: It has some goal in mind. If that goal is stabilization, the Fed will ease monetary policy whenever the economy looks as if it is weakening. Or if the goal is stable prices, the Fed will tighten whenever inflation looks as if it is increasing.

policy rule
Consistent pattern in economic policy.

Placing the individual policy action in the context of a policy rule is important, because it tells us whether or not the action comes as a surprise. As we have seen in the case of the Friedman–Phelps critique of the "tradeoff," the consequences of a policy action may depend a great deal on whether or not it is expected. So if we ignore the policy-rule context when analyzing a tax cut or a monetary expansion, we are making the same sort of mistake as was made in postulating a Phillips-curve tradeoff.

THE IMPLICATIONS OF RATIONAL EXPECTATIONS

The second element of the rational-expectations critique is the assumption that expectations are rational: Firms and households take all available information into account when forming their expectations.[17] In particular, they will use what they know about the rule that is guiding economic policy. This means that most policy actions will *not* come as a surprise. For example, if the Fed eases monetary policy whenever the economy looks as if it is weakening, then at the first sign of weakening people will *expect* the Fed to ease policy. Because the easing is expected, its effect on the economy will be different from what it would have been had it come as a surprise.

A second consequence of rational expectations is that the same policy action may have quite different effects in the context of different policy rules. We saw an example of this when we looked at the expectations effect of a change in the quantity of money in Chapter 28. If the Fed is pursuing an interest-rate target, an announcement of larger than expected monetary growth should not affect people's expectations about short-term interest rates. However, if the Fed is following a monetary-growth target, the announcement of larger than expected monetary growth may suggest future tightening by the Fed to get monetary growth back on target. The result of this will be a rise in interest rates: The expectation of higher interest rates in the future will raise interest rates now.

---

[17]See the discussion of different types of expectations in Chapter 28.

THE LUCAS CRITIQUE OF ECONOMETRIC MODELS

The dependence of behavior on expectations and the dependence of expectations on policy rules have serious implications for the ability of econometric models to predict the effects of changes in economic policy. Econometric models are estimated from data gathered during a particular historical period when particular policy rules were in effect. An econometric model estimated under one rule is therefore of limited use in predicting the behavior of the economy under a different rule.

The Phillips-curve tradeoff is one example of this principle. The original Phillips curve was estimated from data gathered in a period in which policy did not take the Phillips curve into account and was not trying to exploit the implicit tradeoff between inflation and unemployment. When policy did try to exploit the tradeoff, expectations of inflation took this into account and the Phillips curve itself changed.

More generally, if the policy rule changes, the econometric *model* changes too. That is, if we recalibrate the model under the new policy rule, the results will be different. The shift in the Phillips curve is just one example of this more general phenomenon. Recognition of this fundamental problem with econometric models is known as the **Lucas critique**.

Lucas critique
Argument that an econometric model estimated under one policy rule will be of limited use in predicting the effects of a different policy rule.

IS POLICY INEFFECTIVE?

The rational-expectations critique has led some economists to doubt that policy can be of any use at all in stabilizing the economy. This view is based on theoretical results showing that in some economic models *no* anticipated policy can have any effect on the economy; only unanticipated policy can have an effect. Any policy conducted according to a rule will be anticipated and therefore ineffective. Only a policy that is random and arbitrary will be unanticipated and therefore have an effect. But such a random policy can only *reduce* the stability of the economy. Thus any attempt to stabilize the economy is futile. For example, anticipated changes in inflation should have no effect on unemployment, even in the short run (in other words, the short-run Phillips curve is vertical). This school of thought is known as the **New Classical Economics**.

New Classical Economics
School of economic thought that questions the ability of any economic policy to stabilize the economy.

Other economists do not accept that stabilization policy must necessarily be totally ineffective. They argue, backing up their argument with different economic models of their own, that even fully anticipated policy can have real effects on the economy. For example, because wages and prices are not changed continuously, even anticipated changes in inflation can have effects in the short run.[18] The school of economists that accepts the rational-expectations critique but believes nonetheless that stabilization is possible is known as the **New Keynesian Economics**.

New Keynesian Economics
School of economic thought that accepts the rational-expectations critique but also believes that economic policy can be effective.

[18]We saw another example in Chapter 28 when we noted that even a fully anticipated inflation will generally have real effects.

31.8 THE DISILLUSIONMENT WITH STABILIZATION POLICY

By the late 1970s, then, there was fairly wide disillusionment with simple Keynesian ideas about stabilization. On the one hand, the rational-expectations critique had cast serious doubts on the theoretical and econometric basis for such policies. On the other hand, the economy was performing increasingly poorly under policies that bore at least some resemblance to the Keynesian recipe. The time seemed ripe for a change in policy. It came in 1979. In the next chapter we shall see what the new policy was and how it fared.

SUMMARY

- Stabilization policy is controversial. Keynesians believe it is both necessary and feasible. Monetarists believe that it is unnecessary and unfeasible.

- Keynesians assume that investment is relatively insensitive to the interest rate and that money demand is sensitive to it. They also assume that the aggregate supply curve is flat in the short run.

- Under the Keynesian assumptions, a demand shock, such as a fall in the desire to invest, will reduce total expenditure and set off a spiral of falling income and expenditure. Output and employment will fall significantly.

- Total expenditure can be stabilized by offsetting fiscal expansion. Fiscal policy is potent under these assumptions.

- Under these same assumptions monetary policy is ineffective, although it can play a useful supporting role by accommodating fiscal policy and reducing crowding out.

- Monetarists assume that investment is sensitive to the interest rate and that money demand is not. They also assume that the short-run aggregate supply curve is steep.

- Under Monetarist assumptions, a demand shock has little effect on total expenditure and income, and even less on output and employment. Thus stabilization policy is unnecessary.

- Under these same assumptions, fiscal policy is ineffective and monetary policy is potent.

- The two main instances of deliberate fiscal expansion to stabilize the economy were the New Deal public-works programs and the Kennedy tax cuts.

- Monetary policy after World War II evolved into a policy of pegging the interest rate. This was consistent with the Keynesian view that the role of monetary policy is to accommodate fiscal policy.

- The proper timing of stabilization policy is difficult because of lags in data, recognition, implementation, and effectiveness. It is also difficult to gauge the proper amount of stimulus. Monetarists believe these difficulties make attempts to fine-tune the economy futile.

- Politically, expansion is more popular than contraction, and this gives stabilization policy an inflationary bias. Moreover, an interest-rate peg that accommodates fiscal policy also accommodates supply shocks, increasing their inflationary effect.

- The Bretton Woods system of fixed exchange rates led to the export of the U.S. inflation of the 1960s and 1970s to other countries. Under floating exchange rates, inflation in one country need not be affected by inflation in others.

- Keynesians saw in the Phillips curve a tradeoff between inflation and unemployment. Monetarists denied the existence of this tradeoff.

- Friedman and Phelps argued that because the Phillips-curve relationship relies on inflation being unanticipated, changes in inflation only reduce unemployment in the short run.

- The rational-expectations critique takes the Friedman-Phelps argument further. It argues that the effect of policy actions in general depends on whether or not they are anticipated.

- The two main elements of the rational-expectations critique is (1) an insistence that policy be examined in terms of policy rules rather than in terms of individual actions, and (2) an assumption that expectations are rational.

- The Lucas critique of econometric models implies that a model estimated under one policy rule will be of limited use in predicting the effects of a different policy rule.

- The New Classical Economics denies that anticipated policy can have any effect on the economy. The New Keynesian Economics accepts the rational-expectations critique but believes nonetheless that policy can be effective.

KEY TERMS

crowding out	fine-tune	policy rule
monetary accommodation of fiscal policy	Phillips curve	Lucas critique
Treasury–Federal Reserve Accord	Friedman–Phelps critique	New Classical Economics
interest-rate peg	rational-expectations critique	New Keynesian Economics

DISCUSSION QUESTIONS

1. Korea and Taiwan responded to the first OPEC price shock in very different ways. Korea followed an accommodating monetary policy; Taiwan did not accommodate. Use aggregate demand and aggregate supply curves to illus-

trate the different implications of the two policies. Which country would you expect to have had more of a problem with inflation?

2. Why do Monetarists believe that stabilization policy is unnecessary and impossible to carry out?

3. How do Monetarists and Keynesians differ in their assumptions about the economy? What are the implications of these different assumptions for (a) the stability of the economy in the face of demand shocks, (b) the relative effectiveness of fiscal and monetary policy, (c) the tradeoff between inflation and unemployment?

4. "The record of the 1960s and 1970s shows that the Keynesian policy prescription does not work." Discuss.

5. The payment of interest on checking deposits is permitted, and there is an increase in the demand for money. Compare the effect on the economy under Keynesian and Monetarist assumptions.

6. The Fed increases the quantity of money through open market operations. Compare the effect on the economy under Keynesian and Monetarist assumptions.

7. Under a system of fixed exchange rates, inflation in one country is exported to other countries. What effect will a recession in one country have on other countries?

8. In what ways do expectations affect the impact of economic policy? Give examples.

9. What is the difference between an interest-rate target and an interest-rate peg?

SOFTWARE EXERCISES FOR THIS CHAPTER

Title: Policy

This computer exercise challenges you to use the tools of monetary and fiscal policy to try to stabilize the economy. The exercise allows you to choose which goals to emphasize in your particular policy approach. See your instructor if you wish to use this program.

Title: Monkey

This computer exercise is a quiz that tests your knowledge of the Monetarist/ Keynesian debate. It should help you to sharpen your understanding of the differences between these two schools of thought. See your instructor if you wish to use this program.

BIBLIOGRAPHY

Fischer, Stanley, and Rudiger Dornbusch, *Macroeconomics*, New York: McGraw-Hill, 1987.

Friedman, Milton, and Anna Jacobson Schwartz, *A Monetary History of the United States 1867–1960*, Princeton: Princeton University Press, 1963.

Hall, Robert E., and John B. Taylor, *Macroeconomics: Theory, Performance, and Policy*, New York: Norton, 1988.

Laidler, David, "The Legacy of the Monetarist Controversy," *Review of the Federal Reserve Bank of St. Louis* March-April 1990, 49-64.

Lucas, Robert E., Jr., "Econometric Policy Evaluation: A Critique," *Carnegie Rochester Conference Series on Public Policy 5* (Autumn 1976), 19–46.

Lucas, Robert E., and Thomas J. Sargent, *After Keynesian Macroeconomics.* In *After the Phillips Curve: Persistence of High Inflation and High Unemployment*, Boston: Federal Reserve Bank of Boston, 1978, 49–72.

Meulendyke, Ann-Marie, "A Review of Federal Reserve Policy Targets and Operating Guides in Recent Decades, *FRBNY Quarterly Review* Autumn 1988, 6–17.

Sargent, Thomas J., "Rational Expectations and the Reconstruction of Macroeconomics," *Quarterly Review of the Federal Reserve Bank of Minneapolis 4* Summer 1980, 15–19.

Taylor, John B., *The Role of Rational Expectations in the Choice of Monetary Policy.* In *Monetary Policy Issues in the 1980s*, Kansas City: Federal Reserve Bank of Kansas City, 1982.

APPENDIX TO CHAPTER 31

THE KEYNESIAN–MONETARIST DEBATE IN TERMS OF THE ISLM MODEL

The effects of the differing Keynesian and Monetarist assumptions about the sensitivity to the interest rate of investment and of money demand can be expressed quite clearly in terms of the ISLM model.

From Chapter 26, the equation of the IS curve is

$$Y = \frac{1}{\{1 - b\,(1 - t) + g\}}\,[a + (c - d\,i) + \overline{G} + (f - h\,i)]. \qquad [31A.1]$$

The equation for the LM curve is

$$Y = \frac{M - (x - z\,i)}{k}. \qquad [31A.2]$$

(For an explanation of the various symbols, see Chapter 26.)

The sensitivity of investment to the interest rate is represented by the constant d in Equation 31A.1. Keynesians assume that d is small; Monetarists assume that it is large. As we saw in Chapter 26, anything that increases the number that multiplies the interest rate, i, in the IS curve makes it flatter. So the greater is d, the flatter is the IS curve. The sensitivity of money demand is represented by the constant z in Equation 31A.2. Keynesians assume that z is large; Monetarists assume that it is small. As we saw in Chapter 26, anything that increases the number that multiplies i in the LM curve makes it flatter. So the greater is z, the flatter is the LM curve.

We can therefore express the Keynesian and Monetarist assumptions in terms of their implications for the slopes of the two curves:

The Keynesian assumptions:

1. The IS curve is relatively steep.
2. The LM curve is relatively flat.

829

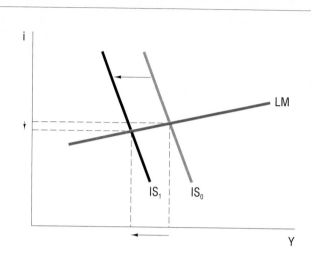

E X H I B I T 31A.1

A FALL IN THE
DESIRE TO INVEST:
THE KEYNESIAN
CASE

Under Keynesian assumptions,
a fall in the desire to invest
leads to a large reduction in
equilibrium income and a small
reduction in the equilibrium
interest rate.

The Monetarist assumptions:

1. The IS curve is relatively flat.
2. The LM curve is relatively steep.

Exhibit 31A.1 shows the IS and LM curves under Keynesian assumptions. Because of the relative steepness of the two curves, the shift to the right of the IS curve from IS_0 to IS_1 as a result of a fall in the desire to invest (a fall in autonomous expenditure) has a large effect on income and a small effect on the interest rate. For similar reasons, fiscal policy will have a large effect on income. Monetary policy moves the LM curve to the left or right. Given the relative slopes of the two curves, such movements will have little effect on either income or the interest rate.

Exhibit 31A.2 shows the IS and LM curves under Monetarist assumptions. The IS curve is now flat and the LM curve is steep. The IS curve shifts to the left in Exhibit 31A.2, as a result of a fall in the desire to invest, by exactly the same amount as it does in Exhibit 31A.1. However, because the relative steepness of the two curves is reversed, there is now a large effect on the interest rate and a small one on income. Similarly, fiscal policy now has little effect on income: Because of the steep LM curve, shifting the IS curve does not affect income much. On the other hand, monetary policy now has a substantial effect. Movements of the LM curve now have little effect on the interest rate and a large effect on income.

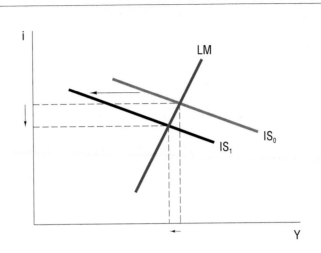

E X H I B I T 31A.2

A FALL IN THE
DESIRE TO INVEST:
THE MONETARIST
CASE

Under Monetarist assump-
tions, a fall in the desire to
invest has a larger effect on the
equilibrium interest rate and a
smaller effect on equilibrium
income.

CHAPTER 32

THE MONETARIST EXPERIMENT AND AFTER

During the 1960s and 1970s the Fed pegged the interest rate in a monetary policy that could be seen as Keynesian. Pegging the interest rate accommodates fiscal policy, which Keynesians see as the primary instrument of stabilization. As we saw in Chapter 31, Keynesian stabilization policy ran into increasing difficulties in the 1970s. By 1979 these difficulties had come to a head, and in October of that year there was a major change in policy. The Fed pursued the new policy, which could loosely be described as Monetarist, for three years, until increasing difficulties with its implementation caused the Fed to abandon it. Since 1982 the Fed has followed a more eclectic policy, not easily characterized as either Keynesian or Monetarist.

In this chapter we shall look at the events leading up to the Monetarist experiment of 1979–1982, at the nature of the new policy, and at the problems with its implementation. We shall then look at the nature of monetary policy since 1982, at how well it has fared, and at some issues of monetary policy that remain to be resolved.

32.1 THE CRISIS OF 1979

The goal of U.S. monetary policy in the late 1960s and 1970s was an uncertain mixture of stabilizing output and fighting inflation. The Fed generally pegged the interest rate, initially caring little about the rate of monetary growth that resulted. As the rate of inflation rose, monetary growth received increasing attention, until in 1975 a congressional resolution required the Fed to announce publicly its annual targets for monetary growth. The Fed, however, routinely failed to hit these targets. As a result, in the Humphrey–Hawkins Act of 1978, Congress required the chairman of the Board of Governors to appear before it twice yearly—in February to present and explain the Fed's monetary targets, and in July to report on how closely those targets were being met.

833

Given the accommodating nature of monetary policy, the first OPEC oil-price shock of 1973 resulted in a serious bout of inflation (see Exhibit 32.1A). Monetary tightening in 1974–1975 restrained the inflation, but it also caused a sharp recession. This experience left the Fed gun-shy. Consequently, when inflation began to rise again in 1978 (partly as the result of a second oil-price shock), the Fed slowed monetary growth only gradually to avoid precipitating another recession. As a result of this reluctance to tighten, monetary growth in early 1979 was running at over 10%, substantially above the target range of 3%–6%. In July inflation topped 13%.

Rising inflation and rapid monetary growth were not the only problems facing the Fed. There were also difficulties with the dollar. Recovery from the 1974–1975 recession had been more rapid in the United States than in Japan and Europe, and U.S. imports had expanded more rapidly than its exports, creating a trade deficit. This was also the period in which U.S. banks were rapidly increasing their overseas lending, putting pressure on the U.S. capital account. As a result of these pressures, the dollar fell from early 1977 to late 1978, particularly against the German mark, and stabilized only when foreign central banks intervened to prevent its further decline (see Exhibit 32.1B). By the summer of 1979 there was renewed downward pressure on the dollar.

In an attempt to restore international confidence in U.S. monetary policy and in the dollar, in July 1979 President Carter appointed Paul Volcker as the new chairman of the Board of Governors. At the time Volcker was president of the New York Fed, and it was well known that he had argued in the FOMC for more aggressive tightening, even at the cost of higher interest rates. Volcker was well known to the international financial community, having been Treasury undersecretary for monetary affairs during the transition from fixed to floating exchange rates in the early 1970s.

The immediate tightening that followed Volcker's appointment was not enough to satisfy the foreign central bankers who were propping up the value of the dollar. When Volcker met his foreign colleagues at a meeting of the International Monetary Fund in Belgrade in October 1979, they were outspoken in their criticism. Volcker hurried back to Washington and called an extraordinary weekend meeting of the FOMC. At that meeting the committee agreed unanimously on a major shift in monetary policy. There would be further tightening, but, far more important, there would also be a change in the way monetary policy was conducted. Instead of controlling monetary growth through an interest-rate target, the Fed would now target monetary growth directly.[1]

---

[1]The press release issued after the October 6 meeting listed the following changes: (1) An increase in the discount rate from 11% to 12%; (2) an 8% reserve requirement on managed liabilities, designed to slow bank lending; (3) "greater emphasis" on the growth of reserves, less on the federal funds rate (the federal funds rate would be allowed to fluctuate between 11.5% and 15.5%, a much wider range than the customary one of less than a single percentage point); (4) the discount rate would be managed to discourage excessive borrowing.

EXHIBIT 32.1

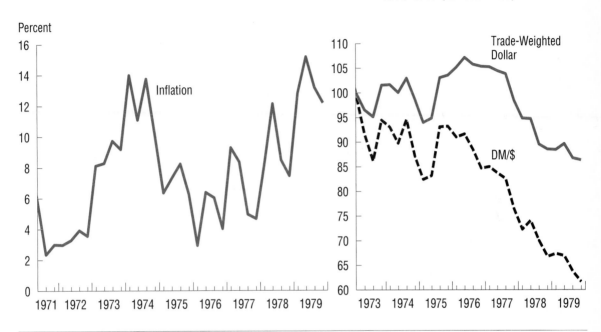

A. CPI INFLATION, QUARTERLY, 1971–1979

B. EXCHANGE RATES, QUARTERLY, 1973–1979 (1973: I = 100)

Source: *Economic Report of the President*, various issues.

32.2 THE MONETARIST POLICY PRESCRIPTION

The new policy represented a turning away from a Keynesian view of monetary policy toward a Monetarist one. Let us review the Monetarist position.

Monetarists believe that attempts to stabilize or fine-tune the economy are misguided. First, the economy needs no help: Demand shocks, such as changes in the desire to invest, have little effect on total expenditure. Second, there are "long and uncertain lags" in the effects of policy on the economy. These lags make it impossible to assess correctly the timing and the extent of policy intervention. Monetarists do not believe in a tradeoff between inflation and unemployment. The proper concern of monetary policy, they believe, is not to stabilize output, but to stabilize the price level.[2]

---

[2]See Chapter 31 for a discussion of the differences between Monetarists and Keynesians in terms of differing beliefs about the sensitivity of investment and money demand to changes in interest rates and about the slope of the aggregate supply curve.

As we saw in Chapter 27, the Monetarist theory of aggregate demand is the Modern Quantity Theory. We can state this in terms of the equation of exchange:

$$MV = PY,$$ [32.1]

where M is the quantity of money, V is velocity, P is the price level, and Y is output.[3] When the economy is changing over time, this relationship may be rewritten in terms of rates of growth:

$$g_M + g_V \cong g_P + g_Y,$$ [32.2]

where g_M is the rate of growth of the quantity of money, and so on.[4]

Long-run price stability can be ensured by setting g_M so that $g_P = 0$. For example, if output grows at 3% and velocity increases at 1%, then money must grow at 2% to keep the price level stable. According to the Modern Quantity Theory, the rate of growth of output and the rate of change of velocity are largely independent of monetary growth. As a result, g_Y and g_V in Equation 32.2 can be regarded as being fixed.[5]

Although such a policy will ensure price stability in the long run, random fluctuations in velocity and output may cause the price level to fluctuate in the short run. However, Monetarists do not believe that policy should try to offset these random fluctuations. Because of the long and uncertain lags in the effects of monetary policy, they feel that any such attempt would likely do more harm than good.

Implementing a policy of steady long-run monetary growth is easy, at least in principle. Assuming, as Monetarists do, that the money multiplier is stable, or at least predictable, then all we need do is ensure that monetary base grows at a rate consistent with the desired rate of growth of the quantity of money. If the money multiplier is constant, then 2% growth of the quantity of money requires 2% growth of monetary base. Regular open market purchases can easily achieve the target rate of growth of monetary base.[6]

---

[3]See Chapter 22, Section 22.2, for an explanation of the equation of exchange.

[4]See Chapter 28, Section 28.1, for an explanation of the transition from Equation 32.1 to Equation 32.2.

[5]See Chapter 27, Section 27.3, for an explanation of the Modern Quantity Theory and of its views on velocity.

[6]Monetarists are against any short-run meddling in the form of "defensive" open market operations (see Chapter 20, Section 20.3). They believe that financial markets are best left to adjust on their own to short-term disturbances.

32.3 THE "MONETARIST EXPERIMENT" OF 1979–1982

Monetary policy took a turn in the Monetarist direction in October 1979, but we shall see that it fell considerably short of the Monetarist prescription of steady monetary growth. Before we examine the conduct of this new policy, however, let us look at its consequences.

THE CONSEQUENCES OF THE NEW POLICY

Inflation, although it did not respond immediately, started to fall rapidly in 1982 (see Exhibit 32.2A). It fell from double digits to the 3%–5% range and has remained there since. The decline in the exchange rate of the dollar, which had precipitated the change in policy, was reversed almost immediately, and the value of the dollar continued to climb for several years (see Exhibit 32.2B).

The tightening of monetary policy led, however, to a major worldwide recession. In the United States unemployment rose to levels not seen since the Great Depression. The number of jobless increased by some 3 million (see Exhibit 32.2C). The loss of output was estimated at $500 billion; real output per capita fell 5%. The housing industry was particularly hard hit, and about 2.6 million houses that would normally have been built were not.

The tightening of monetary policy was not the only policy change at the time. The Reagan administration, which came to office in 1981, also initiated a major change in fiscal policy. Taxes were cut substantially, with no corresponding cut in expenditure, causing a substantial increase in the federal deficit. The increase in government borrowing came just as the supply of loanable funds was being reduced by monetary tightening. The result was a steep rise in interest rates. The combination of expansionary fiscal policy with tight monetary policy provided economists for the first time with a conclusive test of the relative potency of monetary and fiscal policy. Monetary policy won hands down.[7]

The recession in the United States was exported to the other major economies. Rising interest rates in the United States, and falling U.S. imports as a result of the fall in income, put strong upward pressure on the dollar, which rose substantially. Foreign central banks resisted the fall in their exchange rates by tightening their own monetary policy and raising their interest rates. The effect of the tightening and of the fall in their exports to the United States was to drive their own economies into recession.[8]

---

[7]In terms of the ISLM model, monetary policy shifted the LM curve to the left, while fiscal policy shifted the IS curve to the right. The interest rate should definitely rise, but the effect on equilibrium income is, in principle, uncertain. If the LM curve is steep and the IS curve flat as the Monetarists claim, income should fall. That is what happened.

[8]This exporting of recession through the defense of exchange rates parallels the exporting of inflation that we discussed in Chapter 31.

As we saw in Chapter 30, a switch from an interest-rate target to a monetary-growth target should increase the volatility of interest rates. However, the extent of the increase came as a surprise (see Exhibit 32.2D), and it contributed to a series of financial crises. Monetary growth, which should have been stable under a monetary-growth target, was not (see Exhibit 32.2E). We shall see why presently.

THE CONDUCT OF MONETARY POLICY 1979–1982

The conduct of monetary policy under the new rules proved problematic. At the FOMC meeting of October 6, 1979, the target for monetary growth was set at 4.5%. Although monetary growth was actually below target for the rest of the year, at 3.2%, there was relatively little response to this tightening on the part either of output or of inflation. In fact, inflation continued to rise. Interest rates, of course, rose steeply, and the prime rate hit a record 15.5%. Monetary growth continued into 1980 at or below target, while interest rates continued to rise.

A sudden surge in bank lending early in 1980, despite the monetary tightening, panicked the Carter administration into imposing credit controls. In March the Fed instructed banks to limit their loan expansion to an annual rate of 6% to 8% (it had been proceeding at a 20% rate). In addition, the Fed imposed a 3% surcharge on discount loans to discourage bank borrowing of reserves, raised the 8% reserve requirement on increases in managed liabilities to 10%, and imposed a 15% reserve requirement on additional assets of money market mutual funds.

The effect of this restriction of credit on economic activity was dramatic. Industrial production fell sharply, at a 17% annual rate, and the unemployment rate climbed from 6.3% to nearly 8% in a few months. However, 1980 was an election year, and engineering a major recession is hardly the best way for an incumbent president to get reelected. The administration quickly canceled the credit controls. The Fed eased monetary policy sharply. Where was the Fed's much-vaunted independence? Although the Fed's response was political, its motivation may have been more a fear of being accused of deliberately sabotaging Carter's reelection than an actual desire to have him reelected. In any event, the fed funds rate plunged from a peak of 19.5% to below 10%.[9]

With the election safely over and Carter defeated nonetheless, the Fed resumed tightening late in the year, and it continued a tight policy into 1982. Inflation began to fall in early 1982, but unemployment continued to rise steadily. The Fed gradually began to ease. Once again, there was little immediate response, and by October the unemployment rate was approaching 11%. In desperation, the Fed abandoned its monetary-growth targets and eased policy sharply to bring down interest rates. The economy quickly recovered and unemployment fell rapidly. Its confidence in monetary-growth targets shaken, the Fed returned to its old practice of targeting the fed funds rate. The "Monetarist experiment" was over.

---

[9]For a fuller description of the monetary policy of 1980 and its results, see Chapter 24, Section 24.4.

EXHIBIT 32.2

MACROECONOMIC STATISTICS, 1979–1982

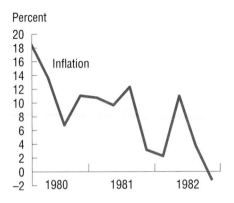

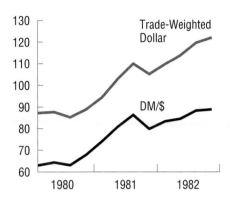

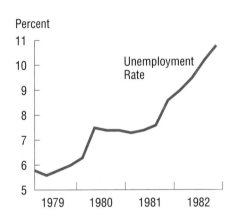

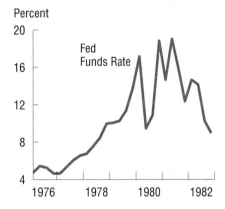

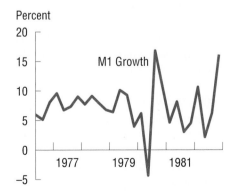

Source: *Economic Report of the President*, various issues.

EXHIBIT 32.3

TARGETS, GOAL,
AND LINKAGES

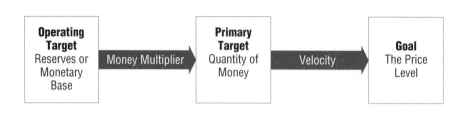

32.4 | DIFFICULTIES OF IMPLEMENTATION

Monetary policy in the 1979–1982 period hardly followed the Monetarist recipe of steady monetary growth. But the reason was not entirely a lack of good intentions: There proved to be serious difficulties in implementing the Monetarist prescription.

Exhibit 32.3 illustrates how policy is supposed to work. The goal is the price level. The **primary target** is what we have until now called simply *the target*: In this case, it is the quantity of money. The primary target is linked to the goal through velocity, according to the equation of exchange. Because the Fed has no immediate control over the quantity of money, it needs an **operating target** over which it does have immediate control and which is linked to the primary target. Possible candidates for operating target include reserves and monetary base. These are linked to the quantity of money—the primary target—by the money multiplier.

The experience of the 1979–1982 period revealed problems with each part of this policy package—with the primary and operating targets, with the two links, and with the goal.

primary target
Variable in terms of which monetary policy is formulated.

operating target
Variable directly controllable by monetary policy and related to the primary target.

THE PRIMARY TARGET

Problems with the primary target included difficulties in finding an appropriate definition of the quantity of money, difficulties in measuring that quantity, and difficulties in distinguishing between long-run and short-run changes in it.

DEFINING MONEY   For a monetary-growth target to be operational, we must be able to measure the quantity of money and know how fast it is growing. Before we measure it, we must decide what to include in our definition of money. The definition we have used in our theoretical discussions corresponds to M1—currency in the hands of the public plus checking deposits. The Fed has published estimates of M1 since 1944.

M1 became increasingly out-of-date as a measure of the quantity of money in the late 1970s as a result of financial innovation. At that time M1 included only checking deposits at commercial banks. As we saw in Chapter 10, however, this was the time of rising interest rates and the invention of various types of "hidden checking deposit." Overnight repos, NOW accounts, and money market mutual funds all made their appearance, but none were included in M1. As an example of how misleading the Fed's definition of money had become, M1 actually declined in the fourth quarter of 1978, suggesting that monetary growth was slowing and that lower inflation could be expected. In fact, inflation accelerated. Although checking deposits at commercial banks were falling, other transactions accounts, not included in M1, were rising rapidly. Indeed, checking deposits at commercial banks were falling precisely *because* firms and households were transferring money into other, more attractive types of transactions account.

In 1980 the Fed recognized these changes and revised its definition of M1. The new definition included NOW accounts and similar transactions accounts, both at banks and at thrifts, as well as traveler's checks.[10] One can quibble with this new definition: It leaves out other hidden deposits like overnight repos, fed funds bought, and overnight Eurodollars, as well as pseudodeposits like money market mutual funds and money market deposit accounts. However, the real point is not whether the current definition is right or wrong, but rather that it is hard to find a good definition of something corresponding to the abstract notion of "money." Any definition is bound to become obsolete, as financial intermediaries invent new forms of money. Indeed, in this respect, the switch to a policy of targeting monetary growth could hardly have come at a worse time. It coincided with the crest of a wave of financial innovation and deregulation.

In addition to its estimates of M1, the Fed also publishes estimates of broader monetary aggregates—M2 and M3. Their precise definitions and the amounts of the various aggregates are shown in Exhibit 32.4. Basically, M2 adds to M1 some more of the hidden deposits not included in M1, plus small savings and time deposits. M3 adds to M2 large time deposits.

MEASURING MONEY Having decided on a concrete definition of money, the next step is to measure how much of it there is. This too turns out to be difficult. The Fed gathers its data from banks and other financial institutions and from the U.S. Treasury and foreign central banks. Some information is received weekly, some less frequently. Since reports on the monetary aggregates must be published weekly, missing data need to be estimated. (Revisions are issued periodically, as missing data come in and errors are corrected.)

With such a tight publication schedule, errors are frequent. For example, in the two weeks following the Fed's announcement of its new commitment to controlling monetary growth, the growth of M1 seemed to accelerate. Each week, when the numbers were announced, fears of further tightening led to near panic on Wall Street. Paper losses in the bond market exceeded $65 billion. It turned out later that the "growth" of M1 was actually a data error. Because of

---

[10]The new definition also excluded demand deposits due to foreign banks and foreign official institutions on the grounds that these are used for Eurodollar transactions (as we saw in Chapter 11) rather than for domestic transactions.

confusion over filling in new forms, someone at Manufacturers Hanover had misreported the bank's deposits for two weeks in a row. This reporting error caused the Fed to overestimate M1 by some $3.7 billion—roughly 1%.

SEASONAL ADJUSTMENT   The rate of growth of the quantity of money changes substantially from week to week and from month to month. When is such a change significant? For example, suppose M1 has been growing at 0.5% per month (a 6.2% annual rate), but in December it rises instead by 2% (a 26.8% annual rate). Should we be concerned? Perhaps not. There is usually a surge in the demand for money in the weeks before Christmas. Similar seasonal disturbances also result from summer vacations, tax filings, and tax refunds.

seasonal adjustment
Process of filtering out seasonal fluctuations to determine the underlying rate of growth.

The process of filtering out such seasonal fluctuations to see whether the underlying growth rate has really changed is called **seasonal adjustment**. This is done by looking at what happened at similar times in previous years. For example, if monetary growth in December is normally 1% above the November number, our 2% growth rate is not so alarming.

Seasonal adjustment has its problems too. Seasonal patterns may change. For example, when the Fed used interest-rate targets, seasonal fluctuations in money demand caused the quantity of money to vary. When it switched to monetary targets, more variation could be expected in interest rates and less in the quantity of money.[11] As a result, the old method of seasonal adjustment became out-of-date. However, until some experience with the new policy had accumulated, it was hard to know what the new seasonal pattern would look like.[12]

Because of all these difficulties, the weekly or even monthly monetary-growth figures say very little about what is really going on. Annual figures are needed for a reliable estimate. But can we afford to wait a whole year to find out whether targets are being achieved? And although the Fed repeatedly denied that it was influenced by the short-term figures, the markets believed otherwise. The markets paid close attention to weekly monetary-growth announcements. Fed watchers believed the Fed would react to deviations from target growth rates by tightening or easing to get back on target, and this would cause interest rates to rise or fall. This expectations effect was so strong that announcements of unusually large monetary growth often led to sharp *rises* in short-term interest rates as the market anticipated monetary tightening. At the time, suggestions were made that the figures be released less frequently, in order to prevent the weekly gyrations in interest rate that they were causing.

[11]See Chapter 30 for an explanation of the different effects of interest-rate and monetary-growth targets.

[12]Another factor that complicates seasonal adjustment is the different seasonal patterns of demand deposits and time deposits. If NOW accounts are used to a significant extent as time deposits, as seems likely, then adding NOWs to M1 will alter the seasonal pattern.

M1	**$ 794.7**
Currency	221.9
Traveler's checks	7.4
Demand deposits	279.7
Other checkable deposits	285.7
M2	**$3,221.7**
M1	794.7
Overnight RPs and Eurodollars	74.9
MMF balances (general purpose and broker/dealer)	313.1
MMDAs (unadjusted)	487.9
Savings deposits	409.0
Small time deposits	1,142.1
M3	**$4,043.3**
M2	3,221.7
Large time deposits	558.2
Term RPs and Eurodollars	161.1
MMF balances (institutions only)	102.3
Monetary Base	**$ 281.9**
Currency	221.9
Reserves	60.0

EXHIBIT 32.4

COMPONENTS OF THE MONETARY AGGREGATES AND MONETARY BASE AND THEIR LEVELS (IN BILLIONS OF DOLLARS, SEASONALLY ADJUSTED, DECEMBER 1989)

Source: *Federal Reserve Bulletin.*

THE OPERATING TARGET

It is hardly practical to instruct the System Account Manager to achieve a particular growth rate of M1. He cannot know on a day-to-day basis what M1 is (as we have seen, even the weekly figures are a poor guide). Hence he cannot know immediately whether he is hitting his target or not. Moreover, if he finds he is off target, there is not much he can do right away to get M1 back on track. Open market operations will eventually affect M1, but they do not provide immediate control. The day-to-day conduct of open market operations therefore needs some sort of operating target. This operating target should be something about which the System Account Manager has good day-to-day information, over which he does have immediate control, and which bears as close a connection as possible to M1. Each of the possible candidates has its drawbacks.

MONETARY BASE The simplest operating target is monetary base. As we saw in Chapter 20, the Fed has no problem either monitoring it or regulating its amount.[13] The problem, rather, is with the connection between monetary base and the primary target, M1. Remember that monetary base, B, consists of bank reserves, R, plus currency in the hands of the public, C:

$$B = R + C. \qquad\qquad [32.3]$$

The reason that the connection between monetary base and M1 is problematic is the mysterious behavior of C.

In September 1989 the amount of currency in the hands of the public was about $220 billion. The population was about 250 million. If we divide the amount of currency by the number of people, we get $880 in cash for every man, woman, and child, or about $3,500 in cash per family of four. Surely these numbers are way too high? To find out, the Fed conducted a survey. It found that only 12% to 14% of all the currency supposedly "in the hands of the public" was actually held by households. This gives a more plausible figure of about $400 for the cash held by a family of four.[14]

So where is the rest? Firms hold some in their cash registers, but most remains unaccounted for. One possibility is that currency is tied up in illegal activities. For example, when the Colombian drug cartel sells a shipment of cocaine to its distributors, checks and credit cards are not accepted: Terms are strictly cash and carry. Indeed, a standard indicator used by law enforcement agencies to gauge the extent of illegal activity in an area is the excess of cash taken in by the local Fed branch over the amount of cash that it dispenses. Miami and Los Angeles usually head the list. However, crime probably accounts for only a small part of the missing currency.

Most of the missing currency is probably in hoards held by individuals in foreign countries. In many developing and Communist countries, the value of the domestic currency is uncertain and the holding of foreign securities impractical. As a result, many people keep their assets in the form of hoards of U.S. dollars. For example, when the safe-deposit boxes of a small branch bank in Israel were destroyed in a fire, it was believed that millions of dollars in U.S. currency had gone up in smoke.

The demand for currency, then, is not much related to legal economic activity in the United States, and it can be somewhat unpredictable. For example, the demand for currency grew much faster than expected in the 1970s. This lack of predictability makes monetary base a poor operating target. If the Fed sets a growth rate for monetary base and there is a surge in the demand for currency, reserves will grow more slowly than intended, and so will M1.

For example, suppose that $B = 100$, $R = 20$, and $C = 80$. In order to expand the money supply by 5%, B is increased to 105, on the assumption that the increase will be split between R and C in the same proportion as existing mon-

---

[13]As we saw in Chapter 20, various factors unrelated to the Fed's own actions can cause changes in the quantity of monetary base, but the Fed can offset them with defensive open market operations.

[14]Comparing these results with the results of earlier surveys, the Fed found that currency use by households had increased. This is probably because withdrawing cash has become easier as a result of the spread of automatic teller machines.

etary base. That is, R is expected to increase to 21 and C to 84. Suppose, however, that C increases by more than expected, to 88. That leaves only $105 - 88 = 17$ of monetary base for R. As a result, deposits will contract and M1 will fall rather than rise by the intended 5%.

A real-world example of the problem was provided by the Carter credit controls of 1980. These placed restrictions on the use of credit cards. As a result, much more currency was withdrawn from banks. The consequent fall in reserves was a major factor in the sharp drop in M1 and the resulting plunge in economic activity.

RESERVES   If monetary base is unsuitable as an operating target, how about reserves? The obstacle to using reserves as the operating target was the method of reserve accounting in use at the time. That method, *lagged* reserve accounting, differed from the method in use today, *contemporaneous* reserve accounting. Under contemporaneous reserve accounting, which we examined in Chapter 20, banks are required to hold reserves during a two-week maintenance period to cover deposits held in a more or less contemporaneous two-week computation period. Under lagged reserve accounting, banks were required to hold reserves during a one-week maintenance period to cover deposits held in a one-week computation period, *two weeks earlier.*

Lagged reserve accounting made it difficult to use reserves as an intermediate target. As we saw in Chapter 21, banks make loans largely according to demand, and borrow the reserves they need in the fed funds market or from the discount window. With lagged reserve accounting, they do not have to acquire the additional reserves to cover new loans immediately. Rather, they expect to do so two weeks later. Now suppose the Fed sets a reserve target for a given week of $50 billion and that it turns out that the amount of reserves required by the banking system is $51 billion (calculated on the basis of deposits held two weeks previously). The fed funds rate will shoot up as banks scramble for reserves that are simply not there. They can, of course, turn to the discount window. However, if the Fed sticks to its reserve target, it will offset any discount lending with open market sales. In these circumstances there is just no way for banks to meet their reserve requirements.

Recognizing this problem, the Fed did not use total reserves as its operating target, but used instead **nonborrowed reserves**—total reserves less discount borrowing. For our numerical example, if the nonborrowed reserve target is $50 billion and banks need $51 billion, they can borrow the extra $1 billion from the discount window, and the Fed will *not* offset this with open market sales. The fed funds rate will nonetheless go up: Banks are rationed in their discount borrowing, and, as we saw in Chapter 21, they will go to the discount window only as a last resort. The rise in the fed funds rate will cause banks to raise the rate on their loans, reducing the demand for loans, and the amount of deposits will shrink. This will lead to a reduced demand for reserves two weeks later.

As a result of lagged reserve accounting and the use of nonborrowed reserves as an operating target, there was a two-week cycle in reserves, monetary growth, and interest rates. The current system of contemporaneous reserve accounting

nonborrowed reserves
Total bank reserves less discount borrowing.

was introduced largely to eliminate this cycle. However, by the time the new procedure was implemented in 1984, the Fed was no longer targeting reserves, and the reserve accounting procedure had become irrelevant.

The Fed had some difficulty controlling nonborrowed reserves. The Fed does not observe reserves on a continuous basis as it does, say, the fed funds rate. It knows the amount of reserve deposits, but vault cash is at best reported weekly. So the Fed had to predict what reserves would be during the coming week and conduct open market operations accordingly. The predictions were not too accurate, and therefore neither was the Fed's success in hitting its target.[15]

THE LINK BETWEEN RESERVES AND MONEY

The connection between the operating target, reserves, and the primary target, M1, is the money multiplier. As we saw in Chapter 19, the size of the money multiplier depends on the currency/checking-deposit ratio, on the time-deposit/checking-deposit ratio, and on reserve ratios. We have already seen that the behavior of the currency/checking-deposit ratio was unpredictable. The behavior of the time-deposit/checking-deposit ratio was also erratic due to the changes going on in the types of time deposit and checking deposit available. As you can see from Exhibits 21.5 and 21.6 in Chapter 21, both of these ratios were particularly unstable in this period.

Reserve ratios too proved to be a problem. Just after the Fed switched to monetary-growth targeting, the Monetary Control Act of 1980 instituted a number of major changes in reserve requirements.[16] These changes were phased in gradually over the next seven years and continually altered the money multiplier in complicated and not entirely predictable ways, making the Fed's task considerably more difficult. In setting its reserve-growth targets, the Fed tried to adjust for these changes, but it was not too successful.

As we saw in Chapter 21, the actual reserve ratios in the money multiplier depend both on reserve requirements and on excess reserves. The latter also proved to be a source of instability. Excess reserves had been falling steadily for many years as banks learned to manage their reserve positions more closely. In 1980 this trend reversed and excess reserves began to grow. Quite probably the reason was the extension of Fed reserve requirements to many more institutions, typically less skilled than member banks at managing their reserves. Excess reserves also fluctuated quite widely (see Exhibit 21.4).

All these factors combined to reduce the stability of the money multiplier. As you can see from Exhibit 21.7, the M1 multiplier behaved much more erratically from 1979 on.

---

[15]There were also problems with the seasonal adjustment of nonborrowed reserves. See note 16.

[16]Under the new law, all depository institutions became subject to the Fed's reserve requirements. Before, the Fed's reserve requirements applied only to Federal Reserve member banks, so when deposits shifted from a member bank to a nonmember bank or to a thrift, the multiplier changed. Also under the new law, time deposits, except for NCDs, were no longer subject to reserve requirements. The change in reserve requirements altered the seasonal pattern of reserves, making seasonal adjustment more difficult.

EXHIBIT 32.5

M1 VELOCITY, 1945–1980; 1981–1989

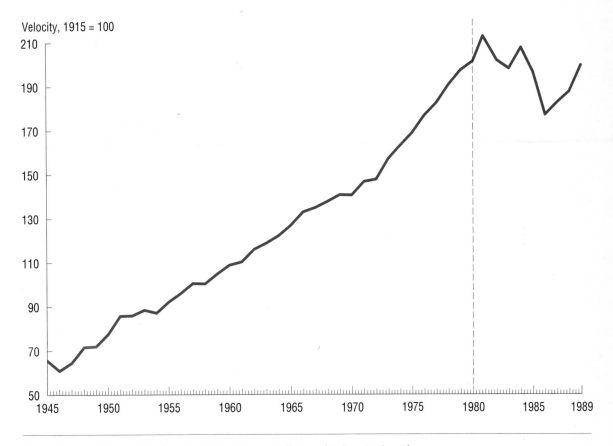

Source: *Economic Report of the President; Federal Reserve Bulletin;* and Robert Gordon, *The American Business Cycle: Continuity and Changes,* Chicago: Univerity of Chicago Press, 1986.

THE LINK BETWEEN MONEY AND SPENDING

The primary target—the growth rate of the quantity of money—should be set at a level that achieves the desired goal—say, stable prices. But what level is that? As we have seen, Monetarists rely on Equation 32.2 to determine the required growth rate. The growth rate of the quantity of money is set so as to be consistent with the inflation goal.

For this procedure to work, the growth rate of velocity must be stable. Before 1979 it was. For the previous 20 years velocity had grown at an almost constant 3% (see Exhibit 32.5). During that period, because velocity was so regular in its behavior, whenever the growth of M1 slowed or accelerated, so did the growth of total spending and so of economic activity, much as the Modern Quantity Theory

E x h i b i t 32.6

OPPORTUNITY COSTS
OF CHECKING
DEPOSITS

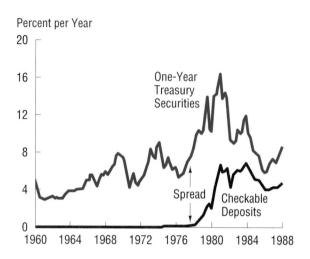

Source: Board of Governors, Federal Reserve System.

predicts. However, this regularity in the behavior of velocity ended in 1981 (see Exhibit 32.5). With it went any clear connection between monetary growth and the behavior of output and prices.

Why this drastic change in the behavior of velocity? Remember that velocity depends on the desire of firms and households to hold money balances. When the demand for money increases, velocity falls. Money balances used to pay no interest. So, as interest rates rose steadily through the 1950s, 1960s, and 1970s, improvements in cash management led to shrinking money balances and steadily rising velocity.[17]

However, as you can see from Exhibit 32.6, after 1980 the opportunity cost of checking deposits dropped sharply. The opportunity cost is the difference between the rate on nonmonetary liquid assets, represented here by T-bills, and the interest paid on checking deposits. Until the late 1970s, the latter rate was zero. But after the deregulation of 1980, NOW and other interest-bearing checking accounts became universally available. As money market rates started to come down in 1981, the opportunity cost shrank rapidly, and the amount of interest-bearing checking deposits mushroomed accordingly.

Money demand not only increased, it also became more sensitive to changes in market interest rates. One explanation for this increased sensitivity is that a large part of NOW accounts probably represents asset rather than transactions balances. Because the rates on NOW accounts do not vary much as market rates change, when market rates rise, people shift these asset balances out of NOW

[17]See Chapters 9 and 10 for a discussion of these improvements in cash management.

EXHIBIT 32.7

VELOCITY, 1915–1989

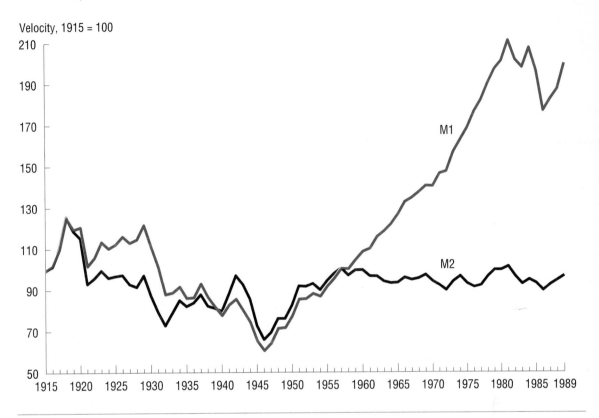

Source: *Economic Report of the President; Federal Reserve Bulletin;* and Robert Gordon, *The American Business Cycle: Continuity and Changes,* Chicago: Univerity of Chicago Press, 1986.

accounts and into money market deposit accounts or money market mutual funds. Since these latter are not included in M1, this shift represents a change in the demand for money.

In a historical context, the regular behavior of M1 velocity from 1945 to 1980 seems to have been the exception rather than the rule (see Exhibit 32.7). That exceptional regularity seems to have been the result of a coincidence of factors—the prohibition of payment of interest on checking deposits, the steadily rising trend in interest rates, and a monetary policy that minimized short-run interest-rate fluctuations. As all these factors have since changed, there seems little reason to expect that M1 velocity will ever again be so stable.

As a result of this breakdown in the stability of M1 velocity, there have been suggestions that M2 should be used as the primary target instead. Indeed, as Exhibit 32.7 shows, M2 velocity has changed much less over the long run than M1 velocity. However, as this exhibit also shows, M2 velocity has always been volatile in the short run, so the short-run connection between M2 and spending has been weak. Even if the long-run stability of M2 velocity were to hold up under an M2 target, these short-run fluctuations in M2 velocity could have substantial real effects on the economy.

THE GOALS

When monetary policy adopted price stability as its primary goal, it was understood that this would mean higher and more volatile interest rates and a squeeze on total spending. However, the magnitude of these effects came as a surprise.

THE EFFECTS ON INTEREST RATES AND EXCHANGE RATES   From the inception of the new policy until the Fed started to ease in mid-1982, both short-term and long-term interest rates shot up to unprecedented heights. This rise in interest rates had a number of serious consequences.

As interest rates in the United States rose relative to those in other countries, the exchange rate of the dollar rose steadily, reversing the downward trend that had played an important role in causing the change in policy (see Exhibit 32.2B). The rise in the value of the dollar put pressure on U.S. manufacturers, who found it increasingly difficult to compete in international markets. It also worsened the plight of LDC borrowers who had borrowed in U.S. dollars and found the value of their liabilities increasing in terms of their own currencies.

The rise in interest rates, together with the ensuing recession, had powerful and long-lasting effects on financial institutions, as we saw in Chapter 17. It did enormous damage to the thrift industry, and it brought on the crisis in LDC debt that continues to weaken the balance sheets of the money center banks.[18]

WHY WAS THE REAL EFFECT OF THE DISINFLATION SO SEVERE?   That a tightening of monetary policy should lead to a recession is not entirely surprising. However, the recession of 1980–1982 was much more severe than expected. One reason was that monetary policy was much tighter than intended. Monetary-growth rates were set in the expectation that velocity would continue to increase. But velocity fell instead. In 1981, for example, the target range for M1 was 6.0%–8.5%. If velocity had continued to rise at a 3% rate, this range would have allowed spending to increase at a rate of 9.0%–11.5%. However, instead of rising 3%, velocity *fell* somewhat, so the target range was consistent with spending growth below 6.0%–8.5%. To make things worse, monetary growth in 1981 came in under target, at only 5.1%.

The severity of the recession was evidence against the New Classical view of the Phillips-curve tradeoff. As we saw in Chapter 31, according to that view, only unexpected changes in inflation have any effect on unemployment. So if people had believed that the new policy would bring down inflation, there should have

---

[18]See the discussion in Chapter 12, Section 12.5.

been no rise in unemployment. That is, if the policy were credible, it should have had no real effect on the economy. The fact that unemployment did rise so sharply can be interpreted in one of two ways. Either the policy was not credible, or the New Classical view is wrong and even expected increases or decreases in inflation can affect economic activity, at least in the short run. That is the position of the New Keynesian school.

So the experiment in monetary policy of 1979–1982 demonstrated problems in all aspects of the Monetarist prescription. Achieving a monetary-growth target proved difficult in practice, and the link between the target and the price-stability goal proved unreliable, with serious consequences for the economy. As a result of these problems, policy underwent a second sharp change in 1982.

32.5 | MONETARY POLICY SINCE 1982

The new policy, which continues in force today, retains the Monetarist goal of price stability. However, it does not pursue this goal in the Monetarist fashion, by targeting monetary growth. Instead, it targets the interest rate. Let us take a closer look at the new policy.

THE GOAL

The primary goal of the new policy is price stability. It is not clear, however, *how much* price stability. The disinflation of 1979–1982 brought the inflation rate down from double digits to the 3%–5% range Is this a low enough rate of inflation? It certainly was not in the past. The Nixon administration imposed wage and price controls in 1971 when inflation rose to a then intolerable level— about what it is now.

The problem is that further reduction in the inflation rate will necessitate further monetary tightening, and this may cause a recession. So far the Fed has shown little stomach for the fight, protecting the gains it has made rather than trying to force inflation down further. In 1989 Representative Neal of North Carolina introduced a resolution directing the Fed to reduce inflation to zero within five years and then to keep it there (see "H. J. Res. 409" on page 853). Chairman Greenspan made sympathetic noises, but the resolution was not adopted.

Is zero inflation really worth the cost? Some economists believe so. They point to the distortions caused by inflation and to the advantages of stable exchange rates, which are possible only when all major countries have stable price levels. They argue that the long-run benefits of zero inflation outweigh the short-term costs of achieving it. Other economists attach less weight to these long-run benefits and more to the short-term costs of monetary tightening in terms of unemployment and lost output. They favor the status quo or even an increase in inflation if necessary to prevent an increase in unemployment.

INDICATORS OF FUTURE INFLATION　　Monetary policy now aims directly at the price-stability goal, with no monetary-growth target in between. But inflation responds only with a long lag to changes in policy. Because of this lag, tightening or easing may go on for too long, *causing* instability of the price level rather than preventing it. We therefore need some **indicator** of future inflation—something that will tell us now what inflation will be in the future. In recent years the Fed has looked at a variety of potential indicators.

indicator
Variable used to predict the future value of some other variable.

One possible set of indicators consists of various measures of real economic activity—the rate of growth of output or how near the economy is to potential output.[19] The rationale for seeing these as indicators of inflation is essentially the Phillips curve: When labor markets tighten and the economy approaches capacity, wages and prices tend to rise. But using real economic activity as an indicator of inflation is not without its drawbacks. First, it assumes that potential output grows at a constant rate, and that when this is exceeded, the economy is "overheating." This assumption may not be correct: Potential output may fluctuate for reasons that have nothing to do with inflationary pressure. If they do, responding to these fluctuations with a change in monetary policy may be inappropriate. Second, responding to these measures as indicators of future inflation comes very close to the old policy of trying to stabilize output and employment—a policy that has supposedly been discredited and abandoned.

Another potential set of indicators consists of various financial variables. One such is the slope of the yield curve. As we saw in Chapter 29, under some assumptions a rising yield curve indicates expectations of rising interest rates. If real interest rates are assumed constant, expectations of rising nominal rates mean expectations of rising inflation. In a similar fashion, under certain assumptions, exchange-rate movements and forward premiums may reflect expectations of future inflation rates. If all these assumptions are accepted, and if we believe that financial markets have some skill at predicting inflation, then these indicators may be of value.

Some prices respond more rapidly to inflationary pressure than do others. Commodity prices seem to respond much faster than the CPI or the GNP deflator. The price of gold seems particularly sensitive. One reason is that some people see gold as a good hedge against inflation, so that when fears of inflation increase, the demand for gold goes up and its price rises. So commodity prices and the price of gold are also potential indicators of future inflation.

Monetary aggregates, even if their relationship to inflation has become too unsteady for them to be used as actual targets, may be useful as indicators. An indicator called P^* (pronounced "P-star"), which relies on this long-term connection, has received considerable attention at the Fed lately, even though some economists regard it with skepticism.

P^* is based on the long-run Quantity Theory. It is the answer to the following question: If no further disturbances occurred and the economy were allowed to settle down to its long-run equilibrium, what would the price level be? Suppose M2 is currently $3 trillion. The long-run velocity of M2 is about 1.65, so

---

[19]See Chapter 27 for an explanation of potential output.

H. J. RES. 409

101ST CONGRESS
1ST SESSION

H. J. RES. 409

Directing the Federal Open Market Committee of the Federal Reserve System to adopt and pursue monetary policies leading to, and then maintaining, zero inflation.

IN THE HOUSE OF REPRESENTATIVES

SEPTEMBER 25, 1989

Mr. NEAL of North Carolina introduced the following joint resolution; which was referred to the Committee on Banking, Finance and Urban Affairs

---

JOINT RESOLUTION

Directing the Federal Open Market Committee of the Federal Reserve System to adopt and pursue monetary policies leading to, and then maintaining, zero inflation.

Whereas zero inflation will reduce interest rates to, and maintain them at, their lowest possible levels;

Whereas zero inflation will promote the highest possible sustainable level of employment;

Whereas zero inflation will generate the maximum sustainable rate of economic growth;

Whereas zero inflation will encourage the highest possible rate of savings and investment, thereby boosting productivity and enhancing our standard of living;

Whereas zero inflation will stimulate efficiency in production, thereby maximizing our competitiveness in world trade;

Whereas zero inflation will help stabilize the economy and minimize risk and uncertainty in economic decisionmaking, thereby facilitating long-term planning and investment;

Whereas zero inflation renders the economy more productive and efficient by abolishing the need to devote resources, time, and energy to predicting inflation and coping with the consequences of inflation;

Whereas zero inflation minimizes the risk and reduces the severity of recession; and

Whereas inflation is essentially a monetary phenomenon which, over reasonable periods of time, can be adequately controlled by the monetary policies of the Federal Open Market Committee of the Federal Reserve System: Now, therefore, be it

1 *Resolved by the Senate and House of Representatives*
2 *of the United States of America in Congress assembled,*
3 That—
4   (1) the Federal Open Market Committee of the
5 Federal Reserve System shall adopt and pursue mone-
6 tary policies to reduce inflation gradually in order to
7 eliminate inflation by not later than 5 years from the
8 date of the enactment of this legislation and shall then
9 adopt and pursue monetary policies to maintain price
10 stability;
11   (2) inflation will be deemed to be eliminated when
12 the expected rate of change of the general level of
13 prices ceases to be a factor in individual and business
14 decisionmaking; and

1   (3) the Board of Governors of the Federal Re-
2 serve System shall explain, in its semiannual monetary
3 policy report to the Congress, the relationship of its
4 plans for monetary policy, including the ranges for
5 growth or diminution in the money and credit aggre-
6 gates, to the achievement and maintenance of price
7 stability over time.

○

---

long-run spending would be 1.65 × $3 trillion, or $4.95 trillion. To find the long-run price level, we need to divide long-run spending by potential output. Potential output is estimated by fitting a 2.5% trend line to actual output. If potential output is $4.1 trillion (at 1982 prices), the long-run price level, P^*, is $4.95 trillion/$4.1 trillion = 1.21.

E X H I B I T 32.8

THE PRICE LEVEL
AND P^*, 1984–1989

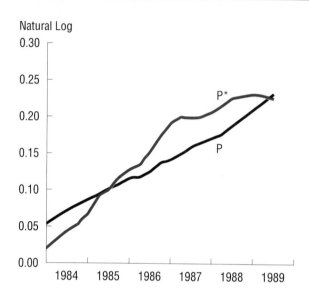

Source: Federal Reserve Bank of Cleveland, September 1989.

P^* is then compared to the actual price level, P. Suppose P is currently 1.25. Since P^* is below P, if there were no further disturbances to the economy, the price level would tend to come down in the future. Hence an easing of monetary policy is indicated to keep prices stable. If, on the other hand, P^* were above P, prices could be expected to rise, and tightening would be indicated. Of course, the validity of these conclusions depends on the stability of long-run M2 velocity and on the stability of the rate of growth of output. The recent behavior of P^* is shown in Exhibit 32.8.

CHECK STATION 1   **M2 is $3.2 trillion, M2 velocity is 1.65, potential output is $4.2 trillion, and the price level is 1.20. According to P^*, should monetary policy be eased or tightened?**

THE TARGET

In October 1982 the Fed abandoned short-run targeting of M1 in favor of "long-run monetary and credit aggregate objectives." What that meant in practice was that instead of setting nonborrowed reserves to achieve an M1 target, the Fed set nonborrowed reserves directly in response to goals.

In 1983 the Fed changed its operating target from nonborrowed reserves to borrowed reserves. Although this sounds like a minor change, it is significant.

EXHIBIT 32.9

TOTAL RESERVES, 1976–1987

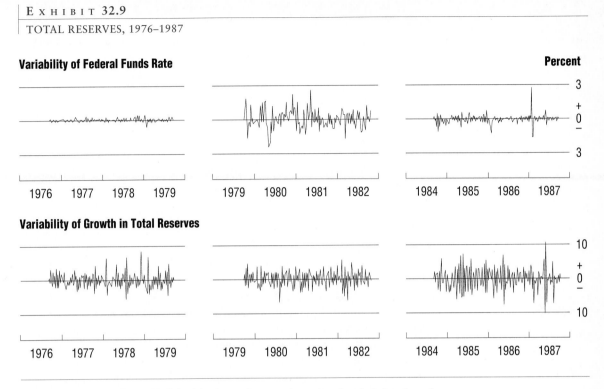

1. Changes in the average weekly federal funds rate (in percent) are plotted as deviations from the mean change over the period.
2. The weekly growth rates of total reserves (in percent) are plotted as deviations from the average weekly growth rate over the period.

Source: *Federal Reserve Bulletin*, July 1988, pp. 424, 426, 427.

Borrowed reserves are reserves lent to banks via the discount window.[20] As we saw in Chapter 21, banks borrow more from the discount window, other things equal, when the fed funds rate rises. Therefore a policy that targets borrowed reserves in effect targets the fed funds rate. Anything that causes the fed funds rate to rise will cause borrowed reserves to increase. To bring borrowed reserves back on target the System Account Manager will have to increase the supply of reserves by conducting open market purchases; this will also bring the fed funds rate down again. So, effectively, the Fed has returned to its old (pre-1979) operating target—the fed funds rate.

Notice from Exhibit 32.9 that as a result of the switch in operating target, the volatility of the fed funds rate was reduced considerably and that of the growth in total reserves was increased somewhat.

[20]Adjustment and seasonal credit only; extended credit to banks in trouble is not included in the definition of borrowed reserves.

HOW THE NEW POLICY HAS WORKED

Exhibit 32.10 shows the important economic variables from 1979 to 1989. You should refer to these graphs as we proceed.

The substantial easing of monetary policy that began in late 1982 led to a rapid recovery of the economy: The unemployment rate fell from nearly 11% to 8% within a year. In fact, the recovery was so rapid that by late 1983 the Fed was already worried that growth was "excessive"—an indicator of renewed inflationary pressure. The Fed therefore began to tighten gradually, and then more forcefully in 1984. Growth slowed, but the rise in interest rates contributed to the financial crisis in the summer of that year, the climax of which was the collapse of Continental Illinois. In response to the financial crisis, the Fed eased and brought interest rates down again.

Beginning in late summer 1985, the Fed became increasingly concerned with the continuing rise in the exchange rate of the dollar. As part of an agreement with other central banks in September of that year to bring down the value of the dollar, the Fed eased policy and lowered interest rates further. The exchange rate did indeed fall sharply and continued to fall into 1988. As a result of the easing, output growth picked up its pace in late 1986.

By February 1987 the Fed and the other central banks were worried that the dollar had fallen too far, and they announced that they would prevent any further decline. To do this, there was a tightening of U.S. monetary policy, with a rise in U.S. interest rates, combined with an easing abroad. The Fed, increasingly worried about the rapid pace of output growth and the supposed increase in inflationary pressure, tightened further during the summer. The consequent rise in interest rates contributed to a plunge in bond prices and to the stock market crash in October 1987.

In response to the crash, the Fed eased rapidly. It switched temporarily to a direct fed funds target from a borrowed-reserves target, allowing as much discount borrowing as needed to provide emergency finance. Once the crisis was over, however, the Fed resumed tightening.

This policy continued into early 1989. By then, a *rising* dollar and *slowing* growth were once again concerns, and the Fed began to bring interest rates down again. By early 1990 signs of renewed inflationary pressure put an end to the easing. The economy seemed balanced on the edge between inflation and recession, with the Fed uncertain whether to ease or tighten.

Throughout this period the erratic behavior of the monetary aggregates that we noted earlier continued. In 1987 the Fed stopped publishing target ranges for M1 growth altogether, citing "uncertainties about its underlying relationship to the behavior of the economy and its sensitivity to a variety of economic and financial circumstances. . . ."[21] At the same time the Fed widened its target ranges for M2 and M3.

---

[21]Monetary Policy Report to Congress, *Federal Reserve Bulletin*, April 1987.

EXHIBIT 32.10

MACROECONOMIC STATISTICS, 1979–1989

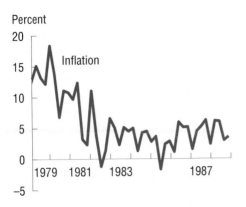

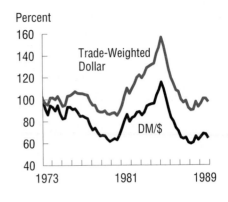

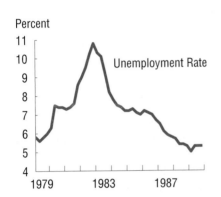

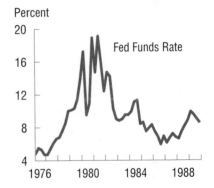

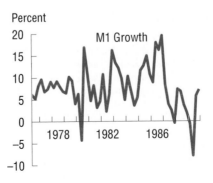

Source: *Economic Report of the President*, various issues.

M1 velocity has declined since 1982, with no clear trend. "Other checkable deposits" (NOW accounts, etc.) have proven very sensitive to interest rates: They mushroomed as money market rates fell from 1984 to early 1987, then fell off sharply as rates started to rise again. After the crash of 1987, they grew rapidly again as rates fell. M2 velocity still fluctuates about its pre-1980 average, but it continues to be very sensitive to interest rates. In 1987 and 1988 the growth rates of M1 and M2 dropped sharply, and Monetarists expressed concern about an impending recession, but none materialized.

In terms of results, the new policy seems to have done quite well. Both inflation and unemployment have remained low. Indeed, the economic expansion since 1982 is the longest peacetime expansion on record.

32.6 | THE FUTURE OF MONETARY POLICY

What is the future of monetary policy? Recent experience has taught us a number of important lessons and raised several major questions.

FINANCIAL STABILITY ALWAYS COMES FIRST

While monetary policy may be guided in the long term by such broad goals as price stability, in the short term the Fed's first concern remains the stability of the financial system. We have seen repeatedly that whenever the safety and stability of the financial system have been threatened, the Fed has responded with direct intervention and with an immediate easing of monetary policy. Once the crisis is over, the Fed resumes it long-term policy. The financial crises of 1982 and 1984, the crash of 1987, and the "minicrash" of 1989 all provide recent examples.

The paramount importance of the Fed's role as lender of last resort was brought out in Federal Reserve testimony before the Bush Commission in December 1983:

> A basic continuing responsibility of any central bank—and the principal reason for the founding of the Federal Reserve—is to assure stable and smoothly functioning financial and payments systems. These are prerequisites for, and complementary to, the central bank's responsibility for conducting monetary policy as it is more narrowly conceived. Indeed, conceptions of the appropriate focus for "monetary policy" have changed historically, variously focusing on control of the money supply, "defending" a fixed price of gold, or more passively providing a flow of money and credit responsive to the needs of business. What has not changed, and is not likely to change, is the idea that a central bank must, to the extent possible, head off and deal with financial disturbances and crises. . . . The [lender of last resort] functions are in addition to, and largely predate, the more purely "monetary" functions of engaging in open market and foreign exchange operations and setting reserve requirements;

historically, in fact, the "monetary" functions were largely grafted onto the "supervisory" functions, and not the reverse.[22]

THE INCREASING IMPORTANCE OF INTERNATIONAL CONSIDERATIONS

Recent experience has shown the increasing extent to which international considerations shape and constrain U.S. monetary policy.

Since the breakdown of the Bretton Woods system in the early 1970s, exchange rates have fluctuated wildly, both in the short run and in the long (see Exhibits 32.1B and 32.10B). These fluctuations have created a great deal of uncertainty in financial markets. For international investors, exchange-rate risk has become a dominant concern. The fluctuations in exchange rates have also had drastic effects on the international competitiveness of particular industries in different countries, with resulting pressure for barriers to protect domestic industries from international competition. This pressure for protection threatens the continued growth of international trade.

As we saw in the previous section, these swings in exchange rates have become an increasing preoccupation of monetary policy. More and more, central banks have intervened in foreign-exchange markets to affect exchange rates, and the need to do so has often conflicted with the pursuit of other goals. However, there has been no consistent policy. The major central banks muddle along from one crisis to another—first driving the dollar up, then down, then up again.

There have been proposals to replace this chaos with some new system of fixed exchange rates. Of course, a necessary precondition for this would be equality of rates of inflation across the major economies, preferably at a rate of zero. Exchange rates cannot remain fixed if price levels change at different rates. Fixed exchange rates would therefore require substantial coordination of monetary policy across the major economies. The major central banks, particularly the Fed, seem reluctant to commit themselves to any such loss of "independence." However, in practice, informal coordination does seem to have increased.

There is a movement toward fixed exchange rates within Europe. As part of the movement toward full economic integration by 1992, there has been discussion of a possible monetary union. The Delors Committee recommended an eventual single currency—equivalent to fixed exchange rates. Under this proposal, there would be a single policy-making authority, to be called the European System of Central Banks (immediately nicknamed the "EuroFed"), that would function rather like the Federal Reserve System. Policy would be made by a central authority, then implemented by national central banks playing a role similar to that of the regional Federal Reserve Banks in the United States.

---

[22]From "Federal Reserve Position on Restructuring of Financial Regulation Responsibilities," quoted in Charles Goodhart, *The Evolution of Central Banks*, MIT Press, 1988.

WHAT TO DO ABOUT SUPPLY SHOCKS?

A major question about future monetary policy is how it will respond to any future supply shock like the oil-price shocks of 1973 and 1979.[23] Will the Fed stick to its goal of price stability or will it accommodate the shock to prevent a recession? In the absence of any clear commitment to a policy rule, we have no idea how the Fed will respond. It will all depend on the personalities and on the politics of the moment. A repeat of the inflation–recession cycles of 1973–1975 and 1978–1982 cannot be ruled out.

RULES VERSUS DISCRETION

The uncertainty about the response to supply shocks is an example of the more general uncertainty about the Fed's future actions. Many economists believe that this uncertainty could be removed by the Fed's committing itself to a clearly stated goal. For example, the Fed might commit itself to achieving zero inflation, or a particular growth rate of monetary base, or exchange-rate stability. It could then set a policy rule consistent with that goal and adhere to that rule without deviation.

The advantage of such a firm rule is that it provides an anchor for people's expectations and thus reduces uncertainty. If people knew, for instance, that the price level in the year 2020 was going to be more or less the same as it is now, it would make their financial decisions much simpler and safer. Because of this reduced uncertainty, they would be more willing to save and to lend, and the level of interest rates would probably be lower. This would mean more investment and faster economic growth. The removal of exchange-rate risk would have similar beneficial effects on international trade and international capital flows.

The disadvantage of a firm rule is that it prevents monetary policy from changing when such a change might, in fact, be beneficial. For example, had the Fed been formally committed to an M1-growth rule when M1 velocity went haywire in 1982, the consequences for the economy would have been severe. The question, of course, is whether or not the advantages of a rule on balance outweigh the disadvantages. Obviously, it helps to choose the right rule. Unfortunately, there is little agreement among economists as to what the right rule might be.

Moreover, the decision between rule and discretion is not made entirely on its merits. The Fed is a bureaucracy, and there are substantial bureaucratic advantages to not being committed to a clearly stated goal or to a firm policy rule (see "The Fed Has No Clothes").

The troubles with both the Keynesian and the Monetarist approaches to monetary policy have to some extent discredited both. The result has been

---

[23]As this book was going to press, the Iraqi invasion of Kuwait was driving up oil prices once again, and pressure was growing for the Fed to lower interest rates to prevent a recession.

THE FED HAS NO CLOTHES

by Milton Friedman

Every now and then a reporter asks my opinion about "current monetary policy." My standard reply has become that I would be glad to answer if he would first tell me what "current monetary policy" is. I know, or can find out, what monetary actions have been: open-market purchases and sales and discount rates at Federal Reserve Banks. I know also the federal funds rate and rates of growth of various monetary aggregates that have accompanied these actions. What I do not know is the policy that produced these actions.

The closest I can come to an official specification of current monetary policy is that it is to take those actions that the monetary authorities, in light of all evidence available, judge will best promote price stability and full employment—i.e., to do the right thing at the right time. But that surely is not a "policy." It is simply an expression of good intentions and an injunction to "trust us."

Such a "policy" can be used to judge present actions or anticipate future actions only through informed conjecture based on empirical extrapolation of past reactions of the Fed to a variety of stimuli, and analysis of the beliefs and attitudes of the participants in the decision-making process—that is, by statistical extrapolation and psychoanalysis. And, of course, there is a sizable and remunerative industry in the financial community engaged in reading the Federal Reserve tea leaves.

I hasten to add that the present situation is not unique. On the contrary, it has persisted for nearly the entire 74-year life of the Federal Reserve System. The only exception was from the outbreak of World War II to 1951, when the Fed followed an announced policy of pegging interest rates on federal government securities. For the rest, the Fed has consistently resorted to statements of good intentions both with respect to the future and with respect to its past actions. It has claimed credit for good results and blamed forces beyond its control—generally fiscal policy—for any bad outcomes. And this avoidance of accountability has paid spectacular dividends. No major institution in the U.S. has so poor a record of performance over so long a period as the Federal Reserve, yet so high a public reputation.

[Under an alternative policy of a constant rate of monetary growth,] the news media would have paid far less attention to the Federal Reserve System. No poll would have designated the Chairman of the System as the second most powerful person in the country and far fewer people would know his name or the names of the other members of the board. The able people now earning high salaries reading the Fed tea leaves would be earning equally high salaries engaged in more productive activities. Similarly, it would be hard to attract individuals of the caliber of Arthur Burns or Paul Volcker or Alan Greenspan to serve as chairman. Why not, they might well say, "turn such a boring job over to a computer." And, indeed, why not? It's my own favorite recipe for improving monetary performance.

Source: Excerpted with permission from Milton Friedman, "The Fed Has No Clothes," *The Wall Street Journal*, April 15, 1988. Mr. Friedman is a Senior Research Fellow at the Hoover Institution and Professor Emeritus of Economics, University of Chicago.

something of an intellectual vacuum. The lack of consensus among economists has left the Fed free to do pretty much as it wants. No one school of economists today has the authority to exert much pressure on the Fed to follow any particular course of action. The policy the Fed has chosen to follow—a goal of price stability and an interest-rate target—has performed quite well, but doubts remain about the future.

SUMMARY

- Increasing inflation and an exchange-rate crisis led the Fed to tighten monetary policy and to switch to a monetary-growth target in October 1979. This represented a turning away from Keynesian ideas and toward Monetarist ones.

- The Monetarist prescription for monetary policy is that it should pursue a goal of price stability by pegging monetary growth at a constant level.

- The new policy did target monetary growth but certainly did not hold it constant. Both monetary growth and interest rates were quite volatile under the new policy.

- Inflation was brought down and the fall of the dollar reversed, but only at the cost of a severe recession.

- The new policy proved difficult to implement. The quantity of money proved hard to define and to measure. A good operating target proved difficult to find, and the connection with the quantity of money (the money multiplier) proved unreliable. The stability of velocity broke down, so that the link between target and goal proved unreliable too.

- As a result of these problems and of its failure to resuscitate the economy by slow easing, the Fed abandoned monetary-growth targeting in 1982 and returned, effectively, to an interest-rate target. The Fed retained price stability as its primary goal.

- The long lag between target and goal necessitates an indicator of future inflation. Some possible indicators are real economic growth, financial indicators, commodity prices, and P^*.

- Monetary policy since 1982 has been reasonably successful in that higher inflation and recession have both been avoided.

- International considerations and coordination of policy with other major economies have become increasingly important.

- In the absence of any clear commitment by the Fed to a firm policy rule, the future of monetary policy is uncertain. No one knows, for example, how it will react to another supply shock.

KEY TERMS

primary target

operating target

seasonal adjustment

nonborrowed reserves

indicator

DISCUSSION QUESTIONS

1. Keynesians claim that in the 1979–1982 period Monetarism failed. Monetarists respond that it was never tried. What are the arguments on each side?

2. What were the difficulties in implementing the Monetarist prescription for monetary policy?

3. How did the Monetarist experiment help to resolve some of the disputes among opposing schools of economists?

4. How did the changes occurring in the financial system—innovation and deregulation—make the implementation of a Monetarist monetary policy more difficult?

5. Should the Neal resolution relating to zero inflation be accepted? Discuss the pros and cons.

6. Why does the Fed need an indicator of future inflation? What are the possible indicators? Discuss their merits.

7. What are the advantages and disadvantages of the Fed's committing itself to a firm policy rule?

BIBLIOGRAPHY

Christiano, Lawrence J., "P*: Not the Inflation Forecaster's Holy Grail," *Quarterly Review of the Federal Reserve Bank of Minneapolis* Fall 1989, 3–18.

Duprey, James N., "How the Fed Defines and Measures Money," *Federal Reserve Bank of Minneapolis Quarterly Review* Spring-Summer 1982, 10–19.

Friedman, Benjamin M., "Lessons on Monetary Policy from the 1980s," *Journal of Economic Perspectives* 2 (3, Summer): 51–72, 1988.

Friedman, Milton, and Anna Jacobson Schwartz, *A Monetary History of the United States 1867–1960*, Princeton: Princeton University Press, 1963.

Hein, Scott E., and Mack Ott, "Seasonally Adjusting Money: Procedures, Problems, Proposals," *Economic Review of the Federal Reserve Bank of St. Louis* November 1983, 16–25.

Hetzel, Robert L., "Monetary Policy in the Early 1980s," *Economic Review of the Federal Reserve Bank of Richmond* March/April 1986, 20–32.

Judd, John, and John Scadding, "The Search for a Stable Money Demand Function," *Journal of Economic Literature* 20:3 (September): 993–1023. 1982.

Mahoney, Patrick I., "The Recent Behavior of Demand Deposits," *Federal Reserve Bulletin* April 1988, 195–208.

Roberds, William, "Money and the Economy: Puzzles from the 1980s' Experience," *Economic Review of the Federal Reserve Bank of Atlanta* September/October 1989.

Walter, John R., "Monetary Aggregates: A User's Guide," *Economic Review of the Federal Reserve Bank of Richmond* January/February 1989, 20–28.

Wicksell, Knut, *Lectures on Political Economy*, translated by E. Classen, London: Routledge & Kegan Paul, 1935 [1906].

APPENDIX A
FINANCIAL TABLES

TABLE 1

FUTURE VALUE FACTORS

The amount you will have n periods from now if $1 earns compound interest of i per period; that is, $(1 + i)^n$.

Period	1%	2%	3%	4%	5%	6%	7%	8%	9%	10%
1	1.010	1.020	1.030	1.040	1.050	1.060	1.070	1.080	1.090	1.100
2	1.020	1.040	1.061	1.082	1.103	1.124	1.145	1.166	1.188	1.210
3	1.030	1.061	1.093	1.125	1.158	1.191	1.225	1.260	1.295	1.331
4	1.041	1.082	1.126	1.170	1.216	1.262	1.311	1.360	1.412	1.464
5	1.051	1.104	1.159	1.217	1.276	1.338	1.403	1.469	1.539	1.611
6	1.062	1.126	1.194	1.265	1.340	1.419	1.501	1.587	1.677	1.772
7	1.072	1.149	1.230	1.316	1.407	1.504	1.606	1.714	1.828	1.949
8	1.083	1.172	1.267	1.369	1.477	1.594	1.718	1.851	1.993	2.144
9	1.094	1.195	1.305	1.423	1.551	1.689	1.838	1.999	2.172	2.358
10	1.105	1.219	1.344	1.480	1.629	1.791	1.967	2.159	2.367	2.594
11	1.116	1.243	1.384	1.539	1.710	1.898	2.105	2.332	2.580	2.853
12	1.127	1.268	1.426	1.601	1.796	2.012	2.252	2.518	2.813	3.138
13	1.138	1.294	1.469	1.665	1.886	2.133	2.410	2.720	3.066	3.452
14	1.149	1.319	1.513	1.732	1.980	2.261	2.579	2.937	3.342	3.797
15	1.161	1.346	1.558	1.801	2.079	2.397	2.759	3.172	3.642	4.177
16	1.173	1.373	1.605	1.873	2.183	2.540	2.952	3.426	3.970	4.595
17	1.184	1.400	1.653	1.948	2.292	2.693	3.159	3.700	4.328	5.054
18	1.196	1.428	1.702	2.026	2.407	2.854	3.380	3.996	4.717	5.560
19	1.208	1.457	1.754	2.107	2.527	3.026	3.617	4.316	5.142	6.116
20	1.220	1.486	1.806	2.191	2.653	3.207	3.870	4.661	5.604	6.727
21	1.232	1.516	1.860	2.279	2.786	3.400	4.141	5.034	6.109	7.400
22	1.245	1.546	1.916	2.370	2.925	3.604	4.430	5.437	6.659	8.140
23	1.257	1.577	1.974	2.465	3.072	3.820	4.741	5.871	7.258	8.954
24	1.270	1.608	2.033	2.563	3.225	4.049	5.072	6.341	7.911	9.850
25	1.282	1.641	2.094	2.666	3.386	4.292	5.427	6.848	8.623	10.83
26	1.295	1.673	2.157	2.772	3.556	4.549	5.807	7.396	9.399	11.92
27	1.308	1.707	2.221	2.883	3.733	4.822	6.214	7.988	10.25	13.11
28	1.321	1.741	2.288	2.999	3.920	5.112	6.649	8.627	11.17	14.42
29	1.335	1.776	2.357	3.119	4.116	5.418	7.114	9.317	12.17	15.86
30	1.348	1.811	2.427	3.243	4.322	5.743	7.612	10.06	13.27	17.45

Period	12%	14%	15%	16%	18%	20%	24%	26%	28%	30%
1	1.120	1.140	1.150	1.160	1.180	1.200	1.240	1.260	1.280	1.300
2	1.254	1.300	1.323	1.346	1.392	1.440	1.538	1.588	1.638	1.690
3	1.405	1.482	1.521	1.561	1.643	1.728	1.907	2.000	2.097	2.197
4	1.574	1.689	1.749	1.811	1.939	2.074	2.364	2.520	2.684	2.856
5	1.762	1.925	2.011	2.100	2.288	2.488	2.932	3.176	3.436	3.713
6	1.974	2.195	2.313	2.436	2.700	2.986	3.635	4.002	4.398	4.827
7	2.211	2.502	2.660	2.826	3.185	3.583	4.508	5.042	5.629	6.275
8	2.476	2.853	3.059	3.278	3.759	4.300	5.590	6.353	7.206	8.157
9	2.773	3.252	3.518	3.803	4.435	5.160	6.931	8.005	9.223	10.604
10	3.106	3.707	4.046	4.411	5.234	6.192	8.594	10.09	11.81	13.79
11	3.479	4.226	4.652	5.117	6.176	7.430	10.66	12.71	15.11	17.92
12	3.896	4.818	5.350	5.936	7.288	8.916	13.21	16.01	19.34	23.30
13	4.363	5.492	6.153	6.886	8.599	10.70	16.39	20.18	24.76	30.29
14	4.887	6.261	7.076	7.988	10.15	12.84	20.32	25.42	31.69	39.37
15	5.474	7.138	8.137	9.266	11.97	15.41	25.20	32.03	40.56	51.19
16	6.130	8.137	9.358	10.75	14.13	18.49	31.24	40.36	51.92	66.54
17	6.866	9.276	10.76	12.47	16.67	22.19	38.74	50.85	66.46	86.50
18	7.690	10.58	12.38	14.46	19.67	26.62	48.04	64.07	85.07	112.5
19	8.613	12.06	14.23	16.78	23.21	31.95	59.57	80.73	108.9	146.2
20	9.646	13.74	16.37	19.46	27.39	38.34	73.86	101.7	139.4	190.0
21	10.80	15.67	18.82	22.57	32.32	46.01	91.59	128.2	178.4	247.1
22	12.10	17.86	21.64	26.19	38.14	55.21	113.6	161.5	228.4	321.2
23	13.55	20.36	24.89	30.38	45.01	66.25	140.8	203.5	292.3	417.5
24	15.18	23.21	28.63	35.24	53.11	79.50	174.6	256.4	374.1	542.8
25	17.00	26.46	32.92	40.87	62.67	95.40	216.5	323.0	478.9	705.6
26	19.04	30.17	37.86	47.41	73.95	114.5	268.5	407.0	613.0	917.3
27	21.32	34.39	43.54	55.00	87.26	137.4	333.0	512.9	784.6	1193.
28	23.88	39.20	50.07	63.80	103.0	164.8	412.9	646.2	1004.	1550.
29	26.75	44.69	57.58	74.01	121.5	197.8	512.0	814.2	1286.	2015.
30	29.96	50.95	66.21	85.85	143.4	237.4	634.8	1026.	1646.	2620.

TABLE 2

PRESENT VALUE FACTORS

The value today of $1 due in n periods time if the periodic interest rate is i; that is, $\dfrac{1}{(1+i)^n}$.

Period	1%	2%	3%	4%	5%	6%	7%	8%	9%	10%
1	0.9901	0.9804	0.9709	0.9615	0.9524	0.9434	0.9346	0.9259	0.9174	0.9091
2	0.9803	0.9612	0.9426	0.9246	0.9070	0.8900	0.8734	0.8573	0.8417	0.8264
3	0.9706	0.9423	0.9151	0.8890	0.8638	0.8396	0.8163	0.7938	0.7722	0.7513
4	0.9610	0.9238	0.8885	0.8548	0.8227	0.7921	0.7629	0.7350	0.7084	0.6830
5	0.9515	0.9057	0.8626	0.8219	0.7835	0.7473	0.7130	0.6806	0.6499	0.6209
6	0.9420	0.8880	0.8375	0.7903	0.7462	0.7050	0.6663	0.6302	0.5963	0.5645
7	0.9327	0.8706	0.8131	0.7599	0.7107	0.6651	0.6227	0.5835	0.5470	0.5132
8	0.9235	0.8535	0.7894	0.7307	0.6768	0.6274	0.5820	0.5403	0.5019	0.4665
9	0.9143	0.8368	0.7664	0.7026	0.6446	0.5919	0.5439	0.5002	0.4604	0.4241
10	0.9053	0.8203	0.7441	0.6756	0.6139	0.5584	0.5083	0.4632	0.4224	0.3855
11	0.8963	0.8043	0.7224	0.6496	0.5847	0.5268	0.4751	0.4289	0.3875	0.3505
12	0.8874	0.7885	0.7014	0.6246	0.5568	0.4970	0.4440	0.3971	0.3555	0.3186
13	0.8787	0.7730	0.6810	0.6006	0.5303	0.4688	0.4150	0.3677	0.3262	0.2897
14	0.8700	0.7579	0.6611	0.5775	0.5051	0.4423	0.3878	0.3405	0.2992	0.2633
15	0.8613	0.7430	0.6419	0.5553	0.4810	0.4173	0.3624	0.3152	0.2745	0.2394
16	0.8528	0.7284	0.6232	0.5339	0.4581	0.3936	0.3387	0.2919	0.2519	0.2176
17	0.8444	0.7142	0.6050	0.5134	0.4363	0.3714	0.3166	0.2703	0.2311	0.1978
18	0.8360	0.7002	0.5874	0.4936	0.4155	0.3503	0.2959	0.2502	0.2120	0.1799
19	0.8277	0.6864	0.5703	0.4746	0.3957	0.3305	0.2765	0.2317	0.1945	0.1635
20	0.8195	0.6730	0.5537	0.4564	0.3769	0.3118	0.2584	0.2145	0.1784	0.1486
21	0.8114	0.6598	0.5375	0.4388	0.3589	0.2942	0.2415	0.1987	0.1637	0.1351
22	0.8034	0.6468	0.5219	0.4220	0.3418	0.2775	0.2257	0.1839	0.1502	0.1228
23	0.7954	0.6342	0.5067	0.4057	0.3256	0.2618	0.2109	0.1703	0.1378	0.1117
24	0.7876	0.6217	0.4919	0.3901	0.3101	0.2470	0.1971	0.1577	0.1264	0.1015
25	0.7798	0.6095	0.4776	0.3751	0.2953	0.2330	0.1842	0.1460	0.1160	0.0923
26	0.7720	0.5976	0.4637	0.3607	0.2812	0.2198	0.1722	0.1352	0.1064	0.0839
27	0.7644	0.5859	0.4502	0.3468	0.2678	0.2074	0.1609	0.1252	0.0976	0.0763
28	0.7568	0.5744	0.4371	0.3335	0.2551	0.1956	0.1504	0.1159	0.0895	0.0693
29	0.7493	0.5631	0.4243	0.3207	0.2429	0.1846	0.1406	0.1073	0.0822	0.0630
30	0.7419	0.5521	0.4120	0.3083	0.2314	0.1741	0.1314	0.0994	0.0754	0.0573

Period	12%	14%	15%	16%	18%	20%	24%	26%	28%	30%
1	0.8929	0.8772	0.8696	0.8621	0.8475	0.8333	0.8065	0.7937	0.7813	0.7692
2	0.7972	0.7695	0.7561	0.7432	0.7182	0.6944	0.6504	0.6299	0.6104	0.5917
3	0.7118	0.6750	0.6575	0.6407	0.6086	0.5787	0.5245	0.4999	0.4768	0.4552
4	0.6355	0.5921	0.5718	0.5523	0.5158	0.4823	0.4230	0.3968	0.3725	0.3501
5	0.5674	0.5194	0.4972	0.4761	0.4371	0.4019	0.3411	0.3149	0.2910	0.2693
6	0.5066	0.4556	0.4323	0.4104	0.3704	0.3349	0.2751	0.2499	0.2274	0.2072
7	0.4523	0.3996	0.3759	0.3538	0.3139	0.2791	0.2218	0.1983	0.1776	0.1594
8	0.4039	0.3506	0.3269	0.3050	0.2660	0.2326	0.1789	0.1574	0.1388	0.1226
9	0.3606	0.3075	0.2843	0.2630	0.2255	0.1938	0.1443	0.1249	0.1084	0.0943
10	0.3220	0.2697	0.2472	0.2267	0.1911	0.1615	0.1164	0.0992	0.0847	0.0725
11	0.2875	0.2366	0.2149	0.1954	0.1619	0.1346	0.0938	0.0787	0.0662	0.0558
12	0.2567	0.2076	0.1869	0.1685	0.1372	0.1122	0.0757	0.0625	0.0517	0.0429
13	0.2292	0.1821	0.1625	0.1452	0.1163	0.0935	0.0610	0.0496	0.0404	0.0330
14	0.2046	0.1597	0.1413	0.1252	0.0985	0.0779	0.0492	0.0393	0.0316	0.0254
15	0.1827	0.1401	0.1229	0.1079	0.0835	0.0649	0.0397	0.0312	0.0247	0.0195
16	0.1631	0.1229	0.1069	0.0930	0.0708	0.0541	0.0320	0.0248	0.0193	0.0150
17	0.1456	0.1078	0.0929	0.0802	0.0600	0.0451	0.0258	0.0197	0.0150	0.0116
18	0.1300	0.0946	0.0808	0.0691	0.0508	0.0376	0.0208	0.0156	0.0118	0.0089
19	0.1161	0.0829	0.0703	0.0596	0.0431	0.0313	0.0168	0.0124	0.0092	0.0068
20	0.1037	0.0728	0.0611	0.0514	0.0365	0.0261	0.0135	0.0098	0.0072	0.0053
21	0.0926	0.0638	0.0531	0.0443	0.0309	0.0217	0.0109	0.0078	0.0056	0.0040
22	0.0826	0.0560	0.0462	0.0382	0.0262	0.0181	0.0088	0.0062	0.0044	0.0031
23	0.0738	0.0491	0.0402	0.0329	0.0222	0.0151	0.0071	0.0049	0.0034	0.0024
24	0.0659	0.0431	0.0349	0.0284	0.0188	0.0126	0.0057	0.0039	0.0027	0.0018
25	0.0588	0.0378	0.0304	0.0245	0.0160	0.0105	0.0046	0.0031	0.0021	0.0014
26	0.0525	0.0331	0.0264	0.0211	0.0135	0.0087	0.0037	0.0025	0.0016	0.0011
27	0.0469	0.0291	0.0230	0.0182	0.0115	0.0073	0.0030	0.0019	0.0013	0.0008
28	0.0419	0.0255	0.0200	0.0157	0.0097	0.0061	0.0024	0.0015	0.0010	0.0006
29	0.0374	0.0224	0.0174	0.0135	0.0082	0.0051	0.0020	0.0012	0.0008	0.0005
30	0.0334	0.0196	0.0151	0.0116	0.0070	0.0042	0.0016	0.0010	0.0006	0.0004

TABLE 3

ANNUITY FACTORS

The value today of a stream of payments of \$1 per period for the next n periods if the periodic interest rate is i; that is, $\dfrac{1}{i}\left[1 - \dfrac{1}{(1+i)^n}\right]$.

Period	1%	2%	3%	4%	5%	6%	7%	8%	9%	10%
1	0.9901	0.9804	0.9709	0.9615	0.9524	0.9434	0.9346	0.9259	0.9174	0.9091
2	1.970	1.942	1.913	1.886	1.859	1.833	1.808	1.783	1.759	1.736
3	2.941	2.884	2.829	2.775	2.723	2.673	2.624	2.577	2.531	2.487
4	3.902	3.808	3.717	3.630	3.546	3.465	3.387	3.312	3.240	3.170
5	4.853	4.713	4.580	4.452	4.329	4.212	4.100	3.993	3.890	3.791
6	5.795	5.601	5.417	5.242	5.076	4.917	4.767	4.623	4.486	4.355
7	6.728	6.472	6.230	6.002	5.786	5.582	5.389	5.206	5.033	4.868
8	7.652	7.325	7.020	6.733	6.463	6.210	5.971	5.747	5.535	5.335
9	8.566	8.162	7.786	7.435	7.108	6.802	6.515	6.247	5.995	5.759
10	9.471	8.983	8.530	8.111	7.722	7.360	7.024	6.710	6.418	6.145
11	10.37	9.787	9.253	8.760	8.306	7.887	7.499	7.139	6.805	6.495
12	11.26	10.58	9.954	9.385	8.863	8.384	7.943	7.536	7.161	6.814
13	12.13	11.35	10.63	9.986	9.394	8.853	8.358	7.904	7.487	7.103
14	13.00	12.11	11.30	10.56	9.899	9.295	8.745	8.244	7.786	7.367
15	13.87	12.85	11.94	11.12	10.38	9.712	9.108	8.559	8.061	7.606
16	14.72	13.58	12.56	11.65	10.84	10.11	9.447	8.851	8.313	7.824
17	15.56	14.29	13.17	12.17	11.27	10.48	9.763	9.122	8.544	8.022
18	16.40	14.99	13.75	12.66	11.69	10.83	10.06	9.372	8.756	8.201
19	17.23	15.68	14.32	13.13	12.09	11.16	10.34	9.604	8.950	8.365
20	18.05	16.35	14.88	13.59	12.46	11.47	10.59	9.818	9.129	8.514
21	18.86	17.01	15.42	14.03	12.82	11.76	10.84	10.02	9.292	8.649
22	19.66	17.66	15.94	14.45	13.16	12.04	11.06	10.20	9.442	8.772
23	20.46	18.29	16.44	14.86	13.49	12.30	11.27	10.37	9.580	8.883
24	21.24	18.91	16.94	15.25	13.80	12.55	11.47	10.53	9.707	8.985
25	22.02	19.52	17.41	15.62	14.09	12.78	11.65	10.67	9.823	9.077
26	22.80	20.12	17.88	15.98	14.38	13.00	11.83	10.81	9.929	9.161
27	23.56	20.71	18.33	16.33	14.64	13.21	11.99	10.94	10.03	9.237
28	24.32	21.28	18.76	16.66	14.90	13.41	12.14	11.05	10.12	9.307
29	25.07	21.84	19.19	16.98	15.14	13.59	12.28	11.16	10.20	9.370
30	25.81	22.40	19.60	17.29	15.37	13.76	12.41	11.26	10.27	9.427

Period	12%	14%	15%	16%	18%	20%	24%	26%	28%	30%
1	0.8929	0.8772	0.8696	0.8621	0.8475	0.8333	0.8065	0.7937	0.7813	0.7692
2	1.690	1.647	1.626	1.605	1.566	1.528	1.457	1.424	1.392	1.361
3	2.402	2.322	2.283	2.246	2.174	2.106	1.981	1.923	1.868	1.816
4	3.037	2.914	2.855	2.798	2.690	2.589	2.404	2.320	2.241	2.166
5	3.605	3.433	3.352	3.274	3.127	2.991	2.745	2.635	2.532	2.436
6	4.111	3.889	3.784	3.685	3.498	3.326	3.020	2.885	2.759	2.643
7	4.564	4.288	4.160	4.039	3.812	3.605	3.242	3.083	2.937	2.802
8	4.968	4.639	4.487	4.344	4.078	3.837	3.421	3.241	3.076	2.925
9	5.328	4.946	4.772	4.607	4.303	4.031	3.566	3.366	3.184	3.019
10	5.650	5.216	5.019	4.833	4.494	4.192	3.682	3.465	3.269	3.092
11	5.938	5.453	5.234	5.029	4.656	4.327	3.776	3.543	3.335	3.147
12	6.194	5.660	5.421	5.197	4.793	4.439	3.851	3.606	3.387	3.190
13	6.424	5.842	5.583	5.342	4.910	4.533	3.912	3.656	3.427	3.223
14	6.628	6.002	5.724	5.468	5.008	4.611	3.962	3.695	3.459	3.249
15	6.811	6.142	5.847	5.575	5.092	4.675	4.001	3.726	3.483	3.268
16	6.974	6.265	5.954	5.668	5.162	4.730	4.033	3.751	3.503	3.283
17	7.120	6.373	6.047	5.749	5.222	4.775	4.059	3.771	3.518	3.295
18	7.250	6.467	6.128	5.818	5.273	4.812	4.080	3.786	3.529	3.304
19	7.366	6.550	6.198	5.877	5.316	4.843	4.097	3.799	3.539	3.311
20	7.469	6.623	6.259	5.929	5.353	4.870	4.110	3.808	3.546	3.316
21	7.562	6.687	6.312	5.973	5.384	4.891	4.121	3.816	3.551	3.320
22	7.645	6.743	6.359	6.011	5.410	4.909	4.130	3.822	3.556	3.323
23	7.718	6.792	6.399	6.044	5.432	4.925	4.137	3.827	3.559	3.325
24	7.784	6.835	6.434	6.073	5.451	4.937	4.143	3.831	3.562	3.327
25	7.843	6.873	6.464	6.097	5.467	4.948	4.147	3.834	3.564	3.329
26	7.896	6.906	6.491	6.118	5.480	4.956	4.151	3.837	3.566	3.330
27	7.943	6.935	6.514	6.136	5.492	4.964	4.154	3.839	3.567	3.331
28	7.984	6.961	6.534	6.152	5.502	4.970	4.157	3.840	3.568	3.331
29	8.022	6.983	6.551	6.166	5.510	4.975	4.159	3.841	3.569	3.332
30	8.055	7.003	6.566	6.177	5.517	4.979	4.160	3.842	3.569	3.332

APPENDIX B

ANSWERS TO CHECK STATION QUESTIONS

CHAPTER 5

1. (p. 88)

ASSETS		LIABILITIES AND NET WORTH	
Savings account	$ 15,000	Mortgage	$100,000
Checking account	5,000	Credit card debt	7,000
House	200,000	Car loan	15,000
Pension plan	100,000	Net worth	218,000
Car	20,000		

2. (p. 90) Jakes's balance sheet after the loan is:

ASSETS		LIABILITIES AND NET WORTH	
Previous assets		Previous liabilities & NW	
Demand deposit at		Loan from	
Solid State	$200,000	Solid State	$200,000

3. (p. 91)

ASSETS		LIABILITIES AND NET WORTH	
Reserves		Demand deposits	$20m
Cash	$ 0.5m		
Deposit at Fed	11.3m		
Loans	10.2m	Equity	2m

4. (p. 93) For every $1,000,000 in loans, you will earn on the good loans

$$0.14 \times \$900,000 = \$126,000,$$

and lose on the bad ones

$$0.10 \times \$100,000 = \$10,000,$$

leaving you with $116,000 or 11.6%. Your profits are, therefore,

$$\pi = (\$10.2m \times 0.116) - (\$10m \times 0.08) - \$100,000 = \$283,200.$$

5. (p. 94) The best contractual rate is 14%.

Contractual Rate	Percent of Loans That Default	Percent of Loan Recovery	Realized Rate
12	10	95	10.30
13	12	95	10.85
14	12	90	11.12
15	15	85	10.50
16	20	75	7.80

6. (p. 101) Raising equity to $1.0 million would raise the equity-to-loan ratio to 10.2% from its current 6.4%:

ASSETS		LIABILITIES AND NET WORTH	
Reserves		Demand deposits	$10m
Cash	$0.5m		
Deposit at Fed	0.7m		
Loans	9.8m	Equity	1.0m

You could increase equity either by retaining some of the bank's earnings or by adding another $400,000 of your own money or that of other investors.

CHAPTER 6

1. (p. 113)

2. (p. 114)

A. $100 × (1 + 0.12) = $112.00.

B. $100 × (1 + 0.08) = $108.00.

C. $90.91 × (1 + 0.10) = $100.00.

3. (p. 115)

A. $100 × (1 + 0.12)^2 = $125.44.

B. $120 × (1 + 0.15)^2 = $158.70.

C. $10,000 \times (1 + 0.12)^{20} = \$96,462.93.$

D. $\$384.54 \times (1 + 0.10)^{10} = \$997.40.$

4. (p. 117)

A. 0%.

B. $P = \dfrac{\$10,000}{1.06} = \$9,433.96.$

C. $P = \dfrac{\$1,000}{1.15} = \$869.56.$

5. (p. 118)

A. $P = \dfrac{\$100}{(1.06)^2} = \$89.00.$

B. $P = \dfrac{\$1,000}{(1.10)^3} = \$751.31.$

6. (p. 121)

A. $P = \dfrac{\$120}{(1.10)} + \dfrac{\$1,120}{(1.10)^2} = \$1,034.71.$

B. $951.23; \$1,000.

7. (p 123)

A. $\$9,500 = \dfrac{\$1,000}{(1 + i)^1} + \dfrac{\$1,000}{(1 + i)^2} + \cdots + \dfrac{(\$1,000 + \$10,000)}{(1 + i)^{10}} \; ; \; i = 10.84\%.$

B. $\$902.25 = \dfrac{\$70}{(1.11)^1} + \dfrac{\$70}{(1.11)^2} + \dfrac{(\$1,070)}{(1.11)^3} \; .$

8. (p. 125)

A. $\$56,500 = \dfrac{\$10,000}{(1.12)^1} + \dfrac{\$10,000}{(1.12)^2} + \cdots + \dfrac{\$10,000}{(1.12)^{10}} \; .$

B. $\$20,000 = \dfrac{\$1,000}{0.05} \; .$

9. (p. 128)

A. $0.02\% = \dfrac{7.3\%}{365}$.

B. $1 + \text{periodic rate} = (1.1025)^{1/2}$; periodic rate $= 5\%$; APR $= 10\%$.

10. (p. 129)   The periodic rate is

$$\frac{\$10,000 - 9,857.40}{\$9,857.40} = \frac{\$142.60}{\$9,857.40} = .0145 \text{ or } 1.45\%.$$

The effective annual rate is 9%:

$$(1.0145)^6 = 1.09 = 1 + \text{effective annual rate.}$$

11. (p. 131)   Periodic rate is 2.4%: $(1 + \text{periodic rate})^4 = 1.10$

$$P = \frac{\$300}{(1.024)} + \frac{\$300}{(1.024)^2} + \frac{\$300}{(1.024)^3} + \frac{\$10,300}{(1.024)^4} = \$10,221.92.$$

12. (p. 131)   Periodic rate $= 9\%/12 = 0.75\%$. The annuity factor for 0.075%

and 360 periods is $\dfrac{1}{0.0075}\left[1 - \dfrac{1}{(1.0075)^{360}} \right] = 124.28.$ So the monthly

payment is $\dfrac{\$120,000}{124.28} = \$965.56.$

CHAPTER 10

1. (p. 252)

Cash	−$1.5m		
Deposit at Fed	+1.5m		
Loans	+$0.2m	Deposits	+$0.2m
Deposit at Fed	−$10,000	Deposits	−$10,000
Deposit at Fed	−$190,000	Deposits	−$190,000
Deposit at Fed	+$10m	Deposits	+$10m

CHAPTER 12

1. (p. 310)

A. $\dfrac{\$1,000,000}{(1.12)^2} = \$797,194.$

B. $-10 \times \dfrac{0.005}{1.115} = 0.045.$

2. (p. 311)

A. $V_1 = \dfrac{\$5m}{(1.09)} = \$4.59m;\ V_2 = \dfrac{\$3m}{(1.09)^2} = \$2.53m;\ V_3 = \dfrac{\$2m}{(1.09)^3} = \$1.54m;$

$A = \$4.59m + \$2.53m + \$1.54m = \$8.66m$

$d_A = \left[1 \times \dfrac{4.59}{8.66} + 2 \times \dfrac{2.53}{8.66} + 3 \times \dfrac{1.54}{8.66} \right] = 1.65.$

B. $\dfrac{\Delta A}{A} = -1.65 \times \dfrac{0.002}{(1.09)} = -0.0030;\ \Delta A = -\$8.66m \times 0.0030 = -\$26,200.$

3. (p. 312) $\Delta E = - (2.5 \times \$11.2m - 1.3 \times \$10.3m)\ \dfrac{0.003}{1.101} = -\$39,809.$

CHAPTER 13

1. (p. 323) Buy a contract (or contracts) for $976,562.50 per contract. If you are right, the spot price will be $987,876.55 and your profit will be $11,314.05 per contract. If rate is 15%, the spot price will be $965,662.89 and your loss will be $10,899.61 per contract.

2. (p. 326) A. NCD repayment is $1,000,000 (1.10)^2 = \$1,210,000.$

Loan Rate at End of Year 1	Return on Sequence of Two Loans	Profit at End of Second Year (loan repayment – NCD repayment)
12%	$1,000,000 (1.12) (1.12)= $1,254,400	$1,254,400 – 1,210,000 = $44,400
17%	$1,000,000 (1.12) (1.17)= $1,310,400	$1,310,400 – 1,210,000 = $100,400
7%	$1,000,000 (1.12) (1.07)= $1,198,400	$1,198,400 – 1,210,000 = –$11,600

B. Metropolis could hedge by buying T-bill futures:

Rate on T-Bills at Year End	Price of T-Bill at Year End	Profit on Futures	Total Profit (profit on loan + profit on futures)
9%	$1m/1.09 = $917,431	$917,431 – 917,431 = $0	$44,000 + 0 = $44,000
14%	$1m/1.14 = $877,193	$877,193 – 917,431 = –$40,238	$100,400 – 40,238 (1.15) = $54,126
4%	$1m/1.04 = $961,538	$961,538 – 917,431 = $44,107	–$11,600 + 44,107 (1.05) = $34,712

3. (p. 335)

A. Loss = DM12.5m x .09 $/DM = $1,125,000.

B. Could hedge by buying a put option.

C.

Strike Price	Cost of Hedge (premium for 12.5m)	Loss If Mark Falls to 50¢
54	0.0017 x 12.5m = $21,250	$12.5m x .04 = $500,000
55	0.0029 x 12.5m = $36,250	$12.5m x .05 = $625,000
56	0.0039 x 12.5m = $48,750	$12.5m x .06 = $750,000

CHAPTER 19

1. (p. 516) $90,000; $90,000; $100,000; $10,000.

2. (p. 518)

BANKING SYSTEM			
Reserves	10,000,000	Checking deposits Old	10,000,000
Loans	90,000,000	New (at all banks)	90,000,000

3. (p. 519)

A. $\dfrac{1}{r} = \dfrac{1}{0.1} = 10$.

B. $D = \dfrac{15m}{0.3} = 50m$.

4. (p. 520) *Immediate effect:*

COCONUT GROVE

Reserves	−5,000	Checking deposits	−5,000

Eventual effect:

BANKING SYSTEM

Reserves	−5,000	Checking deposits	−25,000
Loans	−20,000		

5. (p. 521)

A. $C = 0.1 \times \$36.7m = \$3.67m$; $R = 0.2 \times \$36.7m = \$7.33m$; $C + R = \$3.67m + \$7.33m = \$11m$.

B. $D = \dfrac{1}{0.05 + 0.1} \times \$11,000,000 = \$73.3m$.

6. (p. 522)

A. $T = 2 \times \$27.5m = \$55m$.

B. $C = 0.1 \times \$27.5m = \$2.75m$; $R_D = 0.2 \times \$27.5m = \$5.5m$; $R_T = 0.05 \times \$55m = \$2.75m$;
$C + R_D + R_T = \$11m$.

7. (p. 527)

A. $M = 2.75 \times \$12m = \$33m$.

B. $m = \dfrac{1 + 0.20}{0.20 + 0.12 + 0.03 \times 3} = 2.93$.

8. (p. 528)

A. $m2 = \dfrac{1 + 0.1 + 2}{0.1 + 0.2 + 0.05 \times 2} = 7.75$.

B. $m2 = \dfrac{1 + 0.1 + 3}{0.1 + 0.2 + 0.05 \times 3} = 9.11$.

9. (p. 529) Changes that result from a $500,000 decrease in monetary base:

	Change	Equation Used
Demand deposits (ΔD)	−$1,125,000	19.28
Time deposits (ΔT)	−$2,500,000	19.16
Reserves against checking deposits (ΔR_D)	−$250,000	19.2
Reserves against time deposits (ΔR_T)	−$125,000	19.15
Currency held by public (ΔC)	−$125,000	19.8
Quantity of money ($\Delta D + \Delta C$)	−$1,375,000	19.22
Monetary base ($\Delta R_D + \Delta R_T + \Delta C$)	−$500,000	19.18

APPENDIX TO CHAPTER 19

1. (p. 536) $\Delta T = t \times \Delta D = 2 \times \$1m = \$2m.$

CHAPTER 20

1. (p. 543)

THE FED			
U.S. Securities	−$200m	Deposits Metropolis	−$200m

METROPOLIS			
Deposit at Fed	−$200m	Deposits XYZ Securities	−$200m

CHAPTER 21

1. (p. 562)

Required reserves = 0.03 × $6.5b + 0.12 × $7.9b = $1.143b.
Required amount
in Fed deposit = $1.143b − 0.29b = $853m.

2. (p. 568) An increase in excess reserves would decrease the money multiplier and decrease M1 if R remained the same.

CHAPTER 22

1. (p. 584)

$$V_{annual} = \frac{\$5,233 \text{ billion per year}}{\$798 \text{ billion}} = 6.56 \text{ per year.}$$

Monthly velocity is 6.56/12 = 0.55 per month.

2. (p. 586) $1,500.

3. (p. 589)

$$M_{tr}^D = \sqrt{\frac{5 \times 20,000}{2 \times 0.05}} = \$1,000.$$

4. (p. 590) None.

CHAPTER 23

1. (p. 605) The variables in the equation of exchange will go from

Before: $1.5b × 2/3 = $1.0b = $1 × 2m + $100 × 1,000 + ...

to

After: $750m × 2/3 = $500m = $0.50 × 2m + $50 × 1,000 + ...

2. (p. 606) The real price of bread is 1/100 bicycle; of a canoe, 50 bicycles.

3. (p. 608)

$$1 + r = \frac{1 + 0.07}{1 + 0.05} = 1.019; \; 1 + r = \frac{1 + 0.07}{1 - 0.05} = 1.126; \; 1 + r = \frac{1 + 0.07}{1 + 0.0} = 1.07.$$

CHAPTER 24

1. (p. 622)

Household saving increases by $15 million, equal to the reduction in consumption expenditure. The remaining $20 million increase in asset balances comes at the expense of lending: Households increase their money holdings rather than their holdings of securities.

CHAPTER 25

1. (p. 635)

A. At an exchange rate of 150¥/$, these prices are consistent with purchasing power parity.

B. The yen price of a dancing lesson on the Island is $50 × 150¥/$ = ¥7,500, less than the price on the Atoll. This is not, however, inconsistent with purchasing power parity, because dancing lessons are *not* traded goods.

2. (p. 636)

A. Opening the Island's loanable funds market lowered the equilibrium interest rate. As a result, household lending fell and borrowing for investment increased.

B. If Atoll investors are willing to lend on the Island, then the initial interest rate there must be higher than on the Atoll. The loss of loanable funds will drive up the interest rate on the Atoll. Total lending of Atoll households (to both loanable-funds markets combined) will increase, and borrowing for investment on the Atoll will fall.

3. (p. 646)

No, purchasing power parity does not hold. As a result of the appreciation of the dollar, Island traded goods are generally less expensive than Atoll traded goods. We expect purchasing power parity to be re-established in the long run, but short-run deviations from it are common.

4. (p. 648)

A. 90¥/$.

B. 180¥/$.

CHAPTER 26

1. (p. 668) $0.63 \times (-200) = -\$126$ million.

2. (p. 669) $-0.05 \times (-200) = \$10$ million.

3. (p. 670)

$E_3 = (70 + 0.63 \times 1,037) + 120 + 200 + (30 - 0.05 \times 1,037) = \$1,021m$; income for Month 4 is $1,021m.

4. (p. 670)

An increase in investment would cause a parallel shift of the expenditure line upwards. The level of income at which income and expenditure are in balance would rise.

5. (p. 672)

A. $\Delta T = 0.1 \times 71.4 = \$7.14m$. This is much less than the $30 million increase in government expenditure.

B. $\Delta Y = 2.381 \times (-10) = -\$23.81$.

6. (p. 677)

$\Delta Y = 2.381 \times (-800) \times (-0.02) = \$38.1m.$

7. (p. 680)

$\Delta Y = 1,000 \times 0.01 = \$10m.$

8. (p. 682) From Equation 26.17 net exports decrease:

$$\Delta X = (-0.05) \times 24.4 = \$1.22m.$$

CHAPTER 27

1. (p. 696)

A. This increases available labor and shifts the aggregate supply curve to the right.

B. This is an improvement in technology, which shifts the aggregate supply curve to the right.

C. The same as (B).

APPENDIX TO CHAPTER 27

1. (p. 711)

A. This shifts the IS curve to the right, increasing equilibrium income and so expenditure at a given price level. The aggregate demand curve shifts to the right.

B. This increases the multiplier, shifting the IS curve to the right (and flattening it). The result is a shift to the right of the aggregate demand curve.

C. This moves the LM curve to the right, shifting the aggregate demand curve to the right too.

CHAPTER 28

1. (p. 717)

A. $1.10 + 0.03 \cong g_P + 0.02$, so $g_P = 0.11$.

B. $g_M + 0.03 \cong 0.0 + 0.02$, so $g_M = -0.01$.

2. (p. 723) $i = .04 + .05 = .09$.

3. (p. 726) The real supply of loanable funds was reduced, driving up the real interest rate.

4. (p. 730)

The yearly rate of change of the yen/dollar exchange rate will be 2% − 4% = −2%. After ten years the yen/dollar exchange rate will have fallen to $(1 - 0.02)^{10} \times 155 = 127¥/\$$.

CHAPTER 29

1. (p. 755)

A. $(1 + 0.07)^3 = (1 + 0.06)^2 (1 + i_2^f); i_2^f = 9\%$.

B. $5.75\% \cong \dfrac{5\% + 6\% + 6.25\%}{3}$.

2. (p. 756)

A. Short-term rates are expected to fall initially then rise.

B. $i_2 \cong \dfrac{5\% + 6\%}{2} = 5.5\%; i_3 \cong \dfrac{5\% + 6\% + 6\%}{3} = 5.7\%$.

3. (p. 758)

A. A negative term premium is indeed possible in principle. It would signify a "solidity premium" on long-term securities: A preference, other things equal, for longer-term securities.

B. $i_2 \cong \dfrac{5\% + 6\%}{2} + 0.2\% = 5.7\%$;

   $i_3 \cong \dfrac{5\% + 6\% + 6\%}{3} + 0.3\% = 6.0\%$.

4. (p. 761) $e_1^f = 200¥/\$ \times \dfrac{(1 + 0.10)}{(1 + 0.05)} = 209.52¥/\$$.

5. (p. 766) $\dfrac{e_1^e - e}{e} = i_1^f - i_1^\$ = 11.8\% - 8.5\% = 3.3\%$;

   $\dfrac{e_1^e - e}{e} = i_1^{DM} - i_1^\$ = 8.8\% - 8.5\% = 0.3\%$.

6. (p. 768)

The real rate in the United States is $8.5\% - 5\% = 3.5\%$. If the currency premiums are zero, then the real rates in the other countries are also 3.5%. The expected rates of inflation are therefore:

United States	5.0%
Japan	3.1
United Kingdom	8.3
Germany	5.3
Canada	7.9

CHAPTER 31

1. (p. 820)

$$\frac{W}{2} = 150 \text{ base-period dollars; } W = \$300.$$

$$\frac{\$300}{1.8} = 167 \text{ base-period dollars.}$$

CHAPTER 32

1. (p. 854) $P^* = 3.2 \times 1.65/4.2 = 1.26$. Since this is higher than the current price level, monetary policy should be tightened to restrain inflation.

GLOSSARY

absorption Total expenditure by households, firms, and the government.

accrued interest Interest accumulated on a bond since the last coupon payment.

adaptive expectations Expectations that are based only on past and current values of a variable.

adjustable-rate mortgage (ARM) Mortgage on which the interest rate adjusts with market interest rates.

adjustment credit Discount lending for short periods of time.

adverse selection Tendency, in losing customers, to lose the best ones.

agencies Securities issued by certain agencies of the federal government.

aggregate demand curve Curve showing the demand for output at different price levels.

aggregate demand for money Average money holdings for all economic agents.

aggregate supply curve Curve showing the prices firms will charge at different levels of output.

American option Option that may be exercised anytime up to the contract's expiration date.

amortized loan Security that promises a series of equal payments.

announcement effect Effect on expectations of an announcement of a change in the discount rate.

annual coupon rate Stated annual rate used to calculate the periodic coupon rate.

annuity Security that promises a series of equal annual payments.

anticipated inflation Inflation that is expected by most people.

appreciation Increase in the exchange rate of one currency against another.

ask (offer) price Price at which a market maker will sell a security.

asset management Management of a financial institution's asset structure to provide liquidity.

asset motive Holding money as a store of value.

assets Items of value that a business owns.

automated clearinghouse Clearing of payments through banks' exchange of computer-tape records.

automated teller machine (ATM) Card-operated facility for making bank deposits and withdrawals.

autonomous consumption Consumption expenditure that is independent of the level of income.

autonomous expenditure Expenditure that is independent of the level of income.

autonomous net exports Part of net exports that is independent of income.

average annual yield to maturity Single interest rate at which the present value of a bond's coupon and principal payments equals its market price.

balance on capital account Net foreign investment and lending in the United States.

balance on current account Cumulative balance on goods, services, and transfers.

balance of payments Cumulative balance on current and capital accounts.

balance sheet Financial statement that lists a firm's assets, liabilities, and net worth.

balance of trade Difference between merchandise exports and imports.

bank credit card Card allowing holder to purchase goods on credit extended by issuing bank.

bank money Bank liabilities such as bank notes and deposits that are used as money.

bank notes Promissory notes issued by a bank that are payable to bearer on demand; acceptable as money.

bank repo Arrangement to convert a deposit automatically into a repo overnight.

bank run Withdrawal of deposits simultaneously by many of a bank's customers.

banker's acceptance Short-term credit instrument issued by an importer's bank that guarantees payment of an exporter's invoice.

banker's banks Regional service centers jointly owned by groups of small banks.

banking panic A run on many banks simultaneously.

banks Financial institutions that accept deposits and make loans.

barter Direct exchange of goods for goods without the use of money.

Basel concordat 1974 agreement that each central bank should be responsible for the foreign subsidiaries of its own bank.

basis point One-hundredth of 1% in the yield of an investment.

basis risk Risk that the price of the instrument being hedged will be different from the price of the instrument in the futures contract.

bearer receipts Receipts conveying ownership to the person in possession of them.

bearer security Security for which possession is primary evidence of ownership.

bid price Price at which a market maker will purchase a security.

bills Securities of short maturity promising a single payment.

BIS capital standards Requirements for setting equity ratios, established by the Bank for International Settlements.

bond mutual fund Fund that pools the investments of a large number of people and purchases bonds.

book entry security Security that exists only as a computer record.

book value Face or par value with no consideration for market value; accounting value of a bank.

bracket creep Movement to a higher tax bracket caused by rising income.

break-even interest rate Interest rate above which a project is unprofitable and below which it is profitable.

Bretton Woods New Hampshire town where the post–World War II system of fixed exchange rates and the International Monetary Fund were established by international agreement in 1944.

bridge bank Temporary, government-owned bank resulting from direct FDIC assistance to a failed bank.

broker market Market in which large blocks of federal funds are lent.

brokered deposits Large amounts of money divided into small portions for deposit with a number of banks.

call option Option to buy.

callable Redeemable by issuer at face value before maturity.

capacity utilization rate Measure of the employment of physical capital in the economy.

capital gain Gain from the sale of an asset at a price higher than the original cost.

capital loss Loss from the sale of an asset at a price below the original cost.

capital market Market for financial claims with maturities greater than one year; the long-term financial market.

carry Difference between the interest rate a dealer pays for financing and the interest rate it receives on the securities it owns.

central bank Official institution with broad responsibilities for a nation's payment system; established to help maintain the liquidity of private banks.

chain banking Ownership of two or more banks by an individual or group without the benefit of a holding company.

check An order to a bank to pay out of a deposit.

check card Bank-issued card guaranteeing payment, presented by bank customers when writing a check.

CHIPS Clearing House Interbank Payment System, a clearing system for wire transfers.

clearing Exchange of checks between banks in which checks deposited at one bank are set off against those deposited at another.

clearing bank Bank that executes trades for a securities dealer or broker.

coins Pieces of metal of certified weight and purity that circulate as money.

coinsurance Percentage of a loss paid by the insured.

collateralized Having a borrower's property pledged as a guarantee that a loan will be repaid.

collateralized mortgage obligation (CMO) Security backed by pass-throughs that pays principal and interest like bonds.

commercial bank Financial intermediary that specializes in taking demand deposits and in making loans to business firms.

commercial mortgage Private loan secured by commercial property.

commercial paper Short-term, unsecured debt of corporations and financial institutions.

commodity money Something that is used as money and is also bought and sold for its value as a commercial product.

commodity standard Exchange rates fixed in terms of a commodity.

compensating balance Required minimum balance that a borrower must maintain at a bank, usually in a checking account.

competitive bid Bid for the purchase of a new Treasury issue that specifies a price.

compounding Calculation of interest on interest already earned.

compounding period Period over which interest is calculated.

computation period Two-week time period for calculating a bank's required reserves.

consolidated balance sheet Balance sheet reporting the financial condition of a number of separate entities as if they were a single unified economic entity.

Consumer Credit Protection Act of 1968 (Truth in Lending Act) Legislation requiring lenders to provide borrowers with accurate information about the cost of credit.

consumer price index (CPI) Index that measures the cost of living for a typical urban family.

consumption function Relationship of consumption spending to the level of income.

continuing loan-supply effect Increase in real supply of loanable funds due to increased bank lending.

contractual rate Rate that is charged.

convertibility Capability of being exchanged for a specified equivalent, as another currency or security.

convertible bonds Bonds that may be converted into stock at the option of the investor at a predetermined price.

core capital Book value of stock plus retained earnings.

correspondent balances Zero-interest deposits that a respondent holds with its correspondents.

correspondent bank Large bank that provides a smaller bank with special services.

correspondent market Market in which correspondents convert respondent deposits into federal funds loans.

correspondent relationship Interbank relationship involving deposits and various services.

cost-of-living adjustment (COLA) Clause in a wage contract requiring that wages be raised over the life of the contract to reflect change in the consumer price index.

cost–push inflation Inflation resulting from spiraling increases in wages and prices.

covered interest arbitrage Trading strategy that exploits differences between implicit forward exchange rates and actual forward exchange rates.

credit risk Risk that borrowers will not repay their loans.

crowding out Reduction in the amount of investment owing to government borrowing.

currency/checking-deposit ratio Ratio of publicly held currency to checking deposits.

currency drain Loss of reserves caused by depositors withdrawing cash.

currency premium Quantity reflecting the market's relative preference for securities denominated in one currency over those denominated in another.

currency swap Exchange of payments in two different currencies.

daily settlement Daily payment of gains or losses on a futures contract.

daylight overdraft Amount of money lent interest-free during the business day; overdraft during the business day.

dealer loan Loan that a securities dealer obtains from a bank for the purpose of buying securities.

dealer repurchase agreement Arrangement whereby a dealer sells government securities and simultaneously contracts to buy them back at a specified time and price.

dealers Individuals or firms that act as market makers by quoting bids and offers on securities.

debenture Corporate security backed by the general credit of the issuing firm.

debit card Card authorizing the debiting of the holder's checking account with each transaction.

debt contract Contract stating agreement by the borrower to pay the lender fixed dollar amounts at regular intervals until a specified date when the final payment is made.

deductible Initial amount of a loss paid by the insured.

default To fail either to make interest payments on schedule or to pay off the amount owed when the financial instrument matures.

defined benefit plan Pension plan wherein a company promises a certain level of retirement benefits and funds the plan to cover those benefits.

defined contribution plan Pension plan wherein a company contributes a fixed amount annually for each employee.

definitive money Money that is not convertible into anything else.

demand deposits Funds placed in banks that are payable on demand and transferable by check.

demand for money (M^D) Average amount of money held.

demand–pull inflation Inflation caused by more money chasing the same quantity of goods.

deposit poor Having a lot of loan opportunities relative to deposits.

deposit rich Having a lot of deposits relative to loan opportunities.

depreciation Decrease in the exchange rate of one currency against another.

derivative securities Futures and options in stocks and stock indexes.

direct lending Lending by ultimate lender to ultimate borrower with no intermediary.

direct placement Sale of a security directly to investors without a public issue.

dirty float Exchange rate determined by supply and demand but with occasional central-bank intervention.

discount loan A bank's borrowing from the Fed.

discount rate Rate charged for borrowing from the Fed.

discount window When borrowing from the Fed, one is said to be going to the discount window.

disintermediation Shifting from bank-intermediated lending to lending in the direct market.

disposable income Total household income less taxes.

dissaving Spending more than income.

diversification Process of acquiring a portfolio of securities that have dissimilar risk–return characteristics such that the overall portfolio risk is reduced.

dual banking Banking regulated by both the state and the federal governments.

due-on-sale provision Mortgage contract stipulation that the mortgage must be repaid if the property is sold.

duration Measure of the sensitivity of the value of an asset or a liability to changes in interest rates.

duration gap Difference between asset duration and liability duration times the ratio of liability market value to asset market value.

dynamic hedging (portfolio insurance) Hedging a stock portfolio by trading in index futures.

economic rent The excess of price over the costs required to provide a service.

economies of scale Declining average cost of operation as the scale of operation is increased.

economies of scope Reduction in costs resulting from engaging in complementary activities.

Edge Act corporations Subsidiary corporations set up by U.S. commercial banks to engage in international banking.

effective annual rate Interest accrued at the end of the year as a percentage of the principal amount.

effective reserve ratio The ratio of reserves to deposits, both regular and disguised.

eligible paper Paper acceptable as collateral for a bank's borrowing from the Fed.

Employee Retirement Income Security Act of 1974 (ERISA) Legislation requiring employers to offer pension plans to their workers.

Equal Credit Opportunity Act of 1974 Legislation prohibiting discrimination in credit evaluation.

equation of exchange Expression of the relationship between the quantity of money and expenditure.

equilibrium interest rate Interest rate at which the quantity of loanable funds demanded equals the quantity supplied.

equity contract Contract representing a claim to a share in the net income and in the assets of a business.

equity-to-loan ratio Ratio of the amount of a bank's equity to the amount of its loans.

Eurobonds Bonds denominated in a currency other than that of the country in which they are issued.

Eurocurrency deposits and loans Deposits and loans in any currency other than that of the country in which the bank is located.

Eurodollar market Market for dollar-denominated deposits and loans in financial institutions outside the United States.

Eurodollars Dollar-denominated deposits held in foreign banks.

Euroequities Equities issued by firms in a country other than their own.

European option Option that may be exercised only on the contract's expiration date.

excess reserves Cash in the vault or deposits at the Fed that exceed the amount of reserves required by law.

exchange-rate risk Risk associated with fluctuations in the exchange rate between different currencies.

exercise (strike) price Predetermined price at which an option is surrendered and the underlying transaction takes place.

expectations theory Theory that assumes that borrowers and lenders care only about expected yields.

expiration date Date at which an option contract terminates.

explicit interest Interest paid to depositors.

extended credit Discount lending for lengthy time periods.

externalities Costs of harmful side effects of a firm's activity that are borne by others and not by the firm.

extrapolative expectations Expectations that in the future the value of a variable will continue its present trend.

Fed Federal Reserve Banks.

Fed float The difference in amount between items in process of collection and deferred credit items.

Fed funds market Market in which banks borrow reserves from other banks.

Federal Deposit Insurance Corporation (FDIC) Government agency established to insure deposits in commercial banks up to a specified amount.

Federal Open Market Committee (FOMC) Chief policy-making body of the Federal Reserve System.

Federal Reserve Act of 1913 Legislation that established the Federal Reserve System.

Federal Reserve Banks The 12 banks that make up the central bank of the United States.

Fedwire Communications network that links major-bank computers to the Fed's computers.

fiat money Money created by government order.

finance companies Financial intermediaries that borrow in order to make consumer, mortgage, and business loans.

financial assets Property that represents loans, such as savings accounts and bonds.

financial futures contract Contract for the future delivery of securities.

financial intermediary Institution that borrows by issuing its own securities and relends the funds it raises.

fine-tune To stabilize an economy by continuous, small-scale fiscal and monetary manipulations.

Fisher equation Equation stating that the nominal rate of interest approximates the expected real rate plus the expected rate of inflation.

fixed capital Finance needed for long-term investment in machinery or buildings.

fixed costs Bank's costs that do not vary directly with the amount of deposits or loans.

fixed exchange rate Nonfluctuating exchange rate that is determined by central banks.

fixed-rate mortgage Mortgage that is amortized by fixed monthly payments over the life of the loan.

fixed-rate payer A party to a swap who agrees to make fixed payments in exchange for LIBOR.

floating-rate loans Loans whose interest rate is adjusted periodically as market rates change.

floating-rate payer A party to a swap who agrees to pay LIBOR in exchange for fixed payments.

flow of funds accounts Record of the amounts borrowed and lent among the various sectors of the economy.

FOMC policy directives Federal Reserve policy decisions sent to the New York Fed for execution.

foreign exchange Conversion of U.S. dollars into the currencies of other countries.

foreign-trade effect Effect on aggregate demand caused by change in the relative price of foreign and domestic goods.

forward transaction in foreign exchange Agreement to buy or sell a foreign currency in the future at a price agreed upon now.

forward transactions Transactions in which two parties agree in advance on the terms of a trade to be carried out at a specified future time.

fractional-reserve banking Banking in which only a fraction of a bank's deposits is held in the form of liquid reserves, with the balance lent out to earn interest.

franchising Granting a right to a company to market the franchisers's goods or services in a specific territory, using the franchise name and methods.

freely floating exchange rate Exchange rate determined solely by supply and demand.

free-rider problem Problem of one investor bearing all the cost of research that can also be used by other investors.

Friedman-Phelps critique Argument that the Phillips-curve relationship relies on inflation being unanticipated.

future value Value at a time in the future, including accumulated interest, of an amount invested earlier.

futures contract Contract to buy or sell securities in the future at a price agreed upon in the present.

General Account U.S. government's checking deposit at the Federal Reserve Banks.

general obligation bonds Bonds backed by the ability of the issuing authority to levy taxes; repayable from general tax revenue.

giro payment Bank service allowing direct transfer of funds among account holders.

GNP implicit price deflator Price index based on the basket of final goods and services produced by the economy.

goodwill Difference between the market value of a bank and its book value.

gross national product (GNP) All of the goods and services produced by the economy during a year.

hedge Protect against risk.

hedgers Traders who take a position in futures to offset the risk they face from having a position in the underlying commodity.

holding company Corporation formed for the purpose of owning or holding stock in other corporations.

household sector One of the decision-making divisions of the economy, composed of all individual households.

implicit forward exchange rate Rate that would equalize the expected return from securities in different currencies.

implicit forward interest rate Rate required in the future to equalize expected yields on bills of different maturities.

implicit interest Interest in the form of services provided.

in the money Above the exercise price.

income multiplier The ratio of income to autonomous expenditure.

index arbitrage Simultaneous trading in index futures and in the underlying stocks to exploit price differences.

indexation Linkage of payments to a published price index.

indicator Variable used to predict the future value of some other variable.

indirect lending Lending by ultimate lender to financial intermediary that then relends to ultimate borrower.

indivisible costs Items of cost that cannot easily be divided.

inflation Continuing and sustained rise in prices over a substantial period of time.

inflation-expectations effect Increase in nominal interest rate because of an increase in expected inflation.

inflation rate Percentage change in prices over a period of time.

inflation risk Risk that the realized real interest rate on a loan will be changed by unanticipated inflation.

inflation "tax" Money's loss of value due to rising prices.

inflation-tax effect Decrease in real supply of loanable funds due to the inflation "tax."

initial public offering (IPO) First issue of a corporation's stock.

inside market Market in which primary dealers trade among themselves.

insider trading Use of privileged information by a corporation's employees or agents to profit from trading the corporation's securities.

insolvent Having an excess of liabilities over assets.

insurance company Financial intermediary that sells insurance policies and uses the proceeds to make loans.

insurance policy Type of security that provides protection against loss or costs in return for payment of premiums.

interest Fee paid by a borrower to a lender for the use of the lender's money.

interest rate Cost of borrowing expressed as a percentage of the principal.

interest-rate effect Effect on aggregate demand caused by changes in interest rate.

interest-rate parity Equality of actual and implicit forward exchange rates.

interest-rate peg Monetary policy that pegs interest rates at a fixed level.

interest-rate risk (market risk) Risk associated with changes in market interest rates.

interest-rate swap Exchange of fixed-rate payments for floating-rate payments.

interest-rate target Monetary policy specified in terms of a desired level of some interest rate.

internal funds After-tax profits that are retained by the business and not distributed to stockholders.

international banking facilities (IBFs) Banking subsidiaries that may operate in the Eurocurrency market from within the United States.

International Monetary Fund (IMF) International organization established in 1944 to monitor exchange rates and to promote orderly international financial conditions.

inverted yield curve Yield curve that shows yields falling with maturity.

investment banks Financial institutions engaged in underwriting or brokering publicly traded corporate securities.

investment company Financial institution that raises funds to acquire a diversified portfolio of financial instruments by selling stocks or shares of ownership in that portfolio.

investment function Relationship of investment to the interest rate.

investment-grade bonds Bonds with a rating of Baa or BBB or above.

IO strip Type of mortgage strip that is sold with a right to receive all of the interest payments on a portfolio of pass-through securities.

IS curve Graph showing the levels at which income and expenditure are in balance for different values of the interest rate.

junk (high-yield) bonds Bonds with a rating below Baa or BBB.

law of one price Principle that market forces ensure that the price of a good will tend to be the same in different locations.

lease Contract whereby equipment is lent to a firm for a specific fee and time period.

legal tender Money that the government requires a creditor to accept in discharge of debts.

lender of last resort Financial institution that stands ready to lend to banks in times of crisis.

letter of credit Financial instrument issued by the importer's bank that obligates the bank to pay the exporter a specified amount once certain conditions are met.

leverage Use of borrowed money to make an investment.

leverage ratio Ratio of the total amount of an investment to funds actually supplied by an investor.

leverage requirement Requirement based on the unweighted sum of a bank's assets.

leveraged buyout (LBO) Purchase of a corporation's outstanding stock that is financed by issuing debt.

liabilities A firm's debts.

liability management Management of a financial institution's liability structure to provide liquidity.

LIBOR London Interbank Offered Rate, the rate at which Eurocurrency banks lend to one another.

life-cycle pattern of saving Pattern of borrowing and repayment, saving and dissaving through a lifetime.

life insurance Insurance that pays off on the death of the policyholder.

lifes Companies that sell life insurance.

limited liability Responsibility for payments of business debts that does not extend to the owners' personal assets.

line of credit Arrangement whereby a financial institution guarantees that a business can borrow up to a specified maximum amount of funds during a period of time.

liquid Capable of ready conversion into cash.

liquidity Access to ready cash.

liquidity risk Risk that convertibility into cash may be either impossible or very expensive.

LM curve Graph showing the combinations of income and interest rate for which money demand equals the quantity of money.

loan certificates Certificates used for interbank payments in place of cash.

loan covenants Clauses in a lending contract that limit the borrower's behavior in various ways.

loan participation Respondent's assumption of part of a correspondent's loan.

loan-supply effect Decrease in interest rate due to increased bank lending.

loan syndications Groups of banks that share the risk in making single large loans.

loanable funds market Market for funds that lenders are willing to make available to borrowers.

long Actually holding the commodity.

Lucas critique Argument that an econometric model estimated under one policy rule will be of limited use in predicting the effects of a different policy rule.

macroeconomic aggregate Measure of some variable for the economy as a whole.

maintenance margin Predetermined level of a margin account that must be maintained by the client.

maintenance period Two-week time period over which a bank's actual reserves are calculated.

margin Performance bond required of each party in a futures contract.

margin account Cash or collateral deposited by a client with a broker to protect the broker from loss on a contract.

margin call Broker's request for more collateral to bring a client's margin account up to maintenance margin.

marginal propensity to consume Amount consumed out of each additional dollar of income.

marginal propensity to import Amount imported out of each additional dollar of income.

marked to market Daily updating of a futures contract to the current price.

market maker Someone standing ready to buy and sell securities at declared prices.

market price Price actually paid for a security.

market risk Risk that changes in market interest rates or in exchange rates will lead to a capital loss.

market value Present value of an amount or amounts due, calculated at the market interest rate; amount for which a bank can be sold.

market yield Annual interest rate calculated from the market price.

marketable Capable of being sold to another person.

matching maturities Matching the maturity of the liabilities used to fund a loan with the maturity of the loan to be funded.

means of payment Object of value whose transfer constitutes final payment and concludes the transactions.

medium of exchange Something that, by its transfer from buyer to seller, allows a sale to proceed.

merchant banking Use of an investment bank's own money to retain part ownership of a bought-out company.

minimum efficient scale Point at which the diseconomies of scale balance the economies.

Modern Quantity Theory Theory of the short-run effects of an increase in the quantity of money; favored by Monetarists.

Monetarists Economists who stress the importance of controlling the quantity of money.

monetary accommodation of fiscal policy Monetary policy that minimizes the effect of fiscal policy on interest rates.

monetary base Quantity of definitive money used to determine the money multiplier.

monetary-growth target Monetary policy specified in terms of a desired rate of monetary growth.

monetary policy Deliberate control of the money supply to achieve economic goals.

money Any generally accepted means of payment that will be taken in exchange for goods and services.

M1 Narrow definition of money, consisting only of means of payment.

M2 Definition of money that includes both means of payment (M1) and time deposits.

money broker Financial institution that manages brokered-deposit accounts for large investors.

money center banks Largest banks located in major financial centers and involved in international banking and the financial markets.

money market The short-term financial market.

money market deposit account Account with limited check-writing privileges that pays a market rate of interest.

money market mutual fund Pool of a large number of small accounts for the purpose of investing in diversified portfolios of money market securities.

money multiplier, m Ratio of the total quantity of money to the quantity of monetary base.

moral hazard Tendency of the insured to take more risk because he has insurance.

moral suasion The Fed's use of informal means to restrict bank lending.

mortgage Long-term loan secured by real estate.

mortgage-backed bonds Long-term bonds collateralized by portfolios of mortgages.

mortgage-backed securities (MBSs) Securities backed either by insured or by conventional mortgages.

mortgage banking companies Companies that originate and service insured mortgages.

mortgage bond Mortgage that is issued publicly and that can be traded.

mortgage strip Type of real estate mortgage investment conduit that divides pass-through payments into interest payments and principal payments.

multibank holding company Corporation that owns more than a single bank.

municipal bonds (munis) Bonds sold by state and local governments.

naive expectations Expectations that the future will be the same as the present.

narrow banks Banks allowed to invest only in safe liquid assets.

national income accounting Definition and measurement of macroeconomic aggregates.

natural rate of unemployment Level of unemployment resulting from new workers coming into the labor force and from normal turnover.

negotiable certificate of deposit (NCD) Time deposit with a fixed maturity that can be bought and sold.

negotiated order of withdrawal (NOW) account Time deposit that allows checking.

net export function Relationship of net exports to the interest rate and to income.

net worth (equity) Net ownership value of a firm.

New Classical Economics School of economic thought that questions the ability of any economic policy to stabilize the economy.

New Keynesian Economics School of economic thought that accepts the rational-expectations critique but also believes that economic policy can be effective.

nominal balance Amount of money held measured in dollars.

nominal GNP Dollar value of final goods and services produced by the economy.

nominal interest rate Interest rate measured in money terms.

nominal price Price measured in terms of dollars, as distinct from real price, which is measured in opportunity cost.

nonbank bank Financial institution that accepts deposits but does not make loans.

nonbank office Financial institution that does not accept deposits.

nonbank subsidiaries Companies wholly owned by bank holding companies but having no banking functions.

nonborrowed reserves Total bank reserves less discount borrowing.

noncompetitive bid Bid for the purchase of a new Treasury issue that does not specify a price.

normal yield curve Yield curve that shows yields rising with maturity.

notional principal Amount of the underlying loans in an interest-rate swap.

off-balance-sheet banking The making of commitments by a bank that do not appear on its balance sheet.

Office of Thrift Supervision (OTS) Federal agency established in 1989 to assume the regulatory functions of the Federal Home Loan Bank Board.

One-bank holding company Corporation that owns only a single bank.

on-us clearing Clearing of a check at the bank on which that check is drawn.

open economy Economy in which foreign trade and international lending play major roles.

open interest Number of futures contracts outstanding at a specific time.

open market operations The purchase or sale of government securities by the Federal Reserve.

operating target Variable directly controllable by monetary policy and related to the primary target.

option contract Agreement that allows the purchase or sale of a specified quantity of an asset at a specified price until the expiration date.

options on futures Options to buy and sell futures rather than the underlying commodity or asset.

out of the money Below the exercise price.

over-the-counter (OTC) market Secondary market in which dealers at different locations stand ready to buy and sell securities.

overdraft Automatic loan to cover payment in excess of the depositor's balance.

overline Correspondent's assumption of part of a respondent's loan.

pass-through security Direct share in a pool of mortgages; principal and interest payments on the pool are passed through to the purchaser of the security.

payout Complete liquidation of a failed bank.

Pension Benefit Guaranty Corporation (PBGC) Federal agency that insures the assets of defined benefit pension plans.

periodic rate Rate per compounding period.

perpetuity Annuity that is payable forever.

Phillips curve Graphic representation of the relationship between inflation and unemployment.

point-of-sale transfer system System that links stores' cash registers directly to bank computers.

points Percentage of the face value of a mortgage charged by the lending bank as a fee.

policy loan Loan to the policyholder of an amount up to the cash value of the life insurance policy.

policy rule Consistent pattern in economic policy.

pool To collect a number of different financial assets into a single unit.

PO strip Type of mortgage strip that is sold with a right to receive all of the principal payments on a portfolio of pass-through securities.

potential employment Amount of labor employed if everyone willing to work at current pay can find a suitable job.

potential output Level of output that can be produced with available technology and natural resources, with capital utilized at full capacity, and with labor at potential employment.

precautionary motive Holding money for use for unanticipated expenditures.

preferred-habitat theory Theory of the term structure that assumes borrowers and lenders care about both maturity and expected yield.

premium Price paid by an option buyer for the rights acquired.

prepaid card Purchased card that is used to make payments for certain services.

prepayment Repayment of a loan before it matures.

present value Discounted value today of some amount due in the future.

price-level-adjusted mortgage Mortgage in which monthly payments increase as the price level rises.

primary dealers Securities dealers that are large enough and sound enough to be a trading partner with the Fed.

primary market Financial market in which securities are sold when they are first issued.

primary target Variable in terms of which monetary policy is formulated.

prime rate Base rate for bank lending.

principal Amount of money borrowed or loaned, excluding interest.

private placement Long-term loan made to a firm by a financial intermediary.

program trading Use of computers to track and control equities trading.

property/casualty insurance All insurance other than life insurance: automobile, homeowners, transportation, liability, and health.

public issue Securities sold to the public at large.

purchase and assumption A failed bank is purchased and its liabilities are assumed by another bank.

purchasing-power parity Equivalence of a price for traded goods expressed in one currency to its price expressed in another currency.

put option Option to sell.

Quantity Theory of Money Theory of the long-run effects of an increase in the quantity of money.

quiet bank run A massive loss of funds due to lenders of bought funds declining to roll over their lending.

rate of inflation Rate of growth of the price level in an economy.

rating agencies Investment advisory firms that rank bonds according to the perceived probability of their default.

rational expectations Expectations that take into account all available information.

rational-expectations critique Argument that the effect of economic-policy actions depends on whether or not they are expected.

real assets Property that provides a return or that may increase in value, such as real estate or works of art.

real balance Amount of money held measured in purchasing power.

real estate mortgage investment conduit (REMIC) Type of collateralized mortgage obligation that splits up the cash flow on a mortgage in various ways.

real GNP Nominal GNP divided by the GNP deflator; a measure of real output.

real interest rate Interest rate measured in terms of purchasing power.

real price Price in terms of opportunity cost.

realized rate Rate that is actually obtained.

realized yield Annual rate of interest that is actually earned on an investment.

reciprocity Mutual granting of privileges.

refinance position Method of funding a loan when the maturity of the loan is longer than the maturity of the liabilities used to fund it.

regional banks Medium-sized banks located in regional financial centers.

regressive expectations Expectations that in the future the value of a variable will return to the norm.

Regulation Q Federal Reserve regulation that set an interest-rate ceiling on deposits.

reintermediation Shifting from bank-intermediated lending to other intermediaries.

reinvestment position Method of funding a loan when the maturity of the liabilities used to fund the loan is longer than the maturity of the loan itself.

reinvestment risk Risk associated with reinvestment at uncertain interest rates.

repricing Resetting the interest rate.

repurchase agreement (repo) Simultaneous arrangement to sell securities and to repurchase them later at a specified time and price.

required reserve ratio Minimum ratio between reserves and deposits that financial institutions are required to maintain.

required reserves Minimum amount of reserves a financial institution must hold.

reserves Funds that a bank holds in the form of vault cash and deposits at the Fed.

Resolution Trust Corporation (RTC) Federal agency established in 1989 to oversee the liquidation of insolvent thrifts.

respondent bank Small bank that receives special services from a larger bank.

retail bank Bank that does most of its business with households and small firms.

return on equity (ROE) Percentage return on money invested.

revenue bonds Bonds repayable only from the specific revenue of the project they finance.

reverse repurchase agreement (reverse repo) Simultaneous arrangement to buy securities and to resell them later at a specified time and price.

revolving credit Credit arrangement whereby a business can borrow, re-pay, and reborrow as it sees fit during a period of time.

risk-adjusted assets Total assets cal-culated by assigning risk weights to each type of asset.

rolling over Repaying a debt by fur-ther borrowing.

Rule 415 SEC rule that permits shelf registration.

Rule 144a SEC rule that permits trading in private placements among large financial institutions.

running a book in repos Making a market in repos and reverse repos by reversing in securities from some cli-ents and repoing them out again to others.

saving Spending less than income.

savings Wealth gained through saving.

savings bank (thrift) Financial insti-tution that specializes in taking time deposits and in making loans to households.

savings banks and savings and loans (S&Ls) Financial institutions origi-nally established to accept savings deposits and to make loans to households.

seasonal adjustment Process of fil-tering out seasonal fluctuations to de-termine the underlying rate of growth.

secondary dealers Dealers that buy securities from primary dealers and sell them to the public.

secondary market Financial market in which previously issued securities are traded, such as the New York Stock Exchange.

secured debt Debt backed by a spe-cific asset.

Securities and Exchange Commission (SEC) Federal agency that regulates the securities markets and securities brokers and dealers.

Securities Investor Protection Corpo-ration (SIPC) Private insurance agency that protects the retail cus-tomers of securities brokers.

securitization Practice of converting loans into tradable securities.

security Financial instrument repre-senting ownership or debt that pro-vides a claim to the borrower's future income.

segmented-market theory Theory that markets at different maturities are completely separate.

seigniorage Difference between the value of money and its cost of production.

selling at a discount Selling at a price below face value.

selling at par Selling at a price ex-actly equal to face value.

selling at a premium Selling at a price above face value.

service companies Subsidiaries of thrifts that may engage in activities not allowed to thrifts.

settlement by offset Closing out a futures contract with an offsetting trade rather than through delivery.

shelf registration Corporation's registration of a new stock issue with the SEC as long as two years before selling it.

shell branches (booking centers) Small branch offices, mostly in the Caribbean, that have no contact with the public and whose activities are limited to transactions in the Euro-dollar market.

short Expecting to purchase a spe-cific commodity.

short position Position based on borrowing securities and selling them.

simple deposit multiplier Factor by which total reserves are multiplied to arrive at total deposits.

sovereign lending Lending to governments.

Special Drawing Rights (SDRs) Li-abilities of the International Monetary Fund that serve as international fiat money.

specialists Broker-dealer firms that organize the market in specific stocks by matching buy and sell orders.

speculative motive Holding money for use as protection from capital loss on long-term assets.

speculators Futures traders who have no position in the underlying commodity.

spot price Price of a commodity that is to be delivered immediately.

spot transaction Transaction in which the trade occurs immediately.

standby letter of credit Bank's guar-antee that it will lend an issuer of commercial paper the money to pay off maturing paper.

stated annual rate Periodic rate multiplied by the number of com-pounding periods in the year.

sterilized intervention Central-bank use of open market operations to off-set the monetary effects of exchange-rate intervention.

store credit card Card issued by a store authorizing purchase of goods on credit.

store of value Something that holds value over time.

superregionals Large non-money-center banks that have expanded across state lines.

suspension of convertibility Limita-tion of the amounts depositors can withdraw daily from a bank.

systemic risk Risk relating to the possibility that the failure of one bank will cause the failure of other banks.

T-account Simple accounting statement that lists only the changes that occur in balance sheet items.

term life policy Policy that pays off only if the policyholder dies.

term premium Quantity reflecting relative preference of borrowers and lenders for one maturity over another.

term structure of interest rates Relationship between interest rates at different maturities.

third-country banker's acceptances Banker's acceptances used in international trade that does not involve the United States.

thrifts Generic term for a savings bank or a savings and loan.

time deposit Interest-bearing savings accounts that have a specified date of maturity or that require notice before withdrawal.

time-deposit/checking-deposit ratio Ratio of time deposits to checking deposits.

time draft Negotiable financial instrument payable a specified number of days after the date of the draft.

time line Graphic representation of amounts promised and their due dates.

total capital Core capital plus supplemental capital.

trade credit Time that one business will allow another business to pay for goods or services purchased.

trading profits Profits realized from buying and selling securities.

tranches Classes of bonds that have specific claims on the payment stream of a collateralized mortgage obligation.

transactions motive Holding money for use as means of payment.

transferable (negotiable) Transferable from one person to another so that the title passes to the transferee.

traveler's check Type of insured bank note purchased from a bank or other issuer, refundable from the issuer if lost.

Treasury strips Government bonds broken up and traded as separate coupon and principal payments.

Treasury tax and loan accounts (TT&Ls) U.S. government accounts at local banks.

Treasury–Federal Reserve Accord 1951 agreement that freed the Fed from its obligation to peg interest rates on Treasury securities.

unanticipated inflation Inflation that is not expected by most people.

underwriter An investment firm that purchases new securities from an issuer for a price negotiated in advance and then resells them.

unit of account Specific measure in which a price or value is expressed.

unit bank Bank consisting of a single banking office.

universal banks Banks that are permitted to engage in any activity they wish.

unsecured debt Debt backed only by the general credit of the borrower.

usury ceilings Legal limits placed on the interest rates that banks may charge.

variable costs Bank's costs that vary directly with the amount of deposits or loans.

velocity Speed at which money circulates in the economy.

venture capital Equity funding by a specialized institution that usually demands some control over the firm in which it invests.

warehouse banking The storage and safekeeping of depositors' money.

wealth effect Effects on aggregate demand caused by net gains and losses on nominal assets and liabilities.

whole life policy Life insurance policy that includes a saving plan.

wholesale bank Bank characterized by large transactions with major corporations, government, and other financial institutions.

with recourse With a bank guarantee against default.

working capital Finance needed to cover the expense incurred in the production and sale of a product or service.

yield curve Graphic representation of the relationship between yield and maturity of Treasury securities.

zero-coupon bonds Single-payment securities having a long maturity.

INDEX

Marginal glossary terms and the page on which they are defined appear in boldface type.

Banks (continued)
  costs, 176–177
  and deposit insurance reform, 470–475
  equity-to-risk assets of, 473
  failure of, 443–446
  financial futures use by, 331–332
  interdependence among, 466
  investment, 106, 107n
  loan losses and, 102n
  matching needs of, 285
  and money market, 207–250
  off-balance-sheet activities of, 475
  profitability and size of, 175–180
  as profit-making businesses, 87–102
  regulatory classes of, 490
  reserves, 177–178
  retail, 280
  savings, 46
  services of, 87, 245–246
  size differences of, 280–285
  stock prices of (1984), 464
Bank safety, 71, 427–452
  history of, 435–441
Barter, 62–63
Basel concordat, 450
Basis point, 342
Basis risk, 329
Baumol, William, 588
Baumol-Tobin formula, 588–589, 610n
Bean, L. L., 348
Bear Creek Valley Bank (Phoenix, Oregon), 445
Bearer receipts, 68
Bearer security, 145
Becketti, Sean, 421
Beehler, Paul J., 738
Belongia, Michael T., 352
Benefit plan, 359–360
Benfield, James, 75
Benson, John N., 206
Benston, George J., 486
Berger, A. N., 83n
Berlin, Mitchell, 59, 508
Bernanke, Ben, 393
Bevill, Bresler, and Schulman, 167
Bid price, 37, 146
Bids, for Treasury issues, 151
Big Bang (1986), 502
Bills
  market price of, 133–134
  of maturity less than one year, 128–129
  one-year, 115–118
  Treasury, 148
BIS (Bank for International Settlement) capital standards, 476
Black market, 274
Black Monday, 152
Black Thursday, 322
Bodie, Zvi, 360n
Bond market, 44
Bond mutual fund, 46, 361–362, 363
Bonds (securities), 31, 144, 353–354
  convertible, 377
  coupon, 118–123, 135–136
  coupon period of, 129–131
  flower, 149n
  mortgage-backed, 410
  plastic, 418–419
  secondary market for, 367

Book-entry securities, 146, 159
Booking centers, 258
Book value, 99, 289
Boorman, John, 110
Bordo, Michael D., 601, 658
Borg Warner, 381
Borrowers, 300–301
Borrowing, 12–13. *See also* Circular flow model
  alternatives to, 210–219
  and liability management, 288–289
  timing of, 563
Borrowing and lending
  cost of, 53
  by sector, 28
Bourse Game, 273
Bovenzi, John F., 452
Bracket creep, 741
Branch, Rene O., 308
Branching laws, 195
Brandt, William, 187
Brazil, 718
Break-even interest rate, 22
Bretton Woods, 661
  collapse of, 817–818
Brewer, Elijah, III, 486
Brewer, O. Gordon, Jr., 752
Bridge bank, 445
Britain, 52
  savings rate of, 16
British Petroleum, 380
Brokered deposits, 456–457
Broker market, 232
Brokers, 156–157
Brumbaugh, R. Dan, Jr., 486
Budget, inflation and, 740–742
Budget deficit (1979–1985), 655
Bundesbank (West Germany), 797
Bureau of Labor Statistics (BLS), and buying habits, 692
Burlington Industries, 381
Burns, Arthur, 861
Bush Commission (1983), 858
Bush, George, and Fed, 795
Business failures, 732

Cagan, Phillip, 575
Callability, 146
Call option, 333
Calomiris, Charles W., 486
Calvi, Roberto, 266
Campeau, 370
Canada, 52, 199, 202–204, 224
  banking in, 173, 301–302
  deposit insurance in, 441
  deregulation in, 501
  government bond rates in, 765
Canceled checks, 81
Cantillon, Richard, 584
Capital
  and BIS standards, 476–478
  fixed, 17
  venture, 378
  working, 15
Capital account, balance on, 642
Capital gain, 35
Capital loss, 35
Capital market, 208, 353–393
  borrowers in, 355–357

  crashes and, 389–390
  for debt, 362–376
  globalization of, 385
  lenders in, 357–362
Capital requirements, and deposit insurance, 472–475
Capital utilization rate, 695
Cargill, Thomas F., 508
Carron, Andrew S., 486
Carry, 160–161
CARS (automobile loans), 418
Carter, Jimmy, 838
Cash management, 586–589, 738
Cash transactions, 82, 83
CATS, 120
Caves, Richard E., 658, 772
CD. *See* Certificate of deposit
Celeste, Richard, 449
Central bank, 73, 431–433
  rating of, 797
Certificate of deposit (CD), 45, 113
Chain banking, 185–186
Chain index, 692n
Chain of intermediation, 223, 224n
Chance, Don M., 352
Chase Manhattan, 166–167, 222
Check, 66–67, 72, 77–80, 83
  clearing, 66–67
  float, 545–546
Check card, 78
Check clearing, 66–67
  and float, 545–546
Checking banks, 471
Checking deposit, 559, 569
  and bank lending, 523–525
  equations and, 535–536
  opportunity costs of, 848
Cheesebrough-Pond, 380
Chemical Bank, 81, 348, 738
CHIPS (Clearing House Interbank Payment System), 77, 83
Christiano, Lawrence J., 863
Chrystal, K. Alec, 277
Circular flow model, 596, 618–619, 664
  of Island economy, 579–583
  Keynesian view and, 802–810
  and loanable funds market, 615, 616–622
  money demand in, 596
  of open economy, 638–640
Cirrus ATM network, 79
Citibank, 222, 241, 281–284
  balance sheet of, 283
  Bourse Game of, 273
  sources and uses of funds, 284
Citicorp Centers, 187
Citizens Savings and Loan Association (Grand Prairie, Texas), 469
Clair, Robert T., 206
Classen, E., 863
Classical Quantity Theory, 604n, 706
Clearing, 67, 78–79
Clearing bank, 157–158
Clearinghouse associations, 436–437
  and bank safety, 429
Cloakroom banking, 66n
Closed economy, 615
  deficit spending and, 647
  monetary expansion in, 652–653
CMA (Cash Management Account), 222

Coinage Act (1792), 65
Coins, 63–64, 74, 75
   history of, 65
   dollar, 75
Coinsurance, 434
COLAs, 740
Cold War, 255
Collar, 334n
Collateralization, of mortgage, 398–399
Collateralized, 17
Collateralized mortgage obligation (CMO), 414
Columbia Savings and Loan (Beverly Hills, California), 407, 470
COMEX, 503
Commerce, expansion into banking, 496
Commercial bank, 46
   investment banks and, 493–497
   securities activities of, 496
Commercial banking
   in American colonies, 67
   deposit insurance crisis and, 453–486
Commercial mortgage, 362
Commercial paper, 213–216
   advantages to bank, 237–239
   and loan, 239
   outstanding, 215
   and short-term lending, 220
   standby letter of credit, 236
   underwriting, 237
Commercial paper market, and money market mutual funds, 222
Commodity Futures Trading Commission, 492
Commodity money, 63
Commodity standard, 659–660
Comparative advantage, and swaps, 339–340
Compensating balance, 39, 236
Competition, 53
   in banking, 454–456
Competitive bid, 151
Competitive Equality Banking Act (1987), 186
Compounding, 114–115
Compounding period, 126
Computation period, 560–562
Conditional prediction, 815n
Connecticut, 192
Consol (security), 125
Consolidated balanced sheet, 101–102
Consumer bank, 186
Consumer Credit Protection Act (1968), 489
Consumer loans, 301
Consumer price index (CPI), 692, 740
Consumer Savings Bank (Worcester, Mass.), 244
Consumption function, 667
   Keynesian, 666–668
Contemporaneous reserve accounting, 845–846
Continental Illinois Bank, 289n, 348, 504
   failure of (1984), 330, 331, 445, 462–464
Continuing loan-supply effect, 726
Contracts
   debt, 33
   equity, 33
   loan, 33–34
Contractual rate, 92
Convertibility, 70–71
Convertible bonds, 377
Cook, Timothy Q., 227, 250, 277

Core capital, 476
Core deposit, 294
Cornell, Pamela, 417
Corporations
   financing of, 356
   borrowing and, 210–219
Correspondent balances, 181
Correspondent bank, large bank as, 285
Correspondent market, 232
Correspondent relationship, 180–182, 183, 264n
   and interstate banking, 196–198
Cost efficiency, 51
Cost-of-living adjustment (COLA), 692
Cost-push inflation, 718
Costs
   bank, 176–177
   determinants of, 694–696
   fixed, 92
Coupon bonds, 118–123
   investing in, 135–136
   market yield on, 122–123
Coupon securities, 144
   yield curve for, 756n
Covered interest arbitrage, 761–763, **762**
CPI inflation (1971–1979), 835
Crash of 1987, 389–390
Credit, 15, 62, 64, 80–82
   adjustment, 551
   assessing, 40
   bank card, 80–82, 83
   extended, 551
   as medium of exchange, 589–590
   store card, 80
Credit agencies, 147
Credit cards, nonbank competitors, 497
Credit Control Act (1969), 554
Credit controls, 554, 845
Credit risk, 279
   managing, 300–303
   and swaps, 340, 342
Credit scores, 301
Crisis of 1979, 833–834
   Monetarist policy for, 835–838
Crowding out, 804, 811
Cumming, Christine M., 508
Currency, 844
Currency/checking-deposit ratio, 520–521, 569–570
Currency drain, 520
Currency outstanding, 539
Currency premium, 766
Currency swaps, 344–345
Current account, 643
   balance on, 642
Curves, yield, 149–150
Customer's acceptance, 267–270

Dai-Ichi Kangyo, 190
Daily settlement, 326
Data lag, 813
Davis, K. T., 59, 110, 179n, 206, 277, 452
Daylight overdraft, 161, 504–506, 567
Dealer loan, 160
Dealer repurchase agreements (REPOS), 212–213, 214
Dealers, 152–156, 158
   becoming, 158–166
Debenture, 365–366, 400–401

Debit card, 80
Debt, 62
   subordinated, 476
   of U.S. Treasury, 144
   unsecured, 363–368
Debt contract, 33, 34
Debt market, 362–376
   and Eurobonds, 371–373
   and municipal bonds, 373–376
   secured debt, 362–363
Debt underwriters, 367
Deductible, 434
Default, 32, 42, 238n, 731n
Default risk, hedging of, 346
Deferred payment, money and, 65
Deficit spending, 644–647
   government, 620, 621
Defined benefit plan, 359–360
Defined contribution plan, 359–360
Definitive money, 74, 513, 537–538
   factors affecting, 549–550
Delors Committee, 859
Demand, aggregate, 698–701
Demand and supply, aggregate, 591–613
Demand deposits, 45, 229–235
Demand for money M^D, 585–586. *See also* Money demand
   aggregate, 594–596, **595**
   in circular flow model, 596
   effects of increase in, 620–622
   factors affecting, 592
   frequency of payment and, 586–587
   and ISLM model, 683
   velocity and, 597–598
Demand-pull inflation, 718
Demographics, 14
Deposit insurance, 32, 39n, 440–441, 456–457
   crisis in, 453–486
   and moral-hazard problem, 433–435
   reforming, 470–475
   reserves, 443
Depository Institution's Deregulation and Monetary Control Act (DIDMCA) (1980), 181n, 242, 401, 406
Deposit poor, 281
Deposit rates, 208–210
Deposit rich, 280
Deposits. *See also* Deposits by type
   of checks, 523–525
   clearing, 67
   and currency drain, 520–521
   demand, 45
   and loans, 89–91
   ratio of currency to checking, 569
   setting rates for, 93
   time, 45, 521–523
   tracing through banking system, 532–534
Depreciation, 650
Deregulation, 380–381, 492–497
   FDIC arguments for, 500
   of financial markets, 493
   international, 499–502
   of S&Ls, 469
Derivative securities, 387–389
Developing countries, 52
DIDMCA. *See* Depository Institution's Deregulation and Monetary Control Act
Direct debt, 42

Federal National Mortgage Association (Fannie Mae), 147, 410
Federal Open Market Committee (FOMC), 541, 791, **792**
Federal Reserve Act, (1914), 437
Federal Reserve Banks, 73
  borrowing at, 465
  consolidated balance sheet, 538
Federal Reserve notes, 70
Federal Reserve System (Fed), 437–441
  Board of Governors, 791
  and crisis of 1979, 833–834
  current role of, 858–859, 860
  and deregulation, 499
  income of, 554
  independence of, 796–798
  instruments of, 537–557
  policy of, 856–858, 861
  pressures on, 794–796
  regional banks, 791–792
  role of, 503–506
  structure of, 789–793
  transactions information from, 747
Federal Savings and Loan Insurance Corporation (FSLIC), 147, 441
Fed float, 545–**546**
Fed funds, 629
Fed funds market, 96, 232
  and open market operations, 565
Fed funds rate, 784, 812
Fed money, 76
Fedwatchers, 746, 747
Fedwire, 76–77, 83
  overdraft, 504n, 505
Fees, for services, 92n
Felgran, Steven D., 352
Fergusson, Adam, 1, 6
Fiat money, 74
Finance companies, 216, 217
Financial assets, 50
Financial futures, 295
  currently available, 329–330
  delivery date of, 328n
Financial futures contract, 320–325
  most widely traded, 321
Financial Institutions Reform, Recovery and Enforcement Act (1989) (FIRREA), 478–481
Financial instruments, and risk, 317. *See also* specific instruments
Financial intermediary, 44–48, 49
  bank as, 45–46, 49, 69
  government, 48, 49
  insurance companies as, 47–48, 49
  investment companies, 46, 49
  regulators of, 491
  S&Ls as, 401
Financial markets. *See also* Capital market; Money market
  deregulation of, 493
  fragmented, 55–56
  inflation and, 730–737
  integration of, 54–56, 348–349
  long-run, 208
  regulation of (1990s), 487–508
  regulators of, 491
  short-term, 208
Financial stability, 858–859

Financial system, 10–31
  differences across countries, 52
  efficiency of, 50–56
  stabilization of, 781
Financing
  of long-term investment, 17
  of production, 15
Fine-tuning, 815
Firms
  behavior of, 14–18
  as borrowers, 31, 355–357
First and Second Banks of the U.S., 173–174
First Bank System Inc., 295
First Executive (Los Angeles, Calif.), 371
First Interstate Bank of Los Angeles, 182, 184
First National City Bank of New York. *See* Citibank
First RepublicBank (Dallas, Texas), 464n, 467
First Union (North Carolina), and interstate banking, 197
Fiscal policy
  Keynesian role of, 804
  Monetarist view of, 810–811
  monetary accommodation of, 804–807
Fischer, Stanley, 688, 828
Fisher, Irving, 30, 601, 613
Fisher equation, 723, 728, 748–749
Fixed capital, 17
Fixed costs, 92, 175, **176**
Fixed exchange rate, 653
Fixed-rate mortgage, 395
Fixed-rate payer, 338
Fleet Financial Group of Providence, 192
Float, 545–546, 738
  dirty, 653
Floating-rate loans, 262, 296–297
Floating-rate payer, 338
Flower bonds, 149n
Flow of funds account, 28
Fluctuations, 778–780
FOMC policy directives, 792
Ford Motor Company, 496
Ford Motor Credit Company, 348
Foreclosure, 399
Foreign banking, structure of, 171–175
Foreign banks
  assets of in U.S., 188
  legal restrictions and, 187–189
Foreign exchange, 271–275
Foreign exchange market, 273–274, 632–633, 637–638
  central-bank intervention in, 653–654
  and deficit spending, 644–646
Foreign-exchange speculation, 460
Foreign-exchange transactions, 544
Foreign trade, 253
  financing, 267–270
Foreign-trade effect, 699
Forward exchange rate, 761–763
Forward transaction, 271–272, **317**–318
Fractional-reserve banking, 68–71, **69**, 427, 428–429, 515–518
Fragmented markets, 55–56
France, 52
Franchising, 182
Frankel, Jeffrey A., 658, 772
Franklin, Benjamin, 65
Franklin National, 460, 465n, 503

Franklin Savings Association, 407
Fraud, and bank crisis, 459
Freddie Mac. *See* Federal Home Loan Mortgage Corporation
Freely floating exchange rate, 653
Free reserves, 812n
Free-rider problem, 35
Free Trade Agreement, 501
French, George E., 308
Friedman, Benjamin N., 863
Friedman, Milton, 110, 452, 604n, 630, 700, 709, 718, 719n, 796, 799, 820, 828, 861, 863
Friedman-Phelps critique, 820–821
Full-bodied token money, 74n
Funding, internal and external, 17, 356–357
Futures, 317–332
  options on, 335
  trading complications, 326–330
Futures contract, 295
Futures exchanges, 320
  listings of, 321n
Future value, 114

GAAP (generally accepted accounting procedures), 468
Gain, capital, 35
Galbraith, John Kenneth, 6, 110
Garcia, Gillian G., 508
Garman, William, 449
Garner, C. Alan, 772
Garn-St. Germain Act (1982), 193, 242, 243, 406
Gaubert, Thomas M., 469
General Account, 546-547
General Motors Acceptance Corporation (GMAC), 218
General obligation bonds, 373–374
General Theory of Employment, Interest, and Money, 663, 801
Germany
  banking in, 177n
  hyperinflation in, 1–2, 718, 719n
  monetary union of (1990), 611–612
  reunification, and interest rates, 768–769
  savings rate of, 16
Gibson, Katharine, 244n
Gilbert, R. Alton, 250, 452, 508
Giro payment, 78
Glass-Steagall Act (1933), 209, 237, 243, 372, 488, 498. *See also* Deregulation
GMAC, 496
GMAC Mortgage, 411n
GNP, 629
GNP implicit price deflator, 692
Going public, 376
Gold, 73
  and SDR certificate accounts, 547–548
Golden parachute, 475
Gold reserves, 439–440
Gold standard, 660–661
Goodfriend, Marvin, 557, 575
Goodhart, Charles, 71n
Goodman, Laurie, 352
Goodwill, 99
Government
  as borrower, 357
  deficit spending by, 620, 621